T0348765

HANDBOOK OF REGIONAL AND URBAN ECONOMICS

VOLUME 3

# HANDBOOKS
# IN
# ECONOMICS

7

*Series Editors*

## KENNETH J. ARROW
## MICHAEL D. INTRILIGATOR

**ELSEVIER**

**AMSTERDAM · LAUSANNE · NEW YORK · OXFORD · SHANNON · TOKYO**

# HANDBOOK OF REGIONAL AND URBAN ECONOMICS

## VOLUME 3
## APPLIED URBAN ECONOMICS

*Edited by*

**PAUL CHESHIRE**

*London School of Economics and Political Science*

and

**EDWIN S. MILLS**

*Northwestern University*

1999
**NORTH-HOLLAND**
AMSTERDAM · LAUSANNE · NEW YORK · OXFORD · SHANNON · TOKYO

Elsevier
Radarweg 29, PO Box 211, 1000 AE Amsterdam, The Netherlands

First edition 1999

Library of Congress Cataloging in Publication Data
A catalog record from the Library of Congress has been applied for.

ISBN Volume 3: 0-444-82138-4
ISBN Set (1, 2 & 3): 0-444-87971-4

Printed and bound in the United Kingdom
Transferred to digital print 2009

# INTRODUCTION TO THE SERIES

The aim of the *Handbooks in Economics* series is to produce Handbooks for various branches of economics, each of which is a definitive source, reference, and teaching supplement for use by professional researchers and advanced graduate students. Each Handbook provides self-contained surveys of the current state of a branch of economics in the form of chapters prepared by leading specialists on various aspects of this branch of economics. These surveys summarize not only received results but also newer developments, from recent journal articles and discussion papers. Some original material is also included, but the main goal is to provide comprehensive and accessible surveys. The Handbooks are intended to provide not only useful reference volumes for professional collections but also possible supplementary readings for advanced courses for graduate students in economics.

# CONTENTS OF THE HANDBOOK

# VOLUME II: URBAN ECONOMICS
## E.S. MILLS, Editor

# CONTENTS OF VOLUME 3

## PART II: URBAN MARKETS

*Chapter 39*
## Urban Labour Markets

GRAHAM R. CRAMPTON

*Chapter 40*

Urban Housing Markets: Theory and Policy    1559

CHRISTINE M.E. WHITEHEAD

## PART III: URBAN DEVELOPMENT AND DEVELOPING COUNTRIES

*Chapter 43*
## Urbanization in Transforming Economies                               1673
CHARLES M. BECKER and ANDREW R. MORRISON

*Chapter 45*

## Poverty in Developing Countries                                                              1865

ERNESTO M. PERNIA and M. G. QUIBRIA

## PART IV: URBAN SECTORS

*Chapter 46*

### Urban Transportation 1937

KENNETH A. SMALL and JOSÉ A. GÓMEZ-IBÁÑEZ

*Chapter 47*

Sorting and Voting: A Review of the Literature on Urban Public Finance    2001

STEPHEN ROSS and JOHN YINGER

*Chapter 34*

# INTRODUCTION: APPLIED URBAN ECONOMICS

PAUL CHESHIRE

*London School of Economics*

EDWIN S. MILLS

*Northwestern University, Evanston*

This volume is a follow-up to the earlier *Urban Economics*, Vol. 2 of *Handbook of Regional and Urban Economics*, edited by Edwin Mills. The earlier volume, published in 1987, focused on urban economic theory. This new handbook, in contrast, focuses on applied urban research. The difference is of course in emphasis. The earlier volume was by no means entirely concerned with theoretical research and this one is by no means entirely concerned with applied research.

There have certainly been important theoretical developments during the last decade, and these are surveyed at appropriate places in this volume. But there has also been an outpouring of high quality applied research in urban economics, as in other specialities. The reasons for the rapid growth of applied research are not difficult to identify: better theoretical frameworks within which applied research is undertaken; better econometric techniques and software; more and better data; and, probably most important, ever cheaper and more widely distributed computing power within the research community that provides easier access to, and analysis of, data.

Anyone too young to have lived through the computer revolution in doing applied research should read Alfred Marshall and Simon Kuznets. Neither of course considered himself an urban specialist, but both had deep interests in the formation and functioning of urban complexes. Marshall had few hard facts to work with, but he was an extraordinarily perceptive observer of how the world worked. Kuznets was a compulsive statistical analyst, all done on desk calculators, and he squeezed incredible insights out of meagre data. It is almost daunting how well the urban and other insights of these two geniuses have withstood the test of time. They continue to provide a lesson for researchers about the very basics of good applied work: it derives from theoretical insight and a careful, even frugal, concern for data. Are these data appropriate for answering the questions that theory suggests are relevant? There is a danger as well as an advantage in more easily available datasets. The analysis undertaken is sometimes determined by the nature of the data available rather than vice versa.

Data and research output now move around the world at the speed of light, and thousands of scholars in dozens of countries can access the US census and many other data sources. Not only is more high quality applied research being done, but also it is now being done in many more institutions than it was a decade or two ago. The computer has reduced the inequality among academic institutions in their capability to do applied research.

Selection and classification of topics for inclusion in this Handbook has inevitably depended on the editors' perceptions of subjects on which important research has been undertaken. It also depended on the availability of authors who were able and willing to write critical surveys on large amounts of international research. We have tried to include authors, and to have them survey research, from a variety of countries. But there is still a US bias in applied urban research, partly due to the availability of data and computers, but also because of the sheer size of the US research community.

We have divided the 15 essays in this Handbook into four parts.

Part I surveys basic spatial and spatially related research. Cheshire (Chapter 35) surveys research on urban systems and their changing characteristics. The distribution of city sizes has long intrigued researchers. Recent work suggests that there are significant technical and definitional issues and that the way these are resolved has an important influence on the conclusions reached by particular studies. Nevertheless, the regularity of the distribution has stood up to examination pretty well. Explanations fall into two groups: those that try to generate the precise distribution and those that simply explain why there are cities of varying size. Since most of the latter rely on agglomeration economies in some form, this leads on to a brief survey of work on this topic. There is also an important body of research dealing with the changing distribution of population and economic activity between the parts of urban systems: both at the city level—suburbanisation; and between cities of different sizes. This chapter concludes by reviewing trends in urban development since 1980.

White (Chapter 36) focuses on the increasingly important and well-studied subject of multicentric urban areas. Subcentres, usually some distance from central business districts (CBDs), are smaller versions of CBDs and typically have similar mixtures of business activities. They basically represent suburban clusters of service sectors, that have followed residents and manufacturing firms to the suburbs. They provide the advantages of proximity that are the prime function of CBDs, and enable workers living in the suburbs to commute shorter distances and avoid and mitigate the congestion of innercity streets.

Gyourko, Kahn and Tracy (Chapter 37) survey the voluminous literature on the quality of life and environmental quality in urban areas. Quality of life measurement has both popular and academic components. Popular measures are deficient in that they fail to distinguish between endogenous and exogenous influences or to take account of the equalising effects of migration. Academic measurement has become increasingly sophisticated, based on important theoretical work published a decade or so ago. But this work is highly data intensive and so far—at least in its theoretically most rigorous form—it has been entirely confined to US cities. The slightly pessimistic conclusion of this chapter is that the sheer data intensity of this work means that further development may be slow.

Finally, Eberts and McMillen (Chapter 38) analyse the important relationships between urban infrastructure and urban agglomeration economies. Agglomeration economies are the benefits of urban concentrations that accrue externally to firms and possibly entire sectors. They result partly from profit-motivated clustering of firms and partly from government capital facilities, typically referred to as infrastructure—transportation and communication facilities, and some public utilities. The hallmark of research during recent years has been the careful measurement of returns to infrastructure capital.

Part II surveys literature on specific urban markets. Crampton (Chapter 39) looks at studies of urban labour markets. This is a vast field where the boundaries between urban labour market research, and labour market research in general, are not always clearly drawn. The obvious spatial aspects of labour markets form the first set of areas surveyed in this chapter, i.e., the interrelationship between residential and workplace location, mobility and search. The second set of issues surveyed relate to the various types of stratification of labour markets by skill, gender and family status and how these factors influence labour market outcomes and behaviour.

Whitehead (Chapter 40) reviews research on housing markets. This chapter concentrates on the literature that has analysed the role of those specific attributes of housing, including its locational specificity and durability, that render housing markets both distinctive and urban. It focuses on housing market research in the developed world. There has now been a substantial number of studies of housing demand of increasing sophistication. We cannot be sure, but it does seem that quite secure knowledge has been gained in this area—in both how to do such studies, and in terms of the magnitudes of the resulting estimates of key relationships such as price and income elasticities of demand. The durability of housing makes its supply distinctive with research distinguishing between the determinants of new housing supply and investment in the existing stock. After briefly surveying aggregate models of housing markets and the interaction between housing and labour markets, the chapter concludes with a review of housing policy research.

Hedonic analysis of housing markets is left to a separate chapter by Sheppard (Chapter 41). Although now associated with work on housing markets, this technique had its roots in the Boston vegetable market in the 1920s. Sheppard shows how the technique has developed into an invaluable and increasingly sophisticated analytical tool, not only for housing markets but also for markets in urban land, the analysis of environmental goods and local public finance. Again, this is an area in which research has developed and more recent research has demonstrably learned from the collective efforts of earlier researchers. Certain techniques and approaches have emerged as clearly to be favoured. Sheppard concludes his survey by suggesting some areas in which development should have occurred but as yet has not decisively done so.

Like Sheppard, Evans (Chapter 42) finds origins much older than might have been expected. Looking at work on land use regulation, he demonstrates a striking continuity in both the goals and instruments of British land use planning over more than 400 years to contain the growth of London (and later, other cities) by prohibiting development beyond the existing limit of the urban area. The strikingness of this continuity is only exceeded by that of its failure—400 years of continuous failure. Evans surveys the still quite small but increasing volume of research on urban land markets and their regulation by governments. Land use zoning in its various guises is one of the most widespread of all urban policies, yet almost everywhere it has significant effects on relative prices and induces a variety of perverse incentives. In addition, Evans surveys the increasing literature on interventions intended to increase the supply of urban land.

Part III is devoted to studies of urban development and problems in developing countries. Some of the material in Parts I and II is as relevant to both developing and high income countries, but the chapters in Part III focus specifically on developing countries. Much of the outpouring of research on urbanisation in developing countries has not only been made possible by data collection at the World Bank, but it has also been sponsored by this organisation. It is sad that the World Bank has not only abolished its small but highly productive urban research group, but also de-emphasised research on sectors that are critical to urban growth and to the well-being of urban residents. Becker and Morrison (Chapter 43) survey the trends in developing country urbanisation and in analysis of the causes, correlates and consequences of such urbanisation. It is not yet widely appreciated that both population and urban growth have decelerated markedly in most developing countries. Malpezzi (Chapter 44) surveys the superb work, mostly of World Bank origin, on urban housing in developing countries. The remarkable consensus that emerges from the World Bank analysis is that housing demand parameters are remarkably similar among most countries, even though purchasing power and housing costs differ greatly. Housing supply parameters differ greatly among countries, depending of course on technology and on materials availability, but mainly on the extent to which governments have permitted conversion of land from rural to urban uses, housing development, and housing financial institutions. These are the keys to understanding why housing quality varies more than can be accounted for by income variation and why house prices vary among countries from 3 to 15 times the annual incomes of urban residents. Pernia and Quibria (Chapter 45) provide a masterful survey of poverty and its study in developing countries. Poverty incidence has declined in almost all developing countries, and serious poverty has almost disappeared in high income countries of east and southeast Asia, such as South Korea, Taiwan, Singapore and Malaysia.

Part IV contains papers on specific urban problems and sectors. There is some arbitrariness in the assignment of papers between Parts II and IV, but all subjects surveyed in Part IV have a strong government and government policy component in most countries. Again, much of the content of the papers in Part IV is relevant to developing countries, but the papers have a high income country orientation. Small and Gómez-Ibáñez (Chapter 46) survey the sophisticated literature on urban transportation. In no sector have US governments caused as much resource misallocation as in urban transportation. The predominant wastes result from overinvestment in fixed rail transit systems, underpricing of road use and wasteful government ownership of bus systems. Yinger and Ross (Chapter 47) survey local public economics. They summarise what has been learned from the voluminous literature on the Tiebout hypothesis and from the provincial ways that local governments are financed in the US

What do we know now about urban economics as a result of applied research undertaken during the last decade or two? The answer surely is 'a great deal', although there is very obviously much more we would like to know. Even within their own fields, our authors could only survey the body of research that had been done. Evans, for example, reviews a great deal of work on the impact of land use regulation on housing. There has been substantial progress here and urban economists enjoy a significant degree of consensus on the economic impact of this activity. Yet, Evans provides no account of the impact of regulation on urban uses of land other than housing. These impacts are likely to be at least as significant as they are on housing since we know that land cannot be costlessly substituted out of either production or service activities. If we compare communities in the US and UK that are as comparable as possible except for the constraints their systems of land use regulation place on the supply of land, we observe that the price of retail land is up to 100,000 times higher in the most constrained community. Evans can provide no evidence on the economic impact of such a level of constraint, however, because no research has been done.

In areas where applied research has been done, in contrast, there has been much useful progress. On the basic spatial structure of urban areas, we have much better measurement of the extent of dispersion or suburbanisation from urban cores. We know that dispersion has been a worldwide phenomenon and, although governments can influence it, their many attempts to stop it have so far done much more harm than good. We have better estimates of the relative dispersion of various employment sectors and the reasons for employment dispersion. We have important insights into the roles of subcentres in the dispersion process, although there is still much to be learned about subcentres. We know that not only radial highways but also radial fixed rail transit systems promote dispersion. Indeed, American opponents of what they refer to pejoratively as 'sprawl' ignore the fact that London was among the world's most dispersed metropolitan areas long before auto commuting became important, and that an important reason for this is its century-old fixed rail commuter system that extends far from the core. Indeed, London if functionally defined, despite intensive regulatory efforts over 400 years, is more dispersed than Los Angeles, the favourite "whipping boy" of US critics of low density development. The degree of relative—and in several cases, absolute—recentralisation observed in many European cities during the 1980s did not reflect any new policies. The evidence suggests that it reflected economic and social changes which generated new patterns of incentive.

Despite recent high quality research, there is as yet no consensus about measures of the quality of life in metropolitan areas. Indeed, the entire concept may be a "will-of-the-wisp", and rankings of metropolitan areas may depend on details of people's utility functions. Although most explanations of the remarkable stability of the size distribution of metropolitan areas in many countries have been in terms of production cost, it is certainly consistent with the possibility that preference functions for the disaggregated factors which contribute to peoples' perceptions of the quality of life, at least in relation to the sizes of metropolitan areas, differ among people and that preferences change only very slowly, at least in a gross sense.

The precise nature of agglomeration economies is still something of a mystery. Proximity of diverse activities and the densities permitted by the ability to substitute capital for expensive land certainly economise on transportation, including commuting, costs. Here, as with land use regulation, the research we do not have could provide the key. For data reasons all quantitative studies have been confined to production activities. Yet, some of the most pronounced agglomeration economies (and 80% or more of economic activity in large cities) are—if the actual location concentrations are a guide—in service sectors. Wholly new "industrial districts" have emerged in the past 15 years in some cities—the media district in London's Soho area is an example. But these new urban concentrations have been in nonmanufacturing activities—the up to 80% of economic activity that had to be excluded from the analysis of agglomeration economies.

Exactly how proximity economises on communication costs, especially in the computer age, is still an open question, although it may be related to value added at intermediate stages of production (with resulting "inventory" costs of transport) and on the form of the communication. Bespoke information, particularly where a degree of uncertainty and trust is involved, still requires face-to-face communication, whereas the transmission of bulk information internally within an organisation, is virtually costless.

A metropolitan area without government-provided infrastructure—especially that related to transportation and some utilities—is inconceivable. But social returns to recent government infrastructure investments have been mixed, at least in the US. Fixed rail commuter systems—certainly in the low density context of US cities—have provided little or no social returns. There seem few reasons why the recent "darlings" of local governments, such as convention centres or sports stadiums, should not be left to the private sector.

Labour markets are an area of applied economics where there has been intense activity and considerable progress in the past 25 years. Much has been learned in the context of urban labour markets; for example, with respect to "spatial mismatch", the interaction of housing and labour markets; or how labour market adjustment mechanisms rapidly diffuse the impact of localised events. There is still much work that needs to be done, however, particularly on some of the most characteristically urban aspects of labour markets. Labour market search processes are still imperfectly understood, especially as they relate to both spatial scale and skill and employment status. There is still much to be done in terms of understanding workplace and residential choice and how those interact in terms of commuting patterns. New work here would be likely to provide fresh insights into the interaction of labour and housing markets.

An analogous situation exists with respect to housing markets. Enormous progress has been made on issues which respond to the application of advances in general economic theory and econometric technique. Less progress has been made on other issues which relate peculiarly to housing: its durability, spatial specificity and the institutional regime within which national housing markets operate. With respect to the spatial specificity of housing, it is strange, as Sheppard remarks, that while a central principle of urban economic theory is that the price of land will vary with respect to location, and housing, as well as having a specific location, occupies land, with very few exceptions studies of housing markets have ignored both land and location. Research is, however, starting to address this issue with some success.

History and institutional differentiation are important in housing markets but even more so perhaps in the context of land use regulation. Many aspects of late twentieth century urbanisation are still explained by the logic of pre-industrial warfare. The cities of Britain ceased to be threatened by siege in Tudor times so the incentive to enlarge the space enclosed by the walled city disappeared. The response was suburbanisation—villas in the heights of Islington and Hampstead, and ghettos to the low-lying downwind, east of London. The reaction to these developments was strict but ineffective regulation to try to impose containment. The desire for containment was probably motivated as much by distributional concerns—to protect the villa owners from the encroachment of the city—as with anything else. In Paris, still threatened with siege, the walls expanded and the rich retained their urban presence and developed a strong urban culture supported by urban amenities. The incentive for the influential to develop policies for containment did not arise, and in the late twentieth century the rich of Paris are still overwhelmingly concentrated in the urban core; and Paris, though still high density, has grown by continuous expansion of its built-up area rather than by the leap-frogging process that has ensured that functional London now covers most of southeast England. The Netherlands came into existence through the public provision of land via drainage. Local governments were obligated to provide land for development and this is still reflected in the country's system of land use regulation. Despite a density of population that is twice that of the UK, land for housing remains, as a result, very much cheaper. US cities achieve their leap-frogging and low densities by allowing new communities to incorporate (and so retaining a near perfectly elastic supply of urban land) but then providing a substantial incentive via the fiscal system to develop at the lowest density.

Relative to its status 20 years ago, urban research has perhaps made more progress in understanding developing rather than high income countries. We now have a much better understanding of the factors that generate rural-urban migration. Migration studies have shown that people move from rural to urban areas in developing countries for much the same reasons that they do in high income countries, i.e., to obtain better education and because more and better jobs can be found in urban than in rural areas. Migration is on a much larger scale in developing than in developed countries. We have also learned that migration and urban growth have slowed as population growth has slowed and low productivity agriculture has shrunk. The urban shares of total population in newly emerging countries such as Brazil or Korea have recently approached those in high income countries. Urban growth in such countries is hardly faster than in high income countries.

A remarkable amount has been learned about urban housing in developing countries. Urban housing prices and rents are typically much higher relative to incomes in developing than in high income countries. The reasons are counterproductive government housing policies. Some, such as controls on conversion of land from rural to urban uses are shared with developed countries. Others, such as a lack of legal infrastructure that permits binding contracts between landlords and tenants, the refusal to permit private financial markets to develop enforceable modern mortgages, land use controls that prohibit the only housing that low income residents can afford, and restrictions on development of private housing development companies, are more specific to developing countries. Governments, as they traditionally do, blame high rents and prices on greedy landlords and speculators.

Urban poverty has declined even more than would be inferred from overall measures of economic growth in many developing countries. Improved nutrition and water quality and improved education and health care appear to be the reasons. Poverty rates have stagnated or increased mainly in countries in which violence and political breakdown have occurred—much of the former Soviet Union, parts of tropical Africa and the southeast Asian peninsula. By far the most important contribution to falling poverty rates is rapid economic growth. The extent to which the poor share in the early stage of economic growth varies among countries, but there is no record of economic growth causing a decrease in the living standards of the poorest 10 or 20% of the population in any developing country.

Urban transportation issues are also better understood than they were 10 or 20 years ago. On this subject, virtually all the progress since the early 1970s has been applied, and there has been a great deal of it. Many careful studies have estimated the extent and cost of road congestion. Congestion means the excess of marginal over average social cost of additional road users and indicates a need for additional investment and/or congestion pricing. All careful studies conclude that additional fixed rail commuter systems are unjustified in the low densities of US metropolitan areas, but there is disagreement as to what are optimum investments: certainly much better traffic control systems and much better— preferably privatised—bus systems. The extent to which new and expanded roads are justified is controversial. Undoubtedly, the best strategy is careful benefit-cost studies of each major proposal. Such studies are rare, in part because of the ideological nature of the debate.

Poverty rates have also decreased in most developed countries during the last decade or two—the US and UK being the most important exceptions. Much more is now known about the socioeconomic characteristics of the poor in many countries, certainly including the US. More is probably known in the US than in any other country about the spatial and racial characteristics of the poor. Much of the US research has focussed on the plight of the poor people, especially poor minorities resident in central cities.

US studies have shown that the best nursery for future poverty is to have poor and poorly educated parents, and especially to be raised in a single-parent household. It is also now known that, other things being equal, the probability that children will be poor, be school dropouts, acquire criminal records, and have teenage pregnancies is greater if they are raised in poor neighbourhoods. Aside from improving educational programmes that poor children can access, not much is yet known about government programmes that can alleviate poverty. There is no academic consensus as to whether existing or modified government transfer programmes increase or decrease poverty. Again, the ideological intensity of the debate places objective analysis beyond mere mortals.

Yinger and Ross show that we now know almost all there is to know about conceptual aspects of the Tiebout hypotheses. Applied work has been considerable; we know that typical suburban communities have Tiebout-like characteristics, but we still do not know how Tiebout-like they are and what causes some to be more Tiebout-like than others. An important outstanding issue is whether, or not, suburban Tiebout-like characteristics depend on police-power land use controls in relatively high income communities.

Housing is more than half of all urban real estate and endless research is justified. More estimates of demand for aggregated housing, however, ought to be assigned low priority in many countries. More important is what governments should do, or stop doing, to improve the functioning of housing markets. Many scholars worry about the availability of housing that relatively low income residents can afford. At upwards of 15%, housing constitutes the largest single item of consumer expenditure in most countries. But while research into regulation of utilities, energy and transport operation is voluminous, there have been far fewer studies of how governments cause housing costs to be excessive: greenbelts, growth controls, other land use controls, rent controls, controls on conversion of land from rural to urban uses, excessive restrictions on private housing finance organisations, failure to develop legal infrastructure for housing property rights and contract enforcement, and so on.

In the US, securitisation has moved owner-occupied debt and rental debt and equity financing from neighbourhood financial institutions to national and international bond and stock markets. The benefits have been enormous. Benefits presumably would be even greater in other countries, especially in relatively small newly industrialising countries in east and southeast Asia. What is not understood is why this innovation has been so slow to spread.

Every urban issue is better understood in high income rather than developing countries. As noted, we can now be confident that most people, both the poor and the nonpoor, migrate from rural to urban areas for a similar mix of reasons in developing and high income countries. Most developing country governments adopt many policies to slow rural-urban migration, especially of the poor. The worst policies are those that try to increase labour productivity in agriculture. The result is sometimes to lower food prices, which is desirable, but often, because they are accompanied by protection, such policies increase food prices. They always reduce farm employment, as rapid agricultural productivity growth has done in high income countries. High productivity agriculture is of course important, but it is not an appropriate policy to slow rural-urban migration. The second worst policies are those that promote rural industrialisation. Internal transportation is poor in most developing countries and most industries must be located in large, preferably port cities to survive. A third set of misguided policies is to limit the construction of the only housing that the urban poor can afford. Both governments and scholars should direct their attention to policies that can improve the housing, health, education and productivity of the urban poor. Reduced controls on private urban business development should be an important component of any justifiable set of government actions.

As Pernia and Quibria show, we now know much more about poverty levels and incidence in developing countries than we did a decade or two ago. Economic growth is, of course, the best long run antipoverty policy. But the incidence of poverty correlates only moderately with levels of development or income, however measured. It should now be possible to undertake careful comparative studies among developing countries to deepen insights as to the determinants of poverty. The fact that high literacy rates and high levels of educational attainment are important strategies for poverty reduction even in quite low income countries is strongly suggested by historical data in Korea and Taiwan. Opening up educational and employment opportunities to girls and women are important in raising income levels, reducing birth rates, reducing infant mortality and generally promoting family well-being.

Even among high income countries, poverty rates do not correlate strongly with measures of real income levels or growth rates. Again, comparative studies are needed. The US has been a puzzle for two decades. It has experienced almost no decrease in poverty rates despite economic growth rates that are typical of most other OECD countries, and very high income levels. Although the US probably spends as large a fraction of its GDP on transfers as most OECD countries, the US safety net may leak more than those of some other countries. Although studies by those who believe the US transfers promote dependence and poverty have been justifiably criticised by economists, it seems premature to conclude that transfer programmes do not have adverse incentive effects, either in the US or other OECD countries. Presumably, careful cross-sectional studies could shed light on the issue.

Could cross-national studies also shed light on the public economics of local governments? US scholars undertake cross-sectional studies within the US, made feasible because the sovereignty of states permits considerable variation in the sizes and functions of local governments among states. But the US, Switzerland, Germany, Canada and Australia are the only federal systems among OECD countries. Are local services and infrastructure provided more efficiently in the nonfederal OECD countries than in the federal countries? Are there efficiency differences between all, or northern European countries and others, independent of their constitutional structure?

Finally, we should say that any enterprise such as this depends absolutely on the devotion and expertise of the authors. To those authors who met our frequent requests and deadlines we offer our sincere thanks. Despite their best efforts the book still took far longer to complete than originally intended. To those same authors and to our tolerant editor we offer our thanks for their forbearance.

# PART I

# SPATIALLY RELATED RESEARCH

*Chapter 35*

# TRENDS IN SIZES AND STRUCTURES OF URBAN AREAS

PAUL CHESHIRE*

*London School of Economics*

## Contents

* I am grateful to Charles Leven for reading an earlier draft of this chapter and for his helpful comments. The author is naturally responsible for any remaining errors, whether of fact or omission.

*Handbook of Regional and Urban Economics. Edited by P. Cheshire and E.S. Mills*

## Abstract

This chapter reviews the literature dealing with systems of cities and the patterns of development within such systems. It starts with the longstanding question of the distribution of city sizes, both in relation to how this distribution can be described and, given the form that it takes, how that form can be explained. Such explanations frequently invoke various sorts of agglomeration economies and so some of the literature relating to these is included here. The chapter then surveys the literature that examines patterns of development within urban systems, and then work at a more disaggregated level on suburbanisation. The chapter concludes with a summary of research into recent patterns of urbanisation, including relative recentralisation.

## 1. Introduction

This chapter surveys a wide and disparate set of literature. One unifying theme is that it is not concerned with the location or growth of individual cities but with systems of cities; types of cities or settlements, such as large compared to small cities, or metropolitan compared to nonmetropolitan areas; or core cities compared to suburbs. It excludes such literature, therefore, as Krugman (1993), which is concerned with modelling the factors that influence the growth of individual cities. It also excludes studies of particular cities, their history or development.

Although it identifies the origins of some of the more important themes and ideas, the main emphasis is on the relatively recent literature, since about 1975 or 1980. Given the very wide range of themes surveyed there is no pretence of including all contributions; the aim has been to include the main ideas and the main approaches and to evaluate some of the key contributions.

Section 2 starts with a review of the literature on the distribution of city sizes. The first issue, addressed in Section 2.1, is whether, or not, the evidence shows that there is such a distribution—at least in the sense of a universal distribution conforming to some simple form. The Pareto distribution applied to the urban

over 60 years ago, and both demonstrated that the city size distribution could be represented as a Pareto distribution:

$$y = Ax^{-\alpha} \tag{2.1}$$

or

$$\log y = \log A - \alpha \log x, \tag{2.2}$$

where $x$ is a particular population size, $y$ is the number of cities with populations greater than $x$, and $A$ and $\alpha$ are constants. Singer (1936) further argued that just as in Pareto's case of incomes, the coefficient $\alpha$ was a useful measure of the form of the distribution, in this case an index of metropolitanisation, measuring the relative roles of smaller and larger types of agglomeration in a settlement system.

Zipf (1949) is now frequently credited with originating interest in applying the Pareto distribution to city sizes but his contribution was less original, if more specific. He proposed that the distribution of city sizes could not only be described as a Pareto distribution but that it took a special form of that distribution with $\alpha = 1$, and $A$ corresponding to the size of the largest city. This is the often quoted "rank size" rule, that is, the rule (perhaps proposition would be a better word) that the population of any city multiplied by its rank in the urban hierarchy, is equal to the population of the largest city. This leaves open the question: how do we identify the set of cities that constitute an urban hierarchy or system?

The 1950s and 1960s saw a flurry of research activity exploring and testing this apparent law of city size distributions. Allen (1954) extended the number of countries analysed to 46 and looked at changes over time. Madden (1956) examined the changing distribution of city sizes within one country, the US, from 1790 to 1950, concluding that although the urban system increased immensely in extent and size, and cities changed their rank within the hierarchy, the form of the distribution itself showed remarkable stability. Berry (1961), in a 38-country cross-sectional comparison, classified national city size distributions into three groups. The first group, including 13 countries, fitted the rank size rule; the second group, of 15 countries, had "primate" (that is, dominated by their largest city) urban hierarchies; and the remaining countries had a distribution of city sizes between these two. He then related these differences to levels of economic development.

From the late 1950s, attention tended to move to explanations of why city size distributions conformed to the rank size rule and, in particular, trying to show nonconformity (Vining, 1955) or conformity (Beckmann, 1958) with central place theory (see below). It was not until Rosen and Resnick's (1980) contribution that there was renewed interest in the form of the distribution of city sizes and the question of the extent to which, and why, the distribution varied between countries. Rosen and Resnick observed that "the rank size rule implies a Pareto exponent of unity" and then investigated the value of this exponent for a sample of 44 countries. This investigation produced a set of estimates ranging from 0.81 (Morocco) to 1.96 (Australia). The simple mean was 1.14, with the exponent in almost three-quarters of the countries exceeding unity.

Although it could be argued that they originated none of them, all the central questions relating to the city size distribution came together in Rosen and Resnick's (1980) study, which is perhaps why it is the one to which nearly all later studies refer. Not only did they address the issue of whether, or not, the rank size rule was a statistically valid description of the urban hierarchy, they also provided a more systematic analysis than had previous attempts, of why the form of the distribution differed across countries. Previous studies had relied more on the classification of the distributions, on the basis of their estimated $\alpha$ values, into more or less homogeneous diagnostic groups. At the same time, Rosen and Resnick provided some analysis of how cities should be defined and how the city size distribution—or at least the estimated value of the "Pareto exponent"—was influenced by the definition of city. They also provided some analysis of the effect on the parameter estimate of changing the lower size threshold for including a given settlement within the urban hierarchy; and they briefly raised the question of how an urban system might be most appropriately defined. This last question, however, has been largely neglected. Vapnarsky (1969) is one of the few to address it. National boundaries have normally provided the definition. Vapnarsky argued, however, that an urban system should be defined in terms of the degree of interdependence between its component cities and its independence of other urban systems. He then used this definition to derive propositions about changes that should be expected when previously independent urban systems become integrated.

With respect to the definition of "city", there are essentially two choices: the administrative city or some functionally defined urban area. Most writers argue that the "entire metropolitan area is the most desirable choice" (Rosen and Resnick, 1980) but, particularly in international cross-sectional studies, this judgement has usually been ignored. Data availability has constrained studies to use administrative cities (e.g., Rosen and Resnick, 1980; Alperovich, 1984, 1988, 1993b; Parr, 1985). Rosen and Resnick (1980) started their analysis by conducting a sensitivity test by estimating the parameters of the Pareto distribution for six countries for which there were data for both functionally defined metropolitan areas and administrative cities. The values of the Pareto exponent showed greater variation when estimated on administrative, rather than functional definitions, and the value was in all cases smaller (suggesting greater primacy or metropolitanization, that is greater concentration of population in larger cities) when estimated for the functional areas. In addition, given the criteria that they had suggested for conformity to the rank size rule that $\alpha = 1$, functionally defined metropolitan areas appeared to conform to the rank size rule much more closely than did administrative cities. The mean value for the six estimates of $\alpha$ for functional metropolitan areas was 0.995, compared to 1.181 in the case of administrative cities; and the estimated value of $\alpha$ for the functionally defined areas was closer to 1 in five of the six cases. A more recent study for Japan (Osada, 1997) for the three decades from 1960 provides further support for this finding. While the estimate of $\alpha$ varied little from 1.29 for administrative cities, the estimate ranged from 0.96 for the 1960s to 0.99 for the 1980s for cities defined functionally.

Thus, one immediate conclusion is that not only do most authors agree that on a priori grounds functionally defined metropolitan areas are more appropriate, but the few empirical tests that have been made show that the results are not only sensitive to the criteria on which cities are defined, but that the rank size rule is apparently a better description of the urban hierarchy if applied to functionally defined cities. Yet most cross-sectional comparisons have been constrained by data availability to rely on administratively defined cities.

The second issue addressed by Rosen and Resnick (1980) is that of sample size. On the assumption that national borders[1] appropriately define the set of cities that together constitute an "urban system", they suggested two possible criteria for choosing the sample to which to fit the distribution—a fixed number or a size threshold. Wheaton and Shishado (1981) suggest a third—a size above which the sample of cities accounts for some given proportion of a country's population.[2] Here, again, the evidence presented shows that the results are some-

---

[1] Although echoing Vapnarsky (1969), Rosen and Resnick (1980) raise the question of how, rationally, to define the set of cities: "To achieve consistent results among our samples, we would need to consider more economically rational systems of cities, for example, perhaps the Common Market countries should be considered as a single entity". They conclude, however, that redefining the system of cities is beyond the scope of their study.

[2] One might object to this on the grounds that, since the estimated value of $\alpha$ is a measure of the degree of "metropolitanisation" of an urban system and may also be sensitive to the size of the sample (if, for example, the Pareto distribution is a poorer fit for the bottom tail of the total distribution than for the rest), it introduces a degree of systematic bias into both the estimation of $\alpha$ and its interpretation as a measure of "metropolitanisation". The more metropolitanized an urban system is, the fewer cities will account for a given proportion of the total system's population.

what sensitive to sample size. The impact on the estimated value of $\alpha$ is not, however, as consistent as it is with urban definition. This may reflect the rather limited exploration of the issue, however, compared to some other studies such as Malecki (1980). Guérin-Pace (1995), using an essentially identical form, for example, but exploring varying size cutoffs from 2000 to 100,000 for the French concept of agglomeration (the built-up area that, in France at least, is closely correlated with a functional definition of "city"), finds that not only does the size cutoff influence the estimated value of $\alpha$, but also the conclusion as to whether population was becoming more or less metropolitanised over time. Measured population concentration (measured, that is, in terms of estimates of $\alpha$) had increased for each 50-year time period in France from 1831 to 1982 if all cities over 2000 were analysed. If only cities greater than 50,000 (or 100,000) were included in the sample, however, then at each of the four dates at 50-year intervals population had apparently become less concentrated in the largest cities.[3]

The more detailed studies seem, therefore, to show that estimates of $\alpha$ are sensitive to the sample selection criteria. This implies that the Pareto distribution is not precisely appropriate as a description of the city size distribution. The issue of whether, or not, the Pareto distribution itself was an appropriate form was also raised by Rosen and Resnick (1980) who explored adding quadratic and cubic terms to the basic form. They found indications of both concavity and convexity with respect to the pure Pareto distribution, with more than two-thirds of countries exhibiting an upward concavity. As Guérin-Pace (1995) demonstrates, this particular result is also sensitive to sample selection. Extending the sample to all French cities over 2000, he finds no evidence of concavity for the appropriate time period. Concavity was observed in the nineteenth century, but in the 20th century it was only apparent if the sample was truncated to cities above 100,000.

Another strand of work, associated primarily with Alperovich (1984, 1988, 1989) but also with Kamecke (1990), is the investigation of whether, or not, urban systems really conform to the rank size rule. As Alperovich points out, this is not only a question of whether the distribution of city sizes conforms to the Pareto distribution, nor just, if it does conform, whether, or not, the value of $\alpha = 1$— the criterion adopted by Rosen and Resnick (1980). If the rank size rule is to apply precisely, it also implies that the constant, $A$, is equal to the size of the largest city. In successive articles, Alperovich derives a series of tests for rank size rule conformity and applies them to data for administratively defined cities over 100,000 in 15 countries (1984); to similar data for 17 countries (1988); and

---

[3] This suggests that the results reported in Eaton and Eckstein (1997) may misrepresent the stability of the French urban system over time and the extent to which it conforms to the rank size rule, since they confine their analysis to only the 39 agglomerations that had populations exceeding 50,000 in 1911.

to Metropolitan Statistical Areas (MSA) data for US cities at two dates (1989). This last paper also explores the issue of the sensitivity of rank size rule tests to the sample size. Using the tests suggested in Alperovich (1984), the strict form of the rank size rule advocated is rejected. It is also found that the results are highly sensitive to the sample size. Using the tests developed by Alperovich (1988), framed in terms of relative rather than absolute city sizes, he finds there is less sensitivity to the exclusion of smaller cities and that the rank size rule cannot be rejected when applied to the data for US MSAs in either 1970 or 1980. In absolute terms, however, omitting observations systematically causes estimates of $\alpha$ to increase from 0.95 to 1.6.

An alternative procedure for testing whether the rank size rule is an appropriate statistical description of the city size distribution—or, more precisely, the size distribution of 318 US MSAs in 1980—is proposed by Hsing (1990). He suggests that instead of fitting the simple log linear Pareto distribution, the more general functional form suggested by Box and Cox (1964) should be applied. This reduces to a log linear form when the estimated transformation parameters approach zero. At least for the data to which the Box–Cox function is applied by Hsing, the transformation parameters prove to be significantly different from zero and the implied "Pareto coefficient", $\alpha$, is estimated to be 0.86 compared to 0.97 for the simple log linear form. Thus, the evidence examined in this way suggests both that the rank size rule does not (precisely) hold and that the simple Pareto distribution itself is not entirely appropriate.

Cameron (1990), although writing at the same time as Hsing (1990), develops both these ideas. Her main thrust, however, is that while refinement of the estimation of the exact value of the $\alpha$ parameter of a Pareto distribution of city sizes is a worthwhile endeavour, "not much structural modelling has been undertaken". Wanting more than curve fitting, she argues that while a robust description is desirable, it is mainly desirable so that we know more precisely what it is that theory and empirical investigation should be seeking to explain.

Cameron (1990) raises a somewhat technical objection to the way of investigating the reasons for variation in the form of the distribution of city sizes across countries used by Rosen and Resnick (1980), and subsequently by Alperovich (1993b). They made the estimated $\alpha$ values dependent on a number of independent variables—such as income level, industrial value added as a proportion of GDP, railway mileage and overall population density. Cameron's objection is that this is statistically invalid. Since $\alpha$ values are points without variance, the "true" values cannot be observed. Cameron's substantive contribution is, however, the recognition that if just estimates of $\alpha$ are the variable to be explained, it is impossible to include characteristics of individual cities as part of the explanation of the overall distribution of city sizes. Drawing on recent work investigating the distribution of income, she explored one-stage structural models with normal and nonnormal errors, accommodating truncated size distributions. These make it possible to include variables measuring the characteristics of specific cities: age of the settlement, distance from nearest city, whether, or not, it is a port and whether, or not, it is in New England. These other variables significantly condition the size of individual cities. This finding leads her to conclude that rather than simply comparing country specific variables in investigations of why city size distributions vary, we should simultaneously be analysing what factors systematically determine the size of particular cities. In other words, variations in city size distributions across countries reflect not just national factors but also the characteristics of the individual cities that constitute a particular urban system.

## 2.2. *Explanations of the distribution*

Both Tinbergen (1968) and Krugman (1996), having noted the regularity of the distribution of city sizes, grapple with the issue but fail to come up with a wholly satisfactory explanation. Tinbergen (1968) develops a model derived from central place theory but including manufacturing industry as well as services. Krugman (1996) falls back on random processes, combined with the interaction of a non-homogeneous physical landscape (that determines the size of hinterlands on the basis of transport cost minimising routes) and economies of scale.

Alperovich (1993b) argues that there are two near-universal conclusions that can be reached on the basis of the numerous studies of city size distributions. Despite the qualifications discussed above, it does seem reasonable to agree with the first of these—that the Pareto distribution is a reasonably accurate representation of the city size distribution for many countries—certainly for the upper tail of the distribution. The evidence as to whether, or not, the exponent approximates 1 is not quite so clear-cut. Alperovich's view is that a second near-universal conclusion is that it varies considerably both between countries and through time. Krugman (1996), however, concludes from the evidence that estimates of the exponent tend to be quite close to 1 and—appealing to Rosen and Resnick's (1980) results—get closer to 1 the more carefully metropolitan areas are defined.[4] Certainly, without having internationally comparable studies that have used functionally defined metropolitan areas, it is hard to conclude positively that

---

[4] Apart from Rosen and Resnick's (1980) results there are those of Osada (1997). In addition, it may be worth noting that values of the Pareto exponent estimated for functionally defined core cities of the 10 country European Community of 1981—treating all the core cities as a single urban system—were 1.04 for 1951 and 0.96 for 1981 (Cheshire and Gorla, 1987).

the exponent is often very far from 1. This implies a more substantive objection to studies that have attempted to explain international variation in estimates of the value of the exponent, based on administratively defined cities, than the technical objection raised by Cameron (1990).

Explanations of the form of the city size distribution fall into two main types: those that are based on economic relationships or models—urban systems theories—and those that are essentially stochastic. The former, in turn, can be divided between variants of central place theory and models that rest on economies of scale, agglomeration and differential transport costs. Development of central place theory as a formal explanation of the distribution of city sizes—associated originally with Christaller (1933), and developed in a somewhat more formal way, more in tune with economic modes of thought[5] by Lösch (1940)—seems to have lapsed following the work of Beckmann (1958) and Beckmann and McPherson (1970). Certainly, central place theory implies the existence of cities of varying sizes but it is unclear what mechanism would drive a central place system to generate a size distribution of the form observed (see, for example, Leven, 1968).

The same point can be made for the alternative approaches developed independently by Evans (1972) and the more complete and better known work of Henderson (1974, 1977, 1986, 1987, 1988). Evans's model has two sectors—each of which is heterogeneous—manufacturing and business services with the output of business services, entirely sold as an input to manufacturing. There are costs of commuting so rents and labour costs vary with city size. Transport costs of the output of manufacturing are zero, while those of business services are assumed to be infinite. This is probably the original model in this vein to assume two sectors—one of traded and one of nontraded, goods. The assumption of a sector that is traded without transport costs is convenient in the study of urban systems, although inappropriate in modelling the location of particular cities.

In Evans's (1972) model, business services are assumed to be produced subject to economies of scale but, because of the assumption with respect to transport costs, they are produced in all manufacturing locations (i.e., cities). Manufacturing firms are assumed to vary in their combination of inputs, and so the profit maximising location for any firm will vary with respect to city size. Low wage, labour intensive firms making limited use of business services—such as textiles—will locate in smaller cities. At the other extreme, firms that use large

---

[5] The only difference of substance, as opposed to treatment, that the present author has ever been able to find between the models of Christaller (1933) and Lösch (1940) is that Christaller assumes that the spatially distributed units of demand, the farmsteads, are continuously distributed through space, whereas, Lösch assumes that they are discretely distributed. This results in Christaller's market areas having an infinite set of possible orientations, whereas, those of Lösch have only a finite set.

quantities of high wage labour and business services and less space relative to other inputs—such as headquarters functions, banking and financial complexes—will locate in the largest cities. Cities are then viewed as coalitions of firms with firms locating—either by a deliberate or a natural selection process—in the coalition of firms (or "city") which minimises their costs. From this can be derived a hierarchy of city sizes. Evans (1972) then explores the welfare implications of the model and the impact of falling transport costs for commuting.

Henderson (1987) provides a review of models of urban systems in the context of a general equilibrium model of an economy and synthesises much of his own work to that date. His own model shares some features with that of Evans (1972) but does not differentiate between "manufacturing" and "business services", and allows residents to relocate between cities as they tradeoff the diseconomies of city size against the higher wages generated in larger cities as a result of economies of scale. Equilibrium is the outcome of real welfare being equalised across all cities as a result of this process. If cities are too large for optimal welfare then this creates the potential of development profit and an incentive to develop new cities. Cities of different sizes result from the assumption that external economies are industry specific so that firms in a given industry tend to cluster in cities of particular sizes as they, like residents, tradeoff the diseconomies of larger cities against (in the case of firms) the lower operating costs of clustering to obtain external economies from complementary activities. "The size distribution of cities is not an accident of nature but is directly linked to the regional composition of output and production conditions" (Henderson, 1988).

This model generates empirical questions: for example, whether, or not, particular industries tend to cluster in cities of a particular size. These are extensively investigated—primarily in the context of the US and Brazil—in Henderson (1988) and some supporting evidence is found. Nevertheless, the model does not predict that the city size distribution will follow a Pareto distribution, far less that the exponent will be close to 1. Nor does it plausibly explain the persistence of a stable size distribution of cities over extended periods of time: in the US since the nineteenth century for certain; in Japan for most of the twentieth century (Eaton and Eckstein, 1997; Osada, 1997); and—with somewhat less stability—in France (Guérin-Pace, 1995; Eaton and Eckstein, 1997) since the early years of the nineteenth century, while in all three countries industrial mix and technology changed radically.

Stochastic models could be said to take the opposite view to Henderson. The size distribution of cities is an accident of nature. They come closer, however, to producing a distribution of city sizes that conforms to a Pareto distribution, although they run into trouble generating an exponent close to 1 and, less clearly, in generating a stable Pareto distribution in which the individual components change rank significantly as cities are observed to do. Various writers have proposed a variant of the law of proportionate growth whereby the elements of a system grow at a constant rate relative to the system as a whole (see, for example, Nordbeck, 1971). To allow for changes in city rank, a stochastic component can be incorporated in the growth rate of any given city. Vining (1977) showed that a log linear distribution could result from a balancing of positive autocorrelation of urban growth rates over time with a negative correlation between growth rates and size. Simon (1955) suggested a model whereby urban growth occurred as a series of discrete increments or discontinuous steps. Each increment might with a fixed probability constitute a new city, or attach itself to an existing city with the probability of it becoming a part of an existing city proportionate to the size of the city in question. As Krugman (1996) points out, however, even this model does not satisfactorily predict the observed outcome. Since the probability that a new discrete increment to urban growth will form a new city must be close to zero, and the exponent is close to 1, this appears to imply that the urban population is infinity. This only does not actually happen because of an integer constraint. There are no half cities twice as large as the largest, nor quarter cities four times as large as the largest.

However, there would appear to be more fundamental objections to stochastic models as explanations of the city size distribution. They are not only nihilistic, in the sense that they entirely abstract from economic or social processes; but they also amount to no more than saying, in the end, that the city size distribution is, as it is, because it is. It would appear to be more realistic and no less helpful to "explain" the distribution of city sizes in terms of people's preferences for living in different sized cities. It would not be very hard to specify a distribution of such preferences that explained the size distribution of cities; although since the existence of such preferences would be as hard to validate as it would be easy to specify, such an explanation would have a similar degree of elegant circularity.

## 2.3. Looser definitions of urban hierarchy

The extent to which the literature briefly reviewed above has had as its explicit focus explanations not just of why cities are of different sizes but why the distribution of city sizes conforms to a particular form, varies from author to author. Simon (1955), Beckmann (1958), Tinbergen (1968), Beckmann and McPherson (1970) or Krugman (1996) were explicitly interested in finding explanations for the "rank size rule". Henderson (1988) or Evans (1972) were interested in rather less precise definitions of the "urban hierarchy".

Other authors, however, have been interested in what might be considered a much simpler question: why are cities not all the same size? This question, in turn, has been linked to investigations of the existence and form of agglomeration economies, subdivided between economies of localisation (internal to the industry but external to the firm) and economies of urbanisation (external to both the firm and the industry).[6] A useful survey of the literature on agglomeration economies and a comparison of empirical results is provided by Selting et al. (1994). Many studies embodying measures of agglomeration economies, however, focus only tangentially on the issue of the distribution of city sizes. Some, for example, such as Nakamura (1985), Henderson (1986) or Sveikauskas et al. (1988), are really more relevant to industrial economics. They investigate why productivity in given industries varies between cities of different sizes and try to distinguish between the respective roles of urbanisation economies (resulting from city size alone), and localisation economies (resulting from the size of a given industry in a particular city).

These and other studies are faced with a significant problem of endogenous variables. Finding suitable instruments is not straightforward. As Henderson (1986) puts it, in the context of the model that he is estimating "... unfortunately our situation is not a traditional one ... own industry employment, local wage rates, taxes, and city population are jointly determined". He devises instruments, but, given the spread of industries being examined, they are not industry specific and the 2SLS results are downplayed. In the OLS results on which the conclusions are mainly based, localisation economies are significant across a range of industries with urbanisation economies significant only in printing and publishing in Brazil, and in nonmetallic minerals in the US. Nakamura (1985), using a somewhat more elaborate set of instruments and with measures of capital (unavailable to Henderson), finds evidence for both localisation economies— particularly in heavy industries—and urbanisation economies in light industry.

Sveikauskas et al. (1988) focus exclusively on one industry—food processing. Although restricting the scope of their study, they argue the gains more than offset for this restriction. It allows the use of both a more appropriate form for the production function—the translog form employed by Chan and Mountain

---

[6] It has been argued that there are not just production economies of agglomeration but also agglomeration economies in consumption and in the labour market. Alperovich (1993a) shows that not only is unemployment in Israel negatively related to city size but so, too, is the incidence of prolonged spells of unemployment. Equally, of course, it has been argued that there are diseconomies associated with increasing city size (see Richardson, 1973).

(1983)—to distinguish the effects of technical progress from those of economies of scale and the construction of instruments specifically appropriate to a particular industry (in this case the availability of materials inputs), as well as a wider range of data. When applying the model estimated by Henderson (1986) to their data, they largely replicate his results. Employing the translog production function, and their more sophisticated instruments and data (including direct measures of capital and output prices), however, produces sharply different results. Economies of localisation in food processing disappear but there is strong evidence of significant urbanisation economies in the industry. Although highly particular to their context, these results are valuable for the methodological care and the attention to economic logic that they embody.

Others have employed a production function approach to measure productivity changes over time between size groups of urban areas, and between urban and nonurban areas, to understand better the redistribution of manufacturing between the largest, medium sized and nonurban areas that occurred particularly during the 1970s. The work of Carlino (1985) and Moomaw (1985) falls into this category. Fogerty and Garofalo (1988) straddle this literature and the investigation of agglomeration economies in their own right. They find some of the most persuasive evidence of any study of the importance not only of localisation and urbanisation economies but also of the specific significance of density of employment in contributing independently to such agglomeration economies. As they point out "since the two approaches [localisation and urbanisation economies] are not mutually exclusive, our treatment of agglomeration economies incorporates both". This possibility has been widely ignored by other writers.

Nearly all the studies attempting to estimate agglomeration economies have used a production function approach. Some have been strictly cross-sectional on the argument that it is only on that basis that agglomeration economies can be reliably distinguished from technical progress. Others have been based on time series data—an advantage of which may be that it is more reasonable to assume that industrial composition is constant through time than invariant through space. With very few exceptions—Nakamura (1985) who dealt with Japanese cities is one such[7]—the studies have been of US MSAs, although Henderson (1986, 1988) compared these with Brazilian cities. In almost all cases, evidence of agglomeration economies has been found, although the estimates of the extent of such economies and the comparative importance of economies of localisation compared to those of urbanisation, has varied considerably. The more careful

---

[7] Begović (1992), who analysed the cities of the former Yugoslavia, could be construed as another, but he did not use a production function approach.

studies seem to point towards the existence of both localisation and urbanisation economies. The weight of evidence these studies provide is certainly consistent with an equilibrium for urban systems in which there is significant variation in the size of individual cities.

Apart from the normal problems associated with the estimation of production functions, two particular problems dog efforts to estimate agglomeration economies. The first is the simultaneity problem that makes it very difficult to disentangle the separate contribution of city and industry size from the overall variation in productivity associated with increasing city size. The second is that all econometric studies of agglomeration economies uniquely consider manufacturing industry. Given the data problems involved in producing credible estimates of production function parameters at the city level, this is understandable. Because of both the importance of the service sector in cities and its rapid growth since the 1960s, however, the focus on manufacturing means that perhaps three-quarters of the economic activity of urban economies in mature countries is excluded from the analysis. In addition, more qualitative studies of certain service activities, such as those of Dunning (1969) or Goddard (1973) of the City of London or Saxenian (1993) of Silicon Valley, suggest agglomeration economies are particularly important in some service sectors.

It is difficult to draw a precise line between work that should be classified as attempting to explain city sizes and work that touches on the issue but is primarily concerned with other issues. Nevertheless, if a line must be drawn, then the studies briefly reviewed above probably fall into the latter category. So too, must a number of other studies that have explored other aspects of agglomeration economies. Begović (1992), for example, claims that the positive relationship between city size and the diversity of its industrial structure reflects the existence of economies of localisation which vary between, but not within, industries. The increasing diversification of urban economies as city size increases is an idea that goes a long way back in the literature. Clark (1945) appears to have been the first to have taken a systematic interest. Although Begović (1992) does not develop an explicit model, he does provide empirical evidence that not only did economic diversification increase with city size in the former Yugoslavia but as city size increased, the share of manufacturing in total employment significantly decreased, while that of most services, especially business and technical services and wholesaling, significantly increased. If business and technical services are inputs into manufacturing this suggests an analogy with the work of Sveikauskas et al. (1988), who argued that in distinguishing between economies of localisation and urbanisation in food processing it was necessary to offset for the availability of raw materials. That is true of all sectors, so in principle in all attempts to distinguish between localisation and urbanisation economies one should standardise for the availability of business and technical services. The availability of these, it would appear, is itself a function of city size.

Apart from this empirically oriented work directed to sources of difference in city sizes, there is also a thread of theoretical work investigating the reasons why cities differ in size. Fujita (1989), Abdel-Rahman (1990), Abdel-Rahman and Fujita (1990, 1993), Alperovitch (1995) and Fujita and Mori (1997) are some of the more recent contributors. The earlier work of Abdel-Rahman and of Fujita are variations on previous themes: the varying role of urbanisation economies and economies of localisation in determining city sizes. Abdel-Rahman and Fujita (1990), for example, use a monopolistic competition approach, including external economies, and work out a partial equilibrium set of results. Abdel-Rahman (1990), again within a partial equilibrium framework, considers a model with two industries; one with economies of urbanisation and one with economies of localisation, generating two city types—one with urbanisation economies dominant and one with localisation economies dominant. The underlying assumptions are a Löschian plane with unfilled space, spaceless production in city Central Business Districts (CBDs), but land consumed for residential purposes with consequent commuting costs. These costs play a significant role in determining city size and interact with economies of scale or scope. In equilibrium, the two industry ("diversified") city will only be larger than the single industry ("specialised") city if at least one of the two industries exhibits decreasing returns.

Abdel-Rahman and Fujita (1993) develop a rather similar model within a general equilibrium framework. Equilibrium conditions are derived and their features are explored. There are two industries each with an element of fixed labour costs (labour being the only factor), but that element is allowed to vary if both industries are located within a single city because of potential economies of joint production resulting from shared overhead costs, such as infrastructure or a common input. Three possible city systems emerge: (1) only specialised cities with only one good produced per city; (2) only diversified cities producing both goods; or (3) both diversified and specialised cities (although the solution is such that in this last case one of the two goods will always be produced in a diversified city). The framework is one of competition, with developers maximising surplus but free entry ensuring that surplus is driven to zero. Total national population is given and the familiar equilibrium conditions emerge with the value of labour productivity and utility equal across households and cities. The model is elegantly worked but the results are mainly unsurprising. Equilibrium city size increases with the extent of "labour overhead" costs in the industries; the total number of specialised cities increases as expenditure shares on the good produced increases, total population increases and fixed costs of production ("labour overhead") decreases. Equilibrium wages rise with city size as commuting costs increase. In the outcome with both diversified and specialised cities, diversified cities will always be larger than specialised cities, because if the fixed costs associated with joint production were less than the fixed costs of either industry individually, all production would occur in a diversified city.

The most novel contribution is the way in which the impact of variations in commuting costs is explored. As commuting costs increase, the range of parameter values within which diversified/specialised cities exist systematically varies. As commuting costs decrease, diversified cities are more likely to emerge as the cost of city size falls. It is shown that if commuting costs are set to zero—the cities become spaceless—the results parallel those of the industrial organisation literature and the conditions under which there will be combinations of single- and multiproduct firms.

Fujita and Mori (1997) analyse a rather different problem: how new cities come to be born in an expanding urban system and the form the resulting distribution of cities will take. The forces driving their model are growth and agglomeration economies interacting with transport costs. As the system expands, it becomes profitable at some point, for new cities to form so as to take advantage of the increasing extent of uncontested market demand at the outer limits of the current range of the initial city. Since the model is very much in the spirit of central place analysis, it is perhaps not surprising that it can be shown that such an expanding system would generate an urban system consistent with classical central place theory.

The point of entry into the issue of city size adopted by Alperovitch (1995) seems very different. It is to explore the relation between intraurban income inequality and city size. This is done within the framework of a far less fully developed general equilibrium model than that used by Abdel-Rahman and Fujita (1993). The model builds on the results of Upton (1981) and Henderson (1988). After reviewing the literature that empirically finds income inequality increasing with city size in the US, but not varying significantly with city size in Canada, Alperovich develops a model in which either outcome is possible but depends on the consumption patterns of workers with varying endowments of human capital. The model involves two types of industry, one producing traded goods subject to industry but not firm level economies of scale, and the other producing nontraded goods such as housing and transport services (although it could also, presumably, include urban amenities and cultural services). Competition ensures that the price of traded goods is the same everywhere but, following Henderson (1988), wages and the price of nontraded goods rise with city size.

Workers are then assumed to be divided between groups within which human capital and consumption patterns are constant, but between which they vary. Even though the proportionate representation of these groups may be constant across cities, since the price of nontraded goods is higher the larger the city, if consumption patterns vary systematically between groups, the equality of income distribution—measured by the Gini coefficient—will also vary between cities. If households with high incomes have relative preferences for nontraded goods (the price of which rises with city size), but lower income households have relative preferences for traded goods, inequality will rise with city size, and vice versa. Thus, in a sense preferences enter into explanations of varying city sizes.

A very different approach to explaining variations in the size distribution of urban systems is adopted by Ades and Glaeser (1995). This harks back to one of the questions explored by Rosen and Resnick (1980) but avoids the technical objection of Cameron (1990), by simply adopting the log of the population in the main city in each country as their dependent variable. Although they do not explore the relationship, the log of the population in the biggest city relative to national urban population must be closely correlated with the estimate of $\alpha$—the Pareto exponent. It is also a direct measure of "metropolitanisation" or "primacy". In an eclectic approach they combine insights from modern trade theory with quantitative political science, commonsense and historical case studies. They include in their cross-sectional analysis of 85 countries data for 1970–1985.[8] Their independent variables include a set similar to those used by Rosen and Resnick (1980), such as the proportion of the country's labour force employed in sectors other than agriculture and GDP per capita. They also include the log of population in urban areas other than the main city, a dummy for whether, or not, the main city is also the capital and the land area of the country. Drawing on the argument advanced by Krugman and Livas (1992), they also include the ratio of trade to GDP. Krugman and Livas argued that since international firms sold on a more-or-less equal basis to both the hinterland and to the main city, costs of imported goods would vary relatively less between the main city and the hinterland than those of domestically produced goods. The latter, because of economies of scale, agglomeration economies and transport costs, would be sold at an advantage in the largest cities. Therefore, countries that engaged in more trade protection would tend to have more dominant main cities relative to their urban systems than countries with freer trade. Ades and Glaeser (1995) then develop a series of arguments to the effect that the main city will tend to be

---

[8] More detailed models are estimated for 70 and 50 countries for which a greater range of data are available. These largely confirm the findings for the larger sample.

more dominant the more political instability there is in a country and the more authoritarian is its regime. Factors cited include the comparative safety of life in the main city compared to the outlying hinterland, the importance of proximity to influence peddling (that increases with more dictatorial regimes), and the incentives for dictatorial regimes to favour their main cities at the expense of their outlying hinterlands in both their tax treatment and supply of publicly provided goods (circuses).

Strong empirical evidence is found to support their hypotheses. Main cities tend to be 41% larger if they are also capitals; the size of the main city increases with the total land area of a country; an increase in trade relative to GDP equal to one standard deviation is associated with a 13% increase in the size of the main city; countries with dictatorial regimes have main cities 45% larger than those with nondictatorial regimes; and one coup per year is on average associated with an increase in main city size of 2.4%. The more detailed analysis of the subsample of countries for which there was a wider range of data suggests that both the level of tariff protection and trade as a proportion of GDP separately influence the size of the main city in the expected way. They also support the hypothesis that the development of the transport system is an influence on the degree of primacy of a country's urban system. The size of the main city falls in countries as their transport system becomes more highly developed. The implication appears to be that lower transport costs are associated with a more dispersed urban population.

Because of problems of endogeneity and causality the authors re-estimate some of their main models using instruments and testing the timing of events. This last test suggests that if a country becomes a dictatorship then its main city grows relative to the rest of its urban system. These relationships are then illustrated with case studies of archetypal main cities from different eras: classical Rome, London in 1670, Edo in 1700, Buenos Aires in 1900 and Mexico City at present.

## 3. Economic geographical approaches

The eclectic approach of Ades and Glaeser (1995) combines elements of economic analysis, political theory and economic geography (old and "new"). There is, however, also a rather different approach to investigating urban systems and patterns of development. This has been adopted by some working within a broadly defined economic framework, but is more associated with urban geographers. It is not directed towards investigating the system of cities, in the sense of the distribution of city sizes, but to explaining—or at least classifying—the patterns of urban development.

As originally developed by Hall and Hay (1980), Klaassen et al. (1981), van den Berg et al. (1982) or van den Berg (1987), it was conceived of as a theory of the "stages of urban development". City regions were defined as functional urban regions (FURs) using criteria developed from those used by Berry (1973) to define his daily urban systems for the US. A set of core cities were defined in terms of employment concentrations, including all contiguous local areas with densities of jobs exceeding a given threshold; then a hinterland for each urban core was defined on patterns of commuting. FURs were intended to coincide with a city's field of economic influence to provide economically self-contained city regions.

Hall and Hay (1980) argued that a given FUR passed through successive stages of development. These stages were defined in terms of the relative rates of population growth of the core city, its hinterland and the FUR as a whole. The initial stages of urban development were seen as those associated with population centralisation. During the first such stage the core city grew relative to the hinterland, but both lost population in overall terms because of migration from the FUR as a whole to the main metropolitan centre. Continued development was seen as being characterised by centralisation within the FUR, first with the core city gaining population in absolute terms, while both the hinterland and the FUR overall continued to decline, then with the FUR and subsequently the hinterland turning to positive growth but with the rate of growth in the core city always exceeding that in the hinterland. These stages of centralisation were then seen as giving way first to relative decentralisation, as the growth rate of the hinterland exceeded that of the core, then to absolute decentralisation, and finally to decentralisation and loss with overall decline in both core and hinterland, but that decline being more rapid in the core.

This sequence was tested against data collected for all the FURs of Western Europe for three periods, 1950–1960, 1960–1970 and 1970–1975. The analysis showed that there was a tendency for FURs to exhibit such patterns of development. Van den Berg et al. (1982) developed a very similar set of ideas, although their "stages" were ordered differently, starting with the core city growing and this growth more than compensating for population loss from the hinterland so that the FUR overall showed population gain. They also argued that the pattern was not so much one of stages that came to a halt with urban decline and decentralisation, but one of cycles. Decline and decentralisation was then followed by urban recentralisation and a new cycle begun. This idea was developed in more detail by van den Berg (1987).

Cheshire and Hay (1989) argued that the stages of urban development did not constitute a theory, but rather a classificatory device. This revealed a set of facts about the pattern of urban development that theory needed to explain. They also updated the western European FUR analysis to 1980 and showed that the patterns observed by Hall and Hay (1980) and van den Berg et al. (1982) had continued. The urban system had continued to move towards decentralisation, with decentralisation being observed in the largest city regions first and tending to "move" from the cities of northern Europe to those of the south. They also argued that these patterns did not reflect deterministic patterns inevitable in the development of urban systems; but rather the particular balance of a set of socioeconomic forces prevailing in western Europe during the time period studied. These forces included the ongoing capitalisation of low productivity European agriculture leading to a rural-urban flow of migrants, the size of which was proportionate to the share of the agricultural labour force in the wider regional economy. In the context of growing industrial employment, which halted around 1960 in northern Europe but continued through until the late 1970s in the south, this produced urban growth and centralisation. A counteracting urban-rural flow was associated with the forces driving the decentralisation of those sectors—chiefly manufacturing—that handled goods in bulk; there was a further flow of residential decentralisation, driven mainly by rising incomes and employment decentralisation. As economies matured, which in a European context was equivalent to moving northwards, these decentralising forces interacted with potential flows of recentralisation driven by the relative growth of service activities. In service sectors, relative price changes did not inevitably determine decentralised locations. In addition, economic and demographic changes associated with rising female participation rates and falling average household sizes had played a role. These changes meant that the advantages of decentralised locations relative to centralised ones in northern European cities were, by about 1980, changing as access to the labour market became relatively more significant and space consumption relatively less significant in determining household locations.

Because the overall balance of these forces had altered by the mid-1980s, it was argued that future patterns of European urban development would not necessarily reflect the steady movement towards decentralisation that they had from 1950 to 1980. More varied patterns should be expected reflecting the particular characteristics of individual cities. Cheshire (1995) then updated the analysis for the FURs of western Europe to 1990. This showed that the regular trend towards decentralisation had, indeed, changed during the 1980s, with much more variation and an increase in the number of city regions in northern Europe exhibiting recentralisation. Where recentralisation had occurred it appeared possible to relate this to the characteristics of the particular cities.

An alternative approach to understanding patterns of urban development was developed by Andersson (1985) and Suarez-Villa (1988). Andersson (1985) argued that one should view urban development as an evolutionary process. He identified four major stages in the modern era, each connected with a logistical revolution that reduced key costs affecting transport, the costs of transactions, the costs of coordinating production activities and, most recently, the costs of information. These, he argued, were associated with a set of discontinuous extensions of urban systems from the local, to the national, international and finally to the emergence of a global urban hierarchy. Suarez-Villa (1988), in a wide ranging but ultimately not wholly focussed review, attempted to link both the distribution of city sizes (again measured by the Parato exponent, $\alpha$) and their individual patterns of centralisation and decentralisation to an evolutionary view of economic development. These two papers, however, do not seem to have stimulated further development of this approach.

## 4. Intraurban patterns of development and change

There is a further body of literature exploring, at a more disaggregated level, patterns of intraurban (in the sense of the metropolitan or city region) differential growth and the growth of particular types of cities compared to others. Two main threads can be distinguished. There is a line of work that has, as its focus, the changing distribution of people and jobs within large metropolitan areas. The theoretical core is provided by the classical model of urban structure and land use originating with Wingo (1961), Alonso (1964) and developed by Muth (1969), Mills (1972) and Evans (1973). This line of work has used the articulated theory of residential location contained in that model to examine the changing distribution of resident population within cities, paying particular attention to changing income,[9] although other explanatory variables have also been included. Following the logic of the classical urban model the dependent variable has often been the population density function (the origins of which—as with a number of the quantitative tools of spatial analysis—can be traced to the work of Clark (1951). The theoretical explanation of intraurban employment location is less complete,

---

[9] Margo (1992) suggests that over 40% of suburbanisation of population from US central cities between 1950 and 1980 could be attributed to rising incomes. This estimate was based on the results of a logit model explaining the distribution of households between the central city and suburban rings in 1950. The resulting coefficients were used to simulate the degree of suburbanisation that would have been expected by 1980 given the actual increase in incomes observed.

so the investigation of changes in the location of jobs at this spatial level had a less well articulated theoretical framework. Broadly, these two related bodies of work can be thought of as the study of suburbanisation. One of its recurring questions has been whether, in suburbanisation, the process is led by the decentralisation of jobs, or the decentralisation of people (Steinnes, 1977, 1982).

The second main area of work is the study of changes in the distribution of people and jobs between settlements of varying size, and between metropolitan areas on the one hand, and nonmetropolitan areas—or rural ("ex-urban") areas–on the other. Theoretically, this works tends to be more ad hoc than that on suburbanisation but constitutes, nevertheless, a far larger volume of material.

It is the work on suburbanisation, however, that is reviewed first in this section. As indicated above, a central question has been whether "people follow jobs" or "jobs follow people". Perhaps the most complete investigation of this is provided by Thurston and Yezer (1994). Building on the initial work of Bradford and Kelejan (1973), Steinnes (1977, 1982), Cooke (1978, 1983) and Mills (1992), they estimate a model using annual data in which the value of the population density gradient at time $t$ is determined by the annual percentage change in total population, income and transport investment, the percentage of white population in the central city in time $t$, by the value of the population and employment density gradients in the previous period and by a time trend. City specific effects are eliminated by including a dummy for each city.[10] Compared to previous studies, the main missing independent variable is a measure of crime in the central city (suburbs). This had been found to be significant in Bradford and Kelejan (1973), Grubb (1982) and by Palumbo et al. (1990).

The strength of the Thurston and Yezer (1994) study, however, is that they used as their dependent variable what is probably the theoretically most appropriate measure—the value of the population density gradient; they employed annual data, and had a much more detailed and exhaustive set of employment sectors. They also had a carefully evaluated measure of transport investment. Not being a direct measure of the theoretically appropriate variable, travel costs, however, this still had problems. Although it had the expected sign (unlike in a number of earlier studies), it was not significantly associated with the rate of population suburbanisation. The advantage of using annual data is that it allows much more precise measurement of lags and potentially gives greater insight into causality, where the response in one sector to changes in another is rapid. The advantages of greater and exhaustive sectoral disaggregation of employment are considerable. Location theory predicts that intraurban locational requirements will vary

---

[10] Rather curiously Thurston and Yezer (1994) dismiss these as "of no particular importance".

between industries, as will the locational response to changes in transport technology/costs (see, for example Anas and Moses, 1978). Including an exhaustive (or nearly—agriculture and extractive industry employment was excluded) set of sectors greatly reduces the problem of omitted variables bias.

The findings of Thurston and Yezer (1994) are broadly supportive of theory and much more successful in identifying the relationship between population and employment suburbanisation than was the case with previous studies. They found that in US cities rising incomes were significantly associated with population suburbanisation, but that population growth and its ethnic composition was not significantly related to changes in the population density gradient. They also found evidence of significant relationships between employment and residential segregation. There was only evidence supportive of the "jobs follow people" view, however, with respect to employment in retail and services. Evidence for the interrelationship between decentralisation of employment in construction and transport, communications and public utilities, supported the interpretation that investment in suburban infrastructure facilitated subsequent population suburbanisation. In manufacturing, the results supported the earlier and apparently anomalous results of Steinnes (1977). Suburbanisation of manufacturing employment was significantly related to slower population suburbanisation. This is consistent with Steinnes's original interpretation: that manufacturing industry generates negative externalities from which people tend to remove themselves as their incomes rise, since an alternative way of representing the result is that increased concentration of manufacturing in the central city increases the rate of population suburbanisation.

The second body of work referred to above probably originates with Beale (1975), although it was given an international dimension and much wider currency with the work of Berry (1976), Vining and Strauss (1977), Leven (1978), Vining and Kontuly (1978) and Vining and Yang (1979). The literature consists of a large number of empirically oriented studies that try to establish the facts; and a far smaller body of more theoretically oriented work attempting to explain these facts. In brief, the "facts" are that, starting sometime in the 1960s, a process began of population dispersal from the large metropolitan areas. This was matched by a reversal of previous patterns of depopulation in rural areas. In the 1970s, for example, there was in Britain an almost perfect positive relationship between measures of how rural a region was and its rate of population growth (Champion, 1989). This pattern went far beyond suburbanisation or decentralisation and was associated with a strong growth of smaller cities and "ex-urban" communities. Although originally noted in the US, it appeared also in other mature industrial countries at about the same time (Leven, 1978; Vining and Kontuly, 1978).

It was realised quite early that there should be some connection between the shift in population and employment towards smaller cities and nonmetropolitan areas and changes in the spatial structure of costs (Anas and Moses, 1978) and/or productivity (Vining and Kontuly, 1977). Efforts to estimate relative changes in productivity were problematic, however, partly for lack of time series data on capital stock by area type. This hindered the development of credible estimates of total factor productivity growth. Such data were constructed for US cities and states by Fogarty and Garofalo (1982) and Garofalo and Malhotra (1985), and were used in studies of productivity growth in large MSAs between 1957 and 1977 in Fogarty and Garofalo (1988) and for 1959 to 1982 in Beeson (1990). These studies all related only to manufacturing.

As discussed above, Fogarty and Garofalo (1988) found strong evidence supporting the existence of both economies of scale internal to the industry (localisation economies), and of economies of scale related to city size (economies of urbanisation). In addition, they found evidence of specific economies of employment density as measured by the manufacturing employment density gradient and the density of manufacturing employment in the central city. Together with this evidence of various agglomeration economies, they also established a significant negative relationship between city age and its manufacturing productivity as well as significant regional variations. They did this on the basis of estimating a Variable Elasticity of Substitution production function for manufacturing for a pooled time series dataset across the 13 MSAs, for which they had both capital stock data and manufacturing employment density gradients (from Mills, 1972). This fitted the data well, with all coefficients having the expected signs. Since the functional form estimated for both city size and employment density was quadratic, it was possible to estimate values of the employment density gradient ($-0.5$) and city size (population 2.9 million) which were associated with maximum total factor productivity in manufacturing.

These strong results on agglomeration economies compared to previous studies (such as, for example, Moomaw, 1985) did not provide an explanation of either decentralisation or the shift of manufacturing employment and population to smaller cities. Indeed, they suggested these were seemingly "irrational" and associated with a slowdown of productivity growth. As they acknowledge, however, maintenance of productivity advantages in large cities could have been offset by growing cost disadvantages in private inputs or public goods, or in both. Their analysis related essentially to physical relationships between inputs and outputs. Indeed, since manufacturing is a very heterogeneous sector, there could have been composition effects within it with those subsectors enjoying the strongest productivity advantages in large cities remaining there as other subsectors relocated, or differentially grew in smaller cities or nonmetropolitan areas.

Beeson (1990) addressed the issues far more directly, although since the methodology is significantly different from that employed by Fogarty and Garofalo (1988), the results cannot be compared directly. The basic methodology as devised by Denison (1979) and Kendrick and Grossman (1980) is to account for output changes at a national level; and as subsequently adapted by Hulten and Schwab (1984), is to analyse differences in regional manufacturing performance between the Sunbelt and Snowbelt regions of the US. This means that although the same capital stock data are used as in Fogarty and Garofalo (1988), a substantially different model is estimated. The model assumes no agglomeration economies associated with spatial structure and any economies of scale are reflected in a Hicks-neutral shift parameter. Total factor returns are estimated essentially as a residual, since the contribution to changes in output of changes in inputs, other than land, can be measured directly (with some quite strong assumptions).

The economic space of the US is then divided into 45 large MSAs (each with $2 billion or more value added in manufacturing in 1978), and areas outside the MSAs. The MSAs of New England are excluded from the analysis because of lack of data on capital stock, but there is a further division between the large MSAs and non-MSAs of four regions: the Manufacturing Belt (as defined by Beeson (1990)), South, West and West North Central. The main findings are that there was, in fact, a nontrivial gain in total factor productivity in the large MSAs relative to the non-MSA areas between 1959 and 1978. This accounted for an estimated 70% of their growth in manufacturing output. The growth of output in the non-MSAs relative to the large MSAs over the period was accounted for by the increase in inputs, especially capital. Breaking it down into subperiods showed that the main growth of relative productivity in the large MSAs was in the period 1965–1973, but this coincided with the strongest relative gain in factor inputs in the non-MSA areas and the strongest shift of value added away from the large MSAs. The overall gap between value added growth in the large MSAs relative to the non-MSA areas was reduced very substantially between 1965–1973 and 1973–1978 in all regions except the Manufacturing Belt, where it widened sharply.

It may be argued that these findings still leave the issue of causation wide open. Beeson's (1990) results are not inconsistent with a combination of relative cost changes favouring the areas outside the large MSAs, leading to a shift of investment to such areas despite the increasing productivity advantages of the large MSA economies. Indeed, it would even appear possible that the shift of

investment to the areas outside the large MSAs partly caused their increased productivity advantages because of the composition effect in manufacturing activity
that it induced. In that context, it may be worth noting that the timing of the
greatest gains in relative productivity in the large MSAs coincided with their
greatest period of relative loss of factor inputs.

## 5. Some recent trends

Because of the limitations on data availability, the work done on recent trends in
cities is, not surprisingly, more descriptive than analytical. Demographic data—
especially for the small areas necessary to investigate changes at the urban level—
are the most widely available, up-to-date and straightforward to interpret. Since
recent trends necessarily rely on up-to-date information their study tends to rely
on demographic data. Except where noted, the work discussed in this section uses
straightforward tabulations, or variants of the devices employed by researchers
such as Vining and Strauss (1977) or Hall and Hay (1980). Nevertheless, analysis
of trends in sizes and the distribution of the urban populations to 1990 or 1991 are
available for western Europe (Cheshire, 1995), Australia (Maher, 1993), Canada
and the US (Bourne, 1995); and to 1994 for the US (Long and Nucci, 1995).

Although, as Bourne (1995) suggests, it represents a diverse landscape of
change, some patterns do appear. In mature economies, suburbanisation was
almost universal from the 1950s, but in the US and in some of the countries
of northern Europe, such as the UK, not only did decentralisation accelerate in
the 1970s but it took a new form. Tales of the revival of rural areas (starting
with Beale, 1975) may have turned out to be oversimplifications or related to an
ephemeral phenomenon. Much of the growth in nonmetropolitan areas in the US
appeared, on close examination (Vining and Strauss, 1977), to have been in rural
counties contiguous to metropolitan areas and, therefore, more of an extension
of suburbanisation to ex-urban fringe counties. It was not so much a question
of a rural revival as of "the cities moving to the countryside" (Leven, 1978).
Nevertheless, even though it may not have lasted, there were remote rural areas
that experienced growth during the early 1970s for the first time in the twentieth century. The growth of population in US nonmetropolitan areas combined
increased from 2.5% in the 1960s to 14.4% in the 1970s while, between the same
two decades, growth of population for the US as a whole declined from 13.4
to 11.4%) (Bourne, 1995). Within metropolitan areas, there was a substantial
dispersion of people to less densely populated counties (Long and Nucci, 1995)
and the central cities compared to the suburbs did markedly worse, not only in

terms of population growth but also on economic indicators such as employment, migration and relative property price changes (Linneman and Summers, 1993; Jensen and Leven, 1997). There was a sense in which, not only in the US, the 1970s represented a "clean break with the past".

Breaks, however, do not necessarily continue. The first commentators to note some urban population revival were Cheshire (1987) in Europe, and Long and DeAre (1988) and Frey (1993) in the US. In some of the large FURs of northern Europe, such as London (Champion and Congdon, 1987) and Copenhagen (Matthiessen, 1983), the maximum rate of outflow of migrants from the core cities was observed in 1971 or 1972. Although loss continued, the rate of loss from migration fell continuously until about 1980, and positive migration gain was observed for a few years in the early 1980s. Dangschat (1993) reports that the population of inner West Berlin, which had declined continuously from 1950, began to increase in 1985 and continued to do so until and including 1991. Annual data on changes in the concentration of population for three categories of area in the US—all counties, Bureau of Economic Analysis (BEA) Economic Areas, and BEA Metropolitan Economic Areas (broadly identifiable with FURs)—show similar patterns (Long and Nucci, 1995). From the first year for which the necessary data became available, 1970, concentration was falling in all three types of area. The county based index was the earliest to show a change of trend. It began to move towards concentration in the second half of the 1970s. Positive concentration began to occur between 1982 and 1983. This was quickly followed by positive concentration appearing in the indices for the other two types of areas. Concentration in all three, however, peaked in the mid- to late 1980s. By 1990 to 1991, all three were showing that population deconcentration was present again.

Somewhat more analytical approaches—but including data only to 1990 or 1991—have been adopted by Cheshire (1995) and Jensen and Leven (1997). Cheshire showed that the steady movement towards decentralisation in the largest FURs of western Europe (those with populations of more than one-third of a million) that had been observed gathering pace in each decade from 1950 to 1980, partially reversed in the 1980s. The percentage of core cities gaining population increased between 1975–1981 and 1981–1991 from 22 to 47% in northern Europe and from 40 to 48% in France and northern Italy. Decentralisation continued to spread to the cities of the south of Europe.

The change in trends in European cities was more in terms of relative changes than of absolute ones. Looking at patterns of "turnaround"—that is, the difference in rates of population change between core cities and hinterlands in the 1980s compared to the 1970s—there were many cases where a strong turnaround was observed but the FUR continued to lose population overall. Glasgow was such a city. In the 1980s, however, the rate of loss was much higher from the hinterland or suburbs than from the city core. Nevertheless, those cities in northern Europe with the strongest turnaround tended to share characteristics; they were significantly more likely to be medium sized than the very largest cities (defined as those FURs with a core city exceeding 200,000). Cities with stronger amenities, historic cores and strong service sectors were also more strongly represented. In the UK, for example, Oxford, Cambridge and Canterbury were the three cities with the most significant turnaround. Overall, the message appeared to be that urban recovery and recentralisation was partial and selective and likely to be related to the growth of service employment, falling household sizes and increased labour force participation rates.

Jensen and Leven (1997) show that on the basis of rather strong assumptions, relative rates of change in the measure of quality of life (QOL), developed by Blomquist et al. (1988), can be calculated from data available for central cities and for the metropolitan area as a whole. They derived a simple model. This implied that if house prices in the core are rising, or wages are falling relative to the metropolitan area as a whole, then the QOL of the central city is relatively rising: and when net migration into, or labour supply in, the central city is rising relative to the metropolitan area as a whole, similarly the QOL of the central city is rising relative to the metropolitan area. The advantage of this approach is that since it rests on revealed preference, it can be applied in the absence of information on amenities contributing directly to QOL. Not only are there strong assumptions, however, but not all the appropriate data were available. Particularly, wages for homogeneous labour were unavailable and they had to proxy this with family incomes, offset with a crude measure of changes in human capital. They then calculate the values for these changes in relative QOL for the 25 largest MSAs combined and for each decade from 1950 to 1990.

The results are quite strong and consistent. All indicators except the wage proxy point in the same direction and show statistically significant changes in the relative position of central cities compared to the metropolitan areas. Between the 1970s and 1980s there was a sharp change of trend in central city house prices compared to those in the metropolitan areas and rather less sharp changes in trend in the other indicators. The Jensen and Leven (1997) analysis supports the view that there was significant improvement in the central cities of the 25 largest US MSAs during the 1980s compared to the 1970s. Their tests of significance are invalid for individual MSAs, although the data suggests that there was substantial variation.

The general conclusion of this section is that despite the fact that the experience of individual cities seems to have become more varied, internationally, at least within the industrialised/post-industrial countries for which there have been studies, there is stronger evidence of a predictable pattern than might be expected, given the diversity and variety of cities. It is not that all cities move in the same direction, or that all cities of a particular size grow or decline. It is rather that patterns which are identified in one country have a remarkable tendency to appear in others—either simultaneously, or with some more or less a predictable delay. Explanations of these patterns have been offered but are sofar less than wholly convincing. There are problems with respect to theory and the availability of appropriate data. The fact that there are patterns suggests, however, that explanations are possible. In other words, this chapter can conclude with the recommendation beloved of researchers: more research is needed.

# References

Abdel-Rahman, H.M. (1990), "Agglomeration economies, types and sizes of cities", Journal of Urban Economics 27:23–45.

Abdel-Rahman, H.M. and M. Fujita (1990), "Product variety, Marshallian externalities and city size", Journal of Regional Science 30:165–183.

Abdel-Rahman, H.M. and M. Fujita (1993), "Specialisation and diversification in a system of cities", Journal of Urban Economics 33:189–222.

Ades, A.F. and E.L. Glaeser (1995), "Trade and circuses: explaining urban giants", The Quarterly Journal of Economics CX:195–227.

Allen, G.R.P. (1954), "The 'courbe des populations': a further analysis", Bulletin of the Oxford University Institute of Statistics 16:179–189.

Alonso, W. (1964), Location and Land Use: Toward a General Theory of Land Rent (Harvard University Press, Cambridge).

Alperovich, G.A. (1985), "Urban spatial structure and income: new estimates", Journal of Urban Economics 18:278–290.

Alperovich, G.A. (1988), "A new testing procedure of the rank size distribution", Journal of Urban Economics 23:251–259.

Alperovich, G.A. (1989), "The distribution of city size: a sensitivity analysis", Journal of Urban Economics 25:93–102.

Alperovich, G.A. (1993a), "City size and the rate and duration of unemployment: evidence from Israeli data", Journal of Urban Economics 34: 347–357.

Alperovich, G.A. (1993b), "An explanatory model of city-size distribution: evidence from cross-country data", Urban Studies 30:1591–1601.

Alperovich, G.A. (1995), "The relationship between income inequality and city size: a general equilibrium model of an open system of cities approach", Urban Studies 32:853–862.

Anas, A. and L. Moses (1978), "Transportation and land use in the mature metropolis", in: C.L. Leven, ed., The Mature Metropolis (D.C. Heath, Lexington).

Andersson, A.E. (1985), "The four logistical revolutions", Presidential address to the 32nd North American Congress, Regional Science Association.

Auerbach, F. (1913), "Das Gesetz der Bevölkerungskoncentration", Petermanns Geographische Mitteilungen 59:74–76.

Beale, C.L. (1975), The Revival of Population Growth in Non-Metropolitan America (US Department of Agriculture, Washington DC), ERS 605.

Beckmann, M.J. (1958), "City hierarchies and distribution of city size", Economic Development and Cultural Change VI:243–248.

Beckmann, M.J. and J.C. McPherson (1970), "City size distribution in a central place hierarchy: an alternative approach", Journal of Regional Science 10:25–33.

Beeson, P.E. (1990), "Sources of the decline of manufacturing in large metropolitan areas", Journal of Urban Economics 28:71–86.

Begović, B. (1992), "Industrial diversification and city size: the case of Yugoslavia", Urban Studies 29:77–88.

Berry, B.J.L. (1961), "City size distributions and economic development", Economic Development and Cultural Change 9:573–587.

Berry, B.J.L. (1973), Growth Centres in the American Urban System (Ballinger, Cambridge, MA).

Berry, B.J.L. (1976), Urbanisation and Counterurbanisation (Sage, Beverly Hills).

Berry, B.J.L. and W. Garrison (1958), "Alternative explanations of urban rank-size relationships", Annals of American Geographers 48:83–91.

Blomquist, G.C., M.C. Berger and J.P. Hoehn (1988), "New estimates of the quality of life in urban areas", American Economic Review 78:89–107.

Bourne, L.S. (1995), Urban Growth and Population Redistribution in North America: A Diverse and Unequal Landscape, Major Report 32 (Centre for Urban and Community Studies, University of Toronto).

Box, G.E.P. and D.R. Cox (1964), "An analysis of transformations", Journal of the Royal Statistical Society, Series B 26:211–243.

Bradford, D. and Kelejian, H. (1973), "An econometric model of flight to the suburbs", Journal of Political Economy 81:566–589.

Cameron, T.A. (1990), "One stage structural models to explain city size", Journal of Urban Economics 27:294–307.

Carlino, G.A. (1985), "Declining city productivity and the growth of rural regions: a test of alternative explanations", Journal of Urban Economics 18:11–27.

Champion, A.G. (1989), Counterurbanisation: The Changing Pace and Nature of Population Deconcentration (Edward Arnold, London).

Champion, A.G. and P. Congdon (1987), "An analysis of the recovery of London's population change rate", Built Environment 13:193–211.

Chan, M.L.W. and D.C. Mountain (1983), "Economies of scale and the tornquist discrete measure of productivity growth", Review of Economics and Statistics 65:663–667.

Cheshire, P.C. (1987), "Economic factors in urban change: European prospects", Discussion Papers in Urban and Regional Economics, Series C, No. 30 (University of Reading).

Cheshire, P.C. (1995), "A new phase of urban development in Western Europe? The evidence for the 1980s", Urban Studies 32:1045–1063.

Cheshire, P.C. and G. Gorla (1987), "The effects of Western European integration on Europe's urban system", paper given to the XXVII European Congress of Regional Science, Athens.

Cheshire, P.C. and D.G. Hay (1989), Urban Problems in Western Europe: an Economic Analysis (Unwin Hyman, London).

Christaller, W. (1933), Die zentralen orte in Süddeutschland, Jena: Verlag Gustav Fischer: published in English (1966) as The Central Places of Southern Germany (Prentice-Hall, Englewood Cliffs, NJ).

Clark, C. (1945), "The economic functions of a city in relation to its size", Econometrica 13:97–113.

Clark, C. (1951), "Urban population densities", Journal of the Royal Statistical Society, Series A 114:490–496.

Cooke, T. (1978), "Causality reconsidered: a note", Journal of Urban Economics 5:538–542.

Cooke, T.W. (1983), "Testing a model of intraurban firm relocation", Journal of Urban Economics 13:257–282.

Dangschat, J.S. (1993), "Berlin and the German system of cities", Urban Studies 30:1025–1051.

Denison, E.F. (1979), Accounting for Slower Economic Growth: The United States in the 1970s (The Brookings Institution, Washington DC).

Dunning, J.H. (1969) "The city of London: a case study in urban economics", Town Planning Review 40:207–232.

Eaton, J. and Z. Eckstein (1997), "Cities and growth: theory and evidence from France and Japan", Regional Science and Urban Economics 27:443–474.

Evans, A.W. (1972), "The pure theory of city size in an industrial economy", Urban Studies 9:49–77.

Evans, A.W. (1973), The Economics of Residential Location (Macmillan, London).

Fogarty, M.S. and G.A. Garofalo (1982), "Estimates of the returns to scale in the manufacturing sector of older cities: how important are capital stock estimates?", paper given to the Western Regional Science Association Meeting, Santa Barbara.

Fogarty, M.S. and G.A. Garofalo (1988), "Urban spatial structure and productivity growth in the manufacturing sector of cities", Journal of Urban Economics 23:60–70.

Frey, W.H. (1993), "The new urban revival in the United States", Urban Studies 30:741–777.

Fujita, M. (1989), Urban Economic Theory: Land Use and City Size (Cambridge University Press, Cambridge).

Fujita, M. and T. Mori (1997), "Structural stability and evolution of urban systems", Regional Science and Urban Economics 27:300–442.

Garofalo, G.A. and D.M. Malhotra (1985), "The impact of changes in input prices on net investment in US manufacturing", Atlantic Economic Journal 13:52–63.

Goddard, J. (1973), Office Location in Urban and Regional Development (Oxford University Press, Oxford).

Grubb, W. (1982), "The flight to the suburbs of population and people, 1960–1970", Journal of Urban Economics 11:348–367.

Guérin-Pace, F. (1995), "Rank-size distribution and the process of urban growth", Urban Studies 32:551–562.

Hall, P.G. and D.G. Hay (1980), Growth Centres in the European Urban System (Heinemann Educational, London).

Henderson, J.V. (1974), "The sizes and types of cities", American Economic Review 64:640–656.

Henderson, J.V. (1977), Economic Theory and the Cities (Academic Press, New York).

Henderson, J.V. (1986), "Efficiency of resource usage and city size", Journal of Urban Economics 19:47–70.

Henderson, J.V. (1987), "General equilibrium modelling of systems of cities", in: E.S. Mills, ed., Handbook of Regional and Urban Economics, vol. II, Urban Economics (North-Holland, Amsterdam).

Henderson, J.V. (1988), Urban Development: Theory, Fact and Illusion (Oxford University Press, New York).

Hsing, Y. (1990), "A note on functional forms and the urban size distribution", Journal of Urban Economics 27:73–79.

Hulten, C.R. and R.M. Schwab (1984), "Regional productivity growth in U.S. manufacturing, 1951–1978", American Economic Review 74:152–162.

Jensen, M.J. and C.L. Leven (1997), "Quality of Life in Central Cities and Suburbs", Annals of Regional Science 31:431–449.

Kamecke, U. (1990), "Testing the rank size rule hypothesis with an efficient estimator", Journal of Urban Economics 27:222–231.

Kendrick, J.W. and E.S. Grossman (1980), Productivity in the United States: Trends and Cycles (The John Hopkins University Press, Baltimore).

Klaassen, L.H., W.T.M. Molle and J.H.P. Paelinck (eds) (1981), Dynamics of Urban Development (Aldershot, Gower).

Krugman, P. (1993), "First nature, second nature and metropolitan location", Journal of Regional Science 33:129–144.

Krugman, P. (1996), "Confronting the mystery of urban hierarchy", paper given to the TCER-NBER-CEPR trilateral conference, Economics of Agglomeration, Tokyo.

Krugman, P. and R. Livas (1992), "Trade policy and the third world metropolis", NBER Working Paper No. 4238.

Leven, C.L. (1968), "Determinants of the size and form of urban areas", Regional Science Association: Papers XXII:7–19.

Leven, C.L. (1978), The Mature Metropolis (D. C. Heath, Lexington, MA).

Linneman, P.D. and A.A. Summers (1993), "Patterns and Processes of Employment and Population Decentralisation in the United States, 1970–1987", in: A.A. Summers, P.C. Cheshire and L. Senn, eds., Urban Change in the United States and Western Europe: Comparative Analysis and Policy (The Urban Institute Press, Washington DC, pp. 87–144).

Long, L. and D. DeAre (1988), "U.S. population redistribution: a perspective on the nonmetropolitan turnaround", Population and Development Review 14:433–450.

Long, L. and A. Nucci (1995), "The 'Clean Break' revisited: is US population again deconcentrating?", Mimeo (US Bureau of the Census).

Lösch, A. (1940), Die räumliche ordnung der Wirtschaft, Jena: Gustav Fischer, Published in English as Lösch, A. (1954), The Economics of Location (Yale University Press, New Haven).

Madden, C.J. (1956), "Some indicators of stability in the growth of cities in the United States", Economic Development and Cultural Change 4:236–452.

Maher, C. (1993), "Recent trends in Australian urban development: locational change and the policy quandary", Urban Studies 30:797–825.

Malecki, E.J. (1980), "Growth and change in the analysis of rank-size distributions: empirical findings", Environment and Planning B 12:41–52.

Margo, R.A. (1992), "Explaining the postwar suburbanisation of population in the United States: the role of income", Journal of Urban Economics 31:301–310.

Matthiessen, C.W. (1983) 'Settlement change in Denmark", in: C.W. Matthiessen, ed., Urban Policy and Urban Development in the 80s; Danish Experience in a European Context (University of Copenhagen).

Mills, E.S. (1972), Studies in the Structure of the Urban Economy (John Hopkins University Press, Baltimore).

Mills, E.S. (1992), "The measurement and determinants of suburbanisation", Journal of Urban Economics 32:377–387.

Moomaw, R.L. (1985), "Firm Location and City Size: Reduced Productivity Advantages as a Factor in the Decline of Manufacturing in Urban Areas", Journal of Urban Economics 17:73–89.

Muth, R.F. (1969), Cities and Housing (Chicago University Press, Chicago).

Nakamura, R. (1985), "Agglomeration economies in urban manufacturing industries: a case of Japanese cities", Journal of Urban Economics 17:108–124.

Nordbeck, S. (1971), "Urban Allometric Growth", Geografiska Annaler 53B:54–67.

Osada, S. (1997), "The development of the Japanese urban system, 1970 to 1990", paper presented to Economic Geography Graduate Workshop (London School of Economics and Political Science).

Palumbo, G., S. Sacks and M. Wasylenko (1990), "Population Decentralisation within metropolitan areas: 1970–1980", Journal of Urban Economics 27:151–167.

Parr, J.B. (1985), "A note on the size distribution of cities over time", Journal of Urban Economics 18:199–212.

Richardson, H.W. (1973) The Economics of Urban Size (Saxon House, Farnborough).

Rosen, K.T. and M. Resnick (1980), "The size distribution of cities: an examination of the Pareto law and primacy", Journal of Urban Economics 8:165–186.

Saxenian, A.L. (1993), Regional Networks: Industrial Adaptation in Silicon Valley and Route 128 (Harvard University Press, Cambridge, MA).

Selting, A., C. Allanach and S. Loveridge (1994), "The role of agglomeration economies in firm location: a review of the literature", Staff papers (Department of Agriculture and Applied Economics, University of Minnesota).

Simon, H. (1955), "On a class of skew distribution functions", Biometrika 42:425–440.

Singer, H.W. (1936), "The 'courbe des populations': a parallel to Pareto's law", Economic Journal 46:254–263.

Steinnes, D. (1977), "Causality and intraurban location", Journal of Urban Economics 4:69–79.

Steinnes, D. (1982), "Do 'people follow jobs' or 'jobs follow people'?: a causality issue in urban economics", Urban Studies 19:187–192.

Suarez-Villa, L. (1988), "Metropolitan evolution, sectoral economic change, and the city size distribution", Urban Studies 25:1–20.

Sveikauskas, L., J. Gowdy and M. Funk (1988), "Urban productivity: city size or industry size", Journal of Regional Science 28:185–202.

Thurston, L. and A.M.J. Yezer (1994), "Causality in the suburbanisation of population and employment", Journal of Urban Economics 35:105–118.

Tinbergen, J. (1968), "The hierarchy model of the size distribution of centres", Papers and Proceedings of the Regional Science Association 20:65–68.

Upton, C. (1981), "An equilibrium model of city sizes", Journal of Urban Economics 15:15–36.

Van den Berg, L. (1987), Urban Systems in a Dynamic Society (Gower, Aldershot, UK).

Van den Berg, L., R. Drewett, L.H. Klaassen, A. Rossi and C.H.T. Vijverberg (1982), Urban Europe: A Study of Growth and Decline (Pergamon Press, Oxford).

Vapnarsky, C.A. (1969), "On rank size distributions of cities: an ecological approach", Economic Development and Cultural Change 17:584–595.

Vining, R. (1955), "A description of certain spatial aspects of an economic system", Economic Development and Cultural Change 3:147–195.

Vining, D.R. (1977), "The rank size rule in the absence of growth", Journal of Urban Economics 4:15–29.

Vining, D.R. and T. Kontuly (1977), "Increasing returns to city size in the face of an impending decline in the size of large cities: which is the bogus fact?", Environment and Planning A 9:59–62.

Vining, D.R. and T. Kontuly (1978), "Population dispersal from major metropolitan regions: an international comparison", International Regional Science Review 3:49–73.

Vining, D.R. and A. Strauss (1977), "A demonstration that the current deconcentration of population in the United States is a clean break with the past", Environment and Planning A 9:751–758.

Vining, D.R. and C.H. Yang (1979), "Population dispersal from core regions: a description and tentative explanation of the patterns of 17 countries", in: T. Kawashima, ed., Urbanisation Processes: Experiences of Eastern and Western Countries, vol. 2 (Pergamon Press, Oxford).

Wheaton, W.C. and H. Shishado (1981), "Urban concentration, agglomeration economies and the level of economic development", Economic Development and Cultural Change 30:17–30.

Wingo, L. (1961), Transportation and Urban Land (Resources for the Future, Washington DC).

Zipf, G.K. (1949), Human Behaviour and the Principle of Least Effort (Addison-Wesley, Reading, MA).

*Chapter 36*

# URBAN AREAS WITH DECENTRALIZED EMPLOYMENT: THEORY AND EMPIRICAL WORK

MICHELLE J. WHITE*

*University of Michigan*

## Contents

* I am grateful for comments from Charles Becker, Paul Cheshire, Ken Small, John Yinger and Stephen Ross. I am also grateful for research support from the Economic Policy Research Unit, Copenhagen Business School, Copenhagen, Denmark, where I was a visitor while writing this chapter.

*Handbook of Regional and Urban Economics. Edited by E.S. Mills and P. Cheshire*

## Abstract

This chapter discusses theoretical and applied research in urban economics on decentralized cities, i.e., cities in which employment is not restricted to the central business district. The first section discusses informally the incentives that firms face to suburbanize. The next section summarizes the theoretical literature on decentralized cities, including both models which solve for the optimal spatial pattern of employment and models in which the spatial pattern of employment is exogenously determined. In other sections, I discuss rent and wage gradients in decentralized cities and review the empirical literature testing whether, or not, wage gradients exist in urban areas. A section covers the question of whether people follow jobs or jobs follow people to the suburbs and the last section discusses the "wasteful" commuting controversy.

**Keywords:** Suburbanization, polycentric (urban) models, monocentric (urban) models, wage gradients, decentralized cities, wasteful commuting

## 1. Introduction

Although urban economists often assume that employment in urban areas is concentrated at the central business district (CBD), in actuality urban employment has been suburbanizing for a long time. The best evidence available over a long timespan comes from the two-point density gradients for employment and population first estimated by Mills (1972, Chap. 3) and updated by Macauley (1985). Two-point population density gradients are calculated by solving for the exponential function that fits the two observations of population density and average distance from the CBD for the central city and the suburbs. Two-point employment density gradients are calculated by the same procedure using data for the employment density. The resulting density gradient measures the percentage decrease in population or employment density per mile of distance from the CBD, where a smaller density gradient indicates greater suburbanization. For 18 metropolitan areas in the US, the average density gradients in 1948 were 0.58 for population, compared to 0.68 for manufacturing employment, 0.88 for retailing employment, 0.97 for service employment and 1.00 for employment in wholesaling. For the same metropolitan areas in 1977/80, the figures were 0.24 for population, 0.32 for manufacturing, 0.30 for retailing, 0.38 for services and 0.37 for wholesaling. The decline over the period was 59% for population, 53% for manufacturing employment, 66% for retailing employment, 61% for service employment and 63% for wholesaling. Thus, while population was, and still is, more suburbanized than employment, employment (except in manufacturing) has been suburbanizing faster than population. Overall, the levels of suburbanization of employment and population are converging, with manufacturing and retailing employment the closest to convergence.[1]

In this chapter, I discuss theoretical and applied research in urban economics on decentralized cities, i.e., those in which employment is not restricted to the CBD. In Section 2, I discuss informally the incentives that firms face to stay at the CBD versus to move to the suburbs. In Section 3, I summarize the theoretical literature on decentralized cities. Separate subsections deal with (a) models that derive the optimal spatial location pattern for employment, and (b) models that assume an exogenously determined spatial location pattern for employment and explore its effects on other aspects of resource allocation in urban areas. In Section 4, I discuss the basic model of rent and wage gradients in a decentralized city. In Section 5, empirical research testing for whether, or not, wage gradients exist in urban areas is reviewed. Section 6 discusses the empirical literature on whether population suburbanization follows employment suburbanization or vice versa, i.e., do jobs follow people or people follow jobs? Section 7 discusses and appraises the controversy concerning whether, or not, more commuting occurs in decentralized cities than in urban economic models predict.

A few notes on terminology. Incommuting refers to radial commuting that is toward the CBD in the morning, while outcommuting refers to radial commuting that is away from the CBD in the morning. Circumferential commuting refers to any commuting journey that begins and ends on different rays from the CBD. The original urban models in which all jobs are located at the CBD are often referred to as monocentric models, but this term has also been applied to models in which some jobs are located outside the CBD, as long as jobs remain more centralized than housing and all commuting is incommuting. Nonmonotonic or polycentric models are then those in which employment is decentralized and at least some outcommuting and/or circumferential commuting occurs. In this chapter I refer to all models in which there is non-CBD employment as decentralized urban models.

---

[1] Mills also finds similar results for a smaller sample of US metropolitan areas over a longer time period.

## 2. Why do firms suburbanize?

The original urban models assumed that all jobs were located at the CBD. This assumption made for tractability—an important consideration. It was also appealing since, historically, CBDs tended to develop at a transportation node, usually a port. Firms located at the CBD minimized the cost of goods transportation since doing so was valuable because workers could walk but goods could not. A CBD location also allowed firms access to power and utilities that originally were only available near the CBD.

Now consider the basic factors that cause employment in cities to move out of the CBD. Suppose a hypothetical firm is located at the CBD but is considering moving to a more suburban location. Firms that consider moving out of the CBD face tradeoffs since some costs rise while others fall. As long as the firm's move causes its workers' commuting distances to fall, then workers save on commuting costs and the firm can capture some of this savings in the form of lower wages. Second, the price of land declines at a decreasing rate with the distance from the CBD. Therefore, firms that move out of the CBD benefit from lower land costs which allow them to trade capital for land, i.e., they occupy low, horizontal buildings instead of tall, vertical buildings. Third, goods transportation costs may decline since the firm avoids the traffic congestion of the CBD. Fourth, loss of agglomeration economies at the CBD may cause the firms' productivity to fall. Finally, other costs faced by firms may also change when they move to the suburbs. Costs related to information technology—which are changing rapidly—are an example. Consider these factors individually.

First, firms have an incentive to suburbanize because they can pay lower wages, which workers are willing to accept because they commute less. Since wages are the largest single cost for many firms, this is likely to be an important consideration. However, the extent to which suburbanizing allows firms to pay lower wages depends on labor demand and supply. Suppose all firms are initially located at the CBD and workers commute along straight lines connecting their homes and their workplaces.[2] An arbitrary firm $X$ moves from the CBD to a new location five miles south of the CBD, shown as point $A$ in Fig. 1. All other firms still remain at the CBD. At its new location, suppose firm $X$ hires only workers who live further out than the firm in the same direction away from the CBD, i.e., along the line segment $Aa$. Therefore, all the firm's workers save 10 miles of commuting per day by shifting from CBD jobs to jobs at firm $X$. If

---

[2] A more realistic model would take the specifics of the transportation network into account, so that workers would commute from their homes to their workplaces along existing road or rail networks. This modification would not change the general results discussed here.

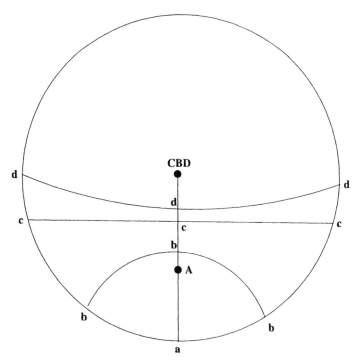

Fig. 1. Commuting regions when a firm moves from the CBD to point A.

the daily wage at the CBD is $w^*$ and the cost of commuting per mile is $t$, then workers will be willing to work at $A$ for a daily wage of $w^* - 10t$ and the firm can save $10t$ per worker per day by moving. However, only workers who live along line segment $Aa$ will be willing to work at $A$ for this wage; all others prefer to continue working at the CBD. Now suppose firm $X$ wishes to hire more workers than are willing to work for it at the wage $w^* - 10t$. If it raises its wage above $w^* - 10t$, then its commuting region will expand from the line segment $Aa$ in Fig. 1 to a larger region such as that enclosed by the line $bbb$. At the higher wage, some workers commute to firm $X$ from homes that are not on the same ray from the CBD as firm $X$ (i.e., they commute circumferentially) and a few workers outcommute.[3] As firm $X$ continues to raise its wage, its commuting region continues to get larger. Now suppose the suburban firm pays the same wage $w^*$ as CBD firms. Then its commuting region will be the area below the

---

[3] Commuting is still along straight lines connecting workers' residences and their workplaces, but the commuting routes are no longer radial. The outer boundary of the urban area also bulges outward in the area closest to the suburban firm, but this effect is not shown in Fig. 1.

horizontal line *ccc*, which bisects the line segment connecting the CBD and point
*A*. If firm *X* pays a higher wage than $w^*$, then its commuting region will be the
area below an upward curving line such as *ddd*. However, even if firm *X* pays
higher than the CBD wage $w^*$, its commuting region will be smaller than the
CBD firms and restricted to workers who live in the southern region of the urban
area. Thus, firms that move out of the CBD can pay lower wages only if their
commuting regions shrink from covering the entire urban area to covering just
a region around their suburban sites. If suburban firms are relatively large and
have relatively high demand for labor, then they may have to pay wages as high
or higher than CBD firms.[4]

Now suppose an additional firm *Y* moves out of the CBD. As long as there
are no agglomeration economies outside of the CBD, firm *Y* has an incentive
to locate north rather than south of the CBD. This is because if firm *Y* locates
north of the CBD, then it will gain from the same wage reduction (discussed
above) in connection with firm *X*. But if firm *Y* locates south of the CBD, then it
must compete with firm *X* for labor and both firms will have to pay higher wages.
Thus, as firms suburbanize, they have an incentive to locate in different directions
around the CBD and, in particular, to avoid suburban regions that already have
high concentrations of firms.

Now consider the firms' gain from suburbanizing due to the lower cost of
suburban land. The extent to which the firms' land costs fall in the suburbs also
depends on the workers' commuting patterns. Suppose we change the previous
model by assuming that all workers commute via a fixed rail network, that consists of radial lines leading out from the CBD in different directions. Firm *X*
again plans to move out of the CBD. Only sites located near public transit stations
would be plausible suburban locations for firm *X*, since workers must be able to
walk to work from the station. But this means that the supply of suburban sites
suitable for use by firm *X* is limited to sites close to transit stations and the price
of these sites is high because their accessibility makes them valuable for high
density residential use. These factors reduce firm *X*'s gain from suburbanizing.
In addition, the gain to firm *X* from reduced wages at suburban locations is also
small in this case, because only workers who live along the same radial transit
line as firm *X*'s suburban location have shorter commuting journeys when they
commute to firm *X* rather than to the CBD. (If workers must travel to the CBD
along one transit route and then outcommute to firm *X* along another transit
route, then they will be unwilling to work at firm *X* if it pays less than the wage

---

[4] See Wieand (1987) and White (1988b) for discussion.

at the CBD.) Thus, firms gain little due to lower land costs or wages in the suburbs when workers commute by fixed rail transit systems.

But now suppose that workers begin to commute by car and the road network is more dense than the fixed rail network. As a result, firm $X$ is less restricted in its choice of suburban sites because workers who commute by car can reach sites that are inaccessible by public transit. The resulting increase in the supply of suburban sites suitable for non-residential use lowers the firms' cost of land, which increases their gain from suburbanizing. In addition, the region from which workers are willing to commute to suburban firms at any given wage also increases and, therefore, wage costs in the suburbs fall. These trends are self-reinforcing. As more workers commute by car, suburban firms' labor supply increases, which makes it more attractive for firms to suburbanize. But as more firms suburbanize, an increasing proportion of suburban jobs becomes inaccessible to workers unless they commute by car, so that more workers shift from commuting by public transit to commuting by car.

Let us turn now to transportation costs other than commuting costs. While the monocentric model assumes that firms export their output from the urban area via a transportation node located at the CBD, in fact the transportation node is now more likely to be an airport or a circumferential freeway surrounding the urban area, both of which are located in the suburbs. Thus, firms that move to the suburbs are likely to gain because they avoid the cost of transporting goods to and from the congested CBD. However, some types of firms may be better off remaining at the CBD. Suppose firms sell to customers who are located in the urban area rather than outside and/or they buy from suppliers who are located in the urban area. Also assume that these customers or suppliers are uniformly distributed around the CBD. Then transportation costs are minimized if the firm stays at the CBD. These firms tend to lose customers or suppliers if they move to the suburbs.

Now consider agglomeration economies and their effect on the employment location pattern in urban areas. These are difficult to measure and there is little agreement as to how they work. One assumption that has been used widely in the literature to represent agglomeration economies is that each firm in an urban area transacts with every other firm in the urban area and the cost of these transactions depends on the distance between pairs of firms.[5] This assumption obviously implies that there is a gain from urban area's firms being concentrated at a CBD, since the centralized location pattern reduces the distance between firms. While this model is useful as a starting point, it has some counterintuitive implications.

---

[5] See Capozza (1976), O'Hara (1977), and Ogawa and Fujita (1980).

Suppose we compare two urban areas having a different number of firms. Then the smaller urban area will have an advantage over the larger because total transactions costs among a smaller number of firms are lower. Thus, larger urban areas are predicted to have lower rather than higher agglomeration economies. But this goes against the notion that higher agglomeration economies are responsible for the existence of larger cities. An alternative approach, used by Henderson (1977) and Straszheim (1984) in the urban context and also commonly used in other fields, assumes that production is characterized by external increasing returns as the number of firms or the number of jobs in the city rises.[6] This gives larger cities an advantage over smaller ones which offsets their disadvantage of higher aggregate commuting costs. However, this approach has the drawback that the level of agglomeration economies is the same all over the urban area, regardless of where firms locate. It might be useful to combine these two approaches, since the latter represents the gain from more firms being present in an urban area, while the former represents the cost of capturing these gains through interactions among firms.

What about the issue of how agglomeration economies vary within an urban area? A variation of the external increasing returns approach, used by Wieand (1987), makes agglomeration economies depend on the number of firms located at particular employment sites. Thus, firms located at the CBD benefit from a high level of agglomeration economies, but firms located at a suburban employment subcenter that is smaller than the CBD benefit from a lower level of agglomeration economies. A more general version of this approach is used by Fujita and Ogawa (1982), who allow the level of agglomeration economies to vary continuously over space, depending on the density level of firms at each location. These approaches are useful in exploring what type of firm location pattern is efficient in a decentralized urban area.

It should also be noted that agglomeration economies may differ for different types of firms. For example, computer firms benefit from locating in the "Silicon Valley" area of San Francisco/San Jose because these firms can hire skilled computer engineers without having to bear the costs of their training. But the computer firms themselves are stretched along at least a 20-mile region, which suggests that they do not need to locate close together to benefit from agglomeration economies. In other industries, firms may benefit from being close together because individual firms can closely observe and react to the behavior of competitors. Agglomeration economies also occur across types of firms, for example, job

---

[6] Firms' production function is multiplied by a shift variable $N^\alpha$, where $N$ equals the number of firms or jobs in an urban area and $\alpha > 1$.

Table 1

Profit variations for two firms locating at two alternative sites

|  |  | Firm 2 | |
|  |  | A | B |
| Firm 1 | A | 5, 2 | 1, 2 |
|  | B | 1, 1 | 3, 3 |

sites are more attractive to workers when there are shops and restaurants nearby. These agglomeration economies seem to require proximate location. In general, there has been little research on how agglomeration economies operate within urban areas and how they affect firm location patterns.

An important implication of agglomeration economies, when applied to issues of location within an urban area, is that they may cause development to occur at inefficient locations. Consider a simple model in which there are two alternative sites for a subcenter in a particular urban area or portion of an urban area. The two sites, denoted $A$ and $B$, are both adjacent to freeway intersections. There are two firms, denoted 1 and 2. While either or both firms may locate at either site, agglomeration economies make both firms better off if they locate at the same site. Table 1 shows both firms' profits from locating at each site. Firm 1 makes a profit of 5 at site $A$ and a profit of 3 at site $B$ if both firms locate at the same site, but firm 1 makes a profit of only 1 if the two firms locate at different sites. Firm 2 makes a profit of 3 at site $B$ and a profit of 2 at site $A$ if both firms locate at the same site, but it makes a profit of only 1 if the two firms locate at different sites. If firm 1 moves first and chooses site $A$, then firm 2 will also choose site $A$ and the outcome will be economically efficient since the sum of both firms' profits (7) is maximized. However, if firm 2 moves first and chooses site $B$, then firm 1 will also locate at site $B$. In this case, the outcome will be economically inefficient since the sum of both firms' profits (6) is lower than if they both located at site $A$. The game has multiple equilibria, of which only one is economically efficient. If the game were played many times in different regions by different firms, then we would expect subcenters to develop at a mixture of efficient sites like $A$ and inefficient sites like $B$. Because the model has multiple equilibria, it is difficult to predict in advance where suburban subcenters will develop.[7]

---

[7] Obviously firm 1 can bribe firm 2 to choose site $A$ even if firm 2 moves first. But firm 1 may not be present when firm 2 makes its move and, once firm 2 has chosen site $B$, the costs of moving may exceed the gains from both firms being located at site $A$ rather than site $B$.

Finally, a much-discussed issue affecting firms' incentives to suburbanize is the rapid development of information/communications technology, including use of computers, the internet, high-volume telephone/fax services, picture phones and video conferencing. Many of these new technologies are likely to affect the relative advantage of the CBD versus suburban locations. One example is that when mainframe computers became available, many banks moved their data-processing operations out of the the CBD to suburban sites, because use of computers made it possible to supervise these operations without locating them at their headquarters. But, with high volume telephone lines and personal computers, this type of work can now be done by workers at home, workers living in small towns, or workers located overseas. Video conferencing also substitutes for face-to-face contact and, therefore, reduces the accessibility advantage of being at the CBD. In general, the implications of these new technologies for firm location patterns have not been carefully thought out.

To summarize, firms' incentives to suburbanize are quite complicated and at least some parts of the story are not well understood. Different types of firms are likely to be affected differently depending on the factor intensities of their production processes. Thus, manufacturing firms benefit strongly from suburban locations, because they can spread out their assembly lines horizontally and accommodate their workforces with large surface parking lots. In contrast, specialized service firms and/or headquarters operations may prefer to stay at the CBD where they can observe their competitors and have face-to-face meetings with suppliers or customers located in all directions.

## 3. Theoretical models of decentralized cities

Suppose suburban locations are more profitable for at least some urban firms than CBD locations. In this case, what overall spatial pattern of employment will develop?; is it economically efficient?; and what are its effects on other aspects of resource allocation in urban areas? There are actually two versions of these questions. In one, the main issue is how agglomeration economies and commuting costs affect the optimal and actual spatial patterns of employment and residences in urban areas. The city is assumed to be built from scratch, so there is no presumption that a CBD will exist. In the second, some firms are assumed to move to exogenously determined suburban locations, but the change is incremental and the historic CBD remains. The main focus is on examining the effects of firm suburbanization on residential location and other aspects of resource allocation in cities. I refer to these two literatures as models of endogenously versus exogenously determined employment location. They are discussed separately below.

## 3.1. Models with endogenously determined employment location

Consider the optimal spatial location pattern for firms in an urban model with no history. The earliest approach to this problem was by Mills (1972: chap. 5). Mills analyzed a model of an urban area in which identical firms produce a good using a fixed amount of land, and housing is also produced using a fixed amount of land. Identical workers commute to the firms at a constant cost per unit of distance traveled. Output produced by firms is transported to the CBD, where it is exported, and the cost of goods transport is also constant per unit of distance. The optimal allocation of land to production and housing is the allocation which minimizes the sum of goods transport costs plus workers' commuting costs. Mills (1972) shows that there are two efficient solutions: the "segregated" solution in which land around the CBD is devoted exclusively to production while land surrounding the production area is devoted exclusively to housing, and the "integrated" solution in which production and housing are mixed at all urban locations. The segregated solution holds when the cost of goods transport is high relative to the cost of commuting, since locating production in the CBD minimizes the cost of transporting goods. The integrated solution holds when the cost of commuting is high relative to the cost of goods transport, since commuting is eliminated when all workers work at home. Mills also shows that in this model, the market equilibrium solution is economically efficient.[8]

I documented above the fact that employment has tended to suburbanize more rapidly than population in US cities over the past several decades. This suggests that urban areas in reality have moved from approximating the "segregated" solution to approximating the "integrated" solution in Mills' model. This suggests that the cost of goods transportation must have fallen relative to the cost of commuting—a testable hypothesis.

The paper by Fujita and Ogawa (1982) uses assumptions similar to those of Mills (1972), but adds agglomeration economies to the model. Fujita and Ogawa analyze a straight-line city. Identical firms are again assumed to produce goods using fixed amounts of land and labor and to transport the goods to the CBD for export. The level of agglomeration economies depends on the density of firms at particular locations and may be constant all over the urban area or may differ at different locations. Workers each occupy a constant amount of land and the

---

[8] See Braid (1988) for a dynamic version of Mills' model.

costs of commuting and transporting goods to the export node are both constant per unit of distance. Fujita and Ogawa (1982) solve numerically for the equilibrium outcome, assuming that firms enter the city until profits fall to zero. Because the costs of commuting and of goods transport trade off against variable agglomeration economies, a number of different land use patterns may occur. If agglomeration economies are high at the CBD and decline with distance from the CBD, then firms concentrate at a single CBD surrounded on both sides by housing. If agglomeration economies are constant at all locations and the cost of commuting is high relative to the cost of goods transportation, then a dispersed land use pattern occurs in which all workers work at home. Another possible outcome is an "incompletely mixed urban configuration", in which the center of the urban area is occupied by mixed firms and housing, surrounded on both sides by regions occupied exclusively by firms, while the outer regions of the urban area are occupied exclusively by residences. Workers occupying the central region work at home, while workers occupying the exclusively residential regions commute to firms located in the exclusively business regions. Finally, other possible outcomes include two employment subcenters without a CBD and a CBD plus two subcenters. In all of the solutions, the left and right sides of the urban area are symmetric.[9]

In a model with agglomeration economies, equilibrium outcomes are likely to be inefficient since individual firms ignore the effects of their behavior on the overall level of agglomeration economies and therefore on other firms' costs. Henderson and Slade (1993) extend Fujita and Ogawa's model by making it into a game between two developers. This introduces another set of reasons why the equilibrium outcome may differ from the optimal outcome.[10] In their model, one of the developers develops the lefthand side of the city and the other develops the righthand side. Each builds a development that contains a residential neighborhood and a business district (land uses are not allowed to mix). When the city is small, it is efficient for both developers to locate their business districts at the inner edge of their respective territories, so that they merge and the combined city has a CBD. As the city increases in size, the costs of goods transportation and commuting rise faster than agglomeration economies, so that eventually it becomes efficient for the business district to split in two.

---

[9] Fujita and Ogawa (1982) do not investigate whether, or not, the equilibrium land use outcome differs from the optimal outcome. But in a later paper, Ogawa and Fujita (1989) discuss the relationship between equilibrium versus optimum land allocations in a similar model.

[10] See also Tauchen and Witte (1984), who analyze equilibrium versus optimum land use allocations in a model of a CBD with agglomeration economies. They show that an inefficient number of firms enters the urban area in the equilibrium outcome. Helsley and Sullivan (1991) investigate the possibility that different employment subcenters could have different production technologies or could have external effects.

At that point, each developer locates its business district at approximately the center of its territory, with residential neighborhoods on both sides, so that there are two equal sized business districts—one on each side of the city. However, Henderson and Slade (1993) show that when there are two developers, they have an incentive to split the CBD prematurely, i.e., the split occurs at a lower than optimum population level. The reason is that each developer takes account of the agglomeration economies realized by firms in its half of the city, but ignores the agglomeration economies realized by firms in the other half. Thus Henderson and Slade's model provides an example of how strategic considerations, combined with agglomeration economies, may cause the spatial layout of the urban area to be inefficient. In a sequential version of their model, they provide another example of how strategic considerations may distort the spatial layout of the city. In that model, the first developer to enter makes its development inefficiently large in order to capture first mover advantages; while the second developer then makes its development inefficiently small. The result is that the two sides of the city are asymmetric, which is inefficient.

A recent model by Anas and Kim (1994) also examines the equilibrium spatial location pattern in a discrete version of a straight-line city. Anas and Kim do not assume that there are external agglomeration economies, but they make an assumption that urban firms sell their output directly to the households who live in the urban area. These shopping interactions between firms and households are similar to the transactions between pairs of firms that formed the basis of early models of urban agglomeration economies. Workers (or their families) thus take shopping trips to buy from firms, as well as making commuting trips. Because goods produced at different locations are assumed to be spatially differentiated, workers demand them all, although they have the highest demand for goods produced by nearby firms. The model also incorporates traffic congestion and endogenous congestion tolls. The results is a dispersed land use pattern: both jobs and housing are present in all regions of the urban area, although the density level of both is highest at the center because of greater accessibility. The dispersed location pattern occurs for a combination of two reasons: first, congestion and congestion tolls make it worthwhile to reduce travel costs by mixing firms and households and, second, when firms transact with households, they have an additional incentive to mix with households so as to reduce the length of shopping trips.

These models have given us a much improved understanding of how agglomeration economies, congestion, the costs of commuting and of goods transportation, and strategic considerations interact to determine the spatial layout of employment in urban areas. The basic factors that cause firms to benefit from congregating at a central point—the CBD—are external agglomeration economies and the cost of goods transportation being high relative to the cost of commuting. As cities increase in size, the CBD becomes congested, which raises both commuting costs and goods transportation costs. Eventually these factors overwhelm the gains from agglomeration economies and make it more efficient for some or all firms to suburbanize. When firms suburbanize, the models just discussed suggest that it is economically efficient for suburban employment to develop at more than one location because this pattern reduces workers' commuting costs. Assuming that at least some firms suburbanize, two basic location patterns are possible: firms may disperse to isolated suburban locations, or they may congregate in one or more discrete suburban subcenters on each side of the CBD. (If models of one-dimensional cities were translated into two dimensions, then an additional location pattern would be one or more ring subcenters.) Factors that tend to cause the dispersed suburban location pattern include high commuting costs, lack of agglomeration economies once firms leave the CBD, firms' demand for land and labor being very price elastic, firms being fairly pollution-free so that households are willing to live near them, and firms selling their output directly to households, which necessitates shopping trips. An additional consideration that emerges from the literature is that firms may not actually locate in the most economically efficient land use pattern, both because individual firms have an incentive to ignore their effects on the level of agglomeration economies and because of strategic considerations.

### 3.2. Models with exogenously determined employment locations

In these models, the set of possible employment location within the urban area is exogenously determined. Wages at suburban employment locations may be either exogenously or endogenously determined. The models focus on how workers decide where to live and work and the resulting spatial patterns of land rents, population densities and commuting regions. In one sense, models with exogenously determined employment locations are special cases of the previous set of models in which the employment location pattern is endogenously determined and optimal versus actual employment patterns can be compared. However, the difficulty of solving models with endogenous employment locations usually means that these models focus on the tradeoff between agglomeration economies and transportation costs and they assume away most other issues. Models with exogenous employment patterns often focus instead on modeling other issues in the context of a decentralized urban area, such as the spatial location pattern when there are multiple household types, the effect of gasoline taxes on employment suburbanization or the effect of zoning regulations that limit development.

The earliest model of a decentralized urban area was that of White (1976). In her model, firms may locate either at the CBD or a constant number of miles away from the CBD in any direction. All firms are initially located at the CBD, but some move to the suburbs because they export their output from the urban area and the cost of doing so is lower in the suburbs. As discussed above, firms that suburbanize have an incentive to spread themselves out in all directions around the CBD, so that the suburban employment locations become a ring subcenter. Workers are assumed to commute along straight lines between their homes and their workplaces. If the wage at the ring equals the CBD wage minus twice the workers' cost of commuting between the ring and the CBD, then all commuting in the model is radial incommuting. All workers located between the CBD and the ring commute to the CBD, while workers located further out than the ring are indifferent between working at the CBD or the ring. But now suppose the wage at the ring rises above this level. Then there will be three commuting regions: a circular region around the CBD composed of workers who commute to the CBD, a doughnut-shaped region around it but inside the ring subcenter composed of suburban workers who outcommute to jobs at the ring, and an outer doughnut-shaped region beyond the ring composed of workers who incommute to jobs at the ring. As long as firms are spread evenly around the ring subcenter, no circumferential commuting occurs. In this situation, the land rent gradient and population density both fall with distance from the CBD, then rise to a local maximum at the subcenter and then fall again beyond the subcenter. Because White's (1976) model did not incorporate agglomeration economies, the optimal location for the ring subcenter was entirely outside the CBD's commuting region.

Sullivan (1986) also considered an urban area with a CBD and a ring subcenter. But rather than making the wage pattern exogenous, he assumed that firms at both locations have downward sloping labor demand functions. This allows wages to be determined endogenously by the condition that labor supply must equal labor demand at each employment location. In Sullivan's model, firms located at the CBD are assumed to be subject to agglomeration economies, while firms at the subcenter are not. His model, which is solved numerically, shows how wages at the two employment locations are linked via the land market. For example, suppose demand for labor at the CBD shifts outward. Then the wage at the CBD rises and some workers who live between the CBD and the subcenter shift from working at the subcenter to working at the CBD. This causes the CBD's commuting region to become larger and the subcenter's commuting region to become smaller. The backward shift in labor supply to the subcenter causes the subcenter's wage to rise. Thus, wages at the two employment locations tend to move together.[11]

Ross and Yinger (1995) consider an urban model in which there are firms both at the CBD and at either a point or a ring subcenter. Like Sullivan (1986), they assume that firms have downward sloping demands for labor, so that wages at each employment location are determined endogenously. Ross and Yinger solve for a closed form solution to their model and they focus on examining comparative statics results and whether, or not, these results are the same in a decentralized urban model as in a model with only CBD employment. Although their model has no agglomeration economies, their comparative statics results are similar to those found by Sullivan (1986), i.e., exogenous shocks cause wages at both employment locations to move in the same direction and a change in wages at one employment location causes wages to change in the same direction at the other. An increase in the exogenous utility level of urban residents is shown unambiguously to raise wages at both employment locations. But because the direct effect of the increase in utility and the indirect effect of the increase in utility via wages have opposing effects on land rents, the direction of the effect on land rents cannot be signed.[12]

Wieand (1987) analyzes a similar model with a CBD and a point subcenter, but he assumes that both employment locations have agglomeration economies and he allows the location of the subcenter to vary. He assumes that the level of agglomeration economies at each subcenter depends on the number of jobs at that subcenter, so that firms at the CBD are more productive as long as the CBD contains more firms. Given that establishing a subcenter is worthwhile, Wieand (1987) explores the question of the optimal subcenter location. He finds that if the subcenter will contain only a small number of jobs, then it is optimal for it to locate near the outer boundary of the urban area; while if the subcenter will be large, then it is preferable for it to locate near the CBD. This is because the further the subcenter is located from the CBD, the fewer the number of workers willing to commute to it for any given wage. If the subcenter contains few firms, then the small commuting region is not a drawback and the best location for it is near the urban periphery where land costs are low. But if the subcenter contains many firms, then it is better for it to remain near the CBD where it can attract more workers for any given wage. Wieand (1987) also points out that if the total population of the urban area is fixed, the establishment of a suburban subcenter

---

[11] Sullivan (1986) also considers the effects of land use controls in the CBD or the residential areas.

[12] Yinger (1992) explores a similar model in which workers commute along a network of radial and circular roads, rather than along straight lines between their homes and workplaces.

causes problems for the CBD since its loss of jobs causes loss of agglomeration economies and the nearby population density also falls.[13]

In White (1990), a simulation model is used to explore public policy concerns about long commuting trips by analyzing the extent to which policy measures that encourage more firms to suburbanize would reduce commuting. An urban model that originally has two suburban point subcenters is assumed to add two additional point subcenters located further out and, for comparison, an urban area that originally has a ring subcenter is assumed to add an additional one located further out. The model has no agglomeration economies, but congestion raises commuting costs near the CBD and the subcenters. The model is designed to allow any number and any spatial configuration of subcenters to be simulated. The main result of the simulation is that adding two additional suburban point subcenters or an additional suburban ring subcenter reduces workers' average commuting journey length by about 15–50%—more for the ring subcenters than the point subcenters.[14]

In Hotchkiss and White (1993), a simulation model is used to explore an urban area where there are multiple household types—two-worker households, "traditional" households with one male worker, and female-headed households. Wages at each of the employment locations are exogenously determined (male workers are assumed to earn more than female workers). The purpose of the model is to explore the spatial implications of such social trends as the high divorce rate, the increasing rate of labor force participation by married women, and the increasing dispersion of income within urban areas that these two trends cause. In general, two-worker households outbid other households for sites that are most accessible to their job locations, traditional households occupy the most suburban sites and female-headed households occupy the intermediate distances. Because high income households occupy central rather than suburban locations, the spatial allocation more closely resembles a European rather than an American city.[15] An increase in the cost of commuting causes a reduction in the number of female-headed households in the urban area, and a decrease in wages for female workers causes traditional households to replace two-worker households in the urban area. Thus, the model suggests that seemingly unrelated policy

---

[13] The Wieand (1987) model implies a testable hypothesis that firm or subcenter size should vary inversely with distance from the CBD. To the author's knowledge, this hypothesis has not been tested empirically.

[14] Even four subcenters is probably too few to realistically represent a large urban area. See Giuliano and Small (1991) for a discussion of how to identify employment subcenters. They find 32 subcenters in the Los Angeles metropolitan area.

[15] These results suggests that to get the typical spatial location pattern of a large US city, explicit disamenities of living near the center of the city would need to be introduced into the model.

changes can have important spatial implications. Hotchkiss and White (1993) also introduce a random component to wages, that allows the model to represent worker/household heterogeneity. The effect of introducing even a small random component is that the commuting region boundaries become very fuzzy. All household types occupy sites all over the urban area (instead of occupying sites only in their particular commuting regions) and the number of different household types represented in the urban area increases. Randomness in income greatly dampens the responsiveness of the model to exogenous shocks.

Finally, the paper by Sivitanidou and Wheaton (1992) also explores a model in which there are two employment locations, but firms compete with households for land. One subcenter is allowed to have a cost advantage in production over the other and relative wages at the two subcenters are determined endogenously. The goal of the model is to determine to what extent differences between the two subcenters are capitalized as differences in commercial land rents versus differences in wages. The authors first show that if the two subcenters have the same costs, then the urban area is symmetric and both subcenters have identical size, wages and commercial land rents. Also the residential land rent patterns around them are identical. Now suppose subcenter $A$ has a cost advantage over subcenter $B$. Then, firms in subcenter $A$ expand by offering higher wages. This leads to an expansion in subcenter $A$'s commuting area, which bids up residential land rents around subcenter $A$. Because firms compete with households for land, the expansion of subcenter $A$ also raises commercial land rents. Thus, the cost differentials between subcenters lead to both higher wages and higher commercial and residential land rents at and around the subcenter that has the cost advantage. Now suppose again that the two subcenters have equal cost, but zoning imposes a binding restriction on the land area of subcenter $A$. Then commercial land rents at subcenter $A$ rise above those at subcenter $B$, but subcenter $A$'s wages fall below those of subcenter $B$. Because of the zoning restriction, commercial land rent at subcenter $A$ is higher than (rather than equal to) land rent for residential land just adjacent to subcenter $A$. Residential land rent around subcenter $A$ is also lower than that around subcenter $B$, which means that workers are willing to work for lower wages at subcenter $A$ because their land costs are lower. Thus, zoning restrictions on one subcenter lead to that subcenter having higher rents, but lower wages. The authors conclude that differences in commercial rents across subcenters within an urban area may not accurately measure differences in the subcenters' productivity.

Models in which the spatial pattern of employment is exogenously determined obviously cannot be used to analyze what spatial location pattern is efficient, but they can be used to analyze other implications of decentralized employment in a more realistic setting. Future research, perhaps using numerical techniques, may be able to combine the strengths of both sets of models.

## 4. Rent and wage gradients in decentralized urban areas

When jobs decentralize, the structure of an urban area becomes much more complicated. To start with, all urban areas—monocentric and decentralized—have rent gradients that relate the price of land to distance from the CBD. Rent offer curves describe how much each household is willing to pay for land at each location, and the market rent gradient is the upper envelope of all households' rent offer curves. In the monocentric city, rent offer curves and the market rent gradient always decline at a decreasing rate with the distance from the CBD.[16] But in the decentralized city, households' rent offer curves may be affected by workers' job locations and this may affect the shape of the market rent gradient. Decentralized cities also have a wage gradient, that relates wages to distance from the CBD for identical jobs. Workers living at particular residential locations have a wage offer curve that indicates the minimum amount they must be paid to be willing to work at any job location. The lower envelope of workers' wage offer curves is the market wage gradient. The characteristics of individual workers' wage offer curves and the market wage gradient, both of which may be affected by where workers live, need to be established. In this section I explore how rent and wage gradients in decentralized cities are determined and how they relate to each other.[17]

Suppose an urban area has an employment pattern consisting of a CBD and suburban firms that are dispersed at isolated locations in all directions around the CBD. Residential distance from the CBD is denoted $u$ and workplace distance from the CBD is denoted $v$. All workers are assumed to incommute, so that their commuting distance is $u - v$. Wages per day are $w(v)$, the out-of-pocket cost of commuting is $m$ per mile, and the speed of commuting is $1/s$. Since there is no congestion, the cost of commuting a mile in each direction is always $2(sw(v) + m)$. Each household has one worker. Suppose the rent on land per unit is denoted $r(u, v)$, land consumption per household is $l(u, v)$ and hours of leisure consumption are $h(u, v)$. Households' rent offer curves must satisfy the property:

$$r_u(u, v) = \frac{-2(sw(v) + m)}{l(u, v)}, \tag{4.1}$$

[16] See Mills and Hamilton (1989).

[17] The main references for this section are Straszheim (1984) and White (1988a).

and workers' wage offer curves must satisfy the property:

$$w_v(u, v) = \frac{-2(sw(v) + m)}{24 - 2s(u - v) - h(u, v)},\tag{4.2}$$

where the subscripts denote partial derivatives. Equation (4.1) looks familiar from the analysis of the monocentric city: it says that land rents fall with residential distance at a rate equal to the cost of commuting a mile further from the CBD divided by the households' demand for housing. However, the presence of terms depending on $v$ in Eq. (4.1) suggests that the rent offer curve may be affected by workers' job locations. Equation (4.2) is the wage offer curve. It says that the rate of change in the wage at which workers are willing to work for firms located further from the CBD equals the cost of commuting a mile further per day divided by the number of hours of work, where the latter equals 24 minus time spent commuting $(2s(u - v))$ minus time spent in leisure. The presence of terms in $u$ in the equation suggests that the wage offer curve may be affected by workers' residential locations.

Since the rent offer curve has the same form as in the monocentric city case, individual households' rent offer curves in decentralized cities must always have a negative slope and must always decline at a decreasing rate with distance. Now consider whether and how individual households' rent offer curves vary with job location by differentiating Eq. (4.1) with respect to $v$. The result is:

$$\frac{\partial r_u}{\partial v} = \frac{-1}{l(u, v)}[2sw_v + r_u l_v].\tag{4.3}$$

The signs of $w_v$ and $r_u$ are both negative, but the sign of $l_v$—the change in land consumption when job location becomes more suburbanized but residential location remains constant—is ambiguous. The most likely case is that $l_v$ is positive, because when workers spend less time commuting (job location shifts outward while residential location remains fixed), they save money and are likely to increase consumption of both land and other goods. In this case, the sign of $\partial r_u / \partial v$ must be positive. Then households' rent offer curves become flatter as workers' job locations become more suburbanized. Since the market rent gradient is the upper envelope of households' rent offer curves, this means that the rent gradient in the decentralized city will decline more slowly than the rent gradient in a monocentric city. In addition, households in the decentralized city will tend to segregate into different residential areas depending on their workers' job locations. For example, suppose that jobs are located only at the CBD and a ring subcenter $v'$ miles from the CBD, while residences are located everywhere.

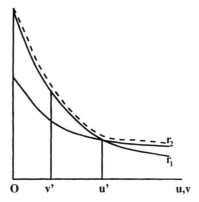

Fig. 2. Rent offer curves of households whose workers work at the CBD and at $v'$, and the market rent gradient.

Figure 2 shows the rent offer curve $r_1$ of households whose workers work at the CBD, and the rent offer curve $r_2$ of households whose workers work at $v'$. The market rent gradient, shown as a dashed line, is the upper envelope of the two rent offer curves. The boundary between the two rent offer curves occurs at $u'$, where $u' > v'$. Households whose workers hold CBD jobs live in the inner residential area between $u = 0$ and $u'$, while households whose workers work at $v'$ live in the outer residential area further out than $u'$.[18]

If we combine the rent and wage offer curves, Eqs. (4.1) and (4.2), we can determine the relative rate at which the wage offer curve falls with distance from the CBD compared to the rent offer curve, or,

$$\frac{w_v/w}{r_u/r} = \frac{rl}{wn}, \tag{4.4}$$

where $n = 24 - 2s(u - v) - h(u, v)$ denotes hours of work. The rate of decline of the wage offer curve relative to the rent offer curve equals the ratio of the rent on land to total earnings. If the ratio of land rent to earnings is approximately constant, then the wage offer curve—like the rent offer curve—is predicted to decline at a decreasing rate with distance from the CBD. In the US, households spend about 20% of their incomes on land and housing combined and the cost of land is approximately one-quarter of the combined cost. Therefore, $rl/wn \simeq (0.2)(0.25) = 0.05$, suggesting that on average urban wages decline with distance from the CBD at only about 5% of the rate at which urban land

---

[18] Because all workers incommute to their jobs, the rent gradient declines monotonically and does not have a local maximum at $v'$.

rents decline. This figure is probably higher in Europe. Nonetheless, because the fraction of earnings spent on land rent is low, the wage offer curve is predicted to decline quite slowly with distance from the CBD. Therefore, measuring it empirically turns out to be difficult.

Finally, consider whether and how individual workers' wage offer curves vary with residential location by differentiating Eq. (4.2) with respect to $u$. The result is

$$\frac{\partial w_v / \partial u}{w_v} = -\frac{n_u}{n}. \tag{4.5}$$

The percentage change in the slope of the wage offer curve when workers move their residential locations a mile further out, but keep their job locations fixed, equals minus the percentage change in hours of work when workers move their residential locations a mile further out. Since $w_v$ is negative, the sign of $\partial w_v / \partial u$ is the same as the sign of $n_u$. The sign of $n_u$ is ambiguous, but the most likely case is that it is negative, since when workers spend more time commuting (residential location shifts outward while job location remains fixed), they are likely to compensate by reducing both the number of hours of leisure and the hours of work. In this case, $\partial w_v / \partial u$ must be negative and workers' wage offer curves become steeper as their residential locations become more suburbanized. Suppose there are only two residential locations, consisting of rings located at distances $u^*$ and $u^{**} > u^*$, while jobs occur at all locations. Figure 3 shows the wage offer curve $w_1$ of the group of workers living at $u^*$ and the wage offer curve $w_2$ of the group of workers living at $u^{**}$. The market wage gradient, shown as a dashed line, is the lower envelope of the two curves. Workers living at $u^*$ take jobs located between $v = 0$ and $v''$, while workers living at $u^{**}$ take jobs located further out than $v = v''$. The market wage gradient has a negative slope and becomes steeper with distance from the CBD.[19]

We have shown that the decentralized urban area has a market wage gradient that relates wages to workplace location, in addition to having a market rent gradient that relates the price of land to residential location. The prediction that urban wages vary with distance from the CBD is one of the major testable hypotheses of the urban model. In the model just discussed, only incommuting was assumed to occur and wage gradients were therefore downward sloping.[20] However, as discussed in Section 1, when suburban firms have high labor demand, they must raise wages in order to attract enough workers. This causes

[19] See White (1988a) for further discussion.

[20] Note from Fig. 3 that the theoretical urban model has no prediction for the sign of the second derivative of the market wage gradient, although the wage offer curves have declining slopes.

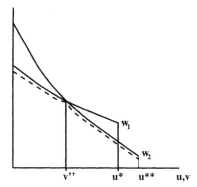

Fig. 3. Wage offer curves of workers who live at $u^*$ and $u^{**}$, and the market wage gradient.

wage gradients to become less negative, or even to turn positive, and it also causes outcommuting to occur. Flat or positive wage gradients are most likely to occur in a particular subregion of an urban area, since they are caused by firms at a large subcenter offering high wages in order to expand their commuting regions.

## 5. Empirical evidence concerning urban wage gradients

One of the major empirical hypotheses generated by the urban model with decentralized employment is that wages for otherwise identical jobs vary with distance from the CBD. In general, the urban model predicts that wages decline with distance from the CBD, but wages could be constant, or even rise, with distance if there is concentrated suburban employment. Rising wage gradients are likely to occur only in a particular direction from the CBD.

The theory predicts that researchers attempting to measure urban wage gradients will confront several problems. First, as discussed above, finding evidence of wage gradients is likely to be difficult since wages decline at a much slower rate than rent as distance from the CBD increases. Second, finding a sample of jobs and workers that are identical except for distance from the CBD is difficult. But if observations of nonidentical jobs or workers are used to estimate wage gradients, then the results may reflect location-specific job differences or location-specific differences among workers rather than a true wage gradient. For example, police jobs are likely to be less dangerous in the suburbs than the central city because suburban crime rates are lower. This factor would tend to cause police wages in the central city to rise relative to police wages in the suburbs. An estimated wage gradient for police wages that did not control for crime rates would therefore decline too steeply. As another example, suburban teachers tend to be more experienced than central city teachers and, as a result, their wages are higher. An estimated wage gradient for teachers that did not control for experience might therefore be flat or even positively sloped, when the true wage gradient would have a negative slope. Third, suppose a metropolitan area has a negative wage gradient in one direction away from the CBD, but a positive wage gradient in another direction—perhaps reflecting the presence of a large subcenter in that direction. Then, if a single wage gradient were estimated for the entire metropolitan area, it would probably result in no gradient being found.

An additional problem with the empirical literature on urban wage gradients is that it combines tests of two distinct hypotheses under the same name. One literature tests for a relationship between wages and distance from the CBD. The other literature tests for a relationship between commuting journey length and wages. The latter relationship results from the hypothesis that workers are willing to commute further in return for higher wages, just as they are willing to commute further in return for lower housing prices. Evidence supporting the commuting journey/wage relationship has sometimes been interpreted as providing support for the hypothesis that wages decline with distance from the CBD (see, for example, Madden, 1985), but this conclusion is not always correct. For example, suppose wages rise rather than fall with distance from the CBD in a particular city. Then suppose a set of workers who outcommute to their jobs is used to test the commuting journey/wage relationship. These workers would have the predicted positive relationship between commuting journey length and wages, even though wages rise rather than fall with distance from the CBD. An alternate possibility is that wages fall and then rise with distance from the CBD in a particular city. In this case, an empirical test of the commuting journey/wage relationship using randomly selected workers might fail to find a relationship at all. In what follows, I survey only papers that directly test the wage/distance from the CBD relationship.[21]

Because of lack of availability of data on workplace location, many of the papers that test for the existence of wage gradients have used data that the authors collected specifically for the purpose. An early effort was that of Rees and Shultz (1970), who collected data on wages, job characteristics, and job location as part of a study of the Chicago labor market. They compared wages in the CBD (the Loop) to those in the region south of the CBD and in the regions north and west of the CBD, for workers in both white and blue collar jobs. At the time of their study,

---

[21] See Crampton (Chap. 39, this volume) for a discussion of papers on the commuting journey/wage relationship.

the region south of the Loop contained most of the Chicago metropolitan area's heavy industry, while the regions north and west were mainly residential. Rees and Shultz (1970) found that wages in the north/west region were significantly lower than at the CBD for both blue and white collar occupations. But wages in the south region were higher than at the CBD for blue collar occupations and not significantly different from the CBD for white collar occupations. Their evidence is consistent with the theoretical model discussed above in that wages rise with distance from the CBD in the region of Chicago where jobs are plentiful but workers living nearby are scarce, so that suburban employers need to raise wages in order to induce enough workers to commute to suburban jobs. In contrast, wages fall with distance from the CBD in the regions of the metropolitan area where workers are plentiful and jobs are scarce.

A more recent study by Eberts (1981) also used data from Chicago. Eberts obtained wage data for employees of 100 municipalities in all regions of the Chicago metropolitan area. He estimated regressions explaining the log of wages as a function of the log of the municipality's distance from the CBD for five categories of public sector workers: police, fire, administration, clerical and public works. These data have the drawback that they are for municipalities rather than individual workers, but job characteristics and workers' average characteristics may vary across municipalities. As discussed above, these variations may bias the estimate wage gradients either upward or downward. In fact, Eberts (1981) finds that that the wage/distance from the CBD relationship is negative for all five categories of workers and statistically significant for all except fire. The elasticity of wages with respect to distance was about $-0.2$ for public works and police employees, and $-0.3$ for administration and clerical. The absolute decrease in monthly wages per mile of distance was $24 for administration, $10 for clerical, $12 for police and $9 for clerical (in 1974 dollars). Despite these problems, Eberts' results provide some support for the hypothesis that urban wage gradients are negatively sloped.

More recent studies of urban wage gradients have taken advantage of the Public Use Microsample (PUMS) of the 1980 US Census of Population and Housing. This dataset includes all the information collected as part of the US Census of Population for a large sample of individual households. For each worker, it indicates whether the worker's job location is in the CBD, the rest of the central city or in any of a set of suburban zones, where the number of suburban zones varies between 1 and 28 for different metropolitan areas.

Ilhanfeldt (1992) uses PUMS data for Philadelphia, Detroit and Boston (the metropolitan areas having the largest number of zones) to estimate urban wage gradients separately for a variety of occupational groups and for white versus

African-American workers. Commuting journey length was measured by straight-line distance from the largest town within each zone to the CBD. Ilhanfeldt's main results come from estimating wage gradients for white workers in seven job categories in the three metropolitan areas. Of these 21 wage gradients, 18 have negative slopes, and 15 of the 18 are statistically significant. The remaining three wage gradients have positive slopes but are not statistically significant. Thus, Ilhanfeldt's results also support the hypothesis that wages decline with distance from the CBD. The rate of decline is approximately 1% per mile of additional distance from the CBD—a figure suggested as reasonable by Mills and Hamilton (1989).[22] For African-American workers, Ilhanfeldt (1992) estimated 14 wage gradients and found that only two were negative and statistically significant, while one was positive and statistically significant and 11 were not significantly different from zero. Thus, African-American workers appear to have flatter wage gradients than white workers. African-American workers are more likely to live in the central city than white workers, so that if they faced the same negative wage gradients as white workers, they would find it less worthwhile to commute to suburban jobs. Finally, Ilhanfeldt tested whether, or not, wage gradients differed for male versus female workers. He found no significant differences between male versus female black workers, while he did find a significant difference by gender for white workers only for the professional/managerial category, where the wage gradient for women was significantly more negative than for men workers. The general finding of no gender differences in wage gradients is probably not surprising since if male and female workers occupy the same job categories and are paid equal wages, then they must face the same market wage gradient. The finding of different wage gradients by race suggests that white workers tend to take different jobs than African-American workers.

McMillen and Singell (1992) also use PUMS data to estimate urban wage gradients, but they use the information in the PUMS to infer individual workers' job location choices. For each of seven cities, they estimate two simultaneous probit equations explaining whether workers choose jobs in the central city versus the suburbs, and whether they choose residences in the central city versus the suburbs. From the probit equation explaining workplace location, they predict the utility-maximizing workplace location for each worker in the sample, in miles from the CBD. They then assume that the utility-maximizing workplace location can be used as a proxy for workers' actual workplace location. Finally, they use the proxy for workplace location, combined with data on workers' wages and

---

[22] Ilhanfeldt (1992) also found that the slope of the wage gradients became flatter (less negative) as distance from the CBD increased. This result is consistent with, although not predicted by, the theory discussed above. It may reflect the fact that average commuting speeds are greater in the suburbs than in the central city.

other characteristics, to estimate an urban wage gradient. The estimated wage gradient is negative and statistically significant for their base city, Detroit, and the results for five of their six other cities are not significantly different from those found for Detroit.

Thus, despite important data limitations, the literature on urban wage gradients finds surprisingly strong support for the hypothesis that wages for otherwise similar jobs decline with distance from the CBD

## 6. Suburbanization: Do jobs follow workers or workers follow jobs?

At the beginning of this chapter, I documented the long-term trend toward suburbanization of both population and employment. A controversy in urban economics concerns the issue of causation: does the spatial pattern of population in a metropolitan area depend on the spatial pattern of employment, or does the employment pattern depend on the population pattern? As discussed above, the urban models literature made widespread use of the assumption that the spatial pattern of employment is exogenously determined—either because all jobs are assumed to be located at the CBD, or because employment is decentralized but its spatial pattern is exogenously specified. This implicitly assumes that the residential location pattern is determined by the employment location pattern, rather than the reverse. The direction of causation issue is testable and a literature has developed that attempts to test whether jobs follow workers or workers follow jobs.

Before examining this literature, however, it seems worthwhile to note that the assumption of the urban models literature that employment location is exogenously determined is mainly made for convenience. In the early models, understanding the economics of residential location within urban areas was difficult enough by itself, and the problem was made much more tractable by assuming away the need to explain employment location. Since then, economists have worked on explaining the pattern of firm location within urban areas and have made progress, but our understanding of firm location remains sketchy relative to our understanding of residential location. Furthermore, theoretical models that explain both simultaneously remain highly simplified and static rather than dynamic, as the discussion in Section 3.1 suggests. Thus, while the empirical question of whether jobs follow people or people follow jobs is interesting and important in its own right, the empirical models do not provide a test of any hypothesis of the theoretical model. The theoretical model itself has not developed to the point where it provides clear predictions on this issue.

Steinnes (1977) was the first to test the causation issue. His technique was to estimate a two-equation simultaneous model using a pooled time-series cross-section dataset. Suppose $P_{i,t}$ denotes the proportion of metropolitan area population located in the central city in city $i$ in period $t$, and $E_{i,t}$ denotes the proportion of metropolitan area employment located in the central city in city $i$ in period $t$. In the first equation, the dependent variable is $P_{i,t}$ and the independent variables are the lagged values $P_{i,t-1}$ and $E_{i,t-1}$, plus other exogenous variables that affect the population pattern. In the second equation, the dependent variable is $E_{i,t}$ and the independent variables are the lagged values $E_{i,t-1}$ and $P_{i,t-1}$, plus other exogenous variables that affect the employment pattern. The test of the "people follow jobs" hypothesis is whether, or not, the coefficient of $E_{i,t-1}$ in the equation explaining $P_{i,t}$ is statistically significant and positive, which would indicate that greater suburbanization of employment causes greater suburbanization of population in the following period. The test of the "jobs follow people" hypothesis is whether, or not, the coefficient of $P_{i,t-1}$ in the equation explaining $E_{i,t}$ is statistically significant and positive.

Steinnes (1977) tested the model separately for manufacturing, service and retail employment. The results for manufacturing and services supported the "jobs follow people" hypothesis, while the results for retail employment supported the "people follow jobs" hypothesis. Cooke (1978) redid Steinnes' estimation using residential and employment density gradients (rather than proportion located in the central city) as his measures of the extent of suburbanization. He also found that employment follows population, although the results for manufacturing employment were more significant than those for retail and service employment. Mills and Price (1984) also found that jobs follow people in a model explaining population and employment density gradients and using data from the 1960 and 1970 Censuses of Population.[23] However, Thurston and Yezer (1994), also explaining density gradients but using annual data from the Local Personal Income Series of the US Department of Commerce, found evidence that jobs follow people in the services and retail sectors, but did not find evidence supporting causality in either direction for five other employment sectors

An interesting recent paper on this issue is that of Boarnet (1994). Rather than using metropolitan areas as observations, Boarnet uses data from 365 municipalities in northern New Jersey and, rather than explaining levels of population and employment, he explains the changes in municipal population and employment between the years 1980 and 1988. Thus, Boarnet focuses the analysis on

---

[23] The main conclusion of the Mills and Price (1984) paper is that adding to the model a set of variables measuring central city problems—crime, race and taxes—does not add any explanatory power to the basic model explaining suburbanization of population and employment.

the submetropolitan area level. For each municipality $i$, Boarnet defines a labor market consisting of all other municipalities in the sample. Each municipality is weighted by $1/d_{ij}^{\beta}$, where $d_{ij}$ is the distance between municipality $i$ and municipality $j$ and $\beta$ is a separately estimated parameter that indicates how labor market relationships across municipalities decay with distance. Employment in municipality $i$'s labor market area is defined as the weighted sum of employment in all the other municipalities in the sample, and population in municipality $i$'s labor market area is defined as the weighted sum of population in all the other municipalities in the sample. Thus, an individualized labor market is defined for each municipality.

In Boarnet's model, the change in population in municipality $i$ between 1980 and 1988 depends on the change in employment over the same period in municipality $i$'s labor market area, the lagged value of population in municipality $i$, the lagged value of employment in municipality $i$'s labor market area, and other control variables. The change in employment in municipality $i$ similarly depends on the change in population in the labor market area surrounding municipality $i$, the lagged value of employment in municipality $i$, the lagged value of population in municipality $i$'s labor market area, and other control variables. The two equations are estimated using simultaneous techniques. Boarnet's results indicate that the change in the municipal employment level is significantly related to changes in the population of the labor market area, but the change in the municipal population level is not significantly related to changes in employment in the labor market area.

Thus, Boarnet's results, like earlier papers, provide support for the hypothesis that jobs follow people, but not vice versa. Since Boarnet's test uses municipalities within a particular metropolitan area rather than more aggregated metropolitan area data, his results suggest that the hypothesis that jobs follow people holds for explaining both overall spatial patterns across metropolitan areas, and more detailed spatial patterns within metropolitan areas.

Boarnet's work is unlikely to represent the final word on this subject, but nonetheless his results and those of previous authors seem sensible and intuitively appealing. If we think about the problem from the viewpoint of the theoretical considerations discussed above, it seems clear that the employers' location decisions are tied to the spatial pattern of population. Employers benefit from moving to the suburbs because they can pay lower wages, but only if the move results in workers having shorter commutes. Therefore, the gain to an employer from suburbanizing depends on the density of population near the intended suburban location and on the employer's level of demand for labor. As shown by Wieand (1987), a small firm can benefit from locating near the periphery of the urban area because it only needs to hire a small number of workers, but a large firm has an incentive to remain close to the CBD, since otherwise the high cost of attracting many workers to the suburban site may more than offset the large firms' other gains from suburbanizing. Thus, the gains to firms from suburbanizing are directly linked to the distribution of population: firms have an incentive to follow—but not to lead—workers to the suburbs. In contrast, households gain from moving to the suburbs regardless of the spatial distribution of employment. Even if all firms were located at the CBD, households would still benefit from moving to the suburbs because workers' longer commutes are compensated by lower housing prices—the basic tradeoff of the urban economic model. Thus, it should not be surprising that empirical studies have tended to find that jobs follow people, while people do not follow jobs. The assumption in the theoretical urban models literature that the spatial distribution of employment is exogenous and determines the spatial distribution of population (i.e., people follow jobs) was, and is, merely a convenient simplification that made difficult models easier to solve. Future work in urban economics needs to devote more attention to modeling firm location choice, so that the simplification will no longer be necessary.

## 7.  Are commuting patterns in decentralized cities "wasteful"?

Hamilton (1982) raised the question of whether, or not, commuting in US metropolitan areas is inefficient. He argued that 10 times more commuting actually occurs in metropolitan areas than is predicted by urban economic models, from which he concluded that 90% of urban commuting is "wasteful". He concluded, therefore, that urban economic models have little predictive power.

   In order to measure how much commuting occurs in metropolitan areas beyond what is predicted by urban economic models, we need to first establish how much commuting is predicted by urban economic models and is therefore efficient. In theory, we would do this by first establishing the optimal spatial location pattern for each metropolitan area for housing, jobs and roads (which might vary across metropolitan areas because of factors such as differing amounts of land being available for urban use or differing distributions of jobs across industries). Then the efficient commuting pattern would minimize the total commuting time required for the metropolitan area's workers to travel from its houses to its jobs.

   But as the previous discussion suggests, urban economic models in fact provide incomplete guidance on these issues. While the model of residential location in metropolitan areas has been extensively researched, the model of firm location in metropolitan areas is still under development and, in particular, the role of agglomeration economies is not well understood. Similarly, the problem of the optimal allocation of land to roads is also relevant and research in this area is also rather sketchy. Thus, in order to measure the efficient amount of commuting, we need to understand whether and how the spatial allocation of land uses in cities is inefficient.

But suppose we wish to proceed anyway and, in order to do so, we make the simplifying assumption that the actual spatial allocation of land uses prevailing in metropolitan areas is efficient. Then the efficient amount of commuting is defined as the minimum amount that would be required for the metropolitan area's workers to travel from its existing housing stock to its existing jobs along its existing roads.

Hamilton's (1982) method of calculating the efficient amount of commuting was based on Mills' (1972) two-point density gradients for population and employment in US metropolitan areas. From the density gradient for population, Hamilton calculated the average distance of houses from the CBD for each of the metropolitan areas in Mills' sample. And from the density gradient for employment, he calculated the average distance of jobs from the CBD in the same metropolitan areas. The difference between them, he argued, is the average minimum commuting journey length required for workers in each metropolitan area to travel from its housing to its jobs. Hamilton then compared this average minimum commuting journey length figure to data on the average actual commuting journey length in each metropolitan area and found that the ratio was 1:10.

Hamilton's (1982) calculation of the average minimum commuting journey length differs from actual minimum commuting journey length for two reasons. First, his calculations assume that houses and jobs are both uniformly distributed in all directions around the metropolitan area's CBDs. This assumption is implicit in the use of density gradients, that treat the metropolitan area as though it can be represented by a one-dimensional ray from the CBD because it is identical in all directions around the CBD. Thus, Hamilton's method ignores the possibility that a metropolitan area's jobs and houses may not be uniformly distributed around the CBD. But if the distributions of jobs and houses around the CBD are not uniform, then they may differ from each other and, therefore, at least some workers must commute circumferentially. But circumferential commuting raises the minimum amount of commuting in the metropolitan area. Since Hamilton's calculations of the minimum average commuting journey length treat the distributions of jobs and housing around the CBD as identical, his method therefore overstates the proportion of urban commuting that is "wasteful". Second, Hamilton's method assumes that all workers commute along straight lines from their houses to their jobs. But actually, workers must commute along the existing road network. If roads are not straight, then the minimum amount of commuting in the metropolitan area rises. The assumption that all commuting journeys occur along straight lines also causes Hamilton's calculations of the proportion of urban commuting that is "wasteful" to be biased upward.[24]

White (1988b) proposed that both the problem of jobs and housing being differently distributed around the CBD and that commuters must travel along the existing road network, could be solved by using an assignment model to calculate the minimum average commuting journey length. An assignment model requires that a metropolitan area be divided into zones, and that we know (1) the commuting journey length between each pair of zones, (2) the number of residences in each zone, and (3) the number of jobs in each zone. The model then calculates an assignment of each worker to a job and residence that minimizes the aggregate amount of commuting for all workers in the metropolitan area. Because of the zonal structure, the assignment model can take into account any spatial distributions of jobs and houses around the CBD. Also, because the characteristics of the existing road network determine the commuting journey length between each pair of zones, the assignment model takes account of the fact that commuting journeys must be made along actual rather than straight-line roads.

Suppose we also know the number of workers who actually commute in each direction between each pair of zones. Conceptually, we can think of the model as starting from the existing allocation of workers to jobs and housing and then making any trades of job or housing assignments that would allow aggregate commuting to be reduced, keeping the number of jobs and houses in each zone fixed. For example, suppose worker *A* lives at the CBD and works five miles south, while worker *B* works at the CBD and lives 10 miles south. Then the total commuting could be reduced by 10 miles if workers *A* and *B* traded either jobs or houses. Efficient trades tend to reduce the amount of outcommuting and circumferential commuting that occurs. Circumferential commuting cannot be eliminated completely as long as the distributions of jobs and housing around the CBD differ from each other. But outcommuting can be eliminated completely as long as employment is less suburbanized than housing. Thus, efficient commuting patterns tend to involve relatively more incommuting, less outcommuting and less circumferential commuting than actual commuting patterns.

White (1988b) used data from the 1980 US Census of Population to calculate the average minimum commuting journey length for 25 US metropolitan areas.

---

[24] Hamilton's (1982) commuting calculations were in terms of distance, but later researchers used commuting time. See Hamilton (1990) and Small and Song (1992) for discussion of the effects of using commuting distance versus time.

For these areas, the total number of zones ranges from five to 32, where the CBD is a separate zone for the purposes of workplace location, but not residential location.[25] Census data on how many workers actually travel from each zone to every other zone are used to calculate the average actual commuting journey length. Comparing these figures, White found that the average actual amount of commuting was only about 10% greater than the average minimum amount of commuting.

Table 2 gives the matrix of actual commuting and optimal commuting flows for the Buffalo metropolitan area, which has four suburban zones plus the central city (zone 1) and the CBD. The lefthand column in both panels gives the number of housing units in each zone and the top row in both panels gives the number of jobs in each zone. (All figures are in thousands.) The top panel gives the optimal assignment of workers to jobs and housing units and the bottom panel gives the actual assignment. In the optimal assignment, all jobs in the CBD are occupied by residents of the central city, whereas, in reality 62% of CBD jobs are held by suburban residents. Thus, the optimal assignment eliminates long incommuting journeys. Except in zone 4, all jobs in the four suburban zones are held by residents who live in the same zone, while the remaining suburban residents mainly commute to jobs in the central city.[26] Thus, most outcommuting and circumferential commuting journeys are also eliminated. Although Buffalo has only a few zones, the results are typical of the pattern for cities having a greater numbers of zones.

A problem with using the assignment model is that as long as commuting journeys within zones are shorter than those between zones, within-zone commutes are treated as efficient and the assignment model does not change them. However, if individual zones are relatively large, then additional trades within zones would probably reduce commuting further. But the Census provides commuting data only for a relatively small number of zones within each metropolitan area and, in addition, the central city is a single zone even when it constitutes a large fraction of the metropolitan area. In later papers, Cropper and Gordon (1991) and Small and Song (1992) applied the assignment model to much more detailed transportation data for particular metropolitan areas. Cropper and Gordon (1991) used data for Baltimore that divided the metropolitan area into 498 zones; while Small and Song (1992) used data for Los Angeles–Long Beach that divided the metropolitan area into 706 zones. Cropper and Gordon found that the actual average commuting journey length in Baltimore was two-and-a-half times as high as

---

[25] The zones for these data are the same as the zones in the PUMS data.

[26] Zone 4 includes Niagara Falls, a suburban subcenter.

Table 2

Optimal versus actual commuting patterns in Buffalo (1980)

| | | | Optimal commuting pattern Jobs (000) | | | | | |
|---|---|---|---|---|---|---|---|---|
| | | | CBD | 1 | 2 | 3 | 4 | 5 |
| | | | 37 | 146 | 13 | 184 | 32 | 49 |
| Housing units | 1 | 116 | 37 | 79 | 0 | 0 | 0 | 0 |
| (000) | 2 | 20 | 0 | 7 | 13 | 0 | 0 | 0 |
| | 3 | 241 | 0 | 57 | 0 | 184 | 0 | 0 |
| | 4 | 26 | 0 | 0 | 0 | 0 | 26 | 0 |
| | 5 | 59 | 0 | 4 | 0 | 0 | 6 | 49 |
| | | | Actual commuting pattern Jobs (000) | | | | | |
| | | | CBD | 1 | 2 | 3 | 4 | 5 |
| | | | 37 | 146 | 13 | 184 | 32 | 49 |
| Housing units | 1 | 116 | 17 | 70 | 2 | 25 | 1 | 1 |
| (000) | 2 | 20 | 2 | 7 | 5 | 7 | 0 | 0 |
| | 3 | 241 | 18 | 65 | 6 | 142 | 6 | 4 |
| | 4 | 26 | 1 | 3 | 0 | 6 | 26 | 6 |
| | 5 | 59 | 2 | 2 | 0 | 4 | 9 | 29 |

the minimum average commuting journey length, while Small and Song's results for Los Angeles-Long Beach indicated a ratio of 3. Both of these results are between Hamilton's (1992) actual-to-minimum commuting journey length ratio of 10, and White's (1988b) actual-to-minimum commuting journey length ratio of 1.1. Thus, there is evidence that much more commuting occurs than the minimum amount required for workers to commute between a metropolitan area's existing houses and its existing jobs, but the best evidence suggests that the ratio of actual to minimum commuting is 2.5:3 rather than 2.5:10.

But does any of this demonstrate that commuting beyond the minimum in metropolitan areas is inefficient or "wasteful"? To address this question, consider what the assignment model omits. One problem is that many households contain two workers and they may choose seemingly inefficient commuting patterns in order to live together. Suppose one spouse works at the CBD and the other in the suburbs and they minimize their combined commuting by living between their two jobs. Therefore, one spouse outcommutes. The assignment model is likely to trade away the outcommuting journey, since the procedure does not take account of the spouses' desire to live together. As another example, suppose an African-American worker lives near the CBD but works in the suburbs. Again, the assignment model will tend to eliminate the outcommuting journey, but in actuality the worker's household may remain at its current residential location because it faces race discrimination in suburban housing markets, or prefers to live in a more familiar environment. Or suppose a worker who lives south of the CBD finds a new job north of the CBD, but remains in the same residential location. This might be because (1) the cost of moving is high, (2) the worker does not expect to keep the new job for long, and/or (3) the worker's household likes the schools or parks in its current neighborhood and makes many (nonwork) trips to them. The assignment model ignores these factors and tends to trade away long circumferential commuting journeys. Finally, all jobs and houses are not identical. Some trades might reduce commuting but would allocate high income workers to small apartments and/or low income workers to large houses; while other trades would allocate high skill workers to low skill jobs and vice versa. All these examples, with the exception of the one involving race discrimination in housing markets, suggest that households choose some amount of commuting beyond the minimum. Such choices are economically rational and efficient as long as households receive other benefits in return for commuting more, and that they voluntarily choose the combination of the longer commute and the other benefits. Nothing in the "wasteful commuting" controversy proves that commuting beyond the minimum is inefficient.

The first model that attempted to allow for any of these factors is Cropper and Gordon (1991). They estimate a multinomial logit model explaining residential location choice as a function of individual household and neighborhood characteristics, and commuting journey length. Using this model, they calculate the utility level of each household in their sample if the household were to locate in each of a set of zones. Then, when the assignment model is used to calculate minimum aggregate commuting, an extra constraint is imposed for each household that the household cannot be moved to a residential zone where it achieves a lower utility level than at its current residential zone. Additional corrections prevent African-American households from being reassigned to zones that are less than 10% African-American, prevent two-worker households from being split up, and allow for differences between the location choices of owner versus renter households. Thus, the Cropper–Gordon model corrects for at least some of the factors that in actuality lead households to choose longer commutes. However, the results suggest that these corrections make relatively little difference. The ratio of actual-to-minimum commuting is 2.0 for owners and 2.4 for renters when the relocation constraints are imposed, compared to 2.3 and 2.8, respectively, when no constraints are imposed. One possible reason for the constraints having little effect is that, in many cases, the same commute-reducing effect can be obtained by workers trading either jobs or houses. Cropper and Gordon's (1991) constraints mainly reduce possible trades of houses, so that the assignment process can obtain the same commute-minimizing result by trading jobs. The results of imposing the constraints might be greater, therefore, if additional constraints on trading jobs—such as workers with high skills not being allowed to trade jobs with workers with low skills—were imposed.

A more recent paper by Kim (1995) divides urban households into those with one-worker and those with two-workers. He runs separate assignment models for one-worker and two-worker households. For the former, both jobs and residences can be traded to reduce commuting but, for the latter, only jobs can be traded so that spouses are not separated. Kim uses data for Los Angeles-Long Beach which divide the metropolitan area into approximately 1500 zones. He finds surprisingly low actual-to-minimum commuting ratios: 1.5 for one-worker households and 1.26 for two-worker households.[27]

Overall, the "wasteful" commuting controversy has shown that workers on average commute no more than about three times the minimum required by the spatial distributions of jobs and housing and the actual road networks in their metropolitan areas. Imposing constraints to reflect the fact that not all trades of housing or jobs to minimize commuting are economically beneficial reduces the ratio to about 1.5–2. Given the low marginal cost of travel in the US, where automobiles and gasoline are lightly taxed and there are few road tolls, this amount of extra commuting seems rather low. It would be interesting to have comparable results for cities in Europe, where the marginal cost of travel is much higher and much more commuting is via public transport.

## References

Anas, A. and I. Kim (1994), "General equilibrium models of polycentric urban land use with endogenous congestion and job agglomeration", Journal of Urban Economics 40:232–256
Boarnet, M. (1994), "The monocentric model and employment location", Journal of Urban Economics 36:79–97.
Braid, R.M. (1988), "Optimal spatial growth of employment and residences", Journal of Urban Economics 24:227–240.
Capozza, D. (1976), "Employment/population ratios in urban areas: a model of the urban land, labor and goods markets", in: G.J. Papageorgiou, ed., Mathematical Land Use Theory (Lexington Books, Lexington, MA).
Cooke, T. (1978), "Causality reconsidered: a note", Journal of Urban Economics 5:538–542.
Crane, R. (1995), "The influence of uncertain job location on urban form and the journey to work", Journal of Urban Economics 39:342–356

---

[27] Also see Crane (1995) for a discussion of how uncertainty concerning job locations would affect the ratio of actual-to-minimum commuting.

Cropper, M. and P. Gordon (1991), "Wasteful commuting: a re-examination", Journal of Urban Economics 29:2–13.

Eberts, R.W. (1981), "An empirical investigation of intraurban wage gradients", Journal of Urban Economics 10:50–60.

Fujita, M. and H. Ogawa (1982), "Multiple equilibria and structural transition of non-monocentric urban configurations", Regional Science and Urban Economics 12:161–196.

Giuliano, G. and K.A. Small (1991), "Subcenters in the Los Angeles region", Regional Science and Urban Economics 21:163–182.

Hamilton, B. (1982), "Wasteful commuting", Journal of Political Economy 90:1035–1053.

Hamilton, B. (1990), "Wasteful commuting again", Journal of Political Economy 97:1497–1504.

Helsley, R.W. and A.M. Sullivan (1991), "Urban subcenter formation", Regional Science and Urban Economics 21:255–276.

Henderson, J.V. (1977), Economic Theory and the Cities (Academic Press, New York).

Henderson, J.V. and E. Slade (1993), "Development games in non-monotonic cities", Journal of Urban Economics 34:207–229.

Hotchkiss, D. and M.J. White (1993), "A simulation model of a decentralized metropolitan area with two-worker, 'traditional' and female-headed households", Journal of Urban Economics 34:159–185.

Ilhanfeldt, K.R. (1988), "Intra-metropolitan variation in earnings and labor market discrimination: an econometric analysis of the Atlanta labor market", Southern Economic Journal 55:123–140.

Ilhanfeldt, K.R. (1992), "Intraurban wage gradients: evidence by race, gender, occupational class, and sector", Journal of Urban Economics 32:70–91.

Kim, S. (1995), "Excess commuting for two-worker households in the Los Angeles metropolitan area", Journal of Urban Economics 38:166–182.

Macauley, M. (1985), "Estimation and recent behavior of urban population and employment density gradients", Journal of Urban Economics 18: 251–260.

Madden, J.F. (1985), "Urban wage gradients: empirical evidence", Journal of Urban Economics 18:291–301.

McMillen, D. and L.D. Singell (1992), "Work location, residence location and the intraurban wage gradient", Journal of Urban Economics 32:195–213.

Mills, E.S. (1972), Studies in the Structure of the Urban Economy. (Johns Hopkins University Press, Baltimore).

Mills, E.S. and B. Hamilton (1989), Urban Economics (Scott, Foresman, Glenview, IL).

Mills, E.S. and R. Price (1984), "Metropolitan suburbanization and central city problems", Journal of Urban Economics 15:1–17.

Muth, R. (1969), Cities and Housing (University of Chicago Press, Chicago).

Ogawa, H. and M. Fujita (1980), "Equilibrium land use patterns in a nonmonocentric city", Journal of Regional Science 20:455–475.

Ogawa, H. and M. Fujita (1989), "Nonmonocentric urban configurations in a two-dimensional space", Environment and Planning A 21:363–374.

O'Hara, J.D. (1977), "Location of firms within a square central business district", Journal of Political Economy 85:1189–1207.

Rees, A. and G.P. Schultz (1970), Workers and Wages in an Urban Labor Market (University of Chicago Press, Chicago).

Ross, S. and J. Yinger (1995), "Comparative static analysis of open urban models with a full labor market and suburban employment", Regional Science and Urban Economics 25:575–605.

Sivitanidou, R. and W.C. Wheaton (1992), "Wage and rent capitalization in the commercial real estate market", Journal of Urban Economics 31:206–229.

Small, K. and S. Song (1992), " 'Wasteful' commuting: a resolution", Journal of Political Economy 100:888–898.

Steinnes, D. (1977), "Causality and intraurban location", Journal of Urban Economics 4:69–79.

Straszheim, M. (1984), "Urban agglomeration effects and employment and wage gradients", Journal of Urban Economics 16:187–207.

Sullivan, A.M. (1986), "A general equilibrium model with agglomerative economics and decentralized employment", Journal of Urban Economics 20:55–75.

Tauchen, H. and A.D. Witte (1984), "Socially optimal and equilibrium distributions of office activity: models with exogenous and endogenous contacts", Journal of Urban Economics 15:66–86.

Thurston, L. and A. Yezer (1994), "Causality in the suburbanization of population and employment", Journal of Urban Economics 35:105–118.

Wieand, K. (1987), "An extension of the monocentric urban spatial equilibrium model to a multi-center setting: the case of the two-center city", Journal of Urban Economics 21:259–271.

White, M.J. (1976), "Firm suburbanization and urban subcenters", Journal of Urban Economics 3:323–343.

White, M.J. (1988a), "Location choice and commuting behavior in cities with decentralized employment", Journal of Urban Economics 24:129–152.

White, M.J. (1988b), "Urban commuting is not 'wasteful' ", Journal of Political Economy 96:1097–1110.

White, M.J. (1990), "Commuting and congestion: a simulation model of a decentralized metropolitan area", Journal of the American Real Estate and Urban Economics Association 18:335–368.

Yinger, J. (1992), "Urban models with more than one employment center", Journal of Urban Economics 31:181–205.

*Chapter 37*

# QUALITY OF LIFE AND ENVIRONMENTAL COMPARISONS

JOSEPH GYOURKO*

*The Wharton School, University of Pennsylvania*

MATTHEW KAHN

*Columbia University*

JOSEPH TRACY

*Federal Reserve Bank of New York*

## Contents

* We thank Glenn Blomquist, Charles Leven and Jerry Hausman for helpful comments on previous drafts. Naturally, the usual caveat still applies.

*Handbook of Regional and Urban Economics. Edited by E.S. Mills and P. Cheshire*

## Abstract

Recent research into the urban quality of life (QOL) is reviewed and analyzed, with a special emphasis on the estimation of implicit prices of environmental attributes. New work has incorporated traditional concerns of urban theory into QOL analyses, as well as increased our understanding of specification bias problems in hedonic estimations. However, empirical research into the QOL finds itself at a crossroads, as the large city-specific error components in the underlying wage and housing expenditure hedonic specifications result in imprecise measurement of overall QOL values and rankings. Amassing higher quality databases to deal with this problem should be high on the agenda of those interested in this research program.

**Keywords:** Hedonics, quality of life, environmental

## 1. Introduction

Measuring the quality of life (QOL) across urban areas has been an important research program in urban economics, since Rosen (1979) and Roback (1980, 1982) showed how to identify implicit market prices of local amenities that can serve as the weights in the construction of QOL indexes. Bartik and Smith (1987) provide an excellent review of the early theoretical and empirical work from this research project in the *Handbook of Regional and Urban Economics* (see Chap. 31, this volume). Our review takes up the story where theirs left off, beginning with work published in the mid-1980s.

Significant conceptual advances in this literature have been made over the last decade. They include the incorporation of traditional concerns of urban theory such as compensation for distance from the central business district (Hoehn et al., 1987) and agglomeration effects (Blomquist et al., 1988) into the Rosen/Roback framework. There also have been contributions showing how local governments can influence the QOL through their own taxation and service provision decisions (Gyourko and Tracy, 1989b, 1991). While interesting in their own right, these theoretical advances have also helped improve our understanding of specification bias problems, that are particularly important when the researcher's interest is on specific capitalization results, rather than the overall QOL. In addition, this new work has expanded our knowledge of the extent of differential capitalization in land versus labor markets.

We also focus on research into the estimation of implicit prices of environmental attributes. This work is particularly relevant to QOL research for several reasons. First, the environment is a significant component of the local trait set. Second, both cross-city and within-city data have been used to generate implicit price estimates, and the differences in results are helpful in understanding the strengths and weaknesses of the empirical work on the overall QOL that relies exclusively on cross-city data. In addition, the greatest experimentation with non-hedonic valuation methods has occurred in the environmental area. Assessing the relative strengths and weaknesses of the varying valuation methodologies yields interesting insights into the QOL literature that, heretofore, has relied on revealed preference techniques.

Despite all these developments, we believe that empirical research into the QOL presently finds itself at a crossroads. This is because recent work by Gyourko and Tracy (1989a,b, 1991) reports the presence of large city-specific error components in the underlying wage and housing expenditure hedonic specifications estimated to determine the local trait prices. After carefully controlling for these error components, it turns out that overall QOL values and rankings are imprecisely estimated. The level of imprecision is such that much better descriptions of local amenity and fiscal conditions, plus superior controls for housing, worker and job quality, are needed to minimize the impact of these city-specific error components. Amassing higher quality databases in the face of budget cutbacks at the key data collection agencies of many national governments will be a difficult and time-consuming process, but it should be high on the agenda of those interested in such research.

Nevertheless, we are far from pessimistic about the prospects for this research program. Progress can be made in other ways and on other fronts. One that we discuss at length in Section 6 involves relaxing the key equilibrium assumption underlying virtually all existing work in the area. The assumption that the researcher is viewing local land and labor markets in states of long-run equilibrium in any cross-section of data is what permits the equating of estimated trait prices with their true market values. The violence done to QOL estimates by this very convenient assumption is unknown, but Cheshire and Hay (1989) and Greenwood et al. (1991) have taken the first steps towards informing us.

The chapter is organized as follows. A brief exposition of the Rosen/Roback model is provided in Section 2. Section 3 then discusses the implications of recent econometric developments in estimating the QOL. This is followed by detailed analyses of three major studies that estimated the QOL across a number of metropolitan areas. Section 5 provides a separate review of the role of the environment in the QOL, as well as a discussion of alternative valuation techniques. Section 6 then focuses on the challenge of integrating mobility into QOL analyses. A brief summary concludes the chapter.

## 2. Theoretical underpinnings[1]

At the heart of the Rosen/Roback framework is a compensating differential model in which workers and firms compete for scarce sites, with wages and rents adjusting so that, in equilibrium, the marginal worker and firm are indifferent among locations. A representative worker-resident is assumed to consume land-housing services, $N$, and a composite commodity, $C$, which is traded at a common price (the numeraire) across cities. Residents living in city $j$ also consume a bundle of pure amenities $A_j$ (e.g., good weather) and government services, $G_j$, that are locally produced (e.g., public safety). The amenity and service package available in city $j$ is taken as exogenous by all potential worker-residents to that city, with the utility for representative worker-resident $i$ living in city $j$ given by,

$$U\{C_i, N_i; A_j, G_j\}. \tag{2.1}$$

The gross-of-tax cost of a unit of the consumption commodity is $(1 + s_j)$, where $s_j$ is the combined state and local sales tax rate. The gross-of-tax rental rate for a unit of land-housing services is $(1 + t_j)n_j$, where $t_j$ is the local property tax rate

---

[1] The model presented in this section includes some, but not all, of the conceptual advances made to the Rosen/Roback structure since the mid-1980s. If data limitations prevented empirical confirmation of a recent conceptual innovation, we do not include it in the model specification below. Specifically, Hoehn et al. (1987) endogenizing of city size and population and introduction of compensation for travel distance from the central business district (CBD) are not modeled. The same holds for agglomeration effects introduced by Blomquist et al. (1988). We refer readers interested in those specific comparative statics to the two articles.

and $n_j$ is the local land rental rate. The worker-resident's net-of-tax wage rate is given by $(1 - z_j)W_j^g$, where $z_j$ is the combined state and local income tax rate and $W_j^g$ is the local gross wage.[2]

Assuming that each worker-resident inelastically supplies one unit of labor, the budget constraint for the worker-resident is given by,

$$(1 + s_j)C_i + (1 + t_j)n_j N_i \leq (1 - z_j)W_j^g + I_i, \tag{2.2}$$

where $I_i$ represents nonwage income.[3]

Conditional on a city location, the following indirect utility function arises from the worker-resident's maximization of Eq. (2.1) subject to Eq. (2.2):

$$V_{ij} = V\{(1 - z_j)W_i^g, (1 + t_j)n_j, (1 + s_j), I_i; A_j, G_j\}. \tag{2.3}$$

Amenities enter the indirect utility function only through their impact on a worker-resident's utility. Services, in contrast, enter the indirect utility function both through their impact on a worker-resident's utility and through their associated impact on the gross- and net-of-tax prices faced by the worker-resident.

Assuming costless mobility and full information about the amenity and fiscal attributes of each city, long-run equilibrium requires that the marginal worker-resident be indifferent to her city location,[4] with wages and land rentals adjusting so that,

$$V^* = V_{ij} \qquad \text{for all } j. \tag{2.4}$$

Turning to the firm's location decision, profits conditional on locating in city $j$ are given by,

$$\pi_{ij} = Y_i\{A_j, G_j\} - (1 + t_j)n_j N_i - W_j^g L_i - (1 + s_j)M_i, \tag{2.5}$$

where $Y_i$ is the total revenues that are a function of the city's amenity and fiscal attributes through their impact on the production (and distribution) function, $L_i$

[2] For simplicity, all workers are treated as equally productive. Empirical applications include variables that attempt to control for productivity differences across workers.

[3] For simplicity of exposition, this specification of the budget constraint assumes that the state taxes only wages. No fundamental conclusions are altered if more complex descriptions are employed.

[4] If workers are homogeneous in preferences, then the arbitrage condition implies equalizing differences that will be exact for all worker/residents. If workers are heterogeneous in preferences, then the equalizing differences will be exact only for the marginal worker. See Roback (1988).

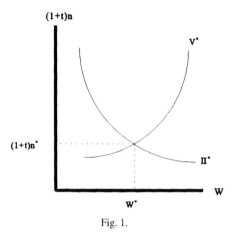

Fig. 1.

represents the firm's labor usage, and $M_i$ is the firm's intermediate input usage.[5] Given a city location, the firm's maximization problem yields the following indirect profit function,

$$\Pi_{ij} = \Pi_i\{W_j^g, (1+t_j)n_j, (1+s_j); A_j, G_j\}. \tag{2.6}$$

Again, assuming costless mobility and full information, the long-run equilibrium requires that the marginal firm is indifferent to its city location. This requires that wages and land rentals adjust to impose the following arbitrage condition:

$$\Pi^* = \Pi_{ij} \qquad \text{for all } j. \tag{2.7}$$

The long-run equilibrium wage and land rentals are found by solving the two arbitrage conditions as illustrated in Fig. 1's familiar representation.

The reduced form wage equation is obtained by isolating the gross-of-tax land rental in Eq. (2.4) and Eq. (2.7), equating the two expressions, and solving for $W_j^g$ so that,

$$W_j^g = W\{(1+s_j), z_j, I, A_j, G_j; V^*, \Pi^*\}. \tag{2.8}$$

The reduced form equation for the gross-of-tax land rental $(1+t_j)n_j$, which we denote as $R_j$, is obtained in a similar fashion so that,

[5] Equal residential and commercial property tax rates are presumed in Eq. (2.2) and Eq. (2.5), but the model is unaffected if different tax rates are allowed. We also abstract from restrictive zoning that might introduce a wedge between residential and commercial rents. In this sense, the model probably is more applicable to larger, more heterogeneous cities than to smaller, relatively homogeneous suburbs.

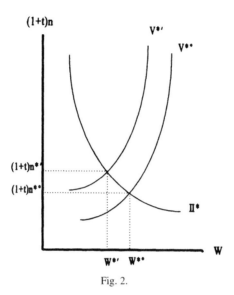

Fig. 2.

$$R_j \equiv (1 + t_j)n_j = N\{(1 + s_j), z_j, I, A_j, G_j; V^*, \Pi^*\}. \tag{2.9}$$

The comparative statics of the model yield several insights into wage and land rental capitalization. The first implication of the model is *full* capitalization of property tax differentials into land rentals. That is, increases in the property tax, $t$, that are not offset by added services or amenities (or other tax reductions) are fully capitalized into land prices:

$$\left.\frac{\partial n}{\partial t}\right|_{z,s,I,A,G} = -\frac{n}{(1-t)} < 0,$$

$$\left.\frac{\partial W}{\partial t}\right|_{z,s,I,A,G} = 0. \tag{2.10}$$

Pure amenities by definition have no explicit market price. They are implicitly priced in the labor and land markets through capitalization into wages and rentals as shown in Eq. (2.11),

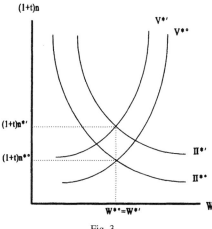

Fig. 3.

$$\left.\frac{\partial n}{\partial t}\right|_{t,s,z,I,G} = \frac{-\dfrac{V_A}{V_R} + \dfrac{V_W}{V_R}\dfrac{\Pi_A}{\Pi_W}(1-z)}{D} > 0,$$

(2.11)

$$\left.\frac{\partial W}{\partial A}\right|_{t,s,z,I,G} = \frac{\dfrac{1}{V_W(1-z)}\left[-V_A + V_R\dfrac{\Pi_A}{\Pi_R}\right]}{D} \gtrless 0,$$

where $D = 1 - (V_W/V_R)(\Pi_R/\Pi_W)(1-z) > 0$, and $V_k$ and $\Pi_k$ are the first partials of the indirect utility and profit functions with $V_W > 0$, $V_R < 0$, $V_A > 0$, $V_G > 0$, $\Pi_W < 0$, $\Pi_R < 0$, $\Pi_A \geq 0$, and $\Pi_G \geq 0$.

These results imply that sites in cities with better amenity characteristics, among other things, will be rationed through higher land prices and an indeterminate shift in wages. If the amenity does not directly affect firm revenues, $\Pi_A = 0$, then wages will fail to help ration scarce sites. In this case, the amenity is capitalized in both wages and rentals (see Fig. 2). If the amenity is productive, $\Pi_A > 0$, then land rentals increase by even more than in the first case, and the wage effect is indeterminate (see Fig. 3, in which the assumed shift in the firm's indirect profit curve leaves the wage unaffected). Smaller (larger) shifts in the firm's indirect profit curve would result in wages falling (rising) in response to the higher amenity level.

The analysis of government service provision parallels that for amenities because the explicit prices for government services (income, sales, and property taxes) are held constant, while the level of government services varies (see Eq. (2.12)). This type of variation in the data is possible if local governments vary in their efficiency at delivering services.

$$\left.\frac{\partial n}{\partial G}\right|_{t,s,z,I,A} = \frac{-\dfrac{V_G}{V_R} + \dfrac{V_W}{V_R}\dfrac{\Pi_G}{\Pi_W}(1-z)}{D} > 0,$$

$$\left.\frac{\partial W}{\partial G}\right|_{t,s,z,I,A} = \frac{\dfrac{1}{V_W(1-z)}\left[-V_G + V_R\dfrac{\Pi_G}{\Pi_R}\right]}{D} \gtrless 0.$$

(2.12)

Two more comparative static results relate to changes in the income and sales tax rates. Higher income ($z$) and sales ($s$) tax rates, holding service levels constant, lead to lower land rentals. Since the income tax rate does not affect the firm's indirect profit function, a higher rate also leads to higher gross wages. In contrast, if firms use intermediate goods, then higher sales tax rates can lead to higher or lower gross wages. These results are summarized in Eq. (2.13).

$$\left.\frac{\partial n}{\partial z}\right|_{t,s,I,A,G} = \frac{\dfrac{V_W}{V_R}\dfrac{W^g}{(1+t)}}{D} < 0,$$

$$\left.\frac{\partial W}{\partial z}\right|_{t,s,I,A,G} = \frac{\dfrac{W^g}{(1-z)}}{D} > 0,$$

(2.13)

$$\left.\frac{\partial n}{\partial s}\right|_{t,z,I,A,G} = \frac{-\dfrac{V_s}{V_R} + \dfrac{V_W}{V_R}\dfrac{\Pi_s}{\Pi_W}(1-z)}{D} < 0,$$

$$\left.\frac{\partial W}{\partial s}\right|_{t,z,I,A,G} = \frac{\dfrac{1}{V_W(1-z)}\left[-V_s + V_R\dfrac{\Pi_s}{\Pi_R}\right]}{D} \gtrless 0.$$

Full prices for amenities and fiscal attributes of cities are constructed from these capitalization results as follows. Define $P_k$ as the full price for the $k$th city attribute, $Z_k$, with,

$$P_k = \frac{\partial n}{\partial Z_k} - e\frac{\partial W}{\partial Z_k},$$

(2.14)

where $e$ denotes the "exposure" of the marginal household to the labor market.[6] The next step in constructing a QOL index value is to use the equilibrium assumption to equate prices with values. In this case, the value of city $j$ is the sum of its attributes multiplied by their full prices.

$$QOL_j = \sum_k P_k Z_{jk}. \tag{2.15}$$

Obviously, the link between the price observed for an attribute and the value placed on the attribute is central to the QOL methodology (see Evans, 1990), and is a topic we return to at the end of the chapter.

## 3. Recent econometric developments in estimating the quality of life

### 3.1. Specification bias problems and the interpretation of capitalization results

All empirical work is subject to specification bias, and recent research suggests that there are special concerns in QOL analyses because of the difficulty of properly controlling for all taxes and the levels of effective service provision (Gyourko and Tracy (1989a,b; 1991)). For example, the reduced form comparative statics for government services parallel those for amenities *only* if all relevant taxes are included in the reduced form equations. In addition, public sector rent-sharing can bias the capitalization results for amenities by creating explicit prices for them if local unions appropriate some of the locational rents through the collective bargaining process via agreements that permit overstaffing or pay wage premia.

Consider how the comparative statics for $G$ would change if all taxes are not controlled for in the reduced form wage and land rental equations. To keep the analysis simple, let the locality vary only the local property tax rate in order to adjust its tax revenues. This gives rise to the following relationship between government services and the property tax rate.

$$t_j = T(G_j; B_j, \Theta_j), \tag{3.1}$$

where $B_j$ is the property tax base in the city, and $\Theta_j$ is an efficiency parameter. While the local property tax rate depends on the level of local services, variations

---

[6] The assumption is that each household owns one residential site in the community, but may have a varying degree of exposure to the labor market. For example, a retired household would have $e = 0$, a single earner household $e = 1$, and a dual earner household $e = 2$.

in rates across communities having the same level of services can exist due to differences in tax bases and efficiency levels of the governments.

Failure to control for the explicit tax price associated with a produced government service, as distinct from a nonproduced amenity, generates the following capitalization results (Gyourko and Tracy, 1989b, 1991):

$$
\begin{aligned}
\left.\frac{\partial n}{\partial G}\right|_{I,A} &= \left.\frac{\partial n}{\partial G}\right|_{t,I,A} + \left.\frac{\partial n}{\partial t}\right|_{I,A,G} \frac{\partial t}{\partial G} \\
&= \left.\frac{\partial n}{\partial G}\right|_{t,I,A} - \frac{n}{(1-t)} \frac{\partial t}{\partial G},
\end{aligned}
$$

$$
\begin{aligned}
\left.\frac{\partial W}{\partial G}\right|_{I,A} &= \left.\frac{\partial W}{\partial G}\right|_{t,I,A} + \left.\frac{\partial W}{\partial t}\right|_{I,A,G} \frac{\partial t}{\partial G} \\
&= \left.\frac{\partial W}{\partial G}\right|_{t,I,A}.
\end{aligned}
$$

(3.2)

Note that the land-rental capitalization effect now involves two terms. The first reflects the pure capitalization of the government services holding their explicit tax prices constant. The second captures the compound effect of a pure property tax rate increase holding services constant multiplied by the increase in the property tax rate due to the higher level of services. Given the increase in property tax rates due to the higher service level, the sign of the second term is negative for land rentals and zero for wage rates (because the property tax rate effect is fully capitalized into land-rentals with no spillover to local wages—see Eq. (2.10)). Thus, the second effect acts to offset the first for land rentals, lowering the observed level of capitalization. However, there is no similar effect on wage capitalization. A consequence of the failure to fully control for taxes, then, is to bias the relative capitalization effects of locally produced services toward wages.

Bias can also result from failing to properly control for all taxes when public sector unionization leads to the sharing of locational rents between union members and other community residents. Assume that unions attempt to organize in areas where the potential return is the highest, so that the level of public sector unionization increases on average with the size of the locational rents. Furthermore, let amenities comprise a significant component of locational rents. Then, as we increase the level of amenities by moving across cities, we also are increasing the level of public sector unionization, $\partial U/\partial A > 0$, where $U$ represents the local public sector unionization rate. The measured capitalized value of amenities in this case is given in Eq. (3.3).

$$
\frac{\partial n}{\partial A}\bigg|_{I,G} = \frac{\partial n}{\partial A}\bigg|_{t,I,G} + \left[\frac{\partial n}{\partial U}\frac{\partial U}{\partial A}\right],
$$

$$
\frac{\partial W}{\partial A}\bigg|_{I,G} = \frac{\partial W}{\partial A}\bigg|_{t,I,G} + \left[\frac{\partial W}{\partial U}\frac{\partial U}{\partial A}\right].
$$

(3.3)

For land rentals, the first term on the righthand side is positive and reflects the total value of the increased amenity level. However, the second term on the right-hand side is negative, reflecting the combined effects of increased rent-sharing and allocative inefficiency associated with the increased union rent-seeking associated with the higher amenity level. For wages, the sign of the first term is ambiguous while that of the second is positive.[7]

In the extreme, if the *entire* value of the additional amenity level is appropriated by local unions, then the capitalized value of the amenity differential is zero. In that case, collective bargaining has completely transformed the implicit price for the amenity into an explicit price, because the cost of local public sector rent-sharing must be financed through a combination of higher taxes and/or lower service levels.

## 3.2. Group effects in the wage and housing data

The data used in QOL studies typically involve microlevel observations on many workers and homes within a given labor or housing market area. Researchers need to be cognizant of the possibility that the wage and house price hedonic regression residuals may contain city-specific error components (i.e., group effects). Ordinary least squares (OLS) estimations, that do not control for these group effects, will lead to reported standard errors of the trait prices that are biased downward (see Moulton, 1986, 1987). Naturally, this is important for testing specific hypotheses about capitalization, and we show below that it is also relevant for calculating the standard errors of the QOL rankings.

Consider the following specification forwages for worker/resident $i$ in city $j$,

$$
\ln W_{ij} = X_i\beta_1 + Z_j\beta_2 + u_{ij}, \qquad u_{ij} = \alpha_j + \epsilon_i, \tag{3.4}
$$

where $X_i$ is a vector of individual worker traits and industry/occupation controls, $Z_j$ is a vector of city amenity/fiscal characteristics, and $u_{ij}$ is the composite

---

[7] See Gyourko and Tracy (1989b) for details.

error term. The composite error term is the combination of a city-specific error component, $\alpha_j$, and an individual-specific error component, $\epsilon_i$. The city-specific error component is common to all workers in the city, and represents systematic uncontrolled differences in worker quality across cities, systematic uncontrolled differences in amenity/fiscal characteristics across cities, and/or common demand/supply shocks to the local labor market.

Similarly, let the local land rental for household $i$ in city $j$ be modeled as follows:

$$\ln n_{ij} = H_i \gamma_1 + Z_j \gamma_2 + \nu_{ij}, \qquad \nu_{ij} = \delta_j + \eta_i, \tag{3.5}$$

where $H_i$ is a vector of individual housing structural traits, and $\nu_{ij}$ is the composite error term. The composite error term again is the combination of a city-specific error component, $\delta_j$, and a house-specific error component, $\eta_i$. The city-specific error component is common to all houses in the city, and represents systematic uncontrolled differences in house quality across cities, systematic uncontrolled differences in amenity/fiscal characteristics across cities, and/or common demand/supply shocks to the local housing market.

If $\sigma_\alpha^2 > 0$ and $\sigma_\delta^2 > 0$, then the composite error terms across workers and across houses within the same city are correlated, violating the OLS independence assumption. The magnitude of the bias imparted to the standard errors of the estimated trait prices when independence is violated depends on the "design effects" present in the data (Kish, 1965). The design effect for the $j$th city is defined as follows:

$$d_j = 1 + (m_j - 1)\rho, \tag{3.6}$$

where $m_j$ is the number of workers (houses) in the sample from the $j$th city, and $\rho$ is the common correlation coefficient between the composite errors for workers (houses) within the city. In our example, these correlations are given by the ratio of the variance of the city-specific error components to the total variance of the composite error terms.

The simplest case to analyze is where the size of each city is the same and the righthand side variables vary only between groups (i.e., there are only $Z$ variables in the model). In this case, the ratio of the true variance of $\beta_2$ to the OLS variance estimate equals the design effect.[8] The presence of city-specific error components generates design effects greater than one. The extent of the downward bias in the

---

[8] See Tuenkloek (1981) for the derivation of the correct variance/covariance matrix.

OLS-based standard errors depends on the size of the city groups in the data and the size of $\rho$.[9]

A second implication of the presence of group effects is that the definition of a city's QOL becomes ambiguous. Assume the city-specific error components represent left-out amenity/fiscal attributes of a city. If data were available on these attributes, then implicit prices could be estimated and the attributes would be included in the calculation of the QOL. In the absence of data on the attributes, their impact on a city's QOL could be determined as follows:

$$QOL = \sum_k P_k Z_{jk} + \delta_j - e \cdot \alpha_j. \tag{3.7}$$

However, if the city-specific error components represent largely uncontrolled for worker and housing quality, then they should *not* be included in the QOL calculation. Given the inherent ambiguity regarding the source of the city-specific error components, it is prudent to always examine the sensitivity of the QOL rankings to include or exclude the city-specific error components.

Testing for the presence of group effects can proceed along the lines suggested by King and Evans (1986), who proposed the following Lagrange multiplier (LM) test for the null hypothesis $H_0$: $\sigma_\alpha^2 = 0$, versus the alternative hypothesis $H_1$: $\sigma_\alpha^2 > 0$,

$$LM = \frac{\sum_j (m_j \bar{u}_j)^2 - \sum_i \sum_j u_{ij}^2}{\sigma^2 \left[ 2 \left( \sum_j m_j^2 - N \right) \right]^{1/2}}, \tag{3.8}$$

where $\sigma^2 = u'u/N$. Under the null hypothesis, the LM statistic is asymptotically distributed as a standard normal. An advantage of this test is that it only requires the OLS residuals, which makes it easy to utilize as a diagnostic test.[10]

If the null hypothesis is rejected, then a random effects estimator should be used in lieu of the OLS. It is important, though, following estimation of the

---

[9] Generalizing the model to allow for differing city sizes and/or variables that vary within each city ($X$ and $H$) still results in a downward bias in the OLS standard errors. See Scott and Holt (1982), Pfefferman and Smith (1985) and Moulton (1986).

[10] If the aim of the empirical exercise is to generate consistent estimates of the coefficients on the worker and/or house quality variables, and the amenity/fiscal variables are of no independent interest, then a fixed effects estimator can be used in lieu of random effects. This approach is much simpler in that no data on a location's amenity/fiscal attributes are required. See Kahn (1995).

random effects model, to run a specification test to establish whether, or not, the city-specific error components are correlated with the righthand side variables in the model. If this is the case, then random effects will produce inconsistent coefficient estimates. The standard procedure is to carry out a Hausman test for a significant difference between the fixed and random effects coefficients on the variables that have within-group variation. If the test rejects the null of no correlation, then instrumental variable random effects procedures can be used (see Hausman and Taylor, 1981).

The presence of group effects also has important implications for the precision of the QOL rankings. The QOL ranking for a given city is a nonlinear function of the hedonic coefficient estimates and the distribution of all city amenity/fiscal attributes. This makes simulation methods for calculating standard errors more tractable than analytic methods. The intuition for the simulation methods is as follows. The researcher would like to draw a new sample of data from the "population", and re-estimate the hedonic coefficients. The new coefficient estimates can then be used to construct a new QOL ranking. Repeating this process will generate a distribution of QOL rankings for each city. A measure of the standard error of a given city's QOL ranking is the standard deviation of this empirical distribution.

This process can be approximated by simulating new draws of the hedonic coefficients based on their estimated joint distributions. In the estimation process above, we assumed a normal distribution for the composite error terms. This implies coefficient vectors that also have a normal distribution, $V(\beta)$. Rather than redrawing samples of data, one can redraw coefficient vectors from their assumed distribution. This saves considerably on computation time relative to bootstrap methods for resampling of the data.[11]

The limited research on this issue suggests that the precision of QOL rankings is considerably less than researchers and decision-makers would like. Using the 1980 *Census of Population and Housing* data on workers for 125 cities, Gyourko and Tracy's (1989b) results imply that the OLS standard errors for the wage hedonic prices were biased downward by a factor of 2.4 on average. Gyourko and Tracy's (1991) paper, also using the 1980 *Census of Population and Housing* data, suggested that the OLS standard errors for the housing hedonic prices were biased downward by a factor of 2.8 on average.

---

[11] Very briefly, since $V(\beta)$ is a positive semidefinite matrix, there exists a unique *lower* triangular matrix $C$ such that $V(\beta) = CC'$. Let $\beta^i$ denote the $i$th simulated coefficient vector and $\xi^i$ a vector (with dimension matching $\beta$) of standard normals. Then $\beta^i$ can be simulated as, $\beta^i = \beta + C \cdot \xi^i$, where $\beta$ are the original hedonic coefficient estimates. The number of simulations should be increased until the implied standard errors of the QOL rankings do not change at an acceptable level of significance between separate simulation exercises.

The impact of city-specific error components on the precision of the hedonic prices, directly affects the precision of the QOL estimates derived from these prices. The average standard error of the rankings based on random effects is 16.9 versus an average of 8.6 for the rankings based on OLS. Given the 130-city sample size, this implies that it is impossible to differentiate among cities at standard confidence levels unless the comparison is between cities ranked in the top and bottom 20 of all cities.

The limitations of existing studies are further amplified when one compares the QOL rankings with and without the city-specific error components included. Assuming that the city-specific error components, $\alpha_j$ and $\delta_j$, primarily represent systematic unobserved worker and house quality differences across cities implies that these error components should be excluded from the QOL calculation. In contrast, assuming that these error components primarily represent left-out city attributes implies that they should be included in the QOL calculation as given by Eq. (3.8). In Gyourko and Tracy (1991), the simple correlation between the two sets of rankings is 0.63. However, the mean absolute change in rankings is 27 with a standard deviation of 21. The housing and wage error components are positively correlated, $\rho = 0.14$ (0.10) when weighted by the number of housing (wage) observations. This positive correlation is consistent with the error components reflecting primarily left-out worker and housing quality, but does not preclude the left-out amenity/fiscal variable explanation.[12]

One solution to this problem is better quality data on worker, housing and city characteristics. The impact of the error components on the estimation results is minimized as the error components themselves are minimized. However, most QOL studies have a limited number of urban areas to work with, which places a severe constraint on the potential number of urban attributes that can be controlled in the wage and housing specifications. Given the difficulties in improving the quality of cross-sectional data used to estimate urban QOL, an important question is the degree to which panel data could alleviate the error components problems discussed above. Unobserved workers and housing quality differences that are time invariant can be differenced out in panel data. However, the problem in QOL applications is that the urban attributes, $Z_j$, are differenced out as well. Moreover, there is likely to be little real variation in most urban attributes over short time periods. The measured variation in the data is likely to be heavily

---

[12] A plausible story is that workers of higher quality will demand higher quality housing. This would imply a positive correlation between the city error components. Left-out amenity/fiscal variables that are valued by workers but not firms would imply a negative correlation. However, if firms also value the amenity/fiscal variables, then the sign of the correlation is indeterminate.

contaminated with measurement error. Panel data, then, do not provide a useful alternative to improved cross-sectional data.

## 4. New estimates of the quality of life: results, comparisons, and analysis

Over the past decade there have been three major QOL estimation projects within the Rosen/Roback tradition that use market prices of local traits as weights in index construction: Blomquist et al. (1988), Gyourko and Tracy (1991) and Stover and Leven (1992). Other recent efforts to estimate compensating differentials arising from city attributes include Hoehn et al. (1987), Roback (1988) and Voith (1991). However, they are not discussed here because they did not compute a single QOL index value for each locality. In addition, research on other approaches (e.g., Cheshire and Hay (1989)) and on mobility and the QOL (e.g., Greenwood et al. (1991)) is dealt with in Section 6. Various organizations also publish QOL rankings that use survey data or some ad hoc weighting scheme. Boyer's (1983) *Places Rated Almanac* and the Mobil Oil Corporation's *1989 Mobil Travel Guide* are good examples of that genre.[13]

### 4.1. Blomquist et al. (1988): "New estimates of the quality of life in urban areas"

This study spurred renewed interest into research on the urban QOL. The empirical work is based on a large cross-section of 253 counties within 185 metropolitan areas in the US taken from the 1980 *Census of Population and Housing*. The authors' underlying theoretical model is one in which each urban area has two counties, and they derive new and interesting comparative static results with respect to the impact of agglomeration effects associated with productivity effects of the size of the urban area. While Blomquist et al. (1998) report substantial intrametropolitan area differences in the QOL for 10 of the 38 urban areas for which they have observations on multiple counties, it is unclear how having amenity variation both within and across urban areas impacts on either the individual trait valuations or the overall QOL rankings. It would be useful to know if the price of (say) their superfund site trait would be substantially different if

---

[13] It should be noted that the three studies to be reviewed below all estimate reduced form wage and housing hedonic price equations. Consequently, they do not test the basic assumption of the Rosen/Roback model that labor and land markets are interrelated. Haughwout (1993) estimates structural versions of these equations using three-stage least squares and finds strong evidence supporting the Rosen/Roback assumption. The elasticity (standard error) of the wage with respect to changes in housing costs is 0.59 (0.02), while the elasticity of housing costs with respect to the wage is 0.73 (0.02).

they had only used metropolitan area-level data for the 185 urban areas in their sample, and whether any such differences were large enough in aggregate to materially impact the QOL values or rankings of these metropolitan areas.

Blomquist et al. (1998) amassed data on 13 local traits, that included 11 climate and environmental attributes that could be considered pure amenities, and two others (a teacher-pupil ratio and violent crime rate to proxy for the quality of educational services and public safety, respectively) that are better described as locally produced characteristics. Their six environmental traits included a rich set of controls for superfund sites, landfills, and waste treatment and discharge sites that had not been used in previous QOL analyses.

The authors employ a Box–Cox search procedure in estimating reduced form hedonic wage and housing expenditure equations within an OLS framework. The results indicate that their 13 local traits are jointly significant, both statistically and economically. The full range of QOL values is $5146, implying that in equilibrium the marginal household residing in the lowest rated county (St. Louis, MO) requires that amount in terms of higher wages and/or lower housing expenditures per year to be indifferent to living in the highest rated county (Pueblo, CO).

Their results for individual trait prices almost always have the correct sign in the sense that locating in an area with more of some obvious "bad" is associated with compensation in the form of higher wages and/or lower land prices. Their pollution-related findings are discussed in some detail in the next section, and we refer the readers interested in other specific trait prices in this (and the other two articles) to the papers themselves.

Blomquist et al. (1988) also report substantial labor market capitalization of the local amenities, suggesting that firm and worker competition for scarce sites does impact on both local land and labor markets. They also present the results of calculations of subindexes based on subsets of variables. Those findings strongly suggest that a top- (bottom-)ranked county need not be highly (poorly) rated on all amenity dimensions. For example, the rank correlation between the subindex based on their seven climate controls and the overall index is 0.63. The analogous correlation between their environmental subindex and the overall index is only 0.21.

### 4.2. Gyourko and Tracy (1991), "The structure of local public finance and the quality of life"

This paper uses the same 1980 *Census of Population and Housing* data and many of the same climate, but not environmental, amenity variables in Blomquist et al.

(1988). An important difference in the two studies is that the geographic unit of observation in Gyourko and Tracy (1991) is the central city of the metropolitan area. This was chosen so that a richer set of tax and service fiscal controls could be matched to a specific political jurisdiction.[14] Gyourko and Tracy (1991) also differs from Blomquist et al. (1988) in the use of a random effects estimator to account for potential group effects in the data.

Despite these differences in data, specification and econometric technique, the signs on the individual trait prices, especially the pure amenity variables, are almost always the same as in Blomquist et al. (1988). The amenities also are jointly significant in statistical and economic terms in both papers. And, both sets of results indicate that substantial compensation for amenity differentials occurs via wages in the labor market. The full range of QOL values across the 130 cities in Gyourko and Tracy's (1991) sample is $8227. This is larger than in Blomquist et al. (1988), but outliers drive that difference. The interquartile range of QOL values is only $1484.

An important contribution of this paper is its documentation that local fiscal environments also are important determinants of the QOL, suggesting that cities may have more control over their local QOL than was previously thought. Consistent with the basic theoretical prediction of the expanded model, variations in effective property tax rates appear to be fully capitalized into land prices. Except for the impact of corporate taxes, their results provide empirical support for the tax capitalization comparative statics in Eqs. (2.10) and (2.13). The full prices estimated for police, fire and health services each have the theoretically anticipated signs, with the police and health service proxies being statistically significant. Of the service vector variables, only the price of the student-teacher ratio has the wrong sign and its value is very low ($-$27).[15] The impact of rent-sharing with successful public sector unions on the local QOL is found to be small on average, but other work suggests substantial capitalization effects into land prices for cities with very high unionization rates among their public sector employees.[16]

---

[14] The material differences in fiscal conditions that existed between a central city and its typical suburb in 1980 (not to mention the extensive heterogeneity across suburbs) would have led to significant errors-in-variables problems had counties or metropolitan areas been the geographical unit of observation.

[15] Unfortunately, the different data, geographical units of observation, and specifications make it infeasible to do a simple comparison of the full prices of the two service controls common to Blomquist et al. (1988) and Gyourko and Tracy (1991). Such a comparison would be helpful in order to gauge whether, or not, the estimated full prices of produced services are smaller when taxes are not controlled for, as the model outlined in Section 2 implies should be the case.

[16] What little capitalization Gyourko and Tracy (1991) do find occurs in the land market, not the labor market. Gyourko and Tracy (1989b, c) focus solely on the impact of local public sector unionization on land

The interquartile range for the aggregate contribution of the seven tax/service fiscal variables in Gyourko and Tracy (1991b) is $1188, compared to $1372 for the 11 pure amenity variables. In addition, they find that fiscal differentials account for at least one-fifth of the variation in quality-adjusted housing expenditures that can be explained by all city-specific variables, and at least one-half of the variation in quality-adjusted wages that can be explained by all city-specific variables.

In an OLS regression estimation done for comparison purposes with the previous literature, Gyourko and Tracy find that including the fiscal and public union controls is associated with a 16.2 mean absolute change in ranks compared to a specification that only includes pure amenities.[17] The bias, then, on the overall QOL ranking from omitting the fiscal variables is substantial.

Perhaps even more important are the findings of this paper suggesting how fragile the QOL rankings estimates are. Moving from an OLS to a random effects estimation is associated with a 10.2 mean absolute change in ranks. In QOL value terms, the mean change is $391 and the standard deviation about that mean is $320. Not only are the rankings different when group effects are controlled for, they are much less precisely estimated.

The issue of how to treat group effects increases the uncertainty regarding the reliability of the results. Gyourko and Tracy (1991) computed QOL rankings that presumed the group effects were entirely composed of omitted city characteristics. When compared to the random effects-based results that did not price out the group effects, the mean absolute change in ranks associated with fully pricing these group effects was 27, with a standard deviation of 20 about that mean change. In general, the largest decreases (increases) in a city's rank were due to observed wages being higher (lower) than predicted.

---

values, using different metrics for identifying cities that are likely to be subject to successful rent-seeking. Gyourko and Tracy (1989c) look at median house prices for 36 cities using the 1976 *American Housing Survey* data. Rent-sharing cities are defined as those whose local public sector employees were paid wage premia in excess of one standard deviation above the mean, with the wage premia being calculated using microdata on public sector workers drawn from the May 1977 *Current Population Survey*. Median house values were found to be 28% lower in the rent-sharing cities. Gyourko and Tracy (1989b) examined median house prices in a larger sample of 90 cities using the 1983 *County and City Data Book* information. Rent-sharing cities in this study were identified as those whose public sector union organization level was at least one standard deviation above the average (i.e., above 67%). This study reports that house values were 12% lower on average in the rent-sharing cities. We interpret the findings of these three papers as indicating that relatively little rent-sharing with local public unions occurs on average (at least between 1976 and 1983), but that there are significant effects on home prices in very highly unionized towns.

[17] The standard deviation about that mean change was 15.2.

### 4.3. *Stover and Leven (1992), "Methodological issues in the determination of the quality of life in urban areas"*

Stover and Leven (1992) work within the Rosen/Roback framework to derive an alternative functional form that is used to reestimate QOLs using the Blomquist et al. (1988) data. A key motivation of their approach is concern about the reliability of hedonic wage equation estimates due to the difficulty of controlling for job and worker characteristics. Stover and Leven (1992) also believe that the dependent variable in a housing hedonic is superior because it measures the service flow from the durable good, while wages understate a worker's total compensation.

These authors assume that both land and labor markets are in equilibrium (a standard Rosen/Roback assumption), and that each market fully reflects the values of local amenities as well as conditions in the other market. This gives rise to wage and land rental specifications that take the following form: $n = n\{Z, W\}$ and $W = w\{Z, n\}$. These specifications differ from the reduced form specifications described earlier in that they include the price from the other market.

Stover and Leven (1992) demonstrate that the full price for the $k$th city attribute, $Z_k$, based on their single equation housing expenditure hedonic, is given by the following expression:

$$P_k = -n_w w_n \frac{dn}{dZ_k} - n_w w_{z_k}, \tag{4.1}$$

where the first term, $-n_w w_n dn/dZ_k$, represents the direct impact of $Z_k$ on land rentals. The second term, $-n_w w_z$, is the indirect impact of $Z_k$ on land rentals and reflects feedback from the labor market.[18]

In interpreting the direct impact of $Z_k$ on land rentals, the partial derivative $n_w$ reflects a pure income effect on the demand side because only amenities are compensating in their model. Thus, it should be greater than zero if housing is a normal commodity. The partial derivative $w_n$ is assumed to be positive as it reflects a compensating differential for the increased cost-of-living associated with an increase in land rents. Naturally, they are interested in land rentals that rise due to a better amenity package ($dn/dZ_k$). In interpreting the indirect impact on land rentals reflected in the second term on the righthand of Eq. (4.2), an increase in some $Z_k$ affects wages as shown in the partial derivative $w_z$. This feeds back into the land market through the $n_w$ term discussed above.

---

[18] Obviously, a single wage hedonic also could be specified, but that is not the preferred option given Stover and Leven's worries about the quality of wage data and job/worker trait controls.

Stover and Leven (1992) actually estimate a hedonic equation in housing expenditures of the following type via the OLS:

$$\ln n_{ij} = H_i \gamma_1 + Z_j \gamma_2 + L_j \gamma_3 + \upsilon_{ij}, \; \upsilon_{ij} = \delta_j + \eta_i, \tag{4.2}$$

where the vector $H_i$ controls for heterogeneity in housing quality, $Z_j \gamma_2$ proxies for $-n_w w_n \, dn/dz$, and $L_j \gamma_3$ proxies for $-n_w w_z$. They define $L_j$ as follows:

$$L_j = \frac{1}{p_j} \sum_i \frac{W_{ij}}{E(W_{ij})}, \tag{4.3}$$

where $p_j$ is the number of worker observations in jurisdiction $j$, $W_{ij}$ is the wage of the $i$th worker in community $j$, and $E(W_{ij})$ is the predicted wage of that same worker based *only* on worker and job traits.

While Stover and Leven (1992) estimate Eq. (4.3) using Blomquist et al.'s (1988) data for 253 counties, the two studies' reported QOL values differ dramatically. For example, the Spearman rank correlation of the two sets of rankings is essentially zero (0.004).[19] The authors interpret these results to imply that one-dimensional QOL rankings are very sensitive to model specification, and they presumably believe that their rankings based on the single equation housing expenditure hedonic are superior.

Stover and Leven's (1992) desire to reduce reliance on relatively noisy wage hedonics is understandable. Unfortunately, the estimation strategy used in this paper does not appear to be a reliable substitute for the traditional method. The reported QOL calculations still rely on imperfect worker/job controls in an underlying wage equation, still reflect the influence of uncontrolled for group effects, and may suffer from endogeneity bias problems. These points can be illustrated by rewriting their wage premium variable $(L)$ in terms of the components of a worker's wage as given above by Eq. (3.4),

$$L_i = \frac{1}{p_j} \sum_i \left[ \frac{X_i \beta_1 + Z_j \beta_2 + \alpha_j + \epsilon_i}{X_i \beta_1} \right]$$

---

[19] Stover and Leven (1992) also estimate QOL values using a single wage hedonic (with an added control for rent premiums analogous to $L$). The rankings generated from that estimation are negatively correlated (Spearman rank correlation of $-0.57$) with those from their housing expenditure hedonic. This is troubling given that their model predicts identical rankings from the two specifications. If the problem is that hedonic wage estimates are noisy as the authors suggest, that would suggest little or no correlation between the rankings generated from the housing versus wage specifications. It does not account for the strong negative correlation between the two.

$$= 1 + (Z_j \beta_2 + \alpha_j) \frac{1}{p_j} \sum_i \frac{1}{X_i \beta_1} + \frac{1}{p_j} \sum_i \frac{\epsilon_i}{X_i \beta_1}$$

$$\approx 1 + (Z_j \beta_2 + \alpha_j) \frac{1}{p_j} \sum_i \frac{1}{X_i \beta_1}, \tag{4.4}$$

where the last step uses the fact that $E(\epsilon) = 0$ and that $\epsilon$ is independent of $X$.

Equation (4.5) shows Stover and Leven's (1992) "wage premium" variable to be a function of the wage equation group error term ($\alpha_j$) and the city-specific variable effects on wages ($Z_j \beta_2$). Note that misspecification of the wage regression through inadequate controls for worker quality will lead to a misspecification of $L_j$ if workers sort by quality into different housing markets.[20] Furthermore, Stover and Leven are implicitly assuming that the $\alpha$'s reflect left-out amenity/fiscal characteristics. If the $\alpha$'s arise from common demand and/or supply shocks to the local labor market or if they reflect systematic mismeasurement of worker/job quality, then $L_i$ will not measure the pure impact of amenities on wages as assumed in their model. Finally, if the group error components from the wage and land rental regressions are correlated, then $L_i$ is endogenous, leading to further bias in the QOL estimates.

## 4.4. Conclusions

Recent empirical work shows that there is still no quick technical fix to the problems of large group effects in the data or hedonic wage and housing equations estimated with imperfect worker, job, and housing quality controls. These really are data problems and probably will have to be solved by amassing higher quality data. Given the considerable effort that Blomquist et al. (1988) and Gyourko and Tracy (1991) expended to construct their local databases, and the fact that better worker, job, or housing quality controls are not likely to be produced in an era of declining budgets at key data collection agencies, the likelihood of superior data soon appearing to solve the problem that empirical literature finds itself in, seems low.

Amid that pessimistic conclusion, we can suggest a diagnostic that should help in distinguishing whether, or not, the group effects reflect, on balance, the unobserved heterogeneity in worker and housing quality or unmeasured city traits. We begin by using the estimated hedonic coefficients on worker and housing quality to construct an estimate of the average observed quality of workers

---

[20] In this case, the misspecification is picked up in the error component, $\alpha_j$.

and housing stock by jurisdiction. Next, we construct a matrix of rank correlations between the predicted worker quality, the predicted housing stock quality,
the local QOL, the wage group error components, and the housing group error
components. If the group error components primarily reflect systematic unobserved quality effects, then we would expect them to be more correlated with the
observed worker and housing quality rankings than with the QOL rankings. If the
group error rankings are uncorrelated with the observed quality rankings, then it
is unlikely that the group error components reflect unobserved systematic quality
differences.

## 5. The value of the environment and the urban quality of life—a detailed analysis

Modern societies' growing concerns about the environment makes research into
the value of environmental attributes worthy of interest in its own right. Most
important for this chapter are the significant implications and insights this burgeoning literature provides for research into the urban QOL. More varied data
have been used to estimate the prices of environmental attributes. Section 5.1
presents a comparison of results generated from cross-city data typical of that
used in QOL research with those based on within-city data. In addition, the
environmental literature includes price estimates for a wider variety of attributes
than have been controlled for in the QOL literature. The findings here suggest
that QOL researchers should expand their list of environmental attributes to be
priced. Finally, there has been greater experimentation with nonhedonic valuation methods in the environmental area. This provides the opportunity to assess
the benefits and costs of valuation methodologies different from the revealed
preference techniques followed in the QOL literature.

*5.1. Environmental hedonic prices: cross-city and within-city data and results*

Cross-city studies of the valuation of nonmarket environmental goods have been
stimulated by the availability of microdata from the 1980 *Census of Population
and Housing* and the 1977 *Current Population Survey*, with Roback (1982),
Blomquist et al. (1988), Gyourko and Tracy (1991) and Clark and Nieves (1994)
estimating house price hedonic and wage regressions where the unit of observation is a person, and the geographical unit of analysis is some measure of the
urban area (e.g., the central city, county or Metropolitan Statistical Area [MSA]).
These studies effectively assume away local public goods measurement error

because they presume that local amenities, including environmental attributes, are constant within a city. This is a strong assumption most likely to hold for climate variables but not for local air quality.

It is useful to begin with a discussion of the results for climate controls in the Blomquist et al. (1988) and Gyourko and Tracy (1991) studies.[21] Gyourko and Tracy (1991) find that individuals are compensated for more cooling and heating degree days, and humidity, but pay for more sunshine. They report that rainfall lowers house price and wages (the wrong sign) so that on net, rain is not capitalized because the house price and wage capitalization cancel out. In terms of dollar amounts, Gyourko and Tracy (1991) estimate that people receive $676 compensation for 1000 extra cooling degree days and $503 for 1000 extra heating degree days. Blomquist et al. (1988) report estimates of $360 and $80, respectively. To put the magnitude of these estimates in perspective, Gyourko and Tracy (1991) report that people are compensated $82.67 for one more standard deviation of violent crimes per capita, while they are compensated $567.8 for one more standard deviation of cooling degree days. This suggests that their climate estimates are very large. One possible explanation is that climate variables are proxying for costs of home heating and air conditioning that are capitalized into home prices.

In addition to climate, air pollution as proxied by ambient particulates is a common proxy in hedonic analysis. Particulates are often included in hedonic specifications because the Environmental Protection Agency has created a database to monitor which cities are not in compliance with the Clean Air Act. In addition, there is ample epidemiological evidence documenting the morbidity and mortality risks of being exposed to high levels of this pollution (Ostro, 1987; Portney and Mullahy, 1990; Ranson and Pope, 1995). For particulates, Blomquist et al. (1988) report a full price of −$0.36 per microgram per cubic meter, while the Gyourko and Tracy (1991) estimate is −$2.74.[22] In 1982, the standard deviation for particulates as measured from over 1000 county ambient

[21] Environmental attributes comprise roughly half of Blomquist et al.'s (1988) location-specific public goods. They include particulates, superfund sites, effluent discharges, landfill waste, and treatment storage and disposal sites. Of this broader set of environmental controls, Gyourko and Tracy (1991) only include a control for particulate matter. However, Gyourko and Tracy (1991) report that the remaining five Blomquist et al.'s environmental variables are jointly insignificant in a random effects specification estimated on a subset of 90 cities.

[22] An earlier reference point is Roback's (1982) cross-city study based on the 1973 *Current Population Survey*. Particulate levels were significantly higher in 1973 than in 1980. If people have preferences that feature diminishing marginal returns with respect to air quality, then we would expect that the hedonic price would have been higher in a study based on the 1970s data than the 1980s data. Roback (1982) reports OLS estimates in which particulates are significant in two out of her four specifications, but the *t*-statistics indicate that all four estimates would likely have been insignificant if city-specific group effects had been estimated.

monitoring stations was 14.2. Thus, these hedonic particulates estimates are very small compared to the climate estimates.

In addition to climate and air quality variables, environmental researchers have used the cross-city approach to measure the capitalization of hazardous waste sites. For example, Clark and Nieves (1994) employed the 1980 *Census of Population and Housing*, to find that proximity to a superfund site is an positive amenity with a price of $58. Blomquist et al. (1988) report that it is a disamenity with a price of −$107—using the same data.

In sum, these cross-city studies provide strong evidence that environmental variables are capitalized, but also suggest the price estimates are highly sensitive to specification—an issue emphasized in Graves et al. (1988).[23]

The most obvious alternative to cross-city analysis is to use data for a single city. If available, the latter is attractive because the researcher typically has access to more disaggregated geographic information. For example, census tract-level data allows the researcher to merge on tract-level environmental exposure, reducing the measurement error problems affecting inference from cross-city studies. Another advantage is that working within a single city controls for local business cycle effects (Topel, 1986).

One obvious disadvantage of within-city data is that only the prices of attributes that vary within the city can be identified. Another is that intracity hedonic wage regressions cannot be estimated because detailed data on where people work within the city generally is unavailable. A third potential problem with intracity studies is spatial sorting on unobservables. The best quality homes may be in the best city neighborhoods. The typical hedonic rental study based on the 1980 *Census of Population and Housing* data has rather crude controls for housing structure. The data do not indicate the actual square footage or condition of the unit. If suppliers build nicer units in terms of unobservables in the nicer parts of the city, then the econometrician will overestimate the value of the QOL. Moreover, low environmental quality in a neighborhood may proxy for low quality of housing structure.

A large number of within-city hedonic house price regression studies have focused on the price of particulates. Smith and Hwang (1995) use meta-analysis techniques to summarize multiple studies of housing capitalization between 1967 and 1988, with each city-specific hedonic home regression study representing a data point to explain variation in estimated prices across cities over time. Based on their sample of over 80 hedonic studies, Smith and Hwang (1995) report

---

[23] Rosen (1979) stressed that multicollinearity between local public goods decreases the likelihood of separating out marginal effects of individual local public goods.

a median reduction in home prices of $20, and a mean reduction of $100 per microgram per cubic meter ($1980).

Hedonic home regressions also are a natural methodology for quantifying how capitalization of an attribute such as proximity to hazardous sites changes over time. This environmental attribute has been examined using both cross- and within-city data. The cross-city approach does not control for distance from the site. Instead, a count of total sites within a city's borders is constructed. Thus, noxious sites are assumed to be a pure local public bad (e.g., Blomquist et al., 1988 and Clark and Nieves, 1994). Kohlhase (1991), Kiel and McClain (1995) and Michaels and Smith (1990) offer intracity studies to test this. Given the size of MSAs, the impact of such noxious facilities seems more likely to be seen in intracity studies.

Kohlhase (1991) is particularly instructive in this regard. She uses the Houston housing data of 1976, 1980 and 1985 to explore how the coefficient on distance from a hazardous waste site changes over time as new information about the site is revealed. Using price data before and after the hazardous site has been placed on the National Priority List (NPL) in 1985, she shows that distance was not a valued amenity until after the site was placed on the NPL. After the announcement, distance became an amenity. The peak marginal price of an extra mile of distance was $2364, which declines to zero at a distance of 6.2 miles. Her findings illustrate the importance of not simply using how many toxic sites are in a county as a proxy for toxic waste exposure—as is typically done in cross-city studies.[24]

The Kohlhase (1991), Kiel and McClain (1995) and Michaels and Smith (1990) studies employing within-city data have also made progress in investigating how "new news" about site toxicity gets capitalized differentially into housing prices at different radius distances from the site. Repeated cross-sectional regression yields insights into the speed with which the perception of environmental hazards is capitalized into price. The siting of a hazardous site can change a community's QOL, induce outmigration, and depress home prices.

Kiel and McClain (1995) studied how the siting of an incinerator in north Andover (Massachusetts), affected the prices of 2600 single family homes. They collect data on the prices of homes sold in the area between 1974 and 1992.

---

[24] Kohlhase (1991) also reports the interesting finding that a site's rank on the NPL list is not capitalized. That is, higher ranked sites do not command a deeper discount. Kohlhase interprets this as evidence that people are unable to differentiate information. A different possible interpretation is that being ranked high on the NPL list has two offsetting effects. A high rank should indicate that your home is near a more dangerous site, but counterbalancing this is an increased likelihood that the site will be cleaned up before sites that are lower on the list.

They then partition calendar years 1974–1992 into several subintervals. The first interval represents the prerumor (no site) stage. In the next stage, news of the proposed project leaks, so that with positive probability the incinerator will be sited in the vicinity. Next the project is constructed but is not online. In this phase the probability of start-up is one, but the exact timing is uncertain. Following this stage, the plant comes online. The impact of each of these stages is explored by estimating a hedonic specification for each. Distance from the incinerator is statistically insignificant through the rumor stage, and is insignificant at the 5% level in the construction phase. Only when the incinerator is online and ongoing is it capitalized. In addition, Kiel and McClain (1995) find a larger peak impact than Kohlhase (1991) at $8100 per mile.[25]

Only a few hedonic studies exist of compensation for water pollution, unlike air quality or the location of superfund sites, no national monitoring system exists to measure water quality differentials across space.[26] Feenberg and Mills (1980) use the Harrison and Rubinfeld (1978) within-city data on the Boston area and augment their specification to include proxies for water pollution that include the water's oil level and turbidity. They find that both have a statistically significant impact on home prices. Surprisingly, Feenberg and Mills do not find strong evidence that beach-front property values decrease the most when nearby water becomes polluted. At the cross-city level, Blomquist et al. (1988) proxied for water pollution using NPDES effluent discharges and found that it lowered rentals. Both Gyourko and Tracy (1989b, 1991b) and Blomquist et al. (1988) found a large coastal affect in their cross-city studies.[27]

## 5.2. *Limitations of capitalization studies of environmental quality*

In estimating Eq. (3.4), researchers assume that people take the stock of environment in a location as exogenously determined. For climate, this is certainly a reasonable assumption. Yet environmental quality, such as clean streets and low smog, may be produced through high expenditures on local services and

[25] Use of within-city data also permits examination of an interesting incidence question—whether, or not, proximity to a hazardous site has different effects depending on the quality of the house. In a study of the Boston real estate market, Michaels and Smith (1990) examine whether, or not, the distance from a hazardous site (interacted with whether, or not, it has been placed on the NPL list) is differentially capitalized into four submarkets based on home quality.

[26] Water regulators have focused on measuring whether individual polluters are in compliance with emissions rather than with measuring spatial variation in water quality.

[27] In addition to quantifying the value of reduced air, waste and water pollution, the environmental QOL literature has also focused on the impact of low probability environmental outcomes. Interesting examples of such small probability events are earthquakes or cancer caused by proximity to electric lines. See, for example, Brookshire et al. (1985) for an analysis of earthquake risk premiums in San Francisco and Los Angeles.

resulting higher local taxes. Examples include frequent garbage collection, large expenditures for vehicle emissions testing, or transfers to high polluting junk-car owners in return for scrapping the vehicle (see Kahn, 1995). Unfortunately, no QOL or other hedonic papers have explicitly modeled that environmental quality is a byproduct of economic activity, regulation and citizen actions.[28]

The implications for the QOL is that the researcher may not estimate the full value for environment if the empirical specification ignores taxes and limitations on behavior. Some environmental attributes are produced through costly actions by local populace, with citizens paying via taxes, lost time or lost utiles due to limitations on one's activities. If such unfunded mandates are not demanded by the local citizens, then in the extreme case, wages could be high and rents low in clean areas to compensate for the pain of achieving the standard.

In a similar vein, citizens have gained more control over their environmental consumption through the growth of explicit markets. The Clean Air Act Amendments of 1990 created a pollution-permit market in sulfur dioxide. Before this market existed, real estate prices around the Adirondacks in upstate New York might be lower because of Ohio-produced acid rain. If citizens in this area could buy pollution permits from Ohio power plants and retire them, this yearly expenditure would lead to improved acid rain levels in New York. However, rents may not rise by much because people who move there would recognize that they must pay a per-capita share for the permits. If permits expand for other environmental factors such as vehicle emissions, implicit capitalization should fall and hedonic techniques would only reveal a fraction of the full payment for environmental goods.

This discussion also highlights the limitations of hedonic prices for issues such as policy analysis. Simply put, the hedonic price indicates how much one pays, conditional on a spatial distribution of environmental quality. It provides no insight as to who paid explicitly or implicitly to achieve any given spatial distribution of environmental quality. Only if the distribution of environmental quality were exogenously determined would the hedonic price indicate total environmental payment. When environmental quality is produced through regulation, taxes and limitations on individual behavior, or increased international trade with nations that specialize in the polluting sector, then it is quite possible that "hedo-

---

[28] For example, changes in air quality may reflect transport regulation or the decline of manufacturing. Henderson (1996) and Kahn (1997) document the relationship between air quality levels and manufacturing activity. If industry declines over time in a major city, then air quality could increase sharply while house prices in a vicinity around these plants might decline due to the decrease in employment opportunities.

nic" payments for environmental quality would be dwarfed by implicit regulatory expenditures and lost quasirents by workers and firms.[29]

## 5.3. Econometric issues

Recent work on hedonic econometric issues of environmental attributes focused on the usual suspects: functional form, model specification and measurement error. For example, Stock (1991) uses nonparametric kernel estimation to study the discount in Boston home prices caused by proximity to a hazardous waste site. He finds smaller estimates of home discounts using nonparametric methods over the standard Box–Cox hedonic specifications.

On the specification front, not enough research has followed up Rosen's (1979) discussion on the problem of multicollinearity of local public goods. In cross-city studies, it is crucial that researchers attempt to estimate parsimonious specifications using random effects estimation and to study the sensitivity of the findings to specification changes. Graves et al. (1988) provide an important specification test on hedonic regressions studying robustness of price estimates to omitted variables, function form and outliers.

An underexplored issue in hedonic regression estimation is expectations of changes in local public goods, and local taxes. Cross-city studies have implicitly assumed that migration costs are zero and that people move to a city for a single period and then reoptimize. The possibility that forward-looking consumers expect that local public goods may change in the future and that this is capitalized into home prices but not rents, has not been developed. For example, Blomquist et al. (1988) and Gyourko and Tracy (1991) assume that the local public goods provision level is in the steady state. Among other benefits, this assumption allows them to increase degrees of freedom by pooling renters and

---

[29] Hedonic capitalization is relevant in analyzing claims of environmental racism. Recent studies have found that minority groups are more likely to be exposed to higher levels of pollution than whites (see Hamilton, 1993, 1995). Howerver, there are two key outstanding issues in the waste siting and race literature. First, from an efficiency perspective, where is the social cost minimizing location for sites? Second, conditional on an efficient site location decision, what transfers, if any, should be made to compensate the home owners exposed to increased levels of pollution? If the siting decision is reached by a majority voting process, then the political process may yield lower transfers to the affected home owners than the mythical benevolent planner would have made in achieving a Hicksian pareto improvement with compensation.

In the extreme case of no offsetting transfers, hedonic estimates of the implicit capitalization of noxious sites represent the dollar value of the environmental burden that the majority is shifting on to the minority home owners. If transfers are generated by the political process, then their form will determine the impact on the measured capitalization. Lump-sum transfers to the original home owners will have no effect on capitalization, while transfers that are paid out over time will tend to mitigate the capitalization. Evidence of environmental racism requires data on *both* the extent of capitalization and the lack of initial compensating transfers to the affected community.

owners. However, there certainly are environmental amenities that will be expected to change over time (e.g., noxious facility sitings and water or air quality). Given data on rentals and home prices for the same geographical locations, future work should separately estimate rental and home price regressions and explicitly test the cross-equation restrictions that the implicit prices are equal.[30] Datasets such as the Toxic Release Inventory could be used to study how new information about exposure to environmental hazards is capitalized in the rental and housing markets.

## 5.4. Alternative valuation methods

The QOL approach identifies the marginal person's environmental valuation. Researchers are also interested in estimating the distribution of a population's willingness to pay for a given environmental good. Kolstad (1991) provides an excellent review of the variety of techniques for learning about environment demand. Contingent valuation is a straightforward method for learning about environmental valuation. The contingent valuation method describes a hypothetical environmental scenario and polls people on their willingness to pay for increased environmental quality. The hardest part of contingent valuation appears to be designing the actual questionnaire. A good survey must not "lead the witness" and must provide sufficient information to elicit a careful answer from a sample of respondents that is representative of the US population. A key problem is that surveyed individuals do not face a binding budget constraint when stating their responses.[31]

Hedonics and contingent valuation have been jointly applied in studies comparing revealed preference data and stated preference data for the same set of respondents to study the consistency of the two samples.[32] These cross-validation studies tend to be more believable because they are studying well-defined and understood environmental phenomena, such as sickness from air pollution and access to water recreation.

Brookshire et al. (1982) estimate hedonic regressions within Los Angeles using data on 684 surveyed home sales. Controlling for neighborhood effects and home characteristics, they report statistically significant impacts of nitrogen dioxide and particulates on home prices. They then survey each community

---

[30] Abelson and Markandya's (1985) noise pollution study is a rare example of separately studying capitalization rates by tenure mode.

[31] Detailed discussions of its strengths and weaknesses are presented in Mitchell and Carson (1989), Cummings et al. (1986) and Hausman (1993), with Portney (1994) providing an excellent summary of the recent debate on this methodology's merits.

[32] For an air quality example based on Israeli data, see Shecter and Kim (1991).

to generate their willingness to pay for pollution reduction. Brookshire et al. (1982) report evidence in favor of the hypothesis that the increase in rent that a household would face if pollution were reduced by a standard deviation is greater than a household's willingness to pay for a standard deviation reduction in pollution. This finding is consistent with economic theory because utility maximizing households (with heterogenous preferences for air quality) will sort across the equilibrium price gradient and locate to reach their highest indifference curve. At a given individual's optimal location, it must be the case that willingness to pay for a nonmarginal increase in air quality is less than what one would have to pay (as indicated by the hedonic housing gradient).[33]

Another approach for valuing pollution reduction is to directly estimate its health impact and then impute a dollar value to pollution-induced morbidity and mortality. This "direct" approach has been the focus of a growing number of papers using microdata to estimate pollution's role in a health production function. Using microdata such as the 1979 *National Health Interview Study*, these studies quantify pollution's impact while controlling for personal attributes and habits, such as smoking and quantify pollution's impact. (Portney and Mullahy, 1986; Krupnick et al., 1990).

Portney and Mullahy (1986) use data from the 1979 *National Health Interview Survey* and spatially merge ambient ozone data. This merger yields a database that includes personal attributes such as whether, or not, one smokes, standard demographic characteristics and ambient air quality. Portney and Mullahy use as a health proxy the number of respiratory related restricted activity days (RRAD) during a two-week recall period. They estimate poisson models of RRAD counts and find that ozone's coefficient is positive and statistically significant.[34] A 10% decline in ozone would yield 22.19 million RRAD per 110 million cases. Based on different scenarios on the health impact and the dollar damage of experiencing a RRAD, the authors estimate per person per year benefit of .$0.04–4 for a 10% reduction in ozone. Due to data limitations, this study implicitly assumes that no citizens engage in self-protection against ozone exposure and that there is no migration selectivity across cities.

---

[33] An interesting extension of this merger between stated willingness to pay through contingent valuation and hedonic estimates would be to survey how people actually vote on environmental initiatives (Deacon and Shapiro, 1975; Kahn and Matsusaka, 1997). With microdata on individual voting patterns and a person characteristics, a structural discrete choice model could be fitted to obtain estimates of the marginal willingness to tradeoff income for publicly provided environmental goods.

[34] Portney and Mullahy (1986) report estimates of ozone's *t*-statistic that vary between 1.97–3.2. While apparently statistically significant, the authors are likely to have underestimated their regression's standard errors because they have not controlled for the fact that observations from the same MSAs are likely to have correlated error terms (Moulton, 1986).

Krupnick et al. (1990) create a 1979 database consisting of 290 families who have children in school. These families kept a diary for 182 days. The authors' goal was to quantify daily ozone's impact on the probability of having a respiratory symptom the next day. The authors aggregate 19 respiratory diseases into a single dummy variable indicator and estimating a Markov transition matrix of the probability of having a respiratory condition on any day as a function of air quality, personal characteristics (such as smoking), and previous day's health and time spent inside. The authors find a small, statistically significant effect that a 1% increase in ozone raises the frequency of symptoms by 0.11%. In 1979, the average Los Angeles resident suffered 76 days of having some cold symptom. Their 0.11 elasticity indicates that if ozone levels fell by 50% between 1980 and the present, then the average Los Angeles citizen has experienced a 4.2 day reduction in respiratory symptoms. If individuals are willing to pay an average of $25 to avoid such an episode, then the per-capita yearly benefits of the reduction ozone would be $100 each. The relationship between direct health study estimates and hedonic valuation estimates would be an interesting research path.

A second literature directly connecting health and pollution has studied pollution's impact on seeking medical care (Gerking and Stanley, 1986; Dickie and Gerking, 1991). These authors estimate discrete choice models of whether, or not, an individual sought medical care in the last year. Controlling for demographics, preexisting conditions and the price of health care, the authors document the positive impact of ozone on seeking medical care. Gerking and Stanley (1986) find that a bid of $24.5 engendered a 30% reduction in ozone, based on the St. Louis sample. Dickie and Gerking (1991) use Los Angeles data in Glendora and Burbank to estimate a similar medical care demand probit with the econometric innovation of allowing for person-specific random effects. The sample consists of full-time workers who are not current smokers and oversamples people with respiratory problems. Dickie and Gerking (1991) find that reducing Glendora's ozone pollution from 117 days to 0 pphm willing to pay $170–210 dollars a year.

While health-based methods have increased our understanding of pollution valuation, they complement but should not replace the hedonic approach. Estimation of health production functions requires representative samples of the population and information on population self-protection. For example, if the econometrician does not observe that people stay inside on highly polluted days then she may conclude that ozone has very low costs for society as measured by sickness. The health production literature has not modeled individual locational choice and population sorting. Such sorting is a function of the equilibrium housing price gradient and individual preferences. A further issue with health studies is that to create a proxy for health capital (the dependent variable) is not easy. Krupnick et al. (1990) aggregate over 15 different health conditions into a single health proxy. If the person's specific losses from these various conditions differ, then this increases the difficulty of assigning a dollar value to the health losses from increased pollution exposure. Given estimates of pollution's health impact, a researcher would still need to impute the value of lost time and borrow from the value of life literature to arrive at the dollar cost of pollution.

## 6. The challenge of relaxing the equilibrium assumption in quality of life analyses

A key feature of the QOL methodology is the assumption that measured implicit prices reflect marginal valuations for marginal worker/households in the data. This assumption hinges on the equilibrium assumption that these worker/households are indifferent to their choice of location at the current implicit prices. Given the methodological importance of this assumption, it is vital to test its validity, adjust price estimates for any possible departures from equilibrium, and explore estimation strategies that do not rely on the equilibrium assumption.

Few papers have addressed this issue. Cheshire and Hay (1989) propose a new methodology that does not rely on the equilibrium assumption. As in the traditional hedonic approach, their first step is to identify a set of Z variables that are believed to affect the QOL. Their next step involves a significant departure from the hedonic approach in that wages and house prices are *not* used to calculate weights for the Z variables. Instead, a group of "experts" is selected who are asked to identify cities having the "worst" and "best" urban environments.[35] Discriminant analysis is used to determine weights for the Z variables that best explains the experts' classifications. The coefficients from the discriminant analysis were then used to create an index for *all* cities in the sample. This approach remains agnostic as to how the experts form their opinion about the cities they are asked to classify. An important issue for study is how sensitive the weights are to the particular set of experts selected, as the Cheshire and Hay (1989) methodology represents a significant departure from the original goal of Rosen/Roback to rely on market data rather than expert opinion.

Researchers who wish to continue in the Rosen/Roback tradition will need to develop tests of the equilibrium assumption, and possibly methods for relaxing the assumption. The first step in that process involves a careful understanding of the likely implications of the equilibrium assumption, which would seem to

---

[35] European experts were asked to classify cities in their home country.

suggest that systematic patterns of intercity migration should not appear in the data. However, the Rosen/Roback framework does not assume that households are homogeneous in their preferences and/or exposure to the labor market. Thus, the presence of substantial intercity household migration does not necessarily indicate that the key underlying equilibrium assumption is being violated.

In fact, the equilibrium price assumption is consistent with three *life-cycle* motivations for migration (see, Linneman and Graves, 1983). First, household preferences for amenities and services such as mild weather and education services are likely to vary over the life-cycle, so that if attribute prices remain relatively constant through time, certain households may relocate to a new city in order to achieve a more preferred local trait bundle. Second, changing household exposure to the labor market over the life-cycle can also be associated with equilibrium migration.[36] An incentive exists for households that are reducing their exposure to the labor market to relocate in cities with a higher mix of those attributes that are capitalized relatively more in the labor market. Third, capital market imperfections make it difficult for the household to perfectly smooth its consumption as its real income changes over the life-cycle. Consequently, as real income rises, a household may choose to relocate in order to consume a more desired amenity/fiscal bundle.[37] An additional equilibrium explanation for migration is spatial mismatch. As individuals enter the labor market and form new households, they may find that their current location is not optimal. Given the equilibrium set of prices for amenity/fiscal attributes, a move is required to

[36] If all city attributes were proportionally priced in both the land and labor markets, then changing labor market exposure would change the price level but not the *relative* price levels of city attribute bundles. Households, therefore, would face no incentive to migrate. Such proportionality is unlikely to exist in practice. The basic model suggests that nonproductive (to firms) attributes will be relatively more capitalized into wages.

[37] Using the 1980 *Census of Population and Housing*, Graves and Waldman (1991) and Gyourko and Tracy (1991) report findings consistent with the life-cycle labor market exposure motivation for migration. Graves and Waldman (1991) regress the net inmigration (and net inmigration rate) of the elderly on the wage capitalization variable from the QOL calculation for each of the 253 counties in Blomquist et al. (1988), and report positive and significant coefficients. When they repeat this exercise using the net inmigration of prime age households they find either insignificant or negative coefficients. Gyourko and Tracy (1991) calculate the implied net subsidy (positive or negative) to a retired household for each of 130 cities based on the assumption that retired households value the amenity/fiscal bundle in the same manner as the marginal household. They then construct the share of "retired" households for each of the cities in their sample. The simple unweighted correlation between the retirement employment share and the net subsidy is 0.15 (with a probability value of 0.08 under the null hypothesis that $\rho = 0$). Weighting cities by their total number of labor market participants increases the correlation to 0.35 (with a probability value of 0.001). Linneman and Graves (1983) find empirical support for migration induced by likely changes in preferences for amenity/fiscal attributes and changes to real income. Their study examines the determinants of both job and geographic mobility using microdata drawn from the *Panel Study of Income Dynamics*. For the 1971–1972 period, they find that 13% of households changed residences while 9% changed jobs. Roughly one-third of job changes also involved a residence change. They model the decision to change job and/or residence using a multinomial logit framework, and find significant mobility effects induced by changes in family size and real income.

maximize their utility. An analogy in labor markets is the notion of frictional unemployment due to the spatial mismatch of currently unemployed workers and job vacancies.[38]

The discussion in this section has so far assumed that local amenity/fiscal bundles do not change over time. This is not the case as Inman's (1995) description of the changing fiscal fortunes of the nation's 40 largest cities clearly shows. Changes in the local fiscal environment, particularly unanticipated ones, are potentially important to the task of reconciling QOL work with observed migration behavior. Consider the effect of an unexpected negative shock to a city's fiscal attributes. If the shock is common knowledge (e.g., a visible tax increase without any added services), we would expect to see land rentals and wages adjusting as described earlier. After the adjustment period, the marginal household would have no incentive to leave the city, although migration could still occur by inframarginal households if there are heterogenous preferences. On the other hand, if information problems exist and potential entrants to the city are unaware of the fiscal shock or underestimate its magnitude, then prices would not fully reflect the new fiscal bundle and residents would face gains from migration.

The conclusion that should be reached from the discussion so far is that attempts to measure the extent of disequilibrium in attribute prices by exploiting migration data must take care to distinguish equilibrium from disequilibrium reasons for migration.

Most of the migration research that involves the QOL tends to focus on another issue—namely, the importance of QOL differences in explaining migration flows.[39] Virtually no work, except that by Greenwood et al. (1991), has attempted to address what we view as a critical issue of how migration data can be used to assess the reasonableness of the equilibrium assumption used to construct QOL indexes. Because future research on this topic will undoubtedly build on this study, a closer look at their paper is necessary.

---

[38] Linneman and Graves (1983) label this motive "residential search", and list it as a disequilibrium explanation. We prefer to include this with the other equilibrium motives since it is consistent with equilibrium pricing in the Rosen/Roback framework.

[39] Sjaastad (1962) and Muth (1971) both argue that migration is primarily a response to economic incentives in labor markets. Migration reflects the flow of human capital across geographic boundaries as it searches out its highest valued use. More recently, Topel (1986) and Greenwood and Hunt (1989) arrive at the same basic conclusion. Berger and Blomquist (1992) argue that QOL issues matter in the choice of a destination given a move, but are secondary in the initial decision to move. Muesser and Graves (1995) argue that the relative importance of economic incentives versus QOL are likely to vary by time period.

Greenwood et al. (1991) start with the assumption that net migration to an area is a function of the relative net present value (NPV) of labor market earnings available in the area and the relative amenity bundle.

$$nm_{jt} = h \left\{ \text{NPV} \left( \frac{Y_{jt}}{\bar{Y}_t} \right), \left( \frac{A_j}{\bar{A}} \right) \right\},$$  (6.1)

where $nm_{jt}$ is the net migration to location $j$ in year $t$, $Y_{jt}$ is potential labor market earnings in location $j$ for a standardized unit of labor in year $t$, $\bar{Y}_t$ is the average potential labor market earnings in the labor market in year $t$, $A_j$ is the amenity bundle in location $j$, and $\bar{A}$ is the average amenity bundle available in the market. Amenity and economic motivations for migration suggest that each first derivative of $h$ is positive.

Several simplifying assumptions are made to allow estimation of this net migration equation. First, growth rates of potential incomes across areas are assumed to be equal so that all net present values can be replaced by current relative incomes. Second, a Cobb–Douglas functional form is specified for $h$, where the coefficient on relative amenities is assumed to equal one. Adding a stochastic error term gives the following estimating equation for the log of net migration:

$$\ln nm_{jt} = \ln \left( \frac{A_j}{\bar{A}} \right) + \lambda \ln \left( \frac{Y_{jt}}{\bar{Y}} \right) + \epsilon_{jt}.$$  (6.2)

Annual data for 50 states and Washington, DC between 1971–1988 were used in this analysis. The net migration and relative income potential variables are constructed by the authors.[40] The relative amenity set is left to be picked up as a location's fixed-effect. The coefficient $\lambda$ is estimated using an instrumental

---

[40] Net migration for year $t$ is defined as the sum of the "natural labor force" (NLF) in year $t - 1$ plus "economic migration" in year $t$ divided by $\text{NFL}_{t-1}$. Economic migration is defined to be the difference between the actual civilian population under the age of 65, and the estimated civilian population under the age of 65 in the absence of migration. This estimated population is calculated by using 1970 cohort counts by state extrapolated for intervening years using cohort-specific birth and death rates (adjusted so that the increments across cohorts match with the gross birth and death rates by state), apportioning international migrants by state, and subtracting all military personnel and their dependents. The natural labor force is calculated by applying cohort-specific labor force participation rates (adjusted to eliminate discouraged worker effects) to cohort-specific population counts, and summing across cohorts. The state relative income variable is constructed by deflating an estimate of the adjusted state nominal wage rate by a cost-of-living index. The state nominal wage is constructed using the Bureau of Economic Analysis (BEA) data on total industry wages divided by average annual employment. This nominal wage is then adjusted for any state and local income and sales taxes. If income and sales taxes are capitalized in both land and labor markets, then fully adjusting wages in the construction of the relative income measure involves an overadjustment. The cost-of-living index is constructed by Greenwood et al. and include an adjustment for regional housing prices.

variables (IV) procedure to correct for any endogeneity problems. The set of instruments is taken from a larger model presented elsewhere, and is not discussed in the paper. The IV coefficient estimate (standard error) for $\lambda$ is 0.21 (0.01). This is consistent with the extensive literature finding a positive connection between migration and economic incentives in the labor market. The data also strongly reject the restriction that all states share a common intercept.

To get at the issue of disequilibrium pricing, Greenwood et al. define the "equilibrium relative income" $(RY^*)$ for a location to be the level of relative income that would imply *no* net migration for the area. The difference between $RY^*$s and the actual relative incomes is taken as a measure of the extent of disequilibrium in the market. Using the state fixed-effect estimates, the measured relative income for the state and the estimate of $\lambda$, an estimate (and 90% confidence interval) for $RY^*$ is constructed for each location. For six states and the District of Columbia, they find the actual relative income outside the 90% confidence interval for the equilibrium relative income.[41] On face, little evidence of disequilibrium pricing is suggested by the data.

It should be noted that a number of important assumptions are implicitly being made in the above formulation. First, amenities are treated as time invariant. While this is likely for true amenities such as climate, it is less likely for fiscal attributes.[42] The functional form assumptions also rule out the equilibrium life-cycle explanations for migration. Amenities enter the migration decision only as a single index, effectively ruling out equilibrium migration due to preference changes for specific amenities over the life-cycle. The Cobb–Douglas assumption further rules out any interactions between income and the demand for amenities—in particular, the potential that real income increases over the life-cycle can induce migration as households purchase a better set of amenities.[43]

The fixed effects estimation strategy is also quite restrictive. While it obviates the need for data on specific amenities by location, it clouds the interpretation of the findings because the fixed effects estimates will pick up, not only relative differences in net migration due to differences in amenity/fiscal characteristics across states, but also *any* other characteristics of states that generate systematic differences in net migration that are unrelated to relative income differences. To

---

[41] Greenwood et al. do not report an overall test for disequilibrium pricing. In addition, the confidence intervals for the relative equilibrium income levels should be wider than reported by Greenwood et al. due to the constructed nature of the relative income variable.

[42] It is clear from the text that Greenwood et al. are thinking of "environmental" characteristics as the center of their analysis.

[43] The sample selection excludes individuals over the age of 65 years. This will mitigate some of the life-cycle migration effects in the data used in the estimation.

attribute 100% of these fixed effects to amenities is speculative. The equilibrium relative income calculation, however, *directly* depends on this assumption.

These caveats aside, the basic intuition of the Greenwood et al. (1991) study is appealing—any significant differences between actual and equilibrium prices creates incentives to relocate. Future research on this important topic should build on this underlying insight.

## 7. Conclusions

Recent research has clearly enriched our knowledge of the urban QOL. Conceptual innovations have incorporated traditional concerns of urban economics, such as distance from the urban core and agglomeration effects into the Rosen/Roback framework. The importance of the local fiscal conditions to the overall QOL and to specific capitalization results has also been made clear. The burgeoning field of environmental economics continues to contribute to our knowledge of the value of key local traits, in addition to yielding insights about data quality and basic strategy with respect to estimating the overall QOL.

Nevertheless, empirical research into the urban QOL stands at an important crossroads. Controlling for the large location-specific group effects in the data shows individual trait prices and overall QOL indexes to be much less precisely estimated than suggested by the OLS-based results. Dealing effectively with the challenge posed by this issue requires understanding that this primarily is a data problem. In particular, there appears to be no econometric or methodological solution on the horizon. Data on more urban areas will help, and richer databases that more fully describe local amenity, environmental and fiscal conditions are absolutely necessary.

More technical advances are needed with respect to relaxing the key underlying equilibrium assumption in the Rosen/Roback framework. Greenwood et al. (1991) have taken the first steps in this direction, and we believe that more fruitful progress can be made while data quality are slowly improved.

## References

Abelson, P.W. and A. Markandya (1985), "The interpretation of capitalized hedonic prices in a dynamic environment", Journal of Environmental Economics and Management 12:195–206.

Bartik, T.J. and V.K. Smith (1987), "Urban amenities and public policy", in: E.S. Mills, ed., Handbook of Regional and Urban Economics, Chap. 31 (Elsevier Science Amsterdam).

Beeson, P. and R. Eberts (1989), "Identifying productivity and amenity effects in interurban wage differentials", The Review of Economics and Statistics 71:443–452.

Berger, M.C. and G.C. Blomquist (1992), "Mobility and destination in migration decisions: the roles of earnings, quality of life, and housing prices", Journal of Housing Economics 2:37–59.

Blomquist, G.C., M.C. Berger and J.P. Hoehn (1988), "New estimates of quality of life in urban areas", American Economic Review 78:89–107.

Boyer, R. (1983), Places Rated Almanac (Rand McNally, Chicago).

Brookshire, D.S., M.A. Thayer, W.D. Schultze and R.C. d'Arge (1982), "Valuing public goods: a comparison of survey and hedonic approaches", American Economic Review 72:165–177.

Brookshire, D.S., M.A. Thayer, J. Tschirhard and W. Schultze (1985), "A test of the expected utility model: evidence from earthquake risks", Journal of Political Economy 93:369–389.

Cheshire, P.C. and D.G. Hay (1989), Urban Problems in Western Europe: an Economic Analysis (Unwin Hyman, London).

Clark, D. and L. Nieves (1994), "An interregional hedonic analysis of noxious facility impacts on local wages and property values", Journal of Environmental Economics and Management 27:235–253.

Cummings, R.G., D.S. Brookshire and W.D. Schulze (1986), Valuing Environmental Goods: An Assessment of the Contingent Valuation Method (Littlefield, Adams, Rowman and Allanheld, Totowa, NJ).

Deacon, R.T. and P. Shapiro (1975), "Private preference for collective goods revealed through voting on referenda", American Economic Review 65:943–955.

Dickie, M. and S. Gerking (1991), "Willingness to pay for ozone control:inferences from the demand for medical care", Journal of Environmental Economics and Management 21:1–16.

Ehrenberg, R. and J. Schwarz (1986), "Public sector labor markets", in: O. Ashenfelter and R. Layard, ed., The Handbook of Labor Economics (North-Holland, Amsterdam).

Epple, D. and A. Zelenitz (1981), "The implications of competition among jurisdictions: does Tiebout need politics?", Journal of Political Economy 89:1197–1217.

Epple, D., A. Zelenitz and M. Visscher (1978), "A search for testable implications of the Tiebout hypothesis", Journal of Political Economy 86:405–425.

Evans, A.W. (1990), "The assumption of equilibrium in the analysis of migration and interregional differences: a review of some recent research", Journal of Regional Science 30:515–531.

Feenberg, D. and E. Mills (1980), Measuring the Benefits of Water Pollution Abatement. Studies in Urban Economics (Academic Press, New York).

Freeman, R. (1986), "Unionism comes to the public sector", Journal of Economic Literature 24:41–86.

Garen, J. (1988), "Compensating wage differentials and the endogeneity of job riskiness", Review of Economics and Statistics 70:9–16.

Gerking, S. and L. Stanley (1986), "An economic analysis of air pollution and health: the case of St. Louis", Review of Economics and Statistics 68:115–121.

Graves, P.E. and D.M. Waldman (1991), "Multimarket amenity compensation and the behavior of the elderly", American Economic Review 81:1374–1381.

Graves, P., J. Murdoch, M. Thayer and D. Waldman (1988), "The robustness of hedonic price estimation: urban air quality", Land Economics 64:220–242.

Greenwood, M.J. and G.L. Hunt (1989), "Jobs versus amenities in the analysis of metropolitan migration", Journal of Urban Economics 25:1–16.

Greenwood, M.J., G.L. Hunt, D.S. Rickman and G.I. Treyz (1991), "Migration, regional equilibrium, and the estimation of compensating differentials", American Economic Review 81:1382–1390.

Gyourko, J. and J. Tracy (1989a), "The importance of local fiscal conditions in analyzing local labor markets", Journal of Political Economy 97:1208–1231.

Gyourko, J. and J. Tracy (1989b), "Local public sector rent-seeking and its impact on local land values", Regional Science and Urban Economics 19:493–516.

Gyourko, J. and J. Tracy (1989c), "On the political economy of land value capitalization and local public sector rent seeking in a Tiebout model", Journal of Urban Economics 26:152–173.

Gyourko, J. and J. Tracy (1991a), "Public sector bargaining and the local budgetary process", Research in Labor Economics 12:117–136.

Gyourko, J. and J. Tracy (1991b), "The structure of local public finance and the quality of life", Journal of Political Economy 99:774–806.

Hamilton, J. (1993), "Politics and social costs. Estimating the impact of collective action on hazardous waste facilities", Rand Journal of Economics 24:101–121.

Hamilton, J. (1995), "Testing for environmental racism, prejudice, profits, political power?", Journal of Policy Analysis and Management 14:107–132.

Harrison, D. and D. Rubinfeld (1978), "Household prices and demand for clean air", Journal of Environmental Economics and Management 5:81–102.

Haughwout, A.F (1993), "Measuring the impact of fiscal policy:a theoretical and empirical examination", working paper (Princeton University).

Hausman, J.A. and W.E. Taylor (1981), "Panel data and unobservable individual effects", Econometrica 49: 1377–1398.

Hausman, J. (1993), Contingent Valuation: A Critical Assessment (North Holland, Amsterdam).

Henderson, J.V. (1985), "The Tiebout model: bring back the entrepreneurs", Journal of Political Economy 93:248–264.

Henderson, J.V. (1996), "The effects of air quality regulation", American Economic Review.

Hoehn, J.P., M.C. Berger and G.C. Blomquist (1987), "A hedonic model of interregional wages, rents and amenity values", Journal of Regional Science 27:605–620.

Inman, R. (1995), "Do you know how much money is in your public purse?" Federal Reserve Bank of Philadelphia. Business Review, pp. 19–30.

Kahn, M. (1995), "A revealed preference approach to ranking city quality of life", Journal of Urban Economics. 38:221–235

Kahn, M. (1997), "Particulate pollution trends in the United States", Regional Science and Urban Economics. February, Vol. 27.

Kahn, M. and J. Matsusaka (1997), "Who votes for the environment? Evidence from California voter initiatives", Journal of Law & Economics.

Kiel, K. and K. McClain (1995), "House prices during siting decision stages: the case of an incinerator from rumor through operation", Journal of Environmental Economics and Management 28:241–255.

King, M.L. and M.A. Evans (1986), "Testing for block effects in regression models based on survey data", Journal of the American Statistical Association 81:677–679.

Kish, L. (1965), Survey Sampling (John Wiley, New York).

Kohlhase, J.E. (1991), "The impact of toxic waste sites on housing values", Journal of Urban Economics 30:1–26.

Kolstad, C. (editor) (1991), Measuring the Demand for Environmental Quality (North Holland Press, Amsterdam).

Krupnick, A., W. Harrington and B. Ostro (1990), "Ambient ozone and acute health effects: evidence from daily data", Journal of Environmental Economics and Management 18:1–18.

Linneman, P. and P.E. Graves (1983), "Migration and job change: a multinomial logit approach", Journal of Urban Economics 14:263–279.

Michaels, R. and V. Kerry Smith (1990), "Market segmentation and valuing amenities with hedonic methods: the case of hazardous waste sites", Journal of Urban Economics 18:223–242.

Mitchell, R.C. and R.T. Carson (1989), "Using surveys to value public goods: the contingent valuation method" (Resources for the Future, Washington, DC).

Mobil Oil Corporation (1989), Mobil Travel Guide.

Moulton, B.R. (1986), "Random group effects and the precision of regression estimates", Journal of Econometrics 32:385–397.

Moulton, B.R. (1987), "Diagnostics for group effects in regression analysis", Journal of Business and Economic Statistics 5:275–282.

Muesser, P.R. and P.E. Graves (1995), "Examining the role of economic opportunity and amenities in explaining population redistribution", Journal of Urban Economics 37:176–200.

Muth, R.F. (1971), "Migration: chicken or egg?", Southern Economic Journal 37:295–306.

Ostro, B.D. (1987), "Air pollution and morbidity revisited: a specification test", Journal of Environmental Economics and Management 14:87–98.

Pfefferman, D. and T.M.F Smith (1985), "Regression models for grouped populations in cross-section surveys", International Statistical Review 53:37–59.

Portney, P.R. (1994), "The contingent valuation debate: why economists should care", Journal of Economic Perspectives 8:3–17.

Portney, P.R. and J. Mullahy (1986), "Urban air quality and acute respiratory illness", Journal of Urban Economics 20:21–38.

Ranson, M. and C. Pope (1995), "External health costs of a steel mill", Contemporary Economic Policy April:86–101.

Roback, J. (1980), "The value of local urban amenities: theory and measurement", Ph.D. dissertation. University of Rochester.

Roback, J. (1982), "Wages, rents, and the quality of life", Journal of Political Economy 90:1257–1278.

Roback, J. (1988), "Wages, rents, and amenities: differences among workers and regions", Economic Inquiry 26:23–41.

Rosen, S. (1974), "Hedonic prices and implicit markets: product differentiation in pure competition", Journal of Political Economy 82:34–55.

Rosen, S. (1979), "Wage-based indexes of urban quality of life", in P. Mieszkowski and M. Straszheim, eds., Current Issues in Urban Economics (Johns Hopkins University Press, Baltimore).

Scott, A.J. and D. Holt (1982), "The effect of two-stage sampling on ordinary least squares methods", Journal of the American Statistical Association 77:848–854.

Sjaastad, L.A. (1962), "The costs and returns of human migration", Journal of Political Economy 70:80–93.

Smith, V.K. and Ju Chin Huang (1995), "Can hedonic models value air quality? A meta-analysis", Journal of Political Economy 103:209–227.

Stock, J. (1991), "Nonparametric policy analysis: an application to estimating hazardous waste cleanup benefits", in: P. Barnett, ed., Nonparametric and Semiparametric Methods in Economics and Statistics.

Stover, M.E. and C.L Leven (1992), "Methodological issues in the determination of the quality of life in urban areas", Urban Studies 29:737–754.

Topel, R.H. (1986), "Local labor markets", Journal of Political Economy 94:S111–S144.

Voith, R. (1991), "Capitalization of local and regional attributes into wages and rents: differences across residential, commercial and mixed-use communities", Journal of Regional Science 31:127–145.

*Chapter 38*

# AGGLOMERATION ECONOMIES AND URBAN PUBLIC INFRASTRUCTURE

RANDALL W. EBERTS

*W. E. Upjohn Institute for Employment Research, Kalamazoo*

DANIEL P. McMILLEN

*Tulane University, New Orleans*

## Contents

*Handbook of Regional and Urban Economics. Edited by E.S. Mills and P. Cheshire*
© *1999 Elsevier Science B.V. All rights reserved.*

## Abstract

This chapter reviews the theoretical and empirical literature on agglomeration economies and urban public infrastructure. Theory links the two concepts by positing that agglomeration economies exist when firms in an urban area share a public good as an input to production. One type of shareable input is the close proximity of businesses and labor, that generates positive externalities which in turn lower the production cost of one business as the output of other businesses increases. The externalities result from businesses sharing nonexcludable inputs, such as a common labor pool, technical expertise, general knowledge and personal contacts. Another perhaps more tangible type of shareable input is urban public infrastructure. Public capital stock, such as highways, water treatment facilities, and communication systems, directly affect the efficient operation of cities by facilitating business activities and improving worker productivity.

The literature has devoted considerable attention to both topics, but not together. Studies of agglomeration economies in several countries find that manufacturing firms are more productive in large cities than in smaller ones. Studies of the effect of infrastructure on productivity show positive, but in some cases statistically insignificant, effects of public capital stock on productivity. Most of these studies are at the national and state levels. Only a handful of studies have focused on the metropolitan level, and even fewer have estimated agglomeration economies and infrastructure effects simultaneously. Results from studies that include both types of shared inputs suggest that both spatial proximity and physical infrastructure contribute positively to the productivity of firms in urban areas. More research is needed to explore the interrelationships between urban size and urban public infrastructure and to open the "black box" of agglomeration economies and estimate how the various other factors associated with urban size affect productivity.

**Keywords:** Agglomeration economies, urban public infrastructure, productivity, optimal city size

## 1. Introduction

Agglomeration economies and public infrastructure play central roles in urban economics. The traditional textbook explanation of the existence and size of cities uses agglomeration economies (e.g., O'Sullivan, 1996 and Blair, 1991). Small cities can be explained by internal scale economies in production, in that larger establishments are more efficient than smaller ones. The large scale of operation attracts workers who subsequently establish a small community near the plant in order to minimize their commuting costs. Agglomeration economies explain the next stage of urban development: how company towns can further develop into large industrial cities. Simply stated, the activities of dissimilar businesses (and households) generate positive externalities that lower the production costs of one establishment as the output of other businesses increases. The externalities result from businesses sharing nonexcludable inputs, such as a common labor pool, technical expertise, communication and transportation networks.

Urban public infrastructure is one such shareable input that directly affects the efficient operation of cities, particularly large cities, and thus promotes the realization of agglomeration economies. Without an efficient highway system and adequate water and sewer capacity, for example, the positive gains achieved from the close proximity of people and businesses could be completely offset by the gridlock of the movement of people and goods and the inability to meet the basic needs of densely populated areas. Therefore, cities of identical size may experience different levels of productivity from agglomeration economies because of differences in the size and quality of their public infrastructure.

The literature has devoted considerable attention to both topics, but rarely together. Estimates of agglomeration economies gained considerable attention in the US during the 1970s and early 1980s. Interest in the effect of public infrastructure on productivity, primarily at the national and state level, followed shortly thereafter. However, few studies combined both effects in their analysis of urban productivity and even fewer recognized the importance of public infrastructure in achieving agglomeration economies.

Most of the agglomeration studies cited in this chapter were written during a period in which large population centers in the US were growing more slowly than smaller cities. Between 1970 and 1978, for example, metropolitan areas with more than 3 million residents grew only 9%, while metropolitan areas of less than 250,000 people grew 137% (Carlino, 1982). Some large metropolitan areas even lost population, particularly in the northeast. The New York City metropolitan area lost 5% of its population between 1970 and 1976. During the same period, metropolitan areas of at least one million people lost manufacturing employment faster than smaller metropolitan areas (Moomaw, 1980; Vining and Koutuly, 1977).

Observing that large US cities were stagnating in size, many researchers and policy makers believed that some cities were too large, claiming that the nation's largest cities were less livable and less economically viable and contributed more than proportionately to the nation's social problems (Sundquist, 1970). They proposed policies to give favorable tax breaks to businesses in smaller cities, and to channel federal infrastructure dollars away from large cities to smaller ones.

Against this backdrop of population trends and policy proposals, a wave of estimates of the net productivity advantages of large cities were conducted. The first estimates showed a substantial productivity advantage of large cities over smaller ones. Sveikauskas (1975) reported that a doubling of city size would yield a 6% increase in manufacturing productivity. Estimates of Segal (1976) and Fogarty and Garofalo (1978) were even larger—8 and 10%, respectively. Such estimates suggest that the New York City MSA, with its 9.5 million people in 1975, would be at least 50% more productive than an MSA of 50,000 people. Some researchers used these estimates to infer an optimal size city based on the economies and diseconomies associated with city size. Carlino (1982), for example, estimated the optimal size city to be 3.6 million people during the 1957–1969 period and 3.4 million during the 1970s. Some researchers viewed these estimates to be too large and inconsistent with the casual evidence of population and employment trends, and subsequent studies set out to resolve these inconsistencies.

Interest in the empirical relationship between public infrastructure and economic development in the US was first generated, not in the urban literature, but in the national productivity literature. The 1970s and 1980s saw not only slow growth or even declines in large urban areas, but also a sharp decline in national productivity. Several articles and books were influential in associating the national productivity decline to a decline in public infrastructure investment. Choate and Walter's (1983) alarming commentary on US infrastructure, entitled *America in Ruins*, fostered the public's perception of crumbling roads and bridges. Aschauer's (1989) large estimates of the marginal product of public capital, ranging from 0.38 to 0.56, fueled the debate. His results implied that public infrastructure was woefully neglected. The high estimated returns promised that government capital would pay for itself in terms of higher output within a year. To some, this finding appeared to be a costless panacea for future growth; to others, these results engendered much scepticism and consequently generated a series of papers seeking to understand what was behind these large estimates. This "third deficit", as Munnell (1990) referred to it, was linked to the celebrated but perplexing productivity slowdown in the 1970s and to lagging real wages. Congress established the National Council on Public Works Improvement (1988) to conduct an in-depth assessment of the state of public infrastructure and come up with policy recommendations. The Council recommended that the nation should double its investment in public infrastructure. Other government agencies, including the Federal Highway Administration and the Corps of Engineers, sponsored research to explore the relationship between public infrastructure and productivity, primarily at the state and national level.

During this period, few researchers explored the effects of public infrastructure at the metropolitan level.[1] From a research and policy perspective, this neglect makes little sense. First, public infrastructure is a key factor in facilitating the benefits of agglomeration and in easing the congestion associated with large cities. Second, public infrastructure is an important input into the production process (and in the household utility function) independent of its associated effects with agglomeration economies. Third, much infrastructure investment is concentrated at the metropolitan area level, where the interaction between infrastructure and economic activity takes place. Infrastructure, like agglomeration economies, is a spatial construct, and linking the actual public infrastructure facility (e.g., a highway segment and network) to its users is important. This spatial correspondence is less distinct at the state and national level. Finally, state and local governments are responsible for most of the expenditures on the nation's infrastructure. Upwards of 85% of total US nonresidential public capital is put in place by state and local governments, with local governments assuming a large part of that responsibility.[2]

This chapter reviews the theoretical and empirical literature on agglomeration economies and urban public infrastructure. Theory links the two inextricably by suggesting that agglomeration economies exist when firms in an urban area share a public good as an input to production. Clearly, public infrastructure is one such

---

[1] The exceptions were Dalenberg (1987), Eberts (1986) and Deno (1988). The primary reason for the lack of research at the metropolitan level is the difficulty in constructing suitable measures of public capital stock. Most research on the productivity effects of public capital stock uses the perpetual inventory technique to estimate capital stock. This approach requires a long investment series, that is not readily available. The only metropolitan and city public capital stock estimates using this approach for the US were constructed by Eberts et al. (1986). Considerably more studies of infrastructure's effect on economic activity have been conducted at state level. Most have used a dataset constructed by Alicia Munnell (1990) using Census of Government data. However, for agglomeration studies, state-level estimates are considered too aggregated given that agglomeration economies are urban specific effects (Calem and Carlino, 1991, among others also make this argument).

[2] Local governments have a similarly large role in many European countries. Seitz (1993) reports that local governments are responsible for investing 70% of (the former West) Germany's share of total public investment.

sharable input. Also, as argued above, public infrastructure facilitates the benefits of agglomeration economies. For example, one suggested source of agglomeration economies is the city's role as an "urban warehouse", which allows firms to carry lower inventories. A warehouse hardly is feasible without public investment in roads, bridges, and other local infrastructure.

The organization of the chapter is as follows. We begin in Section 2 with a review of the theoretical literature. The review follows the literature's chronological development from descriptive studies of agglomeration economies, to use of agglomeration economies in explaining the existence and growth of urban area, to studies of the microfoundations of agglomeration economies. In Section 3, we review empirical studies of agglomeration economies. We begin with the most common type of study, which uses production functions to provide quantitative estimates of agglomeration economies. We then discuss econometric problems with the traditional methodology and highlight alternative estimation strategies. A review of the literature on public infrastructure—that is mostly empirical—is presented in Section 4. Section 5 offers some conclusions and suggestions for future research.

## 2. Agglomeration economies and urban theory

### 2.1. Descriptive analysis

Until recently, the literature on agglomeration economies was largely descriptive. The traditional analysis divides economies of agglomeration into three categories: (1) internal scale economies; (2) economies that are external to the firm but internal to the industry; and (3) economies that are external to both the firm and industry but occur because industry concentrates in an urban area. The second category of agglomeration economies is called "localization economies", and the third category "urbanization economies".[3] Although the categories are not mutually exclusive, they have different implications for the nature of an urban area's economic activity.

---

[3] This categorization appears to have entered the urban/regional literature through Hoover (1937), who uses the terms "localization" and "urbanization" and discusses their role in industrial concentration. Hoover credits the idea to Ohlin (1935), who also defines three categories of economies that lead to concentration of industry: "(1) economies of concentration of industry in general, (2) external economies of concentration of a particular industry, and (3) internal large-scale economies of a producing unit" (Ohlin, 1935: p. 203). Adam Smith (1776) and Alfred Marshall (1890) also have extensive discussions of the advantages of urban areas for industrial location, although without a neat categorization and with an emphasis on internal scale and localization economies.

### 2.1.1. Internal scale economies

Internal scale economies are the most familiar category to economists. They exist when expanding production at some given site lowers a firm's unit costs. The classic example is Smith's (1776) pin factory, in which a firm's growth enables it to take advantage of division of labor. Workers' skills increase through repetition, that lowers production costs. Internal scale economies also are attributed to the existence of indivisible inputs, that occurs when an input has a minimum efficient scale. Other examples include the ability to take advantage of bulk purchases at a site and the more efficient use of specialized machinery. Internal scale economies allow a large firm to underprice its smaller competitors, that may compensate for the additional shipping costs that necessarily occur by concentrating production in a single location. Large-scale manufacturing establishments such as steel production and automobile assembly are obvious examples of industries with significant internal scale economies. Such establishments lead to the formation of a "company town": steel in Gary, rubber in Akron, glass in Toledo, chocolate in Hershey or aircraft manufacture in Seattle.

### 2.1.2. Localization economies

Localization economies occur when a firm's unit costs are lower in an urban area that includes many firms in the same industry. The scale economy is external to the firm (so that firms remain small), but internal to the industry (so that industrial concentration is high in an urban area).[4] As with internal scale economies, specialization may create localization economies as greater city size permits firms within an industry to concentrate on one type of production.

Localization and internal scale economies also can differ. Marshall (1890) presents the classic treatment of localization economies:

> When an industry has thus chosen a locality for itself, it is likely to stay there long: so great are the advantages which people following the same skilled trade get from near neighbourhood to one another. The mysteries of the trade become no mysteries: but are as it were in the air, and children learn many of them unconsciously. Good work is rightly appreciated, inventions and improvements in machinery, in processes and the general organization of the business have their merits promptly discussed: if one man starts a new idea, it is taken up by others and combined with suggestions of their own; and thus it becomes the source of further new ideas. And presently

---

[4] The assumption that economies are external to the firm is important in making a competitive market system compatible with aggregate increasing returns to scale. See Chipman (1970). Mergers can transform external economies into economies that are internal to the new, larger firm.

subsidiary trades grow up in the neighbourhood, supply it with implements and materials, organizing its traffic, and in many ways conducing to the economy of its material. (Marshall, 1890: p. 225)

This passage clearly illustrates textbook "labor-market economies", "communication economies", and the role of localization economies in stimulating innovation emphasized by Jacobs (1969).

Labor-market economies are a much-emphasized source of localization economies. An example is the computer industry in Silicon Valley (Santa Clara County, California). Software firms in Silicon Valley are typically quite small, suggesting the absence of internal scale economies. Start-up costs are small, but the risks are high. Firms routinely fail, and their employees look for new jobs elsewhere. By concentrating employment in one area, firms can easily find the skilled employees they need to start a new operation, and workers can quickly find employment after an enterprise fails. Matching costs are low when industry concentrates in one area.

One firm's internal scale economies may lead to another industry's localization economies. Shipping costs may lead to a substantial cost advantage to locating near the large firm if its output is an input to the industry's production process. An example from O'Sullivan (1996) is high technology firms, that purchase electronic components from large suppliers. Even if the high technology firms have no localization economies of their own, they may cluster near the producer of electronic components to reduce their cost of obtaining nonstandardized electronic parts.

Although traditionally most emphasis is placed on manufacturing in the urban/regional literature, localization economies also may exist in retail establishments by allowing customers to comparison shop. The tendency of car dealers to cluster together is an obvious example. Similarly, restaurants cluster near each other to take advantage of other restaurants' overflow of customers and facilitate comparison shopping for those customers who are undecided in where to eat. A localization economy exists because small establishments in the same industry find it profitable to locate near one another. A similar argument lies behind the idea of "communication economies": firms locate near each other to reduce the cost (both to themselves and their customers) of obtaining information. An important role of communication economies is to increase the rate of technological innovation in urban areas.

### 2.1.3. Urbanization economies

Urbanization economies occur when economies are external to both the firm and industry. Thus, small establishments find it profitable to locate in an urban area even when there are no cost advantages to geographic concentration for their industry. This category is something of a "residual": if we cannot explain a firm's location in an urban area by other types of agglomeration economies, then it must enjoy an urbanization economy. In keeping with its status as a residual, little effort is given to explaining the existence of an urbanization economy, the typical statement being that urbanization economies occur for the same reasons as agglomeration economies but the benefits are not concentrated at the industry level.

Goldstein and Gronberg (1984: p. 92) suggest that "an example of urbanization economies is specialized services in large urban areas that do not exist in smaller areas. In a rural area, a manufacturing firm which operates a fleet of trucks must have on hand its own mechanics, or use local 'general' mechanics. In a large urban area, the firm can draw upon firms which specialize in maintenance of large trucks". The city acts as an "urban warehouse", that allows a small firm to specialize its production without providing all required services. Public infrastructure is another obvious source of urbanization economies: by providing good highways, public utilities, communication facilities and the like, an urban area significantly lowers the cost to all firms of doing business in an urban area.

Note the subtlety of the distinction between localization and urbanization economies. An urban area that is near a cheap source of electricity may attract an industry that is energy-intensive, and thus have a localization economy. Alternatively, it may attract small, unrelated firms for which electricity is a large component of total costs, and then have an urbanization economy.

Similarly, Mills and Hamilton's (1994) application of the law of large numbers as an example of agglomeration economies does not yield a clear distinction between economies of localization and urbanization:

> Sales of output and purchases of inputs fluctuate in many firms and industries for random, seasonal, cyclical, and secular reasons. To the extent that fluctuations are imperfectly correlated among employers, an urban area with many employers can provide more nearly full employment of its labor force than can an urban area with few employers. Likewise, a firm with many buyers whose demand fluctuations are uncorrelated will have proportionately less variability in its sales than a firm with few buyers. It can hold, therefore, smaller inventories and employ smoother production scheduling. (Mills and Hamilton, 1994: p. 20)

## 2.1.4. Modeling implications

The discussion of agglomeration economies suggests that firms enjoy cost and production advantages in urban areas. The usual approach is to include as an argument in the production function one of the following arguments: (1) output of the firm, to represent internal scale economies; (2) output of the industry, to represent localization economies; and (3) population or output of the urban area, to represent agglomeration economies. The approach taken depends on the type of firm that is being modeled, but for the urban area as a whole there is no reason to focus on just one of the three approaches as all may exist simultaneously.

Just as constant returns production leads to an unreasonable implication that cities are unnecessary, agglomeration economies produce an unrealistic world in which all production activity takes place at one site unless there are limits to agglomeration's benefits. Smith (1776) argued that division of labor is limited by the size of the market. Modern urban economists focus on various diseconomies of city size: congestion costs, high wages, high land and housing prices, pollution, crime, etc.[5] The important point for subsequent subsections is that a complete theoretical or empirical model specification should recognize both the benefits and costs of agglomeration.

## 2.2. Theoretical models of urban areas

The first general equilibrium model of an urban economy is presented in Mills (1967), which also provides a treatment of agglomeration economies that serves as a model for much subsequent research. Mills models an urban area with three activities: (1) the production of an export good; (2) intracity transportation, that uses costly land to transport workers to the city center; and (3) housing, that is produced under conditions of constant returns to scale. For our purposes, the most important activity is the first, for the possibility of increasing returns to scale in production leads to the city's existence. The output of the export good is represented by $X$, that is produced by combining land ($L$), labor ($N$), and capital ($K$) according to the following generalized Cobb–Douglas production function:

$$X = AL^{\alpha} N^{\beta} K^{\gamma}. \tag{2.1}$$

The degree of scale economies depends on $H = \alpha + \beta + \gamma$. Increasing returns to scale are implied if $H > 1$, whereas, constant returns to scale exist if $H = 1$. Mills leaves unspecified the source of the scale economies. Equation (2.1) is

---

[5] An extensive discussion of the benefits and costs of agglomeration is presented in Richardson (1973).

an aggregate production function, and the source of the scale economy (when $H > 1$) may be any of the three traditional sources.

The amount of land devoted to transportation limits city size in Mills' (1967) model. He assumes that the amount of land in transportation at any site is proportional to the number of passenger miles at the site. Increases in population associated with large employment in the export sector then lead to a diseconomy in transportation:

> Suppose we consider the possibility of doubling the population of a city by doubling the height of every building. If this were feasible and if twice as many people now traveled between each pair of points as before, then it would lead to just twice the demand for transportation as before. But if transportation requires land as an input, it must use more land after the doubling of population than before. Thus, some land previously used for buildings must now be used for transportation, thus requiring new buildings at the edge of the city. But the edge of the city has now moved out, and some people must make longer trips than before, requiring more transportation inputs. Thus, a doubling of the city's population requires more than doubling transportation inputs. (Mills, 1967: p. 199)

More recent studies of individual urban areas have followed in Mills' tradition, while being more precise about the source of the agglomeration economy. For example, Sullivan (1983) develops a general equilibrium model of an urban economy, providing a detailed analysis of production in the export sector. He assumes that the export sector's production is characterized by the following unit cost function:

$$C = C(P_K, P_L(u), P_T(u)) \cdot \phi(Z), \qquad \phi(Z) = (Z_0/Z)^g, \qquad (2.2)$$

where $P_K$ = the price of capital, $u$ = distance from the city center, $P_L(u)$ = the price of labor, $P_T(u)$ = the price of land, $\phi(Z)$ = the scale-economy function, $Z_0$ = an exogenous parameter, $Z$ = aggregate export output, and $g$ = the degree of increasing returns. If $g = 0$, the export sector is characterized by constant returns to scale, whereas, $g > 0$ implies increasing returns to scale. Since a large number of firms exists in Sullivan's city and the scale-economy function depends on total industry output, the agglomeration economies are those of localization. As in Mills (1967), city size is limited by decreasing returns to transportation caused by land requirements.

Mills' model represents a single city. In a pathbreaking and influential series of writings, Henderson (1974, 1982a, b, 1983, 1985, 1988) models a system of cities, each of which specializes in an export good subject to localization economies. The export good is produced using labor and capital. The production function is,

$$X = Ag(N)\hat{N}_0^\alpha \hat{K}_0^{1-\alpha}, \tag{2.3}$$

where $A$ and $\alpha$ are parameters, $X$ is traded good output, $\hat{N}_0$ and $\hat{K}_0$ represent local employment of labor and capital, and $N$ is the number of city residents. Scale effects are Hicks-neutral, and are represented through the function $g(N)$, with $g'(N) > 0$. The localization economy leads to city existence, and provides an incentive for firms in an industry to locate in the same urban area.[6] Similar to Mills (1967), city size is limited by the land required for transportation services.

Public infrastructure plays an important role in the model. Additional infrastructure reduces commuting time for a given number of residents, freeing labor for housing production. This, in turn, reduces the price of housing and allows firms to pay lower wages. In this way, public investment in transportation technology stimulates growth. However, by focusing only on transportation investment, the model does not take into account the direct role of public infrastructure in reducing firm costs, that the empirical literature emphasizes.

Henderson's (1985) model implies that each city specializes in the production of one export good. Specialization occurs for two reasons. First, costs fall as additional firms in an industry locate in a given urban area, providing an incentive for firms within one industry to locate in the same metropolitan area. Second, locating in different cities is cheaper for any two industries because sharing a location across industries has no cost advantage, and the additional commuting raises costs for both industries. The model produces a system of specialized cities, whose size depends on the size of the local industry. Industries with high degrees of localization economies lead to large cities. For a given level of demand, an increase in the degree of an industry's localization economy leads to a smaller number of cities, each of which is larger than before. For a given level of localization economy, an increase in demand for an industry's product leads to a larger number of cities that specialize in the industry.

The emphasis on localization economies has important implications. First, it explains why all production does not take place in just a small number of extremely large cities, as is implied by simple models with urbanization economies.

---

[6] Moomaw (1985) provides the comparative statics results for a single firm that chooses cities on the basis of this form of production function, with wages that rise with city size. He finds that an increase in the productivity gradient or a decrease in the wage gradient leads a firm to choose a large city size. With a homogeneous production function, a general increase in wages across cities also leads a firm to prefer large cities. A general increase in factor productivity (i.e., an increase in $g(N)$) has an ambiguous effect on city-size choice.

Second, industrial specialization is predicted to be the norm within metropolitan areas. Third, equilibrium in a system of cities includes different city sizes, with wages and costs of living rising with city size. Finally, it is critical in empirical work to disaggregate estimated urban-area production functions by industry type.

Henderson's studies have greatly influenced subsequent theoretical work. For example, Abdel-Rahman (1990a) employs a similar analysis to model a system of two cities, a one-product city with only localization economies, and a two-product city that has both localization and urbanization economies. The localization economy specification is similar to Henderson's. Abdel-Rahman (1990a) establishes that both types of cities can exist simultaneously in equilibrium. He also shows that the two-product city is larger than the one-product city if either industry has decreasing returns in production. With either constant or increasing returns, the one-product city—the one with localization economies only— is larger.

Henderson's systems approach also can explain the growth of subcenters of employment within a metropolitan area. For example, Henderson (1988) outlines a model with two types of industries, both of which are subject to localization economies. Natural resources are a critical input in the first type of industry, tying the industry to a small set of locations. The second type of industry is "footloose", but is drawn to areas near the other industry's locations to reduce costs of intercity trade. The result is "multinucleated" metropolitan areas composed of numerous different cities.

Helsley and Sullivan (1991) take an alternative approach to subcenter formation. This paper shows Henderson's influence, but the specification of agglomeration economies is more similar to Mills' (1967). Helsley and Sullivan (1991) consider a metropolitan area with two locations—the city and a subcenter. In the simplest form of the model, the production function is the same in both locations, but the central city forms first, providing an advantage in the level of urbanization economy. Subcenters arise from the tradeoff between agglomeration economies and diseconomies in transportation. As a city grows, the central city firms enjoy increasing urbanization economies, but commuting becomes increasingly costly. The optimal growth pattern involves an initial period of exclusive central city development, followed by formation of a subcenter when "diseconomies in transportation reduce the social value of central city labor below the social value of subcenter labor" (Helsley and Sullivan, 1991: pp. 258–259). When the subcenter forms, the city enters a period of exclusive subcenter development where no employment is added to the central city. Later, employment growth is split between the two locations.[7]

Unlike many studies, Helsley and Sullivan's (1991) analysis is explicitly dynamic. The dynamics of agglomeration economies form a new growth area for both theoretical and empirical research (e.g., Hanson, 1996; Henderson, 1988; Mori, 1997; Palivos and Wang, 1996; Sasaki and Mun, 1996; Walz, 1996). Henderson (1988) argues that urbanization economies are most important in the early stages of an industry's development, causing the industry to locate in the largest cities. As an industry grows, it may move to smaller cities, with localization economies becoming the dominant force. An example is the Silicon Valley computer industries, that began in the San Francisco Bay Area due to the urbanization economies associated with a large city with electronic firms and major universities. As the industry grew, localization economies became significant. Now, the industry is so large that ample levels of localization economies can be enjoyed in other locations (e.g., Austin, Texas and Portland, Oregon).

Mori (1997) also analyzes the dynamics of urban development when firm location is driven by agglomeration economies. In Mori's model, agglomeration economies are generated by consumers' demand for variety and scale economies in the production of manufacturing goods. Large cities offer more variety in consumption, that attracts workers who increase the demand for manufactured goods. The increased demand supports a greater number of specialized manufactured goods in large urban areas. A large city develops as transport costs decline, because manufacturing firms can support a larger market area while enjoying the agglomeration economies of large cities. But large urban areas pay higher shipping costs on average for agricultural goods. As the urban area grows, some firms may find it worthwhile to locate in the agricultural hinterland, producing another city. Other firms follow to take advantage of agglomerative forces in the new, smaller city. The smaller city may continue to grow as the increased agglomeration economies lead more firms to enter. Eventually, the cities may merge, producing a "megapolis".

## 2.3. Microfoundations of agglomeration economies

In early theoretical studies, metropolitan area population or industry employment serves as a shift factor for the production function. The source of the productivity

---

[7] Anas and Kim (1996) take another approach to modeling subcenter formation. They assume that consumers prefer to shop in areas with many stores. Subcenters develop when these "shopping externalities" are strong relative to the cost of traffic congestion. Henderson and Mitra (1996) provide a fascinating analysis of the development of "edge cities"—cities with large diversified employment centers in suburban areas.

gain is left unspecified. Early analyses of the microfoundations of agglomeration economies, such as Hoover (1937) and Chinitz (1961), were largely descriptive. Recently, theorists attempted to provide more formal microfoundations to the earlier literature.

Goldstein and Gronberg (1984) provide a useful framework for analyzing sources of agglomeration economies. They build on the economies of scope literature developed by Panzar and Willig (1981) to provide a formal framework for analyzing agglomeration economies. Economies of scope exist for a firm if it is less costly to produce a variety of products within one firm than to produce each product in separate firms. Similarly, "agglomerative economies exist when it is less costly to combine two or more product lines in one urban area (*but not necessarily one firm*) than to produce them in different areas" (Goldstein and Gronberg, 1984: p. 97, italics in the original).

Goldstein and Gronberg derive conditions under which (1) urban areas exist and consist of multiproduct firms; (2) urban areas consist of single-product firms; (3) firms produce multiple products but have no incentive to locate in urban areas; and (4) the economy consists of single-product firms that have no incentive to locate in urban areas. Economies of agglomeration exist when producing at one site is cheaper than at multiple sites. Economies of scope exist when total costs are lower for multiple-output than for single-output firms producing the same outputs.

Goldstein and Gronberg's (1984) most important contribution is to identify the sufficient condition for the existence of agglomeration economies. The condition is identified in their proposition 2, which states that economies of agglomeration exist when production costs are lower for each firm when they locate in one area rather than apart.[8] The key is the existence of a sharable input; Goldstein and Gronberg's examples include storage facilities, machine repair shops and training centers for skills. However, their analysis does not explicitly incorporate the spatial distribution of firms. Abdel-Rahman and Fujita (1993) show that Panzar and Willig's (1981) condition for the formation of multiproduct firms docs not extend directly to the formation of multiproduct cities. Diseconomies in urban transportation imply that two specialized cities may have lower overall costs than a single diversified city even when economies of scope produce cost advantages to mutiproduct firms. Nonetheless, Goldstein and Gronberg's (1984) study provides a useful framework for analyzing the benefits of agglomeration.

---

[8] "For any nontrivial partition of $N$ over space, there are economies of agglomeration if and only if the cost of producing the resources to be shared by others is strictly subadditive over space" (Goldstein and Gronberg, 1984: p. 101).

The Goldstein and Gronberg classification closely matches the previous descriptive literature. Economies of agglomeration exist when an urban area provides an input that lowers costs for all firms. A key input is public infrastructure—roads, airports, training facilities, universities, etc. If costs are lowered for only one industry, we have localization economies. If costs are lowered for all firms, we have urbanization economies. Note that the cost advantage may or may not enter directly through productivity gains, as assumed in the preceding theoretical models (other than Sullivan, 1983). For example, a sharable input that lowers the cost of obtaining labor enters the cost and profit functions instead of the production function. This line of reasoning suggests that empirical researchers should consider using a cost function specification rather than the more traditional production function approach.

Other studies directly attempt to model the microfoundations of specific agglomeration economies. An early example is Sullivan (1986), who models a city with two employment sectors. Manufacturing enjoys a traditional localization economy that depends on aggregate manufacturing output. Similarly, an office sector is subject to a localization economy that depends on aggregate office-sector output. However, another source of office-sector agglomeration economies is incorporated into the model: workers in the sector must make costly trips to a central market each day "to interact with the representatives of other firms; these employees exchange information and market their products" (Sullivan, 1986: p. 60). The information is not available to a firm that locates outside of the city, and is more costly to obtain the farther a firm is from the central business district (CBD). Office workers have an incentive to locate near each other in the CBD to reduce the cost of face-to-face contact; this proximity represents a form of sharable input. Sullivan's (1986) model incorporates the "communication economies" that many authors use to justify the existence of agglomeration economies. Sullivan does not attempt to explain why both manufacturing and offices exist in the same city when separate cities would reduce overall commuting costs. Perhaps manufacturing establishments are office customers, and nearby locations reduce transaction costs.

Helsley (1990) models the role of cities in spreading information. In his simple linear city, each firm produces a single output $q$ according to a constant-returns firm-level production function with a Hicks-neutral shift factor that depends on the level of knowledge:

$$q(u) = g[a(u)]f[l(u), n(u)], \tag{2.4}$$

where $u$ is distance from the city center, $l(u)$ is land, $n(u)$ is a nonland input, and $a(u)$ represents the "level of knowledge" at location $u$. Each firm produces knowledge as a by-product of producing $q$:

$$x(u) = \beta q(u), \qquad \beta > 0. \tag{2.5}$$

Knowledge is a public input, but declines with distance according to the decay function $\gamma(z, u)$, that represents the portion of $x(u)$ that remains at $z$. This function reaches a peak at $z = u$ (where $\gamma(u, u) = 1$), and declines symmetrically for $z > u$ and $z < u$ with $|z - u|$. The level of knowledge at location $u$ is $a(u) = \int_{u_0}^{u_1} \gamma(u, z) x(z) \, dz$, where $u_0$ and $u_1$ are the endpoints of the linear CBD. The key result is that "the level of knowledge, land rent, and output and factor intensities achieve unique maxima at the center of the CBD in equilibrium and decline as distance from the center of the CBD increases" (Helsley, 1990: p. 400). Productivity is highest at the city center, and at every location is related positively to the number of firms in the CBD.

Another often-cited source of agglomeration economies is improvements in the labor market as city size increases: in large cities a firm is more likely to find the skilled workers it requires, and workers are more likely to find suitable employment. Helsley and Strange (1990) model the matching process between firms and workers.[9] The productivity of workers, whose skills exactly match their job is $\alpha$, and a loss of $\beta$ per unit distance in the characteristic space, is caused by having skills other than $\alpha$. Let $x$ be the address on the unit circle of firms' job requirements, while $y$ is the address of workers. Then the output of the match $(x, y)$ is $\alpha - \beta|x - y|$. Firms do not observe the skills of workers before choosing a city, and workers do not observe the job requirements of firms. Both groups know the number of firms and workers in each city, and assume that skills and job requirements are random draws from a uniform distribution on the unit circle. The expected quality of the match between firms and workers increases with city size, which confirms the intuition of previous descriptive studies.

This simple but clever formulation leads to important insights:

> First, the agglomeration economy has the characteristics of a local public good. A firm entering a city improves the expected quality of the match between job requirements and skills for all workers, leading to a positive

---

[9] Kim (1989, 1990, 1991) provides a similar analysis, while allowing firms to train workers who have low skills. Abdel-Rahman and Wang (1995, 1997) develop a two-sector (high versus low skill) model with a matching process in the skilled labor market. A hierarchical system is developed in which a single large metropolis contains all skilled workers, while peripheral regions include unskilled workers. The advantage to the high-skill firms of a single location is the increased efficacy of the labor market.

> ex ante relationship between wages, productivity, and city size .... Second, there are two externalities associated with firm location .... One is the conventional productivity externality. If a firm enters a city, it improves the productivity of all workers, but it considers only its own profits. This externality causes a city to contain too few firms under free entry. The other externality arises from spatial competition and the heterogeneity of workers and firms. An entrant to a city reduces the labor market areas, and hence profits, of incumbent firms, but considers only its own profits. This competition externality leads to too many firms under free entry. The competition externality dominates in our model. Third, equilibrium city sizes are not optimal ... [and] the zero profit number of firms is not efficient. (Helsley and Strange, 1990: pp. 190–191)

In Goldstein and Gronberg's (1984) framework, the efficacy of the labor market is a form of public input that is sharable by all firms in Helsley and Strange's (1990) cities.

In a subsequent paper, Helsley and Strange (1991) provide a rigorous explanation of the agglomeration economies that Mills and Hamilton (1994) call "statistical in nature". The basis is an urban area served by a single bank, that allocates credit to different investment projects. Some projects succeed but others fail. When a project fails, the bank gains possession of an immobile and specialized asset. The value of the asset to the bank is its salvage value, that depends on its value in its second best use. The second-best value is higher in large cities because when a wide variety of firms exists there is a higher probability of a good match between the initial firm's capital requirements and those of other firms.

Again, Helsley and Strange summarize the implications well:

> Agglomeration economies arise because the expected second best use of an immobile asset is worth more in a large city than in a small one. This means that resource productivity rises with city size in two ways: used assets are better matched and risk is reduced .... [C]ity size provides borrowers with external collateral on loans. This external collateral is a public input in urban capital markets: it is impossible to exclude borrowers from utilizing the external collateral, and its use by one borrower does not limit its use by others. The external collateral associated with greater city sizes resembles the public inputs that Goldstein and Gronberg discuss. (Helsley and Strange, 1991: pp. 97–98)

Another important implication of this paper is that large cities contain more types of economic activities than small cities because "bad states of nature are less costly" (p. 110).

Several studies (e.g., Abdel-Rahman, 1990b, 1996; Abdel-Rahman and Fujita, 1990; Dobkins, 1996; Mori, 1997) focus on the advantages that large-city diversity provides. Abdel-Rahman (1990b) develops a model in which production of a traded good depends on miscellaneous intermediate goods. The key result is that the number of intermediate inputs produced in a city is an increasing function of city size, which implies that larger cities produce a greater variety of goods. City size is larger as labor requirements fall. If labor requirements vary with industrial structure, city sizes can differ in equilibrium. Unlike most studies, that explain the formation of specialized cities, Abdel-Rahman's (1990b) model produces a system of cities with diversified industrial structures.[10]

## 3. Estimates of agglomeration economies

The most common approach to estimating the productivity advantages of urban areas uses a production function aggregated to the metropolitan level. The base is a production function that is similar to those used in theoretical studies:

$$y_{ij} = g(S_j) f(K_{ij}, L_{ij}, G_{ij}, Z_{ij}), \tag{3.1}$$

where $y_{ij}$ represents output for the $i$th firm in the $j$th city, and $K$, $L$, $G$ and $Z$ represent capital, labor, public infrastructure and other inputs. We include public infrastructure $(G)$ as an input in the production function to show the importance of including both measures of agglomeration and public infrastructure. As described more fully in Section 4, studies typically include either agglomeration measures or public capital but rarely do they include both.

The production function, $f(\bullet)$, is often but not always assumed to exhibit constant returns to scale and may exhibit increasing returns to scale when public infrastructure is included as an input. The shift factor, $g(S_j)$, represents scale economies, with $g' \geq 0$. Scale, $S_j$, is measured by either metropolitan employment or population to represent urbanization economies, or industry employment

---

[10] Fujita and Krugman (1995) use a related approach to explain city existence. In their model, each worker consumes a homogeneous agricultural good and a variety of differentiated manufacturing goods. Manufacturing goods have internal scale economies, and are costly to ship. Workers prefer to live in large cities because a greater number of manufacturing goods is available for consumption. The migration of workers to the city lowers wages, attracting more firms. The result is a diversified city surrounded by an agricultural hinterland. The model has not been extended to include a system of cities.

or output to represent localization economies. It is also possible for either $g$ or $f$ to differ by city, industry or both. The error term that is added to Eq. (3.1) is most often assumed to be multiplicative.

Early studies ignored $g(S_j)$, and attempted to determine whether, or not, $f(\bullet)$ exhibited increasing returns to scale. Although these studies did find evidence of increasing returns, the absence of limits on the degree of increasing returns implies unrealistically that all employment should take place in one city. Later studies either attempted to estimate Eq. (3.1) directly or use $S$ to explain differences in labor productivity $(y/L)$ across metropolitan areas.

Moomaw (1981) criticizes such studies (in particular, Sveikauskas, 1975 and Segal, 1976) for not incorporating their production function into a broader model of firm behavior so that factor prices could be taken into account. He contends that higher factor prices in larger cities offset the gross productivity advantages found in the two studies, and shows that the effect of higher wages in larger cities reduces Sveikauskas' and Segal's estimates of agglomeration economies by half. Most subsequent studies integrate factor prices into production functions either through deriving and estimating demand equations or through factor share equations.

The use of cost functions rather than production functions in some later studies results in part from the recognition that wages and other factor prices vary with city size and affect net productivity advantages (Henderson, 1986). In addition to being more consistent with the theory of agglomeration, estimating a cost function has several econometric advantages over estimating a production function (see Friedlaender, 1990).

Other issues that arise in empirical estimation are evident in Eq. (3.1). What is the appropriate functional form? What is the proper unit of analysis? What is the proper specification of agglomeration economies? How should urban size be measured? What inputs should be included in the analysis? How should public infrastructure be included in the analysis? Is the production function or its dual cost function the most appropriate basis for the analysis or should the analysis be based on an equilibrium model of local labor and land markets?[11]

This section summarizes the empirical literature on agglomeration economies. Each of the above issues is addressed, with the exception of public infrastructure, that is discussed in Section 4.

---

[11] For example, if an agglomeration economy provides a cost advantage to locating in a city, firms will enter the city until wages rise to the point of zero profits. The increased wages are a measure of the productive advantages offered by the city.

## 3.1. Functional form of the production function

The majority of the empirical research is based on production functions. Table 1 summarizes many of the studies published since 1973. The production function approach owes its origin primarily to Mills (1967), who first put forth an aggregative model based on a production function to explain the effects of spatial concentration on productivity. Most of the studies using the production function framework found a positive relationship between their specification of the shift factor, interpreted by many as agglomeration economies, and city size. The magnitude of these estimates varies by model specification and other factors. Unfortunately, because studies differ in the way they specify agglomeration economies and report their findings, it is not possible to compare estimates directly of all the studies included in this chapter. It is still instructive, however, to highlight the major differences among the specifications.

Most empirical studies have adopted a flexible functional form for the production function. Moomaw (1981), in his critique of two early empirical estimates of agglomeration economies, points out the problems with a restrictive functional form, such as a Cobb–Douglas. In particular, "efficiency gains with larger population or output gains because of particular city characteristics result in parallel shifts in the isoquants with no change in their slope. Hence, the optimal input ratio is not altered by changes in efficiency or in city characteristics" (p. 685). Subsequent studies have adopted a variant of the generalized translog production function, specified in per worker terms to reduce multicollinearity problems. Nakamura (1985) specifies a per labor variant of a translog production function, in which agglomeration is entered as $g_i(P_j) = \alpha_1 P_j^{\alpha_p}$. He then estimates the production relationships by estimating the production function and $n - 1$ share equations. Considerable work in the area of production function estimation supports the use of generalized functional forms over specific forms such as the CES and the Cobb–Douglas (see, Fuss and McFadden, 1979).

Assuming separability between intermediate inputs and primary factors of production, Eq. (3.1) represents a value-added production function of typical firm $i$ in city $j$. Firms are assumed to be perfectly competitive and choose the optimal mix of private inputs by equating the marginal product of each input to its price. In a perfectly competitive world, firms exhibit internal constant returns to scale with respect to the privately provided inputs, and a firm's revenue is distributed completely to the private inputs.

These assumptions are not met in the presence of agglomeration economies because firms earn economic rents by generating productivity externalities. Factors whose productivity has been enhanced by agglomeration externalities re-

Table 1

Studies using production functions to estimate agglomeration economies

| Author | Unit of analysis | Specification | RHS Inputs | Agglomeration — Localization | Agglomeration — Urbanization | Agglomeration effects — Localization | Agglomeration effects — Urbanization | Other variables |
|---|---|---|---|---|---|---|---|---|
| Mera (1973) | Japan 9 regions, 1954–1963 pooled | Log linear output per worker production function | Labor, private capital, land | Industry employment | | Postive and significant | | Social overhead capital |
| Shefer (1973) | US two-digit manufacturing industries in MSAs 1958 and 1963 | CES output per worker production function with first-order conditions | Wage | Returns to scale at industry aggregation | Returns to scale at MSA aggregation | Positive and varies widely across industries | Population elasticity about 0.20 | |
| Aberg (1973) | Sweden manufacturing cross section | CES output per worker | Wage | | Population density | | Positive and significant | |
| Kawashima (1975) | US three-digit manufacturing in MSAs 1958 and 1967 | CD output per worker production function | Employment, (1-payroll) | | Population (quadratic) | | Population elasticity 0.20 in 1967; Optimal urban population 5.95 million | |
| Sveikauskas (1975) | US two-digit manufacturing in MSAs | CES output per worker production function | Employment, education | | Population | | 6% with each doubling of population | |
| Segal (1976) | US manufacturing in MSAs, 1958–1972 | CD output per worker production function | Employment, private capital, education, age, %race, %female | | Population | | MSAs > 2 mil had RTS 8% higher than others | |
| Fogarty and Garofalo (1978) | US manufacturing in MSAs | Output per worker production function | Employment, private capital | | Population | | 10% with each doubling of population | |
| Carlino (1979) | US two-digit manufacturing in MSA, 1957–1972 | Labor factor usage equation | Wage regressed on output, labor; RTS regressed on agglomeration variables | MSA Ind. employment/national ind. employment | Economies: number of reporting units; Diseconomies: population Population (log linear) | Positive and significant for 5 of 19 industries | Economies for 12 of 19 industries; Diseconomies for 10 of 19 | |
| Moomaw (1981) | US manufacturing in MSA (same as Segal, 1976) | Capital/labor | Capital/labor regressed on population, regions | | | | 2.7% with each doubling of population | |
| Carlino (1982) | US manufacturing in MSAs 1957–1977 | Factor usage equation | Wage regressed on output, labor | | Population (quadratic) | | Optimal population size 3.6 million | |

| Study | Method | Dependent | Employment measure | Agglomeration measure | Localization result | Urbanization result | Controls |
|---|---|---|---|---|---|---|---|
| Moomaw (1983)<br>US two-digit manufacturing in MSAs 1977 | Value added | Value added/hour regressed on population, regions | Production worker hours | No. of businesses; manufacturing employees per capita | Positive and significant for some industries | Positive and significant for some industries | Highway expenditures educational quality |
| Nakamura (1985)<br>Japan two-digit manufacturing for cities, 1979 | Translog production function estimated with labor share equation | Private capital, employment | Industry employment (log linear) | Population (log linear) | 4.5% with each doubling of population | 3.4% with each doubling of population | |
| Henderson (1986)<br>US two-digit manufacturing, 1972<br><br>Brazil, two-digit manufacturing, 1970 | US: labor factor usage equation from translog production function<br>Brazil: cost function | US: wage<br><br>Brazil: wage, price of capital | Industry employment (quadratic) | Population (log) | Large localization effects | No significant effect | |
| Tabuchi (1986)<br>Japan two-digit manufacturing in cities, 1980 | Labor factor usage equation | Wage | | Population density as capital augmenting | | 4.3% with each doubling of population | |
| Beeson (1987)<br>US manufacturing in states, 1953–1973 | Components of TFP from translog production function | Hours, private capital stock | | Population gravity index | | TFP components related to agglomeration but offsetting | |
| Fogarty and Garofalo (1988)<br>US manufacturing in MSAs, 1957–1977 | TFP from translog production function | Hours, private capital stock | | Manufacturing central density population, age of city | | All three measures are significant and have correct sign | |
| Calem and Carlino (1991)<br>US manufacturing in MSAs, 1957–1978 | Production function in equilibrium model with labor supply and demand | Employment | | RTS partitioned in population groups | | Increasing RTS up to population of 2 million | Fixed effects control for public capital |

ceive compensation higher than they would have in the absence of the agglomeration economies. As a result, private investment in a local labor market is suboptimal. Economic rents may dissipate as businesses expand or additional companies and households move into an area in response to the economic rents. The degree to which they fall depends on the marginal contribution of an additional business to agglomeration economies versus diseconomies.

## 3.2.  Level of aggregation

The specification of agglomeration economies is determined by the level of aggregation of the production function. Ideally, in order to capture all three types of agglomeration economies, one would prefer to estimate production relationships at the establishment level. In this way, one could include the internal rates of return of establishments, the economies of close proximity to other establishments in the industry, and the advantage accrued from the level of all economic activities within the metropolitan area. However, establishment-level data are difficult to obtain.[12] Studies have estimated production functions using data aggregated to the metropolitan level, and many have estimated production functions for two- or three-digit industry classifications within metropolitan areas.[13] A few studies have examined intensively specific industries, such as the study by Appold (1995) of the US metal working industry, or the analysis by Sveikauskas et al. (1988) of the US food processing industry.[14]

Nakamura (1985) and Henderson (1986) point out that localization and urbanization economies can be distinguished by estimating an industry-level production function. As mentioned above, localization economies are external to a firm but internal to an industry at a given location. Nakamura (1985) and Henderson (1986) derive the measure for localization economies differently, but end up estimating it as the coefficient associated with the industry-level employment. Nakamura starts with the assumption that localization economies are associated with industry-wide output, whereas, Henderson specifies localization economies as directly related to industry-level employment. By transforming the production function into per employee terms, Nakamura's specification approximates

[12] The one source of such data for the US is the Longitudinal Research Datafile, maintained by the US Bureau of the Census. To our knowledge, no one has used these data to estimate agglomeration economies in the US.

[13] No attempt was made here to summarize the differential effects of agglomeration economies, since an initial assessment found little consistency across studies.

[14] The results are mixed: Appold (1995) found no localization advantages for the metal working firms while Sveikauskas et al. (1988) found localization economies for food processing plants. Other studies show wide variation in localization effects across two-digit manufacturing sectors.

Henderson's except that each coefficient estimate in Nakamura's formulation is scaled by $(1 - \alpha_s)$, where $\alpha_s$ is the coefficient on the industry employment variable.

Both studies measure urbanization economies as the urban area's population, since these economies are external to the industry but internal to the metropolitan area. Nakamura's (1985) estimates, based on Japanese data, show significant urbanization economies and even greater localization economies. Nakamura also finds a distinct effect among types of industries: firms in light industries benefit more from urbanization economies while firms in heavy industries benefit more from localization economies. Henderson's (1986) estimates for manufacturing industries in Brazil and the US find no urbanization economies but do find localization economies. Henderson interprets his results to imply that "... resources in manufacturing are generally not more productive in larger cities—they may even be less productive. Rather, resources in any industry are more productive in places where there is more of similar activities" (p. 66).

## 3.3. Specification of agglomeration economies

Agglomeration economies are measured either as parallel shifts in the production function (a shift in $g(S)$ in Eq. (3.1), referred to as Hicks-neutral technical change), or as differences in the returns to scale of the production function $f(\bullet)$ (measured by the summation of the coefficients on the inputs). In either case, these two parameters are specified as a function of city size (or other surrogates of agglomeration economies).[15] Moomaw (1983), in his critique of Carlino's (1978) use of the returns-to-scale approach, points out the difference in the two approaches. Assume a Cobb–Douglas production function,

$$y_j = g(S_j) L_j^\alpha K_j^\beta \tag{3.2}$$

where $y_j$, $L_j$, $K_j$ denote output, labor and capital in the $j$th metropolitan area. $g(S_j)$ is the Hicks-neutral productivity, $\alpha$ and $\beta$ are the output elasticities of labor and capital, respectively. The returns-to-scale approach takes $\delta = \alpha + \beta$ as the measure of agglomeration economies of metropolitan areas. The estimated parameter is regressed against population or other scale measures to determine whether, or not, there is a systematic relationship with $\delta$ and the measure of scale. The other approach is to use the shift parameter $g(S_j)$, expressed as a

---

[15] Studies, such as Shefer (1973), Carlino (1978, 1982), Beeson (1983, 1987) and Calem and Carlino (1991), find a positive relationship between returns to scale and city size. Mera (1973), Kawashima (1975), Sveikauskas (1975), Segal (1976), Moomaw (1981), Nakamura (1985) and Henderson (1986), for example, show that city size is positively correlated with a neutral shift in the production function.

function of scale, to estimate agglomeration economies. Moomaw (1983) points out that the two measures of agglomeration are not independent. For output to vary unambiguously with $\delta$, $g(S_j)$ must be constant across metropolitan areas. Similarly, for output to vary unambiguously with the shift parameter, $\alpha$ and $\beta$ must be constant across metropolitan areas. Variables assumed to control for differences in the Hicks-neutral technical change and/or returns to scale must be included in the estimation (Moomaw, 1983; Henderson, 1986). If not, the estimates of agglomeration economies are biased.

Carlino (1978) did not control for differences across cities in the production function shift parameter, and thus his estimates could be biased. Moomaw (1983) accounts for differences in the Hicks-neutral technical change across cities by including measures of highway infrastructure, labor quality, regional dummy variables and states with right-to-work laws. If population scale is not a good surrogate, then the population variables will be either negative or not statistically significant. Moomaw (1983) finds that, depending on the industry, productivity ranges from negative values to statistically insignificant to positive values. For some industries, the population variable is strengthened by the additional variables. He interprets these results to suggest that population scale has a separate role in measuring agglomeration economies. He concludes that population scale, entered into the production function as a shift parameter is an appropriate measure of agglomeration.

In adopting the Hicks-neutral technical change, one assumes that agglomeration economies affect both capital and labor equally. However, Henderson (1986) and Tabuchi (1986) suggest that agglomeration economies may affect capital and labor differently. Following Mera (1973), Tabuchi (1986) posits that urban productivity may be more capital saving than labor saving if social overhead capital, for example, is used intensively in big cities. Conversely, agglomeration economies may be more labor augmenting if human capital is positively associated with city size.[16] Tabuchi was unable to estimate directly the different effects because of the lack of industry-level private capital stock for Japanese urban areas. On the other hand, Henderson's (1986) data for Brazil include prices for both capital and labor. Based on these estimates, Henderson concludes that external economies are Hicks-neutral in their impacts on capital and labor.

Beeson (1987) and Fogarty and Garofalo (1988) approach the decomposition of productivity into several components differently by estimating the growth of total factor productivity (TFP) rather than the level of TFP. TFP is defined as

[16] Tabuchi's (1986) distinction between labor- and capital-augmenting agglomeration economies, particularly as it relates to public infrastructure investment, underscores the importance of including public infrastructure in estimates of agglomeration economies.

output growth less the weighted contribution of input growth, and can be derived from estimates of a production function (or cost function). Assuming that an industry's production function takes the general form $Y = F(X, T)$, TFP is defined as $\dot{Y} - \sum_i \pi \dot{X}_i$, where the dot represents the time derivative. In this expression, $\dot{X}$ denotes the growth rate of the private input, $\pi$ is the output share of the $i$th private input, and $T$ is time. Beeson (1987) decomposed this formulation of TFP growth into its components of technical change and returns to scale. Each component was then regressed on variables reflecting agglomeration economies. The drawback of this approach, at least as executed by the two authors, is that factor prices are not incorporated into the model. As a result, the models may offer estimates of agglomeration economies that are biased upward.

Specifying the growth rate of total factor productivity and its components offers an additional element of agglomeration economies. Sveikauskas (1975) and Kaldor (1970) promote the importance of dynamic benefits of urban concentration over the static advantages of specialization. Kaldor argues that agglomeration economies is more than large-scale production but rather the cumulative advantage from the growth of an industry itself. These advantages result from "the development of skills and know-how, the opportunities for easy communication of ideas and experience, the opportunity of every-increasing differentiation of processes and specialization in human activities" (p. 340). In addition, as stated by Calem and Carlino (1991), the use of pooled data allows the identification of technical change and returns to scale, without relying on the usual control variables.

## 3.4. Alternative measures of urban size

The urban area population is the standard measure of urban size in studies of urbanization economies.[17] Studies incorporate this measure into the production functions in one of two ways: (1) they include population directly in the production function; or (2) they estimate the parameters of the production function without population and then regress these estimated parameters on population and other relevant variables (Carlino, 1979). In either case, population is typi-

---

[17] Henderson (1986) argues that while the degree of urbanization economies may vary by industry, only the size of the city, not its industry structure, affects the extent or level of scale effects relevant to firms in each industry. Subsequent studies, such as Fogarty and Garofalo (1988), argue that intraurban spatial structure is important in explaining agglomeration economies. They test the importance of spatial structure using Mills' (1972) estimates of the manufacturing density gradient. Using pooled cross-section time series data for 13 metropolitan areas, they find that the decline of the manufacturing central density and flattening in the density gradient reduced growth in manufacturing output by more than 1% per year.

cally entered in a nonlinear form. Many adopt an exponential functional form (Nakamura, 1985).

$$g_i(P_j) = \alpha_1 P_j^{\alpha_p}.$$

This relationship converts to a tractable log-linear specification. With $\alpha_p < 1$, agglomeration advantages continuously increase with respect to population, but at a diminishing rate. Other specifications allow for a constant elasticity of productivity with respect to city size, a kink in the constant elasticity formulation, and a declining elasticity. Using these three specifications, Moomaw (1983) found that the appropriate functional form varies by industry. Other studies, notably Kawashima (1975), assume that there is an optimal city size in which the marginal urbanization advantage reaches zero. These studies use a quadratic specification to reflect this inverted U-shaped relationship.

Although population is widely used as a surrogate for agglomeration economies, some others do not find it to be an appropriate measure. For example, Carlino (1978) considers population to be associated more with diseconomies than with economies of agglomeration. Congestion, crime, supplier bottlenecks and reduction in the availability of industry specific resources, are a few of many factors that negatively affect business productivity. Carlino considers these factors to overwhelm the positive effects associated with agglomeration economies. As discussed in Section 3.3, instead of including population directly in the production function as a shift parameter, Carlino interprets internal returns to scale as a measure of agglomeration economies. Using combined time-series and cross-section data, he estimates a returns-to-scale parameter and then regresses it on population and population squared. Finding no statistically significant relationship, he assumes that returns to scale are a function of four variables: (1) average firm size in the industry, that is intended to measure internal economies of scale; (2) the location quotient of the industry, that measures localization economies; (3) the total number of manufacturing establishments, proxying urbanization economies; and (4) population, that captures urbanization diseconomies. All variables are measured for the entire metropolitan area. Carlino (1978) finds that the urbanization economies and diseconomies have the expected signs and are statistically significant. From this result, he concludes that population is a better proxy for urbanization diseconomies than for urbanization economies. However, Moomaw's (1983) criticism that Carlino's estimates may be biased still holds and may affect his conclusions.

## 3.5. Factor prices and cost functions

Factor prices have been shown to vary across cities of different sizes, which in turn affect the demand for factors of production. Moomaw (1983) shows that as city size increases equilibrium requires the percentage increase in productivity to equal the percentage increase in wages multiplied by labor's share. Ignoring the effect of city size on wages may overstate the productivity advantages of large cities. Since Moomaw's critique appeared, most of the studies have incorporated wages into the estimation equations by introducing a labor demand function or by estimating factor share equations along with production functions. The labor demand equations typically specify wages as a function of output, price of capital (when available), population, and regional or state dummy variables. Calem and Carlino (1991) also include a labor supply function to capture the effect of urban amenities on wages. Omitting the supply equation, they argue, would likely bias the estimates, although they do not offer estimates comparing the two specifications.

A more complete specification of including factor prices to model firm behavior is the use of the cost function. As discussed in the previous theoretical section, few studies have used cost functions, although the theoretical models of agglomeration economies are more in line with this specification. Henderson (1986) estimates both a translog production function and a translog cost function using data from Brazil, and finds similar results.

## 3.6. Omitted variables

Estimates of production functions, or cost functions, at the metropolitan level are plagued by missing variables. Theory calls for a production function to include all inputs that contribute to production. These factors include inputs provided by the firm, such as labor, private capital, land and intermediate products (if the value of output and not value added is used). In addition, a firm's production process may be affected by externalities generated by other firms or economic activity within the area that are not completely reflected in the factor prices. Other inputs are publicly provided for which a firm does not pay directly, such as roads and highways, education, water treatment and distribution, and police and fire protection. If these variables have a substantial effect on output (or cost), then the omission of any one variable would bias the estimated contribution of the others.

Moomaw's (1981) critique of the empirical study by Sveikauskas (1975) focuses on the problem of omitting private capital stock. Sveikauskas posits a CES production function with private capital and labor as inputs and agglomeration economies as measured by the Hicks-neutral technical change. Since estimates of private capital are unavailable, Sveikauskas substitutes labor productivity for the Hicks-neutral technical change. However, if capital intensity is correlated with population (and uncorrelated with other independent variables), then the estimates of agglomeration economies (as measured by the coefficient on the population variable) are biased upward. In a later paper, Moomaw (1983) shows that including a proxy for capital intensity reduces the population elasticity from 0.048 to 0.015.[18] He explains that "this estimate implies that the largest MSA has a more plausible 12 percent Hicks-neutral productivity advantage over the smaller one" (p. 537). The 12% estimate is compared with the 50% productivity advantage when capital intensity is not included.

Land is another important input in urban production activities that is rarely included in the estimation of production functions or cost functions. Land prices are difficult to obtain for industrial sites. Housing prices are more readily available for metropolitan areas and may provide a reliable proxy for industrial land prices. However, housing prices may be correlated with wages and introduce multicollinearity in the estimation. Labor market equilibrium conditions dictate higher wages in areas in which agglomeration economies have increased land prices. The omission of land may also bias the returns to scale estimate. The sum of scale parameters in the industry production function that includes only capital and labor necessarily do not correspond with the exact measure of internalized localization economies (Nakamura, 1985: p. 109). Although considered important by many authors, none of the papers surveyed in this chapter, except for Mera (1973), included the quantity or price of land in the estimation equation, primarily because of lack of data.

Public infrastructure is also typically omitted from the agglomeration studies, as mentioned earlier. Public investment in highways and water treatment and distribution and in human capital development is recognized as important to a firm's productivity decisions, but difficult to measure. Infrastructure investment can reduce agglomeration diseconomies due to traffic congestion, insufficient water and sewer infrastructure, or shortage of qualified workers. Section 4 describes in more detail the literature on the productivity effects of public infrastructure.

---

[18] Moomaw (1983) estimates various production function specifications for two-digit industries and finds that the effect of adding variables to the production function differs across industries.

## 3.7. Wage and rent equations

Another approach to estimating agglomeration economies is to relate city size to wages and rents. An extensive literature exists on this topic, that grows considerably larger if one includes studies of the effect of site-specific characteristics on wage and rents. The purpose of this subsection is to offer a flavor of this work rather than to provide a detailed survey of the literature.

Roback (1982) provides a useful framework for understanding the equilibrium conditions of both labor and land markets. She begins with the premise that households and firms compete in both local markets. Site-specific characteristics, that could include agglomeration economies, enter into the household's utility function and the firm's cost function. Differences in site-specific amenities across cities are then capitalized in wages and land prices. For example, consider a household utility function and firm cost function to be functions of rent and wages. The cost curve is downward sloping and the household indirect utility curve is upward sloping in $(r, w)$ space. If agglomeration economies increase firm productivity in a larger city, but does not affect the household's valuation of the city, the cost curve shifts outward moving along the household indirect utility curve, raising wages and rents. This shift represents an expansion of business due to the productivity advantage of the larger city. As a result, demand for labor and land increases, raising both prices.

Rauch (1993) focuses on the relationship between spatial proximity and human interaction. He argues that the sharing of knowledge and skills of workers through formal and informal interaction increases total factor productivity. Citing a paper by Jovanovic and Rob (1989), Rauch offers the example of workers enhancing their human capital by exchanging ideas. As the overall level of education rises in a local labor market, the probability increases that a random pairwise interaction between any two workers will lead to the exchange of ideas and skills that improves human capital for both workers. This enhanced interaction will lead to a more productive and higher paid work force. If this interaction is between entrepreneurs, then it should lead to greater diffusion of innovations, that raise business productivity. As Rauch mentions, Jacobs (1969) offers many concrete examples of how the interaction between highly educated or experienced workers and entrepreneurs generate significant external economies that enhance productivity.

*3.8. Spatial arrangement of cities*

Most investigations of agglomeration economies have been internal to an urban area. Yet, several authors, including von Böventer (1970), Carlino (1978) and Richardson (1979), assert that the interaction of economic agents in neighboring cities may generate net productivity advantages within the system of cities. Beeson (1987) tests this proposition using a two-stage process. First, average annual growth rates of total factor productivity, technical change, and scale economies are estimated for the manufacturing sector of US states. Second, these estimates are regressed on several measures of agglomeration economies internal to an urban area and a gravity index that reflects the externalities between cities and between cities and their hinterlands. Beeson finds that the spatial arrangement of cities in the region is an important determinant of both scale economies and the rate of technical change.

# 4. Public infrastructure

Interestingly, the literatures pertaining to agglomeration economies and the productivity effects of public infrastructure remain disconnected. Most studies that investigate agglomeration economies ignore the contribution of public infrastructure to productivity. Although the concept of agglomeration is based on reduction in transport costs and the ease of shipping goods and communicating ideas and imparting skills and knowledge, it is the exception rather the rule that studies of agglomeration economies consider public infrastructure. By omitting an infrastructure variable, the vast majority of studies assume that services from public capital stock do not vary across cities of similar size. If infrastructure per capita is higher in larger cities than in smaller ones, estimates of agglomeration economies could be biased upward.

That is not to say that the productivity effects of public infrastructure have been ignored. On the contrary, a large and growing literature has emerged on the effects of public infrastructure on business cost and productivity.[19] However, only a handful of studies have merged the two factors when analyzing productivity effects. This section describes the literature on public infrastructure and productivity and then examines the studies that have included both infrastructure and productivity effects.

---

[19] See McGuire (1992) and Gramlich (1994) for reviews of the literature on public infrastructure and productivity.

## 4.1. Infrastructure as a public input

Public infrastructure can affect the economic activity of a metropolitan area through several channels: (a) as an unpaid factor of production; (b) enhancing productivity of other inputs; (c) attracting inputs from elsewhere; and (d) stimulating demand for construction of infrastructure and other services. In keeping with our focus on productivity when discussing agglomeration economies, the treatment in this section will concentrate on the first channel.

As an unpaid factor of production, public infrastructure has private good characteristics, except that it is not provided through a market process, does not have a market-determined price and is not paid for on a per-unit basis. Its private good characteristics generally result from congestion. In the case of highways, as the number of businesses in a region expands, increased use of a facility of fixed size results in congestion, that effectively reduces the total amount of highway services available to each firm. Thus, from the firm's perspective, the level of public input is fixed, unless the facility is continually underutilized. Having many characteristics of a private input, the unpaid-factor type of public input is entered into the production process in the same way as private inputs. Because firms, by definition, do not pay directly for the public input, they initially earn profits or rents according to the value of the marginal product of the public input. Additional firms move into the region until the rents are dissipated and capital earns a competitive rate of return.[20]

To include public infrastructure into a production function, assume that manufacturing firms in a metropolitan area can be aggregated into a manufacturing sector and characterized by the same production as in Eq. (3.1), repeated here:

$$y_{ij} = g(S_j)f(K_{ij}, L_{ij}, G_{ij}, Z_{ij}), \tag{4.1}$$

where $y_{ij}$ is gross output; $K$, $L$ and $Z$ are private capital, labor and other privately-provided inputs and $G$ is public capital stock. The Hicks-neutral technical change as a function of city size is denoted by $g(S)$. Dual to the production function is a total cost function that can be divided into a restricted variable cost function and a quasifixed portion:

$$CT = A(S)CVR(Q, \mathbf{P}, G) + p_g G + p_a A + T, \tag{4.2}$$

where $CT$ is total cost, $CVR$ is variable cost, $\mathbf{P}$ is a vector of prices of privately provided inputs, $p_g$ is the price of public capital, $p_a$ is the price of land, $A$ is

---

[20] Eberts and Stone (1992) estimate that in long-run equilibrium, the benefits of public capital investment in metropolitan areas are almost completely offset by the higher taxes to finance the investment.

the land input and $T$ represents taxes. As discussed above, the cost function has advantages to the production function.

## 4.2. Estimates

Eberts (1986) estimates the direct effect of public capital stock on manufacturing output and the technical relationships between public capital and the other production inputs. Public capital stock is estimated using the perpetual inventory technique for each of 38 US metropolitan areas between 1958 and 1978. With this method, capital is measured as the sum of the value of past investments adjusted for depreciation and discard. Public capital stock includes highways, sewage treatment facilities and water distribution facilities within the MSA. Eberts estimates a translog production function with value added as output, hours of production and nonproduction workers as the labor input, and a value measure of private manufacturing capital stock as private capital.

Eberts (1986) finds that public capital stock makes a positive and statistically significant contribution to manufacturing output, supporting the concept of public capital stock as an unpaid factor of production. Its output elasticity of 0.03 is small relative to the magnitudes of the other inputs: 0.7 for labor and 0.3 for private capital. It follows that the magnitude of the marginal product of public capital is also small relative to the marginal product of private capital.[21]

Dalenberg (1987), using the same public capital stock as Eberts (1986), estimates a cost function, with public capital stock as a quasifixed input, for 31 MSAs for the years 1976 to 1978. He finds that a 10% increase in public capital stock is associated with a 2% decrease in manufacturing costs. This shadow price is close to the average imputed price of private capital, suggesting that the average return to public capital is on par with that of private capital. Dalenberg (1987) computes a shadow price for public capital for each of the 31 MSAs. Comparing the shadow price of public capital with the imputed price of private capital (as a proxy for the opportunity cost of investing) indicates that 26 of the 31 MSAs have public capital stock at least as great as the desired level.

Deno (1988) estimates a profit function for 36 MSAs from 1970 to 1978, using the same public capital stock as Eberts (1986) and Dalenberg (1987). To take account of the shared nature of public capital, Deno (1988) multiplies the public capital stocks by manufacturing's share of total metropolitan population. He finds that output strongly responds to public capital: the output elasticities of water, sewer and highway infrastructure are 0.08, 0.30 and 0.31, respectively.

---

[21] With respect to technical relationships, Eberts (1986) and Dalenberg (1987) find that public capital and private capital are complements.

Unlike those of Eberts and Dalenberg, Deno's estimates suggest a significant underinvestment in public capital stock.

In general, these estimates of the effect of public capital stock on output are smaller than those found at the state and national level. Some argue that the more disaggregated studies cannot pick up the broad externalities generated by the networks of public capital stock, such as the US interstate highway system. However, another explanation argues that national time-series estimates and state pooled cross-section time-series estimates are subject to estimation bias. The national time series estimates are plagued by nonstationarity and spurious correlation. Correcting for nonstationarity, Tatom (1991) finds that the effect of public infrastructure on output is negative and statistically insignificant. State-level estimates are criticized because of unexplained differences across states. Holtz-Eakin (1992), using a state fixed-effects model, finds that the strong effect of infrastructure diminishes or disappears if the state-specific effects are taken into account. McGuire (1992), on the other hand, finds a strong positive and statistically significant effect of public capital stock on output under several specifications, including a Cobb–Douglas production function with state fixed and random effects.

Another criticism of state and national studies is the question of causality. Does public infrastructure affect output, or does output affect public infrastructure? At the metropolitan level, Duffy-Deno and Eberts (1989) test the direction of causation between infrastructure and output by positing two equations: a production function and a demand equation for public capital. Their findings suggest that the causation runs mostly from infrastructure capital to output growth. They also find a smaller elasticity of output with respect to public capital when the demand for public capital is taken into account.

Attention in Europe has also been drawn to the effect of public infrastructure on output. Similar to the US, few studies have focused on metropolitan areas.[22] Seitz (1993) is an exception. He estimates the effect of public infrastructure investment on manufacturing cost for 85 (former West) German cities between 1980 and 1989. Public capital stock is estimated by applying the perpetual inventory method to city-specific outlay data from 1969 to 1989, but using starting values estimated from state-specific data. His cost elasticity estimate with respect to public capital is $-0.127$. This estimate is smaller than that obtained by

---

[22] Many more studies of the effect of public infrastructure on output have been conducted for European countries, but these have focused on regional or national levels of aggregation. Berndt and Hansson (1991) conclude that public infrastructure in Sweden reduces private productions costs. Using data from the UK, Lynde and Richmond (1992) find an average elasticity of output with respect to public capital of 0.20, that is within the range of many national-level studies for the US.

Dalenberg (1987) for the US, but is remarkably similar given different governmental structures and national histories. In addition, Seitz (1983) includes city population and taxes in the estimation, that Dalenberg (1987) did not include.

US metropolitan-level studies, or most of the other studies, have not incorporated taxes into the estimation. However, doing so may increase the estimated effects of public infrastructure on output, particularly if local public infrastructure is financed through a distortionary tax. Jorgenson calculates that every $1 raised by taxes extracts $1.45 from the private sector, with the additional $0.45 resulting from the distortion of economic activities. Tax financing by local jurisdictions would probably cause greater distortion because of the mobility of firms and households among jurisdictions. Therefore, the combined net effect of infrastructure and taxes (when taxes are excluded) would be lower than the individual effect of infrastructure on productivity if taxes were included separately in the estimation.

### 4.3. Studies including both agglomeration effects and public infrastructure

The studies by Mera (1973), Moomaw (1983), Calem and Carlino (1991) and Seitz (1993) are exceptions to the general tendency not to include measures of both agglomeration and public infrastructure simultaneously in an analysis or the productivity. Mera (1973) highlights the importance of public infrastructure in achieving agglomeration economies and includes the level of employment as a measure of localization economies. He contends that "the higher per capita income in high-density areas can be explained by both savings in social overhead capital cost and increased efficiency of inputs" (p. 318). Cities with more investment in social overhead capital, defined by Mera as all capital improvement with social implications, will have less diseconomies and greater net productivity for a given city size. Therefore, including measures of public infrastructure in the production (cost) function identifies the separate contributions of agglomeration economies and public capital stock to productivity advantages of larger cities. Mera finds positive and statistically significant effects of both employment and social overhead capital on the productivity of broad industries for Japanese regions.

Moomaw's (1983) analysis includes a measure of transportation infrastructure along with a population variable that measures net agglomerative effects. He finds that for several two-digit industries, the transportation variable is positive and statistically significant, indicating that public infrastructure, even when included in an equation with population, has a positive effect on the productivity of some US industries within metropolitan areas. Adding public infrastructure to the equation reduces the magnitude of the elasticity of population only slightly.

Calem and Carlino (1991) also recognize that infrastructure and resource endowment are likely to affect urban productivity. They acknowledge the difficulty in measuring these factors, but they also recognize the potential bias of omitting these factors. To circumvent the measurement problem, Calem and Carlino estimate metropolitan-level production functions using a fixed-effects approach. Entering cross-sectional dummy variables accounts for differences in the level of the output, holding inputs constant, across US cities.

Seitz (1993) explicitly models and estimates the effect of both public infrastructure investment and agglomeration economies on private sector productivity within urban areas in Germany. He incorporates measures of public infrastructure and agglomeration economies within a translog specification of a cost function. Public infrastructure, recorded on a per capita basis, is estimated by applying the perpetual inventory method; agglomeration economies are measured by the total employment in each city. His estimates indicate significant but decreasing agglomeration economies and a cost elasticity of public infrastructure of 0.127.

## 5. Conclusions

The two strands of empirical research discussed in this chapter portray an urban landscape in which the productivity of firms vary by city size and the level of investment in public infrastructure. The considerable attention given to these two topics in the last three decades has been generated by concerns about the economic and social well-being of cities, particularly in the US, and by asking what role government can take in promoting a more efficient spatial distribution of economic activities. Studies in several countries find that manufacturing firms are more productive in large cities than in smaller ones, and in cities with a larger stock of public infrastructure. Studies covered in this chapter found positive agglomeration and infrastructure effects in the US, Germany, Sweden, Japan and Brazil. For the most part, the results hold up under various specifications of production relationships and measures of agglomeration, and even when measures of public infrastructure and agglomeration economies are entered simultaneously in production functions (or cost functions).

One of the shortcomings of this literature, and a fruitful area for future research, is the general failure to consider the effects of agglomeration economies and public infrastructure simultaneously. As the theoretical papers clearly demonstrate, the two effects are closely related. Urban infrastructure is a shared input that provides the means by which the close spatial proximity of economic activities can lead to increased productivity for all parties. The dynamics of this process is another area that deserves further attention. Only recently have studies started to explore the length of time cities take to respond to economic shocks. Moreover, the literature gives us little insight into whether, or not, the productivity advantages of cities of different sizes and infrastructure investment have changed since these topics were first introduced.

# References

Abdel-Rahman, H.M. (1990a), "Agglomeration economies, types, and sizes of cities", Journal of Urban Economics 27:25–45.

Abdel-Rahman, H.M. (1990b), "Sharable inputs, product variety, and city sizes", Journal of Regional Science 20:359–374.

Abdel-Rahman, H.M. (1996), "When do cities specialize in production", Regional Science and Urban Economics 26:1–22.

Abdel-Rahman, H.M. and M. Fujita (1990), "Product variety, Marshallian externalities and city size", Journal of Regional Science 30:165–183.

Abdel-Rahman, H.M. and M. Fujita (1993), "Specialization and diversification in a system of cities", Journal of Urban Economics 33:189–222.

Abdel-Rahman, H.M. and P. Wang (1995), "Toward a general-equilibrium theory of a core-periphery system of cities", Regional Science and Urban Economics 25:529–546.

Abdel-Rahman, H.M. and P. Wang (1997), "Social welfare and income inequality in a system of cities", Journal of Urban Economics 41:462–483.

Aberg, Y. (1973), "Regional productivity differences in Swedish manufacturing", Regional and Urban Economics 3:131–156.

Anas, A. and I. Kim (1996), "General equilibrium models of polycentric urban land use with endogenous congestion and job agglomeration", Journal of Urban Economics 40:232–256.

Appold, S.J. (1995), "Agglomeration, interorganizational networks, and competitive performance in the U.S. metalworking sector", Economic Geography 71(1):27–54.

Aschauer, D.A. (1989), "Is public expenditure productive?", Journal of Monetary Economics 23:177–200.

Aydalot, P. and D. Keeble. (1988), High Technology Industry and Innovative Environments: The European Experience (Routledge, London).

Beeson, P.E. (1983), "Essays in regional productivity", unpublished Ph.D. thesis (Department of Economics, University of Oregon).

Beeson, P.E. (1987), "Total factor productivity growth and agglomeration economies in manufacturing 1959–1973", Journal of Regional Science 27:183–199.

Berndt, E. and B. Hansson (1991), "Measuring the contribution of public infrastructure capital in Sweden", NBER Working Paper, No. 3842.

Blair, J.P. (1991), Urban and Regional Economics (Irwin, Boston).

Calem, P.S. and G.A. Carlino (1991), "Urban agglomeration economies in the presence of technical change", Journal of Urban Economics 29:82–95.

Carlino, G.A. (1978), Economies of Scale in Manufacturing Location: Theory and Measurement (Martinus Nijhoff, Leiden, The Netherlands).

Carlino, G.A. (1979), "Increasing returns to scale in metropolitan manufacturing", Journal of Regional Science 19:363–373.

Carlino, G.A. (1982), "Manufacturing agglomeration economies as returns to scale: A production function approach, Papers of Regional Science Association 50:96–108.

Chinitz, B. (1961), "Contrasts in agglomeration: New York and Pittsburgh", American Economic Review 51:279–289.

Chipman, J.S. (1970), "External economies of scale and competitive equilibrium", Quarterly Journal of Economics 84:347–385.

Choate, P. and S. Walter (1983), America in Ruins (Duke Press Paperbacks, Durham, NC).

Dalenberg, D. (1987), "Estimates of elasticities of substitution between public and private inputs in the manufacturing sector of metropolitan areas", Ph.D. dissertation (University of Oregon).

Deno, K.T. (1988), "The effect of public capital on U.S. manufacturing activity: 1970 to 1978", Southern Economic Journal 55:400–411.

Dobkins, L.H. (1996), "Location, innovation and trade: The role of localization and nation-based externalities", Regional Science and Urban Economics 26:591–612.

Duffy-Deno, K. and R. Eberts (1989), "Public infrastructure and regional economic development: A simultaneous equations approach", Working Paper No. 8909 (Federal Reserve Bank of Cleveland).

Eberts, R.W. (1986), "Estimating the contribution of urban public infrastructure to regional economic growth", Working Paper No. 8620 (Federal Reserve Bank of Cleveland).

Eberts, R.W. and J. Stone (1992), Wage and Employment Determination in Local Labor Markets (W.E. Upjohn Institute for Employment Research Monograph).

Eberts, R.W., D. Dalenberg and C.S. Park (1986), "Public Infrastructure Data Development for NSF", mimeo (University of Oregon).

Fogarty, M.S. and G.A. Garofalo (1978), "Environmental quality-income tradeoff functions with policy applications", paper presented at the Southern Regional Science Association Meeting.

Fogarty, M.S. and G.A. Garofalo (1988), "Urban spatial structure and productivity growth in the manufacturing sector of cities", Journal of Urban Economics 23:60–70.

Friedlaender, A.F. (1990), Comment: "How does public infrastructure affect regional economic performance?", in: Is There a Shortfall In Public Capital Investment?, pp. 108–112.

Fujita, M. and P. Krugman (1995), "When is the economy monocentric?: von Thünen and Chamberlin Unified", Regional Science and Urban Economics 25:505–528.

Fuss, M. and D. McFadden (1979), Production Economics: A Dual Approach to Theory and Application (North-Holland, Amsterdam).

Goldstein, G.S. and T.J. Gronberg (1984), "Economies of scope and economies of agglomeration", Journal of Urban Economics 16:91–104.

Gramlich, E.M. (1994), "Infrastructure investment: A review essay", Journal of Economic Literature 32:1176–1196.

Hanson, G.H. (1996), "Agglomeration, dispersion, and the pioneer firm", Journal of Urban Economics 39:255–281.

Helsley, R.W. (1990), "Knowledge and production in the CBD", Journal of Urban Economics 28:391–403.

Helsley, R.W. and W.C. Strange (1990), "Matching and agglomeration economies in a system of cities", Regional Science and Urban economics 20:189–212.

Helsley, R.W. and W.C. Strange (1991), "Agglomeration economies and urban capital markets", Journal of Urban Economics 29:96–112.

Helsley, R.W. and A.M. Sullivan (1991), "Urban subcenter formation", Regional Science and Urban Economics 21:255–275.

Henderson, J. (1974), "The size and type of cities", American Economic Review 64:640–656.

Henderson, J. (1982a), "The impact of government policies on urban concentration", Journal of Urban Economics 12:280–303.

Henderson, J. (1982b), "Systems of cities in closed and open economies", Regional Science and Urban Economics 12:325–350.

Henderson, J. (1983), "Industrial bases and city sizes", American Economic Review 73:164–168.

Henderson, J. (1985), Economic Theory and the Cities, 2nd ed. (Academic Press, New York).

Henderson, J. (1986), "The efficiency of resource usage and city size", Journal of Urban Economics 19:47–70.

Henderson, J. (1988), Urban Development (Oxford University Press, New York).

Henderson, J.V. and A. Mitra (1996), "The new landscape: Developers and edge cities", Regional Science and Urban Economics 26:613–643.

Holtz-Eakin, D. (1992), State-Specific Estimates of State and Local Government Capital (Syracuse University Working Paper).

Hoover, E.M., Jr. (1937), Location Theory and the Shoe and Leather Industries (Harvard University Press, Cambridge).

Jacobs, J. (1969), The Economy of Cities (Random House, New York).

Jovanovic, B. and R. Rob (1989), "The growth and diffusion of knowledge", Review of Economic Studies 56:569–582.

Kaldor, N. (1970), "The case for regional policies", Scottish Journal of Political Economy 17:337–347.

Kawashima, T. (1975), "Urban agglomeration economies in manufacturing industries", Papers of the Regional Science Association 34:157–175.

Kim, S. (1989), "Labor specialization and the extent of the market", Journal of Political Economy 97:692–705.

Kim, S. (1990), "Labor heterogeneity, wage bargaining, and agglomeration economies", Journal of Urban Economics 29:160–177.

Kim, S. (1991), "Heterogeneity of labor markets and city size in an open spatial economy", Regional Science and Urban Economics 21:109–126.

Lynde, C. and J. Richmond (1992), "The role of public capital in production", The Review of Economics and Statistics 74:37–44.

Marshall, A. (1890), Principles of Economics, 8th ed. (1977 reprint) (Macmillan Press, London).

McGuire, T.J. (1992), "Highways and macroeconomic productivity Phase Two", Report to Federal Highway Administration, US Department of Transportation (Volpe national Transportation Systems Center, US Department of Transportation).

Mera, K. (1973), "Regional production functions and social overhead capital:An analysis of the Japanese case", Regional and Urban Economics 3:157–186.

Mills, E.S. (1967), "An aggregative model of resource allocation in a metropolitan area", American Economic Review 57:197–210.

Mills, E.S. (1972), Studies in the Structure of the Urban Economy (Johns Hopkins University Press, Baltimore).

Mills, E.S. and B.W. Hamilton (1994), Urban Economics, 5th ed. (Harper Collins, New York).

Moomaw, R.L. (1980), "Optimal firm location and city size: Productivity vs. wages", Urban Institute Working Paper 1447-1.

Moomaw, R.L. (1981), "Productivity and city size: A review of the evidence", Quarterly Journal of Economics 96:675–688.

Moomaw, R.L. (1983), "Is population scale a worthless surrogate for business agglomeration economies?", Regional Science and Urban Economics 13:525–545.

Moomaw, R.L. (1985), "Firm location and city size: Reduced productivity advantages as a factor in the decline of manufacturing in urban areas", Journal of Urban Economics 17:73–89.

Mori, T. (1997), "A modeling of megalopolis formation: the maturing of city systems", Journal of Urban Economics 42:133–157.

Munnell, A., editor (1990), "Is there a shortfall in public capital investment?" Conference Series No. 34 (Federal Reserve Bank of Boston).

Nakamura, R. (1985), "Agglomeration economies in urban manufacturing industries: a case of Japanese cities", Journal of Urban Economics 17:108–124.

National Council on Public Works Improvement (1988), Fragile Foundations: A Report on America's Public Works, Final Report to the President and Congress.

Ohlin, B. (1935), Interregional and International Trade (Harvard University Press, Cambridge).

O'Sullivan, A.M. (1996), Urban Economics, 3rd ed. (Irwin, Boston).

Panzar, J.C. and R.D. Willig (1981), "Economies of scope", Pap. Proc., American Economic Association 71:268–272.

Palivos, T. and P. Wang (1996), "Spatial agglomeration and endogenous growth", Regional Science and Urban Economics 26:645–669.

Rauch, J.E. (1993), "Productivity gains from geographic concentration of human capital: evidence from the cities", Journal of Urban Economics 34:380–400.

Richardson, H.W. (1973), The Economics of City Size (Lexington Books, Lexington).

Richardson, H.W. (1979), "Optimality in city size, systems of cities and urban policy", Regional Economics (University of Illinois Press, Chicago).

Roback, J. (1982), "Wages, rents, and the quality of life", Journal of Political Economy 90:1257–1278.

Sasaki, K. and Se-Il Mun (1996), "A dynamic analysis of multiple-center formation in a city", Journal of Urban Economics 40:257–278.

Segal, D. (1976), "Are there returns to scale in city size?", Review of Economics and Statistics 58:339–450

Seitz, H. (1993), "The impact of the provision of urban infrastructures on the manufacturing industry in cities", paper presented at the 33rd European Congress of the Regional Science Association, Moscow, Russia.

Shefer, D. (1973), "Localization economies in SMSAs: A production function analysis", Journal of Regional Science 13:55–64.

Smith, A. (1776), The Wealth of Nations (1976 reprint) (University of Chicago, Chicago).

Sullivan, A.M. (1983), "A general equilibrium model with external scale economies in production". Journal of Urban Economics 13:235–255.

Sullivan, A.M. (1986), "A general equilibrium model with agglomerative economies and decentralized employment", Journal of Urban Economics 20:55–74.

Sundquist, J.L. (1970), "Where shall they live?", The Public Interest 18:88–100

Sveikauskas, L.A. (1975), "The productivity of cities", Quarterly Journal of Economics 89:393–414.

Sveikauskas, L., J. Gowdy and M. Funk. (1988), "Urban productivity: city size or industry size", Journal of Regional Science 28(2):185–202.

Tabuchi, T. (1986), "Urban agglomeration, capital augmenting technology, and labor market equilibrium", Journal of Urban Economics 20:211–228.

Tatom, J. (1991), "Should government spending on capital goods be raised?", Review of the Federal Reserve Bank of St. Louis 72:3–15.

Vining, D.R., Jr. and T. Kontuly (1977), "Increasing returns to city size in the fact of an impending decline in the size of large cities: which is the bogus fact?" Environmental and Planning A 9:59–62.

von Böventer, E. (1970), "Optimal spatial structure and regional development", Kyklos 23:903–924.

Walz, U. (1996), "Transport costs, intermediate goods, and localized growth", Regional Science and Urban Economics 26:671–695.

# PART II
# URBAN MARKETS

*Chapter 39*

# URBAN LABOUR MARKETS

GRAHAM R. CRAMPTON

*University of Reading, U.K.*

## Contents

*Handbook of Regional and Urban Economics. Edited by E.S. Mills and P. Cheshire*
© *1999 Elsevier Science B.V. All rights reserved.*

**Abstract**

The large research literature in urban labour market analysis is reviewed, with the emphasis ranging from attempts to model aggregate simultaneous interactions between residential and workplace location to more modern econometric work researching individual labour market behaviour. The job search process is central to the operation of the labour market, yet research is hampered by variable data availability and the limited observability of the search mechanism. Individual responses to major employer relocations have been recently studied, especially the substitutability of the move or quit decision, and relationships to race and gender.

The variation of commuting patterns by income and professional status has also been analysed, and the functioning of the dispersed service-dominated modern urban labour market raises challenging research issues including willingness to search and commute over substantial areas, interacting with family circumstances and expected job security.

The continued growth in all developed economies of female labour force participation and numbers of female-headed households have raised the importance of urban labour market research focusing on gender, including the economic understanding of patterns in the length of the female journey to work.

Study of the influence of racial segregation on outcomes in the urban labour market has a longer history, with the "spatial mismatch hypothesis" having developed a large literature since the 1960s. With higher quality microdata and modern computational power and econometric techniques, statistical research has advanced considerably. Similar spatial relationships between race and labour market and commuting outcomes are also intrinsic to the European urban labour market, and have received particular attention from British, Dutch, Austrian and

French researchers. The chapter concludes with an overview of contrasts between inter- and intraurban labour market adjustment processes.

**Keywords:** Dual labour market, gender, ghetto, high technology, job search, local labour market area (LLMA), logit, mismatch, quit, reservation wage, skill, unemployment duration, vacancy, wage gradient, youth unemployment

## 1. Definitional and introductory issues

### 1.1. Introduction

This chapter attempts to provide an integrated overview of the enormous applied literature in urban labour market analysis. The most obvious starting point for a subdivision of the subject was between inter- and intraurban labour market adjustment mechanisms, but these have been covered by way of conclusion (Sections 8 and 9), following discussion of other phenomena that have played a prominent part in the urban labour market research field in recent years. The development of research into simultaneous modelling of residential and workplace location, for example (Section 2), although at the heart of our empirical understanding of urban labour market evolution, has been hampered by data problems as well as the complexity of the role played by commuting within the urban location decision. To some degree, the discrete empirical detail provided by move and quit data (Section 3) has provided more useful insights than attempts to model residential and job location data in full generality.

The study of labour market search mechanisms is another area on which attention has been focused in recent years (Section 4), although this is still at quite a preliminary stage, given its complexity and the limited observability of search processes. The trend in the labour market as a whole towards expansion of the professional and service sector at the expense of industrial jobs has raised the importance of studying the impact of skill and status variations on labour market behaviour (Section 5). In addition, the sustained growth in all developed economies of female labour force participation has turned the better understanding of the relationships between family structure, or gender and urban labour market outcomes (Section 6), into a more central part of urban economics.

The "spatial mismatch hypothesis" is one of the more long-established problem areas within urban labour market research (Section 7), and focused on the labour market implications of residential segregation by race. In this area, the seminal articles are now nearly 30 years old. The level of sophistication in the econometric analysis of the mismatch hypothesis has grown substantially, and European trends in ethnically diverse migration has sustained the interest in and importance of this area. Regrettably, in this area as with most of this chapter we found it difficult to extend the review much beyond the US and UK literature. A limited amount of analysis of urban labour market conditions in various European countries (e.g., France, Netherlands, Austria) has been published in accessible English language sources, but this is a direction in which international academic communication could be improved.

Overall, the sheer size of publicly available comprehensive data sources in the US has given American researchers a considerable advantage, especially in the development of microeconomic applied research. Standards of econometric modelling have been set which relatively little of the European work has approached, till recently. Continued improvements of uniformly defined European data sources, perhaps through Eurostat, may offer the potential to improve this situation.

## 1.2. Local labour market: definitions and operational problems

A number of the key issues in urban labour markets that will be discussed in greater detail in the course of this chapter have arisen in connection with attempts to define local labour markets operationally. These include the variation of search areas and willingness to commute with the skill and economic status of workers, or the possibility that local labour market areas (LLMAs) once defined may be "dynamic". That is, they may be overtaken by macroeconomic events and rapidly become less relevant and accurate for policy purposes.

An early awareness was found in Goldner (1955) of the likelihood that low status workers may function with smaller LLMAs, stressing both the demand side and search motives:

> Unskilled workers being unspecialised, are more likely to encounter an acceptable job nearer to where they live. Skilled workers have to work

for employers using their specialised skills among a far flung group of establishments

(Goldner, 1955: p. 122)

A more theoretical early paper by Termote (1978) extended the Lösch model of central place and urban hierarchy by including personal commuting costs. Many features of the Lösch hierarchy remain, but the variation of wage rates with urban centre size, required to compensate for commuting costs, would bring about greater dispersion of urban centre size than in the basic model, and the familiar neatly nested hexagonal pattern would not be stable.

European empirical research on local labour market operation has been handicapped by the rather varied nature of the commuting data available. Austrian data was used by Baumann et al. (1988). They addressed important issues such as how to operationalise *nondisjoint* (i.e., overlapping) spatial labour markets, and stressed the importance of estimating the parameters and regionalisation jointly.

An Israeli example came from Felsenstein (1994). This was a study of the effect of the widespread Israeli practice of employers paying commuting costs, either in the form of free bus provision, or liberal car expenses. Felsenstein found that this had helped to bring about a surprisingly extensive spatial labour market for low skill labour, strengthened by the low *residential* mobility of Israeli labour. His results were backed up by empirical estimation of the operation of spatial labour markets for the Lod Airport and Haifa subcentres.

Most British work on LLMAs has been geared towards continued definition or modification of the travel to work areas (TTWAs) used for the reporting of unemployment rate statistics, and for the implementation of regional policy. A weakness of these areas is perhaps the insistence on an exhaustive allocation of all land areas, including nonurban land.

A minimum commuting self-containment level of 75% was introduced (Smart, 1974), and further work (Coombes and Openshaw, 1982) extended the definitions to distinguish between high density multinodal metropolitan areas and free-standing towns. In principle, the data-user should:

... select the one which is more appropriate to its purpose.

(Coombes and Openshaw, 1982: p. 148)

Other British work has focused on the variability over the business cycle of LLMAs (Ball, 1980). This may be caused by a mixture of demand-side factors such as labour-hoarding by firms, who may shed in recession the shorter-commute part of their labour force, with the supply motive of workers searching over a wider area when unemployed. The spatial pattern of "opportunities" is constantly changing, inducing changes in both *search* and commuting. Areas of search rather than areas of commuting may be the most appropriate conceptual base for LLMAs and:

> ... it seems inappropriate to measure unemployment rates and delimit Assisted Areas (for policy purposes) on the basis of travel habits of the employed alone.
>
> (Ball, 1980: p. 137)

## 2. Residential and workplace location

### 2.1. *Employment subcentres and the wasteful commuting controversy*

Given the coverage of this part of the subject elsewhere in this volume (see White, Chap. 36), we have omitted any review material for this section to avoid duplication.

### 2.2. *Simultaneous modelling of residential and workplace location*

The simultaneous modelling of residential and workplace outcomes constitutes the most complete aspiration of applied urban labour market research, although there is still a long way to go before fully convincing estimated models are available using modern econometric techniques. To a great extent, this area of research has been data-driven. A review concluded:

> ... The major stumbling block may not be model development but model estimation and testing, since the spatially disaggregated panel microdata best suited to this analysis will be difficult to find and expensive to develop.
>
> (Simpson and Van Der Veen, 1992: p. 60)

The principal issues in the field of workplace and residential modelling have been first, what plays the primary role in urban adjustment processes. That is, is it possible to generalise about whether the employment distribution "drives" the residential distribution, or vice versa? Second, the question remains of compensation in the labour market for commuting distance, and the extent to which estimations of such compensation interact with the operation of the urban housing market.

Early work on workplace and residential location emerged from the enormous urban transportation studies of the 1960s. Kain (1962) summarised, in the light of the (then new) monocentric urban model, broad patterns revealed by a large stratified sample of Detroit households. However, despite its size, this was a single cross-section dataset with no evidence on moves or other dynamic adjustment.

Beesley and Dalvi (1974) discussed an early version of the labour offer curve from a fixed residence, with the acceptable wage rising with additional commuting distance, and presented simple analysis of British Census data on the journey to work by local authority. Possible interactions between car ownership, search, and the commuting pattern were also mentioned.

Other simple empirical approaches included Steinnes (1977), who used Census aggregates on population and broad employment categories for a pooled sample of 15 large US MSAs, and claimed to find evidence that causality runs from residence to employment, at least for certain sectors of employment, including manufacturing. Gera and Kuhn (1980a, b) used Canadian Census data, with tracts aggregated into zones. They found some suggestive evidence that there may be a U-shaped relationship between a zone's Central Business District (CBD) distance and the average commuting distance to that zone.

Some studies of zonal subaggregate data (e.g., Boarnet (1994)) included the econometric modelling of spatial autocorrelation, and used maximum likelihood techniques rather than ordinary least squares (OLS). Boarnet also found evidence that it was more clearly the case that employment change was endogenous than population change. This would seem to agree with Mills' (1986) finding that, as between US central cities and suburbs, "jobs follow people" much more than "people follow jobs".

Vickerman (1984) used British journey to work data for London and the outer metropolitan local authorities and conducted OLS and two stage least squares (2SLS) estimations with net incommuting as the dependent variable, and employment and migration endogenous. These estimates followed a thoughtful theoretical discussion of the problems of simultaneous modelling of intraurban moves of residence or workplace or both, including considerations of various motives for *not* moving (e.g., search and then conclude the net gain is negative, search and then give up, do not search at all). From survey evidence on a separate sample of about 1000 households, Vickerman concluded that, if anything, employment factors were more likely to influence a residential move than vice versa, although,

> ... there is little immediate connection between the two and adjustments are not made in an obviously fully optimising manner.
>
> (Vickerman, 1984: p. 26)

Some empirical research has used microsurvey data, often in subaggregated form, to address these issues. Siegel (1975) estimated an ambitious six-equation 2SLS model using San Francisco data stratified by race, life-cycle and housing tenure, but given limited sample sizes results were fairly inconclusive.

Andrulis (1982) was among the first to use the Michigan Panel Study on Income Dynamics, focusing on the impact of risk aversion on residence or work-place moves. The innovative use of personal and financial indicators as proxies successfully identified risk aversion effects on various move decisions, with a multivariate logit analysis of their probabilities

The sequential and hierarchical nature of the interdependencies between resi-dential migration, commuting, and the regional labour market was represented in a nested logit model developed by Evers and Van Der Veen (1985). This is esti-mated using microdata in a 40-region breakdown of the Netherlands, in the light of their perception of the Dutch trend (which may indeed by quite widespread) for interregional commuting to rise and migration to decline.

As part of the developing body of research using microsamples of quite im-pressive size, Simpson (1987) analysed survey data from Toronto, with a 400-zone breakdown of the area. However, journey to work detail is only produced for distance from city centre to job, or centre to home, not the actual com-mute. Simpson believed strongly that intraurban commuting patterns, especially their variation with income or status, can only be properly modelled through understanding labour market search.

The 2SLS analysis of the Toronto microdata showed that local employment conditions in a large urban area, in the form of (jobs/resident worker) ratios for the zones in which people live appear to play a bigger role in labour market outcomes for lower status workers, reinforcing Simpson's (1987) view that ex-tensive job search is more important higher up the skill hierarchy. He admitted that longitudinal panel data was needed for proper study of the *sequential* nature of workplace and residential choice, and of migration.

The subsequent literature review by Simpson and Van Der Veen (1992) also touched on the interrelationships with the location decisions of firms in a de-centralised urban area, especially relevant for firms employing large numbers of higher skilled workers.

One of a series of papers by Zax (1991a), all using the same microdata source from an individual large Detroit firm, focused on a related issue, namely, the extent to which workers expect commuting time to be compensated in the form of a higher real wage, and whether, or not, this compensation would be even greater if workers were also paying a high price for housing services. A very simple test of this takes the form of including interaction terms of commuting time with crude proxies for the price of housing services, in OLS regressions to explain real earnings. Commuting time is lagged to "make it exogenous". The interaction terms were indeed successfully found, suggesting that previous estimates that ignored them may have been biased. A link with other sections of this chapter is provided with the finding that white males are wage-compensated for commuting at much better rates than white or black females, perhaps because of better labour market bargaining power.

## 3. Moves and quits, using micro and subaggregate data

### 3.1. Empirical modelling of intraurban moves and/or quits in workplace and job-related residential change

Recent development of empirical research in intraurban migration has shown a trend towards greater rigour both in theoretical and econometric analysis. There has also been a greater readiness to analyse the large microdatabases, with modern econometric software geared towards survey and panel data.

Older literature, around 100 empirical studies, was ably reviewed by Quigley and Weinberg (1977). They offered some useful insights relevant to modern research in their stress on the role of search and information (both free and costly) in moves. A Bayesian approach interpreted the role of information as being to revise the prior expected distribution, and possibly lead to no action, further search, or a move. They also stressed that the mobility and search thresholds may differ considerably.

Empirical inconsistencies can also arise from the difficulty of separating household characteristics which affect housing demand at the same time as moving costs (e.g., family size or income).

Weinberg (1979) himself provided one of the best examples of survey-based microanalysis of intraurban mobility. Data on over 3000 San Francisco Bay Area households were analysed in pooled time series/cross section form, with a range of simultaneous estimation techniques for joint residential and job move probabilities. Weinberg successfully found that workplace change and residential move each affect the other, with additional expected effects from age (reducing both move probabilities) and housing or labour market tightness. Interdependence between workplace and residential moves was especially evident for whites, and was much weaker for other ethnic groups. These results parallel evidence elsewhere in this chapter.

Such detailed intraurban work was emerging at the same time as mainline labour economics publications on applications of maximum likelihood logit techniques to inter-MSA moves, such as Bartel (1979), which reiterated the important role played by job tenure in reducing job move probabilities.

A series of studies of migration using British Census migration data from 1971 and concentrating on London emerged in the 1980s. Gordon and Vickerman (1982) proposed a national 112-zone British migration model, with the London metropolitan area modelled in greater detail than the rest of the country. Three superimposed migration streams, with three separate distance decay parameters, were included. These represented the complex mixture of short distance intra-labour market moves, regional spatial choice, sometimes but not always with both job and residence move, and long distance moves for job-related motives. Factor analysis techniques were then used to identify motives for moves. However, the explicit separation of the three migration streams was subject to the weakness that the distance decay parameters were, in effect, imposed through "experimentation and choice", and nonlinear methods to estimate them were unsuccessful.

Gordon and Lamont (1982) used this migration model as part of an ambitious 11-equation simultaneous model, with in- and outmigration under the three separate streams discussed above, together with net commuting, employment growth, unemployment, house building and owner-occupied house prices all treated as endogenous. There are also 19 exogenous variables contributing to 2SLS and 3SLS estimations, making this one of the largest efforts at structural modelling of an intraurban labour and housing market adjustment model. Policy implications include:

> ... clear conclusions at least about the irrelevance of localised job creation
> for the solution of pockets of high unemployment in the inner city.
>
> (Gordon and Lamont, 1982: p. 259)

An example of more recent British work on migration stressing the disparate nature of migration flows came from Boyle (1994), using 1980–1981 Census migration flows in England and Wales. In contrast to a simultaneous model, Boyle analysed a large migration flow matrix between the major urban districts and the rest of the country. A partially constrained Poisson model yielded residuals giving insights on "bright lights effects" and "remote rural" choices.

A number of microstudies using survey data have used various forms of logit or probit estimation, and sample sizes ranging from 500–4500. Linneman and Graves (1983), using data on the Panel Study of Income Dynamics, set up a joint logit structure with six related probabilities (job change or not, no residential change, residential change between counties or not). Significance testing is done by means of a $\chi^2$ test for whether, or not, a variable affects the *whole* joint probability structure, thus automatically incorporating the "adding up constraint" implicit in probability analysis. Separate impacts for education level, wage level, and length of job tenure are related, but may well be opposite in direction (e.g., the partial effect of education may raise the job change probability, but wage and job tenure reduce it).

British work using microdata series is represented by Congdon (1987), who presented a multinomial logit model focusing on residential migration within and away from London, and the interdependence with employment and housing tenure change. Interesting insights were obtained on the role of the individual education level, which tended to increase mobility between residence and between employers, but reduce mobility between industries.

Modern econometric work using US microdata on an individual Detroit firm was contributed in a series of papers by Zax (1991b, 1994) and Zax and Kain (1991, 1996) extended this in a piece of theory and literature review. These papers explore the phenomenon of the "move or quit" choice operating as a form of spatial substitution. There are also striking racial differences in the move or quit responses to lengthy commute times, and black workers were much less likely to either move or quit, leading to suggestions that for them there is:

> ... irremediable spatial disequilibrium ...

> (Zax and Kain, 1991: p. 164)

Zax (1994) also emphasised that job and residential change could be *complements* in long-distance moves, but substitutes in shorter-distance intraregional moves, so that pooling these data was inappropriate.

## 4. The role of job search

### 4.1. Labour market search mechanisms

The development of the theory of labour market search originated as part of the microfoundations of macroeconomics, and only recently have urban economists begun to apply these concepts to the operation of urban labour markets. Mortensen's (1970) original paper developed the theory of the reservation wage, with a new concept of optimality of search in the context of a stochastic wage distribution. Macroeconomic implications including the Phillips curve emerged from this search formulation, however, no attempt was made to include spatial considerations in the search process. A later comprehensive survey by Mortensen (1986) of the labour market search literature also failed to hint at a spatial element in the modelling of such search behaviour.

One of the first attempts to introduce a spatial aspect into the job search and vacancy contact problem was by Seater (1979), soon taken further empirically by Barron and Gilley (1981) and Chirinko (1982). Seater made use of Pontrya-gin dynamic optimisation techniques to develop a very basic theory of optimal labour market activity over space. A simple model produced the optimal number of vacancies $N$ contacted as a function of total search time $S$, total number of employers $B$, and total number of vacancies $V$:

$$N \sim \frac{V}{B^{2/3}} S^{2/3}. \tag{4.1}$$

$V$ of course will vary cyclically for macroeconomic reasons. The model *generated* an implication of diminishing returns to search, whereas, many earlier papers had just *assumed* this. This conclusion resulted from the less productive nature of searching further away from the residence. The empirical estimations of the power of search time in the formula giving the number of vacancies contacted (two-thirds in the simple theory above) was then an issue of research interest, with a value below unity implying diminishing returns to search. There was also the implication that equiproportional increases in total vacancies and firms would raise the number of vacancy contacts, implying certain "economies of labour market density" in the biggest urban areas.

Barron and Gilley (1981) were able to estimate the Seater model using micro-survey data. The "density of potential employers" was only crudely proxied by a MSA dummy, and the exponent on search time came out at 0.45, confirming diminishing returns to scale, although the spatial content as such is minimal. In a separate econometric model, Barron and Gilley also presented maximum likelihood estimates of a multinomial logit formulation with the employment probability as the dependent variable.

An alternative empirical effort to model labour market search with a simple spatial content was made by Chirinko (1982), using maximum likelihood estimation of a Poisson distribution format on Current Population Survey data. This is sensible given that the number of employer contacts is of course a nonnegative integer. The decreasing returns to search are simply represented by a (negative) quadratic term in total search time, and spatial density of potential employers again simply proxied with a MSA dummy. This paper also made an early contribution to the "different methods of search" debate (see Section 4.2). However, one naturally looks for a spatial job search format extending beyond a MSA dummy.

Simpson (1980) was perhaps the first substantial paper to apply search theory ideas to the urban labour market and try to identify their outcome empirically, extended later in Simpson (1992). The principal issue addressed here was the relationship between skill or education level and the spatial extent of job search. This can potentially explain the seemingly paradoxical tendency for higher income workers to commute longer distances, even to nonCBD jobs (i.e., not just for residential decentralisation reasons).

The data used in the Simpson (1980) study is a large sample of London household interviews. The problem is to confirm empirically whether, or not, for labour market search reasons, higher income people are willing to commute on average further, despite valuing their travel time more highly, and in a way in which commuting distance is not separately compensated by lower property prices. The London data also confirm the quantitative importance of job turnover (about twice as frequent on average) relative to residential change, so that "choice of job search area" from a predetermined residence will normally affect a significant proportion of the labour force, whether searching unemployed or on-the-job.

The intensity of search (part of which is represented by greater search area) is then thought to rise with skill and education level, despite the cost of search also being higher. This is because of differences in productivity of search, formality of search method, or the urgency of accepting an early offer.

The principal difficulty in econometrically modelling search mechanisms in the urban labour market is the degree to which job search models and Alonso–Muth type residential location models generate similar predictions with respect to the variation of skill/education/income and commuting distance. That is, within the search mechanism itself, a simultaneity exists of commuting distance from a fixed residence generating demand for wage compensation, and higher wage jobs themselves being associated with more extensive search. This is complicated by the familiar monocentric residential location mechanism of compensation for commuters by lower property prices at greater CBD distance.

Simpson's (1980) micro-London data, despite the impressive sample size, had centre-job and centre-residence detail, without the journey-to-work trip itself. 2SLS techniques were applied to these linear distance variables, with skill segmentation dummies trying to capture the suggested impacts of skill level on commuting. These models were further developed in Simpson (1987, 1992).

More recent empirical work on the urban labour market search and job matching mechanisms has focused on appropriate modelling of large microsamples. O'Regan and Quigley (1993) were mainly concerned with the relative importance of family in the formation of informal information networks especially for youths. With a logit model of the probability of employment of youths, using a large microsample from the biggest US MSAs, the most explicitly locational element is the role of "central city residence", that had a negative relationship with the youth employment probability. As is quite common in such studies, the statistical restriction to "youths living at home" largely removes the problem of the possible endogeneity of residential location. The positive impacts of parent or sibling being employed were found and discussion was provided of rival explanations, such as unobserved heterogeneity in the "taste for work". Alternatives are the possibility of "mimicking behaviour", or the more immediate impact in the city of the illicit and informal economy.

Rouwendahl and Rietveld (1994) studied the Dutch urban system with a sample of some 4000 households. Indeed, the macroeconomic buoyancy of the labour market in the late 1980s made the rising average commuting distances actually found rather surprising. The authors suggested that, apart from a cheapening in the real price of fuel, a trend towards a more professional labour market was probably the principal explanation. ML estimates were produced, with an assumed lognormal distribution of commuting distance. Dummy variables showed the effects of family structure on equilibrium commuting distances, and the impact of urban density with dummies for urbanisation level. A separate "changes" subsample revealed the possible presence of disequilibrium, in that a recent change of employer tended to produce a longer commute.[1] A rival explanation, of course, is that frequent job changes at the "top end" of the professional labour market may use a stable residence as the base of a flexible approach to a series of jobs, at substantial average commuting distance, and this may have rapidly grown in importance in the 1980s.

The strong impact confirmed by Rouwendahl and Rietveld (1994) of household structure and numbers of children is also particularly relevant in understanding commuting patterns. Rouwendahl (1998) extended the theoretical treatment of search within the urban labour market, and generated "wasteful commuting" phenomena as a result of optimising behaviour by both employers and workers.

There have been other significant research contributions in this area using Dutch data. Russo et al. (1996) focused on the employer's search activity and analysed a microdatabase of filled vacancies, testing three alternative maximum likelihood functions to examine the relationship between recruitment distance for each vacancy and the characteristics of the job and the hiring firm. A consistent

---

[1] The printed coefficient in Table 6, p. 1555, is a typographical error, confirmed in correspondence with J. Rouwendal.

and significant tendency was found for jobs with a higher level of education or specific experience to involve wider recruitment areas, but larger firms also recruited over a wider area. Previously unemployed applicants also were recruited from significantly greater distances, more of a labour supply factor.

Van Ommeren et al. (1997) made use of a Dutch longitudinal microdata set to study the commuting behaviour of individuals and relate it through maximum likelihood estimations to their age, education, family status, and search-specific factors such as the expected job offer arrival rate (an indicator of the relative rareness of their skills) and whether they changed job the previous year (and hence may be only partially adjusted). The theoretical prediction that people who expect to receive more job offers will generally not have to accept a long commute was strongly confirmed. The role of family structure was confirmed by the finding that individuals with an employed working spouse also tended to commute significantly further. Even with all the age, education, family status, job change and search variables accounted for, males still tended to commute significantly further.

## 4.2. Some theoretical extensions to spatial labour market search models

In addition to these empirical efforts to gain insight into labour market search, there have been a number of theoretical efforts. Much of this work, while developing search theory ideas, does so in a context in which commuting plays no role, so that the relevance is more to an interurban than intraurban context.

For example, a series of papers by Rogerson and MacKinnon (1981, 1982), and MacKinnon and Rogerson (1980), developed a Markov chain formulation of the transmission of vacancies between locations, with a role for adaptive interregional adjustment of "perceived vacancies" and an information transmission mechanism proxied by lagged migration. Simulations endogenously represent vacancy chains, and combined with exogenous private or public sector vacancies produce cycles in migration flows. In Rogerson and MacKinnon (1981), the emphasis was on the contrast between contracted versus speculative migration, and Rogerson and MacKinnon (1982) developed policy prescriptions on spatially selective advertising.

Another theoretical contribution to spatial labour market search modelling, mainly oriented towards selective migration phenomena, came from Maier (1985, 1987). He suggested that many of the assumptions of standard search models were empirically weak. For example, the knowledge of the wage distribution may itself be accumulated through search. There is no reason why such models should not be relevant to intraurban moves, as is Maier's discussion of the theoretical need to include the "precision of information" itself as a variable. Maier (1987) took this discussion somewhat further, and incorporated a distance-related cost of search into a sequential search model, with a migration decision to be taken at each stage. It could thus be rational to search first, then as the expected return to further search falls, to migrate and search again around the destination. These models comprise interesting and difficult attempts to inject some spatial content into Mortensen-type search theory.

### 4.3.  Racial differences in labour market search activity

A number of empirical studies have been done using microdata bases and attempting to construct estimates of labour market search processes in which the race of an individual affects either search behaviour or the outcome of search. Rather than focusing directly on the outcome of ghettoisation, more general empirical studies of search have race as simply one explanatory variable usually in nonlinear hazard models.

The early work in this area of the literature was by Holzer (1986, 1987, 1988) who formulated models of the choice of search method and level of reservation wage suitable for comparisons between racial subsamples. Holzer (1986) used panel data on nonstudent youths and constructed models of the impact of self-reported reservation wages on duration of unemployment and the wages actually received. This carried certain implications over the degree to which unemployment is actually "voluntary". It might be noted that whereas the theory of the reservation wage is highly nonlinear, the estimates presented were of a rather straightforward log-linear specification, although there is no evidence of misspecification.

Interesting insights were gained about the comparative search behaviour of blacks and whites. Among the control variables in regressions to explain unemployment duration were simple spatial variables which may proxy local labour demand (region and urban residence dummies) as well as personal supply side factors such as schooling and even "presence of a library card". The main empirical finding was that the impact of a higher reservation wage on longer unemployment duration was found to be more severe for blacks than for whites, whereas the impact of the reservation wage on the actual wage received was found to be stronger for whites than for blacks. These results were striking evidence of racial factors in hiring (with many personal characteristics controlled for). A separate insight was that the severity with which the reservation wage increases unemployment duration for blacks is more marked for the black *unemployed* (i.e., those actively searching) than it is for the black *nonemployed* (i.e., those not economically active at all, some of whom may be living off illicit activity).

The same sample was used by Holzer (1987) to study the racial detail of the use of different search methods by white and black youth. The main objective was to study the use of search using direct contacts compared to indirect methods using state agencies or newspapers. This paper also reviewed labour market search theory in terms of the conditional probabilities, firstly of whether a search technique is used, then whether an offer is received given the techniques used, then whether the offer is accepted. The principal interracial difference related to the rather low black use of informal (i.e., direct contact) search methods, and the question of whether this indicated poor "networking", a low intensity of search, or an acknowledgement that racial discrimination in hiring is less likely through formalised hiring procedures such as agencies.

In Holzer (1988), a more detailed presentation of the same empirical study included a theoretical model of job search. The theory generated comparative statics results showing the impact on choice of search method of the search method cost, productivity, the level of nonwage income and the overall level of the wage offer distribution. Simultaneous probit estimations were provided using a small microsample, and detail on search methods used, as well as "employability" characteristics of individuals and urban residence.

Although this work left one hoping for replicated studies with really large data sets, it did shed light on questions crucial for the operations of urban labour markets.

> In particular, we need to increase our understanding of why search methods vary in productivity across individuals who differ in personal characteristics, such as race and family background.
>
> (Holzer, 1988: p. 18)

The same National Longitudinal Survey (NLS) Youth Cohort data source with linked Census data, was used by Holzer, Ihlanfeldt and Sjoquist (1994). The restriction to a youth sample has the effect of substantially removing the endogeneity of the residential location decision, since youths living at home normally have a residential location decided by parents. The principal objective of this empirical approach was to attempt to identify the impact of MSA-wide job decentralisation on the commuting distances of individuals, using a labour market search model, including the effect of car ownership.

Only simple OLS estimates are offered based on merging micro and metropolitan-wide evidence. The main findings were that black and inner city youths do experience longer travel times to work, but this is partly the effect of lower car ownership. It was also found that rapid job decentralisation by itself may not cause longer commuting distances, but it does tend to result in lower employment rates and longer unemployment duration among inner city blacks. This is clearly closely related to the spatial mismatch debate.

A further contribution (Ihlanfeldt, 1997) was based on a detailed microstudy of the degree to which blacks and whites accurately knew where the best job opportunities were in the Atlanta metropolitan area. He found that the blacks were worse informed, although information levels in general were poor. A logit model of labour market knowledge suggested that central city residential location contributed to making blacks badly informed, so that policies directed towards improving the knowledge and efficiency of the labour market may be more cost-effective than subsidised reverse commuting.

In terms of search activity, it was found that longer distance willingness to commute (and implied longer distance search) did affect wage positively and unemployment duration negatively. Of course, there were simultaneities with car ownership, which results from higher wages and so through cheaper search costs extends the area of search. The policy suggestion is that if public transport is strikingly slower and more restricted in its routes than the private car, public transport subsidy would not be an appropriate policy strategy.

The most detailed recent effort at incorporating spatial factors into a Mortensen-type job search model was by Rogers (1997). Using a remarkable spatially detailed microdata set of unemployment insurance claims in Pennsylvania over 1980–1986, a logit model partly based on the work of Nickell (1979) was formulated, with the probability of leaving unemployment affected by a range of labour market, demographic and policy variables, but with an access to employment index in addition.

ML estimation found that the access-weighted employment growth was indeed a significant variable in explaining the leaving—unemployment hazard. The race dummy variable was included but found to be insignificant; it may be partly collinear with a wide range of education and industry characteristics. The implication appears to be that "access matters more than race".

## 5. Implications of the changing structure of skill and status

### 5.1. Variation in labour market behaviour with respect to skill, status and income

Most applied work studying urban labour market behaviour of specific groups has focused on questions of gender, family structure and race (covered below in Sections 6 and 7). However, a small number of papers have tried to produce useful generalisations about the operations of modern urban labour markets with reference to the general skills and status distribution of workers. In more recent work, much of the focus has been on the working of a mobile "high tech" labour market in a single large urban area.

One of the earliest efforts, however, by Wheeler (1969), was a general study of travel to work patterns by skill and status of workers commuting into the Pittsburgh CBD. The fairly modest level of awareness of gender in commuting at that time is revealed by the stress by Wheeler on the apparent paradox that average commuting distance for women seemed to be fairly low (i.e., "distance friction was high") despite their over-representation in higher status (white collar) occupations. In contrast, the distance frictions for (mainly male) operatives and labourers were fairly low. However, little attempt was made to incorporate in detail the economics of residential location.

A more spatially specific study of high tech labour came from Scott (1992a), as a detailed extension of a wider research programme to refine the understanding of large, modern urban "industrial districts" (Scott, 1988). In the 1992a paper, Scott conducted a questionnaire survey of engineers and scientists employed at three Lockheed plants in the Los Angeles metropolitan area. There was a strong overall sense of a large and complex agglomerated "local" labour market, at metropolitan area scale. Job information was acquired partly by personal contact through friends and relatives, partly through well-known interdependent contacts with Southern Californian universities and colleges. Interindustry moves within the high tech occupation range suggested agglomeration-specific skills. One striking finding was the relative *unimportance* of distance to work in the decision of whether to move residentially. The distributions of distances to work in the final Lockheed job location were compared for residential movers and nonmovers using a Kolmogorov–Smirnoff test and found to have no significant difference. Although a modest sample size may weaken some of his conclusions, an interesting picture was built up of a highly mobile and qualified type of urban labour market evolution in which labour market agglomeration economies:

> ... reduce job search and recruitment costs by facilitating the retrieval of local labor market information at low marginal cost.
>
> (Scott, 1992a: p. 112)

These ideas were among the ingredients of policy-related discussions of the role of high technology agglomerations in regional development (Storper and Scott (1992), Scott (1993)).

Turning to status-related labour market behaviour as revealed by migration, Herzog et al. (1986) focused on a subsample of US high tech workers, and compared their migration decisions with lower grade workers in a large microsample from the 1980 Census using a logit model. The policy orientation of the paper was towards how high tech workers can best be attracted to an area. Comparisons of high tech and other migrants revealed that the high tech workers were more mobile overall, and their decision to migrate was sensitive to age, children and transportation access. There were some tricky simultaneity issues. For instance, high average house prices were found to promote out-migration, and local taxes were used as a cost of living proxy, and both of these variables are the result of simultaneous processes. Personal characteristics of out migrants (not very amenable to policy) turned out to be more important than metropolitan area as explainers of the out-migration decision. This however may be because personal characteristics were much more accurately measured, on a disaggregated microbasis.

### 5.2. Dual urban labour markets, the urban underclass, and the changing structure of labour demand

The last decade has seen the development of a number of alternative approaches to the study of labour markets from a more conceptual, political economy viewpoint. Given the fact that these approaches do not generally make use of econometric or other applied economic techniques, and usually develop their arguments based on descriptive detail or recent historical evidence, we will restrict ourselves to a brief outline. Several of these sources contribute alternative evolutions of the urban labour market from the theory of the dual labour market, much discussed in the 1970s. Piore and Sabel (1984) was one of the first popular formulations of the flexible specialisation theory of industrial organisation. The main emphasis in their work was on the industrial structure implications of computerisation in production materials handling, and the greater flexibility in the urban labour market it required. International comparisons of the US with four alternative "faces" of flexible specialisation stressed the contrasts in centralised planning (France), teamwork and community structure (Germany and Japan), and organic mutability (Italy).

The spatial evolution of the post-industrial economy constitutes one element of modern spatial political economy. Another is the analysis of the role of explicit or implicit management of labour through "spatial division" as developed by Marxist economic geographers such as Massey (1994).

A further body of empirical work analysing the economic geography of the urban labour market under industrial and post-industrial capitalism has been in the research either by or stimulated by Scott (1988) and Scott and Storper (1986). Scott (1988) provided a descriptive account of the whole urban labour market of Southern California, and provided a wider level of detail than the high tech focus of Scott (1992a).

A more traditionally liberal-minded view of where the "dual labour market" paradigm had evolved by the mid 1990s was provided by recent discussions between Jencks and Peterson (1991), Peterson (1992) and Wilson (1987, 1992). A more sociology-based view of modern urban labour market problems in the major US inner cities has focused on the understanding of the "urban under-class" (Peterson (1992)). Concentration is on the evolving long-term nature of the "paradox of the perpetuation of poverty" through the 1970s and 1980s, given the continuation of sustained macroeconomic growth. Peterson's principal policy interest is on the need to provide a more effective national welfare policy.

Of the elements spelled out by Wilson (1987, 1992) in "The Truly Disadvantaged", Peterson stressed certain trends of the last two decades impacting on the operation of urban labour markets. These included the sharp rise in proportion of female-headed households, an adverse movement in labour force participation and earnings possibilities particularly for young blacks, and a significant shift in the relative location of poverty, from rural areas to the larger central cities.

Wilson (1987, 1992) developed the influential paradigm of "The Truly Disadvantaged" by stressing the dual problem of marginal economic position and social isolation in highly concentrated poverty areas. Relative to the analysis of the 1960s and 1970s there is more explicit emphasis now on the:

> ... increasing polarisation of the labour market into low wage and high wage sectors, (and) innovations in technology ...
>
> (Wilson, 1992: p. 640)

Also, it is more common in current work to acknowledge that joblessness is as likely now to take the form of nonparticipation in the labour market as it is of unemployment as such.

In some cases, the same economists who contributed to thinking on trends in urban labour markets in the 1970s have revised and extended their analysis for modern readership. Harrison (1974, 1994) is a leading example whose recent popular interpretation of trends in urban labour markets has stressed the substantial recent rise in "contingent" (part-time, temporary or contract) labour, which now in the US constitutes about one quarter to one third of the civilian labour force. In the current form of the dual labour market, a "contingent" labour force may play a prominent part, even in Silicon Valley.

Nevertheless, other surveys show that a substantial proportion of US part-time workers accept this category voluntarily, often because of family responsibilities. The principal advantage to the employer of part-time or temporary workers lies in avoidance of fringe benefits. These are an attractive incentive for full-time staff due to their untaxed or tax-deferred status.

However, the *earnings* distribution as a whole even for full-time workers has become more unequal, a trend which itself has generated a large literature (Levy and Murnane, 1992). The *income* distribution (with earnings and other income) has received rather less attention, though there are indications that there are substantial international variations even in the trends. The most striking rises in inequality have been in the US, UK and New Zealand. Madden (1996) has also contributed a study of changes in the incidence of poverty in the US over 1979–1989 for the 181 largest metropolitan areas. She found that the rate of increasing concentration in the central cities of poverty was greatest in those metropolitan areas in which it had the highest starting values. Higher Gini coefficients for the metropolitan income distribution were associated with a higher metropolitan poverty rate, but a more even spread of poverty between city and suburbs.

A final trend in Harrison's contemporary interpretation of trends is the global nature of modern industrial organisations and the search for corporate efficiency through conglomerates concentrating on their main product areas and divesting non core business, in many cases in suburban "brownfield" locations. Of more immediate relevance to urban labour markets, Harrison also referred to the "dark side" of industrial districts, with complex ethnic divisions in employment.

Holzer's findings on labour market search activity were discussed above (Section 4.3), but he has added to this with a large telephone survey of employers in four major US metropolitan areas, over 3000 employers in all (Holzer, 1996). His conclusions on the employment problems of blacks and Hispanics in American cities are lent authority by the scale of this survey, but the policy implications are familiar. These include raising high school graduation rates, improving basic cognitive and interactive skills, and the lower willingness of central city resident blacks to apply for and commute to suburban jobs. (The latter factor seemed to be much less significant for Hispanics). Holzer's sharpest concern is over the acceptance by Federal Government in the late 1990s of "welfare to work" policies which might exacerbate the imbalance between job availability and numbers of low-skill workers.

## 6. Impact of gender, family structure and demographic factors on urban labour market behaviour

### 6.1. Theoretical contributions

The earliest rigorous development in theoretical understanding of the role of family structure and demographic factors in urban labour markets was by Madden (1977a). She formulated a model in which wage discrimination by sex could emerge through optimising behaviour in a spatial labour market with multi-worker households. A family utility function, itself a relatively unusual concept, was included in a fully worked out model of an urban labour market with spatially separated firms and leisure time arguments for both husband and wife. Theoretical results were developed on the causes of a lower wage elasticity of supply of labour for married women. The lower elasticity of supply for married female labour gives a degree of monopsony power to local firms, so that wage differences by gender are profit maximising.

A related theoretical treatment by White (1977) was restricted to an assumption of suburban women workers and CBD men, and developed a model of urban structure using Cobb–Douglas utility functions including leisure times. As usual, a Lagrangian treatment produced a full income constraint which generated a valuation of commuting time at the full wage rate.

However, adjusting for experience and education, US women's wages are by now within observational error of men's, so that US gender inequality in terms of job-specific wage rates is low. It is possible that inequality in hiring and promotion is the main research objective deserving further attention in this area.

A policy application of theoretical work on family structure and labour market behaviour is to the enforcement of equal pay policies between genders. Frank (1978) for example, discussed Affirmative Action Programs from the point of view of the two-professional-worker family job search problem. Such families find their job search problems easier to solve in larger urban labour markets, and are thus biased towards such cities to the disadvantage of employers in small labour markets. As a result, simple hiring proportions, or the quotas which may be associated with them as a policy may not be a fair test of Affirmative Action policies.

A useful review of the state of understanding of gender and urban labour markets, in the light of rising female labour force participation (LFP) rates, was provided by Madden and White (1980), discussed in Chapter 36 of this volume by Michelle White. Their principal emphasis was on the implications of urban spatial structure in continuing gender differences, or in the weakening over time of familiar patterns of wage discrimination or job choice by gender. For example, if women simply dislike long distance commuting more than men, the trend towards higher female LFP in white collar service jobs might strengthen the forces of gentrification. But women searching for jobs close to fixed suburban residences will promote suburbanisation of jobs through providing a high quality and possibly cheaper labour force.

Other work on family structure and urban labour market behaviour has either been of an empirical nature, or has pursued a theoretical approach through simulation, as in Hotchkiss and White (1993). They set up a model of spatial allocation in a city with three household types, which are given separate Cobb–Douglas utility functions and treated endogenously in an urban structure with a CBD and two subcentres. Realistic patterns of desegregation of the spatial pattern of household types are obtained, and stochastic wage distributions are assumed.

## 6.2. *Empirical research on gender, family structures and urban labour markets*

The detailed study of gender in urban labour markets has been closely associated with the analysis of sex discrimination and other causes of wage differences by gender in the economy as a whole. Sex discrimination can be assessed in a similar way to racial discrimination (with which it may be mixed in complex ways). Recently, more feminist viewpoints have focused on the manner in which urban commuting patterns can help to generate or reinforce "occupational sex segregation".

One of the earliest high quality papers on the subject of wage differentials by gender in the economy as a whole was by Oaxaca (1973). This work only incidentally included MSA size category as an explanatory variable in wage equations attempting to separate the influences of occupational concentration from that of different wages for equal work in explaining overall wage differentials. These wage equations were estimated using a microsample from the 1967 Survey of Economic Opportunity. Oaxaca concluded that the index of sex discrimination derived from residuals of reduced form wage equations accounted for over half the wage differentials by sex. But it is *not* unequal pay for equal jobs which is the main ingredient, but rather the concentrations of women in low paid jobs which produces the large overall wage differentials. Even with this detailed and sophisticated formulation, the dynamic contribution of women's failure to invest in human capital (or denial of the opportunity) is difficult to identify separately.

Another large US longitudinal microsample was used by Madden (1977b), and the focus here was on the empirical estimation of local monopsony effects in the urban labour market. These results comprised OLS estimations with the worktrip time dependent, and produced suggestive results that married women have a lower wage elasticity of trip time than men, indicating the possibility of a more localised urban labour market for married women. However, difficulties remained over the separate analysis of the participation decision and hours of work in the labour supply decision.

Madden (1981) used yet another US microdata source, the Panel Survey of Income Dynamics. Again, the empirical analysis of work trip length was the principal econometric content, though the overall context was expressed in two directions. Firstly, the study of the policy impact of job-creation programmes requires care where labour markets are spatially constrained, as the author suggests they are for married women. Secondly, the impact on urban structure of the sustained rise in female LFP requires analysis.

The empirical evidence found by Madden (1981) suggested that work trip lengths tend to vary positively with the wage and also with residential distance from the CBD, but negatively with city size, controlling for household structure and gender.

The study was perhaps weakened by the absence of information on job location itself, so that no clear separation was made between the traditional monocentric trade-off and wider search areas to high status jobs in the suburbs. However, there is some good discussion of the important role of the expected turnover rate of residence and job, in that residential location decisions are always implicitly dynamic. But the *unobserved* nature of search and job or residence turnover expectations remain as serious difficulties.

The question of the impact on urban structure of rising female activity rates was further examined by Hekman (1980), who tried to "rescue" the Alonso model from the criticisms of Wheaton (1977) by stressing the higher female LFP rates found in lower income households. (Wheaton (ibid) had constructed simulations of the trade-off model with realistic parameters indicating that there was little difference in the slope of the bid rent curves for different groups). A more general theory of the family labour market produces relationships between female LFP, CBD distance and male earnings. The impact of the male wage on female LFP is quantitatively important, affecting the familiar elasticity conditions governing the household's bid rent curve slope:

> ... the income elasticity of housing demand can be less than the elasticity of transportation cost with income by a considerable margin while the bid-rent curve still becomes flatter at higher incomes.
>
> (Hekman, 1980: p. 810)

The findings of Simpson on urban labour market search in decentralised urban economies have been discussed elsewhere (Section 4.1), but in Simpson (1982) he made use of the same London Census data to analyse variations in female unemployment and married female activity rates across the London Boroughs. This work is subject to the usual reservations about spatial sub-aggregates and resulting problems of simultaneity bias; where substantial jurisdictions comprise the basic data these can be quite damaging. Concentrations of "male" and "female" jobs at Borough level were found to have expected (though nonlinear) effects on married female activity and unemployment rates. The policy relevance concerned the importance of information dissemination and informal networks especially for the unskilled.

American research using area sub-aggregates on unemployment and LFP rates includes Lillydahl and Singell (1985) who ran simple OLS regressions on 1980 urban Census tracts (which are very small compared to jurisdictions). This work is also subject to the customary criticisms of empirical analysis of Census tract averages including ethnic and educational characteristics. Some endogeneity problems also inevitably arise (such as those associated with using "average commute" as an explanatory variable).

Perhaps the most stimulating finding is that although the *total* unemployment rate had little relationship with distance from the city centre in the five MSAs, there seemed to be a tendency for *female* unemployment rates to rise with CBD distance, as did *teenage* unemployment rates. In contrast, *male* unemployment showed a tendency to fall with distance from the city centre, and male LFP to rise. This would indicate that suburban employment opportunities in some large cities may be "pro-male", and local job search around a suburban residence may favour male workers.

A much larger more sophisticated empirical analysis by Singell and Lillydahl (1986) used a large microsample of in two-earner households. They addressed the central issue of "family economics" in the urban labour market, namely the extent to which, in a two-worker household, the female's job may be treated as secondary, and the male's as primary. This may carry the implication that

... the larger the male/female earnings gap, the greater the incentive to locate the residence closer to the male's job location.

(Singell and Lillydahl, 1986: p. 122)

They presented a three equation system, with wage, home value, and commute time treated as endogenous, estimated by two stage least squares. The presence of a "moved" dummy in the "commute time" equation seemed to confirm that residential choice is based more heavily on the male's job location. Other family structure variables, such as the presence of children, had expected results. This was also one of the largest microsamples which made a success of estimating a simultaneous system including firstly the "returns to commuting" (i.e., longer commutes causing a higher wage), and secondly the "cost of commuting", (i.e., the higher wage causing higher time valuation and an incentive to reduce commuting). The interaction of these opposite forces with the discrete "move" decision, and family job priorities, goes to the heart of modern urban labour market research, and deserves further work.

A different approach to the wage equation was taken by Madden and Chen Chiu (1990), using the 5% Public Use Micro Sample (PUMS) of the 1980 US Census. Limiting themselves to Detroit and Philadelphia, they estimated zone-specific wage equations, separated by race and gender. The intention was to identify and compare the intraurban wage variability of men and women. If the wage variability for women were in fact greater, then constraints on female commuting or residential mobility could be more damaging for them and could contribute to male/female overall wage differentials. They found that conversely there was evidence that for whites, the male coefficient of variation was higher, though this was not true for blacks. There was however found to be a greater spatial concentration of "top jobs" for women. The paper also included a theoretical treatment of urban labour market behaviour for the two-earner household (with commuting time as usual priced at full wage rate), with simulations for Detroit and Philadelphia.

A number of papers from a more geographical point of view have adopted a more explicitly feminist approach to urban commuting and labour market outcomes [Hanson and Johnston (1985), Hanson and Pratt (1988), Johnston-Anumonwo (1988), Nelson (1986)]. This research has used quite substantial microsurvey data, but has limited the empirical analysis to analysis of variance.

Hanson and Johnston (1985) using Baltimore home interview data found that, contrary to some preconceptions, gender commuting distance differences were not greatly influenced by household responsibility or even part-time versus full-time status. Shorter journey to work distances were best explained by women's lower incomes and a greater use of the bus in commuting, which may also restrict women to smaller job search areas. Perhaps studies such as this are most useful in summarising evidence on "stylised facts", such as the stronger tendency for working women to both live and work in the central city, for there to be more female headed households in the city, and for women to commute shorter distances even within the same income class as men.

A similar approach was taken by Hanson and Pratt (1988) using special Census runs for a specific town, Worcester Massachusetts. An attempt was made to identify "... women's spatial entrapment" (p. 199), based on average journey to work times for sub-aggregates of the labour force. In addition, full time and part time workers were aggregated. However, there is a result of some interest. *Male* average journey to work times were longer to a suburban job (by 9 minutes) and from a suburban residence (by 6 minutes), compared to males living or working in the central city, and compared to all female subgroups.

A closely related piece of work, using a small subsample of the same data was done by Johnston-Anumonwo (1988). It likewise tried to identify the degree to which

> ... in addition to the better researched socio-demographic characteristics like labour force attachment and household responsibility, journey to work characteristics contribute to occupational sex segregation.
>
> (Johnston-Anumonwo, 1988: p. 138)

The sample was divided into "female" or "male-dominated" jobs, using national employment patterns. One interesting finding was that women in "female-dominated" jobs had significantly shorter journey to work times, and were more likely to work in suburban Worcester. In contrast, women from households with no children were more likely to work in "male" or gender-integrated jobs. The analysis ran quickly into small sample sizes when cross-tabulations were attempted. It was one of very few examples of microsurvey evidence on a single metropolitan area. A similar focus on a single metropolitan area, but the much bigger one of San Francisco–Oakland was provided by Nelson (1986) in the modern "political geography" style.

A more explicit discussion (from a male perspective) of the "patriarchal constraints hypothesis" was provided by Gordon et al. (1989a), using national US microdata. They confirmed the finding that female worktrips were shorter than male worktrips, even after standardising for a wide range of job and personal characteristics. Thus, although the ranking of average journey to work distance was very similar between men and women, women still had shorter average journey to work within each occupational class. There was also a trend over 1977–1983 towards shorter journey to work trips, which the authors associated with job dispersal.

This paper did not address the causes of male wage premia for a given occupation, but did suggest the likelihood that higher wage possibilities for each occupation would induce wider search areas and consequently greater average worktrip distance:

> If the total wage and benefit package is consistently higher for males at the occupational specific level, it may be more worthwhile for men to adopt a spatially more extensive search area in seeking a suitable job than for women.
>
> (Gordon et al., 1989a: p. 508)

Almost all of the above research on gender and urban labour markets was based on US data. Comparisons making use of the urban experience of Paris was provided in a series of papers by Fagnani and colleagues (Fagnani, 1983, 1984, 1990; Brun and Fagnani, 1994). The 1984 descriptive survey of commuting patterns in the Ile de France region focused on "... strategies to reconcile work with family life". Women's jobs in the Ile de France are strongly concentrated in the City of Paris, and the female LFP for the region is well above the national average.

The survey showed that male/female differences in commuting distances are only slight for the intraParis and reverse commute Paris-suburbs trips, but the male average distance was greater for the conventional inwards radial worktrip. In addition, the differences were even greater with respect to commuting *times*, largely explained by women's greater use of public transit. The unequal access to cars by gender was especially damaging for low income jobs in the outer suburbs. Fagnani (1984) presented a descriptive data analysis for mature women in the Ile de France. Again the work found that the single female heads of household were much more likely to be in professions or top management and to reside in the city of Paris:

> ... the higher a woman rises in the socio-occupational hierarchy, the more she can offer herself the "luxury" of not abiding by social conventions.
>
> (Fagnani, 1984: p. 145)

There appears to be an identifiable Parisian female professional elite whose single status plays a role both in their career and in their choice of central city residential location.

Fagnani (1990) used a national French sample of women in couples with children under age 17. She found that although the more highly educated of these women had a higher LFP rate, these educated women tended to work *less* in Greater Paris than in smaller urban centres. This tendency for the stresses of mixing job, commuting and care of school age children to be more severe in the largest cities, inducing career interruption there, is an interesting finding highly relevant in a period of steadily rising female LFP. The paper also contains the results of a smaller sample of personal interviews with women with children, presenting more information on the process of career interruption for professional women. This work should perhaps be read in the context of the long standing French concern with the country's relatively low fertility rate. Finally, Brun and Fagnani (1994) presented the results of a questionnaire survey of Ile de France households, plus some detailed interviews. This work was more a study of contrasting lifestyles of gentrification versus suburban living.

## 7. Spatial mismatch—residential segregation by race in cities, and its implications for earnings and employment differences by race

### 7.1. Original formulation

The original seminal research on the relationship between racial segregation in US cities and poor employment outcomes for blacks was by Kain (1968), and is now a familiar part of the early development of applied urban economics. Using home interview data aggregated into workplace zones, from Area Traffic Studies for Detroit and Chicago dating back to the early 1950s, Kain was able with simple OLSA regression to find a significant impact of residential concentration on employment concentration of blacks by zone, separate from the decay effects of distance from the city's black ghetto. Even higher levels of significance were found when the sample was disaggregated by occupation or industry. The policy implication was that:

> ... continued high levels of Negro unemployment in a full employment economy may be partially attributable to the rapid and adverse (for the Negro) shifts in the location of jobs.
>
> (Kain, 1968: p. 197)

Most of the derivative research which has since emerged developing the same concept has either used more sophisticated data than was available to Kain, better econometric techniques, or has tried to widen the concept of "access" beyond the cost of possible journeys to work. There were some fairly immediate follow-ups to Kain's original work, which questioned the robustness of his findings with respect to specification (Offner and Saks (1971)) or the measure of racial segregation (Masters (1974, 1975)). The results were also dependent on the data set used.

Kain and Meyer (1970) presented a clear policy-oriented analysis of the view of the time, shared by the McCone Commission on the Watts riot, that

> inadequate and costly public transportation currently existing throughout the Los Angeles area ... handicaps them in seeking and holding jobs.
>
> (Kain and Meyer, 1970: p. 76)

The view that poor physical access to suburban job concentrations, caused partly by low car ownership and partly by the inevitably focused radial nature of public transit, led Kain and Meyer to propose a range of flexible and innovative service improvements to public transit, stressing small vehicle and demand-activated transportation possibilities suitable to low density employment distributions. Inspired by this research and lobbying, the US Department of Transportation experimented with free-reverse-commuting bus trips, but the results were poor and the experiments were ended in embarrassment.

It is relevant that older used cars are cheap in the US, and vehicle costs for inner-city—suburban worktrips may normally be lower than bus fares if a modest allowance is made for the value of time saved by reverse commuting (against the main flow) by automobile. Mills and Lubuele (1997) also observed that in the US labour market conditions of the mid-1990s (which admittedly were not typical) there was excess demand for sales and clerical workers in both inner cities and suburbs.

At the text book level of urban economics, incorporation of spatial mismatch ideas was rapid. Kalachek (1973) stressed the likelihood that negative spatial mismatch impacts were more severe amongst single persons, teenagers and married women. Kalachek also anticipated later research by stressing the role played by informal networks in disseminating information about potential jobs. The policy choice at that time was seen as being between subsidising transport to the suburban job concentrations, versus job creation programmes closer to low income residential areas. He favoured the transport improvement approach, partly because of flexibility (with bus infrastructure) and evenness of application.

## 7.2. *More detailed research on racial segregation in urban residential models*

Stimulated by the detailed study of "racial ghettos" which had developed as part of both the study of urban housing markets and the spatial mismatch in urban labour markets, a body of research developed on racial segregation. Some of this work was largely theoretical, e.g., Yinger (1976), who took Bailey's (1959, 1966) original "border-minimising" model of the ghetto further, by showing that residential racial instability could be a built-in and permanent feature of the urban housing market, if any subgroup of the population actually preferred racial mixing. This meant that some form of "institutionalised discrimination" was inevitable (e.g., through minimum lot zoning) if stability in racial composition was to be the outcome.

Courant and Yinger (1977) reviewed theoretical models of ghettos and extended them by incorporating more realistic income distributions. They called for better modelling of ghettos through simultaneous modelling of race and residential demand, incorporation of high search costs (both for housing and for labour), and the possibility of collusive or institutionalised discrimination. The relatively small numbers of highly concentrated racial ghettos, which tend to be quite stable in location, are the stylised facts needing good theoretical explanations.

Straszheim (1980) was the first to provide an integrated model of housing and labour market discrimination with respect to race including hiring policy parameters such as a "black quota". The resulting nonlinear differential equation provided simulation results on how hiring practices interact with the spatial pattern of job opportunities. The possible positive wage gradient effects was studied empirically using data from San Francisco. Evidence was presented that these effects are strongest for less educated blacks, who are also more segregated residentially.

The explicit detailed study of segregation has not attracted so much attention recently. One exception came from Miller and Quigley (1990), who used an entropy technique to study segregation by race and household type for San Francisco, with entropy:

$$H = - \sum_{i,t} \rho_{it} \log \rho_{it}, \tag{7.1}$$

where $i$ represents either household type or race subgroups and $t$ tracts. A maximum of $H$ would then be an equal distribution and $H$ below this measures the degree of segregation. Miller and Quigley found that segregation by race was indeed greater than by household type, and both weakened slightly over

1970–1980. Another interesting finding was that the level of racial segregation measured by these entropy indices in the suburbs was lower than in the central city.

## 7.3. *Reviews and descriptive evidence lying behind spatial mismatch studies*

The research on the locational detail of the spatial mismatch process has been formulated in the context of more general work on racial aspects of urban labour markets. It is perhaps worth commenting on these first.

By the late 1970s in the US, the issue of black/white average wage convergence was worthy of analysis. Smith and Welch (1979) used Current Population Survey data to suggest factors which could be influencing this labour market convergence. These included "cohort effects" as younger, better educated blacks became more numerous, the effects of Affirmative Action Programmes, and long term regional trends such as the urbanisation of the South and black migration to the North. They concluded that the role of Affirmative Action was probably small, and urbanisation *within* the South was a much more important factor in furthering the job prospects of blacks.

One difficulty which emerged was that of distinguishing between "life cycle" or career effects and the "cohort" effects, which operate as a labour force "vintage" phenomenon. The life cycle effects could be properly tested only by microlongitudinal data.

The particular life cycle stage which has received separate detailed research attention concerns the problem of youth unemployment. It emerged in the early 1980s that a serious problem was developing with respect to youth joblessness relative to prime age male unemployment. The paper by Wachter and Kim (1982), and the detailed discussion of it by Gordon (1982) revolved around the effects of "cohort overcrowding", the declining role of military service, the role of the minimum wage or welfare payments on youth reservation wage rates. Gordon suggested that switching occurred into full time school or the informal or illicit sector, but it was difficult to distinguish the demand side from the pure supply side effects of the reservation wage. Bureau of Labor Statistics data showed the importance of youth unemployment "while in school" and the implied role of school as a "substitute job" is somewhat deflating from a human capital point of view.

By the mid 1980s, review material such as Kasarda (1985) on the position of racial minorities in urban labour markets was suggesting a deterioration, that the dynamics of urban change had:

... altered the capacity of America's older cities to offer entry-level jobs and socially upgrade disadvantaged resident groups.

(Kasarda, 1985: p. 34)

The dynamics of urban change partly took the form of the dramatic growth over 1965–1985 of the modern urban service sector at or near the CBD. Informational services grew faster still, especially in the largest cities, placing strong emphasis on numeracy, literacy, and high motivation. The white population was declining rapidly in the biggest cities. Kasarda's (1985) evidence from the C.P.S tapes of 1969, 1977, 1982 showed that while average unemployment rates for all educational groups had increased, the gaps between the better and worse educated had widened, and the same had happened for labour force nonparticipation rates. The scale of economic marginalisation for minority groups, especially in the large northern US cities, had become more severe. As suggested by Mills and Lubuele (1997), wage inequality as such has increased by similar amounts for blacks and whites over 1980–1997. A major reason for widening black wage disparities between inner cities and suburbs is migration of higher wage blacks to the suburbs.

Jencks and Mayer (1989) provided further discussion of the status of the spatial mismatch hypothesis in the late 1980s. They acknowledged the evidence of Kasarda on the widening of city–suburb differences in black labour market outcomes, but they suggested that the role of selective city–suburb migration was both important and difficult to estimate without good longitudinal data. In addition, there were built-in simultaneities between individual job status and the neighbourhood of residence, with each affecting the other. The earnings of blacks living in the suburbs would be much affected by unmeasured heterogeneity so that empirical measures of the role of commuting cost, which anyway might play a modest role, may be statistically unreliable. Jencks and Mayer also stressed the difficult mixture of demand and supply side factors in the spatial mismatch process. The demand side factors involved the impact of racial discrimination in hiring, either pro-black in the ghetto or pro-white in predominantly white suburbs. Supply side factors included the role of search and information costs and commuting costs from the ghetto.

A review of the status of the spatial mismatch hypothesis by Holzer (1991) confirmed that the decentralisation of jobs and residents continued as did declines in manufacturing employment. Although black suburbanisation was slowly rising, blacks were lagging Hispanic and Asian Americans in this respect. It was also true that on average, employed blacks still had longer commute times than employed whites and this might have some measurable relationship with the poorer job access at neighbourhood level suffered by blacks. There seemed also to be some evidence for a positive wage gradient for less-educated blacks commuting to the suburbs.

Holzer concluded that spatial mismatch effects could be identified for black youth employment, but only if, firstly, microlevel Census data were used, and secondly, separate estimates were produced for blacks and whites. If anything, spatial mismatch was growing more relevant over time:

> But uncertainty remains over the magnitude and existence of these effects.
> (Holzer, 1991: p. 119)

It appeared clear that the severity of spatial mismatch phenomena varied between metropolitan areas, as one might expect discriminatory attitudes to do. The developing empirical concentration on the youth labour market was welcome, partly because their employment problems were more severe.

### 7.4. *Empirical research on the spatial mismatch*

A substantial econometric literature has accumulated on the estimation of spatial mismatch models, almost all American. The detailed empirical work by Harrison (1972a, 1972b), on what became known as the "race versus space" question attempted to measure whether the economic disadvantage suffered by blacks was the result of labour market discrimination or their residential location. Harrison provided one of the first large scale analyses of microdata, on 30,000 households including 4000 adult workers in poverty areas of the 12 largest MSAs. The (1972a) paper provided OLS estimates of differential returns to black and white education. Also, evidence on median male earnings mean unemployment and occupational status suggested that the nonpoverty areas of the central city fared somewhat better than the suburbs, though there are causal simultaneities between economic status and residential location. He concluded by making the case for ghetto-based demand side policies as the most effective way of strengthening black economic status.

The same data source was used in Harrison (1972b) to compute microeconomic OLS regressions on the payoff to education and training for residents of city poverty areas, the city remainder, and the suburbs. The similarity in outcomes between suburbs and "city remainder" led Harrison to criticise policies (such as those promoted by Kain after the original spatial mismatch research) promoting black suburbanisation, on the grounds that suburban ghettos may be just as inaccessible from centres of job growth.

Perhaps Harrison was unduly pessimistic in feeling that policies to assist non-whites in moving to the suburbs were ineffective; such surburbanization by better off nonwhites was rapid during the 1980s (Mills, 1997).

Danziger and Weinstein (1976) took the estimation of spatial mismatch phenomena further using a sample of 1970 Census Employment Service data from three cities. They tried to resolve the issue of commuting cost differentials for ghetto residents accessing suburban jobs. Using a reduced form wage equation, the differential between the actual suburban wage and the imputed wage (with characteristics controlled for) would be positive if commuting compensation was paid. This was also compared with hypothetical cash and time commuting differentials. Danziger and Weinstein concluded that the evidence was consistent with labour market imperfections at wage rates which do not compensate for commuting.

A further dimension was added by Myers and Phillips (1979) in stressing the search and reservation wage mechanisms lying behind spatial mismatch. If minority workers were searching from a suburban residence, search costs may result in the reservation wage being higher and unemployment duration longer. The original study estimated wage and job offer probabilities controlling for many characteristic and labour market variables, including the duration of search. Tentative evidence emerged of a positive suburban wage premium. But there was evidence that black workers were more likely to be hired in suburban tracts with large black populations. Raphael (1998) used 1980–1990 Census tract data for the San Francisco Bay Area to explain the relationships between changing accessibility of employment and the employment rates of black and white youths. This produced evidence that racial differences in youth employment rates were significantly explained by changing job access.

The simultaneity problem intrinsic in modelling the relationship between personal characteristics, education, occupation and earnings was directly addressed by Vrooman and Greenfield (1980), using a small microsample. A recursive structural model was proposed and estimated for 6 sample subgroups. The strength of this work was the explicit separation in an income formula of the type:

$$Y_{ij} = \sum_k \beta_{jk} X_{ijk}, \tag{7.2}$$

where $j$ denotes a labour force segment, $k$ denotes a characteristic factor, and $i$ the individual. Racial differences in the coefficients $\beta$ were then referred to as "overt" discrimination (e.g., the payoff to a year of education), whereas differences in $X$ were "institutional" discrimination (e.g., differences in amounts of education completed). One striking conclusion was that black males and females experience very different levels of discrimination in spatial terms, confirming that discrimination is more complex than race itself. Black males were shown to suffer both overt and institutional discrimination regardless of where they reside.

A similar focus but with a much more authoritative data set was offered by Price and Mills (1985). Using microdata from the 1978 Current Population Survey, they estimated a large reduced form with ln(Net Earnings) as dependent variable, in an effort to quantify the degree to which race or city residence affect the marginal valuations of characteristics, the reduced form intercept, or both. They found that, with all possible personal characteristics controlled for, black city earnings were 21.6% and black suburban earnings 15.6% below those for an equivalent white suburban worker. City residence alone therefore imposed a net wage penalty of 6% for blacks and 8% for whites, assuming there were no significant unobserved variables.

Price and Mills concluded that a large part of the 50% or so earnings premium of suburban whites over city blacks is accounted for by the beneficial valuation characteristics enjoyed by suburban whites (which includes the payoff to education). There was a wage penalty for city residence for blacks, but at around 6% it was fairly small, and similar to that of whites. As with the Vrooman and Greenfield study, there was no possibility of analysing spatial detail or commuting costs beyond the city/suburb level.

Virtually all of this body of research on spatial mismatch is based on US experience, but McCormick (1986) showed that similar effects were also evident in racially mixed areas in Britain. Asian or West Indian minority workers in Greater London had 25% longer commute times than similar white workers. In the West Midlands for manual workers the difference in average commuting distance was up to 35%. McCormick presented instrumental variable estimates using both commuting distance and time as the dependent variables, with earnings and car use treated as endogenous. Strongly significant racial dummy variables were consistently found, agreeing with a theoretical model in which nonwhites adjust to lower job offer possibilities by means of wider search areas and greater willingness to commute.

An ambitious attempt to use simultaneous equations techniques at an MSA-wide level came from Galster (1987). Previous studies, he suggested, had not handled the simultaneity problem well. He developed a four equation simultaneous model, in which the endogenous variables comprised the black/white median income ratio, degree of centralisation of jobs, an index of occupational dissimilarity, and indices of housing discrimination from a US (H.U.D) Housing

Market Practices Survey. The system was estimated using two stage least squares, supported by a Hausman specification test.

A microstudy of spatial mismatch using the percentage of blacks employed by industrial firms, related to the distance from the principal black ghetto, was carried out by Leonard (1987) and tested using Federal Contract Compliance data, focusing on a comparison of Chicago and Los Angeles. A strong distance effect was found for both Chicago and Los Angeles, but Leonard suggested that the spatial mismatch phenomenon was more damaging in Chicago because of more intense segregation there. Average commuting times were substantially lower in Los Angeles. Zax (1990) provided another test of spatial mismatch phenomena using evidence from a single large Detroit company which decentralised to Dearborn. Clearly, after the move some black employees had moved to new suburban mixed or ghetto neighbourhoods, added to those who commuted "down the rent gradient". With the firm's suburbanisation, black commute times altered from being shorter than those for whites (with given characteristics) to being longer. The paper did not really address the simultaneous interaction with longer term residential location decisions, indicated by the finding that black commute times to the suburban workplace decreased with age and job tenure.

One of the most ingenious attempts to put some empirical detail on the costs of spatial mismatch was carried out by Hughes and Madden (1991). Using micro Census data for three cities, estimates were constructed of both rent and wage gradients, with the intention of estimating the incidence of *sub-optimality* induced by the residential patterns of both whites and blacks, for the fully employed labour force. Hughes and Madden were able to offer estimates of sub-optimality of the spatial distribution of jobs, given the residential pattern, or of residences given the jobs, or of both unconstrained. Although significance testing was not attempted, they found that the pattern of black residences given the jobs was actually better than that for whites, though the pattern of black jobs, given the residences, did impose suboptimalities. As a result they agreed with the modern view that differences in access in terms of information may be more important than commuting cost access.

The mid 1980s saw discussions of US spatial mismatch at a disaggregated level being dominated by the sheer scale of black youth unemployment. An influential paper by Ellwood (1986) estimated that, if nonemployment was included along with unemployment, about half of all black teenagers out of school were "looking for work but can't find it". The spatial mismatch problem could be most simply put as—would spatially rearranging jobs, with aggregate demand fixed, have beneficial effects on black unemployment? Ellwood's study focused on Chicago, and experimented with three alternative access measures for each zone. A series of weighted OLS regressions found that access measures in fact played a rather weak role in explaining the employment rate.

These results have been criticised (e.g., by Ihlanfeldt and Sjoquist, (1990)) for the absence of race subsampling, and the zone level subaggregates approach. Ellwood felt however that he had supported the view that the impact of access on wage rates was too small to play the dominant role claimed for it, and that

> Race, not space, remains the key explanatory variable.
>
> (Ellwood 1986: p. 149)

He offered a range of alternative tests, questioning the overemphasis given to access. For example, comparisons of the two main areas of black residence in Chicago, the South and West side ghettos, offered a "natural experiment" in the importance of access on labour market outcomes, given that the West side was substantially more accessible to blue collar employment concentrations. In fact, he found little difference in the unemployment or employment rate outcomes for the two areas, apart from the West side area having shorter average travel times. Leonard's (1986) discussion of Ellwood's paper stressed the fact that the impact of access (distance to the ghetto) on black employment share may be rising in the 1980s as

> ... black employment collapsed in the direction of the ghetto.
>
> (Leonard, 1986: p. 189)

Another recent paper questioning the importance of racial differences in job access made use of national US data on journey to work times and distances (Gordon et al., 1989b). Using a $\chi^2$ test, they found they could not reject a hypothesis of the same distribution of work trip *distances*, and the authors claimed that this discredited both the "ghetto trap" (or spatial mismatch) hypothesis, as well as the suggestion that "poorer meant shorter" in commuting distance, though in theory these two phenomena could have cancelled each other out. The commuting time evidence is probably dominated by questions of transit vs. auto use. The authors would find much agreement in concluding that:

> Structural unemployment is a much more complex problem than inaccessibility to jobs.
>
> (Gordon et al., 1989b: p. 325)

## 7.5. Some recent research using microsamples

Finally, a series of papers using microsamples has attempted to estimate the role of job access and race in the context of the much weaker US job market of the 1980s. Ihlanfeldt (1988) used 1980 Public Use Micro Sample (PUMS) data on Atlanta ("one of the most segregated cities in the US") and found that white wage premia were paid in some "labour shortage suburbs" in service sector jobs, but that black wage premia were also paid in blue and white collar jobs in the outer suburbs.

Ihlanfeldt and Sjoquist (1989) used 1978 microdata, with complementary MSA Census data, to estimate annual earnings of central city residents *net* of commuting costs. This is related to an index of decentralisation of low skill jobs, and a number of human capital variables. They found a significant negative effect of low skill job suburbanisation on the net wage for both black and white central city men, but not for black women. This raised the issue of the degree to which black women may substitute for teenagers in terms of labour demand. They also found no support for the idea that the more segregated a city, the more the adverse effect on the net wage. The paper also offered probit estimates of the move probability, and found that low skill job suburbanisation was a significant move-promoter for whites but not for blacks.

Ihlanfeldt and Sjoquist (1990) switched back to using microdata for a specific city, Philadelphia. They tried to improve significantly on earlier studies of access effects by using mean travel time for zones, and presenting logit estimates on samples of youths or adults by race. The authors found the adverse impact of mean journey to work time on employment probability, together with a number of the personal and family characteristics variables and comparative runs for Chicago and Los Angeles were offered. The issue remains that estimates of the access effect are trying to separate out a labour supply mechanism, which itself mixes commuting cost and information decay considerations, from racial discrimination forces which are largely demand side. Single equation specifications will always be open to this weakness.

The PUMS 1980 data was also used by Ihlanfeldt and Sjoquist (1991a) to address three alternative explanations of black wage discrimination. Firstly, there is the suggestion that white dominated areas have "better jobs", secondly the conventional spatial mismatch mechanism of racial residential mix affecting the hiring of blacks, and thirdly the possible tendency for black workers to be biased towards the public sector, the so-called "sheltered workplace" hypothesis. Ihlanfeldt and Sjoquist used this data set of over 200,000 observations in 9 major metropolitan areas. They used a multinomial logit technique for employment by occupation category with the percentage black residents in the area as the principal racial variable, in addition to education, experience and a range of other dummy variables. A Wald test was used to test the significance of the black residence variable on the occupational hiring pattern. The main finding was that black males are more likely to get managerial or sales jobs, the higher the percentage of black residents. The "sheltered workplace" hypothesis, however, was not supported.

Further use of logit regression technique using the 1980 PUMS data was provided in Ihlanfeldt and Sjoquist (1991b), who focused on teenagers living at home in central cities. Average commuting times by private car were estimated to low wage jobs and used as the principal index of job access. Other labour market variables were included at an MSA level, such as indices of occupations suitable for youths, and a ratio of numbers of low education white females to youths to indicate competitiveness between these types of labour supply. These additional variables gave the single equation specification a strong supply side orientation. Ihlanfeldt and Sjoquist concluded that equalising access time to jobs between blacks and whites would reduce the probability-of-employment gap by about 19–23%.

Recent ideas on testing the importance of access for youth employment have shifted towards attempts to quantify informational or networking elements of access, rather than the spatial. O'Regan and Quigley (1991) also used the 1980 PUMS data and found that the importance of parent or sibling working could itself represent both beneficial network and information effects, mixed with the role of family values and culture. They also constructed isolation indices to represent the level of social isolation within races, and these functioned well empirically. They identified a large increase since 1970 in the spatial concentration of US urban poverty, and the social and informational isolation associated with this has identifiable labour market impacts. The programmes implied by such findings, rather than the transportation or job creation orientation stressed in the 1970s, involve the difficult task of:

> ... improving the social connections of poor black youth.
>
> (O'Regan and Quigley, 1991: p. 291)

## 8. Interurban differentials in labour market outcomes

### 8.1. Interurban variation in unemployment rates and durations

The interurban study of unemployment rates has raised a number of research issues. These include the roles labour force characteristics, city size, the time lag structure, and microsurvey evidence.

Firstly, the "characteristics approach", used subaggregate data on labour force attributes to explain unemployment rates, mainly from a supply side viewpoint (Metcalf, 1975; Evans and Richardson, 1981). Such work relied on OLS estimates, with little attempt made to represent the simultaneities. In addition, Metcalf's (1975) paper, based on English County Boroughs, was criticised for treating near-contiguous areas as independent, a problem well addressed by Evans and Richardson (1981). The unsurprising conclusion was that urban areas with higher proportions male unskilled in the labour force had higher male unemployment rates. Newly arriving immigrant workers had selected those urban areas or regions offering better labour market opportunities. The Evans and Richardson (1981) extensions showed that the characteristics "explanation" for unemployment became weaker the more self-contained were the labour markets studied.

Work using British Census data focusing on youth and adult male unemployment (Layard, 1982) found an elasticity of 0.6 for youth unemployment against the adult rate in a cross-section of English cities. This paper addressed macroeconomic labour market issues of the variation of the youth/adult unemployment ratio over time, without offering much spatial detail, or simultaneous labour market insights.

City size and unemployment rates have also received a modest level of attention. Vipond (1974) provided one of the first papers to use Census data to compute OLS estimates of the relationships between male or female unemployment rates and city size. Some of the sample cities were very much *not* self-contained labour markets. Vipond did suggest an interesting tendency in Britain for male unemployment rates to rise with city size to a maximum, and female rates to fall to a minimum in cities of around 1/2 million population. A useful discussion of the "pros and cons of size" suggested bigger urban labour markets may, in addition to efficient search, generate adverse impacts through employers feeling no need to hoard labour in downturns. Sirmans (1977) re-estimated and revised these specifications, using more modern techniques to account for possible interactions between the male and female urban labour markets.

More recent work on this question by Alperovich (1993) used Israeli data and focused on both the rate of overall and long term unemployment. The suggestion was that urbanisation economies may be more clearly evident in the avoidance of long term unemployment. Israeli urban areas varying in age structure and average educational level, did show a tendency to have a lower rate of long term unemployment for bigger urban areas.

A modest number of papers have considered interurban unemployment differentials using microdata. One of the most influential of these was Marston (1985) who stressed that unemployment differentials can be seen as representing either disequilibrium, the result of limited mobility and adjustment, or the equilibrium result of amenity preferences. Marston presents time series estimation for aggregate unemployment rates in 30 US MSAs. He estimated a dynamic model using iterative nonlinear methods. His results suggested that unemployment differentials would in fact disappear quite quickly through migration flows, if there were no amenity or other differences to sustain them:

> ... the main component of area unemployment rate differentials is a local equilibrium component, in that it persists much longer than the time necessary to eliminate it through migration.
>
> (Marston, 1985: p. 66)

The paper then used a large sample of microdata from the 1970 PUMS to obtain probit estimates in which the dichotomous unemployment variable was explained by a combination of human capital, amenity, and purely economic variables. In this equilibrium equation, the higher wage compensates for higher risk of unemployment as do higher amenity levels. Despite the formidable size of the data base, there is still a combination of equilibrium and dynamic mechanisms, which are difficult to model effectively.

A study by Moffitt (1985) focused more closely on the dynamics of unemployment using maximum likelihood methods with a sample of completed unemployment spells over 1978–1993. The impacts of the exhaustion of unemployment insurance on the "ending spell" hazard was successfully estimated, as were racial differences. Kaplan–Meier statistics showed the "spike" in the hazard over time especially at the unemployment insurance exhaustion point. Moffitt also raised the issue of positive duration dependence of the job-finding hazard, which interacts with the time pattern of unemployment insurance, also addressed by Bailey (1994) with a Weibull hazard model, estimated using a sample of over 12,000 aged 14–21. The concentration on youth was important because of "job habit formation", and the adverse impacts of concentrated youth unemployment. Positive duration dependency for the "leave unemployment" probability was found, and a range of 30 independent variables were used to try to minimise the bias caused by unobserved heterogeneity. These included factors such as recent moves and mortgaged housing capital. Positive duration dependence itself partly reflects "job shopping" by less risk averse young people, and the exhaustion of savings. Finally, a British paper by Elliott and Theodossiou (1992) focused on the distribution of the time structure of completed periods of unemployment, for a sample of about 1000 adults in the city of Aberdeen. Lorenz curves and Gini coefficients were calculated and revealed a clear minority who suffered disproportionately from frequent spells.

The problem of the distributed lag structure in fluctuations in unemployment between urban areas has yet to receive much detailed research attention. Gordon, in two papers (1985a,b) suggested that there has in effect been a "modelling vacuum" in studying the complex patterns of lags arising in the spatial transmission of employment and unemployment differentials. The recent slowdown in UK migration as a result of higher unemployment rates has weakened interurban and regional supply adjustments. In particular, the cyclical sensitivity of unemployment was highest in high unemployment regions. Through a very imperfectly understood spatial adjustment, unemployment responds to adjacent interregional change with a distributed lag, even if employment has no lag, or only a discrete lag:

> ... it is clear that rather more complex models are required, which incorporate explicitly the supply-side adjustment process.
>
> (Gordon, 1985b: p. 855)

## 8.2. Wage rates—interurban differentials

There are formidable data problems in standardising occupationally specific wage rates for local price levels. Early papers addressed the issue of to what extent earnings or unemployment could tend to equilibrium, depending on a range of amenity variables.

For instance Reza (1978) used an orthogonal regression technique to model the systematic variation of average earnings and unemployment, with interurban efficiency and amenity differences acting as "shift variables". Cropper and Arriaga-Salines (1980) produced a simultaneous model of real wage determination (normalised for nonproperty prices) for 28 US MSAs. This treats employment and air pollution endogenously, and led to empirical estimates of the willingness to pay for specific reductions in $SO_2$. Ehrenberg and Goldstein's (1975) model was on municipal wage rates. Using a cross-section of US cities, reduced form estimates identified the influences of public sector unions, the form of municipal government (specifically "city manager" cities vs. others), and possible monopsony power of local government.

More recent research on interurban or interregional labour market outcomes, has also provided detailed discussion of US/Europe differences in the adjustment mechanism (Blanchard and Katz (1992)). The authors found that in America labour mobility is the dominant adjustment mechanism in generating convergence in relative wages and unemployment rates:

> ... transitory changes in growth lead to transitory fluctuations in relative unemployment and wages.
>
> (Blanchard and Katz, 1992: p. 52)

There have been examples in the US (e.g., the Massachusetts boom and bust) where the adjustment process was inefficient, through excessive labour mobility and imperfect capital markets. In particular, the response of job creation to movements in wages appears weak. In post-Single Market Europe, the efficiency of labour mobility is much lower, so that unless there is more wage flexibility:

> ... shocks will have larger and longer lasting effects in relative unemployment in Europe.
>
> (Blanchard and Katz, 1992: p. 56)

Interurban studies of wages geared towards the demand side have included the influential work of Glaeser et al. (1992), which focused on mechanisms through which knowledge spillovers can affect wage differentials. Three paradigms included a Marshall–Arrow–Romer intraindustry spillover process, Porter-style competitive innovation, and Jane Jacobs urbanisation externalities working through diversification. A 31 year time series of employment and wage growth in major US cities for the major industries in each MSA is used for OLS estimates of city-industry observations. The sample is inevitably biased towards "mature" industries. Of the alternatives, they rejected the strong version of Marshall–Arrow–Romer knowledge spillovers. If anything they lend support to a Jacobs-type tendency for urbanisation externalities to promote industrial diversification. The models however have a reduced form character, and:

> ... many of our findings can be explained by a mechanical model in which industries grow where labor is cheap and demand is high.
>
> (Glaeser et al., 1992: p. 1151)

## 8.3. Quality of life indicators

The important development of urban quality of life measures and their detailed empirical estimation is discussed in detail elsewhere in this volume by Gyourko, Kahn and Tracy (Chapter 37). There are interactions between quality of life analysis and urban labour market phenomena, both inter- and intraurban which makes this a fertile research area receiving active interest in the 1980s and 1990s in both Europe and the US.

Cheshire and colleagues (1986, 1990, 1995, 1996), in a series of innovative papers extending urban quality of life analysis to the countries of the European Union, designed a "problem index" (an inverse of quality of life) using discriminant analysis based on a "training set" of European Functional Urban Regions (FURs). This work is discussed in detail elsewhere in this volume, but it is worth recalling that unemployment and in-migration rates are included in the urban area attributes, a weighted average of which made up the problem index, which as a result was geared much more towards the labour market components of quality of life than the compensations operating through the housing market. European-wide data on the housing market would be virtually impossible to collect reliably, so that European replications of the US models discussed above would be very difficult. The body of research put together by Cheshire and colleagues is, perhaps, most useful in identifying medium to long term patterns of change in European urban welfare, using the problem index, and speculating on the impact of urban policy by analysing problem score residuals, in addition to the awareness of problems of growth as well as of decline.

## 9. Intraurban wage and unemployment differences

### 9.1. Wage gradient estimation

Considering the established place this relationship has in urban economics, there have been relatively few studies of the variation of wage rates by location within urban areas. Moses' (1962) seminal theoretical paper developed the idea of the wage rate for a standard unit of labour declining with CBD distance so as to preserve equilibrium between workers commuting inwards to jobs at different radial distances. More substantial suburban employment subcentres would modify this (Ravallion (1979) and Madden (1985)).

The problem has been the difficulty of standardising occupations so that the wage rate itself was well-defined. Supply side characteristic variables also play a role, as does the difficulty over which measure of distance or accessibility to use for an employer.

The first substantial empirical urban study of labour markets was the Rees and Schultz (1970) monograph, based on detailed evidence for Chicago. Even here, there was little spatial detail as such, but substantial insight on alternative job search methods. Given its focus on the impact of gender on commuting distance, the volume is as relevant to Sections 4 and 6 of this chapter as to the wage gradient issue. It makes use of microdata to shed light on the commuting distance/wage relationship, for a range of manual occupations which may be simpler to study for wage gradients given the weaker role of salary structures. A consistent positive effect of commuting distance on the wage rate is found, though this is understood more as a compensation for commuters to relatively inaccessible suburban subcentres, than a monocentric wage gradient.

In the Wachter (1972) study of the Boston, Massachusetts labour market, the focus was more on the dynamics of change in the wage distribution over the business cycle, for an individual urban labour market. This was most immediately in evidence in the narrowing of wage dispersion under boom conditions. A suburban wage premium for female clerical workers was evident, though this lost significance as the late 1960s boom developed. No evidence of wage premia was found in other worker subgroups, though sample sizes may have been too small for results to be robust.

Empirical work on New York City and Toronto was provided by Scott (1988). He showed that production worker wage rates had become higher in the suburban rings of these cities, though it is difficult to separate the role of compensation for commuting from that of labour shortage at suburban employment subcentres. Labour turnover rates were higher in New York City than in the suburban ring, implying that job stability and seniority played a part in addition to spatial factors.

Eberts (1981) was one of the few who tested the wage gradient in a monocentric form. Eberts limited himself to five subgroups of Chicago area municipal employees, estimating a reduced form with wage rates explained by CBD distance together with labour demand and supply characteristics interacting with distance. The estimation technique used a Box–Cox transformation and maximum likelihood techniques. Eberts found a significant wage gradient for four of the five labour groups, and a typical wage-distance elasticity was around 0.2–0.3. The restriction to homogeneous municipal labour groups was useful, but the wage gradient interacted with unionisation and the size of the municipal government.

The theoretical treatment of the wage gradient in a model of optimal residential location choice was outlined by Madden (1985), who included hours of work, demographic variables and rent levels in microestimates using recent residence or job movers in the Panel Survey of Income Dynamics. Her model had the change in commuting distance as the dependent variable, affected positively by the wage rate, and although housing rents entered the theory, empirically they were proxied by residential distance. Madden claimed that:

> ... these results provide clear evidence of the existence of wage gradients.
> (Madden, 1985: p. 300)

In effect, this work is also a contribution to the simultaneous modelling of residential and workplace choice. One of Madden's strongest findings is that the impact of wage change on work trip change is much greater for household heads who job-change only, suggesting that job search and labour market flexibility from a fixed residence may dominate dynamic wage gradient modelling.

Ihlanfeldt (1992) made use for three major urban areas (Philadelphia, Detroit, and Boston) of the workplace and wage detail available in the 1980 PUMS, and estimated wage gradient equations incorporating Box–Cox transformations. He found that the predictions of the monocentric model were confirmed consistently for white workers. However, as we have discussed elsewhere, black workers were more likely to "reverse commute" from central city to suburb, and where job concentrations were located in the suburbs, the monocentric model would predict wage gradients sloping the other way (positively with CBD distance). Only patchy evidence was found for this, not surprising given the localised nature of the job concentrations. This was the only paper which focused clearly on the common ground between wage gradients and racial segregation in US cities.

## 9.2. *Intraurban differentials in unemployment*

The empirical study of variation of unemployment rates between different jurisdictions of a large urban area is one of the easier targets for urban labour market research, and London has received close attention.

Metcalf and Richardson (1980) conducted OLS cross-sectional regressions using London Borough Census data on male unemployment rates which were well explained by a mixture of supply side (age, % married, % unskilled) and demand side (relative number of male redundancies preceding 1971) variables. Although it provided some reinforcement of the view that demand side shocks "ripple out" quickly across a large and well-connected urban labour market, there is a rather uncomfortable mixture of demand and supply side factors, and little attention to disequilibria and the full simultaneous operation of the urban labour market.

Cheshire (1979) also provided a sharp and insightful discussion of the London urban labour market, with special reference to the urban policy instruments under discussion in Britain in the late 1970s, the development of which had not shown much awareness of urban labour market processes. The role of a "trap" mechanism for the poorest subgroups for example, could easily be oversimplified:

> It was not the lowest socio-economic groups who might have been trapped that suffered relatively the most unemployment in the GLC area, but the higher groups.
>
> (Cheshire, 1979: p. 37)

It also should always be kept clearly in mind that:

> 'Spatial' inequality may thus be just another and rather unimportant dimension of social inequality. It may consequently be best relieved by policies aimed at greater social equality.
>
> (Cheshire, 1979: p. 41)

Other research addressing intraurban unemployment patterns has included Vipond's papers (1980, 1984) on the Sydney area. This relates to gender patterns of labour market outcomes, as revealed by Australian Census data for local male and female unemployment rates. Vipond found, particularly for the less buoyant recent period, that once skill level, the migrant proportion, and lack of mobility were accounted for, there was a *positive* unemployment gradient with CBD distance for both males and females. This would seem to indicate the weakness of suburban employment development, which may itself be overtaken by events.

American research along these lines has tended to be rare, perhaps because of very large central cities in labour market data. Madden and Stull (1991) offered an alternative approach, based on data for 1500 households in metropolitan Philadelphia. This microsample showed how the buoyant growth of the late 1980s bore fruit in reduced poverty incidence, and sharp improvements in relative incomes of black and Hispanic families. Over the 1980s there was a significant rise in the employment/population ratio, with only limited in- migration response. This real labour market outcome improvement was not dissipated in wage rate rises, and there was strong evidence (as discussed by Cheshire (1979)) of the prime importance in urban labour markets of real macroeconomic factors.

## 10. Conclusions

One finishes a survey of this substantial part of the field of applied urban economics by being impressed by some things but disappointed by others. The use of modern computing power and econometric technique has been coupled (at least in the US) with microdata samples of substantial size to make enormous advances in the sophistication of empirical analysis of urban labour market phenomena. A more limited amount of research of comparable quality has been carried out by Dutch, British, or French researchers.

However despite these advances in analytical and computational power, the estimated models are only as good as the data they analyse, and many labour market phenomena of importance are simply not observable anyway. For example, the activity of job search itself is largely nonobservable, merely its successful outcome; likewise the internal "politics of the family" which affects the commuting, move and quit behaviour of cohabiting partners. The vast complexity of labour market behaviour once location is added to other relevant variables sometimes defeats analysis. A plea for more high quality microlevel data becomes ever more appropriate, as labour market problems are given more priority politically. It would be comforting to think that Eurostat as well as the European national governments might get to work on providing the kind of longitudinal microdata which would encourage better understanding of the urban labour market in Europe, where residential move rates tend to be lower than in the US, and the role of welfare benefit payments generally higher.

Among the trends, shared in varying measure by all countries, which emerged over the time span covered by this survey are the tendency for greater earnings inequality, partly as a result of the growth of a more advanced service sector. The higher earning elite has become relatively richer, but often in parallel with shorter job tenure and higher job aspirations by their domestic partners, both of which then become incorporated in their labour market decisions. At least this part of the labour market is normally well caught by data samples.

There has also been a trend towards further deterioration in the labour market position of those youths and members of disadvantaged ethnic groups who have not thrived in the state education system. In the US, suburbanization of blacks has proceeded apace, but a large underclass has still been left behind in central city areas where total formal employment has often been stagnant. The issue of "nonemployment" as distinct from unemployment again raises the problem for economists that important processes are taking place beyond the reach of observed data. Cultural and social forces have always been somewhere on the stage of the urban labour market, and may be progressively playing a greater role.

Within the reach of empirical research there are perhaps two major issues which have continued to receive detailed attention, and will no doubt continue to do so. The first is the question of the compensation for commuting distance, its interaction with the extent and intensity of search for jobs, and the parallel interaction with spatial variation of house prices. In practice, analysis of this has been made more difficult by the additional roles of family structure and the career aspirations of men and women, and the continuing question of spatial mismatch and residential segregation of ethnic subgroups.

Even more difficult is the study of long term individual labour market behaviour, in which personal characteristics, earnings, education, and occupation all affect and are affected by location in a metropolitan area. Good research of these dynamic phenomena depend largely on the size and quality of the data bases available. Some high quality research has emerged in the last 20 years, but a great deal more in the way of empirical foundations for labour market and welfare policies can be achieved especially in Europe.

# References

Alperovich, G. (1993), "City size and the rate and duration of unemployment: Evidence from Israeli data", Journal of Urban Economics 34:347–357.

Andrulis, J. (1982), "Intra-urban workplace and residential mobility under uncertainty", Journal of Urban Economics 11:85–97.

Bailey, A.J. (1994), "Migration and unemployment duration among young adults", Papers in Regional Science 73:289–307.

Bailey, M.J. (1959), "Note on the economics of residential zoning and urban renewal", Land Economics 35:288–292.

Bailey, M.J. (1966), "Effects of race and other demographic factors on the values of single family homes", Land Economics 42:215–220.

Ball, R.M. (1980), "The use and definition of travel-to-work areas in Great Britain: some problems", Regional Studies 14:125–139.

Bane, M.J. and D.T. Ellwood (1994), *Welfare Realities: From Rhetoric to Reform* (Harvard University Press, Cambridge, Massachusetts).

Barron. J.M. and O. Gilley (1981), "Job search and vacancy contacts: Note", American Economic Review 71:747–752.

Bartel, A.P. (1979), "The migration decision: what role does job mobility play?", American Economic Review 69:775–786.

Bartik, T.J. (1994), "The effects of metropolitan job growth on the size distribution of family income", Journal of Regional Science 34:483–502.

Baumann, J., M.M. Fischer and U. Schubert (1988), "A choice-theoretical labour market model: empirical tests at the mesolevel", Environment and Planning A 20:1085–1102.

Beesley, M.E. and M.O. Dalvi (1974), "Spatial equilibrium and the journey to work", Journal of Transport Economics and Policy 8:197–222.

Blanchard, O. and L. Katz (1992), "Regional evolutions", Brookings Papers on Economic Activity 1:1–61.

Blomquist, G.C., M.C. Berger and J.P. Hoehn (1988), "New estimates of quality of life in urban areas", American Economic Review 78:89–107.

Boarnet, M.G. (1994), "The monocentric model and employment location", Journal of Urban Economics 36:79–97.

Bound, J. and H.J. Holzer (1993), "Industrial shifts, skill level and the labor market for white and black males", Review of Economics and Statistics 75:387–396.

Boyle, P. (1994), "Metropolitan out-migration in England and Wales, 1980–81", Urban Studies 31:1707–1722.

Brun, J. and J. Fagnani (1994), "Lifestyles and locational choices: a case study of middle-class couples living in the Ile-de-France region", Urban Studies 31:921–934.

Burridge, P. and I.R. Gordon (1981), "Unemployment in the British metropolitan areas", Oxford Economic Papers 33:274–297.

Cheshire, P.C. (1979), "Spatial labour markets; a critique of the inner area studies", Urban Studies 16:29–43.

Cheshire, P.C. (1990), "Explaining the recent performance of the European Community's major urban regions", Urban Studies 27:311–333.

Cheshire, P.C. (1995), "A new phase of urban development in western Europe? The evidence for the 1980s", Urban Studies 32:1045–1063.

Cheshire, P.C. and G. Carbonaro (1996), "Urban economic growth in Europe", Urban Studies 33:1111–1128.

Cheshire, P.C., G. Carbonaro and D.G. Hay (1986), "Problems of urban decline and growth in EEC countries: or measuring degrees of elephantness", Urban Studies 23:131–149.

Chirinko, R. (1982), "An empirical investigation of the returns to job search", American Economic Review 72:498–501.

Cloutier, N.R. (1997), "Metropolitan income inequality during the 1980s: the impact of urban development, industrial mix, and family structure", Journal of Regional Science 37:459–478.

Congdon, P. (1987), "The interdependence of geographical migration with job and housing mobility in London", Regional Studies 22:81–93.

Coombes, M.G. and S. Openshaw (1982), "The use and definition of travel-to-work areas in Great Britain: some comments", Regional Studies 16:141–149.

Courant, P. and J. Yinger (1977), "On models of racial prejudice and urban residential structure", Journal of Urban Economics 4:272–291.

Crampton, G.R. (1990), "Commuting between local authorities in England and Wales: Econometric evidence from the 1981 Census", Journal of Urban Economics 28:204–222.

Cropper, M.L. and A.S. Arriaga-Salinas (1980), "Inter-city wage differentials and the value of air quality", Journal of Urban Economics 8:236–254.

Cropper, M.L. and P.L. Gordon (1991), "Wasteful commuting: a reexamination", Journal of Urban Economics 29:2–13.

Danziger, S. and M. Weinstein (1976), "Employment location and wage rates of poverty area residents", Journal of Urban Economics 3:127–145.

Eberts, R.W. (1981), "An empirical investigation of intra-urban wage gradients", Journal of Urban Economics 10:50–60.

Ehrenberg, R.G. and G.S. Goldstein (1975), "A model of public sector wage determination", Journal of Urban Economics 2:223–245.

Elliott, R.F. and I. Theodossiou (1992), "The inequality of unemployment experience in a local labour market", Urban Studies 29:783–797.

Ellwood, D.T. (1986), "The spatial mismatch hypothesis: are there teenage jobs missing in the ghetto?", in: R.B. Freeman and H.J. Holzer, eds., The Black Youth Employment Crisis (University of Chicago Press, Chicago).

Evans, A.W. and R. Richardson (1981), "Urban unemployment: interpretation and additional evidence", Scottish Journal of Political Economy 28:107–124.

Evers, G.H.M. and A. van der Veen (1985), "A simultaneous nonlinear model for labour migration and commuting", Regional Studies 19:217–229.

Fagnani, J. (1983), "Women's commuting patterns in the Paris region", Tijdschrift voor economische en sociale geografie 74:12–24.

Fagnani, J. (1984), "Marital status and occupational structures in the Ile-de-France region", Urban Studies 21:139–148.

Fagnani, J. (1990), "City size and mothers' labour force participation", Tijdschrift voor economische en sociale geografie 81:182–188.

Felsenstein, D. (1994), "Large high-technology firms and the spatial extension of metropolitan labour markets: some evidence from Israel", Urban Studies 31:867–893.

Frank, R.H. (1978), "Family location constraints and the geographic distribution of female professionals", Journal of Political Economy 86:117–130.

Freeman R.B. and H. Holzer (1986), The Black Youth Employment Crisis (University of Chicago Press, Chicago).

Galster, G. (1987), "Residential segregation and interracial economic disparities: a simultaneous equations approach", Journal of Urban Economics 21:21–44.

Gera, S. and P. Kuhn (1980a), "Job location and the journey to work: an empirical analysis", Journal of Socio-Economic Planning Science 14:57–65.

Gera, S. and P. Kuhn (1980b), "An empirical model of residential location and the journey to work in a metropolitan area", Journal of Socio-Economic Planning Science 14:67–77.

Glaeser, E.L., H.D. Kallal, J.A. Scheinkman and A. Schleifer (1992), "Growth in cities", Journal of Political Economy 100:1126–1152.

Glaeser, E.L., J.A. Scheinkman and A. Schleifer (1995), "Economic growth in a cross-section of cities", Journal of Monetary Economics 36:117–144.

Goldner, W. (1955), "Spatial and locational aspects of metropolitan labour markets", American Economic Review 45:111–128.

Gordon, I.R. (1985a), "The cyclical sensitivity of regional employment and unemployment differentials", Regional Studies 19:95–110.

Gordon, I.R. (1985b), "Distributed lags in local responses to fluctuations in unemployment", Environment and Planning A 17:845–856.

Gordon, I.R. (1996), "Family structure, educational achievement and the inner city", Urban Studies 33:407–423.

Gordon, I.R. and D. Lamont (1982), "A model of labour market interdependencies in the London region", Environment and Planning A 14:237–264.

Gordon, I.R. and I. Molho (1995), "Duration dependence in migration behaviour: cumulative inertia versus stochastic change", Environment and Planning A 27:1961–1975.

Gordon, I.R. and R.W. Vickerman (1982), "Opportunity, preference and constraint: an approach to the analysis of metropolitan migration", Urban Studies 19:247–261.

Gordon, P., and H.W. Richardson (1996a), "Employment decentralization in US metropolitan areas: is Los Angeles an outlier or the norm?", Environment and Planning A 28:1727–1744.

Gordon, P., and H.W. Richardson (1996b), "Beyond polycentricity: the dispersed metropolis, Los Angeles 1970–90", Journal of the American Planning Association 62:289–295.

Gordon, P., A. Kumar and H.W. Richardson (1989a), "Gender differences in metropolitan travel behaviour", Regional Studies 23:499–510.

Gordon, P., A. Kumar and H.W. Richardson (1989b), "The spatial mismatch hypothesis: some new evidence", Urban Studies 26:315–326.

Gordon, R.J. (1982), "Comment on: Time series changes in youth joblessness", in: R.B. Freeman and D.A. Wise, eds., The Youth Labor Market Problem: Its Nature, Causes and Consequences (University of Chicago Press, Chicago) pp. 189–198.

Gottfries, N. and B. McCormick (1995), "Discrimination and open unemployment in a segmented labour market", European Economic Review 39:1–16.

Gottschalk, P. and R. Moffitt (1994), "The growth of earnings instability in the US labor market", Brookings Papers on Economic Activity 2:217–272.

Green, A.E. and D.W. Owen (1990), "The development of a classification of travel-to-work areas", Progress in Planning 34:1–92.

Gruver, G.W. and L.A. Zeager (1994), "Steady-state labor turnover as optimal household behaviour", Journal of Regional Science 34:75–90.

Gyourko, J. and J. Tracy (1989), "The importance of local fiscal conditions in analyzing local labor markets", Journal of Political Economy 97:1208–1231.

Gyourko, J. and J. Tracy (1991), "The structure of local public finance and the quality of life", Journal of Political Economy 99:774–806.

Hamnett, C. (1994), "Social polarisation in global cities—theory and evidence", Urban Studies 31:401–424.

Hanson, S. and I. Johnston (1985), "Gender differences in work-trip length: explanations and implications", Urban Geography 3:193–219.

Hanson, S. and G. Pratt (1988), "Spatial dimensions of the gender division of labor in a local labor market", Urban Geography 9:180–202.

Hanson, S. and G. Pratt (1992), "Dynamic dependencies—a geographic investigation of local labor markets", Economic Geography 68:373–405.

Hanson, S. and G. Pratt (1995), Gender, Work and Place (London, New York: Routledge).

Harrison, B. (1972a), "Education and underemployment in the urban ghetto", American Economic Review 62:796–812.

Harrison, B. (1972b), "The intrametropolitan distribution of minority economic welfare", Journal of Regional Science 12:23–43.

Harrison, B. (1974), Urban Economic Development: Suburbanization, Minority Opportunity, and the Condition of the Central City (Urban Institute, Washington, DC).

Harrison, B. (1994), Lean and Mean: The Changing Landscape of Corporate Power in the Age of Flexibility (Basic Books, New York).

Hekman, J. (1980), "Income, labor supply and urban residence", American Economic Review 70:805–811.

Herzog, H.W., A.M. Schlottman and D.L. Johnson (1986), "High technology jobs and worker mobility", Journal of Regional Science 26:445–459.

Hochman, O. and H. Ofek (1977), "The value of time in consumption and residential location in an urban setting", American Economic Review 67:996–1003.

Holzer, H.J. (1986), "Reservation wages and their labor market effects for white and black male youth", Journal of Human Resources 21:157–177.

Holzer, H.J. (1987), "Informal job search and black youth unemployment", American Economic Review 77:446–452.

Holzer, H.J. (1988), "Search method use by unemployed youth", Journal of Labor Economics 5:1–20.

Holzer, H.J. (1991), "The spatial mismatch hypothesis: what has the evidence shown?", Urban Studies 28:105–122.

Holzer, H.J. (1994), "Black employment problems: new evidence, old questions", Journal of Policy Analysis and Management 13:699–722.

Holzer, H.J. (1996), What Employers Want: Job Prospects for Less-Educated Workers (Russell Sage Foundation, New York).

Holzer, H.J., K.R. Ihlanfeldt and D.L. Sjoquist (1994), "Work, Search and Travel Among White and Black Youth", Journal of Urban Economics 35:320–345.

Hotchkiss, D. and M.J. White (1993), "A simulation model of a decentralized metropolitan area with two-worker, 'traditional', and female-headed households", Journal of Urban Economics 34:159–185.

Hughes, M.A. and J.F. Madden (1991), "Residential segregation and the economic status of black workers: new evidence for an old debate", Journal of Urban Economics 29:28–49.

Hyclak, T. (1996), "Structural changes in labor demand and unemployment in local labor markets", Journal of Regional Science 36:653–663.

Ihlanfeldt, K.R. (1988), "Intrametropolitan variation in earnings and labor market discrimination: an economic analysis of the Atlanta labor market", Southern Economic Journal 55:123–140.

Ihlanfeldt, K.R. (1992), "Intraurban wage gradients—evidence by race, gender, occupational class and sector", Journal of Urban Economics 32:70–91.

Ihlanfeldt, K.R. (1997), "Information on the spatial distribution of job opportunities within metropolitan areas", Journal of Urban Economics 41:218–242.

Ihlanfeldt, K.R. and D.L. Sjoquist (1989), "The impact of job decentralisation on the economic welfare of central city blacks", Journal of Urban Economics 26:110–130.

Ihlanfeldt, K.R. and D.L. Sjoquist (1990), "Job accessibility and racial differences in youth employment rates", American Economic Review 80:267–276.

Ihlanfeldt, K.R. and D.L. Sjoquist (1991a), "The role of space in determining the occupations of black and white workers", Regional Science and Urban Economics 21:295–315.

Ihlanfeldt, K.R. and D.L. Sjoquist (1991b), "The effect of job access on black youth unemployment: a cross sectional analysis", Urban Studies 28:255–265.

Jencks, C. (1992), Rethinking Social Policy: Race, Poverty and the Underclass (Harvard University Press, Cambridge, Massachusetts).

Jencks, C. (1994), The Homeless (Harvard University Press, Cambridge, Massachusetts).

Jencks, C. and S. Mayer (1989), "Residential segregation, job proximity and black job opportunities: the empirical status of the spatial mismatch hypothesis", in: M. McGeary and L. Lynn, eds., Concentrated Urban Poverty in America (National Academy Press, Washington, D.C.).

Jencks, C. and P.E. Peterson (1991), The Urban Underclass (Brookings Institution, Washington, D.C.).

Johnston-Anumonwo, I. (1988), "The journey to work and occupational segregation", Urban Geography 9:138–154.

Kain, J.F. (1962), "The journey to work as a determinant of residential location", Papers and Proceedings of the Regional Science Association 9:137–160.

Kain, J.F. (1968), "Housing segregation, negro employment, and metropolitan decentralization", Quarterly Journal of Economics 82:175–197.

Kain, J.F. and J. Meyer (1970), "Transportation and poverty", The Public Interest, Winter.

Kalachek, E.D. (1973), "Ghetto dwellers, transportation and employment", in: D.W. Rasmussen and C.T. Haworth, eds., The Modern City (Harper and Row, New York) pp. 72–80.

Kalachek, E.D. and F. Raines (1976), "The structure of wage differences among mature male workers", Journal of Human Resources 11:484–506.

Kasarda, J.D. (1985), "Urban change and minority opportunities", in: P.E. Peterson, ed., The New Urban Reality (Brookings Institution, Washington, D.C.).

Kim, S. (1995), "Excess commuting for two worker households in the Los Angeles Metropolitan Area", Journal of Urban Economics 38:166–182.

Layard, R. (1982), "Youth unemployment in Britain and the United States", in: R.B. Freeman and H.J. Holzer, eds., The Black Youth Employment Crisis (University of Chicago Press, Chicago) pp. 499–531.

Leonard, J.S. (1986), "Comment on D.T. Ellwood's paper", in: R.B. Freeman and H.J. Holzer, eds., The Black Youth Employment Crisis (University of Chicago Press, Chicago and London) pp. 185–190.

Leonard, J. (1987), "The interaction of residential segregation and employment discrimination", Journal of Urban Economics 21:323–346.

Levy, F. and R.J. Murnane (1992), "U.S. Earnings levels and earnings inequality: a review of recent trends and proposed explanations", Journal of Economic Literature 30:1333–1381.

Lillydahl, J.H. and L.D. Singell (1985), "The spatial variation in unemployment and labour force participation rates of male and female workers", Regional Studies 19:459–469.

Linneman, P. and P.E. Graves (1983), "Migration and job change: a multinomial logit approach", Journal of Urban Economics 14:263–279.

MacKinnon, R.D. and P. Rogerson (1980), "Vacancy chains, information filters, and interregional migration", Environment and Planning A 12:649–658.

Madden, J.F. (1977a), "A spatial theory of sex discrimination", Journal of Regional Science 17:369–380.

Madden, J.F. (1977b), "An empirical analysis of the spatial elasticity of labor supply", Papers and Proceedings of the Regional Science Association 39:157–171.

Madden, J.F. (1981), "Why women work closer to home", Urban Studies 18:181–194.

Madden, J.F. (1985), "Urban wage gradients: empirical evidence", Journal of Urban Economics 18:291–301.

Madden, J.F. (1996), "Changes in the distribution of poverty across and within the US metropolitan areas 1979–1989", Urban Studies 33:1581–1600.

Madden, J.F. and L. Chen Chiu (1990), "The wage effects of residential location and commuting constraints on employed married women", Urban Studies 27:353–369.

Madden, J.F. and W.J. Stull (1991), Work, Wages and Poverty—Income Distribution in Post-Industrial Philadelphia (University of Pennsylvania Press, Philadelphia).

Madden, J.F. and M.J. White (1980), "Spatial implications of increases in the female labor force: a theoretical and empirical synthesis", Land Economics 56:432–446.

Maier, G. (1985), "Cumulative causation and selectivity in labour market oriented migration caused by imperfect information", Regional Studies 19:231–241.

Maier, G. (1987), "Job search and migration", in: M.M. Fischer and P. Nijkamp, eds., Regional Labour Markets (North-Holland, Amsterdam) pp. 189–204.

Marston, S.T. (1985), "Two views of the geographic distribution of unemployment", Quarterly Journal of Economics 100:57–79.

Massey, D. (1994), Spatial Divisions of Labour, 2nd edn. (Macmillan, London).

Masters, S.H. (1974), "A note on John Kain's 'Housing segregation, negro employment, and metropolitan decentralization' ", Quarterly Journal of Economics 88:505–519.

Masters, S.H. (1975), Black-White Income Differentials: Empirical Studies and Policy Implications (Academic Press, New York).

McCormick, B. (1986), "Employment opportunity, earnings, and the journey to work of minority workers in Great Britain", Economic Journal 96:375–397.

Merriman, D. and D. Hellerstein (1994), "Compensation for commutes in the land and labor markets: some evidence from the Tokyo metropolitan area", Journal of Regional Science 34:297–324.

Merriman, D., T. Ohkawara and T. Suzuki (1995), "Excess commuting in the Tokyo Metropolitan Area: measurement and policy simulations", Urban Studies 32:69–85.

Metcalf, D. (1975), "Urban unemployment in England", Economic Journal 85:578–589.

Metcalf, D. and R. Richardson (1980), "Unemployment in London", in: A.W. Evans and D. Eversley, eds., The Inner City: Employment and Industry (Heinemann, London) pp. 193–203.

Miller, V.P. and J.M. Quigley (1990), "Segregation by racial and demographic group: evidence from the San Francisco Bay Area", Urban Studies 27:3–21.

Mills, E.S. (1986), "Metropolitan central city population and employment growth during the 1970s", in: M.H. Peston and R.E. Quandt, eds., Prices, Competition and Equilibrium (Barnes and Noble, Lanham, Maryland).

Mills, E.S. (1992), "The measurement and determinants of suburbanization", Journal of Urban Economics 32:377–387.

Mills, E.S. and L.S. Lubuele (1997), "Inner cities", Journal of Economic Literature 35:727–756.

Moffitt, R. (1985), "Unemployment insurance and the distribution of unemployment spells", Journal of Econometrics 28:85–101.

Molho, I. (1995), "Spatial autocorrelation in British unemployment", Journal of Regional Science 35:641–658.

Moore, B. and P. Townroe (1990), Urban Labour Markets: Reviews of Research, Department of the Environment (HMSO, London).

Mortensen, D. (1970), "Job search, the duration of unemployment and the Phillips curve", American Economic Review 60:847–862.

Mortensen, D. (1986), "Job search and labor market analysis", in: O.C. Ashenfelter and R. Layard, eds., Handbook of Labor Economics (Elsevier, Amsterdam) pp. 849–919.

Mortensen, D. and C.A. Pissarides (1994), "Job creation and job destruction in the theory of unemployment", Review of Economic Studies 61:397–416.

Moses, L. (1962), "Towards a theory of intra-urban wage differentials and their influence on travel patterns", Papers and Proceedings of the Regional Science Association 9:53–63.

Myers, S.L. and K.E. Phillips (1979), "Housing segregation and black employment: another look at the ghetto dispersal strategy", American Economic Review, Papers and Proceedings 69:298–302.

Nelson, K. (1986), "Female labor supply characteristics and the suburbanization of low-wage office work", in: A. Scott and M. Storper, eds., Production, Work, Territory (Allen and Unwin, London) pp. 149–171.

Nickell, S.J. (1979), "Estimating the probability of leaving unemployment", Econometrica 47:249–266.

Oaxaca, R. (1973), "Male-female wage differentials in urban labor markets", International Economic Review 14:693–709.

Offner, P. and D.H. Saks (1971), "A note on John Kain's 'Housing segregation, negro employment, and metropolitan decentralization' ", Quarterly Journal of Economics 85:147–160.

Oi, W. (1976), "Residential location and labor supply", Journal of Political Economy 84:S221–247.

O'Regan, K.M. (1993), "The effect of social networks and concentrated poverty on black and hispanic youth unemployment", Annals of Regional Science 27:327–342.

O'Regan, K.M. and J.M. Quigley (1991), "Labor market access and labor market outcomes for urban youth", Regional Science and Urban Economics 21:277–293.

O'Regan, K.M. and J.M. Quigley (1993), "Family networks and youth access to jobs", Journal of Urban Economics 34:230–248.

O'Regan, K.M. and J.M. Quigley (1996), "Teenage employment and the spatial isolation of minority and poverty households", Journal of Human Resources 31:692–702.

Peterson, P.E. (1992), "The urban underclass and the poverty paradox", Political Science Quarterly 106:617–637.

Pickles, A. and P. Rogerson (1984), "Wage distribution and spatial references in competitive job search and migration", Regional Studies 18:131–142.

Piore, M. and C.F. Sabel (1984), The Second Industrial Divide (Basic Books, New York).

Price, R. and E.S. Mills (1985), "Race and residence in earnings determination", Journal of Urban Economics 17:1–18.

Quigley, J.M. and D.H. Weinberg (1977), "Intra-urban residential mobility: a review and synthesis", International Regional Science Review 2:41–66.

Raphael, S. (1998), "The spatial mismatch hypothesis and black youth joblessness: evidence from the San Francisco Bay Area", Journal of Urban Economics 43:79–111.

Ravallion, M. (1979), "A note on intra-urban wage differentials", Urban Studies 16:213–215.

Rees, A.E. and G.P. Schultz (1970), Workers and wages in an urban labor market (University of Chicago Press, Chicago).

Reid, C.E. (1985), "The effect of residential location on the wages of black women and white women", Journal of Urban Economics 18:350–363.

Reza, A.M. (1978), "Geographical differences in earnings and unemployment rates", Review of Economics and Statistics 60:201–208.

Rogers, C.L. (1994), "Job search and unemployment duration: implications for the spatial mismatch hypothesis", Journal of Urban Economics 42:109–132.

Rogerson, P. and R.D. MacKinnon (1981), "A geographical model of job search, migration, and unemployment", Papers of the Regional Science Association 48:89–102.

Rogerson, P. and R.D. MacKinnon (1982), "Interregional migration models with source and interaction information", Environment and Planning A 14:445–454.

Rosen, S. (1979), "Wage-based indexes of urban quality of life", in: P. Mieszkowski and M. Straszheim, eds., Current Issues in Urban Economics (Johns Hopkins Press, Baltimore) pp. 74–104.

Ross, S.L. (1998), "Racial differences in residential and job mobility: evidence concerning the spatial mismatch hypothesis", Journal of Urban Economics 43:112–135.

Ross, S.L. and J. Yinger (1995), "Comparative static analysis of open urban models with a full labor market and suburban employment", Regional Science and Urban Economics 25:575–605.

Rouwendal, J. (1994), "Search theory, spatial labour markets and commuting", Journal of Urban Economics 43:1–22.

Rouwendal, J. and P. Rietveld (1994), "Changes in commuting distances of Dutch households", Urban Studies 31:1545–1557.

Russo, G., P. Rietveld, P. Nijkamp and C. Gorter (1996), "Spatial aspects of recruitment behaviour of firms: an empirical investigation", Environment and Planning A 28:1077–1094.

Sassen, S. (1991), The Global City—New York, London, Tokyo (Princeton University Press, Princeton, N.J.).

Schafer, R. (1978), "Metropolitan form and demographic change", Urban Studies 15:23–33.

Scott, A.J. (1988), Metropolis: From the Division of Labor to Urban Form (University of California Press, Berkeley).

Scott, A.J. (1992a), "The spatial organisation of a local labor market: employment and residential patterns in a cohort of engineering and scientific workers", Growth and Change 23:95–114.

Scott, A.J. (1992b), "Low wage workers in a high technology manufacturing complex", Urban Studies 29:1231–1246.

Scott, A.J. (1993), Technopolis: High Technology Industry and Regional Development in Southern California (University of California Press, Los Angeles).

Scott, A.J. and M. Storper (1986), eds., Production, Work, Territory: The Geographical Anatomy of Industrial Capitalism (Allen and Unwin, London and Winchester, Massachusetts).

Seater, J. (1979), "Job search and vacancy contacts", American Economic Review 69:411–419.

Siegel, J. (1975), "Intrametropolitan migration: a simultaneous model of employment and residential location of white and black households", Journal of Urban Economics 2:29–47.

Simpson, W. (1980), "A simultaneous model of workplace and residential location incorporating job search", Journal of Urban Economics 8:330–349.

Simpson, W. (1982), "Job search and the effect of urban structure on unemployment and married female participation rates", Applied Economics 14:153–165.

Simpson, W. (1987), "Workplace location, residential location and urban commuting", Urban Studies 24:119–128.

Simpson, W. (1990), "Starting even? Job mobility and the wage gap between young single males and females", Applied Economics 22:723–737.

Simpson, W. (1992), Urban Structure and the Labour Market (Clarendon Press, Oxford).

Simpson, W. and A. van der Veen (1992), "The economics of commuting and the urban labour market", Journal of Economic Surveys 6:45–62.

Singell, L.D. and J.H. Lillydahl (1986), "An empirical analysis of the commute to work patterns of males and females in two-earner households", Urban Studies 23:119–129.

Sirmans, C.F. (1977), "City size and unemployment: some new elements", Urban Studies 14:99–101.

Smart, M.W. (1974), "Labour market areas: uses and definition", Progress in Planning 2:239–383.

Smith, J. and E. Welch (1979), "Race differences in earnings: a survey and new evidence", in: P. Mieszkowski and M. Straszheim, eds., Current Issues in Urban Economics (Johns Hopkins Press, Baltimore) pp. 40–73.

Steinnes, D.N. (1977), "Causality and intra-urban location", Journal of Urban Economics 4:67–79.

Steinnes, D.N. and W.D. Fisher (1974), "An econometric model of intraurban location", Journal of Regional Science 14:65–80.

Storper, M. and A.J. Scott (1992), Pathways to Industrialization and Regional Development (Routledge, London).

Stover, M.E. and C.L. Leven (1992), "Methodological issues in the determination of quality of life in urban areas", Urban Studies 29:737–754.

Straszheim, M. (1980), "Discrimination and the spatial characteristics of the urban labor market for black workers", Journal of Urban Economics 7:119–140.

Termote, M. (1978), "Migration and commuting in Lösch central place system", in: R. Funck and J.B. Parr, eds., The Analysis of Regional Structure: Essays in Honour of August Lösch (Pion, London).

Van Ommeren, J., P. Rietveld and P. Nijkamp (1996), "Residence and workplace location: a bivariate duration model approach", Geographical Analysis 28:315–329.

Van Ommeren, J., P. Rietveld and P. Nijkamp (1997), "Commuting: in search of jobs and residences", Journal of Urban Economics 42:402–421.

Veen, A. van der, and W. Simpson (1991), "Compensation for commuting in the Netherlands: Do skilled workers receive more?" Paper presented at the European Congress of the Regional Science Association, Lisbon.

Vickerman, R.W. (1984), "Urban and regional change, migration and commuting—the dynamics of workplace, residence and transport choice", Urban Studies 21:15–29.

Vipond, J. (1974), "City size and unemployment", Urban Studies 11:39–46.

Vipond, J. (1980), "Intra-urban unemployment differentials in Sydney, 1971", Urban Studies 17:131–138.

Vipond, J. (1984), "The intra-urban unemployment gradient: the influence of location on unemployment", Urban Studies 21:377–388.

Vrooman, J. and S. Greenfield (1980), "Are blacks making it in the suburbs? Some new evidence on intra-metropolitan spatial segmentation", Journal of Urban Economics 7:155–167.

Wachter, M.L. (1972), "Wage determination in a local labor market: a case study of the Boston labor market", Journal of Human Resources 7:87–103

Wachter, M. and C. Kim (1982), "The time series changes in youth joblessness", in: R.B. Freeman and D.A. Wise, eds., The Youth Labor Market Problem: Its Nature, Causes and Consequences (University of Chicago Press, Chicago and London), pp. 155–185.

Wales, T. (1978), "Labour supply and commuting time", Journal of Econometrics 8:215–226.

Weinberg, D. (1979), "The determinants of intra-urban household mobility", Regional Science and Urban Economics 9:219–246.

Wheaton, W.C. (1977), "Income and urban residence: an analysis of consumer demand for location", American Economic Review 67:620–631.

Wheeler, J.O. (1969), "Some effects of occupational status on work trips", Journal of Regional Science 9:69–78.

White, M.J. (1976), "Firm suburbanization and urban subcenters", Journal of Urban Economics 3:323–343.

White, M.J. (1977), "A model of residential location choice and commuting by men and women workers", Journal of Regional Science 17:41–52.

White, M.J. (1988), "Location choice and commuting behaviour in cities with decentralized employment", Journal of Urban Economics 24:129–152.

White, M.J. (1990), "Commuting and congestion: a simulation model of a decentralized metropolitan area", Journal of the American Real Estate and Urban Economics Association 18:335–368.

Wilson, W.J. (1987), The Truly Disadvantaged: The Inner City, the Underclass, and Public Policy (University of Chicago Press, Chicago).

Wilson, W.J. (1992), "Another look at 'The Truly Disadvantaged'", Political Science Quarterly 106:639–656.

Wilson, W.J. (1997), "When work disappears", Political Science Quarterly 111:567–595.

Yinger, J. (1976), "Racial prejudice and racial residential segregation in an urban model", Journal of Urban Economics 3:383–406.

Zax, J.S. (1990), "Race and commutes", Journal of Urban Economics 28:336–348.

Zax, J.S. (1991a), "Compensation for commutes in labor and housing markets", Journal of Urban Economics 30:192–207.

Zax, J.S. (1991b), "The substitution between moves and quits", Economic Journal 101:1510–1521.

Zax, J.S. (1994), "When is a move a migration?", Regional Science and Urban Economics 24:341–360.

Zax, J.S. and J.F. Kain (1991), "Commutes, quits and moves", Journal of Urban Economics 29:153–165.

Zax, J.S. and J.F. Kain (1996), "Moving to the suburbs: do relocating companies leave their black employees behind?", Journal of Labor Economics 14:472–504.

*Chapter 40*

# URBAN HOUSING MARKETS: THEORY AND POLICY

CHRISTINE M.E. WHITEHEAD

*London School of Economics*

## Contents

*Handbook of Regional and Urban Economics. Edited by E.S. Mills and P. Cheshire*
© *1999 Elsevier Science B.V. All rights reserved.*

## Abstract

This chapter examines certain of the developments in the application of economic theory and in empirical and policy analysis with respect to housing markets in general and urban housing markets in particular. The majority of the material refers to US and UK experience with some English language contributions related to other, mainly European, countries.

The main thrust of the chapter is to clarify how the particular attributes of housing, especially those of durability and locational specificity, have been introduced into microeconomic models of housing. On the demand side analysis concentrates on estimates of price and income elasticities and the results that arise from different mode specifications. On the supply side there is emphasis on the importance of distinguishing the factors determining new supply from those which affect investment in the existing stock. Overall housing market analysis is also divided into that which applies to the market as a whole and the very different issues, particularly with respect to market segmentation, which dominate urban models.

Turning to housing policy the chapter clarifies the different approaches taken to analysis, measurement and evaluation of policy in Europe and America and examines in detail developments with respect to particular examples of policy concern, including market versus administrative allocation, housing and labour markets, the impact of local taxation and rent control.

**Keywords:** Housing, housing markets, housing demand, housing supply, housing policy

## 1. Introduction

The literature on housing, even that on urban housing economics, covers an immense range of topics and approaches. This is, in part, because of the complex nature of the good housing, in part, because of the wide ranging interaction between housing with other elements of the urban economy, and, in part because of the extent of government intervention in housing systems at both national and local level. Moreover, while the comparative static paradigm is dominant, particularly in the American literature, housing is also an important element in behavioural, structural and Marxist approaches to economic decisions and development. The outcome of this is that the literature tends to look eclectic, with each contribution adding to understanding but often opening up more complexities rather than generating an obviously coherent body of knowledge.

It is not possible effectively to cover this range of material within a single chapter. Nor, indeed, is it necessary, particularly because there have been a number of detailed reviews of different elements of the literature at intervals over the last decades. Rather the approach taken here is to build on this material to examine trends in the way in which housing, particularly urban housing, has been addressed in the economics and related literature and then to clarify the areas where our understanding provides a basis for examining particular policies affecting urban housing and the impact that these have had on the housing system.

The rest of this first section concentrates on these earlier reviews, bringing out the main strands of analysis. Section 2 then examines basic housing market relationships, concentrating on the findings with respect to the nature of housing, the factors determining demand and supply and models of the marketplace both national and local. Section 3 then draws on these results to examine a range of questions that have been central to the English language literature on housing policy.

An early overview of progress in the positive economics of housing was that by Quigley (1979). This concentrated on clarifying the special characteristics of housing, the demand for housing as a composite good and its components, certain aspects of the economics of the supply of new construction and to a much lesser degree the supply of the existing stock. Quigley pointed out very clearly that the literature even then was going in two directions: on the one hand, greater econometric sophistication and better use of data enabling more secure estimates of relatively simple relationships; and, on the other, greater emphasis on specific relationships which tended to require more complex and narrowly based models which tended to reduce the potential generalisation. He also pointed out how much more advanced was the material on demand, and to a lesser extent price, than that on supply. It is worth adding that in that review the role of government in housing markets was treated entirely separately and very much more descriptively (Weicher, 1979).

The distinction between more tightly drawn theoretical analysis and greater econometric sophistication was further delineated in the housing chapters of the earlier handbook in this series (Mills, 1987). This included a survey by Arnott of theoretical contributions which set out developments in the competitive theory of housing markets, particularly with respect to durability and filtering. The conclusion was however quite negative arguing that, because there was no well defined alternative approach able to include imperfect competition thus sophistication had little to offer policy makers. The survey of the empirical literature by Olsen (1988) again stressed the relative extent of work on demand rather than supply, as well as the potential for empirical work made possible by the large scale data sets generated for the Housing Allowance Experiment and the Annual Housing Survey. Other chapters, notably that by Kain, examined the value of the computer simulation urban housing market models developed by the Urban Institute and the NBER (De Leeuw and Struyk, 1975; Struyk, 1976; Ingram, 1977; Bradbury et al., 1977). The availability of these large data sets has been an important driver in research significantly affecting the ways in which understanding of American housing markets have developed.

A major review of the housing economic literature, concentrating more on housing market models and less on both urban structures and large scale empirical analysis, was published at much the same time (Smith et al., 1988). This still found it necessary to set out general empirical information about the American market (without reference to any other country) before detailing the state of existing knowledge with respect to the treatment of particular characteristics, notably durability, heterogeneity, spatial fixity and slow and costly adjustment. The growing body of material on the impact of inflation and the economic cycle on housing markets was also discussed. Finally, the role of government was acknowledged and a wide range of positive economic analyses of particular programmes, notably those relating to zoning, rent regulations and the impact of taxation were included.

The conclusions of this review were remarkably similar to those of Quigley a decade earlier: that housing is a complex product, whose special characteristics need to be incorporated into formal models, but that the resulting range of attributes and relationships cannot then all be dealt with within a single framework. The result was seen to be a growing range of models addressing specific elements of the housing market, almost all within a traditional comparative static framework, and almost all concentrating on positive analysis. The bibliography included was vast and, although the importance of institutional realism was noted in the text, wholly North American in its orientation.

Published before the review, but not included there, was what is now argued to be a seminal work by Poterba (1984). This innovative contribution placed housing as an asset into a general equilibrium framework, where the emphasis is on the equalisation of risk adjusted rates of return. The immediate problem addressed was that of the impact of tax subsidies on demand for housing and market behaviour. This analysis treated housing within a competitive framework as basically a financial asset. As such it necessarily excluded much of the depth of understanding associated with a more characteristics based approach. In particular it excluded most elements relating to spatial fixity and slow adjustment. On the other hand it provided far greater predictive capacity than most earlier material. It is not therefore surprising that this approach has found favour within more formal housing market analysis and that much of the housing market material published in the early 1990s has taken this as a starting point.

In the early 1990s a further, far more urban and spatially oriented, review was included in the text by Rothenberg et al. (1991). The work itself emphasised local housing markets, spatial segmentation and substitutability on the one hand and the consumption/asset decisions of consumers on the other. The extensive literature review first examined the different approaches used in spatially based models, ranging along a spectrum from those which assume housing is a one dimensional good which can be addressed within a simple comparative static framework to those which emphasise richer specifications of housing and neighbourhood attributes, which tend to be addressed through simulation approaches. It then reviewed the literature on demand for housing overall, as well as for individual attributes, before discussing the complexities of the supply and allocation of both the new and existing stock. The outcome emphasised local and locational factors and the resultant range of sub-markets with partial substitutability and then examined individual actors' decisions and the rich variety of interactions that these can generate. The substantive research then attempted, using cross area data, econometrically to establish the key parameters on local housing markets, stressing the degree of substitutability between these markets. By doing so the authors argued that they are offering a quantum leap forward in both theoretical and empirical understanding—but interestingly link that to the Quigley review (Quigley, 1979) and other research undertaken in the 1970s (Bradbury et al., 1977; Rabianski and Spitzer, 1978) rather than to that of the 1980s. Inherently this approach depends heavily on hedonic price analysis, the subject addressed in Chapter 41.

All the reviews so far discussed are American in their origin. There are no similarly extensive reviews covering European research and experience. The nearest equivalents are those by Maclennan (1982) and Maclennan et al. (1987) which mainly emphasise the importance of housing sub-markets and search behaviour within the context of a Lancastrian characteristics approach to definitions of housing (Lancaster, 1979).

One important lesson from these wide-ranging reviews is that there is an agreed body of knowledge relating to certain basic housing market relationships but beyond this there are a variety of different and partial approaches. Another is that the vast majority of work undertaken in the field sees government as one actor modifying specific market relationships rather than, as is the case in many European countries, as a pervasive influence on the way in which the housing system operates. This in turn places the emphasis on comparing outcomes across localities, while in the European context far greater importance is placed on analysing the impact of national policies on the operation of the housing system as a whole rather than on how these policies impact at the local level (Maclennan, 1982; Meen, 1989, 1996).

## 2. The basic market relationships

### 2.1. What is housing?

A fundamental question in analysing urban housing markets is how to treat the good housing. There are two general approaches: housing is a unidimensional product which bears a specific, evaluable, relationship with other urban variables; or housing is a multidimensional product where the emphasis is on the way in which these different dimensions interact with one another and what determines the output and price of these different elements and thus overall equilibrium. There is a further strand which sees housing as an element within more fundamental ideas of position, class struggle etc. but this is not one which finds much favour in traditional economic analysis (Ball, 1981, 1983).

A starting point for the first approach is the article by Muth in Harberger (1960). Here the unit of measurement is taken to be "that quantity of service yielded by one unit of housing stock per unit of time" (p. 32) where the stock is measured by its constant dollar value and price is determined for a standard unit. It is this approach which is carried forward into the seminal work by Muth (1969) in which he argues that "my usage of the term price of housing is perfectly analogous to the meaning more readily attached to the term price of food namely the expenditure required to obtain a given "market basket" of food and related items". This approach matched well with that of Alonso (1964), Mills (1967) and others working on the development of access/space models of urban areas. By assuming normal substitution effects between space and structure and further assuming competition in the construction market it was possible to develop predictions about the spatial relationships of density and price. The first comprehensive attempt at testing these relationships was that by Muth himself (1969) using data from forty-six cities. Thereafter there were a large number of attempts to develop different aspects of the model. Some of these examined specific relationships (e.g., White, 1977, which examines the convexity of population density functions as a test of the standard model). Others introduced particular additional attributes into the market, notably by Evans (1973) which incorporated neighbourhood external effects and McDonald (1979 and 1981) which considered the asset structure of urban housing and the mechanics by which housing is demolished and redeveloped within the urban area. Inherently the main organising principle was the relationship of housing to urban structure rather than the operation of urban housing markets themselves.

The other end of the scale in looking at the good housing is that grounded in Lancaster's characteristics approach (1966, 1979) (although, as is shown in Chapter 41 this approach preceded Lancaster's contribution by more that thirty years). This emphasises the heterogeneity of the housing product which makes it possible to evaluate different bundles of attributes within the same total expenditure package. The assumption here is that households value goods by their characteristics and that a well operating market will generate different groupings of characteristics in relation to relative costs. The approach was described formally by Rosen (1974) setting out a model of demand, supply and competitive equilibrium. It is this approach that lies at the base of the hedonic price approach (discussed in detail in Chapter 41). It is also fundamental to both analytic and simulation approaches to modelling urban and housing market structures such as those undertaken, in the US context, by Kain and Quigley (1970), Ingram et al. (1972) and others summarised in Ingram (1977). In the European context, the range of articles in Stahl (1985) and the model by Rouwendal (1989) mainly take a similar approach within the context of modelling residential location.

Much of the work on housing as a set of characteristics is concentrated on the interpretation of fully adjusted equilibrium. Another strand of analysis, mainly based in Europe, has queried the extent to which such stringent assumptions can be applied to housing markets, particularly because of the durability of housing and the slow adjustment of the market, but also because of the extent of supply gaps and the quality of information available to consumers and suppliers alike. Maclennan (1977, 1982) in particular has stressed the problems of using the hedonic approach in markets where there are significant constraints on adjustment.

Analysis which takes as its starting point the complexity of the good housing, in terms of spatial fixity, durability and externality as well as physical attributes of the dwellings, tends not to concentrate on an urban modelling approach but rather to emphasise the considerable potential for market failure in housing markets and therefore the rationale for government intervention in these markets (Hills, 1991; Whitehead, 1993).

## 2.2. The demand for housing

The analysis of demand started with the measurement of income and thereafter price elasticities. In both cases the story is one where initial estimates were seen to generate unrealistically high and low estimates respectively. More recent analyses suggest that these early elasticity measures were inadequately founded in theory and suffered from technical deficiencies in estimation. As a result these approaches have now been continually refined so that they generate results that are more in line with general expectations. The treatment of the economic determinants of household formation and their impact on the demand for housing has been much less formally examined (Smith et al., 1984).

Income elasticities are particularly important with respect to both urban structure and housing policy. The starting point is the work by Reid (1962) in which, using Friedman's permanent income hypothesis and aggregate data, she found that the income elasticity of demand might be nearer two than the usually assumed value of unity or below. Starting with Lee (1964, 1968) much of the work thereafter has been concentrated on refining both specification and testing, in particular to take account of the problem that what is observable is expenditure rather than price and quantity separately (de Leeuw, 1971 and 1976). Household level studies have tended to result in far lower income elasticities. In particular Polinsky (1977) showed how separating out transitory income, interpreted as variance within aggregate estimates, allowed a better specification of permanent income while Polinsky and Ellwood (1979) took account of spatial variations in measured prices to improve the estimates of both price and income elasticities.

An equally important question has been whether and how income elasticities vary with level of income. Ihlanfeldt (1982) suggested elasticities were higher for higher income groups, while Hansen et al. (1996) using Lorenz curves shows, income elasticity to be less than unity at all levels. Finally, problems associated with the equilibrium assumptions have also been a matter of concern, with some arguing that only recent moves should be included (Maclennan, 1982; Hanushek and Quigley, 1982), while others suggest little difference between movers and nonmovers (Goodman and Kawai, 1984).

Initial UK analyses tended to stress the importance of tenure, for instance Byatt et al. (1973), which suggested that the elasticity was higher for owner-occupation than for the private rented sector. A second area of concern in the UK context was the impact of financial constraints on the individual household's capacity to adjust housing expenditure to desired levels. King (1980), for instance, showed that, while measured income elasticities were still inelastic, without constraints income elasticity would be much closer to unity. Later work by Meen (1996), where the emphasis is on improved estimation of long-run supply, generates income elasticities as high as 1.25.

In the comparative context the detailed work undertaken at the World Bank (Mayo, 1981; Mayo and Malpezzi, 1985; Jimenez and Keane, 1984) tends to suggest that income elasticities are reasonably constant across countries, that there are significant differences between those for rental and owned housing and that governmental and other constraints are important in limiting adjustment.

Estimates of price elasticities presented similar, closely related, problems. Early unit cost based measures tended to generate estimates ranging from $-0.3$ to $-0.7$ in the United States (De Leeuw, 1971; Maisel et al., 1971). Estimates based on appraisal data suggested the upper end of the range (Polinsky, 1977; Polinsky and Elwood, 1979). Using grouped data tended to increase both income and price elasticities in comparison to individual observations but still generated estimates of a similar order (Rosenthal, 1989). Excluding tenure choice is agreed to bias both price and income elasticities upwards (Gillingham and Hagemann, 1983). These and other authors have also argued that elasticities vary with income (Friedman and Weinberg, 1981), while Harrington (1989) suggested that taking a lifetime intertemporal approach generates a wider range of price parameters.

An important question from the point of the view of the operation of housing markets is the extent to which income and price elasticities, as well as cross elasticities of demand, vary across different attributes. Early studies based on hedonic approaches suggested significant differences in both price and income elasticities between different attributes (Kain and Quigley, 1975; King, 1976, 1977; Witte et al., 1979; Follain and Jimenez, 1985). These studies use a range of approaches, for instance, Awan et al. (1982) and Parsons (1986) which estimated an Almost Ideal Demand System developed by Deaton and Muellbauer (1980) across a range of attributes, Ball and Kirwan (1975, 1977) which took account of space and structure and Boehm (1982), which examined the demand for dwelling size and quality in relation to tenure choice. All these studies tend to suggest that income and price elasticities vary considerably across the ranges of attributes that have been identified, notably with respect to space, structure and environment as do cross elasticities of demand with respect to substitute and complementary attributes.

Later work has evaluated price and income elasticities within wider analysis of urban areas. In the USA these differential estimates are crucial to the analysis of segmented markets (Rothenburg et al., 1991). In the UK, Cheshire and Sheppard (1995, 1998) suggest particularly high income elasticities of demand, as well as larger price elasticities because of the capacity to adjust between attributes within an analysis of the impact of land use planning on demand and house prices.

An area of particular concern with respect to demand is that of tenure choice. The American literature tends to treat the decision as dependent simply upon economic and demographic variables with particular emphasis on price differentials between tenure (Kain and Quigley, 1972; Struyk, 1976; McDonald, 1979; Megbolugbe and Linneman, 1993). Later developments have concentrated on the determination of the user cost of housing, taking account of both local and national taxation policies as well as inflationary expectations within the context of life cycle models (Kearl, 1979; Hendershott, 1980; Follain, 1982; Wheaton, 1985; Goodman, 1988). Similar studies have been undertaken in Australia where the inclusion of user costs have significantly improved goodness-of-fit (Bourassa, 1995). There has been growing emphasis on portfolio aspects of tenure choice (Haurin and Lee, 1989; Follain and Ling, 1988; Haurin, 1991; Pollakowski and Wachter, 1990; Meyer and Wiend, 1996) and on the positive linkages between decisions about quantity and tenure (Gillingham and Hagemann, 1983; Henderson and Ionnides, 1983, 1986, 1989; Borsch-Supen and Pollakowski, 1990).

In the European context, far more of the emphasis has been on constraints on tenure choice arising from financial restrictions and rent regulation as well as the relationship between the market and administratively allocated social housing. King (1980) for instance, stressed the nature of the joint decision between quantity and tenure in a system where there was rationing in both of the two main tenures. Ermisch et al. (1996) using data for 1988 and 1989 when financial rationing for owner-occupation had almost disappeared, found aggregated price elasticities ranging from −0.35 to 0.44.

As models have become more comprehensive both income and price elasticities tend to be generated as an element of the analysis, rather than being the object of central concern (Rothenberg et al., 1991; DiPasquale and Wheaton, 1994; Pain and Westerway, 1996). The implied values generally appear relatively similar to those already discussed. The main conclusion must be that on the demand side both income and price elasticities are generally less than one but vary between tenures, income and demographic groups as well as between different housing attributes.

## 2.3. Housing supply

One of the most important attributes of housing is the fact that new supply forms only a very small proportion of the total supply of housing at any given time and that the overall supply of housing is modified not just by new building but also by improvement and conversion of the existing stock on the one hand and depreciation of that stock on the other. Equally new housing supply is made up of both land and structure, which means that the analysis of housing supply must be linked both to the operation of land markets and the organisation of the construction industry. It is perhaps not surprising therefore that, for both technical and data reasons, models of supply appear to have made relatively little progress as compared to those dealing with demand (Quigley, 1979; Olsen in Mills, 1987).

### 2.3.1. The supply of new housing

The American literature tends to emphasise the supply of housing services. This supply combines land and nonland inputs (the housing stock of various qualities, energy etc.) into a production function for homogeneous housing services (Muth, 1973). The interaction of this available stock of housing with the demand for that stock determines the price of housing services and therefore the extent to which new supply can be expected to be forthcoming. de Leeuw and Ekanem (1971) is the usual starting point for analysis of the responsiveness of supply to price. This used cross-sectional data to estimate a reduced form equation where the assumption was that long-run supply was in equilibrium. The results which suggested very low price elasticities of supply, have been strongly criticised on both empirical and theoretical grounds (see, e.g., Follain, 1979; Quigley, 1979; Olsen in Mills, 1987). Direct estimates of rental supply using simultaneous techniques have been made by Rabianski and Spitzer (1978) and, as part of the Housing Allowance Supply Experiment, by Rydell et al. (1982). These in turn have been criticised on technical and other grounds (Olsen in Mills, 1987). Later cross-sectional work by Stover (1986) and more formal modelling approaches by Smith (1989) suggested that the long-run supply elasticity is close to infinite, a result consistent with time series analyses by both Muth (1960) and Follain (1979).

   A rather different approach is that which attempts to look at the speed and location of response. Bradbury et al. (1977) for instance, in a model emphasising the importance of vacancy and competition from other land uses in determining responsiveness, looked at responses over a ten-year period in Boston. At the same time Ozanne and Struyk (1978) were examining supply elasticities in the same area within the existing stock. Rothenberg et al. (1991) argued that most of the empirical difficulties could be traced to the lack of an unambiguous measure of the quantity and quality of new provision. Relying on sub-market analysis and a cross area model they analysed both the speed and location of adjustment. They found quite rapid rates of adjustment across most markets to the point that the medium term supply elasticity was close to infinity. The evidence from the United States thus suggests that market supply is potentially very responsive to changes in demand, both in terms of new building and within the existing stock.

British contributions to the literature on supply and housing markets tend both to give less emphasis to cross-sectional analysis (in part because of a paucity of the necessary locally based data) and more to the flow of new building, rather than the stock of housing services. The provenance of these models is usually that of estimating investment at the national level, as an input into wider macro-economic analysis (Hendry, 1984; Meen, 1989).

Early econometric models tended to distinguish construction costs, credit availability and land costs as determinants of new supply (Whitehead, 1974; Hadjimatheou, 1976). They typically found that borrowing constraints and land prices were relatively insignificant in determining that supply, although this may in part have been a result of the quality of the aggregate data. Later models have incorporated formal optimisation decisions by builders as well as more appropriate error correction and forward looking techniques which emphasise the importance of expectations (Tompkinson 1979; Ericsson and Hendry 1985 and particularly Tsoukis and Westaway, 1994). Dynamic models of economics with credit constraints help to explain cycles in durable asset investment including residential property (Kiyotaki and Moore, 1997).

Models of new construction generally assume rising supply functions in order effectively to estimate supply (Tsoukis and Westaway 1994). Work by Ericsson and Hendry (1985), Dicks (1990), Giussani and Hadjimatheou (1990 and 1991) for instance, all incorporate rising supply functions. Later work by Shea (1993) and Ozanne (1996) have tested the assumption within a more general framework.

In the USA, Poterba (1984) made a similar assumption that supply curves slope upward when he incorporated a simple equation relating investment to costs of production, credit availability for builders and the price of alternative projects in order to estimate levels of construction. Topel and Rosen (1988) on the other hand avoided the problem by emphasising the importance of adjustment costs with respect to supply. This generated differences between the short and long run responsiveness to supply, with a best estimate of the long run supply elasticity, measured as the responsiveness of investment to a permanent price increase, of around 2.8. Neither model finds much evidence suggesting construction costs are significant in determining this response. DiPasquale and Wheaton (1994) in a paper on housing market dynamics at the aggregate level argue for a stock adjustment approach of the type first put forward by Muth (1969) and similar to that employed in the UK literature. Applying this suggests both slow adjustment and a long run price elasticity of supply of around 1.2 in the USA. The work by Tsoukis and Westaway (1994), which built heavily on Topel and Rosen's approach when examining the UK data, suggested a much lower long-run elasticity of housing starts with respect to a permanent price increase, of around unity.

This model also finds no evidence that turnover in the housing market influences starts. Again the findings are somewhat different to the US where it has been suggested that quantity signals in the form of vacancies play a relevant part in determining the construction decision (Arnott in Mills, 1987) but that, anyway, new construction reacts slowly to both market prices and vacancy rates (Wheaton, 1990).

There is now growing interest in the UK in examining spatial interactions with respect to both housing starts and house prices. Meen (1996) in particular has clarified the conditions under which it is possible to consider national markets independently from spatial structure, based on the standard aggregation conditions of whether markets are homogenous, dependant and convergent. While he suggests that the evidence points to the need to treat housing markets as a set of inter-related local or regional markets, using a Poterba style model for the English regions, he found that housing starts equations were remarkably similar across regions and hence construction could be characterised as a national market.

Another important issue in the context of new construction is the treatment of the impact of land markets and the planning system on the provision of new housing. In the US there is a long tradition of analysis of the impact of zoning in land and housing markets (e.g., Grieson and White, 1981; Mark and Goldberg, 1986) detailed in Chapter 42. The model by Mayo and Sheppard (1991, 1996) examines the effect of stochastic development controls and suggests that there may be situations in which increases in demand could impact more on the price of vacant land than on developed land, resulting in a reduction in current supply. In the UK context Cheshire and Sheppard (1989) examined the impact of land use controls on supply and access to housing to two areas one with tight controls, the other less constrained. Bramley (1993) estimated a cross-section model across local authorities suggesting that land availability at the district level impacts significantly on housing output. Monk et al. (1996) examined the processes by which the planning system modifies supply and price over the economic cycle to reduce effective output levels in a range of areas with different levels of constraint. Later work by Pryce (forthcoming) compares responsiveness in boom and slump and finds evidence of a backward bending supply curve in periods of boom. The research estimates average price elasticities of supply of 0.58 in the boom and 1.03 in the slump as well as considerable variation between districts. All the evidence so far available therefore suggests that, even where supply of new construction is very elastic in the medium term, the attributes of the land market are extremely important in determining both the rate of response and the overall supply elasticity.

### 2.3.2. Investment in the existing stock

Additional supply is made up not just of new units but also of maintenance, improvement and conversion. Often these have been treated as part of the over-all supply of housing services to make the analysis reasonably tractable. The basic approach is one of developing rules for optimal maintenance or the mix of operating and capital inputs (Ingram and Kain, 1973; Ingram and Oron in Ingram, 1977; Meyer, 1981). Some have regarded the decision as similar between landlords and owner-occupiers (e.g., Ozanne and Struyk, 1976; Segal, 1979). Others have stressed the importance of utility rather than profit maximising and the superiority of owner-occupation in this context (Struyk, 1976; Meyer, 1981, Galster, 1981 and 1987). Studies of maintenance expenditure all suggest that the extent of maintenance is related to the age of the structure and of the owner, income and neighbourhood factors. Studies of rehabilitation and conversion are less well founded, in part because of data difficulties. Characteristics of occu-pants, dwellings and neighbourhood all appear to be relevant to these decisions (Galster, 1981; Meyer, 1981, 1985), although owners' expectations about the area may be more important than current conditions (Taub et al., 1984; Galster, 1987). An interesting model of household decision (Potepan, 1989) found that, in a fixed mortgage rate environment, the probability of improving rather than moving was positively associated with increasing current interest rates and neg-atively associated with increases in current income. In the UK context, a number of authors have examined the choice between extension and moving within a tightly constrained planning system (Gosling et al., 1993; Seek, 1983). What is clear from these studies is that the approaches taken are far less strongly located in formal modelling, involve very large and detailed data sets and suggest that a simple rate of return based analysis does not adequately reflect the complexity of behaviour.

Rothenberg et al. (1991) reach a rather different conclusion on the basis of a full scale urban housing model. They take account of both the potential for dif-ferent technological transformation possibilities and for different implicit prices across local sub-markets and types of investment while continuing to assume a basic optimising approach to individual decision. They suggest that, both across areas and within a specific urban area, relative rates of return provide good predictions of structural improvement.

There has been considerable emphasis in the US on the analysis of abandonment, demolition and replacement based on market decision making starting from Davies and Whinston (1961), Rothenberg (1967, 1983) and Stegman, 1972.

This process has been a subject of far less interest in Europe where dwellings tend to last longer, where abandonment is anyway very rare and where governments usually play an important directive role in slum clearance and replacement. Again the models are fundamentally straightforward, involving comparisons of net present value between options, including that of abandonment. Results stress the importance of neighbourhood conditions and the tax environment (Sternlieb and Burchall, 1973; White 1986). Within the UK context a similar approach has been applied to the public sector choice between rehabilitation and renewal with respect to particular projects. Here the emphasis has been on both cost minimisation (Needleman, 1969) and on wider cost benefit approaches (Kirwan and Martin, 1972). Private sector decisions about improvement are more often addressed in the context of housing and finance market imperfections on the one hand and government policy on the other.

## 2.4. Housing markets

So far we have discussed specific elements of the housing market and of urban housing markets in particular. In so doing it has often been the case that extreme assumptions have had to be made about the way in which the market actually operates, for instance hypothesising that the conditions for long-run competitive equilibrium exist in either a single market or a set of sub-markets.

Questions about whether housing markets can be effectively analysed in this way lie at the forefront of the evaluation of empirical analysis and their relevance for policy determination. Again there is a tension between incorporating adjustment processes and introducing other, perhaps more realistic, assumptions about the attributes of housing. Much of the analysis of adjustment has occurred within aggregate models of the housing market while that introducing additional attributes of housing occurs in the context of urban analysis.

### 2.4.1. Aggregate models of the housing market

At the aggregate level the majority of analyses have concentrated on price determination, price adjustment and the impact on investment. The starting point for these models in both the US and the UK has been housing as part of the macroeconomy (Grebler and Maisel, 1963; Arcelus and Meltzer, 1973; Whitehead, 1971, 1974). Yet clearly results at the aggregate level impact significantly on urban housing markets, notably in terms of the incentive to invest in and maintain the quality of the housing stock. They are also important with respect to the speed of adjustment, the impact of macro variables on housing decisions and the robustness of equilibrium assumptions.

The possibility of a collapse in real house prices as a result of demographic changes has generated new interest in aggregate housing market models in the US. Mankiw and Weil (1989, 1992) were the first to put forward a model suggesting that lower rates of new household formation and an ageing population would result in a 40% fall in real house prices. Their results have been contested by, among others, Englehardt and Poterba (1990), Hamilton (1991), Holland (1991) Hendershott (1991) and Woodward (1991). DiPasquale and Wheaton (1994) used the question as a starting point for the reevaluation of this type of approach, generating a stock flow model with price and output adjustment. The strong conclusion was that prices in the owner-occupied market adjust slowly, in contrast to the general assumptions of instantaneous market clearing, with the implication that housing markets operate in ways that are far different from other financial assets.

Aggregate models incorporating adjustment mechanisms have been fundamental to the developments in housing market analyses in the UK, notably in the 1990s by Meen (1990, 1993, 1996b), Milne (1991) and Muellbauer and Murphy (1994, 1997), although the usual starting point here has been the impact of finance market liberalisation as well as fundamental demographic and income relationships.

A rather different approach at the aggregate level has been that of evaluating the efficiency of housing in an asset market. The starting point here was the article by Poterba (1984) which postulates a rational expectations approach to housing in an efficient asset market. A range of studies of the North American evidence in Hendershott and Hu (1981), Case and Schiller (1989, 1990), Mankiw and Weil (1991), Poterba (1991) and, in the Canadian context, Clayton (1996, 1997), all suggest that the arbitrage conditions do not hold at a given point in time, so that excess returns can be maintained for long periods. This does not necessarily negate the basic Poterba model, as long as market behaviour converges to the basic equation over both time and space (Meen, 1996). However, this may be an heroic assumption. Housing market efficiency has also been discussed in the context of Tokyo (Ito and Hirono, 1993) and Britain (Evans, 1995).

Nontraditional models of housing market disequilibrium concentrate on the extent to which house prices can be regarded as the sole determinant of supply and the speed of the supply adjustment (Fair, 1972; Eubank and Sirmans, 1979;

Rosen and Smith, 1983; Hendershott and Haurin, 1988). All tend to suggest that other factors, notably the vacancy rate, sales rates, financial market and macro-economic variables can be significant (Arnott, 1989; Kaserman et al., 1989). None suggest that instantaneous adjustment is a reasonable assumption.

In this context there has been considerable interest in the question of transactions costs, notably with respect to demand. Chinloy (1980) for instance incorporated a range of implicit and explicit costs many of them related to financing, Goodman (1995) examined the differences in these costs between owners and renters while Read (1991) looked at national rates of vacancies. A range of studies has shown that these costs affect mobility as much, if not more than, the benefits of these moves (Hanuschek and Quigley, 1978; Weinberg, Friedman and Mayo, 1981). In the UK context, Muellbauer and Murphy (1996) have suggested that these can impact on market behaviour to generate important non-linearities in house prices.

### 2.4.2. *Urban housing models*

The first formal general equilibrium model of the urban housing market was that put forward by Muth (1969). This assumed utility maximisation and perfect competition to make it possible to determine and describe the long run stationary state with respect to prices and densities. Muth's approach has been developed in the theoretical literature to take more detailed account of space and thus residential location, the durability of housing and optimal maintenance and quality. In the context of monocentric cities important developments and syntheses have been put forward by Evans (1973), MacDonald (1979), Wheaton (1979) and Henderson (1985). Durability was introduced by Fujita (1976), Anas (1978) and Arnott (1980) among others with different assumptions about the capacity to adjust the existing stock generating more complex sets of spatial structures. Finally, demolition and replacement was introduced (Brueckner, 1981), all within a spatial general equilibrium framework.

The life cycle of the dwelling has also been examined first aspatially (Sweeney, 1974a, b), then including both space and the capacity to improve the dwellings (Arnott et al., 1983) and finally embedding the supply model in a stationary general equilibrium monocentric city model (Arnott et al., 1986). These models, while increasing in theoretical strength, all include strong and unrealistic assumptions in order to generate clear-cut predictions about investment and spatial patterns. Even so, there is some empirical evidence to support the basic predictions. However, the relative importance of these relationships as compared to those arising from more complex but less tractable approaches taking account of historical patterns, infrastructure, transport and neighbourhood is less clear (Evans, 1973; Whitehead and Odling-Smee, 1975; Maclennan, 1982).

While certain aspects of adjustment within the existing stock have been incorporated into this general equilibrium approach (Edell, 1972; Lowry, 1960), richer analyses of the filtering process tend to be less formally based, starting from the empirical inductive approach of Hoyt (1939). In this context filtering has been defined in terms of households moving into better housing as a result of new construction (Lansing et al., 1969; Watson 1973); dwellings deteriorating over time (Muth, 1973; Margolis, 1982); dwellings becoming less desirable over time and thus tending to house lower income and excluded groups (Leven et al., 1976; Vandell 1981); and in the more formal models as prices of existing units of constant quality that deteriorate over the longer term (Sweeney, 1974a, b). Unlike the majority of the work discussed so far these models have been used to analyse the impact of government policy in the form of public housing and subsidies for moderate income households. Results vary, with Sweeney (1974a, b) among others concluding that benefits do filter down while, for instance, Olsen (1969) and Ohls's (1975) simulation approaches suggest there are no benefits, except to those directly affected. Their results depend upon models based on Hoyt's (1939) empirical inductive approach.

Empirical studies have tended to provide fairly general evidence about neighbourhood dynamics rather than strict tests of the filtering hypothesis (Grigsby, 1963; Davis, 1974; de Leeuw and Struyk, 1975). However the results generally support the hypothesis that significant filtering with respect to dwellings does occur (Weicher and Thibodeau, 1988).

A closely related issue with more obviously spatial connotations is whether the urban, or indeed the national, housing system should be modelled as a single market or as a set of related sub-markets (Meen and Andrew, 1998). Indeed Grigsby's (1963) conceptual starting point for his filtering approach was a partitioning of the stock by substitutability by households, based on patterns of residential mobility. This compares with later filtering models which assume hierarchical partitioning (Sweeney 1974a, b).

In principle a distinction can be made between those approaches which assume that, at least in the long-run, the overall market will equilibrate, in which case it is basically a study in product differentiation, and those where the emphasis is on market imperfections and adjustment processes which tend to suggest that disequilibrium will prevail. In the American literature much of the material relates to defining submarkets through evidence on price or to the price adjustment process (Goodman, 1981; Reece, 1988; Rothenberg et al., 1991). Others have looked at natural rates of vacancy in a way comparable to labour market analysis (Gabriel and Nothaft, 1988; Read, 1991). In the UK there has been more emphasis on the extent to which the existence of submarkets implies recurrent or permanent disequilibrium (Maclennan et al., 1987; Maclennan and Tu, 1996) and the factors that tend to generate submarkets (Hancock and Maclennan, 1990; Tu 1997). One area of concern has been whether sub-markets should be characterised as spatial or attribute based. Here there appears general agreement from a range of different approaches that the second is the more appropriate (Rothenberg et al., 1991; Maclennan and Tu, 1996). Meen (1996), for instance, suggests that markets should be defined by appropriately aggregating sub-markets on the basis of coefficients, not space. This in turn implies that coefficient homogeneity may be more likely to occur over areas with similar socio-economic groupings than as a result of spatial contiguity.

The main conclusions from this discussion of markets is that, not surprisingly, housing markets are more complex than can be described by simple, single market, competitive equilibrium models. However the more complex the model, the more difficult it is either to generate predictions or to test them effectively. Empirical analyses are limited, particularly by the extent and quality of data. Only in the US has it been possible to undertake large scale analyses and simulations. These tend to confirm expected general relationships but are often not strongly grounded in theory (Arnott in Mills, 1987; Anas and Arnott, 1994). There remains a dichotomy between the theoretical developments and the capacity to test the resultant hypotheses empirically, even in the US. In Europe understanding of market mechanisms tends to have weaker theoretical foundations and to be tested in a more partial fashion. The strength there lies more in the development of national housing markets models, the relationship between housing and the wider economy and, in this context, the evaluation of policy (Buckley, 1982; Buckley and Ermisch, 1982; Meen, 1989, 1996; Muellbauer and Murphy, 1996; Englund et al., 1995).

## 3. Urban housing policy

The approach to analysing housing policy is very different in America and Europe. In the American literature the government and particularly local government, is seen as one actor that modifies private investment decisions through taxation, subsidy and quantitative constraints. The impacts of these policies are then traced through market behaviour. Few question whether the mainstream theory of competitive equilibrium discussed in this chapter is appropriate to policy analysis. Arnott (in Mills, 1987) is unusual when he argues that "the highest priority item on the research agenda in the economic theory of housing markets is the development of imperfectly competitive and non-competitive models of the housing market" (p. 985). Most of the emphasis in later research has in fact gone the other way, improving the theoretical base but in the context of competitive equilibrium rather than market failure and welfare analysis.

Second, the American literature emphasises local market analysis both because of limited federal intervention in housing and the fact that policies are mediated and initiated by local government in many different ways. The Experimental Housing Allowance Program undertaken in the 1970s is a good example in that it was intentionally implemented in only a small number of areas allowing relatively easy comparison with similar areas where no subsidy was available (Bradbury and Downs, 1982; Friedman and Weinberg, 1981 and 1982). The Experimental Housing Allowance Program generated important empirical results with strong policy implications. On the demand side the experiment included a range of different subsidies to selected households in six cities for a three year period. The outcome was far lower price elasticities of demand than had been predicted but relatively large price elasticities of supply ensuring that the majority of benefits went to consumers. The supply experiment which lasted for ten years and was available to all eligible landlords included a minimum quality requirement which effectively raised standards at relatively low cost (Rydell, 1976; Rydell et al., 1982; Lowry, 1983).

Equally rent control, dwelling-based taxation, housing assistance to low income families and zoning and planning controls are all fundamentally local policies which can thus be evaluated by comparison across areas (Apgar, 1990; Malpezzi and Green, 1996; Galster, 1997). In this context, Galster, for instance, has argued that the demand side approach to subsidy will normally be superior to supply side housing assistance because of the capacity of sub-markets to respond effectively (Galster, 1997). Anas and Arnott (1994) generate similar conclusions within a dynamic-equilibrium simulation model of Chicago. Critics of this approach from a European angle, argue both that the range of objections is too narrowly defined and that the outcome depends more on the specifics of the subsidy (Yates and Whitehead, 1998).

A third important element in the American approach to policy analysis is the emphasis placed on the costs of government intervention, the extent of administrative failure and the evaluation of alternative policies in terms of these costs (Weicher, 1979; Nesslein, 1982, 1988; Apgar, 1990; Galster, 1997).

In Europe housing has been seen far more as a fundamental part of national social policy throughout much of the century. This impacts on what is seen as relevant theory, as well as on the approach to policy analysis. In particular the starting point tends to be that of market imperfection, the relevance of welfare economics and the rationale of government intervention (Maclennan, 1982; Whitehead, 1984; Turner et al., 1977).

Second, the emphasis on housing as part of welfare and social policy means that there has been large scale intervention at the national level, including considerable emphasis on direct provision of housing as well as large scale supply subsidies and controls on the pricing and financing of housing (Maclennan and Williams, 1990a, b; Boelhouwer and van der Heijden, 1992, 1993; Turner and Whitehead, 1993). These policies are generally national in character and, while often mediated by local government, apply across all jurisdictions. It is not normally politically acceptable to apply policies to specific areas as was done in the US with the Housing Allowance Experiment. Instead policies apply either across the country as a whole or to relevant categories of households, providers or localities. Policy analysis tends either to be undertaken at the national level or through case studies of the impact of particular programmes on local housing conditions rather than the operation of the market. Moreover because of the scale and type of intervention much of the analysis is tenure rather than market driven (Freeman et al., 1996; Boelhouwer and van der Heijden, 1993).

It is impossible in a review chapter of this kind to give more than a flavour of the types of policy issues that are relevant to the economics of urban housing markets, particularly as the approaches are so different between countries. Here we touch on four areas of current debate: market versus administrative provision; the relationship between housing and labour markets; the impact of local taxation on house prices; and the impact of rent control on investment in rental housing. The impact of zoning and land use planning on housing provision and prices is another issue of particular importance, but is discussed in detail in Chapter 42.

Two areas of concern have not been included: the relationship between racial segregation and housing markets, which is seen as of particular importance in the US context and the impact of housing tax expenditures on housing demand which is seen as of more national the urban interest. Both are well covered in the literature (Yinger, 1979; Smith et al., 1988; Wood, 1988; Lundqvist, 1988; Englund et al., 1995).

## 3.1. Market versus administrative provision

A fundamental question in the policy debate is whether housing provision should be market based or should be provided through government directly or with the assistance of supply subsidies. Three interlinked questions arise in this context:

is it need or demand which is relevant in the provision of low income housing; should subsidies be made available to supply, often with associated administrative allocation; and, more fundamentally, whether housing is essentially a private good, which can be more effectively provided through the market or whether market failures are such as to make social sector provision more desirable.

As we have already seen, in the American literature the approach is almost entirely market-based. This allows policy analysis to be undertaken within the context of clearly formulated microeconomic models or in simulations of local housing markets (Rothenberg et al., 1991; Anan and Arnott, 1994). As such policy analysis remains firmly based in the positive economics of housing. This is in strict contrast to much of the European literature where, at least until the 1980s, housing was seen as a social good where it is the government's role both to determine minimum acceptable standards and then to ensure that the identified needs are met (Maclennan and Williams, 1990b; Hills, 1991; Whitehead, 1991). The need for government intervention is evaluated using demographic forecasts, the likely provision by the market and the standards to be achieved (Holmans, 1995). Only in the last few years has this analysis been placed more formally within the framework of economic and econometric models, examining determinants of household formation, a medium term model of the housing market and the cost effectiveness of private and public approaches to social housing provision (Peterson et al., 1998) and sustainable homeownership (Meen 1998).

Since the mid 1970s, however, there has been considerable pressure to move towards a more market based approach providing assistance to households to enable them to purchase or rent their own homes (Maclennan and Williams, 1990b; Turner and Whitehead, 1993). Studies have examined both the rationale for such a policy shift in terms of the economic principles underlying concepts of need and affordability (Whitehead, 1991; Hancock, 1993), and the impact of these changes on operation of housing systems (Hills et al., 1990; Boelhower and van der Heijden, 1993; Turner et al., 1996). Equally there have been analyses of both the rationale and the impact of privatisation policies with respect to both the housing stock and finance for social housing (Whitehead, 1993; Turner and Whitehead, 1993). While this strand of the literature is firmly embedded in economic analysis, examining, for instance the nature of the good housing, aspects of market imperfection and the relative impact of different forms of intervention, the vast majority of the research is either simply an economic input into a wider policy debate or a description of outcomes. Almost none of the material is based on either detailed formal models or strongly based empirical analysis.

## 3.2. Housing and labour markets

An important aspect of the social provision of housing is that the output is allocated to households by administrative rather than market mechanisms. This has impacts on household behaviour and on the nature of local housing and urban systems. The question which has been much discussed in the UK literature has been the impact of administrative allocation on mobility and ultimately employment. Hughes & McCormick (1981, 1985, 1987, 1990) have examined migration behaviour, comparing outcomes with the United States and with the UK, between council tenants and equivalent owner-occupiers. They show that council house tenants tend to migrate less often that those in the market sector and when they do move it is likely to be for housing rather than labour market reasons. More generally administrative allocation, rent controls and subsidies to owner-occupation are all shown adversely to affect the operation of the labour market (Bover et al., 1988). Earlier work by, for instance, Gordon and Lamont (1982), tended to point to tenure as an important determinant of differential unemployment at the local level. In the 1990s, much of the discussion has turned to tenure polarisation, social exclusion and urban regeneration rather than to interaction with the labour market per se.

## 3.3. The impact of local taxation

The impact of local taxation on house prices and community satisfaction has been an area of considerable interest in both North America and Europe. In the American literature much of the discussion has concentrated on Tiebout (1966) style analysis, evaluating the impact of the mix of expenditure and taxes on demand and price (Oates, 1969; Yinger, 1982; Wheaton, 1993). A survey of these approaches can be found in Yinger et al. (1988), which also includes estimates of the impact of tax reassessment, suggesting capitalisation in house prices of around 15–25%. Mieszkowski and Zodrow (1989) examines the impact of local expenditure and shows it to have an important impact on property values.

The UK, with its local taxation changes from property taxes to person-based taxes to a mixture of the two provides an interesting case study. Work for the Department of the Environment suggested on the basis of relative demand and supply elasticities subject to a range of constraints, uncertainties and transaction costs, that the impact of the change from property to person-based taxation would be of the order of 5% of total house prices (Department of the Environment, 1988). Hughes (1989a, b), using a similar approach, suggested a much larger impact.

There has been considerable interest in examining the relationship between local taxation and house prices in Sweden, where it has been an important element in the question of tenure neutrality in taxation as well as in the impact of taxation reform on house prices and output (Turner et al., 1996; Englund et al., 1995).

### 3.4. Rent control and its impact on the provision of rented housing

The impact of rent controls on the operation of the housing market has been the subject of more theoretic and empirical analysis on both sides of the Atlantic than almost any other housing topic. Many countries in Europe introduced rent controls during the 1914–1918 war with constraints continuing in varying degrees throughout the century (Arnott, 1988). In the US certain cities, notably New York, have had long experience of controls as well as periods of decontrol (Gyourko and Linneman, 1990; Ault and Saba, 1990). There have been detailed studies in countries around the world (e.g., Cheung, 1979 for Hong Kong; Malpezzi, 1986 for Cairo).

Early work concentrated on setting out the analytic framework in which to analyse the impact of rent control particularly on housing as an investment but also on prices in other markets (Frankena, 1975; Olsen, 1969; Cheung, 1975; Fallis and Smith, 1984; Kempner and Fine, 1989) as well as on empirical analyses of simple relationships (e.g., Olsen, 1972; Stegman, 1982). Much of this work has been criticised as being based on too simple models and on casual empiricism (Olsen, 1988).

One area where there has been considerable development both of theoretical models and empirical analysis is that of the impact of rent control on maintenance investment (Frankena, 1975; Dildine et al., 1974; Olsen, 1969, 1988; Albon and Stafford, 1990; Kutty, 1995, 1996). These have tended to suggest that there will be a deleterious effect on both quality and the life of the building but that better formulated policies can limit or even reverse these effects. Empirical studies have generated more results although the majority suggest reduced investment and increased dereliction (Cheung, 1975; Gyorko and Linneman, 1990). What they do suggest very strongly is that the specifics of controls are important in determining the extent and nature of landlord response.

In Europe and elsewhere much of the discussion on rent control has been subsumed into a wider discussion of the incentives and disincentives associated with the provision of privately rented housing (van der Heijden and Boelhouwer, 1996; Yates, 1996; Crook and Kemp, 1996) and of the attributes of private rented accommodation for landlords, tenants and investment (Whitehead, 1996). Again the analyses tend to be based on implicit models and to provide a general description of trends, incentives and constraints, rather than tests of more formal hypotheses.

## 4. Conclusions

A telling criticism of the current position of comparative housing market analysis can be found in the review by Renaud (1994) of Hårsman and Quigley (1991), which provides a comparative analysis of seven countries written by "highly regarded housing and urban economists". In this review Renaud suggests that we have gone a long way in understanding how housing markets are structured and what causes the failures and successes of particular policies. However, housing economics has not yet achieved a synthesis which allows effective comparison across countries within a simplified analytic framework.

This may be an overgenerous view of our understanding even at the national and local level. The areas where housing economics has always been strong have further improved over the last decade since the last major reviews (Mills, 1987; Smith et al., 1988). In particular income and price elasticities are more clearly founded in both theory and high quality econometric analysis. Considerable progress has been made in understanding the adjustment processes at national level and the extent and impact of market segmentation at the local level. Acting mainly as if the conditions necessary for competitive equilibrium apply has also enabled large strides to be made in policy analysis.

The overall result is that a great deal of progress has been made by applying general developments in economic and econometric theory to the specifics of the housing market, even when there is concern about both the suitability of assumptions and the quality and range of data available. At the national level treating housing as an asset among other financial assets reflects developments in the general finance market and increases our understanding of how housing investment decisions are made. Similarly the application of investment decision analysis has improved understanding of the operation of the market for existing housing and of the filtering process in particular.

However the limitations of this approach are also clear. Housing markets are inherently imperfect and addressing such imperfections at best one at a time may well be all that is possible but does not adequately reflect the complexity of relationships, especially in countries where government has played a large part in provision and allocation. Equally the inter-relationship between housing and land markets makes the development of robust supply side estimates particularly intractable, especially in countries where housing land is in relatively short supply.

The criticisms made by Arnott (in Mills, 1987) thus still apply perhaps even more strongly. Our understanding of imperfect markets, the impact of concentration of ownership and of monopolistic power remains extremely limited, even in the context of market models, let alone policy analysis. The transfer of both theoretical and econometric techniques from the US to European analysis has, if anything, lessened economists' interests both in developing understanding of imperfect markets and in more normative questions. What can be done in analytic terms and therefore meet peer group criteria is tending to dominate what may be more relevant to the more nationally organized, regulated and constrained markets of Europe.

In the policy context these comments apply even more strongly. Theory and policy analysis have undoubtedly come far closer together over the two decades since they were treated separately by Quigley (1979) and Weicher (1979). The extent of empirical analysis of the outcomes of policy has expanded enormously. However, technical developments continue to be based on the competitive market paradigm, which is far more relevant in the US than the European market.

In the US literature the emphasis in policy assessment is almost always on efficiency. Even here it is sometimes difficult to distinguish how far the conclusions, for instance that public sector housing generates welfare losses, demand side subsidies are better than supply side, local taxation and rent control distort the operation of the market, arise from the nature of the assumptions rather than from detailed understanding of what actually occurs. In Europe where the range of policies is far wider and the influence of government all pervasive, not only is the dichotomy even more difficult to address but the objectives are also more widely defined. The result is perhaps greater understanding of the complexity of institutions and inter-relationships but considerably less analysis that is strongly founded in theory. Everywhere the gap between what the housing economist is aiming to provide and what policy makers require remains very large. The result is that the vast majority of analyses tend to be seen as both too practical to satisfy technical criteria and too abstract to satisfy the policy makers. Perhaps these problems are inherent in the nature of housing as both a social and a market good.

The last decade has been a period of rapidly increasing sophistication in economic analysis both with respect to housing markets at the national level and in terms of our understanding of local markets and housing as a durable asset. It is less clear that there has been equivalent progress in the availability of suitable data which, in itself, impacts heavily on the types of questions that are researched. The areas where the least progress has occurred are the far more intractable problems of how effectively to address questions of market failure and to model and evaluate the interaction between government and the housing market.

# References

Albon, R.P. and D.C. Stafford (1990), "Rents control and housing maintenance", Urban Studies 27:233–240.

Alonso, W. (1964), Location and Land Use (Harvard University Press, Cambridge, MA).

Anas, A. (1978), "Dynamics of urban residential growth", Journal of Urban Economics 5:66–87.

Anas, A. and R.J. Arnott (1994), "The Chicago prototype housing market model with tenure choice and its policy implication", Journal of Housing Research 5:23–90.

Apgar, W.C. (1990), "Which housing policy is best?", Housing Policy Debate 1:1–32.

Arcelus, F. and A.H. Meltzer (1973), "The markets for housing and housing services", Journal of Money Credit and Banking 1:78–99.

Arnott, R. (1980), "A simple urban growth model with durable housing", Regional Science and Urban Economics 10:53–76.

Arnott, R. (1988), "Rent control: the international experience", Journal of Real Estate Finance and Economics 1:3.

Arnott, R. (1989), "Housing vacancies, thin markets and idiosyncratic tastes", Journal of Real Estate Finance and Economics 2:5–30.

Arnott, R., R. Davidson and D. Pines (1983), "Housing quality maintenance and rehabilitation", Review of Economic Studies 50:467–494.

Arnott, R., R. Davidson and D. Pines (1986), "The spatial aspects of housing quality, quantity and maintenance", Journal of Urban Economics 19:190–217.

Ault, R. and R. Saba (1990), "The economic effects of long-term rent control: the case of New York City", Journal of Real Estate Finance and Economics 3:25–41.

Awan, K., J.C. Odling-Smee and C.M.E. Whitehead (1982), "Housing attributes and the demand for private rented housing", Economica 49:183–200.

Ball, M. (1981), "The development of capitalism in housing provision", International Journal of Urban and Regional Research 5:145–177.

Ball, M. (1983), Housing Policy and Economic Power (Methuen, London and New York).

Ball, M. and R. Kirwa (1975), The Economics of an Urban Housing Market, Bristol Area Study (Centre for Environmental Studies, London).

Ball, M. and R. Kirwan (1977), "Accessibility and supply constraints in an urban housing market", Urban Studies 14:11–32.

Boehm, T. (1982), "A hierarchical model of housing choice", Urban Studies 19:17–31.

Boelhower, P. and H. van der Heijden (1992), Housing Systems in Europe (Delft University Press, Delft).

Boelhower, P. and H. van der Heijden (1993), "Housing policy and housing finances in seven European countries", in: B. Turner and C.M.E. Whitehead, eds., Housing Finance in the 1990s, SB56 (The National Institute for Building Research, Gävle).

Börsch-Supan, A. and H. Pollakowski (1990), "Estimating housing consumption adjustments from panel data", Journal of Urban Economics 27:131–150.

Bourassa, S.C. (1995), "A model of housing tenure choice in Australia", Journal of Urban Economics, 37:161–175.

Bover, O., J. Muellbauer and A. Murphy (1988), "Housing, wages and UK labour markets", Oxford Bulletin of Economics and Statistics 51:97–136.

Bradbury, K. and A. Downs, eds. (1982), Do Housing Allowances Work? (Brookings Institution, Washington, DC).

Bradbury, K., R. Engle, O. Irvine and J. Rothenberg (1977), "Simulation estimates of supply and demand for housing location in a multizoned metropolitan area", in: G.K. Ingram ed., Residential Location and Urban Housing Markets, pp. 51–86 (Lippincott, Ballinger for National Bureau of Economic Research, Cambridge, MA).

Braid, R. (1981), The short run comparative statistics of a rental housing market", Journal of Urban Economics 10:280–310.

Bramley, G. (1993), "The impact of land use planning and tax subsidies on the supply and price of housing in Britain", Urban Studies 30:5–30.

Brueckner, J. (1981), "A dynamic model of housing production", Journal of Urban Economics 10:1–14.

Buckley. R.M. (1982), "A simple theory of the UK housing sector", Urban Studies 19(3):303–312.

Buckley, R. and J. Ermisch (1982), "Government policy and house prices in the United Kingdom: an econometric analysis", Oxford Bulletin of Economics and Statistics 44:273–304.

Byatt, I.C.R., P. Holmes and D.W. Laidlaw (1973), "Income and the demand for housing: some evidence for Great Britain", in: Parkinson, ed., Essays in Modern Economics (Longman, London).

Case, K.E. and R. Schiller (1989) "The efficiency of the market for single family homes", American Economic Review 79:125–137.

Case, K.E. and R.J. Schiller (1990), "Forecasting prices and excess returns in the housing market", Journal of the American Real Estate and Urban Economics Association 18.

Cheshire, P. and S. Sheppard (1989), "British planning policy and access to housing", Urban Studies 26:469–485.

Cheshire, P. and S. Sheppard (1995), "On the price of land and the value of amenity", Econometrica 62:247–267

Cheshire, P. and S. Sheppard (1998), "Estimating the demand for housing, land and neighbourhood characteristics", Oxford Bulletin of Economics and Statistics 60(3):357–382.

Cheung, S.N.S. (1975), "Roofs or stars: the stated intent and actual effects of a rents ordinance", Economic Inquiry 13:1–21.

Cheung, S.N.S. (1979), "Rent control and housing reconstruction:the post-war experience of pre-war premises in Hong Kong", Journal of Law and Economics 22(1):27–53.

Chinloy, P. (1980), "An empirical model of the market for resale homes", Journal of Urban Economics 7:279–292.

Clayton, J. (1996), "Rational expectations, market fundamentals and housing price volatility", Real Estate Economics 4:441–470.

Clayton, J. (1997), "Are house price cycles driven by irrational expectations?", Journal of Real Estate Finance and Economics 14:341–364.

Crook, A.D.H. and P.A Kemp (1996), "The revival of private rented housing in Britain", Housing Studies 1:51–68.

Davies, G. (1974), "An econometric analysis of residential amenity", Urban Studies 11:217–225.

Davies, O. and A. Whinston (1961), "The economics of urban renewal", Law and Contemporary Problems 26:105–117.

Deaton, A. and J. Muellbauer (1980), "An almost ideal demand system", American Economics Review 70:312–326.

de Leeuw, F. (1971), "The demand for housing: a review of cross-section evidence", Review of Economics and Statistics 53:1–10.

de Leeuw, F. (1976), "The demand for housing: a review of the cross-sectional evidence", Review of Economics and Statistics 53:1–10.

de Leeuw, F. and N.F. Ekanem (1971), "The supply of rental housing", American Economic Review 61: 806–817.

de Leeuw, F. and R. Struyk (1975), The Web of Urban Housing (Urban Institute, Washington).

Dicks, M. (1990), "A simple model of the housing market", Bank of England Discussion Paper, No. 49.

Dildine, L.L., F.A. Massey and R.E. Worth (1974), "Dynamic model of private incentives to housing maintenance", Southern Economic Journal 40:631–639.

DiPasquale, D. and W.C. Wheaton (1992), "The cost of capital, tax reform and the future of the rental housing market", Journal of Urban Economics 31:337–359.

DiPasquale, D. and W.C. Wheaton (1994), "Housing market dynamics and the future of house prices", Journal of Urban Economics 35:1–27.

Edell, M. (1972), "Filtering in the private housing market", in: M. Edel and J. Rothenberg, eds., Reading in Urban Economics, pp. 204–215 (Macmillan, New York).

Engelhardt, G.V. and J.M. Poterba (1990), "House prices and demographic change: Canadian evidence", Regional Science and urban Economics 21:539–546.

Englund, P., P.H. Hendershott and B. Turner (1995), The Tax Reform and the Housing Market (National Institute of Economic Research Economic Council, Stockholm).

Ericsson, N.R. and D.F. Hendry (1985), "Conditional econometric modelling: an application to new house prices in the UK", in A.C. Atkinson and S.E. Feinberg, eds., A Celebration of Statistics (Springer-Verlag, Berlin).

Ermisch, J., J. Findlay, and K. Gibb (1996), "The price elasticity of demand for housing in Britain: issues of sample selection", Journal of Housing Economics 5:64–86.

Eubank, A.A. and C.F. Sirmans (1979), "The price adjustment mechanism for rental housing in the United States", Quarterly Journal of Economics 93(1):163–168.

Evans, A.W. (1973), The Economics of Residential Location (Macmillan, London).

Evans, A.W. (1995), "The property market:ninety per cent efficient", Urban Studies 32:5–29.

Fair, R.C. (1972), "Disequilibrium in housing models", Journal of Finance 27:207–221.

Fallis, G. and L.B. Smith (1984), "Uncontrolled prices in a controlled market: the case of rent controls", American Economic Review 74:193–200.

Follain, J.R. (1979), "The price elasticity of the long-run supply of new housing", Land Economics 55:190–199.

Follain, J.R. (1982), "Does inflation affect real behaviour?: the case of housing", Southern Economic Journal 48:570–582.

Follain, J.R. and E. Jimenez (1985), "Estimating the demand for housing characteristics: a survey and critique", Regional Science and Urban Economics 15:77–107.

Follain, J.R. and D.C. Ling (1988), "Another look at tenure choice, inflation and taxes", Journal of the American Real Estate and Urban Economics Association 16(3):207–229.

Frankena, M. (1975), "Alternative models of rent control", Urban Studies 12:303–308.

Freeman, A., A. Holmans and C.M.E. Whitehead (1996), Is the UK Different? International Comparisons of Tenure Expenditure and Subsidy (Council of Mortgage Lenders, London).

Friedman, J. and D.H. Weinberg (1981), "The demand for rental housing:evidence from the housing allowance demand experiment", Journal of Urban Economics 9:311–331.

Friedman, J. and D.A. Weinberg (1982), The Economics of Housing Vouchers (Academic Press, New York).

Fujita, M. (1976), "Spatial patterns of optimal growth", Journal of Urban Economics 3:193–208.

Gabriel, S.A. and F.E. Nothaff (1988), "Rental housing markets and the natural vacancy rate", Journal of the American Real Estate and Urban Economics Association 16:343–353.

Galster, G. (1981), "A neighbourhood interaction model of housing maintenance and quality changes by owner-occupants", Regional Science Perspectives 11:29–48.

Galster, G. (1987), Homeowners and Neighbourhood Reinvestment (Duke University Press, Durham, NC).

Galster, G. (1997), "Comparing demand side and supply-side housing policies: market and spatial perspectives", Housing Studies 12:561–577.

Gillingham, R. and R. Hagemann (1983), "Cross-sectional estimation of a simultaneous model of tenure choice and housing services demand", Journal of Urban Economics 14:16–39.

Giussani, B. and G. Hadjimatheou (1990), "House prices: an econometrics model of the UK", The APEX Centre Economics Discussion Paper No.1.

Giussani, B. and G. Hadjimatheou (1991), "Modelling regional house prices in the UK", Regional Science 70:201–219.

Goodman, A.C. (1981), "Housing submarkets within urban areas:definitions and evidence", Journal of Residential Science 21:175–185.

Goodman, A.C. (1988), "An econometric model of housing price, permanent income, tenure choice and housing demand", Journal of Urban Economics 23(1):327–353.

Goodman, A.C. (1995), "A dynamic equilibrium model of housing demand and mobility with transactions costs", Journal of Housing Ecotiomics 4:307–327.

Goodman, A.C. and M. Kawai (1984), "Replicative evidence on the demand for owner-occupied and rental housing", Southern Economic Journal 50:1036–1037.

Gordon, I.R. and D. Lamont (1982), "A model of labour market interdependencies in the London region", Environment and Planning A 14:237–264.

Gosling, J., G. Keogh and M. Stabler (1993), "House extensions and housing market adjustment: a case study of Wokingham", Urban Studies 30:1561–1576.

Grebler, L. and S.J. Maisel (1963), "Determinants of residential construction: a review of present knowledge", in: D. Suits et al., eds., Impacts of Monetary Policy (Prentice Hall, Englewood Cliffs).

Grieson, R.E. and J.R. White (1981), "The effects of zoning on structure and land markets", Journal of Urban Economics 10:27–85.

Grigsby, W. (1963), Housing Markets and Public Policy (University of Pennsylvania Press, Philadelphia).

Gyourko, J. and P. Linneman (1990), "Equity and efficiency aspects of rent control: an empirical study of New York City", Journal of Urban Economics 26:54–74.

Hadjimatheou, G. (1976), Housing and Mortgage Markets (Saxon House, Farnborough).

Hamilton, B.W. (1991), "The baby boom, the baby bust and the housing market: a second look", Regional Science and Urban Economics 21:547–552.

Hancock, K. (1993), "Can't pay, won't pay: or economic principles of affordability", Urban Studies 30(1):127–145.

Hancock, K. and D. Maclennan (1990), Housing Price Monitoring Systems and Housing Planning in Scotland (Central Research Unit, Scottish Office, Edinburgh).

Hansen, J.L., J.P. Formby and W.J. Smith (1996), "The income elasticity of demand for housing: evidence from concentration curves", Journal of Urban Economics 39:173–192.

Hanushek, E. and J. Quigley (1978), "An explicit model of intra-metropolitan mobility", Land Economy 54:411–429.

Hanushek, E. and J. Quigley (1979), "The dynamics of the housing market: a stock adjustment model of housing consumption", Journal of Urban Economics 6:90–111.

Hanushek, E. and J. Quigley (1980), "What is the price elasticity of renewal?", Review of Economics and Statistics 62:449–454.

Hanushek, E. and J. Quigley (1982), "The determinants of housing demand", in: J. Vernon Henderson, ed., Research in Urban Economics, vol. 2, pp. 221–242 (JAI Press, Greenwich, Corin).

Harrington, D.E. (1989), "An intertemporal model of housing demand: implications for the price elasticity", Journal of Urban Economics 25(2):230–246.

Hårsman, B. and J. Quigley, eds., (1991), Housing Markets and Housing Institutions: An International Comparison (Kluwer Academic, Boston, Dordrecht, London).

Haurin, D.R. (1991), "Income variability, home-ownership and housing demand", Journal of Housing Economics 1(1):60–74.

Haurin, D.R. and K. Lee (1989), "A structural model of the demand for owner-occupied housing", Journal of Urban Economics 26:348–360.

Hendershott, P. (1980), "Real user costs and the demand for single-family housing", Brookings Papers on Economic Activity, vol. 2, pp. 401–444 (Washington DC).

Hendershott, P.H. (1991), "Are real estate prices likely to decline by 47%?", Regional Science and Urban Economics 21:553–563.

Hendershott, P.H. and D.R. Haurin (1988), "Adjustments in the real estate market", Journal of the American Real Estate and Urban Economics Association 16:

Hendershott, P. and S.C. Hu (1981), "Inflation and extraordinary returns on owner-occupied housing: some implications of our capital allocation and productivity growth", Journal of Macroeconomics 3:177–203.

Henderson, J.V. (1985), Economic Theory and the Cities (Academic Press, Orlando).

Henderson, J.V. and Y.M. Ioannides (1983), "A model of housing tenure choice", American Economic Review 73:98–113.

Henderson, J.V. and Y.M. Ioannides (1986), "Tenure choice and the demand for housing", Economica 53:231–246.

Henderson, J.V. and Y.M. Ioannides (1989), "Dynamic aspects of consumer decisions in housing markets", Journal of Urban Economics 26:212–230.

Hendry, D.F. (1984), "Econometric modelling of house prices in the UK", in: D.F. Hendry and K.F. Wallis, eds., Econometrics and Quantitative Economics (Basil Blackwell, Oxford).

Hills, J. (1991), Unravelling Housing Finance (Oxford University Press, Oxford).

Hills, J., F. Hubert, H. Tomann and C.M.E. Whitehead (1990), "Shifting substitution for bricks and mortar to people", Housing Studies 5:147–167.

Holland, S.A. (1991), "The baby boom and the housing market: another look at the evidence", Regional Science and Urban Economics 21:565–571.

Holmans, A.E. (1995), Housing Demand and Need in England 1991–2011 (Joseph Rowntree Foundation, York).

Hoyt, H. (1939), Structure and Growth of Residential Neighbourhoods in American Cities (Federal Administration, Washington DC).

Hughes, G.A. (1989a), "The poll tax and the housing market", The Economic Review September:10–13.

Hughes, G.A. (1989b), "The switch from domestic rates to the community charge in Scotland", Fiscal Studies 10:1–12.

Hughes, G.A. and B. McCormick (1981), "Do council house policies reduce mobility between regions?", Economic Journal 91:919–937.

Hughes, G.A. and B. McCormick (1985), "Migration intentions in the UK: which households want to migrate and which succeed", Economic Journal 95:113–123.

Hughes, G.A. and B. McCormick (1987), "Housing markets, unemployment and labour market flexibility in the UK", European Economic Review 31:615–645.

Hughes, G.A. and B. McCormick (1990), "Housing and labour market mobility", in J. Ermisch, ed., Housing and the National Economy (National Institute of Economic and Social Research, London).

Igarashi, M. (1991), "The rent vacancy relationship in the rental housing market", Journal of Housing Economics 1.

Ihlanfeldt, K.R. (1982), "Property tax incidence on owner-occupied housing: evidence from the Annual Housing Survey", National Tax Journal 35:89–97.

Ingram, G.K., ed. (1977), Residential Location and Urban Housing Markets (Ballinger, Cambridge Mass).

Ingram, G.K. and J.F. Kain (1973), "A simple model of production and the abandonment problem", American Real Estate and Urban Economics Association Journal 1:79–106.

Ingram, G.K., J.F. Kain and J.R. Ginn (1972), The Rental Prototype of the NBER Urban Simulation Model (National Bureau of Economic Research, New York).

Ito, T. and K. Hirono (1993), "Efficiency of the Tokyo housing market", NBER Working Paper No. 4382.

Jimenez, E. and D. Keane (1984), "Housing consumption and permanent income in developing countries: estimates from panel data in El Salvador", Journal of Urban Economics 15:172–194.

Kain, J.F. and J.M. Quigley (1970), "Measuring the value of housing quality", Journal of the American Statistical Association June:532–547.

Kain, J. and J. Quigley (1972), "Housing market discrimination, home-ownership and savings behaviour", American Economic Review 62:263–277.

Kain, J.F. and J.M. Quigley (1975), Housing Markets and Racial Discrimination (National Bureau of Economic Research, New York).

Kaserman, D.L., J.L. Trimble and R.C. Johnson (1989), "Equilibrium in a negotiated market: evidence from housing", Journal of Urban Economics 26(1):30–42.

Kearl, J.R. (1979), "Inflation, mortgages and housing", Journal of Political Economy 87(5):115–1138.

Kempner, J.L. and M.E. Fine (1989), "The high cost of rent control", Journal of Real Estate Finance and Economics.

King, A.T. (1976), "The demand for housing", in: N. Terleckyj, ed., Household Production and Consumption (National Bureau of Economic Research, New York).

King, A.T. (1977), "The demand for housing: a Lancaster approach", Southern Economic Journal 43:1077–1087.

King, M.A. (1980), "An econometric model of tenure choice and the demand for housing as a joint decision", Journal of Public Economics 14:137–159.

Kirwan, R. and D. Martin (1972), The Economics of Urban Residential Renewal and Improvement, Working Paper CES WP77 (Centre for Environmental Studies, London).

Kiyotaki, N. and J.E. Moore (1997), "Credit cycles", Journal of Political Economy 105:211–248.

Kutty, N.K. (1995), "A dynamic model of landlord reinvestment behaviour", Journal of Urban Economics 37:212–237.

Kutty, N.K. (1996), "The impact of rent control in housing maintenance: a dynamic analysis incorporating European and North American rent regulations", Housing Studies 11:69–88.

Lancaster, K.J. (1966), "A new approach to consumer theory", Journal of Political Economy 74:132–157.

Lancaster, K. (1979), Variety, Equity and Efficiency (Basil Blackwell, Oxford).

Lansing, J.B., C.W. Clifton and J.N. Morgan (1969), New Homes and Poor People: a Study of Chains of Moves (Survey Research Centre, Ann Arbor).

Lee, T.H. (1964), "The stock demand elasticities of non-farm housing", Review of Economics and Statistics 49:82–89.

Lee, T.H. (1968), "Housing and permanent income", Review of Economics and Statistics 50:480–490.

Leven, C., J. Little, H. Nourse and R. Read (1976), Neighbourhood Change (Praeger, New York).

Linneman, P. (1985), "An economic analysis of the home-ownership decision", Journal of Urban Economics 17:230–246.

Lowry, I.S. (1960), "Filtering and housing standards: a conceptual analysis", Land Economics 36:362–370.

Lowry, I.S. (1983), Experimenting with Housing Allowances: The Final Report of the Housing Assistance Supply Experiment (Oelgechlager, Gunn and Hain, Cambridge, MA).

Lundqvist, L.J. (1988), Housing Policy and Tenures in Sweden, the Quest for Neutrality (Gower/Avebury, Aldershot).

Maclennan. D. (1977), "Some thoughts on the nature and purpose of house price studies", Urban Studies 14:39–71.

Maclennan, D. (1982), Housing Economics (Longman, Harlow).

Maclennan, D. and R. Williams, eds. (1990a), Affordable Housing in Britain and America (Joseph Rowntree Foundation, York).

Maclennan, D. and R. Williams, eds. (1990b), Affordable Housing in Europe (Joseph Rowntree Foundation, York).

Maclennan, D., M. Munro and G. Wood (1987), "Housing choice and the structure of the housing submarket", in: B. Turner, J. Kemeny and L. Lundquist, eds., Between State and Market Housing in the Post Industrial Era, pp. 26–51 (Almquist and Wicksell International, Stockholm).

Maclennan, D. and Y. Tu (1996), "The microeconomics of local housing market structure", Housing Studies 11:387–406.

Maisel, S.J., J.B. Burnham and J.S. Austin (1971), "The demand for housing: a comment", Review of Economics and Statistics 53:410–415.

Malpezzi, S.J. (1986), Rent Control and Housing Market Equilibrium: Theory and Evidence from Cairo, Doctoral Dissertation (George Washington University).

Malpezzi, S.J. and R. Green (1996), "What has happened at the bottom of the US housing market?", Urban Studies 33:1807–1820.

Mankiw, N.G. and D.N. Weil (1989), "The baby boom, the baby bust and the housing market", Regional Science and Urban Economics 19:235–258.

Mankiw, N.G. and D.N. Weil (1992), "The baby boom, the baby bust and the housing market", Regional Science and Urban Economics 21:573–579.

Margolis, S. (1982), "Depreciation of housing: an empirical consideration of the filtering hypothesis", Review of Economics and Statistics 64:90–96.

Mark, J.H. and M.A. Goldberg (1986), "A study of the impacts of zoning on housing values over time", Journal of Urban Economics 20: 257–273.

Mayo, S.K. (1981), "Theory and estimation in the economics of housing demand", Journal of Urban Economics 10:95–116.

Mayo, S.K. and S. Malpezzi (1985), Housing Demand in Developing Countries, WP-733 (The World Bank, Washington DC).

Mayo, S.K. and S. Sheppard (1991), "Housing supply and the effects of stochastic development control", Discussion Paper in Economics, Oberlin.

Mayo, S.K. and S. Sheppard (1996), "Housing supply under rapid economic growth and varying regulatory stringency: an international comparison", Journal of Housing Economics 5:274–289.

McDonald, J.F. (1979), Economic Analysis of an Urban Housing Market (Academic Press, New York).

McDonald, J.F. (1981), "Capital-land substitution in urban housing: a survey of empirical estimates", Journal of Urban Economics 9:190–211.

McLeod, B. and J. Ellis (1982), "Housing consumption over the family life cycle: an empirical analysis", Urban Studies 19:177–185.

Meen, G. (1989), "The ending of mortgage rationing and its effects on the housing market: a simulation study", Urban Studies 26:240–253.

Meen, G. (1990), "The removal of mortgage market constraints and the implications for econometric modelling", Oxford Bulletin of Economics and Statistics 52.1:1–24.

Meen, G. (1993), The Treatment of House Prices in Macroeconometric Models (Department of the Environment, London).

Meen, G. (1996a), "Spatial aggregation, spatial dependence and predictability in the UK housing market", Housing Studies 11:345–372.

Meen, G. (1996b), "Ten propositions in UK housing macroeconomics: an overview of the 1980s and early 1990s", Urban Studies 33:425–444.

Meen, G. (1998), "Modelling sustainable home-ownership: demographics or economics", Urban Studies 35(11):1919–1934.

Meen, G. and M. Andres (1998), Modeling Regional House Prices, A Review of the Literature (Department of Environment, Transport & the Regions, London).

Megbolugbe, I. and P. Linneman (1993), "Home ownership", Urban Studies 30:659–682.

Mendelsohn, R. (1977), "Empirical evidence on home improvements", Journal of Urban Economics 4:459–468.

Meyer, N. (1981), "Rehabilitation decisions in rental housing", Journal of Urban Economics 10:76–94.

Meyer, N. (1985), "The impacts of lending, race and ownership on rental housing rehabilitation", Journal of Urban Economics 17:349–374.

Meyer, R. and K. Wiend (1996), "Risk and return to housing, tenure choice and the value of housing in an asset pricing context", Real Estate Economics 24:113–132.

Mieskowski, P. and G.R. Zodrow (1989), "Taxation and the Tiebout model", Journal of Economic Literature 27:1098–1146.

Mills, E.S. (1967), "An aggregative model of resource allocation in a metropolitan area", American Economic Review 57:197–210.

Mills, E.S. ed. (1987), Handbook of Regional and Urban Economics (North Holland, Amsterdam).

Milne, A. (1991), Incomes, Demography and UK House Prices, LBS Centre for Economic Forecasting, Discussion Paper 39-90.

Monk, S., B.J. Pearce and C.M.E. Whitehead (1996), "Land use planning, land supply and house prices", Environment and Planning A 28:495–511.

Muellbauer, J. and A. Murphy (1994), "Explaining regional house prices in the UK", mimeo (Universities of Oxford and Durham).

Muellbauer, J. and A. Murphy (1997), "Booms and busts in the UK housing market", Economic Journal 107:1701–1727.

Muth, R.F. (1960), "The demand for non-farm housing", in: A. Harberger, ed., The Demand for Durable Goods, pp. 29–96 (University of Chicago Press, Chicago).

Muth, R.F. (1969), Cities and Housing (University of Chicago Press, Chicago).

Muth, R.F. (1973), "A vintage model of the housing stock", Paper of the Regional Science Association 30:141–156.

Muth, R.F. (1988), "Housing market dynamics", Regional Science and Urban Economics 18:345–356.

Needleman, L. (1969), The Economics of Housing (Staples Press, London).

Nellis, J.G. and J.A. Longbottom (1981), "An empirical analysis of the determination of house prices in the UK", Urban Studies 18:9–22.

Nesslein, T.S. (1982), "The Swedish housing model: an assessment", Urban Studies 19:235–246.

Nesslein, T.S. (1988), "Housing: the market versus the welfare state model revisited", Urban Studies 25:95–108.

Oates, W.E. (1969), "The effects of property taxes and local public spending on property values: an empirical study of tax capitalisation and the Tiebout hypothesis", Journal of Political Economy 77:957–971.

Ohls, J. (1975), "Public policy towards low income housing and filtering in housing markets", Journal of Urban Economics 2:144–171.

Olsen, E.O. (1969), "A competitive theory of the housing market", American Economic Journal Part 1, 59:612–621.

Olsen, E.O. (1972), "An econometric analysis of rent control", Journal of Political Economy 80:1081–1100.

Olsen, E.O. (1988), "What do economists know about the effect of rent control on housing maintenance?", Journal of Real Estate Finance and Economics 295–307.

Ozanne, L. (1996), "Do supply curves slope up? the empirical relevance of the critique of product economics", Cambridge Journal of Economics 20:749–762.

Ozanne, L. and R. Struyk (1976), Housing from the Existing Stock (Urban Institute, Washington DC).

Ozanne, L. and R. Struyk (1978), "The price elasticity of supply of housing services", in L. Bourne and J.R. Hitchcock, eds., Urban Housing Markets: Recent Directives in Research and Policy (University of Toronto Press, Toronto).

Pain, N. and P. Westerway (1996), Modelling Structural Change in the UK Housing Market (National Institute of Economics and Social Research, London).

Parsons, G.R. (1986), "An almost ideal demand system for housing attributes", Southern Economic Journal 53:347–363.

Peterson, W., C. Pratten and J. Tatch (1998), An Economic Model of the Demand and Need for Social Housing (Department of Environment, Transport and the Regions, London).

Polinsky, A.M. (1977), "The demand for housing: a study in specification and grouping", Econometrica 45:447–461.

Polinsky, A.M. and D.T. Ellwood (1979), "An empirical reconciliation of micro and grouped estimates of the demand for housing", Review of Economics and Statistics 61:199–205.

Pollakowski, H.O. and S.M. Wachter (1990), "The effects of land use constraints on house prices", Land Economics 66:315–324.

Potepan, M.J. (1989), "Interest rates, income and home improvement decisions", Journal of Urban Economics 25:282–294.

Poterba, J.M. (1984), "Tax subsidies to owner-occupied housing: and asset market approach", Quarterly Journal of Economics 99:729–752.

Poterba, J.M. (1991), "House price dynamics: the role of tax policy and demography", Brookings Papers in Economic Activity 2:143–203.

Pozdena, R.J. (1988), The Modern Economics of Housing: a Guide to Theory and Policy (Quorum Books, Greenwood Press).

Pryce, G. (in press) "Constructive elasticities and land availability", Urban Studies.

Quigley, J. (1979), "What have we learned about urban housing markets?", in: P. Mieszkowski and M. Straszheim, eds., Current Issues in Urban Economics, pp. 391–429 (John's Hopkins, Baltimore).

Rabianski, J. and J. Spitzer (1978), "A two-sector cross-section econometric model of the 1970 housing stock", Growth and Change 9:2–8.

Read, C. (1991), "An equilibrium model of advertising and natural vacancies in a spatially differentiated housing market", Journal of Housing Economics 1.

Reece, B.F. (1988), "The price adjustment process for rental housing: some further evidence", Journal of the American Real Estate and Urban Economics Association 16:411–418.

Reid, M. (1962), Housing and Income (University of Chicago Press, Chicago).

Renaud, B. (1994), "Book review", Journal of Housing Economics 3:156–163.

Rosen, K.T. (1974), "Hedonic prices and implicit markets: product differentiation in pure competition", Journal of Political Economy 82:34–55.

Rosen, K.T. and L.B. Smith (1983), "The price adjustment process for rental housing and the natural vacancy rate", American Economic Review 73:779–786.

Rosenthal, L. (1989), "Income and price elasticities of demand for owner-occupied housing in the UK: evidence pooled cross-sectional and time series data", Applied Economics 21:761–775.

Rothenberg, J. (1967), The Economics of Urban Renewal (Brookings Institute, Washington).

Rothenberg, J. (1983), "Housing investment, housing consumption and tenure choice", in: R. Grieson, ed., The Urban Economy and Housing (Lexington Books, Lexington).

Rothenberg, J., G.C. Galster, R.V. Butler and J. Pitkin (1991), The Maze of Urban Housing Markets (University of Chicago Press, Chicago).

Rouwendal, J. (1989), Choice and Allocation Models for the Housing Market (Kluwer Academic Publishers, Dordrecht).

Rydell, C.P. (1976), "Measuring the supply response to housing allowances", Papers of the Regional Science Association, 37:31–57.

Rydell, C.P., K. Neels and C.L. Barnett (1982), Price Effects of a Housing Allowance Program R-2720HUD (Rand Corporation, Santa Monica).

Seek, N. (1983), "Adjusting housing consumption: improve or move", Urban Studies 20:455–469.

Segal, D. (1979), The Economics of Neighbourhood (Academic Press, New York).

Shea, J. (1993), "Do supply curves slope up?", Quarterly Journal of Economics 108(1):1–32.

Smith, J.W. (1989), "A theoretical analysis of the supply of housing", Journal of Urban Economics 26:174–188.

Smith, L.B. et al. (1984), "The demand for housing, headship rates and household formation: an international comparison", Urban Studies 21:407–414.

Smith, L.B., K.T. Rosen and G. Fallis (1988), "Recent developments in economic models of housing markets", Journal of Economic Literature 26:29–64.

Stahl, K. (1985), Microeconomic Models of Housing Markets (Springer-Verlag, Berlin).

Stegman, M. (1972), Housing Investment in the Inner City: The Dynamics of Decay (MIT Press, Cambridge).

Stegman, M.A. (1982), The Dynamics of Rental Housing in New York City (Rutgers University, New Jersey).

Sternlieb, G. and B. Burchall (1973), Residential Abandonment: The Tenement Landlord Revisited (Rutgers University Press, New Brunswick, NJ).

Stover, M. (1986), "The price elasticity of supply of single family detached housing", Journal of Urban Economics 20:331–340.

Straszheim, M. (1975), An Econometric Analysis of the Urban Housing Market (National Bureau of Economic Research, New York).

Struyk, R.J. (1976), Urban Home-ownership (DC Heath, Lexington).

Struyk, R.J. and M. Bendick (1981), Housing Vouchers for the Poor: Lessons from a National Experiment (The Urban Institute Press, Washington DC).

Sweeney, J.L. (1974a), "A commodity hierarchy model of the rental housing market", Journal of Urban Economics 1:288–323.

Sweeney, J.L. (1974b), "Quality commodity hierarchies and housing markets", Econometrica:147–167.

Taub, R., G.D. Taylor and D. Durban (1984), Paths of Neighbourhood Change (Chicago University Press, Chicago).

Tiebout, C.M. (1966), "A pure theory of local expenditures", Journal of Political Economy 64:416–424.

Tompkinson, P. (1979), "A model of housebuilder's supply behaviour", Applied Economics 11:195–210.

Topel, R. and S. Rosen (1988), "Housing investment in the United States", Journal of Political Economy 96:718–740.

Tsoukis, C. and P. Westaway (1994), "A forward looking model of housing construction in the UK", Economic Modelling 11:266–279.

Tu, Y. (1997), "The local housing sub-market structure and its properties", Urban Studies 34:337–353.

Turner, B., J. Kemeny and L.J. Lundqvist (1977), Between State and Market: Housing in the Post-Industrial Era (Almqvist and Wiksell International, Göteborg).

Turner, B. and C.M.E. Whitehead (1993), Housing Finance in the 1990s, SB56 (The National Institute for Building Research, Gävle).

Turner, B., C.M.E. Whitehead and J. Jacobsson (1996), "Comparative housing finance", in: Bostadspolitik 2000 Statens offentliga utredningar 1996: 156 (SOU, Stockholm).

van der Heijden, H. and P. Boelhouwer (1996), "The private rented sector in Western Europe: developments since the Second World War and prospects for the future", Housing Studies 11(1):13–34.

Vandell, K. (1981), "The effects of racial composition in neighbourhood succession", Urban Studies 18:315–333.

Watson, C.J. (1973), Household Movement in West Central Scotland, Occasional Paper No 26 (Centre for Urban and Regional Studies, Birmingham).

Weicher, J. (1979), "Urban housing policy", in: P. Mieszkowski and M. Stroszheim, eds., Current Issues in Urban Economics, pp. 469–508 (John's Hopkins, Baltimore).

Weicher, J. and T. Thibodeau (1988), "Filtering and housing markets", Journal of Urban Economics 23:21–40.

Weinberg, D.H., J. Friedman, and S.K. Mayo (1981), "Intraurban residential mobility: the role of transaction costs, market imperfections and disequilibrium", Journal of Urban Economics 9:332–348.

Wheaton, W.C. (1979), "Monocentric models of urban land use: contributions and critiques", in: P. Mieszkowski and M. Straszheim, eds., Current Issues in Urban Economics, pp. 107–129 (John's Hopkins University Press, Baltimore).

Wheaton, W.C. (1985), "Life-cycle theory, inflation and the demand for housing", Journal of Urban Economics 18:161–179.

Wheaton, W.C. (1990), "Vacancy, search and prices in a housing market matching model", Journal of Political Economy 98:1270–1292.

Wheaton, W.C. (1993), "Land capitalisation, Tiebout mobility and the role of zoning regulations", Journal of Urban Economics 34.

White, M.J. (1977), "On cumulative urban growth and urban density functions", Journal of Urban Economics 4:104–112.

White, M.J. (1986), "Property taxes and urban housing abandonment", Journal of Urban Economics 20:312–330.

White, M.J. and L. White (1977), "The tax subsidy to owner-occupied housing: who benefits?", Journal of Public Economics 7:111–126.

Whitehead, C.M.E. (1971), "A model of the UK housing market", Bulletin of Oxford University Institute of Economics and Statistics 33:245–266.

Whitehead, C.M.E. (1974), The UK Housing Market: An Econometric Model (Saxon House, Farnborough).

Whitehead, C.M.E. (1984), "Privatisation and housing", in: J. Le Grand and R. Robinson, eds., Privatisation and the Welfare State (Allen and Unwin, London).

Whitehead, C.M.E. (1991), "From need to affordability", Urban Studies 8:871–886.

Whitehead, C.M.E. (1993), "Privatising housing: an assessment of UK experience", Housing Policy Debate 4:101–139.

Whitehead, C.M.E. (1996), "Private renting in the 1990s", Housing Studies 11:7–12.

Whitehead, C.M.E. and J. Odling-Smee (1975), "Long run disequilibrium in the housing market", Urban Studies 12:315–318.

Witte, A., H. Sumko and H. Erikson (1979), "An Estimate of a structural hedonic price model of the housing market: an application of Rosen's theory of implicit markets", Econometric 47:1151–1174.

Wood, G. (1988), "Housing tax expenditures in OECD countries: economic impacts and prospects for reform", Policy and Politics 16.

Wood, G. (1991), Taxation and Housing, National Housing Strategy Background Paper No. 5 (AGPS, Canberra).

Woodward, S.E. (1991), "Economists' prejudices: why the Mankiw–Weil story is not credible", Regional Science and Urban Economics 21:531–537.

Yates, J. (1996), "Towards a reassessment of the private rental market", Housing Studies 11(1):35–50.

Yates, J. and C.M.E. Whitehead (1998), "In defence of greater agnoticism: a response to Galster's 'Comparing demand side and supply side housing policies' ", Housing Studies 13(3):415–424.

Yinger, J. (1979), "Prejudice and discrimination in the urban housing market", in P. Mieszkowski and M. Straszheim, eds., Current Issues in Urban Economics (John's Hopkins, Baltimore).

Yinger, J. (1982), "Capitalization and the theory of local public finance", Journal of Political Economy 90:917–943.

Yinger, J., H. Bloom, A. Börsch-Supan and H. Ladd (1988), Property Taxes and House Values: the Theory and Estimation of Intra-Jurisdictional Property Tax Capitalisation (Academic Press, San Diego, CA).

*Chapter 41*

# HEDONIC ANALYSIS OF HOUSING MARKETS

STEPHEN SHEPPARD*

*Oberlin College, Ohio*

## Contents

* I would like to thank Joseph Gyourko, Paul Chesire and Ed Mills for helpful comments on an earlier draft of this chapter.

*Handbook of Regional and Urban Economics. Edited by E.S. Mills and P. Cheshire*

## Abstract

This chapter examines the hedonic analysis of housing markets. These techniques have been widely applied in studies of the demand for housing attributes and environmental amenities. The chapter discusses the theoretical foundation of hedonic analysis, the use of hedonic estimates of demand for welfare analysis, the empirical difficulties that arise in such studies, and some of the methods for overcoming these difficulties.

**Keywords:** Housing attribute demand, Hedonic prices

## 1. Introduction

Imagine, for a moment, that you are a private investigator or market researcher studying the demand for food. You have a particular disadvantage, however, in that you have been banned from entering the local grocer. You have found a place outside where you can sit and photograph shoppers as they approach the checkout counter, and from these photographs you can pretty much tell what foods each customer has purchased (although some items may be obscured in the shopping basket) and the total cost of all items combined. By bribing a contact at the local bank, you are able to find out each shopper's income. That is all the information you have. From this, can you infer the demand for eggs? Can you determine how much households would be willing to pay to remove sugar import quotas?

Such a difficult assignment is essentially what is undertaken in the hedonic analysis of housing markets. We have no direct observations of attribute prices. We have somewhat imprecise observations of what attributes are purchased. We have reasonably good observations of what is spent for the entire bundle, and how much income the household has. From this we attempt to answer some important questions.

Housing and residential construction are of central importance for determination of both the level of welfare in society and the level of aggregate economic activity. In many economies a residence represents the most valuable single asset owned by most individuals, and a very large share of total household wealth.

In all economies the share of income spent on housing represents a very large fraction of total expenditure. It is thus to be expected that economists would devote considerable effort towards understanding the structure of the demand for housing and equilibria in these markets.

The first difficulty that arises in this effort stems from the obvious heterogeneity of the product. To attempt a comparison between the price of houses in China and Chile, or between housing prices in 1996 and 1946 requires us to address the similarity and appropriateness of making such a comparison. We observe a low-income central city resident who pays $500 per month for housing, while the more affluent suburban family in the same city has a monthly expenditure of $1500. Can we conclude that the central city resident is lucky and faces a price of housing lower than in the suburbs? More subtly, suppose we observe that these residences are really very different. Are the different choices made by the two households attributable to different incomes, different preferences, nonmarket constraints on choice, or differences in the effective prices of the attributes that characterize each house? To answer such questions, we have no choice but to undertake hedonic analysis of the market.

The important work of Griliches (1961, 1971) did much to introduce hedonic analysis and techniques for dealing with commodity heterogeneity to a wider audience of economists. Griliches and many others have rightly referred to the work of Court (1939) as an early pioneer in the application of these techniques, as well as the first to apply the term "hedonic" to analysis of prices and demand for the individual sources of pleasure—the attributes which combine to characterize heterogeneous commodities. A decade before the appearance of Court's work, however, the study of Waugh (1929) appears to be the first to provide a systematic analysis of the impact of "quality" on the price of a commodity. Waugh characterizes quality using a variety of observable attributes, and estimates the implicit price of each of these attributes. Not only is the study the first to estimate what we now call a "hedonic price function", it is an important early application of multivariate statistical techniques to economics. It nicely illustrates the way in which hedonic analysis was, and is, an important source of econometric innovation for the profession.

This chapter reviews several aspects of the hedonic analysis of housing markets, focusing broadly on the theoretical foundation of such analysis followed by the practical implementation. Within each of these areas, we consider the issues which affect the determination and estimation of implicit prices for housing attributes, as well as the difficult problems which confront the use of these prices to estimate the demand for characteristics.

This reflects a basic dichotomy which is also present in the literature. There is a large body of work that focuses more or less exclusively on inference of the implicit prices of housing and environmental characteristics. Such information is of considerable value in the construction of price indices which take proper account of changes in the quality of the goods produced, and also in estimating or forecasting values of real estate assets. A second branch of the literature uses these implicit prices to estimate the structure of household demand for housing attributes, and to evaluate the welfare consequences of changes in attribute prices or environmental quality.

There have been several excellent surveys of all or important parts of this literature. The papers by Mayo (1981), Follain and Jimenez (1985), Palmquist (1991) and others provide particularly useful accounts of the progress made in this area, and one might "review" this area of urban economics by simply referring the reader to these. The discussion below, in addition to highlighting some of the more recent contributions in this area, provides an alternative view of some of these developments.

## 2. Theoretical foundation

Before discussing the actual estimation and use of hedonic models of housing markets, we begin with a discussion of some of the theoretical constructs that are the foundation of this approach. We begin with some preliminary remarks concerning "implicit markets" before turning to discussion of hedonic price functions and the structure of demand for housing attributes.

### 2.1. Implicit markets

The notion of implicit markets denotes the process of production, exchange, and consumption of commodities that are primarily (perhaps exclusively) traded in "bundles". The explicit market, with observed prices and transactions, is for the bundles themselves. Such a market, however, might be thought of as constituting several implicit markets for the components of the bundles themselves. This is of particular importance when the bundles are not homogeneous, but vary due to the varying amounts of different components that they contain.

There are at least two possible perspectives to take on implicit markets, that differ more in their emphasis and orientation than in the final theory whose development is thus motivated. On the one hand, we might regard the demand for all goods—even those that appear to be homogeneous—as not being based on the goods themselves but on the characteristics they embody. The household purchases these goods and uses them as a type of 'input', transforming them into utility, the level of which depends on the quantity of characteristics embodied in the goods purchased. This approach, motivated at least in part by the work of Lancaster (1966), tends to place particular emphasis on household production and the properties of household demand for the (sometimes unobservable) characteristics.

An alternative view emphasizes the idea that some goods are usefully combined and thought of as being traded in a single "market", but they are quite heterogeneous—automobiles, workers and houses are all reasonable examples. Such markets are incapable of being analyzed with the usual economic models because they are not characterized or even approximated by a single price, but rather by a range of prices that depend on the quality of the commodity or the characteristics it contains. The hedonic approach attacks this difficulty by asserting that these goods, while globally heterogeneous, are composed of aggregates of (more or less) homogeneous parts, and while the aggregate bundle may not have a common price, the component attributes do (or at least have a common price structure). The hedonic approach provides a methodology for identifying the structure of prices of the component attributes (estimation of the hedonic price function). Analysis of demand can then proceed using these prices, estimating a demand system in which the attributes are treated as goods. This involves an implicit assumption that a variety of aggregate bundles are available in the market so that consumers can choose any bundle of attributes they wish, being constrained only by their incomes and the price of the resulting bundle.

If we let $Z$ represent a vector of quantities of these attributes that differentiate the commodities, the hedonic approach starts by recognizing that first, each consumer may consume a different commodity, in the sense that each consumer may consume a unit of the good with a different amount of $Z$ embodied. Second, each consumer may pay a different price for the good, so that a range of marginal prices may exist that, in general, depend on the quantity of $Z$.

## 2.2. Hedonic price functions

Hedonic price functions are estimated for two primary reasons: (1) for use in construction of overall price indices that account for changes in the quality of goods produced; and (2) as an input in the analysis of consumer demand for attributes of heterogeneous goods. To understand the appropriate estimation techniques and problems, and to interpret the results, we must begin with an understanding of how a market for heterogeneous goods can be expected to function, and what types of equilibria we can expect to observe.

We begin with a recapitulation of the basic theory of hedonic markets. Consumers are assumed to derive utility from consumption of a commodity that embodies a vector $Z$ of $J$ different characteristics, plus consumption of a composite good $Y$. They have fixed income $M$ and face a price function $P(Z)$ that gives the price of the heterogeneous good (that we refer to as housing) as a function of the embodied characteristics $Z$. The preferences of the household are represented by the utility function

$$u = u(Z, Y, \alpha), \tag{2.1}$$

where $\alpha$ is a vector of observed and unobserved parameters which characterize the preferences of the household. Households are therefore assumed to be fully characterized by an income $M$ and parameter vector $\alpha$, with distribution over possible values described by the joint probability $f(\alpha, M)$.

From the utility function (2.1) we can derive the amount that a household would be willing to pay for a house as a function of the embodied characteristics, given the income and achieved utility level for the household. This household "bid rent" function $\beta(Z, M, u, \alpha)$ is defined implicitly by:

$$u = u(Z, M - \beta, \alpha) \tag{2.2}$$

The derivative of the bid rent function $\partial \beta / \partial Z_i$ gives the rate at which the household would be willing to change expenditure on a house as characteristic $i$ increases, while holding the utility level constant. This is the inverse of the compensated demand curve.

The household chooses a house with characteristics $Z$, and consumption of composite commodity $Y$, to solve:

$$\max_{Z,Y} u(Z, Y, \alpha) \quad \text{subject to } M \geq P(Z) + Y. \tag{2.3}$$

First-order conditions for this problem require that,

$$\frac{u_i}{u_Y} = P_i \forall i, \tag{2.4}$$

where subscripts indicate partial derivatives so that $u_i = \partial u / \partial Z_i$ and $P_i = \partial P / \partial Z_i$. The derivative $P_i$ is usually referred to as the *hedonic price* of characteristic $i$, and the function $P(Z)$ as the *hedonic price function*.

Combining the first-order conditions in Eq. (2.4) with implicit differentiation of Eq. (2.2) yields the familiar result that optimal choice of a house is characterized by equality between the slope of the bid rent and the hedonic price for each characteristic:

$$\frac{\partial \beta}{\partial Z_i} = \frac{u_i}{u_Y} = P_i. \tag{2.5}$$

This observation is part of the justification of the hedonic approach to analysis of markets, for it indicates that if we can "observe" (or estimate) the hedonic price for a characteristic and the choice made by the consumer, then under the assumption of optimizing behavior the observation provides local information about the consumer's preferences or willingness to pay for attributes in the neighborhood of the observed choice. In this sense, the problem seems similar to the standard analysis of consumer behavior, in which observed choices and prices provide local information about consumer preferences, and given sufficient data we can hope to make accurate inferences about consumer behavior and price determination. As we shall see below, the hedonic market problem is substantially more complex.

To complete the model, we must provide an explanation for the determination of the hedonic price function $P$. For this we introduce producers of the heterogeneous good who are characterized by cost functions $C(Z, N, \gamma)$ that depend on the characteristics $Z$ of the houses supplied, the number $N$ of such houses built, and a vector $\gamma$ of parameters that characterize each producer. Thus, the profit of a producer is given by,

$$\pi = P(Z) \cdot N - C(Z, N, \gamma). \tag{2.6}$$

There are a variety of producers, and their distribution is described by the probability density $g(\gamma)$. Each of these producers is assumed to take the price function $P(Z)$ as given and solve,

$$\max_{Z,N} P(Z) \cdot N - C(Z, N, \gamma). \tag{2.7}$$

The first-order conditions for solution of this require that,

$$P_i = C_i \forall i \tag{8a}$$
$$P(Z) = C_N. \tag{8b}$$

Thus, each producer equates the marginal cost of each characteristic to its hedonic price, and builds houses until the marginal cost of building another house (of type $Z$) is equal to the value of the house $P(Z)$. There will typically be a large number of housing producers active in the market, with sellers of existing housing consisting of a special type of producer with $N = 1$ and a cost function $C(.)$ that is determined by the costs and technology of house repair and remodeling.

Equilibrium in this market for heterogeneous goods requires a hedonic price function $P(Z)$ that equates supply and demand for every type of house $Z$. This equilibrium is conventionally represented as a locus of tangencies between a series of marginal cost curves, $C_i$, and the derivatives $\beta_i$ of the bid rent curves. In general, as pointed out in Epple (1987) inter alia, the equilibrium price function depends on the distributions $f(\alpha, M)$ and $g(\gamma)$. This dependence has also been discussed in the context of labor markets in Tinbergen (1959) and Sattinger (1980).

This dependency is clear when one considers extreme examples. Suppose that there are a variety of consumers but only one type of producer, so that $g(\gamma)$ is degenerate. In this case, the equilibrium will have only a single $C_i$ for each characteristic, and all $\beta_i$ will be tangent to it. An equilibrium hedonic price function would be the cost function $C$. In general, then, the equilibrium hedonic price function depends on the distribution of consumers and producers. It is possible to endogenize the distribution $g$ using a zero profit condition to generate "entry" and "exit" of house producers who behave as described above, increasing or decreasing the density of each producer type $\gamma$ until a type of "long run" equilibrium condition is met.

This provides a theoretically coherent foundation for explaining the relationship between the price of a house (or other heterogeneous good) and the characteristics it possesses. It describes the actions of market participants, and provides equilibrium conditions in which these actions combine to determine the hedonic price relationship. Furthermore, it does so in a way that underscores the potential usefulness of observing this relationship. Apart from the difficulties in actually carrying out the estimation required for this "observation", there are still some gaps that have been addressed by researchers or provide opportunities for future research.

The gaps that seem of greatest relevance in the present context relate to aspects that set the market for houses apart from the markets for other heterogeneous commodities, such as breakfast cereals or automobiles. Some of these aspects are shared with a few other markets, but in any event are not incorporated into the standard formulations of hedonic models of housing markets. Consider the following features of housing markets:

- *Housing markets involve search*: It is costly to collect information concerning the characteristics embodied in a particular structure, and as a result there is uncertainty about the exact nature of the hedonic price function. A consumer purchases a house by examining a sequence of structures, eventually beginning the process of making offers on properties (possibly continuing to sample) and continuing until the expected increase in utility from continued search is less than the cost. In this sense, the housing market is similar to other "matching" type markets such as the labor market.

- *Housing markets are intrinsically spatial*: Houses involve varying quantities of land, and possess particular locations. Many empirical studies do not even include location as a characteristic of the house, let alone take advantage of the special nature of this characteristic. The special nature arises when all (or most) relevant local amenities have been accounted for, so that the only factor that distinguishes one location from another is the transport costs. In this case, the bid rent curve for locations with greater accessibility is determined by the transport cost function.

- *Housing markets involve both new and existing homes*: Perhaps the most significant difference between housing and other heterogeneous goods markets is the importance of the sale of existing (previously produced) goods. The share of house sales accounted for by new construction is relatively small in almost all housing markets. Consumers can substitute between them, and seek out the type, whether new or old, that maximizes utility. While this poses no problem for the consumer side of the market, how should this factor be incorporated into the supply side of the market?

In addition to the observations made above, we can also question whether, or not, the "hedonic approach" itself has any testable implications. Are there observations that could be made concerning the implicit price of housing attributes that would refute some or all of the theory outlined above? One issue concerns the convexity of the hedonic price function. This in turn translates into the convexity of the consumer's budget set, that would, if violated, make problematic the first-order characterization of consumer choice outlined in Eq. (2.4) above.

In a restrictive setting (all attributes and commodities perfectly divisible) Jones (1988) shows that in equilibrium, hedonic price functions must be convex. He also shows that in this setting they must be linearly homogeneous. In practice, most estimated hedonic price functions satisfy convexity (see Anderson, 1985), but a great many fail to satisfy the homogeneity restriction.

## 2.3. Structure of demand and welfare evaluation

A primary reason for undertaking hedonic analysis of housing markets is to understand the structure of demand for housing attributes and environmental amenities. Such understanding is essential for predicting the response to changes in the housing market and for providing welfare estimates of the costs and benefits associated with such changes. In this section, we explore some of the properties that can be expected of such demand, and the way in which these properties inform and constrain the application of hedonic analysis. In this context, we begin with a consideration of the extent to which "demand functions" can be derived within the hedonic framework, and which properties these relationships might be expected to exhibit. We then discuss the way in which these relationships might be applied to evaluate the welfare consequences of changes that affect the prices of attributes or the levels of environmental amenities.

### 2.3.1. *Properties of attribute demand*

Because the hedonic price of an attribute is typically not constant, an ambiguity arises in presenting housing "demand" within the context of a hedonic model. If we know the structure of preferences for housing and environmental characteristics, we can present the demand functions that would characterize a household with those preferences if they faced constant prices. Alternatively, we can present behavioral functions that represent the choices that would be made by a utility maximizing household, as a function not of hedonic prices, but rather of the parameters of the hedonic price function. The first would present quantities chosen by the household as a function of "prices" and income. The second presents choices as a function of the parameters which determine the hedonic price function and income.

The first has the advantage of presenting household choice as a function of income and prices in a structure which is reassuringly (but deceptively) familiar. By presenting a representation of household choice in a conventional structure, demand functions which express household choice as a function of prices and income allow calculation of price and income elasticities that facilitate comparison of demand for housing with the demand for other goods. Unfortunately, such comparisons can be misleading since households do not, in fact, face linear budget constraints.

The second technique, that presents household choice as a function of income and the parameters of the hedonic price function has the advantage of providing (subject to the limits of estimation) a quantitative description of actual household behavior. Unlike the "linearized" demand functions, these would provide accurate descriptions of household responses to changes in the hedonic price function. There are two difficulties with these "hedonic demands" that account, perhaps, for the infrequency with which they appear in applied research. First, they can be somewhat difficult to estimate, since they will almost always necessitate the use of nonlinear models. Second, they are difficult to use in developing what might be called a "housing market heuristic". For example, we often confront changes in housing markets, such as an increase in household incomes or a change in the availability of land for residential development, that are expected (and typically do) have clear qualitative consequences for hedonic prices. It can be difficult to translate these into qualitative predictions of housing attribute demand using the "hedonic demands", and quite easy to do so with the "linearized demands".

The ease with which such a heuristic is developed, however, is of little benefit if it is fundamentally misleading. Our first question, therefore, is to inquire as to the usefulness of estimating these linearized demands. We shall see below that estimation of this type of "demand" provides a technique for estimating the structure of preferences, that is a principal objective of hedonic analysis of housing markets, and from which the more complete "hedonic demands" can be derived analytically. There are a variety of properties that demand functions possess in the conventional setting, and we inquire as to those that might be expected to carry over to the linearized demands derived for a consumer facing a nonlinear budget. In the subsection that follows, we consider problems that arise in using the linearized demands for welfare analysis in housing markets.

Suppose that we proceed along the lines suggested by Rosen (1974), and implemented in a number of studies, taking estimated hedonic prices as if they were actual prices, combining them with household income and observed household choices to estimate the structure of demand. We might attempt this by postulating a parametric form either for the utility function or, equivalently, for the expenditure function, and then derive a demand function for each attribute of the form,

$$q_i(P_1, \ldots, P_J, M, \alpha). \tag{2.9}$$

We could then proceed to estimate this in the form of a share equation with an additive error term,

$$w_i = \frac{P_i \cdot q_i(P_1, \ldots, P_J, M, \alpha)}{M} + \varepsilon. \tag{2.10}$$

There are two important problems with this strategy: the first concerns the estimation technique and lack of stochastic independence between the "variables" $P_i$ and the error term $\varepsilon$. This issue has received a great deal of attention and is discussed more completely in Section 3.2 below. The second problem concerns the appropriateness of this approach when the budget set faced by the household is potentially nonlinear due to the nonlinearities that may be present in $P(Z)$.

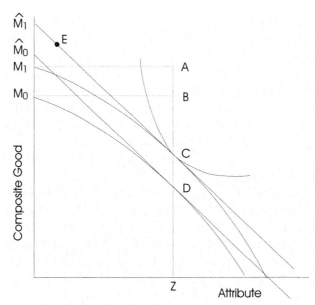

Fig. 1. Hedonic budget lines and consumer choice.

To understand the importance of the nonlinearity, consider Fig. 1. Here we see two "budget lines". The budget line is defined by the equality

$$Y = M - P(Z), \tag{2.11}$$

where we assume that the hedonic price function is convex so that the household's budget set will be convex. As long as the hedonic price function is independent of household income (which will in general be true if sellers of houses are price-takers) the budget lines themselves are "quasilinear"—the slope of the budget line is $-P'(Z)$ and independent of consumption of the composite good. Thus, the distance $(A - C) = (B - D) = P(Z)$, and $\widehat{M_1} - \widehat{M_0} = M_1 - M_0 = (C - D)$.

A household with income $M_1$, facing hedonic price $P(Z)$ and making choice $C$ exhibits the same behavior as a household with income $\widehat{M_1}$ facing an attribute price that is constant and equal to $\partial P / \partial Z$. As discussed in Section 2.2, the first-order conditions for household choice imply a tangency between the indifference curve, the true budget line $M_1$, and the linearized budget line $\widehat{M_1}$ at the point $C$. Provided that preferences are strictly convex, demand will be a function, and the linearized demand will be the same as the hedonic demand.[1]

---

[1] A discrepency clearly arises if preferences are not *strictly* convex. While a point such as $E$ in Fig. 1 would not be an element of hedonic demand, it could be an element along with point $C$ in linearized demand

Thus, if we want to estimate the structure of household preferences by estimating household demand for attributes, we can take as data the hedonic prices $P_i = \partial P(Z)/\partial Z_i$, and the actual household choices, but we must use income level $\widehat{M} = M - P(Z) + \sum_{i=1}^{J} P_i \cdot Z_i$. Based on this data, the structure of demand can be estimated.

Such demand is what Murray (1983) refers to as "mythical" demand, stressing that the resulting estimated demands are those that would obtain if the consumer faced linearized prices. While the demand functions might be "mythical", there is nothing mythical about the household preferences that can be inferred from the estimated demands. If a parametric form for demand functions is chosen to facilitate integrability, then we can determine the parameters of a utility or expenditure function directly from the estimated demand systems. For example, if a generalized CES (as in Quigley (1982) or Follain and Jimenez (1983)) or almost ideal demand system (as in Cheshire and Sheppard (1998) or Parsons (1986)) is applied, then the parameters of the utility or expenditure function are directly obtainable from estimates of the demand.

It is important to qualify the interpretation of the estimated demands and preferences by recognizing that households subject to nonlinear budget constraints do not exhibit the same behavior as households subject to linear constraints, even if (locally) the linear and nonlinear budgets are equivalent. In this sense, the "linear approximation" demands are not so much mythical as erroneous, with the error depending on the nonlinearity of the hedonic prices and the preferences of the household.

Conventional demands derived from linear budget constraints exhibit a variety of standard properties that have proven useful in applied demand analysis. These can be used either as the basis of tests of the model, or potentially as a source of "nonsample" information to improve the quality of estimates when, for example, sample data exhibit colinearity. Which of these properties are preserved in the linearized demands?

The study by Turnbull (1994) derives some properties of overall housing demand in a context that explicitly considers the endogenous location choices that determine the spatial structure of housing consumption. This paper (along with related studies such as Blackley and Follain (1987), DeSalvo (1985) or Turnbull (1993)) establish clearly that demand for housing is affected in important ways by endogenous location choice, and that such demand does not possess the same properties as conventional demand. In particular, the "law of demand" may be

---

if the indifference curve had a flat portion that was colinear with the linearised budget constraint $\widehat{M}_1$. While of minor theoretical interest, this is of minimal relevance in applications since estimation of demand functions already requires the assumption of strictly convex preferences.

violated for housing even if housing is not an inferior good. Turnbull derives sufficient conditions to rule this out, and shows that with convex equilibrium rent functions this is less likely to occur near the urban periphery. The fact that it can occur at all might make one despair at using these properties to test or inform housing demand estimates. While the analyst might seek comfort in the fact that the analysis focuses on location choice, the difficulty is much more general.

The problem arises because of the endogeneity of prices, and the potential for a household to respond to a pattern of price increases by not only altering the amount of space they consume, but also their location (and, hence, the price of space and their effective income). In a nonspatial setting, an almost identical problem arises, in which an increase in the general price of an attribute can generate not only a change in the consumption of that attribute, but also a reconfiguration of the entire dwelling and neighborhood. In general, this will change the marginal price of the attribute under consideration, and the final adjustment in consumption of the attribute may be quite unexpected.

The most complete treatment of this problem (surprisingly rarely cited in the hedonic literature) has been provided by Blomquist (1989), who investigates the general properties exhibited by demands that are obtained by maximizing a strictly quasiconcave differentiable utility function subject to a general nonlinear budget constraint $M \geq P(Z, \theta)$, where $\theta$ is a vector of parameters of the hedonic price function.[2] Blomquist assumes that $P$ is strictly increasing in $Z$ and differentiable, and is such that a unique differentiable solution exists to the household optimization problem. Clearly, it is sufficient for this if $P$ is convex. Let $Z_i(M, \theta, \alpha)$ represent the hedonic demand for housing attribute $i$, that is the $i$th component of the solution to the problem,

$$\max_{Z,Y} u(Z, Y, \alpha) \quad \text{subject to } M \geq P(Z, \theta) + Y. \tag{2.12}$$

For a fixed $(M^*, \theta^*)$, we have well defined household choice given by $Z_i(M^*, \theta^*, \alpha)$, and can define the linearized demand $Z_i^L(\widehat{M}, p)$ as the $i$th component of the solution to the problem,

$$\max_{Z,Y} u(Z, Y, \alpha) \quad \text{subject to } \widehat{M} \geq p'Z + Y, \tag{2.13}$$

where

$$p_i = \frac{\partial P(Z_i(M^*, \theta^*, \alpha), \theta^*)}{\partial Z_i} \quad \text{and} \quad \widehat{M} = \sum_{i=1}^{J} p_i \cdot Z_i(M^*, \theta^*, \alpha).$$

---

[2] Blomquist (1989) does not refer to $P$ as a "hedonic price" function. The focus of his paper is oriented towards complex tax schedules or wage functions.

Let $S$ represent the Slutsky matrix of substitution terms derived from the linearized demands $Z^L$, and let $H^P$ represent the matrix of second derivatives of the hedonic price function with typical element given by,[3]

$$H^P_{i,j} = \frac{\partial^2 P(Z_i(M^*, \theta^*, \alpha), \theta^*)}{\partial Z_i \partial Z_J}. \tag{2.14}$$

Blomquist (1989) shows that there is a well-defined link between the income effects of the true hedonic demand and the income effect of the associated linearized demand. The relation is given by,

$$\frac{\partial Z}{\partial M} = (I - S \cdot H^P)^{-1} \frac{\partial Z^L}{\partial \widehat{M}}. \tag{2.15}$$

This elegant formulation illustrates how the curvature of the true budget constraint (captured via $H^P$), and the curvature of preferences (captured via $S$), interact to produce a complex relation between the estimated income effects of the linearized demand and the income effects that can be expected of a utility maximizing household. A similar expression allows evaluation of the impacts of a change in the parameters $\theta$ that determine the hedonic price function. Define a vector $H^P_\theta = (\partial^2 P)/(\partial Z_i \partial \theta_j)$, whose $i$th element gives the impact on the hedonic price of attribute $i$ of a change in parameter $\theta_j$. Taking

$$A = S \cdot H^P_\theta - \frac{\partial P}{\partial \theta_j} \frac{\partial Z^L}{\partial \widehat{M}}, \tag{2.16}$$

we can write the impact of the parameter $\theta_j$

$$\frac{\partial Z}{\partial \theta_j} = (I - S \cdot H^P)^{-1} A. \tag{2.17}$$

Again, we see the possibility of expressing the actual change in household attribute demand as a function of the structure of linearized demand (via $S$ and the "income effect" component of $A$), the curvature of the budget constraint, and the way in which the parameter in question affects the budget constraint.

This analysis demonstrates that there is nothing problematic or incorrect in estimating linearized demands using the derivatives of the hedonic price function as prices and using the modified income $\widehat{M}$ defined in Eq. (2.13). Not only is

---

[3] Clearly this matrix comprises the first $J$ rows and columns of the hessian matrix of the hedonic price function.

such a procedure capable of providing estimates of the parameters of the utility or expenditure function, but the true comparative statics of hedonic demand in the neighborhood of the equilibrium choice can be obtained by applying Eqs. (2.15) and (2.17).

This analysis is not, however, always helpful in constraining or informing the estimation of the linearized demands. Some writers (such as McConnell and Phipps, 1987) prefer to avoid the term "demand" altogether, since the "correct" hedonic demands do not depend on prices (but rather on the parameters of the hedonic price function), and the linearized demands that do depend on prices are "mythical". Whatever terminology is preferred, it is clear that it is (at least in principle) possible to infer the parameters of attribute demand directly from observations of household choices and hedonic prices.

The primary difficulty that confronts such inferences is the nonlinearity of the household budget set. Although it increases the complexity of analysis, this difficulty is surmountable. For example, the analysis of Ohsfeldt and Smith (1990) derives exact expressions for calculating elasticities taking into account the nonlinearity of household budgets. Their research makes an insight which will be important in the discussion of welfare analysis below: that "linearized" elasticities underestimate the substitution that occurs between housing attributes and nonhousing goods.

### 2.3.2. Welfare analysis

Consider two examples of analysis that might constitute plausible goals for application of hedonic analysis of housing markets: (1) evaluation of the welfare effects of housing regulation; and (2) anticipation of the consequences of an increase in income on housing demand. We continue to assume that the hedonic price function is convex, so that household choice sets are also convex.

Figure 2 illustrates the situation of a householder having income $M_1$ who achieves the maximum utility level $U_1$ by purchasing a house with quantity $Z_1$ of the attribute. Suppose that a constraint on household behavior requires them instead to purchase quantity $Z_3$ of the attribute.[4] This forces them to utility level $U_0$ and it could be reasonably said to generate a welfare cost whose income equivalent is $M_1 - M_0$.

Suppose we utilize the standard expenditure function derived from the preferences we have estimated using "linearized" budgets and adjusted income as outlined above. From the estimated expenditure function, we could parametrize

---

[4] We might call this example "large lot zoning", except that strictly speaking such a system wide regulation would also change the equilibrium hedonic price function $P(Z)$. Perhaps the extra required painting of a home with "historic" designation would be an appropriate interpretation.

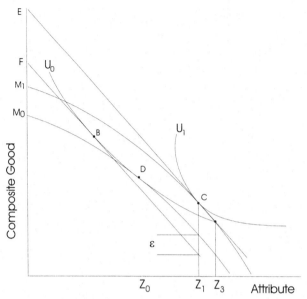

Fig. 2. Estimated attribute demand can overstate welfare costs.

utility to determine utility levels $U_1$ and $U_0$. We might then try to estimate the welfare cost using this expenditure function, and the estimate would be $E(P_Z, U_1) - E(P_Z, U_0) = E - F$ in Fig. 2, where the hedonic price of the attribute $P_Z$ is held constant. What relation does this estimate have to the correct magnitude $M_1 - M_0$?

As indicated in Fig. 2, the welfare loss estimated from the conventional expenditure function is usually *greater* than the true welfare cost, and the error is indicated by $\varepsilon$. This error results from the convexity of the hedonic budget constraint and the failure of the usual technique using traditional expenditure functions to account for the endogeneity of price. This is related to the observation noted by Ohsfeldt and Smith (1990) that nonlinearity of the budget generates greater substitution between housing attributes and nonhousing goods (the composite commodity).

One circumstance in which the traditional approach gives an exact evaluation is if there is "zero income effect" in demand for the attribute. In such an unlikely case, the utility maximizing choice for a household facing the reduced income level $M_0$ would involve no change in the quantity of the attribute, and the change in total expenditures would equal the equivalent change in income.

The nonlinearity of budgets also has implications for forecasting the response of house attribute demand to a change in household income. Again referring to Fig. 2, the estimated demand structure would lead us to expect an increase in attribute demand from $Z_0$ to $Z_1$ to be generated by an increase in income of $E - F$. In fact, demand will be somewhat more income elastic, with this change in attribute demand being generated by the smaller increase in income of $M_1 - M_0$. Clearly, the accuracy of approximation obtained using the conventional "linear budget" constructs to analyze household choice in a hedonic framework depends on the structure of preferences and the curvature of the hedonic price function.

Similar problems arise when we seek to evaluate the impact of a change in the hedonic price function. Of course, there are a wide variety of possible changes, but suppose we consider an "increase" in the hedonic price in which, at every level of attribute consumption, the hedonic price increases so that the budget line is "steeper". Such a situation is illustrated in Fig. 3, where the budget line produced by the hedonic price function is rotated downwards by the price increase. The household responds by changing from optimal choice $B$ to choice $C$. It is reasonable to seek to measure the variation in income that is equivalent to this price change.

Figure 3 indicates that if the hedonic attribute prices were kept constant but income were reduced by $M_1 - M_0$, then the effect on welfare would be the same as the increase in attribute price. Using a conventional measure of the welfare effect based on the expenditure function would give $E - F$ as the change in income that is equivalent to the price increase. As indicated, this overestimates the actual welfare effect by $\varepsilon$. The accuracy of the approximation will depend on the nonlinearity of the hedonic price function and the structure of preferences.

Thus, a basis exists for using estimated hedonic prices and modified income levels to estimate the structure of demand. A variety of econometric difficulties confront such estimation, and these are discussed in Section 3.2. To be most useful, a parametric form could be chosen that is explicitly derived from an underlying expenditure or utility function, but in this respect hedonic analysis of house attribute demand is no different from other types of demand analysis.

Bartik (1988) provided a comprehensive guide to accurate measurement of benefits from changes in house attributes or environmental amenities using hedonic price models. The methods discussed implicitly provide a way to estimate the error $\varepsilon$ in the linearized welfare measure noted above. Although difficult to implement, it is possible to obtain an exact welfare measure. In practice, many studies communicate the approximate welfare measure, but it is important to note that this is at best an approximation.

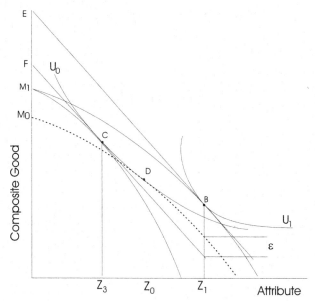

Fig. 3. Measuring welfare effects of a price change.

## 2.4. *Hedonic price indices*

Before proceeding to discuss implementation of hedonic analysis of demand, we note that a great deal of interest focuses purely on the use of estimated hedonic price functions for the construction of price and quantity indices. Indeed, such indices have been the primary motivation for much of the hedonic literature, particularly that which begins with Griliches (1961). There have been a variety of interesting contributions in this area, including a relatively comprehensive method for constructing price indices presented in Feenstra (1995). Comparisons of some of the alternative methods used for estimation have been presented by Meese and Wallace (1997).

## 3. Implementation

### 3.1. *Estimation of hedonic price functions*

As mentioned in the introduction, the pioneering study by Waugh (1929) represented not only the first attempt to estimate a hedonic price function, but also a very early application of multivariate techniques to the analysis of economic

data. It is perhaps surprising that one of the first applications of multiple regression should be a problem that is in fact very difficult. This may account
for the continued attention that the problem draws from econometricians and
applied economists. Estimation of hedonic prices confronts the economist with
a rich sampling of the standard difficulties that arise in estimation using cross-
section data. These include choices of the proper parametric specification—both
of functional form and of variables to be included—coping with colinearity and
ill-conditioned data, potential heteroscedastic and nonnormal errors, regressors
subject to measurement error, and maximum likelihood estimation of relationships that are nonlinear.

Confronted with these difficulties, a variety of approaches are possible. We
review here some approaches that appear to be most useful or promising, along
with the traditional ones. Choosing an estimation methodology cannot be done
independent of consideration of the particular data sources available and the objectives of the analysis. For example, the "best" approach to use will generally
depend on whether the estimated hedonic price function is to be used to infer
the implicit prices of attributes, or simply to forecast or appraise the value of
individual properties.

We first discuss the traditional parametric approaches in which a specific
functional form is chosen, and the parameters that define it are estimated. This is
followed by noting the alternative nonparametric or semiparametric approaches
that make inferences about the implicit prices of attributes without imposing a
priori a functional relation between the total price of the house and the quantities
of attributes which characterize it.

### 3.1.1. Parametric approaches

From the early work of Waugh (1929), Court (1939) and Griliches (1961) to
the most recent studies, the standard approach to estimation of the hedonic price
function has been to adopt some form of parametric approach. This means that
the analyst must choose a functional form whose actual values are determined by
a finite number of parameters. The estimation then proceeds by selecting those
parameter values resulting in a hedonic price function that gives the "best fit" to
the data.

This procedure has evolved in several ways, as allowed by the constraints
of computation technology, the availability of data, and the understanding of
the nature of the statistical problems involved. Studies such as those of Ridker
and Henning (1967), Kain and Quigley (1970), Harrison and Rubinfeld (1978),
Goodman (1978) and Linneman (1981), tended to rely on linear or logarithmic
parametric forms that performed reasonably well and were computationally fea-

sible to estimate. In the 1980s, beginning with the work of Linneman (1980), hedonic studies began to use more flexible functional forms obtained by applying the Box–Cox transformation, either to housing prices or nondichotomous attribute quantities. This transformation uses a single parameter $\lambda$ to transform the variable $x$ as follows:

$$x^{(\lambda)} = \begin{array}{ll} (x^{\lambda} - 1)/\lambda & \text{if } \lambda \neq 0 \\ \ln x & \text{if } \lambda = 0 \end{array} . \tag{3.1}$$

The model proceeds by expressing transformed price as a linear or quadratic function of transformed attribute quantities, with the transformation parameters being possibly different between the variables, and estimated along with the other parameters.

Although more complicated to estimate, particularly using computationally simple techniques (as noted by Spitzer (1982) and further investigated by Blackley et al. (1984a)), increased computing power eventually made maximum likelihood estimation of such models relatively straightforward, even with a large number of attributes. Combined with the analysis of Halvorsen and Pollakowski (1981) that identified some particularly strong features of models based on the Box–Cox transformation, many studies began, and still do, rely on this sort of parametric approach.

This approach is not, however, free of all difficulties. A problem observed by Cassel and Mendelsohn (1985) is that focus on traditional model specification criteria that emphasize the predictive capability of the model, is not always appropriate in estimating a hedonic model. If the model is estimated for the sole purpose of predicting total house values, then choosing the parametric form that gives the best possible "fit" is quite appropriate. Often, however, the objective of estimating a hedonic price function is to determine the implicit prices of attributes. For this objective, minimization of the squared prediction error may be quite inappropriate, and a model that "fits the data" well in this sense may be less satisfactory than another with less predictive power but more stable parameter estimates.

The interesting paper of Cropper et al. (1988) investigates precisely this issue. They simulate housing market equilibria using housing stock data from an actual urban area and varying the parameter of the household utility functions. They then determine analytically the true equilibrium price functions, and the prices of structures can be used to estimate hedonic price functions and marginal bids, comparing the estimates obtained from different functional forms with the "true" values. They evaluated linear, log-linear, quadratic, linear and quadratic Box–Cox models, and obtained several surprising results. Models were evaluated not by how well they fit the data, but by how accurately they estimated true marginal bids. When all valuable attributes were observed, and without measurement error, the model that was linear in Box–Cox variables performed the best, while the quadratic Box–Cox performed the worst.

When some important attributes were omitted or observed imprecisely, the simpler forms such as linear Box-Cox and logarithmic forms were the most accurate. They attribute this, at least in part, to the fact that in quadratic forms, each hedonic price depends on more coefficients than in the more nearly linear cases.

Related to the issue of the parametric form of the hedonic price function are issues of which variables to include and the way in which they should enter. Consider, for example, the role of lot size or land area. Examination of any standard presentation of urban economic theory reveals the central role played by models of land value determination. One might reasonably assert that a central principal of urban economics is that the price of land will vary with location, and this varying land price is what produces the varying types and intensity of land use in cities.

Given this observation, it is surprising how many hedonic models lack either a variable for land area, or a variable that explicitly identifies the location of the structure.[5] Some studies, such as the interesting analysis of Laakso (1997), include location explicitly and land implicitly via a separate variable that measures the density of structures. Very few models explicitly incorporate a land value function that depends on location. Two exceptions are Jackson et al. (1984) and Cheshire and Sheppard (1995). Both of these studies are able to obtain reasonable estimates of the value of land in residential use, and to reject the hypothesis that this value is constant over locations. Recent research by Colwell and Munneke (1997), who studied prices of vacant land, also show that land prices are most definitely not constant over locations.

While it is commonplace to justify adoption of a flexible form for estimation of a hedonic price function by observing that "theory places few restrictions" on the form, there are at least *some* restrictions. As observed above, urban economic theory suggests that the form should include land values that depend on location. Furthermore, Jones (1988) show that in equilibrium the hedonic price functions should be convex. This guarantees convexity of consumer budget sets and, with convexity of preferences, establishes continuity properties of house-hold attribute demand. Although Anderson (1985) develops and applies a test of hedonic function convexity, it is again surprising how few subsequent studies

---

[5] Even worse, some studies lack both.

have applied this simple test. At this point the study of Colwell and Munneke (1997) is worth mentioning again because in examination of prices of vacant land they obtain concavity of the price function for land. Whether, or not, this holds more generally for land as an attribute in housing markets has not been widely investigated.

A third way in which theory might suggest appropriate restrictions on the parametric structure of the hedonic price function estimated concerns public goods or environmental amenities. Parsons (1990) argues for weighting local public goods and neighborhood amenities by lot size, based on land market equilibrium and the fact that consumption of these amenities is limited by available land for residential consumption. While his argument depends on an assumption that consumption of these attributes is nonexclusive (and therefore may not be appropriate for some local attributes such as schools or parks), for a great many environmental amenities his analysis suggests a reasonable theoretical constraint on the parametric specification for hedonic models.

*Specification.* Many of the issues raised above might be viewed under the general heading of "model specification" for the hedonic price function. Over the past decade, this topic has generated considerable interest amongst econometricians. Several studies have considered techniques for testing or evaluating alternative specifications for the hedonic price function. Among these are Butler (1982), Milon et al. (1984), Dubin and Sung (1990), Burgess and Harmon (1991) and Craig et al. (1991).

This last paper is interesting because it introduces a new test that is particularly appropriate in the setting of hedonic estimation. They apply the test to housing market data to test for the systematic nonlinearities in the relationship between structure price and attribute quantity. In addition to testing for the appropriateness of nonlinearities in the functional form, the test can also provide an indication of important omitted variables. Interestingly (and a propos the comments above about the need to include land area that varies with location), their analysis identified an inability to "discover a specification for lot size which ... passes" the test they derive. Whether a specification that did not impose spatially invariant land value would pass was not tested.

*Colinearity and error structure* Two econometric problems that seem intrinsic to estimation of hedonic price functions are colinearity or ill-conditioned data and lack of stochastic independence between observations. The first problem has received considerable attention in the literature. Only recently has the second begun to be addressed.

It seems natural to expect colinearity to pose a problem for the estimation of hedonic prices. Because of similarity in the preferences of households, and limits on the technology of house construction, there are intrinsic limits to the extent of variance of attributes that we are likely to observe. The more limited this variance is (and the greater the extent to which the variables tend to move together), the less will be the precision with which model parameters are estimated. This is a particular problem for hedonic estimation where the precision of parameter estimation is important for obtaining accurate estimates of attribute prices.

As is reasonably widely known (see for example, Belsley and Welsch, 1980), there is really only one way to "solve" the problem of colinearity—get more information. This information might come from larger or richer data sources. Alternatively, we might turn to formal ways of incorporating nonsample information into our estimates using some sort of Bayesian technique. Recent studies by Knight et al. (1993) and Gilley and Pace (1995) applied and evaluated this approach. The first study uses the Monte Carlo techniques to evaluate Bayesian versions of Stein-like estimators and shows that according to several criteria, the approaches based on nonsample data empirically dominate least squares approaches.

The study by Gilley and Pace (1995) is particularly important because it illustrates an innovative use of information that should be available in almost all applied settings. As noted in Section 2.2 above, equilibrium in an implicit market involves a tangency between consumer bid functions and producer cost functions. Thus, the hedonic price should be equal to both the household marginal willingness-to-pay (Eq. (2.4)) and also the marginal cost of making the attribute available (Eq. (2.8)). In many markets there are standard construction cost data sources that give some estimate of the marginal cost of attribute supply. While these would apply primarily to new construction, they may constitute a valuable source of nonsample information that can be used to inform a prior distribution in a Bayesian estimation procedure.

The spatial structure of housing markets has been noted above, and is obvious to anyone engaged in the analysis of the housing market. This might lead one to be concerned about spatial linkages between errors in hedonic price models, that is, a lack of stochastic independence between observations, in which the error of an observation is correlated with those observations that are located nearby. In analogy with the common time series difficulty, this problem is termed spatial autocorrelation and, if present, leads to similar difficulties as those in time series models.

The presence of this problem and possible corrections have been investigated by Dubin (1988, 1992a) and Can (1992). Alternative estimation strategies that account for the spatial autocorrelation are seen to be warranted, and the results suggest that models that account for these types of spatial structure are likely to produce more reliable results.

### 3.1.2. Non-parametric approaches

An alternative to specification of a parametric functional form for the hedonic price function is to adopt a non- or semiparametric approach to estimation, that attempts to infer attribute prices directly from the data without benefit of an assumed functional relationship. The difficulty that arises in the application of these techniques is the extremely large amounts of data required (formally, the slow rate at which these estimation techniques converge to the true value as sample size increases).

Feasible estimates can be obtained, however, by using approaches that consider truly nonparametric combinations of simple parametric forms. Papers that have investigated this approach include Knight et al. (1993), Pace (1993, 1995) and Anglin and Gencay (1995). These approaches turn out to be much more robust to specification and measurement error than many parametric estimates, although they can be considerably more computationally complex to estimate.

The analysis of Pace (1995) suggests in particular that semiparametric estimates of hedonic price functions seem to suffer fewer incorrectly signed parameters—a common problem with colinear data. Even more interesting, the study of Anglin and Gencay (1995) compares a parametric estimator with a semiparametric one. The parametric model was easily rejected in tests that compare it to the semiparametric. Furthermore, this was not for a poorly specified parametric model, but one that passed a variety of standard tests of model specification. This suggests that considerable gains in accuracy may be available by utilizing semiparametric techniques for estimating hedonic price functions.

### 3.2. Estimation of demand for housing attributes

Estimation of the demand for any heterogeneous good such as housing presents a variety of difficult problems, some of which are rarely encountered in other economic contexts. It is perhaps a peculiar attribute of the literature concerning estimation of demand for housing attributes that, during the past decade, much of it has been obsessed with clarifying the problem of endogeneity of price.

Partly, this stems from a peculiarity in the development of the literature, in which the problem of estimating the demand for housing attributes was originally thought to represent a "garden variety" simultaneous equations problem.[6] That this was not so was realized relatively quickly, but it took nearly a decade to produce a clear exposition of exactly how the price endogeneity problem differed from the variety one finds in the usual economist's "garden".

What is peculiar about this is that while there have been a variety of papers that discussed and clarified the nature of the problem, there have been few that used actual housing market data to illustrate how much difference a proper accounting of the problem made to final estimates. In part this was no doubt due to the difficulty of producing estimates that do take proper account, but in part, it was also due to the somewhat limited intersection between the set of economists interested in elucidating proper econometric practice, and the set of economists seeking to use hedonic analysis as a tool for understanding markets or conducting policy analysis.

A second peculiar aspect has been the enthusiasm with which the "lack of consistency" due to failure to use a proper instrumental variables technique has been criticized, while other sources of bias receive little in the way of repeat attention. Most obvious of these other sources has been the failure to include almost certainly relevant variables in hedonic models, particularly the structure location. Again, there is a pragmatic explanation: an individual economist might be expected to be able to adopt different estimation techniques that could improve estimation and account for price endogeneity. An individual researcher is unlikely to be able to compel release of actual (rather than pseudo) census tract numbers in the *American Housing Survey*.

Economists have become accustomed to accepting data as they find it, warts and all. They then agonize about how optimally to analyze these data, even if the reduction in error obtained from this optimization is trivial compared to the error caused by the structure of (or omissions from) the data. This occupational hazard applies with particular force to practitioners in the hedonic modeling area. A reader of the literature could be forgiven for getting the impression that studies that neglected location, land area and all local public goods, would be welcomed if only they incorporated a maximum-likelihood instrumental variables technique that accounted for price endogeneity. In fact, of course, there is little to recommend adoption of an estimation technique that achieves consistent estimates if it is applied to an obviously misspecified model.

---

[6]  As characterized in Rosen (1974).

### 3.2.1. Identification and endogeneity

The most widely perceived difficulty afflicting estimation of demand for housing attributes is the "identification" problem that arises because of the endogeneity of attribute prices. Although the problem is technically one of identification, it is useful to avoid confusion with the econometric difficulties faced when attempting to estimate the parameters of demand and supply simultaneously. This sort of "conventional" simultaneity was first noted as a potential problem by Freeman (1979), and alluded to in Rosen (1974). For studies based on cross-sectional data with units of observation large enough to influence market prices, such difficulties may indeed arise. Most hedonic studies, however, are based on datasets with observations of individual household decisions and incomes.

For estimates based on individual data, the first response might be to argue that there is no problem in estimation (other than the usual ones of specification and dealing with nonlinear structures). The individual demands or "marginal benefit functions" are determined taking the hedonic prices as exogenous. The situation would seem to be similar to that depicted in Fig. 4. Here we see a three dimensional surface representing the individual demand function that gives the quantity of attribute desired as a function of household income and the hedonic price of the attribute. A few of the many available data points are indicated, and these may be used to determine the demand function using relatively standard maximum likelihood methods.

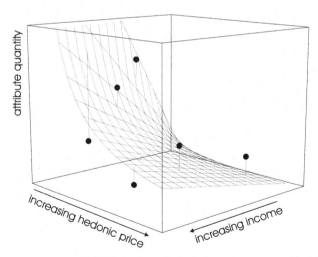

Fig. 4. Estimation of hedonic demand.

This perspective (that at least implicitly lies at the foundation of a very large literature) holds that since we have observations of individual behavior, along with the prices and incomes that have produced that behavior, we can estimate the structural equations of household demand as long as we are willing to assume that a common preference ordering determines the decisions of all households. All that is required are data in which there is linearly independent variation in income and hedonic prices, and the estimates will be readily obtained.

The first objection to this perspective is the simple one that the hedonic prices are not known with certainty, but must be estimated. The stochastic nature of the relation between attribute quantities and house price will impart some uncertainty to the estimated hedonic prices. To this, one might reply that demand estimation is a classic "errors in variables" problem, and that as long as the hedonic price function has been correctly specified, the parameters will be consistently estimated and for large samples we need not worry. Of course, for finite samples any hypothesis testing we might wish to do with our demand estimates will be troubled by variance estimates that are biased downwards, but in principle, these could be corrected by using the covariance matrix for parameters of the hedonic price function to obtain an estimate of the covariance structure for the hedonic prices. This approach, however, cannot by itself compensate for violations of the Gauss–Markov conditions, and produces consistent estimates only if the errors in hedonic prices (and "linearized income") are independent of the error terms in the demand functions. This is precisely the core of the problem.

The problem is easily seen in Fig. 5. In the upper portion of the figure, a hedonic price function $P(Z)$ is shown with a household bid function for the attribute $Z$ that is tangent at point $B$ so that the household would demand $Z_1$ units of the attribute given this price structure.[7] The object of hedonic analysis is to obtain an estimate of the actual demand or marginal benefit function drawn as a solid line in the lower portion of Fig. 5. For example, we might assume additive error $\varepsilon$ and estimate

$$Z = \beta_0 + \beta_1 \cdot P_Z + \varepsilon, \tag{3.2}$$

using the observed household consumption and the estimated hedonic price function to determine the hedonic prices $P_Z$. In the case illustrated, the parameter $\beta_1$ is negative, and we try to obtain an estimate $\widehat{\beta_1}$. When the error $\varepsilon$ is near zero, we observe the household consuming $Z_1$ and infer from the hedonic price function that the price which produces this behavior is the slope of $P(Z)$ at point $B$.

---

[7] Alternatively, the hedonic price function could be used to construct a budget line, and the bid function would be an indifference curve tangent to the budget line at $B$.

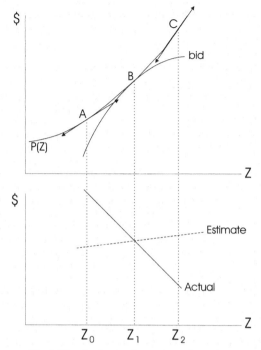

Fig. 5. Biased estimates from price endogeneity.

When $\varepsilon$ is negative, we observe household consumption of an attribute level such as $Z_0$. At this consumption, we infer a hedonic price that is the slope of $P(Z)$ at point $A$, which is less than the true slope of the household bid curve and, hence, less than the true level of the household demand function. When $\varepsilon$ is positive, we observe $Z_2$ and infer a hedonic price that is the slope of $P(Z)$ at point $C$. The result is an estimated household demand that, as indicated in Fig. 5, is too low for negative $\varepsilon$ and too high for positive $\varepsilon$—we are simply tracking the slope of the hedonic price function.

This is essentially the problem observed by Brown and Rosen (1982). If no correction is made for price endogeneity, demand estimates may be determined entirely by the hedonic price function itself. The estimate $\widehat{\beta}_1$ is biased upwards, and is inconsistent since increasing the sample size does nothing to eliminate or change the correlation $\rho$ between the error $\varepsilon$ and the hedonic price $P_Z$. Letting $\sigma_\varepsilon$ and $\sigma_{P_Z}$ denote the standard deviation of $\varepsilon$ and $P_Z$, respectively, we have,

$$\text{plim}\widehat{\beta}_1 = \beta_1 + \rho \frac{\sigma_\varepsilon}{\sigma_{P_Z}}. \tag{3.3}$$

For strictly convex hedonic price functions, the correlation $\rho$ is positive and we obtain inconsistent demand estimates whose slopes are biased upwards. For more complex (and realistic) demands with several attributes, and linearized income which is also correlated with $\varepsilon$, the formula for the bias is more complex but the basic intuition remains unchanged: *the correlation between estimated hedonic prices and errors in measured demand behavior leads to inconsistent estimates of the structure of demand.*

There are a variety of possible responses to this problem, but most of the recent literature on estimation of housing demand begins with this basic observation. Thus, the analyses of Blomquist and Worley (1982), Brown and Rosen (1982), Murray (1983), Diamond and Smith (1985), Ohsfeldt and Smith (1985), Bartik (1987b), Epple (1987) and McConnell and Phipps (1987) all share a common initial theme: with individual household data, there is no structural simultaneity; the difficulty arises because the endogeneity of prices gives rise to correlation between the random error in the model and the "independent variables". This results in inconsistent estimates.

The required response to such a problem is to devise consistent, "instrumental variables" estimates of those variables which appear on the righthand side of the structural equations. Thus, for example, in Eq. (3.2) we need to identify variables that are uncorrelated with $\varepsilon$ which can be used to provide a consistent estimate of $P_Z$. This estimate is then used in subsequent stages of the procedure to estimate attribute demand. More generally, we identify instruments that permit estimation of all of the hedonic attribute prices and linearized income.

Three basic approaches exist to obtain such instruments. First, we may be able to find or construct other variables that are independent of the errors, but sufficiently correlated with hedonic prices to provide admissible instruments. Second, we might take advantage of nonlinearities that exist in actual hedonic price and marginal benefit relations to identify the models (essentially using transformations of the variables as instruments). Third, we might use other variables that occur in the structural equations to obtain a set of instruments for consistently estimating hedonic prices.

The third method is familiar from its use in solving the identification problem and estimating models in which there is true simultaneity. Its application is stressed as a potential solution in several of the papers cited above, and is illustrated in the righthand portion of Fig. 6. In the upper righthand quadrant of the figure, we see two budget curves associated with hedonic price functions from two different markets.[8] In one market, the observed household has income

---

[8] We know these are two different markets because the budget lines are not vertically parallel.

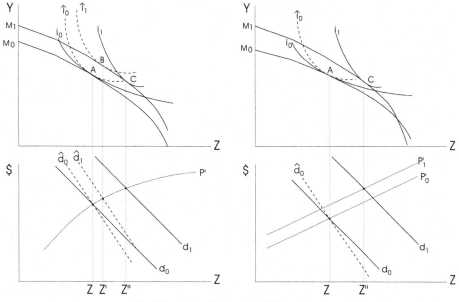

Fig. 6. Data from single and multiple markets.

$M_0$ and optimally chooses attribute level $Z$ indicated by tangency $A$. The problem is to distinguish between the alternative demand structures $d_0$ and $\widehat{d_0}$ generated respectively by preferences $i_0$ and $\widehat{i_0}$. This is possible because of the exogenous variation in price schedules. In the second market, the observed household has income $M_1$, and the choice of attribute level $Z''$ at tangency $B$ serves to identify the demand structure and preference. This approach, is recommended inter alia by Brown and Rosen (1982), Diamond and Smith (1985), Ohsfeldt and Smith (1985), Bartik (1987b) and Epple (1987).

There are two primary difficulties with actually applying this "multiple market" approach. The first is theoretical, the second practical. From a theoretical perspective, estimation of demand from multiple markets requires the assumption of a common demand structure in all markets covered. If these markets are from multiple time periods, we must assume constant preferences over time (as well as cross-sectionally). More problematic, if the markets are from widely separated urban areas, we must assume that households have a common preferences structure across all areas. Given the wide variety of environmental amenities, available public goods and social structures that characterize each urban area, this may be regarded as a possible source of specification error. Related to this point is a problem noted by Diamond and Smith (1985): in a world in which households can choose among several urban areas to live, the urban area itself may well be endogenous and not serve as a valid instrument.

From a practical perspective the difficulties are even larger. There are almost no individual level datasets that are comparable across a large number of urban areas and available to the public. There are none[9] in Europe or Asia. In the US, there are two potential data sources: the *American Housing Survey* and property market data available from local tax authorities or through real estate listing services. The first of these is available at very low cost and includes a large number of variables for about 30 metropolitan areas. The difficulty is that it does not include location. This makes it impossible to estimate a "land value" component in the hedonic price function, although there are some accessibility variables that provide information on the journey to work and mode of transport used. The second data source contains much better information concerning location (since property address is included), but typically contains no detail concerning the occupants. In particular, it does not contain household income, nor does it include any data on the age or structure of the occupants. It might be possible (given sufficient resources) to survey a sample of properties to determine values for these other important variables.

Most of the "multiple market" studies done have used the *American Housing Survey*.[10] These studies were severely constrained by the nature of the data available. None of these included location, despite the theoretical importance of location in determining the value of land and the relatively large proportion of residential construction costs accounted for by land. None included more than eight attributes, with such obviously important factors as local school quality or accessibility to parks and open space never appearing in any study. These limitations arise because of the limited data available, and might be corrected in the future. At present, however, it is rather difficult to understand the attraction of seeking to correct one sort of bias (arising from endogenous prices) by introducing bias of another sort (severe specification error by failing to include important attributes). This is particularly true when other approaches exist that might solve the problem.

The second approach mentioned above relies on imposition of mostly untestable restrictions of nonlinearity on both the hedonic price function and the structure of demand. This approach is illustrated in the lefthand side of Fig. 6. In the top left quadrant, we see two budget sets drawn from the same hedonic market but generated by the two income levels $M_0$ and $M_1$. At the lower income

---

[9] None, at least, known to the author.
[10] See inter alia, Parsons (1986).

level, the household makes optimal choice of attribute level $Z$ determined by the tangency $A$. As before, the problem is to distinguish between the demand structure $d_0$ and $\widehat{d_0}$ generated respectively by preferences $i_0$ and $\widehat{i_0}$.

To get an intuitive feel for the problem, imagine that we restrict attention to *only* these two possible preference structures. While it might be impossible to distinguish between these two demand structures at income level $M_0$, they may be readily distinguished at other price-income combinations. If households have preferences that generate indifference curves $\widehat{i_0}$ and $\widehat{i_1}$, then at income level $M_1$ the optimum will be at tangency point $B$ and they will choose attribute level $Z'$. If they have preferences that generate indifference curves $i_0$ and $i_1$, their optimum will be defined by point $C$ with attribute level $Z''$. Subject to the constraint that household demand structures are one of these two types, we only need data with sufficient variation in hedonic prices and household incomes to identify demand.

Of course, it is hardly satisfactory to restrict households to having one of two possible preference orders, but given sufficient variation in incomes and hedonic prices we can impose much less severe restrictions. The analysis of McConnell and Phipps (1987) provides a complete discussion of the restrictions required for identification of preference parameters in this case, and the discussion in Epple (1987) is also usefully comprehensive.

These sources underscore the difficulty, but not the impossibility, of identifying hedonic demand estimates from single market data. If there is sufficient variation in the data to permit unique maximum likelihood estimates of parameters, that alone can be argued to ensure local identifiability. The studies by Quigley (1982) and Kanemoto and Nakamura (1986) pursue variations on this second approach. By restricting attention to a particular class of preference ordering and functional forms for the hedonic price function, they solve for and estimate the parameters of the preference function.

The first of the three approaches to price endogeneity mentioned above was to find or construct other variables that are correlated with hedonic prices faced by the household, but not correlated with the error terms of the demand (or marginal benefit) functions. In one sense, this obvious approach is what is being done in the multiple market approach as well: other variables (that index or characterize the particular hedonic markets) are used to construct instruments that are then used to obtain consistent estimates of variables on which the demand functions depend. The usual approach when applying this method to true simultaneous equation models is to rely on other variables in the structural equations, and most of the discussion on the "multiple market" approach has followed this tradition.

Restricting the search to other structural variables, however, makes the problem very difficult. Thus, McConnell and Phipps (1987) argue that if some attribute is not included in the hedonic price function, it will be impossible to create instruments that are not correlated with the error. The analysis of Bartik (1987a) makes this argument most forcefully, arguing that unless unobserved variability in preferences is assumed not to exist, it will be impossible to construct valid instruments for consistent estimation of household attribute demand. His argument proceeds by examples, however, and is restricted implicitly to an assumption that the source of instruments are other variables that appear in the structural equations of the model.

Are such variables the only source of instruments to which we might turn? Surely that depends on the stochastic structure of the application, but in principle one need not restrict attention to only these variables. It is helpful to keep in mind that our problem is not one of a truly simultaneous equation system. Consistent estimation of the hedonic demand for $J$ attributes requires that we obtain consistent estimates of the $J$ hedonic prices (and hence also linearized income) that define the budget set of the household. For this we need $J+1$ or more instruments that are uncorrelated with the error in household attribute demand, but which are not so weak as to give extremely imprecise (even if consistent) estimates of the actual hedonic prices.

Murray (1983) makes a variety of interesting suggestions concerning possible instruments, and recently Cheshire and Sheppard (1998), have pursued the idea of using the average attribute prices paid by "similar" households as instruments. There are numerous dimensions along which one might define similarity, and they consider two: (1) taking those households that occupy the locations that are nearest to the household, and taking those households that have chosen to consume similar houses (including both the attributes and location). For the latter concept of similarity, they construct an index that measures the Euclidean distance in characteristics space weighted by consumption shares. For both geographic distance and characteristics space distance, they experimented using as instruments the prices paid by the two "nearest" households in their sample.

Whether, or not, such an approach is likely to provide a valid set of instruments is, as noted above, dependent on the stochastic specification of the model.[11] If these errors come from simple measurement error on the quantities of attributes, then consideration of prices paid by similar households might provide good instruments as long as the measurement errors were uncorrelated between observations. Whether, or not, this is true will naturally depend on the attribute and the nature of the market, but fortunately it is relatively straightforward to

---

[11] This particular importance of stochastic specification is in addition to the important considerations identified by Horowitz (1987).

test for instrument admissibility. Gourieroux and Monfort (1995) present a test of unknown linear constraints based on asymptotic least squares, and show how to apply it as a test of instrument admissibility.

Suppose we seek to estimate a hedonic demand, $Z_i$, that depends on hedonic prices $P_k$ and linearized income $\widehat{M}$ (see Eq. (2.13) above):

$$Z_i = \beta_0 + \sum_{k=1}^{J} \beta_k \cdot P_k + \beta_M \cdot \widehat{M} + \varepsilon. \tag{3.4}$$

Suppose we have a set of $K > J$ instruments $\Psi$ for the $T$ observations of $P_k$ and $\widehat{M}$, and we wish to test the validity of these instruments. That is, we wish to test the hypothesis that

$$\mathrm{plim}_T \frac{1}{T} \sum_{t=1}^{T} \Psi_t \cdot \varepsilon_t = 0, \tag{3.5}$$

where the $\varepsilon_t$ error terms have common variance $\sigma_\varepsilon$. A test statistic for this hypothesis is

$$\xi_T = \frac{1}{\widehat{\sigma}_\varepsilon} \widehat{\varepsilon}' \Psi (\Psi' \Psi)^{-1} \Psi' \widehat{\varepsilon}, \tag{3.6}$$

where $\widehat{\varepsilon}$ is the vector of residuals from the two-stage least square estimate obtained using $\Psi$ as instruments. A remarkable feature of this statistic is that it is equal to the product of the sample size $T$ and $R^2$, the coefficient of determination obtained from regressing the two-stage least squares residuals $\widehat{\varepsilon}$ on the set of instruments $\Psi$. The statistic $\xi_T$ is distributed $\chi^2$ with $K - J$ degrees of freedom under the hypothesis of admissibility.

This is completely intuitive: we have as an estimate of the (unobserved) error the residuals $\widehat{\varepsilon}$. Validity of the instruments $\Psi$ requires that they be independent of these errors. If the variables $\Psi$ are able to explain the variation in $\widehat{\varepsilon}$, then it seems unlikely that $\Psi$ and $\varepsilon$ will be independent.

Using this test, Cheshire and Sheppard (1998) found that the combined characteristics distance instruments are admissible for use in estimating the hedonic demand for land area and open space amenities. They found that the geographic distance instruments are admissible for all of the characteristics for which they had data. The geographic distance based instruments were somewhat weaker, although both provided demand system estimates with acceptable (in sample) accuracy.

Thus, a potentially reasonable procedure for applied analysis using single market data would be to estimate hedonic demand using an instrumental variables procedure such as two-stage least squares, taking as instruments the hedonic prices that confront the households with the nearest locations. A possible variation on this idea would be to average several nearby households, possibly weighting the average by distance. This approach, of course, requires that the location of the households is part of the available data, but this is almost surely required for proper specification of the model in any event. If it is not available, proximity or similarity based on other household characteristics might serve the same role.

If the data are available, it would be quite reasonable to combine these approaches. Use of nonlinear functional forms, with data from several urban areas, taking as instruments the hedonic prices faced by the nearest households would be defensible on several grounds. Data from multiple markets will always be helpful, and increase the in-sample variability in income and hedonic prices, and will therefore generally produce more accurate estimates. The point is that multimarket data are not the only approach to estimation of such demand. Tolerating a severely misspecified model in order to access data from several housing markets is unlikely to be a reasonable strategy.

### 3.2.2. Specification

In estimating household hedonic demand or marginal bid functions, there are three basic approaches that have appeared in the literature. First, and probably least reliable, is to simply estimate some reasonably flexible nonlinear demand that depends on (linearized) household income and attribute hedonic prices. The difficulty with this is the lack of connection between the estimated demand and a preference ordering which presumably generates it.[12]

A preferable approach is to estimate a demand structure derived from an explicit utility or expenditure function. For example, the studies by Quigley (1982) and Kanemoto and Nakamura (1986) undertake this as a possible solution to the price endogeneity problem discussed above. Without regard to whether, or not, their technique is the best solution to price endogeneity, they do certainly obtain estimable demand functions derived from an explicit preference ordering. An alternative is to use a demand system derived from a flexible expenditure function. The "almost ideal demand system" presented in Deaton and Muellbauer (1980) is used in Parsons (1986) and Cheshire and Sheppard (1998).

---

[12] As noted, for example, by McConnell and Phipps (1987) in discussing the example used by Brown and Rosen (1982).

While some techniques have been proposed for estimating compensating and equivalent income variations directly from hedonic price functions (see Horowitz (1984)), general welfare analysis will typically require more detailed knowledge of the household expenditure functions. This is most directly obtained by estimation of a completely specified demand system.

### 3.2.3. Comparison with discrete choice approaches

Before ending our discussion of attribute demand estimation using hedonic techniques, it is worth noting an alternative approach to valuing house attributes using the "discrete choice" approach developed by McFadden (1977), and more completely presented in Ellickson (1981) and Lerman and Kern (1983). This approach uses the basic hedonic model of implicit markets to develop a multinomial discrete choice model of residential choice in which the amount by which increasing an attribute raises the probability that a particular house is chosen conveys information about the value the household attaches to that attribute. While the discrete choice model has fewer problems to deal with in terms of price endogeneity and demand specification, it avoids these problems by imposing considerable structure (implicit in the discrete choice modeling itself) on the nature of household preferences.

This discrete choice approach provides an alternative to hedonic demand estimation, and the study presented in Cropper et al. (1993) compares the two approaches. The study concludes that for small "marginal" changes in attributes, the traditional hedonic approach using a hedonic price function that is linear in Box–Cox transformed variables provides more accurate evaluation. This advantage is lost, however, for large changes in attribute quantities.

## 4. Conclusion

Hedonic analysis of housing markets is an important part of the toolbox of applied urban economics. The technique has been evolving over some 70 years of econometric practice and economic understanding, and has become very important in the past 25 years.

The theory can be presented in a formal way based on theories of implicit markets, and it is possible to infer the parameters of household demand from observations of household choices and the implicit prices they face. Implementation of this approach, however, forces confrontation with a variety of difficulties.

Most of the problems associated with estimation of the hedonic price function itself are conventional, even if not easily solved. Models should be specified so that they correspond to the restrictions implicit in the theory of urban housing markets. Estimation must confront inadequate data, and make use of whatever information sources are available.

Use of these hedonic prices to estimate the structure of demand brings more difficulties, many of which have been only poorly understood. In addition to the usual problems of model specification and measurement error, the nonlinearity in household budgets implies endogenous determination of attribute prices. A variety of strategies for meeting the challenge of endogeneity have been presented, ranging from use of multiple market data to construction of alternative "nonstructural" instrumental variables for prices and income. Whatever approach is adopted, it is clear that accurate estimation requires some explicit acknowledgment of the endogeneity, although the actual quantitative significance of the problem may in some cases be modest.

## References

Anderson, J.E. (1985), "On testing the convexity of hedonic price functions", Journal of Urban Economics 18:334–37.

Anglin, P.M. and R. Gencay (1995), "Semiparametric estimation of a hedonic price function", Discussion paper, University of Windsor, University of Windsor Working Paper.

Bartik, T.J. (1987a), "Estimating hedonic demand parameters with single market data: the problems caused by unobserved tastes", Review of Economics and Statistics 69:178–80.

Bartik, T.J. (1987b), "The estimation of demand parameters in hedonic price models", Journal of Political Economy 95:81–88.

Bartik, T.J. (1988), "Measuring the benefits of amenity improvements in hedonic price models", Land Economics 64:72–83.

Belsley, D.A., K.E. Belsley and R.E. Welsch (1980), Regression Diagnostics, Identifying Influential Data and Sources of Collinearity (Wiley, New York).

Blackley, D.M. and J.R. Follain (1987), "Tests of locational equilibrium in the standard urban model", Land Economics 63:46–61.

Blackley, P., J. Follain and J. Ondrich (1984), "Box–Cox estimation of hedonic models: how serious is the iterative OLS variance bias?", Review of Economics and Statistics 66:348–353.

Blomquist, G. and L. Worley (1982), "Specifying the demand for housing characteristics: the exogeneity issue", in: D.B. Diamond and G.S. Tolley, eds., The Economics of Urban Amenities, Chap. 4, pp. 89–102 (Academic Press, New York).

Blomquist, N.S. (1989), "Comparative statics for utility maximization models with nonlinear budget constraints", International Economic Review 30:275–296.

Brown, J.N. and H.S. Rosen (1982), "On the estimation of structural hedonic price models", Econometrica 50:765–768.

Burgess, J.F. and O.R. Harmon (1991), "Specification tests in hedonic models", Journal of Real Estate Finance and Economics 4:375–393.

Butler, R.V. (1982), "The specification of hedonic indexes for urban housing", Land Economics 58:96–108.

Can, A. (1992), "Specification and estimation of hedonic housing price models", Regional Science and Urban Economics 22:453–474.

Cassel, E. and R. Mendelsohn (1985), "The choice of functional forms for hedonic price equations: comment", Journal of Urban Economics, 18:135–142.

Cheshire, P. and S. Sheppard (1995), "On the price of land and the value of amenities", Economica 62:247–267.

Cheshire, P. and S. Sheppard (1998), "Estimating the demand for housing, land, and neighbourhood characteristics", Oxford Bulletin of Economics and Statistics 60:357–382.

Colwell, P.F. and H.J. Munneke (1997), "The structure of urban land prices", Journal of Urban Economics 41:321–336.

Court, A.T. (1939), "Hedonic price indexes with automotive examples", in: The Dynamics of Automobile Demand (General Motors, New York).

Craig, S.G., J.E. Kohlhase and D.H. Papell (1991), "Chaos theory and microeconomics: an application to model specification and hedonic estimation", Review of Economics and Statistics 73:208–215.

Cropper, M.L., L.B. Deck and K.E. McConnell (1988), "On the choice of functional form for hedonic price functions", Review of Economics and Statistics 70:668–675.

Cropper, M.L., L. Deck, N. Kishor and K.E. McConnell (1993), "Valuing product attributes using single market data: a comparison of hedonic and discrete choice approaches", Review of Economics and Statistics 75:225–232.

Deaton, A. and J. Muellbauer (1980), "An almost ideal demand system", American Economic Review 70:312–326.

DeSalvo, J.S. (1985), "A model of urban household behavior with leisure choice", Journal of Regional Science 25:159–174.

Diamond, D.B. Jr. and B.A. Smith (1985), "Simultaneity in the market for housing characteristics", Journal of Urban Economics 17:280–292.

Dubin, R.A. (1988), "Estimation of regression coefficients in the presence of spatially autocorrelated error terms", Review of Economics and Statistics 70:466–474.

Dubin, R.A. (1992), "Spatial autocorrelation and neighborhood quality", Regional Science and Urban Economics 22:433–452.

Dubin, R.A. and C.H. Sung (1990), "Specification of hedonic regressions: non-nested tests on measures of neighborhood quality", Journal of Urban Economics 27:97–110.

Ellickson, B. (1981), "An alternative test of the hedonic theory of housing markets", Journal of Urban Economics 9:56–79.

Epple, D. (1987), "Hedonic prices and implicit markets: estimating demand and supply functions for differentiated products", Journal of Political Economy 95:59–80.

Feenstra, R.C. (1995), "Exact hedonic price indexes", Review of Economics and Statistics 77:634–653.

Follain, J. and E. Jimenez (1983), "The demand for housing characteristics in developing countries", Discussion Paper WUDD 43 (The World Bank Water Supply and Urban Development Department).

Follain, J.R. and E. Jimenez (1985), "Estimating the demand for housing characteristics: a survey and critique", Regional Science and Urban Economics 15:77–107.

Freeman, A.M. (1979), "Hedonic prices, property values and measuring environmental benefits: a survey of the issues", Scandinavian Journal of Economics 81:154–173.

Gilley, O.W. and R.K. Pace (1995), "Improving hedonic estimation with an inequality restricted estimator", The Review of Economics and Statistics 77:609–621.

Goodman, A.C. (1978), "Hedonic prices, price indices and housing markets", Journal of Urban Economics 5:471–484.

Gourieroux, C. and A. Monfort (1995), Statistics and Econometric Models, Vol. 2 (Cambridge University Press, Cambridge).

Griliches, Z. (1961), "Hedonic price indexes for automobiles: an econometric analysis of quality change", The Price Statistics of the Federal Government, No. 73.

Griliches, Z. (1971), Price Indexes and Quality Change: Studies in New Methods of Measurement (Harvard University Press, Cambridge, MA).

Halvorsen, R. and H.O. Pollakowski (1981), "Choice of functional form for hedonic price equations", Journal of Urban Economics 10:37–49.

Harrison, D.J. and D.L. Rubinfeld (1978), "Hedonic housing prices and the demand for clean air", Journal of Environmental Economics and Management 5:81–102.

Horowitz, J.L. (1984), "Estimating compensating and equivalent income variations from hedonic price models", Economics Letters 14:303–308.

Horowitz, J.L. (1987), "Identification and stochastic specification in Rosen's hedonic price model", Journal of Urban Economics 22:165–173.

Jackson, J.R., R.C. Johnson and D.L. Kaserman (1984), "The measurement of land prices and the elasticity of substitution in housing production", Journal of Urban Economics 16:1–12.

Jones, L.E. (1988), "The characteristics model, hedonic prices, and the clientele effect", Journal of Political Economy 96:551–567.

Kain, J.F. and J.M. Quigley (1970), "Measuring the value of housing quality", Journal of the American Statistical Association 65:532–548.

Kanemoto, Y. and R. Nakamura (1986), "A new approach to the estimation of structural equations in hedonic models", Journal of Urban Economics 19:218–233.

Knight, J.R., R.C. Hill and C.F. Sirmans (1993), "Estimation of hedonic housing price models using nonsample information: a Monte Carlo study", Journal of Urban Economics 34:319–346.

Laakso, S. (1997), Urban Housing Prices and the Demand for Housing Characteristics (ETLA, The Research Institute of the Finnish Economy, Helsinki).

Lancaster, K. (1966), "A new approach to consumer theory", Journal of Political Economy 74:132–157.

Lerman, S.R. and C.R. Kern (1983), "Hedonic theory, bid rents, and willingness-to-pay: some extensions of Ellickson's results", Journal of Urban Economics 13:358–363.

Linneman, P. (1980), "Some empirical results on the nature of the hedonic price function for the urban housing market", Journal of Urban Economics 8:47–68.

Linneman, P. (1981), "The demand for residence site characteristics", Journal of Urban Economics 9:129–148.

Mayo, S.K. (1981), "Theory and estimation in the economics of housing demand", Journal of Urban Economics 10:95–116.

McConnell, K.E. and T.T. Phipps (1987), "Identification of preference parameters in hedonic models: consumer demands with nonlinear budgets", Journal of Urban Economics 22(1):35–52.

McFadden, D. (1977), "Modeling the choice of residential location", Discussion Paper 477 (Cowles Foundation).

Meese, R.A. and N.E. Wallace (1997), "The construction of residential housing price indices: a comparison of repeat-sales, hedonic-regression and hybrid approaches", Journal of Real Estate Finance and Economics 14:51–73.

Milon, J.W., J. Gressel and D. Mulkey (1984), "Hedonic amenity valuation and functional form specification", Land Economics 60:378–387.

Murray, M.P. (1983), "Mythical demands and mythical supplies for proper estimation of Rosen's hedonic price model", Journal of Urban Economics 14:326–337.

Ohsfeldt, R.L. and B.A. Smith (1985), "Estimating the demand for heterogeneous goods", Review of Economics and Statistics 61:165–171.

Ohsfeldt, R.L. and B.A. Smith (1990), "Calculating elasticities from structural parameters in implicit markets", Journal of Urban Economics 27:212–221.

Pace, R.K. (1993), "Nonparametric methods with applications to hedonic models", Journal of Real Estate Finance and Economics 7:185–204.

Pace, R.K. (1995), "Parametric, semiparametric, and nonparametric estimation of characteristic values within mass assessment and hedonic pricing models", Journal of Real Estate Finance and Economics 11:195–217.

Palmquist, R.B. (1991), "Hedonic methods", in: J.B. Braden and C.D. Kolstad, eds., Measuring the Demand for Environmental Quality, pp.77–120 (Elsevier Science, Amsterdam).

Parsons, G.R. (1986), "An almost ideal demand system for housing attributes", Southern Economic Journal 53:347–363.

Parsons, G.R. (1990), "Hedonic prices and public goods: an argument for weighting locational attributes in hedonic regressions by lot size", Journal of Urban Economics 27:308–321.

Quigley, J.M. (1982), "Nonlinear budget constraints and consumer demand: an application to public programs for residential housing", Journal of Urban Economics 12:177–201.

Ridker, R.G. and J.A. Henning (1967), "The determinants of residential property values with special reference to air pollution", Review of Economics and Statistics 49:246–257.

Rosen, S. (1974), "Hedonic prices and implicit markets: product differentiation in pure competition", Journal of Political Economy 82:34–55.

Sattinger, M. (1980), Capital and the Distribution of Labor Earnings (North-Holland, Amsterdam).

Spitzer, J.J. (1982), "A primer on Box–Cox estimation", Review of Economics and Statistics 64:307–313.

Tinbergen, J. (1959), "On the theory of income distribution", in: L.M.K.L.H. Klaasen and H.J. Witteveen, eds., Selected Papers of Jan Tinbergen (North-Holland, Amsterdam).

Turnbull, G.K. (1993), "The substitution theorem in urban consumer theory", Journal of Urban Economics 33:331–343.

Turnbull, G.K. (1994), "Housing demand properties in the monocentric market form", Regional Science and Urban Economics 24:253–263.

Waugh, F.V. (1929), Quality as a Determinant of Vegetable Prices (Columbia University Press, New York).

*Chapter 42*

# THE LAND MARKET AND GOVERNMENT INTERVENTION

ALAN W. EVANS*

*The University of Reading, UK*

## Contents

\* I am indebted to the Leverhulme Trust for financial support in the completion of this survey.

*Handbook of Regional and Urban Economics. Edited by E.S. Mills and P. Cheshire*

**Abstract**

Two kinds of government intervention in the land market are considered. The first is the control of development, of which the most studied form is zoning, but we also consider the designation of conservation areas and the effects of growth controls. Growth control may raise the price of land, allowing an infrastructure charge to be made or growth may be limited by charging impact fees. The second kind of intervention aims to increase the supply of land, either by direct action, as in the Netherlands, through compulsory purchase or eminent domain, or through the reallocation of land ownership as in land readjustment schemes.

**Keywords:** Land, planning, government, zoning, conservation

## 1. Introduction

In this chapter we aim to survey the effects of government intervention in the market for land. This intervention may be of two kinds. The more usual kind in market economies involves the imposition of controls of some type on the uses to which a piece of land can be put, either by zoning or some other means, so restricting the freedom of action of the owner of the land. This is surveyed in the first half of the chapter. The second half deals with the second kind of intervention that aims to bring forward land for development where it is thought that landowners would hold back and be unwilling to sell their land for development at the market price. This may involve compulsory purchase of the land by an agent of government, or the public supply of land for development, as in the Netherlands, or the reallocation of land ownership as occurs in Japan, Germany and elsewhere. For lack of space the consequences of government control of land in the socialist economies are not considered, nor are the changes which have occurred because of the creation of land markets in these countries in the 1990s.

Intervention may be by central or local government, and therefore, at either a national or local level, but will usually be intended to be part of the implementation of a plan for the future physical development of an area. We largely exclude consideration of the effects of differing forms of taxation of land, that is, we are interested in physical controls on, and planning for, land use rather than fiscal measures. The latter are usually imposed at a national level and for fiscal or equity reasons, and even though they may have an impact on the local land market, they are not our primary interest. In practice, of course, as we will see, it may be very difficult sometimes to draw a clear dividing line between physical controls and fiscal measures, so that we will, on occasion, cross to the other side of this particular frontier.

It should also be obvious that our main interest is in the secondary, and usually unforeseen, effects of government intervention. It is uninteresting if the controls achieve their stated objectives. If, for example, a local government restricts the development of an area of land for residential use, then we are not interested, qua economists, in the fact that the land is so developed. We are interested, however, if, as a result, through the economic system, prices rise or fall as a consequence in that area or elsewhere, and if these price changes have consequential effects on development elsewhere, and we are particularly interested if the economic system frustrates the intended operation of the planning restriction. In this we operate on a well-known principle—"Dog bites man" is not news, "Man bites dog" is.

That intervention can have unforeseen effects has been known, but largely disregarded, by planners for a long time. Abercrombie (1945: p. 29), in his plan for the future of Greater London after the second World War, reports on the impact of the laws introduced in the sixteenth century to control the physical expansion of the City of London, in effect an early form of urban growth control or green belt. In the words of the proclamation of 1580, "her Majestie [Elizabeth I] . . . doth straightly command all manner of Persons . . . to desist and forbeare from any new buildings of any house or tenement within three miles of any of the gates of the said cittie of London . . . where no former House hath been known to have been in the memory of such as are now living".

The ban was extended to 7 or 10 miles from the city and continued during the reigns of the Stuarts and the Commonwealth of Cromwell "but ultimately avoidance of the Law became widespread as Cromwell and the Kings preferred to accept the payment of fines rather than to see that the buildings were demolished and all attempts to control growth lapsed" (Abercrombie, 1945: p. 29f). In the period after it was introduced it was noted that houses already in existence in the area covered by the ban on development were often subdivided or extended by digging out cellars. It was also noted that the ban was often flouted by people constructing new houses in the area, but that these new dwellings were of a temporary, jerry-built nature because the owners anticipated they would have to be demolished when they were eventually identified as illegal. From an economic point of view, it is obvious (even though Abercrombie does not provide the information) that the constraint on expansion had been followed by a continuing excess demand for housing and hence rising prices, because the price of housing in the area had risen enough to make the cost of excavation worth bearing and the risk of demolition worth taking.

This question of the risk of incurring a penalty if a regulation is disobeyed is important. In the Elizabethan case, there was clearly a risk of discovery which was significant, but not very high, since a temporary building was worth constructing and presumably had a reasonable, if short, anticipated life. If it had been known that discovery would be immediate and certain, no such houses would have been built. If the regulation was not enforced at all then a properly constructed permanent house would have been built. So the same regulation may have different effects at different times and under differing enforcement regimes.

Many of the studies to which we refer report on the research carried out in the US within an approximately homogeneous legal system, but even here Fischel (1990) suggested that some knowledge of the enforcement regime is important in gaining an understanding of its economic effects. Within this system it has been suggested by Wallace (1988) and McMillen and McDonald (1991, 1993), that zoning follows the market, i.e., the pattern of land use that occurs after a system of land use regulation and planning is imposed may be exactly what would have occurred without such a system, only in a more ordered fashion, the land use regulatory system therefore providing a kind of imprimatur. This will happen, it is argued, because political pressure will tend to ensure that land values are maximised, if only to maximise local government revenues from property taxes.

In other legal systems different principles may apply. The British system can be placed at one extreme, where land use regulation is enforced (and enforceable) against the pressure of market forces, where the fiscal system gives no encouragement to local authorities to maximise revenue from property taxes, and where deliberate flouting of the rules by would-be developers is likely to result in financial penalties and demolition. Near the other extreme is the Italian system, where land use controls exist but may often be ignored or flouted, and where amnesties in 1985 and 1994 allowed illegally constructed buildings to be legalised on the payment of a fine (Ave, 1996: p. 49f). Since the fines were not set too high to ensure that people paid them, the result was that controls appeared to be, to say the least, highly flexible. It may be noted that environmental pressure groups strongly opposed such amnesties on the grounds that each one that was announced reduced the degree to which people were willing to abide by the existing physical controls. Moreover, the amnesty/fines system tends to transform a system of physical controls into a fiscal system, since the result is a system where nonconforming uses are, in effect, allowed provided a payment is made, with a consequent loss of the possibility of fine tuning that can occur with a physical planning system (but with greater benefit to the Treasury).

## 2. Zoning

There have been two recent surveys of the empirical literature on the economic effects of municipal zoning in the US. One, more recent and explicitly on this subject is by Pogodzinski and Sass (1991), and the other, on the related topic of growth controls is by Fischel (1990) and summarised in Fischel (1989). In the circumstances, this topic does not need to be dealt with at length, since this would mean covering the same ground as these authors, and their work can be readily assessed by those wishing to study the topic in more depth. The aim of these topics in this chapter is therefore to summarise their findings and, where possible, draw attention to non-North American literature, since the two surveys limit themselves to US and Canadian work.

In general, researchers have found it difficult to measure the extent of the external diseconomies or externalities caused by nonconforming land uses, at least in part, it has been argued, because the reallocation of land uses caused by zoning would have been intended to reduce the extent and impact of these externalities and because it is difficult to find an urban area where there is not a zoning system in place. In this respect the position in Houston, Texas, is of interest. In Houston, there are districts with zoning ordinances, districts with systems of covenants, and districts without either. Speyrer (1989) found that property values were lower in the latter, and that buyers were prepared to pay a substantial premium for properties covered by either covenants or zoning. Thus, zoning must achieve something, from the local property owners' point of view, even though, as Speyrer points out, "premiums paid for land use restrictions do not imply such restrictions may be optimal . . . gains may be small compared with the losses incurred by excluded groups" (Speyrer, 1989: p. 128). An alternative interpretation of the position was put forward by McDonald (1995) after the voters of Houston had narrowly voted in 1993 against a proposed zoning plan. In general, low income areas voted against zoning while middle income areas voted in favour. McDonald (1995) suggests that this was primarily because zoning was perceived, by both groups, as a means of keeping out the (low income) "riffraff". An alternative interpretation might be that the negative externalities minimised by zoning are given less weight by low income families, i.e., the presence of a factory might be perceived as a wholly unwelcome intrusion in a middle income suburb, but considered more as a source of employment in a low income area.

Much empirical work has been devoted to trying to discover the effect of "nonconforming uses" on neighbouring property values, and as part of this work there has been a considerable discussion on the correct area or range over which externalities might be considered to have an impact. So, it is argued, those studies which find that such uses have little or no impact may do so because they are considering property values within too large an area or at too great a distance. A key study in this respect is that by Li and Brown (1980), even though it was not concerned with zoning or government regulation as such, but was explicitly concerned with the range over which external diseconomies have an effect and, as a further problem, with disentangling the negative effects of any diseconomy from the positive effects of proximity. For example a factory or commercial centre may reduce land values nearby because of noise, pollution or congestion, but may also increase land values because of a shorter journey to work or shop. So, in an early and, for obvious reasons, unpublished study (presented to the first UK Urban Economics Conference in 1971), the researcher found it impossible to ascertain any negative effects of noise from a main road because, insofar as property values were concerned, these negative effects were swamped by the positive advantages of proximity to the road and its bus routes. The achievement of Li and Brown (1980) was to carefully specify the distance relationships so as to fully allow for the possible negative and positive effects, and to show that the two effects could be distinguished provided the distance decay rates of these effects differed. It seems to be established that commercial and industrial uses do have a negative impact on the value of housing in the vicinity, but a few such uses may be acceptable in an area because they provide opportunities for shopping and employment. Furthermore, the presence of (multifamily) higher density housing may reduce the value of lower density (single family) housing. A study by Cheshire and Sheppard (1995)—using British data, details of housing transactions in the towns of Reading in southern England and Darlington in northeast England—found more evidence of amenities being valued than disamenities. Property values were increased as a result of being in the catchment areas of the more highly regarded schools and the existence of open space nearby, whether accessible or not. More recent work (Cheshire and Sheppard, 1997) reports evidence that industrial activities imposed external diseconomies which were minimised by planning controls. Furthermore, this effect was redistributive, although they found that the effects of planning with respect to accessibility to open space was regressive.

One of the difficulties of measuring the impact of zoning is the separation of what one might call the impact of quality from quantity. So, with respect to residential densities it was established some years ago (Mirrlees, 1972), that there is a likelihood of market failure and that, in the absence of appropriate zoning mechanisms, density controls or ownership by a single landowner, land will be developed at too high a density. The zoning of land at a lower density than would occur in a competitive land market with many landowners should, therefore, raise land values to a Pareto optimal level. But suppose that, possibly because of political pressure, too much land is zoned at the lower densities, or the zoned density is in fact too low, then the supply of land at these lower densities will be too great, property values may be lower than the optimum, and indeed may be lower than they would be had there had been no intervention. In this case, the finding of an empirical study might be that zoning is inefficient, whereas the correct conclusion would be that incorrect zoning is inefficient.

One problem, as noted by Pogodzinski and Sass (1991), is that zoning may be carried out for at least three different reasons. First, to try to minimise the impact of external diseconomies—externality zoning, second, to try to exclude poorer households—exclusionary zoning, and third, to try to reduce taxes for the existing residents by expanding the tax base (relative to expenditure)—fiscal zoning. While these can be distinguished conceptually they may be difficult to distinguish empirically. Does a city lay down a large minimum lot size to exclude the less wealthy or to deal with a possible market failure? Possible explanations may also be complicated by interactions. So Bates and Santerre (1994) found a positive correlation between the area of land zoned for residential use and minimum lot size. Interactions of this kind need not be limited to zoning instruments. Lenon et al. (1996) found considerable interdependence between zoning, taxing and spending levels for towns in Connecticut, both within towns, and between competing, i.e., nearby, towns, and the analysis of these various kinds of interdependencies and interactions would appear to be a fruitful area of current research.

There is one point that could be made on the considerable body of North American work surveyed by Fischel (1990) and Pogodzinski and Sass (1991). Virtually all of this empirical work on the economics of zoning uses hedonic methods to carry out cross-sectional analyses of differences in the price of housing or land between different locations at a point in time. The first such study was carried out by Crecine et al. (1967), and their paper seems to have defined the research agenda, or at least the rules, by which this particular game was to be played. Their conclusions, from a study of property values in Philadelphia, almost certainly helped in this. They found that externalities were not important, nor indeed statistically significant, in determining differences in property values. So the objective of later researchers appears to have become that of either refuting or confirming this particular result. Methodologically, this could only be done conclusively by using similar data and hedonic price studies, and showing that there must have been either some peculiarity in the data used by Crecine et al., or an error in their methodology. In effect, the objective became one of measuring differences in property values rather than the measurement of the magnitude of social costs of externalities.

It might be asked what else could have been done. And the answer is that there are a number of methods that might be used to assess the cost of an externality, and it is this, after all, that is of primary interest. One approach was that used by Ihlanfeldt and Boehm (1987) in a study that was an exception to the rule. They used the results of a survey in which households had been asked to rank the over-all quality of their neighbourhood, and explored the relationships between this quality ranking and the perceived or actual characteristics of the neighbourhood. The most obvious alternative approach would be to use contingent valuation methods and ask people how much they would be willing to pay to be rid of an external diseconomy, or how much they would require to be compensated for it. Such methods are used frequently in discussions of the rural environment. Indeed, it is odd to peruse almost any issue of the journal *Land Economics*, and to see numerous papers on the social costs and benefits of rural conservation using contingent valuation methods alongside other papers on urban externalities using, exclusively, hedonic methods. Of course, contingent valuation methods are more suitable for the analysis of the environment in rural areas because of the absence of properties into which the value of the environment can be capitalised. The views of those living elsewhere, therefore, have to be taken into account. But the persistent methodological division implies that in the urban case the environment is only important to those living nearby while in the rural case the benefits are felt by those living elsewhere.

The fact that contingent valuation methods can be used was demonstrated by Willis and Whitby (1985) in an attempt to evaluate the social costs and benefits of planning control. They asked people for their valuation of the green belt around the Tyne and Wear conurbation in northern England at the core of which is the city of Newcastle-on-Tyne. They found that the social value of the then existing green belt was greater than its cost, but that the benefit of a proposed widening of the belt, which has since been carried out, would be less than the social cost.

The argument implicit in the US studies is that the social cost of a "non-conforming use" must be identifiable using hedonic methods, if it is of any importance. Much of the argument has been methodologically along the lines laid out by Lakatos (1970: p. 100), with the example of a planet that is predicted to exist but an empirical study fails to locate. The prediction is not necessarily considered to be refuted. It is the empirical study that is claimed to be at fault, and much more sophisticated studies may be carried out to try to confirm the planet's existence. In this case the failure by earlier researchers to find evidence of price differences resulting from externalities was not considered as refuting the hypothesis that externalities exist and cause social costs. Rather, it was argued that the earlier research must be at fault and that, with better specification of what was at issue, the effects of the externalities would be ascertained, and so this respecification and clarification is what has been carried out.

The concentration of the researchers on the static relationships between house prices and externalities may, however, have resulted in the neglect of more complex reasons for the voters' apparent preference for zoning (Houston excepted). One is the "slippery slope" argument. It may well be that the presence of a single factory in a suburban area may have a negligible impact on house prices in its immediate vicinity, and this impact may be difficult to identify among all the other influences on property values, given the imperfections of the property market. And it may be true, therefore, that the population of an area would not mind one or even two factories in the area, but it may still be true that they do not want several factories in the area. They will not want their housing to be surrounded by industry. And, therefore, it may well be that the perceived way to prevent this is to vote for a zoning regulation that excludes *all* factories. So even though an economic researcher may argue that the evidence shows that one factory is unimportant, the voters' perception is that they have to bar the door against any one factory to prevent it from becoming the thin end of a wedge used to prise the door open to many. One of the town planning arguments is that planning increases certainty, and in this the voters may agree with the planners.

There is a further point here that can be argued with respect to the numerous American studies of the economics of zoning using hedonic price studies and that is the lack of what one might call consistency in these studies. One researcher may fit an equation to the data for a city or a number of cities. In the report of the research results, stress will be laid on the sign and magnitude of one of the coefficients, and it may be noted that the sign or the significance of the coefficient differs from that found by some earlier researcher with the implication that this refutes the earlier findings. But it is, to say the least, not unknown for the signs and magnitudes of other coefficients to differ and for these differences to be ignored, even though the whole paper could have been given another title and the stress laid on these other differences. To demonstrate this, one need only look at the question of whether, or not, the number of governments in an urban area affects the price of land and housing there. It is hypothesised that the smaller the number of jurisdictions the more likely it is that they can, and will, act monopolistically. Hamilton (1978) proposed and tested this hypothesis using the 1960 Census data for census tracts in 13 urban areas in the northeastern US. Fischel (1980) argued that Hamilton's measure of zoning power (MSA jurisdictions/MSA population, or a dummy if number of jurisdictions less than four) was misleading, first, because the cities with few jurisdictions were all in New England, and second, because the number of jurisdictions in a Standard Metropolitian Statistical Area was misleading since the data should relate to the Urbanised Area (UA) so that the UA jurisdictions/UA population would be the correct measure. Using these measures, and the 1970 Census data, Fischel found the monopoly zoning hypothesis to be "not proven".

Two later papers discuss determinants of interurban house prices (Ozanne and Thibodeau, 1983), and interurban land prices (Manning, 1988), and include measures of monopoly zoning power as independent variables. Data for the first paper were from the 1974–1976 *Annual Housing Survey* and data for the second were from the 1980 Census. In both these studies, the variable is highly significant but both use MSA jurisdictions despite the strictures in Fischel's paper, to which neither refers. We do not know, therefore, whether the significance of the measure of monopoly zoning in their later work is because they are using an incorrect measure, or using later data and the situation has changed over time, or their equations are more carefully specified. Manning (1988), for example, includes a measure of the high "real income tail" to take account of the way in which taxes and inflation may interact to reduce the cost of housing for high income households, and this was highly significant. But this variable was itself introduced by Gottlieb (1965), only to be neglected until Manning's (1988) apparent rediscovery of it. A later paper by Thorson (1996) goes some way towards settling the question in that he takes account of the points made by Fischel (1980), and carefully specifies his equations taking account of the specifications used by others such as Manning (1988), and shows that "zoning power is associated with higher housing prices for both 1980 and 1990", arguing that inflation and population changes since 1970 account for the increase in the importance of zoning power since that date.

It would seem better if there were an attempt at consistency, taking cognisance of the argument in the econometrics of time series studies that later research should be able to encompass the earlier results in order to demonstrate the superiority of the later formulation. So, for example, with respect to house price studies, the model formulated by Giussani and Hadjimatheou (1990) is shown to encompass the model set out by Hendry (1984). Because researchers using urban data are using cross-sectional analyses involving different cities and dates, it is impossible to follow this principle literally, but the paper by Thorson (1996) shows what should be done in the case of interurban property price studies. With intraurban house and land price studies, a check-list of what might be expected in a hedonic study of house prices could be used. One effort in this direction is by Andersson, who explicitly considers the relationship between what others have already found and what he would therefore expect to find in his study of the Swedish cities of Malmo and Lund (Andersson, 1994), and of the condominium market in Singapore (Andersson, 1997).

## 3. Conservation areas and historic districts

One form of zoning that should be considered on its own terms is the designation of an area as worthy of conservation and preservation, with as little as possible alteration, either because of its historic interest or its architectural or environmental interest. From an economic point of view, it is not immediately clear what the effect should be on the value of the properties within the designated area. In the first place, one would expect that the value of properties in the area would be higher than elsewhere because of the characteristics which make the area worthy of designation. Nevertheless, this enhanced value might be small and not statistically observable, particularly if the characteristics of the area are not valued by those who might be expected to live there normally. Furthermore, since designation usually restricts the ability of owners to alter properties in ways they might wish, but which would be regarded as altering the character of the area, this feature would tend to reduce the value of properties. On the other hand, designation ensures that other owners cannot alter the character of their properties and so ensures that the favourable environment is preserved when it might otherwise change. Because of designation, it follows that a purchase of a property in the area becomes slightly less risky because the favourable environment, for which a premium has to be paid, becomes more secure and less likely to be degraded.

With respect to the designation of individual buildings, we would expect their value to fall since the owner's ability to alter the building is restricted, but there is no compensating guarantee that the surrounding environment will not be altered for the worse. Hence, Asabere et al. (1994) found that local designation of buildings in Philadelphia was "associated with a 24% price decrease". On the other hand, as we would expect, empirical evidence with respect to the designation of conservation areas is mixed. In Baltimore, Maryland, for example, Ford (1989) found that designation of an area as a historic district resulted in prices being higher than one would expect, while, on the other hand, Asabere et al. (1989)

found in Newburyport, Massachusetts, that historic district designation did not raise prices, although certain historic architectural styles did result in premium prices being paid for individual houses. Gale (1991), reviewing the evidence, concluded that, on balance, historic district designation did not appear to result in higher prices, but that there was some evidence that the prices of buildings in historic districts were more "robust' in that they were less volatile than expected.

An interesting study is that carried out by Schaeffer and Millerick (1991). They analysed property prices in an area of Chicago that had been designated as a National Historic District. Such designation, in fact, imposes few controls on existing owners and occupiers, but may allow some tax benefits, particularly for income producing buildings. The authors found that buildings within the designated area appeared to have increased in value as a result of the designation. Within the National Historic District, however, two smaller areas were designated as Chicago Historic Districts. Such designation limits the ability of the owners to alter or further develop their properties, and the value of properties within these two districts appeared to have been reduced as a result, almost certainly below their value if they had merely been in a National Historic District, although property values still seemed to be higher than if they had not been in any form of Historic District.

The research by Schaeffer and Millerick (1991) draws attention to the importance of the precise conditions attached to the designation of buildings in a conservation area. If the implication is only that the ability of the owners to alter their buildings is restricted then this may or may not result in an increase in the price of the properties. The effect may also vary from property to property. The house that has already been extended in the conservation area may increase in value because the surroundings are less likely to change. On the other hand, the value of a house may fall if it has a garden or yard that could have been developed but where development is now unlikely to be permitted. The effects may also vary from area to area. If the characteristics of the properties are valued by the local population, preservation may also be valued, but if preservation is imposed, as it were from outside, and the residents do not value the style of the area, no matter how historically interesting it is, then prices are unlikely to increase and may even fall. Again, if designation as a historic district is accompanied by tax advantages then prices are likely to increase to capitalise the financial benefits resulting from designation. Lack of any such fiscal advantages is more likely to lead to a fall in value.

## 4. Growth controls

As well as the survey of the empirical evidence on the economics of zoning by Pogodzinski and Sass (1991), there has also been an even more complete survey of the empirical evidence regarding the growth controls in the North American context by Fischel (1990) to try to answer the question "Do growth controls matter?" In the end, after an extensive survey summarised in Fischel (1989), he concludes that they do, that growth controls do limit development, and so affect, at the least, land and property prices.

The discussion by Fischel (1990) is, in one way, an excellent illustration of the problem of surveying worldwide evidence. His survey covers only studies relating to North American cities. He reviews a large body of fairly sophisticated econometric work which has been carried out in order to discover whether, or not, there is a price differential caused by the existence of land use controls. The implication of the structure of the argument is that any price differential is so small that sophisticated techniques are necessary to reveal its existence. Japanese researchers had a related problem of identification. Given that Japanese land prices are high, can these high prices be attributed to planning controls, in particular the designation of Urban Control Areas to limit development? Takeuchi et al. (1994) conclude that the Urban Control Areas have been effective in limiting development around the three largest cities (Tokyo, Osaka, Kanagawa) and, therefore in causing higher prices, but they have been ineffective elsewhere. Oizumi (1994) attributes the land price boom of the 1980s to speculation fuelled by the finance industry, but, on the other hand, since planning controls reduce the elasticity of supply and so increase price volatility, they too will make some contribution to fuelling speculation.

In Korea and the UK, on the other hand, planning controls, in particular the green belts around the major cities, were, to economists at least, obvious causes of high land and property prices. So, in Korea, "the opportunity cost of home-ownership ... was 40% of income in Seoul, and even higher in other large cities" (Malpezzi and Mayo, 1987). This could be attributed to the shortage of land, as demonstrated by Son and Kim (1998) who estimated negative exponential land price functions for Korean cities for both residential and agricultural land, and by comparing the resulting pairs of functions concluded that urban land was in short supply in almost every city in the Capital Region, and that the shortage was mainly attributable to artificial scarcity caused by land use regulations.

In the UK, with a planning control system and green belts around major cities, at the time that the Fischel's (1990) survey was published, the price of land in the green belt round London was approximately $5000 per hectare if it was in agricultural use, but, if planning permission for residential development could be obtained then the price of the same land would have jumped to $1 million, even possibly $2 million, per hectare. No sophisticated econometric analysis of any kind was necessary to confirm that there growth controls did matter and that planning had not followed the market.

Curiously, although this might be obvious to economists, what was necessary at that time was an extremely unsophisticated discussion of basic rent theory. Planners and politicians remembered from their early studies of economics that Ricardian rent theory demonstrated that "the price of land is high because the price of corn [or housing] is high and not vice versa" but had forgotten, or never realised that the proof of this conclusion depended on the assumption made by Ricardo that the supply of land was fixed. Therefore, the price of land for housing was not only determined by the price of housing (and so by the demand for housing), but would be affected by any increase in the supply of land for housing through a relaxation of some kind in the stringency of planning controls. This basic and, one would have thought, elementary theoretical point was debated in at least two quasijudicial appeals against refusals to grant planning permission for major developments, at some length and considerable cost, since it involved both leading and junior counsel, on both sides, and expert witnesses. Curiously, the same lack of understanding appears to have been true of Korea. Kim (1994) comments that "very few people in Korea seem to realise that green belt policy and other up-tight control of urban land use is a critical contributing factor to high prices of urban land and housing". Just as in Britain, "many people and even some experts put the blame on 'speculators' " (Kim, 1994: p. 6).

The empirical work undertaken in the UK has therefore taken forms other than trying to demonstrate the existence of a self-evident (to economists) price differential. So, Cheshire and Sheppard (1989) compared the land markets of Reading, in southern England, which they identified as one of the urban areas most constrained by planning controls, and Darlington in northeast England, identified as one of the least constrained. They used hedonic methods to model the two housing markets, but then sought to identify what would be the effect on the Reading housing market of reducing the degree of planning constraint to a level equivalent to that in Darlington, or of removing constraints altogether. If all constraints were removed they found that the area of the town would increase by some 50%, but that this would mostly be an expansion in garden space, since the reduction in house prices, because of the increase in land supply, would result in people buying larger houses with much larger gardens or in moving from apartments to houses. Because of the expansion in the quantity of housing purchased, they found that the average price paid for a house would fall substantially but that people would take advantage of this fall to buy bigger houses occupying more land, so would only spend some 5% less on housing. In their most recent paper, Cheshire and Sheppard (1997) calculate the cost of containment as equivalent to 'a tax on household incomes of around 10%". They also estimate that the benefits associated with containment tend particularly to favour upper income groups.

It is evident that while the question at issue for American researchers has been whether, or not, land use controls affect land use, the question at issue for British researchers has been, given that land use controls affect land use, what are their other unforeseen effects, and what would be the effect on land use and the wider economy if they were relaxed? The former question will be considered later, the latter question, as we have shown, was considered by Cheshire and Sheppard (1997) and answered using a simulation based on the hedonic price approach. An entirely different approach to the question has been taken by Bramley (1993a, b). He collected data for each of 80 local planning areas in southern and central England relating to 1988. Using these observations he set up a three equation model. In the first equation, the dependent variable is the (average) price of housing in each authority, as a function of the environmental and socioeconomic characteristics of the authority and the housing output (amount of housing constructed) in the year. In the second equation, the dependent variable is the housing output for each authority as a function of the land price, planning policies (including planning permissions) and land availability. In the third equation, the dependent variable is the flow of planning permissions in each local authority area as a function of land price, planning policy and land availability. While the adjusted $R^2$ for the first two equations are reasonably high at 0.65 or more, that for the third equation is only 0.18, indicating the difficulty of modelling what is essentially a political process.

Having set up the model, Bramley (1993a, b) uses it to simulate the effect of various policy changes, in particular, the effect of substantially increasing the amount of land made available for housing. The American studies, and the simulation by Cheshire and Sheppard (1997), generally assume that the supply of land for development is elastic, the sole limitation on development, in the British case, being the absence of permission for development. If this permission is available then it is assumed that, in the longer run if not in the short, the land will be developed if its price, when developed and allowing for the cost of infrastructure, exceeds the price of land in agricultural use, i.e., land is always used for that purpose which will yield the highest current rent. There are several reasons why this might not be so in the short or medium term which are rehearsed by Neutze (1987) and to which we shall refer again later—owners may have an attachment to the site that makes them unwilling to sell, they may be uncertain about the future and hold their land as a kind of option, and, not least, they may speculate as to the price currently available and the price that they might obtain later. It is this feature of the land market, the inelasticity of the supply of land for urban development, that is an important feature of Bramley's results. What he found was that a substantial release of land as available for development would have little sustained impact on house prices—after a few years these prices would only have fallen by some 5%, and the output of housing would only have increased by some 10%.

Now, it may be that not too much reliance should be placed on Bramley's (1993a, b) model when it is used for the simulation of changes that are supposed to occur over substantial periods of time, at least because it is based on cross-sectional data (see Evans, 1996; Pryce, 1997). Nevertheless, Bramley's findings are of interest. In his simulation, the increase in supply is supposed to occur because the local authorities designate a greater amount of land as available to be developed, and this is represented as an alteration in the variable "structure plan provision for housing". But in his empirical analysis Bramley finds an extremely weak relationship between this "structure plan provision" and the output of housing. One might have expected the coefficient to be close to one if there was a close relationship between the allocation of land for development by planning authorities and the development of this land by developers. In fact, the coefficient is much less than one. Most of the effect of any increase in structure plan provision for new housing is therefore dissipated in what Bramley calls an "implementation gap". Land may be declared to be available for development by planning authorities but this does not mean that landowners will sell it immediately for development or that developers will immediately buy it. Each will respond in their own time, rationally seeking to maximise benefits within their own time horizon.

The evidence relating to the economic effects of the designation of urban growth boundaries (UGBs) in the state of Oregon is relevant to this argument. Studies by Knaap (1985) of the Portland UGB and by Nelson (1985) of the Salem UGB both found that four years after designation of the UGBs the price of nonurban land within a UGB was higher than that outside the UGB. Since the UGBs were designed and intended to meet the demand for urban land for 20 years, this evidence indicates that even with a presumed 16-year supply of development land available within a UGB, together with a presumption that at the end of the 16 years the UGB would be relaxed, there was still a significant price effect.

Taken together, the British and Oregon evidence demonstrates that a constraint on the availability of land for development need not be completely binding to have an economic impact. The land designated as available for development may not be developed immediately even though its price is considerably higher than it would otherwise be because of the existence of the constraint. Moreover, because the price of land is higher, the development that does take place will use the land more intensively.

## 5.  Planning gain and impact fees

As we have noted, while there has been some discussion and considerable economic research to discover whether, or not, the imposition of growth controls in and around US cities has resulted in increased property values, in the UK the difference between the value of a site without permission to develop and its value with permission to develop has become so great over the years, certainly in southern England, that it could not be ignored. In particular, it could not be ignored by the local planning authorities who were granting planning permission, and, in the process, giving the landowners substantial increases in value. The observation by the local authorities that planning permission could be worth a considerable sum of money has therefore led, over the past 25 years or so, to what have come to be called "planning gain" agreements. Under such an agreement, the developer agrees to certain conditions which both reduce the value of the permission and transfer some of the benefits to the local authority. Initially, these agreements mainly involved the designation of part of the site for some public use, e.g., an open space or a road improvement, later they included the construction of a building on the site that might be handed over to the local authority, e.g. a community centre or housing for low income households. By the 1980s they had widened in scope to include payments for facilities elsewhere in the area that might have only a tenuous relationship with the proposed development, e.g., part of the cost of a swimming pool in a nearby town.

It is interesting to note that, as the British system has moved from a system of wholly physical controls to one involving fiscal elements, so the same movement has occurred in the US as local authorities have buttressed exclusionary zoning by the levying of so-called impact fees, fees which are represented as covering the cost to the city of the additional population or development. The shift has occurred for different reasons in the two countries, however. In Britain, the local authorities have recognised, in a manner any economist would understand and applaud, that there is no point in giving anything away free if you can obtain something you want in exchange. In the US, on the other hand, it would appear that the wish is to prevent further development in an area and to use fiscal methods when physical controls have been perceived as being less than fully successful. So Gyourko (1991) reports evidence from the Wharton Urban Decentralisation Project that "among the cities which impose impact fees, there is a statistically significant positive correlation between the amount of the fee and the rating of its exclusionary strength [and the] amount of the fee is significantly negatively correlated with the respondents' ratings of the exclusionary strength of other growth control devices including ordinances and building permit restrictions. Thus, it appears that some cities may have turned to fees after other restrictive policies did not work as well as desired" (p. 244).

Because planning gains in Britain are subject to ad hoc negotiation between the local planning authority and the developer, and because they vary in level, type and cost, from development to development, little empirical research has been carried out into their magnitude and effect. It does appear, however, that, as one might expect, the cost of planning gain is borne by the landowner in reduced land values, rather than being borne by the developer or passed on to the purchaser of the property. To exemplify this, one should note that in the late 1980s it became standard practice for a developer to purchase an option to buy a piece of land and then seek planning permission. One of the conditions of the option would often be that the cost of planning gain, that had to be conceded in order to increase the probability of obtaining permission, would result in a lower price being paid to the landowner for the land in the event of permission being granted and the option to buy being exercised.

In the US and Canada, on the other hand, because within any local authority the level of the impact fee is set and standardised, some empirical work has been carried out to ascertain the incidence of the fees. Singell and Lillydahl (1990) report a study of house prices in Loveland, Colorado, over a period including July 1984 when fees to developers were increased by $1182 over and above the level of the traditional water and sewage fees. They found that the price of both new and old houses increased after July 1984, indeed by substantially more than the amount of this impact fee.

In a later study of the effects of changes in impact fees in three Toronto suburbs, Skaburski and Qabeer (1992) also found that property prices rose by more than the amount of the impact fees. They found that "each dollar ... increase in the fee results in a $1.88 increase in lot prices when the growth rate is zero" but that the extent of forward shifting is reduced by growth so that, "when the region is growing at the study period's average rate of 2.33 per cent a year, each dollar increase in development impact fees leads to a $1.23 increase in lot prices" which they estimate corresponds to the impact fee plus the administrative cost (p. 663).

Since land was available for development in the areas studied, the finding that the amount of the impact fee was passed on to the buyers of new properties is theoretically plausible, as is Singell and Lillydahl's (1990) finding that the increased price of new properties resulted in higher prices for older houses. If the supply of land is elastic, one would expect the fee and any increase in the fee to be passed on to buyers.

In other contexts, however, the impact fee may not be passed on at all, but borne by the landowner. Skaburkis (1990) points out that in a housing boom such as occurred in Vancouver in the early 1980s when prices doubled within two years (and then halved), the impact fee is unlikely to be passed on to the buyers because the price of housing is demand determined. In these circumstances the response is likely to be a reduction in the prices offered by developers to landowners. Similarly, in Britain, in southern England at least, since the price of land is determined by demand because the supply is fixed by the local planning authorities, as opposed to land being freely available at a price set by the owners of agricultural land, any form of impact fee is likely to reduce the price of land for development, rather than passed on in the form of higher house prices.

## 6. Growth controls matter

Planning gain, as a benefit being traded by developers in exchange for being given planning permission for a development, would not have become normal in England if the controls on the availability of land for development had not been so stringent, relative to demand, so as to cause the price of land with planning permission to be higher than its price without it. Planning gain is thus one of the unforeseen effects of intervention to restrict the supply of land for development, as market forces cause changes in behaviour, in particular as economic activities change in response to the higher price of land and of property.

These consequences should not be ignored, although they are little studied, for they are very evident in countries such as Korea and England where land use controls have been stringently enforced. The high price of land ensures, for example, that urban land is used intensively, and Evans (1988) has shown that the housing market in England has been significantly affected. Over the years the price of housing that uses land extensively (single storey, detached houses) has risen faster than the price of housing that uses land intensively (apartments, terrace housing). As a result, the construction of the former has fallen relative to construction of the latter; for example in 1969, 12% of dwellings constructed in the private sector were single storey houses, but the proportion had fallen to about

6% 20 years later. Moreover, because demand is greater in southern England so that controls are relatively more stringent and land prices higher, virtually no single storey houses are constructed while they have been a significant proportion of the new housing stock in northern England, and still more important in Northern Ireland where land use constraints have been much more relaxed than in Britain (Adair et al., 1991). Monk et al. (1996) conclude from their study of the operation of the planning system in southern England, that it "tends to generate a narrower range of housing types and densities than would be expected if the market were allowed to operate more effectively" (p. 509).

The pressure to use land intensively has affected commercial uses, but the evidence as to the intensity of use of shops or offices is more anecdotal. Other consequences are also evident. The controls on the growth of the larger cities have prevented contiguous physical expansion, and deterred people from living there because of the high price of housing, but jobs still exist there, and this leads to commuting across the green belt. This has been evident with respect to London, and has also been noted with respect to Seoul. Kim (1993) reported that a survey by the Korea Transport Institute found that "about 600,000 people living outside Seoul's green belt commuted to work or to school in Seoul every day in 1987". He estimated that "the additional cost due to longer commuting would be about W 1 billion per day" (about $1.4 million), and remarked that "it is ironic that green belts, which are designed to contain urban sprawl, in fact result in dispersed development beyond their outer edges, thereby raising social costs" (Kim, 1993: p. 65).

In Britain because planning permission is worth acquiring, it has been worth spending money and resources to acquire it. So, in addition to "planning gain" accruing to local authorities, developers have often incurred substantial sums of "rent seeking expenditure" to try to persuade local planning authorities and the central government if necessary, that planning permission should be given. This may be in the form of public relations costs or in the hiring of barristers, consultants, and expert witnesses to support the application in any inquiry.

Planning controls may also have macroeconomic effects. Malpezzi and Mayo (1997: p. 387) report that the price elasticity of the supply of housing is exceptionally low in Korea and in Malaysia, which also has tight planning controls, when compared with the supply elasticities in Thailand and the USA. With respect to the UK, Monk et al. (1996) observe that, because planning constraints reduce the elasticity of supply, the land-use planning system in the UK exacerbates cycles in house and land prices (p. 509). It has also been argued that they have significantly slowed the growth of the UK economy (Evans, 1988), and although this would be difficult to prove, nevertheless, given that local authorities have deliberately set out to restrict the growth and movement of firms (Evans, 1992), it would also seem difficult to deny. We have already noted that, in any event, Cheshire and Sheppard (1997) estimate the static costs of containment in southern England as equivalent to a 10% tax on incomes. The oddity is that because macroeconomists have little interest in town planning, planning controls are rarely cited by economists as one of the causes of the slow rate of growth of the British economy. The interesting question lies in explaining why one of the fastest growing economies in the world, Korea, should share stringent planning controls with one of the slowest growing economies in the world.

One difference between the two economies lies in the field of housing finance. As house prices have risen in the UK it has become evident that homeowners have saved less because they have perceived that their wealth has risen. The sophisticated system for financing the purchase of housing allowed people to borrow almost all the cost of the property so that households purchased housing early in life and the rented sector declined. On the other hand, the less sophisticated Korean system for financing house purchase did not permit households to purchase a home until they had saved a very high proportion of the cost. So in Korea, households were encouraged to save a high proportion of their income in order to get on the house price escalator, while in Britain, households, once on the house price escalator, were discouraged from saving by the rising value of their home, because of inflation and land use controls. Between, say, 1970 and 1990, it was quite possible for the value of someone's home in Britain to increase by more than the total amount received (net of taxes, etc.) from their employers so that any saving out of income would have affected their net wealth very little. On the other hand, on the credit side, the housing finance system in Britain has resulted in loans on the security of housing being a significant source of finance for new entrepreneurs, particularly in southern England where house prices increased the most (Black et al., 1996).

## 7. The supply of land

Up to this point we have considered only the effects of government controls on the use of land, or, more precisely, controls on the supply of land for a particular use, and, in the case of impact fees and planning gain, the effects of taxes or payments which reinforce these land use controls. Furthermore, our analysis to date implies that the land market can be treated as a competitive market, indeed a perfectly competitive market, without doing too much disservice to the facts, or distorting the implications of the results obtained.

But, as is increasingly realised, the market for land—or to be exact, the market for urban land—is not a perfectly competitive market. Assuming that it is may result in investigators reaching false conclusions, and, in the context of this chapter, failing to realise the reasons for various forms of government intervention in the land market which would seem to be intended to ease rather than to restrict the supply of land for some use. The land market is a highly imperfect market— the good being sold, a piece of real estate, is not a homogeneous product, there are relatively few buyers and sellers involved in trading pieces of real estate that might be regarded as homogeneous products, and the buyers and sellers do not have full information about the alternatives available, particularly alternative future states (Evans, 1995).

Real estate has a particular characteristic that distinguishes it from other kinds of asset, indeed it could be described as its defining characteristic. It is fixed in location. This is easily forgotten by economists schooled in the neoclassical tradition in which all factors of production can be treated identically. It is not, of course, necessary to go as far as the classical economists and construct a theory of land rent and land pricing that is entirely different from that relating to capital and labour, but it is necessary to recognise this intrinsic difference. It is, after all, not forgotten by the owners and buyers of land. From it follow two other features of real property—the implications of contiguity or relative location for land as a production good, which we will look at shortly, and its peculiar status as a consumption good. In many places and at many times, real property has been regarded as a better kind of asset to own than other, movable, assets. This seems to be implicit in the use of the terms "real" estate, "real" property. Real estate cannot be stolen like gold, jewellery or money. Nor can it be concealed. It follows that in a stable society subject to the rule of law, land may be preferred as an asset, particularly when its ownership may confer wealth and power. (In an unstable society, of course, portable valuables may be preferred to land and property.) Many nineteenth century novels could be cited in support of this view, but perhaps Trollope's *Framley Parsonage* may serve as an example. At a less exalted level, and closer to the present day, one could cite the British Conservative government's policies of the 1980s that encouraged people to become homeowners because it was felt that this would lead them to become responsible citizens (and, also of course, it was hoped, become more likely to vote Conservative).

Whether this judgement was politically correct or not, certainly it is evidence that land is, in some way different. The economic implication is that people become attached to their property and their home and may be reluctant to sell at what would be presumed to be the market price (Dynarski, 1986). This attachment may be sentimental or social, but it has an economic effect in that most people are not prepared to sell the real estate that they own for the "market price", but only at some higher price that compensates them for losing possession; indeed some may state that they are unwilling to sell at any price, and this may indeed be true. An elderly couple with little ability to spend money may be reluctant at any price to move away from their home but may prefer to "end their days" there. Empirical evidence on the position was gathered some time ago as part of the investigations carried out for the Roskill Commission on the Third London Airport. They surveyed householders to find out whether, or not, they would be willing to sell at the assessed market price and, if not, how much more they would require. In other words, what was the consumer surplus attached to occupation of their current house. Eleven per cent of the sample were willing to sell at the market price and 8% would not have been willing to sell at any price. While some of the householders required very little to induce them to sell—for 15% of the sample the consumer surplus amounted to less than 15% of the value of their house—"the overall average excess over market price for the sample as a whole [was] 39 per cent" (GB Commission, 1970: p. 373).

Economically these preferences can be represented as implying that the supply curve for land for a particular use in a particular area slopes upwards (Evans, 1983; Neutze, 1987). Of course, as Neutze points out, people may be reluctant to sell at the going market price for other reasons. First, as Titman (1985) shows, this may be because of uncertainty about the future. The ownership of a piece of developable land is like the ownership of an option to develop. Development of any kind, however, incurs a substantial capital cost and fixes the use of the land for the foreseeable future. Therefore, this option can, in effect, be exercised by any owner only once, but the option itself has value, until it is exercised and development takes place. The "market price" of the land, even if it is the value of the land in the highest yielding current use may not be enough to tempt the owner to sell, or to develop; waiting may be preferable.

Second, as Neutze (1987) demonstrates, the owners of land may "speculate" about the future and may withhold their land from some currently profitable development in the belief, the possibly quite correct belief, that a different and more profitable development will become viable at some time in the future. Once again, development, because it incurs a high capital cost and because of the equally high cost of demolition and redevelopment, closes off the possibility of this more profitable future development.

The supply curve for land for a particular use, on the basis of the above evidence and argument, can be regarded as upward sloping. Suppose then we consider the position with respect to, say, the market for land for urban development in a zone on the periphery of a city during a particular period with respect to the land in agricultural use (Evans, 1983), where the upward sloping supply curve represents the supply of land for sale for development.

Some land would normally be sold to other farmers, because, say, the owners wished to retire from farming and so were willing to sell at the ruling agricultural market price (or less). A demand for land for urban development would result in the price of land for development being bid up above the agricultural use price. The premium will encourage some other landowners to sell who otherwise would not. Thus, more land will be sold for development than would be sold for agricultural use and it will be sold at the higher price necessary to encourage landowners to sell.

Nevertheless, in the period, it is probable that only some of the land that might be sold for development actually will be sold. The rest will not be sold but will remain in agricultural use, because the price offered is not enough to induce the owners to sell. Furthermore, there is no reason why the pieces of land sold for development should be contiguous. As a result, in the absence of government intervention, there will be urban sprawl and scattered development as noncontiguous pieces of land are developed and intervening pieces are not. It should be noted that scattered development is not necessarily nonoptimal from an economic point of view. Scattered development does not completely fix the pattern of development for the future and gives flexibility. Scattered development does appear to be nonoptimal, however, and governments have intervened to try to control and minimise its extent.

One reaction has been to define green belts, urban growth boundaries or some other physical control to limit the extent of sprawl by limiting the area of land available for development. The results of this kind of limitation on the availability of land have been discussed earlier in this chapter. The price of the land that is available for development is raised. The land that might have been developed further from the urban area is now unavailable and the demand for land closer to the city is therefore higher. The price of land for development rises as does the quantity of land developed during the period in the area where it is permitted.

An alternative government reaction is that of the governments of Sweden and the Netherlands. In both cases it has been government policy for many years to buy up agricultural land that it was anticipated would be developed in the foreseeable future. Therefore, as urban growth occurs, the land adjacent to the city on which building should take place to maintain an orderly pattern of development is land that is already in public ownership. Land for development is, in effect, supplied to developers "off the shelf" at a market price that allows only for the cost of acquiring the land at the agricultural use price and the cost of any infrastructure. The process is discussed in detail by Duncan (1985) in the case of Sweden, and by Needham (1992) in the case of the Netherlands.

The paper by Needham (1992) is of particular interest in that he gives information on the cost of providing infrastructure (pp. 679f), and therefore sheds light both on the operation of the policy and also, along the way, on the possible different meanings of "the price of land". Land in agricultural use (towards the end of the 1980s) was sold at between DFL2 and DFL5 per square metre, depending on soil properties. When municipalities acquired rural land for urban development they paid (at the beginning of the 1980s) about DFL10 per square metre. Thus, some compensation was paid to the seller, in part because the seller may often have been otherwise unwilling to sell—Needham suggests that DFL10 was close to the price that would be paid if powers of compulsory purchase (i.e. eminent domain) were to be exercised. The evidence suggests (but this time for the 1970s) that the cost of servicing this land, i.e., the infrastructure cost, was about DFL40 per square metre. Serviced land was sold to developers for housing at a price of about DFL100 per square metre (1970s figures again), but it would appear that the municipalities could in fact only sell on about half of the land that they bought, because the rest was used for roads and other community uses. The figures, even allowing for the differences in the periods for which the data on prices were obtained, suggest that municipalities did not try to make a profit but merely covered their costs as they sold land on to developers. Thus, land could be bought for DFL10 and sold for DFL100 and either of these prices would be "the price of land". The information is an explanation of the considerable range in quoted market prices, and a warning to researchers to take special care in using statistics on "the price of land".

Even taking the small compensation element into account, since the municipalities pass on the land at cost price, it is clear that the price of land for development is significantly lower than it would have been if green belts, or some other form of physical growth control, had been imposed.

It should also be noted that this form of intervention does not lead to windfall gains for developers who appear to be buying land from the municipalities at a lower price than they would otherwise have to pay. It is the greater availability of land for development which allows the land price to be lower, and if the developers supply housing in a competitive market the result is that their costs are lower and, hence, the price of housing should be lower. Certainly the evidence indicates that the cost of land is a much smaller proportion of the cost of housing in these two countries than it is elsewhere. For example, Duncan (1985: p. 322f) notes that in the 1970s the plot prices as a proportion of selling price of housing ranged between 15 and 27% in England and Wales, whereas they ranged between 1 and 4% in Sweden.

As mentioned earlier, there is a second feature of the land market which follows from the characteristic of land that it is fixed in location, and that is that the location of one piece of land relative to another can be important. So one might be able to advertise for capital to build a railway, widen a road, construct an office park or develop an industrial or housing estate and accept any funds subscribed—one might also be able to advertise for labour and accept any with the necessary skills that might apply—but one cannot advertise for land in the same way. The pieces of land necessary to build a railway would have to form a continuous strip, there is only one piece of land that could be used to widen the road, the pieces of land for the office park or the industrial or housing estate have, at the least, to be contiguous. This feature of the land market may be relatively unimportant if large areas of land are owned or controlled by single landowners, whether individuals, companies or trusts, but it becomes of great importance if the ownership of land is fragmented. Now, it is possible that a would-be developer may wait and painstakingly acquire all the various pieces of land necessary to carry out a development at the right location of the scale needed to achieve all the possible economies. The earlier analysis suggests that some sites will come on the market, that others may follow in due course, but that it may be necessary to pay higher prices to some owners in order to induce them to sell, given either their attachment to the property or their expectations about its future value. Some developers do this. Nevertheless, it is well known that if some owners discover that theirs is the key property necessary to complete the scheme then they may attempt to exercise their apparent monopoly position by holding out for an excessive price—"price gouging" as it is called in the US. Moreover, as Eckart (1985) has shown, even if the developer were to negotiate with all the owners at the same time, very great fragmentation of ownership may result in a higher price being asked in total as each small owner operates a strategy that their site is such a small proportion of the whole that they might as well ask for a high price. Because of this, some developers may operate using a number of "front" companies with each one apparently buying separately so that it is not apparent that there is a single overall buyer until the whole site has been acquired. This is not possible in many cases. The local authority that wishes to widen a road has to acquire a particular site and both it and the site's owner know this. The owner has a monopoly and could use it, and it is for this reason that governments have powers of compulsory purchase or eminent domain which allow them to force the supply of land for a particular use where, for one reason or another, the public interest is felt to be involved.

Empirical (as opposed to theoretical) research into the economics of eminent domain is scarce. Indeed, a search of the *Social Science Citations Index* suggests that there may be only one published paper, a study by Munch (1976) of eminent domain in the acquisition of land for urban renewal in three areas of Chicago between 1962 and 1970. She found the price paid was, on average, nearly 40% greater than the predicted market value, thus implying some recognition that sellers' reserve prices were likely to be higher than the market value. Some sellers sold voluntarily, and others were subject to the legal process of eminent domain with the price being settled by the court. In the former case, prices were 45% higher than the predicted market value and in the latter case, they were only 25% higher. Munch argued that since the prices for compulsory sales were settled in the courts there was scope for influencing the price paid through legal argument. Since the amount and quality of legal assistance that sellers might use would depend on the total amount at stake, small owners would be at a disadvantage relative to large owners. This implied, Munch said, that the prices obtained by the sellers of large properties would be higher than the prices obtained by the sellers of small properties and this is what she found. Nevertheless, it seems remarkable that the differences were as great as they appeared to be. She concluded that, under eminent domain, "high-valued properties systematically receive more than market value and low-valued properties receive less than market value" (Munch, 1976: p. 495). While one might accept that small sellers who went to court did badly, it seems odd that they should do worse than might be expected from an open market sale as well as from a voluntary sale to the government authority. Although the property market is an imperfect one, this would indicate both a lack of information among a group of sellers who might have been expected to be in communication and that their legal avisers were also giving faulty advice (since one would have expected that with better information and advice small sellers would not have gone to court).

As already stated, there is a scarcity of empirical research on this topic, and a number of questions need to be answered. Even within the US setting the question arises as to whether, or not, Munch's (1976) results are replicable. There are also further questions as to the operation of compulsory purchase under different legal jurisdictions. To what extent are her results location specific? What appears to be the same form of intervention may take different forms in different places. So in Italy (Ave, 1996: pp. 69–77) and Taiwan, the price paid for land purchased compulsorily is substantially lower than the market price. On the other hand, in the UK the price paid for residential properties is greater than the market price to include an element of compensation for disturbance. What is meant by compulsory purchase is important because its threat is often present when apparently voluntary agreements are made for the sale of land under schemes arranged by governments, whether central or local. So, in the discussion above of the system of advance purchase operated in the Netherlands, it was indicated that the price at which land was sold to the local governments was close to the price at which it would be compulsorily purchased. Thus, the compulsory purchase price, plus (or minus) any differences in legal costs, provides an upper bound to the price that might be agreed in any "voluntary" agreement.

The threat of legal coercion is also present in the schemes for the readjustment of land ownership which exist in some countries such as Germany and Taiwan. Under such schemes, an agreement is reached with and by the landowners in an area that some land will be allocated for roads and other infrastructure in an area, as laid out in a proposed plan. If this amounts to, say, one-third of the land area, then each landowner is allocated a share of the remaining land equal to two-thirds of the area of their original land holding, but in a single unit (if the holding was previously split as it might be in Taiwan), and of a shape, size and location suitable for development, for example, rectangular and bordering a planned road. Each owner is then in a position to sell his or her landholding for development. (A description of the process in Germany, where it is called replotting or *Umlegung* is given by Dieterich et al., 1993.)

Such land readjustment schemes are unknown in the UK or the US, possibly because in both countries, but for different historical reasons, agricultural land holdings are relatively large so that it is unnecessary to put together small peasant landholdings to obtain sites of a reasonable size for urban development. In countries where social, constitutional or agricultural factors have encouraged the splitting up of the landholdings amongst numerous owners, powers to encourage land reallocation are more necessary.

Once again, however, there will be differences between countries so that apparently similar schemes will differ in their operation. As noted earlier, the pressure on landowners to reach an agreement may be backed by government powers to force an agreement if one is not reached voluntarily. But in Germany land may be compulsorily purchased while in Taiwan a scheme of land reallocation may be imposed on the landowners. On the other hand, the land readjustment schemes adopted in Japan are wholly voluntary, apart from anything else because of strong public opposition to land expropriation. "Between 1955 and 1975 the Japan Housing and Urban Development Corporation exercised the power only six times" (Hebbert and Nakai, 1988: p. 42). Land readjustment, however accounts for over 20% of urban land supply (Hebbert and Nakai, 1988: p. 25), both in urban promotion areas and in urban control areas. In the latter, schemes are used by landowners to get around the presumption against urban development outside the major cities. If a scheme for land readjustment is agreed within an urban control area then it has to be permitted to proceed (Hebbert and Nakai, 1988: p. 60), the landowners then selling off some land to cover the costs of the infrastructure and the creation of the scheme, and reallocating the remainder among themselves, which they may either choose to sell at that time or continue to hold on to as an asset that it is hoped will appreciate in value. This practice encourages urban sprawl since only a few sites may be sold for development at the time that the ownership of the land is reallocated. The rest will be farmed or left vacant, with a few sites sold each year as and when the owners need to realise capital.

Land readjustment schemes are used to put together sites for urban development which were previously used for agriculture. In all countries, similar problems of site assembly occur within urban areas where ownership is fragmented and a reordering of the pattern of land use and ownership would be desirable. For this reason, powers of compulsory purchase or eminent domain are available to government or state authorised activities such as utilities. In most developed economies, such powers were used to force through schemes of urban renewal or slum clearance in the period after World War II, particularly in cities that had suffered extensive bomb damage. In Britain, in the 1970s and 1980s these powers have been used to promote the redevelopment of the commercial centres of cities by the local authority, using its powers of compulsory purchase, in partnership with a private developer, building and operating a new shopping or commercial centre. As we have already noted, however, there has been little or no economic research into either the effects, efficiency or equitability of these schemes.

## 8. Conclusions

This survey has been limited to looking at research into government intervention in the land market in the market economies. Of course land was allocated according to government directives and plans in the former communist countries, but this was not really intervention in the market because no market existed. Recently, of course, the situation has changed as, in the former communist countries of eastern Europe, governments have tried to ensure the creation of markets where none existed before, and in China where, within an overtly communist state, some kind of simulacrum of a land market is being created, and where the apparent price of land must be determined prior to the market coming into existence. Previously the view had been that, in effect, land had no value, with the result that the pattern of land use came to differ significantly from the pattern in the market economies. Bertaud and Renaud (1997) demonstrate that Moscow has a "perverse" population density gradient because households are concentrated at the periphery, and that low intensity industrial uses occupy prime central areas. The process of adjustment to differentiated land prices is likely to be lengthy. As Li (1997) notes, "government intervention in the operation of the land market can leave behind an inflexible system that cannot react to the market system immediately, even after a market mechanism is created" (Li, 1997: p. 165). It is almost certainly too early to survey research into this topic and, anyway, to do so would lengthen this survey excessively.

Of the conclusions which can be drawn from this survey of government intervention in the land markets of the market economies, the main one must surely be that there is a disproportion in the research effort allocated to the various topics discussed. The major part has been devoted to the analysis of the economics of zoning and growth controls in cities in the US. In part, of course, this is inevitable given that there are more academic economists in the US than elsewhere, but the disproportion is such that there must be other factors. One such is surely the relative ease with which data on house prices can be obtained and analysed, coupled with the view, which we noted, that hedonic price methods seem to have been regarded as almost the only acceptable way in which the economics of zoning could be researched. So there are almost no studies of zoning using contingent valuation methods, despite their continued use in the study of the economics of the rural environment. Is it also significant that there is only one empirical study, using any method, of the economics of eminent domain and that this, which was certainly not the last word on the subject, was published 20 years ago? It would appear to be a topic that could equally well be researched. Presumably, however, the collection of sufficient accurate data to generate tenable conclusions would be costly and time consuming, and the absence of other research deters rather than encourages exploration of the topic.

I am aware, therefore, that a different survey could have been written, one which updated the previously published surveys of the economics of zoning by Pogodzinski and Sass (1991) and of growth controls by Fischel (1990), and that such a survey, in covering 95% or more of the published research would have been regarded as normal and acceptable. Instead the existence of these recent surveys has allowed the coverage of other topics in more detail, indicating in this way more the areas where research might be carried out than those where it has been carried out.

Because the forms of government intervention, and the operation of land markets vary from country to country, and even within countries, this survey is certainly incomplete. I only hope that this incompleteness will encourage others to research the problems of government intervention in the land market in their own countries and in their own way.

## References

Abercrombie, P. (1945), Greater London Plan 1944 (HMSO, London).

Adair, A.S., J.N. Berry and W.S. McGreal (1991), "Land availability, housing demand and the property market", Journal of Property Research 8:59–67.

Andersson, D.E. (1994), Households and accessibility: an empirical study of households' valuation of accessibility to one or more concentrations of employment or services, University of Reading Discussion Papers in Urban and Regional Economics, No. 97.

Andersson, D.E. (1997), Hedonic Prices and Center Accessibility: Conceptual Foundations and an Empirical Hedonic Study of the Market for Condominium Housing in Singapore (Department of Infrastructure and Planning, Royal Institute of Technology, Stockholm).

Asabere, P.K., G. Hachey and S. Grubaugh (1989), "Architecture, historic zoning, and the value of homes", Journal of Real Estate Finance and Economics 2:181–193.

Asabere, P.K., F.E. Huffman and S. Mehdian (1994), "The adverse impacts of local historic designation: the case of small apartment buildings in Philadelphia", Journal of Real Estate Finance and Economics 8:225–234.

Ave, G. (1996), Urban Land and Property Markets in Italy (UCL Press, London).

Bates, L.J. and R.E. Santerre (1994), "The determinants of restrictive residential zoning: some empirical findings", Journal of Regional Science 34:253–263.

Bertaud, A. and B. Renaud (1997), "Socialist cities without land markets", Journal of Urban Economics 41:137–151.

Black, J., D. De Meza and D. Jeffreys (1996), "House prices, the supply of collateral, and the enterprise economy", Economic Journal 106:60–75.

Bramley, G. (1993a), "The impact of land use planning and tax subsidies on the supply and price of housing in Britain", Urban Studies 30:5–30.

Bramley, G. (1993b), "Land use planning and the housing market in Britain: the impact on housebuilding and house prices", Environment and Planning A 25:1021–1051.

Cheshire, P.C. and S. Sheppard (1989), "British planning policy and access to housing: some empirical estimates", Urban Studies 26:469–485.

Cheshire, P.C. and S. Sheppard (1995), "On the price of land and the value of amenities", Economica 62:247–267.

Cheshire, P.C. and S. Sheppard (1997), Welfare economics of land use regulation, Research Papers in Environmental and Spatial Analysis, No. 42 (Department of Geography, London School of Economics, London).

Crecine, J.P., O.A. Davis and J.E. Jackson (1967), "Urban property markets: some empirical results and their implications for municipal zoning", Journal of Law and Economics 10:79–100.

Dieterich, H., E. Dransfeld and W. Voss (1993), Urban Land and Property Markets in Germany (UCL Press, London).

Duncan, S. (1985), "Land policy in Sweden: separating ownership from development", in: S. Barrett and P. Healey, eds., Land Policy: Problems and Alternatives, Chapter 15 pp. 308–344 (Gower, Aldershot).

Dynarski, M. (1986), "Residential attachment and housing demand," Urban Studies 23:11–20.

Eckart, W. (1985), "On the land assembly problem", Journal of Urban Economics 18:364–378.

Evans, A.W. (1983), "The determination of the price of land", Urban Studies 20:119–139.

Evans, A.W. (1988), No Room! No Room! (Institute of Economic Affairs, London).

Evans, A.W. (1992), Town Planning and the Supply of Housing. The State of the Economy, 1992 (Institute of Economic Affairs, London).

Evans, A.W. (1995), "The property market: ninety per cent efficient?", Urban Studies 32:5–29.

Evans, A.W. (1996), "The impact of land use planning and tax subsidies on the supply and price of housing in Britain: a comment", Urban Studies 33:581–585.

Fischel, W.A. (1980), "Zoning and the exercise of monopoly power: a reevaluation", Journal of Urban Economics 8:283–293.

Fischel, W.A. (1989), "What do economists know about growth controls: a research review", in: D.J. Brower, D.R. Godschalk and D.R. Porter, eds., Understanding Growth Management (The Urban Land Institute, Washington, DC).

Fischel, W.A. (1990), Do Growth Controls Matter? (Lincoln Institute of Land Policy, Cambridge, Mass.).

Ford, D.A. (1989) "The effect of historic district zoning on single-family home prices", Journal of the American Real Estate and Urban Economics Association 17:353–362.

Gale, D.E. (1991), "The impacts of historic district designation: planning and policy implications", Journal of the American Planning Association 57:325–340.

GB Commission on the Third London Airport (1970), Papers and proceedings, Vol. VII (HMSO, London).

Giussani, B. and G. Hadjimatheou (1990), "Econometric modelling of UK house prices", Cyprus Journal of Economics 3:36–57.

Gottlieb, M. (1965), "Influences on value in urban land markets", Journal of Regional Science 6:1–16.

Gyourko, J. (1991), "Impact fees, exclusionary zoning, and the density of new development", Journal of Urban Economics 30:242–256.

Hamilton, B.W. (1978), "Zoning and the exercise of monopoly power", Journal of Urban Economics 5:116–130.

Hebbert, M. and N. Nakai (1988), How Tokyo grows: land development and planning on the metropolitan fringe. Suntory-Toyota International Centre for Economics and Related Disciplines, Occasional Paper No 11 (London School of Economics).

Hendry, D.F (1984), "Econometric modelling of house prices in the United Kingdom", in: D.F. Hendry and K. Willis, eds., Econometrics and Quantitative Economics (Blackwell, Oxford).

Ihlanfeldt, K. and T.P. Boehm (1987), "Government intervention in the housing market: an empirical test of the externalities rationale", Journal of Urban Economics 22:276–290.

Joseph Rowntree Foundation (1994), Inquiry into Planning for Housing (Joseph Rowntree Foundation, York).

Kim, K-H. (1993), "Housing policies, affordability, and government policy: Korea", Journal of Real Estate Finance and Economics 6:55–71.

Kim, K-H. (1994), Controlled developments and densification: the case of Seoul, Korea. Discussion Paper, Dept of Economics (Sogang University, CPO Box 1142, Korea).

Knaap, G-J. (1985), "The price effects of urban growth boundaries in metropolitan Portland, Oregon", Land Economics 61:26–35.

Lakatos, I. (1970), "Falsification and the methodology of scientific research programmes", in: I. Lakatos and A. Musgrave, eds., Criticism and the Growth of Knowledge (Cambridge University Press, Cambridge).

Lenon, M., S.K. Chattopadhyay and D.R. Heffley (1996), "Zoning and fiscal interdependencies", Journal of Real Estate Finance and Economics 12:221–234.

Li, L-H. (1997), "Privatization of the urban land market in Shanghai", Journal of Real Estate Literature 5:161–170.

Li, M.M. and H.J. Brown (1980), "Micro-neighbourhood externalities and hedonic housing prices", Land Economics 56:125–141.

Malpezzi, S. and S.K. Mayo (1987), "User cost and housing tenure in developing countries", Journal of Development Economics 25:197–220.

Malpezzi, S. and S.K. Mayo (1997), "Getting housing incentives right: a case study of the effects of regulation, taxes, and subsidies on housing supply in Malaysia", Land Economics 73:372–391.

Manning, C.A. (1988), "The determinants of intercity home building site price differences", Land Economics 64:1–14.

McDonald, J.F. (1995), "Houston remains unzoned", Land Economics 71:137–140.

McMillen, D.P. and J.F. McDonald (1991), "Urban land value functions with endogenous zoning", Journal of Urban Economics 29:14–27.

McMillen, D.P. and J.F. McDonald (1993), "Could zoning have increased land values in Chicago?" Journal of Urban Economics 33:167–188.

Mirrlees, J.A. (1972), "The optimum town", Swedish Journal of Economics 74:114–135.

Monk, S., B.J. Pearce and C.M.E. Whitehead (1996), "Land-use planning, land supply and house prices", Environment and Planning A 28:495–511.

Munch, P. (1976), "An economic analysis of eminent domain", Journal of Political Economy 84:473–497.

Needham, B. (1992), "A theory of land prices when land is supplied publicly: the case of the Netherlands", Urban Studies 29(5):669–686.

Nelson, A.C. (1985), "Demand, segmentation and timing effects of an urban containment program on urban fringe land values", Urban Studies 22:435–443.

Neutze, G.M. (1987), "The supply of land for a particular use", Urban Studies 24:379–388.

Oizumi, E. (1994), "Property finance in Japan: expansion and collapse of the bubble economy", Environment and Planning A 26:199–214.

Ozanne, L. and T. Thibodeau (1983), "Explaining metropolitan housing price differences", Journal of Urban Economics 13:51–66.

Pogodzinski, J.M. and T.R. Sass (1991), "Measuring the effects of municipal zoning regulations: a survey", Urban Studies 28(4):597–621.

Pryce, G. (1997) Construction Elasticities and Land Availability (Centre for Housing Research and Urban Studies, University of Glasgow).

Schaeffer, P.V. and C.A. Millerick (1991), "The impact of historic district designation on property values: an empirical study", Economic Development Quarterly 5:301–312.

Singell, L.D. and J.H. Lillydahl (1990), "An empirical examination of the effect of impact fees on the housing market", Land Economics 66:82–92.

Skaburskis, A. (1990), "The burden of development impact fees", Land Development Studies 7:173–185.

Skaburskis, A. and M. Qabeer (1992), "An empirical estimation of the price effects of development impact fees", Urban Studies 29:653–667.

Son, J-Y., and K-H. Kim (1998), "Analysis of urban land shortages: the case of Korean cities", Journal of Urban Economics 43:362–384.

Speyrer, J.F. (1989), "The effect of land-use restrictions on market values of single-family houses in Houston", Journal of Real Estate Finance and Economics 2:107–113.

Takeuchi, K., K. Nishimura, D-K. Lee and H. Ikegeuchi (1994), "Land prices and Japanese city planning: evaluating the effects of land use control", in: B. Koppel and D. Young Kim, eds., Land Policy Problems in East Asia—Toward New Choices (East-West Center, and Korea Research Institute for Human Settlements: Kyounggi-Do, Korea, Honolulu).

Thorson, J.A. (1996), "An examination of the monopoly zoning hypothesis", Land Economics 72:43–55.

Titman, S. (1985), "Urban land price under uncertainty", American Economic Review 75:505–514.

Wallace, N.E. (1988), "The market effects of zoning undeveloped land: does zoning follow the market?", Journal of Urban Economics 23:307–326.

Willis, K.G. and M.C. Whitby (1985), "The value of green belt land", Journal of Rural Studies 1:147–162.

# PART III

# URBAN DEVELOPMENT AND DEVELOPING COUNTRIES

*Chapter 43*

# URBANIZATION IN TRANSFORMING ECONOMIES

CHARLES M. BECKER*

*University of Colorado at Boulder*

ANDREW R. MORRISON

*Inter-American Development Bank*

## Contents

* We are deeply grateful to Omar Bello, Christopher Grewe, Ramon Key, Stephen Malpezzi and Edwin Mills, all of whom gave extensive and valuable comments on earlier versions of this manuscript. All errors, omissions and misinterpretations, however, are our own.

*Handbook of Regional and Urban Economics. Edited by E.S. Mills and P. Cheshire*

## Abstract

The past half-century has witnessed a dramatic change in the way in which people live. Fifty years ago, only a small proportion of the less developed world lived
in cities, and world poverty was overwhelmingly rural. In 1950, less than one-
fifth of the population of the "third world" was urban; in the next five years or
so, a majority of developing countries' populations will be urban. This dramatic
social change has captured the attention of development economists and, to a
lesser degree, urban economists. This chapter examines what has been learned in
a variety of areas. Section 1 discusses the stylized patterns of urbanization in the
developing world, while Section 2 turns to models of third world city growth and
their empirical estimates, discussing partial equilibrium models, general equilibrium models, economy-wide computable general equilibrium (CGE) models,
demographic-economic perspectives, and household migration modeling. Section 3 considers the impact of government policies on urbanization. Particular
attention is devoted to structural adjustment policies, urban biases in public expenditures, and issues unique to (ex)-socialist economies. Section 4 examines
structural impediments to urban development, including labor and land markets, transportation issues, public finance and social infrastructure concerns, and
urban spatial structure. The final section looks at the macroeconomic impacts

of urbanization—on wage gaps and income distribution, demand patterns and economic efficiency.[1]

**Keywords:** Urbanization, economic development, rural–urban migration, labor markets in developing countries

## 1. Patterns of urbanization in developing countries

Given the vast literature on migration and urbanization in developing countries, it is perhaps surprising that so little is known about actual patterns. The seminal work with respect to urban growth (the rate of increase of urban population) and urbanization (referring to increases in the proportion of a nation's population living in urban areas) remains the Preston report (United Nations, 1980). While a great deal has happened in the intervening years, aside from periodic UN publications on urbanization rates and levels there has been no systematic effort to track actual patterns of urbanization. This is unfortunate on two counts: first, there have been substantial departures in recent patterns from those in the past; and second, it is unlikely that all of these patterns are captured adequately in existing databases.

### 1.1. Urbanization patterns and data issues

Broad trends are shown in Table 1. The urban populations of developing countries grew at about 4.7% annually during the 1950s and at about 4.0% during the 1960s. What happened thereafter is a matter of some debate. Estimates through the early 1990s suggest that urban growth rates accelerated somewhat in the 1970s, perhaps to 4.4%, and remained quite high in the 1980s. But the most recent estimates by international agencies indicate much more moderate urban population growth, both in the 1980s, and, more surprisingly, in the 1970s (only 3.6%, according to World Bank (1995).

The extent of disagreement is disconcerting, especially to those inclined to regard as inviolately factual anything printed by authoritative international agen-

---

[1] This survey should be regarded as a complement to Lucas' (1997) survey of internal migration in developing countries for the *Handbook of Population and Family Economics.*

Table 1

Patterns of urbanization, 1950–1995 (all figures are in percentages)

| Region | 1950 | 1960 | 1970 | 1975 | 1980 | 1990 | 1995[e] | 1995 | 2015[e] |
|---|---|---|---|---|---|---|---|---|---|
| Proportion of population living in urban areas | | | | | | | | | |
| Less developed regions | 16.7 | 21.8 | 25.8 | 28.0 | 30.5 | 36.5[e] | 43.5[e] | 37.6 | 50.5 |
| Latin America | 41.2 | 49.4 | 57.4 | 61.2 | 64.7 | 70.7 | 75.2 | 74.2 | 82.1 |
| East Asia excl. China and Japan | 28.6 | 36.3 | 47.5 | 53.4 | 58.8 | 67.5 | 73.0 | 36.9 | 51.7 |
| China | 11.0 | 18.6 | 21.6 | 23.3 | 25.4 | 31.1 | 38.6 | 30.2 | 46.9 |
| South Asia | 15.6 | 17.8 | 20.4 | 22.0 | 24.0 | 29.1 | 36.1 | | |
| Africa | 14.5 | 18.2 | 22.8 | 25.7 | 28.8 | 35.7 | 42.5 | 34.4 | 47.2 |
| Middle Africa | 14.6 | 18.1 | 25.2 | 29.7 | 34.4 | 43.6 | 51.6 | 33.2 | 46.6 |
| East Africa | 5.5 | 7.5 | 10.7 | 13.2 | 16.1 | 22.7 | 29.4 | 21.7 | 34.1 |
| West Africa | 10.2 | 13.5 | 17.3 | 19.6 | 22.3 | 28.6 | 35.9 | 36.6 | 52.3 |

| Region | 1950–1960 | 1960–1970 | 1970–1975 | 1975–1980 | 1980–1990 | 1990–1995 | 1975–1995 | 1995–2025 |
|---|---|---|---|---|---|---|---|---|
| Annual average urban population Growth rates (%) | | | | | | | | |
| Less developed regions | 4.68 | 3.94 | 3.95 | 4.06 | 4.02[e] | 3.76[e] | 3.7 | 3.1[e] |
| Latin America | 4.57 | 4.21 | 4.01 | 3.86 | 3.56 | 3.06 | 3.0 | 1.9 |
| East Asia excl. China and Japan | 4.16 | 5.20 | 4.52 | 4.00 | 3.33 | 2.36 | 3.2 | 2.5 |
| China | 6.84 | 3.15 | 3.17 | 3.32 | 3.29 | 3.25 | 4.2 | 3.0 |
| South Asia | 3.37 | 3.91 | 4.01 | 4.33 | 4.47 | 4.27 | | |
| Africa | 4.42 | 4.85 | 4.97 | 5.10 | 5.00 | 4.56 | 4.4 | 4.1 |
| Middle Africa | 4.07 | 5.71 | 5.56 | 5.40 | 5.04 | 4.40 | 4.1 | 4.6 |
| East Africa | 5.37 | 6.06 | 6.95 | 6.87 | 6.39 | 5.59 | 5.8 | 5.0 |
| West Africa | 4.97 | 4.87 | 5.10 | 5.34 | 5.43 | 5.21 | 5.3 | 4.5 |

*Source:* United Nations (1980: Tables 5, 6); final two columns: United Nations (1996: Tables 1–2).

cies. These agencies, however, have to use census data, and these are collected only every decade or so, typically around the beginning of a new decade. Given that processing often takes three years or more, it is fairly natural that large revisions to world statistics occur at mid-decade.

Data on the proportion of populations living in urban areas tend to be less volatile. In part, this is simply because it is a stock rather than a flow measure. But it also reflects the fact that much of the error in predictions of city growth is caused by erroneous estimates of population growth rates, rather than mistaken assessments of the geographical distribution of population. On the other hand, the overall level of urbanization in developing countries is even more sensitive to definition of "developing", since wealthier "developing" countries are far more urban than their poorer counterparts.

Estimates also have been muddied in recent years by the inclusion of data from a considerable number of countries which had not reported (or not reported accurately) earlier. Most of these are from the current or former socialist bloc, and it should be clear that, even now, many of these official statistics are implausible.[2] In these cases, historical "pass" systems and other forms of population control have begun to break down, but censal data continue to reflect official locations of residence.

Ironically, then, we may know less about world urbanization today than we did 15 years ago. But two key patterns are clear: (1) the developing world continues to urbanize, but it is doing so at a slower pace than in the 1950s and 1960s; (2) excluding China and east Asia, urban growth in the early 1990s is slower than in the 1970s; it is also slower than in the 1980s for all regions except for east Asia.[3] Thus, Preston's (1979: p. 196) claim that "The rate of change in the proportion urban in developing countries is not exceptionally rapid by historical standards; rather it is the growth rates of urban population that represent an unprecedented phenomenon" is somewhat less valid today than it was two decades ago. Urban growth rates remain very high, but they have slowed significantly in many regions.

A final note on forecasts. Earlier forecasts of urbanization appear to have been on the high side, especially in Africa, south Asia and China. The Preston Report (United Nations 1980; Preston, 1979) had 42.5% of Africans living in cities by 1995 (revised down to an implied 37.3% in a UN 1991 re-estimate cited in Lucas, 1997); more recent estimates by the United Nations (1996) place the actual figure at 34.4%. Forecasts for south Asia and India suffer from similar problems. For "less developed regions" as a whole, the United Nations (1980) forecasted an increase in urbanization from 1980 to 1995 by 13%, to 43.5%

---

[2] It stretches credulity that the urban population of a country like Vietnam is only growing at 2.7 to 3.1% (with background total population growth of 1.6 to 2.1%), given the obvious mushrooming of major cities and the very low initial urbanization rate. China's official and actual urbanization levels may be similarly distorted, especially if one considers that most of the official urban growth was "achieved mainly through the transformation of villages into new-style cities and towns, rather than through migration of residents from rural to established urban areas" (Young and Deng, 1997: p. 5).

[3] If one accepts the veracity of official Chinese data. Zhu (1996) suggests that recent growth may be far larger than official figures suggest, as official figure miss much or all of the "floating population". Individuals are registered as "agricultural" or "nonagricultural;" perhaps surprisingly, Zhu's (1996: p. 11) empirical results from a microsurvey are that people from agricultural households are more likely to migrate to urban areas. The interpretation offered is that such people face more limited opportunities at home, and therefore must migrate to enhance earnings. The finding by Young and Deng (1997) that political regime changes did not appear to directly affect urban growth in China also merits notice.

urban. The United Nations (1996) revised estimates for 1995 indicated a rise of only 7.1%—a dramatic revision.

There are clear demographic explanations for these large prediction errors. In times of considerable behavioral change across cohorts, such as during the past decade, simple, highly aggregated, a behavioral demographic accounting models are subject to huge forecasting errors. Behavioral economic models and more sophisticated demographic frameworks perform better, and one might expect a combined approach to do better still.

## 1.2. The great fertility deceleration and components of urban growth

One of the primary reasons for overestimating urban growth rates has been the recent decline in world fertility rates. Previous studies indicate that, for developing countries as a whole, somewhat less than half of the increase in urban population is due to migration from rural areas (see United Nations, 1996, 1980; Preston, 1979; Gregory, 1986; Ledent, 1982a); the remainder is due to natural population increase in urban areas. In Preston's survey, 61% of developing countries' urban population growth was due to natural increase, and this share was expected to rise with time. The United Nations (1996) study of urbanization compares 30 countries between the 1960s and 1970s and 19 countries between the 1970s and 1980s; it shows migration's contribution to urban growth declining over time for most countries.

If one is willing to make the assumption that crude birth rates are identical in urban and rural areas, then it is possible to provide a simple decomposition of urban growth.[4] This decomposition appears in Table 2, which provides estimates of the urban net inmigration rate (net change in rural-urban migrants as a fraction of base urban population) both for regional aggregates, as well as for a small number of Asian, Latin American and African countries which are at the forefront of the economic and/or demographic transitions. Compared with 1970-1980, the period 1980–1993 was one of decreasing urban net inmigration in Africa, Latin America and south Asia, but of rising inmigration in east Asia. Among the east Asian "tigers", however, the (unweighted average) inmigration rate declined, albeit not to a very low rate.

Population growth is a different matter. Growth rates have been stable in south Asia and Africa (where they actually rose in the 1980s relative to the 1970s). In contrast, population growth rates have declined by one-third or more in east Asia and Latin America from the 1970s to the early 1990s; it is clear that large

---

[4] These UN data reported above are based on separate estimates of urban and rural fertility, and such data are available in consistent form only for a limited number of countries and years.

Table 2

Sources of urbanization: Population growth versus rural-urban migration (all figures are in percentages).

| | 1970–1980 | | | | 1980–1993 | | | | 1990–1995 | | | |
|---|---|---|---|---|---|---|---|---|---|---|---|---|
| | Total fertility rate (1970) | Urban pop. growth rate | Total pop. growth rate | Rural-urban immigration rate | Total fertility rate (1993) | Urban pop. growth rate | Total pop. growth rate | Rural-urban immigration rate | Total fertility rate (2000) est. | Urban pop. growth rate | Total pop. growth rate | Rural-urban inmigration rate |
| **Low Income countries** | **5.9** | **3.6** | **2.1** | **1.5** | **3.6** | **4.2** | **2.0** | **2.2** | **3.3** | – | **1.8** | – |
| Kazakstan | 3.5 | 2.0 | 1.3 | 0.7 | 2.5 | 1.7 | 1.0 | 0.7 | 2.3 | 1.2 | 0.5 | 0.7 |
| **Sub-Saharan Africa** | **6.6** | **4.8** | **2.7** | **2.0** | **6.2** | **4.8** | **2.9** | **1.8** | **5.6** | **4.4** | **2.9** | **1.5** |
| Botswana | 6.7 | 9.4 | 3.5 | 5.7 | 4.8 | 7.6 | 3.4 | 4.1 | 4.2 | 7.0 | 3.1 | 3.8 |
| Côte d'Ivoire | 7.4 | 6.4 | 4.0 | 2.3 | 7.3 | 5.2 | 3.7 | 1.4 | 6.6 | 5.0 | 3.5 | 1.4 |
| Kenya | 8.1 | 8.1 | 3.6 | 4.3 | 5.2 | 7.0 | 3.3 | 3.6 | 4.0 | 6.8 | 3.6 | 3.1 |
| Zimbabwe | 7.3 | 5.8 | 3.0 | 2.7 | 4.9 | 5.6 | 3.2 | 2.3 | 4.2 | 5.0 | 2.6 | 2.3 |
| *Upper income African average* | | *7.7* | *3.5* | *3.8* | | *6.4* | *3.4* | *2.8* | | *6.0* | *3.2* | *2.6* |
| **Latin America/Caribbean** | **5.2** | **3.6** | **2.4** | **1.2** | **3.1** | **2.7** | **2.0** | **0.7** | **2.7** | **2.5** | **1.6** | **0.9** |
| Brazil | 4.9 | 4.1 | 2.4 | 1.7 | 2.8 | 2.5 | 2.0 | 0.5 | 2.5 | 2.7 | 1.7 | 1.0 |
| Mexico | 6.5 | 4.0 | 2.8 | 1.2 | 3.1 | 3.1 | 2.3 | 0.8 | 2.6 | 2.8 | 2.1 | 0.7 |
| Venezuela | 5.3 | 4.8 | 3.4 | 1.4 | 3.2 | 3.3 | 2.5 | 0.8 | 2.8 | 2.8 | 2.3 | 0.5 |
| *Upper income Latin American avg.* | | *4.3* | *2.7* | *1.4* | | *3.0* | *2.3* | *0.7* | | *2.8* | *2.0* | *0.7* |
| **South Asia** | **5.8** | **3.8** | **2.3** | **1.5** | **4.0** | **3.3** | **2.1** | **1.2** | **3.6** | – | **2.2** | – |
| India | 5.5 | 3.7 | 2.2 | 1.5 | 3.7 | 3.0 | 2.0 | 1.0 | 3.2 | 2.9 | 1.9 | 1.0 |
| **East Asia** | **5.7** | **3.4** | **1.9** | **1.5** | **2.3** | **4.2** | **1.5** | **2.3** | **2.2** | – | **1.2** | – |
| China | 5.8 | 3.0 | 1.8 | 1.2 | 2.0 | 4.3 | 1.4 | 2.9 | 1.9 | 4.0 | 1.1 | 2.9 |
| Indonesia | 5.3 | 4.9 | 2.3 | 2.5 | 2.8 | 4.8 | 1.7 | 3.0 | – | 4.5 | 1.6 | 2.9 |
| Korea | 4.3 | 5.1 | 1.8 | 3.2 | 1.7 | 3.6 | 1.1 | 2.5 | 1.8 | 2.9 | 1.0 | 1.9 |
| Thailand | 5.5 | 5.1 | 2.7 | 2.3 | 2.1 | 2.7 | 1.7 | 1.0 | 2.1 | 2.5 | 1.1 | 1.4 |
| *Upper income east Asian average* | | *5.0* | *2.3* | *2.7* | | *3.7* | *1.5* | *2.2* | | | | |

*Sources*: World Bank (1995), World Resources Institute (1996: Table A.1). Comparable 1995 urbanization rates from the Population Reference Bureau (1997).

declines will continue in the coming years, given that total fertility rates are now at or below replacement in east Asia.

Consequently, declining fertility is currently the major source of decelerating urban population growth in east Asia and Latin America, while declining urban inmigration rates are the larger source of slowing urbanization in Africa and (to the extent that changes are taking place) south Asia. The east Asian pattern shows clearly both in China and in the "tigers": during the current decade, migration is likely to account for two-thirds or more of total urban growth. In Latin America and south Asia, much lower migration rates and much higher population growth rates prevail, so that natural population growth will be the main source of urban population growth in both regions. This is especially true in the most advanced Latin economies, which have urbanization levels comparable to those in the most developed countries.

The emerging African pattern may be that of its relatively prosperous and stable nations, which appear to be entering a fertility transition. Migration and natural population growth appear to be roughly comparable in importance, although the role of migration is decreasing. Moreover, while still quite high (6.0%), annual urban population growth in prosperous Africa has declined considerably from the 1970s.

There is good reason to believe that declining population growth will continue. Declines in population growth rates have been modest thus far. World Bank (1995) reports that for all low income countries, the weighted average annual growth rate was 2.1% in the 1970s, 2.0% from 1980–1983, and is projected to be 1.8% for 1993–2000), but should accelerate for two reasons. First, *demographic momentum* has largely maintained population growth thus far: for low income countries, the weighted crude birth rate declined from 39 births per thousand people in 1970 to 29 births per thousand in 1993 (the decline is only from 45 to 40 if China and India are excluded). But the total fertility rate, defined as the expected number of children a woman will bear, applying current cohort-specific birth rates, fell from 5.9 in 1970 to 3.6 in 1993. A rising share in the total population of women of child-bearing ages during the past 25 years thus maintained the crude birth rate, but in the coming decades, the impact of declining fertility will not be so offset by the momentum created by past high fertility.

Second, the *mortality component* of the "demographic transition" has been largely completed. The decline in the crude birth rate by 11 births per thousand was largely offset by a fall in the crude death rate from 14 to 10 per thousand (and from 19 to 13 for low income countries other than China and India, more than offsetting the birth rate decline). These declines reflect health care improvements which raise life expectancies and limit deaths, especially from contagious diseases. However, as populations age, increasing mortality from chronic disease begins to compensate (especially as many of the "easy gains" already have been realized), so that further crude death rate declines are likely to be more moderate.

In short, the developing world overall is moving into a more mature stage of the demographic transition, with sharply declining population growth rates. Thus, while the contribution of migration to urban growth eventually must decline, the combined effects of the demographic transition and rapid economic growth in much of the transforming world's cities virtually ensure that migration's role will be large in the coming decades.

## 1.3. Survey themes

There is little doubt that the nature of urbanization is in the midst of major change. Education and infrastructure projects of the preceding three decades have led to much greater integration of economies today than ever before. Thus, the stylized facts are changing—but differently in different places, to such a degree that it is a terrible mischaracterization to write of a single "third" or "developing" world. Hereafter, we therefore refer to economies other than in advanced capitalist nations as *transforming*—for nearly all are undergoing major change. We further distinguish them in two ways: whether they have *integrated* or *segmented* labor and other factor markets, and, affirming the distinction made more than two decades ago by Chenery and Syrquin (1975), whether countries are *large, small and open*, or *small and inward-looking*. The essay obviously will not make constant reference to which of the six categories a model or empirical finding is appropriate, but will make these distinctions as necessary. Clearly, other delineations are possible as well; among these, high and low economic growth regimes might be the most critical. Prolonged rapid growth seems strongly associated with growing economic integration, however, and for purposes of analyzing human mobility we prefer to emphasize the latter feature.

A second theme which appears throughout the chapter concerns the need to develop a new set of "stylized facts", for the traditional ones are surely dated. The explosion of microhousehold and firm datasets gives us information of almost unimaginable detail. In the coming pages, we argue that much of the new information is inconsistent with the "informed impressions" which guide model builders and policymakers alike. At the same time, the gap between microstudies and aggregate models appears to be growing, and we see efforts at reconciliation to be of critical importance. A related theme is that economic models of urbanization need to connect with models of demographic change, especially given the dramatic transitions underway in many societies.

Finally, we believe that economic models of urban growth are correct to remain focused on the role of migration. As noted, there are good reasons to believe that it will continue to be the dominant source of growth in China and east Asia, and will play an important role everywhere except for Latin America.[5] Second, economic analysis focuses on marginal decisions, and it seems plausible spatial living decisions react more immediately to economic incentives than do fertility decisions in transforming economies.

## 2. Models of city growth and empirical estimates

### 2.1. *Urban labor markets: empirical microfoundations*

This section discusses three topics related to the functioning of urban labor markets: inequality in urban labor markets, the relationship between educational attainment and labor force outcomes, and the performance of urban labor markets during economic adjustment programs. These aspects of urban labor markets have important implications for urbanization in terms of incentives for potential migrants and the efficiency of production processes in urban areas.

### 2.1.1. *Inequality in urban labor markets: segmentation and discrimination*
Perhaps the first observation to be made about urban labor markets in transforming economies is that they are generally characterized by a very unequal distribution of income by the standards of developed countries. This is true both within the urban sector and in comparing urban and rural incomes (for figures see Lecaillon et al. (1984) and Kahnert (1987)). We will critically examine the ability of two paradigms—segmented labor markets and labor market discrimination— to explain the observed income inequality in urban labor markets.[6]

The most common explanation of income inequality in urban areas is that labor markets are segmented into formal and informal sectors. The informal sector is populated with small firms, employing labor-intensive factor mixes, that are not covered by government labor legislation (e.g., social security taxes and minimum wage legislation). This sector is an important source of employment;

---

[5] And even in Latin America, migration will continue to be important in the region's poorer, more rural countries.

[6] Much of the observed income inequality clearly is due to unequal human capital endowments. We focus on this relationship in Section 2.1.2.

estimates for Latin America range from a low of 19% of the economically active in urban areas in Uruguay to a high of 39% in Peru (Infante and Klein, 1991: p. 126). Informal labor markets are also important sources of employment in Africa and in some Asian countries.[7]

Labor markets are segmented because workers in one sector (the protected or formal sector) earn higher wages than identical workers in the other sector (the unprotected or informal sector). Neoclassical economic theory suggests that such a wage gap should be competed away by informal workers moving to the formal sector, but the theory of segmented labor markets argues that mobility is extremely limited between the sectors. Note that the mere existence of wage gaps between formal and informal sectors is not sufficient evidence to prove segmentation; mobility must be limited as well.

One of the most common—and commonly misused—techniques for identifying segmented labor markets is to estimate wage equations for a sample of workers in each labor market segment. A typical set of wage equations would be:

$$\ln W_f = \alpha_f + \beta_f X + \eta_f; \qquad \ln W_I = \alpha_I + \beta_I X + \eta_I, \tag{2.1}$$

where $W$ is the wage rate, the subscripts $f$ and $I$ represent formal and informal sectors, respectively, $X$ is a vector of human capital characteristics, $\alpha$ is a constant, $\beta$ is a vector of coefficients that captures the return to human capital, and $\epsilon$ is a random error term. The conventional interpretation is that if $\beta_f > \beta_i$ for some or all of the estimated coefficients then labor market segmentation is present, since returns to human capital in the formal sector exceed those in the informal sector.

This is an incorrect interpretation for two reasons. The first problem with this approach is that there may be a selection process not captured in the regressions. Gindling (1991) corrects selection in his investigation of segmentation in San Jose, Costa Rica, by estimating multinomial logit selection equations that allocate workers to the private formal, public formal and informal sectors.[8] He finds that many of the coefficients in the selection equations, including education, sex, age, head of household and marital status, are statistically significant predictors

---

[7] Sethuraman (1981) provides an early but very comprehensive estimate of the share of the urban labor force working in the informal sector for a long list of cities. His estimates for the late 1970s are worth listing here: Abidjan (31%), Lagos (50%), Kumasi (60–70%), Nairobi (44%), Calcutta (40–50%), Ahmedabad (47%), Jakarta (45%), Colombo (19%), Singapore (23%), Sao Paulo (43%), Rio de Janeiro (24%), Bogota (43%), Guayaquil (48%), Mexico City (27%) and Caracas (40%).

[8] Gindling is not the only researcher to note that the conventional approach is subject to selectivity bias. Gronau (1973) and Magnac (1991) also offer intelligent discussions of this issue.

of sector of work.[9] A second problem with the regression framework sketched is omitted variable bias, which may vary in severity by sector. In particular, very few wage equations, especially for transforming economies, contain a measure of workers' innate ability.[10] If the bias introduced from omitting a measure of ability were of the same magnitude in both equations, the omission would not affect a comparison of estimated coefficients between the equations. But there is no assurance that ability is equally important in formal and informal sectors without actually including it as a regressor and measuring its impact on wages.

More fundamentally, much of the literature on segmented labor markets can be criticized for being overly descriptive: the "explanation" for intersectoral wage gaps actually explains very little. Wage gaps arise because of segmentation, but unless the determinants of segmentation are explored, the causal determinants of wage gaps remain unidentified (Morrison, 1994: p. 355). Two broad classes of explanations for intersectoral wage gaps have been offered. The first focuses on the role played by institutions in creating the wage gaps, while the second argues that wage gaps are created by the profit maximizing decisions of firms.

Not surprisingly, the institutions cited as being important causes of intersectoral wage gaps vary significantly over countries. For three central American and Caribbean nations, Fields and Wan (1989) identify the following institutions as being most responsible for intersectoral wage gaps in the late 1980s: above-market public sector wages (Costa Rica), a restrictive labor code (Panama), and trade unions (Jamaica). Morrison (1994) identifies minimum wage legislation, social security coverage, and level of public employment as being important determinants of interindustry wage gaps in Ecuador. Svejnar (1989) focuses on the role played by public enterprises and labor legislation, particularly tripartite bargaining frameworks.

Intersectoral wage gaps need not be caused by institutions or government intervention, though; wage gaps may occur as a result of unilateral decisions by firms due to efficiency wage considerations. To the authors' knowledge, only one paper has examined the empirical relevance of efficiency wage theory for urban labor markets in transforming economies.[11] Abuhadba and Romaguera (1993), using data from Brazil, Chile, Uruguay and Venezuela, find that interindustry

---

[9] Interestingly, the selection correction term is not statistically significant in his wage equations. In other words, even though the assignment of a worker to a sector is not random, the probability of a worker being assigned to a given sector is not correlated with the error term of that sector's wage equation (Gindling, 1991: p. 596).

[10] They do contain a measure of school attainment, but this is not a good measure of ability. For more on the distinction between ability, years of schooling and human capital, see Section 2.1.2 below.

[11] Riveros and Bouton (1994) examine the theoretical applicability of efficiency wage theories to transforming economies, while bemoaning the lack of empirical evidence. They, however, offer no evidence of their own.

wage differentials are strongly correlated across different occupations within industries. This casts doubt on the labor turnover and shirking models, since turnover or shirking costs should be more similar within occupations than within industries. Their evidence, however, is consistent with the gift-exchange model, in which workers are paid higher wages in exchange for greater work effort.

Labor market segmentation is not the only factor generating inequality in urban labor markets. Labor market discrimination may also play an important role. Discrimination occurs when a worker's job prospects or pay after obtaining a job are affected by some personal characteristic unrelated to productivity, such as gender, race or religion. There are two strands in the economic theory of discrimination: (1) discrimination due to employers', coworkers', or society's "tastes", and (2) statistical discrimination.[12] While these two categories of discrimination are often treated as distinct, this may not be the case: "If employers base hiring decisions on average endowments (statistical discrimination), is it because information-gathering about particular candidates is costly, or because employers simply wish to use averages to rationalize their prejudices?" (Birdsall and Sabot, 1991: p. 3).

The methodology used to test for the presence of labor market discrimination is well developed, but only recently has it begun to be applied to urban labor markets in transforming economies.[13] Ashenfelter and Oaxaca (1991: pp. 46–48) report the findings of a set of studies that examine labor market discrimination in transforming economies. Gross earnings differentials (expressed as log wages) between males and females are 29% in Tanzania, 120% in the formal sector in Brazil, 341% in the informal sector in Brazil, and 85% in Nicaragua.[14] Of these gross differentials, 17, 113, 99 and 71%, respectively, are attributable to labor market discrimination; the remainder are due to differential human capital endowments. Gross wage differentials are also reported between Africans (blacks) and non-Africans (Asians) in Tanzania (112%) and between scheduled and non-scheduled castes (untouchables) in Delhi (17%). Of these gross wage differentials, 78 and 54%, respectively, are attributable to labor market discrimination.

There are, however, several articles which examine the applicability of efficiency wage theory to *rural* Indian labor markets (see Rodgers, 1975; Bliss and Stern, 1978, Part II).

[12] As Birdsall and Sabot (1991) note, "tradition" may confine women to working in family businesses or household production, or segregate castes by occupation or industry. Tradition may be viewed as a societal taste for discrimination. Statistical discrimination occurs when employers generalize a certain group's "average" behavior to all members of the group, e.g., a higher likelihood of leaving the labor force is ascribed to an individual woman, since women in general have higher rates of voluntary separation from the labor force.

[13] The standard methodological references are Blinder (1973), Oaxaca (1973) and Brown et al. (1980).

[14] The samples are from urban labor markets, with the exception of Nicaragua. In the case of Nicaragua, the sample is taken from the national labor market.

Clearly, discrimination is responsible for generating much inequality in labor markets, but no facile generalizations can be made. Labor market discrimination against women in Tanzania is quite low, while it is quite significant in Brazil and Nicaragua. Race and caste discrimination seem severe in both Tanzania and India. But both gross wage differentials and discrimination matter: while labor market discrimination in Delhi (at 54% against untouchables) is severe, this percentage is applied to gross wage differential of "only" 17%. For that matter, it is difficult to generalize even within a country. Discrimination against blacks in Tanzania is severe, but discrimination against women is relatively mild—women earn about 5% less than similarly qualified men because of labor market discrimination. One important conclusion should be emphasized, though. Labor market segmentation and human capital explanations have received much more attention than discrimination as forces generating inequality in the labor markets of transforming economies. The evidence presented here suggests that discrimination is a serious handicap for women and minority groups in certain countries.

Before proceeding, we should note that sectoral concepts glibly used both in theoretical and empirical papers often translate poorly into on-the-ground reality. This is especially important in analyzing segmentation, since a precursor to finding segmented markets is to define the appropriate segments. Grootaert's (1992) preferred distinguishing characteristic is the degree of legal protection afforded workers. Even sorting according to this characteristic does not prevent the informal sector from having many components, including self-employed skilled workers, young workers acquiring skills of value in either the formal or informal sectors, unskilled self-employed, and unskilled employees. Given this informal sector heterogeneity, null findings of segmentation are perhaps unsurprising.

Mead and Morrison (1996) find that correlation of firm size with physical assets, human capital of firm owners, firm registration, conformance to labor regulations, conformance to standards and other regulations, and payment of taxes vary markedly across seven countries (Algeria, Ecuador, Jamaica, Niger, Swaziland, Thailand and Tunisia).

Telles (1993) examines labor market segmentation in urban Brazil, defining categories according to whether workers are paying into and hence covered by the social security system. Three categories of informal sector workers are defined (and distinguished in the analysis): the "protected" self-employed, all paid domestic workers, and all "unprotected" workers; everyone else is defined as a formal sector worker. Yamada (1996) in his study of urban Peru defines the informal sector to include all self-employed plus workers employed on flexible contracts where the employer can alter the wage rate at will. He performs a Heckman–Lee correction for self-selection, noting that those with high entrepreneurial ability will choose informal sector work, and compares predicted earnings in informal sector versus public and private formal sector jobs. Informal sector work actually provided an income premium relative to the private formal sector both in 1985 and 1990; the public sector appeared to offer a protected premium in 1985, but by 1990 after a period of pronounced depression, its workers were at a strong disadvantage. Yamada's work, with its emphasis on sectoral selection as well as thoughtful sectoral definitions, provides powerful evidence against crude segmentation. On the other hand, it is difficult to claim that no labor market imperfections exist in transforming economies, or that all of the returns to distinguishing features reflect differing capacities: rather, the nature of imperfections is complex, and it is not evident that their crude depiction in modeling is a second best solution.

Funkhouser (1997) examines labor market segmentation in Guatemala, and also corrects for self-selection—which greatly increases the formal/informal sector difference in returns to education (12 versus 6%, respectively). Much of the earnings gaps in Guatemala can be tied to gender and indigenous/nonindigenous differences; broadly speaking, these are more important than differences among (and are generally maintained within) the formal private, formal government, and informal sectors.

## 2.1.2. Education and labor market outcomes

Education has two important impacts on the functioning of urban labor markets. First, educational expansion has the potential to increase workers' productivity. Second, the structure of the educational system and the rate at which it expands have important consequences for income distribution. In this section, both links are explored.

One way to gauge the impact of education on workers' productivity is by estimating wage equations. Hundreds of studies have employed Mincerian wage equations to derive the return to investments in education. Psacharopoulos (1993: p. 7) aggregates these country-level results into the following regional averages for the social return to education:[15]

|  | Primary | Secondary | Higher |
|---|---|---|---|
| Sub-Saharan Africa | 24.3 | 18.2 | 11.2 |
| Asia | 19.9 | 13.3 | 11.7 |
| Europe/Middle East/North Africa | 15.5 | 11.2 | 10.6 |
| Latin America/Caribbean | 17.9 | 12.8 | 12.3 |
| OECD | 14.4 | 10.2 | 8.7 |
| World | 18.4 | 13.1 | 10.9 |

[15] Return figures are for the "latest year"; for most countries this is during the 1980s.

One might think that estimating the productivity-enhancing effects of education would be as simple as reading the coefficients from Mincerian wage equations. After all, wages are equal to the marginal revenue product of labor in a neoclassical world. Unfortunately, two complications stand in the way.

The first is the screening hypothesis, which argues that additional years of education do not improve individuals' productivity; they just signal to firms that these workers have more innate ability. If the screening hypothesis is correct, the social benefit of education identified by the wage equation approach will suffer from an upward bias. The solution to this problem is to include measures of innate ability, human capital (skills), and years of education in the wage equation.[16]

The second problem with the estimates produced by a wage equation is that they do not correct for cohort effects (Knight and Sabot, 1990: p. 41). In other words, the assumption is that the returns to education identified by the wage equation are available to current school leavers. If, for example, the returns to primary education have fallen over time (as is almost certainly the case in sub-Saharan Africa), then current primary school leavers cannot expect to reap the returns identified by a wage equation which includes individuals from older cohorts. The solution to this second problem is to interact dummies for cohorts with the other explanatory variables. Cohen and House (1994) find strong cohort effects in Khartoum, where formal sector employment growth has expanded very slowly. It seems plausible that such cohort effects would be weaker in rapidly growing economies where demand keeps apace with supply.

Knight and Sabot (1990) offer an insightful analysis of the impact of educational policy on urban labor market outcomes in Kenya and Tanzania.[17] The datasets used are exceptionally rich; collected from surveys of wage earners in Nairobi and Dar es Salaam, they include measures of individuals' cognitive skill (as a measure of the amount of human capital imparted by schooling), reasoning ability (as a measure of innate ability), and years of schooling (to test the screening hypothesis). Thus, Knight and Sabot are able to test directly the applicability of the screening hypothesis. They find some support for the screening hypothesis, but what students actually learn in the classroom is a more important determinant of future income than the number of years of schooling completed.

---

[16] Such stringent data requirements are unlikely to be met in many transforming economies, though.

[17] They term the comparison a "natural experiment" because the countries are structurally very similar, but pursued strikingly different educational policies upon obtaining independence. Kenya embarked upon a rapid expansion of secondary education, including allowing private secondary schools to open. Tanzania, on the other hand, stringently limited access to secondary schooling, using a manpower planning approach to avoid excess supply of secondary school leavers.

Another contribution of Knight and Sabot's work is a correction of the wage equation estimates for cohort effects. The conventional measurement of the return to primary education is 17%, but the return available to current school leavers is only 12%. This significant difference is largely due to the "filtering down" of secondary school graduates, i.e., the most attractive jobs formerly filled by primary school graduates are now filled by secondary school graduates (Knight and Sabot, 1990: p. 42). The rate of return to secondary school, on the other hand, is not affected by correcting for cohort effects; it remains 13%.

A more general problem with Mincerian wage equations concerns their interpretation, though these problems are mitigated with thoughtful econometric techniques (such as correction for sectoral selection bias) and good datasets. Nevertheless, it takes something of a leap of faith to ascribe the full effect of human capital variables to human capital effects, especially when selectivity, screening, credentialism and cohort effects are not accounted for. An example of the sort of careful work which does inspire confidence is provided by Lam and Schoeni's (1993) work on Brazil. Returns to schooling decline by one-fourth to one-third when family background measures are included, a finding consistent with Behrman and Wolfe's (1984c) study of 500 sister pairs from Nicaragua. Lam and Schoeni's most memorable finding, though, is that the schooling of a man's father-in-law has a larger effect than own father's schooling, which they take as an indication of assortive mating.

The other important effect of educational expansion on urban labor markets is its impact on the distribution of income. Two potentially opposing effects must be considered. The first is the compression effect. Education expansion compresses the premium on education by: (1) reducing wages in occupations that employ educated individuals, and (2) causing more educated workers to filter down into jobs formerly occupied by less-educated individuals, reducing more educated individuals' average wages in relation to the less-educated (Knight and Sabot, 1990: p. 28). The composition effect, by changing the educational composition of the labor force, may either increase or decrease wage inequality.[18] Educational expansion is likely to increase wage inequality only if the composition effect increases inequality *and* if this effect dominates the compression effect. In practice, this is likely to happen only in the very early stages of economic development. Educational expansion not only increases the productivity of labor, but also is likely to make labor market outcomes more equitable.

---

[18] If the initial number of educated workers is small, an increase in their number is likely to increase wage inequality. After some critical point is passed, however, further increases in the number of educated workers will decrease wage inequality.

## 2.1.3. *Economic crisis, adjustment and urban labor markets*

Economic adjustment programs, including both stabilization and structural adjustment programs, have had important impacts on urban labor markets.[19] The role of assigned to labor markets in an adjustment program is clear: if wages fall sufficiently in response to a decrease in demand, then a reduction in expenditure can be accomplished without a substantial reduction in national output. Of course, the line between "fall sufficiently" and "fall disastrously" may be all too fine; if wages fall too far, aggregate demand will collapse and national output will fall as well (Horton et al., 1994: p. 4).

Have urban wages been flexible in the face of economic adjustment? Overwhelming evidence suggests that they have. In Latin America in 1989, real wages in large enterprises were 93% of their 1980 levels. Wage declines in small enterprises, the public sector, and the informal sector were much greater; 1989 real wages were only 70, 70 and 58% of their 1980 levels, respectively (Infante and Klein, 1991: p. 132). Even these significant declines pale compared to the collapse of real wages in African formal sectors. The percentage declines from the real wage peak (usually in the early- to mid-1970s) to trough (in the early 1980s) ranged from a high of 95% in Uganda to a "low" of 32% in Kenya. The unweighted average for the seven sub-Saharan countries was 61% (Weeks, 1995).

There is not much agreement whether the substantial wage declines cushioned the effects of adjustment on employment, or whether wage declines caused further, multiplied falls in output (Horton et al., 1994: p. 20). There is somewhat more agreement that wage declines (and possible employment losses) in formal sectors caused increasing informalization of LDC urban labor markets. In Latin America, for example, the informal sector's share of the urban labor force rose from 25 to 31% in the 1980s (Infante and Klein, 1991: p. 123).[20] Evidence on wage trends in informal sector employment is hard to come by, but the combination of exchange rate devaluation (accompanying adjustment) and entry of workers into the sector strongly suggest that informal wages fell as a result of economic crisis.

---

[19] Structural adjustment programs are designed to restore external balance and, in the long run, achieve positive economic growth. Structural adjustment programs, at least in theory, differ from stabilization programs, which were designed to reestablish external balance in the short run via demand compression (Conway, 1994: p. 267).

[20] The urban unemployment rate in Latin America rose from 6.9% (1980) to 10.9% (1985) (Portes, 1989: p. 27). Is this evidence that real wage declines were not large enough? It is difficult to determine. Certainly labor should not bear the entire cost of adjustment; in addition, as mentioned above, a too severe decline in wages will constrict aggregate demand and reduce output.

## 2.2. Aggregate partial equilibrium migration models

The literature on the aggregate determinants of urbanization may be divided into work (a) which looks at the determinants of the proportion of population living in urban areas, and (b) which models aggregate migration flows. The former is close to the Chenery and Syrquin (1975) patterns of development literature, and is largely motivated by the same forces which drive computable general equilibrium models. That urbanization invariably accompanies economic development is virtually indisputable. Both a brief survey of findings in this regard and one of the latest sets of findings is provided in Moomaw and Shatter (1996), who use a pooled dataset for 90 countries for 1960, 1970 and 1980. Urbanization rises strongly with per capita income, industrialization, trade orientation, and foreign capital inflows. No time trends emerge at the world level.

*Patterns based on neoclassical and gravity frameworks.* Economists have long recognized the strong link between urbanization and economic growth. The starting point may be taken as the two-sector labor market model, in which inter-sectoral labor mobility operates to equate real wages in rural and urban activities. Forces which increase the value of urban marginal products ("pull" factors, including capital formation, technological progress, and demand growth) or decrease rural labor's value of marginal product ("push" forces) create disequilibria, to which labor migration is an equilibrating response. The actual speed of migration will depend on the strength of the disequilibrating forces and on costs of mobility.

Consequently, the standard aggregate migration models are broadly consistent with neoclassical economic theory (and with "gravity" models which appeal to an alleged analogy with the physical world). The rate of rural-urban migration can be written as a function of push, pull, and cost variables. The most common formulation is to use migration probability (defined as number of migrants from one region to another, divided by the population of the source region) as the dependent variables. A good example of this type of study is Greenwood (1971), who contrasts urban-urban and rural-urban interstate migration in India. He finds that distance is a greater deterrent for rural-urban than urban-urban migrants. Rural migration rates increase with destination per capita income, but also rise with origin per capita income, a finding replicated in many, although not all, other studies. Standard arguments for this finding include the claims that one needs a certain level of family income in order to finance migration and job search, and that the better off also have better contacts in cities, and tend to have more education.[21] In a rather striking finding based on aggregate data, Velenchik (1993) finds that male interregional migration in Côte d'Ivoire declines with origin per capita cash income, but rises with origin per capita food production. Velenchik's interpretation is that migration is motivated by a demand for marketed goods: raising agricultural productivity without simultaneously improving rural transportation and marketing infrastructure may simply release constraints on migration of young adults.

Aggregate migration studies also indicate that people are more inclined as well to migrate toward densely populated regions (presumably because they have more contacts, though the precise rationale is rather "obscure", to repeat Mazumdar's characterization).

In short, aggregate studies tend to be consistent with neoclassical migration models, and the basic findings reported in Mazumdar (1987) a decade ago remain intact. Three serious problems exist with this aggregate empirical work, although: (i) a formal model is rarely specified, so that problems of potential omitted variables are ignored; (ii) attention is rarely devoted to stock/flow concerns, so that one often finds flow measures (such as migration) being regressed on levels, without attention to the implied lag structure; and (iii), the functions actually estimated are consistent with a wide variety of competing models. It is also difficult to interpret magnitudes of coefficients, as opposed to signs, since the terms used in aggregate empirical work are all highly imperfect instruments for actual explanatory variables.

*Harris–Todaro models.* Two seminal works by Todaro (1969) and Harris and Todaro (1970) (hereafter referred to as HT) modified neoclassical labor market models by hypothesizing the existence of a fixed, above equilibrium urban wage. Migration is an increasing function of the expected income gain from migration, itself a function of relative wage rates and the probability of obtaining a formal sector (FS) job, $p$:

$$M_{R \to U} = \phi(pW_U - W_R). \tag{2.2}$$

This probability was alternately specified by Todaro in flow terms as the rate of job creation divided by the number of urban unemployed, and by HT as a function of the stock of urban employed relative to the entire urban labor force. The

---

[21] Other studies of this type include Barnum and Sabot (1977), who find that Tanzanian migration rates rise with urban wages and decline with rural earnings, as does Byerlee et al.'s (1976) study of Sierra Leone and Beals, Levy and Moses' (1967) work on Ghana. However, House and Rempel (1980) and Rempel (1981) find that Kenyan migration rates rise with origin earnings as well as destination—though Barber and Milne (1986) find standard push and pull effects for Kenya instead. The origin unemployment rate is a standard push factor, though destination unemployment effects are not always negative.

specification of $p$ affects some policy implications, but, in either case, predicts the presence of a group of unemployed urban workers, as there will be excess demand for high wage jobs, as long as turnover and job growth offer some hope to the currently unemployed.

The HT equilibrium is one in which individuals behave rationally, but migration carries additional social costs as long as the rural marginal product of labor is not zero. Creation of a new urban job will be likely to induce more than one migrant, thereby adding to unemployment as well, and, under some circumstances, the urban unemployment rate. On the other hand, "an increase in agricultural income will induce reverse migration with no diminution of industrial output" (Harris and Todaro, 1970: p. 132). Migration restriction will therefore raise total GDP in the HT model, though, of course, it will harm rural dwellers.

The HT paradigm, especially as it accumulated increasingly realistic modifications, caused economists to turn from traditional neoclassical (or classical, in the Lewis (1954) surplus labor model sense[22]) explanations of urbanization as depending on relative rates of capital accumulation, productivity growth, and price movements spurred by changing demands. Wage and job creation policies clearly mattered as well, as did differential provision of social infrastructure. HT appeared to explain the unemployed and underemployed so visible in cities in the transforming world, and at the same time challenged the notion that high wages in the cities would inevitably control urbanization by limiting job growth.

HT models also appeared to generate empirical support at the aggregate level.[23] Cole and Sanders' (1985) simultaneous equations model across Mexican states of net inmigration, modern sector wages, migrant employment probability, and agricultural poverty lends strong support to the HT paradigm. Migration rises strongly with modern sector wage and the probability of finding a job (as well as the urbanization level); it falls with destination rural poverty and the cost of providing a workplace in the informal sector. Banerjee and Kanbur's (1981) study of male migration across Indian states finds expected attraction and push effects,

---

[22] The surplus labor versus neoclassical rural sector distinction is not terribly important. Bhatia (1979) extends HT to a rural surplus labor economy. His findings (1979: p. 409) are:

Result 1 An increase in expected urban wage will lead to outmigration from agriculture whether work hours on the farm are fixed or flexible ...

Result 2 ... for a given increase in rural wage, flexible hours in farming will cause larger outmigration than in the HT model ...

Result 4 ... for a given, small increase in expected urban wage, the presence of surplus labour will lead to a larger outmigration than in Result 2.

[23] This paper does not deal with the econometric problems encountered in estimating aggregate migration functions, but there are many. Among the more obvious, but rarely recognized, is that interregional net migration coefficients must sum to zero, as pointed out by Greenwood and Hunt (1984). Data problems abound as well.

but also finds that origin poverty incidence is a deterrent to migration. The HT variable—a measure of the expected income differential—also has the expected sign, though it is only significant at the 10% level.

*The neoclassical reaction: empirics, education, and wage exogeneity.* HT and their successors represented the dominant paradigm from 1970 through the mid-1980s, and they remain highly influential today. While the HT model provided an elegant explanation of urban labor markets in crisis, the evidence amassed by the late 1980s clearly made the model inapplicable to most transforming societies. As Kannappan (1984: p. 55), a leading HT critic, writes, "Prevailing dualisms represent aggregation of urban employment which founder on the reality of its richness and diversity".

Indeed, problems with the dualistic, segmented HT framework abound. Earnings distributions in formal (FS) and informal (IFS) activities overlap considerably, and many studies fail to find a large FS premium for comparable workers. Furthermore, while such a premium almost certainly has existed at various times and places (see Section 4.1 below), there is very strong evidence that this gap has declined, especially in troubled economies in Africa and elsewhere.[24] Nor is there evidence that unemployment rises with wage gaps in transforming economies, as HT predicts: the converse may well be the case.

Further evidence does not suggest prolonged unemployment in many developing country cities or particularly high rates (Kannappan, 1988; Kahnert, 1987) outside collapsing economies. Kannappan also cites evidence of substantial movement from formal to informal sector employment in Thailand. Banerjee's (1983, 1986) detailed household study of Indian migrants confirms these impressions: skills gaps and information gaps matter, but migrants for the most part do not head for cities in hopes of obtaining a prize FS job; rather, they end up in jobs—and fairly quickly, at that—similar to those enjoyed by their urban family and contacts. Indeed, some 54% of rural-urban migrants in Banerjee's study virtually had urban jobs lined up for them upon arrival, debunking the "probabilistic" notion of job search.

An obvious weakness with HT is its assumption of urban formal sector wage exogeneity. We address this further below, but the point worth noting here is that it is not difficult to generate endogenous wages for a variety of noninstitutional reasons. Indeed, one of the most valuable outcomes of HT was the spark it set off

---

[24] In an important paper, Jamal and Weeks (1988) document the "vanishing" formal sector premium over rural (and IFS) activities; further evidence of gap narrowing is summarized in Becker et al. (1994).

among labor economists, who were challenged to generate a wage gap within a neoclassical framework.

Among the responses to HT were those which emphasized educational level as a screening device. Barnum and Sabot (1977) examine Tanzanian migration from 1955–1970 and find rural-urban male migration rates for those with some secondary schooling (Standard 5–8; the differential is even greater for those with high school education) to be about six times greater than those with only primary schooling, and 20 times as great as for those without any schooling. By the late 1960s, the likelihood of finding a job within four months had fallen considerably for all groups, but those with secondary education still had dramatic advantages in terms of finding a job and also received much higher wages. Using aggregated data, the HT expected wage term is highly significant, but so is education.

For Kenya (the country which originally inspired the HT model), Collier and Bigsten (1981), using microdata from the late 1970s, find evidence of wage flexibility, substantial increases in screening in response to rising educational standards, and falling unemployment rates among those least likely to obtain formal sector jobs. In a study of Venezuelan interstate migration, Levy and Wadycki (1974: p. 387) find that those with secondary education are far "more responsive than the uneducated to variables which represent the costs and benefits of migration".

Sabot (1979) and his associates synthesize these results into a "queuing" model of migration. As growth of formal sector jobs with wages above what can be earned in informal activities is outstripped by growth in the supply of secondary school leavers, educated workers "filter down" and take increasingly less skill-using jobs. Potential migrants with less education are crowded out, and migrate only to take advantage of competitive, unskilled formal or informal sector jobs. Collier (1979) generalizes this framework to a model for Tanzania in which the perceived probability of finding a job depends on anticipated duration, and in which rural labor supply conditions matter. In effect, his model accommodates both the education-based arguments and HT, but he concludes that shifting supply forces and changing employment probability perceptions are the main forces driving inmigration.

This paradigm suggests that stable equilibria will occur at low rates of open unemployment. Migration will exceed new job opportunities mainly when information is unclear—that is, when rapid economic changes are taking place. Lengthy job searches will not persist, though, nor will random turnover give new hope to those without the requisite qualifications.

*Urbanization models based on individual city formation.* Urban economists have devoted far less attention to migration and urbanization in transforming economies than development economists, but they have hardly ignored the topic. Some have approached the problem by constructing Mills–Muth monocentric models, and, through a leap of aggregation faith, making inferences about the pace of overall urbanization and urban inmigration. Brueckner (1990) follows this path most explicitly. Since monocentric city models require (a) identical utility across regions and within the city, and (b) urban land rents equal to rural land rents $r_a$ at the city boundary less the kilometers from the center, equilibrium is defined by:

$$y_a = y - tx(P, y, t, r_a),$$

where $t$ is the commuting cost per km, $P$ is city population, and $y$ and $y_a$ are urban and rural incomes, respectively. This equation can be inverted and solved for equilibrium city population $P^*$. A standard stock adjustment framework thus gives:

$$P^* = f[P^*(Y, y_a, t, r_a) - P_0] \qquad \frac{\partial P^*}{\partial y}, \frac{\partial P^*}{\partial r_a} > 0 > \frac{\partial P^*}{\partial Y_a}, \frac{\partial P^*}{\partial t}, \qquad (2.3)$$

where $P_0$ is initial population. In contrast to other aggregate models, Brueckner emphasizes rural land rents and urban commuting costs. In his formulation, nominal incomes are exogenous in both sectors, though it should be noted that equilibrium requires $y > y_a$, since urban residents bear additional commuting costs. To estimate the model, a Cobb–Douglas agricultural production function implies that $r_a$ is proportionate to output per hectare, while an international public transit dataset exists for $t$. Unfortunately, neither of these variables are significant in the cross-country regressions: urban/rural per capita income and lagged population dominate the regressions. But measurement of the rent and commuting cost variables is difficult, and they may well be important.

*Microevidence.* A host of studies based on microdata confirm that the cost-benefit calculus posited both by HT and neoclassical paradigms is of central importance to the migration decision. A point of departure is Mazumdar's (1987) warning a decade earlier that returns to migration must be related to an individual's potential earnings at his/her origin, and not to incomes of nonmovers. One of the most careful studies is Falaris (1987), who considers migration behavior for nearly 11,000 Venezuelan men. He estimates a predicted wage based on the individual's characteristics, rather than just using mean wages in origin and destination areas.

He also goes a step further, correcting for selectivity in the wage equations. The selection correction matters: migrants earn on average higher wages than would observationally identical people drawn at random from the population (Falaris, 1987: p. 440). That said, wage and distance enter with expected signs, and highly significantly.[25]

Of course, not all studies based on microdata are supportive of HT. Using data from the *Malaysian Family Life Survey*, Blau (1986) finds that the likelihood of moving from employee to self-employed status is considerably greater than the reverse for men older than 27; moreover, for migrants to urban areas the likelihood of being self-employed *rises* with time since migration.

Fuller Lightfoot and Kamnuansilpa ("FLK", 1985) suggest that migration at the individual level is a complex phenomenon hardly driven simply by relative earnings considerations. In their study of migration from northern Thailand, migration was largely circular, and most village residents declared a strong preference for rural life. Past migration experience appears to generate a taste for (or tolerance of) migration, and that, plus having urban contacts, tends to be both directly important and influential in forming positive evaluations (where the cost-benefit calculus occurs) and making plans to move. Their work indicates (a) that specific villages or regions are likely to develop propensities to migrate, and (b) that migration may have a self-feeding process (as yet ignored in aggregate models).

Microsurveys typically have detailed information on community characteristics at the origin or destination, but rarely both, unless they involve census data and consider crude regional characteristics. One exception is Aratme (1992), who analyzes internal migration in the Philippines using the *Philippine Migration Survey*. Aratme finds that education, wealth, and the presence of relatives in Manila are all valuable in securing formal sector employment for male migrants; for females, formal sector is positively associated with mother's formal sector employment, but negatively associated with father's formal sector employment. Most interestingly, and casting doubt on a key HT assumption, prearrangement in Manila turns out to be more important for securing informal than formal sector jobs.

Bigsten (1996) also provides careful corrections to problems which arise in an origin-based survey, where he examines estimates of the number of hours worked in urban activities for clusters of households. Corrections to standard probit regressions include a Heckman sample selection correction to impute wages

---

[25] Another interesting finding from Falaris is that, by estimating a nested logit model, it appears that Venezuelan states are perceived as clusters with intracluster similarities. If this perception is generally accurate, then it would imply that standard regressions with unadjusted distance terms are potentially biased.

for those not presently employed for wages, as well as an iterative procedure to correct for simultaneity of hours worked and proportion of households with a migrant away in urban areas. Bigsten's findings are striking, and somewhat at variance with those from Asia and Latin America. Neither rural land pressure nor local economic potential appear to influence migration: potential urban income appears to be the overwhelmingly dominant force.

Other stylized facts from microstudies include the following. The incentives generated by the household and community structures appear to matter enormously. Outmigration often rises with education, but not invariably: in Ecuador, the least educated young women tended to migrate, presumably to enter domestic service and other jobs at the low end of the urban service sector (Bilsborrow et al., 1987). Land holdings tend to have mixed effects as well. As with education and origin income, greater family land ownership is associated with relaxed migration (and job search) financing constraints, but also with a higher opportunity cost. Amenities associated with rural infrastructure have mixed effects as well: their absence represents a "push" factor, but poorer infrastructure is associated with greater remoteness, and hence greater difficulties in arranging migration, especially if it is likely to be circular. Migration also tends to diminish with rural job opportunities and marriage, and rises with the household's effective labor supply (Bilsborrow et al., 1987). As Findley (1987) emphasizes, household and community variables are strongly interactive, so that linear or even loglinear specifications without interaction terms are likely to miss a great deal. Her work on the Philippines suggests that outmigration will rise with agricultural commercialization—except for those communities where social and economic infrastructure is weak. She also finds (Findlay, 1987: p. 185) that in "communities with little previous migration, the lower- and upper-class families are more likely to migrate than the middle-class families, but in communities with much previous migration, this differential is reversed".

In short, the microstudies typically offer little in the way of clear implications for aggregate studies, much less policy measures. They *do* tend to find that individuals and households respond to incentives: it is the incentives which vary enormously across contexts. The glib interpretation of the vast micromigration literature (and consistent with a few studies, such as Bigsten, 1996) is that the myriad variables and contexts represent much random noise that can be ignored at aggregate levels—but this statement is one of faith rather than an empirical assessment, and, as we indicate below, may well be wrong.

## 2.3. Analytical general equilibrium models

HT models spurred several attempts to generate high and low wage sectors within a competitive environment. Three themes merit pursuit here: efforts to endogenize wages, work which extends the HT model to include product markets and international trade, and general equilibrium models based on monocentric city models.

*Endogenous wages: labor turnover, efficient search, and efficiency wages.* The endogenous wage literature in turn has several branches. By far the most influential is Stiglitz's (1974) seminal piece (also written in Nairobi) which advances a "labor turnover" model. In this paradigm, an urban modern sector's total labor costs depend both on the wage bill and on the costs $T$ of training new workers, since the existing force quits at rate $q$. This quit rate in turn depends on the firm's wage relative to the expected urban wage, its wage relative to prevailing rural earnings, and to the urban unemployment rate $U$—and is decreasing in each argument. Thus, the firm's wage bill may be written as

$$w_u L_u + q \left( \frac{w_u}{E w_u}, \frac{w_u}{w_r}, U \right) \cdot T \cdot L_u \equiv w_u^* L_u. \tag{2.4}$$

Firms will take $U$ and the general urban wage rate parametrically, and then choose $w_u$ to minimize $w_u^*$. The simple rule which follows is that "marginal savings in turnover costs must be equal to the extra wage costs" (Stiglitz, 1974: p. 199).

Assuming that modern sector firms can buy loyalty and that quitting is costly to the firm, then firms will offer a wage above $w_r$ (but not $E w_u$ in equilibrium, since firms are identical), and in consequence a natural urban wage premium will occur—leading to HT-like unemployment, though under a more sophisticated turnover regime than the random turnover assumed by Harris and Todaro. The scope for unemployment is also more limited, since its presence directly inhibits quits, which in turn means fewer new jobs, and hence less inmigration.

Beyond the turnover equation and an intersectoral wage ratio

$$\frac{w_u}{w_r} = \phi \left( \frac{1}{1-U} \right), \qquad \phi' > 0. \tag{2.5}$$

Stiglitz (1974) has neoclassical production functions and competitive behavior in both urban and rural areas. Relative to the socially optimal urban wage, the competitive $w_u$ is too high because firms fail to recognize that they cannot outbid other firms. On the other hand, it is too low because they consider neither the endogeneity of $w_r$ nor the effect of their actions on $U$. Stiglitz asserts that the first effect is likely to dominate, though the matter is uncertain theoretically. In any event, the socially optimal urban wage will still exceed the rural wage.

The labor turnover perspective moves attention from institutional forces which cause high wages, and instead focuses on labor market characteristics. If an economy is highly dualistic in the sense that modern sector production involves substantial accumulation of job-specific skills which cannot be acquired outside the firm, then $w_u$ will be high. It seems plausible that quits will be less sensitive to market conditions during periods of rapid economic growth, while high profits in those periods may also raise the opportunity costs of quits to the firm in terms of foregone profits (captured in $T$). During stagnant periods, on the other hand, urban unemployment might even fall as $q$ approaches a lower bound, especially if $w_r$ is low and falling.

Turnover rates in transforming economies are often very low, especially in African countries for which the models were first formulated. East Africa in 1970 may have had turnover rates comparable to those in the US (Collier and Lal, 1980: p. 42), but more recent evidence (for example, Knight and Sabot, 1990: p. 171) suggests that these rates have fallen greatly, presumably in response to economic difficulties and the rapid increase in educated labor.

A second reason for endogenous intersectoral wage gaps is "expense preference" by managers. The expense preference model (Williamson, 1964) posits that the payment of higher wages to workers allows managers to reduce their effort level, by reducing the need for monitoring, oversight and training. This model has not yet been applied to urban labor markets of transforming economies.

Costly turnover and expense preference are not the only factors which may impel firms to pay wages above workers' reservation prices. Bliss and Stern (1978) argue that firms may pay additional wages to ensure that their workers are physically capable of working—that is, they pay a "nutrition premium" (see also Deolalikar (1988)). More broadly, Stiglitz (1976) proposes an "efficiency wage" hypothesis, which claims that a worker's productivity rises with his or her wages. This effect may stem both from greater capacity (some of the additional income goes to more and better food, some may go to more reliable transport to work, and some may go to education) and effort. Recently, Bencivenga and Smith (1997) provide a model in which a formal sector wage generates under-employment in a three-sector, two-labor type model. Put simply, formal sector firms are compelled to offer both high and low productivity workers the same wage, and cannot (perfectly) monitor performance. Migrants can either search for formal sector jobs or work in the informal sector, where high quality workers are more productive. An equilibrium which attracts some good workers must also be one with some informal sector underemployment in order to compensate for adverse selection and somewhat discourage low quality migrant workers. In all cases, HT-like unemployment can emerge as a result of endogenous wage-setting—as will rural-urban migration of those willing to endure a considerable spell of unemployment in order to gain access to a high-wage job.

*Endogenous wages: rent-seeking models.* Knight and Sabot (1988) recognize that public enterprises, which have dominated many African modern sectors for the past 25 years, are under pressure to provide employment regardless of needs. But one should not regard this as limited to Africa: evidence that large enterprises are pressured into employing an above optimal number of workers in order to limit unemployment can be cited from Turkey (Knight and Sabot, 1988), the former Soviet Union, China, Latin America, Korea and Indonesia[26]—indeed, it is hard to list transforming countries where such pressure does or did not exist.[27] In a small simulation model, Knight and Sabot (1988) show that an overly expansionary government employment policy will actually exacerbate HT unemployment, though under different labor supply conditions this finding could be reversed.

The next question is to ask what will happen if wages rather than public employment become endogenous. Calvo (1978) modifies HT by assuming union power in the formal sector, although only within the context of a small, open economy (fixed product prices). In a similar vein, Becker and Morrison (1993) provide a simple three-sector model of a stereotypical African economy which is neoclassical in the urban traditional and agricultural sectors, and in which urban modern (UM) employers act as rational profit maximizers. However, organized labor is able to capture a share of UM value added; this share depends on government's share in total output, the unemployment rate, the degree of protection from foreign competition, the government budget deficit as a share of GDP (indicating the public sector's financial flexibility), the size of foreign capital inflows (on the assumption that foreign firms are more susceptible to political pressure), and the balance of trade (as an indicator of the health of the domestic UM sector, since access to imports is a key determinant of production and profitability).

---

[26] Lumbantoruan (1997) analyzes frontier cost functions for state-owned and private industrial enterprises (mainly textile firms) in Indonesia, and finds that there is no significant difference in efficiency levels: most firms are highly inefficient regardless of ownership. This finding can be attributed to the fact that few firms are truly private in the sense of being independent of government or immune to its pressures; for a variety of political reasons, government has also encouraged firms to build capacity (and employ) way beyond market needs, so that optimal production scale is rarely reached.

[27] Privatization programs underway in many countries are changing this panorama.

Calvo, Becker–Morrison and other rent-seeking models generate a UM wage above the perfectly competitive equilibrium level, and hence HT unemployment and "excess" migration occur. The real message of Becker–Morrison is a much more sobering one, though: empirical estimations at the aggregate level can in principle distinguish among Harris–Todaro, perfectly competitive neoclassical, rent-seeking, and Brueckner's monocentric city-based models of UM labor market behavior. In practice, though, very weak data bases and nonrobust sensitivity to minor changes in specification make the various specifications in effect observationally equivalent. In other words, one's choice of aggregate model must be based on assessment of plausibility of assumptions or on model implications unrelated to migration and urbanization.

Becker et al. (1994) strongly lean to a rent-seeking paradigm for African labor markets for its consistency with time series trends. African economies have been characterized by falling real UM wages, which cannot be explained by HT. In a neoclassical world, falling wages would normally be accompanied by falling average product as well, along with rising employment (if due to supply increases). But in six of 15 countries for which the authors had data, wages fell but productivity did not: this could be the case if demand declines were observed, but in all six cases UM employment actually increased. Furthermore, the magnitude of the urban wage declines was far greater than the declines in rural per capita output, which should anchor urban wages in a neoclassical model.

*Migration models: dynamics, product markets and trade*. Bennett and Phelps (1983) design a neoclassical two-sector, small, open economy model in which households have money (or other liquid assets). Their model contains goods markets' equilibria, fixed exchange rates but an explicit trade balance statement, labor-leisure choices, exogenous urban labor demand due to an above-equilibrium wage, and urban wage dependence on the cost of living. With an implicit government budget constraint, their framework provides an exceptionally lucid presentation of the impact of short-run macropolicies on a developing economy, and in particular on rural-urban migration. Key comparative static results include the finding that urban public works employment will have a total employment impact less than one, and possibly less than zero. Export taxes on the rural good affect the urban sector through a falling domestic price level, but of course hurt the rural economy. A rise in tariffs on urban goods raises output prices but not workers' living costs (consisting of rural food), so protectionism is bound to expand cities. Devaluation raises prices of both urban and rural goods, but most plausibly the net effect is to increase urban labor demand. Devaluation is also less costly than the other measures considered (tariffs, rural export taxes, urban employment subsidies and public works programs) in terms of rural jobs lost per urban job created.

Becker and Morrison (1988) employ a model of an African economy that is similar in many respects, building on the basic HT fixed urban modern sector wage hypotheses. Unlike Bennett and Phelps (1983), they have neither money nor an explicit labor supply choice; they do, however, build in a balance of payments constraint, an endogenous exchange rate, and goods markets. Becker and Morrison (1988) further include a traditional urban sector $T$, along with agriculture $A$ and the urban modern UM sectors, and consider the consequences of imported goods used as intermediate inputs rather than simply being competitors with UM outputs. They also permit $T$ goods to be used as intermediates by UM. The model predicts an uncertain effect on migration from raising the UM wage for standard Harris–Todaro reasons. Government demands are urbanizing, as are foreign capital inflows. Trade effects are similar to those in Bennett and Phelps (1983), except that protectionism plays an ambiguous role, since it both raises UM costs and diminishes foreign competition.

The Becker–Morrison formulation is useful in part for explicitly laying out the erstwhile implicit assumptions undertaken in single equation migration or urban growth regressions. These equations can be generated as a reduced form, but only from highly restrictive models. Becker and Morrison estimate the model for a cross section of sub-Saharan African countries and find a very tenuous link between urban population growth and UM employment growth. This result is disturbing for all models which posit industrialization and modern sector growth as the primary engine of urbanization. Indeed, while Becker and Morrison (1988) do find that growth of government, GDP and the rate of urban capital formation matter in expected ways, rural push factors also turn out to be very important.

## 2.4. Computable general equilibrium (CGE) models

During the past 25 years, a vast range of CGE models of developing economies has been produced. Most, but not all, lack spatial content. Of those with spatial content, some contain urban and rural locations for different sectors, but do not seriously model spatially related forces. CGE models with detailed spatial structure appear to be limited to Kelley and Williamson (1984), itself an outgrowth of Kelley et al. (1973), and Kelley and Williamson's successors, Becker et al. (1992). The general structure of CGE models is well known, and need not be repeated here. We instead focus on what makes the Kelley and Williamson and Becker et al. models unique and the insights they present into the urbanization process.

CGE models enable economists to describe economies in a more sophisticated way than one can handle analytically. As analytical solutions cannot be obtained for systems typically in excess of 100 nonlinear equations, parameter values must be assigned to the functional forms and exogenous variables, and the model must be solved numerically. Typically, most of the specific equations cannot be estimated econometrically either. The standard solution procedure is therefore to take whatever econometric estimates are available from the literature and then solve the others by forcing the simulated model to replicate a "benchmark" year.

In effect, CGEs trade accuracy in estimation for complexity in specification. Despite their complexity, CGEs are of no use in assessing the effects of short-run events: after all, by construction, they replicate equilibria, not disequilibria. CGE models are of greatest value when complex, second round effects are likely to be important. Indeed, one can view CGE models as providing a test of whether indirect effects are important in the sense of frequently overriding direct (partial equilibrium) effects; the experience of Kelley and Williamson (1984) and Becker et al. (1992) is that this often is the case. In the case of urbanization, the relative increases of land rents and wage rates play key roles in determining migration, and analytically tractable models inherently miss much of this. Interplay between traded and nontraded goods sectors in urban and rural areas is best modeled in a CGE framework, as is determination of output prices.

Both Kelley and Williamson (1984) and Becker et al. (1992) are fairly small CGE models. Becker et al. model India with 10 sectors and over 100 equations and a 1960 benchmark, and then seek to explain economic history for the period 1960–1981. In contrast, Kelley and Williamson describe a "representative developing country" (RDC)—one that is small and open, based on the era 1960–1973, and characterized by rapid growth. Since the Indian economy is only semi-open and has had historically low growth rates, the models together offer insights into how closed and open economies are differently affected by forces driving urbanization.

Both models assume competitive markets, albeit regionally segmented in the case of land and (Becker et al., 1992) capital. Becker et al. contain a rural economy with agriculture, services and manufacturing (with far more employment its urban counterpart for most of the period), public services, and housing. The urban economy contains modern manufacturing, modern services, an informal sector, public services, and both high and low quality housing. The model thus captures dualism in production and demand, as well as a sophisticated statement of government behavior. A main limitation of both models is the exogeneity of demographic behavior, although this is addressed in an aspatial context by Kelley and Schmidt (1988).

In the Kelley and Williamson (1984) open economy, urban manufacturing is the engine of growth, reflecting both infinitely elastic demands and strong backward linkages relative to other sectors. The simulated 1960s is an era of a growing skilled wage premium, rapid urban manufacturing growth (its employment share rises from 12% in 1960 to 18% in 1973), and substantial but slower informal sector growth (its national employment share rises from 10 to 13%). City growth during the 1960s occurs at an annual rate of 4.7%, with a net urban inmigration rate of 2.1%. Real urban land prices more than double between 1960 and 1973; along with skilled labor shortages, this helps brake urban growth. Rising population growth naturally causes cities to grow more rapidly, but actually markedly reduces the urbanization rate. The story is simple: per capita output falls as capital/labor ratios decline; Engel effects thereby raise the relative price of food.

Kelley and Williamson (1984) also find that the external environment after the 1973 OPEC shock was markedly less favorable for urbanization. Their simulations forecast an increase in the urbanization rate for their RDC from 33% in 1960 to 40% in 1970, and then to 68% by 2000 given the OPEC shocks—and to 78% in their absence. Overall, city growth and inmigration rates peak in 1973 (or around 1980 in the absence of OPEC), and then decline fairly rapidly. As their comparison (Kelley and Williamson, 1984: pp. 156–167) shows, urban growth takes place at a more rapid pace in Kelley and Williamson than virtually any of the pure demographic forecasts.

Turgid India turns out to be quite a contrast from the dynamic small open economies captured by Kelley and Williamson. Urbanization rises from 14% in 1960 to 24% in 2001 in the benchmark run (see Becker et al., 1992: p. 167) and 30% in the stable run (without the OPEC shock); even by 2060, India is only half urbanized. Needless to say, these simulations generate much slower growth than most of the (apparently excessive) purely demographic runs.[28] Indian city growth declines from annual rates in excess of 5% in the mid-1960s to about 4% in the 1970s and early 1980s to under 3% in the 1990s.

The relatively closed nature of the Indian economy is inherently less favorable for rapid urban growth than is a small open economy. Rapid total factor productivity (TFP) growth and capital accumulation in urban sectors are choked off by rising prices of food and other rural inputs, as well as by rising rents and wages. The more closed the economy, the less distinctive are manufacturing and agriculture as traded goods' sectors. Thus, while unbalanced TFP and world price

---

[28] Only Mohan's (1985) smaller CGE model and Rogers (1984) produce urbanization rates close to the low rates forecast by Becker et al. (1992). See Becker and Morrison (1993: p. 70).

shifts (which filter through to the Indian economy via Armington equations) continue to play important roles in Becker et al. (1992), they are of far less relative importance than in the Kelley and Williamson (1984), RDC model. Factors central to India's low urban growth rate include its low manufacturing TFP growth rate, low rates of foreign capital inflows, rising imported raw materials prices, and low rate of overall TFP growth. Modest savings rates do not help, but are clearly exacerbated by low foreign investment rates and low capital productivity. About one-third of the slowdown in urban growth following the early 1960s can be attributed to unfavorable environmental conditions (including TFP change); the rest is due to the large and undynamic agricultural sector.

The Becker et al. (1992) simulations contain several important messages for students of urbanization. India appears to have become increasingly sensitive to exogenous shocks over time, mainly because its structure is shifting toward activities (urban manufacturing and modern services) capable of responding to opportunities. Migration restriction has very small GDP impacts in the Indian context, but does have the anticipated neoclassical distributional effects, and as a whole is highly inegalitarian.

GDP is a poor measure of welfare, especially in fragmented and distorted economies. Growth of government is unambiguously urbanizing and harmful to the poor: governments consume skill-intensive goods and, depending on how their growth is funded, may reduce capital formation. Sophisticated policies of all types have unanticipated consequences which may swamp the direct effects. More critically, *the underlying economic environment crucially determines the impacts of various policies: impact multipliers in 1981 India often differ strikingly from those for 1960 India, and both differ even more from those in the Kelley and Williamson small, open economy.* Perhaps most importantly, though, there is a clear policy direction for India-like economies: welfare of the poor is most enhanced, as Mellor (1976) has long asserted, if agriculture and labor-intensive employment creation policies are followed.[29] Its urbanization impacts are ambiguous, but its welfare consequences are not.

A final model worth mentioning is Adelman and Robinson (1978a, b). Parameterized for 1968 and historically simulated over 1968–1972 for Korea, it is superficially similar in structure to Kelley and Williamson (1984). In practice it differs greatly because of the greater degree of disaggregation (four firm size groups in each of 29 sectors; 15 household categories; and 6 skill levels). With a migration statement based on urban/rural wage gaps and competitive product

---

[29] Job creation policies need not be activist; they may be as simple—and as effective—as a benign policy environment which does not articificially lower the price of capital.

and factor price determination elsewhere, the model offers distributional insights unobtainable from Kelley and Williamson (1984) or Becker et al. (1992).

A key finding of Adelman and Robinson concerns the distributional effect of rural-urban migration. Had migration not taken place, the simulation 9 years out (Adelman and Robinson, 1977) would have yielded a Gini coefficient of 0.598 and a bottom quintile income share of 1.2%—far worse than the baseline simulation values of 0.457 and 5.0%, respectively. As they write (Adelman and Robinson, 1988b: p. 21), "rural-urban migration is beneficial to the poor and detrimental to the rich. It improves the distribution of income, increases overall productivity of the economy, and reduces poverty". As in the other CGE models, migration restriction counterfactuals have little immediate impact on GDP, but are highly inegalitarian. On the whole, though, migration unambiguously raises GDP in Adelman and Robinson, since urban activities enjoy a considerable productivity advantage over rural pursuits.

## 2.5. Demo-economic approaches

Virtually all recorded migration patterns show strong patterns by age, and frequently by gender. Figure 1 provides unweighted average net urban inmigration rates for 10 Asian, 13 African and 14 Latin American countries.[30] Inmigration rates peak strongly for both genders, especially for African men and women. But for all regions, the inmigration rates for 15–29-year-olds are far larger than for other age groups. Rural outmigration rates show a similar peaking pattern.

Figures 2 and 3 show urban inmigration and rural outmigration rates for one country, Korea, at roughly 5-year intervals from 1960–1985. Korea exhibits a peculiar double spiking for men at ages 15–19 and 25–29; the intervening lull reflects nearly universal, lengthy military service. For both sexes, the pattern is one of exceptionally high migration, with urban inmigration rates gradually diminishing for a given age group over time following the 1966–1970 peak. In contrast, rural outmigration rates do not appear to be systematically diminishing: on the contrary, for males aged 5–19 and 40–69 they peak during 1980–1985; and for all females aged over 5, except those 25–29 and 75+, the highest recorded rate was during 1980–1985. This difference between in- and outmigration rates reflects the rapid urbanization of the country, coupled with high and rising outmigration rates.

---

[30] We are indebted to Christopher Grewe for generating the figures in this chapter, as well as for calculating the migration rates which underlie them. In order to avoid making fairly arbitrary assumptions on region-specific birth rate patterns, migration rates for those born during intercensal periods (age 0–9) were not computed. Computation methodology by residual inference is discussed in Becker and Grewe (1996).

### Asian Female Net Urban In-Migration Rates

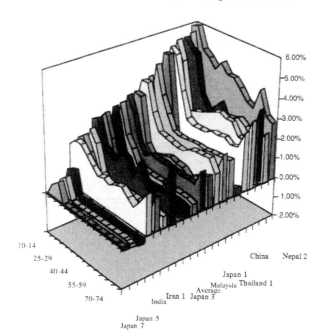

### Korean Female Net Urban In-Migration

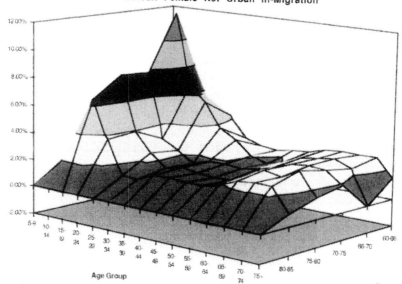

Fig. 1. Age-specific net rural–urban migration rates, 1960s–1980s.

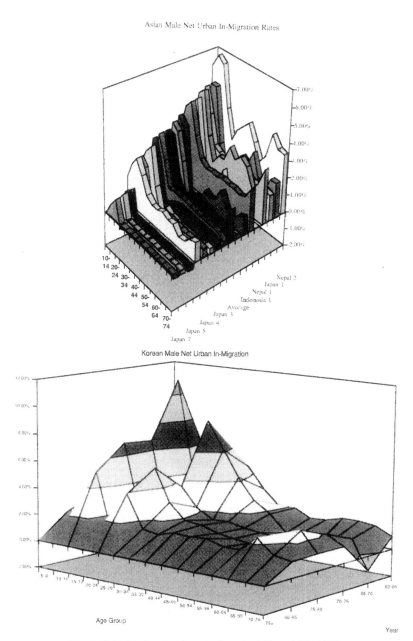

Fig. 2. Net urban in-migration rates by cohort, Korea 1960–1985.

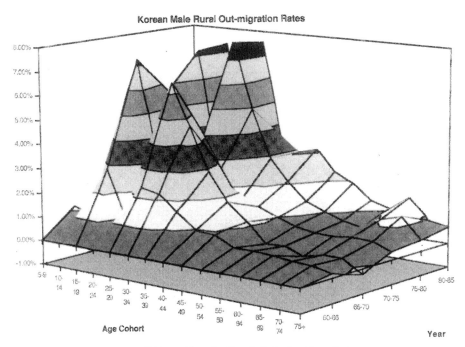

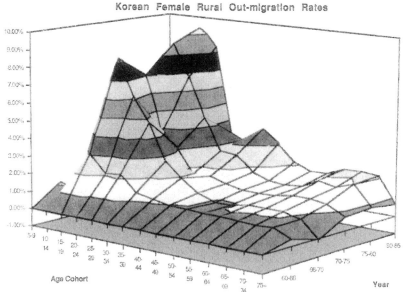

Fig. 3. Net rural out-migration rates by cohort, Korea 1960–1985.

At the microlevel, all migration studies include demographic (household characteristic) variables. Unfortunately, as is apparent from our survey thus far, most aggregate economic models do not include demographic forces (the main exception is Adelman and Robinson (1978)). This would not be problematic if demographic forces remained constant over time, but we know that dramatic shifts have occurred; hence, so have cohort weights (Becker and Morrison, 1993; Becker and Grewe, 1996). In particular, the relative sizes of those cohorts at greatest risk to migrate began growing, with roughly a 15 year lag, once the mortality component of the demographic transition set in from country to country. Between 1960 and 1975, crude death rates declined at an annual rate of just under 1% in Africa, 0.4% in south Asia, 2.5% in Latin America, and 4.3% in east Asia; since most of these dramatic gains in mortality reduction took place in infant and child mortality, the population of surviving children grew rapidly and eventually became a large cohort of surviving young adults. In short, even if cohort-specific migration rates had remained constant over time, changing cohort weights would have given rise to an increase in aggregate migration rates from roughly 1965–1985 relative to past (and future) periods.

In fact, not only did the share of young adults rise in many populations: there were even more spectacular increases in those young adults most likely to migrate, namely those with secondary educations. Secondary school enrollment ratios grew at an annual rate of 4.94% between 1965–1970 and 6.75% from 1970–1975 (implying even more rapid secondary school population growth: see Becker and Morrison (1993)) in transforming economies. While some secondary school leavers would have displaced less educated migrants, it seems plausible that the overall effect of rapid education growth would be to increase total migration rates.

Until the censuses around 1990 were reported, it was impossible to generate a sufficiently large cross-country dataset to determine whether, or not, migration patterns of different cohorts were indeed driven by very different forces. Generating these data from UN *Demographic Yearbooks* is now straightforward, though. Empirical work by Becker and Grewe (1996) employing SUR regressions for an African sample find that primary education has a strong, positive effect on the migration of nearly all groups. Growth of government attracts male migrants under, but not over, 40 years. Social services attract women and male migrants except for those aged 20–34. Improved rural conditions (proxied for by change in calories per capita) cause migration to increase for all male groups except those aged 20–29; measures of rural income growth, however, encourage migration among all groups. Broadly speaking, female cohorts are more attracted by social service variables and less by economic variables than their male counterparts.

These findings should be taken as a first rather than last word, but a key point emerges: different forces matter to different groups.

The lack of attention to demographic forces in understanding urbanization derives neither from its omission in classic works (e.g., Sjaastad, 1962), nor from lack of emphasis by economic historians or demographers. Nor, for that matter, have past *North-Holland Handbook* chapters ignored the topic, since Williamson (1988a) emphasizes migrant age selectivity. Williamson (1988b) emphasizes the "young adult bias" of England's cities during the industrial revolution, and their parallel relatively low dependency ratios. Furthermore, the age distribution of migrants from the countryside to English cities was overwhelmingly of young working age people: by the 1980s, two-thirds of all inmigrants were aged 15–29. This age selectivity enabled urban labor force participation rates to rise, and actually curbed total rural inmigration, both immediately, and in the longer run via the inmigration of adults of child-bearing years.

Demographic forces are also important determinants of natural rates of population in urban areas. Williamson (1988b) finds that in the 1970s for developing economies as a whole, 29.4% of urban and 26.0% of rural populations were in the 20–39 year age group, respectively. *These differing age structures imply that, even if urban total fertility rates are considerably below rural TFRs, urban crude birth rates may differ little from rural CBRs.* In short, it is clear that age selectivity plays a key role in urbanization patterns, both by affecting relative sizes of the population at greatest risk to migrate and by compensating for rural-urban TFR differentials.

### 2.6. Migration of women and families

*The "new economics of labor migration".* Rural-urban migration thus far has been presented largely as an implicitly permanent event undertaken by full-time workers, accompanied perhaps by their families. We know, however, that much migration takes place for quite different reasons, and that the relevant decision-making units may be large, extended families rather than individuals. By now a wealth of literature on the migration decision-making process at the microlevel has emerged, and it can only be cursorily summarized here (as noted above, the Lucas (1997) survey treats this topic in far greater detail, as does Massey's (1990) survey). The economist perhaps most responsible for the "new economics of labor migration" is Stark (see Stark (1991) for a collection of major papers, Stark and Bloom (1985) for an overview, and Katz and Stark (1986b) for a formal statement of rational low-earnings migration due to risk aversion), though the new paradigm may be traced to Stiglitz (1969).

The point of departure is that migration is an instrument used in an optimizing framework by a rural household. As such, the models are neoclassical in spirit, but go far beyond "representative workers" in complexity. Most of the models have little immediate implications for aggregate migration and urbanization patterns, though one certainly can derive case-specific implications. Perhaps most importantly, many of these models predict that migration will occur even in the absence of vast opportunity differentials. This approach also predicts that social structure, rural landholding structure, and the nature of capital markets will have significant impacts on migration behavior—hypotheses not yet well examined at the aggregate level (but see Morrison (1994) for an aggregate migration model that includes capital markets). Most fundamentally, the new approach regards migration as the outcome of a (generally) cooperative game involving many players, rather than stemming from an individual's calculus of discounted expected net benefits.

As Stark has emphasized, rural households can manage risk by sending at least one migrant to an urban area if this results in a lower variance of household income. This "portfolio management" approach to family placement will involve having some family members migrate to cities, even if no anticipated income gains exist, as long as risk (proxied for by the variance of household income) is reduced. Massey (1990) finds that the empirical work as a whole is quite supportive of the risk diversification hypothesis.

The subject becomes still more interesting when one considers that migrants do not have legal obligations to remit a portion of their income in the event that they are successful in the cities. Family migration decisions under imperfectly altruistic behavior then become a cooperative game, with migration curtailed to the extent that household members do not devise mechanisms to ensure that potential migrants' incentives are the same as the household's collective interests. While it is obvious that origin families have an interest in sending members to cities, having them earn high salaries, and then remitting substantial amounts, it is far less obvious what induces these migrants to behave cooperatively. Stark and Katz (1985) conceive of remittances as an insurance premium. The origin household provides initial support for job search activity and living costs by the migrant, and will provide subsequent support in the event of job loss. And, as Lucas and Stark (1985, 1988) have also emphasized, potential bequests and the origin household's partial control over the migrant's origin property rights both help reduce moral hazard problems. Beyond direct economic incentives, the migrant's "social status, prestige and honor" are all influenced greatly by the origin family: there is social opprobrium attached to being labeled an outcast by one's family, and few people would truly ignore this.

Finally, Lucas and Stark have emphasized that households are most likely to fund those who have already demonstrated altruistic behavior beforehand, as this reduces enforcement costs. Conversely, children are more likely to send large remittances to families which have demonstrated altruistic behavior in the past. Such mutual altruism reduces contract enforcement costs (and perceived outcome variance)—in a sense, it defines a family.

*Conflict: alternatives to the unitary household.* Attempts to develop alternatives to a unitary household model, in which all individuals cooperate for the good of the household unit, has come from two ideologically distinct groups: (1) neo-classical microeconomists who wish to deconstruct the household, often using noncooperative game theory, and (2) feminist and institutional economists who emphasize normative and structural features of the household (Katz, 1997).

While they have not yet been applied to migration models, there have been three types of noncooperative games applied to household bargaining. The first is a Cournot–Nash approach, which unlike unitary household and cooperative models, finds that outcomes hinge on the distribution of current income among family members (Katz, 1997: p. 14; Woolley, 1993; Lundberg and Pollak, 1993). The second noncooperative approach is an alternating offer framework (Rubenstein, 1982) in which offers and counteroffers are made sequentially by the parties involved in bargaining. Fleck (1997) has examined the implication of this type of model for female labor force participation and wages; a logical extension would be to migration modeling. The third type of model to examine intrahouse-hold modeling is the principal-agent family of models, in which one household member has an advantage in influencing outcomes because of his ownership of productive assets (Katz, 1997: p. 15). While this approach has been used to examine the division of labor in West African agriculture (Chawla, 1993), it has not yet been applied to migration modeling.

*Migration of women and families.* As Banerjee (1982) details in his study of migrants to Delhi, a wide range of migration patterns coexist simultaneously: some men migrate with their families; some do not; others migrate prior to marriage; and a substantial number have no family members at the point of origin. Beyond India and conservative Moslem societies, the range of migration is still greater: the data underlying Fig. 1 show that female migration rates typically exceed male migration rates in Latin America and the Philippines, and the migration of single women is common in much of Africa, Indonesia, and southeast and east Asia as well.

Hugo (1993), Singelmann (1993) and United Nations (1993) provide exceptionally detailed overviews of female migration patterns across the developing world. Overall, women who migrate to cities are relatively less likely to be married (Bilsborrow (1993) and United Nations (1993), than their stayer counterparts—though in most transforming economies, most female migrants over 15 are married, and marriage-related reasons for migration are important everywhere, and dominate in many countries (United Nations, 1993). This pattern is changing in southeast Asia, where export-oriented manufacturing jobs are largely held by women. As Hugo's survey details, the fertility of migrant women appears to fall, though whether this reflects migration selectivity, disruption of desired child-bearing patterns, or adaptation to new conditions and expectations remains an unsettled debate. It seems likely that women tend to migrate shorter distances, on average, than men (United Nations, 1993). As the United Nations Secretariat notes, rural-urban migration only accounts for a small proportion of total migration in most transforming economies, so that characteristics of the former may differ markedly from those of all migrants. In assessing motives, one must also heed Bilsborrow's (1993) more general point that many surveys question only heads of households, who are typically men—and who may well misrepresent motives for the migration behavior of female relatives. Indeed, there are many social constraints that may lead to systematic underreporting of female migration, especially when it is economically motivated.

Lauby and Stark (1988) examine the *Philippines' 1976 Status of Women Survey* (SWS), and conclude that women are *more* likely than men to migrate, generally alone, for family reasons. The data clearly indicate that women in the Philippines head to cities for stable, but low-paid work. Relative to nonmigrants, migrant women are more likely to be wage workers, regardless of destination.[31] Female migrants tend to enter easily obtained low-pay, low-skill, dead-end jobs, but nonetheless earn substantial amounts relative to origin family incomes.

Very high rates of female labor force participation are unusual, however, especially outside of Latin America and parts of southeast Asia, making economic studies of women far more complicated than studies of men. One cannot simply estimate conditional earnings functions and then estimate economic migration functions with predicted gaps as the main explanatory variables. For one thing, labor force participation and fertility decisions are simultaneously determined. Moreover, as live birth outcomes are far from guaranteed, the resulting model should be dynamic, rather than a static net present value representation. Cross-

---

[31] Lauby and Stark (1988) conjecture that migrants have poorer access to information and network capital needed to successfully start one's own business.

tabular evidence strongly suggests that, in many cultures, women migrate in search of suitable husbands. Rosenzweig and Stark (1987) have shown that cross-village migration by brides is used as a strategy in parts of rural India in order to reduce risk, since the ties created by marriage also serve as an insurance contract.

Behrman and Wolfe (1984a; see also 1984b) for more detail on the earnings functions) use a study of 4000 Nicaraguan women from 1977–1978 to consider three different types of female migration: labor market flows, "demographic marriage market" considerations (probability of having a male companion), and "economic marriage market" forces, or "expected earnings from a companion given regional labor market considerations and assortive mating". For rural-urban migration of women, the incentive effects of female migration and employment probabilities were all significant for migration to Managua (but not other cities), and had the "right" sign in all cases. The economic and marriage market effects were insignificant for migration to other cities; economic marriage effects were highly significant in determining migration to Managua, but had the "wrong" sign.

Cinar's (1994) study of women in Istanbul documents the importance of "economic marriage market" effects. Over 71% of female respondents in a random survey gave economic reasons as the main cause of migration, with the majority identifying husband's job needs as the most important cause.

Donato's (1991) study of female migration from Mexico to the US finds that economic factors dominated. As with many other microstudies, those with past migration experience were far more likely to migrate again. The likelihood of a woman's migration increased with education and being from an entrepreneurial family; it was deterred by origin, land ownership and the presence of other adults in the household. These variables had dramatic impacts (as did US amnesty law coverage): women without a business background, no education, and no past migration experience (and no residence eligibility) had less than a 2% chance of migrating; those with 6+ years education and a business had a 56% chance of migrating even if they had no past migration experience. On the whole, though, women were less likely to migrate than comparable men.

In her work on migration from northeastern to southeastern Brazil (with appropriate selectivity correction), Puente Cackley (1993) examines expected wage differentials for both husband and wife among married couples. The coefficient for husband's expected wage differential was seven times that of the wife's; however, both variables were significant at reasonable levels. The wage differential effect for never married men and women did not differ greatly, and in both cases the significance levels were far higher than for either married partner. Overall, it seems plausible that earnings opportunities for married women are a less important factor in migration decision than are wage differentials for men, or unmarried women. Nevertheless, part of the large difference may simply reflect specification error, since labor force participation and fertility decisions are inextricably linked for married women.

Phongpaichit's (1993) work on female migration to Bangkok, based on the *1982–1989 Thai Labor Force Surveys* and *1988 Survey of Migration to Bangkok Metropolis*, provides a detailed picture of industrial employment-oriented migration. By the late 1980s, as many as 60% of migrants arriving in Bangkok were women; the majority of both men (72%) and women (65%) reported that finding work was the main reason for migration. Labor force participation rates were extremely high for both genders, but especially for young female migrants. For female migrants aged 11–19, the reported participation rate was 78.7%; for those 20–29 it was 78.0%, and fell below 75% (50%) only for migrant women over 50 (60) years. Remittances also appear to be higher for women migrants, indicating stronger ties to home families, and perhaps greater residual authority by families over women migrants.

Toward the opposite end of the spectrum is the Senegal River Valley of western Mali, with insignificant industrial employment, and a traditional culture in which female migration for economic reasons is somewhat shameful, as is work for pay anywhere. As Findley and Diallo (1993) find, female migration in this setting consists largely of those women with the lowest status in the household being sent to "visit" kin outside the village of origin. In this setting, women were only half as likely as men to migrate, and migrated for shorter distances. The bottom line, though, is that economic factors do appear to matter in Mali as well as in Thailand—as do many similar social constraints and obligations.

It is difficult to draw clear conclusions from this brief sampling of women's migration. Empirical findings appear to indicate that women migrate largely for economic reasons: if the studies discussed above are representative, then one may conclude that, outside conservative Moslem and Hindu societies, women's rural-urban migration is *primarily* driven by her direct economic considerations, both at the individual and family level. With the rapid industrialization of many transforming economies, new urban employment opportunities are emerging for women, and migration flows for this purpose now compete with marriage- and family-based migration, and with migration based on the expectation of working in domestic service or in urban commerce. Since the degree of a woman's involvement in her individual or a family's migration decision varies with the nature of migration (Bilsborrow, 1993; United Nations, 1993), it seems likely as well that women's inputs will rise in coming years as well. Together with rapidly declining fertility in Asia and parts of Latin America and Africa, the nature of women's migration in the coming decades will be quite different from that of the past half-century.

## 3. Impacts of public policy on urban growth

### 3.1. Structural adjustment

#### 3.1.1. The structure of structural adjustment

Before the 1980s and the emergence of the debt crisis, the World Bank devoted the majority of its resources to project lending. In the 1980s, however, structural adjustment loans, designed to support structural adjustment programs, became an important element of the World Bank's lending. Between 1980 and 1987 the World Bank made adjustment loans of over $15 billion to 51 countries. These adjustment loans included structural adjustment loans (51 for a total of $5.9 billion) and sectoral adjustment loans (70 for a total of $9.35 billion) (McCleary, 1991). In 1990 alone, 29 countries received either structural adjustment loans, sectoral adjustment loans, or both (Greenaway and Morrissey, 1993).

The World Bank disburses these loans conditional upon a government's agreement to pursue certain policy reforms. *Trade reforms* (e.g., tariff liberalization, reduction of quantitative restrictions, improving the incentive structure for exports) were the most important condition, comprising 28% of all conditions for loans between 1980 and 1988. *Reform of public enterprises* accounted for 16% of all conditions, and *fiscal reform* and *agricultural policy reform* each accounted for 11%.[32] Other, less frequently imposed conditions include (in descending order) modifications of: *budget and public expenditure, energy, industry* and *exchange rate policy*.[33]

In discussing the probable impact of structural adjustment programs (SAPs) on urbanization, three key points must be made at the outset. First, any effect of structural adjustment programs (SAPs) on urbanization is purely incidental; SAPs have more immediate policy concerns in mind—principally restoring external and internal macroeconomic balance. Second, the design of SAPs varies somewhat by region. In sub-Saharan Africa the emphasis has been on reforming agriculture and public institutions, while in highly indebted countries the emphasis has been on trade and financial policies (McCleary, 1991: pp. 200–201).

---

[32] McCleary (1991: p. 201). These percentages are based on an in depth study of 51 loans in 15 transforming economies.

[33] Exchange rates targets are infrequently specified in World Bank structural adjustment programs because they are considered the province of the International Monetary Fund.

To the extent that the different components of SAPs have distinct impacts on urbanization, we should not expect the effect of SAPs to be identical across countries. Third, while SAP policies themselves are important, the outcomes produced by SAPs may be more crucial determinants of urbanization. Thus, the decline in wages produced by SAPs (see Section 2.1.3) is likely to have a more important impact on urbanization than either trade reform or the reform of public enterprises, though these policies will themselves affect wages. Finally, and quite soberingly, there is almost no empirical literature which examines the impact of SAPs on urbanization rates. The reasons are simple: the research would of necessity need to be cross-sectional in nature, and within this structure it is difficult to: (1) develop cross-country measures of the strictness of SAP programs; (2) to control for other factors that shape urbanization rates; and (3) interpret the impact of SAPs, given that dependable urbanization rates only can be calculated over intercensal intervals, which typically last much longer than a SAP.

### 3.1.2. Impacts of SAPs on urbanization

Given the lack of empirical studies of the impacts of SAPs on urbanization, this section must of necessity contain predictions based on simple theoretical models, rather than empirical testing.[34] By and large, the policy reforms during SAPs can be expected to slow the growth of the largest cities.[35] *Trade reforms*, including reduction of quantitative restrictions, reduction of import duties and introduction of export incentives, have sounded the death knell for the strategy of import substitution. Since the vast majority of import-substituting production and employment is found in the largest of cities, a shift away from import substitution likely will make the largest cities less attractive to both current residents and potential migrants (Portes, 1989: pp. 33–34).[36] Export incentives will stimulate the production of tradable goods, which for the most part takes place in rural areas and secondary cities.[37] *Fiscal reform* most frequently involves an attempt to increase tax collections. Here the impact on urbanization hinges on the "reach" of national government; if taxing authority extends little beyond the boundaries

---

[34] Counterfactual exercises conducted within the framework of CGE models also imply that SAPs will slow urbanization, since they show that closed economies tend to have slower urbanization rates than more open economies (see Section 2.4).

[35] Much of the impact of SAPs on urbanization occurs because of SAPs impact on urban labor markets; for a discussion of this impact, see Section 2.1.3.

[36] As Portes (1989: pp. 33–34) notes, the implantation of an export-oriented growth model in Latin America has been accompanied by growth of industries outside of the region's large cities, such as commercial agriculture, forestry, mining and product assembly.

[37] This is true for most transforming economies. For those producing primarily manufactured exports, however, export incentives will favor increased urbanization.

of the capital city, fiscal reform—to the extent it is successful—will make the capital a relatively less attractive place to locate for firms and consumers. If, on the other hand, the government's taxing agency has national reach, fiscal reform will have little spatial impact.

The *reform of public enterprises* is often a key element of *budget reform*, since the closure or sale of money-losing state-owned enterprises is one step in reducing budget deficits. The closure of public firms results in immediate employment losses, and privatization is often preceded by reductions in employment to make the firms more attractive to potential buyers. These firms are located predominantly in the largest urban areas, so the employment losses serve to make these areas less attractive places to live.[38] Other elements of budget reform include reduction of subsidies for food and public services; these actions also have their principal impact in the largest cities. *Agricultural policy* and *exchange rate reform* are both designed to increase production of tradable goods, the first specifically in the agricultural sector and the second economy-wide. Given the structure of production in most transforming economies, these reforms likely will slow urbanization.[39]

It is difficult to gauge the impact of the *decrease in investment* (associated with SAPs) on urbanization. To the extent that the investment is public investment and there is urban bias in investment expenditure (see Section 3.2), the decrease in investment spending may slow urbanization.[40] The effect of a decrease in private investment on urbanization depends on the spatial distribution of private investment. Since data on the spatial distribution of private investment in transforming economies are rare, it is impossible to make any generalizations.

The *improvement in the current account* associated with SAPs is clearly urbanizing. Most rural areas are net producers of foreign exchange, while urban areas are net users of foreign exchange.[41] The improvement in the current account loosens the import constraint on urban areas, both for producers and consumers.

---

[38] It is important to note that the eventual impact on employment and incomes is larger than the initial impact, since there will be multiplier effects on the production of other firms. Proponents of privatization would argue that in the long run private ownership will lead to increased output and employment in privatized firms.

[39] Note that agro-processing is often an urban industry. In the African context, growth of agro-processing is likely to stimulate the growth of secondary cities (Becker et al., 1994).

[40] There is ample evidence that as public budgets are squeezed, capital expenditure is reduced to a greater extent than current expenditure (Greenaway and Morrissey, 1993: p. 252).

[41] The magnitude of the gap between rural and urban areas presumably has declined with the demise of import substitution industrialization, though.

## 3.2. The urban bias thesis

As the name implies, the urban bias thesis (Lipton, 1976) describes ways in which the government favors producers and consumers in urban areas at the expense of rural residents. According to the urban bias thesis, government policies typically have been biased against agriculture in three ways: (1) macroeconomic policy (mainly trade and price policies) distorted economic signals, raising non-agricultural value-added above what it would have been at world prices; (2) governments have allocated investment funds in urban infrastructure projects without regard for the higher rates of return available in nonurban areas; and (3) public employment has been expanded in urban areas—especially in capital cities—to a degree not justified by any conceivable efficiency criteria (Becker et al., 1994: p. 94).

Lipton (1993; p. 233), originator of the urban bias thesis, has stressed the need to distinguish between two types of urban-biased policies: price policies and expenditure policies. This distinction is crucial, since price distortions—in the form of below-market prices for agricultural output, and above-market prices for urban-produced goods—have been greatly reduced in recent years, largely as a result of structural adjustment programs. But the mere reduction of price distortions does not imply the elimination of urban bias: the government may react by spending more money on goods and services produced in urban areas, leaving urban bias intact (Braverman and Kanbur, 1987: p. 1180). Indeed, Lipton (1993: p. 248) argues that price distortions are not the main source of urban bias. He suggests that expenditure biases are exacerbated by an economic structure in which multiplier effects—backward and forward linkages—are far stronger in urban than rural areas, while price biases are compounded by rural mark-ups due to poor transport, and limited competition among wholesalers and retailers. In a sense, rural neglect rather than specific policies lies at the heart of his indictment.[42] Nor can there be any doubt that health care and education are considerably better in urban than rural areas nearly everywhere; there is also considerable evidence that urban children are better fed than their rural counterparts (see World Resources Institute, 1996: p. 10).

---

[42] This claim, however, does not have clear empirical support. Lipton's thesis implies that urbanization could easily stunt rural development, a proposition at variance both with neoclassical spatial economics and Loschian central place theory. Shukla (1996: Chap. 10) relates rural *nonfarm* employment across districts in Maharashtra to local urbanization, and finds a fairly strong positive connection, even controlling for measures of rural infrastructure, capital, credit access, value of crop production, and Government rural development expenditures. It is difficult to read her work without getting the sense that at least secondary cities spark rather than stifle rural development opportunities.

But how can price and expenditure bias be measured? The measure of price bias employed in some empirical studies is the ratio of local to world prices for farm products. This measure has three serious problems. First, it does not account for any price bias favoring urban-produced products. Second, as Timmer (1993) points out, domestic prices for commodities tend to change less—and less frequently—than do international prices; thus, much of the variation in this ratio results from changes in international market conditions (including variation in exchange rates), not from conscious governmental policy decisions. Third, the mere existence of price controls on agricultural output does not necessarily lower agricultural incomes, since these controls can often be side-stepped by farmers who sell their produce in black markets (Bates, 1993: p. 227). Furthermore, as Braverman and Kanbur (1987) illustrate, general equilibrium effects of price distortions may completely reverse the partial equilibrium effects. Expenditure bias is no easier to measure, since without a well-specified social welfare function there is no clear reason to prefer one spatial distribution of expenditure over another on welfare grounds. Indeed, given certain conditions, urban bias may be the socially optimal policy.[43]

Given these severe measurement problems, the major contribution of this literature is not to produce a precise measure of bias; rather, it is to focus attention on the fact that macroeconomic and sectoral policies shape urbanization patterns. In a distortion- and externality-free economy, urbanization must be welfare-improving, since it reflects the utility-maximizing behavior of rational economic agents. In such an environment, the optimal city size—much discussed in the urban economics literature—is whatever size results from the maximizing behavior of individual agents. Urban-biased policies introduced by governments probably have led to more rapid urban growth than would otherwise have been the case.[44]

"Overurbanization" per se is not the problem, though; the problem is urban-biased policies which respect neither static nor dynamic comparative advantage, and consequently imply efficiency losses for countries that pursue them. Indeed,

---

[43] Arnott and Gersovitz (1986), for example, build a model in which urban-biased expenditure is socially optimal, because some public goods (e.g., education, medical care and electricity) are more costly to provide in rural than in urban areas. Note, however, that different models would give quite different results. A model which included congestion and pollution costs in urban areas, for example, would generate an optimal policy rule involving rural expenditure bias.

[44] Although, as Williamson (1988: p. 442) points out, no studies have documented empirically the link between urban-biased policies and faster urbanization. Malpezzi's (1990) efforts to link urban growth to a measure of price distortion found virtually no correlation, a finding consistent with Becker and Morrison (1988). In addition, urban-biased policies need not always attract more migrants to the city. Policies that artificially raise urban firms' profitability by subsidizing capital may result in less labor demand, not more.

perhaps the healthiest approach to the topic is the political economy rational choice approach taken by Bates (1993) and, though couched in terms of social class competition, Lipton (1993). They see the underlying problem as that of unequal political power, especially in nondemocratic, nonpluralistic polities. In this setting, the transition from urban-biased policies characteristic of developing societies to rural-biased policies prevalent in advanced capitalist economies can be explained by shifting political power (and coalitions), as well as declining costs in meeting infrastructure and other needs of rural communities.

## 3.3. Special problems of (ex)-socialist countries

A large proportion of people inhabiting the world's poorer countries live in countries which experienced prolonged periods of communist rule. According to Population Reference Bureau (1997), some 1.733 billion people live in current or former communist states; this number accounts for 37% of the 4.666 billion inhabitants of the "less developed" world. While the economic aspects of communism are in various stages of abandonment, the legacy continues to exert a profound impact.

Urbanization has been a quite different experience under communism, which has also given rise to urban patterns and problems dissimilar to those in economies even with mild market orientations. The critical distinction is not that urban growth has been abnormally slow, although it has been in Vietnam and China until recently, but rather the manner in which it has been formed and channeled. The communist structure has also greatly influenced post-communist patterns. This section will examine first the former Soviet Union and then turn to China; for reasons of space, eastern Europe, Indochina and Cuba will not be discussed.

### 3.3.1. Urbanization in the former USSR
Soviet urbanization was reasonably rapid, and followed necessarily from the regime's determination to industrialize rapidly. Agricultural collectivization also generated population concentration in rural areas, so that much of the rural Soviet Union had densely settled towns and villages.

The collapse of the Soviet Union accelerated and accentuated several demographic tendencies already underway. The most important of these are declining life expectancy, especially among men, and the appearance of shocking middle-aged male mortality rates. At the same time, fertility has declined, dramatically so in the ethnically Slavic regions. After peaking at 2.2 during the early Gorbachev years, Russian total fertility rates (TFRs) declined to about 1.35 in 1995 (Andreev et al., 1997: p. 43); in much of the former USSR, crude death rates also exceed crude birth rates. While immigration to Russia from other republics of the former USSR has roughly maintained its population thus far, Andreev et al.'s projected population declines in the next 30 years range from 2 to 32 million, depending on the demographic scenario employed. Becker and Hemley's (1998) simulations based on demo-economic forecasts give little reason to adopt the less pessimistic scenario, barring a miraculous economic recovery.

Nor are these projected population declines likely to be evenly distributed. Andreev et al.'s "medium" projections are for an overall 1995–2025 population decline in Russia of 10.9%. While not broken down by rural and urban areas, the largest declines are for the heavily urbanized Northwest ($-20.6\%$), Central ($-22.7\%$), Volga-Vyatsk ($-15.4\%$) and Ural ($-13.5\%$) regions. Although TFRs in cities like Moscow and St. Peterburg are very low (1.01 for St. Petersburg: see Safarova (1996)), it appears likely that inmigration spurred by their economic recovery will ensure population growth.[45] Rather, the greatest population losses are likely in: (1) northern and far east industrial cities (ASW (1997: p. 27) report that 15% of the population left Magadan oblast in 1994 alone); (2) defense cities such as Novosibirsk, St. Petersburg and Ekaterinburg, where demand for core products has vanished; and (3) heavy industrial "company towns", that produced goods uneconomically or for which demand has collapsed.

Ethnic-based migration began in a significant way during the mid-1980s, when the first decentralization of Soviet power was accompanied by growing regional nationalism. It accelerated following the break-up of the Soviet Union, and was especially great in the republics on the periphery of the Soviet Union. Unsurprisingly, outmigration was greatest from the heavily ethnically Russian large cities of these republics. In Kazakstan (United Nations Development Programme, 1996: Chap. 3), ethnic Slavs, Germans and Tartars make up 90% of emigrants.

Nor is this emigration unique to countries like Kazakstan and Uzbekistan, where strongly nationalistic policies are being imposed. The capital of the Kyrgyz Republic, Bishkek, saw its population decline from 640 thousand in 1992 to 594 thousand in 1995, a loss of 7.3% of the total population (and 14% of the Russian and 63% of the German populations, respectively: see Natskomstat, 1995).

---

[45] The process will nonetheless be traumatic. Safarova's (1996) simulations for St. Petersburg for the period 1995–2005 indicate a 5.2% population decline for St. Petersburg under an *optimistic* scenario. But this decline occurs almost entirely among children under 15 (indeed, the elderly population continues to grow), who are projected to fall by 32%, and hence from 19% to 13% of the population.

*Kazakstan emigration, 1993–1995.*

|  | 1993 | 1994 | 1995 | 1996 |
|---|---|---|---|---|
| Net emigration/thousand population | 13.2 | 24.5 | 14.4 | 10.6 |
| ethnic Russians | 20.3 | 42.7 | 22.5 | 17.1 |
| ethnic Ukrainians | 19.1 | 38.5 | 21.1 | 16.0 |
| ethnic Germans | 128.4 | 160.2 | 190.5 | 147.0 |
| Population change: urban Kazakstan (000) |  | −161 | −72 |  |
| net births |  | 34 | 18 |  |
| net population movement |  | −195 | −90 |  |
| Population change: rural Kazakstan |  | −33 | −43 |  |
| net births |  | 80 | 65 |  |
| net population movement |  | −113 | −108 |  |

Throughout the communist world, governments sought to control population movements via an internal passport and residence authorization systems. The Soviet permit (*propiska*) system was declared unconstitutional in the waning days of the Soviet period (Willikens and Scherbov, 1995: p. 215), but in much if not most of the ex-Soviet Union it remains in force today. It is generally agreed that this system did not control urbanization, although it undoubtedly did divert population from Moscow and other elite cities, and, of course, had unjust and devastating consequences for many individuals. Its general impact was not to absolutely prevent movement of people, but to raise the effective price for large numbers, creating a dualistic urban population structure, divided into those with formal residency privileges, and those who had to pay for housing and other services. In the post-Soviet period, the *propiska* system has weakened, and the advantages conferred by having residence authorization have gradually declined, so that one would expect considerable migration in response to the past disequilibrium. Such a pattern may take some time to emerge, however. As Shakhotko (1996: pp. 132–133) finds in her exceptionally informative study of Belarus, net rural-urban migration there has declined dramatically, falling from over 70,000 in 1988 to less than 8000 in 1995—a pattern reflecting soaring urban unemployment, growing poverty, and privatization of the housing market (forcing newcomers to pay market prices for apartments). Thus, despite falling birthrates (and hence a natural population decline of 1.1%), the rate of population decline in rural Belarus has actually slowed, while urban population growth, despite a natural population increase of 0.5% in 1995, has virtually stagnated, since international emigration offsets inmigration.

At the same time, deteriorating urban living conditions and job opportunities appear to have given rise to net urban outmigration to rural areas (Willikens and Scherbov, 1995: p. 217). This pattern is clearly noticeable during the period initially following the collapse of the Soviet Union; whether it has continued in more recent years as urban food supplies have improved remains to be seen.

Soviet housing policies were dictated by the principal that investments should go first to industry and defense, leading to appalling crowding and low quality throughout the Soviet period. Populist efforts to construct more mass housing began under Khrushchev and were followed by the construction of sturdier but depressingly homogeneous and seemingly endless apartment complexes on the outskirts of large Soviet cities during the Brezhnev era. The construction spurt at the end of the Gorbachev era was marked by deteriorating standards as the economy weakened.

Because housing was in chronically short supply and was tied to one's job, labor mobility was severely constrained throughout the Soviet period. So was urban fertility: based on cross-oblast regressions, Becker and Hemley (1998) have estimated that an increase in 15 $m^2$ of living space (a one-third increase in mean urban apartment size) would lead to an extra birth per household.

Failure to allocate land via a market mechanism also led to growth of Soviet cities in concentric rings, with vast amounts of unused land throughout the city. A very low proportion of built-up area is used for residential land. In contrast, vast amounts of even the largest cities are used for industrial sites (31.5% of Moscow, as compared with 5% of Paris) and railroad lines. In large part due to the absence of an efficient land market, obsolete industrial areas rather than residential areas dominate land use just beyond the city center. Because housing construction is determined by enterprise wealth and success in obtaining space, *housing and land consumption per person do not decrease exponentially with distance from the city center*. Residential densities do tend to fall, but not consistently, with distance from the center (Bertaud and Renaud, 1994; Bertaud and Kolko, 1994).

Such patterns obviously add to infrastructure costs, especially in a society where urban heating and hot water is centrally generated and then piped to apartment complexes throughout the city. Excellent but very costly metro lines in many large cities have enabled population dispersal, but further growth will require further large infrastructure investments.

There are indications that market forces are beginning to have an impact in the post-Soviet era. Maddala et al. (1993) examined Moscow land price gradients, and found that they were becoming increasingly steep over time. With the privatization of housing stock, emergence of significant private housing construction, and the growing disassociation of housing from employment, normal rent gradients seem likely to emerge in the former Soviet Union. On the other hand, mechanisms for land transfer remain seriously stunted, as do efforts to recover the costs of social infrastructure provided by local governments.[46]

There is certainly evidence of rapidly appreciating property values in real terms in desirable areas of major cities (for example, see Kaganova and Berezin, 1993). Indeed, it seems likely that these prices exceed long run equilibrium values, since increases in the housing stock remain constrained, albeit now more by the tiny new levels of housing construction and existing shortages rather than by prohibition of housing sale and transfer.

### 3.3.2. Urbanization in the People's Republic of China

China offers a fascinating contrast, as it is characterized by a rapidly growing economy proceeding from a much less developed and more rural base. Like the USSR, China sought to control its population via an internal passport system—in this case, by issuance of urban "grain ration" cards. But economic growth here has led to pressure for an urban explosion rather than to dying industrial cities, as in the former Soviet Union.

China's economic and regional policies have been characterized by dramatic lurches (for a summary, see Young and Deng, 1997). During and prior to the Great Leap Forward (1958–1960), public policy focused on industrialization and hence on urbanization. Food shortages in the early 1960s caused a shift to an "agriculture first" policy, during which 20 million urban residents were sent to the countryside. They were joined by another 30 million during the anti-urban Cultural Revolution years 1966–1976. The Four Modernizations program that commenced in 1978 ushered in a period of rapid agricultural and industrial growth, along with a growing market orientation; unsurprisingly, urban growth has accelerated since then.

Given these political lurches, China's urbanization rate grew from roughly 13% in the mid-1950s to 20% in 1960, then declined to 17% during the cultural revolution period, and has since recovered to 26–27% (Young and Deng, 1997). These, and indeed all aggregate numbers for China should be viewed as approximate, however, since Chinese definitions of "cities" and "towns" are politically-based, and also changed radically in 1984. The broad patterns are

---

[46] As of 1989, only 2.5% of Soviet household incomes were devoted to apartment rents or "communal services" (Renaud, 1993: p. 15). Comparable figures elsewhere in eastern Europe ranged from 1.0% in Romania to 7.1% in Hungary.

quite clear, though, as is the fact that urbanization has been forcefully suppressed in China.[47]

The fascinating finding by Young and Deng (1997), however, is that the political regime did not matter directly. Rather, estimating a disequilibrium model of supply and demand for urban labor, they find that food supplies have been the critical determinant of urban growth (and these, of course, have been greatly influenced by political policies). They find as well that agricultural sector constraints rather than industrial demand have been the driving force in population movements throughout the communist period; the real achievement of the Deng era, in that light, has been to create agricultural surpluses sufficient to enable rapid urban and industrial growth.

The emphasis in recent years on rural industrialization and spatial decentralization (following, and at times inconsistent with another policy of favoring coastal cities) has resulted in the surging growth of new urban areas.[48] Migration patterns have been affected in curious ways as well. Zhu (1996) examines rural outmigration at the household level, and most of the results for China are unexceptional.[49] But migration is actually more likely for people who are registered as agricultural workers; even though they cannot hope for an urban grain card, they also have even more relatively constrained opportunities at home. Goldstein et al. (1991) find that migration to Shanghai (based on the 1984 Shanghai Floating Population Study), arguably the most desirable location in China, is mainly

---

[47] The most definitive account of the roles of reclassification and rural-urban migration in affecting Chinese urban population growth is given by Goldstein (1990). The 1987 1% National Survey reported an increase in China's urban population share from 20.6% in 1982 to 46.6% in 1987 according to Goldstein (1990), and from 20.8 to 36.9% according to Yi and Vaupel (1989); the 1990 Census, however, reported an urban share of only 26.4% (see Chang (1994)). Despite the presence of a large unregistered population, this smaller figure seems more plausible (World Bank 1997 estimate for 1995 is 30%). The 1984 reclassification led to an increase in the "agricultural" population of cities from 33% in 1982 to 50% in 1987, indicating that many of the new urbanites were in fact peasants—although, of course, many people designated as "agricultural" were engaged in urban services and manufacturing. Nonetheless, as Goldstein terms it, there undoubtedly has been a "ruralization" of China's cities. An extreme case is that of "the newly created city of Zibo, in Shandong Province ...Zibo's 1987 population of 2.4 million was 66% agricultural .... These 2.4 million are all counted as part of China's 1987 urban population defined by residence within city boundaries". (Goldstein, 1990: p. 677). Ma (cited in Ma and Fan, 1994: p. 1640) estimates that boundary enlargement accounted for 49.5% of 1982–1987 urban population growth, and migration accounted for 46.3%—but that urban population grew by only 46 million, a figure vastly different from the increases reported by Goldstein of 116 million in cities and 181 million in towns for the same period.

[48] Perhaps even more than Soviet planners, Chinese planners have been taken by notions of growth poles and leading regions. Since the Deng era, special economic zones have also been in favor; in effect, this gives a rationale for favored treatment to coastal regions.

[49] Zhu (1996) finds that the likelihood of migration is greater for men; it rises with education, number of relatives in the city, family size and per capita income, land ownership (an asset measurement), and the level of village socioeconomic development; it rises and then falls with age; it declines with the household dependency ratio, marriage, the number of people engaged in farming, and the extent of village industrialization.

for reasons other than immediate employment. Most "temporary" or "floating" migrants to Shanghai are in fact long-term, and were related to household heads already in Shanghai. Reunion with family, education and urban amenities were more important than work; only about 30% of Shanghai's temporary migrants were in the 15–34 year age group.[50] Indeed, much of the growth in Shanghai's labor force comes from workers who live in nearby rural communities and commute. This "pendulum population" is important throughout China's large cities (see, for example, Ma and Fan, 1994), who report that 27.6% of the *daytime* urban population of Jiangsu Province consists of rural workers who commute mainly by bicycle).[51] Corroborating evidence for China as a whole based on the 1995 1% survey is provided by Zhang et al. (1997).

Thus, even more than in the post-Soviet Union, urban segmentation is emerging in response to ineffective population movement control. Vast differences in welfare exist between favored urban dwellers, in terms of incomes, social services, and secure access to food supplies.[52] Rural inequality is also striking, as restricted factor movements prevent intrasectoral as well as intersectoral equalization. In more prosperous regions, households have the ability to fund part-time or permanent urban job searches by otherwise productive adults, and the result has been the creation of a vast "floating" or "temporary" urban population. No one knows just how large this is (see Henderson, 1988; Goldstein, 1990; Wang, 1994; Chan and Yang, 1997); Wang reports that it may account for 20% of total urban employment; figures of 80–100 million are commonly given (Chan and Yang, 1997). As Cai (1997) documents for Shandong province, nearly two-thirds of migrants are self-employed, or work in private or collective enterprises; two-thirds of workers with urban residency permits work for state enterprises. There is general agreement, however, that this unregistered population has grown

[50] Restricted migration, young workers confined largely to members of the "pendulum population", and low fertility rates imply that populations of cities like Shanghai (where TFRs have ranged from 1.1–1.3 for the past 20 years) will age very rapidly in the years to come. Chen et al. (1997) forecast that by 2025, one-third of Shanhai's population will be over 60 years of age.

[51] Both these workers and migrants to Jiangsu's towns appear to be motivated overwhelmingly by work prospects. Ma and Fan's regression analysis based on a survey of 190 towns in Jiangsu Province indicates that land scarcity is an important push factor, while employment prospects in township and village enterprises (TVEs) are the major attraction – especially as this employment does not require state approval. The combination of greater stringency in state control of large cities and explosive TVE employment growth has led to more rapid growth of China's towns and smaller cities than its largest cities in recent years, even discounting definitional changes.

[52] Oi (1993) reports a mean urban:rural income ratio of 2.42 for China, well above many other east Asian countries. Beyond wages, she also reports that subsidies account for 39% of Chinese urban income (Oi, 1993: p. 144).

greatly in recent years, causing recent urbanization and urban growth rates to be understated.[53]

But even given this understatement, the limited extent of rural-urban migration since the 1978 reforms until the 1990s remains striking. The 1987 1% survey, which asked migration questions for the first time, found that only 30.5 million people moved residences in the preceding five years, implying that an annual permanent migration rate of only 0.6% (Ma and Fan, 1994: p. 1630)— and, in their study of Jiangsu Province, they find that only 48% of these migrants are from villages to towns or cities). The 1990 national census also collected migration information, as did the 1988 Two Per Thousand Fertility Survey, that covered the floating population as well. This latter survey enabled Liang and White (1996) to infer interprovincial migration rates as far back as 1950, and confirms low long distance mobility (the 1965–1984 average gross migration rate was 0.3%). This rate rose to 0.43% in the latter half of the 1980s, while 1985–1988 gross inmigration rates for economically surging destinations such as Sichuan (9.7%), and Shandong (8.0%) were much higher.[54] Liang and White also confirm the virtually universal pattern that young adults have the highest propensity to move: the distinguishing feature of China has not been migration motive, but rather its government's ability to suppress much of the drive. Figures from the 1995 1% survey, however, indicate an acceleration in rural-urban (city and town) migration: the data from Zhang et al. (1997) imply an annual net inmigration rate of 1.45% for 1990–1995. Chan and Yang (1997), however, argue that the floating population has probably risen from about 50 million in 1990 to 90 million in 1995, implying a gross urban inmigration rate of about 2.4%, and a net inmigration rate of about 1%.[55]

---

[53] Recent migrants, primarily of the floating variety, also differ from base populations (and probably earlier migration streams) in terms of gender, especially to towns. Historically, male workers were allowed to move place of employment, but could not take their families out of rural areas. This restriction was relaxed with respect to towns in 1984; the 1982–1987 sex ratio (100*females/males) of town migrants was only 81, as compared with a sex ratio of 107 for migrants to cities, and a base town population sex ratio of 116 (Goldstein, 1990).

[54] However, the 1987 1% National Survey (which defined residents as those who reported having lived in a location for more than six months, or who had official registration) indicates that 80% of migrants move *intraprovincially* (Goldstein, 1990). This inclusive survey finds that 1982–1987 net migration to cities was 5.8 million, and to towns was 7.2 million. These imply annualized inmigration rates of 0.8% for cities and 2.3% for towns, respectively, using base populations (which one recalls are vastly different than terminal populations because of definitional changes). These data suggest that migration to towns has been an important phenomenon (and has probably increased in the 1990s). Migration from cities to the countryside is rare, since it would entail potential loss of urban registration, itself a valuable asset.

[55] One should not discount the possibility that these large estimates are nonetheless vast underestimates. Rawski and Mead (1998) discount census figures and official data on agricultural labor force, and in place construct estimates of farm employment based on crop area and estimated labor inputs, by province. Their

Some of China's urban problems are similar to the Soviet ones; others are not. Like the Soviet Union, much Chinese urban land was not allocated by any market or efficiency-based principles, although a much larger proportion of new growth involves costly land acquisition in China. As in the Soviet Union, China starved its cities of infrastructure and, until recently, such infrastructure as was constructed was planned and implemented by the central government. This policy greatly constrained urban growth. In the past two decades, however, significant decentralization of power has enabled local governments to undertake infrastructure projects of their own.[56] Their response to decentralization of authority and responsibility has become gradually more effective. Initially, much land was handed out virtually freely (for a detailed study of Shenzhen, see Zhu, 1994); unsurprisingly, the consequences were local government revenue shortages, excess demand for land, and low utilization rates of new allocations. Indeed, in Shenzhen, industrial land "hoarded" exceeded industrial land developments around 1990; obviously, incentives for corruption in such a system were enormous. Need for local government revenues and aversion to giving land to foreign investors, however, today appear to be generating price-based land allocation systems in at least part of China.

Oi (1993) argues that relative rural living standards have risen with economic liberalization, especially at the outset of the reforms, as they were felt first in the countryside. This rural growth does not signify movement away from an "urban bias", however—indeed, she does not perceive a deliberate bias toward cities or countryside, but rather a need by the Chinese Communist Party to maintain a prosperous and complacent urban population. Rather, the "bottom-up" revenue-sharing system and abandonment of the compulsory unified grain procurement system (because by 1983–1984, record harvests depressed market prices below the state price) generated an environment of local autonomy and relaxation of rural controls. Pressed for revenues, local governments pushed the development of "township and village enterprises" (TVEs) rather than agricultural expansion, however, leading to exceptionally rapid growth of industries in rural China. Thus, despite decollectivization, net income from grain production appears to have

---

figures, and similar Chinese ones, suggest that 75–100 million fewer people are employed in agriculture than the 330 million reported for 1993. Official data at the same time appear to markedly undercount employment in construction, transport, and trade, both rural and urban. Moreover, some "rural" areas may well have sufficiently high densities of nonagricultural activities that they would be more accurately classified as urban.

[56] As Wang (1994) details, local governments have responded by requiring developers to provide "rent-in-kind" as they build new factories or housing. The ultimate incidence of such quasi-taxes is hard to determine, since government officials grant rent-generating privileges to developers at the same time, and since many construction projects are contracted on a cost-plus basis. One clear consequence is that it provides local officials with a powerful reason to encourage local growth, since existing enterprises and households cannot be similarly taxed.

fallen during 1984–1988 by perhaps 15% (Oi, 1993: p. 135), while by 1988 the majority of *rural* output was industrial rather than agricultural, and 24 percent of the rural labor force was employed in TVEs. To reiterate, it is clear that "rural" and "urban" designations in the Chinese contexts have quite different meanings than elsewhere.

Chinese cities are not as residentially decentralized as post-Soviet ones, partly because of lower industrialization and greater land pressure, but mainly because commuting methods (mainly bicycles) necessitate higher densities and proximities to jobs. Consequently, as Bertaud and Kolko (1994) note, Chinese cities have structures similar to those in market economies, though for quite different reasons.[57]

A distinct feature of Chinese development, continued in the reform era, has been the relative autarky of its provinces. Due partly to poor interregional infrastructure, partly in reaction to national pricing policies which sought to achieve "primitive socialist accumulation" (in Preobrazhenkii's words) by extracting surpluses from the producers of primary products, partly in reaction to self-sufficiency drives, and partly because of trade and factor movement restrictions (Cai, 1997), China's regions and cities are far less integrated than one would expect.[58] In consequence, cities are also less specialized (Henderson, 1988a): in contrast, Soviet cities were probably overly specialized.

As China continues to develop rapidly, it seems likely that its overall urbanization and urban structure will increasingly resemble those of other poor but rapidly industrializing market economies. Economic growth will not remove all of the existing inefficiencies, but it will make their consequences less pronounced.

## 4. Selected urban challenges: land use, transportation, public finance and environment

### 4.1. Urban land use and land markets

In discussing urbanization in the transforming world, one usually thinks of labor market models and imperfections, and occasionally of capital markets. Yet the impressionistic evidence is that the greatest market failures actually occur with

---

[57] Like Soviet enterprises, Chinese enterprises have incentives to appropriate as much land as possible, however. Wang (1994: p. 279) reports that, in consequence, some 19% of total urban land in Guangzhou City lay idle. More recent imposition of land fees has caused some reduction in idle holdings, but these fees do not generally reflect full opportunity costs.

[58] Growing autonomy has not reversed the situation; rather, many regions have erected protectionist barriers against producers from other provinces (Wang, 1994: p. 270).

respect to land. This section focuses strictly on the problems associated with land use imperfections: housing issues are the subject of Malpezzi's work (Chapter 44, this volume).

To start with, governments' roles in urban land markets tend to be terribly confused. Justifiable rationale for government intervention are to correct market failures, to compensate for externalities, or to achieve welfare redistribution (for a nice statement, see Dowell and Clarke (1991)). But while there is much need on all three counts, government interventions are rarely welfare enhancing: on the contrary, there is substantial evidence that in much of the world, they make all three problems worse.

Even in the absence of government intervention, urban land markets suffer from severe problems. Perhaps most critical is an *absence of well-defined property rights* for households and businesses. In many transforming economies, multiple property right systems coexist simultaneously in an ill-defined manner. Formal (Western) property registration is often restricted to upper income housing and formal sector enterprises; it may coexist with traditional, indigenous systems (sometimes codified legally), and almost certainly much housing and small businesses will be governed by extra- or semi-legal arrangements which, nonetheless, have fairly widespread acceptance.

Somewhat surprisingly, the economist's obvious answer to the problem of ill-defined property rights (register everything quickly and clearly) is not always appropriate. Formal land registration is expensive, especially if done precisely, and may be perceived by many as a mechanism for alienating them from their land and dwellings. Management design strategists suggest that adding more legal authorization to existing semi-official institutions for resolving disputes and authorizing these bodies to define titles and property rights to units when owners wish to sell will have more relevance and be more readily accepted.

A thorough survey of urban land policies is provided in Farvacque and McAuslan (1992). They detail the painfully difficult journey toward legal property status which ends up effectively excluding all those without considerable resources and patience. They also discuss several reasons for unclear land titling and the absence of straightforward policies (beyond self-interested supply restrictions by powerful officials). Skilled labor constraints surely matter: legal systems in many countries are nearly paralyzed by excess demand, and at the same time government capacity is often severely limited. Centralized management in much of the developing world adds to skill constraints by requiring the involvement of many layers in making land use (or other) decisions. Registration and development authorization thereby becomes needlessly time consuming and civil servant labor-intensive. Complex and contradictory laws subject to sporadic enforcement add to difficulties, as do weak, small-scale capital markets. Unless one has a great deal to gain by formal authorization and has considerable resources to wield, the consequence is likely to be failure to obtain the required authorization— necessitating recourse to informal means of acquisition. But manufacturing and construction enterprises thus constrained are also unlikely to grow beyond a modest size, thereby restricting economic growth of potentially dynamic firms. The powerful and well-connected, on the other hand, will be tempted to seek "special" authorizations and concessions, thus circumventing the impractical formal process.

Poorly defined property rights and ill-designed government interventions are astonishingly costly. *Poorly defined property rights ensure that lower value structures are constructed, thereby reducing densities, which in turn increase total urban space requirements, consequently raising unit infrastructure costs, increasing commuting costs and diverting land from other valued uses.* This problem is especially acute in Africa (where up to one third of urban households engage in some farming: see Becker et al., 1993), but is pervasive elsewhere as well.[59] Just how great the costs of misallocated land and uncertain property rights are is difficult to determine, and a comprehensive study remains to be done. Dowall and Clarke (1991: p. 2) cite a World Bank estimate that land use and housing restrictions cost Malaysia about 3% of its GDP annually, and Malaysia is hardly the worst offender—nor are all of the costs enumerated in this section included in that study. Data from Kampala, Uganda indicate that in 1992, some 56% of total city land was devoted to agriculture (Maxwell, 1995); moreover, since only 20% of urban farmers owned the land they tended, input utilization and crop choice were suboptimal. Moreover, because of the dependence of the poor on urban farming for food supplements (and in Kampala there is a strong linkage between urban farming and nutritional status of children in lower income classes), efficiency-oriented measures may have disastrous social consequences.

As Aina's (1992) study of Lagos finds, the exact implications of a given mix of land tenure laws tend to be complicated. Nigeria sought to merge colonial and customary legal practices in the Land Use Act of 1978, which, not surprisingly, was virtually inaccessible to the poor. Its practical consequences seem to be to

---

[59] Rakodi's (1988) study of Zambia reports similar figures, and also that in some squatter areas, roughly 75% of squatter households have plots. While the income from household plots only amounted to 10–15% of food budgets, these savings were important for the poor. Maxwell (1995) in his study of Kampala, Uganda, found that 35% of households engaged in agricultural production. As in Zambia, urban farming in Uganda is overwhelmingly done by women in order to enhance food security; only 2.5% of Kampala's farmers were commercially oriented. Maxwell's study also finds that the likelihood of farming *rises* with a household's length of residence in the city: it is not an activity particularly associated with recent migrants, who in fact are likely to lack access to convenient plots.

add legal authority to the already considerable power of landlords in poor neighborhoods, which in turn has brought additional tenure insecurity to low income neighborhoods. In cities with rapid economic change but still incomplete property rights, landowners may find it useful to permit high density but impermanent housing on large tracts until they develop the land for "formal sector" purposes. This pattern is not inherently inefficient; rather, the inefficiency arises because land markets are not well enough established to permit lower income groups to obtain long-term contracts. As the landlord is, in effect, the enforcing agent as well, there is no mechanism that permits poor tenants to enter into long term contracts with confidence. One therefore finds scattered neighborhoods of very high housing density and very low quality, even though total urban density is likely to be inefficiently low.

Jimenez (1985) develops a model of land tenure choice that incorporates the cost that insecure tenure imposes on urban squatters. In his model, both squatting and nonsquatting households maximize an indirect utility function which contains income and the price of housing. Squatters have two possible budget constraints: one if they maintain possession of their land, and the other if they are evicted by the landowner. If they are evicted, they face the additional costs of moving and obtaining housing in the formal sector. Squatters maximize expected utility, which is a weighted average of the utility they will obtain in the two states of the world (eviction and no eviction), where the weight is given by the probability of eviction. Squatters are able to lower the probability of eviction by engaging in (costly) community organization.

A second model by Hoy and Jimenez (1991) formalizes the disincentive to improvements in housing stock caused by insecure tenure. The model provides insight into squatters' decisions whether or not to improve their dwellings and landlords' decisions whether or not to evict squatters. In this model, the stylized sequence of events is:

> (1) Squatters invade a plot of land. (2) The landowner chooses a value of deterrence activity (to deter investment in housing stock, since a more valuable housing stock is more expensive to remove) and a ... rate of eviction. (3) Squatters choose a level of housing stock conditional on the cost of eviction and the expected eviction rate. (4) The state of the world is realized. (5) The landowner implements his eviction rate (Hoy and Jimenez, 1991: pp. 82–83)

The principal implication of this model is that the Coase theorem is not appropriate in the case of squatter settlements.[60]

Not surprisingly, the market price of squatter dwellings is lower than that of equivalent dwellings with secure land tenure. Using data from a sample of metro Manila households, Friedman et al. (1988) find that an average squatter dwelling would sell for 23% more if it had tenure security.[61] This finding has an important policy implication: governments can create wealth for the poor simply by providing secure land tenure.

Three superb papers on Jakarta (Bertaud, 1989; Dowall and Leaf, 1990; Ferguson, 1992) provide a detailed analysis of the spatial consequences of land use policies there. As in Lagos, areas of very high density coexist with underutilized space in the core city (DKI Jakarta). A segmented housing market exists, in part because the process of titling land is extremely lengthy and quite expensive, if one considers the required bribes. But formal registration is necessary to undertake housing developments which can be funded by bank loans or whose occupants can get mortgages from the National Housing Bank. While poor neighborhoods and villages (kampungs) have benefitted considerably from public upgrading projects in the past decade, they generally remain outside the formal registration system, and tenure rights are much less secure than in the formal sector. As in Lagos, the result is to discourage housing investment—in effect, households and landlords substitute away from risky assets (unsecured housing) to safer investments.

Insecure property rights also mean residents do not tend to be reimbursed at full value for their land as it is acquired ("appropriated" might be more apt) for development. Naturally, there is a considerable value placed on secure tenure, as Dowall and Leaf find in their hedonic regressions for Jakarta.[62] Jakarta in the late 1980s was characterized by a very steep land price gradient relative to Bangkok, Karachi, Latin American or Western cities, largely due to poor road infrastructure. Close access to a major road increased property values by about Rp57, 429 m$^2$, or slightly more than 50%. Formal land titling further increased

---

[60] The Coase theorem implies that the "observed rate of evictions is just right. Evictions (would) occur only if the value of land use to squatters is less than the sum of the alternative development value to the landowner less the costs of evictions … since squatters would outbid any competing use of the land if indeed they valued it more" (Hoy and Jimenez, 1991: p. 79). The Coase Theorem fails because of significant imperfections in the market for land.

[61] Older squatter dwellings are valued more highly than newer ones, holding dwelling characteristics constant. Presumably age of dwelling is negatively correlated with eviction risk.

[62] Garr's (1996) study of squatting in a cemetery in central Java also finds that investments in these dwellings appears to rise with perceived security of tenure. Willingness to pay for metered water and electricity (quite possibly in part for the implicit property rights thereby conferred) also coincided with expansionary policies by the local public utilities, which appeared undeterred by clear lack of formal title.

property values by Rp22, 060 m$^2$ for low infrastructure and Rp32554 m$^2$ for high infrastructure land, or about 19.4% and 19.0%, respectively. Returns to secure title appear to be especially great at the city fringe, where kampungs are at greatest risk of being swallowed up. Given these empirical estimates, it seems obvious that formal land registration and improved road networks would be of great value to all classes. But titling would also restrict potential capital gains to developers, a far more influential group than kampung residents.

As Ferguson (1992: p. 12) discusses, the process of property development authorization in Indonesia further exacerbates land underutilization. Roughly, a developer submits a site plan and development schedule along with financial documentation. Once a development permit is granted, other developers cannot acquire and develop land in the permitted area without the consent of the original developer. Property owners on the site do not have to sell (though there is "national interest" pressure to do so, especially on those without formal title) to the redeveloper immediately, and, in practice, the process of conversion is often a lengthy one. This gradual acquisition means that much land will sit idle or in temporary uses for substantial periods while the developer amasses the financial means to buy out all initial holders.

To the social costs thus created must also be added the costs of delays due to the lengthy development approval process (2.67 years on average, according to Ferguson (1992: p. 27)), formal and "informal" fees, and costs due to restricted land supply. Ferguson's rough estimate is that all of these costs together inflate construction project costs by about 34% in DKI Jakarta. None of these comments should be taken as Indonesia-specific; Jakarta's patterns are typical rather than atypical of cities in transforming (and many industrialized) countries. Rather, the point here is that urban land policies have not contributed to poverty reduction.[63]

The literature on land use restrictions contains considerable recognition of their rationality from the point of view of those agents who impose them (see Dunkerley et al., 1980). As Tewari and Kumar (1986) note, the largest beneficiaries of Indian rent control laws are senior civil servants. Tewari and Kumar also suggest (but do not formally model) the possibility that rent controls may be efficient in a setting of limited government capacity. In their study of Bangalore, they find that eviction is difficult, but that both landlord and tenant have mutual threats, since the court system is paralyzed. Thus, the setting encourages landlord and tenant to create a cooperative game. Furthermore, the ease of bribing officials

---

[63] In general, Indonesia has been one of the most successful countries in the world in terms of combating dire poverty; land use policy just has not been one of the policy instruments employed.

and limited applicability of laws ensures that the expected net present value of rental payments under rent control need not be greatly restricted.

The inefficiencies of rent control arise in other areas. The system ensures considerable nominal price stickiness and locks people into housing for inefficiently long stays. Sticky nominal rents also discourage landlords from making repairs, and hence lead to accelerated housing stock deterioration. Potential arbitrariness of government officials adds as well to the riskiness of housing investment, thereby reducing total supply.

An issue periodically raised concerns government land banking (see Rivkin in Dunkerley et al., 1980; Farvarcque and McAuslan, 1992). Some governments have sought to acquire urban land in advance of development, with the aim of selling it off subsequently at low prices to users whose objectives are consistent with those of urban planners. Its main justification would be an absence of land and capital markets, though the presence of substantial government intervention here would seem to stunt development of the former. Land banking is obviously a tempting cover for favoritism and corruption; to our knowledge, no studies have been produced which attest to its efficacy. Hannah et al. (1993) provide a nice study of an extreme case, Korea. They looked at five "development projects" in which the government acquired (via eminent domain, but at market prices given existing zoning) sites, provided them with infrastructure and rezoned them according to a master plan, and then sold parcels off to developers. The discounted return to this activity for the government ranged from 70 to 550%—but the restrictive policies that make such returns possible are also responsible for creating an average annual real (CPI deflated) 1974–1989 land price increase of over 12% in Seoul.

It should be noted as well that not all market distortions have clear welfare impacts. Consider the case of lot size zoning restrictions, which are common in Pakistan and other countries. In an aspatial model, restrictions on land consumption by the wealthy will cause land prices to fall and raise welfare of the poor. But as Pasha (1992) elaborates, the consequences are indeterminate in a standard spatial model. If the wealthy live in or near the CBD, then lot restrictions will cause total city size to decline, lowering both commuting costs and rents paid by the poor. But if the wealthy live on the periphery, then restrictions will cause them to increasingly compete with the poor for central land, raising rents and commuting costs, and therefore lowering welfare of the poor.

Land use patterns are determined by more than conscious government policy; as Ingram and Carroll (1981) emphasize, they are also influenced by the age of the city and by transportation technology. Briefly, improved transport infrastructure and rising automobile ownership enable suburbanization—while rising incomes in transforming economies will lead to rapid growth of demand for residential space. Consequently, the traditional pattern in which high income groups are centrally located in the cities of transforming economies is gradually disappearing, while elite, low-density suburbs spring up. Similar decentralization over time is observed for Korean cities (Follain et al., 1979). They estimate land—nonland input substitution elasticities, find them to range from 0.41 to 0.67, and note that this implies decentralization and relatively rapid land price increases away from central areas as real income growth generates housing demand growth. Their model further implies that density gradients should respond less to urban growth when land's value share in total housing services is very high, as is the case in east Asia.

Employment decentralization appears to be accompanying residential decentralization as well, though the former remains more concentrated in CBDs. For example, Henderson et al. (1995b) find evidence of strong population decentralization for the Jakarta region metropolitan area from 1980 to 1990, which they attribute to massive population growth, dramatic transport improvements (though there is little doubt that Jakarta remains characterized by underinvestment in urban mass transit), conversion of residential to commercial land near the city center,[64] and rising real incomes. Manufacturing employment appears to have decentralized even more dramatically, though, as of 1986, only 43% of the metropolitan area's formal sector manufacturing employment was outside Jakarta city (DKI Jakarta) boundaries; by 1991, this figure had risen to 56%, and 73% of all corporate sector plant births in the metropolitan area were in suburban regions. In fact, during this five year period, employment density gradients roughly halved from $-0.35$ to $-0.19$; the emergence of manufacturing nodes on transport spokes and radial connections also caused the adjusted $R^2$ to fall from 0.38 to 0.08. In fact, spatial dispersal of manufacturing occurred simultaneously with spatial concentration in the region's 61 districts (*kecamatan*): the Hirschman–Herfindahl index rises from 0.53 to 0.58.

As discussed above in Section 3.3, some work has been done on the urban structure of nonmarket cities. In addition to socialist cities, there is also a literature on colonial cities (briefly surveyed in Becker et al., 1994). Porter's (1993) treatment of South African cities is unique to our knowledge in providing a formal economic model. As he describes it, "South African cities are inverted" in the sense that the rich live close to the CBD, while the poor endure small plots, poor infrastructure and services, *and* long commutes, since *apartheid* forced them to

---

[64] Henderson et al. (1995b) treat Jakarta as a circular city, and pinpoint the National Monument, Monas, as the city center. Results might have differed slightly had they regarded Jakarta as a semicircle and taken the port area and historic center, Kota, as the CBD.

the periphery. Nor, for that matter, is there any free-riding by the poor in the Tiebout sense of consuming public services but not fully bearing the cost via local taxes, since nearly perfect zoning is enforced. Rent gradients in the *apartheid* city decline, but only within racially homogeneous areas: in general, given total land constraints, unit land rents were higher in distant historically nonwhite areas than in white residential areas near the CBD.

With the initially gradual and then accelerating collapse of *apartheid*, spatial patterns have begun to change. White suburbanization began even prior to the end of *apartheid*, as growing white urban populations and increased automobile ownership simultaneously put pressure on expansion and provided the means for low cost commuting from distant suburbs. With the breakdown of *apartheid*, pressure for white (and wealthy nonwhite) suburbanization is enhanced, but removal of other spatial restrictions may generate substantial industrial suburbanization, possibly taking with it substantial nonwhite workers. Reductions in the fiscal independence of exclusive suburbs will decrease incentives for income-based racial segregation, though it may accelerate the development of very distant private enclaves. To some extent, the changes in South Africa are an extreme case of what has been happening elsewhere, as wealthy and politically powerful groups seek better living standards for themselves without having to pay for services for all, as the Tiebout model predicts. In the coming decade, South Africa's cities will lose many of their distinctive features; at the same time, spoke and radial freeway systems will help other large cities in transforming economies acquire some South African attributes in terms of increasingly effective economic segregation.

In concluding this section, it should be noted that ample evidence exists that land prices are growing very rapidly in the cities of successfully transforming economies. But the evidence does *not* indicate that land prices are growing at a systematically more rapid rate in the largest cities (see Ingram, 1980), although land prices are of course at a much higher level in big cities than in small ones. Nor, within large cities, does it appear that land prices are rising most rapidly in CBDs. On the contrary, Ingram's review of Korean and Colombian cities finds a tendency for land value gradients to decline over time in every city examined, dramatically in the case of Bogota.[65] Declining land price gradients are also a common finding in Dowall and Leaf's (1990) study of south Asian cities. In

---

[65] A detailed study of Bogota appears in Dowall and Treffeisen (1991). They focus in particular on the emergence of subcenters beyond the CBD. They also find a substantial elasticity of substitution between capital and land ($\sigma = 0.69$, which is toward the upper bound for estimates from the US), indicating considerable variation throughout the city in land use intensity. Dowall and Treffeisen find that a multicentric approach does not improve goodness-of-fit over a monocentric model when population density gradients are estimated, but that it does improve when land price gradients are examined.

most cases, this is driven by an expansion of urban infrastructure, which raises the value of land on the periphery of large cities and in smaller towns, thereby creating conditions favorable to urban decentralization.

## 4.2. Urban transport

Building transportation infrastructure is costly, and most transforming countries have tried to avoid huge outlays, with the exception of showcase projects. Intra- and intercity roads often have not received the attention warranted, leading to "excessive" concentration in favored major cities, and hindering urban decen- tralization. Until recently, many public transportation systems also were state- owned, so that general budget crunches meant deteriorating bus and rail services, regardless of the public's potential demand.

Urban transport problems probably have been greatest in the poorest coun- tries and in countries experiencing exceptionally rapid urban growth. In Africa, collapsing government capacity has meant minimal road repairs even in capital cities, resulting in slower traffic and more rapid vehicle deterioration (Becker et al., 1994). As noted above, unclear property rights have made African cities more decentralized than they otherwise would have been, thereby exacerbating urban transport demands and increasing commuting costs.

The consequences of inadequate transportation networks are several. *Poor in- tercity transportation* limits horizontal integration and urban specialization (see Henderson, 1988a with reference to China). Rural-urban migration is also de- terred, at least from distant areas. While policymakers are not generally unhappy with this outcome, it has the very negative consequence of preventing pockets of dire rural poverty from being eliminated (World Bank, 1988: p. 6). Furthermore, poor intercity transportation limits development of secondary cities, increasing the primacy of the city system.

*Poor intraurban transport infrastructure* has complex effects. In cities with weak road systems, the relatively wealthy tend to live in or near the CBD, leaving the poor to the unserviced periphery (and squatter areas throughout the city). In transforming country cities where road systems have improved (Jakarta and Abidjan are good examples), though, the wealthy appear to suburbanize quite rapidly. Poor roads make for long commuting times for the poor, and transport constraints must lock many workers, especially women, into informal activities which involve less commuting.

During the past 15 years, a large number of studies of urban transport prob- lems in transforming countries have been carried out, especially by the World Bank (see World Bank, 1986, 1988; also Transportation Research Board, 1997;

Barrett, 1988; Armstrong-Wright, 1986; Thomson, 1983). The problems are widely recognized and there seems to be a reasonable consensus with respect to policy prescriptions.

A set of World Bank studies of individual cities has provided important insights into the critical role of urban transport, and has outlined several low cost steps which can improve existing systems. Among the major stylized facts:

- Modal choice varies greatly across cities in the transforming world. Buses account for more than half of all trips (other than walking) in a Armstrong-Wright's (1986) study in 17 of 26 large cities in market transforming countries. Buses were the most important form everywhere save Amman (where private automobiles accounted for 44% of all trips, and "paratransit"—small passenger transport vehicles operating informally—accounted for 26%), Bogota (where rail/subway lines and buses each accounted for 34% of trips), Kuala Lumpur (automobiles accounted for 37%), Manila (paratransit accounted for 59%), and Nairobi (automobiles accounted for 45% of all trips). In China and Indochina, bicycling accounts for the majority of trips, and is also widespread in south Asia.

- Cost per passenger kilometre appears to vary more with quality of service and labor costs than with public/private ownership (though this is another inadequately researched topic, and Barrett (1988) finds that public companies have unit costs about twice that of private bus firms in west Africa). However, it is unambiguous that the revenue/cost ratio is far greater for private than for publicly owned bus companies across all continents (Armstrong-Wright, 1986: p. 46; Barrett, 1988).

- Rapid rail transit (subway or elevated rail) systems invariably fail to cover costs in transforming countries (and in nearly all industrialized nations). This mainly reflects staggering construction costs, especially of underground lines. Operating revenue as a fraction of total costs ranged from 19% for the Sao Paulo metro to 35% for the Caracas metro.

- In Asia and Latin America, the incidence of motorization is rising (as one would expect, since the income elasticity of demand almost certainly exceeds unity). The incidence is falling in much of Africa, however, as real incomes continue to decline. Virtually everywhere, motorization and private automobile ownership incidence is higher in capitals than in secondary cities. Traffic problems are considerably exacerbated by conflicting uses, and, in particular, large numbers of nonmotorized vehicles and street vendors competing with automobiles and motorcycles for scarce road space.

- In the absence of public transportation, most urban Africans must walk. As Barrett (1988: p. 3) notes, "those least able to afford public transportation are the ones that live furthest from the principal employment centers". Affordable transportation is thus closely linked to poverty traps in Africa, south Asia, and parts of Latin America. In large cities in transforming countries, 5–10% of household income is typically spent on transportation, and for the urban poor this figure can be even higher (15–16% in the Calcutta and New Delhi figures cited in World Bank, 1986: p. 7).

- Urban transport problems are greatest in the largest cities, since mean journey distance rises with size, as jobs and housing become more distant. Low densities in small cities mean that parking and congestion are minor problems, while people tend to live on or near a small number of main roads, which can be easily served by public transport. Densities and hence complexities rise disproportionately with city size; hence, so do expenditures on transportation. Nor is it surprising that urban transport problems are greater in lower income megacities, since dramatic solutions tend to be unaffordably expensive (World Bank, 1986), and since road space tends to be a smaller proportion of land area (Transportation Research Board, 1997). Estimates of regional GDP costs of traffic jams (which range from 0.4% in Seoul to 2.1% in Bangkok: see World Resources Institute, 1996: p. 25) show no clear pattern against per capita income, since wealthier cities have better transport infrastructure—but the lost time of commuters has higher value.

- Decentralization of large "megacities" to outlying areas and to secondary cities is inhibited largely by fears of inadequate transportation and other infrastructure (Hamer, 1984: p. 53). Decentralization of enterprises strongly follows expanded transportation networks virtually everywhere (Choe and Song, 1985: p. 41 provide a detailed discussion of this in the case of Seoul's manufacturing enterprises).

- Despite disincentives via high costs of commuting and at times poor residential services, suburbanization of higher income groups is becoming increasingly prevalent. Punpuing's (1993) study of commuting by employed people in Bangkok finds that predicted commuting time rises strongly with years of education (or home ownership, which is highly correlated with education and income) and age. Surprisingly, commuting length and time were not affected by gender. In effect, very high commuting costs in Bangkok appear to be offset by highly income elastic demand for environmental amenities that are found only on the outskirts of the city.

- Both intraurban and intercity transportation infrastructure is expensive, and a major drain on national budgets. Many cities devote 15–25% of their budgets to their transport systems (World Bank, 1986). Less construction-intensive urban transport investments, however, have extremely high rates of return (in the 25–75% range: Barrett (1988: p. 26)), even without fully accounting for positive externalities.

- There is significant scope for realizing cost recovery for government expenditures on urban transport systems. The main constraints, especially to user fees, but also to vehicle and fuel taxes, are political. *Demand management* steps such as higher vehicle and fuel taxes, road pricing, area licensing, and parking restraints have long been advocated for traffic control reasons as well. In contrast, *transport subsidies* tend to be self-defeating, as they imply greater excess demand, unsustainable budget deficits, and hence ultimately reduced public transport services.

- Throughout the transforming world, the highest return public investment activities regarding urban transport are those that raise the efficiency of bus services. Measures that improve private automobile efficiency have the lowest return (and are the most regressive).

- Poor financing structures mean chronic deficits and shortages for state-owned bus companies. This results in huge subsidies in wealthier nations, or bus systems in which a high proportion of the fleet lies idle for want of spare parts.

Several points of *road and traffic management* bear mention:

- Vehicle operating costs tend to be far greater than road construction and maintenance costs. Nevertheless, the lack of cost recovery now typical of most transforming countries ensures that publicly-provided infrastructure is not supported by the (mainly private) beneficiaries. Existing arrangements thus virtually guarantee underinvestment in road infrastructure. Moreover, maintenance typically suffers during recessions, so that road conditions tend to be worst in slowly growing or declining economies.[66]

- Urban road capacity can be enhanced in the short run by several inexpensive measures: improving maintenance, segregating different modes of transport, creating one-way street networks, integrating traffic signal schemes, and eliminating street trading are among the important steps here. Improved footpaths and sidewalks are also critical, since they keep pedestrians off roads. At least in much of Africa, inefficient road use rather than lack of capacity is the main cause of congestion (Barrett, 1988). These management steps are all far cheaper than new road construction but traffic and parking management require political determination.

---

[66] As World Bank (1988: p. 18) notes, private trucking or bus firms may not complain about poor roads, since the high depreciation rates which result also create barriers to entry from potential competitors.

- It should come as no surprise that traffic management steps actually taken often tend to come at the expense of the poor. Traffic flow in Jakarta has improved in the past decade, despite considerable growth in automobile ownership, following the banning of nonmotorized vehicles (bicycle-rickshaw *becaks* and pushcarts) and animals from the streets. A more egalitarian policy would have been to have restricted automobiles and encouraged more public buses, but this would have been at variance with Jakarta's new sophistication; moreover, such a noncar-friendly policy might have jeopardized the new express tollway and limited the market for a national car—projects both run by President Suharto's children.

- Enhancing bus and paratransit capacity and speeds implies improved maintenance, creation of high-speed express bus networks, upgraded bus transfer depots, construction of reserved bus lanes, and paving and drainage of primary roads to improve access to low income areas (Barrett, 1988: p. 17). Subsidized bicycle purchase schemes may also have merit.

- Ultimately, traffic and transportation demand management is integrally related to *land use management* and *automobile use policies*. The recommended design structure for megacities is one of a "regional polynucleated development pattern, with relatively high density outlying nodes connected to the center by high capacity road and bus service" (Transportation Research Board, 1997). Low density sprawl is difficult to serve other than by individual vehicles and invariably adds to mean commuting distances. Unfortunately, as we have seen, there are powerful forces working against efficient density levels in many countries. Indeed, developers rarely have to pay the associated infrastructure costs of new housing or other construction projects; since these costs are rarely recaptured in property taxes either, there is an effective government subsidy implied for new construction.

In short, in much of the transforming world, there are conditions that create transport demand above a socially efficient level. Worse, they coexist with other conditions that repress supply to inefficiently low levels. Worst of all, while socially efficient moves would help the poor, they lack political support in much of the transforming world; hence, more expensive and less efficient options tend to be undertaken.

### 4.3. Public finance and service provision

The existing level of public service provision is often quite low in transforming economies. For the countries the United Nations characterizes as "low human development", only 72% of urban residents had reasonable access to safe drinking water, while only 55% had access to sanitary means of excreta and waste disposal as of the early 1990s (United Nations, 1994: p. 149).

In any discussion of the provision of urban public services, an important question is, "Who is doing the providing?" Is it the central government, the municipal government, or private firms? The level of responsibility assumed by local governments for public service provisions varies greatly. Municipal governments in Bogota, Calcutta, Jakarta, Nairobi and Seoul have primary responsibility for water supply, sewerage, primary education, as well as highways and roads. In other cities, such as Tehran, Lagos, Lima and Kinshasa, municipal governments have few responsibilities.[67] Not surprisingly, given the varied responsibilities of local governments, the allocation of local expenditures across public services also varies enormously. Expenditures on water provision range from 5.7% of the municipal budget in Ahmadabad to 26.1% in Bogota; expenditures on education vary from 1.1% in Cali to 29.3% in Madras; other public services show equally large variation (Bahl and Linn, 1992: pp. 20–27).

Although the range of services provided varies greatly across cities, most local governments do generate the majority of revenue to finance local public services. Of the 22 municipal budgets examined by Bahl and Linn for the 1980s, only two (Gwangju, Korea and Tunis, Tunisia) had less than 50% of total expenditures financed with locally raised revenue; the mean share was 72%. These revenues are generated primarily through user charges, license fees and locally-collected taxes; the property tax is the most important revenue instrument. The share of locally-generated revenue has increased significantly in many transforming countries, including China, India and South Korea (Kojima, 1992).

Not surprisingly, income elasticities of demand for water, sewerage service, electricity, telephones, garbage disposal, education and health services are positive (Linn, 1982: p. 632). Thus, as incomes rise, so will the demand for public services. Even in the absence of economic growth, population growth, especially in large urban areas, may lead to increased demand for public services. Income and population are not the only determinants of demand for public service; the price charged for these services also matters. In particular, pricing public services below the marginal cost of provision is problematic for at least two reasons: it will limit the ability of public service utilities to undertake capital expenditures that would expand service to more users, and below-cost pricing is an inefficient

---

[67] In Tehran, local government—while having primary responsibility for highways and roads—has secondary responsibility for water and sewerage, and no responsibility for primary education. Lagos has only secondary responsibility for water and sewerage; Lima has no responsibility for secondary schooling and only secondary responsibility for highways and roads; and Kinshasa has no responsibility for water, sewerage or primary schools.

way to subsidize the consumption of the poor, since higher income groups also benefit from the subsidy.

Recent studies have also found substantial willingness-to-pay for urban public services (for a brief survey, see Crane and Daniere (1997)). While not true in every city for every good, WTP for many services is sufficient to induce supply from small-scale private producers (where permitted). In these cases, substantial gains to market liberalization exist (enhancing competition and enabling producers to realize scale economies); elsewhere, returns to public infrastructure investments are often quite high. Even very poor households tend to have considerable demand for public services. Altaf and Hughes (1994), for example, estimate a mean WTP of 4% of household expenditure for sewer access in Ouagadougou, Burkina Faso. As anticipated, WTP rose with household income, education, and whether all housing compound members were relatives. The Ouagadougou study also suggested that an effective and cooperative government could expand supply by creating conditions for the emergence of private firms which would invariably use far less sophisticated (but also far cheaper) technologies.

These findings have been mirrored in southeast Asia. Crane (1994) reports that only 20% of Jakarta's residents get their water from municipal connections; the rest obtain their water either from groundwater wells, from public hydrants, or, for fully one-third of the population (Crane and Daniere, 1997), from vendors who resell hydrant water. In Crane's survey from North Jakarta (where groundwater is increasingly saline, making private wells of little use), only 13% of households enjoyed municipal connections: the vast majority bought water from vendors, spending an average of 7.5% of their income in the process. Given an expenditure elasticity of demand for water estimated at 0.03 and a price elasticity of around −0.5, it is unsurprising that vendors and private hydrant franchise operators (with high costs and considerable spatial market power) price water far—more than 14 times—above the cost through municipal connections. Municipal system expansion and deregulation (permitting resale from connections) would both generate efficiency and equity gains in this case, but problems in arranging a municipal hook-up, especially by the poor, remain the core problem.

Crane et al. (1997) provide hedonic regressions of housing value as a function of structural features, house amenities, and locational amenities. Since marginal prices depend on quantities of characteristics consumed, they use four corrections to remove simultaneity bias, as is now conventional. For Bangkok owners and renters, house amenities linked to public infrastructure (piped water and sewerage) tend to be far more important than structural features. Legal access to electricity alone raises a an owner-occupant's house's value by $869, or about

5%, and raises dwelling value by $100 (1–2%) for squatters. In contrast, electricity access turns out to be worth little at the margin in Jakarta, since nearly all households have access. Access to piped water and in-house toilets are worth more in Jakarta (in the latter case than in Bangkok) than structural characteristics: *in general, high WTP reflects scarcities driven by public infrastructure policy.*

In many and perhaps most cases, inadequate service provision reflects an inability to collect user fees; this, in turn, is linked to limited local government capacities (see Becker et al., 1994). Elsewhere, rents achieved by restricted service provision are attractive both to private and public officials. But the pressures generated by rapid growth make it difficult for even the best intentioned urban authorities to keep up, especially when historic traditions militate against private market solutions.

In the case of sewerage services, the problem is more complex. There is little doubt that sewage treatment is abysmal throughout the developing world (for figures, see Kingsley et al., 1994), or that the health consequences are often severe. But national governments tend to focus on generating economic growth, and defer expensive solutions, especially away from capital cities. At the same time, they assign neither responsibilities nor revenue authority to local governments, which therefore have little incentive or capacity to treat sewage.

## 4.4. Environment

Environmental problems in urban areas of transforming economies often dwarf those found in urban areas of developed nations. Cohen (1993: p. 46) argues that uncollected garbage, heavily polluted air and shortages of clean water have begun to have direct, visible consequences on the health and productivity of urban residents. Indeed, environmental problems are often staggering.[68] In Bangkok, for example, one study estimates that air pollution is causing 900,000 minor headaches per day, 300–1400 excess deaths/year, 200,000–500,000 cases of hypertension per year, and 400,000–700,000 lost IQ points in children per year (Leitmann, 1991). Bangkok is far from an isolated case. Atmospheric pollution often exceeds the levels specified in World Health Organization guidelines in Mexico City, Sao Paulo, Santiago, Ibadan, Lagos, and nearly all the megacities in Asia (including Bombay, Jakarta, Manila and Seoul) (Faiz, 1992: p. 181).

---

[68] A complete review of environmental problems urban areas would include discussion of water pollution, soil degradation and toxic contamination of soils, as well as other forms of environmental damage. It is impossible to discuss the gamut of environmental problems in urban areas in this brief section; consequently, we will use air pollution as the context in which to discuss the causes of environmental damage and some proposed solutions.

Air pollution can be divided into two classes: conventional and greenhouse gases. Conventional pollutants include the immediately harmful elements of motor vehicle and industrial emissions, including carbon monoxide, nitrogen oxide, nonmethane hydrocarbons, sulfur oxides, suspended particulate matter, and lead. Greenhouse pollutants—which as the name implies cause damage to the earth's ozone layer—include carbon dioxide, methane, nitrous oxide and chlorofluorocarbons. While the levels of air pollution in urban areas of industrialized countries have been falling for most pollutants, the reverse is true in transforming countries. Lead emissions from automobiles, for example, are rising sharply in transforming countries. Levels of several pollutants (particulate matter, sulfur dioxide and carbon monoxide) in Taiwan and Korea already exceed those in industrialized nations of similar population size (Faiz, 1992: p. 176). The race to achieve higher recorded economic standards implies disregard for environmental measures. On the contrary, much growth has been energy and transport-intensive, and limited concern has been devoted to the air and water pollution implications. Rapid growth without environmental incentives can have staggering implications, though: total energy use in southeast and east Asia is rising at an annual rate of about 4%; CO, hydrocarbon and particulate emissions from vehicles in already heavily polluted Bangkok are rising at 5% to 6% annually (Kingsley et al., 1994).

Groundwater pollution and water shortages are also growing problems, especially in megacities. Braadbaart and Braadbaart (1997) focus on excessive groundwater mining in Java, but it is a serious problem as well in Bangkok, Hanoi, Dhaka, Manila, Delhi, Mexico City, and many Chinese cities (also see World Resources Institute, 1996: pp. 65–66, and the brief papers by McIntosh and Herrera in Serageldin et al., 1995). Groundwater in many places is a classic public good and metering, while not technically difficult, requires a concerted effort on the part of authorities. Ironically, the absence of meters and illicit pumping together ensure low revenues for municipal water authorities, who then lack the capacity to expand water use monitoring and fee collection, thereby perpetuating a vicious cycle.

A common misconception is that environmental degradation will cease if externalities are fully internalized. This is not necessarily the case, since the value to firms of polluting may exceed the value of the damage caused to other individuals and firms. In other words, there is some economically optimal level of pollution. In the case of urban areas of transforming economies, however, so many environmental negative externalities are not internalized that it is clear that degradation far exceeds its optimal level.

There are two principal causes of externalities: market failure and policy failure. Types of market failure include the lack of a market because of difficulty in identifying or enforcing property rights (e.g., air quality), partial marketing of a resource (e.g., timber from hillsides is sold as firewood, but watershed protection is not sold, and the nonmarketed use is consequently ignored or undervalued), open access to resources (tragedy of the commons), and lack of information about environmental impacts or low cost ways to mitigate or avoid damage. Types of policy failure include subsidies of polluting activities, nonaccountability of public sector polluters, and ineffective management of public lands (World Bank, 1992).

What makes urban areas of transforming economies particularly susceptible to high levels of pollution? Part of the answer clearly lies in the explanations already given. Transforming countries have less complete markets than developed countries, including markets for property rights to environmental commodities. The policy failure represented by nonaccountability of public sector polluters is especially damaging when these polluters are using "dirty" technologies and public sector producers are responsible for large shares of output. But more factors are at work. They include poverty, rapid population growth, and migration. If urban poverty is extensive, society may be quite willing to trade off environmental damage for more rapid economic growth, since the environmental impact may not be felt for many years.[69] Rapid population growth and migration will place severe strains on the environmental carrying capacity of urban areas.

In attempting to control urban pollution, governments of transforming countries face the same choice as governments in industrialized nations: whether to use command and control (direct regulation along with monitoring and enforcement mechanisms) or economic (market-based) strategies to control pollution.[70] The critiques of command and control systems are well known. In particular, the approach has been criticized for being economically inefficient, since it does not allow producers who could reduce pollution at lower cost the opportunity to do so in place of polluters who must undertake more costly reductions in pollution. Economists, not surprisingly, have trumpeted the advantages of the economic approach, which can: (1) promote cost-effective means for achieving pollution targets; (2) encourage development of pollution control technology; (3) provide government with a source of revenue; (4) allow flexibility in pol-

---

[69] In other words, the social discount rate is very high.

[70] Economic instruments include pollution charges (effluent and emission charges, user charges, product charges, administrative charges, and tax differentiation), market creation (marketable permits and liability insurance), subsidies, deposit-refund systems, and enforcement incentives. For a discussion of these instruments, see Bernstein (1993).

lution control technology; and (5) eliminate the necessity for governments to collect large amounts of detailed information.[71] The disadvantages of market-based strategies for transforming economies have been less well publicized. They include a more uncertain impact on environmental quality and the need for sophisticated institutions to implement and enforce them (Bernstein, 1993: pp. 2–3).[72] The latter may be an insurmountable obstacle in the short run in many poorer countries. In any discussion of polices to combat pollution, the most obvious policy instrument should not be overlooked: economic growth. As Beckerman (1992: pp. 490–491) argues, the best way to improve the environment of the vast mass of the world's population may well be via sustained economic growth. At a minimum, it is well established that the poor in developing country cities tend to endure far worse environmental conditions than the comparatively wealthy (see Kingsley et al., 1994), and growing suburbanization of the wealthy suggests that income elasticities of demand for environmental quality exceed unity.

An important question related to optimal city size and external diseconomies is how environmental degradation appears to vary with city size. Few have addressed this matter thoroughly: Shukla and Parikh (1992) provides an important exception. With data on 48 large cities from developed and transforming economies, in many cases delineated further by central city/suburban, and residential/industrial/commercial zone, they provide an exceptionally thorough comparative analysis. They find that particulate levels are 3–5 times as high in developing country cities as in their developed counterparts; the pattern for sulphur dioxide emissions is less clear. For cities in transforming economies, particulate concentration exhibits a tendency to rise with city size up to a population of 4–5 million, and then decrease. The pattern with $SO_2$ is weaker, but concentration shows a slight tendency to rise with city size. Developed country cities have a similar pattern, but the downturn starts at a lower population level (about 1–3 million). For combined regressions (and not controlling for city zone), $SO_2$ measures are related neither to GDP per capita nor to city size; particulate incidence and measures of smoke decline with GDP per capita (though in a U-shape for particulates). Particulates rise with city size in the inverse-U relationship; a similar but weaker pattern is exhibited by smoke.

---

[71] As Yang Suzhen (in Serageldin et al., 1995) discusses, Beijing's municipal government has been among the limited number authorities the transforming economies to level pollution fees, especially at rates which generate substantial revenue.

[72] As Bernstein (1993) notes, any agency given responsibility for implementing pollution control policies must have clear authority, as well as adequate expertise, staff, equipment and funds to carry out its monitoring and enforcement mission.

That air pollution should decline with income is unsurprising, and can be generated (though not unambiguously) by a simple general equilibrium model, as long as clean air is a normal good. That air pollution is greater in larger cities is similarly unsurprising, but the downturn requires some explanation. In part the pattern may reflect employment and output composition: very large cities have higher shares in services than manufacturing than do medium-sized cities. But other forces also may be at work: large cities may be wealthier and politically more powerful, and hence able to demand government subsidies for abatement equipment and measures. In any event, the topic has hardly been touched: Shukla and Parikh's work is the first word, but hardly the last.

## 5. Macroeconomic impacts of urbanization and internal migration

### 5.1. Urbanization, poverty and income distribution

This section only briefly addresses the arguments underlying a longstanding and contentious issue: Does urbanization exacerbate or alleviate poverty in developing countries? The general issue of urban poverty is ably addressed in Chapter 46 of this volume, while Kannappan (1989) also offers a superb survey of poverty and urban labor markets.

*Urbanization and inequality.* Conventional multi-sector models of urbanization and economic growth in the Lewis-Fei-Ranis tradition invariably generate a Kuznets inverted-U curve in which inequality first rises and then declines with economic development. Kaldorean models of inequality based on factor incomes similarly tend to generate rising inequality in early stages of economic growth.[73] The evidence for such an inverted-U is strong, both at the national level and, as Becker (1987) finds, for the urban sector alone. Rising inequality is not generally associated with increasing poverty in Lewis (1954) or other underlying models, however.

More recent work, focusing largely on the east Asian "miracle", casts doubt on the growth-inequality link. Birdsall et al. (1995a) find in cross-sectional work that greater income equality appears to spur rather than hinder economic growth. Two avenues of causality are likely. Rising educational attainment is strongly associated with reduced inequality; it also contributes to economic growth. Reduced fertility also results from rising education; it in turn contributes to rising

---

[73] A nice overview of the literature appears in Birdsall et al. (1995a). Readers of this chapter are assumed to be familiar with basic income distribution theory and patterns.

female earnings and, over a longer period, to tighter labor markets. Since urbanization is linked to lower fertility and improved educational attainment, one would therefore expect it to give rise to greater equality and more rapid growth as well. Indeed, as Birdsall et al. note, these forces all comprise self-reinforcing virtuous circles in the east Asian environment.[74]

One of the longest urban inequality time series is for Indonesia (Firdausy, 1993), where there appears to have been virtually no change in per capita expenditure Gini coefficients from 1964 through 1990. Indonesia's rural Gini coefficient appears to have declined dramatically during this period, however, from 0.34 to 0.25. For urban Indonesia, it appears that inequality increased sharply between the mid-1960s and late 1970s, and then declined throughout the 1980s. Income shares of the bottom 40% mirror this pattern. It is also worth noting that most Javanese cities' Gini coefficients' trends appear to have mirrored the broad national pattern, save for several discrepancies between 1984 and 1990. Among the most important of these is a pattern of rising inequality in urban east Java, which is dominated by booming Surabaya. Surabaya's Gini coefficient rose from 0.35 in 1960 to 0.41 in 1978 to 0.44 in 1990, while Gini coefficients in more established Jakarta, Bandung and Medan were all stable or declining during this period.

Assessing distributional patterns is a tricky matter, especially where systems of mutual obligations exist in extended families. Even defining a "family" of "household" is difficult, especially in polygamous societies. In much of rural and urban Africa, sub-households headed by wives exist in a fairly independent state, but with some mutual obligations to related units and, of course, the husband. Surely, the definition of a "household" in these circumstances will markedly affect distributional and poverty measures. At the same time, measures of individual wage inequality are problematic as well. For example, Terrell and Svejnar (1989: p. 110) in their study of Senegalese industrial workers found that the average formal sector worker fed 10.9 people other than himself. In a sense, it might be apt in such a setting to view intrahousehold migration as taking place in order to equate utilities across space.

---

[74] Other ways Birdsall et al. (1995: p. 20) hypothesize that low inequality might contribute to rapid growth include:

- contributing to political and macroeconomic stability;
- raising $x$-efficiency of low-income workers;
- limiting rural/urban income gaps, which in turn limits rent-seeking migration and raises multipliers from productivity gains;
- inducing increased savings and investments by the poor.

This latter phenomenon will result if the poor (and their businesses) are liquidity constrained: see the analytic model of Birdsall et al. (1995b).

*Urban unemployment and poverty.* Inconsistent definitions across surveys make most economists reluctant to attempt to gauge whether unemployment is rising or falling in a given developing country, much less discerning patterns across countries or in relation to social phenomena. The general impression is that open unemployment is rare in the countryside of transforming societies (though there is also debate as to how hard men work in some of them), as there is always work to do, and it is generally shared by a household's able-bodied members. More-over, even where wage labor predominates, unemployment is a luxury beyond reach of the rural poor: those idle are generally ill or infirm.

Given this picture, unemployment is seen as accompanying urbanization. Who is unemployed in the cities is a more hotly debated issue. Portes (1989) finds strong evidence that urban unemployment rates rose considerably in Latin Amer-ica between the mid-1970s and mid-1980s. He also finds strong evidence of rising informal employment and, more tellingly, female labor force participation (which rose from 31% in 1974 to 44% in 1986 in Bogota and from 33% in 1975 to 45% in 1985 in Montevideo). These patterns and evidence of industrial layoffs indicate that much of the unemployment is likely to have been a middle and lower class phenomenon, rather than reflecting a growing army of idle university graduates.

This picture appears not to apply to Africa (Nafziger, 1988), where open unemployment is concentrated among primary and secondary school leavers or dropouts. The difference may be attributed plausibly to Africa's lower level of economic development, and perhaps to the state's greater control of the formal sector (which makes real wage reductions more likely than layoffs during periods of industrial decline: see Becker and Morrison (1993)). Mazumdar (1981) also argues that very long delays between secondary school graduation and first job characterized Malaysia's unemployment around 1970, in large part because of unrealistic expectations. But such patterns are unlikely to have been maintained in the past decade because of exceptional economic growth.

Fields and Wan (1989) contrast Latin America with east Asia, and find that labor market flexibility in the latter, together with a strong export orientation, has had dramatic effects on poverty reduction, unemployment abatement, and real manufacturing wage increases. Clearly, rapid growth and high inmigration rates need not be associated with adverse consequences for any large group. Nor, for that matter, is there evidence of systematic increases in inequality in east Asia between 1970 and the mid-1980s, while Gini coefficients appeared to be lower by the 1980s than in the 1950s or 1960s.

Rather, government-influenced institutional bargaining with firms over formal sector wages and employment levels (often simultaneously) is increasingly seen as the cause of urban labor market ills in Africa and Latin America (Svejnar, 1989). Economic growth in this setting leads to segmented urban labor markets, with high levels of poverty and unemployment coexisting with a high wage sector. Capital accumulation and attendant urbanization cannot be said to cause unemployment or poverty in these frameworks (with labor market equilibria determined a la Harris and Todaro, 1970; Stiglitz, 1974; Svejnar, 1989, or Becker and Morrison, 1993), but neither is economic development a cure.

*The implication of BHS, Fields and Wan, Svejnar and others is that very different development paradigms are operating in different transforming economies. In those east Asian "miracles" which emphasize the virtuous cycles, economic growth and urbanization mean lower poverty and reduced inequality.*[75] These economies thrive on exports, initially of labor-intensive manufactures, but increasingly of goods with greater skill content. Whether, or not, the growth/inequality linkages are similar elsewhere with different economic structures is less clear, although the Tanzanian-Kenyan contrast highlighted in Knight and Sabot (1990) suggest that they are. Much of the answer can be gleaned from Morley's (1988) framework and analysis of Brazilian inequality. Brazil's growth in the 1970s was both skill-using and heavily urbanizing, which led to rising inequality (though earnings of the poor did increase). This short-run response could be offset by a longer-run supply response, itself determined by an equilibrium reflecting demand for and supply of education. Under elastic supply conditions (east Asia, Kenya), the long run impact will be to reduce inequality; where substantial supply constraints exist (Tanzania, much of Latin America), mitigating supply responses will not occur.

Both rural and urban poverty is influenced heavily by household dependency ratios (for detailed Malaysian evidence, see Mazumdar, 1981). Human capital variables appear to matter virtually everywhere, though there is considerable labor market segmentation in much of the developing world. Moreover, in public sector dominated economies, credentialism and queuing may account for much of the apparent explanatory success of human capital regressions (again, see Mazumdar, 1981). There is strong evidence that in developing and transition

---

[75] It is difficult to completely disregard the Boserup hypothesis explanation as well. It is certainly manifested in writings on rural development through heavily populated East and Southeast Asia. Collier et al. (1987) vividly describe what they term the "urbanization of rural Java", and credit improved intercity (and intervillage) transportation links, together with high population density (and hence both substantial rural demand bases and a large rural labor force) for the rapid nonagricultural growth experienced by rural Java. Interestingly, their survey did not find that electrification played an important role in initial rural development, though it doubtless greatly improved quality of life for many. Rather, transportation access came out as key: "nine of the thirteen villages had between one to two hundred persons migrating each day to work, some being picked up by company buses in their village" (Collier et al., 1987: p. 39). Similar daily migration appears to be taking place in China.

economies, like developed nations, poverty is disproportionately prevalent in female-headed households (for a detailed study of urban Brazil, see Barros et al., 1997). The Brazilian study also links poverty to the relative absence of prime-age male workers, and the presence of child workers, and a high incidence of dependency. Since children in poor and female headed households are more likely to be working and less likely to be in school, poverty will also pass from one generation to the next.

In Indonesia, both urban and rural poverty declined markedly between the mid 1960s and 1990, though some estimates indicate stagnation of the share of the urban population in poverty since 1980. More strikingly, according to official BPS (Biro Pusat Statistik) figures, since 1980 the proportion of the rural population defined as poor (14.3% as of 1990) has actually been less than the comparable urban figure. Firdausy's (1993) detailed study finds that the lowest gains in urban poverty reduction occurred in Aceh (far western Sumatra) and west Kalimantan; both provinces also experienced rising rural poverty. The greatest urban poverty reduction gains appeared to be in Bali, Lampung (southern Sumatra), north Sulawesi, and East Nusatenggara: all four provinces experienced dramatic rural poverty declines as well. Provincial urban poverty does not show any obvious relation to the degree of urbanization, though the rate is lowest in DKI Jakarta.[76]

As in Malaysia, Indonesian poverty appears strongly linked to education. A majority who have not completed primary school are classified as poor; only tiny proportions of those with junior high school or higher education are. Within cities, the poor are overrepresented in agriculture (the occupational sector of 24% of the 1990 urban poor, some four times the occupational incidence of the urban nonpoor) and construction.

The reduction of poverty in Indonesia also appears to reflect the "rural industrialization" of, especially, Java. Collier et al. (1987) examine 13 Javanese villages. Briefly, they find dramatic improvements in education and transport access during the 1970s and 1980s; they also found rapidly growing real wages and employment opportunities *despite* the adoption of many labor-saving techniques in agriculture. Farmers also alleged that migration by and local factory employment of erstwhile farm laborers had led to labor shortages. The greatest gains naturally accrue to those in villages near urban areas, but rural factories were clearly springing up as well. Successful "formal sector" factories in rural

---

[76] Manning (1988) provides a less sanguine view of rural employment and income growth in Indonesia. While not terribly pessimistic, Manning does focus far more on the labor saving nature of agricultural change than do Collier et al. (1987). Furthermore, among the poor access to machines and fertilizers is limited, perhaps leading to rising inequality. Like Henderson and Kuncoro (1994), Manning emphasizes the considerable centralization of Indonesian manufacturing along with the slow growth of agricultural employment.

areas tend to have owners with good marketing contacts and access to capital, however: one should not picture these as informal sector microenterprises taking off.

The situation in Bangladesh, a very poor and densely populated country, is less clear. As Bhadra (1992) discusses, urban poverty as a whole appears to have fallen since Independence and the late 1980s, but the acute poverty may not have (depending on the survey one uses). Given Bangladesh's very high inmigration rates, it is unsurprising that the urban poor are overwhelmingly migrants. As in Malaysia, poverty is linked to the number working (79% have only one member of the household working), and to occupation. A survey of squatters analyzed by Bhadra found that 42% were engaged in transport activities (presumably, rickshaw pulling); another study found that 29% of those classified as urban poor were employed in transport. Construction and other unskilled activities account for most of the rest of the urban poor's occupations. Bhadra (1992: p. 26) also generates a series from 1976/77–1988/89 of Dhaka low income housing rents relative to the food CPI for industrial workers: as food prices rose at an annual rate of 11% while housing rents rose at 20% per annum during this period, he concludes that land and hence housing rent pressures during the urban boom were largely responsible for the persistence of high rates of acute poverty.[77]

Finally, Mitra (1994) regresses estimates of urban poverty incidence by Indian state on labor productivity, industrial per capita income, and a time trend for 1960/61–1973/74. He found positive time trends for all states during this period of economic stagnation, and inconclusive links to productivity and per capita incomes.

## 5.2. Demand patterns and economic structure

Will urbanization affect demand patterns, especially in a manner that matters for macroeconomic policy? From economy-wide CGE simulation studies such as Becker et al.'s (1992) work on India, we know that cities are far more capital- and import-intensive than rural areas. Government is highly urbanizing, both because governments consume urban services (the bureaucracy and formal sector manufactures), and because the goods and services it consumes themselves have urban-oriented demands. Since the urban-orientation (and capital- and import-

---

[77] Food accounted for about 60% and housing for about 15% of expenditures of all urban households during this period (housing's share rose and food's share fell over time as well). Food shares will be higher for the poor, naturally.

intensivity) of consumer demands rise with incomes, real urban-rural income gaps will generate distinct urban and rural consumption patterns.[78]

Elsewhere (see Becker (1997)), we have argued that such differential consumption patterns are likely to be quite important in the highly fragmented economies of the (formerly) socialist world. Existing evidence does not point to a similar situation in developing market economies, though.[79] Grewe (1999), for example, finds quite similar food demand functions across urban and rural areas in Indonesia, and reasonably similar nonfood demand patterns as well.[80] As one might expect, urban consumers tend to exhibit preferences for more import-intensive goods (processed foods, drink flavorings), but the distinctions are not vast.[81]

As Grewe notes, since mean urban incomes in Indonesia are about twice those of rural households (see our earlier warnings about interpreting urban-rural gaps, though), the critical features in differing demand patterns are the underlying Engel forces and income elasticities, not region-specific differences per se.

Perhaps more important is the difference in urban and rural objective functions. As the Singh et al. (1986) discuss, farm households have both consumption and production aspects. Slutsky substitution equations therefore contain both the standard income and substitution effects as well as a "profit effect":

$$\frac{dX_i}{dP_j} = \left(\frac{\partial X_i}{\partial P_j} - X_i \frac{\partial \bar{Y}}{\partial P_j}\right) + \frac{\partial X_i}{\partial Y^*}\frac{\partial Y^*}{\partial P_j}.$$

[78] Differential consumption patterns have important implications for macroeconomic policy, especially in two-gap models in which foreign exchange or capital shortages limit total output. In this case, government re-distributive efforts aimed at shifting demand from foreign exchange or capacity constrained sectors to demand constrained sectors potentially could result in real GDP gains.

[79] Evidence on this point is scanty, due to the fact that very few researchers have examined differences in rural and urban consumption patterns. A possible reason is that if data are good enough to support estimation of region-specific demand functions, then the goods market in such a country probably be sufficiently developed and integrated so that large differences will not exist.

[80] Grewe uses the Susenas dataset on income and consumption patterns in Indonesia, which has microlevel data for over 46,000 households.

[81] Overall expenditure patterns were as follows:

| | Mean household expenditures, Indonesia, 1990 | | | |
|---|---|---|---|---|
| | Urban: Rp. | Percent | Rural: Rp. | Percent |
| Food | 32,178 | 56 | 21,253 | 70 |
| Purchased and other | (30,334) | (52) | (16,552) | (54) |
| Own-produced | (1,834) | (3) | (4,701) | (15) |
| Housing | 10,534 | 18 | 3,562 | 12 |
| All other goods | 15,142 | 26 | 5,679 | 19 |

The term in parentheses contains the standard Slutsky terms, with nominal income kept constant. But rising prices also generate production responses and hence rising real incomes. As Singh et al. (1986: p. 26)) find empirically, these profit effects tend to swamp the standard terms when agricultural prices rise. Again, though, the implications for consumption patterns are a bit vague, as these patterns will depend on specific policy and relative price environments. If growing urban demand raises the relative price of agricultural goods, then one should expect to find trends toward growing consumption shares of domestic farm products in rural households, and declining shares among urban households.

## 5.3. Efficiency impacts

### 5.3.1. Mega-city problem versus agglomeration economies
The face of large urban agglomerations is changing. In 1960, seven of the ten largest cities in the world were found in developed nations. By the year 2010, the United Nations predicts that eight of the ten largest cities will be in developing nations (United Nations, 1993: pp. 13–14). Of the 26 urban agglomerations predicted to have more than ten million inhabitants in 2010, 21 will be in developing nations. Fourteen of these cities will be in Asia, five in Latin America and two in Africa (United Nations, 1993: p. 15).

How should governments respond to continued growth of extremely large cities? One literature, spawned by the United Nations mega-cities project, focuses on the serious challenges produced by further growth, Oberai (1993: 10ff.) identifies five categories of problems facing megacities: rapid growth in population, unemployment and underemployment, poverty and limited access to social services, environmental degradation and fiscal constraints. In a survey of ten Asian mega-cities, Brennan and Richardson (1989: p. 124) classify housing and environmental problems in all of them at least "serious", and often "very severe".[82] To avoid further exacerbation of mega-city problems, most authors of this literature argue that further growth of mega cities should be curtailed.

A much more sanguine view of urban growth is held by those who estimate agglomeration economies—productivity advantages available to firms—offered by urban areas. Agglomeration economies are subdivided into two types: urbanization and localization economies. Urbanization economies accrue to all firms located in a given urban area, while localization economies benefit only firms within a given sector. Factors such as better or cheaper access to intermediate

---

[82] The three-tier classification system of service deficits includes "moderate", "serious" and "very severe" deficits. Only two of the ten cities had moderate water and sewerage deficits; the remaining eight cities had either serious or very severe deficits.

inputs or specialized labor pools and communication among specialists involved in productions fall under the heading of localization economies. Urbanization economies may involve such factors as better developed public services.

While most research on agglomeration economies has focused on developed countries, Henderson (1982a, 1988a) estimated the magnitude of agglomeration economies in Brazilian cities.[83] At the two-digit industry level, Henderson finds little evidence of urbanization economies; he does find, however, significant evidence of localization economies. For most two-digit industries, the elasticity of output with respect to own-industry employment exceeds 0.1.

Shukla (1996) and Mitra (1997) estimate agglomeration economies in India. In Shukla's work, the elasticity of firm output with respect to urban population of the firm's location for two-digit industries range from 0.04 (cotton textiles) to 0.19 (basic metals and alloys), with a mean of 0.09. By implication the TFP for a typical Indian manufacturing will be 51% greater in a city of 1,000,000 than it will be if the same firm locates in a town of 10,000. When agglomeration elasticities are permitted to vary, Shukla finds no maximum value in two of five industries, and large (but unstable) optimum population values in the remaining industries. Broadly speaking, the optima are very sensitive to specification, but the presence of agglomeration economies is sensitive neither to specification nor to agglomeration measure. Distinguishing between urbanization and localization economies appears to improve the model fit; in contrast to Henderson's (1982a) findings for Brazil, Shukla finds that urbanization economies are larger for 11 of 13 industries.

Shukla (1996) also examines the impact of urban infrastructure on regional productivity. Using 63 distinct measures of different types of infrastructure and social service provision plus 15 financial indicators of infrastructural level, she examines translog production functions for five 2-digit industries across the 26 districts of Maharashtra state in India. Different infrastructure and finance measures are typically introduced alternately to avoid problems of multicollinearity, and because of the small sample size. Output elasticities for current budgetary items tend to be high (other than for repair services, they range from zero to as high as 0.74), but causality seems unclear (productive firms, after all, generate more local tax revenue). But reverse causality cannot explain many of the physical infrastructure patterns. As Shukla (1996: p. 95) notes, for the food industry, "—a consumer-oriented, resource-based activity—water supply, power, asphalt roads, and urban market-places appear to significantly enhance

---

[83] Verma's (1986) analysis is state-level. But since she estimates agglomeration economies in manufacturing, a large share of production presumably takes place in urban areas.

efficiency. For Industry 23 (Cotton Textiles)—and established consumer-goods industry—drainage capacity, industrial water consumption asphalt roads, public transport ... and, again, market places have maximum impact". In contrast, for the producer-oriented Metal Products and Parts industry, power consumption, roads and public transport, and telephone connections are most important. While these results can be taken as only suggestive, it is difficult to avoid concluding that the public sector provides complementary capital inputs (water supply, roads, electricity, health and educational facilities tend to be gross complements in the empirical work) and free but valuable substitutes as well to private industries and public enterprises. This infrastructure, as it is likely to be strongly correlated with city size, represents an important component of those amorphous urban agglomeration economies.

Mitra (1997) takes a slightly different approach and estimates translog frontier production functions for Indian firms in two industries, electrical machinery (EM) and cotton and cotton textiles (CCT), and uses city population and city work force as alternative measures of urbanization economies. OLS regressions indicate some but limited support for "U"-shaped urbanization economies for UM, and none for CCT. However, when efficiency indices are calculated from the frontier functions and regressed on size of the plant's home city, the "U"-shaped effect is more significant for EM, and sporadically significant for CCT, though the explanatory power is low. The optimal city size for EM turns out to have a population of 1.5–2.5 million; for CCT the optimal size is 2.5–5.0 million.

The empirical agglomeration literature is highly suggestive but not entirely convincing, largely because of small sample sizes. The works of Henderson, Shukla and others are fascinating, but there is a desperate need for more study based on narrowly defined industries and larger samples. It is also difficult to leave the literature without wondering about causality and possible aggregation biases.

Parallel with the development of the agglomeration literature in urban and regional economics has been an emerging focus over the past two decades on scale economies in the international trade literature. Spatially oriented CGE simulation models such as Markusen and Rutherford (1993) examine industrial production location decisions under conditions of imperfect competition, fixed costs and discrete numbers of plants. While their model examines automobile plant location in North America, the same framework would be applicable to, say, plant location in different types of cities in China or Brazil. Their findings suggest that output growth may be highly sensitive to (a) whether plant sites are fixed or variable, (b) the nature of tariff protection—but not necessarily in a continuous, linear manner, especially if fixed costs or scale economies are substantial.

Livas Elizondo and Krugman (1992) develop a trade-based model of a single giant metropolis, with Mexico City in mind. In their multiregional (Mexico City, Monterrey, USA) trade model with standard intracity commuting costs, significant scale economies and production oriented toward the domestic market drive resources to concentrate in a single location (or small number of locations). Thus, *the rise of huge metropolises and, more general, urban system primacy is the "unintended by-product of import-substituting industrialization"*. Livas Elizando and Krugman's model also includes intercity transport costs (which can be interpreted as well to include trade barriers, and can be solved (in part analytically and in part numerically) for three regions using CES functional forms in a general equilibrium framework, with intersectoral migration over time depending on real wage differentials. Livas Elizando and Krugman find that as Mexico's protectionism toward the US increases, then the population distribution between Mexico City and Monterrey, if initially equal, becomes unstable, and only allocations with all labor in one city are stable. They infer that relatively closed economies have strong backward and forward linkages which give rise to a single large megacity, but "as the economy is open, these forces are weakened and the offsetting centrifugal forces make a less concentrated urban system first possible and then necessary".

In Livas Elizando and Krugman, each firm produces a distinct good ("apparel", $Y$). Hanson (1994) adopts a framework somewhat similar to Livas Elizondo and Krugman, but with two production stages: design (with location-specific external economies) and assembly (which is CRS). Localization economies exist in design, and this generates urban concentration—as long as "Mexico" has sufficient trade barriers to ensure that it both designs and assembles the $Y$ good. If not, then there is no rationale for concentration: in the Mexican setting, resources will flow from integrated plants in Mexico City to assembly plants in northern Mexico, assuming that with free trade design will migrate to the US. The data, in fact, show evidence of such a movement in the past decade; again, protectionism appears to be a major determinant of industrial and population spatial concentration.

Henderson and Kuncoro (1994) focus on the determinants of Javanese industrial centralization with reference to the policy environment rather than spatial agglomeration economies. They argue that firms need access to politicians and government officials, who authorize various activities (such as export and import licenses), and to financial institutions. These needs make large cities, and especially capitals, attractive locations, especially in countries with directed financial markets and weak oversight of politicians and civil servants. In the Indonesian case, financial liberalization appears to have actually generated more spatial centralization, since it expanded financial access to parts of the unincorporated sector, giving them incentive to locate in larger urban areas. Examining firm location by 2-digit industry, and using instruments for plausibly simultaneous variables, conditional logit regressions of the probability of a firm in industry $I$ operating in *kabupaten* (county) $j$ is found to vary inversely with local wage and distance from major metro areas; and to vary positively with local population, quality of electricity infrastructure, past own industry employment, and both maturity and diversity of the surrounding manufacturing environment. The Henderson–Kuncoro findings are consistent with Shukla's (1996) work, and provide further insight into those factors that create agglomeration economies.

Neither the mega-city nor agglomeration economies literature gives a balanced picture of the costs and benefits of continued urbanization, although this balance does exist in Livas Elizando and Krugman-type models. The former focuses on only the costs of continued urbanization, while the latter focuses on only the benefits. In Section 5.3.2 below, we focus on micro- and macroeconomic approaches that attempt to determine whether, or not, city growth is efficient. As each approach is presented, we will be careful to document what concept of efficiency underlies it.

Finally, there is a long literature on the size distribution of urban systems, as well as an often uninformative debate on the optimality of any particular distribution. Rosen and Resnick (1980) provide a good point of departure for the topic: they estimate Pareto distributions of the form $R = AS^{-\alpha}$, where $R$ is the number of cities in a country with population greater than or equal to $S$; $A$ and $\alpha$ are parameters to be estimated. In the special case of the "rank-size rule", $\alpha$ equals unity. Rosen and Resnick find (a) that the Pareto coefficient falls when metropolitan area populations are used instead of city proper populations; (b) that changing the number of cities at times mattered considerably, but not in any systematic way; (c) that the coefficient on the added quadratic terms in the regression

$$\ln R_i = A - \alpha \ln S_i + \beta (\ln S_i)^2,$$

tended to be significant, and also positive in about two-thirds of cases; and (d) that the Pareto coefficient appears to rise (a country's city system becomes less primate) as per capita income and railroad density increase; other economic variables did not appear to matter. Ledent (1990) examines African data, and finds that Pareto coefficients are sensitive to the number of cities included, rising toward unity as the number increases. Ledent finds that primacy declines with a country's population and total area; the role of economic variables tends to depend on the primacy definition (a distributional statistic or population share of the largest city).

Wheaton and Shishido (1981) link city size distributions to classical spatial theory, and in particular to the production efficiency gains associated with urban concentration-induced scale and agglomeration economies, which must be balanced against product and commuter transport costs which rise with concentration. They posit scale economies as increasing with the capital intensity of economic activities as well as the size of the potential market. They use as a measure of urban concentration $H$, the sum of squared population shares of $n$ cities; if all cities are identical, then $H = 1/n$, so that $1/H$ may be thought of as the number of "size-corrected" cities, which will be a function of market size and city scale economies. To this is added the country's physical size and the ratio of central to total government expenditures. The econometric fits prove quite significant for all but government concentration variables; they also predict increasing urban concentration until a per capita income of about $2000 1976 US dollars is reached, or about Venezuela's per capita GDP at that time.

In a 90-country sample for 1960, 1970 and 1980, Moomaw and Shatter (1996) fail to find a relationship between the share of urban population in cities above 100,000 ($M$) and per capita GDP, though they do find a negative relation between the share of the largest city and per capita GDP. Ades and Glaeser (1994) look at urban concentration in a broader context, noting that agricultural-based (and other weight-losing) production invites decentralization, and also focusing on political influences. In their political economy framework, a government allocates resources between (and imposes taxes on) a dominating metropolis and the hinterland, subject to migration as a function of wage differentials. Favoritism toward the metropolis rises with political instability (metropolitan residents are more menacing and effective rioters) and falls with the extent of democracy (the rural masses are more numerous). Cross-country, pooled (over 1970–1985) regressions are run for the logarithm of main city population, with fitted instruments for dictatorship, road density and trade variables to correct for endogeneity. The main city's size turns out to be positively influenced by (a) its status as a capital, (b) the country's land area, (c) per capita income, (d) trade orientation, (e) protectionism—the ratio of import duties to total imports; it falls with (f) road density, and (g) government expenditure on transport. Political variables turn out to be important: "one extra revolution or coup per year increases the average size of the central city by 2.4%", and "dictatorships have main cities that are about 45% larger" than nondictatorships.

Both this work and that of Livas–Krugman and Hanson may be seen as in part building on the earlier theoretical work of Henderson (1982b), who examines the impact of government policies on urban system concentration in an intracity spatial model with agglomeration economies. In free mobility equilibrium, the size of city $j$ will depend on the characteristics of the industry in which it specializes; those for which there is large employment (and hence in which their cities tend to be large) will have to pay higher wages to compensate for higher commuting costs, housing prices, and levels of size-driven disamenities. In equilibrium, government subsidies for production of good $j$ will lead to an expansion of the number of type of cities which produce $j$, rather than a rise in the size of and rents in a particular city, which of course is the outcome if a particular city is favored. It seems reasonable that federal systems of governments will have more cities competing for scarce government-provided infrastructure and other favors, so that decentralization of government should be associated with urban system decentralization, and cross-country empirical work bears this out. The impact of trade restrictions is more complex. For a developing country which exports labor-intensive manufactures $l$ and imports capital-intensive goods $c$, a rise in tariffs will cause the number, or if those are restricted, the size of type $c$ cities to increase. Since equilibrium plant employment may well be greater for type $c$ firms because of greater scale economies, it seems plausible that protectionism will raise urban concentration, as in Livas Elizondo–Krugman and Hanson.

Henderson (1986b) has also addressed the nature of secondary region (or city) development in an environment in which the initially developed site enjoys inverted-U-shaped agglomeration and scale economies. In this setting, population growth (and quite likely economic growth) will generate initial site growth for some time (and hence growing urban concentration if secondary towns exist on the basis of regional commerce and agricultural processing). However, beyond a certain point, secondary regions/cities will emerge. This implied nonlinearity in the determinants of urban concentration unfortunately has been ignored in the empirical literature.

The empirical literature on size distribution suffers from inherent limitations. Even when it is generated from formal models, the regression analysis to date tends to involve fairly arbitrary functional forms and independent variables which might be best described as hopeful instruments for desired but unobserved variables. In consequence, it is impossible to confidently assert that the empirical work provided affirms any of the hypotheses advanced, since the regressions are likely to be consistent with many other hypotheses as well. This, plus an absence of careful modeling and attention to simultaneity issues, may well account for the widely varying empirical patterns.

## 5.3.2. Microeconomic and macroeconomic measures of urbanization's efficiency

The simplest microeconomic measure of whether migration to urban areas increases economic efficiency is whether the migrants involved (on average) realize wage gains after migrating.[84] Under the neoclassical assumption that workers are paid the value of their marginal product, the wage in source areas is an accurate measure of the foregone value of production, and the destination wage earned is an accurate measure of the value of increased production. Efficiency gains occur until wage gaps are eliminated by labor supply shifts.[85] There are at least two problems with this approach. First, if wage gains are obtained only after some period of unemployment or underemployment, how is the resulting destination wage discounted to reflect this? Second, any computation of wage gains based upon sample survey data likely will suffer from severe selection bias. If only workers in destination areas are surveyed, temporary and failed migrants will be underrepresented, and the wage gains from migration will be overstated; if only source regions are sampled, the bias will be in the other direction. Few surveys include both source and destination areas due to the increased cost of doing so.

A second microeconomic approach analyzes whether spells of unemployment cause individuals to migrate. Since the opportunity cost (in foregone output) of an unemployed individual's migrating is zero, any wage increase in the destination is an efficiency gain. There is significant evidence that personal unemployment increases the likelihood of migration, although the magnitude of the effect varies across countries and population subgroups (Herzog et al., 1993: p. 337). To the authors knowledge, no such studies have been done for transforming economies.[86] Finally, a third microeconomic approach measures the extent to which interregional migration is generated by mismatches between the reward structure in a region and an individual's skills. Sorting of individuals according to skills between regions leads to greater allocative efficiency in the distribution of workers. Results from the US support the contention that internal migration increases efficiency (Borjas et al., 1992). Unfortunately, the model has not been applied to transforming economies.

---

[84] All the approaches analyzed in this section measure the contribution of city growth to overall economic efficiency when that growth is caused by internal migration. To the authors' knowledge, no analysis has combined natural population increase with efficiency analysis.

[85] This is the case if there are no costs associated with migration. As Herzog and Schlottmann (1981) have shown for the US, however, the moving, information and psychic costs of migration are nontrivial. Once costs are included, migration will not eliminate completely interregional wage gaps.

[86] Largely, one presumes, because of the questionable relevance of the concept of open unemployment in transforming economies, especially in rural areas.

At the macroeconomic level, three approaches have been used to gauge the efficiency of the internal migration process, but—to the authors' knowledge—only one of these has been applied to urban growth in transforming economies. The first macroeconomic approach computes an efficiency ratio for migration flows, where the ratio is defined as the absolute value of the number of net migrants between two areas divided by the number of gross migrants between the two areas.[87] The usual interpretation of the efficiency ratio is that migration is more efficient the closer is the ratio to one; a higher ratio for a given amount of net migration indicates lower costs incurred in reallocating migrants between regions. Galloway and Vedder (1985), however, develop a simple model in which an optimal population distribution results in an efficiency ratio of zero, calling into question the conventional interpretation of the migration efficiency ratio. If diametrically opposite welfare conclusions can be obtained from the same value of the efficiency ratio, it should be discarded as a measure of migration's efficiency.

A second, more appropriate measure of migration's efficiency is to determine whether migration closes regional wage and unemployment differentials. Evidence that migration reduces differentials supports the contention that migration increases allocative efficiency. For the US, Herzog et al. (1993) cite evidence that migrants move from areas with high unemployment rates. In a simulation exercise (also for the US), Gabriel et al. (1993) find that migration reduces but does not eliminate interregional unemployment differentials caused by a region-specific shock. While the evidence mustered by these authors is convincing, it is not directly relevant to migration to urban areas of transforming economies.

A final approach to measuring the efficiency impact of migration is introduced by Morrison (1993). Using data from Peru, he employs stochastic frontier production functions to calculate the efficiency-adjusted marginal products of labor by productive sector and Peruvian department. For migration flows to Lima between 1976 and 1981, he then calculates foregone production in source regions and production increases in Lima. The net result: internal migration increased migration from 1.9 to 2.1% of 1979 GDP—a considerable efficiency gain.[88] Note that this efficiency gain has elements of both technical and allocative efficiency, since the frontier production function allows for differing degrees of technical

---

[87] If gross migration from region $I$ to $j$ is defined as $M_{ij}$ and gross migration from $j$ to $I$ as $M_{ji}$, then the efficiency ratio would be: $E_{ij} = |(M_{ij} - M_{ji})|/(M_{ij} + M_{ji})$.

[88] The percentages reported are computed at domestic relative prices, but the result remains robust if: (1) gains and losses are calculated at world prices, and (2) negative externalities generated by the migrants in Lima are included in the analysis.

efficiency across departments, while reallocation between sectors of differing productivities constitutes a gain in allocative efficiency.

# References

Abuhadba, M. and P. Romaguera (1993), "Inter–industry wage differentials: evidence from Latin American countries", Journal of Development Studies 30:190–205.

Acsadi, G.T.F., G. Johnson Acsadi and R.A. Bulatao, eds. (1990), Population Growth and Reproduction in Sub-Saharan Africa (World Bank, Washington, DC).

Adams, R.H., Jr. (1992), "The effects of migration and remittances on inequality in rural Pakistan", Pakistan Development Review 31:1189–1206.

Adelman, I. and H. Fetini (1991), "Development strategies and the environment", University of California at Berkeley Department of Agricultural and Resource Economics (CUDARE) Working Paper 587.

Adelman, I. and S. Robinson (1978a), Income Distribution Policy in Developing Countries: A Case Study of Korea (Stanford University Press, Stanford, CA).

Adelman, I. and S. Robinson (1978b), "Migration, demographic change and income distribution in a model of a developing country", Research in Population Economics 1:1–26 (JAI Press).

Adelman, I. and D. Sunding (1987), "Economic policy and income distribution in China", Journal of Comparative Economics 11:444–461.

Adelman, I. and J.E. Taylor (1990), "Is structural adjustment with a human face possible? The case of Mexico", Journal of Development Studies 26:387–407.

Adelman, I. and J.E. Taylor (1991), 'Multisectoral models and structural adjustment: new evidence from Mexico", Journal of Development Studies 29:154–163.

Ades, A.F. and E. Glaeser (1994), "Trade and circuses: explaining urban giants", National Bureau of Economic Research Working Paper No. 4715, Cambridge, MA.

Ahmad, N. (1992), "Choice of location and mobility behavior of migrant households in a third world city", Urban Studies 29:1147–1157.

Ahmad, N. (1993), "Choice of neighborhoods by mover households in Karachi", Urban Studies 30:1257–1170.

Ahmed, A. and I. Sirageldin (1993), "Socio–economic determinants of labour mobility in Pakistan", Pakistan Development Review 32:139–157.

Aina, T.A. (1992), "Land tenure in Lagos", Habitat International 16:3–15.

Akerlof, G. (1982), "Labor contract as partial gift exchange", Quarterly Journal of Economics 97:543–569.

Akerlof, G. (1984), "Gift exchange and efficiency—wage theory: four views", American Economic Review 74:79–83.

Alchian, A. and H. Demsetz (1972), "Production, information cost, and economic organization", American Economic Review 62:777–795.

Alexander, C. and J. Wyeth (1994), "Cointegration and market integration: An application to the Indonesian rice market", Journal of Development Studies 30:303–328.

Alperovich, G. (1993), "An explanatory model of city—size distribution: evidence from cross-country data", Urban Studies 30:1591–1601.

Altaf, M.A. and J.A. Hughes (1994), "Measuring the demand for improved urban sanitation services: results of a contingent valuation study in Ouagadougou, Burkina Faso", Urban Studies 31:1763–1776.

Amano, M. (1983), "On the Harris–Todaro model with intersectoral migration of labour", Economica 50:311–323.

Amis, P. (1984), "Squatters or tenants: the commercialization of unauthorized housing in Nairobi", World Development 12(1):87–96.

Amsden, A.H. (1991), "Big business and urban congestion in Taiwan: the origins of small enterprise and regionally decentralized industry (respectively)", World Development 19:1121–1135.

Andreev, E., S. Scherbov and F. Willikens (1997), The Population of Russia: Fewer and Older (University of Groningen Faculty of Spatial Sciences, Groningen).

Angel, S. and S. Mayo (1993), "Housing: enabling markets to work", World Bank Policy Paper, Washington, DC.

Appleton, S., P. Collier and P. Horsnell (1990), "Gender, education and employment in Côte d'Ivoire", World Bank SDA Unit Working Paper No. 8, Washington, DC.

Aratme, N. (1992), "A study of the occupational mobility of Ilocano migrants in metro Manila, The Philippines", Paper given at the 1992 PAA meetings (University of Chicago, Department of Sociology, Chicago).

Armstrong–Wright, A. (1986), "Urban transit systems", World Bank Technical Paper No. 52 (Washington, DC).

Arnott, R.J. and M. Gersovitz (1986), "Social welfare underpinnings of urban bias and unemployment", Economic Journal 96:413–424.

Aryee, G. (1981), "The informal manufacturing sector in Kumasi", in S. Sethuraman, ed., The Urban Informal Sector in Developing Countries (ILO, Geneva).

Aryeetey-Attoh, S. (1992), "An analysis of household valuations and preference structures in Rio de Janeiro, Brazil", Growth and Change 23:183–198.

Asabere, P.K. (1981), "The determinants of land values in an African city: the case of Accra, Ghana", Land Economics 57:385–397.

Asabere, P.K. and K.O. Banahene (1983), "Population density function for Ghanaian (African) cities: an empirial note", Journal of Urban Economics 14:370–379.

Ashenfelter, O. and R. Oaxaca (1991), "Labor market discrimination and economic development", in N. Birdsall and R. Sabot, eds., Unfair Advantage: Labor Market Discrimination in Developing Countries (World Bank, Washington, DC).

Assadian, A. and J. Ondrich (1993), "Residential location, housing demand and labour supply decisions of one- and two-earner households: the case of Bogota, Colombia", Urban Studies 30:73–86.

Bahl, R. and J. Linn (1992), Urban Public Finance in Developing Countries (Oxford University Press, New York).

Baker, J., ed. (1990), Small Town Arica (Nordiska Afrikainstitutet, Uppsala).

Baker, J. and P.O. Pedersen, eds. (1992), The Rural-Urban Interface in Africa (Nordiska Afrikainstitutet, Uppsala).

Banerjee, B. (1981), "Rural-urban migration and family ties: an analysis of family considerations in migration behaviour in India", Oxford Bulletin of Economics and Statistics 43:321–355.

Banerjee, B. (1983), "The role of the informal sector in the migration process: a test of probabilistic migration models and labour market segmentation for India", Oxford Economic Papers 35: 399–422.

Banerjee, B. (1984a), "Information flow, expectations, and job search: rural-to-urban migration process in India", Journal of Development Economics 15:239–257.

Banerjee, B. (1984b), "The probability, size, and uses of remittances from urban to rural areas in India", Journal of Development Economics 16:293–311.

Banerjee, B. (1986), Rural to Urban Migration and the Urban Labour Market (Himalaya for the Institute of Economic Growth, Bombay).

Banerjee, B. (1991), "The determinants of migrating with a pre-arranged job and of the initial duration of urban unemployment", Journal of Development Economics 36:337–351.

Banerjee, B. and G. Bucci (1994), "On-the-job search after entering urban employment: An analysis based on Indian migrants", Oxford Bulletin of Economics and Statistics 56:33–47.

Banerjee, B. and S.M. Kanbur (1981), "On the specification and estimation of macro rural–urban migration functions", Oxford Bulletin of Economics and Statistics 7:29.

Barat, J. (1989), "A brief review of the development of urban transportation in Brazil", International Journal of Social Economics 16:44–57.

Barber, G.M. and W.J. Milne (1986), "Modeling internal migration in Kenya: an econometric analysis using limited data", Unpublished manuscript (University of Toronto, Toronto).

Barber, G, W. Milne and G. Ongile (1990), "Determinants of urban labour force participation in Kenya", Eastern Africa Economic Review 6:83–93.

Barnum, H.N. and R.H. Sabot (1977), "Education, employment probabilities and rural-urban migration in Tanzania", Oxford Bulletin of Economics and Statistics 39:109–126.

Barrett, R. (1988), Urban Transport in West Africa, Technical Paper No. 81, Urban Transport Series (World Bank, Washington DC).

Barros, R., L. Fox and R. Mendonca (1997), "Female–headed households, poverty, and the welfare of children in urban Brazil", Economic Development and Cultural Change 45:231–257.

Bartlett, W. (1983), "On the dynamic instability of induced—migration unemployment in a dual economy", Journal of Development Economics 13:85–96.

Bates, R. (1993), " 'Urban bias': a fresh look", Journal of Development Studies 29:219–228.

Baydar, N., M.J. White, C. Simkins and O. Babakol (1990), "Effects of agricultural development policies on migration in peninsular Malaysia", Demography 27:97–110.

Beals, R.E., M.E. Levy and L.N. Moses (1967), "Rationality and Migration in Ghana", Review of Economics and Statistics 49:480–486.

Becker, B.E. and Y. Gao (1989), "The Chinese urban labor system: prospects for reform", Journal of Labor Research 10:411–428.

Becker, C.M. (1987), "Urban sector income distribution and economic development', Journal of Urban Economics 21:127–145.

Becker, C.M. (1992), "Demographic cohort shifts and third world urbanization", Paper presented at the 39th North American meeting of the Regional Science Association International, Chicago.

Becker, C.M. (1997), "Enterprise incentives in post-Soviet agribusiness and manufacturing", in R.E. Evenson, ed., Proceedings of the Conference on Attaining Ukraine's Agro-industrial Potential (Yale University Economic Growth Center, New Haven, CT).

Becker, C.M. and C. Grewe (1996), "Cohort-specific rural-urban migration in Africa", Journal of African Economies 5:228–270.

Becker, C.M. and D. Hamley (1998), "Demographic change in the former Soviet Union during the transition perod", World Development 26:1957–1976.

Becker, C.M. and A.R. Morrison (1988), "The determinants of urban population growth in sub-Saharan Africa", Economic Development and Cultural Change 36:259–278.

Becker, C.M. and A.R. Morrison (1993), "Observational equivalence in the modeling of African labor markets and rural-urban migration", World Development 21:535–554.

Becker, C.M., J.G. Williamson and E.S. Mills (1992), Indian Urbanization and Economic Development (Johns Hopkins University Press, Baltimore).

Becker, C.M., A.M. Hamer and A.R. Morrison (1994), Beyond Urban Bias in Africa: Urbanization in an Era of Structural Adjustment (Heinemann, Portsmouth, NH).

Beckerman, W. (1992), "Economic growth and the environment: whose growth? Whose environment?", World Development 20:481–496.

Behrman, J. and A. Deolalikar (1991), "The poor and the social sectors during a period of macroeconomic adjustment: empirical evidence for Jamaica", World Bank Economic Review 5:291–313.

Behrman, J.R. and B.L. Wolfe (1984a), "Micro determinants of female migration in a developing country", Research in Population Economics 5:137–166.

Behrman, J.R. and B.L. Wolfe (1984b), "Labor force participation and earnings determinants for women in the special conditions of developing countries", Journal of Development Economics 15:259–288.

Behrman, J.R. and B.L. Wolfe (1984c), "The socioeconomic impact of schooling in a developing country", Review of Economics and Statistics 66:296–303.

Bell, C. (1991), "Regional heterogeneity, migration, and shadow prices", Journal of Public Economics 46:1–27.

Benabou, R. (1991), "Workings of a city: location, education, and production", National Bureau of Economic Research Technical Paper 113.

Bencivenga, V.R. and B.D. Smith (1997), "Unemployment, migration, and growth", Journal of Political Economy 105:582–608.

Beneria, L. and S. Feldman, eds. (1992), Unequal Burden: Economic Crises, Persistent Poverty, and Women's Work (Westview Press, Boulder and Oxford).

Bennett, J. and M. Phelps (1983), "A model of employment creation in an open developing economy", Oxford Economic Papers 35: 373–398.

Bernheim, B.D. and O. Stark (1986), "The strategic demand for children: theory and implications for fertility and migration", Migration and Development Program, Discussion Paper No. 25 (Harvard University, Cambridge, MA).

Bernstein, J.D. (1993), "Alternative approaches to pollution control and waste management: regulatory and economic instruments", World Bank Urban Management Programme, Urban Management and the Environment Series, No. 3.

Bernstein, J.D. (1994), "Land use considerations in urban environmental management", Urban Management and the Environment series, vol. 12 (World Bank, Washington, DC).

Berry, R.A. and R.H. Sabot (1978), "Labour market performance in developing countries: a survey", World Development 6:

Bertaud, A. (1989), "The regulatory environment of urban land in Indonesia: constraints imposed on the poor", Unpublished manuscript (World Bank, Washington, DC).

Bertaud, A. and B. Renaud (1994), Cities without land markets: lessons of the failed socialist experiment. Discussion Paper 227 (World Bank, Washington DC).

Bertaud, A. and J. Kolko (1994), "West of Los Angeles, east of Budapest: new evidence on residential density patterns", Urban Development Division, Unpublished manuscript (World Bank, Washington, DC).

Bhadra, D. (1992), "Migration and urban poverty: a case study of Bangladesh", Unpublished manuscript (Cornell University, Ithaca, NY).

Bhalla, A.S. (1990), "Rural-urban disparities in India and China", World Development 18:1097–1110.

Bhatia, K.B. (1979), "Rural-urban migration and surplus labour", Oxford Economic Papers 31:403–414.

Bigsten, A. (1996), "The circular migration of smallholders in Kenya". Journal of African Economies 5:1–20.

Bigsten, A., S.K. Mugerwa (1992), "Adaption and distress in the urban economy: a study of Kampala households", World Development 20:1423–1441.

Bilsborrow, R.E. (1993), "Issues in the measurement of female migration in developing countries", in United Nations, ed. Migration of Women in Developing Countries (UN, New York).

Bilsborrow, R.E., T.M. McDevitt, S. Kossoudji and R. Fuller (1987), "The impact of origin community chartacteristics on rural-urban out-migration in a developing country", Demography 24:191–210.

Birdsall, N. and R. Sabot (eds.) (1991), Unfair Advantage: Labor Market Discrimination in Developing Countries (World Bank, Washington, DC).

Birdsall, N., D. Ross, and R. Sabot (1995a), "Inequality and growth reconsidered", Williams College, Center for Development Economics, Research Memorandum RM-142 (Williams College, Williamstown, MS).

Birdsall, N., T. Pinckney, and R. Sabot (1995b), "Inequality, savings and growth", Williams College, Center for Development Economics, Research Memorandum RM-148 (Williams College, Williamstown, MS).

Bissiliat, J. and J. Fenet-Rieutord (1984), Les Villes Secondaires en Afrique: Leur Role at Leurs Fonctions dans le Developpement National et Regional, Phase 1, Senegal, Paris: Agence Francaise pour l'Amenagement et le Developpement a l'Etranger.

Black, D., and J.V. Henderson (1997), "Urban Growth", Unpublished manuscript (Brown University Department of Economics, Providence, RI).

Black, R. (1993), "Migration, return, and agricultural development in the Serra do Alvao, Northern Portugal", Economic Development and Cultural Change 41:563–585.

Blau, D.M. (1986), "Self-employment, earnings, and mobility in peninsular Malaysia", World Development 14:839–852.

Blinder, A. (1973), "Wage discrimination: reduced form and structural estimates", Journal of Human Resources 8:436–455.

Bliss, C. (1992), "The design of fiscal reforms in revenue-constrained developing countries", Economic Journal 102:940–951.

Bliss, C. and N. Stern (1978), "Productivity, wages and nutrition. Part I: the theory", Journal of Development Economics 5:331–362.

Blomqvist, A.G. (1978), "Urban job creation and unemployment in LDCs: Todaro versus Harris and Todaro", Journal of Development Economics 5:3–18.

Boehm, T.P., H.W. Herzog Jr. and A.M. Schlottmann (1991), "Intra-urban mobility, migration, and tenure choice", Review of Economics and Statistics 73:59–68.

Borjas, G., S. Bronars and S. Trejo (1992), "Self-selection and internal migration in the United States', NBER Working Paper 4002 (National Bureau of Economic Research, Cambridge, MA).

Braadbaart, O. and F. Braadbaart (1997), "Policing the urban pumping race: industrial groundwater overexploitation in Indonesia". World Development 25:199–210.

Brandon, C. and R. Ramankutty (1993), Toward an Environmental Strategy for Asia (World Bank, Washington, DC).

Braverman, A. and R. Kanbur (1987), "Urban bias and the political economy of agricultural reform", World Development 15:1179–1187.

Brennan, E. and H. Richardson (1989), "Asian megacity characteristics, problems and policies", International Regional Science Review 12:117–129.

Brown, A.N. (1993), "A note on industrial adjustment and regional labor markets in Russia", Comparative Economic Studies 35:147–157.

Brown, L.A. and A.R. Goetz (1987), "Development-related contextual effects and individual attributes in third world migration processes: a Venezuelan example", Demography 24:497–516.

Brown, R., M. Moon and B. Zoloth (1980), "Incorporating occupational attainment in studies of male–female earnings differentials", Journal of Human Resources 15:3–28.

Brueckner, J. (1990), "Analyzing third-world urbanization: a theoretical model with empirical evidence", Economic Development and Cultural Change 38:587–610.

Burki, A. and Q. Abbas (1991), "Earnings functions in Pakistan's urban informal sector: a case study", Pakistan Development Review 30:695–703.

Button, K., N. Ngoe and J. Hine (1993), "Modeling vehicle ownership and use in low income countries", Journal of Transport Economics and Policy 27:51–267.

Byerlee, D, J.L. Tommy and H. Fatoo (1976), "Rural-urban migration in Sierra Leone", Michigan State University, African Rural Economy Program, African Rural Economy Paper 13 (E. Lansing, MI).

Calvo, G. (1978), "Urban unemployment and wage determination in LDCs: trade unions in the Harris–Todaro model", International Economic Review 19:65–81.

Caces, F., F. Arnold, J. Fawcett and R. Gardner (1985), "Shadow households and competing auspices", Journal of Development Economics 17:5–25.

Campbell, T. (1989), "Environmental dilemmas and the urban poor", in L.H. Jeffrey, ed., Environment and the Poor: Development Strategies for a Common Agenda (Transaction Books, New Brunswick, NJ and Oxford).

Chan, K.W. and Y. Yunyan (1997), "Internal migration in post-Mao China: a dualistic approach". in China Population Association, Symposium on Demography of China, Population Association and IUSSP (Beijing, China).

Chang, K.-S. (1994), "Chinese urbanization and development before and after economic reform", World Development 22:601–614.

Chawla, A. (1993), "Intrahousehold resource allocation: a principal-agent analysis with empirical evidence", Ph.D. Dissertation, Department of Economics, University of Michigan.

Chen J., J. Yafen, and Z. Kaimin (1997), "Development of population aging Shanghai". in China Population Association, Symposium on Demography of China, China Population Association and IUSSP (Beijing, China).

Chenery, H.B. and M. Syrquin (1975), Patterns of Development, 1950–1970 (Oxford University Press, London).

Choe, S.-C. and S. Byung-Nak (1985), "Spatial distribution of industries and important location factors in the Seoul region", Water Supply and Urban Development Department, Discussion Paper UDD 89 (World Bank, Washington, DC).

Cinar, E.M. (1994), "Unskilled urban migrant women and disguised employment: home-working women in Istanbul, Turkey", World Development 22:369–380.

Clark, D. and J. Cosgrove (1991), "Amenities versus labor market opportunities: choosing the optimal distance to move", Journal of Regional Science 31:311–328.

Clark, M.H. (1985), "Household economic strategies and support networks of the poor in Kenya", Water Supply and Urban Development Department, Discussion Paper UDD–69 (World Bank, Washington, DC).

Cleaver, K. (1985), "The impact of price and exchange rate policies on agriculture in sub-Saharan agriculture", Staff Working Paper No. 728 (World Bank, Washington, DC).

Cohen, B. and W. House (1993), "Women's urban labour market status in developing countries: how well do they fare in Khartoum, Sudan?" Journal of Development Studies 29:461–483.

Cohen, B. and W. House (1994), "Education, experience and earnings in the labor market of a developing economy: the case of urban Khartoum", World Development 22:1549–1565.

Cohen, M. (1993), "Megacities and the environment", Finance and Development 30:44–47.

Colburn, F.D. (1993), "Exceptions to urban bias in Latin America: Cuba and Costa Rica", Journal of Development Studies 29:60–78.

Cole, W.E. and R.D. Sanders (1983), "Interstate migration in Mexico", Journal of Development Economics 12:341–354.

Cole, W.E. and R.D. Sanders (1985), "Internal migration and urbanization in the third world", American Economic Review 75:481–494.

Collier, P. (1979), "Migration and unemployment: a dynamic general equilibrium analysis applied to Tanzania", Oxford Economic Papers 31:205–236.

Collier, P. and A. Bigsten (1981), "A model of educational expansion and labor market adjustment applied to Kenya", Oxford Bulletin of Economics and Statistics 43:31–49.

Collier, P. and D. Lal (1980), "Poverty and growth in Kenya", World Bank Staff Working Paper No. 389.

Collier, P. and D. Lal (1986), Labour and Poverty in Kenya 1900–1980 (Clarendon Press, Oxford).

Collier, P., S. Radwan and S. Wangwe (1990), Labour and Poverty in Rural Tanzania (Clarendon Press, Oxford).

Collier, W.L., S.K. Santoso, G. Wiradi and Makali (1987), Economic and Social Transformation of Rural Java (US Agency for Agricultural Development, Jakarta).

Collier, V.C. and H. Rempel (1977), "The divergence of private from social costs in rural-urban migration: a case study of Nairobi, Kenya", Journal of Development Studies 13:

Connolly, P. (1990), "Housing and the state in Mexico", in G. Shidlo, ed., Housing Policy in Developing Countries (Routledge, London and New York).

Conway, P. (1994), "An atheoretic evaluation of success in structural adjustment", Economic Development and Cultural Change 42:267–292.

Cornia, G.-A. and F. Stewart (1991), "Sistema fiscal, ajuste y pobreza (The fiscal system. Adjustment and the poor. With English summary)," Coleccion Estudios CIEPLAN 0:77–106.

Cour, J.-M. (1985), Macroeconomic Implications of Urban Growth: Interaction between Cities and Their Hinterlands, Eastern and Southern Africa Region, Water Supply and Urban Development Region (World Bank, Washington, DC).

Crane, R. (1992), "Voluntary income redistribution with migration", Journal of Urban Economics 31:84–98.

Crane, R. (1994), "Water markets, market reform and the urban poor: results from Jakarta, Indonesia", World Development 22:71–83.

Crane, R. and A. Daniere, with S. Harwood (1997), "The contribution of environmental amenities to low-income housing: a comparative study of Bangkok and Jakarta", Urban Studies 34:1495–1512.

Day, R.H., S. Dasgupta, S.K. Datta and J.B. Nugent (1987), "Instability in rural-urban migration", Economic Journal 97:940–950.

De Cola, L. (1984), "Statistical determinants of the population for a nation's largest city", Economic Development and Cultural Change 33:71–98.

De Cola, L. (1985), "Lognormal estimates of macroregional city-size distributions, 1950–1970", Environment and Planning A. 17:1–16.

de la Paz L., M.H. Izazola, and J.G. de Leon (1993), "Characteristics of female migrants according to the 1990 census of Mexico", in United Nations, ed., Migration of Women in Developing Countries (UN, New York).

Deolalikar, A.B. (1988), "Nutrition and labor productivity in agriculture: estimates for South India", Review of Economics and Statistics 70:406–413.

Dimitriou, H.T. (1990), "Transport and third world city development", in H.T. Dimitriou and G.A. Banjo, ed., Transport Planning for Third World Cities (Routledge, London and New York).

Doan, P.L. and B.D. Lewis (1993), "Growth linkages and urban development in Niger", Growth and Change 24:487–508.

Donato, K.M. (1991), "Current trends and patterns of female migration: evidence from Mexico", unpublished manuscript (Louisiana State University, Department of Sociology, Baton Rouge, LA).

Dowall, D.E. (1992), "Benefits of minimal land-use regulations in developing countries", Cato Journal 12:413–423.

Dowall, D.E. and G. Clarke (1991), "A framework for reforming urban land policies in developing countries", Urban Management Program Policy Paper 7 (World Bank, Washington, DC).

Dowall, D.E. and M. Leaf (1990), "The price of land for housing in Jakarta: an analysis of the effects of location, urban infrastructure, and tenure on residential plot prices", Institute of Urban and Regional Development Working Paper 519 (University of California at Berkeley, Berkeley, CA).

Dowall, D.E. and P.A. Treffeisen (1991), "Spatial transformation in cities of the developing world: multi-nucleation and land-capital substitution in Bogota, Colombia", Regional Science and Urban Economics 21:201–224.

Dunkerly, H., ed. (1983), Urban Land Policy: Issues and Opportunities (Oxford University Press, New York).

Dunkerley, H.B., A.A. Walters, J.M. Courtney, W.A. Doebele, D.C. Shoup and M.D. Rivkin (1978), "Urban land policy issues and opportunities", Staff Working Paper No. 283 (World Bank, Washington, DC).

Dupont, V. (1986), Dynamique de Villes Secondaires et Afrique de l'Ouest (Ostrom, Paris).

Dureau, F. (1987), Migration et urbanisation: Le Case de la Côte d'Ivoire (Ostrom, Paris).

Eaton, J. and Z. Eckstein (1997), "Cities and growth: theory and evidence from France and Japan", Regional Science and Urban Economics 27:443–474.

Edwards, S. and G. Tabellini (1991), "Explaining fiscal policies and inflation in developing countries", Journal of International Money and Finance 10:S16–S48.

Ellis, F. (1984), "Relative agricultural prices and the urban bias model: a comparative analysis of Tanzania and Fiji", Journal of Development Studies 20:28–51.

El Shakhs, S. and H. Amirahmadi (1986), "Urbanization and spatial development in Africa: some critical issues", African Urban Quarterly 1:3–19.

Evans, H.E. (1992), "A virtuous circle model of rural-urban development: evidence from a Kenyan small town and its hinterland", Journal of Development Studies 28:640–667.

Evenson, R.E. and J.A. Roumasset (1986), "Markets, institutions and family size in rural Philippine households", Journal of Philippine Development 13:141–162.

Faini, R. and J. de Melo, eds. (1993), Fiscal Issues in Adjustment in Developing Countries (St. Martin's Press, New York, Macmillan Press, London).

Faiz, A. (1992), "Motor vehicle emissions in developing countries: relative implications for urban air quality", in A. Kreimer and M. Munasinghe, eds., Environmental Management and Urban Vulnerability, World Bank Discussion Paper No. 168.

Falaris, E.M. (1987), "A nested logit migration model with selectivity", International Economic Review 28:429–443.

Fallon, P. (1983), "Education and the duration of job search and unemployment in rural India", Journal of Development Economics 12:327–3440.

Fallon, P. (1985), "The labor market in Kenya: recent evidence". Development Research Department, Labor Market Division (World Bank, Washington, DC).

Fang, C. (1997), "The impact of labour mobility on market development and economic growth", in China Population Association, Symposium on Demography of China, Population Association and IUSSP (Beijing, China).

Farvacque, C. and P. McAuslan (1992), "Reforming urban land policies and institutions in developing countries", Urban Management Program Policy Paper 5 (World Bank, Washington, DC).

Feeney, G., F. Wang, M. Zhou and B. Xiao (1989), "Recent fertility dynamics in China: results from the 1987 one percent population survey", Population and Development Review 15:297–322.

Ferguson, B.W. (1992), "Land markets and the effect of property rights and regulations on development in Indonesia", Unpublished manuscript (Urban Institute, Washington, DC).

Fields, G. (1975), "Rural-urban migration, urban unemployment and under-employment, and job-search activities in LDCs", Journal of Development Economics 2:165–187.

Fields, G. (1982), "Place to place migration in Colombia", Economic Development and Cultural Change 30:539–558.

Fields, G. (1989), "On-the-job search in a labor market model: ex ante choices and ex post outcomes", Journal of Development Economics 30:159–178.

Fields, G. and H. Wan (1989), "Wage-setting institutions and economic growth", World Development 17:1471–1483.

Findlay, S.E. (1987), "An interactive contextual model of migration in Ilocos Norte, the Philippines", Demography 24:163–190.

Findlay, S.E. and A. Diallo (1993), "Social appearances and economic realities of female migration in rural Mali", in United Nations, ed., Migration of Women in Developing Countries (UN, New York).

Firdausy, C.M. (1993), Critical Issues and Policy Measures to Address Urban Poverty in Indonesia, Unpublished manuscript, Seminar on Critical Issues and Policy Measures to Address Urban Poverty (Asian Development Bank, Manila).

Firman, T. (1992), "The spatial pattern of urban population growth in Java, 1980–1990", Bulletin of Indonesian Economic Studies 28:95–109.

Fleck, S. (1997), "Choice or bargain? Married women's labor force participation in Hondurus", Ph.D. Dissertation, Department of Economics, American University.

Follain, J.R. and E. Jimenez (1985), "The demand for housing characteristics in developing countries", Urban Studies 22:421–432.

Follain, J.R., B. Renaud, and G.-C. Lim (1979), "Economic forces underlying urban decentralization trends: a structural model for density gradients applied to Korea", Environment and Planning A 11:541–551.

Foot, D. and W. Milne (1984), "Net migration estimation in an extended, multiregional gravity model", Journal of Regional Science 24:1.

Francis, E. and J. Hoddinott (1993), "Migration and differentiation in western Kenya: a tale of two sub-locations", Journal of Development Studies 30:115–145.

Friedman, J., E. Jimenez and S. Mayo (1988), "The demand for tenure security in developing countries", Journal of Development Economics 29:185–198.

Fujita, M. (1991), "A rational expectations equilibrium model of urban growth and land markets", Journal of Real Estate Finance and Economics 4:225–265.

Fuller, T.D., P. Lightfoot and P. Kamnuansilpa (1985), "Rural-urban mobility in Thailand: a decision-making approach", Demography 22:565–580.

Funkhouser, E. (1997), "Demand-side and supply-side explanations for barriers to labor market mobility in developing countries: the case of Guatemala", Economic Development and Cultural Change 45:341–366.

Gabriel, S., J. Shack-Marquez and W. Wascher (1993), "Does migration arbitrage regional labor market differentials", Regional Science and Urban Economics 23:211–233.

Gaile, G.L. and H.R. Aspaas (1991), "Kenya's spatial dimensions of development strategy", Urban Geography 12:381–386.

Galloway, L. and R. Vedder (1985), "Migration efficiency ratios and the optimal distribution of population", Growth and Change 16:3–7.

Garr, D.J. (1996), "Expectative land rights, house consolidation and cemetary squatting: some perspectives from Central Java", World Development 24:1925–1933.

Gaviria, J., V. Bindlish and U. Lele (1989), "The rural road question and Nigeria's agricultural development", MADIA Discussion Paper 10 (World Bank, Washington, DC).

Geyer, H. and T. Kontuly (1993), "A theoretical foundation for the concept of differential urbanization", International Regional Science Review 15:157–177.

Ghai, D. and S. Radwan, eds. (in press), Agrarian Policies and Rural Poverty in Africa (International Labour Office, Geneva).

Gibbon, P., ed. (1993), Social Change and Economic Reform in Africa (Scandinavian Institute of African Studies, Uppsala).

Gilbert, Alan (1990), "The provision of public services and the debt crisis in Latin America: the case of Bogota", Economic Geography 66:349–361.

Gilbert, Alanon (1990), "Urbanization at the periphery: reflections on the changing dynamics of housing and employment in Latin America", in D. Drakakis-Smith, ed., Economic Growth and Urbanization in Developing Areas (Routledge, London and New York).

Gindling, T. (1991), "Labor market segmentation and the determination of wages in the public, private-formal, and informal sectors in San Jose, Costa Rica", Economic Development and Cultural Change 39:584–605.

Glewwe, P. (1988), "The distribution of welfare in Côte d'Ivoire in 1985", Living Standards Measurement Study, Working Paper No. 29 (World Bank, Washington, DC).

Glewwe, P. and D. de Tray (1988), "The poor during adjustment: a case study of Côte d'Ivoire", Living Standards Measurement Study, Working Paper No. 47 (World Bank, Washington, DC).

Goldstein, A., S. Goldstein and S. Guo (1991), "Temporary migrants in Shanghai households, 1984", Demography 28:275–292.

Goldstein, S. (1990), "Urbanization in China, 1982–1987: effects of migration and reclassification", Population and Development Review 16:673–702.

Goode, R. (1993), "Tax advice to developing countries: an historical survey", World Development 21:37–53.

Goza, F.W., E. Rios–Neto and P. Vieira (1993), "The consequences of temporary out-migration for the families left behind: the case of Jequitinhonha Valley, Brazil", in United Nations, ed., Migration of Women in Developing Countries (UN, New York).

Greenaway, D. and O. Morrissey (1993), "Structural adjustment and liberalization in developing countries: what lessons have we learned", Kyklos 46:241–261.

Greene, D.L. (1978), Multinucleation in Urban Spatial Structure, Unpublished Ph.D. dissertation (Johns Hopkins University, Baltimore).

Greenwood, M. (1971), "A regression analysis of migration to urban areas of a less-developed country: the case of India", Journal of Regional Science 11:253–262.

Greenwood, M. (1985), "Human migration: theory, models and empirical studies", Journal of Regional Science 25:521–543.

Greenwood, M. (1991), "Migration, regional equilibrium, and the estimation of compensating differentials", American Economic Review 81:1382–1390.

Greenwood, M.J. and G.L. Hunt (1984), "Econometrically accounting for identities and restrictions in models of interregional migration", Regional Science and Urban Economics 14:113–128.

Gregory, J. (1986), "Migration and urbanization trends", Nairobi: paper delivered at the IUSSP Seminar on Economic Consequences of Population Trends in Africa.

Grewe, C.D. (1999), Household Demand and Composition in Indonesia, Unpublished Ph.D. dissertation (University of Colorado, Department of Economics, Boulder, CO).

Grimes, O.F. Jr. (1976), Housing for Low Income Urban Families (The Johns Hopkins University Press, Boulder, CO).

Gronau, R. (1973), "The effect of children on the housewife's value of time", Journal of Political Economy 81:S168–S199.

Grootaert, C. (in press), "The position of migrants in the urban informal labour markets of Côte d'Ivoire", Journal of African Economies 1:416–445.

Gruver, G.W. and L.A. Zeager (1993), "Agricultural price policy in a less developed economy with endogenous urban wages", Journal of Economic Development 18:27–41.

Gruver, G.W. and L.A. Zeager (1994), "Steady-state labor turnover as optimal household behavior", Journal of Regional Science 34:75–90.

Gugler, J. (1991), "Life in a dual system revisited: urban-rural ties in Enugu, Nigeria, 1961–1987", World Development 19:399–409.

Gupta, I. and A. Mitra (1997), "Does duration of migration matter? Poverty and occupational choice among slum dwellers in Delhi", Unpublished manuscript (Institute of Economic Growth, Delhi).

Haessel, W.W. (1978), "Macroeconomic policy, investment and urban unemployment in less developed countries", American Journal of Agricultural Economics 60:29–36.

Haggblade, S. and J. Brown (1989), "Farm-nonfarm linkages in rural sub-Saharan Africa", World Development 17:1173–1201.

Hamer, A. (1988a), China Zhejiang: Challenges of Rapid Urbanization, Report No. 6612-cha (World Bank, Washington, DC).

Hamer, A. (1988b), China Urban Housing Reform: Issues and Implement Options, Report No. 8222-cha (World Bank, Washington, DC).

Hamer, A. M. (1984), "Decentralized urban development and industrial location behavior in Sao Paulo, Brazil", Water Supply and Urban Development Department, Discussion Paper UDD 29 (World Bank, Washington, DC).

Hamer, A.M. (1985), "Bogota's unregulated subdivisions: the myths and realities of incremental housing construction", Staff Working Paper No. 734 (World Bank, Washington, DC).

Hamid, N., I. Nabi and A. Nasim (in press), Trade, Exchange Rate, and Agricultural Pricing Policies in Pakistan (World Bank, Washington, DC).

Hannah, L., K.-H. Kim and E.S. Mills (1993), "Land use controls and housing prices in Korea", Urban Studies 30:147–156.

Hansen, B. (1979), "Colonial economic development with an unlimited supply of land: a Ricardian case", Economic Development and Cultural Change 27:611–628.

Hansen, E. (1983), "Why do firms locate where they do?", Water Supply and Urban Development Department, Discussion Paper UDD 25 (World Bank, Washington, DC).

Hansen, K.T. (1982), "Lusaka's squatters: past and present", African Studies Review, 25:117–236.

Hanson, G.H. (1994), "Localization economies, vertical organization, and trade", NBER Working Paper No. 4744 (Cambridge, MA).

Hanson, P. (1933), "Local power and market reform in Russia", Communist Economies and Economic Transformation 5:45–60.

Hardoy, J.-E. and D. Satterthwaite (1986), "Government policies and small and intermediate urban centres", in J.E. Hardoy and D. Satterthwaite, eds., Small and Intermediate Urban Centres: Their Role in Regional and National Development in the Third World (Westview, Boulder, CO).

Harrigan, F. and P. McGregor (1993), "Equilibrium and disequilibrium perspectives on regional labor migration", Journal of Regional Science 33:49–67.

Harris, J. and R. Sabot (1982), "Urban unemployment in LDC's: towards a more general search model", in R.H. Sabot, ed., Migration and the Labor Market in Developing Countries (Westview, Boulder, CO).

Harris, J. and M. Todaro (1970), "Migration, unemployment and development: a two-sector analysis", American Economic Review 60:126–142.

Hay, M.J. (1980), "A structural equations model of migration in Tunisia", Economic Development and Cultural Change 28:345–358.

Hazari, B.R. and P.M. Sgro (1991), "Urban-rural structural adjustment, urban unemployment with traded and nontraded goods", Journal of Development Economics 35:187–196.

Hazlewood, A. (1989), Education, Work, and Pay in East Africa (Oxford University Press/Clarendon Press, New York).

Henderson, J.V. (1979), "The economics of systems of cities", Brown University Working Paper No. 78-22.

Henderson, J. V. (1980), "A framework for international comparisons of systems of cities", World Bank, Urban and Regional Economics Division, Urban and Regional Report No. 80-3.

Henderson, J.V. (1982a), "Urban economies of scale in Brazil", Water Supply and Urban Development Department Discussion Paper UDD–17 (World Bank, Washington, DC).

Henderson, JV. (1982b), "The impact of government policies on urban concentration", Journal of Urban Economics 12:280–303.

Henderson, J.V. (1986a), "Urbanization in a developing country", Journal of Development Economics 22:269–293.

Henderson, J.V. (1986b), "The timing of regional development", Journal of Development Economics 23:275–292.

Henderson, J.V. (1988a), Urban Development: Theory, Fact, and Illusion (Oxford University Press, New York).

Henderson, J.V. (1988b), "General equilibrium modeling of systems and cities", in P. Nijkamp and E. Mills, eds., Handbooks in Regional and Urban Economics, Vol. II, (North-Holland, Amsterdam).

Henderson, J.V. (1994), "Where does an industry locate?", Journal of Urban Economics 35:83–104.

Henderson, J.V. and Y.M. Ioanides (1981), "Aspects of growth in a system of cities", Journal of Urban Economics 10:117–139.

Hercowitz, Z. and D. Pines (1991),"Migration with fiscal externalities", Journal of Public Economics 46:163–180.

Henderson, J.V. and A. Kuncoro (1994), "Industrial centralization in Indonesia", Unpublished manuscript (Brown University Department of Economics, Providence, RI).

Henderson, J.V., A. Kuncoro and M. Turner (1995a), "Industrial development of cities", Journal of Political Economy 103:1067–1090.

Henderson, J.V., A. Kuncoro and D. Nasution (1995b), "The dynamics of Jabotabek development", Unpublished manuscript (Brown University Department of Economics, Providence, RI).

Herzog, H. and A. Schlottmann (1981), "Labor force migration and allocative efficiency in the United States: the roles of information and psychic costs", Economic Inquiry 19:459–475.

Herzog, H., A. Schlottmann and T. Boehm (1993), "Migration as spatial job-search: a survey of empirical findings", Regional Studies 27:327–340.

Hoddinott, J. (1992), "Modeling remittance flows in Kenya", Journal of African Economies 1:206–232.

Hoddinott, J. (1994), "A model of migration and remittances applied to western Kenya", Oxford Economic Papers 46:459–476.

Horton, S., R. Kanbur and D. Mazumdar (1994), "Labor markets in an era of adjustment: an overview", in S. Horton, R. Kanbur and D. Mazumdar, eds., Labor Markets in an Era of Adjustment: Vol. 1, Issues Papers (World Bank, Washington, DC).

Hotchkiss, D. and M.J. White (1993), "A simulation model of a decentralized metropolitan area with two-worker, "traditional", and female-headed households", Journal of Urban Economics 34:159–185.

House, W. (1984), "Nairobi's informal sector: dynamic entrepreneurs or surplus labor?", Economic Development and Cultural Change 32:277–302.

House, W. (1987), "Labor market differentiation in a developing economy: an example from urban Juba, Southern Sudan", World Development 15:877–897.

House, W. (1992), "Priorities for urban labor market research in anglophone Africa", Journal of Developing Areas 27:49–67.

House, W. and H. Rempel (1980), "The determinants of interregional migration in Kenya", World Development 8:25–36.

Hoy, M. and E. Jimenez (1991), "Squatters' rights and urban development: an economic perspective", Economica 58:79–92.

Hugo, G.J. (1993), "Migrant women in developing countries", in United Nations, ed., Migration of Women in Developing Countries (UN, New York).

Hyatt, D.E. and W.J. Milne (1990), "Urban and rural fertility differentials in Kenya: an econometric analysis using micro data", Institute for Policy Analysis Working Paper (University of Toronto, Toronto, ONT).

Imai, K. (1997), "Urban structural change in Asian LDCs' Cities", Unpublished manuscript (University of Colorado Department of Economics, Boulder, CO).

Infante, R. and E. Klein (1991), "The Latin American labour market, 1950–1990", CEPAL Review 45:121–135.

Ingram, G.K. (1980), "Land in perspective: its role in the structure of cities", Urban and Regional Economics Division Urban and Regional Report No. 80-9 (World Bank, Washington, DC).

Ingram, G. and A. Carroll (1981), "The spatial structure of Latin American cities", Journal of Urban Economics 9:257–273.

Ishumi, A.G.M. (1984), The Urban Jobless in Eastern Africa (Scandinavian Institute of African Studies, Uppsala).

Ito, K. (1992), "The reinstatement of local fiscal autonomy in the Republic of Korea", Developing Economies 30:404–429.

Jamal, V. (1984), "Rural urban gap and income distribution: synthesis report of seventeen African countries", Addis Ababa, ILO/JASPA.

Jamal, V. and J. Weeks (1988), "The vanishing rural–urban gap in sub-Saharan Africa", International Labour Review 127:271–292.

Jimenez, E. (1982), "The value of squatter dwellings in developing countries", Economic Development and Cultural Change 30:739–752.

Jimenez, E. (1985), "Urban squatting and community organization in developing countries", Journal of Public Economics 27:69–92.

Jones, G. (1993), "The role of female migration in development", in United Nations, ed., Migration of Women in Developing Countries (UN, New York).

Joshi, H., H. Lubell and J. Mouly (1976), Abidjan: Urban Development and Employment in the Ivory Coast (International Labour Office, Geneva).

Kaganova, O. and M. Berezin (1993), "The market for urban real estate: development tendencies", Voprosy Ekonomiki 1993:7 (in Russian).

Kahimbaara, J. A. (1993), "The convolution of urban planning with tradition in Lesotho, 1928–1991", Environment and Planning A 25(7):100–120.

Kahn, J. and H. Ofek (1992), "The equilibrium distribution of population and wages in a system of cities", Review of Regional Studies 22:201–216.

Kahnert, F. (1987), "Improving urban employment and labor productivity", Discussion Paper 10 (World Bank, Washington).

Kannappan, S. (1983), Employment Problems and the Urban Labor Market in Developing Countries, Graduate School of Business Administration, Division of Research (University of Michigan, Ann Arbor).

Kannappan, S. (1984), "Tradition and modernity in urban employment in developing nations", Regional Development Dialogue 5:55–62.

Kannappan, S. (1988), "Urban labor markets and development", World Bank Research Observer 3:189–206.

Kannappan, S. (1989), "Employment policy and labour markets in the developing nations: a perspective on the state-of-the-art in the 1980s", in Bernard Salome, ed., Fighting Urban Unemployment in Developing Countries (IECD, Paris).

Kannappan, S. (1990), "A heterodox model of employment and labor underutilization: Sri Lanka in 1971 and 1989", Unpublished manuscript, Department of Economics (Michigan State University, E. Lansing, MI).

Kano, H. (1992), "The reorientation of Indonesia's centralized budgetary system", Developing Economies 30:377–403.

Katz, E. (1997), "The Intra-household economics of voice and exit: Evaluating the feminist institutional content of family resource allocation models", Working Paper 97-05, Barnard College, Department of Economics.

Katz, E. and O. Stark (1985a), "Desired fertility and migration in LDCs: signing the connection", Center for Population Studies, Migration and Development Program Discussion Paper 15 (Harvard University, Cambridge, MA).

Katz, E. and O. Stark (1985b), "On fertility, migration and remittances in LDCs", Center for Population Studies, Migration and Development Program Discussion Paper 19 (Harvard University, Cambridge, MA).

Katz, E. and O. Stark (1986a), "On the shadow wage of urban jobs in less developed countries", Journal of Urban Economics 20.

Katz, E. and O. Stark (1986b), "Labor migration and risk aversion in less developed countries", Journal of Labor Economics 41:134–149.

Kelley, A.C. (1991), "African urbanization and city growth: perspectives, problems, and policies", Unpublished manuscript (Duke University Department of Economics, Durham, NC).

Kelley, A.C. and R. Schmidt (1983), "Incorporating demography into general equilibrium modeling", in A.C. Kelley, W.C. Sanderson and J.G. Willamson eds. *Modeling Growing Economies in Equilibrium and Disequilibrium*. Durham, NC: Duke Univ. Press, pp. 317–337.

Kelley, A.C. and J.G. Williamson (1984), What Drives Third World City Growth? A Dynamic General Equilibrium Approach (Princeton University Press, Princeton, NJ).

Kelley, A.C., J.G. Williamson, and R.J. Cheetham (1972), Dualistic Economic Development: Theory and History (University of Chicago Press, Chicago).

Khasiani, S. (1991), "A model of migration motivations: migration valuations and migration dispositions among rural youth in Kenya", Eastern Africa Economic Review 7:27–38.

Kim, S.T., C.S. Jung and K.H. Roh (1991), "Regional economic gap in Korea", Journal of Economic Development 16:145–167.

Kingsley, G.T., B.W. Ferguson, and B.T. Bower with S.R. Dice (1994), "Managing urban environmental quality in Asia", Technical Paper No. 220 (World Bank, Washington, DC).

Klak, T. and M. Holtzclaw (1993), "The housing, geography, and mobility of Latin American urban poor: the prevailing model and the case of Quito, Ecuador", Growth and Change 24:247–276.

Knight, J.B. and R.H. Sabot (1981), "The returns to education: increasing with experience or decreasing with expansion?", Oxford Bulletin of Economics and Statistics 43:51–71.

Knight, J.B. and R.H. Sabot (1982), "From migrants to proletarians: employment experience, mobility, and wages in Tanzania", Oxford Bulletin of Economics and Statistics 44:199–226.

Knight, J.B. and R.H. Sabot (1988), "Lewis through a looking glass: public sector employment, rent-seeking and economic growth", Economics Research Memorandum RM-108 (Williams College Center for Development, Williamstown, MA).

Knight, J. and R.H. Sabot (1990), Education Productivity and Inequality: The East African Natural Experiment (Oxford University Press, New York).

Knowles, J.C. and R. Anker (1981), "An analysis of income transfers in a developing country: the case of Kenya", Journal of Development Economics 8:205–226.

Kojima, R. (1992a), "Introduction (to fiscal decentralization)", Developing Economies 30:311–314.

Kojima, R. (1992b), "The growing fiscal authority of provincial-level governments in China", Developing Economies 30:315–346.

Konadu-Agyemang, K.O. (1991), "Reflections on the absence of squatter settlements in west African cities: the case of Kumasi, Ghana", Urban Studies 28:139–151.

Kreimer, A. and M. Munasinghe, eds. (1992), Environmental Management and Urban Vulnerability, World Bank Discussion Papers, No. 168 (World Bank, Washington, DC).

Krupnick, A.J. (1991), "Transportation and air pollution in urban areas of developed and developing countries", Resources for the Future, Quality of the Environment Division Discussion Paper: QE91–08.

Kulaba, S. (1989), "Local government and the management of urban services in Tanzania", in R. Stren and R. White, op. cit.

Lam, D. and R.F. Schoeni (1993), "Effects of family background on earnings and returns to schooling: evidence from Brazil", Journal of Political Economy 101:710–740.

Lauby, J. and O. Stark (1988), "Individual migration as a family strategy: young women in the Philippines", Population Studies 42:473–486.

Lecaillon, J., F. Paukert, C. Morrisson and M. Germidis (1984), Income Distribution and Economic Development (International Labour Office, Geneva).

Ledent, J. (1982a), "Rural-urban migration, urbanization, and economic development", Economic Development and Cultural Change 30:507–538.

Ledent, J. (1982b), "The factors of urban population growth: net immigration versus natural increase", International Regional Science Review 7: 99–126.

Ledent, J. (1990), "The distribution of city sizes in subSaharan Africa: a cross-sectional analysis", INRS-urbanisation, Unpublished manuscript presented at the 1990 North American meetings of the Regional Science Association (Universite du Quebec au Montreal, Montreal).

Lee, K.S. (1981), "Intra urban location of manufacturing employment in Colombia", Journal of Urban Economics 9:222–241.

Leigland, J. (1993), "Decentralizing the development budget process in Indonesia: progress and prospects", Public Budgeting and Finance 13:85–101.

Leitmann, J. (1991), "Energy-environment linkages in the urban sector", World Bank Urban Management Program Discussion Paper No. 2 (World Bank, Washington, DC).

Lent, G.E. (1978), "Experience with urban land value tax in developing countries", Bulletin for International Fiscal Documentation 32:75–83.

Levy, M.B. and W.J. Wadycki (1974), "Education and the decision to migrate: an econometric analysis of migration in Venezuela", Econometrica 42:377–388.

Lewis, W.A. (1954), "Economic development with unlimited supplies of labour", The Manchester School 22:139–191.

Liang, Z. and M.J. White (1996), "Internal migration in China, 1950–1988", Demography 33:375–384.

Liang, Z. and M.J. White (1997), "Market transition, government policies, and inter-provincial migration in China: 1983–1988", Economic Development and Cultural Change 45:321–339.

Lim, G.C., J. Follain Jr. and B. Renaud (1984), "Economics of residential crowding in developing countries", Journal of Urban Economics 16:173–186.

Lim, J.D. (1993), "Urban growth and industrial restructuring: the case of Pusan", Environment and Planning A 25:95–109.

Lim, L.L. (1993), "The structural determinants of female migration", in United Nations, ed., Migration of Women in Developing Countries (UN, New York).

Linn, J.F. (1979), "Policies for efficient and equitable growth of cities in developing countries", World Bank Staff Working Paper No. 342.

Linn, J. (1982), "The costs of urbanization in developing countries", Economic Development and Cultural Change 30:625–648.

Lipton, M. (1976), Why Poor People Stay Poor: Urban Bias in World Development (Harvard University Press, Cambridge, MA).

Lipton, M. (1984), "Urban bias revisited", Journal of Development Studies 20:139–166.

Lipton, M. (1991), "A reassessment of Kenya's rural and urban informal sector", World Development 19:651–670.

Lipton, M. (1993), "Urban bias: of consequences, classes and causality", Journal of Development Studies 29:229–258.

Livas E.R. and P. Krugman (1992), "Trade policy and the third world metropolis", NBER Working Paper No. 4238 (Cambridge, MA).

Locay, L. (1990), "Economic development and the division of production between households and markets", Journal of Political Economy 98:965–982.

Lodhi, A. and H.A. Pasha (1991), "Housing demand in developing countries: a case-study of Karachi in Pakistan", Urban Studies 28:623–634.

Lovell, P. (1993), "The geography of economic development and racial discrimination in Brazil", Development and Change 24:83–101.

Lowder, S. (1978), "The limitations of planned land development for low-income housing in third world", Urban Studies 30:241–255.

Lubell, H. and C. Zarour (1990), "Resilience amidst crisis: the informal sector of Dakar", International Labour Review 129:387–396.

Lucas, R. (1982), "Determinants of migration decisions", in Migration in Botswana: Patterns, Causes, and Consequences. Final Report of the National Migration Study (Government Printers, Garborone, Botswana).

Lucas, R.E.B. (1997), "Internal migration in developing countries", in M. Rosenzweig and O. Start, eds., Handbook of Population and Family Economics (North-Holland, Amsterdam).

Lucas, R.E.B. and O. Stark (1985), "Motivations to remit: evidence from Botswana", Journal of Political Economy 93:901–918.

Lucas, R.E.B. and O. Stark (1988), "Migration, remittances, and the family", Economic Development and Cultural Change 36:465–482.

Lumbantaruan, H. (1997), "Relative efficiency of public and private enterprises in Indonesia", Boulder, CO: Univ. of Colorado Dept. of Economics, unpubl. Ph.D. diss.

Lundberg, S. and R. Pollak (1993), "Separate spheres bargaining and the marriage market", Journal of Political Economy 101:988–1010.

Ma, L.J.C. and M. Fan (1994), "Urbanisation from below: the growth of Jiangsu, China", Urban Studies 31:1625–1645.

Mabogunje, A. (1983), "The case for big cities", Habitat International 7:

Machado, C.C. and J.F. Abreu (1991), "The elderly mobility transition in Brazil", Paper presented at University of Colorado Program in Population Processes seminar on the Elderly Mobility Transition, Unpublished manuscript.

Maddala, G.S., Y. Toda and N. Nozdrina (1993), "Analysis of sales prices for apartments in Moscow", Voprosy Ekonomiki 1993:7 (in Russian).

Magnac, T. (1991), "Segmented or competitive labor markets", Econometrica 59:165–187.

Malpezzi, S. (1990), "Urban housing and financial markets: some international comparisons", Urban Studies 27:971–1022.

Malpezzi, S. (1991), "Discounted cash flow analysis: present value models of housing programmes and policies", in A.G. Tipple and K.G. Willis, eds, Housing the Poor in the Developing World: Methods of Analysis, Case Studies and Policy (Routledge, New York).

Malpezzi, S. (1993), "Can New York and Los Angeles learn from Kumasi and Bangalore? Costs and benefits of rent controls in developing countries", Housing Policy Debate 4:589–626.

Malpezzi, S. and G. Ball (1991), "Rent control in developing countries", Discussion Paper No. 129 (World Bank, Washington, D.C.).

Malpezzi, S. and S. Mayo (1987), "The demand for housing in developing countries: empirical estimates from household data", Economic Development and Cultural Change 35:687–721.

Malpezzi, S. and S.K. Mayo (1987), "User cost and housing tenure in developing countries", Journal of Development Economics 25:197–220.

Manning, C. (1988), "Rural employment creation in Java: lessons from the green revolution and oil boom", Population and Development Review 14:47–80.

Marcouiller, D., V. Ruiz de Castillo, and C. Woodruff (1997), "Formal measures of the informal-sector wage gap in Mexico, El Salvador, and Peru", Economic Development and Cultural Change 45:367–392.

Markusen, J.R. and T.F. Rutherford (1993), "Discrete plant-location decisions in an applied general-equilibrium model of trade liberalization", NBER Working Paper No. 4513 (Cambridge, MA).

Martin, M.F. (1992), "Urban incomes, worker's democracy and the spring uprising", Review of Radical Political Economics 24:136–165.

Massey, D.S. (1990),"Social structure, household strategies, and the cumulative causation of migration", Population Index 56:33–26.

Mathieu, R. (1982), "Locational analysis of bank funded projects in Ivory Coast, Cameroon, and Mali", Water Supply and Urban Development Department, Discussion Paper UDD 28 (World Bank, Washington, DC).

Mathur, O.P. (1982), "The role of small cities in national development re-examined", in Mathur, ed., Small Cities and National Development (United Nations Centre for Regional Development, Nagoya, Japan).

Mathur, V. and S. Stein (1993), "The role of amenities in a general equilibrium model of regional migration and growth", Southern Economic Journal 59:394–409.

Maxwell, D.G. (1995), "Alternative food security strategy: a household analysis of urban agriculture in Kampala", World Development 23:1669–1681.

Mayo, S.K. and S. Angel (1993), Housing Enabling Markets to Work, A World Bank Policy Paper (World Bank, Washington, DC).

Mayo, S. and D. Gross (1987), "Sites and services—and subsidies: the economics of housing in developing countries", World Bank Economic Review 1:301–335.

Mayo, S., S. Malpezzi, and D. Gross (1986), "Shelter strategies for the urban poor in developing countries", World Bank Research Observer 1:183–203.

Mazumdar, D. (1976), "The urban informal sector", World Development 4:655–679.

Mazumdar, D. (1981), The Urban Labor Market and Income Distribution: A Study of Malaysia (Oxford University Press, New York).

Mazumdar, D. (1983), "The rural-urban wage gap migration and the working of urban labor market: an interpretation based on a study of the workers of Bombay city", Indian Economic Review 18:169–198.

Mazumdar, D. (1987), "Rural-urban migration in developing countries", in E.S. Mills, ed., Handbook of Regional and Urban Economics, vol. II (Elsevier Science Publishers, New York).

Mazumdar, D. (1989), "Microeconomic issues of labor markets in developing countries: analysis and policy implications", Economic Development Institute Seminar Paper No. 40 (World Bank, Washington, DC).

Mbuyi, K. (1989), "Kinshasa: problems of land management, infrastructure and food supply", in R. Stren and R. White, op. cit.

McCleary, W.A. (1991), "The design and implementation of conditionality", in V. Thomas, A. Chhibber, M. Dailami and J. de Melo, eds., Restructuring Economics in Distress: Policy Reform and the World Bank (Oxford University Press, New York).

McCutcheon, L. (1994), "Measuring migrant change: a look at housing in Bogota, Seoul, and Surabaya", Journal of Developing Areas 18:357–372.

Mead, D.C. and C. Morrison (1996), "The informal sector elephant", World Development 24:1611–1619.

Megbolugbe, I.F. (1989), "A hedonic index model: the housing market of Jos, Nigeria", Urban Studies 26:486–494.

Mellor, J. (1976), The New Economics of Growth: A Strategy for India and the Developing World (Cornell University Press, Ithaca, NY).

Mera, K. (1973), "On the urban agglomeration and economic efficiency", Economic Development and Cultural Change 21:309–324.

Mera, K. (1984), "Measuring economic contributions of infrastructure in cities of developing countries", Water Supply and Urban Development Department, Discussion Paper UDD 34 (World Bank, Washington, DC).

Mills, E.S. and C.M. Becker (1986), Studies in Indian Urban Development (Oxford University Press, New York).

Mills, E.S. and J.P. Tan (1980), "A comparison of urban population density functions in developed and developing countries", Urban Studies 17:313–321.

Mitra, A. (1994), Urbanisation, Slums, Informal Sector Employment and Poverty (B.R. Publishing Corporation, Delhi).

Mitra, A. (1997), "Industry, agglomeration economies and urban growth", Unpublished manuscript (Institute of Economic Growth, Delhi).

Mohan, R. (1985), "Urbanization in India's future", Population and Development Review 11:619–645.

Mohan, R. (1986), Work, Wages, and Welfare in a Developing Metropolis: Consequences of Growth in Bogota, Colombia (Oxford University Press, New York).

Montgomery, M.R. (1987), "The impacts of urban population growth on urban labor markets and the costs of urban service delivery: a review", in D.G. Johnson and R.D. Lee, eds., Population Growth and Economic Development: Issues and Evidence, Social Demography Series (University of Wisconsin Press, Madison, WI), pp. 149–188.

Montgomery, M. and E. Brown (1985), Migration and Urbanization in Sub-Saharan Africa, Population, Health and Nutrition Department (World Bank, Washington, DC).

Moomaw, R. (1981), "Productivity and city size: a critique of the evidence", Quarterly Journal of Economics 96:675–688.

Moomaw, R. and A.M. Shatter (1996), "Urbanization and economic development: a bias toward large cities?", Journal of Urban Economics 40:13–37.

Morley, S. (1988), "Relative wages, labor force structure, and the distribution of income in the short and long run", Economic Development and Cultural Change 36:651–668.

Morley, S. (1994), Poverty and Inequality in Latin America: Past Evidence, Future Prospects (Overseas Development Council, Washington, DC).

Morrison, A. (1994), "Are institutions or economic rents responsible for interindustry wage differentials?", World Development 22:355–368.

Morrison, A. (1992), "Inter-industry wage differentials in LDCs: are institutions or economic rents responsible?", Department of Economics Working Paper (Tulane University, New Orleans, LA).

Morrison, A. (1993), "Unproductive migration reconsidered: a stochastic frontier production function framework for analyzing internal migration", Oxford Economic Papers 45:501–518.

Mosley, P., J. Harrigan and J. Toye (1991), Aid and Power: The World Bank and Policy-Based Lending, vols. 1 and 2 (Routledge, London).

Munasinghe, M. (1992), Water Supply and Environmental Management: Developing World Applications (Westview Press, Boulder and Oxford).

Muth, R. (1969), Cities and Housing (University of Chicago Press, Chicago).

Nabi, I. (1984), "Village-end considerations in rural-urban migration", Journal of Development Economics 14:129–145.

Nafziger, E.W. (1988), Inequality in Africa: Political Elites, Proletariat, Peasants and the Poor (Cambridge University Press, Cambridge, UK).

Nakagome, M. (1989), "Urban unemployment and the spatial structure of labor markets: an examination of the "Todaro paradox" in a spatial context", Journal of Regional Science 29:161–170.

Natskomstat National Statistical Committee of the Kyrgyz Republic (1995), Demograficheskii Ezhegodnik Kyrgyzskoi Respubliki 1994 (Natskomstat, Bishkek).

Newbery, DM. (1988), "Road transport fuel pricing policy", Department of Applied Economics, Working Paper: 889 (University of Cambridge).

Niedercorn, J.H. and B.V. Bechdolt, Jr. (1969), "An economic derivation of the 'gravity law' of spatial interaction", Journal of Regional Science 9:2.

Oaxaca, R. (1973), "Male-female wage differentials in urban labor markets", International Economic Review 3:693–709.

Oberai, A.S. (1993), Population Growth, Employment and Poverty in Third-World Mega-Cities (St. Martin's Press, New York).

Ogura, M. (1991), "Rural-urban migration in Zambia and migrant ties to home villages", Developing Economies 29:145–165.

Oi, J.C. (1993), "Reform and urban bias in China", Journal of Development Studies 29:129–148.

Okojie, C.E.E. (1984), "Female migrants in the urban labor market: Benin City, Nigeria", Canadian Journal of African Studies 18:547–562.

Okpala, D.G.I. (1978), "Housing standards: a constraint on urban housing production in Nigeria", Ekistics 240.

Ozo, A.O. (1986), "Residential location and intra-urban mobility in a developing country: some empirical observations from Benin", Urban Studies 23:457–470.

Pachon Munoz, A. and S. de Hernandez (1989), "La Vivienda en Colombia, 1973–1985: La Distribucion Espacial de la Poblacion en las Areas Metropolitanas", Boletin de Estadistica 438:245–258.

Panayotou, T. (1993), Green Markets: The Economics of Sustainable Development (ICS Press for the International Center for Economic Growth and the Harvard Institute for International Development, San Francisco).

Papageorgiou, Y.Y. (1990), The Isolated City State: An Economic Geography of Urban Spatial Structure (Routledge, London).

Park, S.O. (1993), "Industrial restructuring and the spatial division of labor: the case of the Seoul metropolitan region, the Republic of Korea", Environment and Planning A 25:81–93.

Pasha, H.A. (1992), "Maximum lot size zoning in developing countries", Urban Studies 29:1173–1181.

Paul, S. (1992), "Accountability in public services: exit, voice and control", World Development 20:1047–1060.

Payne, G.K. and L. Payne (1991), "Urban land tenure and property rights", Urban Management Program, Unpublished manuscript (World Bank, Washington, DC).

Pchelintsev, O. (1993), "Regional hierarchy under threat: a spatial dimension of the socio-economic crisis in the former Soviet Union and Russia", International Regional Science Review 15:267–280.

Peil, M. (1976), "African squatter settlements: a comparative study", Urban Studies 13:155–166.

Peil, M. (1979), "Housing the poor in West Africa, public and private provisions", Institute of Development Studies Bulletin 10:28–32.

Petrakos, G.C. (1992), "Urban concentration and agglomeration economies: re-examining the relationship", Urban Studies 29:1219–1229.

Petrakos, G. and J.C. Brada (1989), "Metropolitan concentration in developing countries", Kyklos 42:557–578.

Pfister, F. (1982), "Housing improvement and popular participation in the Upper Volta", Habitat International 6:209–214.

Phongpaichit, P. (1993), "The labour market aspects of female migration to Bangkok", in United Nations, ed., Migration of Women in Developing Countries (UN, New York).

Plane, D.A. (1993), "Demographic influences on migration", Regional Studies 27:375–383.

Population Reference Bureau (1997), 1997 World Population Data Sheet (PRB, Washington, DC).

Porter, R. (1993), "Toward an economic theory of the apartheid city", in L. Stetting, K.E. Svendsen and Y. Yndgaard, eds., Global Change and Transformation: Economic Essays in Honor of Karsten Laursen (Handelshojskolens Forlag, Copenhagen).

Portes, A. (1989), "Latin American urbanization during the years of the crisis", Latin American Research Review 24:7–43.

Portes, A. and R. Schauffler (1993), "Competing perspectives on the Latin American informal sector", Population and Development Review 19:33–60.

Preston, S.H. (1979), "Urban growth in developing countries: a demographic reappraisal", Population and Development Review 5:195–215.

Pryor, F.L. (1988a), "Income distribution and economic development in Malawi", Discussion Paper No. 36 (World Bank, Washington, DC).

Pryor, F.L. (1988b), "Income distribution and economic development in Madagascar", Discussion Paper No. 37 (World Bank, Washington DC).

Psacharopoulos, G. (1993), "Returns to investment in education: a global update", World Bank Policy Research Working Paper WPS 1067 (World Bank, Washington, DC).

Puente, C.A. (1993), "The role of wage differentials in determining migration selectivity by sex: the case of Brazil", in United Nations, ed., Migration of Women in Developing Countries (UN, New York).

Punpuing, S. (1993), "Correlates of commuting patterns: a case study of Bangkok, Thailand", Urban Studies 30:527–546.

Quan, Z.X. (1991), "Urbanisation in China", Urban Studies 28:41–51.

Raimondos, P. (1993), "On the Todaro paradox", Economics Letters 42:261–267.

Rakodi, C. (1988), "Urban agriculture: research questions and Zambian evidence", Journal of Modern African Studies 26:495–515.

Rallis, T. (1988), City Transport in Developed and Developing Countries (St. Martin's Press, New York).

Ramsdell, L. (1990), "National housing policy and the favela in Brazil", in L.S. Graham and R.H. Wilson, eds., The Political Economy of Brazil: Public Policies in an Era of Transition, Institute of Latin American Studies Symposia on Latin America Series (University of Texas Press, Austin).

Rauch, J.E. (1989), "Urbanization, underemployment, and the size distribution of income: Harris–Todaro and Kuznets's inverted U", University of California, San Diego Department of Economics Working Paper: 89-39.

Rauch, J. (1993a), "Productivity gains from geographic concentration of human capital: evidence from the cities", Journal of Urban Economics 34:380–400.

Rauch, J.E. (1993b), "Economic development, urban underemployment, and income inequality", Canadian Journal of Economics 26:901–918.

Ravallion, M. and D. van de Walle (1991), "Urban-rural cost-of-living differentials in a developing economy", Journal of Urban Economics 29:113–127.

Rawski, T.G. and R.W. Mead (1998), "On the trail of China's phantom farmers", World Development 26:5.

Reccini de Lattes, Z. and S.M. Mychaszula (1993), "Female migration and labour force participation in a medium–sized city of a highly urbanized country", in United Nations, ed., Migration of Women in Developing Countries (UN, New York).

Redclift, M.R. (1984), " 'Urban bias' and rural poverty: a Latin American perspective", Journal of Development Studies 20:123–138.

Rempel, H. (1981), Rural-Urban Labor Migration and Urban Unemployment in Kenya, International Institute for Applied Systems Analysis (Laxenburg, Austria).

Renaud, B. (1993), "The housing system of the former Soviet Union: does it need market reforms?", Voprosy Ekonomiki 7:14–19 (in Russian).

Richardson, H. (1982), "Policies for strengthening small cities in developing countries", in Mathur, ed., Small Cities and National Development, United Nations Centre for Regional Development (Nagoya, Japan).

Rickman, D. and G. Treyz (1993), "Alternative labor market closures in a regional model", Growth and Change 24:32–50.

Rietveld, P. (1992), "Methods for planning urban facilities in rural areas of developing countries: a comparison of approaches", International Regional Science Review 15:345–356.

Rimmer, P.J. (1987), "The World Bank's urban transport policy: authorized version, revised version", Environment and Planning A 19:1569–1577.

Riveros, L.A. (1990), "Recession, adjustment and the performance of urban labor markets in Latin America", Canadian Journal of Development Studies 11:33–59.

Riveros, L. and L. Bouton (1994), "Common elements of efficiency wage theories: what relevance for developing countries?", Journal of Development Studies 30:696–716.

Rodgers, G.B. (1975), "Nutritionally based wage determination in the low-income labour market", Oxford Economic Papers 27:61–81.

Rodgers, G. (ed.) (1989), Urban Poverty and the Labour Market: Access to Jobs and Incomes in Asian and Latin American Cities (International Labour Office, Geneva).

Rodgers, W. (1991), "The significance of access to land as a determinant of Kenya's interregional migration", World Development 19:921–926.

Rogers, A. (1982), "Sources of urban population growth and urbanization, 1950–2000: a demographic accounting", Economic Development and Cultural Change 30:483–506.

Rogers, A. (1990), "Requiem for the net migrant", Geographical Analysis 22:283–300.

Rogers, A. and J.G. Williamson (1982), "Migration, urbanization, and third world development: an overview", Economic Development and Cultural Change 30:463–482.

Rogers, A. (1984), Migration, Urbanization, and Spatial Population Dynamics (Westview, Boulder).

Rondinelli, D. (1983), Secondary Cities in Developing Countries (Sage, Beverly Hills).

Root, B.D. and G.F. DeJong (1991), "Family migration in a developing country", Population Studies 45:221–233.

Rosen, K.T. and M. Resnick (1980), "The size distribution of cities: an examination of the Pareto law and primacy", Journal of Urban Economics 8, 165–186.

Rosenzweig, M.R. and O. Stark (1989), "Consumption smoothing, migration and marriage: evidence from rural India", Journal of Political Economy 97:905–926.

Ruane, F. (1981), "On modelling the influence of sectoral policies on the spatial concentration of industrial activities", Urban and Regional Economics Division, Development Economics Department Urban and Regional Report No. 81-28 (World Bank, Washington, DC).

Rubenstein, A. (1982), "Perfect equilibrium in a bargaining model", Econometrica 50:97–110.

Sabot, R.H. (1979), Economic Development and Urban Migration: Tanzania, 1900–1971 (Clarendon Press, Oxford).

Sabot, R.H., ed. (1982), Migration and Labor Market in Developing Countries (Westview Press, Boulder, CO).

Sabot, R.H. et al. (1981), "The Structure of wages in Kenya and Tanzania: what role has pay policy played?", Population and Human Resources Division, Discussion Paper No. 81-55 (World Bank, Washington DC).

Sah, R.K. and J.E. Stiglitz (1992), Peasants versus City-Dwellers: Taxation and the Burden of Economic Development (Oxford University Press/Clarendon Press, Oxford).

Safarova, G. (1996), "Reproduction of the population of St. Petersburg: medium-run perspectives", Monitoring sotsialjno-ekonomicheskoi situatsii i sostoyaniya rynka truda S-Peterburga (Press-Analitik, St. Petersburg, Russia) (in Russian).

Salehi Isfahani, D. (1993), "Population pressure, intensification of agriculture, and rural-urban migration", Journal of Development Economics 40:371–384.

Sanyal, B. (1981), "Who get what, where, why and how: a critical look at the housing subsidies in Zambia", Development and Change 12.

Sarris, A.H. and R. van den Brink (1993), Economic Policy and Household Welfare during Crisis and Adjustment in Tanzania (New York University Press for the Cornell University Food and Nutrition Policy Program, New York).

Sarris, A.H. and P. Tinios (1995), "Consumption and poverty in Tanzania in 1976 and 1991", World Development 23:1401–1419.

Sato, H. (1992), "The political economy of central budgetary transfers to states in India, 1972–1984", Developing Economies 30:347–376.

Schmertmann, C.-P. (1992), "Estimation of historical migration rates from a single census: Interregional migration in Brazil 1900–1980", Population-Studies 46:103–120.

Schultz, T.P. (1982), "Lifetime migration within educational strate in Venezuela: estimates of a logistic model", Economic Development and Cultural Change 30:559–594.

Schultz, T.P. (1988), "Heterogeneous preferences and migration: self-selection, regional prices and programs, and the behavior of migrants in Colombia", in T.P. Schultz, ed., Research in Population Economics, vol. 6 (JAI Press, Greenwich, CT).

Schwalbenberg, H.M. (1994), "Economic growth and the rise of protectionism and urban unrest in developing economies", Open Economies Review 5:65–88.

Serageldin, I., M.A. Cohen and K.C. Sivaramakrishnan, eds. (1995), The Human Face of the Urban Environment, Environmentally Sustainable Development Proceedings Series No. 6 (World Bank, Washington, DC).

Sethuraman, S.U. (1981), The Urban Informal Sector in Developing Countries (International Labour Organization, Geneva).

Shabbir, T. (1991), "Earnings functions in Pakistan's urban informal sector: a case study (comment)", Pakistan Development Review 30:704–706.

Shakhotko, L.P. (1996), The Population of the Republic of Belarus at the End of the 20th Century (Republic of Belarus, Ministry of Statistics, Statistical Research Institute, Minsk) (in Russian).

Shapiro, C. and J. Stiglitz (1984), "Equilibrium unemployment as a worker discipline device", American Economic Review 74:433–444.

Shaw, K. (1991), "The influence of human capital investment on migration and industry change", Journal of Regional Science 31:397–416.

Sheppard, E. (1982), "City size distributions and spatial economic change", International Regional Science Review 7:

Shidlo, G., ed. (1990), Housing Policy in Developing Countries (Routledge, London and New York).

Shields, N. (1980), "Women in the urban labor market in Africa: the case of Tanzania", Staff Working Paper No. 380 (World Bank, Washington, DC).

Shixun, G. and X. Liu (1992), "Urban migration in Shanghai, 1950–1988: trends and characteristics", Population and Development Review 18:533–548.

Shukla, V. (1996), Urbanization and Economic Growth (Oxford University Press, Delhi).

Shukla, V. and K. Parikh (1992), "The environmental consequences of urban growth", Urban Geography 13:422–449.

Shukla, V. and O. Stark (1984), "On agglomeration economies and optimal migration", Harvard Institute of Economic Research Discussion Paper 1122 (Cambridge, MA).

Shukla, V. and O. Stark (1990), "Policy comparisons with agglomeration effects augmented dual economy model", Journal of Urban Economics 27:1–15.

Singh, I., L. Squire and J. Strauss, eds., (1986), Agricultural Household Models (Johns Hopkins University Press, Baltimore).

Singelmann, J. (1993), "Levels and trends of female internal migration in developing countries, 1960–1980", in United Nations, ed., Internal Migration of Women in Developing Countries (UN, New York).

Sjaastad, L.A. (1962), "The costs and returns to human migration', Journal of Political Economy 70(Suppl.):80–93.

Smith, J.P., L.A. Karoly and D. Thomas (1992), "Migration in retrospect: differences between men and women", Paper presented at the 1992 Population Association of America meetings, Denver, CO. Unpublished manuscript.

Standing, G., ed. (1991), In search of Flexibility: The New Soviet Labour Market (International Labour Office, Geneva).

Stark, O. (1991), The Migration of Labor (Basil Blackwell, Cambridge, MA and Oxford, UK).

Stark, O. and D. Bloom (1985), "The new economics of labor migration", American Economic Review 75:173–178.

Stark, O. and E. Katz (1985), "A theory of remittances and migration", Harvard University Center for Population Studies, Migration and Development Program Discussion Paper 16 (Cambridge, MA).

Stark, O. and R.E.B. Lucas (1988), "Migration, remittances, and the family", Economic Development and Cultural Change 36:465–481.

Stark, O., M.R. Gupta and D. Levhari (1991), "Equilibrium urban unemployment in developing countries: is migration the culprit?", Economics Letters 37:477–482.

Steel, W. and Y. Takagi (1983), "The intermediate sector, unemployment and the employment-output conflict: a multi-sector model", Oxford Economic Papers 35:423–446.

Stigler, G. (1962), "Information in the labor market", Journal of Political Economy 70:94–105.

Stiglitz, J. (1969), "Rural-urban migration, surplus labour, and relationship between urban and rural wages", East African Economic Review 1:1–27.

Stiglitz, J. (1974), "Alternative theories of wage determination and unemployment in LDCs: the labor turnover model", Quarterly Journal of Economics 88:194–227.

Stiglitz, J. (1976), "The efficiency wage hypothesis, surplus labor, and the distribution of income in LDCs", Oxford Economic Papers 28:185–207.

Stiglitz, J.E. (1982), "The structure of labor markets and shadow prices in LDCs", in R.H. Sabot, ed., Migration and the Labor Market in Developing Countries (Westview, Boulder, CO).

Strassmann, W.P. (1991), "Housing market interventions and mobility: an international comparison", Urban Studies 28:759–771.

Streeten, P. (1987), What Price Food? Agricultural Price Policies in Developing Countries (St. Martin's Press, New York).

Stren, R.E. (1975), Urban Inequality and Housing Policy in Tanzania (University of California, Berkeley. Institute of International Studies, Berkeley, CA).

Stren, R.E. (1978), Housing the Urban Poor in Africa (University of California, Berkeley. Institute of International Studies, Berkeley, CA).

Stren, R. (1982), "Underdevelopment, urban squatting and the state bureaucracy: a case study of Tanzania", Canadian Journal of African Studies 16:67–92.

Stren, R.E. (1989), "Administration of urban services", in R.E. Stren and R. White, eds., African Cities in Crises: Managing Rapid Urban Growth (Westview Press, Boulder).

Stren, R.E. (1992), "African urban research since the late 1980s: response to poverty and urban growth", Urban Studies 29:533–555.

Stren, R.E., ed. (1994a), Urban Research in the Developing World, vol. 2, Africa (University of Toronto Centre for Urban and Community Studies, Toronto).

Stren, R.E., ed. (1994b), Urban Research in the Developing World, vol. 1, Asia (University of Toronto Centre for Urban and Community Studies, Toronto).

Stren, R.E. and R.R. White, eds. (1989), African Cities in Crisis (Westview, Boulder).

Struyk, R.J. (1988), Assessing Housing Needs and Policy Alternatives in Developing Countries, Urban Institute Report, 88-4 (Urban Institute Press, Washington, DC).

Struyk, R.J. and M.A. Turner (1987), "Simulating housing quality changes in developing countries: a tool for policy analysis", World Development 15:1375–1387.

Struyk, R. and M. Turner (1991), "Econometric analysis: measuring the impact of rent controls in urban housing markets", in A.G. Tipple and K.G. Willis, eds, Housing the Poor in the Developing World: Methods of Analysis, Case Studies and Policy (Routledge, New York).

Summers, L. and L. Pritchett (1993), "The structural adjustment debate", American Economic Review 83:383–389.

Svejnar, J. (1984), "The determinants of industrial sector earnings in Senegal", Journal of Development Economics 15:289–311.

Svejnar, J. (1989), "Models of modern-sector labor market institutions in developing countries", World Development 17:1409–1415.

Tanzi, V. (1991), Public Finance in Developing Countries (Elgr., Aldershot, UK).

Tanzi, V. (1992), "Fiscal policy and economic reconstruction in Latin America", World Development 20:641–657.

Telles, E. (1993), "Urban labor market segmentation and income in Brazil", Economic Development and Cultural Change 41:231–249.

Terrell, K. and J. Svejnar (1989), The Industrial Labor Market and Economic Performance in Senegal (Westview, Boulder, CO).

Tewari, V.K. and T.K. Kumar (1986), "Rent control in India: its economic effects and implementation in Bangalore", Water Supply and Urban Development Department, Discussion Paper UDD 91 (World Bank, Washington, DC).

Thobani, M. (1982), "A Nester logit model of travel mode to work and auto ownership", Urban Development Department, Discussion Paper UDD 5 (World Bank, Washington, DC).

Thomson, J.M. (1983), "Toward better urban transport planning in developing countries", Staff Working Paper No. 600 (World Bank, Washington, DC).

Timmer, C.P. (1993), "Rural bias in the east and south-east Asian rice economy: Indonesia in comparative perspective", Journal of Development Studies 29:149–176.

Tipple, A.G. and K.G. Willis, eds (1991), Housing the Poor in the Developing World: Methods of Analysis, Case Studies and Policy (Routledge, London and New York).

Todaro, M.P. (1969), "A model of labor migration and urban unemployment in less developed countries", American Economic Review 59:139–148.

Todaro, M.P. (1971), "Income expectations, rural-urban migration and employment in Africa", International Labour Review 104:387–414.

Tokman, V., ed. (1992), Beyond Regulation: The Informal Economy in Latin America (Lynne Rienner, Boulder, CO).

Transportation Research Board (1997), "Transportation options for megacities of the developing world", Working Paper (National Research Council, National Academy of Sciences, Washington, DC).

United Nations (1980), Patterns of Urban and Rural Population Growth (United Nations, New York).

United Nations (1982), Model Life Tables for Developing Countries (United Nations, New York).

United Nations (1988), World Population Trends and Policies: 1987 Monitoring Report (United Nations, New York).

United Nations (1993), World Urbanization Prospects: The 1992 Revision (United Nations, New York).

United Nations (1994), Human Development Report 1994 (Oxford University Press, New York).

United Nations (1996), "Trends in urbanization and the components of urban growth", Paper presented at the Symposium on Internal Migration and Urbanization in Developing Countries (UN Population Fund, New York).

United Nations Development Programme (1996), Kazakstan Human Development Report 1996 (UNDP, Almaty).

Valentine, T.R. (1993), "Drought, transfer entitlements, and income distribution: the Botswana experience", World Development 21:109–126.

van der Gaag, J. and W. Viverberg (1988), "Wage determinants in Côte d'Ivoire", Living Standards Measurement Study, Working Paper No. 33 (World Bank, Washington, DC).

van der Gaag, J., M. Stelcner and W. Viverberg (1989), "Public-private sector wage comparisons and moon-lighting in developing countries: evidence from Côte d'Ivoire and Peru", Living Standards Measurement Study, Working Paper No. 52 (World Bank, Washington, DC).

van der Hoeven, R. (1984), "Zambia", in W. van Ginnekin and J.-G. Park, eds., Generating Internationally Comparable Income Distribution Estimates (International Labour Office, Geneva).

van Dijk, J., et al., eds. (1989), Migration and Labor Market Adjustment (Kluwer Academic, London).

Varshney, A. (1993), "Introduction: urban bias in perspective", Journal of Development Studies 29:3–22.

Velenchik, A.D. (1993), "Cash seeking behaviour and migration: a place-to-place migration function for Côte d'Ivoire", Journal of African Economies 2:329–347.

Verma, S. (1986), "Urbanization and productivity in Indian states", in E. Mills and C. Becker, eds., Studies in Indian Urban Development (Oxford University Press, New York).

Viverberg, W. and J. van der Gaag (1991), "The private wage sector in Côte d'Ivoire: homogeneity or heterogeneity?" Southern Economic Journal 58:406–423.

Wang, Y. (1993), China: Urban Development Towards the Year 2000 (Hong Kong Institute of Asia-Pacific Studies, Hong Kong).

Wang, Y. (1994), "China: urban development and research towards the year 2000", in R. Stren, ed., Urban Research in the Developing World: Asia (University of Toronto Centre for Urban and Community Studies, Toronto).

Ward, P.M. (1993), "The Latin American inner city: differences of degree or of kind?", Environment and Planning A 25:1131–1160.

Weeks, J. (1995), "Income distribution and its implications for population trends in sub-Saharan Africa", in A. Mafeje and S. Radwan, eds., Economic and Demographic Change in Africa (Clarendon Press, Oxford).

Weiss, A. (1980), "Job queues and layoffs in labor markets with flexible wages", Journal of Political Economy 88:526–538.

Wheaton, W.C. and H. Shishido (1981), "Urban concentration, agglomeration economies, and the level of economic development", Economic Development and Cultural change 30:17–30.

Wheaton, W. (1981), "Housing policies and urban "markets" in developing countries: the Egyptian experience", Journal of Urban Economics 9:242–256.

Whittington, D. et al. (1993), "Household sanitation in Kumasi, Ghana: a description of current practices, attitudes, and perceptions", World Development 21:733–748.

Widner, J.A. (1993), "The origins of agricultural policy in Ivory Coast 1960–1986", Journal of Development Studies 29:25–59.

Williamson, J. (1988a), "Migration and urbanization", in H. Chenery and T.N. Srinivasan, eds., Handbook of Development Economics, vol. I (North-Holland, Amsterdam).

Williamson, J. (1988b), "Migrant selectivity, urbanization, and industrial revolutions", Population and Development Review 14:287–314.

Williamson, O. (1964), Economics of Discretionary Behavior: Managerial Objectives in a Theory of the Firm (Prentic-Hall, Englewood Cliffs, NJ).

Willikens, F. and S. Scherbov (1995), "Demographic trends in Russia", in H. van den Brekel and F. Deven, eds., Population and Family in the Low Countries 1994 (Kluwer Academic, Amsterdam).

Willis, K.G., S. Malpezzi and A.G. Tipple (1990), "An econometric and cultural analysis of rent control in Kumasi, Ghana", Urban Studies 27:241–257.

World Bank (1984), World Development Report 1994 (World Bank, Washington, DC).

World Bank (1986), Urban Transport (World Bank, Washington, DC).

World Bank (1988a), "Report on adjustment lending", Document R88-119 (Washington, DC).

World Bank (1988b), Road Deterioration in Developing Countries (World Bank, Washington, DC).

World Bank (1990), "Report on adjustment lending II: policies for the recovery of growth", document R90-99 (Washington, DC).

World Bank (1991), Urban Policy and Economic Development: An Agenda for the 1990s, A World Bank Policy Paper (Washington, DC).

World Bank (1992), World Development Report 1992: Development and the Environment (World Bank, Washington, DC).

World Bank (1995), World Development Report 1995 (World Bank, Washington, DC).

World Bank Operations Evaluation Department (1993), Evaluation Results for 1991, World Bank Operations Evaluation Study (World Bank, Washington, DC).

World Resources Institute (1996), World Resources 1996–1997 (Oxford University Press, New York).

Yamada, G. (1996), "Urban informal employment and self-employment in developing countries", Economic Development and Cultural Change 44:289–314.

Yi, Z. and J.W. Vaupel (1989), "The impact of urbanization and delayed childbearing in China", Population and Development Review 15:425–446.

Young, D. and D. Honghai (1997), "Urbanization, agriculture and industrialization in China: 1952–1991", Unpublished manuscript (University of Alberta).

Yutopoulos, P.A. (1985), "Middle-income classes and food crises: the 'new' food-feed competition", Economic Development and Cultural Change 33:463–483.

Zhang W., Y. Hongwen and C. Hongyan (1997), "Current changes of China's population", in China Population Association, Symposium on Demography of China (China Population Association and IUSSP, Beijing).

Zhu, B. (1997), "The duration of stay and displacement of the floating population in the urban area: a case study of Shanghai municipality", in China Population Association, Symposium on Demography of China (China Population Association and IUSSP, Beijing).

Zhu, J. (1994), "Changing land policy and its impact on location growth: the experience of the Shenzhen special economic zone, China, in the 1980s", Urban Studies 31:111611–111623.

Zhu, J. (1996), "Multilevel analysis of rural outmigration in Guangdong, China", Paper presented at the Symposium on Internal Migration and Urbanization in Developing Countries (UN Population Fund, New York).

*Chapter 44*

# ECONOMIC ANALYSIS OF HOUSING MARKETS IN DEVELOPING AND TRANSITION ECONOMIES

STEPHEN MALPEZZI*

*University of Wisconsin*

## Contents

* The author is indebted to Edwin Mills, Bertrand Renaud and Christine Whitehead for comments on a previous version, but bears sole responsibility for the chapter's shortcomings.

*Handbook of Regional and Urban Economics. Edited by E.S. Mills and P. Cheshire*

## Abstract

The purpose of this chapter is to survey recent research on housing markets and policy in what used to be called the "second" and "third" worlds. We adopt the labels "transition" economies to refer to countries as disparate as Russia and Vietnam, and "developing" to refer to countries as disparate as Korea and Singapore (arguably now developed) and countries like Mozambique and Laos. It is therefore quite interesting that the bulk of the research surveyed finds that housing market *behavior* is remarkably similar from place to place. Institutions and constraints, particularly the amount of income available for housing and other goods and services certainly do vary dramatically from place to place. And the stakes of how well housing markets work vary from place to place. But these differences in institutions and constraints do not obscure regularities in behavior.

The first major section, on housing markets (Section 2), examines property rights, supply, demand and tenure. Section 3 presents research on the related markets for land, finance and infrastructure. Housing policy is covered in Section 4, including housing subsidy systems, privatization, taxation and regulation. Section 5 concludes with a discussion of current issues and research.

**Keywords:** Housing, urban development, housing finance, land use, regulation, housing subsidies and taxation

**JEL codes:** R14, R21, R31, R38, R51, R52, O12, O18

## 1. Introduction

The purpose of this chapter is to survey recent research on housing markets and housing policy in what used to be called the "second" and "third" worlds. We will adopt the labels "transition" economies to refer to countries as disparate as Russia and Vietnam, and "developing" to refer to countries as disparate as Korea and Singapore (arguably now developed) and countries like Mozambique and Laos, where the adjective "developing" is currently more a wish than a statement of fact. We generally omit research devoted to "first world", "developed" or "OECD" countries, except when such reference is fundamental or unavoidable.[1] Of course much literature relevant to housing in the "second" and "third" worlds can be found in the technical literature on housing which has no particular reference to place or time.[2]

Some would argue—or argued a decade ago–that countries outside the so-called developed or OECD world are so different as to obviate comparisons, or the transferability of research results and methods, across countries. In fact, the bulk of the research below documents that housing market *behavior* is remarkably similar from place to place. Institutions and constraints, particularly the

---

[1] See, among others, Whitehead (Chapter 40, this volume), Shephard (Chapter 41, this volume) and Olsen (1987).

[2] See, for example, Arnott (1987), Olsen (1987) and Smith et al. (1988) for reviews of the relevant technical literature. Also omitted from this chapter is a review of the stylized facts regarding housing markets across countries. See Malpezzi (1990) and Angel and Mayo ((1996) for such a review. Other recent reviews which may be profitably consulted include Hoffman et al. (1991), Gilbert (1992), Rakodi (1992), World Bank (1993) and UN Centre for Human Settlements (1996).

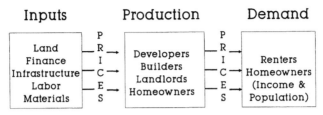

Fig. 1. How housing markets work.

amount of income available for housing and other goods and services certainly do vary dramatically from place to place. And at a different level it could be argued that the stakes of how well housing markets work vary from place to place. But these differences in institutions and constraints should not obscure regularities in behavior.

## 1.1. Conceptual framework

Figure 1 (from Mayo et al., 1986; Malpezzi, 1990) shows a schematic diagram of how the housing market works. Inputs such as land, labor, finance, materials and infrastructure are combined by supply-side agents such as landlords and developers to produce housing services. Homeowners, and to a lesser extent, renters, are also producers, as they maintain and upgrade their houses. Relative prices inform producers of housing services about whether to provide more or less housing, and the input suppliers about providing more or fewer inputs.

Several other important features of housing markets are implicit in Fig. 1. First, transactions within and across "boxes" are possible only to the extent property rights are defined, recognized and enforced. Second, government interventions can have profound effects on the operation of the housing market. Third, fully understanding housing markets requires analysis of key input markets and the regulatory environment, as well as revealed market behavior in the housing market per se.

Every introductory real estate textbook emphasizes a number of other salient features about housing. It is a large share of every country's wealth and productive capital stock. Because its stock price is large relative to incomes, it must be financed. Some households own their own housing capital, others lease it. Housing is fixed in location, extremely durable (slowly depreciating), and can be viewed alternatively as a composite commodity yielding a flow of "housing services", or as a set of individual characteristics.

Each of these interesting features will be discussed in one or more sections below. The section on the basics of the housing market will focus on the second and third "boxes" in our simple conceptual framework; the section on input markets on the first box; and the section on housing policy on the effects of government interventions within and across boxes.

## 2. Housing markets: the basics

This section corresponds roughly to the first two boxes in Fig. 1. Alternatively one could think of this section as examining the usual supply and demand diagram from any principles textbook, or, more properly, multivariate supply and demand *relations*. Housing market analysis is complicated by several facts. First, the system of property rights implicit in any supply and demand diagram cannot be taken for granted. Second, housing is a composite commodity and may be examined in terms of its service flows or stock in some aggregate way, or in terms of individual characteristics. Third, supply in any given period comes from both new construction and modification of the existing stock. Fourth, transactions costs of changing consumption are quite high. Fifth, housing consumption choices are bound up with tenure choices. Sixth, housing markets are a large part of the economy in general and the capital stock in particular, so have strong linkages with its aggregate economy. Each of these points will be discussed at greater or lesser length below.

### 2.1. Property rights

Property rights are sine qua non of housing market development. Until recently, property rights have been much neglected in the "developed" country housing literature, but were somewhat better represented in the "traditional" developing country housing literature.[3] Post-Perestroyka (circa 1989) the topic moved properly to the fore. Some property rights issues are common among countries, and some issues are specific (more or less) to Africa, eastern Europe, or to some other specific region or country.

Property rights may be defined and assigned through a formal legal system, or by custom or tradition.[4] Henceforth we use "law" to refer to both. Two ar-

---

[3] This neglect refers to the housing literature. Economists, political scientists, and of course lawyers have long studied property rights in other contexts. See, for example, Browder (1984), Friedman (1975) and Moynihan (1987).

[4] This section draws from Vandell's contribution to Malpezzi and Vandell (1992). See Jaffe and Louziotis (1996) for another recent review.

eas of law which particularly affect the operation of housing and real estate markets are contract law and land use regulation. Contract law deals with the system that defines and facilitates the transfer of property and property rights, allocates those rights, and settles disputes. In formal systems these functions are associated with such instruments as contracts of sale, leases, easements and rights-of-way, operating agreements, mortgages and deeds of trust, etc. In all countries, rich and poor, some of these functions are also affected by less formal "mores and folkways of society". In many countries, including most of the transition countries and many African countries, these systems are in flux. Land use regulation includes the body of custom, law, regulation and case law which governs the rights to locate certain uses in certain locations and provides standards of development and operation of those uses. Formal instruments include zoning ordinances, building and housing codes, subdivision regulations, private deed restrictions, environmental laws and regulations, etc.

Together, these two areas of the law render operational the notion of ownership, exercise and transfer of rights in real property. A wide range of descriptive studies have examined property rights in Africa (Ault and Rutman, 1979; Kiamba, 1989); in Asia (Bromley, 1989); in Latin America (Betancur, 1987; Gilbert, 1989); and of course formerly socialist countries (Jaffe, 1993; Pejovich, 1990). From that descriptive literature, and from analytic literature such as Alchian and Demsetz (1973), Coase (1960), Demsetz (1967) and Williamson (1975), a clear list of general principles has emerged. In order to maximize the social value associated with rights in real estate, the set of laws and regulations governing their associated property rights must possess certain characteristics. They must be transparent and agreed on by some not-as-yet-well- defined social consensus. They must be enforceable at a reasonable cost, with little or no uncertainty. There must be some general agreement on final arbiter of disputes (most often but not always the state).

Tenant and landlord rights must be well defined, whether with a formal or informal contract. There must be clear remedies for violation by either party. These rights and obligations will generally be freely negotiated between the parties and represent the outcome of a competitive market process. Versacaj (1993) presents a discussion of leases in Russia and shows how the violations of such principles inhibits the market.

In a well-functioning system property rights will be transferrable from seller to purchaser on payment of a consideration (Jaffe and Louziotis, 1996). The bundle of such rights can be largely complete (fee simple, although still limited by land use regulation), or partial, including leasehold. Specific rights include the right to use or modify the use of the real estate, the right to derive income or other benefits from its use, the right to bequeath the ownership interest, the right not to be evicted, etc. Implicit in the contract of sale is not only an obligation to the seller, typically to pay a specific amount for the real estate interest but sometimes a more complex obligation such as to limit future uses or to bequeath the property in a certain way. An explicit or implicit obligation will also exist to maintain the property at a certain level, to maintain a use which is consistent with existing land use regulations, to pay taxes assessed on the basis of property ownership, to give up the property for a preemptive public purpose on payment of compensation, and not disturb or do other damage to neighbors as a result of use. Government constraints may be required to prevent certain adverse market failures or imperfections (such as conflicting land uses or limitations on access or economic productivity) or in cases in which the buyer or seller has excessive market power.

Maximum social return to the housing stock value, generally requires liquidity, or the ease of transfer of real estate interests. Landis (1986) shows that high fees or other rights of entry to the market, restrictions on appropriate purchasers or tenants, unreasonable constraints on use, excessively costly development standards, etc. can be counterproductive. Markets are rendered most efficient to the extent that they are "thick", i.e., there are many transfers and prices/rents are well established (Bikhchandri, 1986). Because the high purchase prices of real estate requires finance for most transactions, maximum benefit is obtained when financing is freely available at market rates. Financial innovations and reforms, discussed below, which enhance the liquidity of the mortgage market, such as the development of the secondary market or securitization, also enhances the liquidity of the real estate market in general. The possibility of foreclosure in the ownership market for the nonpayment of debt or other violation of the obligations of ownership (such as the nonpayment of real estate taxes) is essential for efficient operation (Buckley, 1990) just as is the possibility of eviction in the rental market (Jimenez, 1984).

Property rights profoundly affect not only the efficiency of the housing market; they also profoundly affect other social goals or questions such as the distribution of wealth or income. Concentration of ownership rights may adversely affect on the concentration of wealth and power, as well as reduce the efficiency of the market, especially if quasimonopoly exploitative situations are produced.[5] Solomon and Vandell (1982) discuss alternative conditions under which real estate markets may operate which cause deviation from the competitive ideal.

---

[5] Malpezzi (1994) argues that with a few important exceptions, mainly in taxation, housing policies which are more efficient are also more equitable. The argument can certainly be made with respect to property rights, e.g., the large literature linking land reforms to faster growth.

Many of the biggest property rights and regulatory issues are regarding land. Systems can function with long-term leaseholds as well as with fee simple (Bromley, 1989), but efficient markets require long and enforceable leases. In some countries there is no history or memory of private ownership of or significant use rights over land. Paradoxically, in such countries public landlords (central government, large state enterprises or cities) may have true market power, and do not respond well to external incentives. Moving to a market system has powerful redistributive consequences which will be politically charged (Hegedus et al., 1992; Buckley et al., 1995). More research is certainly required on the essential property rights necessary sufficient for efficient use of land. Most studies of land reforms have focused on agricultural and/or rural land (e.g., Dorner, 1982). Certainly we should study the effects of past major *urban* land reforms just as carefully.

## 2.2. *Housing demand*

In this section we will examine demand in cross-section, as well as demand in the very long run as markets develop. The literature generally finds significant regularities across developing *and* developed countries, although there is a dearth of demand studies from more "middle income" countries and transition economies. Since characteristics demand is treated elsewhere in this volume by Shephard (but see also Quigley, 1982; Kaufmann and Quigley, 1987; Follain and Jimenez, 1985a, b; Gross 1988 for developing country examples), we focus on demand for the composite commodity housing.[6]

Research on housing demand in developing and formerly socialist countries has more or less followed the developed country's literature. The literature on the former group of countries is somewhat more developed than on the latter, partly because only recently have data become available for socialist and formerly socialist countries, and partly because even given a dataset it can be hard to recover true demand parameters from pre-reform "prices".

### 2.2.1. *Early literature*
The literature on housing demand on an international context is too large to review completely. Our selective review is summarized in Table 1. The earliest studies of housing demand were primarily studies which threw off housing estimates as part of larger studies of consumption, as in Lluch et al. (1977) and Howe and Musgrove (1977). These and similar studies are reviewed in Malpezzi and Mayo (hereafter M&M) (1985). Among the first published studies to carefully

---

[6] See also the related literature on "needs analysis", for example Struyk (1987).

analyze housing demand per se were Follain et al. (1980) who studied urban Korea using survey data from 1976; Ingram (1984) who used data from Bogota, Columbia using 1978 data; and Strassman (1980b) who used survey data from Cartagena, Columbia in 1978. These and most of the other studies described below estimate single equation models using least squares, usually stratified by tenure (owners and renters in most cases). A number of the studies experiment with other types of stratification, such as by income, class or location within the city. Ingram's (1984) study of Bogota and Cali is notable because of its careful specification of intrametropolitan location. Jimenez and Keare's (1984) study of Santa Anna and Sonsonate, El Salvador, (1980 data) is notable for its analysis of the effect of using a rough permanent income measure. M&M (1985, 1987a, b) built on these and other studies to estimate a series of simple demand models in 15 cities in eight countries using a simple but consistent specification. We will discuss this study in some detail, partly as a benchmark for a number of fine studies that succeeded it.

*Within* particular markets, M&M generally found that demand is income in-elastic: most estimates using household housing consumption and incomes from cross-section data range between 0.4 to 0.6 or so. *Across* markets demand is elastic: M&M estimated that, using city averages of housing consumption and incomes as the unit of observation, the very long run elasticity ranges somewhere above 1 but less than 1.6 (M&M, 1987a, b). They also found that owner and renter elasticities are surprisingly similar, but the *level* of owner consumption is higher; and the difference increases with income.

M&M's demand results are from developing countries, with a range of per capita GNP at the time of data collection of roughly $300 per capita to $2500 (1981 dollars). Comparing their results to those for developed countries (Mayo, 1981), individual cross-section income and price elasticities *within* markets are similar; but evidence is mixed on the very long run elasticity *across* markets and countries. Time series data on several developed countries is more consistent with a higher very long run elasticity. Microdata suggest that average housing consumption to income ratios are lower for developed countries than for Korea and some other higher income developing countries, implying that the long run elasticity is less than one over some part of the range between the two groups. Data on housing investment analyzed by Burns and Grebler (1977, discussed below) is also consistent with this pattern.

M&M's price elasticity results are less strong. Untangling prices and quan-tities in housing market studies is always problematical. M&M use a simple formulation due to Muth (1971) to estimate price elasticities. M&M estimated this model for Cairo and Beni Suef, Egypt, and for Manila. The model was

Table 1

Summary of selected international housing demand studies

| Author | Location & date | Model, estimation | Key results | Comments |
|---|---|---|---|---|
| Follain et al. (1980) | Urban Korea, 1976 | Cross-section log expenditure model, single equation OLS, stratifed by tenure. | Renter $E_y = 0.12$ for current income, 0.42 for consumption; owner $E_y = 0.21, 0.62$. $E_p$ is near zero for all models. | Other models reported pool tenure, stratify by location. |
| Strassman (1980) | Cartegena, Colombia, 1978 | Cross-section log expenditure model, single equation OLS, stratifed by tenure. | Renter $E_y = 0.78$, owner $E_y = 1.19$. Current income only, no $E_p$ estimates. | Other models stratify by income; $E_y$ generally increases with income but not strictly so. |
| Ingram (1984) | Bogota and Cali, Colombia, 1978 | Cross-section log expenditure model, single equation OLS, stratifed by tenure. Includes distance to workplace. | Renter $E_y = 0.47$ (Cali), 0.72 (Bogota); $E_p = -0.48$ (Cali), $-0.28$ (Bogota). Owner $E_y = 0.76$ (Cali), 0.78 (Bogota); $E_p = -0.44$ (Bogota). | One of few studies explicitly modeling intermetropolitan location. |
| Jimenez and Keare (1984) | Santa Ana and Sonsonate, El Salvador, 1980 | Log expenditure model, single equation OLS, two cross-section panel data, stratifed by tenure. | Renter $E_y = 0.27$ (Santa Ana), 0.42 (Sonsonate); owner $E_y = 1.05$ (Santa Ana). | Permanent income proxied by weighted average of two years' income. |
| Malpezzi and Mayo (1985, 1987) | Data from Colombia, Egypt, El Salvador, Ghana, India, Jamaica, Korea and the Philippines, various dates in the 1970s and the early 1980s | Log expenditure model, single equation OLS, stratified by tenure. | Renter and owner income elasticities, respectively: Bogota, 0.66, 0.75; Cali, 0.44, 69; Cairo, 0.46, 0.17; Beni Suef, 0.51, 0.42; Santa Ana, 0.48, 1.11; Sonsonate, 0.50, 0.79; Kumasi, 0.33, owners NA; Bangalore, 0.58, 0.43; Kingston, 0.16, owners NA; Seoul, 0.45, 0.44; Pusan, 0.31, 0.45; Taegu, 0.44, 0.47; Kwangju, 0.62, 0.41; other Korean cities, 0.54, 0.79; Davao, 0.88, 0.99; Manila, 0.56, 0.57. | Price elasticities estimated for Cairo, Beni Suef and Manila, following Muth (1971); most estimates close to $-1$, but procedure is biased towards $-1$. |
| Ndulo (1986) | Lusaka (1979) | Linear expenditure function. | Owner $E_y = 0.6$ (presumably at means, see text). | Also segments by household size, finds larger households have larger income elasticities. |
| Mehta and Mehta (1987) | Ahmedabad (1985) | Logrithmic expenditure function, by tenure. | Renters, $E_y$ is 0.17 to 0.40, $E_p = -0.8$; owners, $E_y = 0.2$, $E_p = -0.4$ | Also segments by income, generally finds low income households have lower elasticities. |
| Grootaert and Dubois (1988) | Cote d'Ivoire (1979) | Estimate tenure choice, then rental demand equation with selectivity correction. Use hedonic to decompose rent into $P$ and $Q$. | For Abidjan, renter $E_y = 0.37$, $E_p = -0.25$. For other cities, renter $E_y = 0.28$, $E_p = -0.25$. | Selectivity correction has virtually no effect on demand results. Some problem with interpretation of $P$ and $Q$ measures, see text. |
| Shefer (1990) | Indonesia (1978) | Logrithmic expenditure function, by tenure. Uses expenditure to proxy permanent income. Also presents results by city size and income class. | For all renters, $E_y = 0.84$; for all owners, $E_y = 1.17$. | Elasticities generally rise with income class, size of city (with exceptions). |

Table 1

(continued)

| Author | Location & date | Model, estimation | Key results | Comments |
|--------|-----------------|-------------------|-------------|----------|
| Lodhi and Pasha (1991) | Karachi (1987–88) | Linear expenditure functions, segmented by tenure and by formal–informal development. Estimates with current income and consumption (permanent income). | Planned, owners: current $E_Y = 0.58$; permanent $E_Y = 1.20$. Planned renters: current $E_Y = 0.42$, permanent $E_Y = 1.10$. Katchi abadi owners: current $E_Y = 0.06$, permanent $E_Y = 0.12$. Katchi abadi renters: current $E_Y = 0.09$, permanent $E_Y = 0.31$. | |
| Assadian and Ondrich (1993) | Bogota and Cali (1978) | Simultaneous model of housing demand, location, and labor supply. | $E_Y = 0.56$ for head's work income if household has two earners; is 0.95 if there is no other earner. | |
| Lim and Lee (1993) | Urban China, sixth plan (1981–1985) | Log model, province/municipality is the unit of observation. | At provincial level, grouped $E_Y = 1.23$ (wages), 1.32 (household expenditures). At city level, grouped $E_Y = 1.04$ (wages), 1.30 (expendtures). | Limited comparability to other studies because of aggregated data. |
| Arimah (1994) | Ibadan (1987–1988) | Log model, by tenure. | Renter $E_Y = 0.88$; owner $E_Y = 0.56$. | |
| Chou and Shih (1995) | Hong Kong (1991) | Box–Cox model, by tenure. | At meands, renter $E_Y = 0.27$ (transitory income), 0.37 (permanent income). | Tenure choice has no effect on renter demand. |

*Notes:* Most studies present a range of elasticity estimates from alternative specifications; therefore "Key Results" entry in this table contains our judgement of representative point estimates.

estimated separately for owners and renters. Estimates of the price elasticity are close to 1 in absolute value, ranging from $-0.76$ to $-1.08$, with the exception of Manila owners whose price elasticity is estimated to be $-0.4$.

These price elasticity estimates suggest that demand is considerably more elastic than previous estimates in the literature suggest. However, a shortcoming of this model is that a unitary income elasticity is the null hypothesis, because a land price coefficient of zero implies a price elasticity of 1. Note that if land prices are measured with error, the price elasticity is biased towards $-1$. Therefore, the tests of significance of land price coefficients should not be interpreted as tests of zero price elasticity. Neither are they correct tests of unitary elasticity, because the land's share estimate, assumed fixed for the sample, actually has a distribution as well. Testing the micromodel price elasticities under alternative specifications remains high on any agenda for future research.

## 2.2.2. Recent literature

A number of recent studies have extended this earlier literature. Some contributors apply similar models to additional locations, and others contain theoretical extensions. A number of these are also included in Table 1. Table 1 presents point estimates of the income elasticity using various income definitions. Even a casual inspection of Table 1 shows that far fewer studies present price elasticity estimates (compared to many income elasticity estimates). Table 1 also shows that price elasticity estimates are more highly varied. Ndulo (1986) estimates a linear expenditure function for Lusaka, Zambia using data from 1979. He found an owner income elasticity of 0.6. Mehta and Mehta (1989a, b) analyze a logarithmic expenditure function similar to M&M's using data from Ahmedabad, India in 1985. Their estimates are on the low end, with income elasticities around 0.2–0.4, and price elasticities ranging from −0.4 to −0.8. Grootaert and DuBois (1988) estimate a housing demand model for the Ivory Coast using 1979 data, and find income and price elasticities around 0.4 in absolute value. Shefer (1990) examines Indonesia, and obtains some of the higher income elasticity estimates; the owner estimate exceeds 1. Lodhi and Pasha (1991) study Karachi, Pakistan. They segment by tenure. Their estimates are highly variable, but generally elasticities are higher the stronger property rights. Arimah (1994) estimated a model similar in Ibadan, Nigeria and found income elasticities of 0.88 for renters and 0.56 for owners. Chou and Shih (1995) found lower income elasticities in Hong Kong, from 0.27 to 0.37.

Assadian and Ondrich (1993) revisit the Bogota and Calli data that Ingram (1984) studied, but this time estimate a simultaneous model of housing demand, location and labor supply. They find that the income elasticity of demand is much higher (0.95) if there is a single owner in the household; the income elasticity of heads work income is positive but smaller (0.56) for the heads work income of the household has two owners.

Many alternatives to the Muth (1971) factor share model discussed above can be used to estimate price elasticities. One such model uses the method of hedonic indexes to decompose rent (or value) into price and quantity. Grootaert and Dubois (1988) and Malpezzi (in press) are among studies that follow this procedure. Malpezzi's estimates for Cairo are particularly interesting, since they are based on the same dataset used by M&M to apply the Muth (1971) method. Using the Muth factor shares model, M&M estimates the point elasticity to be about −0.9; using the hedonic model Malpezzi (1998) finds an elasticity of −0.5, so the estimated price elasticities are not robust with respect to choice of technique. Grootaert and Dubois (1988) find estimates of the price elasticity range between $-0.5$ and $-0.6$.[7] So point estimates of the price elasticity in developing countries have a substantial range, and if we consider the fact that these estimates themselves have considerable standard errors, we can conclude that our knowledge of price elasticities is far from satisfactory.

Other price elasticity estimates include Follain et al.'s (1982) finding that the price elasticity of demand was near zero in most of their models. Ingram's (1984) study used distance as a proxy for price, and found price elasticities in the range of $-0.28$ to $-0.48$, closer to the low end of the estimates extant.

In formerly socialist economies analysis of demand is hindered by what Renaud terms "planner sovereignty and the standardization of demand". That is to say, households may consume any sort of unit they like, as long as it is a 55 m$^2$ flat. The location of the unit is determined by the planner who is working without a market referent. Location and quality choice are almost totally ignored under the planning system. Furthermore, the price of housing is centrally determined and has nothing to do with whatever variation does exist in quality, size or location. Of course this is a highly stylized view, and in many countries such as Poland and Yugoslavia official production was supplanted or supplemented by a rudimentary market. In other countries such as the former Soviet Union at least in urban areas little if any housing was produced outside "the plan". Furthermore, in many such countries there was variation in quality and location, but it was not allocated by income. Rather, incomes were typically compressed; and valued workers were party officials were compensated by receiving better quality housing (or perhaps a second dacha in the countryside).

Alexeev (1988a, b) documented how these unofficial allocation systems worked in the former Soviet Union. He found income elasticity of demand in the pre-Peristroika Soviet Union range between 0.15 and 0.30, which is somewhat low but not wildly lower than estimates for both developing and developed countries. Buckley and Gurenko (1997) analyzed housing demand in Russia post-Perestroyka in 1992, the last year of the administrative allocation system (see the discussion on privatization below). In contrast to Alexeev's results, Buckley and Gurenko find no relationship between income and housing demand. They claim that there are systematic biases in Alexeev's prior study. They point out Polinsky's (1977) critique that without a price term the income elasticity of demand estimate will be biased; and they conject that, as Polinsky argued, the correlation is positive (but cf. M&M, 1985: p. 33).

---

[7] Grootaert and Dubois (1988) actually estimate a reverse regression with price as dependent variable, although they do not note that in their paper.

Daniel (1985) finds quite high income elasticities of around 1, for Hungary. She also finds that on balance the addition of implicit housing subsidies to wage income as an in kind transfer leads to an increase in the distribution of income.

Other studies of transition economies have examined demand indirectly, through queues (Ciechoncinska, 1990; Andrusz, 1990; Charemza and Quandt, 1990). McMillen and Pogodzinski (1993) point out the often cited tendency for queue to overstate effective demand because of low costs of joining the queues may or may not be correct. They point out that there are requirements for joining queues (e.g., based on family status), which vary with the country involved, but which generally raise costs or present a different cost schedule to different households.

Mayo and Stein (1995) examine these issues with data from Poland in the 1980s. Using aggregate data Mayo and Stein show that housing investment is systematically lower in Poland and several other then-socialist economies, compared to other countries with similar levels of development. They also show that housing output prices are substantially higher than marginal costs in Poland. Taken together these two facts confirm the existence of a shortage in Poland during the 1980s.

Using regional (Voivodship) data, Mayo and Stein (1995) estimate several models that show that housing queues are associated with compensating wage differentials and labor shortages, as well as depressed migration to regions. Pogodzinski (1993) undertakes a similar analysis and generally has similar findings; higher housing queues are associated with larger regional labor shortages in Poland. These queues are analyzed in other countries for example Renaud (1995a, b) examines waiting lists in Russia. Charemza and Quandt (1990) also analyze such queues.

### 2.2.3. Cross-country demand models

So far our review has focused on individual markets. Several studies make systematic comparisons across markets. For example, Lakshmanan et al. (1978) reviewed several (mostly developed country) demand studies, and estimated Engel curves for 31 countries using aggregate time series data. These elasticities were rather high compared to other studies, ranging from 0.38 in Tanzania to 2.3 in the US. They generally found somewhat higher elasticities in higher income countries.

In addition to their city specific estimates, M&M also present a set of cross-city Engel curves, estimated separately for owners and renters. The dependent variable is predicted housing expenditure for a five-person household at each city's mean income or its logarithm; these predictions are from the household level equations discussed above. The income variables are based on the city averages. Incomes and rents are converted to 1981 US dollars by using local CPI and official 1981 exchange rates. Price, and its logarithm, are constructed from the rental price series devised by Kravis et al. (1982).

M&M estimate several variants of this model. The key results are straightforward: in a very long run, housing consumption is income elastic, or at least of unit elasticity. Price elasticities are lower than income elasticities in absolute value. Interval estimates of price elasticities are quite wide. In the M&M sample, which is dominated by developing countries, it does not appear that owners have higher long-run responsiveness to changes in incomes and prices; if anything, the reverse to true. Eight out of nine specifications yield a higher median income elasticity for renters than owners; the differences are not great. This does not mean that within a market renters consume less than owners, but that as cities' economies develop over a very long run, owner and renter consumption patterns increase at a similar pace, ceteris paribus. However, because prices rise with income, and estimated renter price elasticities are also higher than owner elasticities, the net effect of both incomes and prices rising as development proceeds is to increase owner consumption faster than renter consumption through most of the range of the data.

Further evidence on the cross-country price and income elasticities of demand for housing is provided by the UN. International Comparisons Project (ICP, see Kravis et al., 1982). The ICP is a major research effort which makes international comparisons of consumption and prices. As part of that effort, Kravis and his associates use hedonic index methods to decompose rents for similar units into rental price and quantity indexes. These indexes, and indexes of total consumption, are used to estimate simple cross-country demand models, where housing consumption is a function of total consumption and the price per unit of housing services (see their Chapter 9). Kravis et al. found demand to be slightly inelastic with respect to price, and slightly elastic with respect to income demand.

## 2.3. Housing supply

In this section, we will examine aggregate descriptive supply (e.g., Burns and Grebler, 1976, 1977; and related work by Renaud, 1980; Chang and Linneman, 1990; Buckley and Madhusudan, 1984). We also examine certain behavioral evidence on aggregate supply elasticities, and their determinants using data from Korea, Thailand and Malaysia. Finally, we examine supply from the existing stock and filtering (Ferchiou, 1982).

### *2.3.1. Early cross-country research*

Several previous studies have documented cross-country differences in housing investment, notably Howenstine (1957), Kuznets (1961), Burns and Grebler (1976), Strassman (1977), Renaud (1980), Kravis et al. (1982), Annez and Wheaton (1984) and Buckley and Madhusudhan (1984). This section briefly reviews the five papers which test some models or exploratory hypotheses about cross-country differences, namely, Burns and Grebler (1976, 1977), the extensions of their model by Renaud (1980) and Buckley and Madhusudhan (1984), the shelter results of the UN's ICP reported in Kravis et al. (1982), and the model of Annez and Wheaton (1984).

Burns and Grebler's (1976, 1977) study examines the share of housing investment (measured by new residential construction) to gross domestic product, using data from 39 countries, and two time periods. Burns and Grebler regress the share of housing investment against GDP per capita and its square, change in population and its square, and a measure of urbanization, squared. They find evidence that the share of housing investment increases at an early stage of development but on average *declines* past about $1600 per capita GDP (1970 US dollars). Furthermore, although there was a wide variance in their dependent variable at different income levels, their simple model explains that variation quite well, and the turning point is quite sharp and measured with apparently reasonable precision.

Of course this turning point in the share does not imply that the level of housing investment decreases with development, at least throughout the observed range of the data. Presumably there is a direct cross-country relationship between housing investment and consumption, since housing investment is a derived demand. Formal models of the relationship between housing demand and investment could be undertaken in the future, to make the link more precise.

Studies by Renaud (1980) and Buckley and Madhusudhan (1984) have shown the Burns and Grebler (1976, 1977) result to be qualitatively robust. Renaud analyzes time series data from Korea and confirms the nonlinearity of the relationship between the share of housing investment and per capita GDP, but finds the exact turning point to be sensitive to specification. Renaud also considers several additional explanatory variables reflecting financial constraints. In general, the financial variables perform well in some specifications but are not robust, which is not surprising given the measurement difficulties involved and the modest number of degrees of freedom.

Buckley and Madhusudhan (1984) test the effect of additional financial variables, namely, the anticipated rate of inflation, changes in the rate of inflation, and the extent of capital deepening. Their analysis confirms the importance of financial conditions in explaining housing investment. In particular, they find that countries with deeper financial markets invest relatively more in housing ceteris paribus. There is also weak support for the hypotheses that the share of investment (1) is higher in less egalitarian countries, (2) increases with anticipated inflation, and (3) decreases with changes in inflation (presumed unanticipated in their model).

The principal shortcomings of these studies have been discussed at length by the authors themselves. Developed countries are overly represented. Official statistics underestimate total housing investment, because of large informal sectors and because new construction statistics fail to count upgrading, maintenance, and depreciation of existing units. These undercounting errors are doubtless largest for the poorest countries. Because of data problems, Burns and Grebler (1976, 1977), and those who followed them, ignored the effects of relative prices, climate, and other variables (although they were careful to point out these omissions). Finally, these models can be thought of as exploratory reduced forms because there is no explicit behavioral model used to justify the estimating equations.

Annez and Wheaton (1984) address several of these problems. They develop a structural model with five endogenous variables (four stochastic equations and an identity). Their model explains total growth in the housing stock, the officially recorded growth, the average quality of new units, and the cost of construction. The share of new construction to national product, conceptually similar to the Burns and Grebler (1976, 1977) dependent variable, then emerges from the identity: share of investment equals the product of change in stock, average size and cost, divided by GNP.

Annez and Wheaton (1984) assembled data from 24 nonsocialist countries (largely developed), and estimated two variants of this model. The more complete model includes several policy related variables (the share of public housing in total production, credit cost and typical loan-to-value ratios), but could only be estimated for a smaller sample of 20 countries. Key results include the following. When total stock is measured in the number of housing units, its growth is determined by demographic, not economic variables. The reverse is true for the quality of an existing unit. Demographics determine the number of units; incomes and prices determine their quality, The fraction of production officially recorded is positively related to the level of economic development, as expected. Costs also rise with development. There is no evidence of any supply inelasticity; cost is unrelated to share of housing investment. Annez and Wheaton note that their estimates imply that as economies develop, increasing incomes fuel housing demand; but this is in large part offset by increasing prices.

### 2.3.2. Market wide effects on supply

To examine links between the microanalysis of incentives above and aggregate outcomes, M&M (1997a) investigated the aggregate supply of housing in Malaysia, and compared these results to those in two other rapidly growing Asian countries, Korea and Thailand. Generally, Korea has a highly restrictive regulatory framework, especially with respect to land use, redevelopment and finance (Kim K.-H., 1990a, b, 1993; Hannah et al., 1993; Greenet al., 1994). Thailand has a liberal regulatory environment (Angel and Chuated, 1990; Dowall, 1989a, 1991c). The US has a generally liberal regulatory environment (albeit with restrictive environments in selected metropolitan areas, see Malpezzi, 1995b). Thus, M&M (1997a) expected price elasticities of supply to be low in Malaysia and Korea, and high in Thailand and the US.

In all three countries, income per capita grew substantially over the period. M&M (1997a) documented that the relative asset price of housing grew substantially over time in Malaysia and Korea, but not in Thailand. This is consistent with the prior that aggregate supply would be inelastic in the first two countries and elastic in the third. M&M's formal test is based on a simple three-equation supply and demand model, using prior information on demand elasticities to identify the price elasticity of supply from the reduced form coefficients. M&M calculate this elasticity for a range of assumptions, assuming the price elasticity of housing demand to lie in the interval $-0.5$ and $-1$, and following M&M (1987), assuming the long-run income elasticity of demand to be alternately 1.0 and 1.5.[8]

The calculated housing supply elasticities are presented in Table 2. For comparison, supply elasticity estimates for the US based on a similar reduced form estimation procedure using Malpezzi and Maclennan's (1996) results for the US are also provided in Table 2. Again results are as expected. In general, Malaysia and Korea have inelastic supply curves for housing, and Thailand and the US have elastic supply.

Certainly additional research could be undertaken along these lines. M&M use a limited dataset (annual data for three developing countries from 1970 to 1986, and some US data). Analysis of additional countries would be straightforward, given the data. Longer time series would permit examining hypotheses about (e.g.) properties of the errors over time, and coefficient stability. Malpezzi

---

[8] As noted above, M&M (1987) estimated cross-sectional elasticities within markets, and long-run elasticities across markets. Since we are examining long-run phenomena, M&M (1997) used the latter results.

Table 2

Estimated price elasticity of supply, four countries

| | Long-run income demand elasticity = 1.0 | | Long-run income demand elasticity = 1.5 | |
|---|---|---|---|---|
| | Price elasticity of demand=-0.5 | Price elasticity of demand = −1.0 | Price elasticity of demand = −0.5 | Price elasticity of demand = −1.0 |
| *Restrictive regulatory environments* | | | | |
| Malaysia | 0.07 | 0[a] | 0.35 | 0[a] |
| Korea | 0[a] | 0[a] | 0.17 | 0[a] |
| *Liberal regulatory environments* | | | | |
| Thailand | $\infty$[b] | $\infty$[b] | $\infty$[b] | $\infty$[b] |
| US | 13.09 | 12.59 | 19.88 | 19.38 |

[a] Point estimate of price elasticity was negative, market deemed inelastic (see text).
[b] Point estimate of $\gamma_1$ was negative, market deemed elastic (see text).
US estimates constructed using results from Malpezzi and Maclennan (1994), others from Table 1.
For discussion of bounds on income and price elasticities of demand see Malpezzi and Mayo (1987).

and Maclennan (1996) demonstrated that results from such models can be sensitive to time period chosen. Other fruitful extensions would be to develop a stock adjustment model and to disaggregate such analysis by region or metropolitan area.

### 2.3.3. *Supply from the existing stock of housing*

Another under researched area is housing from the existing stock. Other than the few studies surveyed in Ferchiou (1982) and Johnson (1987), very little has been done on filtering and other changes in utilization of the existing stock. There is a useful literature on upgrading, for example, Jimenez (1982). Analysis of the utilization of the existing stock is particularly important in understanding rental markets, as will be discussed below.

In common parlance, as units "filter down", they pass from richer households (owners or tenants) to lower income households. Units can also "filter up", i.e., pass from poor to richer households, if a neighborhood is undergoing "revitalization" or "gentrification". Actually there are at least three different definitions of filtering: (1) change in the income of households living in the unit; (2) changes in price per unit of housing services from a unit; and (3) changes in quantity of housing services from a unit. Green and Malpezzi (1997) elaborate and provide further references.

Most studies of developing country /transition economy filtering fall into categories (1) or (3). Most such studies actually *labelled* filtering are chains of move studies related to filtering concept (1). A number of studies have been done on the upgrading process, which is clearly central to (3), although incomplete. Studies of the relative price of housing at different quality levels (2) are are rare in general and almost unkown in developing/transition economies.

Ferchiou (1982) examines data from Tunisia and Mexico, looking at chains of moves, following Lansing et al. (1969) methodology. Generally Ferchiou finds these chains are of limited duration; he finds that a little over two families take part in a chain of moves before it terminates. Ferchiou notes that this is probably a lower bound estimate, partly because of the limited size of the study area. He also notes that construction of more expensive units initiate longer chains.

Hegedus and Tosics (1991) undertake a similar study for Hungary. Generally, they find short chains, usually less than two moves on average. They find little systematic difference by location or by state/private construction. A conjecture (by this author) is that the shortness of these chains may unsurprising give the shifts in employment and population and repressed demand for housing in formerly socialist Hungary.

Several studies examine filtering using some version of the so-called "stock-user matrix" (Strassman, 1977). These basically cross-tabulate households by income category and dwellings by value or rent. A number of these studies are surveyed by Johnson (1985). Baer and Koo (1994) examine Korea.

### 2.3.4. *Housing upgrading*

A number of papers have investigated the determinants of upgrading behavior in developing countries. Struyk and Lynn (1983) estimate several simple reduced form linear probability models for upgrading squatter housing in Manila's Tondo Foreshore area. Generally, increases in income are associated with higher probabilities of upgrading, and (dichotomously measured) improvement of tenure security increases the probability of upgrading by 0.12–0.27 depending on the model. Increasing income by a standard deviation increases the probability of upgrading by about 0.04.

Struyk (1982) presents a simple reduced form model estimated using metropolitan level data from Korea in the late 1970s. The dependent variable used as a proxy for upgrading behavior is the percentage change in average floor area in the housing stock built prior to the baseline period. Struyk's simple reduced form has a series of variables reflecting the cost of upgrading (proxied by shared units in detached dwellings and population density), and a larger set of variables proxying the potential return on expansion: crowding in the baseline year, growth in households, demolitions, the extent of new construction and conversion, and change in household size.

Generally Struyk (1982) found that the variables reflecting potential return had the expected sign and were significant, but the cost of proxies (such as type or density) were generally not significant. One variable, the extent of new construction, was significant but of the wrong sign; that is high rates of new construction were associated with greater upgrading of the existing stock. Struyk notes that this is consistent with a world in which regulatory and financial constraints impede new construction as an adjustment mechanism, so that in active markets new construction is insufficient to meet demand, and upgrading is a gross complement to new construction rather than a gross substitute for it. The crowding variables work particularly well; for example, a 10% increase in an initial crowding measure is associated with about a 10% increase for upgraded area. Elasticity of average floor area to households is 0.5 and of household size is about 1.5.

Strassman (1980b) presents another upgrading study using data from Cartagena, Columbia. Strassman's paper contains several related analyses. To begin, he assumes a cross-section unitary income elasticity and sets up what is referred to in the literature as a stock-user matrix. That is, households are arrayed by rows where income doubles in each row, and dwellings are arrayed in columns, where the value of the unit doubles in each column. If the elasticity were truly unity and if there were no households out of equilibrium, cells along the diagonal would contain most households matched in corresponding housing units. Unsurprisingly, Strassman found large numbers of households off the diagonal elements. This is consistent with M&M's findings discussed at length above that these elasticities are much lower than 1.

Strassman (1980b) also undertook a simple logit tenure choice model that was based on an ad hoc reduced form of the presence or absence of pipe water and sewage; whether relatives were forwarding remittances, household size, age of household add-in income from sales of property. As in much of the developing country literature, no measure of relative tenure prices was available. Strassman implicitly argues that the availability of infrastructure (water and sewer) is largely exogenous. He finds that the probability of owning is negatively associated with the presence of piped water but positively associated with sewage. He interprets this as evidence that "rather than build an owner a waterless shack on land reclaimed from a marsh, those who can afford it will rent a house or apartment with plumbing". While Strassman does not draw this out further, he seems to be suggesting that very low income households will be owners, albeit of units with little in the way of housing quality or property rights; as their income rise they move first into the formal rental sector, and finally into the formal home-owner sector with infrastructure and utilities. We will return to this hypothesis later. Daniere (1992) and Malpezzi (1986) also find a nonmonatonic relationship between tenure and income.

Other upgrading studies of note include Rakodi (1987).

### 2.4. Tenure choice, tenure security and mobility

This section is closely related to the discussions of property rights and housing demand from above. We will examine forms of housing tenure, the value of tenure (Jimenez, 1982; Hoy and Jimenez, 1991), and tenure choice (Lim et al., 1980; Tipple and Willis, 1992; Strassman, 1982; Zorn, 1988). Having examined one method of changing consumption, upgrading, we examine the other—moving (Strassman, 1991; Zorn, 1988).

#### 2.4.1. Forms of tenure

In much of this review, as in much of the housing market literature in both developed and developing countries, households are classified as either homeowners and renters. As always there is a tradeoff between simplicity and analytical tractability, and realism. Whether, or not, such a gross simplification is sensible depends on the purpose at hand.

There are many elements to consider in tenure as implied by our property rights discussion above. Households can own or rent structures and/or land. Usage rights can be fee simple or leased for short or long terms. Households may or may not hold title or customary rights over adjacent property and common space; they may rent from relatives or the government as well as private landlords. Long-term tenants may be treated differently from recent movers, rent may be paid in cash or in kind, periodically or in a lump sum, or some combination of the two. Lump sum payments may or may not be returned, with or without interest, on leaving the unit. Tenants may or may not receive utilities, maintenance and other services as part of the package. Tenants from family or kinship groups may have different rights than strangers. There are a thousand kinds of informal tenure if there is one.

The above list is confusing but by no means exhaustive. A number of schemes can be suggested to try to categorize tenure forms, or put them in a spectrum. Anglo-American lawyers refer to a "bundle of sticks", that is, that any property right can be broken down into component rights. Particular tenures in particular places can be described in terms of the property rights they comprise. This can facilitate comparison and even ranking. Malpezzi (1992) presents a few simple examples of how such an index of tenure rights can be constructed. Unfortunately, detailed classification and analysis of such property rights remains for future work.

### 2.4.2. *Tenure choice*

Many studies of tenure choice have been carried out in developed countries (e.g., Rosen, 1979; Li, 1977). These studies usually find income and stage of the life-cycle are important determinants of tenure choice, as is the relative cost of owning versus renting.[9] Several studies have examined tenure choice in developing countries.

Lim et al. (1980) examined tenure choice in Korea. Limited by the econometrics of the day, they aggregated a number of tenure categories into owning and renting, and estimated an ordinary least square (OLS) tenure choice model for that simple binary choice. Not surprisingly, the authors found that income was a significant determinant of home ownership.

Several studies followed Lim et al. (1980) in examining Korea. Kim S.-J. (1992) used a hierarchical logit model to study Korea. Whereas, Lim et al. aggregated a number of tenure types into owning versus renting, Kim examines several cases separately. In addition to home ownership, Korea has several types of rental tenures, usually distinguished by their payment schemes. In the most common form, *chonsei* ("key money"), tenants put down a large lump sum deposit. In recent years this can be as much as 40% of the cash value of the unit. At the end of the lease period, the deposit is refunded, but without interest. Other tenants pay periodic rent; and their are mixed forms (deposit and rent). Kim finds both permanent and current income measures, as well as demographic variables, explain tenure choice in Korea.

Tipple and Willis (1991, 1992) examine tenure choice in Kumasi, Ghana. They also disaggregate tenure, by ownership, renters and "family housers" (roughly similar to renters, but not an arm's length transaction). They also distinguish tenure forms by whether the households share services with others or have exclusive use. Using both discriminant and logit models, they find there are more differences between sharing services or not, than between owning or renting per se. Income, wealth and how long households have resided in the city are the primary determinants of tenure.

Daniere (1992) examines tenure choice in Cairo and Manila. She uses a logit model to examine owning versus renting (Cairo); renting, squatting and legal ownership (Manila). Home ownership is strongly associated with income in

---

[9] In the US the tax code has a strong effect on the relative price of tenure, and it varies with income since the chief tax break, the mortgage interest deduction, increases with income. This partly explains the strong demand for home ownership for middle and upper income Americans.

Cairo, but not in Manila. In the latter city, rather, the probability of ownership hardly budges with income; but the probability of renting falls significantly and that of squatting rises. Interestingly, squatters have more in common with owners than with renters.

Grootaert and Dubois (1988) estimate a probit model of tenure choice in Cote d'Ivoire and find that income and lifecycle variables do the bulk of explaining home ownership.

Several studies of Philippine data show the value of tenure. For example, Friedman et al. (1988) estimate hedonic functions for formal and squatter housing. They find that on average a rented squatter unit in Manila would rent for 15% more were it formal; the corresponding owner premium is 25%.

A number of papers have presented evidence that in some cities, large fractions of low income households own in the informal sector; as incomes rise they rent in the formal sector; and the richest again become homeowners. Yet, such patterns have not been scrutinized or explained carefully. Strassman (1980b, c) suggests that availability of services such as piped water may catalyze investment by some households and make the shift to renting such units attractive relative to current owners of informal units without such amenities. In a very stylized version of such a world, we would observe the lowest income households owning very low quality housing, perhaps in the informal sector or with little tenure security; past some threshold, households would begin into a higher quality rental submarket; finally, at higher incomes and (perhaps) overcoming financial constraints, households would be able to purchase such housing.

One variable conspicuous by its absence in most of these studies is the relative price of each tenure form. Constructing such a variable is possible but requires some effort (M&M, 1987b). To a household, the user cost of a rental unit is the periodic rent paid, plus any deposits or key money payments appropriately discounted, plus their own payments to others for housing services (e.g., household maintenance expenditures). User cost for owners is even more complicated, since it must account for financing, depreciation and inflation. User cost is another fruitful area for future research.

### 2.4.3. Mobility

The range of variation in mobility is enormous. Strassman's (1991) survey finds that in a given year less than 3% of households moved in a year in the German Democratic Republic in 1980; in Colombo, Sri Lanka only 5% moved. At the other extreme, in Bangkok, Thailand about 20% moved in a year, and in Seoul, Korea an astounding 43%. Strassman (1991) argues that government interventions in housing markets on balance tend to lower residential mobility. He uses data on rents and prices as a proxy for distortion in the housing market; the higher the house price to income ratio, the lower the mobility rate. The higher the rent to income ratio, the higher the mobility rate.

Strassman's (1991) paper sets an interesting agenda in this area. Among other issues, even in such a simple model it's hard to imagine mobility as endogenous while price is exogenous. And many regulations, such as rent control, that could affect mobility can be measured directly.

In the developed country literature, in addition to income and lifecycle effects, disequilibrium in housing consumption has been emphasized as an explanatory variable for household mobility (e.g., Goodman, 1976; Weinberg et al., 1981). Malpezzi (1986) constructs a measure of housing disequilibrium and uses it as an explanatory variable in a model of planned moves and upgrades using data from Cairo. In the event, neither housing consumption variables nor lifecycle and income variables contribute much to explaining planned moves with that dataset.

Zorn (1988) estimates a joint model of tenure choice and mobility, focusing on transactions costs as well as income and lifecycle. As expected, income is positively associated with moving and owning, but negatively with moving and renting. Transactions costs generally reduce the probability of moving, whatever the tenure.

## 2.5. Housing and the aggregate economy

Housing has strong links to general development, both forward and backward (Malpezzi, 1990; Buckley and Mayo, 1989; Renaud, 1990). In this section, we explore the relationship between housing investment and development; housing investment and the business cycle (including employment); housing policy and structural adjustment; and alternative views of housing as a productive investment.

In policy discussions macroeconomists will sometimes point to housing's allegedly unfavorable incremental capital output ratio (ICOR) as evidence that reducing housing investment will increase growth of the economy. While the ICOR can be derived from a simple Harod Domar growth model, such models abstract from the different useful lives of capital and are of little use in distinguishing between investment in one form of capital over another. At the same time, one can find a housing related literature that strains to find multiplier and externality arguments for investment in housing (see Katsura, 1984, for a survey). Malpezzi (1990) develops the argument that housing investment decisions are generally best made on the basis of internal rate of return/present value criteria, as are investment decisions generally. Generally high and rising prices for housing can be viewed as signals that the market requires additional investment.

A number of papers such as Strassman (1985) have examined whether housings employment multiplier is "favorable", or not. The most careful studies using input/output analysis suggest that after indirect effects have taken into account, housing's multiplier is more or less like other multipliers. Research on the existence of externalities such as Burns and Grebler (1977) or more recent evidence for the US such as Green and White (1995), suggest that while health and education externalities may exist, in many developing and transition economies these are probably dwarfed by the innate economic return to additional housing investment.

This is not to imply that there are no general equilibrium or aggregate effects of housing in these economies. Buckley and Mayo (1989) present some examples. They examine two case studies: Argentine housing policy, with special emphasis on financial linkages, and Polish housing policy, with special emphasis on interactions with the labor market. As of the mid-to-late 1980s, they find the present value of welfare costs of Argentine housing subsidies through the financial system are on the order of 6% of GDP in present value terms. Buckley and Mayo find that Poland's insufficient housing investment and ill-located housing are equivalent to a compensating wage differential or tax of about 10% of labor income in the late 1980s. (Both the Argentine and Polish cases are illustrative; both countries have followed quite different policies in recent years.)

Malpezzi (1990) points out that many people working in the shelter sector are not used to thinking of its investments as productive. This is true of many developing country housing analysts and was certainly true under socialist central planning, where housing was explicitly labeled "nonproductive" and was not even counted in Net Material Product (the socialist analogue of Gross National Product). But of course shelter and infrastructure investments are, in fact, by definition productive: they are investment in an asset that yields a flow of services over time. To label such investment as "consumption", is quite common, but incorrect. The same criteria which governs choice of other investments governs housing. Arguments about externalities, indirect contributions to labor productivity, and employment multipliers obscure this central point. Malpezzi (1990) discusses these issues in some detail, including the role housing market reform can play in structural adjustment.

## 3. Related markets

This section is primarily about the first box in Fig. 1, above. Why examine the input markets for housing, when this is rarely done explicitly for many other goals? Because of its high cost in relation to incomes, housing must be financed. Because of its locational fixity, housing markets are profoundly affected by the operation of land markets, and by infrastructure.

### 3.1. Housing finance

Bertrand Renaud (1984) put it best: "Cities are built the way they are financed". In this section, we will examine housing finance, not only as a key input to housing development (Struyk and Turner, 1986), but also housing finance as a key element in financial development more generally. We will investigate certain systemic and institutional issues (Buckley, 1994; Renaud, 1990), as well as more technical details, such as instrument design (Buckley et al., 1993; Chiquier and Renaud, 1992; Sandilands, 1980). We will examine the effects of trying to run housing finance as a subsidy system rather than as a system for true intermediation (Renaud, 1990, 1993; Buckley, 1991). We will also discuss the key role the evolution of housing finance plays in the reform of formerly socialist economies (Buckley et al., 1993; Renaud, 1991).

Housing is the largest asset owned by most households. Housing is *always* financed, in the sense that virtually all owners of housing capital must pay for their units over several periods. Even households which own their units "free and clear" finance the unit in the sense that holding such a large asset has a financial opportunity cost.

But in most countries only a small share of this potential finance, roughly equal to the value of the underlying assets, is in the form of mortgages or other formal sector finance. Goldsmith (1985) shows that in both developing and developed countries formal sector finance is only a small part of the total.

### 3.1.1. Housing finance and financial development

A large literature now exists, on the relationships between financial development and economic development in general (e.g., Besley, 1995, and references therein). It is well known that financial deepening takes place as countries develop, in general; what is less well known is that as countries develop, the formal housing finance system generally grows faster than finance in general. For example, data from the Housing Indicators Project (Angel and Mayo, 1996) show that mortgage loans average roughly 6% of total formal sector loans for countries with

GNP per capita under $1000. For middle income countries ($1000–10,000 per capita), the average is about 16%. For countries above $10,000, the average is about 25%. Of course there is great variation within groups, but the overall trend is quite clear.

Buckley (1991) illustrates the spillovers that an inappropriate housing finance system can have with the case of Argentina during the 1980s.[10] Almost all housing finance came from two sources: a housing fund based on wage taxes (FON-AVI) and the National Mortgage Bank (BHN). Roughly, FONAVI targeted lower income households, and BHN middle income households. Buckley showed that in the system in place in the 1980s, given that payments are only partially indexed, long grace periods, and poor foreclosure and other recovery practices, only 2–5% of every dollar FONAVI invested was ever recovered. During the period Buckley studied BHN was also largely dependent on central government transfers and forced deposits from local authorities at negative rates. Together FONAVI and BHN transferred about 2% of GNP into a narrow segment of the housing market.

Buckley (1991) used a simple consumer surplus model to demonstrate the ineffiency of such transfers. The present value of the net cost of these distortions approached 6% of GNP, and the large expenditures may have accounted for up to one-third of Argentina's inflation during the period.

Many similar examples are documented in the literature. Sandilands (1980) and Silveira (1989) examine Brazil, another country with experience of a large housing fund.

Early studies of housing finance in developing countries emphasized the role of the deposit taking institutions in housing finance. Implicitly the model for many was the US savings and loan system and to some extent Britain's building society system. However, in developing countries and transition economies as well as in the developed world, the trend has been to move away from deposit taking institutions, and to break the direct link between small scale saving and mortgage lending. Secondary institutions and bond finance are becoming more important as proximate sources of funds (see Renaud, 1995).

### 3.1.2. Housing finance and housing

Of course many studies of housing finance focus on the beneficial effects of a well functioning housing finance system for the housing market (Kim K.-H., 1994; UN Centre for Human Settlements, 1996, Chapter 11; Okpala, 1994). Buckley (1994, 1996) and Malpezzi (1990) shows that the better the housing

---

[10] The current Argentine system is quite different from that described in Buckley (1991) and in these paragraphs.

finance system performs, the lower housing prices relative to incomes. Despite these potential benefits, few developing countries have widespread and success-ful systems of housing finance. Many formerly socialist economies are still strug-gling with financial systems which were mainly conduits and are just developing basic skills in underwriting and intermediation.

Malpezzi (1990) showed a simple positive correlation between house prices and positive real interest rates across countries. While heavily regulated rates are often justified on the grounds of affordability, the simple correlation between regulation suggests that artificially low rates may be tied to inelastic supply and higher prices. While such a link remains to be demonstrated conclusively, an inevitable consequence of keeping mortgage rates below market rates is that loans are rationed.

### 3.1.3. Institutional and systemic issues

Even more that the "real side" of the housing market, housing finance is pro-foundly affected by institutional and systemic features that vary from country to country. A broad range of country-specific detail on these can be found in Boleat (1985), Fannie Mae (1991, 1992), Lea and Bernstein (1995) and numerous issues of *Housing Finance International*. Renaud (1984, 1997) provides useful taxonomies to place some structure on this wealth of detail.

In the Anglophone world, housing finance has been particularly influenced by the Savings and Loan/Building Society model, in which mutual savings in-stitutions mobilized funds from household deposits and onlent the proceeds for mortgages. These systems also tended to rely on heavy government regulation, of these institutions and of the financial system generally. Of course, many countries followed quite different models, as Boleat (1985) among others illustrates. But until the last two decades, many countries instituted so- called "special circuits" for housing finance, whether they followed the Anglophone model or some other. Housing finance was generally cossetted and particularly heavily regulated.

As Diamond and Lea (1992) and Renaud (1997) among others have docu-mented, such special circuits are in decline in developing as well as developed countries.[11] As general financial liberalization proceeds apace, housing finance systems are becoming ever more integrated with financial markets in general. Rather than relying on direct household deposits, more institutions are relying on broader capital markets as sources of funds. Housing finance is less often seen as a mechanism to subsidize housing off-budget; subsidies are increasingly separated from the financial system, and are generally better targeted and more

---

[11] Pre-Perastroyka, transition economies generally had no financial institutions other than conduits that provided whatever funds were required to fulfill the plan.

efficient as a result. Housing finance is becoming more competitive, many specific functions are becoming "unbundled", and actors are making ever more use of modern risk management techniques (Renaud, 1997). Of course some countries are moving faster in this direction than others. Chile is one of several Latin American countries that have made significant progress (Ferguson et al., 1996), while Korea is an obvious example of a country that has yet to tackle housing finance reform in a serious way (Green et al., 1994, Kim K-H., 1990a). India is one example of a country that has seen the growth of market oriented housing finance institutions (the Housing Development Finance Corporation) despite the general slow pace of general financial reform (Munjee, date needed).

While there are certainly common issues, research on housing finance in the transition economies has been colored by the fact that most had no true financial institutions prior to Perastroyka; so-called banks were merely conduits, and had no true intermediation or underwriting functions. Housing finance institutions as understood by market economists were generally nonexistent. Housing finance was often some nontransparent combination of municipal finance and benefit-in-kind subsidy to workers. Representative descriptions can be found in Andrusz (1990), Guarda (1993), Diamond (1992), Renaud (1993b), Thalwitz (1993), Parry et al. (1990) and Buckley and Gurenko (1993).

Building on the experience of developing and developed countries, a number of studies have analyzed the housing finance situation in individual transition economies, and presented models for the development of housing finance systems. Of course, such systemic development must be closely tied to progress in privatization and the development of the "real side" of the market (discussed above, see Struyk, 1996, for example). Todate, the best published "roadmap" for the simultaneous development of housing markets and a housing finance system is the study of Russia's housing market by Renaud et al. (1995). Other useful studies in this regard include Buckley and Gurenko (1995), Buckley et al. (1993) and Struyk and Kosareva (1993).

*3.1.4. Mortgage design and other technical details*
Embedded in any full discussion of housing finance systems and institutions is a wealth of important, often critical, details such as the design of mortgage instruments, the proper roles and regulation of various primary and secondary institutions, insurance, settlement procedures, foreclosure procedures, risk management techniques and of course many regulatory issues. Full discussion of such

a wide range of issues is well beyond the scope of this chapter. Here, we briefly discuss one such issue, namely mortgage design.[12]

In the 1970s and 1980s many developing countries adopted some variation of the long-term fixed rate mortgage as the model instrument for their formal housing finance institutions. In the 1970s, in developing as well as developed countries, high and variable inflation made reliance on such instruments untenable. Some Latin American countries, with formal institutions of significant size and volatile macroenvironments, were among the leaders in moving to adjustable or indexed mortgage instruments.

Buckley and Dokeniya (1989) show how indexation aids financial deepening and, by extension, development. They demonstrate that of the set of major Latin American countries studied during the 1980s, Colombia had the most complete system of indexation and the most stable if not most spectacular financial deepening. Buckley and Dokeniya estimated an augmented aggregate production function which suggested that indexation might have accounted for up to one-third of Colombian growth.

A popular form of mortgage instrument is the so-called dual index mortgage (DIM). The DIM is designed to deal, within limits, with the problems of wages which do not track general price levels contemporaneously. The mortgage balance increases with a general price level, and payments increase with a wage-based price level. Shortfalls in real payments are capitalized into the value of the loan. Chiquier and Renaud (1992) simulate the outcomes of the DIM instrument and compare them to a range of alternative instruments. Their simulations show that even DIMs have their limits; in markets with long periods of high price inflation and stagnant or falling wages, DIMs can also "break". This and other studies, such as Buckley et al. (1993) demonstrate that no instrument can fully substitute for sound macroeconomic policy.

## 3.2. Urban land markets

Of course the starting point for understanding land markets is to refer back to our previous discussion of property rights, and tenure issues. See also Alan Evans' contribution in Chapter 42 of this volume.

Here we examine several other land related issues, especially land pricing, effects of infrastructure, and location. We also discuss development vs. redevelopment, and land development and environmental issues (see Joseph Gyourko's contribution to this volume). We also examine regulatory issues (Bertaud, 1992; Dowall, 1989b; M&M, 1997a).

---

[12] More detailed reviews of such issues can be found in Renaud (1989) and Buckley (1996).

### 3.2.1. *How land markets work*

Much of the developing country literature on urban land markets focuses on the operation of the so-called informal sector. For example, Payne (1989) cites Vernez (1973) and Blaesser (1981) as early and innovative studies of norimally illegal pirate subdivisions or (Piratas).[13] They found that housing investments by lower income households in so-called pirate subdivisions worked much more like a market and was a significant form of capital formation. These studies of Bogota and Medellin were in many ways a forerunner of the large World Bank funded study of Bogota and Cali generally known as the City Study (see Mohan, 1994, and references therein). In the 1970s, Gilbert and Ward (1985) undertook a three-country comparative study of Valencia, Mexico City and Bogota. They also found that so-called land invasions and other extra-legal market mechanisms worked reasonably efficiently under the circumstances. In effect, these pirate subdivisions were able to evade formal regulations which would imply large plot sizes and high development standards inconsistent with the incomes of the bulk of the city's populations. Yonder (1987) finds similar results for Istanbul. Mayo et al. (1982) is a very detailed study of the informal housing market in Cairo and Beni Suef, Egypt. All these studies find that the quality and quantity of housing produced in contravention of strict legal codes is impressive. Moreover, conditional on the income of the occupants, such development is often indistinguishable from formal or legal land development. A number of other studies in this vein (which are unpublished and often hard to find) are summarized in Payne (1989), such as Nayani's (1987) study of Hyderabad, India; Mitra's (1987) study of Delhi; and Benninger's (1986) study of Pune, India.

A number of authors have focused on the development of more formal market mechanisms in developing country cities, or "commodification" as this is often called. Amis (1984) discusses the case of urban Kenya; Mehta and Mehta (1989) discuss Ahmedabad; and Payne (1980) finds similar trends in Ankara, Turkey. These and many related studies are quite consistent with dynamic models of property rights. These authors show that, in both agricultural and urban settings, the form of property rights and the way in which they are traded will develop and change as countries densify and develop.

Some authors, such as Baken and Van der Linden (1993), approach informal land markets (pirate subdivisions and the like) as if they are fundamentally different and not amenable to normal economic analysis. Others, such as Gilbert and Ward (1985) and Malpezzi (1994), argue that (in Payne's words) "it is misleading to stress the distinctiveness of the formal and informal land markets". Malpezzi

---

[13] Some of the following is drawn from Payne (1989).

(1994) argues that there are costs to informality; it is often more difficult to get access to infrastructure, and almost always impossible to use such land or real estate as collateral for mortgage loans. Many studies, including some described above such as Jimenez (1982), show that formal tenure is associated with higher asset prices and investment.

DeSoto (1989) presents a general discussion of the inhibiting effects of excessive regulation on Latin American land development, with special reference to Peru. DeSoto's work is descriptive, yet arresting, and has made more of an impact on the popular press and the general development community than more technical pieces. A series of studies by Alain Bertaud and associates have been among the best studies of such regulatory issues. See Bertaud et al. (1988) and Bertaud and Malpezzi (1994) for discussion of methodology, and see Bertaud and Lucius (1989) and Bertaud (1997) for additional case studies. Other regulatory studies of note include Wadhva's (1983) analysis of India's Urban Land Ceiling Act, and those discussed in Farvaque and McAuslan's (1992) overview paper.

Regulatory and planning issues also arise in socialist land "markets". The quotes remind us that in true socialist economies land is often allocated by non-market means. As Bertaud and Renaud (1994) point out, socialist planners made investment and location decisions under a system in which land had no value, capital had no interest opportunity cost, and energy prices were a tiny fraction of loan prices. Since enterprises could not capture any gain from redevelopment or conversion of land to highest and best use, socialist cities often had a pattern of sprawling industrial plants, often using what would be the highest value and highest density office and residential land use under any kind or market system. French and Hamilton (1979) discuss many of these issues pre-Perestroyka, and Bertaud and Renaud (1994, 1997) illustrate with examples from Russian cities.

Bertaud and Renaud show, for example, that population density in Moscow some 10 miles out is about the same as population density in the center of Paris. The negative population densities exhibited in Moscow and a number of other socialist cities would not be as problematic if it were not for the fact that employment is generally highly centralized (unlike say Los Angeles that has decentralized residential patterns but also highly decentralized employment).

This pattern is changing as Russia and a number of other formerly socialist economies move to the market. Not only are land, housing and other real estate markets emerging, but property rights are becoming assigned de facto, if not de jure, meaning that enterprises can capture the gains from redevelopment. Movement towards world energy prices also encourage a shift in the form of the city. Mozolin (1994) presents a detailed analysis of housing price gradients in Moscow.

Hamer et al. (1993) examines urban land markets in China. Many of the issues in China are conceptually similar, although they are played out against the backdrop of one of the most rapidly growing urban populations in the world. (In contrast to Russia's stable urban population.) The authors point out the short-comings of various land market "reforms" during the 1980s, which focused on control and limiting the size of cities, and to a lesser extent on government revenue and the land needs of state enterprises. Overall allocative efficiency was not highlighted in these reforms. Reform has been pushed further by the growing obviousness of problems arising from poor allocation of land and fiscal problems of both local governments and enterprises. Hamer et al. point out that the post-1979 reintroduction of foreign investment brought in a group of actors accustomed to well defined property rights and market or market-like mechanisms. After 1984, a number of Chinese cities embarked on a range of land use management experiments, including the well known Special Economic Zones in several southern and coastal cities. Less well known are changes such as the creation of profit oriented real estate development companies (mainly publicly owned) which develop commercial real estate and sell at prices including land location premia: and introduction of the range of development fees, taxes and lease premia for specific tenure rights. China is also introducing land and building cadastres which define the location, use and rights of specific parcels. Dowall (1993) provides a convenient summary of some of the recent policy changes and requirements for the new two land markets.

Perhaps the most pathological case of land market regulation in any large country was South Africa's Apartheid system. Turok (1994a, b) presents a concise description. Brueckner (1996) analyzes the welfare gains from dismantling Apartheid in the context of the standard urban model.

### 3.2.2. Land prices across markets and over time

A decade or two ago much of the literature on land price trends in developing countries argued, in fact mainly accepted, that given population and income growth, land prices will rise inexorably and that a corollary of this is that housing prices will show similar increases. See, for example, Evers (1976), Geisse and Sabatini (1982) and Haddad (1982).[14] However, several authors such as Ward et al. (1993) and Angel and Chuated (1990) point out that much of this work suffers from failure to standardize land prices, failure to consider a very long-run time period instead of simply part of the cycle, and sometimes even fail to adjust for general price inflation. The literature that has been emerging more recently has

---

[14] These references are due to Ward et al. (1993).

been more careful in each of these respects, and generally finds that: (a) land prices do not rise inexorably; (b) when they are rising over a long period of time it is often due to specific policies adopted by the public sector; and (c) at least modest increase in house and land prices need not necessarily translate into a one-to-one increase in housing prices. It should also be noted that the pattern of land prices in the aggregate (say average or median price) abstracts from locational differences within the city, as discussed further below.

Gilbert and Ward (1985) found land prices in three Latin American cities rising in real terms during the late 1970s and 1980s, but that the increase was not dramatic. Later research by some of these authors (see Ward et al., 1993) found that during part of the 1980s real land prices fell in Mexico.

Dowall (1989a) and Angel and Chuated (1990) showed that despite rapid population and income growth, land prices in Bangkok rose only modestly in real terms during the late 1970s and early 1980s. Furthermore, even this slight increase in real land prices did not translate into a significant increase in housing prices, as developers were generally free to substitute capital for land and develop more densely (cf. Foo, 1992; Dowall, 1991c).[15] Strassman et al. (1994) found that while land prices were high by international standards in Manila, house prices were closer to the norm. However, the downmarket penetration of the unsubsidized private sector was found to be significantly lower than Bangkok's. Strassman et al., point to a number of public sector policies which keep land prices high, focusing particularly on negligible effective property tax rates, which keeps the holding cost of vacant land low (Strassman et al., do not discuss the opportunity cost).

Peng and Wheaton (1994) also shows that in Hong Kong where land supply is extremely restrictive, increase substitution of capital for land has implied much higher land prices but reasonably stable (in the long run) housing prices. Hannah et al. (1993) show that in Korea land and housing prices rose quite rapidly during periods of high demand. They point to the extremely restrictive land use policies of the Korean government which attempts to limit land and urban use (see also Green et al., 1994).

A number of papers have further investigated the relationship between land prices, housing asset prices and rents, e.g., Lin (1993), Chang and Ward (1993), Chang et al. (1994) and Kim and Suh (1993). Chow and Wong (1997) apply the user cost model to Hong Kong prices, and Renaud et al. (1997) apply the related asset-rental price framework of DiPasquale and Wheaton (1992).

---

[15] With a number of associates, Dowall (1991c) performed similar analyses in some 30 markets. Dowall (1997) provides a review, see also Dowall and Clarke (1991).

Table 3

Land price gradients

| Study | Data | Model | Typical gradient | Comments |
|---|---|---|---|---|
| Asabere (1981) | Kumasi, Ghana 1970–1979 | Individuals, infrastructure whether sold to Ashante/non-Ashante, type of neighborhood, size of plot. | −0.037 | Also found nominal $P_L$ rose 1.1% per month, 1970–1979 (of CPI). |
| Son and Kim (1998) | Korea six cities | Land price gradient greenbelt dummies. | −0.027 (Seoul) to −0.290 (Kwang-ju) | Finds green belt a strongly binding constraint. |
| J. Eckert data reported in Bertaud and Renaud (1994) | Moscow, Russia 1992 | Simple gradient (estimated by this author from graphs). | $Q_1$ 1992: −0.017 $Q_2$ 1992: −0.034 | Moscow is first ever case of steepening gradient as market emerges. (Need to find figures) |
| J. Eckert data reported in Bertaud and Renaud (1994) | Krakow, Poland 1992 | Simple gradient (estimated by this author from graphs). | 1992: −0.10 | (Need to find figures) |
| Dowall (1989) | Karachi, Pakistan 1985 | Dummy for large plots and developed plots. | −0.058 | Large plots sell at large premium and developed plots worth more than twice undeveloped. |

### 3.2.3. Prices within cities

Table 3 presents data from several studies of the pattern of prices within cities. Asabere (1981a, b), Sun and Kim (1994) and Dowall (1989) estimate straightforward negative exponential models with familiar results. Gradients are negative and declining; constraints raise prices; and larger developed plots are worth more. Perhaps most interesting are the studies of formerly socialist markets.

Bertaud and Renaud (1994, 1997) use unpublished data from Joseph Eckert and find Krakow's land price gradient is similar to the US and other developed countries. On the other hand, Moscow's gradient is extremely flat. This is particularly remarkable given the high employment density in Moscow's center. However, Bertaud and Renaud also point out the remarkable steepening of the house price gradient in Moscow over the course of the year in which Eckert collected his data. This may be the first ever case of rent gradient steepening over time, as a true market emerges.[16]

Bertaud and Renaud (1994, 1997) forecast a sharp shift in the relative price of locations during the transition. Their conclusion is

> in cities the process is likely to be seriously disruptive. We can only point here at some of the management issues during this transition to markets . . . .

---

[16] The numerical gradient estimates in Table 2 were constructed by this author from data presented from Fig. 3 of Bertaud and Renaud's (1994, 1997), from Eckert.

Current Russian discussions of the affordability problem of non residential land or a false problem which ignore the necessity of land use transition. By definition the market price of land is affordable to new users. The industrial land may not be affordable, however, to existing users who are asked to pay for it retroactively, but these existing users are precisely those who are using land in an inefficient manner. The affordability dilemma can be solved by recognizing the land equity interest of present land users and then allowing these users to trade freely the land they occupy.

## 3.3. Infrastructure

See also the contributions by Eberts and McMillen (Chapter 38), Small and Gómez-Ibáñez (Chapter 46) in this volume, and World Bank (1994). Here, we will focus on transport, water and sanitation, power and housing.

The provision of infrastructure and related services—transport, water, sanitation and so forth—is a traditional public sector activity, and one of particular importance to low income households. Directly, households benefit from several types of infrastructure through saving time and money (for example, publicly supplied water rates versus user charges) and through improved living conditions. Often, infrastructure investments encourage new construction and upgrading of existing housing, including the provision of more houses to rent. Households also benefit indirectly from infrastructure investments, if these are seen as legitimizing previously illegal or informal settlements (discussed in the previous section).

Like land and finance, infrastructure for housing generally needs to be considered in conjunction with infrastructure for other uses. Roads, electricity, water and sanitation are at some level all shared by households and firms, or are if economies of scale are taken advantage of. In a series of studies of infrastructure in Nigeria, Thailand and Indonesia, Lee and his associates have examined the efficiency losses from inappropriate infrastructure policies, with a particular focus on manufacturing, although many of the arguments can be generalized to other sectors (need more here). See, for example, Anas et al. (1996), Kessides (1993) and Lee et al. (1996).

Government policies on the supply and pricing of urban infrastructure are characterized by various conflicting tendencies. For example, governments have taken the view that (a) water and sanitation (and sometimes other types of infrastructure) are merit goods; (b) infrastructure has significant externalities; (c) low income households may, out of ignorance, seriously underestimate the benefits of improved water and sanitation; and (d) some of these services involve large economies of scale—that is, they are "natural monopolies" or at least require investments too large for the private sector. These views have led to governments' taking the leading role in providing urban infrastructure, but often with under investment, and prices that are too low to recover costs. The result has been severe rationing and chronic problems in maintaining and expanding the stock of urban infrastructure. Therefore, cities are both less efficient and more inequitable than they could be with alternative policies. For the past two decades a large literature exists on the engineering side of a wide range of water and sanitation alternatives, such as Kalbermatten et al. (1980, 1982). Current debates are more about economics.

### 3.3.1. Water and sanitation

Of the possible alternative policies, cost recovery is a contentious issue (Jimenez, 1987). Poor households are widely assumed to be unable or unwilling to pay for improved services; research such as Whittington et al. (1990, 1993), Katzman (1977), McPhail (1993), Warford and Turvey (1974) demonstrates that this is not so. For example, many urban households spend significant amounts of time collecting water from standpipes or wells; in cities with water vendors, people often pay high unit prices for water (Zaroff and Okun, 1984; Okun, 1982). Understanding the demand for water, sanitation, and other urban services also helps to indicate the correct type of technology. For example, the choice between a communal standpipe system and individual house connections depends on the demand for water and the value people place on the time spent in water collection. But given the potentially large externalities involved and the low incomes and often low willingness to pay for sanitation (as opposed to water), others view cost recovery as a secondary goal at best and a potential barrier to sufficient investment (Hardoy et al., 1990).

### 3.3.2. Urban transport

Another key infrastructure element, and one deserving of its own chapter, is transportation infrastructure. Here we only highlight a few key issues and references.

Congestion is endemic in developing countries. Traffic and Lagos, Bangkok and Mexico City, to name only three cities, is legendary. In many cities this increase traffic congestion contributes to additional air pollution. The cities of Eastern Europe and the former Soviet Union, on the other hand, face somewhat different transportation issues in general. Often these cities face much slower population growth, and have more existing transport infrastructure. But given the common repression of automobile ownership under socialist regimes, we can expect large increases in automobile use and dramatic increases in congestion in the decade ahead in many of these cities (see Hall, 1993, and the European Conference of Ministers of Transport, 1995).

A range of research such as Deaton (1984) and Yucel (1975) show transport demand elasticities and modal choice parameters to be broadly similar to those in developed countries. Rules of thumb about price elasticities and the value of travel time transfer reasonably well.

World Bank (1981, 1986) documents the bias towards large infrastructure investments in transport and away from less sexy investments in bus systems, improved maintenance and traffic management. The Urban Edge (1983) for example documents that large investments in fixed rail are often uneconomic in developing country cities. On the other hand, Walters (1979) shows extremely large net social benefits from the introduction of a minibus system to Kuala Lumpur. Barrett (1983), among other references shows the very large returns generally to traffic management improvements in cities. Readers interested in pursuing this important area further could consult World Bank (1986), Thomson (1983) and Dhareshwar (1987).

This short discussion certainly does not do justice to all infrastructure issues. Interested readers should consult Lee (1988, 1992) and Lee and Anas (1992) for example on the costs of deficient communications and electricity generation infrastructure as well as transport infrastructure in Thailand and Nigeria. Lee and colleagues are currently engaged in research on infrastructure and urban productivity in Indonesia.

## 4. Housing policy

This section is primarily about how the elements in Fig. 1, relate to each other. In particular, how government policies profoundly affect these relationships.

The previous discussions of housing markets and related input markets, perforce incorporated some discussion of public policy issues. In this section we examine public policy more systematically. We begin with a stylized history of thinking in the area, in both theory and practice. We examine council/public housing, an idea brought to its ultimate conclusion in socialist countries. We then introduce some alternative policy paradigms, sites and services: (Turner, 1972; Mayo and Gross, 1987), and upgrading: Indonesia's Kampung Improvement Program (KIP), for example (Payne, 1984). We compare and contrast these approaches with what some term the market wide approach and others term the enabling approach (UN Centre for Human Settlements, 1990; World Bank,

1993). We examine the effects of various government interventions: taxes, subsidies and regulations (Hannah et al., 1989). We also discuss current issues of reforming socialist economies and privatization (Struyk, 1996).

## 4.1. "Industrial organization" of the housing market

The "industrial organization" of the housing market can be characterized along several dimensions. First, we can compare and contrast public and private sector roles (see the Costa and van der Borg contribution to this volume). Second, we can consider competition policy (Olsen, 1969; Barlow and King, 1992; Landis, 1983; Maclennan, 1989). Third, we can consider interventions (tax, regulation and subsidy policy), as in Kim J-H. (1990), Dowall (1992), Ondiege (1986), Sanyal (1981) and Yu and Li (1985).

### 4.1.1. Public housing

Developing and developed countries, differ widely in the share and nature of publicly provided and assisted rental housing. Of course, as noted above, virtually all housing of whatever tenure receives some government assistance in some form (and virtually all is also taxed in some way), so "publicly assisted" is surprisingly arbitrary and difficult to define rigorously. Publicly provided usually means that governments or local authorities own and manage rental units, but even here there are gray areas; some nonprofit housing authorities do not fit unambiguously into either public or private definitions; in socialist countries, where does rental housing provided by state enterprises fit in? And partly because of such definitional problems, a consistent data series for cross-country comparisons is surprisingly difficult to construct.

Within market or mixed economies, most countries' public rental or council housing stock is a small percentage of the total (5% or less); most significant exceptions are in developed countries such as the Netherlands (9%); the UK (29%); but Hong Kong (40%). Many centrally planned economies have much greater shares of their housing stock as public rental; for example China's urban housing stock is well over 80% public or enterprise rental.

Even in those countries where public and council housing is not a large share of total housing, the asset value of such housing can be significant, because housing's asset value is large due to its long life, and because a disproportionate number of these units are built on expensive urban land. For example, according to unpublished World Bank estimates some 15,000 public housing units in Ghana have an asset value of about 2% of GNP; yet most are barely maintained and the rents collected are so low that the development corporation which owns the housing is technically insolvent. Privatization as a solution to such problems is discussed below; first a discussion of the relative efficiency of the public and private rental markets is in order.

### 4.1.2. Privatization of public housing

Three kinds of housing related issues have been neglected in the privatization literature. First, when should housing be privatized, or, more precisely, should a change be made in the manner of provision? Second, what concomitant regulatory changes are required for the new delivery system? Third, how can the privatization or other change be implemented? Malpezzi (1990) illustrates the issues and an approach using a simple present value model. Mills (1995) presents an overview of the concomitant changes necessary for privatization. Other useful general references include Clapham (1995), Turner et al. (1992) and Telgarsky and Struyk (1991).

Tomann (1992) discusses the case of eastern Germany. Reunification presents special problems and opportunities. Rather than struggle to develop property rights, legal systems, financial institutions, policy and the like, from scratch, eastern Germany has largely adopted the western system whole. Post-unification, state-owned housing has been transferred to local governments and their subsidiary housing authorities. Ownership of private units is still clouded by 1.3 million claims from pre-communist owners, driving up risk and reducing investment. Rents for sitting tenants are controlled in both private and public markets; units are relet at market rents if tenants turn over, and new construction is exempt; while still low, controlled rents are rising, from 0.3 DM per square meter two years ago to 1.75 DM today for multifamily; for single families rents have risen from 1.2 to 4.9 DM (there are currently about 1.65 DM to the dollar).

Hegedüs and Tosics (1992) discuss Hungarian public housing. This housing has been devolved to local governments, and as in those countries recurrent costs drain local treasuries. Hegedüs and his colleagues laid out a range of privatization options—whether to sell mainly to sitting tenants or to others, at what selling price, and what rents to charge for unprivatized stock.

Despite a slow start in 1988–1989, the privatization effort picked up steam in the 1990s, so that now over a quarter of the public units have been privatized, mostly to sitting tenants. Terms are very favorable to tenants—the authors estimate the selling price is about 15% of market value, with a 40% discount of that sale price for cash, or 10% down with a 15-year 3% mortgage (inflation was 26% in 1992). Hegedüs et al. (1992) predict a wide and rapid shift from rental into home ownership, given such terms and the uncertainty of the future of public rental housing. They note, however, that since receiving the best housing was a large part of the communist elite's compensation, selling public units to sitting tenants at nominal prices, in effect, capitalizes the value of the previous subsidy and exacerbates perceived inequities in the distribution of income and wealth.

Among many other interesting points, the authors discuss the interaction between rent policy and selling price policy. The current situation, with low controlled rents and low selling prices, bleeds local treasuries and (as just argued) perpetuates perceived inequities. If, on the other hand, rents are kept low and selling prices are raised to market levels, privatization will be hindered as households have strong incentives to keep renting. Conversely raising rents while keeping selling prices low encourages privatization. Hegedüs et al. (1992) favor raising both selling prices and rents to market levels, to stem local government losses, and to avoid distorting tenure decisions in either direction. This would also wipe out current subsidies, which could be replaced with more equitable and targeted housing allowances. However, they are not optimistic about the political feasibility of raising rents and selling prices simultaneously.

A different point of view is expressed in Buckley et al. (1995). They argued that moving to market rents is so unlikely for political reasons that the inequities in the current distribution of units should be ignored, especially since the most desirable units had already been privatized, i.e., the worst inequities could no longer be addressed. Another argument they raised in favor of low rent-low price policy was that governments would be hard pressed to come up with the money for housing allowances. They therefore recommended a strategy not too far removed from current practice: keep rents and selling prices low; effectively giving units away would, they argue, allow a faster move to a market. The most detailed and comprehensive roadmap to privatization on a wide scale remains the study by Renaud et al. (1993) for Russia; see also Kaganova (1994) and Kosareva and Struyk (1992).

## 4.2. Subsidies

Subsidies and public actions reduce the cost of something to particular recipients. A common type of subsidy is a payment to someone for a particular purpose—such as an allowance used for rent. But subsidies are also created when government makes rules which change the price that someone has to pay for a good or service—such as rent control.

In most countries, market as well as socialist, the pattern of subsidies that has grown up over time has little to do with explicitly articulated policy objectives. For example, most countries pay some sort of lip service to the notion that housing subsidies should be at least partly targeted to low income households.

But in fact, in most countries larger subsidies go to higher income households, especially when indirect subsidies through the tax and finance subsidies are considered. Similar patterns can be found in most other countries, developing and developed, market and socialist.[17]

In reforming socialist countries tax subsidies are not yet an issue, partly because income tax systems are still poorly developed. Other indirect subsidies, especially to rental housing, have been shown to be large and inefficient (Buckley et al., 1993), and perversely targeted (Daniel, 1983; Alexeev, 1990).

Mayo (1986) makes an important distinction between production and consumption efficiency. Production efficiency refers to the economic value of the unit in relation to the cost of producing it. Consumption efficiency refers to the value the *tenant* places on the unit in relation to its market value. The concepts are equally applicable to rental and other programs.

Empirical evidence suggests that public housing is rarely a very efficient way to increase housing consumption or welfare. In the most complete study to date Mayo (1986) reported that the consumption efficiency of US public housing is about 86% (ratio of benefits to costs), and its production efficiency is only 43% (ratio of value to costs). Another study by Olsen and Barton (1983) that took a more narrow view of production efficiency, reported that US public housing costs 14% more than they were worth. Agrawal (1988) reports that for the 300,000 public housing units in Australia the mean consumption efficiency is 0.75 to 0.68. Daniel (1983) studied the effect of public housing on the distribution of income in Hungary. She found that the ratio of highest to lowest income decile was 1 : 6; for housing consumption, 1 : 12; and for housing expenses per head, 1 : 23. Rents for flats are about 40% of maintenance costs, and about 15–20% of full cost (maintenance, depreciation, and a small profit to finance expansion). The average subsidy is 15% of income (only 10% in lowest decile). She examines the effect on income distribution and finds *"the rented flat as an allowance in kind does not reduce vertical inequality in society, as it should under the declared intentions, on the contrary it augments it"* (emphasis in the original). Her findings suggested horizontal equity is also violated.

Yu and Li (1985) study Hong Kong's public units, which house 40% of its population. In 1980, the rent charged for public units was $10 per square meter; the market rent for comparable units was $56 per square meter. Consumption efficiency is 0.75. A later study by Wong and Liu (1988) found qualitatively similar results. Wong and Liu highlighted the fact that public housing's inefficiency was due to underconsumption by higher income tenants as well as overconsumption

---

[17] See, for example, Agrawal (1988), Piggott (1984), Trollegard (1989) and Nicholson and Willis (1990).

by lower income tenants, and only a fraction of eligible low income tenants obtained public housing, leading to violations of horizontal and vertical equity. Ondiege (1986) carried out a similar study for Kenyan public housing. He found an average deadweight loss of only a little over 2%. But Ondiege also noted the wide variance in outcomes across households, implying poor horizontal equity and perverse vertical equity (the largest benefits go to the richest households). Ravallion (1989) analyzes the welfare costs of stylized housing programs in Indonesia, but is only able to present ex ante costs and benefits under different assumptions of how binding standards would be.

Such welfare analyses are difficult to carry out in transition economies because of the lack of market comparators (e.g., a private market reasonably close to equilibrium that can be used to estimate market prices for units and market demand for households). Papers which present rough magnitudes based on cost data include Wang (1991) and Pudney and Wang (1995).

A related issue that has not received the attention it deserves in developing and transition economies is the extent to which public housing expenditure—for owner occupied or rental units—simply crowds out private. For example, Murray (1983) found that for every 100 public rental housing units built in the US during the 1970s, private construction was reduced by about 85 units.[18] From the studies done so far, in the developed and developing countries, it seems that publicly built housing or subsidized new construction has not given good value for money. But often the largest and most problematic expenditures never appear on the budget.

The dominance of off-budget housing expenditures through the financial system and tax code in developed countries is well known. For example, in the US the value of the mortgage interest deduction tax subsidy alone is at least three times the size of on-budget federal housing expenditures. Off-budget expenditures are often as much, or more, a central feature of housing policies in developing and transition countries. In developed countries tax expenditures receive much of the attention. In developing countries there are often large implicit subsidies in the provision of land for shelter projects, although these are somewhat self-limiting, as large implicit subsidies limit their scale. Such housing finance subsidies are often "off the books"; Buckley and Mayo (1989) discuss the example of Argentina. In transition economies, the subsidy implied by non-market housing systems, already discussed, are large and only partly carried on government budgets.

---

[18] But more recent work by Murray (1993) highlights the fact that the degree of substitution varies markedly by type of housing program.

Another important class of off-budget expenditures related to housing are energy related. These are particularly problematic in the former Soviet and eastern European countries, where residential energy use was unpriced and spectacularly wasteful. Renaud et al. (1993) calculate that Russian residential energy prices are less than 10% of world prices, for example.

Housing allowances require a certain level of administrative capability, as well as reasonably reliable income data. Many countries would have great difficulty with the latter if not the former, given the nature of urban labor markets. Little research has been undertaken on this important practical issue.

## 4.3. Housing market regulation

A number of authors suggest changes in regulation are often among the most pressing areas for reform (Hannah et al., 1989; Dowall, 1992). Regulatory reform can play a key role in the three areas just discussed, i.e., increasing the supply of finance, infrastructure and developable land. Zoning, taxes, rent controls and building standards are other obvious regulatory areas to study for possible change. Governments must carefully weigh the costs and benefits, and the distributional consequences, of regulation. Regulation should strive for a "level playing field" insofar as is practical. Land regulation has already been briefly discussed; we now discuss the issue more broadly, based on a simple framework laid out in Hannah et al. (1989) and M&M (1997a).

### 4.3.1. Subsidies, taxes, regulation, and other interventions: a simple model
Hannah et al. (1989), Malpezzi and Mayo (1997a) and related papers cited therein, point out the obvious fact that government subsidizes, regulates, taxes and otherwise, intervenes in housing markets for a variety of purposes. Each policy intervention can be analyzed in turn by examining how the interventions change the prices and corresponding present values. Present values have the advantage of enabling direct comparisons of the costs and benefits of quite different interventions in different programs. Some interventions impose costs (e.g., land use regulations, taxes, rent controls, building regulations) and some benefits (e.g., land subsidies, tax relief, financial subsidies). Some interventions confer corresponding costs and benefits on different market participants; for example, rent controls benefit some tenants at the expense of landlords (and perhaps some other tenants). Other interventions confer costs and/or benefits on some participants without an obvious corresponding gain or loss elsewhere. For example, some very high infrastructure standards can confer large costs on developers without producing much in the way of benefit for anybody.

While there is nothing technically difficult about doing so, hardly ever are the effects of all the numerous taxes, regulations and subsidies added up. In the US the "user cost" literature takes this approach, usually focusing on the interaction between taxes, inflation and finance.[19] In a number of developing countries, we are beginning to adopt a variant of the same approach.

In this framework, there are three entities from whose point of view housing policies and programs are evaluated: the economy, housing suppliers (or developers) and households. The exact incidence of the various costs and benefits of government interventions can be a subtle issue. For example, although the incidence of the property tax appears straightforward—property owners pay the property tax—some portion of the tax could be shifted to tenants (for rental property) or to the owners of capital generally (if capital markets were well integrated).[20] Incidence can depend on the competitiveness of the market, the state of transactions costs and knowledge in the market, the efficiency of financial markets in a country, and the time frame—in other words, it is rarely settled and unambiguous. Hannah et al. (1989) adopt a simple approach, where the entire cost or benefit is assigned to one participant. They point out that if our knowledge of actual incidence improves, it would not be difficult to build in more sophisticated treatment of incidence.

Hannah et al. (1989) and Malpezzi and Mayo (1997a) use the case of Malaysia to illustrate the simple "incentives model". Malaysia's Special Low Cost Housing Program was designed to induce private developers to build low-cost housing. But analysis using this model demonstrated that despite strong demand, on balance government regulations still cost the developer money, raised costs and reduced supply. Many of these regulations yielded little or no benefit to consumers or anyone else.

Similar models have been applied to Turkey (Baharagolu et al., 1997), Korea (Kim K.-H., 1991) and Ethiopia (Erbach et al., 1996). In each case, the application has highlighted several interventions, especially on the regulatory front, that have had unintended consequences, driving up housing costs, often disproportionately at the low end of the market.

### 4.3.2. Rent control

Roughly 40% of the world's urban dwellers are renters; in many developing country cities, two-thirds or more of the housing stock is rental (Malpezzi and

---

[19] DeLeeuw and Ozanne (1981) and Diamond (1978) provide examples.
[20] See, for example, Aaron (1975) and McLure (1977).

Ball, 1991). A majority of countries have some form of price control on some or all of their rental housing stock.

Rent control is usually thought of as a policy applied to private markets, but publicly provided housing is also subject to controls, and to some of the attendant problems like reduced revenue and maintenance. For example, most urban housing in Russia and China is owned by the government or state enterprises. Rents are based on historical costs and extraordinarily low in real terms. As a consequence, housing subsidies are a huge share of government budgets. Many units are undermaintained because of lack of financing.

Malpezzi and Ball (1991, 1993) document the many different kinds of rent control regimes around the world. For example, one key feature is whether regulations set the level of rents, or control increases in rent. Others include *how* controlled rents are adjusted for changes in costs (with cost pass-through provisions, or adjustments for inflation); how close the adjustment is to changes in market conditions; how it is applied to different classes of units; or whether, or not, rents are effectively frozen over time. Other key provisions that vary from place to place include breadth of coverage, how initial rent levels are set, treatment of new construction, whether, or not, rents are reset for new tenants, and tenure security provisions. Rent control's effects can vary markedly depending on these specifics, and on market conditions, as well as enforcement practices.

A number of rent control cost-benefit studies have been carried out; Malpezzi (1993) and Malpezzi and Ball (1993) review several. For example, in Cairo, Egypt, monthly rents for a typical unit are less than 40% of estimated market rents (Malpezzi, 1986). "Key money" (illegal upfront payments to landlords) and other side payments make up about one-third of the difference. In Amman, Jordan, the static cost of controls is about 30% of estimated market rent; the benefit to the typical tenant is only 65% of cost (Struyk, 1988a).

Rent control can also impose dynamic costs (i.e., undesirable changes in the stock of housing over time). Controls can reduce dwelling maintenance, reduce the useful life of dwellings, and inhibit new construction. Controls provide strong incentives to convert rental units to other uses. These market responses shift the incidence of rent control's costs forward to tenants, over time. It is theoretically possible to design a rent control regime that does not discourage maintenance, and starts with a pricing scheme that rewards maintenance and new construction (Malpezzi, 1986; Olsen, 1988). In practice, revaluation and maintenance inspections are expensive and difficult to organize; and new construction can still be adversely affected by the expectation of future controls.

Given their potential importance, dynamic effects of controls are understudied. For example, no one has yet credibly analyzed the effects of controls on the aggregate supply of housing. Despite many studies which imply controls, qualitatively reduce returns to rental investors, given the myriad ways real world regimes work and ways around controls (legal and illegal) the size of the net aggregate effect on supply remains unknown. Malpezzi and Ball (1993) found that countries with stricter rent control regimes invested less in housing, in the aggregate; but while they controlled for demand (income and demographics), they were unable to control for other constraints on housing markets (e.g., land use constraints, financial constraints). Since these may well be correlated with the strength of controls, precise quantitative measures of the effects of rent controls per se await future research.

The evidence todate casts doubt on controls' effectiveness as income transfer mechanisms. In Cairo and Bangalore, for example, no relationship was found between the benefits gained from reduced rent and household income, because rent control is not well targeted to low income groups. In Kumasi and Rio, benefits were found to be somewhat progressive (Malpezzi and Ball, 1991; Malpezzi, 1986; Malpezzi and Tewari, 1991; Malpezzi et al., 1990; Silveira and Malpezzi, 1991).

Another questionable assumption behind redistribution as a rationale for controls is the notion that landlords are rich and tenants are poor. In Cairo, Kumasi and Bangalore, the income of tenants and landlords was compared; and, while the landlords' median income was higher in all three, there was significant overlap. In Cairo, for example, about 25% of tenants had incomes that were higher than the landlord median, and about 25% of landlords had incomes lower than the tenant median. There is no guarantee the transfers will only occur from high income landlords to low income tenants.

Rent control issues in formerly socialist countries are somewhat different. While construction is now more or less decontrolled, rents on public and private housing are still controlled. For example, in an unpublished presentation, Jan Brzeski explained that in Poland current proposals for rent reform are not based on letting rents seek market levels but on rents based on costs. Each year rents may be increased by a fraction of the difference between current rents and 6% of "replacement costs". Apart from the poor incentives inherent in cost-based systems, in practice these replacement costs are poorly estimated. Tolley (1991) provides a detailed analysis of cost-based rents in the Chinese context.

Generally, tenants in formally socialist countries have very strong security of tenure, although if a tenant dies, and there are no parties with rights of succession to the tenure, private property owners may now repossess the property, resetting rents to market or selling. State rental property was devolved to municipalities.

This has had serious repercussions for municipal finance, as rents do not cover maintenance costs.

Alternatives for decontrol are analyzed in Malpezzi and Ball (1991), following Arnott (1981). In addition to analysis of changes in controls per se, Malpezzi and Ball emphasize the need for collateral reform in land, finance and housing development regulations, for decontrol to work. Decontrol in an inelastic market (due for example to other distortions) will largely raise rents with little supply response, and lead to political pressure for reimposition of controls.

### 4.3.3. Is overregulation systematic?

Much of the discussion on regulation so far in this chapter is in the context of *overregulation*. But regulation per se is neither good nor bad nonetheless, is there a systematic tendency to overregulation? Malpezzi (1990) argues the tendency to overregulate can be explained by (1) the failure to consider costs and benefits, from which follows (2) that every interested party adds his own small regulation which are never considered together (the adding up problem), (3) some overregulation results from a breakdown in exchange between regulators and the regulated (the Coase theorem can be applied here), and (4) regulations are an opportunity for rent seeking behavior/vested interests. Given such overregulation, understanding reduced efficiency is easy: they impose larger transactions costs than benefits. Inequities also follow: the poor are not usually particularly good at rent seeking behavior, and since regulations raise costs and restrict supply, it is the poor who are rationed out first. Regulations on lot size, for example, are not directly binding on the rich.

Other areas are clearly underregulated. The environment is one area in which a consensus is building that more needs to be done. What we have argued above is that our path is clear for *all* regulation: do the cost-benefit of specific regulations; eliminate or modify regulations whose benefits exceed costs; keep, enact or enforce the ones that make the grade. Get the *regulations* right. The superficial inconsistency of arguing for tighter environmental regulations disappears in this framework; even more importantly, we have a tool to discriminate between important and frivolous environmental issues, and policies.[21]

The lesson of a number of studies is that regulation per se is neither good nor bad; what matters is the cost and benefit of specific regulations under specific market conditions. Having said that, it is common for regulations to exceed their costs in developing countries and the former socialist economies as well as in developed countries. In Mexico, for example, the waiting period to obtain

---

[21] See Blinder (1987, Chapter 4).

a building permit is 8–10 months (Shidlo, 1994; Zearley, 1993). In Malaysia, Mexico, and Peru as well as Indonesia, research has documented literally 100 steps or more in the development or house purchase process. Each step increases risk, delays development or purchase, and is often associated with explicit and implicit cash transactions (De Soto, 1989).

A number of countries have recently taken steps to reduce the regulatory burden notably Mexico and Malaysia. Green et al. (1994) document the extraordinary rigid development regulations in Korea. Cook (1984) describes building codes and bye-laws in Africa with a series of recommendations for changes in codes that recognize the progressive step-by-step building methods used in the informal sector. It is often not recognized that given cost constraints as well as climate and materials availability, so-called traditional materials such as mud and wattle adobe or rammed earth are not always inferior materials. Generally, research in this area has argued for codes based on outcomes and performance rather than inputs, paralleling the developed country literature. For example, a well-constructed and maintained house of rammed earth (swish) in Ghana can return 100 years or more service.

## 5. Current issues and research

Reversing the normal order of such a discussion, we go from the specific to the general. First, several "live" housing issues are briefly outlined by geographical region. Because of the size of the countries and the scope of the issues they face, we discuss India and China separately. Next we briefly examine research by "modes of analysis", with particular reference to recent research on comparative indicators. A more general research agenda concludes the chapter.

### 5.1. Taxonomy of countries and stylized "issue triage"

Current research on China focuses on how to reform prices and move from a command and control system to a market oriented system in land and housing markets. Other research points to the severe problems China faces managing a huge money-losing public stock as the private housing market takes off. China's rapid urbanization (see Becker and Morrison, Chapter 43 of this volume) adds further urgency to the research agenda. Even more than in other countries, housing issues in China are tied up with a host of other micro- and macroreform issues, because of housing's link to employment (through enterprise housing) and the fact that a large share of Chinese wages have traditionally been paid in-kind rather than in cash (Tolley, 1991; Renaud and Bertaud, 1989; Hamer, 1996; Fong, 1989; Lim and Lee, 1993; Zhang, 1986).

Much recent research on India focuses on financial innovations such as replacing state directed credit with private and quasiprivate institutions like the Housing Finance and Development Corporation (HDFC). India also urgently needs additional research on the regulatory environment for land and housing. Some empirical research has been undertaken on rent control, but little has been done on land use regulation or the regulation framework for housing finance, apart from mainly descriptive analyses of the Urban Land Ceiling Act (Malpezzi and Tewari, 1991; Mehta and Mehta, 1989; Mohan, 1992; Munjee, (date); Buckley, 1990; Acharya, 1987).

Remarkably little research has been published for other south Asian markets, with the exception of Pakistan. Several papers have examined demand (Pasha and Ghaus, 1988) and land issues, namely, rebulatory issues and the relative roles of public versus land development in Pakistan (Dowall, 1989b, 1991a; Pasha, 1992).

The research agenda in east Asia is somewhat different. Here the focus is on price bubbles and their effects, on households and the aggregate economy (Chang, 1990). Other studies examine the order of liberalization of housing and financial markets, and compares the "tigers" and "semitigers" with slower growth economies like the Philippines and not-yet-liberalizing economies such as Burma. (Bertaud and Malpezzi, 1994; Mayo, (date); Green et al., 1994; Kim K.-H., 1990a, b, 1991a, 1993). Events at the time of this 1997 writing suggest further research on the relationship between property lending, underwriting and development incentives, and the aggregate economy would prove particularly fruitful.

In central and eastern Europe, and the states of the former Soviet Union, research focuses on developing property rights, the distributional consequences of existing subsidies, and different methods of privatization. Issues of political economy loom large here, as does research relevant to the development of true financial intermediaries to replace conduit institutions, and the effects of broader reform dynamics on housing, and vice versa (Sillince, 1990; Hegedus and Tosics, 1991; Daniel, 1989; Renaud, 1995a, b; Alexeev, 1988a; Kosareva and Struyk, 1993; Jaffe, 1989).

Current issues in northern Africa and the mideast include the effects of small but heavily subsidized public housing programs and financial institutions that offer even less transparent subsidies to a selected few households (Tipple, 1993; Dehesh, 1994). Daniere (1992) examines tenure choice, and Struyk (1988b) vacancy rates. Research has been carried out on finance (Landeau, 1987) and the informal sector (Mayo et al., 1980; Payne, 1980; Yonder, 1987). Particularly sensitive and important housing issues arise relative to the development of politically volatile parts of this region, e.g., Gaza and the West Bank.

Despite recent growth in countries such as Uganda, sub-Saharan Africa is still in many respects a region in economic disarray, and the housing market is no exception (Malpezzi and Sa-Aadu, 1996). Analysis of property rights, currently in flux in many countries, is particularly useful (Ault and Rutman, 1979; Asabere, 1981; Mabogunje, 1992; Besley, 1993). Other literature addresses the consequences of extremely disrupted and delclining economies for the housing market (Amis and Lloyd, 1990). Other research focuses on "governance" issues, deep subsidies to small minorities (Awotona, 1987; Megbolugbe, 1983). Many papers make particular reference to South Africa, especially to apartheid's unwinding and the housing market ties to locational issues (Turok, 1994a, b; Brueckner, 1996; Mayo, 1993a, b; Hoek Smit, 1992).

Latin America and the Caribbean have spawned significant research on finance under extreme inflation. Chile's experience with housing under stabilization and structural adjustment is much studied (Morande, 1992; Renaud, 1988; Rojas and Greene, 1995). Squatting and tenure issues also come to the fore (Gilbert, 1983, 1989, 1993). One of the best integrated analyses of housing, land and labor markets in any developing or developed market remains the "City Study" of Bogota and Calli, Colombia (Ingram, 1984; Mohan, 1994).

## 5.2. Modes of analysis/data sources

Twenty years ago, many doubted that market-based models of housing markets had much applicability to developing countries. Furthermore, it has been increasingly clear that in many respects the "distance" between so-called developing countries at middle and low levels of development are often greater than the "distance" between particular pairs of developing countries. To give a simple concrete example, the *World Development Report* reports a US life expectancy of 77 years for the US, which is average for "high income countries". Jamaica, Costa Rica, Sri Lanka and Jordan are just a few of the developing countries with life expectancies over 70 years. Hong Kong, a country until recently often classified as developing, has a life expectancy of 78 years. Contrast these countries with Mozambique, Sierra Leone, Uganda, Senegal and a half dozen other countries with life expectancy under 50 years. One hardly has to develop the idea that the countries we label "transition" are similarly diverse. Among the countries of the former Soviet Union alone, per capita income ranges from around $3000 in Russia to under $500 in Azerbaijan and Tajikistan.

Thus, it is perhaps remarkable that this chapter documents that, in general, market models have been fruitfully applied to so many and diverse places. But the chapter also documents that widely divergent market conditions, institutions and constraints requires a tailoring of models to the particular case at hand. A number of examples now exist of solid case studies of markets, including analysis of household survey data. See especially the studies of Cairo by Mayo et al. (1982), of Indonesia by Struyk et al. (1990), of Bangkok by Angel et al. (1986), and by Dowall (1989a), and of Cameroon by the Government of Cameroon in 1990. References on data collection and study design include Jones and Ward (1993), Tipple and Willis (1991), Malpezzi et al. (1982) and Malpezzi (1984, 1988). Guides to regulatory research include the so-called Bertaud model, and the "Malaysia model" of incentives (Hannah et al., 1989; M&M, 1995), and rent control (Malpezzi and Rydell, 1986; Malpezzi et al., 1988). Examples of institutional and property rights research include Cifuentes et al. (1984), Harsman and Quigley (1991) and Page and Struyk (1990).

### 5.2.1. Recent research on housing indicators

During the past five years, the World Bank and the UN Center for Human Settlements (UN Centre for Human Settlements) has sponsored an ongoing housing indicators program. The aim of this program is to systematically collect more or less comparable data on housing and other urban development outcomes as wide a range of countries as possible. As of this writing, an initial round of data collection has been completed in some 51 countries, and is ongoing in a larger sample. In each country, a set of centrally specified data is collected by a local analyst including rudimentary data on house values, rents, there relationship to incomes, housing output, floor area, the prevalence of unauthorized housing, several housing finance indicators, and information on land development, infrastructure and the regulatory environment. See Angel (1996), M&M (1997b) and especially Angel and Mayo (1996).

### 5.3. A general research agenda

Many elements of the general research agenda are discussed in the preceding paragraphs, and to some extent within the body of the chapter. More research is needed on behavioral parameters and their determinants; particularly on the supply side. Additional research is needed on institutions and the role of governance. There is a large agenda related to property rights. Most of the research surveyed above is static; we need to learn more about dynamics, especially of reform.

Research on property rights remains paramount. Comparative analysis would be greatly facilitated by a careful cross-market categorization and indexation of the specific "sticks" that make up the bundle of property rights. How to measure property rights, how to price them, and their effects on the housing market and on related markets (especially finance) all need further study.

The developing and transition economy literature on tenure choice, tenure security and mobility, could profit by further application of models incorporating the relative user costs of owner-occupied and rental housing.

In housing demand, we clearly know much about the income elasticity of demand and its remarkable stability across countries and markets. Much less is known about the price elasticity of demand, particularly given the difficulty of decomposing expenditure into price and quantity. New research on cross-country demand could have a high payoff. So far, such work has focused primarily on developing countries (M&M). Much remains to be learned about demand in middle and even upper income countries. This is particularly important since many of the emerging markets in eastern Europe and the former Soviet Union fit into the "omitted middle" of little studied countries.

We reiterate Olsen's (1987) lament that so little empirical work has been done on housing supply. Certainly the initial efforts in M&M (1985) and the filtering research of Thompson (1985) and Ferchiou (1982) can be extended and updated.

Research on housing and the aggregate economy can be extended in several directions. For example, little is known systematically about the leading the relationship between housing and the business cycle in developing and former socialist countries.

The research agenda in finance is developing rapidly. Risk management perspectives and more rigorous institutional analyses head the list of current research topics. Studies such as Diamond and Lea's (1993) study of developed countries provide good models for future work in this area. Much of the world is shifting from a housing finance perspective, where special circuits are used to mobilize short-term household deposits for long-term mortgages, to a perspective where housing finance is integrated with broader capital markets. Research on the conditions under which such a shift occurs, and the concomitant costs and benefits, and changes in risk, are high on any agenda.

Research on land markets can be extended in several directions. We still know very little beyond assertions and results from simple theoretical models about such policies as India's Urban Land Ceiling Act.

Most research on developing country and transtion economy housing markets has developed in isolation from analysis of broader real estate markets. In North America, and increasingly in other OECD economies, housing is more and more examined as part of an overall real estate market which also includes commercial uses. This perspective has been largely neglected in the developing and transition country literature. Paradoxically, in developing countries the distinction between housing and commercial property is less distinct than in richer economies, since housing unit and place of work often overlap (ILO, 1995).

The industrial organization of the housing market remains a fertile area for research. Analysis of distributional as well as efficiency outcomes from privatization of public housing in socialist and other countries would remain high on any list. Despite the large literature on the production and consumption efficiencies of public housing vouchers and other programs in the US and a few other countries, remarkably little empirical research has been done in developing countries or the former socialist economies. Even more remains to be done on the analysis of off-budget expenditures, particularly subsidies in the tax and financial systems. Many of these countries have not yet built up large tax expenditures as has the US and other developed countries.

## References

Aaron, H. (1975), Who Pays the Property Tax? (The Brookings Institute, DC).

Aaron, H.J. and G.M. von Furstenberg (1971), "The inefficiency of transfers in kind: the case of housing assistance", Western Economic Journal 9:184–191.

Acharya, B.P. (1987), "The urban land ceiling act: a critique of the 1976 legislation", Habitat International 11:39–51.

Agrawal, N. (1988), "The economic effects of public housing in Australia", The Economic Record 254–267.

Agarwala, R. (1983), Price Distortions and Growth in Developing Countries, World Bank Staff Working Paper No. 575.

Ahmad, N. (1994), "A joint model of tenure choice and demand for housing in the city of Karachi", Urban Studies 31:1691–1706.

Akbar, M. (1990), "Rate of return to investment in housing attributes", Pakistan Journal of Applied Econ. 9:71–92.

Alchian, A.A. and H. Demsetz (1973), "The property rights paradigm". Journal of Economic History 33:16–27.

Alexeev, M. (1988a), "Market vs. rationing: the case of Soviet housing", Review of Economics and Statistics.

Alexeev, M. (1988b), "The effect of housing allocation on social inequality: a Soviet perspective", Journal of Comparative Economics 12:228–234.

Alexeev, M. (1990), "Distribution of ahousing subsidies in the USSR. with some Soviet-Hungarian comparisons", Comparative Economic Studies 32:138–157.

Amis, P. (1984), "Squatters and tenants: the commercialization of unauthorized housing in Nairobi", World Development 12:87–96.

Amis, P. and P. Lloyd (1990), Housing Africa's Poor (Manchester University Press, UK).

Anas, A., K.S. Lee and M. Murray (1996), Infrastructure Bottlenecks, Private Provision, and Industrial Productivity: A Study of Indonesian and Thai Cities, World Bank, Policy Research Working Paper No. 1603.

Andrusz, G.D. (1990), "Housing policy in the Soviet Union", in: J.A.A. Sillince, ed., Housing Policies in Eastern Europe and the Soviet Union (Routledge, New York).

Angel, S. and S. Chuated (1990), "The down-market trend in housing production in Bangkok, 1980–87", Third World Planning Review 12:1–20.

Angel, S. and S.K. Mayo (1996), Enabling Policies and Their Effects on Housing Sector Performance: A Global Comparison. Paper presented to the Habitat II Conference, Istanbul, Turkey.

Angel, S. et al. (1986), The Land and Housing Markets of Bangkok: Strategies for Public Sector Participation, PADCO, Thailand National Housing Authority, and ADB.

Annez, P. and W.C. Wheaton (1984), "Economic development and the housing sector: a cross-national model", Economic Development and Cultural Change 32:749–746.

Antwi, A. (1995), An Economic Perspective of Land Policy Implementation in a Developing Economy: The Case of Accra (Royal Institute of Chartered Surveyors, Ghana).

Archer, R.W. (1989), An Outline of Urban Land Policy for the Developing Countries of Asia (Asian Institute of Technology, Bangkok).

Arimah, B.C. (1992a), "An empirical analysis of the demand for housing attributes in a Third World City", Land Economics 68:366–379.

Arimah, B.C. (1992b), "Hedonic prices and the demand for housing attributes in a Third World city: the case of Ibadan, Nigeria", Urban Studies 29:639–651.

Arimah, B.C. (1994), "The income elasticity of demand in a sub-Saharan African housing market: evidence from Ibadan, Nigeria", Environment and Planning A 26:107–119.

Arnott, R.J. (1987), "Economic theory and housing", in: E.S. Mills, ed., Handbook of Regional and Urban Economics, North Holland, V.2.

Arnott, R. and N. Johnston (1981), Rent Control and Options for Decontrol in Ontario (Ontario Economic Council, Toronto).

Asabere, P. (1981a), "The determinants of land values in an African city: the case of Accra, Ghana", Land Economics.

Asabere, P. (1981b), "The price of land in a chiefdom: empirical evidence on a traditional African city, Kumasi", Journal of Regional Science: 529–539.

Asabere, P.K. and K. Owusu-Banahene (1983), "Population density function for Ghanaian (African) cities: an empirical note", Journal of Urban Economics 14:370–379.

Asabere, K., C.F. Sirmans and P.F. Colwell (1982), "The intensity of residential land use in Accra, Ghana", Journal of Urban Economics 11:190–198.

Ashenfelter, O. and D. Genesove (1992), "Testing for price anomalies in real estate auctions", The American Economic Review 82:501–505.

Assadian, A. and J. Ondrich (1993), "Residential location, housing demand and labor supply decisions of one- and two-earner households: the case of Bogota, Columbia", Urban Studies 30:73–86.

Ault, D.E. and G.L. Rutman (1979), "The development of individual rights to property in tribal Africa", Journal of Law and Economics 22:163–182.

Awotona, A. (1987), "Housing policy in Nigeria—government policies for housing Nigeria's urban poor and the working class: laudable promises, great expectations, colossal failure", Habitat International 11:89–103.

Baer, W.C. (1991), "Filtering and third-world housing policy", Third World Planning Review 13:69–82.

Baer, W. and C. Koo (1994), "Housing turnover in developing nations: the case of Seoul", Journal of Planning Education and Research 13:104–118.

Baharoglu, D., L.M. Hannah and S. Malpezzi (1997), Getting Housing Incentives Right in Turkey, University of Wisconsin, Center for Urban Land Economics Research Working Paper.

Baken, R.-J. and J. Van der Linden (1993), "Getting the incentives right: banking on the formal private sector— a critique of World Bank thinking on low-income housing delivery in third world cities", Third World Planning Review 15:1–22.

Bariandiaran, E. and E. Mills (1983), Macroeconomic Analysis of the Chilean Housing Program, Mimeo.

Barlow, J. and A. King (1992), "The state, the market, and competitive strategy: the house building industry in the United Kingdom, France, and Sweden", Environment and Planning A (UK) 24:3811–400.

Barrett, R. (1983), "A brief review of World Bank experience in traffic management", World Bank.

Barro, R.J. and X. Sala-i-Martin (1995), Economic Growth (McGraw Hill, New York).

Barry, C., G. Casteneda and J. Lipscomb (1994), "The structure of mortgage markets in Mexico and prospects for their securitization", Journal of Housing Research 5:173–204.

Bartone, C. (1990), "Water quality and urbanization in Latin America", Water International 15:3–14.

Bartone, C. (1991), "Environmental challenge in third world cities", APA Journal: 411–415.

Bater, J.H. (1994), "Housing developments in Moscow in the 1960s", Post-Soviet Geography 35:309–328.

Behbehani, R., V. Shetty Pendakur and A. Armstrong-Wright (1984), Singapore Area Licensing Scheme: A Review of the Impact (Water Supply and Urban Development Department, World Bank).

Belkina, T. (1994), "Housing statistics and the condition of the housing sector", Problems of Economics Transition 37:56–71.

Benninger, C. (1986), Formal and Semi-formal Strategies of Land Acquisition. Poona, India (Centre for Development Studies).

Bertaud, A. (1992), "The impact of land-use regulations on land supply, consumption and price", Regional Development Dialogue 13:35–40.

Bertaud, A. (1997), The Spatial Distribution of Population in Cracow: A City's Structure Under the Conflicting Influences of Land Markets, Zoning Regulations and its Socialist Past. Paper presented to the Lincoln Institute of Land Policy Conference on Land Prices, Land Information Systems, and the Market for Land Information (Cambridge, Mass.).

Bertaud, A. and S. Malpezzi (1994), Measuring the Costs and Benefits of Urban Land Use Regulation: A Simple Model with an Application to Malaysia (Center for Urban Land Economics Research, University of Wisconsin).

Bertaud, A. and B. Renaud (1994), Cities Without Land Markets: Lessons of the Failed Socialist Experiment, World Bank Discussion Paper No. 227.

Bertaud, A. and B. Renaud. (1997), "Socialist cities without land markets", Journal of Urban Economics 41:137–151.

Bertaud, A., M.-A. Bertaud and J. Wright (1988), Efficiency in Land Use and Infrastructure Design: An Application of the Bertaud Model, World Bank, INU Discussion Paper.

Bertaud, M.-A. and D. Lucius (1989), Land Use, Building Codes, and Infrastructure Standards as Barriers to Affordable Housing in Developing Countries (World Bank Urban Development Department).

Besley, T. (1993), Property Rights and Investment Incentives: Theory and Microevidence from Ghana (Research Program in Development Studies, Princeton University).

Besley, T. (1995), "Finance, credit and insurance", in: J. Behrman and T.N. Srinivasan, eds., Handbook of Development Economics, vol. 3(A) (Elsevier).

Betancur, J.J. (1987), "Spontaneous settlement housing in Latin America: a critical examination", Environment and Behavior 19:286–310.

Bikhchandri, S. (1986), Market Games With Few Traders, Ph.D. Thesis, Stanford University School of Business.

Binswanger, H.P. and K. Deininger (1993), "South African land policy: the legacy of history and current options", World Development 21:1451–1475.

Blaesser, B.W. (1981), Clandestine Development in Colombia (U.S. Agency for International Development).

Blinder, A. (1987), Hard Heads and Soft Hearts (Excellent chapter on the environment, Addison Wesley).

Boehm, T.P. (1981), "Tenure choice and expected mobility: a synthesis", Journal of Urban Economics 10.

Boleat, M. (1985), National Housing Finance Systems: A Comparative Study. London: Croom Helm.

Briscoe, J. (1984), "Water supply and health in developing countries: selective primary care revisited", American Journal of Public Health: 1009–1013.

Bromley, D.W. (1989), "Property relations and economic development: the other land reform", World Development 17:867–877.

Browder, J.O. and J.R. Bohland (1995), "Patterns of development on the metropolitan fringe: urban fringe expansion in Bangkok, Jakarta and Santiago", Journal of the American Planning Association 61:310–327.

Browder, O.L. (1984), Basic Property Law, Fourth Ed. (West Publishing, St. Paul).

Brueckner, J.K. (1996), "Welfare gains from removing land-use distortions: an analysis of urban change in post-apartheid South Africa", Journal of Regional Science 36:91–109.

Buckley, R.M. (1985), Pricing Federal Credit Programs: An Application of the Option Pricing Perspective to the AID Housing Guaranty Program, Urban Institute Working Paper.

Buckley, R.M. (1990), "Housing finance in India", Mimeo (World Bank).

Buckley, R.M. (1991), "The measurement and targeting of housing finance subsidies: the case of Argentina", Public Finance 46:355–372.

Buckley, R.M. (1994), "Housing finance in developing countries: the role of credible contracts", Economic Development and Cultural Change 42:317–332.

Buckley, R.M. (1996), Housing Finance in Developing Countries (Oxford).

Buckley, R.M. and A. Dokeniya (1989), Inflation, Monetary Balances and the Aggregate Production Function, World Bank, INU Discussion Paper No. 55.

Buckley, R.M. and E.N. Gurenko (1995), Housing Finance in Reforming Economies: Measuring Macro Constraints on Moving to Market (World Bank).

Buckley, R.M. and E.N. Gurenko (1997), "Housing and income distribution in Russia: Zhivago's legacy", World Bank Research Observer 12:19–32.

Buckley, R.M. and R. Madhasudhan (1984), The Macroeconomics of Housing's Role in the Economy: An International Analysis. Paper presented to the American Real Estate and Urban Economics Association.

Buckley, R.M. and S.K. Mayo (1989), "Housing policy in developing countries: evaluating the macroeconomic impacts", Review of Regional and Development Studies 1.

Buckley, R.M. and B. Renaud (1988), Urban Finance in Post-Depression Latin America: The Solvency Status of Urban Borrowers, INU Discussion Paper No. 22.

Buckley, R.M. and R.J. Struyk (1985), An Economic Analysis of AID's Housing Guaranty Program. Urban Institute Working Paper.

Buckley, R.M., B. Lipman and T. Persaud (1993a), "Mortgage design under inflation and real wage uncertainty: the use of dual indexed instruments", World Development 21:455–464.

Buckley, R.M., P.H. Hendershott and K.E. Villani (1993b), Ponzies to Zombies: Housing Finance in Previously Centrally Planned Economies (World Bank).

Buckley, R.M., Z. Daniel and M. Thalwitz (1993c), The Welfare Cost and Transparency of Housing Policy in Socialist Economies: The Hungarian Experience (Urban Development Division, World Bank).

Buckley, R.M., P.H. Hendershott and K.E. Villani (1995), "Rapid housing privatization in reforming economies: pay the special dividend now", Journal of Real Estate Finance and Economics 10:63–80.

Burns, L.S. and L. Grebler (1976), "Resource Allocation to Housing Investment: A Comparative International Study", Economic Development and Cultural Change 25:95–121.

Burns, L.S. and L. Grebler (1977), The Housing of Nations: Advice and Policy in a Comparative Framework (Macmillan, London).

Cairncross, S. and J. Kinnear (1988), Measurement of the Elasticity of Domestic Water Demand: A Study of Water Vendors and their Clients, in Urban Sudan (London School of Hygiene and Tropical Medicine).

Cameroon, Republic of (1990), Evaluation of Real Housing Needs in Cameroon (Ministry of Town Planning and Housing, Yaounde, Cameroon).

Chang, C.-O. and C.W.R. Ward (1993), Forward Pricing and the Housing Market: The Pre-Sales Housing System in Taiwan. Paper presented to the American Real Estate and Urban Economics Association International Conference, Mystic, CT.

Chang, C.-O. and P.P.Y. Lai (1993), Indicators of Real Estate Cycles in Taiwan. Working Paper, National Chengchi University.

Chang, C.-O. and P. Linneman (1990), "Forecasting housing investment in developing countries", Growth and Change 21:59–72.

Chang, C.-O., C.-C. Lin and S.C.L. Farr (1994), A Study of Real Estate Transaction Price in Taipei Metropolitan Area (National Chengchi University).

Charemza, W. and R. Quandt (1990), "Dual housing markets in a centrally planned economy", Kyklos 43:411–436.

Cheung, Y.-L., S.-K. Tsang and S.-C. Mak (1995), "The causal relationships between residential property prices and rentals in Hong Kong: 1982–1991", Journal of Real Estate Finance and Economics 10:23–36.

Chiquier, L. and B. Renaud (1992), Alternative Mortgage Instruments in Distorted Housing Systems: How Useful is the Dual Rate Adjustable Mortgage? (EMTIN Technical Department, World Bank).

Choko, M.H. and C. Guangting, eds., (1994), China: The Challenge of Urban Housing (Meridien, Laval, Quebec).

Chomchan, S. and S. Silapacharanan (1990), Land Use Development in Bangkok and Major Cities: Directions and Problems. Thailand Development Research Institute Foundation, Background Report No. 5-1.

Chou, W.L. and Y.C. Shih (1995), "Hong Kong housing markets: overview, tenure choice, and housing demand", Journal of Real Estate Finance and Economics 10:7–22.

Chow, Y.-F. and N. Wong (1997), Property Value, User Cost, and Rent: An Investigation of the Residential Property Market in Hong Kong (Chinese University of Hong Kong).

Ciechoncinska, M. (1990), "The social image of urban housing—dreams and realities: the case of Poland", Journal of Urban Affairs 12:157–172.

Cifuentes V., J.R. Stevenson and R.L. Paredes (1984), Housing and Urban Development in Bogota: The Institutional Backdrop (World Bank, Washington).

Clapham, D. (1995), "Privatization and the east European housing model", Urban Studies 32:679–694.

Coase, R.H. (1960), "The problem of social cost", Journal of Law and Economics 3:1–44.

Cook, D.B. (1984), "Building codes and regulations in low income settlements", in: P.J. Richards and A.M. Thomson, eds., The Urban Poor: The Provision of Communal Services (Croom Helm).

Daniel, Z. (1983), "Public housing, personal income and central redistribution in Hungary", Acta Oeconomica 31:87–104.

Daniel, Z. (1985), "The effects of housing allocation on social inequality in Hungary", Journal of Comparative Economics.

Daniel, Z. (1989), "Housing demand in a shortage economy: results of a Hungarian survey", Acta Oeconomica 41:157–179.

Daniel, Z. and G. Partos (1989), Housing Reforms in Hungary: History and Lessons of Experience. Paper presented to the Joint Seminar on the Urban Housing Reforms in China, Beijing.

Daniel, Z. and A. Semjen (1987), "Housing shortage and rents: the Hungarian experience", Economics of Planning.

Daniell, J. and R. Struyk (1994), "Housing privatisation in Moscow—who privatize and why", International Journal of Urban and Regional Research 18:510–526.

Daniere, A.G. (1992), "Determinants of tenure choice in the Third World: an empirical study of Cairo and Manila", Journal of Housing Economics 2.

Daniere, A.G. (1994), "Estimating willingness to pay for housing attributes—an application to Cairo and Manila", Regional Science and Urban Economics 26:577–600.

Deaton, A.S. (1984), The Demand for Personal Travel in Developing Countries: Pricing and Policy Analysis. Paper presented at the Transportation Research Board, Washington, D.C.

De Leeuw, F. (1971), "The demand for housing: a review of the cross-section evidence", Review of Economics and Statistics 53:1–10.

De Leeuw, F. and L. Ozanne (1981), "Housing", in: H. Aaron and J. Pechman, eds., How Taxes Affect Economic Behavior (The Brookings Institute, DC).

De Soto, H. (1989), The Other Path: The Invisible Revolution in the Third World (Harper and Row, New York).

Dehesh, A. (1994), "Developmental instability in Iran: its impact on housing since 1962", Cities 11:409–424.

Demsetz, H. (1967), "Towards a theory of property rights", American Economic Review 57:347–373.

Dhareshwar, A. (1987), Transportation Sector Bibliography. World Bank Transportation Department Report TRP8.

Diamond, D.B. Jr. (1978), "A note on inflation and relative tenure prices", Journal of the American Real Estate and Urban Economics Association 6:438–450.

Diamond, D.B. Jr. (1993), "Restructuring housing finance in Hungary", Housing Finance International, December, pp. 10–42.

Diamond, D.B. Jr. and M.J. Lea (1992), "The decline of special circuits in developed country housing finance", Housing Policy Debate 3:747–778.

Diamond, D.B. Jr. and M.J. Lea (1993), "Housing finance in developed countries: an international comparison of efficiency", in B. Turner and C. Whitehead, eds., Housing Finance in the 1990s (Gavle, Sweden: The National Swedish Institute for Building Research).

DiPasquale, D. and W.C. Wheaton (1992), "The markets for real estate assets and space: a conceptual framework", Journal of the American real Estate and Urban Economics Association 20:181–198.

Dorner, P. (1992), Latin American Land Reforms in Theory and Practice (University of Wisconsin Press).

Dowall, D. (1988), "The land and housing market assessment: an important tool", Habitat International 12:135–149.

1850                                                                                    *S. Malpezzi*

Dowall, D. (1989a), "Bangkok: a profile of an efficiently performing housing market", Urban Studies: 327–339.
Dowall, D. (1989b), Karachi Land and Housing Market Study (UNCHS and PADCO, Karachi Development Authority).
Dowall, D. (1991a), "Comparing Karachi's informal and formal housing delivery systems", Cities 8:217–227.
Dowall, D. (1991b), The Land Market Assessment: A New Tool for Urban Management. Jointly published by the United Nations Development Program, The World Bank, and the United Nations Centre for Human Settlements (Habitat).
Dowall, D.E. (1991c), "A second look at the Bangkok land and housing market", Urban Studies 29:25–37.
Dowall, D.E. (1991d), "The Karachi development authority: failing to get the prices right", Land Economics 67:463–471.
Dowall, D. (1992), "Benefits of minimal land-use regulations in developing countries", Cato Journal 12:413–423.
Dowall, D. (1993), "Establishing urban land markets in the People's Republic of China", Journal of The American Planning Association 59:182–192.
Dowall, D.E. (1997), A Retrospective Look at the Land Market Assessment. Paper presented to the Lincoln Institute of Land Policy, Cambridge, November.
Dowall, D.E. and M. Leaf. (1991), "The price of land for housing in Jakarta", Urban Studies 28:707–722.
Eberts, Chapter 38 this volume.
Edwards, M. (1982), "Cities of tenants: renting among the urban poor in Latin America", in: A. Gilbert et al., eds., Urbanization in Contemporary Latin America (Wiley, New York).
Edwards, M. (1990), "Rental housing and the urban poor: Africa and Latin America compared", in: A. Phillip and P. Lloyd, eds., Housing Africa's Poor (Manchester University Press, Manchester).
Erbach, G.E., K. Moges and J.K. Bachmann (1996), Cost Benefit Analysis of Representative Housing Investents (Ministry of Works and Urban Development, Government of Ethiopia).
European Conference of Ministers of Transport (1995), Transport Infrastructure in Central and Eastern European Countries (OECD, Paris).
Evans, A.W. (Chapter 42, this volume).
Evers, H. (1976), "Urban expansion and land ownership in underdeveloped societies", in: J. Walton and L. Masotti, eds., The City in Comparative Perspective (Sage).
Fannie Mae (1991), Housing Finance Arrangements: A Comparative Analysis. Conference Proceedings.
Fannie Mae (1992), Housing Finance for Sustainable Development. Conference Proceedings.
Farvaque, C. and P. McAuslan (1992), Urban Land Policies and Institutions in Developing Countries. World Bank/UNDP Urban Management Program Paper UMP-5.
Ferchiou, R. (1982), "The indirect effects of new housing construction in developing countries", Urban Studies 19:167–176.
Ferguson, B., J. Rubenstein and V. Domingez Vial (1996), "The design of direct demand subsidies for housing in Latin America", Review of Regional and Urban Studies 8:202–219.
Fitzwilliam Memorandum, The (1991), Land Value Changes and the Impact of Urban Policy upon Land Valorisation Processes in Developing Countries. Conclusions of an International Research Workshop at Fitzwilliam College, Cambridge; reprinted in International Journal of Urban and Regional Research 15:623–628.
Follain, J.R. and E. Jimenez (1985a), "Estimating the demand for housing characteristics: a survey and critique", Regional Science and Urban Economics 15.
Follain, J.R. and E. Jimenez (1985b), "The demand for housing characteristics in developing countries", Urban Studies 22.
Follain, J.R. and S. Malpezzi (1980), Dissecting Housing Value and Rent (Urban Institute).
Follain, J.R., G.-C. Lim and B. Renaud (1980), "The demand for housing in developing countries: the case of Korea", Journal of Urban Economics 7.
Follain, J.R., G.-C. Lim and B. Renaud (1982), "Housing crowding in developing countries and willingness to pay for additional space: the case of Korea", Journal of Development Economics 11:249–272.
Follain, J.R., E. Jimenez, S. Malpezzi and S.K. Mayo (1983), "Housing in Korea: recent trends and recurrent problems", in Gill-Chin Lim, ed., Urban Planning and Spatial Strategies in Rapidly Changing Societies (Consortium on Urban and Regional Policies in Developing Countries, Princeton).

Fong, P.K.W. (1989), "Housing reforms in China", Habitat International 13:29–41.

Foo, T.S. (1992), "The provision of low cost housing by private sector developers in Bangkok, 1987–1989—the result of an efficient market?", Urban Studies 29:1137–1146.

French, R.A. and F.E.I. Hamilton, eds., (1979), The Socialist City: Spatial Structure and Urban Policy (John Wiley, Chichester, UK).

Friedman, J., E. Jimenez and S.K. Mayo (1988), "The demand for tenure security in developing countries", Journal of Urban Economics 29:185–198.

Friedman, M. (1975), Contents and Consequences of Real Property. Third ed. (Practicing Law Institute, New York).

Frimpong-Ansah, J.H. (1992), The Vampire State in Africa: The Political Economy of Decline in Ghana (Africa World Press).

Geisse, G. and F. Sabatini (1982), "Urban land market studies in Latin America: issues and methodology", in: M. Cullen and S. Woolrey, eds., World Congress on Land Policy, (1980) (Lexington Books).

Ghosh, P. and R. Mohan (1983), Housing in the National Accounts: A Critical Review of Concepts and Sources. Urban Development Task Force Paper No. S.7, Housing and Urban Development Division, Planning Commission.

Gibb, K. (1992), "Bidding, auctions and house purchase", Environment and Planning A 24:853–860.

Gilbert, A. (1983), The tenants of self help housing: choice and constraint in the housing markets of developing countries", Development and Change 14.

Gilbert, A. (1989), Housing and Land in Urban Mexico (Center for U.S.–Mexican Studies, University College, San Diego).

Gilbert, A. (1992), "Third world cities: housing, infrastructure and servicing", Urban Studies 29:435–460.

Gilbert, A. and A. Varley (1990), "The Mexican landlord: rental housing in Guadalajara and Puebla", Urban Studies 27:23–44.

Gilbert, A. and A. Varley (1991), Landlord and Tenant: Housing the Poor in Urban Mexico (Routledge).

Gilbert, A. and P. Ward (1985), Housing, the State and the Poor (Cambridge University Press, Cambridge).

Gilbert, A., O.O. Camacho, R. Coulomb and A. Necochea (1993), In Search of a Home: Rental and Shared Housing in Latin America (University of Arizona Press, Tucson).

Goldsmith, R.W. (1985), Comparative National Balance Sheets: A Study of Twenty Countries, 1688–1978 (University of Chicago Press, Cambridge).

Gómez-Ibáñez, J. (Chapter 46, this volume).

Goodman, J.L. Jr. (1976), "Housing consumption disequilibrium and local residential mobility", Environment and Planning A 8:855–874.

Government of India (1988a), National Housing Policy (Ministry of Urban Development, New Delhi).

Government of India (1988b), Report of the National Commission on Urbanisation (New Delhi).

Green, R.K. and S. Malpezzi (1997), A Primer on U.S. Housing Markets and Policies. University of Wisconsin, Center for Urban Land Economics Research Working Paper. Forthcoming as a monograph of the American Real Estate and Urban Economics Association.

Green, R.K. and M.J. White (in press), "Measuring the benefits of homeowning: benefits to children", Journal of Urban Economics.

Green, R., S. Malpezzi and K. Vandell (1994), "Urban regulations and the price of land and housing in Korea", Journal of Housing Economics.

Grootaert, C. and J.-L. Dubois (1988), "Tenancy choice and the demand for rental housing in the cities of the Ivory Coast", Journal of Urban Economics 24:95–112.

Gross, D.J. (1988), "Estimating willingess to pay for housing characteristics: an application of the Ellickson bid-rent model", Journal of Urban Economics 24:95–112.

Guarda, G.C. (1993), "Housing finance in Albania", Housing Finance International, December 1993, pp. 5–42.

Gyourko, J. (Chapter 37, this volume).

Gyourko, J. and K. Jaehye Han (1989), "Housing wealth, housing finance, and tenure in Korea", Regional Science and Urban Economics 19:211–234.

Haddad, E. (1982), "Report on urban land market research in Sao Paulo, Brazil", in: M. Cullen and S. Woolrey, eds., World Congress on Land Policy (1980) (Lexington Books).

Hall, D., ed. (1993), Transport and Economic Development in the New Central and Eastern Europe (Belhaven Press, London and Halsted Press, New York).

Hamer, A.M. (1996), The World Bank's Involvement in Urban Housing Reforms in China. Paper presented to the American Real Estate and Urban Economics Association International Conference, Orlando.

Hamer, A.M. et al. (1993), China: Urban Land Management in an Emerging Market Economy (World Bank, Washington, DC).

Hannah, L., A. Bertaud, S. Malpezzi and S. Mayo (1989), Malaysia: The Housing Sector; Getting the Incentives Right. World Bank Sector Report No. 7292-MA.

Hannah, L., K.-H. Kim and E.S. Mills (1993), "Land use controls and housing prices in Korea", Urban Studies 30:147–156.

Hanushek, E. and J. Quigley (1978), "An explicit model of intra-metropolitan mobility", Land Economics 411–429.

Hardoy, J.E. and D. Satterthwaite (1989), Squatter Citizen: Life in the Urban Third World (Earthscan, London).

Hardoy, J., S. Cairncross and D. Satterthwaite, eds. (1990), The Poor Die Young: Housing and Health in Third World Cities (Earthscan Publications, London).

Harsman, B. and J.M. Quigley (1991), Housing Markets and Housing Institutions: An International Comparison (Kluwer Academic Press, Dordrecht).

Hegedus, J. and I. Tosics (1991), "Filtering in socialist housing systems—results of vacancy chain surveys in Hungary", Urban Geography 1:1–18.

Hegedus, J. and I. Tosics (1994), "The poor, the rich and the transformation of urban space", Urban Studies 31:989–993.

Hegedus, J., K. Mark, R. Struyk and I. Tosics (1992), The Privatization Dilemma in Budapest's Public Rental Housing Sector. Paper presented to the American Real Estate and Urban Economics Association international meeting.

Hegedus, J., K. Mark, R. Struyk and I. Tosics (1994), "Tenant satisfaction with public housing management: Budapest in transition", Housing Studies 9:315–328.

Hinds, M. (1990), Issues in the Introduction of Market Forces in Eastern European Socialist Economies. World Bank: Europe, Middle East and North Africa Region Internal Discussion Paper No. IDP-0057.

Hoek-Smit, M. (1992), Housing Supply Systems and Housing Outcomes in Southern Africa. Paper prepared for the American Real Estate and Urban Economics Association/USC International Real Estate Conference, Los Angeles.

Hoffman, M., B. Haupt and R.J. Struyk (1991), International Housing Markets: What We Know; What We Need to Know. Fannie Mae Working Paper.

Howe, H. and P. Musgrove (1977), "An analysis of ECIEL budget data for Bogota, Caracas, Guyaquil and Lima", in: C. Lluch et al., eds., Patterns in Household Demand and Savings (Oxford University Press, Oxford).

Howenstine, E.J. (1957), "Appraising the role of housing in economic development", International Labor Review 75.

Hoy, M. and E. Jimenez (1991), "Squatter rights and urban development: an economic perspective", Econonomica 58:79–92.

Ihlanfeldt, K.R. (1981), "An empirical investigation of alternative approaches to estimating equilibrium demand for housing", Journal of Urban Economics 9:97–105.

International Labour Office (1995), Shelter Provision and Employment Generation. Geneva.

Ingram, G.K. (1984), Housing Demand in the Developing Metropolis: Estimates from Bogota and Cali, Colombia. Staff Working Paper No. 633.

Ingram, G.K. and A. Carroll (1981), "The spatial structure of Latin American cities", Journal of Urban Economics 9:257–273.

International Journal of Urban and Regional Research (1987), Special Volume on Eastern Europe 11.

Ivanicka, K., M. Zubkova, E. Sindlerova and D. Spirkova (1996), Development of Housing Finance in Visegrad Countries. Paper presented to the American Real Estate and Urban Economics Association International Conference, Orlando.

Jaffe, A.J. (1989), "Concepts of property, theories of housing, and the choice of housing policy", Netherlands Journal of Housing and Environmental Research 4.

Jaffe, A.J. (1989), Property Rights and Market Behavior in Eastern European Housing Reforms. Paper presented to the January (1993) meeting of American Real Estate and Urban Economics Association, Anaheim, CA.

Jaffe, A.J. and D. Louziotis, Jr. (1996), "Property rights and economic efficiency: a survey of institutional factors", Journal of Real Estate Literature 4:137–159.

Jimenez, E. (1982a), "The economics of self help housing: theory and some evidence from a developing country", Journal of Urban Economics 11:205–228.

Jimenez, E. (1982b), "The value of squatter dwellings in developing countries", Economic Development and Cultural Change 30.

Jimenez, E. (1984), "Tenure security and urban squatting", Review of Economics and Statistics 66:556–567.

Jimenez, E. (1985), "Urban squatting and community organization in developing countries", Journal of Public Economics 27:69–92.

Jimenez, E. (1987a), Pricing Policy in the Social Sectors: Cost Recovery for Education and Health in Developing Countries (Johns Hopkins University Press).

Jimenez, E. (1987b), "The magnitude and determinants of home improvement in self-help housing: Manila's Tondo project", Land Economics 70–83.

Jimenez, E and D. Keare (1984), "Housing consumption and permanent income in developing countries: estimates from panel data in El Salvador", Journal of Urban Economics 15:172–194.

Johnson, T.E. Jr. (1985), A Study of Upwards Filtering of Housing Stock as a Consequence of Informal Settlement Upgrading in Developing Countries (Graduate School of Design, Harvard University).

Johnson, T.E. Jr. (1987), "Upward filtering of the housing stock", Habitat International 11:173–190.

Jones, G. and P. Ward, eds., (1994), Methodology for Land Market and Housing Analysis (University College Press, London).

Kaganova, O.Z. (1994), On the Program of the Land Policy and Reform of Taxation in the Cities of Russia Proposed by Adherents of Henry George's Ideas. Discussion Paper.

Kalbermatten, J. et al. (1980), Appropriate Technology for Water Supply and Sanitation: A Summary of Technical and Economic Options (World Bank).

Kalbermatten, J., DeAnne Julius, D. Mara and C. Gunnerson (1982), Appropriate Sanitation Alternatives: A Technical and Economic Appraisal (Johns Hopkins University Press).

Karadimov, N. (1992), The Reorientation of Urban Development and Housing Policy in Central and East-European Countries in their Transition to a Market Economy: General and Specific Tendencies and Phenomena of the Experience of the Republic of Bulgaria (Ministry of Regional Development, Housing Policy and Construction, Sofia).

Kasongo, B.A. and A.G. Tipple (1990), "An analysis of policy towards squatters in Kitwe, Zambia", Third World Planning Review 12:147–165.

Katsura, H.M. (1984), Economic Effects of Housing Investment. Urban Institute Contract Report.

Katsura, H.M. and R.J. Struyk (1991), "Selling eastern Europe's social housing stock: proceed with caution", Housing Policy Debate 2:1251–1271.

Katzman, M. (1977), "Income and price elasticities of demand for water in developing countries", Water Resources Bulletin 13:47–55.

Kaufman, D. and J. Quigley (1987), "The consumption benefits of investment in infrastructure: the evaluation of sites and services programs in underdeveloped countries", Journal of Development Economics 25:263–284.

Kessides, C. (1993), The Contributions of Infrastructure to Economic Development. World Bank Discussion Paper No. 213.

Kiamba, M. (1989), "The introduction and evolution of private landed property in Kenya", Development and Change 20:121–148.

Kidokoro, T. (1992), "Development control systems for housing development in southeast Asian cities", Regional Development Dialogue 12:64–87.

Kim, J. (1995), "Demand for rental housing in Korea with some estimation issues", Journal of Urban Planning and Development-Asce 121:57–74.

Kim, J.-H. (1990), "Korean housing policies: review and future directions", in: Hyundai Research Institute, Proceedings of (the) International Housing Conference on Korean Housing Policies, Seoul.

Kim, J.-H. (1991), Housing Program Evaluation Using the Present Value Model: A Korean Experience. Paper presented to the World Bank seminar on Korean Housing Markets and Policy.

Kim, K.-H. (1990a), "An analysis of inefficiency due to inadequate mortgage financing: the case of Seoul, Korea", Journal of Urban Economics 28:371–390.

Kim, K.-H. (1990b), "Housing finance and housing related taxes in Korea", in Hyundai Research Institute, Proceedings of (the) International Housing Conference on Korean Housing Policies, Seoul.

Kim, K.-H. (1993), "Housing prices, affordability and government policy in Korea", Journal of Real Estate Finance and Economics 6:55–72.

Kim, K.-H. (1994), Financing Shelter and Urban Development: Towards Habitat II (UN Centre for Human Settlements, Nairobi).

Kim, K.-H and K.-Y. Kim (1992), Policy for Public Housing Finance in Korea. Paper presented at the International Symposium on Housing, Korea National Housing Corporation, Seoul.

Kim, K.-H. and E.S. Mills (1988), "Korean development and urbanization: prospects and problems", World Development 16:157–167.

Kim, K.-H. and S.-H. Suh (1989), An Analysis of Optimality of Housing Investment in Korea. Paper presented to the Korea International Economic Association.

Kim, K.-H. and S.-H. Suh (1993), "Speculation and house price bubbles in the Korean and Japanese real estate markets", Journal of real estate Finance and Economics 6:73–88.

Kim, S.-J. (1992), "A model of rental housing choices in the Korean market", Urban Studies 29:1247–1263.

Kingsley, G.T. and R.J. Struyk (1990), Institutional Reform and the Housing Sector: Thinking Through the Transition. Urban Institute Working Paper, U.I. Project No. 3941.

Kingsley, G.T. and R.J. Struyk (1992), Progress in Privatization: Transforming Eastern Europe's Social Housing (The Urban Institute for USAID).

Klak, T. and M. Holtzclaw (1993), "The housing, geography, and mobility of Latin American urban poor: the prevailing model and the case of Quito, Ecuador", Growth and Change 24:247–276.

Kornai, J. (1990), The Road to a Free Economy (Norton).

Kornai, J. (1992), The Socialist System: The Political Economy of Communism (Princeton University Press).

Kosareva, N. and R. Struyk (1993), "Housing privatization in the Russian Federation", Housing Policy Debate 4:81–100.

Kosareva, N., O. Pchelintsev and G. Ronkin (1991), "On the path to housing reform—analysis and forecast", Problems of Economics 34:60–82.

Kravis, I.B., A. Heston and R. Summers (1982), World Product and Income: International Comparisons of Real Gross Product (Johns Hopkins University Press).

Kuznets, S. (1961), "Quantitative aspects of the economic growth of nations. VI: long term trends in capital formation proportions", Economic Development and Cultural Change 9:3–124.

Lakshmanan, T.R., L. Chatterjee and P. Kroll (1978), "Housing consumption and level of development: a cross national comparison", Economic Geography 54:222–233.

Landeau, J.-F. (1987), "Tunisia: a case study in analyzing the affordability of mortgage loans", African Urban Quarterly.

Landis, J.D. (1983), How Competitive Are Urban Housing Markets? Ph.D. Dissertation (University of California, Berkeley).

Landis, J.D. (1986), "Land regulation and the price of new housing: lessons from three California cities", Journal of the American Institute of Planners: 9–21.

Larbi, W.O. (1995), The Urban Development Land Process and Urban Land Policies in Ghana (Royal Institute of Chartered Surveyors).

Lea, M.J. and S.A. Bernstein (1995), International Housing Finance Sourcebook 1995 (International Union of Housing Finance Institutions, Chicago).

Lee, K.S. (1988), Infrastructure Constraints on Industrial Growth in Thailand. INURD Working Paper No. 88-2.

Lee, K.S. (1992), "Spatial policy and infrastructure constraints on industrial growth in Thailand", Review of Urban and Regional Development Studies 4.

Lee, K.S. and A. Anas (1992), "Costs of deficient infrastructure: the case of Nigerian manufacturing", Urban Studies 29:1071–1092.

Lee, K.S., A. Anas and G.-T. Oh (1996), Costs of Infrastructure Deficiencies in Manufacturing in Indonesia, Nigeria and Thailand. World Bank, Policy Research Working Paper No. 1604.

Lee, L.-F. and R. Trost (1978), "Estimation of some limited dependent variable models with application to housing demand", Journal of Econometrics: 357–382.

Leibenstein, H. (1966), "Allocative efficiency versus X-efficiency", American Economic Review.

Li, M. (1977), "A logit model of homeownership", Econometrica 45:1081–1097.

Lim, G.-C. (1987), "Land markets and public policy: a Korean case study", Habitat International 11:73–81.

Lim, G.-C. and M.-H. Lee (1993), "Housing consumption in urban China", Journal of Real Estate Finance and Economics 6:89–102.

Lim, G.-C., J.R. Follain and B. Renaud (1980), "The determinants of homeownership in a developing economy", Urban Studies 17.

Lim, G.-C., J.R. Follain, Jr. and B. Renaud (1984), "Economics of residential crowding in developing countries", Journal of Urban Economics: 16:173–186.

Lin, C-C.S. (1993), "The relationship between rents and prices of owner-occupied housing in Taiwan", Journal of Real Estate Finance and Economics 6:25–54.

Linneman, P. (1981), "The demand for residence site characteristics", Journal of Urban Economics: 129–148.

Linneman, P.D. and I.F. Megbolugbe (1994), "Privatisation and housing policy", Urban Studies 31:635–651.

Lira, R. (1989), Viviendas Subsidiadas en Paises en Desarollo: Eficiencia y Movilacion de Recursos (Instituto de Estudios Urbanos, Universidad Pontifica Catolica de Chile).

Lluch, C., A. Powell and R. Williams (1977), Patterns in Household Demand and Savings (Oxford University Press, Oxford).

Lodhi, A. and H.A. Pasha (1991), "Housing demand in developing countries: a case-study of Karachi in Pakistan", Urban Studies 28:623–634.

Mabogunje, A.L. (1992), Perspective on Urban Land and Urban Management Policies in sub-Saharan Africa. World Bank Technical Paper No. 196.

Mackay, C.J. (1996), "The development of housing policy in South Africa in the post apartheid period", Housing Studies 11:133–146.

Maclennan, D. (1989), Privatization, Deregulation and Competition in the British Housing System, 1979 to 1989. Mimeo.

Maddison, A. (1995), Explaining the Economic Performance of Nations (Edward Elgar).

Malpezzi, S. (1984), Analyzing an Urban Housing Survey. World Bank: Infrastructure and Urban Development Department Discussion Paper No. UDD-52.

Malpezzi, S. (1986), Rent Control and Housing Market Equilibrium: Theory and Evidence from Cairo, Egypt. Unpublished Ph.D. Dissertation (The George Washington University).

Malpezzi, S. (1988), Analyzing Incentives in Housing Programs: Evaluating Costs and Benefits with a Present Value Model. World Bank: INU Discussion Paper No. 23.

Malpezzi, S. (1990), "Urban housing and financial markets: some international comparisons", Urban Studies 27:971–1022.

Malpezzi, S. (1991), "Discounted cash flow analysis: present value analysis of housing programmes and policies", in: A.G. Tipple and K.G. Willis, eds., Housing the Poor in the Developing World: Methods of Analysis, Case Studies and Policies, pp. 208–233 (Routledge Publishing).

Malpezzi, S. (1992), Rental Housing in Developing Countries: Issues and Constraints. United Nations Centre for Human Settlements, Rental Housing: Proceedings of an Expert Group Meeting (Nairobi).

Malpezzi, S. (1993), "Can New York and Los Angeles learn from Kumasi and Bangalore? A comparison of costs and benefits of rent controls", Housing Policy Debate 4:589–626.

Malpezzi, S. (1994), " 'Getting the incentives right': a reply to Robert-Jan Baken and Jan Van Der Linden", Third World Planning Review 16:451–466.

Malpezzi, S. (in press), "Welfare analysis of rent control with side payments: a natural experiment in Cairo, Egypt", Regional Science and Urban Economics.

Malpezzi, S. and C.P. Rydell (1986), Rent Controls in Developing Countries: A Framework for Analysis. World Bank, Water Supply and Urban Development Department Discussion Paper No. 102.

Malpezzi, S. and D. Maclennan (1996), The Long Run Price Elasticity of Supply of New Construction in the United States and the United Kingdom. Paper presented to the European Network for Housing Research/American Real Estate and Urban Economics Association Conference, Glasgow, September (1994). Revised, University of Wisconsin, Center for Urban Land Economics Research Working Paper.

Malpezzi, S. and G. Ball (1991), Rent Control in Developing Countries. World Bank Discussion Paper No. 129.

Malpezzi, S. and G. Ball (1993), "Measuring the urban policy environment: an exploratory analysis using rent controls", Habitat International 17:39–52.

Malpezzi, S. and J. Sa-Aadu (1996), "What have African housing policies wrought?", Real Estate Economics.

Malpezzi, S. and K. Vandell (1993), Housing Markets and Policy in Market Economies: Lessons for Formerly Socialist Economies. Paper prepared for the American Real Estate and Urban Economics Association, Mystic, CN, October.

Malpezzi, S. and L. Ozanne (1980), Evaluation of FMRs in the Section 8 New Construction Program: An Application of Hedonic Price Indexes (Urban Institute).

Malpezzi, S. and S.K. Mayo (1987a), "The demand for housing in developing countries", Economic Development and Cultural Change 35:687–721.

Malpezzi, S. and S.K. Mayo (1987b), "User cost and housing tenure in developing countries", Journal of Development Economics 25:197–220.

Malpezzi, S. and S.K. Mayo (1994), A Model Design for a Developing Country Housing Market Study. University of Wisconsin-Madison, Center for Urban Land Economics Research Working Paper.

Malpezzi, S. and S.K. Mayo (1997a), "Getting housing incentives right: a case study of the effects of regulation, taxes and subsidies on housing supply in Malaysia", Land Economics 73:372–391.

Malpezzi, S. and S.K. Mayo (1997b), "Housing and urban development indicators: a good idea whose time has returned", Real Estate Economics 25:1–11.

Malpezzi, S. and V. Tewari (1991), Costs and Benefits of Rent Regulation in Bangalore, India. World Bank, Infrastructure and Urban Development Department Discussion Paper No. 82 (160 pp).

Malpezzi, S., M. Bamberger and S.K. Mayo (1982), Planning an Urban Housing Survey. World Bank: Infrastructure and Urban Development Department Discussion Paper No. UDD-42.

Malpezzi, S. and S.K. Mayo and D.J. Gross (1985), Housing Demand in Developing Countries. World Bank Staff Working Paper No. 733.

Malpezzi, S., S.K. Mayo, R. Silveira and C. Quintos (1988), Measuring the Costs and Benefits of Rent Control: Case Study Design. INU Discussion Paper No. 24.

Malpezzi, S., G. Tipple and K. Willis (1990), Costs and Benefits of Rent Control: A Case Study in Kumasi, Ghana. World Bank Discussion Paper No. 74.

Mathey, K. (1990), "An appraisal of Sandinista housing policies", Latin American Perspectives 17:76–99.

Mayo, S.K. (1981), "Theory and estimation in the economics of housing demand", Journal of Urban Economics 10:95–116.

Mayo, S.K. (1986), "Sources of inefficiency in subsidized housing programs: a comparison of U.S. and German experience", Journal of Urban Economics 20:229–249.

Mayo, S.K. (1990), Housing Finance Development: Experiences in Malaysia and Thailand, and Implications for Indonesia (World Bank).

Mayo, S.K. (1993), Housing Policy Reform in South Africa: International Perspectives and Domestic Imperatives (World Bank).

Mayo, S.K. (1993), South African Housing Sector Performance in International Perspective. Paper presented to the 21st IAHS Housing Congress, Capetown.

Mayo, S.K. and D.J. Gross (1987), "Sites and services—and subsidies: the economics of low cost housing in developing countries", World Bank Economic Review 1:301–335.

Mayo, S.K. and J. Stein (1988), Housing and Labor Market Distortions in Poland: Linkages and Policy Implications. INU Discussion Paper No. 25.

Mayo, S.K. and J. Stein (1995), "Housing and labor market distortions in Poland: linkages and policy implications", Journal of Housing Economics 4:153–182.

Mayo, S.K. et al. (1982), Informal Housing in Egypt (Abt Associates).

Mayo, S.K., S. Malpezzi and D.J. Gross (1986), "Shelter strategies for the urban poor in developing countries", World Bank Research Observer 1:183–203.

Mayo, S.K., S. Angel, M. Heller and W. Stephens (1992), The Housing Indicators Program: Extensive Survey Preliminary Results (Urban Development Division, World Bank).

McLure, C. (1977), "The "new view" of the property tax: a caveat", National Tax Journal.

McMillen, D.P. and J.M. Pogodzinski (1993), Land Use in Planned Economies: A Survey of Eastern Europe. Paper prepared for the American Real Estate and Urban Economics Association International Conference, Mystic, CT.

McPhail, A.A. (1993), "The "five percent rule" for improved water service: can households afford more?", World Development 21:963–973.

Megbolugbe, I.F. (1983), "The hopes and failures of public housing in Nigeria: a case study of Kulende and Adewole housing estates, Ilorin", Third World Planning Review 5:349–369.

Mehta, M. and D. Mehta (1989a), A Report on Housing Finance Systems in Metropolitan Areas of India (USAID, New Delhi).

Mehta, M. and D. Mehta (1989b), Metropolitan Housing Market: A Study of Ahmedabad (Sage Publications, New Delhi).

Merrett, S. (1984), "The Assessment of housing consumption requirements in developing countries", Third World Planning Review 6.

Mills, E.S. (1995), Housing: The Step-Child of the Privatization and Deregulation Movement. Paper prepared for the UNU/WIDER Conference on Human Settlements in the Changing Global Political and Economic Process.

Mills, G., D. Sherwell and M. van Rooyen (1995), "Integrated housing policy in South Africa: cost constraints on built form", Environment and Planning B: Planning and Design 22:5–20.

Mitra, B.C. (1987), Land Supply for Low Income Housing in Delhi (Institute for Housing Studies, Working Paper, Rotterdam).

Mohan, R. (1989), Housing and Urban Development in India: The Need for Innovative Strategies. Mimeo (New Delhi).

Mohan, R. (1992), "Housing and urban development policy issues for the 1990s. 1", Economic and Political Weekly 27:1913–1920.

Mohan, R. (1994), Understanding the Developing Country Metropolis: Lessons from the City Study of Bogota and Cali, Colombia (Oxford University Press, Oxford).

Mok, H.M.K., P.P.K. Chan and Y.-S. Cho (1995), "A Hedonic price model for private properties in Hong Kong", Journal of Real Estate Finance and Economics 10:37–48.

Morande, F.G. (1992), "The dynamics of real asset prices, the real exchange rate trade reforms and foreign capital inflows: Chile, 1976–1989", Journal of Development Economics 39:111–139.

Moser, C.O.N. and L. Peake, eds., (1987), Women, Human Settlements and Housing (Tavistock, London).

Moynihan, C.J. (1987), Introduction to the Law of Real Property. Second Edition (West Publishing Co., St. Paul).

Mozolin, M. (1994), "The geography of housing values in the transformation to a market economy—a case study of Moscow", Urban Geography 15:107–127.

Munjee, N.M. (1992), "Recent developments in Indian housing finance", Housing Finance International.

Murray, M.P. (1983), "Subsidized and unsubsidized housing starts: 1961–1977", Review of Economics and Statistics 65:590–597.

Murray, M.P. (1993), Subsidized and Unsubsidized Housing Stocks 1935–1987: Crowding Out and Cointegration (Department of Economics, Bates College).

Muth, R.F. (1971), "The derived demand for urban residential land", Urban Studies 8:243–254.

Nayani, P. (1987), Process of Illegal Subdivision of Land and Housing Consolidation. New Delhi School of Archictecture, Working Paper.

Ndulo, M. (1986), "Patterns of housing demand in a low income economy: the case of urban Zambia", Eastern Africa Economic Review 2.

Nelson, K.P. (1992), "Housing assistance needs and the housing stock", Journal of the American Planning Association 58:85–102.

Nicholson, M. and K.G. Willis (1990), "The scale and distribution of financial subsidies to owner-occupied households: a comparison", Journal of Economic and Social Measurement 16:71–85.

Okpala, D.C.I. (1985), Urban Low Income Shelter in Africa: A Review of Provision and Delivery Policies, Programmes and Strategies (United Nations Center for Human Settlements, Addis Ababa).

Okpala, D.C.I. (1986), Investments in Human Settlements Development in the National Development Plans of African Economies. Addis Ababa: UNCHS (Habitat) Discussion Paper.

Okpala, D.C.I. (1987), "Received concepts and theories in African urbanization", Urban Studies 24:137–150.

Okpala, D.C.I. (1994), "Financing housing in developing countries—A review of the pitfalls and potentials in the development of formal housing finance systems", Urban Studies 31:1571–1786.

Okun, D.A. (1982), "Financing water supply systems", in: E.J. Shiller and R.L. Droste, eds., Water Supply and Sanitation in Developing Countries (Ann Arbor Science).

Olsen, E.O. (1969), "A competitive theory of the housing market", American Economic Review: 612–622.

Olsen, E.O. (1987), "The demand and supply of housing services: a critical review of the empirical literature", in: E.S. Mills, ed., Handbook of Regional and Urban Economics, vol. 2 (Elsevier, Amsterdam).

Olsen, E.O. (1988), "What do economists know about rent control?", The Journal of Real Estate Finance and Economics 1:295–308.

Olsen, E.O. and D.M. Barton (1983), "The benefits and costs of public housing in New York City", Journal of Public Economics 20:299–332.

Ondiege, P. (1986), Implicit Benefits in the Rental Public Housing Sector in Nairobi. Paper presented to the International Conference of Urban Shelter in Developing Countries, London, September 1–4.

Page, D. and R.J. Struyk (1990), Measuring the Housing Sector: Results from the International Housing Market Survey (The Urban Institute).

Parry, David L., Maya T. Koleva and Eugeni M. Popov (1990), "Bulgarian housing markets and mortgage financing", Housing Finance International, May 1990, pp. 27–30.

Pasha, H.A. (1992), "Maximum lot size zoning in developing countries", Urban Studies 29:1173–1181.

Pasha, H.A. and M.S. Butts (1996), "Demand for housing attributes in developing countries: a case study of Pakistan", Urban Studies 33:1141–1154.

Pasha, H.A. and A. Ghaus (1988), "The demand for housing in Pakistan", Pakistan Journal of Applied Economics 7:83–99.

Payne, G. (1980), "The Gecekondus of Ankara", Process of Architecture 15:78–115.

Payne, G., ed. (1984), Low Income Housing in the Developing World (Wiley).

Payne, G. (1989), Informal Housing and Land Subdivisions in Third World Cities: A Review of the Literature (Centre for Development and Environmental Planning, Oxford Polytechnic).

Peattie, L. (1987), "Affordability", Habitat International 11:69–76.

Pejovich, S. (1990), The Economics of Property Rights: Towards a Theory of Comparative Systems (Kluwer Academic Press, Dordrecht).

Peng, R. and W.C. Wheaton (1994), "Effects of restrictive land supply on housing in Hong Kong: an ecometric analysis", Journal of Housing Research 5:263–291.

Piggott, J. (1984), "The value of tenant benefits from UK council housing subsidies", Economic Journal 94:384–389.

Pinto-Lima, L. (1990), "The financing of housing in Brazil", Housing Finance International 5:25–26.

Pogodzinski, J.M. (1991), "Reform of the Polish housing market: issues and methods", Mimeo.

Pogodzinski, J.M. (1993), The Effect of Housing Market Disequilibrium on the Supply of Labor: Evidence From Poland, 1989–1990.

Pogodzinski, J.M. (1994), "The value of 'full' ownership rights: a Hedonic study of Warsaw", Mimeo.

Polinsky, A.M. (1977), "The demand for housing: a study in specification and grouping", Econometrica 42:1533–1551.

Pollak, R. and T. Wales (1981), "Demographic variables in demand analysis", Econometrica 49:1533–1551.

Pornchokchai, S. (1992), Bangkok Slums: Review and Recommendations (Agency for Real Estate Affairs, Bangkok).

Pudney, S. and L. Wang (1995), "Housing reform in urban China—efficiency, distribution and the implications for social security", Economica 62:141–160.

Quigley, J.M. (1982), "Nonlinear budget constraints and consumer demand: an application to public programs for residential housing", Journal of Urban Economics 12:177–201.

Rakodi, C. (1987), "Upgrading in Chawama, Lusaka: displacement or differentiation?", Urban Studies 25.

Rakodi, C. (1992), "Housing Markets in third world cities: research and policy in the 1990s", World Development 20:39–55.

Rakodi, C. (1995a), "From a settler history to an African present—housing markets in Harare, Zimbabwe", Enviroment and Planning 13:91–116.

Rakodi, C. (1995b), "Housing finance for lower income urban households in Zimbabwe", Housing Studies 10:199–227.

Rakodi, C. and P. Withers (1995), Home ownership and commodification of housing in Zimbabwe", International Journal of Urban and Regional Research 19:250–271.

Ravillion, M. (1989), "The welfare cost of housing standards: theory with application to Jakarta", Journal of Urban Economics 26:197–211.

Renaud, B. (1980), "Resource allocation to housing investment: comments and further results", Economic Development and Cultural Change 28:189–199.

Renaud, B. (1984), Housing and Financial Institutions in Developing Countries. World Bank Staff Working Paper No. 658.

Renaud, B. (1988a), Compounding Financial Repression with Rigid Urban Regulations: Lessons of the Korean Housing Market. World Bank, Infrastructure and Urban Development Department Discussion Paper No. 21.

Renaud, B. (1988b), Housing Under Economic Structural Adjustment in Chile. INURD Working Paper No. 88-3.

Renaud, B. (1988c), "The future of the housing finance system in Korea", Mimeograph.

Renaud, B. (1989a), Affordable Housing, Housing Sector Performance and Behavior of the Price-to-Income Ratio: International Evidence and Theoretical Analysis. Paper Presented to the Center of Urban Studies and Urban Planning, University of Hong Kong.

Renaud, B. (1989b), Understanding the Collateral Qualities of Housing for Financial Development: The Korean "Chonsei" as Effective Response to Financial Sector Shortcomings. INU Discussion Paper No. 49.

Renaud, B. (1990), "Housing affordability and housing finance: an international perspective", in: Hyundai Research Institute, Proceedings of (the) International Housing Conference on Korean Housing Policies, Seoul.

Renaud, B. (1991), Housing Reform in Socialist Economies. World Bank Discussion Paper No. 125.

Renaud, B. (1992), The Housing System of the Former Soviet Union: Why Do the Soviets Need Housing Markets? Paper presented to the Fannie Mae University Colloquium Series, UCLA.

Renaud, B. (1993), "Confronting a distorted housing market: can Korean policies break with the past?", in: L.B. Krause and F.-K. Park, eds., Social Issues in Korea: Korean and American Perspectives (Korea Development Institute, Seoul).

Renaud, B. (1995a), "The real estate economy and the design of Russian housing reforms, Part I", Urban Studies 32:1247–1264.

Renaud, B. (1995b), "The real estate economy and the design of Russian housing reforms, Part II", Urban Studies 32:1437–1451.

Renaud, B. (1997), Financial Markets and the Financing of Social Housing: The View from Developing Countries. Paper presented to the Conference on Social Housing Finance in the European Union, Nunspeet, The Netherlands.

Renaud, B. and A. Bertaud (1989), The Urban Housing Reforms in China: Review of City Experiments and Analytical Issues. Paper presented at the Joint Seminar on Urban Housing Reforms, Beijing.

Renaud, B. and R.M. Buckley (1987), Housing Finance in Developing Countries: A Framework for Bank Operations (World Bank).

Renaud, B. and R.M. Buckley (1988), Urban Finance in Post-Depression Latin America. INU Discussion Paper No. 22.

Renaud, B. and M. Gronicki (1990), Bulgaria: Aide Memoire, World Bank Housing Reconnaissance Mission.

Renaud, B. et al. (1993), Russia—Housing Reform and Privatization: Strategy and Transition Issues. World Bank Sector Report 11868-RU.

Renaud, B., F. Pretorius and B. Pasadilla (1997), Markets at Work: Dynamics of the Residential Real Estate Market in Hong Kong (Hong Kong University Press, Hong Kong).

Rodwin, L., ed. (1987), Shelter, Settlement and Development (Allen and Unwin, London).

Rojas, E. and M. Greene (1995), "Reaching the poor: lessons from the Chilean housing experience", Environment and Urbanization 7:31–50.

Rosen, H.S. (1979), "Housing decisions and the U.S. income tax", Journal of Public Economics 1–23.

Rosen, S. (1974), "Hedonic prices and implicit markets", Journal of Political Economy 177–201.

Salazar-Carrilo, J. and I. Tirado De Alonso (1989), "Housing services in national accounts: the case of Latin America", International Journal for Housing Science and its Applications 13:297–300.

Sandilands, R.J. (1980), Monetary Correction and Housing Finance in Colombia, Brazil and Chile (Gover Publishing, Farnborough, UK).

Sanyal, B. (1981), "Who gets what, where, why and how: a critical look at housing subsidies in Zambia", Development and Change 12:409–440.

Sanyal, B. (1987), "Problems of cost-recovery in development projects: experience of the Lusaka squatter upgrading and site/service project", Urban Studies 24:285–295.

Schlyter, A. (1985), "Housing strategies: the case of Zimbabwe", Trialog 6:20–29.

Shefer, D. (1990), "The demand for housing and permanent income in Indonesia", Urban Studies 27:259–272.

Shephard, S. (Chapter 41, this volume).

Shidlo, G., ed. (1990), Housing Policy in Developing Countries (Routledge).

Shidlo, G. (1994), Housing Regulatory Reform in Mexico. World Bank Infrastructure Note HS-8.

Sillince, J.A., ed., Housing Policies in Eastern Europe and the Soviet Union (Routledge, London).

Silveira, R. (1989), The Evolution of Rent Control in Brazil, 1921–1989. INURD Working Paper No. 89-8.

Silveira, R. and S. Malpezzi (1991), Costs and Benefits of Rent Control in Rio De Jainero. World Bank, Infrastructure and Urban Development Department Discussion Paper No. 83, (97 pp).

Simkins, C., M. Oelofse and D. Gardner (1992), "Designing a market-driven state-aided housing programme for South Africa", Urban Forum 3:13–38.

Small, K.A. and J.A. Gomez-Ibanez (Chapter 46, this volume).

Smith, L.B., K. Rosen and G. Fallis (1988), "Recent developments in economic models of housing markets", Journal of Economic Literature 26:29–64.

Solomon, A. and K. Vandell (1982), "Alternative perspectives on neighborhood decline", Journal of the American Planning Association 45:81–91.

Son, J.Y. and K.H. Kim (1998), "Analysis of urban land shortages: the case of Korean cities", Journal of Urban Economics 43:362–384.

Stedman, S.J. (1992), Botswana: The Political Economy of Democratic Development (L. Rienner Publishers, Boulder).

Strassman, W.P. (1977), "Housing priorities in developing countries: a planning model", Land Economics 53.

Strassman, W.P. (1980a), Guidelines for Estimating Employment Generation through Shelter Sector Assistance (Michigan State University).

Strassman, W.P. (1980b), "Housing improvement in an opportune setting: Cartagena, Colombia", Land Economics.

Strassman, W.P. (1980c), "Shelter improvement in Lima, Peru", Mimeo.

Strassman, W.P. (1982), The Transformation of Urban Housing: The Experience of Upgrading in Cartegena (Johns Hopkins University Press).

Strassman, W.P. (1984), "The timing of urban infrastructure and housing improvements by owner occupants", World Development 12:743–754.

Strassman, W.P. (1985), "Employment in construction: multicountry estimates of costs and substitution elasticities for small dwellings", Economic Development and Cultural Change 33:395–414.

Strassman, W.P. (1991), "Housing market interventions and mobility: an international comparison", Urban Studies 28:759–771.

Strassman, W.P., A. Blunt and R. Thomas (1992), "Land prices and housing in Manila", Urban Studies 31:267–285.

Straszheim, M. (1975), An Econometric Analysis of the Urban Housing Market (NBER).

Struyk, R.J. (1982), "Upgrading existing dwellings: an element in the housing strategies of developing countries", Journal of Developing Areas 17:69–76.

Struyk, R.J. (1987), Assessing Housing Needs and Policy Alternatives in Developing Countries (Urban Institute Press, Washington, DC).

Struyk, R.J. (1988a), The Distribution of tenant benefits from rent control in urban Jordan", Land Economics 64.

Struyk, R.J. (1988b), "Understanding high vacancy rates in a developing country: Jordan", Journal of Developing Areas 22:373–380.

Struyk, R.J. (1993), Implementing Housing Allowances in Russia: Rationalizing the Rental Sector (Urban Institute Press, Washington, DC).

Struyk, R.J., ed. (1995), Economic Restructuring in the Former Soviet Bloc: Evidence from the Housing Sector (Urban Institute Press, Washington, DC).

Struyk, R.J., ed. (1996), Economic Restructuring in the Former Soviet Bloc: Evidence from the Housing Sector (Urban Institute Press, Washington, DC).

Struyk, R.J. and N.B. Kosareva (1993a), "Developing the Russian housing finance system", Housing Finance International 7:2–10.

Struyk, R.J. and N.B. Kosareva (1993b), The Russian Housing Market in Transition. Prepared by the Urban Institute for U.S. Agency for International Development.

Struyk, R.J. and N.B. Kosareva (1994), Transition in the Russian Housing Sector: 1991–1994 (The Urban Institute Press, Washington, DC).

Struyk, R.J. and R. Lynn (1983), "Determinants of housing investment in slum areas: Tondo and other locations in metropolitan Manila", Land Economics 59:444–454.

Struyk, R.J. and M. Turner (1986), Housing Finance and Quality in Two Developing Countries (Urban Institute Press, Washington, DC).

Struyk, R.J., M. Hoffman and H. Katsura (1990), The Market for Shelter in Indonesian Cities (Urban Institute Press, Washington, DC).

Struyk, R.J., K. Mark and J.B. Telgarsky (1991), "Private management for eastern Europe's state rental housing", Journal of Housing Economics 1.

Struyk, R.J., J. Daniell, A. Puzanov and N.B. Kosareva (1993a), Income Adjustments When Raising Rents in Post-Soviet Economies: Housing Allowances or Wage Increases? Analysis for Moscow (Urban Institute Press, Washington, DC).

Struyk, R.J., N.D. Kosareva, Daniell, Hanson and Mikelsons (1993b), Implementing Housing Allowances in Russia. Rationalizing the Rental Sector (University Press of America (UPA), Lanham).

Struyk, R.J., et al. (1994), Implementing Housing Allowances in Russia: Rationalising the Rental Sector (Urban Institute Press, Washington DC).

Telgarsky, J.P. and R.J. Struyk (1991), Toward a Market-Oriented Housing Sector in eastern Europe: Developments in Bulgaria, Czechoslovakia, Hungary, Poland, Romania, and Yugoslavia (Urban Institute Press, Washington, DC).

Tewari, V.K. and T. Krishna Kumar (1987), "Rent control in India: its economic effects and implementation in Bangalore", Nagarlok 19:55–85.

Thalwitz, M. (1993), "Poland: building a new system of housing finance", Housing Finance International, December, pp. 13–42.

Thomson, M.J. (1983), Toward Better Urban Transport Planning in Developing Countries. World Bank Staff Working Paper No. 600.

Tideman, N. et al. (1990), Open letter to Mikhail Gorbachev on land markets in Russia.

Tipple, A.G. (1983), "Housing policy and culture in Kumasi", African Urban Studies 15:17–30.

Tipple, A.G. (1993), "Housing in Algeria—recent research at CAROD—a review article", Third World Planning Review 15:55–62.

Tipple, A.G. (1994), "The need for new urban housing in sub-Saharan Africa—problem or opportunity", African Affairs 93:587–610.

Tipple, A.G. and K.G. Willis (1991a), "Tenure choice in Kumasi, Ghana", Third World Planning Review 13:27–45.

Tipple, A.G. and K.G. Willis, eds. (1991b), Housing the Poor in the Developing World: Methods of Analysis, Case Studies and Policy (Routledge, London).

Tipple, A.G. and K.G. Willis (1992), "Who owns, who rents: tenure choice in a west African city", in: L. Kilmartin and H. Singh, eds., Housing in the Third World: Analyses and Solutions (Concept Publishing, New Delhi).

Tolley, G.S. (1991), Urban Housing Reform in China: An Economic Analysis. World Bank Discussion Paper No. 123.

Tolley, G.S., ed. (In press), Urban Land and Housing Reform in Socialist and Formerly Socialist Countries.

Tomann, H. (1992), Towards a Housing Market in Eastern Germany. Paper presented to the American Real Estate and Urban Economics Association, Los Angeles.

Tomlinson, R. (1992), "Competing urban agendas in South Africa", Urban Forum 3:97–110.

Trollegaard, S. (1989), Distributional Aspects of Housing and Taxation Policies. United Nations, Economic Commission for Europe, Committee on Housing, Building and Planning, monograph.

Turner, B., J. Hegedus and I. Tosics, eds. (1992), The Reform of Housing in Eastern Europe and the Soviet Union (Routledge, London, New York).

Turner, J.F.C. (1972), Freedom to Build (Macmillan, New York).

Turok, I. (1994a), "Urban planning in the transition from apartheid—Part I: the legacy of social control", Third World Planning Review 65:243–259.

Turok, I. (1994b), "Urban planning in the transition from apartheid—Part II: towards reconstruction", Third World Planning Review 65:355–374.

United Nations (1993), Housing Policy Guidelines: The Experience of ECE with Special Reference to Countries in Transition (E.93.II.E.15).

U.N. Centre for Human Settlements (Habitat) (1989), Improving Income and Housing: Employment Generation in Low-Income Settlements (Nairobi).

UNCHS (Habitat) (1990), The Global Strategy for Shelter to the Year 2000 (Nairobi, Kenya).

UNCHS (Habitat) (1996), An Urbanizing World: Global Report on Human Settlements, 1996. New York: Oxford University Press.

UN Centre for Human Settlements, and the World Bank (1993), The Housing Indicators Program—Volume I: Report of the Executive Director (Nairobi).

UN Centre for Human Settlements, and the World Bank (1993), The Housing Indicators Program—Volume II: Indicator Tables (Nairobi).

UN Centre for Human Settlements, and the World Bank (1993), The Housing Indicators Program—Volume III: Preliminary Findings (Nairobi).

UN Centre for Human Settlements, and the World Bank (1993), The Housing Indicators Program—Volume IV: The Extensive Survey Instrument (Nairobi).

Urban Edge, The (1983), Third World Faces Great Subway Debate. World Bank 7.

U.S. Agency for International Development (1981), Housing and Health: An Analysis for Use in the Planning, Design, and Evaluation of Low-Income Housing Programs (U.S. A.I.D).

Valladares, L. do P. (1978), "Working the system: squatter response to resettlement in Rio de Janeiro", International Journal of Urban and Regional Research 2:12–25.

van der Linden, J. (1986), The Sites and Services Approach Reviewed (Gower, Aldershot).

van Vliet, W. (1990), International Handbook of Housing Policies and Practices (Greenwood Press, Westport, CT).

van Vliet, W. and J. van Weesep, eds. (1990), Government and Housing: Developments in Seven Countries (Sage Publications, Urban Affairs Annual Reviews, Vol. 36).

Vandell, K.D. and T.J. Riddiough (1991), On the Use of Auctions as a Disposition Strategy for RTC Real Estate Assets: A Policy Perspective. University of Wisconsin, Department of Real Estate and Urban Land Economics Working Paper.

Vanderporten, B. (1992), "Strategic behavior in pooled condominium auctions", Journal of Urban Economics 31:123–137.

Vernez, G. (1973), Bogota's Pirate Settlements. University of California at Berkeley, Working Paper.

Versacaj, J.P. (1993), "Leasing real estate in the Russian Federation", Real Estate Review: 70–75.

Wadhva, K. (1983), "An evaluation of the urban land ceiling legislation: a case study of Ahmedabad", Nagarlok 15:76–86.

Walters, A.A. (1979), The benefits of minibuses: the case of Kuala Lumpur", Journal of Transport Economics and Policy.

Wang, Y. (1991), "The size of housing subsidies in China", Review of Urban and Regional Development Studies 3.

Ward, P. (1989), "Land values and valorisation processes in Latin American cities: a research agenda", Bulletin of Latin American Research 8:47–66.

Ward, P., E. Jimenez and G. Jones (1993), "Residential land price changes in Mexican cities and the affordability of land for low-income groups", Urban Studies 30:1521–1542.

Warford, J. and R. Turvey (1974), Lahore Water Supply—Tariff Study. World Bank, Public Utilities Report No. PUN 12.

Weinberg, D.H., J. Friedman and S.K. Mayo (1981), "Intraurban residential mobility: the role of transactions costs, market imperfections and household disequilibrium", Journal of Urban Economics 9:332–348.

Wells, J. (1986), The Construction Industry in Developing Countries: Alternative Strategies for Development (Croom Helm).

Wheaton, W.C. (1979), "Public policy and the 'shortage' of housing in Egypt", Mimeograph.

Wheaton, W.C. (1981), "Housing policies and urban 'markets' in developing countries: the Egyptian experience", Journal of Urban Economics 9:242–256.

Whitehead, C. (Chapter 40, this volume).

Whittington, D., J. Briscoe, X. Mu and W. Barron (1990), "Estimating the willingness to pay for water services in developing countries: a case study of the contingent valuation method in Haiti", Economic Development and Cultural Change 38:293–311.

Whittington, D., D.T. Lauria, A.M. Wright, K. Choe, J.A. Hughes and V. Swarna (1992), Household Demand for Improved Sanitation Services: A Case Study of Kumasi, Ghana (UNDP-World Bank Water and Sanitation Program).

Whittington, D., D.T. Lauria, K. Choe, J.A. Hughes, V. Swarna and A.M. Wright (1993), "Household sanitation in Kumasi, Ghana: a description of current practices, attitudes and perceptions", World Development 21:733–748.

Williams, M. and M. Ondera (1982), "Public expenditures on housing in less developed countries", Journal of Economic Development 7:127–133.

Williamson, O.E. (1975), Markets and Hierarchies: Analysis and Antitrust Implications (Free Press).

Willis, K.G. and A.G. Tipple (1991), "Economics of multihabitation: housing conditions, household occupancy and household structure under rent control, inflation and nonmarketability of ownership rights", World Development 19:1705–1720.

Willis, K., S. Malpezzi and G. Tipple (1990), "An econometric and cultural analysis of rent control in Kumasi, Ghana", Urban Studies 27:241–257.

Wong, Y.-C. and P.-W. Liu (1988), "The distribution of benefits among public housing tenants in Hong Kong and related policy issues", Journal of Urban Economics 23:1–20.

Woodfield, A. (1989), Housing and Economic Adjustment (Taylor and Francis for the United Nations, New York).

World Bank (1981), The Road Maintenance Problem and International Assistance (Washington).

World Bank (1986), Urban Transport: A World Bank Policy Study.

World Bank (1990), Ghana Housing Sector Review. Report No. 8099-GH.

World Bank (1992), China: Implementation Options for Urban Housing Reform (World Bank, Washington, DC).

World Bank (1993a), China: Urban Land Management in an Emerging Market Economy (World Bank, Washington, DC).

World Bank (1993b), Housing: Enabling Markets to Work. World Bank Policy Paper.

World Bank (1993c), Russia Housing Reform and Privatization: Strategy and Transition Issues. (By B Renaud et al.) Report 11868-RU, 2 Vols.

World Bank (1994), World Development Report 1994: Infrastructure for Development (Oxford University Press, Oxford).

Yap, K.S., ed. (1992), Low Income Housing in Bangkok: A Review of Some Housing Submarkets. Bangkok, Asian Institute of Technology, HDS Monograph No. 25.

YapiDiahou, A. (1995), "The informal housing sector in the metropolis of Abidjan, Ivory Coast", Environment and Urbanization 7:11–30.

Yonder, A. (1987), "Informal land and housing market: the case of Istanbul", Journal of the American Planning Association 53:213–219.

Yoon, I.-S. (1994), Housing in a Newly Industrialized Economy: The Case of South Korea (Brookfield, Vt., Aldershot, UK and Ashgate, Avebury, Sydney).

Yu, F.-L. and S.-M. Li. (1985), "The welfare cost of Hong Kong's public housing program", Urban Studies 22:33–140.

Zaroff, B. and D.A. Okun (1984), "Water vending in developing countries", Aqua 5:289–295.

Zearley, T.L. (1993), "Creating an enabling environment for housing: recent reforms in Mexico", Housing Policy Debate 4:239–249.

Zhang, J. (1986), Urban Construction Reconsidered: China's Cities, Issues and Solutions. World Bank, UDD Discussion Paper No. 101.

Zorn, P. (1988), "An analysis of household mobility and tenure choice: an empirical study of Korea", Journal of Urban Economics 24:113–128.

*Chapter 45*

# POVERTY IN DEVELOPING COUNTRIES

ERNESTO M. PERNIA and M.G. QUIBRIA*

*Asian Development Bank, Manila*

## Contents

* We would like to gratefully acknowledge the helpful comments of Arsenio Balisacan, Jere Behrman, Douglas Brooks, Malcolm Dowling, Frank Harrigan, S. Iftekhar Hossain, Emmanuel Jimenez, Haider A. Khan, Michael Lipton, Edwin Mills, and S. Rashid. The authors acknowledge the valuable research assistance given by Isabelita Alba and Emma Murray, editorial assistance by Cherry Zafaralla, and secretarial support by Helen K. Buencamino, Zenaida M. Acacio and Anna Liza P. Silverio. The views expressed in the paper are the authors' own and do not reflect the official position of the Asian Development Bank.

*Handbook of Regional and Urban Economics. Edited by E.S. Mills and P. Cheshire*

## Abstract

This chapter begins with the dimensions of the poverty problem in developing countries, and then deals with conceptual and measurement issues. It next discusses the nature, characteristics and correlates of rural and urban poverty. It looks into the issue of gender and poverty, then turns to the relationship between poverty and population growth. It also examines the crucial nexus between economic growth and poverty. Before concluding, the chapter discusses strategies and policies for poverty reduction.

**Keywords:** Deprivation, living standards, human capital, gender, economic growth, development strategy, urban–rural differences

## 1. Introduction

Poverty is an age-old problem. Notwithstanding decades of overall economic growth and official concern about the problem, poverty remains a formidable challenge to governments and the international community. Defining the poor as those whose incomes fall below one US dollar per day, the World Bank estimates that there are about 1.3 billion poor people in all developing countries. Approximately three-quarters are in Asia, one-sixth are in sub-Saharan Africa, and about one-tenth in Latin America, eastern Europe and central Asia, and the residual in the Middle East and north Africa (World Bank, 1996). The number of poor

people has been increasing in Asia, notably in south Asia, although poverty incidence has been declining. The decline in poverty incidence in Asia was greatly
helped by strong economic growth in the region as a whole during the 1980s and
through the 1990s. In the other developing regions, both the incidence and the
numbers of poor people have been on the rise. But, while for sub-Saharan Africa
and Latin America the 1980s had been labeled as a "lost decade", their more
recent economic performances have distinctly improved prospects for poverty
reduction.

Poverty has many dimensions besides income or consumption.[1] Among the
more important ones are health, education, nutrition and gender equality, which
should be incorporated in a more comprehensive poverty indicator. Attempts are
being made toward this end in the Human Development Report (HDR) of the
United Nations Development Programme (UNDP). In various issues of the HDR,
many of these dimensions, as they affect the poverty situation in developing
economies, have been highlighted.

While in east and southeast Asia and the Pacific, life expectancy at birth in
1992 was close to 85% of that in industrial countries, rural access to safe water
and basic sanitation in southeast Asia and the Pacific remains only two thirds of
urban access (UNDP, 1995). In south Asia, despite notable advances in female
literacy over the past two decades, about two-thirds of adult women are still
illiterate, and 80% of pregnant women suffer from anemia (the highest rate in the
world). In Latin America and the Caribbean, notwithstanding remarkable strides
in secondary and tertiary enrollment ratios, less than half of grade 1 entrants reach
grade 5. In sub-Saharan Africa, infant mortality rate was reduced from 165 per
thousand live births to 97 over the past three decades; still, 26 million children
are malnourished and more than 15% of babies are underweight.

Poverty in developing countries has commonly been perceived as a rural problem, mainly due to much larger numbers of people in rural areas where average
earnings are considerably less than those in urban areas. In sub-Saharan Africa
around the late 1980s, rural poverty incidence at about 60% was double that
in urban areas; in Latin America and the Caribbean, rural and urban poverty
incidence were roughly 60 and 36%, respectively; and in Asia (excluding China)
poverty incidence was 47% for rural areas and 34% for urban areas (Tabatabai,

---

[1] It is now widely recognized that there are serious shortcomings in perceiving poverty only in terms of
income or consumption of commodities. Poverty, as a reflection of human ill-being, has many dimensions.
Sen (1985) argues that human well-being extends beyond possession of commodities or generation of utilities;
it should be measured in terms of "functioning" and "capabilities". However, even if one confines oneself to
basic capabilities and human functioning, the task of operationalizing capabilities for measuring poverty is not
an easy one. For more on this issue, see Section 2.

1993). With rapid urbanization, poverty is pervading cities in a very perceptible way. As urbanization accelerates, urban poverty in both absolute and relative terms is likely to increase before it diminishes. In this sense, the burden of poverty is steadily being shifted from the countryside to the cities.[2]

The escalating seriousness of urban poverty was anticipated several decades ago by author and social critic George Bernard Shaw (1913). He wrote about poverty in cities that

> infects with its degradation the whole neighborhood in which they [the poor] live, (and therefore) whatever can degrade a neighborhood can degrade a country and a continent and finally the whole civilized world, which is only a large neighborhood.

He added:

> All the other dishonors are chivalry itself by comparison. Poverty blights whole cities; spreads horrible pestilence; strikes dead the very souls of all who come within sight, sound, or smell of it. What you call crime is nothing: a murder here and a theft there, a blow now and a curse then. What do they matter? They are only the accidents and the illnesses of life. There are millions of poor people, abject people, dirty people, ill-fed, ill-clothed people. They poison us totally and physically; they kill the happiness of society; they force us to do away with our own liberties and to organize unnatural cruelties for fear they should rise against us and drag us down into their abyss. Only fools fear crime; we all fear poverty. (Shaw, 1913, as reproduced in Smith, 1970: p. 65)

This chapter surveys the literature on poverty in developing countries. The survey is somewhat skewed toward studies of Asian developing countries both because of the fact that the incidence of poverty is much higher in Asia than in any other continent—indeed, Asia has more poor people than all other continents combined—and because the authors have more access to, and familiarity with, studies of poverty in developing Asia. Section 2 deals with conceptual and measurement issues, pointing out the necessary caveats in the use of poverty indicators. Section 3 discusses the nature, characteristics and correlates of poverty,

---

[2] This statement is particularly true of the Latin American experience. According to a recent study by Psacharopoulos et al. (1995), poverty rose almost in every Latin American country throughout the 1980s, but it rose much faster in the cities than in the countryside. Psacharopoulos et al. (1995: p. 246) observe: "given that almost the entire increase in population over the decade took place in the cities, ... what we are seeing here is simply a transfer of the poverty problem from the countryside to the cities through migration rather than a real improvement in the conditions in the rural sector".

looking separately at rural and urban poverty. Section 4 focuses on the increasingly topical issue of gender and poverty. Section 5 looks into the relationship between poverty and population growth. Section 6 dwells on the crucial nexus between economic growth and poverty. Drawing on the foregoing analyses, Section 7 discusses strategies and policies for poverty reduction. The final section gives some concluding remarks.

## 2. Conceptual and measurement issues[3]

### 2.1. What is poverty?

Poverty has been described as "a matter of deprivation" (Sen, 1981). This deprivation can be *absolute*, infringing on basic sustenance of life; or it could be *relative*, in relation to the standard of living enjoyed by a reference group in the society with higher incomes. Two concepts of poverty, absolute and relative, reflecting two types of deprivation, have been distinguished in the literature.

Absolute poverty is defined as the inability to attain a minimal standard of living.[4] This notion of minimal standard is, however, not fixed but varies across countries. What is considered an absolute necessity in one country may be considered a luxury in another. As a result, items of consumption which are deemed as luxury in Bangladesh may be considered a necessity in the US. Relative poverty, on the other hand, is defined as the inability to attain a given contemporary standard of living, which is often defined in terms of some indicator of well-being such as the median income. In the US, it was proposed that families with one half of the median income be classified as poor (Fuchs, 1965). Similarly, the poor may be defined, as has been suggested for developed countries, as the lowest four deciles in the national income distribution. There is a disconcerting aspect about this notion of relative poverty, as it seems to predetermine the extent of relative poverty. It has been pointed out, no matter how much income increases, "in the absence of a marked shift toward greater equality in the income distribution the poor, in a relative sense, will always be with us" (Sawhill, 1988: p. 1076). In other words, it may be possible to eradicate absolute poverty, but it is,

---

[3] This section draws on Quibria (1991).

[4] Atkinson (1989) distinguishes between two different concepts of poverty. One is the standard of living concept, where one is perceived as poor if one's total expenditure or the consumption of specific goods falls below a given threshold. The other is the right to a minimum level of resources, where one is perceived as poor if one's income falls below a specified minimum level. In the second approach, the right to a minimum income is critical, and not its disposal. In this chapter, emphasis is on the first approach, which seems to have gained greater acceptability.

however, never possible to eradicate such a type of relative poverty. Despite this nagging aspect about relative poverty, it should be emphasized that it is perfectly legitimate[5]—and, as has been suggested, is consistent with the Rawlsian criterion of justice—for government and policy makers to be concerned with the lower segments of the population in the income scale (Rawls, 1971).

In developing countries today, the term poverty is used essentially to indicate absolute poverty. In developed countries, with increasing material wealth and virtual elimination of hunger, this concept has lost much of its significance. Poverty in most advanced industrial nations is now defined in relative terms as a matter of deviation from social and economic norms.

Finally, it appears that there is some measure of ambiguity about whether poverty should be viewed from a welfarist, or a nonwelfarist perspective. In other words, is it concerned with the level of resources of the poor or with their economic well-being? Sen (1977) argues that the subject should adopt a nonwelfarist approach and focus on the level of resources, not the family's sense of well-being.[6] This perspective, however, has been far from universally adopted.

## 2.2. Poverty line

The poverty line defines the minimum acceptable standard of living for the society. When an individual is poor, he/she has a standard of living that is below the minimum acceptable level. Thus, the definition of the poverty line is based on two concepts: (i) the concept of a standard of living; and (ii) the concept of a minimum acceptable level. The standard of living is a multidimensional concept, which encompasses all the commodities an individual consumes and all the activities in which he or she participates. To define a poverty line that incorporates this multidimensional aspect of standard of living, one ought to specify a minimum acceptable level for all the different dimensions.[7] These dimensions relate to various basic needs such as food, health, education, clothing, fuel and transport.

---

[5] J. Rawls (1971), an American philosopher, presents a systematic moral theory in his book, *A Theory of Justice*, which is in opposition to utilitarianism. The principal hypothesis of the book is that a system is just if and only if it accords with the principles which would be agreed on by rational people making a kind of social contract. The book further argues for principles that emphasize basic liberties and improvement for the worst-off individuals in the society.

[6] In terms of notation, if $y$ indicates income and $u(y)$ the utility from income, then the subject is concerned with $y$ and not with $u(y)$. See Atkinson (1989, Chapter 1).

[7] Although the basic needs approach to poverty is couched in specific commodity terms and adopts a nonwelfarist approach, it can be easily translated into welfarist terms. Or in other words, there is behind the apparent nonwelfarist approach an embedded welfarist perspective. To put it technically, assume $x^0$ specifies the basket of "basic needs" commodities. Then the utility level associated with $x^0$ is $u(x^0)$. By solving the optimizing problem of the consumer, one can define the money metric utility function: $e(p, x^0) = [\min px: u(x) \geq u(x^0)]$, where $p$ is the level of prices.

If a household fails to achieve an adequate level for any one of these basic needs, it is counted as poor. However, there are a number of practical difficulties in implementing this multiple- index approach. To agree on an acceptable level for one item of basic needs is not easy, but to agree on many different items is next to impossible. Furthermore, the failure to satisfy an item of basic needs may arise from individual preference than from stringency of income. A well-to-do household may be considered poor for its idiosyncrasies of preference than for its deprivation due to lack of income. All these difficulties have led to a greater reliance on the single indicator of poverty.

There is a disadvantage in a single index of living standard, often summarized in total household income or expenditure. Income, which includes both savings and dissavings, is in some sense considered a better conceptual measure of living standard. It is argued that it is possible for an individual to choose a level of living below his or her income. But this is decided on volition rather than dictated by a lack of income. In this sense, income should be the indicator of poverty, since it is a measure of the opportunities open to a household and is not influenced by the consumption decisions made.[8] However, there are a number of problems with using income as a proxy of family welfare. First, income data are often unreliable, since there are problems in identifying and assessing production for home consumption and for sale in developing countries. Second, income may understate the level of living. A family may dissave and its current standard of living may exceed current income. Expenditure may then be the more appropriate indicator of welfare. Third, the level of living may exceed income if there is sharing. An elderly parent living with his children may benefit from their expenditures. Fourth, income may, in some instances, overstate the standard of living. This happens when money alone is not sufficient to buy the necessities, for example, when there is rationing or unavailability of goods. For all these reasons, poverty incidence is now calculated not on the basis of household income but household expenditure—in many cases by consumption expenditure of privately supplied goods.

There are two general approaches to arrive at a poverty line at the operational level. One is to determine a bundle of basic goods, consisting of food and non-food items, and then calculate the income required to purchase this bundle at current prices. Denoting the food items by vector $x^f$, purchasable at $p^f$ prices and the nonfood items by the vector $x^{nf}$, purchasable at prices $p^{nf}$, the poverty line is defined as: $\lambda \, (p^f x^f + p^{nf} x^{nf})$ where $\lambda (\geq 1)$ is a provision for inefficient expenditure or waste.

---

[8] This notion is advocated by those who subscribe to the minimum rights approach, as noted earlier.

There are three problems with this approach. First, the notion of a basic good is a matter of value judgment. What will be considered a basic good by one investigator will be deemed as nonbasic by another. Second, some basic goods are provided from the public budget. The Indian norm on the poverty line excludes these public goods, the implicit assumption being that these public goods are provided adequately to all sections of the population. It is, however, questionable whether this is correct, especially in the case of health, education, water supply and sanitation. Third, prices of many commodities vary according to location, year and the socioeconomic status of the consumer. The poor often pay more for an inferior variety; the rich often pay less for a superior variety. These issues are important if comparisons are made over time and space.

The other approach determines the poverty line more directly on the basis of food requirements. It was used by Orshansky (1965) to develop the poverty line for the US and is now widely used for calculating poverty in developing countries. First, the minimum expenditure necessary to satisfy the minimum nutritional intake should be determined. However, the determination of the minimum nutritional intake is a formidable task. Many economists in developing countries working in this area apply the Food and Agriculture Organization/World Health Organization guidelines on minimum "energy requirements". The minimum food expenditure thus calculated is then multiplied by an appropriate proportion to allow for nonfood requirements. In more precise terms, denoting the food items by the vector $x^f$, purchasable at $p^f$ prices, the minimum food expenditure is given by $p^f x^f$. Then the poverty norm becomes: $\theta p^f x^f$ where $\theta (\geq 1)$ is a multiplier to incorporate nonfood items and to allow for inefficient expenditure. But the important and still unresolved issue is, what is the appropriate multiplier? That is, how does one determine $\theta$? Orshansky (1965) used (the reciprocal of) the average ratio of food expenditure to the total expenditure in the population.

There are at least two major problems with the nutrition-based food approach. First, in the case of food requirements, while physiological needs may be a good starting point, it is difficult to determine $x^f$ with any precision. Nutritional needs depend on the location, climate as well as the occupation and age of the individual. They vary from person to person, and even from one day to another for the same person. Therefore, any nutritional statement can only be probabilistic; i.e., at a certain consumption level, there is a certain probability that a particular person is inadequately fed. Second, there is a disparity between expert recommendation and actual consumption. Consider a hypothetical example where an individual chooses to spend her income on things other than meeting her energy requirements, even though she has the means to do so. It can be argued that such individuals are not poor since they could have chosen not to be poor.

This brings us to the issue of an individual's preference in determining her poverty status.[9] If the poverty norm is viewed as a socially determined threshold in regard to some arguments of an individual's utility function, then it is irrelevant whether an individual is below the threshold by choice or force of circumstances.[10] On the other hand, if the poverty norm is viewed as a threshold level of welfare, then all individuals can reach the same level of welfare with different choices, depending on the constraints they face. In this case, individual preferences are irrelevant; the overriding consideration is the level of welfare attained by the individual.[11] According to this perspective, an individual is classified as poor only if the utility maximizing choice does not lead to a welfare level above the poverty threshold. The choices in, and of themselves, are of no significance.

At the empirical level, the method chosen to arrive at the poverty line is often dictated not by the rigor or elegance of one method over another but by the availability of data. To those who work on poverty measures, they would have at their disposal at best an income and expenditure survey and a nutrition survey. Given these data constraints, the empirical implementation of some methods of arriving at the poverty line becomes more difficult than others. In addition, there are a few problems in analyzing household income and expenditure surveys. Most surveys are presented as tabulations of group data, where income shares of households are ranked in deciles or income frequency distributions. As poverty lines rarely occur at the end points of the group data, interpolation between boundaries is often required and different methods of interpolation may lead to different results.

## 2.3. Unit of analysis

In poverty analysis, the unit of analysis should ideally be the individual as it is, in the ultimate analysis, an enquiry into the issue of the welfare of an individual. However, in practice, most empirical studies take the household as the basic unit of analysis.[12] This choice is dictated more by the availability of data than by any other considerations. Income-expenditure data of an individual within a family are very difficult to obtain. There may be members within the family with zero recorded cash income but they may not be without resources. Indeed, records

---

[9] The distinction between the standard of living approach and the minimum rights approach is critical here.

[10] A welfarist approach is implicitly taken here.

[11] That is, if one adopts the minimum rights approach, individual preference is irrelevant. However, if the standard of living approach is adopted, individual preference can make the difference between rich and poor.

[12] There may be many different definitions of a household. The definition which has become increasingly popular is the so-called "kitchen" definition, i.e., people living at the same address with common housekeeping and having a common meal.

of income transfers among family members are difficult to obtain. Besides data, another important consideration for taking the household as the unit of analysis is that it can take into account items of expenditure which have "public good" characteristics for family members. If some assets are indivisible or if there are economies of scale in consumption, then the division of family resources by the size of the household will underestimate the individual level of economic well-being. However, it may be possible that, within the family, there are unequal standards of living between members. There is some empirical evidence which shows disparity in consumption between sexes within the household.[13] In light of this fact, there is some doubt on the use of household as the proper unit of analysis for poverty measurement.[14]

## 2.4. Equivalence scales

The index numbers which relate the poverty lines for different household sizes and types are referred to as *equivalence scales*.[15] These are used to make welfare comparisons between households with different size and demographic characteristics. What cost of living indices are to welfare comparisons for a given household facing different prices, equivalence scales are to the poverty line for comparing poverty across households. While the cost of living indices are based on the assumption of unchanging tastes, equivalence scales are based on the premise of differing tastes between households due to variations in observable characteristics.

Three main approaches have been adopted for the determination of the equivalence scales for different types of households. One is the survey of individual assessments of needs. As the method uses survey questionnaires to elicit household preferences, it introduces a strong subjective element in the construction of equivalence scales. The other is empirical investigation of the expenditure behavior of households. Here again different assumptions about the effect of demographic variables on the cost function leads to different equivalence scales. And still another is the nutritional and physiological studies. The estimated scales are likely to vary considerably across time and space as nutritional needs depend

---

[13] For a discussion of this evidence, see Section 4. If such gender disparities exist, then the conventional measures based on the assumption of an equal distribution of resources between household members may lead to distortions in the true nature and extent of poverty. See also Haddad and Kanbur (1990).

[14] Atkinson (1991) states that there is a strong case for measuring poverty on an individual basis from the minimum rights perspective. It is by posing the poverty problem on an individual basis that important gender issues such as the feminization of poverty can be meaningfully addressed.

[15] Operationally, in most cases an equivalence scale provides a set of conversion factors that are used to convert a household of given size and demographic composition to its adult male equivalent.

Table 1

The Amsterdam scale

| Age group | Male | Female |
|-----------|------|--------|
| Under 14 years | 0.52 | 0.52 |
| 14–17 years | 0.98 | 0.90 |
| 18 + years | 1.00 | 0.90 |

*Source:* Stone (1954).

on climatic and environmental conditions, health and work habits. Needless to emphasize, the different methods used to arrive at such scales can produce very different results.

Table 1 shows the equivalence scale, called the Amsterdam scale, used in a study of consumer expenditure in the UK. In this table, the adult male is the unit of measurement and the other members of the family have been expressed in terms of adult-male equivalents.[16] Poverty studies from developed countries have used a whole range of different scales. The scale for a couple, relative to a single person, ranges between 1.25 to 2.0 (although there is a clustering around 1.6 to 1.7), and that for a child between 0.15 and 0.75 (Atkinson, 1991).

To sum up, poverty studies indicate that there are substantial variations in equivalence scales in terms of how much weight to place on increments to family size. At the one extreme, there are analyses which make full adjustment for family size ignoring economies of scale in producing and consuming household goods and services. Indeed, it has been argued that such a procedure can be defended in the context of developing countries because the poor in developing countries consume mostly goods, such as food and clothing, which have few economies of scale. However, to the extent that scale economies in consumption are important, such a procedure would lead to estimation errors. At the other extreme, there are analyses which make no adjustment for the family size. This no-adjustment method has often been defended in the context of developing countries on grounds of lack of data availability. In this case, the analyst derives a poverty line for a household of "average" size and composition and applies that to

---

[16] As noted earlier, most equivalence scales assign adult females and children a value less than one in terms of adult male equivalent, the reason being that children and females tend to consume less than adult males. It is often assumed that this difference in valuation mirrors a difference in needs as women and children can achieve the same level of well-being by consuming less than adult men.

each household, irrespective of its size and composition. Needless to emphasize, this procedure may result in a large estimation error.[17]

## 2.5. Measurement of poverty

### 2.5.1. Cardinal measurement

All single-index poverty measures count an individual or household to be poor if its income or expenditure falls below a given poverty line. To illustrate these measures, let us assume that there are $n$ households and let the income of unit $i$ be $y_i$. If the incomes are arranged in ascending order and the poverty line is $z$, then:

$$y_1 \leq y_2 \leq y_3 \cdots \leq y_q < z < y_{q+1} \leq \cdots \leq y_n.$$

Denote by $p$ the set of the poor and $q$ the cardinality of the set $p$. That is, there are $q$ units below the poverty line. The most commonly used measure of poverty— the headcount ratio— is the number of income-receiving units as a fraction of the total population. If $q$ is the number of the poor in a population of size $n$, then the headcount ratio is given by $H = q/n$. While it is useful as a summary measure of poverty, it reveals nothing about the depth or severity of poverty. That is, how poor are the poor?[18]

   A group of measures that can address this issue is the poverty gap measures. The poverty gap of an individual $i$ is given by $g^i = (z - y_i)$ and then the aggregate poverty gap is given by

$$g = \sum_{i \in p} (z - y_i).$$

The corresponding poverty gap ratios are denoted by $g^i/z$ and $g/z$. The aggregate poverty gap is often normalized by the number of the poor to obtain the average poverty gap $(g/q)$. Sen (1977) focuses on a slightly different normalization to obtain the income-gap ratio:

$$G = (1/qz) \sum_{i \in p} (z - y_i).$$

[17] For an empirical demonstration on how the different definitions of an "average" household leads to different levels of potential error in poverty estimates, see Bhalla and Vashistha (1988).

[18] The headcount measure has been subject to other criticisms as well. For example, it has been argued that poverty is not really a discrete, either or condition; and as such one does not shed the affliction associated with poverty by crossing an income line (see Watts, 1991). Whether one accepts this criticism depends on one's notion about poverty.

Expressed as a percentage of the poverty line, the income gap ratio measures the proportion by which the average income (or consumption) of the poor would have to increase in order to eliminate poverty completely.

$H$ and $G$ are, in a sense, complementary. $H$ captures the number of people in poverty but not its depth, while $G$ measures the *depth* of poverty but is insensitive to the number involved. Neither measure is sensitive to redistribution of income within poor units. That is, if a dollar of income is taken away from the poorest unit and is given to a richer unit that is still below the poverty line, then $G$ will remain unchanged. In other words, $G$ does not reflect the *severity* of poverty.

Sen (1976) has noted the desirable properties of a poverty measure, which include the sensitivity of the measure to the number of poor, to the depth of poverty, as well as to the distribution of income among the poor. He has formalized the requirements in the following two axioms of *monotonicity* and *transfer*. *Monotonicity axiom* implies that other things remaining the same, a reduction in the income of any poor household will increase the poverty measure. *Transfer axiom* implies that other things remaining the same, a transfer of income between two poor households—from a poorer household to a richer one—will increase the poverty measure. Simply put, any increase in inequality among the poor, due to one or a series of regressive transfers, must be reflected in a higher level of poverty.

It can be readily seen that $H$ violates both these axioms. Since $H$ measures only the number of households under poverty, a fall in the income of any of these households leaves the measure unchanged. It thus runs contrary to the monotonicity axiom. Similarly, $H$ is unaffected by a transfer of income from any poor household to any nonpoor household, and this violates the transfer axiom.

It can be seen by inspection that the income gap measure satisfies the monotonicity axiom but does not satisfy the transfer axiom. A fall in the income of any household under the poverty line will increase the poverty measure. The measure is, however, unaltered by any mean-preserving transfer of income among households below the poverty line. For example, a direct transfer from a poor household to another less poor household will increase the poverty gap of the first household by exactly as much as it will reduce that of the second household, leaving the measure unchanged. In addition, $G$ is insensitive to any change in the number of poor households: if the population below the poverty line were duplicated with the same characteristics, this would leave $G$ unchanged.

Sen (1976) has proposed a distributionally sensitive index which combines the properties of $H$ and $G$ in an ingenious way. This index is given by:

$$S = H[G + (1 - G)d],$$

where $d$ is the Gini-coefficient of income distribution among the poor.[19] Although the Sen index is one of the best known of the poverty indices and has been extensively used in empirical applications, it suffers from a number of deficiencies in practical applications, including a lack of sub-group monotonicity (a concept which is explained in a subsequent paragraph).

A class of additively separable measures, which has been quite widely used in recent years, is that proposed by Foster et al. (1984) (henceforth referred to as FGT). This class of measures is additively separable in the sense that poverty measures by population subgroups can be aggregated to yield a single measure of poverty for the population as a whole. The FGT class of poverty measures is given by:

$$F(a) = (1/n) \sum_{i \in p} (g^i/z)^a \qquad a \geq 0.$$

The FGT class of measures views poverty essentially as a function of the poverty gap ratio, which is raised to a power of $a$, a parameter that reflects concern for this shortfall. The FGT class of measures subsumes a number of commonly used poverty measures as special cases: Note that when $a = 0$, i.e., there is no concern for the depth of poverty, then $F(0) = H$; i.e., the measure becomes the headcount ratio. When $a = 1$, reflecting uniform concern for the depth of poverty, then $F(1) = HG$; i.e., the index reduces to the income gap ratio normalized by the number of households in poverty. When $a = 2$, reflecting heightened sensitivity for the depth of poverty, then

$$F(2) = H[G^2 + (1 - G)^2 C p^2],$$

where $Cp$ stands for the coefficient of variation of income among the poor.[20]

The FGT class of measures is consistent with the monotonicity axiom for $a > 0$ and with the transfer axiom for any $a > 1$. For $a > 2$, the FGT class of measures also satisfies the transfer sensitivity axiom (Kakwani, 1980), which requires that a (regressive) transfer from a poor to a less poor household will result in an increase in the poverty measure, but the rate of increase will be smaller, the higher the initial incomes of the two households. In addition to the above desirable properties, the FGT class of measures has been found to be of great advantage in empirical application.

---

[19] The Gini-coefficient is an aggregate measure of inequality, which can vary from zero to one, the former implying perfect equality and the latter perfect inequality.

[20] Note that the squared coefficient of variation is defined as the variance (where each observation has equal probability) divided by the square of the mean.

As mentioned earlier, the $F(a)$ index has an attractive "decomposability" property, which implies: If a population of $n$ units is divided into $m$ subgroups with the number of units in each subgroup as $n_j$, then the aggregate index $F(a)$ for the entire population is a weighted average of the aggregate indices of the subgroups, the weights being their population shares:

$$F(a) = \sum (n_j/n) F_j(a).$$

The class of additive separable FGT measures is *subgroup monotonic*; i.e., an increase in poverty in any single group, while that of other groups remaining the same, will increase the overall poverty measure. This decomposability property is particularly useful for the purpose of constructing and interpreting poverty profiles. When the subgroups within a population have well- defined socioeconomic characteristics (for example, rural and urban, male and female, or different regions within a country), decomposability enables one to isolate the salient features of the poor. As decomposability permits straightforward estimation of the standard error of the poverty measure, it allows statistical determination of whether, or not, poverty is significantly higher in one group than in another.

### 2.5.2. Ordinal measurement[21]

There is a degree of arbitrariness in any cardinal measure of poverty. This arbitrariness relates to the choice of the poverty line and to the specific functional form of the poverty measure. However, for many purposes, there is no need for precision of a cardinal measure; ordinal ranking of income distributions in terms of poverty will suffice. This ordinal ranking, which does not depend on one particular line or one particular poverty measure, utilizes the technique of stochastic dominance analysis. The following provides an intuitive explanation of the idea behind stochastic dominance analysis.

Consider a range of poverty lines, the maximum being defined by the highest permissible income level. Then poverty has unambiguously declined between two dates (say, before and after the policy change) if the cumulative distribution of income for the latter date lies nowhere above that for the former date over the entire interval up to the maximum allowable poverty line. This is called the first-order dominance condition.[22] If the result is unambiguous, then poverty has declined irrespective of the poverty line and the poverty measures adopted.

---

[21] For technical details, see Atkinson (1989: Chap. 2), Foster and Shorrocks (1988) and Ravallion (1993).

[22] The dominance conditions have been discussed, among others, by Atkinson (1987, 1989) and Foster and Shorrocks (1988). For a nontechnical exposition, see Ravallion (1993).

However, if the cumulative distribution curves intersect within the range of permissible poverty lines, then the results are ambiguous; in other words, it implies that different poverty lines and measures may provide different answers.

If the first-order dominance condition fails, the stronger second- order dominance condition may prove useful. However, to apply this, one needs to impose more structure on the poverty measure. If we restrict our attention to additive measures that reflect the depth of poverty, such as FGT measures for which $a > 1$, the second-order dominance condition states that poverty will have fallen if the area under the old cumulative distribution function is greater than that under the new distribution over the entire range of admissible poverty lines. As is obvious, the second-order dominance condition requires more restrictions than the first- order dominance condition to achieve an unambiguous ranking of distributions.

### 2.5.3. *Caveats on international comparisons*

Different countries arrive at their poverty estimates based on different poverty lines. To make meaningful international comparisons of poverty statistics, one needs to adopt a common poverty line having the same real value across the countries. However, this is easier said than done. Despite improvements and standardization of the methodologies in recent years, household surveys differ across countries in terms of definitions, coverage and quality. Moreover, the official exchange rates do not reflect the real purchasing power of countries, a problem that has, to some extent, been circumvented by the adoption of the purchasing power parity (PPP) exchange rates. Remaining difficulties notwithstanding, several analysts have attempted to make international comparisons of poverty (e.g., Ahluwalia et al., 1979; Kakwani, 1980; World Bank, 1980, 1990; Ravallion et al., 1991).

A recent study (Chen et al., 1993) that assumes a common poverty line across countries indicates that about one fifth of the population in the developing world in the mid-1980s was poor, if a poverty line of $23 per month in 1985 US prices (in purchasing power parity terms) were adopted. If a higher poverty line of $31 per month, i.e., $1 per day, is adopted, the incidence of poverty increases to about one in three. Similar estimates for 1990 indicate that the incidence of poverty has declined slightly over a wide range of poverty lines. However, there is significant variation between regions. The incidence of poverty has risen in both Latin America and Africa while it has fallen in Asia, particularly in east Asia.

## 3. Nature, characteristics and correlates of poverty

It is convenient to examine the nature of poverty by looking separately into rural and urban poverty. Although conceptually convenient, this treatment of the subject is somewhat artificial as rural and urban poverty are two sides of the same problem. They have much in common in terms of their characteristics and etiology. They are also intimately intertwined in that poor people move between rural and urban areas, though primarily from rural to urban areas. Nevertheless, the incidence, depth and severity of poverty differ between rural and urban areas. Moreover, the economics, demography, and politics of poverty are different in the cities from those in the countryside. Accordingly, the analysis of the problem and the formulation and implementation of policies should be differentiated, although coordination is obviously required for best results (Mills and Pernia, 1994).

Poverty incidence is typically lower in urban than in rural areas (Quibria, 1993; Pernia, 1994). Moreover, for a given GNP per capita, the national poverty incidence is lower the more urbanized a country is (Mills and Becker, 1986). In virtually all developing countries, real urban incomes per person are higher than those in rural areas. Rural-to-urban poverty incidence ratios, that allow for rural-urban price differences, are reported for the 1980s to be as high as 5–6 in Kenya and Côte d'Ivoire; moderate at 1.7–2.5 in Thailand and Malaysia; and relatively low at 1.1–1.3 in India, Guatemala and Mexico (Lipton and Ravallion, 1995). Surveys in developing countries indicate that rural-urban migrants generally improve their living standards although they may still be classified as urban poor (Mazumdar, 1987; United Nations, 1994). However, the poorest in rural areas, as well as discouraged migrants who return, are unlikely to be represented among rural-urban migrants, given that migration is an undertaking that involves risks and requires a minimum of capital (Sjaastad, 1962).

Rural-urban migration is theoretically viewed as an equilibrating process that reduces urban earnings and raises rural earnings (Greenwood, 1975; Todaro, 1976). Nevertheless, the excess of urban over rural earnings has tended to persist for decades owing to, among other factors, imperfect labor markets and information, and lack of human capital among the rural poor (Mazumdar, 1987; Lipton and de Haan, 1997). Rural-urban migration tends to increase urban poverty, or at least slow the pace of reduction in urban poverty. Not only are many migrants poor, although perhaps not among the poorest of the rural poor, but also migration exerts a downward pressure on the earnings of both poor and nonpoor urban residents. Rural-urban migration can also contribute to sharper urban inequality even in countries experiencing buoyant economic growth. However, in a dynamic context, rural-urban migration is traditionally viewed as an important mechanism that, on balance, enhances the general well-being of both rural and urban households in the long run.[23] Still, if externalities are taken into account, the improvement in general well-being may be arguable. For instance, the external diseconomies on earlier urban residents (e.g., congestion costs) and on the rural population (e.g., loss of dynamic agents of change) may be greater than the income gains to migrants at the margin.

## 3.1. Rural poverty

Poverty in developing countries has for a long time been largely a rural phenomenon, principally because the majority of the population in these countries is rural-based, earning significantly lower incomes and with relatively less access to public services than their urban counterparts. For example, the proportion of poor people living in rural areas is reported to be about 96% in Kenya, 86% in Côte d'Ivoire, 91% in Indonesia, 80% in India and Thailand, 70% in the Philippines, 66% in Guatemala and 59% in Panama (World Bank, 1990). Despite significant growth in agricultural production and employment over the past three decades, rural poverty has persisted in many developing countries, particularly in sub-Saharan Africa and south Asia. In terms of incidence, anywhere from 40 to 60% of the rural population is considered poor in these countries.

Rural poverty can be characterized in many ways. Among the principal characteristics or correlates are: (i) limited access to land and irrigation facilities; (ii) slow adoption of modern technology; (iii) large dependency burden; (iv) limited human capital; (v) concentration in backward regions; and (vi) concentration among minority and ethnic groups (Asian Development Bank, 1992; Quibria, 1993).

The rural poor usually have very little or no land at all. They also rarely benefit from available irrigation facilities. For instance, in Bangladesh in 1987 the extremely poor owned less than half as much land on average as did the nonpoor at 0.4 versus 0.9 hectares (Hossain et al., 1994). Additionally, the poor had merely one-quarter of their land irrigated while the nonpoor had one-third of their land irrigated. In India, households with no land had a poverty incidence of more than 40% in contrast to those cultivating more than 4 hectares which had an incidence of less than 15% (Dev et al., 1994). In Nepal, land ownership in the hills averaged 0.3 hectares for the poor versus 0.5 hectares for the nonpoor;

---

[23] This is the basic rationale why attempts to stem migration directly tend to be ill-conceived and counterproductive. Admittedly, migration can be "excessive" in terms of social consequences at destination and origin. A better approach to this problem is through indirect measures, such as reforming policies that have undesirable spatial biases and providing alternative destination choices, if not improving basic conditions at origin (Pernia and Paderanga, 1981; Renaud, 1981; Tolley and Thomas, 1987).

in the Terai plains the corresponding figures were 1.1 versus 3.1 hectares (Asian Development Bank, 1992; Quibria, 1994).

Also, in the Philippines, a great majority of poor farmers own small-size rainfed plots or work as tenants (Balisacan, 1995). The situation in Thailand is roughly comparable (Krongkaew et al., 1995). In Sri Lanka, most poor farmers owned less than 0.4 hectares of land, although with adequate rainfall and opportunities for growing and selling high-value crops (e.g., vegetables and fruits) a holding of only 0.1 hectare could provide a household sufficient earnings to escape poverty (Gunatilleke et al., 1994). This suggests that low productivity and unfavorable pattern of land use combine with limited landholding to contribute to rural poverty. In Latin America, the average size of farms diminished from 2.4 hectares in 1950 to 2.1 hectares in 1980 (de Janvry and Sadoulet, 1989). It is in small farms where the bulk of rural poverty in Latin America is concentrated.

Although limited access to land is an important feature of rural poverty, tenurial status is not necessarily an indicator of poverty (Asian Development Bank, 1992). In the Philippines, for instance, tenancy is not significantly related to poverty, but in Bangladesh the opposite appears to be the case. In India, the relatively high income farmers lease land from both large and small landowners. Moreover, it is not at all clear that tenants are slower than owner-operators in the adoption of modern techniques.

Poor farmers are comparatively slow in adopting modern agricultural techniques (Asian Development Bank, 1992; Quibria, 1994a). For example, Bangladeshi poor farmers planted 31% of their land with modern rice varieties compared with 45% in the case of the nonpoor. Similarly, poor Filipino farmers employ agricultural techniques which are antiquated relative to those used by the more affluent farmers. This slowness in the adoption of modern technology stems from several factors, including institutional barriers, a scarcity of information partly due to low literacy among the poor, and a lack of access to credit. These constraining factors affect different types of farmers differently within and among regions of a given country. Hence, there is wide variation across countries in the rate of adoption of modern agricultural techniques.

Poor households are typically large in size and have few income earners relative to nonearners or dependents (Asian Development Bank, 1992; Quibria, 1994a). In Bangladesh, the extremely poor households are slightly smaller in size than the nonpoor households, but they have a larger proportion of dependent children, fewer working males, and a higher child–woman ratio. In Nepal, the poor have larger families and more children but roughly the same share of female-headed households as the nonpoor. In Pakistan, households with many dependents and headed by old persons are likely to be poor. Large family size

Table 2

Indicators of education in developing countries

| | Per cent illiterate (Aged 15+) | | | Gross enrolment ratio (Per cent of school age) | | | | | |
| | | | | Primary | | | Secondary | | |
| | 1959–1963 | 1970 | 1992 | 1960 | 1970 | 1992 | 1960 | 1970 | 1992 |
|---|---|---|---|---|---|---|---|---|---|
| Sub-Saharan Africa | NA | 73 | 50[e] | 58 | NA | 66 | 67 | NA | 18 |
| Benin | 95 | 84 | 77 | 27 | 36 | 66 | 2 | 5 | 12 |
| Burundi | 86 | 80 | 67 | 18 | 30 | 69 | 1 | 2 | 6 |
| Burkina Faso | NA | 92 | 83 | NA | 13 | 31 | NA | 1 | 8 |
| Chad | 94 | 89 | 55 | 17 | 35 | 65 | NA | 2 | 7 |
| Ghana | 73[a] | 69 | 39 | 38 | 64 | 74 | 5 | 14 | 38 |
| Guinea | 93 | 86 | 67 | 30 | 33 | 42 | 2 | 13 | 10 |
| Kenya | 81 | 68 | 26 | 47 | 58 | 95 | 2 | 9 | 29 |
| Madagascar | NA | 46 | 20 | 52 | 90 | 92 | 4 | 12 | NA |
| Mali | 98 | 92 | 73 | 10 | 22 | 25 | 1 | 5 | 7 |
| Mozambique | NA | 78 | 63 | 48 | 47 | 60 | 2 | 5 | 8 |
| Niger | 99 | 96 | 88 | 5 | 14 | 29 | NA | 1 | 6 |
| Nigeria | 85 | 75 | 47 | 36 | 37 | 76 | 4 | 4 | 20 |
| Rwanda | 84 | 68 | 43 | 49 | 68 | 71 | 2 | 2 | 8 |
| Somalia | 99 | 97 | 76 | 9 | 59 | NA | 1 | 6 | 10 |
| Sudan | 87 | 83 | 57 | 25 | 47 | 50 | 3 | 14 | 22 |
| Uganda | 75 | 59 | 41 | 49 | 38 | 71 | 3 | 4 | 13 |
| Zambia | 72 | 48 | 25 | 42 | 90 | 97 | 2 | 13 | 31 |
| Zimbabwe | 61 | 45 | 17 | 96 | 74 | 119 | 6 | 7 | 48 |
| East Asia | NA | NA | 24[e] | NA | NA | 121 | NA | NA | 53 |
| China | 57[a] | 42 | 27 | 109 | 89 | 121 | 21 | 24 | 51 |
| Indonesia | 61 | 46 | 18 | 71 | 80 | 115 | 6 | 16 | 38 |
| Korea, Rep. of | 29 | 12 | 3 | 94 | 103 | 105 | 27 | 42 | 90 |
| Lao PDR | 72 | 65 | NA | 25 | 53 | 98 | 1 | 3 | 22 |
| Malaysia | 47 | 40 | 18 | 96 | 87 | 93 | 19 | 34 | 58 |
| Philippines | 28 | 17 | 6 | 95 | 108 | 109 | 26 | 46 | 74 |
| Taiwan | NA | 15 | 6[d] | NA | 98[c] | 99 | NA | 71[c] | 87 |
| Thailand | 32 | 21 | 6 | 83 | 83 | 97 | 13 | 17 | 33 |
| Viet Nam | NA | 16 | 12[b] | NA | NA | 108 | NA | NA | 33 |
| South Asia | NA | 33 | 54[e] | 46 | NA | 103 | 55 | NA | 41 |
| Bangladesh | 78 | 76 | 64 | 47 | 54 | 77 | 8 | NA | 19 |
| India | 72 | 66 | 50 | 61 | 73 | 102 | 20 | 26 | 44 |
| Nepal | 91 | 87 | 74 | 10 | 26 | 102 | 6 | 10 | 36 |
| Pakistan | 85 | 79 | 64 | 30 | 40 | 46 | 11 | 13 | 21 |
| Sri Lanka | 25 | 23 | 11 | 95 | 99 | 107 | 27 | 47 | 74 |

Table 2

(continued)

| | Per cent illiterate (Aged 15+) | | | Gross enrolment ratio (Per cent of school age) | | | | | |
| | | | | Primary | | | Secondary | | |
| | 1959–1963 | 1970 | 1992 | 1960 | 1970 | 1992 | 1960 | 1970 | 1992 |
|---|---|---|---|---|---|---|---|---|---|
| Latin America & the Caribbean | NA | 24 | 15[e] | 95 | NA | 106 | 93 | NA | 47 |
| Argentina | 9 | 7 | 4 | 98 | 105 | 107 | 23 | 44 | NA |
| Bolivia | 61 | 43 | 19 | 64 | 76 | 85 | 12 | 24 | 34 |
| Brazil | 39 | 34 | 18 | 95 | 82 | 106 | 11 | 26 | 39 |
| Chile | 16 | 11 | 5 | 109 | 107 | 96 | 24 | 39 | 72 |
| Colombia | 37 | 22 | 10 | 77 | 108 | 117 | 12 | 25 | 55 |
| Costa Rica | 80 | 12 | 6 | 96 | 110 | 105 | 21 | 28 | 43 |
| Dominican Republic | 36 | 33 | 19 | 98 | 100 | NA | 7 | 21 | NA |
| Ecuador | 33 | 28 | 12 | 83 | 97 | NA | 12 | 22 | NA |
| El Salvador | 51 | 43 | 30 | 80 | 85 | 78 | 13 | 22 | 25 |
| Guatemala | 69 | 56 | 46 | 45 | 57 | 79 | 7 | 8 | 28 |
| Haiti | 86 | 78 | 57 | 46 | 60 | 56 | 4 | 8 | 22 |
| Honduras | 55 | 47 | 29 | 67 | 87 | 105 | 8 | 14 | 19 |
| Mexico | 35 | 26 | 11 | 80 | 104 | 113 | 11 | 22 | 55 |
| Peru | 39 | 29 | 13 | 83 | 107 | 119 | 15 | 31 | 30 |
| Venezuela | 37 | 15 | 10 | 100 | 94 | 99 | 21 | 33 | 34 |

[a]For 1964. [b]For 1987–1992. [c]For 1980.
[d]Data for Taiwan refer to 1992 illiteracy rate for 6 years old and above.
[e]For 1990.
NA: data are not available
Sources: World Bank (WB), World Development Report 1995 and past issues; UNDP, Human Development Report, 1995; WB, Social Indicators for Development, 1995 and past issues.

with many young children also characterizes poor households in the Philippines. In Thailand, rural poor households are not only large in size and with many young dependents but are also commonly headed by younger persons compared with the nonpoor. Family size, dependency and poverty will be discussed further in Section 5 on poverty and population growth.

The poor are lacking in assets, and even the only asset that they possess— human capital or labor power—is limited. The poor typically have low literacy, lower even in rural than in urban areas. Table 2 shows indicators of literacy and schooling during different periods for various countries in sub-Saharan Africa, Asia and Latin America. It is clear that, at the aggregate level, the poorer countries have had slower educational advancement over time than the better-off countries.

Very few literates among the poor have secondary or higher education (Asian Development Bank, 1992; Quibria, 1994a). In India, more than 70% of heads of poor households are illiterate and less than 3% of them have education above the secondary level. In Indonesia, net school enrollment rates are lower among the poor than among the nonpoor in all age groups, with the disparity increasing with the age of the child. In Bangladesh, Nepal, Pakistan and similar low income countries, rural poor households are also headed by individuals with low literacy or no formal education at all. In the Philippines, Thailand and other middle income developing countries, the poor also have lower educational attainment than the nonpoor, but the difference is smaller than in the lower income countries.

Rural poverty is typically concentrated in regions or provinces with low quality of land, inadequate water control, and limited integration into the market (Asian Development Bank, 1992; Quibria, 1994a). In China, following economic liberalization in 1978, agricultural growth picked up markedly with a consequent reduction in rural poverty. But in areas where land quality was poor, water control limited, and integration into labor and product markets circumscribed, poverty persisted. In India's Bihar state, poverty incidence is 50% higher than the national average and more than twelvefold that in the most prosperous state, Himachal Pradesh. In Pakistan, poverty incidence is higher in Punjab and Baluchistan than in the northwest Frontier Province and Sindh. In the Philippines, the poorest region, Bicol, has 70% more people below the poverty line than the national average, and more than threefold the national capital region's percentage of poor (Balisacan, 1995). In Indonesia, west Nusatenggara's poverty incidence is more than four times that of Jakarta (Tjondronegoro et al., 1994). In Thailand, poverty has traditionally been concentrated in the dry northeast region (Krongkaew et al., 1994). These pronounced interregional variations clearly suggest that a national development strategy must incorporate appropriate regional thrusts.

To the extent that the minority and ethnic groups have limited or no access to common resources and public services, they comprise a large proportion of the poor (Asian Development Bank, 1992; Quibria, 1994a). In India, the so-called scheduled castes and tribes represented more than one-third of the rural poor in 1983 although they accounted for less than one-eighth of the rural population. In many other countries minority ethnic groups usually have a higher poverty incidence than do other social groups or the population as a whole.

### 3.2. Urban poverty

Urban poverty is becoming increasingly prominent and poignant owing to accelerating urbanization and higher urban population growth rates. In the 1980s,

Asia experienced the fastest rate of urbanization among the developing regions: 2.7% yearly compared with average annual rates of 2% in Africa and 1% in Latin America (United Nations, 1992).[24] In the less economically dynamic developing countries, urban poverty incidence ranges from one-fourth to two-fifths, with signs of worsening in certain cases (Mills and Pernia, 1994). In some countries where urban poverty is officially reported to have diminished, visible deprivation is observed by independent analysts to have increased (Mathur, 1994). With inexorable urbanization in the years to come, urban poverty is likely to be a persistent national problem in developing countries.

Most of the characteristics of the rural poor apply, with some modifications, to the urban poor as well (Asian Development Bank, 1994; Pernia, 1994). The urban poor typically: (i) have limited access to resources and services; (ii) possess inadequate human capital; (iii) have large dependency burden; (iv) earn low wages; (v) are preponderant in unorganized and small-scale enterprises (SSEs); and (vi) belong disproportionately to disadvantaged subgroups, living in slum areas. As in the case of rural poverty, these characteristics are common throughout the developing world and across developing regions.

The urban poor usually have little or no physical earning asset. They have also limited access to social services, such as basic education, health and family planning (Gertler and Rahman, 1994). This easily explains why the urban poor have low human capital and measly earnings. Illiteracy continues to be commonplace in cities in Africa and in the poorer countries of Asia and Latin America. In India, for example, illiteracy rates are 20% for urban males and 45% for urban females, compared with 50% for rural males and 80% for rural females (Mathur, 1994). In general, the more education and better health an individual possesses, the better he or she is likely to fare in the labor market.

The incidence of urban poverty is highest in households with the largest dependency ratios (Mills and Pernia, 1994). A high dependency ratio is principally the result of having large numbers of children; additionally, it is due to the presence of many elderly people in the household. Often, the most disadvantaged urban residents are children, their mothers and grandparents in households in which there is no paid worker.

Most urban poor workers earn their income in SSEs. These activities constitute what is frequently referred to as the "urban informal sector". But such a terminology connotes a large gray area and it seems better to view urban labor markets as compromising more than just two categories. A five-way classification

---

[24] This refers to the annual rise in the proportion of the population that is urban, which is to be distinguished from the rate of increase in urban population; the latter is about two to three times the former.

Table 3
Health indicators in developing countries

| | Population per physician | | | Access to safe drinking water | | | | | | | | |
| | | | | Total | | | Urban | | | Rural | | |
| | 1960 | 1970 | 1988–1993 | 1970–1975 | 1980–1985 | 1988–1993 | 1970–1975 | 1980–1985 | 1988–1993 | 1970–1975 | 1980–1985 | 1988–1993 |
|---|---|---|---|---|---|---|---|---|---|---|---|---|
| Sub-Saharan Africa[a] | NA | 31720 | 18480[d] | NA | 25 | 41[b] | NA | 57 | 78[b] | NA | 18 | 27[b] |
| Burkina Faso | NA | 95690 | 57213 | 25 | 67 | 67 | 50 | 43 | 44 | 23 | 69 | 72 |
| Burundi | 98900 | 58570 | 17236 | NA | 26 | 38 | 77 | 98 | 100 | NA | 22 | 34 |
| Ethiopia | 100470 | 85690 | 30560 | 8 | 16 | 18 | 58 | 69 | 70 | 1 | 9 | 11 |
| Ghana | 21600 | 12910 | 23178 | 35 | 49 | 56 | 86 | 72 | 93 | 14 | 39 | 39 |
| Kenya | 10690 | 8000 | 9851 | 17 | 28 | 49[b] | 100 | 61 | NA | 4 | 21 | NA |
| Madagascar | 8900 | 10310 | 8733 | 25 | 21 | 21[b] | 76 | 81 | 62[b] | 14 | 9 | 10 |
| Mali | 35250 | 76580 | 50360 | NA | 53 | 51[b] | NA | 82 | 66[b] | NA | 50 | 49 |
| Niger | 64130 | 45320 | 21177 | NA | 16 | 48 | 29 | 46 | 100 | NA | 10 | 36 |
| Rwanda | 82170 | 60360 | 35141 | 27 | 49 | 59 | 36 | 48 | 100 | 26 | 49 | 52 |
| Uganda | 143290 | 60130 | 73796 | 67 | 61 | 64 | 81 | 79 | 66 | 66 | 60 | 64 |
| Tanzania | 15050 | 9210 | 21681 | 22 | 15 | 15 | 88 | 45 | 45 | 17 | 12 | 12 |
| Zambia | 18220 | 22900 | 24970[e] | 39 | 53 | 52 | 88 | 88 | 75 | 36 | 42 | 46 |
| | 9540 | 13640 | 11431 | 42 | 54 | 59 | 86 | 70 | 76 | 16 | 41 | 43 |
| East Asia[a] | NA | 5090 | 6202[d] | NA | 37 | 67 | NA | 55 | 84 | NA | 26 | 61 |
| China | 8390 | 1500 | 1063 | NA | NA | 71 | NA | NA | 87 | NA | NA | 68 |
| Indonesia | 46780 | 27440 | 7033 | 11 | 38 | 42 | 41 | 43 | 65 | 4 | 36 | 32 |
| Korea, Rep. of | 54140 | 2220 | 951 | 44 | 74 | 78 | 95 | 90 | 91 | 38 | 48 | 49 |
| Malaysia | 7020 | 4310 | 2414 | 34 | 80 | 78 | 100 | 96 | 96 | 6 | 71 | 66 |
| Lao PDR | 53520 | 15160 | 4447 | 41 | 21 | 28 | NA | 28 | 47 | NA | NA | 25 |
| Philippines | 6940 | 9270 | 8037 | 50 | 54 | 81 | 67 | 53 | 93 | 20 | 54 | 72 |
| Taiwan | NA | 2240 | 1323[e] | 44 | 67 | 85 | NA | NA | NA | NA | NA | NA |
| Thailand | 7900 | 8290 | 4421 | 25 | 67 | 72 | 69 | 56 | 57 | 16 | 70 | 85 |
| Viet Nam | NA | 4190 | 2298 | NA | 45 | 50 | NA | 70 | 70 | NA | 39 | 33 |

| | | | | | | | | | | | | |
|---|---|---|---|---|---|---|---|---|---|---|---|---|
| South Asia[a] | NA | 6120 | 3747[d] | NA | NA | 33 | 70 | NA | 71 | 74 | NA | 22 | 67 |
| Bangladesh | NA | 8450 | 5216 | 56 | 56 | 41 | 78 | 22 | 24 | 39 | 61 | 43 | 90 |
| India | 4850 | 4950 | 2446 | 31 | 31 | 56 | 75 | 80 | 76 | 79 | 18 | 50 | 73 |
| Nepal | 73470 | 52050 | 16106 | 8 | 8 | 28 | 37 | 85 | 71 | 62 | 5 | 25 | 38 |
| Pakistan | 5400 | 4670 | 2940[e] | 25 | 25 | 44 | 50 | 75 | 84 | 84 | 5 | 28 | 35 |
| Sri Lanka | 4490 | 5900 | 7140[c] | 19 | 19 | 40 | 60 | 36 | 82 | 80 | 13 | 29 | 55 |
| Latin America & the Caribbean | NA | 2020 | 1043[d] | NA | NA | 65 | 80 | NA | 78 | 90 | NA | 44 | 58 |
| Argentina | 740 | 530 | 330 | 66 | 66 | 56 | 64 | 76 | 63 | 73 | 26 | 17 | 17 |
| Bolivia | 3830 | 1970 | NA | 34 | 34 | 42 | 46 | 81 | 75 | 77 | 6 | 13 | 15 |
| Brazil | 2210 | 2030 | 670 | 55 | 55 | 75 | 96 | 87 | 85 | 100 | 28 | 53 | 86 |
| Chile | 1780 | 2160 | 2149 | 70 | 70 | 87 | 86 | 78 | 100 | 100 | 28 | 22 | 21 |
| Colombia | 2640 | 2260 | 1150 | 64 | 64 | 92 | 86[b] | 86 | 100 | 87[b] | 33 | 76 | 82[b] |
| Costa Rica | 2740 | 1620 | 1030 | 72 | 72 | 91 | 94 | 100 | 100 | 100 | 56 | 83 | 84 |
| Dominican Republic | 8220 | 2299 | 930 | 55 | 55 | 61 | 62 | 88 | 85 | 86 | 27 | 33 | 28 |
| Ecuador | 2670 | 2870 | 957 | 36 | 36 | 57 | 58 | 67 | 81 | 75 | 8 | 33 | 37 |
| El Salvador | 5330 | 4100 | 1560 | 53 | 53 | 50 | 41 | 89 | 76 | 76 | 28 | 40 | 10 |
| Guatemala | 4640 | 3660 | 2270 | 39 | 39 | 58 | 60 | 85 | 90 | 91 | 14 | 39 | 41 |
| Honduras | 12620 | 3720 | 2326 | 41 | 41 | 52 | 64[b] | 99 | 56 | 85[b] | 10 | 49 | 48[b] |
| Mexico | 1830 | 1480 | NA | 62 | 62 | 70 | 78 | 70 | 95 | 89 | 49 | 47 | 49 |
| Peru | 1910 | 1920 | 943 | 47 | 47 | 54 | 58 | 72 | 73 | 78 | 15 | 17 | 22 |
| Venezuela | 1500 | 1130 | 639 | 75 | 75 | 85 | 89 | 92 | 88 | 89 | 38 | 65 | 89 |

[a] Regional data are the weighted average of low- and middle-income countries in the region.
[b] Data are for the period 1987–1992.
[c] For 1981.
[d] For 1988–1991.
[e] For 1990.
NA data are not available.
Sources: WB, World Development Report 1995 and past issues; WB, Social Indicators for Development, 1995;
For Taiwan, Directorate General of Budget, Accounting and Statistics, Social Indicators in Taiwan Area of ROC, 1992.

has been proposed as follows: (i) self-employed; (ii) casual laborers hired by a sequence of employers on a daily contract; (iii) wage workers on longer contracts with SSEs; (iv) high-wage formal sector whose boundary is defined partly by enterprise size and partly by ownership; and (v) public sector where wages are administratively determined (Fields, 1990). Urban poor laborers fall under the first three categories.

Finally, as in the case of the rural poor, the urban poor are disproportionately represented among the disadvantaged subgroups, such as castes and ethnic groups (Asian Development Bank, 1994). Several of them are migrants from the most depressed rural areas. They reside in slums and squatter settlements lacking in basic services such as water and sanitation (Pernia and Alabastro, 1997), as can be gleaned from national data on various developing countries in Table 3. Since these settlements are typically illegal, they are not provided with health services or schools in the same manner as legal neighborhoods (Wegelin, 1994). In most cases, because of government plans to relocate squatters to permanent and legal sites, their settlements are not furnished with even the most basic services or amenities (Mills and Pernia, 1994). This situation may persist indefinitely if governments lack the wherewithal or the will to provide the permanent sites and services, or if the squatters resist being relocated. In many cases, shortly after squatters are relocated to designated legal settlements, they move back to the illegal sites after selling or subleasing the subsidized dwelling provided by the government.

In sum, poverty essentially connotes low earnings which are caused by the lack of ownership of, or access to, physical and human assets. In turn, this is attributable to unequal distribution of physical capital, such as land and basic infrastructure, and of opportunities for investment in human capital. Before discussing the link between economic growth and poverty, we look first at the issues of gender inequality and population growth in relation to poverty.

## 4. Gender and poverty[25]

Some concern has been expressed in recent years regarding "feminization" of poverty, i.e., whether, or not, women are overrepresented among the poor. While data limitations do not permit any unambiguous conclusion, some evidence from developing Asia suggests that there is no significant difference in incomes between male- and female-headed households (see, e.g., Balisacan, 1995, for the

---

[25] This section draws on Quibria (1995b).

Philippines and Krongkaew et al., 1994, for Thailand). There is also no evidence to suggest that females are overrepresented in poor households.

Nevertheless, several studies, particularly from India and Bangladesh, claim that intrahousehold consumption disparity exists between sexes while other studies find no such disparity.[26] A recent paper by Pitt et al. (1990), provides some evidence on discrimination in Bangladesh against females in the distribution of calories. They note, however, that when account is taken of marginal energy expenditures, men undertaking energy-intensive work suffer a "tax" that exceeds that on adult females, indicating some discrimination against males by the household.

There is no evidence of a gender bias in the relatively richer southeast and east Asian countries. Haddad and Kanbur (1990), who investigated the issue of intrahousehold disparity in food consumption and calorie intake in the Philippines, find no significant difference in the incidence of undernourishment among males and females, although the extent (depth) of undernourishment appears to be slightly higher for females. For Thailand and Côte d'Ivoire, Deaton (1989) made a similar investigation, adopting a different methodology based on inference from consumption expenditure rather than direct observation of intrahousehold allocation. He finds a *statistically insignificant* bias in favor of boys in Thailand. Deaton (1995) notes that subsequent studies, which adopt the Deaton- type methodology, by Subramaniam and Deaton in Maharastra (India), Rudd (Taiwan), Ahmed and Murdoch (Bangladesh), and Deaton (Pakistan), all tend to suggest the absence of any discrimination between sexes in household expenditure.

A related body of evidence exists on gender differences in child anthropometric status. The anthropometric status of a child partly reflects his or her food consumption status. Relevant studies on south Asia tend to find that boys enjoy superior anthropometric status, while those on other Asian countries do not confirm the existence of such differentiation between sexes.[27]

Food consumption and anthropometric status are strongly correlated with child mortality. While there is a significant differential in child mortality rates across developing countries, mortality rates for girls exceed those for boys in south Asia (except in Sri Lanka). Sen (1990) has dramatized these gender differences in mor-

---

[26] Studies which indicate such disparities include Agarwal (1986), Banerjee (1983), Behrman (1988a,b), Chen et al. (1981), Sen and Sengupta (1983), Sen (1988) and Taylor and Faruque (1983). Studies which find no such intrahousehold consumption disparity include Basu (1989, 1993), Behrman and Deolalikar (1990), Das Gupta (1987) and Harris (1990). It may be noted that the studies that claim to find gender disparities in intrahousehold consumption do not generally consider possible gender disparities in energy expenditures that might reverse the perceived direction of gender discrimination, as in Pitt et al. (1990).

[27] For a sample of these studies in Asian developing countries, see Senauer et al. (1988) for the Philippines, and Senauer et al. (1986) for Sri Lanka.

tality by arguing that "over 100 million women are missing" in Asia: if gender differences in mortality in Asia and north Africa were identical to those in sub-Saharan Africa, then there would be 100 million more women in the world than are reported today.[28] Sen argues that the bias against women in intrahousehold allocation accounts for a substantial part of this difference in mortality. This intrahousehold allocation encompasses a wide gamut of resources, including food consumption, medical care and other health inputs.

As in food allocation, similar inequities are said to exist between sexes in the availability of medical care.[29] However, Deolalikar (1991) notes that there is little gender bias—if any, it is toward girls—in health care in Indonesia. An indirect evidence of the inequity in health care between sexes is provided by the respective morbidity rates, but available evidence is sparse. Two notable studies in this respect—by Chen et al. (1981) and Deolalikar (1991)—seem to confirm a similar geographical pattern of gender disparity: females have higher morbidity in south Asia while there is no discernible difference in southeast Asia. In a recent study of health status and physical functioning, Strauss et al. (1993) found that women report more problems and at an earlier age than men, despite greater longevity of women; and that females suffer from a greater incidence of functional disabilities than males. While this is true for all ages in Jamaica, it is true for older people in Malaysia and Bangladesh.

Regarding educational attainment, Behrman and Schneider (1994) note widespread inequalities in Asian developing countries. The inequalities in expected years of schooling (given by a weighted average of enrollment rates for primary, secondary, and tertiary levels multiplied by the number of years required for completing the respective levels) are once again more acute in south Asia (ex-

---

[28] To arrive at serious quantitative estimates of "missing women", as Sen (1992: p. 124) has himself noted, requires "proper demographic models of births and deaths", with "clear speculation of the possible counterfactual scenarios". It has been argued that the simple Sen-type calculation, based on comparisons of the crude ratios of women to men in two populations, tends to exaggerate the number of missing women. Klasen (1994) has noted that Sen's estimate is to some extent dependent on the demographic peculiarity of African populations that have a considerably low ratio of males to females at birth. As Coale (1991) has argued, the expected sex-ratio in a nondiscriminating society is not a constant but varies with population growth and the sex-specific mortality pattern in such a population. He notes that in a rapidly growing population, the cohorts of young people far exceed older cohorts, and since males outnumber females by about five to 6% at birth, the male excess will cause the overall sex ratio to tilt in favor of males. Using the Model Tables "west", Coale arrives at a different estimate of 60 million missing women. As Klasen has shown, an alternative counterfactual assumption regarding the expected sex-ratio leads to a different estimate of missing women. He also shows that the application of the Model Life Tables "west" would imply that there is a problem of "missing men" in South Africa, the Indian state of Kerala, and to a lesser extent in sub-Saharan Africa. While the application of sophisticated demographic models may have improved the estimates, the wide divergences among estimates only prove that estimating "missing women" is still far from an exact science.

[29] See, for example, Chen et al. (1981); Kynch and Sen (1983); Taylor and Faruque (1983); Das Gupta (1987); Miller (1981); and Alderman and Gertler (1989).

cept in Sri Lanka) compared with southeast and east Asia. Similar disparities exist in terms of literacy, where men seem to be ahead of women in most developing countries. These disparities are more pronounced in poorer developing countries.[30]

An important policy issue in this regard is: how important are individual preferences, vis-á-vis public policies, in determining the gender gap in schooling attainment and cognitive achievement? If gender gaps reflect essentially individual preferences, then there is little that public policies can do to eliminate or reduce the gap. Recent studies by Alderman et al. (1992, 1993), however, indicate that the gender gap in cognitive achievement in rural Pakistan for the age group 20–25 was about 25% that of males for the same age group. For this age group, nearly 50% of the gender gap could have been reduced by eliminating the inequality in access to single-sex schools. In other words, a large part of the gender disparity reflects a bias in policy rather than individual preferences.

However, if one takes a broader perspective on individual well- being as being determined by economic and noneconomic factors, including one's level of participation in society, then disparity in terms of traditional poverty indicators, as discussed earlier, provides only a partial basis for judgment. In many developing countries, in addition to the disparities in economic indicators between men and women, there are social, cultural and psychological factors which limit women's full participation in societal activities.[31] For example, women often have limited access to employment opportunities, and there is often a considerable differentiation in the nature of jobs held by men and women. Women are generally engaged in inferior jobs—which are unskilled, have low security, and provide less opportunity for advancement.[32] Accordingly, the welfare level being enjoyed by women is likely to be lower than that enjoyed by men. Moreover, as is often suggested, women have to work longer hours as they engage in both wage and nonwage employment, the latter usually consisting of household chores. Ac-

---

[30] Although interesting, cross-country comparison in education is somewhat encumbered by serious data problems. For an in-depth discussion of the quality and reliability of cross-section data on education and labor force, see Behrman and Rosenzweig (1994). In view of the data gaps and the weak foundation that underpin these statistics, Behrman and Rosenzweig caution that the conclusions drawn about the "determinants or consequences of development (based on these data) can be seriously misleading".

[31] Despite substantial variations across countries, it is widely claimed that women suffer from a unique set of constraints, which impinge on important dimensions of human freedom. These constraints, it is claimed, stem partly from biological factors, but mostly from societal values and traditions that tend to constrict women's freedom in assuming their productive role. However, these claims are difficult to subject to any rigorous empirical testing.

[32] However, when limited to poor men and women, whether one can make such a differentiation is an open question.

cordingly, it is argued that women suffer from inequities in the consumption of leisure.

Labor market participation rates for women are generally less than those for men in developing countries. However, this does not imply that women enjoy more leisure and thereby greater welfare than men do. For poorer women, labor force participation entails increased work and reduced leisure but, at the same time, may confer higher self-esteem and greater control over one's destiny. Thus, whether increased labor force participation by women raises their welfare depends on the balance of the conflicting factors and their respective contributions to welfare. It is argued that despite the lower participation rate of women in the labor force, women—especially poor women—work longer and engage in more arduous work (Bardhan, 1993). Given these inequities in the allocation of leisure, women are relatively worse-off than men—in welfare terms—even if they are earning the same level of income.[33]

How does one explain gender differentials in earnings?[34] Women as well as men operate within the context of a number of market and nonmarket institutions besides the family. It is in this context that the differentials between men and women in endowments of assets and their returns have to be explained. The following discusses briefly the implications of gender for poverty in the context of these various institutions.

### 4.1. Access to land and employment

In many developing countries, women appear to be more disadvantaged than men in the land market. For example, among the poor in south Asia, the percentage of landless women is higher than that of landless men (Bardhan, 1993). This has much to do with inheritance laws of many of these countries where the male children inherit most of the family land, but may also reflect the bias in the working of the tenancy market. Female tenants are extremely rare compared to male tenants. The landlords rent out land to tenants who are considered to be adept at land cultivation, physically strong enough to carry out many arduous farm tasks, have good knowledge about details of farming, possess some farm implements, and have access to working capital (for purposes of cost sharing). Although many poor women perform arduous farm tasks, the general perception is that women

[33] An important point of Bardhan's (1993) paper is to argue that females from rural poor households participate in the labor force to a greater extent than their counterparts from the nonpoor households.

[34] Gender differentials in earnings have serious implications for female poverty, if the unit of analysis is the individual. However, if the unit of analysis is the family, and if the family remains intact and pools its resources, wage differentials between men and women have no direct implications for sex differentiation of poverty.

are not particularly suited to become tenants. Therefore, inheritance laws and the general perception of landlords tend to conspire toward excluding women from having access to agricultural land. However, when women have access to land, there is no evidence that they are discriminated against in the contract. The terms of contract are usually uniform across a particular village or locality, with little or no variation between tenants.

Many women, including poor landless women, are engaged in homestead agriculture. This includes vegetable and fish cultivation, poultry and livestock raising, tree plantation, and crop processing. Most poor women have a small homestead, although in the traditional social environments of poor developing countries, they are often more constrained, as compared with poor men, by lack of technical information, extension services, credit, and good seeds (Safilos-Rothschild, 1990; Bardhan, 1995).

Despite increasing participation, it is widely believed that females are generally more disadvantaged than males in labor markets. In many countries, females used to be assigned to specialized farm tasks; but women are increasingly making inroads into operations previously considered to be the exclusive domain of men. This segregation into different sectors of employment may have much to do with physiological and biological differentiation, differential skills and training, and the sociocultural environment of the country. Nevertheless, with economic development, the social environment is undergoing rapid changes in many developing countries.

Labor market discrimination takes many forms, including: wage discrimination—paying differential wages to equally productive workers; employment discrimination—hiring members of a favored group; occupational segregation—the assignment of members of different groups to different jobs; crowding—the confinement of less-favored groups to undesirable occupations; and statistical discrimination—selection of individuals for employment and training on the basis of attributes (such as gender) considered to be related to productivity.

Gender disparity in returns to labor has been the subject of a number of studies. A summary of studies that provides estimates of returns to schooling is given by Psacharopoulos (1988). As Behrman and Zhang (1994) note, these estimates do not necessarily indicate a one-way differential—in some cases, the estimates indicate no substantial disparity in the labor market returns to schooling, but in others they indicate substantial differences favoring either women or men. Behrman and Zhang conclude that, women, generally though not always, have received labor market returns in Asia at least of the same order of magnitude as have men.

A few studies have attempted to decompose the wage differential into differences due to observed human capital and wage discrimination. A study on Taiwan by Gannicott (1986) indicates a gender wage differential of 0.44, of which one third can be attributed to observed human capital and two-thirds to discrimination (i.e., the unexplained residual). While such studies are potentially interesting, as Behrman and Zhang (1994: p. 26) note, many of these suffer from a number of analytical problems that include

> inferring dynamic patterns from cross-sectional data, often mixing the effects on the value of time (the wage rate) with those on hours worked by using earnings, ignoring the impact of grade repetition and school dropout, and ignoring the possibility that individuals' background (e.g., abilities, motivations, habits and family connections) directly increases both their schooling and their labor market earnings, so that schooling in such studies partially represents the effects of unobserved background in addition to the effects of schooling itself.

Foster and Rosenzweig (1993a, b, 1994a, b), in a series of studies, investigate the issue of labor market discrimination in the rural casual labor markets in the Philippines, India and Pakistan. They find that there are significant wage differentials between sexes. Among workers with similar productivity, women are paid less than men because of the lack of information regarding true productivity and statistical discrimination. However, Foster and Rosenzweig do not find the existence of any gender discrimination. On the issue of whether occupational specialization by gender (e.g., the relative concentration of women in weeding) reflects employers' discrimination and monopsony power, they conclude that it reflects comparative advantage rather than gender discrimination (which does not contradict the existence of statistical discrimination).

## 4.2. Access to capital and other related inputs

To make a successful bid as an entrepreneur, one needs access to capital. Most poor women, like poor men, suffer from a lack of collateral, a deficiency common to households with no male members. Even if allowed equal access to formal sector credit, women are likely to be more constrained than men in taking advantage of this access because of the high transaction costs associated with borrowing. This high transaction cost of borrowing (e.g., having to commute to urban centers where formal sector banks are located) derives from the multiple roles women perform and the time constraint they encounter due to household responsibilities. As a consequence of lack of collateral and high transaction costs, women are often shut off from the low-interest formal financial institutions. Moreover, their lower educational attainment poses additional difficulties as most formal sector loans require complex processing of application papers. Furthermore, as compared to poor men, poor women have more limited access to information as well as social connections, an important asset in a traditional economic setting. There are other social, religious and institutional restrictions which also constrain female access. For instance, in many developing countries, particularly Muslim societies, for a female to apply for a bank loan, she needs to have the application cosigned by a male family member (father or husband).

The failure of formal financial institutions to reach the poor, especially the female poor, has led to the emergence of alternative modes of group-oriented financial intermediation. Group-based lending—the Grameen Bank in Bangladesh being the most successful example—has helped to circumvent the need for collateral and to decrease the risk of default and transaction costs by incorporating some form of joint liability and peer monitoring mechanisms (Khandker, 1996). The Grameen Bank, whose loan recovery rate has consistently been above 90%, has by the end of 1993 served 1.8 million borrowers of whom 94% were women, disbursing the equivalent of $311 million and mobilizing about $218 million in savings and deposits (Pitt and Khandker, 1994). Pitt and Khandker find that the credit program of the Grameen Bank, as well as other similar programs in Bangladesh, has contributed toward the reduction of poverty, measured in terms of food as well as consumption per capita, and has increased investment in human capital (in particular, children's school enrollment rate).

Gender bias regarding access to extension services in agriculture as well as other technical information facilities provided by the government has been widely noted (Baxter, 1986; Boserup, 1990; Saito and Spurling, 1991; Safilos-Roths-child, 1990). Besides cultural reasons, there are economic reasons for this gender bias. Schultz (1989) notes that governments often give priority to supporting cash crops for purposes of increasing exports and government revenue. And since these crops are often managed by males, Schultz argues, male farmers get high priority from government agents. In addition, mechanisms inherent in the system can help to perpetuate the existing biases. For example, in Indonesia, the spread of agricultural research results is through "lead farmers" who are expected to share their learning with other farmers (World Bank, 1992). Because few lead farmers are women, despite women's active role in agriculture, they are often excluded from direct access to extension services. As a result, women are more handicapped than men in entrepreneurial activities in agriculture, such as home gardening or cottage industries. Finally, in many developing countries, there are skill training programs, mainly for industrial and service sector activities, offered by governmental and nongovernmental organizations. However, poor women have limited opportunities to take advantage of these programs, sometimes because of the adverse social environment but often because of other household obligations.

## 5. Poverty and population growth[35]

In developing countries many parents are so poor that their fecundity is impaired owing to inadequate nutrition. The more general case, however, is that low income families are larger in size than high income ones, even allowing for higher mortality among the former. The natural consequence is a distribution of consumption that is worse than the distribution of family incomes (Boulier, 1977). There may be attenuating forces such as economies of scale in household consumption, additional work effort on the part of parents, and productive contribution of children net of their consumption needs.[36] But these countervailing effects of family size do not seem to be large and significant enough to matter (Cassen, 1976). Moreover, if small families are in a relatively better position to take advantage of such income-enhancing mechanisms as education and health investments, migration and labor-market mobility, large families would be in a relatively worse position.

The extended family system that is quite common among poor households especially in rural areas may work for or against better income distribution. If the arrangement enables a family to earn in excess of its requirements and thus accumulate physical or human capital, it can be better off. Otherwise, the family would be worse off, and this will be reflected in a further deterioration of income distribution.

The simple intergenerational effect of family size is via parents' income which is a key determinant of an individual's income. Since poor parents have more children than the rich, unequal distribution of income is transmitted intergenerationally by differential fertility (see also Potter, 1979). Cassen (1976: p. 811) adds:

> There are more complex intergenerational effects, such as those that operate through property inheritance if several children can inherit property, then those with more children will divide their property into smaller fractions;

---

[35] This section draws on Pernia (1982) and Deolalikar and Pernia (1993).

[36] It is also argued that the cost to parents of additional children are fairly low if adult equivalence scales are adopted in the computation of cost (Rodgers, 1984).

and if they have less property to start with, or worse, if their property is diminished by sale in their lifetimes while that of the rich increases by purchase, there will be a tendency for the distribution of property to become more unequal over time and therefore probably, the distribution of income also.

The pure demographic effect is also important. An increase in the proportion of low-earning young people, given an age-earning pattern, necessarily results in a higher measure of unequal income distribution (Sirageldin, 1975).

Population growth can also bring about significant changes in the functional distribution of income by raising rents and profits relative to wages. Such alterations in turn invariably worsen personal and household income distributions, given the preponderance of wage earners (Sirageldin, 1975; Boulier, 1977). Additionally, persistent excess labor supply over demand keeps wages from rising in absolute terms. Moreover, as land becomes scarce in agriculture, landowners become increasingly wealthy relative to those who merely provide labor. Through investment in physical and human capital, the wealthy are allowed further upward social mobility (Roumasset and Smith, 1981).

Figure 1 depicts in simple fashion the association between poverty incidence and population growth for a cross section of developing countries on which data are available. The population growth rates have been lagged to reduce the possibility of reverse causality in the relationship, namely, higher poverty incidence inducing faster population growth. The statistical relationship implies that a 1% increase in population growth is associated with a subsequent rise in poverty incidence of about 0.83%.

Recent evidence, as discussed, for example, by Ahlburg (1994), suggests that rapid population growth may influence poverty by affecting the correlates of poverty, such as low wages, lack of human capital, lack of income-earning assets such as land, loss of economic growth, and income inequality as discussed below. Ahlburg notes that there is scant evidence available on the direct impact of population growth on poverty. While many countries with growing populations have shown declining poverty incidence, in several others rapid population growth has made poverty reduction more difficult.

International cross-section data show a direct and strong correlation between the rate of population growth and the extent of income inequality (see, e.g., McNicoll, 1984; World Bank, 1984). This relationship holds with different datasets and model specifications, and persists even after controlling for such variables as level and growth rate of gross domestic product or GDP. The negative effect of population growth on the income shares of the poorest 30 or 40% of households,

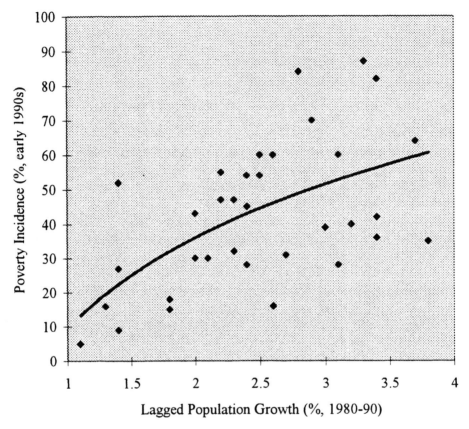

Fig. 1. Poverty incidence and population in developing countries.

in particular, is usually pronounced. Chenery et al. (1974), for example, find that a 1% increment to population growth rate is associated with a 1.6% fall in the income share of the poorest 40% of households. On the other hand, Rodgers (1983) concludes from a cross- sectional exercise that the effects of population growth on inequality are not so important. Nevertheless, a finding similar to that of Chenery et al. (1974) is reported by Ahluwalia (1976), showing, in addition, a positive relation between population growth and the income share of the richest quintile.

Using longitudinal district-level data on population, agricultural production, and infrastructure from north India, Evenson (1984) finds evidence of a worsening functional distribution of income with increasing population density. In districts where population density increased fastest, the poorest groups generally comprising the landless laborers experienced the largest decline in real incomes, while the richest groups, typically large land owners, experienced a sharp increase in the rents paid to them.

There is ample evidence showing that bigger households have larger household incomes but lower incomes per capita than smaller households (e.g., Kuznets, 1976; Lipton and de Haan, 1997). Poverty incidence tends to rise with family size and the evidence is that this relationship is monotonic. In the Philippines, for example, 1975 data showed that only 9% of one-person families were below the poverty line, but the proportion of poor was 34% for four-person families, 52% for six-person families, and 65% for 10-or-more person households (Pernia, 1982). On the whole, poverty incidence was below the average for up to five-member families and above the average for larger-size families. The effects of high fertility on poverty are also documented by village studies in Java (Penny and Singarimbun, 1973) and by an urban study for Kerala (Scott and Matthew, 1983). In rural areas these effects often operate through landlessness,[37] unemployment, and low output or wages, as shown by studies in India, Bangladesh, and the Philippines (Das Gupta, 1978; Arthur and McNicoll, 1978; Kikuchi and Hayami, 1980).

Recent studies in the Philippines and Thailand also show that households with many children are at great risk of being poor and that a high rate of child bearing restricts women's ability to participate in the labor market and contribute to household income (East–West Population Institute, 1993). Using longitudinal household survey data from India, Gaiha and Deolalikar (1993) find that not only are larger families likely to be poor at any given point in time, but they are also likely to experience chronic poverty (defined over nine years of longitudinal data). In other words, an important distinguishing characteristic of chronic poverty viz., households whose incomes fall below the poverty line continuously every year is large numbers of children. To the extent that some proportion of these children represent unwanted births, family planning programs that reduce the number of unwanted births can have a significant effect on the alleviation of chronic poverty.

The fact that large families are generally poor has obvious implications for family welfare. Household budget studies in developing countries typically show that the consumption basket tends to be heavily weighted by items that satisfy such basic human needs as food, clothing and shelter. For the average Filipino family, for example, about 78% of total expenditures are accounted for by these

---

[37] For example, in Bangladesh, landlessness increased from an estimated 7.3% of the farm labor force in 1951 to 26.1% in 1977. Real agricultural wages in the 1970s were allegedly below what they had been in the 1830s (Khan, 1984).

basic necessities, with food alone claiming half of the total (Cabañero, 1978). The food share is higher in rural than in urban areas, and is also larger the poorer and bigger is the household (Valenzona, 1976). Moreover, these studies suggest that a smaller number of children would raise the absolute consumption of a low income household. Thus, increases in household consumption and savings, including investment in human capital, are important opportunity costs of children (Mueller, 1972).

Notwithstanding arguments that high population growth or fertility can have favorable effects on poverty and income distribution (as when families try to cope with poverty by having many children), the empirical evidence on the adverse effects seems overwhelming (Deolalikar and Pernia, 1993). It is often argued that the poor have large families because they perceive the marginal benefit to exceed the marginal cost of an additional child. But such an advantage may be illusory and short-term at best. The fact more often is that, in the long run, families with many children save less and invest less in the human capital (i.e., education, health and nutrition) of their children. Thus, poverty tends to be transmitted intergenerationally. High fertility not only impoverishes a household in the present but significantly increases the likelihood of that household's children being in poverty as adults owing to their scant endowments of human capital, which is frequently the poor's only asset.

Because the poor typically have higher fertility and infant mortality rates than the nonpoor, government efforts at slowing population growth via reductions in both infant mortality and fertility disproportionately benefit the poor. Conversely, a weak population policy, or lack of a population-control strategy, hurts the poor more than the nonpoor. The experience of the more economically and demographically successful developing countries clearly suggests that a family planning program can be highly effective if it is supported or complemented by programs to lower infant/child mortality and promote female literacy and schooling, at least up to the lower secondary level (Deolalikar and Pernia, 1993; Cassen, 1994).

## 6. Poverty and economic growth

In a long-run context, economic growth performance is probably the most robust determinant of poverty trends.[38] Economic growth basically results from the adoption of new or nontraditional technology as well as physical and human

---

[38] There is a large literature on the relationship between economic growth and poverty alleviation. For an interesting discussion, see Bhagwati (1988).

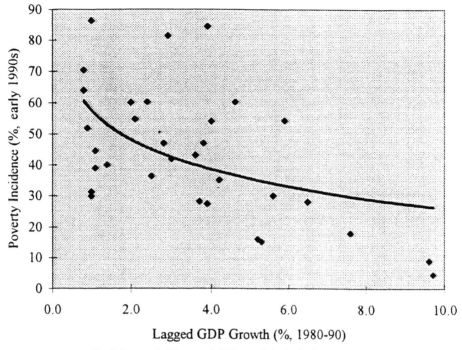

Fig. 2. Poverty incidence and GDP growth in developing countries.

capital accumulation, all of which generate employment opportunities and raise worker productivity and, consequently, earnings (Mills and Pernia, 1994). More-over, economic growth makes available public and private resources that can be used to improve institutions and essential services, particularly education and health care, which are all critically important for the functioning of economic systems and increasing worker productivity.

However, not all types of economic growth can lead to a reduction of poverty to the same degree (Fields, 1995). If the national pie is made bigger, not everyone will necessarily get a larger slice. What is crucial is the extent of participation of the poor in a growing economy. There are principally two mechanisms for such participation. One is improved earning opportunities, and the other is better social services. The latter serves to enhance not only well-being as such but also productivity and income.

The variations in intertemporal economic growth across the world's develop-ing regions, as well as across countries within those regions, explain to a large degree the differences in the extent and severity of poverty among developing

Table 4

Economic growth and poverty in developing regions

(a) Growth of real per capita income in industrial and developing countries, 1960–1991
(Average annual percentage change)

| Country Group | 1960–1970 | 1970–1980 | 1980–1990 | 1990 | 1991[a] |
|---|---|---|---|---|---|
| High-income countries | 4.1 | 2.4 | 2.4 | 2.1 | 0.7 |
| Developing countries | 3.3 | 3.0 | 1.2 | −0.2 | −0.2 |
| Sub-Saharan Africa | 0.6 | 0.9 | −0.9 | −2.0 | −1.0 |
| Asia and the Pacific | 2.5 | 3.1 | 5.1 | 3.9 | 4.2 |
| East Asia | 3.6 | 4.6 | 6.3 | 4.6 | 5.6 |
| South Asia | 1.4 | 1.1 | 3.1 | 2.6 | 1.5 |
| Middle East and North Africa | 6.0 | 3.1 | −2.5 | −1.9 | −4.6 |
| Latin America and the Caribbean | 2.5 | 3.1 | −0.5 | −2.4 | 0.6 |
| Europe | 4.9 | 4.4 | 1.2 | −3.8 | −8.6 |
| Eastern Europe | 5.2 | 5.4 | 0.9 | −8.3 | −14.2 |
| Developing countries weighted population | 3.9 | 3.7 | 2.2 | 1.7 | 2.2 |

(b) Headcount ratios and number of poor in developing countries

| Region | Percentage of population below the poverty line | | Number of poor (Millions) | |
|---|---|---|---|---|
| | 1985 | 1990 | 1985 | 1990 |
| All developing countries | 30.5 | 29.7 | 1,051 | 1,133 |
| South Asia | 51.8 | 49.0 | 532 | 562 |
| East Asia | 13.2 | 11.3 | 182 | 169 |
| Sub-Saharan Africa | 47.6 | 47.8 | 184 | 216 |
| Middle East and North Africa | 30.6 | 33.1 | 60 | 73 |
| Eastern Europe[b] | 7.1 | 7.1 | 5 | 5 |
| Latin America and the Caribbean | 22.4 | 25.5 | 87 | 108 |

Note: The poverty line used here—$370 annual income per capita in 1985 purchasing power parity dollars—is based on estimates of poverty lines from a number of countries with low average incomes. In 1990 prices, the poverty line would be approximately $420 annual income per capita. The estimates for 1985 have been updated from those in World Bank (1990) to incorporate new data and to ensure comparability across years.
[a] Estimates.
[b] Does not include the former USSR.
Source: World Bank (1992), Tables 1.1 and 1.2 (Poverty data based on Ravallion et al. (1992)).

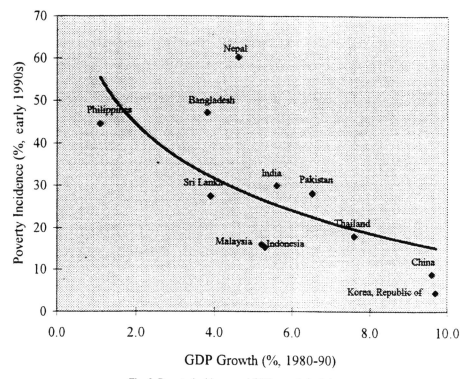

Fig. 3. Poverty incidence and GDP growth in Asia.

countries. The relationship between poverty and economic growth is illustrated in Fig. 2.[39]

In developing Asia, average annual growth in real GNP per capita kept on rising from the 1960s through to the 1980s (Table 4a). This sustained uptrend was especially remarkable in east Asia where real per capita income growth, which was 3.6% yearly in the 1960s, peaked to 6.3% in the 1980s. During the latter part of the 1980s alone, poverty incidence in east Asia was brought down from about 13 to 11% by 1990, with the number of poor people also reduced from 182 to 169 million (Table 4b). In south Asia, where GNP per capita was growing annually at slightly above 3% during the 1980s, poverty incidence dropped from about 52 to 49% in 1990, although the number of poor people rose from 532 to 562 million. By contrast, in sub-Saharan Africa where the growth of incomes per capita were already below 1% per annum in the 1960s and 1970s and turned negative in the

---

[39] As previously, economic growth rates have been instrumented by their lagged values to minimize the possibility of reverse causality. The statistical association has an implied point elasticity at the mean of −0.49.

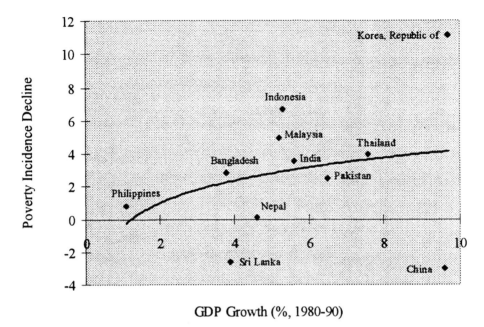

GDP Growth (%, 1980-90)

Fig. 4. Poverty incidence decline and GDP growth in Asia.

1980s, poverty incidence remained unchanged at about 48% during the 1980s and the number of poor increased markedly from 184 to 216 million. Similarly, in Latin America and the Caribbean, per capita incomes also contracted in the 1980s and both poverty incidence and the number of poor people increased significantly, from 22 to 26% and from 87 to 108 million, respectively.[40]

The important association between poverty and economic growth is exemplified more clearly by the experiences of developing countries in Asia, a region which has been the scene of dramatic economic and social transformations. As noted earlier, poverty incidence at a point in time is largely a reflection of previous economic growth performance. This is again illustrated quite clearly with data for several Asian developing countries in Fig. 3. Putting it differently, the rate of reduction in poverty is contemporaneously associated with GDP growth

---

[40] Psacharopoulos et al. (1995) report a similar increase in poverty in Latin America during the 1980s although their numbers are somewhat different from those reported here. The differences, however, are largely due to the differences in the poverty line. Despite the differences, what emerges clearly from their analysis is that there is a strong correlation between growth and poverty reduction. Psacharopoulos et al. note that economies that grew in the 1980s, for example, Colombia and Costa Rica, performed better with respect to poverty reduction and income inequality than those that stagnated. In particular, countries that failed to achieve macroeconomic stability such as Brazil and Peru experienced substantial increases in poverty.

over time, as shown in Fig. 4. This cross-country evidence is indirect, however, inasmuch as individual economies start the growth process at different points and follow different growth paths. For more direct evidence, one needs to examine individual countries. This indicates that economic growth reduces poverty most of the time, although not all the time (Fields, 1995).

There is compelling evidence from the experiences of such newly industrializing economies (NIEs) as Korea and Taiwan and such upcoming NIEs as Malaysia, Indonesia and Thailand that economic growth leads to poverty decline. In these countries poverty incidence has been cut to half or even less in 10–15 years (Table 5). In the Republic of Korea and Taiwan poverty incidence is reported to be below 5%. In Malaysia, Indonesia and Thailand where rapid economic growth has been more recent than in the NIEs, poverty incidence ranges from 15 to 20%. In countries with relatively poor-to-modest economic performance, such as south Asian countries and the Philippines, poverty reduction has been correspondingly slow and somewhat unclear. Poverty incidence in these countries remains at 30–45%. In some cases, the number of poor people, if not the incidence itself, appears to be on the rise.

Economic growth in the NIEs and near-NIEs has not only been rapid and sustained but, more importantly, it has been broad-based and pervasive, that is, reaching the poor as workers and as consumers (World Bank, 1993). Because growth in these economies has been labor-intensive, many job opportunities have been created leading to full or near-full employment and, consequently, rising real earnings. Moreover, a part of the increase in national incomes has been utilized to improve the access of the poor to social services. Since consumption by the poor of these services (education, health, and family planning) is also simultaneously an investment in their human capital, the quality and productivity of their labor have been enhanced.

The development strategy of these successful Asian developing countries basically pursued agricultural development and industrialization policies based on market incentives and outward orientation. The association between outward orientation and sustained economic growth alongside poverty reduction is not accidental (Quibria and Srinivasan, 1993). Sustained economic growth is feasible for a developing country with a limited domestic market only if opportunities in international markets are effectively exploited. A developing country with surplus labor and scarce capital will naturally have a comparative advantage in activities that are labor intensive. Accordingly, a strategy of promoting export-oriented, labor-intensive industries not only ensures sustained growth but also alleviates poverty in both rural and urban areas. Furthermore, an outward oriented,

Table 5

Estimates of poverty incidence in developing countries

People in poverty (head count) (percentage and number)

| | Earlier year/s | Total (%) | Total No. ('000) | Rural (%) | Rural No. ('000) | Urban (%) | Urban No. ('000) | Latest year/s | Total (%) | Total No. ('000) | Rural (%) | Rural No. ('000) | Urban (%) | Urban No. ('000) |
|---|---|---|---|---|---|---|---|---|---|---|---|---|---|---|
| Sub-Saharan Africa | 1977–1987 | 48 | 184392 | 61 | 120085 | 34 | 64308 | 1980–1990 | 54 | 227810 | 65 | 203775 | 23 | 24035 |
| Burundi | 1977–1987 | 84 | 3629 | 85 | 3582 | 55 | 47 | 1992 | 84 | 4900 | 86 | 4700 | 57 | 200 |
| Chad | 1977–1987 | 51 | 2349 | 56 | 2087 | 30 | 262 | 1992 | 54 | 3200 | 56 | 2200 | 51 | 1000 |
| Ethiopia | 1973 | 65 | 16906 | 65 | 15491 | 60 | 1414 | 1992 | 60 | 31900 | 63 | 29300 | 38 | 2600 |
| Ghana | 1977–1987 | 45 | 5507 | 37 | 2844 | 59 | 2663 | 1992 | 42 | 6700 | 54 | 5600 | 20 | 1100 |
| Kenya | 1977–1987 | 48 | 8733 | 55 | 8462 | 10 | 272 | 1990 | 35 | 8661 | 41 | 7527 | 20 | 1134 |
| Madagascar | 1977–1987 | 50 | 4600 | 50 | 3680 | 50 | 920 | 1990 | 39 | 4340 | 37 | 3108 | 44 | 1232 |
| Malawi | 1977–1987 | 79 | 5135 | 85 | 4973 | 25 | 163 | 1992 | 82 | 8400 | 90 | 8200 | 16 | 200 |
| Mali | 1973 | 40 | 2424 | 48 | 2221 | 27 | 203 | 1992 | 54 | 5300 | 60 | 4400 | 37 | 900 |
| Niger | 1973 | NA | NA | 35 | 135 | NA | NA | 1992 | 77 | 2300 | 95 | 2300 | NA | NA |
| Nigeria | 1973 | NA | NA | 90 | 12839 | NA | NA | 1992 | 40 | 46400 | 51 | 37200 | 21 | 9200 |
| Rwanda | 1973 | 88 | 3537 | 90 | 3501 | 30 | 36 | 1992 | 87 | 6490 | 91 | 6400 | 20 | 90 |
| Somalia | 1977–1987 | 50 | 2232 | 40 | 1224 | 70 | 1008 | 1992 | 60 | 5600 | 71 | 4300 | 40 | 1300 |
| Sudan | 1977–1987 | NA | NA | 85 | 13221 | NA | NA | 1992 | NA | NA | 85 | 17500 | NA | NA |
| Zambia | 1978 | NA | NA | NA | NA | 25 | 504 | 1992 | 64 | 5500 | 80 | 4000 | 42 | 1500 |
| East Asia | | | | | | | | | | | | | | |
| China[a] | 1985 | NA | NA | 10 | 79200 | NA | NA | 1992 | 9 | 105000 | 12 | 105000 | NA | NA |
| Indonesia | 1976 | 40 | 54200 | 40 | 44200 | 39 | 10000 | 1990 | 15 | 27200 | 14 | 17800 | 17 | 9400 |
| Korea, Rep. of | 1970 | 23 | 7544 | 28 | 5439 | 16 | 2105 | 1984 | 5 | 1818 | 4 | 602 | 5 | 1216 |
| Malaysia | 1970 | 49 | 5280 | 59 | 4655 | 21 | 625 | 1992 | 16 | 3000 | 22 | 2300 | 8 | 700 |
| Philippines | 1971 | 52 | 19764 | 58 | 14816 | 41 | 4948 | 1991 | 45 | 28039 | 51 | 18072 | 37 | 9967 |
| Thailand | 1975–1976 | 32 | 13360 | 36 | 11760 | 18 | 1600 | 1990 | 18 | 10100 | 21 | 8400 | 10 | 1700 |
| Viet Nam | | NA | NA | NA | NA | NA | NA | 1992 | 54 | 37600 | 60 | 33400 | 30 | 4200 |

| | | | | | | | | | | | | | | |
|---|---|---|---|---|---|---|---|---|---|---|---|---|---|---|
| South Asia | | | | | | | | | | | | | | |
| Bangladesh | 1973–1974 | 73 | 55675 | 74 | 51260 | 63 | 4415 | 1988–1989 | 47 | 48483 | 44 | 42135 | 33 | 6348 |
| India | 1972–1973 | 52 | 291550 | 54 | 244220 | 41 | 47330 | 1987–1988 | 30 | 237670 | 33 | 195970 | 20 | 41700 |
| Nepal | 1979 | 61 | 8498 | 61 | 8113 | 55 | 385 | 1992 | 60 | 12400 | 61 | 11100 | 53 | 1300 |
| Pakistan | 1973–1977 | 43 | 19831 | 43 | 14764 | 42 | 5067 | 1992 | 28 | 35000 | 29 | 24300 | 26 | 10700 |
| Sri Lanka | 1978–1989 | 22 | 3306 | 23 | 2686 | 19 | 620 | 1986–1987 | 27 | 4414 | 31 | 3996 | 12 | 418 |
| Latin America & the Caribbean[b] | 1970 | 40 | NA | 62 | NA | 26 | NA | 1990 | 46 | 194199 | 61 | 70025 | 39 | 124174 |
| Argentina | 1970 | 8 | NA | 19 | NA | 5 | NA | 1992 | 16 | 5200 | 21 | 900 | 17 | 4300 |
| Bolivia | 1973 | NA | NA | 85 | 1627 | NA | NA | 1992 | 60 | 4500 | 86 | 3100 | 36 | 1400 |
| Brazil | 1970 | 49 | NA | 73 | NA | 35 | NA | 1992 | 47 | 72400 | 73 | 25900 | 39 | 46500 |
| Chile | 1970 | 17 | NA | 25 | NA | 12 | NA | 1992 | NA | NA | 25 | 500 | NA | NA |
| Colombia | 1973 | 45 | 10026 | 54 | 5187 | 38 | 4839 | 1992 | 43 | 14400 | 45 | 4400 | 42 | 10000 |
| Costa Rica | 1970 | 24 | NA | 30 | NA | 15 | NA | 1992 | 28 | 900 | 36 | 600 | 20 | 300 |
| Dominican Republic | 1977–1987 | 44 | 2511 | 43 | 1152 | 45 | 1359 | 1992 | 55 | 4100 | 70 | 2000 | 45 | 2100 |
| El Salvador | 1977–1987 | 27 | 1375 | 32 | 947 | 20 | 428 | 1992 | 52 | 2800 | 74 | 2200 | 25 | 600 |
| Guatemala | 1977–1987 | 71 | 5452 | 74 | 3419 | 66 | 2033 | 1992 | 70 | 6900 | 73 | 4300 | 66 | 2600 |
| Haiti | 1977–1987 | 76 | 3957 | 80 | 3078 | 65 | 879 | 1992 | 75 | 5100 | 80 | 3800 | 64 | 1300 |
| Honduras | 1970 | 65 | NA | 75 | NA | 40 | NA | 1992 | 36 | 2000 | 56 | 1700 | 12 | 300 |
| Mexico | 1970 | 34 | NA | 49 | NA | 20 | NA | 1992 | 30 | 26400 | 51 | 11700 | 23 | 14700 |
| Peru | 1970 | 50 | NA | 68 | NA | 28 | NA | 1992 | 32 | 7200 | 75 | 4900 | 14 | 2300 |
| Venezuela | 1970 | 25 | NA | 36 | NA | 20 | NA | 1992 | 31 | 6300 | 61 | 1100 | 32 | 5200 |

[a] Based on income rather than expenditure.

[b] 1970 data for Latin America and the Caribbean refer to per cent of households.

NA: data are not available.

Sources: UNDP, Human Development Report, 1994 and past issues; WB, Social Indicators of Development, 1994 and past issues. For 1970 data for Latin American countries see Altimir (1982).

liberal economic policy environment also encourages the inflow of foreign direct investment in industries that are typically labor intensive and export oriented.

The economic growth policy of the dynamic Asian developing countries has been complemented by a sound social investment policy, particularly in the areas of education, health and family planning, with favorable consequences for the quantity and quality of human capital and overall economic productivity. It is also important to note that such social investment has enhanced the status and productivity of women at home and in the labor market. Moreover, better educated, healthier and more productive women have tended to have fewer and higher quality children, further improving prospects for succeeding generations. Thus, economic growth and human resource development leading to poverty reduction have been promoted in a mutually reinforcing manner, a process aptly referred to as a "virtuous circle" (World Bank, 1990).

Direct poverty alleviation or social safety net programs have been necessary in many countries, especially in certain sectors where chronic poverty exists or in periods of adjustment and transition with the implementation of economic policy reforms. As will be discussed below, these programs have typically involved significant budgetary spending which would have been difficult without rapid economic growth, and probably feasible only with foreign aid or borrowings.

In sum, economic growth that is outward oriented and labor intensive is likely to be also sustained, rapid and broad-based and, hence, poverty reducing. In addition, such growth provides the wherewithal for improved social services and investment in human capital, not to mention direct poverty alleviation programs. This has been the path taken by the Asian NIEs and near-NIEs. Conversely, economic growth that is inward oriented and capital intensive tends to be erratic and weak, with the benefits being captured by the upper income segments of society and limited trickle-down to low income groups. This has been the experience of most of the other Asian developing economies, at least up until the early 1990s. By and large, this conclusion is applicable to the growth and poverty experience of many African and Latin American countries.

## 7. Strategies and policies

In considering policies and strategies toward reducing poverty, it is important to distinguish between two types of poverty: *transient* poverty and *chronic* poverty. Poverty can be a transitory phenomenon as the poor today may become nonpoor tomorrow. Transient poverty can occur for many reasons. Income may be temporarily reduced due to ill-health, unemployment, a wage cut or a bad harvest.

Families may split up, leaving one parent with inadequate income. A sizable number of the poor show upward mobility to the ranks of the nonpoor (this does not mean that this poverty is not a matter of concern but that these people are not part of a permanent "under class").

Such mobility requires careful interpretation. It may arise in connection with the life cycle.[41] If lifetime income is above the poverty level, there is no lifetime poverty for this individual. If the capital market is perfect and if the individual can borrow against future income at a constant interest rate, then he or she can maintain a constant consumption. In this case, by using a consumption-based poverty line, it can be concluded that there is no lifetime poverty. However, if an income-based poverty line is used, there would be an indication of poverty. If capital markets are imperfect (credits are rationed at a fixed interest rate), the individual will not be able to rise above the poverty line. Similarly, the lack of a perfect insurance market may lead to temporary poverty.

Without perfect capital and insurance markets, some people who may be nonpoor on a lifetime basis may face transient poverty. Those who suffer from transient poverty may be helped by transfer and other programs or perhaps by public interventions to remove the relevant market imperfections. But those who are under chronic poverty, either because of lack of assets or lack of employable skills, will not be helped by the possible remedies of market imperfections. They cannot be helped by mere income transfers: they will need more assets, possibly made available through a program of asset redistribution. In an agrarian setting, this may involve a more egalitarian distribution of land, but implementation of land reform programs is fraught with many practical difficulties, as discussed below.

One of the most lively debates about the causes and cures of poverty has focused on the relationship between economic growth and poverty alleviation, which has been discussed earlier. The so-called "trickle-down" view argues that rapid economic growth is both a necessary and sufficient condition for poverty reduction. An opposing view, often referred to as the "basic needs approach", argues that while growth may be necessary, it is by itself insufficient and there is a need for some intervention in favor of the poor.[42] The distinction between chronic and transient poverty can shed some further light on this matter. As far

---

[41] Rowntree (1901) finds that the life of a laborer is marked by five alternating periods of want and comparative plenty, the periods of want being childhood, when he himself had children, and old age.

[42] There is yet another view which argues that the relationship between provision of basic needs and growth need not necessarily be competitive but can be complementary. According to this view, considerations of optimal growth entail some measure of balance between growth and basic needs. See, for example, Quibria (1982).

as transient poverty is concerned, fast growth and economic dynamism can help, but do not have any direct bearing on the problem. As far as chronic poverty is concerned, rapid growth and economic dynamism can help in the long run but require direct intervention in the form of asset transfers as well as investment in human capital formation through education and training.

It is widely agreed now that economywide and sector strategies and policies have significant impacts on levels and trends of poverty, often much greater than the effects of special programs directed at poverty alleviation per se (Quibria and Srinivasan, 1993). These policies include macroeconomic policies (fiscal and monetary), foreign trade and exchange rate policies, sector policies and various income and asset transfer policies.

## 7.1. Macroeconomic policies

There are two types of macroeconomic policies for developing countries: (i) *stabilization* policies that are meant to return the economy to an equilibrium growth path from which it has deviated due to shocks; and (ii) *adjustment* policies that attempt to change the current path of the economy to a new equilibrium path. The two types of policies often use the same instruments such as currency devaluation and fiscal contraction. Sometimes the two types of objectives are intermingled; sometimes adjustment programs are preceded by stabilization programs (Behrman, 1993).

Macroeconomic policies affect the real incomes of the poor, primarily through their impact on the returns to their assets—principally labor, on the prices they face with respect to the goods and services they produce and sell as well as those they buy, and on the transfer incomes they receive. An adjustment program which often relies on devaluation of the domestic currency is likely to increase the price of tradables and decrease the price of nontradables. If the tradable sector is more labor intensive than the nontradable sector, the real wage will rise and the poor whose asset is labor is likely to benefit from such an increase (Behrman, 1993). However, a priori theorizing about the signs and the magnitudes of these effects may be mere speculation. In the final analysis, the issue of the relation between macroeconomic policy and poverty is essentially an empirical one.

However, it is extremely difficult empirically to isolate the impact of macroeconomic policies on poverty. It is expected that during adjustment, economic growth slows down, which in turn exacerbates the poverty problem in the short run; however, in the longer term as economic growth gathers momentum, the poor are likely to be more than compensated for their short-run losses. Nevertheless, while one can expect a dynamic tradeoff between adjustment and poverty, this is far from empirically established.

Distributional changes can also influence the final outcome in this regard. A favorable distributional shift in Indonesia and an unfavorable distributional shift in the Philippines reduced poverty in the former and increased it in the latter (Balisacan, 1995; Ravallion and Huppi, 1991). However, these distributional impacts of adjustment are largely dependent on labor market flexibility, trade and investment regimes, and other economic and social conditions.

Similarly, poverty outcomes also depend on the degree and composition of public expenditure reduction. If public expenditure reduction translates into heavy reduction of social sector spending, it is likely to affect the poor adversely in both the short and long run. However, if the expenditure reduction is accompanied by increasing social sector spending, as has happened in some countries, the adverse effect of slower short-run growth can be more than offset by the prospects of longer-term gains for the poor.

Behrman (1993) reviews the evidence from a cross-country statistical analysis of various indicators of living conditions (in particular, labor and social indicators) in developing countries and how changes in them have been associated with participation in international organization-supported adjustment programs. The cross-country evidence suggests that reduction of economywide distortions, such as overvalued exchange rates and industrial protection, improved the prices of agricultural exportables while only marginally affecting the prices of importables. The short-run supply response was fairly small. However, the adjustment programs had little impact on labor markets and social sectors. There was some evidence that there were some *positive* effects on rural income growth and *negative* effects on longer-run human capital investments. These results are somewhat less deleterious than those often claimed by many skeptics of adjustment programs.

Behrman (1993) also provides an in-depth analysis of three country studies. The Indonesian study indicates that the country experienced a substantial decrease in poverty during 1984–1987 when it undertook a major adjustment program. The poverty reduction that took place reflected in part increased prices for exportable cash crops, and in part increased government support in terms of policies that augmented the consumption of the poor during the adjustment. Finally, Indonesia had rapid growth for two decades before adjustment and investments made during those two decades also paid off during the adjustment.

The Jamaican experience of the mid-1980s suggests very little evidence of the short-run negative effects of adjustment programs on the income and human resources of the poor. The analysis of the Côte d'Ivoire adjustment program in the early 1980s contrasts sharply with that of Indonesia in that poverty is estimated to have risen faster than the rate of fall of mean real per capita income. This suggests a combination of negative growth and more unequal income distribution. Although Côte d'Ivoire had also experienced rapid growth in the 1960s and much of the 1970s, substantial declines in the world prices of its major exports in the late 1970s precipitated the adjustment. The poverty situation was aggravated by the withdrawal of the support prices for exportables grown by the poor farmers.

Finally, it may be noted that structural adjustment policies have received unfavorable reviews from many poverty analysts. A number of studies that claim to show the negative effects of adjustment on poverty (e.g., Cornia et al., 1987) are based on erroneous and simplistic comparisons of poverty indicators "before" and "after" adjustment. If the adjustment is intended to correct a potentially unsustainable situation, then the relevant comparison is between the actual after-adjustment paths of the poverty indicators and the counterfactual paths had there been no adjustment (Srinivasan, 1993). To undertake such an analysis, one requires some manipulation of applied general equilibrium models (see, e.g., Bourguignon et al., 1991, 1992). However, the construction of a counterfactual scenario is dependent on the structure of the model and on the various parameters assumed for the model. While an applied general equilibrium model may be conceptually the ideal tool to explore these issues, it falls short of the ideal in actual applications.[43]

## 7.2. Trade and industrialization policies

The importance of an appropriate trade and industrialization policy in achieving rapid growth and reducing poverty can hardly be overemphasized. In the past, governments in many developing countries adopted a strategy of import substitution and industrialization which entailed adoption of high tariffs; quantitative restrictions and overvalued exchange rates on the one hand; and subsidized credit, electricity, water and other public inputs on the other. This strategy, which was often undertaken to accelerate industrialization and to reduce poverty, more often than not failed to achieve either of the objectives.

---

[43] Some of the problems associated with applied general equilibrium models in this regard were succinctly expressed by Srinivasan (1992: p. 24): "Unfortunately, the models involve many other parameters, and relatively few of the parameters used in the model are derived from econometric analysis of the data from the country being modeled. Besides a pure Walrasian AGE model does not incorporate the fundamental monetary and financial variables of the macroeconomics of stabilization and structural adjustment policies. Eclectic models that combine macroeconomics with Walrasian microeconomics ... appear promising for distributional analysis. However, it is essential, though not simple, to incorporate the "political-economy" of structural adjustment and stabilization in a credible way in such models".

A critical element of trade and industrial policies of the more dynamic developing economies has been that policies did not penalize the traded goods sector. Market forces had to a large extent been allowed to determine the real exchange rate and lead to an efficient allocation of resources. Endowed with abundant labor resources, the Asian NIEs, and later their southeast Asian neighbors, emphasized production and exports of low value- added, labor-intensive manufacturing goods. Their success in exports of labor-intensive manufacturing led to a dramatic reduction in poverty in these countries. Subsequently, however, as labor costs rose, these economies responded by moving up the export product hierarchy.

There are a number of possible routes through which a liberal trading environment contributes to an efficient allocation of resources and rapid growth. In removing barriers to market entry, trade liberalization is a powerful antidote to rent seeking and monopoly. By encouraging greater competition and a more efficient allocation of resources, trade liberalization increases output, investment and employment in sectors where a high degree of competition already exists. Further, trade liberalization creates the opportunity for further specialization and the exploitation of economies of scale where such economies exist. All these contribute to economic growth and poverty reduction.

A strategy of import substitution, based on high tariffs, quantitative restrictions and over-valued exchange rates, often creates an inefficient industrial structure, characterized by a high degree of monopoly and a narrow ownership structure. Without sufficient internal or external competition, this type of industrial structure is conducive neither to growth nor to domestic capital accumulation. It is also true that, on balance, long-term capital, especially in the form of foreign direct investment, is unlikely to be attracted to economies in which there is an array of trading and associated bureaucratic restrictions and regulations. It is no coincidence that economies in southeast Asia that have comparatively liberal trading regimes have demonstrated significant successes in attracting foreign direct investment that contributed in significant ways to the growth and poverty-reduction performance of these countries. Moreover, to the extent that technological progress is embodied in new capital goods produced abroad, growth will be impeded by protectionist regimes that tax or otherwise raise the cost of foreign direct investment or technology licensing.

In sum, trade and industrialization policies of the successful developing economies, in particular those in Asia, were such that they introduced a regime of internal and external competition for these economies, a neutral incentive structure that did not penalize exports, and a conducive economic environment where savings and investment (including foreign) flourished. All these helped to generate not only a high rate of income growth but also a high rate of employment growth that helped to foster a dramatic reduction in poverty.

## 7.3. Land reform[44]

Land reform is often advocated as an effective antidote to poverty. The term *land reform* has been used in many different senses, but in the following it is defined to encompass both land distribution and tenancy reform. The former implies distribution of land from households with holdings higher than a stipulated upper limit to households owning little or no land; the latter entails changing the terms and conditions defining the tenancy contract.

Tenancy legislation appears to have no sound theoretical or empirical basis. Share tenants, who comprise the great majority of agricultural tenants, work hard, maintain the land, and adopt new practices quickly. When laws make tenancy illegal, as the Asian experience indicates, the landlord is found to use wage laborers and this leads to a less efficient arrangement. It is therefore argued that tenancy regulations should be eliminated to allow a wider range of contractual choices and to induce larger farms to lease out more land to the landless (Otsuka, 1993).

To make the tenancy option attractive to the larger landowners and to ensure economic success for the tenants, the latter should be given public support in the form of easy access to capital and technical know-how on farm operation and management. It is argued that rather than suppressing the tenancy market, as many reforms have attempted to do, efforts should be made to make it function efficiently, as a well-functioning tenancy market can contribute to both the equity and efficiency of the rural economy. In particular, tenancy deregulation is expected to open up for the landless tenants the agricultural ladder out of poverty.

As regards redistributive land reform, there is a sound rationale underlying such a policy. First, there is no evidence of significant economies of scale in agriculture; therefore, there can be no general presumption against small farms. For the rice economies of developing countries, the skill-intensive and scale-neutral nature of rice cultivation makes the case for land redistribution even stronger. Second while small farms are at a disadvantage in perceiving and adopting new technology, this difference is not particularly significant empirically. Indeed, the receptiveness of small farmers to extension services dilutes most objections to small farms. Finally the fragmented and oligopolistic nature of the land market in most developing countries further strengthens the case for land reform. In this connection, it has been noted that land reform can affect the local political structure, as it gives "voice" to the poor who are induced to participate in the local

---

[44] This subsection draws on Rashid and Quibria (1995).

government institutions and in the management of local public goods (Bardhan, 1996).

Land reform, which improves distributional equity, appears to have many strong arguments in its favor on grounds of efficiency. The traditional arguments—such as the efficiency wage argument, (in terms of better health and a more effective labor force) and the labor-absorption argument (in terms of the greater labor intensity of small farms)—appear to be well founded. And while the impact of land reform on gender equity or on the environment are uncertain, there is no presumption against land reform on these grounds. On balance, land reform can have a salutary impact on poverty alleviation by promoting social equity.

Despite its putative benefits, land reform has been far from universally adopted. The Asian experience provides a simple answer to this apparent paradox. In Taiwan, land reform was conducted efficiently by an alien military power— a precedent that carries no force for democratic regimes. In the Republic of Korea, land reform was instigated by a military government and succeeded in bankrupting the landlord class. No agricultural surplus was generated to help toward industrialization, and the Republic of Korea's industrial success came over a decade later owing to seemingly unrelated circumstances. In Thailand, land reform has affected marginal farmers, yet the economy has grown rapidly. In Indonesia, no land reform at all has taken place and yet the economy has performed well. The above indicates that land reform is neither necessary nor sufficient for success in economic development or poverty alleviation. In addition, land reform is difficult to implement in democratic societies where landlords tend to exert more political power than tenants and landless farmers.

Finally, in most agrarian societies especially in Asia, while there may exist a marked inequality in terms of land ownerships, there is much less inequality in terms of operational holdings (Otsuka, 1993). This fact tends to weaken much of the equity argument in favor of land reform. Moreover, in many poor countries (such as Bangladesh), the large size of the population makes further redistribution economically infeasible. In these countries, the main plank of antipoverty policy in rural areas needs to be based on enhancing land productivity through new seed-fertilizer and irrigation innovations, and not through further redistribution.

## 7.4. Infrastructure

Infrastructure is the essential underpinning for development. In particular, it contributes in important ways to both economic growth and poverty reduction. Human and physical infrastructure services exert direct and positive impacts on the productivity of the factors of production, namely, land, labor, capital and technology (Jimenez, 1992; World Bank, 1994). In addition, both infrastructure services provide consumption utility that directly enhances well-being and raises living standards.

### 7.4.1. Human infrastructure

The literature on the link between human capital investment and productivity focuses on the effect of education on earnings. Rates of return to education are consistently shown to be superior to rates of return to investment in other physical sectors (Psacharopoulos, 1985). Studies also indicate that returns to education are highest for primary education in which the poor participate to a large extent. These results, however, have been subject to criticism on econometric grounds besides the issue of screening or credentialism. Nonetheless, these findings have generally been accepted and have guided education policy in many developing countries.

Education has other salutary effects as well. It makes workers more favorably disposed to innovation and adaptable to new ways of doing things. More educated farmers, for example, are found to be more productive (Jamison and Lau, 1982). Outside the sphere of the market, better educated mothers are likely to have fewer and healthier children (Cochrane, 1979; Behrman, 1990), besides being more efficient in home production.

Although not as well analyzed, the impacts of health and nutrition on productivity, particularly in the types of activities in which the poor are involved, are also positive and significant (Jimenez, 1992; Strauss and Thomas, 1995). Some studies suggest that the causation runs from education to nutrition, health and family planning, and then to productivity, as education improves understanding of the need for hygiene, proper nutrition and health care (Cochrane et al., 1980). At the same time, better nutrition and health also enhances the capacity to learn. Because of the interactive links among education, nutrition, health and family planning, the net effects on productivity and poverty reduction are difficult to isolate (Behrman et al., 1988). What is important is an understanding of the joint nature of returns to investment in these areas.

Given the critical importance of human infrastructure services for poverty reduction, access of the poor to these services needs to be improved. This can be achieved through better public investment and pricing policies. As Jimenez (1992) points out, public investment policy can be improved by setting priorities better both inter- and intrasectors, directing subsidized public investments into those sectors and subsectors with the highest returns and are primarily utilized by the poor, such as basic education, primary health care and family planning. In addition, resources need to be mobilized in a nondistortionary manner, management and internal efficiency improved, and targeting to the poor sharpened.

Jimenez (1987) further notes that pricing policy which differentiates prices by type of service and type of consumer is considered to be generally more efficient and equitable than low and uniform price policies. Prices should be raised for higher-level services, such as tertiary education and specialized curative health care, which are primarily consumed by the nonpoor. The savings should be directed toward more or better basic services, such as primary education and health care, which benefit the poor.

### 7.4.2. Physical infrastructure

Spending on physical infrastructure is considered part of measured final output. More importantly, however, its role is to raise the productivity of such factors of production as private capital and labor. Better physical infrastructure lowers the costs of production and transaction (Jimenez, 1992; World Bank, 1994). Physical and human infrastructure are thus highly complementary.

Besides their productivity effects, most physical infrastructure services have a direct bearing on well-being and living standards. Bringing water and sanitation services to slum communities can significantly improve living conditions and reduce the health hazards to which the poor are otherwise constantly exposed. A better mass transportation system directly improves the welfare of the poor besides enabling them to increase their earnings. The same is true of electricity provision to poor households.

The access of the poor to basic physical infrastructure services can be improved in three ways (World Bank, 1994). First, there should be greater responsiveness to the needs of the poor through deeper user involvement in the selection, design, construction, operation and maintenance of infrastructure. Such involvement is likely to lead to more modest design and less costly construction, as well as better operation and maintenance, of facilities. This is illustrated in a World Bank study of 121 completed rural water supply projects in Africa, Asia and Latin America, financed by various agencies (Lanjouw, 1995). The study suggests that projects with extensive participation by users in project selection and design have a higher probability of being better operated and maintained.

Second, user fees that correspond to the true cost of infrastructure provision are likely to minimize unnecessary use and wastage of infrastructure services. Moreover, appropriate pricing serves as a signal to the supplier in terms of the kinds and amounts of infrastructure services demanded. A system of user fees instead of price subsidies is likely to be more sustainable and better for poverty reduction in the long run. Many subsidies in practice are misdirected and inefficient. In developing countries, the poor often use fuelwood for cooking and kerosene or candles for lighting, thus leaving them out of subsidized electricity. They also have to buy water from private vendors who charge prices that are often a multiple of those charged by public utility agencies (World Bank, 1988). Within a system of user fees the poor can be protected through block pricing for utilities, whereby higher unit prices are charged at higher consumption levels such that the nonpoor pay full cost (Jimenez, 1992).

Third, while the trend is toward less government intervention and more private sector participation in the economy, poverty reduction efforts will continue to require public sector involvement in planning, budgetary provision, coordination, and monitoring (Lanjouw, 1995). The government's direct role will be called for in the provision of such basic facilities (with limited scope for cost recovery) as rural roads and irrigation systems. The Malaysian experience in privatization is highly instructive. The privatization program enabled the government to shift increased attention and resources to poverty-linked infrastructure. For example, the share of rural roads in the aggregate road network nearly doubled to 32% between 1965 and 1990, and rural poverty incidence declined from 53% in 1973 to 19% in 1989 (Lanjouw, 1995).

## 7.5. Credit

Because poor households usually do not possess any physical capital, credit provision is considered as an important means of alleviating poverty. Siamwalla (1993) suggests three ways in which the poor may benefit from credit: (i) it may enable them to cope with the consequences of poverty; (ii) it may act as a way out of poverty; and (iii) even if credit is not made available directly to them but to nonpoor households in the community, it may create activities with trickle-down benefits to them.

Based on his analysis of rural credit market of developing Asia, Siamwalla (1993) arrives at the following conclusions. First, the provision of credit appears to be ill-suited to deal with the consequences of poverty. More effective mechanisms are those that enhance human capital (basic education, health and nutrition), as mentioned above, and those that reduce the risks faced by the poor, such as public works projects during periods of crop failure or food subsidies in times of natural disasters. In these cases, public intervention is more in the nature of a grant rather than a loan. Second, credit provision seems better suited to assist the poor engage in gainful economic activities that will enable them to move out of poverty. For instance, credit may be used to purchase new tools or adopt new technology to make them more efficient in producing goods for the market. Higher earnings then allow them to make profits and amortize their loans.

Third, while like many other government policies and programs, general provision of credit benefits the richer households, the impact often does not stop there but generates subsequent rounds of effects. These additional or "trickle-down" impacts can benefit the poor by increasing the demand for their labor services or goods they produce. Finally, credit should be regarded as playing merely a supportive role. It can help in poverty alleviation only if there are profitable investment opportunities and viable projects available to the poor. However, if they do not exist, provision of credit is unlikely to alleviate poverty, especially if it is chronic.

It is often suggested that the poor have to rely on informal sector credit at exorbitant terms as they are shut off from formal sector credit owing to lack of collateral. This traditional view about informal credit has been increasingly challenged by economists (Bottomley, 1963; Adams et al., 1984; Ghate et al., 1992) who suggest that the informal credit market is often highly competitive, and therefore informal sector interest rates do not contain monopoly profits but high administrative costs of small loans. Moreover, in many countries, the poorer tenants receive loans from landlords in the context of an interlinked rural transaction where the tenants receive loans at below-market rates (Taslim, 1988) for being involved in other land and/or labor market transactions with the landlord. The exclusion from the formal sector credit that the poor often suffer because of lack of collateral can be overcome by group-based lending, as exemplified by the Grameen Bank in Bangladesh. This type of credit program has achieved almost full recovery, although their impact on poverty alleviation may not be commensurate with their success in loan recovery.

In sum, it is worth recapitulating the distinction between chronic and transient poverty. While transient poverty is often the outcome of market failures, chronic poverty reflects low factor productivity (due to low level of technology) and low levels of physical and human capital. It is therefore widely accepted that while credit can redress transient poverty by addressing market failures, it cannot address chronic poverty unless accompanied by new technological innovations and/or investments in physical and human capital.[45]

---

[45] This view has recently been contested by Hoff (1996) who argues that with imperfect risk markets and constraints on borrowing for consumption needs, poor households can increase their tradeoffs in expected incomes for reduced risks. Therefore, the policies which are designed for short-term poverty alleviation—such as food-for-work programs—can have long- term impacts. These impacts include increased long-term average earnings of the poor and reduction in inequality in asset holdings. While it is clear that credit can help the transient poor from sliding into chronic poverty, it is not clear how it can help reduce chronic poverty.

## 7.6. *Special employment programs*

Two types of special employment programs have commonly been adopted by governments in developing countries, namely, self-employment creation and wage employment. The first allows the poor to obtain income-generating assets, often by extending credit, as discussed earlier, and marketing assistance. The second scheme provides the poor with employment opportunities, typically on rural public works. While basically designed for the poor in rural areas, there is no reason why special employment programs cannot be adapted as tools for alleviating urban poverty as well.

Many self-employment creation schemes, such as India's large Integrated Rural Development Program and Indonesia's BIMAS, extend subsidized credit for the purchase of income-earning assets. However, as pointed out earlier, subsidized credit is often problematic. One problem is that the demand for subsidized credit almost always exceeds the supply and this leads to rationing. When credit is rationed the nonpoor usually have an advantage over the poor. The poor thus end up resorting to loans at market rates, or worse, are forced to borrow from informal lenders who charge usurious rates. Another problem is that subsidized loans often lead to unviable projects, resulting in loan defaults or low repayment rates, as also observed in Africa and Latin America (World Bank, 1990).

Self-employment creation schemes based on unsubsidized credit are generally more successful (Robinson and Snodgrass, 1987). An example is Indonesia's KUPEDES which replaced the BIMAS program. Another example is Bangladesh's internationally well-known Grameen Bank, which has the additional features of being based on group lending and being biased in favor of women. To be successful, self-employment creation programs require targeting which, in practice, is very imprecise and entails high administrative costs. These programs tend to be more successful in more developed areas than in depressed areas where they are particularly needed (Deolalikar, 1994). However, more carefully designed evaluation studies are required for policy guidance on their true effectiveness.

While self-employment creation schemes have the potential to promote long-term entrepreneurship and self-reliance among the poor, wage employment programs are meant to be temporary emergency measures. Traditionally, they have been used during periods of calamity when there is famine or massive unemployment of a transitory nature. Recently, they have also become an important instrument of poverty alleviation in many developing countries (Deolalikar, 1994). Among the known examples of public employment programs for poverty alleviation are India's National Rural Employment Program and its more established and successful Maharashtra Employment Guarantee Scheme. Wage employment schemes have also been adopted in Latin American countries during periods of macroeconomic stabilization and structural adjustment. They have provided appreciable unemployment relief and some stability to incomes of poor households.

One advantage of wage employment schemes is that they contribute to the construction and maintenance of physical infrastructure, such as roads, irrigation, water and sanitation systems. However, as a tool for poverty alleviation, their distinct advantage is in the important aspect of targeting. This is because these schemes pay lower-than-market wages and hence the poor—who do not necessarily have access to those employment opportunities in the market owing to various types of market imperfections—participate through self-selection. As in the case of self-employment programs, however, Deolalikar (1994) notes that there is a need for more empirical research to compare their efficiency and effectiveness in poverty alleviation with those of alternative interventions.

## 7.7. Targeting

It is widely agreed that anti-poverty programs should be cost effective implying that the poor should reap the maximum gain for a given budgetary outlay (or the budgetary outlay should be minimum for a given impact on poverty). One way to achieve this cost-effectiveness is by ensuring that the targeted transfers accrue more to the poor than to the nonpoor. However, this is easier said than done due to administrative and institutional bottlenecks. Given the difficulties associated with observing incomes as well as the incentive effects of means testing required for successful targeting, many transfers to the poor are contingent on correlates of poverty, such as geographical location, land holding or caste, etc.—referred to as *indicator targeting*.

The experience with indicator targeting in reducing poverty has, however, been far from satisfactory and has led to innovative interventions that rely on self-targeting. These schemes create incentives for the poor to participate voluntarily such as the various wage employment and food-for-work programs in south Asia. Similarly, rationing of food by queuing or subsidizing inferior food can be self-targeting. However, these innovations can also fail if the poor cannot access this food because they cannot afford any work loss due to queuing, while the rich can jump the queue. Similarly, some poor people cannot participate in various wage employment and food-for-work programs because of physical disability or old age. Therefore, some poor candidates are screened out along with the nonpoor.

Targeting is beset with other practical difficulties.[46] First, the efficiency rankings of poverty programs are not unique but change with alterations in budgetary outlays. Second, maximum impact on poverty is subject to different interpretations and will depend to a large extent on the poverty measure adopted. Third, cost-effectiveness is often used as the principal criterion for "better" targeting— excluding the nonpoor and including the poor as far as possible. However, "better" targeting does not necessarily imply greater impact on poverty if extensive participation entails high administrative costs and, hence, reduced cost effectiveness. Finally, targeting can be accompanied by an erosion of political support for antipoverty programs. This can happen if the focus of the program in question changes from one of a universal coverage to that of a targeted one (Besley and Kanbur, 1991). However, this political economy perspective is somewhat simplified as the supporters for antipoverty programs cover a broader constituency beyond the direct beneficiaries.

## 8. Concluding remarks

Poverty reduction is the primordial task of development effort in developing countries. Despite its economic dynamism in recent times, Asia is still home to the vast majority of the developing world's poor. At the same time, poor-to-mediocre economic performance largely explains the rise in both the incidence and numbers of people in poverty in sub-Saharan Africa and Latin America. However, these developing regions account for relatively smaller fractions of poor people in all developing countries. This clearly suggests that Asia is the main arena where the assault against poverty will have to be waged.

Although distinct in many respects, the rural and urban poor commonly have: (i) inadequate human capital; (ii) little or no access to physical assets; (iii) large dependency burden; and (iv) unhealthy living environments. Poverty in developing countries has for a long time been largely a rural phenomenon. This is because the majority of population in these countries are rural- based with significantly lower earnings and poorer access to public services than their urban counterparts. However, because of accelerating urbanization, urban poverty is becoming increasingly pronounced and is likely to be the more difficult challenge in the years to come. This means that policy approaches cannot simply shift from rural to urban poverty reduction, but will have to pay closer attention to the dynamic links between rural and urban poverty to be more effective. This in itself is a

---

[46] An overview of various approaches to targeting can be found in Besley and Kanbur (1991).

strong argument for broad-based, labor-intensive economic growth as opposed to narrow, sectoral approaches to poverty alleviation.

It is often argued that women are poorer than men in developing countries and, therefore, there is a need for gender-focused policies on grounds of equity and efficiency. On grounds of equity, redressing gender discrimination is viewed as tantamount to poverty alleviation. On grounds of efficiency, the issue of sub-optimality in investment in human capital due to market failure is seen as more serious for females than it is for males. However, gender equity requires that females participate not only in economic but also in noneconomic dimensions of life. A good deal of gender disparity stems from inequity in intrahousehold allocation of resources. To the extent that intrahousehold allocation is governed by societal norms and values, it cannot be *directly* influenced by the government. Public policy can influence economic factors, through economic incentives and fiscal measures, but not necessarily sociocultural norms and values. This explains why gender inequity has tended to perpetuate itself.

A direct consequence of rapid population growth in developing countries is that low income families are typically larger than high income ones, even allowing for higher mortality among the former. However, because of the interactive links between fertility and poverty, one cannot unambiguously say that high fertility directly results in poverty. Rather, the evidence suggests that rapid population growth may influence poverty by impinging on its correlates or characteristics, such as inadequate human capital, lack of physical assets such as land or tools, and low earnings, or, at the macrolevel, weak economic growth and income inequality. Families with many children tend to save less and invest less in physical assets and, more importantly, in the human capital of their children. This means that poverty tends to be transmitted intergenerationally. Thus, policies to slow population growth—via raising women's education, reducing infant mortality, and promoting suitable family planning programs—disproportionately benefit the poor. Conversely, a nonexistent or weak population policy hurts the poor more than the nonpoor.

The generally accepted view is that, in a long-run context, economic growth performance is the most reliable determinant of poverty trends. For economic growth to make a meaningful dent on poverty it has to be rapid and sustained. In turn, rapid and sustained growth is feasible with economic policies that are market based and outward oriented. For developing countries, such economic growth is almost always labor intensive and broad-based, implying maximum utilization of labor, the poor's principal, if not sole, asset. Not only is economic growth critical for employment generation, it also raises the government's revenue and ability to invest in human and physical infrastructures, which serve to enhance the poor's earning capacity as well as help improve their living standards.

Furthermore, a more healthy fiscal position—due to actual or potential growth—enables the government to make direct but selective short-run interventions to appropriately deal with chronic poverty through, e.g., asset transfer, or transient poverty through "safety nets", e.g., special credit or wage employment. However, special antipoverty programs should be regarded as supplementary, not as substitutes, for growth-inducing policies. To be efficient and cost effective, these programs should be properly targeted. But targeting, to ensure that transfers accrue more to the poor than to the nonpoor, is fraught with administrative and logistical problems. Most targeting techniques—such as individual, geographic, indicator, and self-selection—are less than satisfactory. Nevertheless, it appears that self-targeting is the least administratively cumbersome.

Understanding of poverty can be enhanced with better data emanating from appropriately standardized household income and expenditure surveys in terms of definitions, coverage and quality. Data that are intertemporally and internally consistent as well as cross-nationally comparable would facilitate better measurement, analysis and monitoring of poverty. Likewise, targeting can be improved to make government interventions more successful in supplementing economic growth in the war against poverty. Finally, further work on such other important dimensions of human welfare as health, education, gender equality, and political participation—issues that have important connections with or implications for poverty—will help deepen the understanding of the "true" meaning of development, as well as improve policies and actions required toward its achievement.

# Appendix

Table 1

GNP per capita, real GDP growth, population frowth and change in poverty incidence

| | GNP per capita 1992 (US dollars) | Real GDP growth, 1980–1990 (% annual) | Population growth 1980–1990 (% annual) | Change in poverty incidence (% annual) | |
|---|---|---|---|---|---|
| Sub-Saharan Africa | | | | | |
| Burundi | 210 | 3.9 | 2.8 | 1977–1987/1992 | 0.0 |
| Chad | 220 | 5.9 | 2.4 | 1977–1987/1992 | 0.6 |
| Ethiopia | 110 | 2.0 | 3.1 | 1973/1992 | −0.4 |
| Ghana | 450 | 3.0 | 3.4 | 1977–1987/1992 | −0.7 |
| Kenya | 310 | 4.2 | 3.8 | 1977–1987/1990 | −3.2 |
| Madagascar | 230 | 1.1 | 3.0 | 1977–1987/1990 | −2.5 |
| Malawi | 210 | 2.9 | 3.4 | 1977–1987/1992 | 0.3 |
| Mali | 310 | 4.0 | 2.5 | 1973/1992 | 1.6 |
| Nigeria | 320 | 1.4 | 3.2 | 1973/1992 | −3.0 |
| Rwanda | 250 | 1.0 | 3.3 | 1973/1992 | −0.1 |
| Somalia | NA | 2.4 | 3.1 | 1977–1987/1992 | 2.0 |
| Zambia | 420[a] | 0.8 | 3.7 | 1978/1992 | −0.6 |
| East Asia | | | | | |
| China[b] | 470 | 9.6 | 1.4 | 1985/1992 | 3.0 |
| Indonesia | 670 | 5.3 | 1.8 | 1976/1990 | −6.7 |
| Korea, Rep. of | 6790 | 9.7 | 1.1 | 1970/1984 | −11.1 |
| Malaysia | 2790 | 5.2 | 2.6 | 1970/1992 | −4.9 |
| Philippines | 770 | 1.1 | 2.4 | 1971/1991 | −0.8 |
| Thailand | 1840 | 7.6 | 1.8 | 1975–1976/1990 | −4.0 |
| South Asia | | | | | |
| Bangladesh | 220 | 3.8 | 2.3 | 1973–1974/1988–1989 | −2.9 |
| India | 310 | 5.6 | 2.1 | 1972–1973/1987–1988 | −3.6 |
| Nepal | 170 | 4.6 | 2.6 | 1979/1992 | −0.1 |
| Pakistan | 420 | 6.5 | 3.1 | 1973–1977/1992 | −2.5 |
| Sri Lanka | 540 | 3.9 | 1.4 | 1978–1979/1986–1987 | 2.6 |
| Latin America & the Caribbean | | | | | |
| Argentina | 6050 | −0.5 | 1.3 | 1970/1992 | 3.1 |
| Bolivia | 680 | −0.1 | 2.5 | 1973/1992 | 0.0 |
| Brazil | 2770 | 2.8 | 2.2 | 1970/1992 | −0.2 |
| Colombia | 1330 | 3.6 | 2.0 | 1973/1992 | −0.2 |
| Costa Rica | 1960 | 3.7 | 2.4 | 1970/1992 | 0.7 |
| Dominican Republic | 1050 | 2.1 | 2.2 | 1977–1987/1992 | 2.2 |
| El Salvador | 1170 | 0.9 | 1.4 | 1977–1987/1992 | 6.7 |
| Guatemala | 980 | 0.8 | 2.9 | 1977–1987/1992 | −0.0 |
| Honduras | 580 | 2.5 | 3.4 | 1970/1992 | −2.6 |
| Mexico | 3470 | 1.0 | 2.0 | 1970/1992 | −0.6 |
| Peru | 950 | −0.2 | 2.3 | 1970/1992 | −2.0 |
| Venezuela | 2910 | 1.0 | 2.7 | 1970/1992 | 1.0 |

[a] For 1991.

[b] Poverty incidence decline based on rural poverty incidence.

NA: data are not available.

Sources: WB, World Development Report 1994; UNDP, Human Development Report 1994 and past issues; WB, Social Indicators of Development 1994 and past issues; and Altimir (1982).

# References

Adams, D.W., D. Graham and J. von Pische, eds. (1984), Undermining Rural Development with Cheap Credit (Westview, Boulder, CO).

Agarwal, B. (1986), "Women, poverty and agricultural growth in India", Journal of Peasant Studies 13:165–220.

Ahlburg, D.A. (1994), "Population growth and poverty", in: R. Cassen and contributors, Population and Development: Old Debates, New Conclusions (Transaction Publishers, New Brunswick and Oxford).

Ahluwalia, M.S. (1976), "Inequality, poverty and development", Journal of Development Economics 3:307–342.

Ahluwalia, M.S., N.G. Carter and H.B. Chenery (1979), "Growth and poverty in developing countries", Journal of Development Economics 6:299–341.

Alderman H. and P. Gertler (1989), "The substitutability of public and private medical care for the treatment of children's illnesses in Pakistan", Living Standards Measurement Study (LSMS) Working Paper 56 (The World Bank, Washington, DC).

Alderman, H., J. Behrman, D. Ross and R. Sabot (1992), "The gender gap in cognitive achievement in a poor rural economy", mimeo (Williams College).

Alderman, H., J. Behrman, S. Khan, D. Ross, and R. Sabot (1993), "Public schooling expenditures in rural Pakistan: Efficiently targeting girls and a lagging region", mimeo (Bryn Mawr College).

Altimir, O. (1982), "The extent of poverty in Latin America", Staff Working Paper No. 522 (World Bank, Washington, DC).

Arthur, W.B. and G. McNicoll (1978), "Samuelson, population and intergenerational transfers", International Economic Review 19:241–246.

Asian Development Bank (1992), Asian Development Outlook 1992 (Oxford University Press, Hong Kong).

Asian Development Bank (1994), Asian Development Outlook 1994 (Oxford University Press, Hong Kong).

Atkinson, A.B. (1987), "On the measurement of poverty", Econometrica 55:749–764.

Atkinson, A.B. (1989), Poverty and Social Security (Harvester Wheatsheaf, London).

Atkinson, A.B. (1991), "Comparing poverty rates internationally: lessons from recent studies in developed countries", The World Bank Economic Review 5:3–21.

Balisacan, A.M. (1994), "Chapter on the Philippines", in: M.G. Quibria, Rural Poverty in Developing Asia, Vol. 2 (Asian Development Bank, Manila).

Balisacan, A.M. (1995), "Anatomy of poverty during adjustment: The case of the Philippines", Economic Development and Cultural Change 44:33–62.

Banerjee, N. (1983), "Women and poverty: report on workshop", Economic and Political Weekly 18:1693–1698.

Bardhan, K. (1993), "Women and rural poverty in some Asian cases", in: M.G. Quibria, Rural Poverty in Asia: Priority Issues and Policy Options (Oxford University Press, Hong Kong).

Bardhan, P. (1995), "Research on poverty and development twenty years after, 'Redistribution with Growth' ", in: M. Bruno and B. Pleskovic, eds., Annual World Bank Conference on Development Economics (World Bank, Washington, DC).

Bardhan, P. (1996), "Efficiency, equity and poverty alleviation: policy issues in less developed countries", Economic Journal 106:1344–1356.

Basu, A.M. (1989), "Is discrimination in food really necessary for explaining sex differentials in childhood mortality?", Population Studies 43:193–210.

Basu, A.M. (1993), "How pervasive are sex differentials in childhood nutritional levels in South Asia?", Social Biology 4:25–37.

Baxter, M. (1986), New Developments in Agricultural Extension (The World Bank, Washington, D.C.).

Behrman, J.R. (1988a), "Intrahousehold allocation of nutrients in rural India: are boys favored? Do parents exhibit inequality aversion?", Oxford Economic Papers 40:32–54.

Behrman, J.R. (1988b), "Nutrition, health, birth order and seasonality: Intrahousehold allocation among children in rural India", Journal of Development Economics 28:43–62.

Behrman, J.R. (1990), "The action of human resources and poverty on one another", Living Standards Measurement Study (LSMS) Working Paper 74 (The World Bank, Washington, DC).

Behrman, J.R. (1993), "Macroeconomic policies and rural poverty: issues and research strategies", in: M.G. Quibria, Rural Poverty in Asia: Priority Issues and Policy Options (Oxford University Press, Hong Kong).

Behrman, J.R. and A.B. Deolalikar (1990), "The intrahousehold demand for nutrients in rural South India: individual estimates, fixed effects and permanent income", Journal of Human Resources 24:665–697.

Behrman, J.R. and M.R. Rosenzweig (1994), "Caveat emptor: cross-country data on education and labor force", Journal of Development Economics 44:147–171.

Behrman, J.R. and R. Schneider (1994), "An international perspective on schooling investments in the last quarter century in some fast growing east and Southeast Asian countries", Asian Development Review 12:1–50.

Behrman, J.R. and Z. Zhang (1994), "Gender issues and employment in Asia", Paper presented in the Asian Development Bank Round Table on Employment Creation for Broad-Based Growth (Manila, Philippines).

Behrman, J.R., A.B. Deolalikar and B.L. Wolfe (1988), "Nutrients: impacts and determinants", The World Bank Economic Review 2:299–320.

Besley, T. and R. Kanbur (1991), "Principles of targetting", in M. Lipton and Jacques Van Der Gaag, eds., Including the Poor (The World Bank, Washington, DC).

Bhagwati, J. (1988), "Poverty and public policy", World Development 16:539–555.

Bhalla, S. and P.S. Vashistha (1988), "Income distribution in India: a reexamination", in: T.N. Srinivasan and P.K. Bardhan, eds., Rural Poverty in South Asia (Columbia University Press, New York).

Boserup, E. (1990), "Population, the status of women and rural development", in: G. McNicoll and M. Cain, eds., Rural Development and Population (Oxford University Press, Oxford).

Bottomley, A. (1963), "The costs of administering private loans in underdeveloped rural areas", Oxford Economic Papers 15:154–163.

Boulier, B.L. (1977), "Population policy and income distribution", in: C.R. Frank and R.C. Webb, eds., Income Distribution and Growth in less Developed Countries (The Brookings Institution, Washington, DC).

Bourguignon, F., J. de Melo and A. Suwa (1991), "Distributional effects of adjustment policies: simulations for archetype economies in Africa and Latin America", The World Bank Economic Review 5:339–366.

Bourguignon, F., W. Branson and J. de Melo (1992), "Adjustment and income distribution: a micro-macro model for counterfactual analysis", Journal of Development Economics 38:17–39.

Cabañero, T.A. (1978), "The shadow price of children in Laguna households", Philippine Economic Journal 17:62–83.

Cassen, R. (1976), "Population and development: a survey", World Development 4:785–830.

Cassen, R. (1994), "Population policy: a new consensus", Policy Essay No. 12 (Overseas Development Council, Washington, DC).

Chen, L.C., E. Huq and S. DeSouza (1981), "Sex bias in the family allocation of food and health care in Bangladesh", Population and Development Review 17:55–70.

Chen, S., G. Datt and M. Ravallion (1993), "Is poverty increasing in the developing world?", mimeo (The World Bank, Washington, DC).

Chenery, H.L. et al. (1974), Redistribution with Growth (Oxford University Press for the World Bank and the Institute of Development Studies, University of Sussex, London).

Coale, A.J. (1991), "Excess female mortality and the balance of sexes in the population: an estimate of the number of 'missing females' ", Population and Development Review 17:517–523.

Cochrane, S. (1979), Fertility and education: What do we really know? (Johns Hopkins University Press, Baltimore).

Cochrane, S., D. O'Hara and J. Leslie (1980), "The effects of education on health", Staff Working Papers, No. 405 (The World Bank, Washington, DC).

Cornia, G.A., R. Jolly and F. Stewart (1987), Adjustment with a Human Face (Clarendon Press, Oxford).

Das Gupta, M. (1978), "Production relations and population: Rampur", Journal of Development Studies 14:177–185.

Das Gupta, M. (1987), "Selective discrimination against female children in rural Punjab, India", Population and Development Review 13:77–100.

de Janvry, A. and E. Sadoulet (1989), "Investment strategies to combat rural poverty: a proposal for Latin America", World Development 17:1203–1222.

Deaton, A. (1989), "Looking for boy–girl discrimination in household expenditure data", World Bank Economic Review 3:1–15.

Deaton, A. (1995), "Inequality within and between households in growing and aging economies", in: M.G. Quibria, Critical Issues in Asian Development: Theories, Experiences and Policies (Oxford University Press, Hong Kong).

Deolalikar, A.B. (1991), "Intrahousehold allocation of health inputs and distribution of health outcomes among Indonesian children", in: Robert McNamara Fellowship Program: 10th Anniversary Publication (The World Bank, Washington DC: Economic Development Institute).

Deolalikar, A.B. (1994), "Special employment programs and poverty alleviation", Paper presented at the Asian Development Bank's Development Round Table on Employment Creation for Broad-Based Growth, 12–14 October 1994, Manila, Philippines.

Deolalikar, A.B. and E.M. Pernia (1993), "Population growth in developing Asia: trends and implications for economic growth, ecology and poverty" (Asian Development Bank, Manila).

Dev, S.M., K.S. Parikh and M.H. Suryanarayana (1994) "Chapter on India", in: M.G. Quibria, Rural Poverty in Developing Asia, Vol. 1 (Asian Development Bank, Manila).

Directorate-General of Budget, Accounting and Statistics, Executive Yuam (1992), Social Indicators of the Republic of China (Republic of China).

East-West Population Institute (1993), "Research program on priority health and population issues", Final report submitted to the Asian Development Bank.

Evenson, R.E. (1984), "Population growth, infrastructural development, technology and welfare in rural north India", Paper prepared for the IUSSP Seminar on Population, Food and Rural Development (New Delhi, India).

Evenson, R.E. (1993), "Institutions and rural poverty in Asia", in: M.G. Quibria, Rural Poverty in Asia: Priority Issues and Policy Options (Oxford University Press, Hong Kong).

Fields, G.S. (1990), "Labor market modeling and the urban informal sector: theory and evidence", in: D. Turnham, B. Salome and Antoine Schwartz, eds., The informal sector revisited (OECD, Paris).

Fields, G.S. (1995a), "Income distribution in developing economies: conceptual, data, and policy issues in broad-based growth", in: M.G. Quibria, Critical Issues in Asian Development: Theories Experiences and Policies (Oxford University Press, Manila).

Foster, A. and M.R. Rosenzweig (1993a), "Information flows and distribution in the labor markets in low-income countries", World Bank Economic Review and World Bank Research Observer, Proceedings of the World Bank Annual Conference on Development Economics 1992, pp. 173–203.

Foster, A. and M.R. Rosenzweig (1993b), "Information, learning, and wage rates in low-income rural areas", Journal of Human Resources 28:759–790.

Foster, A. and M.R. Rosenzweig (1994a), "A test for moral hazard in the labor market: contractual arrangements, effort, and health", Review of Economics and Statistics 76:213–217.

Foster, A. and M.R. Rosenzweig (1994b), "Comparative advantage, information and the allocation of workers to tasks: evidence from an agricultural labor market", mimeo (University of Pennsylvania).

Foster, J. and A.F. Shorrocks (1988), "Poverty orderings", Econometrica 56:173–77.

Foster, J.E., J. Greer and E. Thorbecke (1984), "A class of decomposable poverty measures", Econometrica 52:761–766.

Fuchs, V. (1965), "Toward a theory of poverty", Task force economic growth and opportunity: The concept of poverty (U.S. Chamber of Commerce, Washington, DC).

Gaiha, R. and A.B. Deolalikar (1993), "Persistent, expected and innate poverty: estimates for semi-arid rural south India, 1975–1984", Cambridge Journal of Economics 18:409–422.

Gannicott, K. (1986), "Woman, wages and discrimination: some evidence from Taiwan", Economic Development and Cultural Change 39:721–730.

Gertler, P. and O. Rahman (1994), "Social infrastructure and urban poverty", in: E.M. Pernia, Urban Poverty in Asia: A Survey of Critical Issues (Oxford University Press, Hong Kong).

Ghate, P., A. Das Gupta, M. Lamberte, N. Poapongsakorn, D. Prabowo and A. Rahman (1992), Informal finance: Some findings from Asia (Asian Development Bank; and Oxford University Press, Manila).

Glover, D. and K. Kusterer (1990), Small farmers, big business: Contract farming and rural development (St. Martins, New York).

Greenwood, M.J. (1975), "Research on internal migration in the U.S.: a survey", Journal of Economic Literature 13:397–433.

Gunatilleke, G., M. Perera, R.A.M.C. Wanigaratne, R.E. Fernando, W.D. Lakshman, J.K.M.D. Chandrasiri and R.D. Wanigaratne (1994), "Chapter on Sri Lanka", in: M.G. Quibria, Rural Poverty in developing Asia, Vol. 1 (Asian Development Bank, Manila).

Haddad, L. and R. Kanbur (1990), "How serious is the neglect of intrahousehold inequality", Economic Journal 100:866–881.

Harris, B. (1990), "The intrafamily distribution of hunger in south Asia", in: J. Dreze and A. Sen, eds., The Political Economy of Hunger, vol. 1 (Clarendon Press, Oxford).

Hoff, K. (1996) "Comment on 'Political Economy of Alleviating Poverty Theory and Institutions, by Timothy Besley' ", in: M. Bruno and B. Pleskovic, eds., Annual World Bank Conference on Development Economics (World Bank, Washington DC).

Hossain, M., R. Mannan, H.Z. Rahman and B. Sen (1994), "Chapter on Bangladesh", in: M.G. Quibria, Rural Poverty in Developing Asia, Vol. 1 (Asian Development Bank, Manila).

Jamison, D. and L. Lau (1982), Farmer education and farm efficiency (Johns Hopkins University Press, Baltimore).

Jimenez, E. (1987) Pricing Policy in the Social Sectors: Cost Recovery for Education and Health in Developing Countries (The Johns Hopkins University Press for the World Bank, Baltimore).

Jimenez, E. (1992), "Human and physical infrastructure: public investment and pricing policies in developing countries", Paper prepared for the Asian Development Bank's Conference on Development Economics (Manila, Philippines).

Kakwani, N.C. (1980), "On a class of poverty measures", Econometrica 48:437–446.

Khan, A.R. (1984), "Population growth and access to land: an Asian perspective", Paper prepared for the IUSSP Seminar on Population, Food and Rural Development (New Delhi, India).

Khandker, S. (1996), " Grameen Bank: impact, costs, and program sustainability", Asian Development Review, 14:97–130.

Kikuchi, M. and Y. Hayami (1980), "Inducements to institutional innovations in an agrarian community", Economic Development and Cultural Change 29:21–36.

Klasen, S. (1994), " 'Missing women' reconsidered", World Development 22:1061–1071.

Krongkaew, M., P. Tinakorn and S. Suphachalasai (1994), "Chapter on Thailand", in: M.G. Quibria, Rural Poverty in Developing Asia, Vol. 2 (Asian Development Bank, Manila).

Kuznets, S. (1976), "Demographic aspects of the size distribution of income: an exploratory essay", Economic Development and Cultural Change 25:1–94.

Kynch, J. and A.K. Sen (1983), "Indian women: well-being and survival", Cambridge Journal of Economics 7:363–380.

Lipton, M. and A. de Haan (1997), "Poverty in emerging Asia", Background paper for Emerging Asia: Changes and Challenges (Asian Development Bank).

Lipton, M. and M. Ravallion (1995), "Poverty and Policy", in: J. Behrman and T.N. Srinivasan, eds., Handbook of Development Economics (Elsevier Science BV).

Lanjouw, P. (1995), "Infrastructure: a ladder for the poor", Finance and Development 32:33–35.

Mathur, O.P. (1994), "The state of India's urban poverty", Asian Development Review 12:32–67.

Mazumdar, D. (1987), "Rural-urban migration in developing countries", in: E.S. Mills, ed., Handbook of Regional and Urban Economics (Elsevier, Amsterdam; also in World Bank Reprint Series No. 422).

McNicoll, G. (1984), "Consequences of rapid population growth: overview and assessment", Population and Development Review 10:177–240.

Meyer, C.A. (1991), "A hierarchy model of associative farming", Journal of Development Economics 34:371–383.

Miller, B.D. (1981), The Endangered Sex (Cornell University Press, New York).

Mills, E. and C. Becker (1986), Studies in Indian Urban Development (Oxford University Press for the World Bank, Oxford).

Mills, E. and E.M. Pernia (1994), "Introduction and overview", in: E.M. Pernia, Urban Poverty in Asia: A Survey of Critical Issues (Oxford University Press, Hong Kong).

Mueller, E. (1972), "Economic cost and value of children: conceptualization and measurement", in: J.T. Fawcett, ed., The Satisfactions and Costs of Children: Theories, Concepts and Methods (East-West Center, Honolulu).

Orshansky, M. (1965), "Who's who among the poor: a demographic view of poverty", Social Security Bulletin 28:3–32.

Otsuka, K. (1993), "Land tenure and rural poverty", in: M.G. Quibria, Rural Poverty in Asia: Priority Issues and Policy Options (Oxford University Press, Hong Kong).

Penny, D.H. and M. Singarimbun (1973), "Population and poverty in rural Java: some economic arithmetic from Sriharjo", Mimeograph 41 (Cornell International Agricultural Development, Ithaca, New York).

Pernia, E.M. (1982), "Micro-level implications of population growth", in: A.N. Herrin, V.P. Paqueo and E.M. Pernia, eds., Essays on the Economics of Fertility, Population Growth and Public Intervention in a Developing Country: The Philippines, University of the Philippines School of Economics Discussion Paper 8212.

Pernia, E. M., ed. (1994), Urban Poverty in Asia: A Survey of Critical Issues (Oxford University Press for the Asian Development Bank, Hong Kong).

Pernia, E. M. and S. Alabastro (1997), "Aspects of urban water and sanitation in the context of rapid urbanizaton in developing Asia", Economic Staff Paper No. 56 (Asian Development Bank, Manila).

Pernia, E. M. and C. Paderanga (1981), "Philippines: the impact of national policy on urban systems", in: M. Honjo, ed., Urbanization and Regional Development, pp. 149–177 (Maruzen Asia for UNCRD, Nagoya, Japan, Singapore).

Pitt, M. and S. Khandker (1994), "Household and intrahousehold impacts of the Grameen and similar targeted credit programs in Bangladesh", mimeo (The World Bank, Washington, DC).

Pitt, M., M.R. Rosenzweig and Md. N. Hassan (1990), "Productivity, health and inequality in the intrahousehold distribution of food in low-income countries", American Economic Review 80:1139–1156.

Potter, J.E. (1979), "Demographic factors and income distribution in Latin America", Proceedings of the Conference on Economic and Demographic Change: Issues for the 1980s, Helsinki, 1978, Liege: International Union for the Scientific Study of Population I.

Psacharopoulos, G. (1985), "Returns to education: a further international update and implications", Journal of Human Resources 20:583–604.

Psacharopoulos, G. (1988), "Education and development: a review", The World Bank Research Observer 3:99–116.

Psacharopoulos, G., S. Morley, A. Fiszbein, H. Lee and W. Wood (1995), "Poverty and income inequality in Latin America", Review of Income and Wealth 4:245–264.

Quibria, M.G. (1982), "An analytical defense of basic needs: the optimal savings perspective", World Development 10:285–291.

Quibria, M.G. (1991), "Understanding poverty: an introduction to conceptual and measurement issues", Asian Development Review 9:90–112.

Quibria, M.G., ed. (1993), Rural Poverty in Asia: Priority Issues and Policy Options (Oxford University Press for the Asian Development Bank, Hong Kong).

Quibria, M.G., ed. (1994a), Rural Poverty in Developing Asia, vol. 1 (Asian Development Bank, Manila).

Quibria, M.G., ed. (1994b), Rural Poverty in Developing Asia, vol. 2 (Asian Development Bank, Manila).

Quibria, M.G. (1995a), Critical issues in Asian Development: Theories, Experiences and Policies (Oxford University Press for the Asian Development Bank, Hong Kong).

Quibria, M.G. (1995b), "Gender and poverty: issues and policies (with special reference to Asian developing countries)", Journal of Economic Surveys (forthcoming).

Quibria, M.G., and T.N. Srinivasan (1993), "Introduction", in: M.G. Quibria, Rural Poverty in Asia: Priority Issues and Policy Options (Oxford University Press, Hong Kong).

Rashid, S. and M.G. Quibria (1995), "Is land reform passe? With special reference to Asian agriculture", in: M.G. Quibria, Critical Issues in Asian Development: Theories, Experiences and Policies (Oxford University Press for the Asian Development Bank, Hong Kong).

Ravallion, M. (1993), Poverty Comparisons. Fundamentals of Pure and Applied Economics, vol. 56 (Harvard Academic Press, Chur Switzerland).

Ravallion, M. and Huppi, M. (1991), "Measuring changes in poverty: a methodological case study of Indonesia during an adjustment period", World Bank Economic Review 5:57–84.

Ravallion, M., G. Datt and D. Van De Walle (1991), "Quantifying absolute poverty in the developing world ", Review of Income and Wealth 37:345–361.

Ravallion, M., G. Datt and S. Chen (1992), New Estimates of Aggregate Poverty Measures for the Developing World, 1985–89 (The World Bank, Population and Human Resources Department, Washington, DC).

Rawls, J. (1971), A Theory of Justice (Harvard University Press, Cambridge, MA).

Renaud, B. (1981), National Urbanization Policy in Developing Countries (Oxford University Press, Oxford).

Robinson, M. and D. Snodgrass (1987), "The role of institutional credit in Indonesia's rice intensification program", mimeo, Development Discussion Paper No. 248 (Harvard Institute for International Development, Cambridge, MA).

Rodgers, G. (1983), "Population growth, inequality and poverty", Paper prepared for the UN Expert Group on Population, Resources, Environment and Development, Geneva.

Rodgers, G. (1984), Poverty and Population: Approaches and Evidence (International Labour Organisation, Geneva).

Roumasset, J.R. and J. Smith (1981), "Population, technological change and landless workers", Population and Development Review 7:401–420.

Rowntree, B.S. (1901), Poverty: A Study of Town Life (Macmillan, London).

Safilos-Rothschild, C. (1990), "Gender and rural poverty in Asia", Paper prepared for the International Seminar on Poverty Alleviation through Agricultural Projects, Organized by the Economic Development Institute of the World Bank, the Asian Development Bank and the Centre on Integrated Rural Development for Asia and the Pacific.

Saito, K. and D. Spurling (1991), Agricultural Extension and Research for Women Farmers (The World Bank, Washington, DC).

Sawhill, I.V. (1988), "Poverty in the U.S.: why is it so persistent?", Journal of Economic Literature 26:1076.

Schultz, T.P. (1989), "Women and development: objectives, frameworks and policy interventions", mimeo (Yale University).

Scott, W. and N.T. Matthew (1983), Levels of Living and Poverty in Kerala (United Nations Research Institute for Social Development, Geneva).

Sen, A.K. (1976), "Poverty: an ordinal approach to measurement", Econometrica 44:219–231.

Sen, A.K. (1977), "On weights and measures: informational constraints in social welfare analysis", Econometrica 45:1539–1572.

Sen, A.K. (1981), Poverty and Famines (Clarendon Press, Oxford).

Sen, A.K. (1985), Capabilities and Commodities (North Holland, Amsterdam).

Sen , A.K. (1988), "Family and food: sex bias in poverty", in: P. Bardhan and T.N. Srinivasan, eds., Rural Poverty in South Asia (Columbia University, New York).

Sen, A.K. (1990), "More than 100 million women are missing", New York Review of Books 37:61–66.

Sen, A.K. (1992), Inequality Reexamined (Clarendon Press, Oxford).

Sen, A.K. and S. Sengupta (1983), "Malnutrition of rural children and the sex bias", Economic and Political Weekly 18.

Senauer, B., D. Sahn and H. Alderman (1986), "Effects of the value of time on food consumption patterns in developing countries: evidence from Sri Lanka", American Journal of Agricultural Economics 86:920–927.

Senauer, B., M. Garcia and E. Jacinto (1988), "Determinants of the intrahousehold allocation of food in the rural Philippines", American Journal of Agricultural Economics 70:170–180.

Siamwalla, A. (1993), "Rural credit and rural poverty", in: M.G. Quibria, Rural Poverty in Asia: Priority Isues and Policy Options (Oxford University Press for the Asian Development Bank, Hong Kong).

Sirageldin, I.A. (1975), "The demographic aspects of income distribution", in: W. Robinson, ed., Population and Development Planning (The Population Council, New York).

Sjaastad, L. (1962), "The costs and returns of human migration", Journal of Physical Economies 70:80–93.

Smith, W.S. ed. (1970), Bernard Shaw's Plays (W.W. Norton & Co., Inc., New York).

Srinivasan, T.N. (1992), "Income distribution and the macroeconomy: some conceptual and measurement issues", Journal of Philippine Development 19:1–25.

Srinivasan, T.N. (1993), "Rural poverty: conceptual, measurement and policy issues", in: M.G. Quibria, Rural Poverty in Asia: Priority Isues and Policy Options (Oxford University Press for the Asian Development Bank, Hong Kong).

Stone, R. (1954), The Measurement of Consumers' Expenditure and Behavior in the United Kingdom, 1920–38, vol. 1 (Cambridge University Press, Cambridge).

Strauss, J., P. Gertler, O. Rahman, and K. Fox (1993), "Gender and life cycle differentials in the patterns and determinants of adult health", Journal of Human Resources 28:791–837.

Strauss, J. and D. Thomas (1995), "Human resources: empirical modeling of household and family decisions", in: J. Behrman and T.N. Srinivasan, eds., Handbook of Development Economics, vol. 3A (North Holland Publishing Company, Amsterdam).

Streeten, P. (1990), "Poverty: concepts and measurement", Bangladesh Development Studies 18:5–6.

Tabatabai, H. (1993), The Incidence of Poverty in Developing Countries: An ILO Compendium of Data (International Labour Organisation, Geneva).

Taslim, M.A. (1988), "Tenancy and interlocked markets: issues and some evidence", World Development 16:655–666.

Taylor, G. and R. Faruque (1983), Child and Maternal Health Services in Rural India (Johns Hopkins University, Baltimore).

Tjondronegoro, S.M.P., I. Soejono and J. Hardjono (1994), "Chapter on Indonesia", in: M.G. Quibria, Rural Poverty in Developing Asia, Vol. 2 (Asian Development Bank, Manila).

Todaro, M.P. (1976), Internal Migration in Developing Countries: A Review of Theory, Evidence, Methodology and Research Priorities (International Labour Organisation, Geneva).

Tolley, G. S. and V. Thomas, eds. (1987), The Economics of Urbanization and Urban Policies in Developing Countries (World Bank, Washington, DC).

United Nations (1992), World Population Monitoring 1991. Population Studies No. 126. Sales No. E.92.XIII.2.

United Nations (1994), Population Distribution and Migration, Paper prepared for the UN International Conference on Population and Development (Cairo, Egypt).

UNDP (1995), Human Development Report 1995 (Oxford University Press, Oxford).

Valenzona, R. (1976), "Poverty measurement and nutrition", University of the Philippines School of Economics Discussion Paper 76–27.

Watts, H.W. (1991), "An economic definition of poverty", in: D.P. Moynihan, ed., On Understanding Poverty (Basic Books, New York).

Wegelin, E. (1994), "Urban shelter, municipal services, and the poor", in: E.M. Pernia.

World Bank (1994), Social Indicators of Development 1994.

World Bank (1995), Social Indicators of Development 1995.

World Bank (1980), World Development Report 1980 (Oxford University Press, Oxford).

World Bank (1984), World Development Report 1984 (Oxford University Press, Oxford).

World Bank (1988), World Development Report 1988 (Oxford University Press, Oxford).

World Bank (1990), World Development Report 1990 (Oxford University Press, Oxford).

World Bank (1992), World Development Report 1992 (Oxford University Press, Oxford).

World Bank (1993), World Development Report 1993 (Oxford University Press, Oxford).

World Bank (1994), World Development Report 1994 (Oxford University Press, Oxford).

World Bank (1995), World Development Report 1995 (Oxford University Press, Oxford).

World Bank (1996), World Development Report 1996 (Oxford University Press, Oxford).

# PART IV
# URBAN SECTORS

*Chapter 46*

# URBAN TRANSPORTATION

KENNETH A. SMALL

*University of California at Irvine*

JOSÉ A. GÓMEZ-IBÁÑEZ*

*Harvard University*

## Contents

* We are grateful to Pia Koskenoja for research assistance, and to David Anderson, Graham Crampton, Amihai Glazer, Phil Goodwin, Yoshitsugu Kanemoto, Herbert Mohring and Clifford Winston for comments on an earlier draft.

*Handbook of Regional and Urban Economics. Edited by E.S. Mills and P. Cheshire*

## Abstract

We use applied microeconomics to examine several salient problems of urban transportation: traffic congestion, air pollution, the costs of motor vehicle accidents and the future of public transportation. Throughout this chapter, we focus on analytic methods and findings that bear on current policy issues, and on the factual basis for policy analysis. We find that the most promising approaches in each case are narrowly targeted to solving market failures, such as the existence of externalities, and that these approaches are unlikely to alter the overall dominance of automobiles in urban passenger transportation.

**Keywords:** Urban transportation, congestion, pollution, safety, public transit.

## 1. Introduction

The functioning of the transportation sector is central to the functioning of urban economies. Cities exist because they enable people to take advantage of economies of agglomeration, where spatial proximity facilitates productivity-enhancing cooperation. Transportation defines proximity and determines how economies of agglomeration are realized.

Transport costs in themselves are complex. In simplified urban spatial models, transportation cost is usually assumed to be a linear function of distance traveled. In real cities, however, the transport system is composed of a complex network of interdependent links, and there are often economies of scale at the link or network levels. Moreover, the quality of service (speed, frequency, reliability) often matters as much as or more than financial costs.

Given the complexities and nonlinearities of both transport systems and the urban economies they support, it is not surprising that there are so many market failures and such great scope for public intervention. But public policy failures are common too, and many of the issues currently at the forefront of urban transportation policy involve how to make public intervention more beneficial. A key question is the extent to which the market can be relied on, or used as a model for public activities.

In this chapter, we examine the role that economic analysis plays in analyzing such questions. We focus heavily on highway transportation in private vehicles, just as actual travelers do in most modern cities. More specifically, we ask whether or not the policy implications of various market failures in urban transportation affect significantly the overall dominance of motor vehicle travel in cities. This question is salient because many people have argued that travel in private motor vehicles is overemphasized due to a neglect of its full social costs.

We examine policy responses to three such social costs: congestion (and the related issue of investments in infrastructure capacity), air pollution and accidents. In each case, we begin with an assessment of the overall magnitude of the cost, while recognizing that a large magnitude does not necessarily indicate inefficiency. Next, we examine public transit as an alternative to the automobile, taking up the question of the effects and merits of subsidies. We conclude by outlining some key research areas that could help close gaps in our ability to analyze policy.

## 2. Highway infrastructure costs and congestion

The capacity of urban road and street systems is determined in large part by the desire to accommodate peak period flows. Investment decisions thus involve a tradeoff between infrastructure and congestion costs, and so it makes sense to discuss infrastructure expansion and congestion as a single policy issue.

### 2.1. Congestion severity and growth

Road congestion is widely perceived to be one of the most pressing problems of urban transportation (Small et al., 1989; Newbery, 1990; Downs, 1992; National Research Council, 1994). A simple starting point for assessing the problem is to estimate the aggregate costs involved. Several widely cited studies suggest that congestion is responsible for billions of dollars per year in lost time in many of the world's largest metropolitan areas (Lindley, 1987, 1989; Hanks and Lomax, 1991; Quinet, 1994). For example, statistics on the ratios of daily vehicle flows to highway capacity suggest that Chicago was the fifth most congested metropolitan area in the US in 1990, with its population of 7.5 million suffering annual congestion delays of 193 million vehicle hours. Assuming an average value of time of $6.60 per vehicle hour, this works out to $1.27 billion per year in time costs; adding $350 million for extra fuel consumption yields $1.62 billion, or $410 for each registered vehicle, in annual costs.[1] For the US as a whole, Lindley (1989) estimates congestion costs at $16 billion annually, a figure that would be considerably higher today.

Such aggregate congestion cost estimates are a bit misleading, of course, because they usually represent the difference between actual travel times and the times possible if every highway were flowing freely every hour of the day. It would be prohibitively expensive to build enough highways to make free flow possible, and thus a highway system with zero congestion would actually be highly wasteful. A measure of the inefficiency of congestion would be the difference in net social surpluses between current and efficient levels of congestion (Prud'homme, 1997: pp. 5–6).

Is congestion getting worse? The answer depends on how it is measured. On any given set of roads, there is abundant evidence that congestion has become worse in most large cities. For example, of the 50 large US metropolitan areas

---

[1] Total delay, extra fuel consumption, and the ratio of registered vehicles to population are taken from Schrank et al. (1993: Tables 11, 16, 17). We have applied a per person value of time of $6.00 per hour, based on the consensus of studies as reviewed by Small (1992: pp. 43–44) that commuting time is valued at roughly half the wage rate, and multiplied by an assumed vehicle occupancy of 1.1.

studied by Schrank et al. (1993: Table 6), all but three showed an increase between 1982 and 1990 in a "congestion index" that reflects ratios of daily volume to capacity on selected road segments; between 1986 and 1990, the average area suffered an estimated 18% increase in vehicle hours of delay (their Table 14). Anecdotal evidence abounds for increases in congestion on specific roads.[2] London, famous for its all-day traffic congestion, experienced steady declines in average speeds from 1968 through 1990, although this appears to have been reversed by the recession of the early 1990s ("Traffic speeds in central and outer London", 1995).

Speeds faced by the average person, however, have not necessarily declined. US data suggest that average trip times and speeds have changed little since the mid-1970s (Gordon et al., 1991; Gordon and Richardson, 1994). Journey-to-work statistics from the US Census show, for example, that the mean commuting time in the largest 15 metropolitan areas increased only slightly, from 26.0 to 26.6 minutes, between 1980 and 1990.[3] This finding need not conflict with the findings of worsening traffic on specific roads:

> ... not only is there no contradiction but the two phenomena are causally related. Rational commuters will, sooner or later, seek to escape congestion by changing the location of their homes and/or their jobs .... The process is facilitated by the decentralizing location decisions of firms seeking to move closer to suburban labor pools. (Gordon et al., 1991: p. 419)

In other words, people escape worsening congestion by moving homes and jobs to the suburbs—or even to less congested metropolitan areas. Whether or not this is efficient, as argued by Gordon and Richardson (1994) in numerous articles, is quite another question; given that traffic congestion is an unpriced externality, congestion-induced dispersal is a distortion that may or may not be desirable as a second-best adaptation. In either case, the distortion should be counted as one of the costs of congestion (Downs, 1992: p. 2).

---

[2] See for example Meyer (1994), European Conference of Ministers of Transport (1995: pp. 72–76), Levy (1994) and Daniere (1995).

[3] Rosetti and Eversole (1993: Tables 2-1, 4-13). These figures exclude Boston's mean travel time, that increased from 23.4 to 24.2 minutes. The average masks substantial differences: in the largest area (New York: The mean commute time *decreased* by 7.7%, whereas in the second largest (Los Angeles) it *increased* by 11.9%; it also increased in each of the other 13 areas, by an average of 5.4%. Figures are for the Consolidated Metropolitan Statistical Area if there is one, otherwise for the Metropolitan Statistical Area. For recent comparisons, these census data may be more reliable than those from the National Personal Transportation Survey (NPTS), since the survey methodology for the latter changed between the latest two surveys (1983 and 1990), possibly causing the 1990 data to be overweighted with newer cars (Lave, 1996).

Another measure of urban traffic congestion is the ratio of marginal to average time cost for a motorist. This ratio represents the relative external costs since motorists perceive average and not marginal travel times when making their travel decisions. The ratio has been estimated at 2.2 during the peak hour on an arterial highway in Edmonton, Canada (Shah, 1990: p. 15), at 1.9 for an average of 20 Indonesian urban roads (Hau, 1994: Table 2), and at 1.7 for an average morning peak trip in the Minneapolis area (Anderson and Mohring, 1996: p. 28).

Congestion is increasing because automobile ownership and use is growing considerably faster than the road system in most nations. Selected national statistics compiled by the International Road Federation (1980, 1990) are shown in Table 1. Data for urban areas are less readily available, but the trends seem to be the same. In the US, for example, urban automobile use grew 77% from 1980 to 1996, while urban highway mileage grew only 34%.[4]

Car ownership and use are growing especially rapidly in western Europe, causing the gap between European and US ownership rates to narrow. Selected comparisons between the US and the 17 member nations of the European Conference of Ministers of Transport (ECMT) are shown in Table 2. Between 1970 and 1990, per capita ownership grew by 32% in the US, compared to 111% in Europe.[5]

Meanwhile, real annual investment for European land transportation has fallen by some 10% since 1975, to less than 1% of gross domestic product (GDP) (Banister, 1993: p. 348). In the US, the depreciated value of cumulative road investment declined for more than a decade following its remarkable buildup during the 1950s and 1960s.[6]

Lave (1992) has shown that the US car ownership trends are leveling off as they approach one car per driving-age adult. He argues that the recent growth in car ownership has been accelerated by a number of trends that have played out their logical course: increased labor-force participation by women, the spread of driving ability to upper age groups, and rapid growth of young and middle-aged population groups due to the "baby boom" between 1946 and 1964. Indeed, the growth of motor vehicles in use came to a temporary halt during the recession year of 1992, while motor vehicles per capita grew from 0.72 in 1990 to only 0.74

---

[4] US Census Bureau (1998: Table 1020) and the American Automobile Manufacturers Association (1997: p. 65).

[5] Similarly, Pucher (1995a: p. 101) reports that during the decade of the 1980s private car ownership per capita increased faster in almost every European country than in the US, and fastest in those starting with the lowest levels. Pucher also reports results of a survey of 93 European cities by Sharman and Dasgupta (1993), indicating that private car traffic increased by 30–35% per decade in the 1970s and 1980s.

[6] See Winston and Bosworth (1992: Fig. 8-2) and Gramlich (1994: Fig. 3).

Table 1

Motor vehicle ownership and use, and extent of road network, selected nations: 1977–1987

| | Four-wheeled motor vehicles in use (1000s) | | | Road network extent (1000s km) | | | Use intensity (1000s veh-km per km of road) | | |
|---|---|---|---|---|---|---|---|---|---|
| | 1977 | 1987 | Change (%) | 1977 | 1987 | Change (%) | 1977 | 1987 | Change (%) |
| USA | 143,750 | 179,044 | 24.6 | 6,223 | 6,233 | 0.2 | 374.9 | 493.8 | 31.7 |
| France | 19,330 | 26,195 | 35.5 | 801.1 | 804.9 | 0.5 | 355.4 | 467.1 | 31.4 |
| Spain | 7,121 | 12,083 | 69.7 | 221.1 | 318.0 | 43.8 | 277.4 | 270.3 | −2.6 |
| Sweden | 3,326 | 3,626 | 9.0 | 128.9 | 130.9 | 1.6 | na | na | na |
| Hungary[a] | 963.0 | 1,862.1 | 93.4 | 99.61 | 95.23 | −4.4 | 145.5 | 231.2 | 58.9 |
| Turkey | 885.9 | 1,997.4 | 125.5 | 231.7 | 320.6 | 38.4 | 71.7 | 65.3 | −8.9 |
| Tunisia | 188.8 | 442.5 | 134.4 | 21.89 | 27.37 | 25.0 | 106.1 | 182.5 | 72.0 |
| Ethiopia | 21.13 | 41.12 | 94.6 | 23 | 38.99 | 69.5 | na | na | na |
| New Zealand | 1,446 | 1,976 | 36.7 | 92.62 | 93.11 | 0.5 | na | na | na |
| Japan | 32,044 | 49,907 | 55.8 | 1,088 | 1,099 | 1.0 | 314.6 | 499.4 | 58.7 |
| Hong Kong | 185.4 | 300.6 | 62.1 | 1.093 | 1.395 | 27.6 | 3,060.4 | 4,423.7 | 44.6 |
| Brazil | 7,433 | 14,155 | 90.4 | 1,502 | 1,675 | 11.5 | na | na | na |
| Chile | 480.5 | 938.4 | 95.3 | 74.90 | 79.22 | 5.8 | 88.7 | 183.2 | 106.5 |

[a] Use intensity is for 1976, 1986.

na: not available.

*Source*: International Road Federation (1980, 1990: Tables I, IV, V).

Table 2

Per capita passenger car ownership, passenger travel, and road network: the US and 17 European nations

|  | Registered passenger cars per capita | Registered passenger cars per km of road | Annual travel in passenger cars |
|---|---|---|---|
| USA[a] |  |  | (vehicle-km per capita) |
| 1970 | 0.435 | 14.9 | 7194 |
| 1980 | 0.535 | 19.1 | 7858 |
| 1990 | 0.574 | 23.0 | 9759 |
| Change 1970–1980 (%) | 23.0 | 28.2 | 9.2 |
| Change 1980–1990 (%) | 7.3 | 20.4 | 24.2 |
| Europe[b] |  |  | (passenger-km per capita) |
| 1970 | 0.192 | 23.2 | 4895 |
| 1980 | 0.301 | 36.2 | 6800 |
| 1990 | 0.405 | 50.3 | 8891 |
| Change 1970–1980 (%) | 56.8 | 56.0 | 38.9 |
| Change 1980–1990 (%) | 34.5 | 39.0 | 30.8 |

[a] Source for population: US Census Bureau (1994: Table 2). Source for other figures: US Federal Highway Administration (various years: Tables MV-1, MV-201A, VM-1, HM-10).
[b] Member nations of the European Conference of Ministers of Transport (ECMT): Belgium, Denmark, West Germany, Greece, France, Ireland, Italy, Luxembourg, the Netherlands, the UK, Spain, Portugal, Norway, Sweden, Switzerland, Austria, and Finland. For passenger travel, the figures exclude Greece, Ireland and Luxembourg; and the UK includes only Great Britain (populations are adjusted accordingly). Source for population: UN, *Demographic Yearbook* (1975, 1985, 1992); plus Europa Publications, *The Europa World Year Book* (1992), for Great Britain. Source for registered passenger cars: ECMT (1993: Table 3-3-1), for 1970–1980; Banister and Berechman (1993: p. 16) for 1990. (Banister and Berechman's data are from the same source but contain more recent years.) Source for km of road: ECMT (1993: Table 3-2-1); 1989 data are used for 1990. Source for passenger travel: ECMT (1995: p. 30).

by 1995 (US Census Bureau, 1997: Tables 14, 1009). However, congestion also depends on local population growth and on the amount that each vehicle is driven. Trends in usage per vehicle are unclear: in the US, the reported annual distance traveled per vehicle rose from the years 1950 to 1970, declined in 1980, then rose again by 23% to a peak value of 18,700 km in 1993 (American Automobile Manufacturers Association, 1997: p. 64). In other nations, there is more room for continued growth in car ownership since current levels are well below the natural saturation level of one per potential driver.

## 2.2. Financing new infrastructure

Road building programs have not kept pace with vehicle traffic in many developed countries due to a combination of political opposition and financial constraints. Much of the traffic growth has occurred in densely populated urbanized areas, where road construction is not only very expensive but increasingly opposed by environmentalists and by residents of neighborhoods along the proposed right of way. Furthermore, past expansion sometimes relied on taxes whose bases are not growing commensurately with traffic.

In Europe, for example, fuel tax revenues have more than covered highway expenditures in most nations (Pucher, 1995a), but physical constraints and political opposition prevent the expansion of highways in many congested cities. In the US, a major problem has been the historic tie between highway investment funds and fuel tax revenues. Table 3 shows the average US fuel tax rates in nominal and real terms. Since 1960, the real tax rate per vehicle mile has been cut in half as state legislatures have raised nominal tax rates by less than inflation, and as the fleet average fuel efficiency has grown.

One response has been to finance new roads at the time of land development, in the form of fees or exactions charged to the land developers. The rationale

Table 3

Average motor fuel tax rates: US

| Year | Nominal rate (cents/gal) | | | Real rate, 1995 prices[c] (cents/gal) | Effective real rate, 1995 prices[d] (cents/veh-mi) |
|------|---------|-------|-------|---------|---------|
| | Federal[a] | State[b] | Total | | |
| 1960 | 4.0 | 5.9 | 9.9 | 51.0 | 3.56 |
| 1970 | 4.0 | 7.0 | 11.0 | 43.2 | 3.20 |
| 1975 | 4.0 | 7.7 | 11.7 | 33.1 | 2.36 |
| 1980 | 4.0 | 8.3 | 12.3 | 22.7 | 1.42 |
| 1985 | 9.88 | 11.3 | 21.2 | 30.0 | 1.71 |
| 1990 | 10.50 | 15.2 | 25.7 | 30.0 | 1.49 |
| 1995 | 19.37 | 17.1 | 36.5 | 36.5 | 1.73 |

[a] *Source:* US FHWA (1995: Table FE-101A). For 1985 and later, rate shown is a weighted average of different rates applied to gasoline and diesel fuel. The weights are aggregate fuel consumption, from the US FHWA (1990, 1995: Table MF-2); and the US FHWA, *Highway Statistics, Summary to 1985* (1987: p. 9, Table MF-221) (US Government Printing Office, Washington, DC). For 1990, during which the tax rate went up in December, the rate shown is the average by month, i.e., it is 11/12 times the initial rate plus 1/12 times the final rate.

[b] State gasoline and diesel tax revenues (American Automobile Manufacturers Association, 1993: p. 78; 1996: p. 82) divided by motor vehicle fuel consumed (American Automobile Manufacturers Association, 1997: p. 64).

[c] Previous column divided by the consumer price index relative to that for 1995. Price index is from US Census Bureau (1997: Table 752).

[d] Previous column divided by fleet average fuel efficiency in miles per gallon for cars, from the US Census Bureau (1998: Table 1053; 1981: Table 1092) (the latter used for 1960 only).

is that development creates new traffic sources, so the infrastructure to handle these sources can be legitimately charged to the developer. Furthermore, recent evidence suggests that many types of development do not produce enough local revenue to cover the public service costs resulting from the development (Altshuler and Gómez-Ibáñez, 1993: Chap. 6). Altshuler and Gómez-Ibáñez argue that land use exactions are seriously flawed on grounds of equity and efficiency, especially compared to user charges, but that such exactions are preferable to stringent growth controls—which are the only politically feasible alternatives in many cases.

In cities with intense peak-period travel demand, expanding road capacity may not reduce peak congestion much but instead induce more people to travel during the peak. These people constitute a "latent demand" for peak travel that is currently deterred only by the extent of congestion. Capacity expansion still creates benefits in such cases, inasmuch as more people can now exercise their preference for peak-period motor-vehicle travel, but it is unlikely to eliminate peak congestion. Downs (1962) describes this phenomenon as a "fundamental law" of traffic congestion in large cities: expressway traffic will grow to the point that peak expressway travel times are comparable to those on competing arterial streets or transit routes. More generally, empirical evidence suggests that new urban road capacity induces substantial new traffic (SACTRA, 1994; Goodwin, 1996).

If the competition is with public transit service instead of arterial streets, latent demand may be even more prominent. Because transit service is provided under increasing returns to scale when people's waiting times are taken into account (Mohring, 1972), expanding highway capacity may degrade the service that the transit operator can offer economically due to loss of transit riders attracted to the newly expanded highways. So in the new equilibrium, congestion could be worse than before highway capacity was expanded. This phenomenon, sometimes called the "Downs–Thomson paradox", is described by Downs (1962) and Holden (1989); Thomson (1977) and Mogridge et al. (1987) provide suggestive empirical evidence for it from London.

## 2.3. Other supply-side measures

Another response to the inability to finance infrastructure expansion has been to impose measures to utilize existing infrastructure more efficiently. Some of these measures involve controlling demand, which is treated in the next subsection. Others involve physical or operational changes that effectively increase capacity. Such measures, known as transportation systems management (TSM), are logically thought of as part of the investment design problem, and considerable attention has been devoted to them ever since Kain (1970) eloquently portrayed them as a low cost alternative to road widening. Some TSM measures, such as arterial signal timing and ramp metering on expressway entrances, are now routine in many areas and quite effective in modestly augmenting capacity.

One TSM measure now emphasized in many pollution control plans in the US is reserving lanes for high occupancy vehicles (HOVs) such as buses, vans and carpools. HOV lanes are most commonly viewed as demand management policies aimed at enticing more people to form carpools. An equally important function, however, may be to reduce aggregate travel time by speeding-up high occupancy vehicles at the expense of low occupancy ones. In a queuing context, this amounts to imposing a more efficient queue discipline. For example, suppose it takes 2 seconds for each vehicle to pass through a bottleneck. If a four-occupant carpool is moved ahead of 10 single-occupant cars in the queue, the carpool gains 20 seconds while each solo driver loses 2 seconds; therefore, 80 passenger seconds of delay are saved by the carpool at a cost of 20 passenger seconds of additional delay by the solo drivers.

Mohring (1979) and Small (1983) consider both functions of HOV lanes in the cases of urban arterials and expressways, respectively. They find that even accounting for the inconvenience of forming carpools, HOV lanes produce substantial benefits—approximately half those possible from fully optimal pricing. Their calculations assume, however, that no capacity is lost in the process of separating the traffic streams, and that any desired fraction of capacity can be allocated to HOVs. In practice, capacity usually can be allocated only one traffic lane at a time, and this indivisibility reduces the benefits and can make them negative (Dahlgren, 1998). Thus, a key to successful HOV lanes is finding a way not to waste too much of their capacity through indivisibilities; we return to this point when we discuss road pricing in the next subsection.

How cost-effective are HOV lanes? Kain et al. (1992) and Fuhs (1993) review a number of cases of HOV lanes and busways in North America. Kain et al. estimate that construction costs per daily passenger round-trip vary from between $3900 and $10,400 (1988 prices) for new roads, and between $20 and $410 for lane additions to existing roads. (By comparison, their figure for an average of four light rail systems is $38,800.) They also report the favorable early experience of a guided busway, opened in 1986 in Adelaide, Australia, whose specially equipped buses can also travel on regular city streets.

Low capital costs per passenger trip do not guarantee that HOV lanes will reduce traffic congestion, however. On this issue the empirical evidence is mixed but generally not encouraging. Giuliano et al. (1990) estimate, for example, that only about 4% of peak-period workers using a new HOV lane in Orange County, California, joined carpools because of the new lane.

TSM measures may include other direct controls on vehicle movements. Examples include controlled left turn lanes, oneway streets, limitations on curbside parking, and partial or complete bans on vehicles in designated parts of cities. Such vehicle bans are used successfully in many European cities, especially in historic areas with narrow streets (Hass-Klau, 1990). The evidence from Germany and the UK shows that they substantially increase pedestrian volumes and that total retail trade, while sometimes dropping for a time, remains healthy and often increases over a period of a few years (Hass-Klau, 1993).

Recently, a great deal of attention and money have been lavished on intelligent transportation systems (ITS), which attempt to make road travel more efficient using new information technology. Some of these measures are making modest improvements in people's trips by helping them find their way, or by routing them around areas with especially high congestion. However, simulation studies frequently show that once the market penetration of information systems exceeds a critical fraction, further dissemination has little effect on aggregate costs and may even raise them by facilitating routing decisions that minimize private but not social cost (Ben-Akiva et al., 1991; Mahmassani and Jayakrishnan, 1991; Arnott et al., 1991; Emmerink et al., 1996). More ambitious efforts aimed at increasing highway capacity by automating vehicle spacing are still preliminary and appear to be very expensive.

Managing the existing infrastructure more efficiently to increase its person-carrying capacity, then, seems a promising direction for traffic policy, but one with only limited potential beyond current practice.

## 2.4. Demand-side measures for congestion relief

Increasing the supply of highway infrastructure is only one way of dealing with supply–demand imbalance. Another way is to manipulate demand. Terminology is not uniform, but such demand-side measures are often divided into four categories: land use controls, public transit enhancement, transportation demand management and pricing measures.

### 2.4.1. Land use controls

It is natural to look to land use policies as a starting point for influencing travel demand since the demand for transportation is derived from the spatial separation of land uses.

Many urban planners have linked congestion to local imbalances between employment and housing, arguing that high-density employment centers often lack nearby housing suitable for their workers (Cervero, 1989a, b; Nowlan and Stewart, 1991). For this reason, some cities are trying to achieve a closer balance by restricting suburban sprawl, by channeling growth into outlying satellite towns, or by dispersing job growth to locations where residential sprawl has already occurred.

In the US, however, the ratio of jobs to housing is reasonably balanced in most cities, and the imbalances that do occur tend to be eliminated over time by market forces (Giuliano, 1991). Indeed, Small and Song (1992) show that in the Los Angeles region, employment and housing are sufficiently interspersed so that the average commute in 1980 could be reduced by two-thirds without changing land use patterns, just by reallocating workers to different houses. This suggests that factors other than availability of housing are causing people to live at some distance from their jobs. Such factors probably include public services, amenities, racial segregation, frequent job searches (Rouwendal and Rietveld, 1994; Crampton, 1997) and the complexities of job and housing choices by two-worker households (Kim, 1995).

Comparable calculations for Tokyo reveal a pattern of residential choices much more constrained by the available locations of housing (Merriman et al., 1995). Tokyo is a residentially dispersed metropolitan area with strong job concentrations in the central areas. This land use pattern, combined with high public transit usage, produces a much greater average commuting time than in any US city. Furthermore, two-worker families are less common in Japan than in most developed western nations. In such circumstances, the journey to work is more likely to be the dominant consideration in the choice of housing location.

Is there a directly observable link from land use patterns to the amount of road traffic? Newman and Kenworthy (1989, 1991) use data from 32 large metropolitan areas in developed countries to argue that the major determinant of automobile usage is in fact the density of development. They show that metropolitan areas with residential densities above 30–40 persons per hectare, such as those in western Europe and Japan, have much lower levels of automobile usage and rely more heavily on public transportation than their lower density counterparts in Canada, Australia and the US. However, they do not control for the effects of other variables, such as income levels, that might influence the mix of automobile and transit usage (Gordon and Richardson, 1989; Gómez-Ibáñez, 1989).

But even if Newman and Kenworthy (1989, 1991) are right, does their finding lead to useful policy conclusions? High urban densities in Europe and east Asia are probably due to a scarcity of habitable land relative to total population, and to the fact that many of their cities experienced their greatest population growth before the automobile era was fully upon them. More recent development on the peripheries of European cities has densities and patterns of transport use quite similar to those in the US. Thus, it is unclear that international differences in urban densities are primarily policy-driven.

Furthermore, once low density development becomes common it is extremely difficult to reverse. Downs (1992) systematically examines the prospects for using land use regulation to reduce transportation demand in US metropolitan areas. Downs defines a prototype city, complete with suburban subcenters, and applies empirical travel propensities to model various land use changes. He finds only a tiny effect on travel patterns from any regional land use policies that are even remotely politically feasible. In part, this is due to the fragmented governmental structure in US metropolitan areas and the ferocity with which local governments protect their powers of land use planning.

Finally, most advocates of using land use policies to influence transportation choices ignore the information that land markets are providing about economic efficiency. Urban job concentrations have deep roots in agglomeration economies, which in turn underlie the economic functioning of large cities. Although there may well be market failures in land development that prevent optimal land use, heavy-handed regulation that subverts land markets could exact a high cost. There seems to be little empirical research on how business efficiency is affected by policies aimed at limiting the spatial concentration of industry. Given the interest in such policies, their widespread use outside of North America, and their potentially far-reaching effects, such research could have a high payoff.

### 2.4.2. Public transit

Another approach to alleviating congestion is to promote public transportation in the hopes of enticing people not to drive cars during peak periods. The prospects for public transit are discussed in more detail later but, in brief, the experience of using transit improvements to reduce driving is disappointing. Furthermore, there is evidence that most of the drivers diverted to public transit are replaced by drivers who otherwise would travel at other times, take other routes or modes, or not travel at all (Small, 1992a: pp. 112–116). This is another example of the "fundamental law" of traffic congestion discussed above: in large congested cities a very large fraction of potential peak travelers must be enticed into transit before the latent demand for peak highway use is absorbed.

Nor does improving urban mass transit appear to be a very promising way to change land use patterns, especially where transit carries only a small proportion of trips. Small (1985) provides some numerical examples showing that given the current built environment, feasible changes in transportation policy can alter locational decisions so little that they cannot make much difference in urban form. Moreover, radial transit lines create incentives for residential sprawl much like those of radial highways (Gómez-Ibáñez, 1985).

### 2.4.3. *Transportation demand management (TDM)*

TDM is usually defined as policies that aim to directly influence travel behavior, especially for work trips. Pricing measures are sometimes included, but we separate them here because they use a quite different means of influencing behavior. TDM measures are often categorized under the somewhat broader rubric of "transportation control measures" or "congestion management".

One popular approach has been to promulgate regulations requiring employers to reduce peak-period highway use by their workers—for example, by offering preferential parking for carpools, adopting flexible work hours, or permitting employees to work at home or at centers equipped with special-purpose telecommunications. Other measures involve parking limitations, ride-sharing information services, and improvements for bicyclists and pedestrians.

How cost effective is TDM? Reviews of experience by OECD (1994) and Apogee Research (1994) conclude that most of the measures tried had disappointingly small results, and some are very costly to employers and/or travelers. Out of 15 measures reviewed by Apogee Research (1994: pp. 23–29), for example, none of the nonpricing measures was judged to have the potential to reduce regional vehicle travel by as much as 1.5% in a typical US metropolitan area. Furthermore, very few of them achieve trip reductions at a financial cost of less than $1.70 per vehicle round-trip avoided, which is the estimated net cost of a policy requiring that employees pay for parking; often costs are much higher, for example $10.60 (per vehicle round-trip eliminated) for providing bicycle and pedestrian facilities. One exception is ride-sharing information and promotion, which achieves only small reductions in vehicle trips but also incurs only $0.60 in administrative expenses per vehicle round-trip avoided.

Formal empirical studies of TDM measures are scarce. Two of the most well-examined TDM measures are those imposed by the air-quality control agency for the Los Angeles metropolitan area in the 1980s as part of the agency's effort to reduce automobile-related smog. One study, by Giuliano and Wachs (1997), examines the effects of a regulation that required large employers to submit plans for reducing automobile commuting by their employees. Their analysis of the experience of 243 large companies showed that only three incentives offered by employers had a statistically significant impact on average vehicle occupancy for employee work trips during peak periods: information and marketing, subsidies for alternative modes and parking incentives for carpools. ("Parking incentives" consist mainly of preferential parking for carpools, plus some rarely used pricing incentives.)

Brownstone and Golob (1992) also examine the Los Angeles experience, by estimating a disaggregate travel demand model on a sample of over 2000 commuters. They find that two categories of ride-sharing incentives have substantial and statistically significant effects on choice of carpool mode: preferential parking at work and availability of HOV lanes. If every employee in the region were offered preferential parking, for example, they estimate that the number of solo commuters would decline by about 6%.

Thus, it seems that only a few nonpricing TDM measures have a discernible influence on travel behavior, and that these are either prohibitively expensive or have only a limited potential in aggregate. It is probably worth pursuing selected TDM policies but they cannot be expected to have a very large impact.

### 2.4.4. Pricing measures

Most of the policies discussed above elicit only small changes in behavior because they change the relative advantages to travelers of different modes, times, or routes only slightly. Even HOV lanes, potentially a big time saver, do not perform as well as hoped because of the additional time and loss in flexibility involved in sharing rides, especially where trips are dispersed and work schedules are flexible. The policies also do nothing to reduce the attractiveness of peak-hour vehicle use for categories of trips not targeted directly, and thus tend to be undermined by latent demand.

Pricing measures, by contrast, can significantly deter trips of all types, while permitting flexible travel patterns. They encourage people to use ride-sharing or mass transit when feasible, but allow them to switch to the car at other times. A variety of forms of pricing have been proposed and tested, including raising parking charges or charging tolls for use of congested roads.

Parking charges have been studied the most and have considerable potential (Giuliano and Small, 1995). Shoup (1994) reports that parking is free for 99% of all automobile trips in the US. His research on seven case studies from Los Angeles, Washington (DC) and Ottawa, demonstrates that charging realistic market rates for parking in large cities can reduce the proportion of commuters who drive alone by an average of 25%. Shoup has advocated a relatively unintrusive method of charging for employee parking known as "cashing out free parking". Under Shoup's proposal, employers who offer free parking are required to offer an equivalent cash bonus as an alternative. A limited form of cashing out was legislated in California in 1992, but the concept is severely inhibited by US tax laws that exempt free parking—but not cash subsidies—from employees' taxable income.

One disadvantage of using parking charges to reduce congestion is that they do not deter through trips, which may in fact increase to fill the street capacity vacated by former free parkers. Of course, there is a market argument for pricing parking independent of its effect on congestion (as a means of optimizing the use of resources to provide parking spaces). Furthermore, the presence of congestion and tax distortions makes the practice of including free parking as a standard fringe benefit of employment less socially efficient or desirable.

A more direct approach is to price roads at or near marginal congestion cost, a policy known as "congestion pricing". Vickrey's (1955) eloquent advocacy stimulated academic, but little practical, interest in congestion pricing for many decades. Practical interest has arisen recently, however, due to a combination of government needs for additional revenue sources, failures of other measures to reduce congestion, and new technology that makes it feasible to price roads without toll booths (Small et al., 1989: Chap. 5). A thorough, policy-oriented review is provided by National Research Council (1994). Key theoretical treatments include Walters (1961), Vickrey (1969) and Arnott et al. (1993).

Empirical evidence confirms that congestion pricing, even when far from optimally designed, can substantially reduce congestion if the charges are high and well targeted. The most dramatic example is Singapore, where from 1975 through 1994, a peak charge for entering the central area was assessed, first during the morning peak only and then during both morning and afternoon peaks. (Beginning in 1995 the charge was extended to all day on weekdays and a charge system was imposed on two expressways that approach the central area.) The entry charge varied roughly from US$1.50 to 2.50 per day over those years. Peak traffic into the central area was reduced immediately by 47% (Gómez-Ibáñez and Small, 1994: Chap. 3), although there is debate about how much of this was due to other measures such as taxes and quotas on new cars and increases in parking fees. Singapore converted from a system of paper licenses displayed in windshields to electronic collection of charges in 1998 (Phang and Asher, 1997; Phang and Toh, 1997). The electronic system will eventually permit Singapore to vary charges more finely by time-of-day, location and level of congestion.

Low charges or charges that vary little by time-of-day have much less effect. Examples include three Norwegian cities which recently established toll rings around their central areas. The charges (roughly US$0.72 to 1.60 per round-trip) are small relative to incomes and vary little by time-of-day. Effects on traffic have been correspondingly small, probably less than 5%. The most interesting effects are in one of the cities (Trondheim), where the charge is lifted at 5 pm, causing some travellers to delay their trips and some retailers to extend their shop hours (Gómez-Ibáñez and Small, 1994: Chap. 4).

Simulation models also suggest that reasonably fine-tuned congestion pricing policies could significantly reduce congestion (Keeler and Small, 1977; Harvey, 1994; Anderson and Mohring, 1996). Prices would of course vary widely; Harvey (1994: Tables 3–4), for example, estimates average peak period fees of $0.10 and $0.15 per mile for the San Francisco and Los Angeles metropolitan areas, respectively. Harvey's fees are not necessarily optimal but were chosen to reduce congestion to a specified level; they imply roughly $2 and $3 per daily round-trip for a typical worker traveling during the peak in both directions. Harvey also estimates that a $3 per day employee parking fee would have a somewhat smaller effect on overall vehicle travel.

Unfortunately, congestion pricing has not proven to be politically popular. The basic problem is that the efficiency gains for most motorists seem small and uncertain while the charges they will have to pay are large and very visible (Altshuler et al., 1979; Gómez-Ibáñez, 1992; Giuliano, 1992; Rom, 1994). The charges are, of course, a transfer from motorists to the government, and in theory could be rebated in some way so that the motorists would be better off than before. But motorists seldom understand this, or trust that governments will rebate in this way.[7]

It is thus understandable that the more grandiose plans for congestion pricing once advanced in Hong Kong, London, the Netherlands, Stockholm, and Cambridge, England, have been abandoned or delayed. It seems likely that experience in the near future will be limited to small demonstrations or special cases where time-varying prices can reinforce policies adopted for other purposes. Two examples are discussed in the next subsection: one where time-varying tolls are needed to finance new infrastructure, and another where a revenue-neutral change to a time-varying toll structure can solve a well-defined peaking problem on an existing toll road. A third possibility is a concept known as high-occupancy/toll (HOT) lanes, in which unused capacity in an HOV lane is released for single-

---

[7] In other cases the benefits may simply be small because long distance automobile commuters are self-selected from those with relatively low values of time (Calfee and Winston, 1998).

occupant cars for a fee, giving them in effect a time-varying toll since only during the peak period would they need to take the tolled lane at all. The first such facility opened in the Los Angeles area in 1995 (Small and Gómez-Ibáñez, 1998) and the following year some existing HOV lanes near San Diego were converted to HOT lanes (Duve, 1994; Kawada et. al., 1997).

One of the keys to political viability of any road pricing scheme will be to establish a clear link between toll revenues and expenditures on things that citizens want. The Norwegian toll rings were designed to finance an explicit set of infrastructure projects. Equally telling, a planned toll ring for Stockholm, part of a package involving new highways and rail improvements, was at least temporarily abandoned due to public opposition to one of the highway projects being financed by it. Jones (1991) finds that public opinion in London is much more favorable toward road pricing if it is presented as part of a package including improvements to public transportation. Many commentators in the US believe that some or all of the revenues from road pricing would need to be offset by tax decreases for the concept to be viable. Recent survey evidence from the Los Angeles region shows support rising from 40 to 49% when revenue is used to reduce other taxes (Harrington and Krupnik, 1996). Small (1992b) employs the principle of tax offsets as part of an attempt to describe a congestion pricing package that would be Pareto-improving to broad classes of people, in the sense that the average person in each identifiable income class or interest group would be made better off.

## 2.5. Private toll roads

Our review of both supply- and demand-side measures to alleviate congestion is discouraging: most policies seem either ineffective, of limited aggregate potential, too costly, or politically unpopular. It is perhaps natural, then, that policy-makers have increasingly turned to an old institutional arrangement—private highways. This method of providing highways simultaneously addresses supply- and demand-side approaches because a private firm builds the highway and chooses, within limits, the pricing structure. Gómez-Ibáñez and Meyer (1993) review the concept and recent experience in Europe, the US and several developing nations. Viton (1995) shows through simulation that even in competition with subsidized public roads, private roads are financially viable under a wide variety of conditions.

Most developed nations have some toll roads, with some—especially in France and Spain—operated by private companies. Developing and eastern European nations are also turning to private toll roads. In most cases these are intercity roads, but there is increasing interest in private urban roads. Urban toll roads offer greater traffic potential but they also typically cost much more to build and may face severe competition from untolled alternatives in the off peak (Johansen, 1989; Gómez-Ibáñez and Meyer, 1993).

The advantages of private provision can be considerable. By tapping private capital markets and issuing private debt, private roads can provide a way around borrowing contraints that affect some governments, particularly in developing countries. Lower construction and operating costs are another possibility, although the evidence for them is limited (Gómez-Ibáñez and Meyer, 1993: pp. 201–203). Pricing structures that may be politically or legally infeasible for a public roadway are sometimes possible for a private enterprise. Other quite unexpected forms of innovation, such as novel construction methods and routes, may occur as happened in several California proposals. Environmental or other objections to specific sites may in some cases be overcome by private entrepreneurs with the flexibility and motivation to do so; and if a project appears too vulnerable to delay to be economical, the private company may be quicker to cut its losses and abandon the plan before it becomes a costly embarassment.

On the other hand, private ownership can create problems as well. One of these stems from the fact that private roads are usually financed by tolls while public roads are often financed by broad-based taxes. The use of tolls avoids the collection and deadweight losses of taxation, but it also causes an inefficient allocation of traffic between the private toll road and any competing free, or nearly free, alternative routes. The private highway will carry too little traffic which, given that it is of higher quality, will produce greater congestion and higher accident rates overall than if the entire system were optimally managed. Traffic misallocation is especially a problem where tolls are very high, as in Spain and Mexico (Gómez-Ibáñez and Meyer, 1993: pp. 141–142, 156–157; Ruster, 1997). Furthermore, in the presence of free roads the investment signals provided by profitability of a proposed new road link do not accurately reflect its overall effect on welfare (Mills, 1995).

Further problems arise where the owner of a private highway has so much monopoly power that authorities turn to regulation. Will the potential efficiencies of unregulated private enterprise be realized if competition is lacking? Can regulation be imposed without destroying the advantages of flexibility and innovation? Given the resistance to time-of-day pricing of public highways, for example, how likely is it that a public regulatory body would permit such a pricing structure on a regulated highway?

On the last question, there were only two cases as of 1996 of toll roads where congestion pricing was used. One is on the French Autoroute A1 southbound from Lille to Paris, that is operated by a publicly owned but independent road corporation; here a revenue-neutral time-of-day differential, on Sundays only, was introduced successfully in 1992 (Gómez-Ibáñez and Small, 1994: Chap. 5). The other is the new HOT lanes, mentioned earlier, that were built in the median of the existing Riverside Freeway (State Route 91) in the Los Angeles region. A private consortium built these lanes under a franchise agreement with the State of California that allows the consortium flexibility to adjust its time-of-day pricing schedule subject only to a cap on its overall rate of return (Gómez-Ibáñez and Meyer, 1993: pp. 173–176; Fielding, 1994).

The form of franchising is crucial to reaping the advantages of pricing flexibility. European and developing nations have typically regulated toll rates, leading to the usual problems of political interference with economic decisions. For example, France developed an elaborate system of cross-subsidies both within and across its toll road operating companies, public as well as private; the result is that investment decisions do not face any real market discipline, and there is political pressure to charge toll rates that are relatively uniform across the entire country. In contrast, California adopted rate of return regulation for its recent experiment with private highways, which in theory should preserve more incentives for efficiency. A number of researchers are beginning to explore other franchising or regulatory regimes that would protect the public from potential monopoly abuse by the private toll road operator while still preserving the operator's flexibility to implement time-of-day or other congestion pricing regimes (Engel et al., 1997; Fielding and Klein, 1993). Clearly, the best franchising or regulatory framework will depend in complex ways on the specific local context. This is a topic ripe for research using tools from the fields of industrial organization and of law and economics.

## 2.6. Conclusion

Policy toward relieving congestion is at something of an impasse. Expanding capacity by building or widening roads remains the primary response, and is effective to a degree—but road construction cannot keep up with demand in many locations due to high costs and political opposition. The more ambitious schemes for augmenting capacity with information or vehicle-guidance technology appear too expensive and uncertain for near-term application. Transportation systems management and a few selected demand management policies offer economical but modest gains.

Pricing measures are cost effective and have the potential to significantly reduce urban traffic congestion, but politics appears to preclude widespread adoption in the foreseeable future. Nevertheless, two avenues toward the dissemination of road pricing seem to be gradually opening. The first is targeted, limited-purpose projects such as those in France and California which can command support by solving problems peculiar to a local situation in a manner that is viewed as experimental. The second is private highways, to which governments are occasionally turning for financial reasons and which may be allowed pricing flexibility if policy-makers understand its importance. Both avenues lead to small-scale demonstrations of principles and technology. As confidence is gained, technology and financial imperatives will encourage more road operators to experiment with pricing flexibility.

Meanwhile, it may be comforting that congestion is a self-limiting phenomenon. When it gets too bad, people find ways to avoid or mitigate it—perhaps a better car stereo, mobile phone, or relocation outside the congested city core. Some of these measures are harmless enough but others arguably create further negative externalities, a possibility that adds weight to economists' appeals to adopt efficient measures that tackle congestion directly.

## 3. Motor vehicle air pollution

The environmental costs of motor vehicles are another great concern. The air pollution problem is especially well documented and motor vehicles are important contributors to it. In Europe and the US, motor vehicles typically account for 32–98% of national emissions of carbon monoxide (CO), volatile organic chemicals (VOCs, primarily hydrocarbons), and nitrogen oxides ($NO_x$) (Small and Kazimi, 1995: Table 1). Transportation also accounts for an important fraction of emissions of "greenhouse gases", especially carbon dioxide ($CO_2$), that are believed to be having significant long-term effects on the earth's climate (Cline, 1991). Resulting policy issues are discussed by many authors including Button (1993), Hensher (1993), Whitelegg (1993) and Harrington et al. (1995).

### 3.1. Damage estimates

The environmental costs of motor vehicles are hard to measure and, as one would expect, vary according to local conditions. Most of the available estimates are for the health and materials-damage effects of local (or tropospheric) air pollution rather than for the damage from depletion of the ozone layer by greenhouse gases. Reviewing studies from Europe, Australia and the US, for example, Quinet (1994: p. 58) reports that estimated aggregate social costs average around 0.3 and

0.4% of GNP for noise and local air pollution, respectively. Small and Kazimi (1995) estimate health costs from local air pollution caused by the average on-road automobile in the Los Angeles region in 1992 to be $0.03 per vehicle mile using middle-range assumptions. Costs of truck emissions are higher by a factor of 16. The Small-Kazimi estimates are within the rather wide range estimated by McCubbin and Delucchi (1996), who similarly find trucks to be more damaging by a factor of at least 10. In both studies, most of the health costs are from increased mortality due to inhalable particulates, both those directly emitted and those indirectly formed in the atmosphere from VOCs, $NO_x$ and sulfur oxides $(SO_x)$. The rest of the costs are due mainly to minor illnesses from ozone that is formed in the atmosphere from VOCs and $NO_x$.

Estimates of damage from greenhouse-gas emissions are speculative given the extreme scientific uncertainty and the very long-term nature of the effects. Some policy analysts have used the cost of control as a proxy for damage costs, although this is very controversial. The basic idea is that the costs of the emissions control schemes considered in recent international negotiations should, if policy makers are rational, reflect their assessment of what the damage costs are likely to be. One widely discussed emission control scenario involves stabilizing $CO_2$ emissions at 1990 levels by the year 2000 and at 20% below those levels by the year 2010. Manne and Richels (1992) estimate that the marginal $CO_2$ reduction costs implied by such a scenario rise over time and then stabilize at around $208 per ton of carbon in the US (1990 prices). This is more than twice the size of a carbon tax proposed but never implemented in the European Union, and is also within the range of other estimates of carbon taxes required to meet various reductions (Quinet, 1994: p. 49). Updated to 1992 prices, this figure is equivalent to 3.1 cents per vehicle mile for an automobile with the 1992 US average fuel economy (Small and Kazimi, 1995: p. 28). But of course this emissions control scheme is both stringent and arbitrary: the damage costs for greenhouse gases may actually be much lower than these control costs imply (Prud'homme, 1997; Gómez-Ibáñez, 1997).

Policy-makers have been partially successful in improving air quality. In the US, the ambient levels of most pollutants have been reduced steadily since the 1960s, although targets for achieving health-based standards have slipped by decades and there has been little improvement in ozone, for which motor vehicles bear substantial responsibility (Calvert et al., 1993; Harrington et al., 1995). Europe has lagged behind the US in emission controls on motor vehicles (Small and Kazimi, 1995: pp. 9–11). In Japan, high population densities and levels of automobile usage make air pollution a continuing problem. Tangible policies bringing about significant reductions in $CO_2$ emissions, other than the high fuel taxes already in place for other reasons, have yet to be realized in any part of the world.

## 3.2. The relationship between congestion and pollution

Certain transportation policies might reduce both congestion and air pollution since both problems are related to vehicle use. Such policies might also enjoy a broader base of political support (Rom, 1994). However, policies aimed broadly at reducing overall vehicle use often do little to reduce either congestion or pollution, while policies that are well targeted toward one of these problems often address the other only poorly (Hall, 1995). The problem is that congestion is specific to location and time, whereas pollution emissions are specific to vehicle characteristics and driving behavior.

Simulations suggest, for example, that congestion pricing could reduce air pollution but not by enough to excite most environmentalists. Harvey (1994) estimates that fairly high congestion charges in the San Francisco and Los Angeles areas would reduce motor-vehicle VOC emissions by 5.5 and 8.2% and $CO_2$ emissions by 6.5 and 9.2%, respectively. The primary effect of congestion charges is to shift traffic from peak to off-peak rather than to eliminate it altogether. Conversely, emission charges have rather small effects on congestion because they encourage reduced emissions per mile more than reduced travel.

Planners are also less hopeful than before that reductions in congestion will reduce average emissions per vehicle mile. It is true that CO and VOC emissions are higher in stop-and-go traffic. $NO_x$ emissions tend to increase with average speed, however, as do CO and VOCs emissions at speeds above those characteristic of moderately congested expressways. Furthermore, there is great statistical uncertainty in the relationship between emissions and speed, especially for increases from moderate to high average speed (Guensler and Sperling, 1994).

Probably the safest conclusion is that policies aimed at reducing congestion and pollution tend to reinforce each other, but that specific measures targeted toward each goal are necessary for success. Once such measures are identified, it may make political sense to package them together.

## 3.3. Technological controls

Nearly all of the reductions in motor vehicle air pollution achieved so far have been due to mandated reductions in emission rates per vehicle mile. In the US, which requires the most stringent controls, 1993-model new cars were required to emit 95% fewer VOCs and CO, and 75% fewer $NO_x$, than new cars 25 years earlier. California's standards are even stricter, and the schedule fixed by the Clear

Air Act Amendments of 1990 continues a policy of significant reductions. In-use emissions from the fleet at large have declined by smaller but still impressive amounts (Calvert et al., 1993: pp. 38–39).

Further tightening of the already low legal emission standards may not accomplish much. The problem is that the remaining emissions appear to be dominated by three factors that are missed by current enforcement mechanisms. First, a substantial fraction of total emissions now comes from a relatively small number of vehicles, known as "gross polluters", with malfunctioning emissions control systems. Second, large emissions occur during brief episodes in ordinary driving that are inadequately represented in the test procedures, such as rapid acceleration when entering expressway traffic.[8] Third, inspection and maintenance programs fail to accurately identify vehicles out of compliance or to elicit adequate repairs when such vehicles are identified.

Further tightening of emissions standards may have little or no effect on these sources of emissions, which are caused by a combination of the inherent complexity of automotive technology, fraud or laxity during inspections, tampering by vehicle owners, and the limitations of test procedures (Glazer et al., 1995). Furthermore, it is now recognized that previous estimates understated aggregate VOC emissions from mobile sources by a factor of two or three (Small and Kazimi, 1995: pp. 11–12). This, in turn, misled policy-makers to rely excessively on controlling VOCs instead of $NO_x$ as the means of reducing ozone, since the chemistry of ozone formation depends critically on the ratio of VOCs to $NO_x$ in the ambient air (National Research Council, 1991).

It is now possible to measure actual emissions by cars on a highway by measuring light absorption from a roadside laser beam. This technology appears accurate enough to improve existing vehicle inspection programs by, for example, using random roadside screenings to identify vehicles in need of a more thorough inspection (Glazer et al., 1995). It is even possible that such technology could eventually become the basis for direct emission charges.

Another technological approach is to reformulate fuel in order to lower emissions. This policy, which is included in the US Clean Air Act Amendments of 1990, has the advantage that it immediately improves emissions from the entire fleet, not just new cars. Its disadvantages include large investments for refinery conversion, the danger of creating maintenance or performance problems in vehicles designed for different fuel mixes, and possible safety hazards.

---

[8] These episodes are known as "off-cycle" or "open-loop" events. For careful documentation, see Calvert et al. (1993), and references in Small and Kazimi (1995).

Other possibilities include introducing "alternative fuel vehicles" that run on methanol, ethanol, compressed natural gas, electricity, or other more exotic fuels. Such alternative fuels offer one way to reduce emissions, although not necessarily across the board. They also raise new problems such as toxic formaldehyde emissions from methanol and the safe disposal of lead and cadmium from current-generation electric batteries (Lave et al., 1995).

A more drastic approach is to require a proportion of vehicles sold to have zero emissions. California law requires that specified percentages of "zero-emission vehicles" be phased in by vehicle manufacturers, and several other states in the northeast have announced a similar approach. In practice this requires electric cars (whose off-site emissions at the power source are not counted). Aside from the question of whether or not "zero" has any defensible scientific meaning as an emission standard, this regulation is clearly based on a belief in a particular technological solution, and it may ignore some complex behavioral adaptations. For example, electric cars have a shorter range so households purchasing them might use their other, older cars more often (Kazimi, 1997).

Harrington et al. (1995) examine the cost-effectiveness of various policies applied to the US as a whole. Cost-effectiveness is measured, somewhat narrowly, as cost per ton of VOCs removed. Reformulated gasoline and inspection and maintenance programs are relatively cheap ($1900–6000 per ton VOCs removed). The tighter emission standards being implemented by California cost about the same or as much as 10 times more, depending on assumptions. Alternative fuel vehicles are the most expensive, with electric vehicles estimated to entail a cost of $29,000–108,000 per ton VOCs removed. As a point of comparison, the health costs estimated by Small and Kazimi (1995: Table 5) for the Los Angeles region come to $2920 per ton VOCs, with a range of $1240–4080 under various alternative assumptions. To the extent the latter estimates accurately measure people's willingness to pay to breathe less polluted air, it appears that many current measures do not meet a cost-benefit test.

## 3.4. Transportation control measures

Clean air legislation promotes several of the TDM policies also used for congestion relief. In the clean air context they are usually called "transportation control measures", or TCMs, the term used in the US Clean Air Act. Hall (1995) finds that TCMs have only limited ability to reduce motor vehicle travel compared with pricing policies, in agreement with our earlier discussion of TDM policies toward congestion. Employer-based policies are especially ineffective in controlling pollution because work trips are an even smaller proportion of total travel (less than one-fourth in the US) than they are of peak-period travel.

## 3.5. Pricing policies

In theory, one might charge motorists for air pollution on the basis of actual vehicle emissions in use. Assuming this will not be feasible for some time, an approximation would be a fee proportional to distance traveled, with the rate determined by the estimated emissions rates (as measured, for example, by an annual test of the vehicle or by the manufacturer's new-vehicle test results). This proposal would not eliminate the need for more reliable inspections, but it would strongly encourage drivers to minimize their use of high-polluting vehicles. For $CO_2$ emissions, the most direct pricing policy would be a fuel tax whose rate is based on the carbon content of the fuel.

A number of studies have examined the quantitative impacts of pricing policies. Harvey (1994) tests distance- and emissions-based pollution fees in his San Francisco and Los Angeles simulations described earlier. The pollution fees he tests are rather small, about $110 per year per vehicle in Los Angeles, so have correspondingly small effects. Employee parking fees of $3 per day reduce emissions by only around 1.4–2.1%, presumably because the fees affect only the minority of trips that are to or from work and because they fail to discourage new trips from taking advantage of any improvement in travel conditions.

Harvey also tests a gasoline tax increase of $2 per gallon in his San Francisco simulations. Such a tax is equivalent to $670 per ton carbon,[9] more than three times the amount implied by international agreements for $CO_2$ reduction discussed earlier. The gasoline tax increase costs the average vehicle owner around $1000 per year[10] and is predicted to have modest impacts on both vehicle miles of travel (reduced by 8.1%) and on emissions (VOC, CO and $NO_x$ all reduced by around 7.7%). The gasoline tax is a rather blunt instrument for dealing with local pollution, however, because it is not emissions-based. The tax is best targeted for $CO_2$ control, and elicits an estimated 36% reduction in $CO_2$ emissions. This reduction is more than four times the estimated reduction in total vehicle travel because motorists shift toward vehicles and driving patterns that are more fuel-efficient.

---

[9] This is based on 1 ton carbon content for every 335 gallons of refined petroleum product, calculated from Manne and Richels (1992: p. 59).

[10] Based on average annual fuel consumption of 513 gallons per year for US passenger cars in 1993 (American Automobile Manufacturers Association, 1995: p. 66).

Harrington et al. (1995) examine the cost-effectiveness of emissions-based fees as well as the regulatory policies described earlier. They find the fees to be considerably less costly—$1650 per ton of VOCs removed—than any other policies considered with the exception of congestion pricing, which the authors regard as costless because it produces travel-time benefits.

Koopman (1995) simulates the effects of policies calibrated to reduce $CO_2$ emissions in Europe by 10% by the period 2010–2015. One policy is a carbon tax that implies a 21% rise in average gasoline prices. This is compared with three other policies also aimed directly at fuel consumption—fuel taxes, "gas-guzzler" taxes and fuel economy standards—and with car ownership taxes. The policies aimed directly at fuel consumption are found to have very similar overall welfare costs, with the carbon tax having a slight edge. Car ownership taxes are much worse, imposing welfare losses nearly three times as high for the same $CO_2$ reduction. The effects on household behavior are also very different. Taxes on car ownership tend to reduce car ownership, naturally enough. With carbon taxes and other measures aimed directly at fuel use, however, car ownership and use fall only 3.3 and 4.3%, respectively; households respond instead by shifting to more fuel-efficient and smaller vehicles. The fuel or carbon taxes are a relatively minor share of total costs of owning and using cars to begin with, and their share is reduced by the shift to fuel- efficient vehicles (Greene, 1992), further diminishing the incentive to own fewer cars or drive them less.

Another pricing policy is marketable permits, which under certain conditions provides incentives equivalent to those of emission fees. A variety of marketable-permit schemes have been developed (Hahn, 1989), but none has been applied to mobile sources.

*3.6. Conclusion*

Estimates suggest that the marginal social costs of motor vehicle use due to air pollution are a small fraction of the marginal cost of urban driving. Thus, if motorists had to pay for the air pollution damages they cause, total vehicle travel would not be affected much. This finding implies that measures to reduce emissions per vehicle mile are likely to be the most efficient means of motor vehicle air pollution control.

The principal measure for reducing emissions per vehicle mile to date has been to set maximum emissions standards for new vehicles. This has worked reasonably well so far, but further progress will require stronger incentives on individual vehicle owners to maintain their vehicles so as to keep emissions low. Such incentives affect individual drivers in a more direct way than previous policies, and as a result most governments have been reluctant to move in this direction.

The problem of global $CO_2$ pollution is rather different and far more uncertain. Nevertheless, current evidence does not provide a compelling case for drastic across the board reductions in vehicle travel. Rather, incentives for fuel conservation seem called for, and the evidence suggests that the primary response would be through improved fuel efficiency of vehicles. Once again, a technical solution underlies the most promising approach.

## 4. Motor vehicle accidents

Economic theory has not provided the same ready consensus with regard to the problem of motor vehicle accidents that it has for congestion and pollution. Yet the aggregate costs of accidents appear to be far higher than those of pollution, and comparable to those of congestion even in urban areas (Small, 1992a: Table 3.2). The difference in treatment may be due to the elegance with which congestion and pollution can be formulated as externalities. For motor vehicle accidents, the externality formulation is certainly possible (Jansson, 1994), but the nature of the externality in practice is less clear. Meanwhile other potential market failures—arising from insurance, incentives in the legal system, and the like— are prominent. Such issues in the evaluation of motor vehicle accidents make the subject fascinating and potentially very productive for economic analysis.

### 4.1. Magnitude of accident costs

In a widely cited and comprehensive study, Miller (1993) estimates that motor vehicle accidents cost the US $333 billion in 1988, or an average of $0.164 per vehicle mile.[11] In another careful study, Newbery (1988) estimates the total 1984 accident costs in the UK at £26 billion (in 1986 prices) or US$0.22 per vehicle mile.[12] These US and UK estimates correspond to 7 and 5% of GNP, about three to four times higher than the typical estimates of 1.5–2% found by Quinet (1994: pp. 37–39, 58) in a review of other studies—which include rural areas, where accident costs are quite high because higher rural traffic speeds increase accident severity. These cost estimates are relative to a world with no accidents at all, a

[11] Total motor vehicle in the US was 2,025.6 billion vehicle miles, according to the US FHWA (1988: Table M–1).

[12] This applies the 1986 exchange rate of £1 = US$1.47, from US Council of Economic Advisors, Annual Report, 1995, in *Economic Report of the President*, Feb. 1995 (Washington: US Government Printing Office: Table B-112.) Vehicle kilometers traveled are inferred from Newbery's Tables 4 and 5 to be 273.8 billion.

level of safety that would of course be impossible to provide at a reasonable cost to society.

Accident costs are not as heavily dominated by fatalities as are air pollution costs. Fatalities account for only 34% of Miller's US estimates; nonfatal injuries account for 53% (brain injuries being the largest category), and property damage and time delays account for the remaining 13%. In Newbery's (1988) UK study, fatalities and serious injuries each account for 49% of the estimate. The difference may be that Newbery uses a value of life about 50% higher than that used by Miller. Neither study includes insurance administrative costs, which elsewhere have been found to be very large in the US, perhaps two-thirds as large as all property damage (Small, 1992a: p. 78).

Traffic accident fatalities per vehicle mile have dropped steadily throughout the developed world. Between 1970 and 1992 they fell 60% in the US, 65% in Canada, 72% in Japan, and more than two-thirds in eight of the 11 European nations for which data are available (Pucher and Lefèvre, 1996: p. 26). The reduction is thought to be due to a combination of changes including road improvements, efforts to discourage drunk driving, and safety improvements to vehicles. In the US, some would also credit the national 55 mile per hour speed limit enacted in 1974 and repealed in 1996, although Lave (1985) argues that it had little if any positive effect because accident rates are more closely related to variance in speed across vehicles than to average speed.

## 4.2. *Issues in valuation*

Economists have clarified a number of conceptual issues in valuing safety improvements. The most important is the idea of valuing the health consequences by the aggregate of individuals' willingness to pay to reduce the risk of injury or death from accidents. This is now well established in the literature, and replaces the less justified practice of measuring the market value of lost production.

The empirical measurement of willingness to pay, particularly for reduction in risk of death, is reviewed by Kahn (1986), Jones-Lee (1990) and Viscusi (1993), among others. The studies with the best controls for bias seem to yield values for developed nations on the order of $1.5–9.0 million per statistical life, i.e., $1.50–9.00 for a marginal increment of 1 per million in risk of death. Actual practice in valuing statistical lives for purposes of cost-benefit analysis in Europe is summarized in Quinet (1994) and analyzed in EC (1994).

Just how the value of life varies across population groups is an important unsettled question. If it varies inversely with age, as many suspect, that variation would further increase the relative cost of motor vehicle accidents (which kill people across the age spectrum) compared to air pollution (which tends to kill older people from cancer and respiratory diseases).

Another issue is whether or not to add to the individual's willingness to pay an additional amount reflecting the concerns of family and friends. Jones-Lee (1990) suggests that this could add 40 or 50% to the "value of life". There are two arguments for not doing so, but neither is definitive. The first, due to Bergstrom (1982), is that family and friends may place value on the individual's utility rather than just on her health, in which case they would not want to alter her own tradeoffs between health and money:

> to push values of safety beyond the level implied by people's willingness to pay for their own safety would result in an "overprovision" of safety relative to the other determinants of their utility. (Jones-Lee, 1990: p. 42)

Empirical evidence is needed to decide the extent to which family and relatives' altruism is health-specific. The second argument is that the individual may already take her family's and friends' concern for her into account in her own utility function.

The willingness to pay to prevent nonfatal injuries is analyzed carefully by Jones-Lee et al. (1995) based on survey data from the UK. Their results suggest that people are unable to provide reliable answers when asked directly, through what are called "contingent valuation" questions. But credible self-consistent answers are given to more indirect questions which ask people to choose among hypothetical treatments for speficied road injuries, some of which have better probable outcomes than others but ancillary fatal risks. From these questions, the authors make a strong case that the average valuation of a nonfatal injury classified as "serious" in the UK—a weighted average of injuries ranging from some requiring 3–4 months for full recovery to some causing severe permanent disability—is about 9.5% of the valuation of a fatal injury.

## 4.3. The demand for safety

Policy toward motor vehicle safety has often been discussed under the assumption that people do not behave as rational consumers when evaluating safety. However, empirical research has clearly established that people are willing to pay for safety improvements, and is mostly consistent with the conclusion that they evaluate costs and benefits rationally. Examples of this research include studies of the demand for specific safety features on vehicles (Arnould and Grabowski, 1981; Mannering and Winston, 1995), for vehicle models that rank high on an index of crash worthiness (McCarthy, 1990), and for models with good records of actual safety outcomes (Winston and Mannering, 1984).

A related aspect of consumer behavior is the extent to which people may compensate for safer vehicles by engaging in more dangerous behavior—or equivalently, the extent to which they offset safety hazards by being careful. Peltzman (1975) posited that the potentially beneficial effects of government-mandated safety features in new vehicles would be partially or fully offset because drivers would respond by driving more dangerously. (Safety features could even raise accident costs overall if such drivers then injure pedestrians and cyclists more frequently.) Many researchers have tested the "Peltzman effect" empirically; a good example is Chirinko and Harper (1993), who also provide a useful review. A common finding is that compensating behavior occurs but does not fully offset the original safety improvement. Such studies are frequently plagued by problems of changing vehicle mix and by potential endogeneity of the variables measuring the use of safety equipment.

## 4.4. Externalities

For policy purposes it is important to know what portion of accident costs is externalities—that is, how do the marginal costs resulting from a motorist's decisions about when, where, and how to drive compare to his or her perceived private cost? This question entails both conceptual and empirical issues that are far from fully understood. Here, we examine a few such issues that seem to us important and amenable to analysis using available tools of applied microeconomics.

*How do accident costs vary with traffic volumes?* The extent to which accident costs are externalities depends critically on the extent to which accident rates and their severity are affected by traffic volume. The problem is similar to that of congestion; if adding additional vehicles to the traffic stream increases the accident rate per vehicle, then a form of congestion externality exists even if each traveler fully bears the average accident risk (Vickrey, 1968).

Like the relationship between traffic volumes and speeds, the relationship between volumes and accident rates could be a simple static one, or it might depend in complex ways on the dynamics of traffic movements. It may be important to know how different vehicle types or driver behaviors affect costs. At the simplest static level, the question may be reduced to asking what is the elasticity of total accident cost on a road with respect to its traffic volume; if the elasticity exceeds 1, there is a negative externality because each user imposes costs on other users, causing social marginal cost to exceed private marginal cost.

Until recently, most researchers had to make assumptions about the relationship between accident costs and traffic volume since there was little empirical evidence available. Vickrey (1968) argues from impressionistic evidence for an elasticity of 1.5; Jones-Lee (1990) follows official British practice by assuming 1.0 (i.e., linearity); Newbery (1988) splits the difference at 1.25.

Some empirical work is emerging which suggests a more complex story in which the elasticity could actually be less than 1, particularly for accidents serious enough to cause a fatality or injury rather than only property damage. Zho and Sisopiku (1997) find that accident rates on a 26 km segment of an urban expressway in Detroit have a "U"-shaped relation to the volume/capacity ratio; that is, accidents per vehicle mile are lowest at intermediate volumes. But when injury and fatality accidents are broken out separately, accident rates decline fairly dramatically with traffic volume. Similarly, in a Norwejian study of mostly rural roads, Fridstrøm and Ingebrigsten (1991) find an elasticity of only 0.47, implying accident rates decrease with volume.

The problem with measuring the relationship between accident costs and traffic volume is that traffic densities are highly correlated with time-of-day and degree of urbanization, both of which affect accident rates and severities strongly. For example, in Zho and Sisopiku's (1997) study, many of the hours with low volumes are in the evening or on weekends, when visibility and alcohol probably play a role in elevating accident rates. Unfortunately, researchers have not yet done a careful multivariate study of the determinates of accident rates, even though this is obviously a critical issue in measuring safety externalities.

*How much of accident costs are borne by nonmotorists?* Pedestrians and cyclists appear to account for considerably more than half of the motor vehicle deaths in the UK, according to figures reported by Jones-Lee (1990: p. 51). In the US they account for 16% (US Census Bureau, 1995: Table 1033). The government pays for some medical expenses through various programs of health or indigent care. Both of these represent potential externalities if there is no compensation mechanism by which motorists are faced with these costs.

*Does insurance affect users' perceptions of the accident costs resulting from their driving?* It is typical for government publications to include insurance premiums as a fixed cost of driving, as for example in the US Census Bureau (1995: Table 1038). The belief that people do not perceive these costs as being variable underlies "pay at the pump" proposals to convert automobile insurance to a surcharge on the gasoline tax.

However, insurance companies attempt to vary their premiums as closely as possible with actual accident risk. For this reason, annual premiums often depend on age, sex, residential location, prior accident record, and distance traveled for daily commuting to work. The variation with past accident record is so strong that people sometimes pay damages themselves rather than report an accident to their insurance company, for fear of causing dramatic rises in future rates. It is impossible to believe that people are unaware of these considerations. Just how they take the information into account is an empirical question with strong bearing on efficient externality fees. We would argue that where the private insurance market is allowed considerable freedom in varying premiums, the starting assumption should be that all insured costs are perceived as private variable costs by users unless specific evidence to the contrary is produced.

Note that efficiency does not require the user responsible for an accident to pay the actual costs of that accident, as would happen under a tort system with strict liability. All that is required is that the user be faced with the *expected* social cost resulting from his or her decisions. The fact that the user can insure against the random component of accident cost is a legitimate function of insurance and need not interfere with efficient pricing.

If liability insurance is perceived as a variable cost, then the cost of injuries to pedestrians and bicyclists becomes internalized to the motorist to the extent they are reimbursed by the motorist's insurance policy. However, external costs or benefits due to a nonlinear dependence of accidents on traffic remain uninternalized, even if insurance pays up to 100% of the cost of an accident. For example, if party B is fully compensated by party A's insurance because party A was legally liable for the accident, then the costs of that accident are removed from party B's perceived cost of driving; yet if B's presence on the highway increases the overall accident rate, efficiency requires that it be discouraged through some corrective policy such as Pigovian taxation. Under that scenario, such Pigovian taxes would generate more revenue than needed to compensate victims. Such revenue could help offset certain infrastructure costs that are undertaken for safety improvements rather than capacity enhancement. Of course if the elasticity of total accident costs with traffic volumes is less than 1, as the recent empirical research suggests, we should be subsidizing people to drive!

*How do tort and criminal law affect incentives?* The legal system is another way that parties may be charged for accidents resulting from their driving decisions. The literature in law and economics provides a theoretical framework for analyzing such effects; see, for example, Calabresi (1970), Brown (1973), Shavell (1987) and Boyer and Dionne (1987). Empirical work that applies these ideas to motor vehicle accidents is limited, but one interesting study is Calfee and Winston's (1993) analysis of liability damages for pain and suffering. In the case of automobile safety, they find that allowing such damages to be recovered may in fact reduce welfare by forcing drivers as a group to buy insurance that they do not really want.

*Do people seek out a certain level of risk taking?* It is possible that people who drive in an aggressive or dangerous manner are using the road system to express emotions that would otherwise find another outlet. The predominance of young males in accident statistics is certainly suggestive. If so, an evaluation of safety improvements would have to take into account how costly those alternative outlets of destructive behavior would be to society. If they are equally costly, the safety improvement has no net social benefit. To address such a question requires going well outside the usual framework of economic analysis to incorporate psychological motivations for behavior.

### 4.5. Conclusion

Accidents constitute one of the largest costs of motor vehicle use, and one that appears highly susceptible to public policy. Accidents almost certainly entail externalities, although their exact nature and magnitude are largely unknown. Valuing accident costs involves sophisticated concepts and difficult empirical challenges, but researchers seem to be succeeding. The behavior and technology that produce accidents interact strongly with insurance and legal institutions, adding to the challenge of performing accurate analysis of incentives and policy effects. Some types of consumer behavior—such as drunk driving—are probably not entirely rational, and determined regulatory approaches toward them can be quite effective. Others—such as purchase and use of safety equipment—are rational and thus readily susceptible to economic or legal policies designed to fine-tune the incentives acting on individuals.

Three topics seem both important and feasible areas for futher economic analysis. The first is exactly how accident rates and severity vary with traffic volumes. The second is how people perceive insurance costs, and whether, or not, any institutional changes could make those perceptions more consonant with efficiency. The third is the incentives produced by the legal system.

The historical evidence suggests that there is considerable room for addressing accidents with technology and targeted behavioral incentives. We suspect that efficient policies would lead to various adjustments in vehicle mix, technology and driving behavior. At this point there seems little reason to believe that the costs of driving would dramatically rise or that people would adjust by markedly reducing their use of motor vehicles.

## 5. Public transportation

One of the longstanding issues in transportation is the appropriate balance between urban public transportation and the automobile. The term public transportation typically refers to modes that offer service for hire to the general public, such as buses, streetcars, subways and commuter railroads. By contrast, private modes, such as the automobile, are generally available for the use of only one travel party at a time. Although some researchers include taxis among the public modes on the grounds that they are available for hire to the general public, the more general practice is to consider taxis separately, as something of hybrid. Public transportation services may be provided by either private firms or public agencies.

We address a number of issues that have been the topics of intense research and debate. First, we examine current trends and patterns of public transportation ridership, and alternative explanations for them. Next, we consider whether or not it is desirable to subsidize public transportation in order to compensate for the external costs of the automobile or for other reasons. We then take up a question that has great practical importance and continues to provoke controversy: in what circumstances is rail better than bus at providing urban mass transit services? Next, we review and evaluate current moves to rely more heavily on private companies and deregulated markets. Finally, we examine quasipublic and flexible modes known as paratransit.

### 5.1. Trends in ridership and subsidy

Many of these issues have become pressing because public transportation ridership has been declining for decades in the US and many other developed countries. The situation in the US has been particularly well documented, for example by Altshuler et al. (1979), Meyer and Gómez-Ibáñez (1981) and Wachs (1989). In the US, ridership began to decline after World War I as postwar prosperity brought the first major surge in automobile ownership. The decline was interrupted by World War II, when fuel and tires were rationed, but resumed immediately after. By the 1960s, many of the private firms that had provided public transportation services were bankrupt or nearly so.

The threat of further deterioration or outright abandonment of services brought popular pressure for subsidies, usually accompanied by public takeover. In 1964, the federal government began a program of grants for capital expenses, which is alleged to have encouraged the wave of municipal takeovers (Hilton, 1974). In 1974, federal grants were made available to cover operating expenses as well. These federal infusions supplemented state and local taxes, which remained the predominant form of operating aid.

By 1973, the decline in ridership had been halted, probably due to a combination of growing subsidies and the oil shortages which began that year. Subsequently aggregate ridership has grown. Between 1972 and 1992, reported trips by public mass transit increased by 14% nationwide (from 7332 to 8362 million trips per year), although perhaps half of this increase was due to changes in reporting procedures.[13]

Meanwhile subsidies soared. In constant 1992 dollars, the average operating subsidy per passenger trip increased from $0.18 in 1970 to $1.43 in 1992 (Perl and Pucher, 1995: Table 2). Farebox revenues covered only 41% of operating expenses and 31% of total expense by 1992.

Even though ridership has increased, automobile use has increased faster, so that public transportation's share of all trips has continued to decline. According to US Census statistics, for example, the percentage of all workers using public transportation fell from 12.6 in 1960 to 5.1 in 1990 (Rossetti and Eversole, 1993: p. 2-2). In the 39 largest metropolitan areas, the percentage of workers commuting by bus or rail transit or by commuter railroad fell from 11.2 in 1980 to 8.7 in 1990 (Rossetti and Eversole, 1993: pp. 5–11, 5–12).

Many other nations appear to be suffering from similar adverse trends in public transit usage and profitability, although ridership per capita there is still much higher than in the US (Pucher and Lefèvre, 1996: p. 18). Pucher and Kurth (1995: p. 118) report that between 1980 and 1993 transit ridership declined in the UK, Italy, Norway and West Germany, but increased in Austria, Canada, France and the Netherlands. In Canada, however, 1990 was a peak year: absolute ridership fell 11% and per capita ridership fell 20% in the next four years (Perl and Pucher, 1995: Table 1).

Throughout western Europe, North America, and Australia urban public transit is heavily subsidized by the taxpayer (Pucher, 1988: p. 511; Pucher and Lefèvre, 1996: pp. 32–35). The level of subsidy is growing in many countries, which

---

[13] See American Public Transit Association (1987: p. 32; 1993: p. 64; 1995: p. 88). The main problem in reporting transit ridership is the distinction between linked and unlinked trips. An unlinked trip consists of a ride on one transit vehicle, whereas a linked trip may include two or more vehicles connected by a transfer. Measuring patronage by unlinked trips creates misleading comparisons whenever there is a change in the proportion of travelers who transfer, such as occurs on the introduction of a rail transit system supplemented with feeder buses.

is probably the major reason why public transit ridership is still increasing in some of them. To give just two examples, annual real subsidies grew by 45% in Canada between 1980 and 1992, with ridership growing just 7% (Perl and Pucher, 1995: Table 2). In West Germany between 1980 and 1993, annual subsidies increased by 67% in real terms while ridership held essentially constant (Pucher and Kurth, 1995: pp. 118, 126).

Even where public transit ridership has stabilized or increased, moreover, car ownership and use are increasing faster as we demonstrated in Section 2.1. As a result, public transportation's share of total trips is declining in Europe as in the US.

Analogous trends are evident in the newly emerging economies of eastern Europe and in the developing countries of Asia, Latin America and Africa. Pucher (1995b: p. 220) examines four eastern European countries, finding that between 1985 and 1993 public transportation ridership fell dramatically in three (East Germany, Hungary and Poland) and rose in only one (Czechoslovakia). In the developing world, trends are more complex. Transit ridership in the poorest countries is growing fairly rapidly as the population shifts from human or animal-powered modes to motorized modes, primarily bus. In the large cities of such countries, public transportation often accounts for 80% or more of all motorized trips, although a much smaller share of total trips. Among the richer developing countries, however, the transition to motorized forms of travel is nearly complete and the shift from public transportation to the automobile has begun in earnest. Public transportation ridership is often still stable or growing slowly, usually without the aid of significant subsidies. But automobile ownership and use is growing far more rapidly so that public transportation's share of motorized trips, although still higher than in Europe, is falling steadily.

## 5.2. Explaining ridership trends and patterns

One interesting question is whether the long-term decline in public transportation ridership in the US and elsewhere is the result of income growth, demographic trends, and other structural shifts in the economy, or is a consequence of public policies that, intentionally or not, favor the automobile and handicap public transportation. A related question is which of these factors account for differences across countries.

Most researchers agree that rising incomes and the suburbanization of jobs and residences have had powerful effects. Rising real incomes make the door-to-door convenience, privacy, and amenities of the automobile more affordable, while also making labor-intensive services such as transit more costly. Suburbanization of jobs and residences produces a dispersed pattern of travel that is difficult for conventional public transportation to serve.

A variety of empirical evidence supports this theoretical reasoning. Time-series studies consistently suggest that income growth and urban spatial structure are important determinants of ridership. For example, Gómez-Ibáñez (1996) found that ridership changes in the Boston metropolitan area during the 1970s and 1980s could be explained largely by changes in transit fares and services, real incomes per capita, and the number of jobs in the central city. The statistical analysis implies that in those two decades, when there was little new highway construction in the metropolitan area, Boston's transit ridership would have declined by 10–15% if public officials had not reduced fares and improved services. Kain (1997), Liu (1994) and Kyte et al. (1988) obtained similar results in time-series analyses of ridership in Atlanta and Portland, Oregon.

Cross-sectional studies also show that differences in transit ridership are strongly associated with income and spatial structure. Gordon and Willson (1984) examine an international cross-section of 91 cities with light-rail lines, finding that ridership is strongly related to city population density and per capita GNP. Hendrickson (1986) finds that most of the variation in transit ridership across US cities is explained by differences in the number of jobs in the central business district. Analyses of microdata on households also show that household income is a major determinant of travel mode and automobile ownership; the income elasticity of transit usage is typically estimated at $-0.5$ or higher when car ownership is treated as endogenous, as it should for this purpose.[14]

Beyond subsidizing transit fares or services, there seem to be few effective policies to significantly counteract the broad trends working against transit. One possible such policy is to raise fuel taxes. Pucher (1988, 1995a, b) concludes from a country-by-country comparison that Europe's high gasoline taxes are a primary factor in explaining its high transit usage. However, this inference appears to be overturned when multivariate statistical techniques are used. Wheaton (1982) finds that if one controls for differences in income and other variables, Europeans respond to higher gasoline taxes largely by buying more fuel efficient vehicles rather than by owning fewer cars or driving less. Wheaton's finding is consistent with the simulations of the effects of congestion tolls and other measures by Harvey (1994) and Koopman (1995) discussed in Section 3.4.

Another possibility is to promote land use patterns more supportive of public transport use. Newman and Kenworthy (1989, 1991) and others have often

---

[14] Lower absolute values of this elasticity are sometimes estimated in models that include car ownership as well as income variables; but since car ownership responds strongly to income, the full effect on transit ridership is larger (Berechman, 1993: p. 38).

argued that the higher transit usage in European cities is largely due to higher densities and other factors under the control of planners. As noted in Section 2.4, however, other factors besides land use are involved and it may not be desirable or politically feasible to force households and firms into denser locations to achieve only small reductions in automobile use.

## 5.3.  The pros and cons of subsidy

The most obvious method of arresting the decline in transit usage, and the one most widely adopted, is to subsidize transit. Three arguments are often advanced in support of such subsidies. The first is that motorists do not pay the full marginal social costs of automobile use, and thus transit subsidies are necessary to insure that travel choices between public and private modes are not distorted. The better solution would be to price automobile use directly, of course. If it is administratively difficult or politically impossible to correct the mispricing of automobile use, however, then subsidizing automobile's competitor, public transportation, may be a useful second-best corrective.

The second argument is that public transportation is characterized by economies of scale so that fares set at marginal cost will be insufficient to cover total cost. Scale economies are more likely in rail transit than bus transit if only the costs of the public transportation firm are considered. Cost functions of bus firms show only modest economies of scale and then only for very small firms or firms that have excess capacity (Berechman, 1993: pp. 120–127). In contrast, cost functions for rail transit and for multimodal enterprises generally show economies of scale, traffic density or scope (Berechman, 1993: pp. 127–128; Viton, 1992).

Economies of scale can be found in bus as well as rail, however, if one includes the value of time spent by the travelers. The reason is that greater passenger densities permit some combination of more frequent service, greater vehicle utilization, and more direct routes (Mohring, 1972; Turvey and Mohring, 1975; Nash, 1988; Jansson, 1993). This effect is so pronounced that some simulation models have predicted surprisingly large modal shifts to public transit resulting from simultaneous marginal-cost pricing of peak automobile and transit trips (Viton, 1983); the initial effect of much higher peak automobile prices is further accentuated by resulting improvements in transit service quality and/or fare reductions.

The final argument for subsidies is that poor and disadvantaged households tend to be more dependent on public transportation than the rest of the population.

Subsidies therefore may be an important means of aiding these groups or insuring that they have a minimum level of mobility needed to participate in society.

Transit subsidies bring their own problems, however, as reviewed insightfully by Wachs (1989). First, public transportation demand is often fairly insensitive to price or service improvements so that substantial subsidies are needed to have a significant effect on ridership. Estimates of the direct price elasticity of demand generally range from $-0.1$ to $-0.5$ in developed countries with many studies reporting results around $-0.3$; the elasticity of demand with respect to travel time, service frequency or service miles, is perhaps a bit higher in absolute value but less than 1.[15] Estimates of the cross-elasticity of demand for automobile trips with respect to public transportation fares or service are even smaller because only a fraction of transit riders are diverted from automobiles and because the starting base of automobile use is so large (Kemp, 1973). For example, estimates of cross-elasticities for eight Australian cities are all less than 0.02 in absolute value (Dodgson, 1986: Table 4). The modest direct elasticities suggest that the efficiency gains from pricing at marginal cost instead of average cost in the face of increasing returns to scale may be modest. The even smaller cross-elasticities suggest that transit subsidies are a costly way to correct for the mispricing of automobile use.

Another difficulty is that many public transportation riders are not poor or disadvantaged, so that transit subsidies are a relatively inefficient means of re-distributing income (Meyer and Gómez-Ibáñez, 1981). In the smaller and less congested US metropolitan areas, the majority of transport users are generally too poor to own a car or too young, elderly or infirm to drive (Pucher et al., 1983). But in larger and more congested metropolitan areas, many public trans-portation riders are commuters to the central city, who are wealthier than the average metropolitan resident. In both small and large metropolitan areas, more-over, many poor households own cars or use taxis because public transportation, despite subsidies, does not serve well the trips they need to make.

Perhaps the most serious problem is that a large portion of the subsidies is absorbed by reduced productivity or higher wage rates instead of being used to improve service or reduce fares. This is supported by both cross-sectional and time-series studies of transit firms receiving different levels of subsidy. For ex-ample, Bly et al. (1980) examine data on transit subsidies and performance in 59 cities in 17 developed countries between 1966 and 1976. Their analysis suggests that a 1% increase in subsidies was associated with a 0.4–0.6% increase in the

---

[15] See Goodwin (1992: p. 160), Oum et al. (1992: p. 148), Chan and Ou (1978) and Berechman (1993: pp. 38–39).

real costs of providing a vehicle mile of service. They also test specifications in which either the subsidy or productivity variables are lagged; the model performs better when the subsidy variable is lagged, suggesting that the causality was from subsidies to costs rather than vice versa. Anderson (1983), Pucher et al. (1983) and Perry and Babitsky (1986) find similar results in analyses of cross-sections of US public transportation companies, as does Cervero (1984) for a pooled time-series cross-section of California transit systems.

Similarly, Lave (1991) examines costs using annual data from 62 large US bus firms. He finds that unit costs increased by an average of 1.4% per year in the era before federal subsidies were available (1950–1964), compared to 2.1% per year during the decade of federal capital grants (1965–1974) and 3.1% per year when the federal government subsidized both capital and operating expenses (1975–1985). Larger firms experienced more cost inflation, suggesting to Lave that workers at such firms may have used their cities' vulnerability to transit strikes to extract more of the subsidies in the form of higher wages.

How much of subsidy funds have been absorbed by higher costs? For the US, Pickrell (1985a) uses simple accounting identities to calculate that 61% of the increase in real (net of inflation) subsidies between 1970 and 1980 was used to cover an increase in the real cost of providing a vehicle mile of service, while only 14% was used to reduce real fares and 9% to increase the number of vehicle miles of service offered.

There is some evidence that the rate of increase in unit costs has slowed since the mid-1980s, perhaps because taxpayers have become reluctant to finance further subsidy increases. For example, the average operating expense per vehicle hour in the US declined 7% in real terms between 1986 and 1992 (American Public Transit Association, 1993). Similarly, in a detailed study of Boston's public transit system Gómez-Ibáñez (1996) finds that real operating expenses per vehicle hour increased rapidly in the 1970s, but then declined in the 1980s after the state legislature strengthened management's position on key labor contract issues.

## 5.4. Rail versus bus

A related issue is whether or not public transportation enterprises have been relying too heavily on rail rather than bus services as a means of attracting or retaining riders. In the US, for example, rail is favored by the availability of federal capital grants at much more generous terms than operating grants. Since 1964, federal grants have been available to pay up to two-thirds (later 80%) of the cost of local transit capital improvement. Federal operating aid, by contrast, was made available only in 1974, is much less generously funded, and is distributed among cities on the basis of a formula rather than for specific projects.

The fear that capital grants might be distorting local choices was strengthened by the explosion of interest in rail transit projects among US cities. Only one city (Cleveland) built and opened a new rail system between 1945 and 1970. But in the next 25 years, 12 cities opened 14 new rail systems while other cities expanded their older rail systems. Six of the new systems, built in relatively large metropolitan areas such as San Francisco, Washington and Atlanta, use heavy rail technology, in which trains operate on a fully grade-separated right of way. Eight of the new systems use light rail technology, the modern version of a streetcar that draws power from an overhead wire so that trains can operate on city streets in mixed traffic; these were generally opened later and in smaller metropolitan areas such as San Diego, Portland, Buffalo and Sacramento.

Just how high traffic densities have to be to justify rail transit has been a subject of intense debate since Meyer et al. (1965) published an influential study of the comparative costs of bus, heavy rail, and automobile in hypothetical or prototype corridors. They found that if one attempts to hold the quality of service roughly constant across modes, the comparison depends critically on peak corridor passenger volumes. At hourly volumes below 15,000, bus was generally cheaper while at volumes above 30,000, rail was cheaper; at intermediate volumes the comparison could go either way depending on local circumstances. Their results have generally been confirmed by a half dozen other researchers since (see Meyer and Gómez-Ibáñez, 1981: p. 46, or Pickrell, 1985b, for reviews).

As the new rail systems have opened, researchers have been able to analyze actual rather than hypothetical results. Among the more recent studies of this type, the most important is a comparison by Pickrell (1992) of forecast and actual performance of eight recently-opened systems, four heavy- and four light-rail. Ridership was far lower than forecast in the seven systems where such comparisons were possible: by 28% in Washington, DC, and by more than 50% in all the others. In most cases, about half of the ridership shortfall was due to failures to predict accurately various inputs to the forecast, such as downtown employment levels, gasoline prices and transit fares. The balance of the shortfall appeared to be due to errors arising from "...the structure of the forecasting models, how they were employed, or the misinterpretation—or possibly misrepresentation—of their numerical outputs" (Pickrell, 1985b: p. 164). Kain (1990) is less circumspect, as indicated by the title of his paper: "Deception in Dallas: strategic misrepresentation in rail transit promotion and evaluation".

Pickrell also finds that costs were typically far higher than forecast. Capital cost overruns, ranging from 17 to 150%, occurred in all seven systems where comparisons were possible. About half was due to construction delays, the rest to underestimates of the real unit prices of inputs or the quantities of inputs required. Operating costs were also higher than forecast in five of the six cases where such comparisons were possible, in large measure because train speeds were slower than forecast.

Other researchers have examined the experience of individual metropolitan areas that built new rail systems or extensions, and argued that bus improvements would have been a less costly method of attracting or retaining ridership. Kain (1994: p. 16) estimates the demand for transit ridership using time-series data for the Atlanta metropolitan area; he then predicts that between 1980 and 1993 Atlanta could have attracted 9% more ridership at only 37% of the cost if it had reduced fares and improved service on its bus system instead of building its new rail transit system. Using a similar approach, Gómez-Ibáñez (1996) finds that Boston's policy of extending its rail lines further into the suburbs adds $10.68 in new deficit spending per new ride attracted, while a policy of reducing real fares on the existing system would add only $2.60 to the deficit for each new ride attracted.

Nor is there evidence that these costly rail systems have significant impacts on automobile traffic. When the Bay Area Rapid Transit (BART) line opened between San Francisco and Oakland in 1973, 8750 daily automobile trips on the parallel bridge were diverted; but soon after, 7000 new automobile trips appeared on the bridge (Sherret, 1975). Zurich's ambitious regional light rail system, which opened in 1990, has succeeded in substantially increasing transit usage, yet with no observable reduction in traffic flow at the city boundaries (OECD, 1994: p. 97). The reason is probably the "fundamental law" of traffic congestion, discussed earlier: new peak-period motorists soon take the place of those who switch to transit.

Less developed countries are facing a similar debate about the appropriate role of rail and bus transit, although in a context in which the vast majority of travelers are still using public rather than private transportation. Many major metropolitan areas in developing countries have built or planned new rail systems since the late 1960s, when Mexico City opened the first modern heavy rail transit system in the developing world.

A recent survey prepared for Britain's Transport and Road Research Laboratory finds that developing nations have experienced many of the same ridership shortfalls and cost overruns as the US (Halcrow Fox and Associates, 1989; Fouracre et al., 1990). The study examined 21 large cities in developing countries with new rail systems: 13 in full or partial operation and eight under construction or in advanced stages of planning. Of the 13 operational systems, only three (Hong Kong, Porto Allegre and Singapore) were built within 10% of their forecast capital costs while six had overruns of more than 50%. The most common reason for overruns was failure to accurately predict the difficulty of construction in a densely developed urban environment. Similarly, forecast ridership was approximately achieved in only two of the cities (Manila and Tunis), while in the remaining seven cases for which comparisons were possible actual ridership fell short of forecasts by 20–90%. Although the new rail lines are often heavily patronized by international standards—Mexico City has twice as many rail passengers as London—they still capture only 10–20% of all urban passenger trips, and the limited available data suggest no noticeable diversion from automobiles (Halcrow Fox and Associates, 1989: p. 7.11).

On the positive side, three of the 10 cities with complete financial data indicated that fares covered operating costs and made some contribution toward depreciation. Furthermore, 10 of the 13 completed systems are estimated to have produced a social rate of return above 10%, in most cases due to large time savings by bus users who switched to rail. The largest social rates of return (above 15%) were in cities that had high rail patronage and relatively high values of time (Hong Kong and Singapore), or that had moderate patronage and very low construction costs (Cairo). The researchers did not compare the returns on rail investment with those that might have been achieved from improving the bus systems.

## 5.5. Privatization and deregulation

The growth in transit subsidies has encouraged some important experiments in the private provision of mass transit. The hope is that private operators, disciplined by competition, can reduce the costs of providing service and thus cut subsidy requirements. Furthermore, researchers have long pointed to select transit markets that can be served profitably (Viton, 1980; Morlok and Viton, 1985). These experiments have taken a variety of forms: with or without continuation of subsidy, and with or without regulation of entry and fares.

Much urban bus transit has long been privately provided without subsidy in many developing countries, sometimes even in competition with a publicly owned bus company that is subsidized. With a few exceptions, however, the government continues to regulate the routes the private operators serve and the fares they charge (Gómez-Ibáñez and Meyer, 1993: pp. 22–36).

Among the developed countries, private provision is usually accompanied by some subsidies, perhaps at reduced levels. The most common form of private provision is for public officials to contract with a private company to operate all or part of the system while fully specifying service characteristics and fares. The contract is awarded to the firm that bids the lowest subsidy to provide the service required. Often the existing public bus company is not privatized but competes against the private companies in the bidding. The London metropolitan area has had extensive experience with contracting out bus routes beginning in 1985; the percentage of bus service competitively tendered in this way increased from 3% that year to 50% in 1993 (Kennedy, 1995: p. 342). Contracting out has also been increasing slowly in the US since the 1980s (Teal, 1988; Gómez-Ibáñez and Meyer, 1993: pp. 67–70). Sweden has encouraged local authorities to contract out for local bus service, especially after 1988 (Jansson and Wallin, 1991).

Studies suggest that contracting out can reduce costs by around 15–25%. In London, for example, Kennedy (1995: p. 343) estimates that from 1987 to 1992, tendered service cost 16% less to operate than comparable untendered services. Furthermore, London Transport (the public bus company) is thought to have improved its efficiency significantly during this period in an effort to remain competitive and discourage further contracting out. Teal (1991) finds savings in the range of 25–30% among US cities with contracted bus service. Less than one-quarter of the savings came from lower wages, while the rest came from lower fringes, higher productivity, and reduced overhead expenses. Savings of 5–15% are reported in Sweden (Jansson and Wallin, 1991).

Outside London, the UK has experimented with the more radical step of simultaneously privatizing and deregulating local bus services while preserving the possibility of subsidy at local option. The British scheme, which went into effect in October 1986, involved three changes. First, controls on routes and fares were dropped so that a bus company, public or private, could offer virtually any unsubsidized service it liked (subject to providing advance notice and meeting safety requirements). Second, the large public bus companies that dominated the business in most metropolitan areas were set up as separate for-profit corporations, and in many cases were eventually sold to the private sector, often through labor or management buyouts. Finally, local authorities could supplement the unsubsidized service where they thought there was an unmet social need, but only by putting out the requested service to bid. National assistance for such subsidies was simultaneously cut drastically. London was eventually to be subject to similar measures.

The British reforms have been much studied because they represent the most ambitious effort at local transit privatization in developed countries to date— only New Zealand has adopted similar measures, starting in 1991 (Fielding and Johnston, 1992). Results are still being assessed and debated; for two excellent summaries of the literature see White (1995) and Mackie et al. (1995).

The British reforms were clearly successful in one dimension: local bus service increased despite the subsidy cuts. During the first eight years of the reforms, the number of vehicle miles of service increased by 24% in all the deregulated areas and 21% in the major metropolitan areas, where the subsidy cuts were the harshest (White, 1995: p. 71). As of fiscal year 1993/94, commercial (i.e., unsubsidized) service accounted for approximately 85% of mileage. The commercial mileage is more concentrated on high density routes and on the weekdays, however, so there are some times and places where there is less service than before, despite local government efforts to fill the gaps.

In addition, service innovations were stimulated by the bus operators' freedom to design their own commercial services. Particularly striking was the rapid growth in the use of minibuses with 16–25 seats. This development surprised some observers because it reversed a long-term industry trend to substitute capital for labor as real wages increased by, for example, eliminating conductors and increasing the size of the vehicle. Private operators found that the cost-per-seat mile of operating a minibus was not much higher than that of a larger bus. The minibus is cheaper to maintain because it relies on a conventional truck rather than a purpose-built chassie; it also can make more round-trips per day since it stops less frequently for passengers and is more maneuverable. Use of minibuses often increased ridership per seat mile, moreover, because they can operate more frequently and can penetrate housing developments with narrow streets.

The costs of providing a vehicle mile of service declined substantially. Real operating costs per vehicle mile declined by 41.7% in deregulated areas during the eight-year period. Only about one-sixth of the reduction was due to lower hourly wages, which fell about 12%; the balance was due largely to higher productivity, particularly among nonplatform staff (White, 1995: pp. 74–76). According to White and Turner (1990), about one-third of the cost savings per mile was due to the shift to minibuses.

Fares did not decline as expected, however, because all of the savings in cost per vehicle mile were used to offset the subsidy cuts and to increase vehicle mileage. In fact, real fares increased by 22% on average in all deregulated areas and by 44% in the large metropolitan areas, where the subsidy cuts were sharpest (White, 1995: p. 78). In some areas, coordinated ticketing and travel passes were abandoned as competing bus companies declined to continue arrangements.

Table 4

Percentage changes in local bus service characteristics: the UK, 1985/86 to 1993/94

|  | Deregulated areas | | London |
|---|---|---|---|
|  | All areas | Metropolitan areas |  |
| Vehicle miles of service | +24.0 | +20.6 | +24.0 |
| Real cost per vehicle mile | −41.9 | −45.5 | −35.1 |
| Real average fare | +21.6 | +44.4 | +6.7 |
| Passenger trips | −27.4 | −35.5 | −3.0 |

*Source:* White (1995).

Even more discouraging was the substantial reduction in local bus ridership. Ridership fell by 27% in all deregulated areas and 36% in the metropolitan counties. Some decline in ridership would have been expected even in the absence of policy reforms, given that real incomes were rising in the UK. But the rate of ridership loss was greater than in the previous decade, reinforcing the supposition that riders have been made worse off.

Many researchers have attempted to assess who won and lost from privatization and deregulation in the UK and whether, on the whole, social welfare was improved. The key difficulty is to isolate the effects of reforms from the effects of subsidy cuts and other adverse trends.

One approach is to use metropolitan London as a control. White (1990, 1995), Mackie et al. (1995) and others have argued that the policy of gradually contracting out adopted in London proved to be superior to the more sudden and complete privatization and deregulation adopted in the rest of the country. As shown in Table 4, metropolitan London enjoyed as large a service increase and almost as large a unit cost saving as did the deregulated areas, but it suffered much smaller fare increases and losses of patronage.

Such comparisons are suggestive but far from conclusive given the difficulty in controlling for other differences between London and the rest of the country. In particular, government subsidies were cut far less in London, as shown in Table 5. Seven years after deregulation, London transit was still subsidized at 39% of fare receipts, whereas in the other metropolitan areas subsidies had been cut drastically to just 18% of receipts. Employment growth was stronger in downtown London than in the rest of the UK, moreover, and London was probably losing fewer bus riders to automobiles because driving and parking is so much more difficult and costly there.

Table 5

Government revenue support for local bus service: the UK

| | Deregulated areas | | London |
| --- | --- | --- | --- |
| | All areas | Metropolitan areas | |
| 1985/86 | | | |
| Revenue support | 510 | 319 | 207 |
| Passenger receipts | 1944 | 640 | 426 |
| Support as percentage of receipts | 26.2 | 49.8 | 48.5 |
| 1992/93 | | | |
| Revenue support | 237 | 114 | 167 |
| Passenger receipts | 1725 | 626 | 432 |
| Support as percentage of receipts | 13.7 | 18.2 | 38.6 |

Figures are in millions of British pounds at constant 1992/93 prices.
*Source:* UK Department of Transport (1993).

An alternative approach is to compare the actual passenger decline with an estimate of the decline that might have been expected from the combination of exogenous trends and the service reductions and fare increases forced by subsidy cuts. Several researchers assume that the long-term decline in bus ridership was 1.5% per year, for example, and then estimate the ridership losses attributable to reduced subsidies using standard rules of thumb about price and service elasticities. Others have built simple aggregate demand functions to try to estimate the counterfactual scenario (e.g., Mackie et al., 1995). The results appear to be sensitive to reasonable differences in assumptions about the exogenous trend and industry rules of thumb. White (1990) argues that the ridership losses were greater than those one would expect from trends and subsidy cuts alone, so that deregulation and privatization must have worsened the industry's performance; Gómez-Ibáñez and Meyer (1993: pp. 55–58) come to the opposite conclusion.

The British experiment has also rekindled debate over whether or not competition is workable in urban buses. There has been only limited, but often intense, head-to-head competition—Tyson (1989) estimated, for example, that less than 10% of bus passengers have a choice of company. The incumbents have often driven off new entrants and there has been a wave of mergers among incumbents. Some British researchers blame residual regulation for the limited competition (Beesley, 1990; Glaister, 1993), while others believe that competition is inhibited by the inherent advantages of incumbents, such as local knowledge, name recognition and greater financial resources (Evans, 1990, 1991; Mackie et. al., 1995). These incumbent advantages, however, do not appear more serious than those in many other industries where competition is thought to function reasonably well. An alternative explanation is that the network aspects of transit create economies of scale sufficient to make head-to-head competition overly expensive.

Indeed, where competition has broken out it has not necessarily been in the passengers' short-term interests. Competition has most often taken the form of matching or increasing frequencies on routes rather than cutting fares, apparently because passengers find waiting at a bus-stop so inconvenient that they would rather take the first bus that arrives than wait for a bus from the company offering lower fares. Evans (1991), White (1995) and others argue that this results in wasteful duplication of services and uncoordinated schedules, for example buses scheduled slightly ahead of the competitor's so there is little effective reduction in passenger waiting times. White (1990) believes that the large service increases after deregulation did not result in commensurate patronage gains because service competition was wasteful.

A few researchers, such as Dodgson et al. (1992), have begun using game theoretic models to better understand the nature of competition in this industry. Klein et al. (1997) point to the importance of defining the rights to public curb space that private operators are granted as a way of shaping the nature of service competition. How the overall system performs depends much on how smoothly operators mesh their products into an overall system. Whether this can be fostered through regulatory measures, through definition of property rights, or only through public coordination as argued by Nash (1988) is a question ripe for further research.

In sum, the British experience seems to have been neither the panacea that some hoped for nor the disaster that others predicted. Taxpayers clearly gained, and the impact of subsidy cuts on passengers was softened by the significant reduction in unit costs. Whether it would have been better to simply contract out, as in London, rather than take the added step of deregulating entry and fares is harder to tell. With contracting, passengers might not have suffered the risk of some wasteful forms of competition, but they also would not have enjoyed the benefits of service innovations.

## 5.6. *Paratransit and unconventional services*

The difficulties faced by conventional public transit systems have periodically provoked interest in paratransit and other unconventional forms of public transportation. Paratransit is often defined as a cross between conventional fixed-route bus and taxi service. As with bus service, passengers not traveling together often share the same vehicle; but like a taxi, the vehicle may deviate from its route or skip stops for the convenience of its passengers. Paratransit service is usually provided in vehicles smaller than a conventional bus—such as a minibus, a passenger van or an ordinary sedan.

Paratransit services are quite common in the cities of the developing world, where they often carry more passengers than the conventional fixed-route bus systems (Shimakazi and Rahman, 1995). Similar services were also found in US cities in the first decades of this century, but they all but disappeared due to restrictive regulation and competition from the private automobile and conventional taxi and transit services.

Interest revived in the 1970s as a potential answer to the problems that conventional transit faced in serving the dispersed trips of low density suburbs. The idea, christened "dial-a-ride" or "demand responsive transit", was to provide door-to-door service but with vehicle productivity enhanced by using computer- assisted dispatching to schedule vehicles to serve different passengers simultaneously. Demonstrations conducted during the 1970s suggested, however, that the computer algorithms of the time were no better at matching trips than an experienced human dispatcher. Moreover, acceptable matches were less frequent than hoped for so that paratransit productivity and costs were usually no better than those of a taxi (Meyer and Gómez-Ibáñez, 1981: pp. 73–76).

Paratransit services survived during the 1980s, but largely in the specialized role of carrying elderly and handicapped persons unable to use conventional buses or subways. Beginning in 1973, federal law required that public transit agencies receiving federal funds provide services accessible to the handicapped. Many agencies sought to do so by providing specialized paratransit in lift-equipped vans in lieu of more expensive efforts to fit out all their vehicles or stations for the handicapped. These paratransit services usually require reservations 24 hours or more in advance, and often serve only limited destinations as well as a limited clientele. Despite these restrictions, moreover, costs are rarely as low as that of a conventional taxi, even allowing for the more expensive lift-equipped vehicles.

Two recent developments have encouraged transit planners to believe that there may be a wider role for paratransit services in developed countries. First, paratransit has begun to reappear in some markets. The most dramatic development was the near simultaneous appearance of minibus services after the bus deregulation in the UK and of private but illegal "gypsy" van services in competition with conventional buses in parts of New York City and Miami. The British minibuses probably should not be classified as paratransit in that they seldom deviate from their route, unlike the New York and Miami van services. In both cases, however, high frequency services in small vehicles proved attractive to riders and profitable for operators. The fact that these services appeared only after deregulation or illegally also suggests that regulatory barriers may be very important impediments. In the American suburbs, moreover, Cervero (1997) discovered a variety of paratransit-like services have been growing, including shared-ride taxi services, airport limousines and subscription vans to ferry children to after-school activities. These services still account for only a tiny percentage of total trips, but they suggest interesting possibilities.

The second hopeful development is improvements in computing and satellite-based automatic vehicle locating (AVL) systems. Low cost scheduling software linked to geographic information systems is readily available (Stone et al., 1993). Teal (1993) contends that current technology makes us much more likely to realize the promise of dial-a-ride than we were in the 1970s. Nelesson and Howe (1995) argue that instead of providing on-demand door-to-door service, as in the old dial-a-ride, it might be much less expensive and almost as convenient to provide on-demand service to a series of conveniently located telephone-equipped stops or nodes. The potential is still largely unproven but the time seems ripe for a new series of demonstrations.

### 5.7. Conclusion

Conventional public transportation remains an important component of any sizeable urban area. It is especially good at serving certain specific high volume radial commuting flows, circulation in areas with many low income people, and trips to areas with very scarce or expensive parking. Experiments with privatization demonstrate that many of these markets can be profitable and others can be served at reasonable cost with public subsidy.

Public transportation is not well suited, however, for low density suburban service, especially in affluent areas. Nor can it be expected to alter land use patterns sufficiently to create good transit markets where there otherwise are none. Many of the problems of public transportation arise because it is being asked to do too much. The result has often been out-of-control subsidies, inappropriate infrastructure decisions and disappointing performance.

Newer development everywhere tends to take forms that do not produce good transit markets. This raises the question of whether or not newer forms of public transportation can evolve to serve some of these areas. While results to date are not very promising, the private sector success with minibuses and vans and the popularity of taxicabs, even among the poor, provide hints at the possible ingredients for some successful new services. Research on ways to combine flexibility and real-time information to serve medium-density but dispersed trip patterns might have a high payoff for the future.

## 6. Conclusions

Domination of urban transportation by automobile travel continues to spread, and we do not foresee any reversal of this overall trend. Nor does the economic analysis of problems of congestion, air pollution or safety appear to call for solutions in the form of large reductions in total automobile travel. For each of these problems, the most promising policies are targeted narrowly at the problem rather than more broadly at ancillary causes of it; and analysis suggests that the primary responses to such narrowly targeted policies will be technological or specific behavioral changes—such as driving more in off-peak hours, better maintenance of pollution control equipment, and driving only when sober—rather than thoroughgoing alterations to people's way of traveling.

As for public transit, there is ample scope for improving performance and cost-effectiveness. Doing so will improve urban living and may create dramatic increases in transit use in narrowly selected markets. But it will not have much effect on the trend toward overall increases in automobile use.

There are several areas in which additional research might shed light on key uncertainties that affect transportation policy. One is the potential costs of using land use policies to try to affect travel behavior. Interest in land use policies continues despite evidence that they are unlikely to reverse the increasing dominance of automobile travel. In nations where the political system makes effective land use control possible, the response may be to enact more restrictive policies. The research described in this chapter tell us something about the likely effects of land use controls on travel behavior, but we know almost nothing about the costs of such controls to household and firms. For example, how are urban agglomeration economies affected by the different land use patterns that could result from plausible policies?

Another area for research is accidents, since accident costs appear to be a large component of the cost of driving. We do not know what portion of accident costs is external to the individual driver and, therefore, whether there is a strong case for corrective taxes or other forms of public intervention. Further research is needed on how accident and injury rates depend on traffic volumes, on how people perceive variations in insurance costs, and on how people respond to applicable criminal and civil laws.

The valuation of both environmental damage and accidents requires knowledge of how people value changes in the risk of death. Despite considerable consensus about average values, little is known about how these values vary with age. Such knowledge is needed because some risks, such as air pollution, primarily affect the elderly while others, such as accidents, affect all age groups. There is also little empirical evidence on precisely how the concerns of families and friends are reflected in individuals' willingness to pay for risk reduction.

Another obvious area for research is on methods of providing public transportation suitable for today's dispersed land use and travel patterns. So far the experience with paratransit is somewhat encouraging and new technologies might dramatically change the picture. The ability to track vehicles, to gather information about traffic conditions, and to provide users real-time information offers potential improvements to existing types of paratransit and taxi services and may create entirely new market niches. Most research on such technologies has been oriented toward improving the quality of travel by automobile or conventional transit; comparable research on newer forms of transit would help determine their potential.

Finally, privatization and deregulation are currently in favor for both highway infrastructure and mass transit services. Just how well the private sector works in these contexts will depend on the nature of competition in very specific situations involving small numbers of competitors. We need to better understand how private construction firms compete for a franchise to build a highway, and how private bus operators compete for passengers on overlapping routes. An underlying goal would be to show how different rules of the game affect outcomes. By carefully specifying the conditions facing such firms, researchers using existing tools of industrial organization should obtain important insights.

## References

Altshuler, A.A. and J.A. Gómez-Ibáñez, A.M. Howitt (1993), Regulation for Revenue: the Political Economy of Land Use Exactions (Brookings Institution and Lincoln Institute of Land Policy, Washington, DC/Cambridge, MA).

Altshuler, A.A., J.P. Womak and J.R. Pucher (1979), The Urban Transportation System: Politics and Policy Innovation (MIT Press, Cambridge, MA).

American Automobile Manufacturers Association (1993, 1995–1998), Motor Vehicle Facts and Figures (Detroit).

American Public Transit Association (1987, 1993, 1995), Transit Fact Book (Washington, DC).

Anderson, D. and H. Mohring (1996), Congestion Costs and Congestion Pricing for the Twin Cities, Report No. MN/RC-96/32 to Minnesota Department of Transportation, (Department of Economics, University of Minnesota, St. Paul. Minneapolis).

Anderson, S. (1983), "The effect of government ownership and subsidy on performance: evidence from the bus transit industry", Transportation Research A 17A:191–200.

Apogee Research (1994), Costs and Effectiveness of Transportation Control Measures (TCMs): A Review and Analysis of the Literature (National Association of Regional Councils, Washington, DC).

Arnott, R., A. de Palma and R. Lindsey (1991), "Does providing information to drivers reduce traffic congestion?", Transportation Research 25A:309–318.

Arnott, R., A. de Palma and R. Lindsey (1993), "A structural model of peak-period congestion: a traffic bottleneck with elastic demand", American economic review 83:161–179.

Arnould, R. and H. Grabowski (1981), "Auto safety regulation: an analysis of market failure", Bell Journal of Economics 12:27–48.

Banister, D. (1993), "Investing in transportation infrastructure", in: D. Banister and J. Berechman, eds., Transport in a Unified Europe, pp. 347–368 (North-Holland, Amsterdam).

Banister, D. and J. Berechman (1993), "Transport policies and challenges in a unified Europe: introduction", in: D. Banister and J. Berechman, eds., Transport in a Unified Europe, pp. 1–25 (North-Holland, Amsterdam).

Beesley, M.E. (1990), "Collusive, predation, and merger in the U.K. bus industry", Journal of Transport Economics and Policy 24:295–310.

Ben-Akiva, M., A. de Palma and I. Kaysi (1991), "Dynamic network models and driver information systems", Transportation Research 25A:251–266.

Berechman, J. (1993), Public Transit Economies and Deregulation Policy (North-Holland, Amsterdam).

Berechman, J. and G. Giuliano (1985), "Economics of scale in bus transit: a review of concepts and evidence, Transportation 12:313–332.

Bergstrom, T.C. (1982), "When is a man's life worth more than his human capital?", in: M.W. Jones-Lee, ed., The Value of Life and Safety (North-Holland, Amsterdam).

Bly, P.H., F.V. Webster and S. Pounds (1980), "Effects of subsidies on urban public transport", Transportation 9:311–331.

Boyer, M. and G. Dionne (1987), "The economics of road safety", Transportation Research 21B:413–431.

Brown, J. (1973), "Toward an economic theory of liability", Journal of Legal Studies 2:323–350.

Brownstone, D. and T.F. Golob (1992), "The effectiveness of ridesharing incentives: discrete-choice models of commuting in southern California", Regional Science and Urban Economics 22:5–24.

Button, K., (1993), Transport, the Environment and Economic Policy (Edward Elgar, Aldershot, UK).

Calabresi, G. (1970), The Costs of Accidents: A Legal and Economic Analysis (Yale University Press, New Haven, CT).

Calfee, J.E. and C. Winston (1993), "The consumer welfare effects of liability for pain and suffering: an exploratory analysis", Brookings Papers on Economic Activity: Microeconomics, NSI:133–196.

Calfee, J.E. and C. Winston (1998), "The value of automobile travel time: implications for congestion policy", Journal of Public Economics 69:83–102.

Calvert, J.G., J.B. Heywood, R.F. Sawyer and J.H. Seinfeld (1993), "Achieving acceptable air quality: some reflections on controlling vehicle emissions", Science 261:37–45.

Cervero, R. (1984), "Cost and performance impacts of transit subsidy programs", Transportation Research 18A:407–413.

Cervero, R. (1989a), "Jobs-housing balance and regional mobility", Journal of the American Planning Association 55:136–150.

Cervero, R. (1989b), America's Suburban Centers: The Land Use—Transportation Link (Unwin Hyman, Boston).

Cervero, R. (1994), "Making transit work in suburbs", Transportation Research Record, No. 1451, pp. 3–11.

Cervero, R. (1997), Paratransit in America: Redefining Mass Transportation (Praeger, Westport, CT).

Chan, Y. and F.L. Ou (1978), "Tabulating demand elasticities for urban travel forecasting", Transportation Research Record 673:40–46.

Chirinko, R.S. and E.P. Harper, Jr. (1993), "Buckle up or slow down? New estimates of offsetting behavior and their implications for automobile safety regulation", Journal of Policy Analysis and Management 12:270–296.

Cline, W.R. (1991), "Scientific basis for the greenhouse effect", Economic Journal 101:904–919.

Crampton, G.R. (1997), "Labour-market search and urban residential structure", Environment and Planning A 29:989–1002.

Dahlgren, J.W. (1998), "High occupancy vehicle lanes: not always more effective than general purpose lanes", Transportation Research-A.32:99–114.

Daniere, A.G. (1995), "Transportation planning and implementation in cities of the third world: the case of Bangkok", Environment and Planning C: Government and Policy 13:25–45.

Davis, S.C. (1997), Transportation Energy Data Book: Edition 17, Report ORNL–6919 (Oak Ridge National Laboratory, Oak Ridge, TN).

Dodgson, J.S. (1986), "Benefits of changes in urban public transport subsidies in the major Australian cities", The Economic Record 62:224–235.

Dodgson, J.S., C.R. Newton and Y. Katsoulacos (1992), "A modelling framework for the empirical analysis of predatory behaviour in the bus services industry", Regional Science and Urban Economics 22:51–70.

Downs, A. (1962), "The law of peak-hour expressway congestion", Traffic Quarterly 16:393–409.

Downs, A. (1992), Stuck in Traffic: Coping with Peak-hour Traffic Congestion (The Brookings Institution, Washington, DC).

Duve, J.L. (1994), "How congestion pricing came to be proposed in the San Diego region: a case history", in: National Research Council, Vol. 2, pp. 318–333.

Economic Report of the President (1995), Together with the Annual Report of the Council of Economic Advisors (Washington: US Government Printing Office).

Emmerink, R.H.M., E.T. Verhoef, P. Nijkamp and P. Rietveld (1996), "Information provision in road transport with elastic demand", Journal of Transport Economics and Policy 30:117–136.

Engel, E. and R. Fischer and A. Glatovic (1997), "Highway franchising: pitfalls and opportunities", American Economic Review 2:68–72.

EC (European Communities—Commission) (1994), Socioeconomic Cost of Road Accidents, Report EUR 15464 (Office for Official Publications of the European Communities, Luxembourg).

ECMT (European Conference of Ministers of Transport) (1993), Statistical Trends in Transport 1965–1989 (OECD Publications Service, Paris).

ECMT (European Conference of Ministers of Transport) (1995), European Transport Trends and Infrastructural Needs (OECD Publications Service, Paris).

Europa Publications (1992), The Europa World Year Book: 1992 (Europa Publications, London).

Evans, A.W. (1990), "Competition and the structure of local bus markets", Journal of Transport Economics and Policy 24:255–281.

Evans, A.W. (1991), "Are urban bus services natural monopolies?' Transportation 18:131–150.

Fielding, G.J. (1994), "Private toll roads: acceptability of congestion pricing in southern California", in: National Research Council, Vol. 2, pp. 380–404.

Fielding, G.J. and D.C. Johnston (1992), "Restructuring land transport in New Zealand", Transport Reviews 12:271–289.

Fielding, G.J. and D.B. Klein (1993), "How to franchise highways", Journal of Transport Economics and Policy 27:113–130.

Fouracre, P.R., R.J. Allport and J.M. Thompson (1990), The Performance and Impact of Rail Transit in Developing Countries, Research Report No. 278 (Transport and Road Research Laboratory, UK Department of Transport, Crawthorne, Berkshire).

Fridstrøm, L. and S. Ingebrigtsen (1991), "An aggregate accident model based on pooled, regional time-series data", Accident Analysis and Prevention 23:363–378.

Fuhs, C.A. (1993), Preferential Lane Treatments for High-occupancy Vehicles, National Cooperative Highway Research Program, Synthesis of Highway Practice 185 (National Academy Press, Washington, DC).

Giuliano, G. (1991), "Is jobs-housing balance a transportation issue?", Transportation Research Record 1305:305–312.

Giuliano, G. (1992), "An Assessment of the Political Acceptability of Congestion Pricing", Transportation 19:335–358.

Giuliano, G. and K.A. Small (1993), "Is the journey to work explained by urban structure?", Urban Studies 30:1485–1500.

Giuliano, G. and K.A. Small (1995), "Alternative strategies for coping with traffic congestion", in: H. Giersch, ed., Urban Agglomeration and Economic Growth, pp. 199–225 (Springer-Verlag, Berlin).

Giuliano, G. and M. Wachs (1997), "An employer panel for evaluating the effectiveness of trip reduction incentives", in: T. Golob, R. Kitamura and L. Long, eds., Panels for Transportation Planning: Methods and Applications, pp. 129–151 (Kluwer Academic Publishers, Dordrecht).

Giuliano, G., D.W. Levine and R.F. Teal (1990), "Impact of high occupancy vehicle lanes on carpooling behavior", Transportation 17:159–177.

Glaister, S. (1993), "Bus deregulation in Britain", in: J. Carbajo, ed., Regulatory Reform in Transport: Some Recent Experiences (World Bank, Washington, DC), pp. 50–70.

Glazer, A., D.B. Klein and C.A. Lave (1995), "Clean on paper, dirty on the road: troubles with California's smog check", Journal of Transport Economics and Policy 29:85–92.

Gómez-Ibáñez, J.A. (1985), "Transportation policy as a tool for shaping metropolitan development", Research in Transportation Economics 2:55–81.

Gómez-Ibáñez, J.A. (1989), "A global view of auto dependance", Journal of the American Planning Association 57:376–379.

Gómez-Ibáñez, J.A. (1992), "The political economy of highway tolls and congestion pricing", Transportation Quarterly 46:343–360.

Gómez-Ibáñez, J. A. (1996), "Big city transit ridership, deficits and politics: avoiding reality in Boston", Journal of the American Planning Association 62:30–50.

Gómez-Ibáñez, J. A. (1997), "Estimating whether transport users pay their way: the state of the art", in: D.A. Greene, D.W. Jones and M.A. Deluchi, eds., The Full Costs and Benefits of Transportation: Contributions to Theory, Method, and Measurement, pp. 149–172 (Springer-Verlag, Berlin).

Gómez-Ibáñez, J.A. and J.R. Meyer (1993), Going Private: The International Experience with Transport Privatization (The Brookings Institution, Washington, DC).

Gómez-Ibáñez, J.A. and K.A. Small (1994), Road Pricing for Congestion Management: A Survey of International Practice, National Cooperative Highway Research Program, Synthesis of Highway Practice 210 (National Academy Press, Washington, DC).

Goodwin, P. B. (1992), "A review of new demand elasticities with special reference to short and long run effects of price changes", Journal of Transport Economics and Policy 26:155–169.

Goodwin, P.B. (1996), "Empirical evidence on induced traffic: a review and synthesis", Transportation 23:35–54.

Gordon, P. and R. Willson (1984), "The determinants of light-rail transit demand: an international cross-sectional comparison", Transportation Research 18A:135–140.

Gordon, P. and H.W. Richardson (1989), "Gasoline consumption and cities: a reply", Journal of the American Planning Association 55(3):342–346.

Gordon, P. and H.W. Richardson (1994), "Congestion trends in metropolitan areas", in: National Research Council, Vol. 2, pp. 1–31.

Gordon, P., H.W. Richardson and M.-J. Jun (1991), "The commuting paradox: evidence from the top twenty", Journal of the American Planning Association 57:416–420.

Gramlich, E.M. (1994), "Infrastructure investment: a review essay", Journal of Economic Literature 32:1176–1196.

Greene, D.L. (1992), "Vehicle use and fuel economy: how big is the "rebound" effect?", Energy Journal 13:117–143.

Guensler, R. and D. Sperling (1994), "Congestion pricing and motor vehicle emissions: an initial review", in: National Research Council, Vol. 2, pp. 356–379.

Hahn, R.W. (1989), "Economic prescriptions for environmental problems: how the patient followed the doctor's orders", Journal of Economic Perspectives 3:95–114.

Halcrow Fox and Associates (1989), The study of mass transit in developing countries, report prepared for the UK Department of Transport, Transport and Road Research Laboratory, Overseas Unit.

Hall, J.V. (1995), "The role of transport control measures in jointly reducing congestion and air pollution", Journal of Transport Economics and Policy 29:93–103.

Hanks, J.W., Jr. and T.J. Lomax (1991), "Roadway congestion in major urban areas: 1982 to 1988", Transportation Research Record 1305:177–189.

Harrington, W. and A. Krupnick (1996), "Public support for congestion and pollution fee policies for motor vehicles: survey results", working paper, Resources for the Future, Washington, DC.

Harrington, W., M.A. Walls and V. McConnell (1995), "Shifting gears: new directions for cars and clean air", discussion paper 94–26-REV, Resources for the Future, Washington, DC.

Harvey, G.W. (1994), "Transportation pricing and travel behavior", in: National Research Council, Vol. 2, pp. 89–114.

Hass-Klau, C. (1990), The Pedestrian and City Traffic (Belhaven, London).

Hass-Klau, C. (1993), "Impact of pedestrianization and traffic calming on retailing: a review of the evidence from Germany and the UK", Transport Policy 1:21–31.

Hau, T.D. (1994), "Estimation of marginal congestion costs, congestion tolls and revenues for urban road use in Indonesia", in: Proceedings of the International Conference on Advanced Technologies in Transportation and Traffic Management, pp. 77–88 (Centre for Transportation Studies, Nanyang Technological University, Singapore).

Hendrickson, C. (1986), "A note on trends in transit commuting in the United States relating to employment in the central business district", Transportation Research 20A:33–37.

Hensher, D.A. (1993), "Socially and environmentally appropriate urban futures for the motor car", Transportation 20:1–19.

Hilton, G.W. (1974), Federal Transit Subsidies: The Urban Mass Transportation Assistance Program (American Enterprise Institute, Washington, DC).

Holden, D.J. (1989), "Wardrop's third principle: urban traffic congestion and traffic policy", Journal of Transport Economics and Policy 23:239–262.

International Road Federation (1980), World Road Statistics 1975–1979 (International Road Federation, Geneva and Washington, DC).

International Road Federation (1990), World Road Statistics 1985–1989 (International Road Federation, Geneva and Washington, DC).

Jansson, J.O. (1994), "Accident externality charges", Journal of Transport Economics and Policy 28:31–43.

Jansson, K. (1993), "Optimal public transport price and service frequency", Journal of Transport Economics and Policy 33:50.

Jansson, K. and B. Wallin (1991), "Deregulation of public transport in Sweden", Journal of Transport Economics and Policy 25:97–107.

Johansen, F. (1989), "Toll road characteristics and toll road experience in selected south east Asia countries", Transportation Research 23A:463–466.

Jones, P. (1991), "Gaining public support for road pricing through a package approach", Traffic Engineering and Control 32:194–196.

Jones-Lee, M.W. (1990), "The value of transport safety", Oxford Review of Economic Policy 6:39–60.

Jones-Lee, M.W., G. Loomes and P.R. Philips (1995), "Valuing the prevention of non-fatal road injuries: contingent valuation vs. standard gambles", Oxford Economic Papers 47:676–695.

Kahn, S. (1986), "Economic estimates of the value of life", IEEE Technology and Society Magazine 5:24–31.

Kain, J.F. (1970), "How to improve urban transportation at practically no cost", Public Policy 20:335–358.

Kain, J.F. (1990), "Deception in Dallas: strategic misrepresentation in rail transit promotion and evaluation", Journal of the American Planning Association 56:184–196.

Kain, John F. (1997), "Cost-effective alternatives to Atlanta's rail rapid transit system", Journal of Transport Economics and Policy 31:25–49.

Kain, J.F., with R. Gittell, A. Daniere, S. Daniel, T. Somerville and Z. Liu (1992), Increasing the Productivity of the Nation's Urban Transportation Infrastructure, US Department of Transportation report DOT-T-92–17 (US DOT, Technology Sharing Program, Washington, DC).

Kawada, K., S. Lawrence and G. Gastelum (1997), "I–15 congestion pricing project" (San Diego Association of Governments, San Diego, CA).

Kazimi. C. (1997), "Valuing alternative-fuel vehicles in southern California", American Economic Review, Papers and Proceedings 87:265–271.

Keeler, T.E. and K.A. Small (1977), "Optimal peak-load pricing, investment, and service levels on urban expressways", Journal of Political Economy 85:1–25.

Kemp, M.A. (1973), "Some evidence of transit demand elasticities", Transportation 2:25–52.

Kennedy, D. (1995), "London bus tendering: an overview", Transport Reviews 15:341–352.

Kim, S. (1995), "Excess commuting for two-worker households in the Los Angeles metropolitan area", Journal of Urban Economics 38:166–182.

Klein, D.B., A.T. Moore and B. Reja (1997), Curb Rights: A Foundation for Free Enterprise in Urban Transit (Brookings Institution, Washington, DC).

Koopman, G.J. (1995), "Policies to reduce $CO_2$ emissions from cars in Europe: a partial equilibrium analysis", Journal of Transport Economics and Policy 29:53–70.

Kyte, M., J. Stoner and J. Cryer (1988), "A time-savings analysis of public transit ridership in Portland, Oregon", Transportation Research A 22A (5):345–359.

Lave, C.A. (1985), "Speeding, coordination, and the 55 mph limit", American Economic Review 75:1159–1164.

Lave, C.A. (1991), "Measuring the decline in transit productivity in the U.S".", Transportation Planning and Technology 15:115–124.

Lave, C.A. (1992), "Cars and demographics'", Access, 1:4–11 (University of California Transportation Center, Berkeley).

Lave, C.A. (1996), "What really is the growth of vehicle usage?", Transportation Research Record 1520:117–121.

Lave, L.B., C.T. Hendrickson and F.C. McMichael (1995), "Environmental implications of electric cars", Science 268:993–995.

Levy, H. (1994), "China: highway development and management issues, options, and strategies", Report No. 13555-CHA (The World Bank, Washington, DC).

Lindley, J. (1987), "Urban freeway congestion: quantification of the problem and effectiveness of potential solutions", Institute of Traffic Engineers Journal 57:27–32.

Lindley, J. (1989), "Urban freeway congestion problems and solutions: an update", Institute of Traffic Engineers Journal 59:21–23.

Liu, Z. (1994), "What caused rising transit deficits and escalating operating expenses?", paper presented at the annual conference of the Eastern Economic Association, Boston.

Mackie, P., J. Preston and C. Nash (1995), "Bus deregulation: ten years on", Transport Reviews 15:317–339.

Mahmassani, H.S. and R. Jayakrishnan (1991), "System performance and user response under real-time information in a congested traffic corridor", Transportation Research 25A:293–307.

Manne, A.S. and R.G. Richels (1992), Buying Greenhouse Insurance: The Economic Costs of Carbon Dioxide Emission Limit (MIT Press, Cambridge, MA).

Mannering, F. and C. Winston (1995), "Automobile air bags in the 1990s: market failure or market efficiency?", Journal of Law and Economics 38:265–279.

McCarthy, P.S. (1990), "Consumer demand for vehicle safety: an empirical study", Economic Inquiry 27:530–543.

McCubbin, D.R. and M.A. Delucchi (1996), The social cost of the health effects of motor-vehicle air pollution, report #11 in the series: The annualized social cost of motor-vehicle use in the United States, based on 1990–1991 data, report UCD-ITS-RR–96–3 (Institute of Transportation Studies, University of California, Davis).

Merriman, D., T. Ohkawara and T. Suzuki (1995), "Excess commuting in the Tokyo metropolitan area: measurement and policy simulations", Urban Studies 32:69–85.

Meyer, J.R. and J.A. Gómez-Ibáñez (1981), Autos, Transit, and Cities (Harvard University Press, Cambridge, MA).

Meyer, J.R., J.F. Kain and M. Wohl (1965), The Urban Transportation Problem (Harvard University Press, Cambridge, MA).

Meyer, M.D. (1994), "Alternative methods for measuring congestion levels", in: National Research Council, Vol. 2, pp. 32–61.

Miller, T.R. (1993), "Costs and functional consequences of U.S. roadway crashes", Accident Analysis and Prevention 25:593–607.

Mills, G. (1995), "Welfare and profit divergence for a tolled link in a road network", Journal of Transport Economics and Policy 29:137–146

Mogridge, M.J.H., D.J. Holden, J. Bird and G.C. Terzis (1987), "The Downs/Thomson paradox and the transportation planning process", International Journal of Transport Economics (Revista Internazionale di Economia dei Trasporti) 14:283–311.

Mohring, H. (1972), "Optimization and scale economies in urban bus transportation", American Economic Review 62:591–604.

Mohring, H. (1979), "The benefits of reserved bus lanes, mass transit subsidies, and marginal cost pricing in alleviating traffic congestion", in: P. Mieszkowski and M. Straszheim, eds., Current Issues in Urban Economics, pp. 165–195 (The Johns Hopkins University Press, Baltimore, MD).

Morlok, E.K. and P.A. Viton (1985), "Recent experience with successful private transit in large U.S. cities", in: C.A. Lave, ed., Private Transit: The Challenge to Public Transportation, pp. 121–149 (Ballinger, Cambridge, MA).

Nash, C.A. (1988), "Integration of public transport: an economic assessment", in: J.S. Dodgson and N. Topham, eds., Bus Deregulation and Privatisation, pp. 97–118 (Gower, Aldershot, UK).

National Research Council (1991), Rethinking the Ozone Problem in Urban and Regional Air Pollution (National Academy Press, Washington, DC).

National Research Council (1994), Curbing Gridlock: Peak-period Fees to Relieve Traffic Congestion, Transportation Research Board Special Report 242 (National Academy Press, Washington, DC).

Nelessen, A. and L.K. Howe (1995), "Flexible, friendly neighborhood transit: a solution for the suburban transportation dilemma", Working Paper No. 86 (Center for Urban Policy Research, Rutgers University, Piscataway, NJ).

Newbery, D.M. (1988), "Road user charges in Britain", Economic Journal 98: 161–176.

Newbery, D.M. (1990), "Pricing and congestion: economic principles relevant to pricing roads", Oxford Review of Economic Policy 6:22–38.

Newman, P.W.G. and J.R. Kenworthy (1989), Cities and Auto Dependence: A Sourcebook (Gower, Aldershot, UK).

Newman, P.W.G. and J.R. Kenworthy (1991), "Transport and urban form in thirty-two of the world's principal cities", Transport Reviews 11:249–272.

Nowlan, D.M. and G. Stewart (1991), "Downtown population growth and commuting trips: recent experience in Toronto", Journal of the American Planning Association 57:165–182.

OECD (Organisation for Economic Co-Operation and Development) (1994), Congestion Control and Demand Management (OECD, Paris).

Oum, T.H., W.G. Waters and J.-S. Yong (1992), "Concepts of price elasticities of demand and recent empirical estimates", Journal of Transport Economics and Policy 26:139–154.

Peltzman, S. (1975), "The effects of automobile safety regulations", Journal of Political Economy 83:677–725.

Perl, A. and J. Pucher (1995), "Transit in trouble?: the policy challenge posed by Canada's changing urban mobility", Canadian Public Policy 21:261–283.

Perry, J.L. and T.T. Babitsky (1986), "Comparative performance in urban bus transit: assessing privatization strategies", Public Administration Review 46:57–66.

Phang, S-Y and M. Asher (1997), "Recent developments in Singapore's motor vehicle policies", Journal of Transport Economics and Policy 31:211–220.

Phang, S-Y and R. Toh (1997), "From manual to electronic road congestion pricing: the Singapore experience and experiment", Transportation Research E 33:97–106.

Pickrell, D.H. (1985a), "Rising deficits and the uses of transport subsidies in the United States", Journal of Transport Economics and Policy 24:281–298.

Pickrell, D.H. (1985b), "Urban rail in America: a review of the regional planning association study", US Department of Transportation Volpe Center Report No. SS–64V.5–3.

Pickrell, D.H. (1992), "A desire named streetcar: fantasy and fact in rail transit planning", Journal of the American Planning Association 58:158–176.

Prud'homme, R. (1997), "On transport-related externalities", Working Paper No. 97–15 (Observatoire de l'Economie et des Institutions Locales, University of Paris).

Pucher, J. (1988), "Urban travel behavior as the outcome of public policy", Journal of the American Planning Association 54:509–519.

Pucher, J. (1995a), "Urban passenger transport in the United States and Europe: a comparative analysis of public policies", Part 1: "Travel behavior, urban development, and automobile use", Transport Reviews 15:99–117.

Pucher, J. (1995b), "Urban passenger transport in the United States and Europe: a comparative analysis of public policies", Part 2: "Public transport, overall cost comparisons and recommendations", Transport Reviews 15:211–227.

Pucher, J., D. Hendrickson and S. McNeil (1981), "Socioeconomic characteristics of transit riders: some recent evidence", Traffic Quarterly 35:461–483.

Pucher, J. and S. Kurth (1995), "Making transit irresistible: lessons from Europe", Transportation Quarterly 49:117–128.

Pucher, J. and C. Lefèvre (1996), The Urban Transport Crisis in Europe and North America (Macmillan, Basingstoke, UK).

Pucher, J., A. Markstedt and I. Hirschman (1983), "Impacts of subsidies on the costs of urban public transport", Journal of Transport Economics and Policy 17:156–176.

Quinet, E. (1994), "The social costs of transport: evaluation and links with internalisation policies", in: European Conference of Ministers of Transport (ECMT), Internalising the Social Costs of Transport, Publications Service, pp. 31–75 (OECD, Paris).

Rom, M. (1994), "The politics of congestion pricing", in: National Research Council, Vol. 2, pp. 280–299.

Rossetti, M.A. and B.S. Eversole (1993), Journal to Work Trends in the United States and Its Major Metropolitan Areas, 1960–1980. Available from the National Technical Information Service at Springfield, Virginia as Publication No. FHWA-PL–94-012 (Volpe National Transportation Systems Center, US Department of Transportation, Cambridge, MA)..

Rouwendal, J. and P. Rietveld (1994), "Changes in commuting distances of Dutch households", Urban Studies 31:1545–1557.

Ruster, J. (1997), "A retrospective on the Mexican toll road program (1989–1994)", in: The Private Sector in Infrastructure: Strategy, Regulation, and Risk, pp. 117–124 (World Bank, Washington, DC).

SACTRA (1994). Trunk Roads and the Generation of Traffic (Her Majesty's Stationery Office, London).

Schrank, D.L., S.M. Turner and T.J. Lomax (1993), Estimates of Urban Roadway Congestion—1990, Research Report 1131–5 (Texas Transportation Institute, College Station).

Shah, A.M. (1990), "Optimal pricing of traffic externalities: theory and measurement", International Journal of Transport Economics 17:3–19.

Sharman, K. and M. Dasgupta (1993), Urban Travel and Sustainable Development: An OECD/ECMT Study of 132 Cities (Transport Research Laboratory, Department of Transport, Crawthorne, UK).

Shavell, S. (1987), An Analysis of Accident Law (Harvard University Press, Cambridge, MA).

Sherret, A. (1975), Immediate Travel Impacts of Transbay BART. Peat, Marwick, Mitchell & Co. Report TM 15–3–75 to US Department of Transportation (National Technical Information Service, Springfield, VA).

Shimazahi, T. and M. Rahman (1995), "Operational characteristics of paratransit in developing countries of Asia", Transportation Research Record, No. 1503, pp. 49–56.

Shoup, D. (1994), "Cashing out employer-paid parking: a precedent for congestion pricing?", in: National Research Council, Vol. 2, pp. 152–199.

Small, K.A. (1983), "Bus priority and congestion pricing on urban expressways", in: T.E. Keeler, ed., Research in Transportation Economics, Vol. 1, pp. 27–74 (JAI Press, Greenwich, CT).

Small, K.A. (1985), "Transportation and urban change", in: P.E. Peterson, ed., The New Urban Reality, pp. 197–223 (Brookings Institution, Washington, DC).

Small, K.A. (1992a), Urban Transportation Economics (Harwood Academic Publishers, Chur, Switzerland).

Small, K.A. (1992b), "Using the revenues from congestion pricing", Transportation 19:359–381.

Small, K.A. and J.A. Gómez-Ibáñez (1998), "Road pricing for congestion management: the transition from theory to policy", in: K.J. Button and E.T. Verhoef, eds., Road Pricing, Traffic Congestion and the Environment (Edward Elgar, Aldershot, UK).

Small, K.A. and C. Kazimi (1995), "On the costs of air pollution from motor vehicles", Journal of Transport Economics and Policy 29:7–32.

Small, K.A. and S. Song (1992), " 'Wasteful' commuting: a resolution", Journal of Political Economy 100:888–898.

Small, K.A., C. Winston and C.A. Evans (1989), Road Work: A New Highway Pricing and Investment Policy (Brookings Institution, Washington, DC).

Stone, J.R., A. Nalevanko and J. Tsai (1993), "Assessment of software for computerized paratransit operations", Transportation Research Record, No. 1378, pp. 1–9.

Teal, R.F. (1988), "Public transit service contracting: a state report", Transportation Quarterly 42:207–222.

Teal, R.F. (1991), "Issues raised by competitive contracting of bus transit service in the USA", Transportation Planning and Technology 15:391–403.

Teal, R.F. (1993), "Implications of technological developments for demand responsive transit", Transportation Research Record, No. 1390, pp. 33–42.

Thomson, J.M. (1977), Great Cities and Their Traffic (Gollancz, Peregrine Edition, London).

Traffic speeds in central and outer London: 1993–94 (1995), Traffic Engineering and Control 36:101.

Turner, R.P. and P.R. White (1991), "Overall impacts of bus deregulation in Britain", Transport Planning and Technology 15:203–229.

Turvey, R. and H. Mohring (1975), "Optimal bus fares", Journal of Transport Economics and Policy 9:1–7.

Tyson, W.J. (1989), A Review of the Second Year of Bus Deregulation (Association of Metropolitan Counties, London).

UK Department of Transport (1993), Bus and Coach Statistics in Great Britain 1992/93 (Her Majesty's Stationary Office, London).

United Nations (1975, 1985, 1992), Demographic Yearbook (New York: UN).

US Census Bureau (1994, 1995, 1997, 1998), Statistical Abstract of the United States (US Government Printing Office, Washington, DC).

US FHWA (US Federal Highway Administration) (1987, 1988, 1990, 1995), Highway Statistics (US Government Printing Office, Washington, DC).

Vickrey, W.S. (1955), "Some implications of marginal cost pricing for public utilities", American Economic Review, Papers and Proceedings 45:605–620.

Vickrey, W.S. (1968), "Automobile accidents, tort law, externalities, and insurance: an economist's critique", Law and Contemporary Problems 33:464–487.

Vickrey, W.S. (1969), "Congestion theory and transport investment", American Economic Review, Papers and Proceedings 59:251–260.

Viscusi, V.K. (1993), "The value of risks to life and health", Journal of Economic Literature 31:1912–1946.

Viton, P.A. (1980), "The possibility of profitable bus service", Journal of Transport Economics and Policy 14:295–314.

Viton, P.A. (1983), "Pareto-optimal urban transportation equilibria", in: T.E. Keeler, ed., Research in Transportation Economics, Vol. 1, pp. 75–101 (JAI Press, Greenwich, CT).

Viton, P.A. (1992), "Consolidations of scale and scope in urban transit", Regional Science and Urban Economics 22:25–49.

Viton, P.A. (1995), "Private roads", Journal of Urban Economics 37:260–289.

Wachs, M. (1989), "U.S. transit subsidy policy: in need of reform", Science 244:1545–1549.

Walters, A.A. (1961), "The theory and measurement of private and social cost of highway congestion", Econometrica 29:676–699.

Webster, F.V., P. Bly, R.H. Johnston, N. Pauley and M. Dasgupta (1986), "Changing patterns of urban travel", Transport Reviews 6:49–86, 129–172.

Wheaton, W. (1982), "The long run structure of transportation and gasoline demand", Bell Journal of Economics 13:439–455.

White, P.R. (1990), "Bus deregulation: a welfare balance sheet", Journal of Transport Economics and Policy 24:311–332.

White, P.R. (1995), "Deregulation of local bus services in Great Britain: an introductory review", Transport Reviews 15:65–89.

Whitelegg, J. (1993), Transport for a Sustainable Future: The Case for Europe (Belhaven Press, London).

Winston, C. and B. Bosworth (1992), "Public infrastructure", in: H.J. Aaron and C.L. Schultze, eds., Setting Domestic Priorities: What Can Government Do?, pp. 267–293 (Brookings Institution, Washington, DC).

Winston, C. and F. Mannering (1984), "Consumer demand for automobile safety", American Economic Review, Papers and Proceedings 74:316–319.

Zho, M. and V. Sisiopiku (1997), "Relationship between volume-to-capacity ratios and accident rates", Transportation Research Record 1581:47–52.

*Chapter 47*

# SORTING AND VOTING: A REVIEW OF THE LITERATURE ON URBAN PUBLIC FINANCE

STEPHEN ROSS*

*University of Connecticut*

JOHN YINGER

*Syracuse University*

## Contents

* The authors are grateful to Liz Bernhard, Alex Stricker and Jamila Thompson for research assistance and to Graham Crampton, Dennis Epple, Hydeo Konishi, Thomas Nechyba, David Sjoquist and Myrna Wooders for helpful comments.

*Handbook of Regional and Urban Economics. Edited by E.S. Mills and P. Cheshire*

## Abstract

This chapter reviews the literature on the boundary between urban economics and local public finance, defined as research that considers both a housing market and the market for local public services. The first part of the chapter considers positive theories. This part presents the consensus model of the allocation of households to jurisdictions, which is built on bid functions and household sorting, as well as alternative approaches to this issue. It also examines models of local tax and spending decisions, which exhibit no consensus, and reviews research in which both housing and local fiscal variables are endogenous. The second part of the chapter considers empirical research, with a focus on tax and service capitalization, on household heterogeneity within jurisdictions, and on the impact of zoning. The third part considers normative theories about a decentralized system of local governments. This part examines the extent to which such a system leads to an efficient allocation of households to communities or efficient local public service levels, and it discusses the fairness of local public spending. This review shows that the bidding/sorting framework is strongly supported by the evidence and has wide applicability in countries with decentralized governmental systems. In contrast, models of local public service determination depend on institutional detail, and their connections with housing markets have been largely unexplored in empirical work. Ever since Tiebout (1956), many scholars have argued that decentralized local governments have efficiency advantages over centralized forms. However, a general treatment of this issue identifies four key sources of inefficiency even in a decentralized system: misallocation of households to communities, the property tax, public service capitalization and heterogeneity. Few policies to eliminate these sources of inefficiency have yet been identified. Finally, this review explores the equity implications of household sorting and other features of a decentralized system.

**Keywords:** bid functions, sorting, capitalization, Tiebout, decentralized system of government, property tax, community choice, voting

## 1. Introduction

The literature on urban public finance revolves around two questions: How do households select a community in which to live? What determines the level of local public services? To answer these questions, researchers must analyze both the housing market and the market for local public services—and how these two markets influence each other—and therefore must operate on the boundary between urban economics and local public finance. This chapter surveys the literature on this boundary. It covers theoretical work, both positive and normative, that considers both housing and local public services, along with related empirical work. Section 2 presents positive theory, Section 3 reviews empirical research, and Section 4 considers normative analysis. Most of the research on these topics concerns the US, but this review explores both the applicability of existing research to and availability of evidence for other countries.

## 2. Positive theory

The literature focuses on three central conceptual problems: (1) how does the housing market allocate households to communities when local public services and taxes vary from one community to the next?; (2) how do communities select the level of local public services and tax rates? These two problems obviously interact as the people who move into a community become voters. Hence, the third problem is: (3) under what conditions are solutions to the first two problems compatible, that is, when does an urban equilibrium exist? This section addresses the conceptual literature on each of these problems.

## 2.1. *The impact of local fiscal variables on housing prices and community choices*

A broad consensus has emerged concerning the appropriate way to model the first conceptual problem, namely, the allocation of households to communities. This consensus has general applicability to any country with active housing markets, reasonably mobile households, and multiple local governments that exhibit some variation in public service levels or tax rates. It evolved from the central positive insight of Tiebout (1956), namely, that households care about local public services and local taxes and compete for entry into the most desirable communities, and builds on the analytical framework developed in the pioneering work of Ellickson (1971).

The current consensus is contained in similar models presented by Epple et al. (1983, 1984, 1993), Epple and Romer (1989), Henderson (1977, 1991), Pogodzinski and Sjoquist (1985, 1991, 1993), Wheaton (1993) and Yinger (1982, 1985, 1995). It has two components: bidding and sorting.

*Bidding.* Bidding analysis builds on five central assumptions:
1. A household's utility depends on its consumption of housing, public services, and a composite good.
2. Households may differ in terms of income and preferences, but every household falls into a distinct income/taste class.
3. Households are mobile, so that like households must all achieve the same level of utility; this is equivalent to assuming no moving costs.
4. All households who live in a jurisdiction receive the same level of local public services, and the only way to gain access to the public services in a jurisdiction is to buy or rent housing there.
5. A metropolitan area is assumed to contain many local jurisdictions, which have fixed boundaries and vary in their local public service quality and effective tax rates.[1]

Two other assumptions are widely used, but are not central to the logic of the model, namely, that all households are homeowners and that local public services are financed with a local property tax, which sets assessed value equal to market value. More formally, the effective property tax rate, $t$, equals the nominal rate, $m$, multiplied by the assessment to sales ratio, $k$; all existing models assume that

---

[1] This chapter concentrates on models with multiple jurisdictions. Another approach is to examine a single jurisdiction that encompasses an entire urban area. Polinsky and Rubinfeld (1978), Haurin (1980) and Sullivan (1985) examine the effects of changes in property taxes and public services on an open urban equilibrium. Arnott and Mackinnon (1977) and Pasha and Ghaus (1995) examine the effects of such changes in a closed urban equilibrium. Pasha (1990) and Bentick (1996) examine the incidence of a land tax in an urban model.

$k$ is the same for all houses in a jurisdiction. We will briefly consider models with local income taxes instead of property taxes.

Our notation is as follows: $H$ is housing, measured in units of housing services with price $P$; $S$ is the quality of local public services; $Z$ is a composite good with a price of unity; and $t$ is the effective property tax rate. The property tax payment, $T$, equals $t$ multiplied by the value of a house, which is $V = PH/r$, where $r$ is a discount rate; that is, $T = tV = tPH/r = t^*PH$. Thus, a household's budget constraint is $Y = Z + PH(1 + t^*)$.

To capture competition for entry into desirable communities, we express the household problem as a bidding problem: How much would a household bid for a unit of housing in a community with a particular service/tax package? This approach is explicit in Wheaton (1993) and Yinger (1995), and is equivalent to the indirect utility function approach used by Epple et al. (1983, 1984, 1993).[2] To be specific, the household's bidding problem, derived by rearranging the budget constraint, is to

$$\text{Maximize} \quad P = \frac{Y - Z}{H(1 + t^*)}$$
$$H, Z \tag{2.1}$$
$$\text{Subject to} \quad U(Z, H, S) = U^0(Y),$$

where $U^0$ is the level of utility achieved by households with income $Y$.[3] This problem need not include a community budget constraint because a household moving into a community is not concerned with the factors that determine $S$ and $t$, only with the outcome.

In this problem, $S$ and $t$ are treated as parameters, so their impact on bids can be found through the envelope theorem. In particular,

$$P_S = \frac{U_S/U_Z}{H(1 + t^*)} = \frac{MB}{H(1 + t^*)} \tag{2.2}$$

and

$$P_t = -\frac{P}{r + t} = -\frac{P/r}{1 + t^*}, \tag{2.3}$$

---

[2] Ellickson (1971) and Epple et al. (1983, 1984, 1993) talk about "indifference curves" in $[P(1 + t^*), S]$ space, which are the same thing as "bid functions".

[3] For a bid-function approach that adds differences in preferences, see Epple and Platt (1998).

where subscripts indicate partial derivatives and $U_S/U_Z = MB$ is the marginal rate of substitution between $S$ and $Z$, which can be interpreted as the marginal benefit from $S$ in dollar terms.[4]

These two equations provide the principal testable hypotheses to come from the consensus view, namely, that $S$ and $t$ are capitalized into the price of housing. As we will see, Eq. (2.2) provides an incomplete picture of the relationship between observed housing prices and $S$, but the differential Eq. (2.3) fully describes the impact of $t$ on housing prices. Using the initial condition that the before-tax housing price, $\hat{P}$, equals the after-tax price, $P$, when $t = 0$, the solution to Eq. (2.3) yields the well-known formula for property tax capitalization:

$$V = \frac{PH}{r} = \frac{\hat{P}H}{r+t} = \frac{\hat{P}H/r}{1+t^*}. \tag{2.4}$$

*Sorting.* These results describe the housing bids for a single household but do not reveal how different types of households are sorted into jurisdictions. The key to sorting is to recognize that Eq. (2.2), the slope of the bid function with respect to $S$, has a different value for different household types. This leads to a well-known diagram, which is in Ellickson (1971), Henderson (1977), Yinger (1982), Epple et al. (1983, 1984) and Wheaton (1993) and presented here as Fig. 1.[5] Housing suppliers sell to the highest bidder, so observed prices are the envelope of the bid functions, and the group with the steepest bid function wins the competition for housing at the highest value of $S$. The exact boundaries between income classes depend on the heights of the bid functions, not just the slopes. These heights are related in turn to each group's utility level.[6] Nevertheless, the ordering of household types along the $S$-axis depends only on the relative slopes of their bid functions.

This approach implies that heterogeneous jurisdictions are possible. If a jurisdiction provides a value of $S$ at which the bid functions of two groups cross,

---

[4] The first formal derivation of Eq. (2.2) is in Henderson (1977). Equation (2.3) is equivalent to the standard expression for property tax capitalization, which has a long history. See Yinger et al. (1988).

[5] Ellickson (1971), Henderson (1977) and Epple et al. (1983, 1984) draw this figure with $P(1+t^*)$ on the vertical axis, whereas Yinger (1995) and Wheaton (1993) draw it with $P$. As discussed in later footnotes, this difference is inconsequential for sorting, but does influence the role that bid functions play in the analysis. For illuminating sorting, however, drawing the figure with $P$ on the vertical axis makes more sense because $P$ is the price that housing suppliers receive; suppliers will sell or rent to the household type with the highest $P$, not the highest $P(1+t^*)$. Moreover, a focus on $P(1+t^*)$ requires additional analysis, supplied by Epple et al. (1983, 1984) but not Ellickson (1971), to capture the behavior of housing sellers. Henderson (1977) assumes that suburbs can be costlessly created so that $P$ is constant across suburbs. We return to this assumption below.

[6] Readers familiar with urban models will recognize the logic here. In an open urban model, the height of a bid function (over location) is fixed by a group's utility in a system of cities; in a closed model the height is raised (and utility lowered) until there is enough room for all members of the group. See Brueckner (1987).

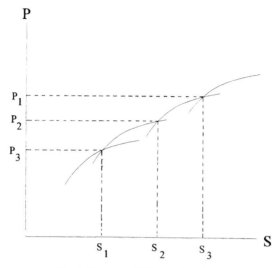

Fig. 1. Consensus bidding and sorting.

both groups are content to live there. In several models, including those of Epple et al. (1983, 1984, 1993), income is modeled as a continuous variable and every jurisdiction contains a range of income classes. In the bid-function approach, therefore, jurisdictions are more homogenous than with a random allocation of households, but may nevertheless be fairly heterogeneous.

Figure 1 also implies that observed differences in housing prices across jurisdictions do not necessarily correspond to a household's willingness to pay for the corresponding service quality differences. When income classes are defined continuously, as in Epple et al. (1983, 1984, 1993), the observed price difference between two communities with adjacent values of $S$ equals the willingness to pay only for "border" or marginal households which are indifferent between residing in either community.[7] In addition, observed price differences between communities with nonadjacent levels of $S$ may not correspond to any group's bid differences.[8]

---

[7] With discrete income classes, one class may fill a jurisdiction, implying that its bid exceeds the bid of every other class. In this case, observed price differences between that jurisdiction and jurisdictions inhabited by other classes, even if they provide adjacent levels of $S$, may not correspond exactly to the bid differences of any group.

[8] Pogodzinski (1988) criticizes Yinger's (1982) claim that capitalization may not be "complete" in the sense that observed price differences may not correspond to some group's bid difference. This strikes us as a semantic disagreement, not a substantive one. From the perspective of the marginal household class, complete capitalization always exists between communities with adjacent values of $S$ (Pogodzinski's claim), but estimated price differences across a range of communities need not correspond to the bid differences of

Most local public services are normal goods, but the standard market mechanisms are not available to allow higher income households to buy more of them. A natural question to ask, therefore, is whether or not bidding alone is sufficient to sustain "matched" sorting, which is defined to exist when higher income households sort into jurisdictions with higher $S$. To answer this question, it will prove convenient to write problem (1) in a somewhat different form, introduced by Wheaton (1993).[9] To be specific, let us assume that both $S$ and $t$ are known functions of some jurisdictional characteristic, say $\tilde{Y}$. We interpret $\tilde{Y}$ as a jurisdiction's median income, but it could, as in Wheaton, be a more general index that incorporated preferences or other factors that boost service quality.

Furthermore, we can simplify the problem by introducing a jurisdiction's budget constraint, ignoring for now nonresidential property and revenue from sources other than the property tax.[10] Because all households in a jurisdiction must pay the same price per unit of housing services, $\tilde{Y}$ affects house value only through its impact on average house size, written $\bar{H}$, and the average property taxbase in the community is $P\bar{H}(\tilde{Y})/r$. On the expenditure side, the cost of public services per household is written $E[S(\tilde{Y}), \tilde{Y}]$. This form recognizes not only that costs increase with the public service quality, $S$, but also, as discussed more fully below, that costs may depend on $\tilde{Y}$ itself. Thus, the jurisdiction's budget constraint is

$$E[S(\tilde{Y}), \tilde{Y}] = t^*(\tilde{Y})P\bar{H}(\tilde{Y}). \tag{2.5}$$

Note that $\partial E/\partial S = MC$ is the marginal cost of $S$.

---

any particular group (Yinger's claim). Moreover, as pointed out in the previous footnote, with discrete income classes a marginal household type may not exist.

[9] Although we use Wheaton's (1993) technique, we do not reproduce his problem, which unlike the rest of the literature, enters land and housing capital as separate arguments in the household utility function. We return to this issue in footnotes 13 and 60.

[10] A budget constraint is not needed to describe how bids change as $\tilde{Y}$ changes—or to look at matched sorting. Without a budget constraint, we can make $S$ and $t$ in Eq. (2.1) functions of $\tilde{Y}$ and use the envelope theorem to derive

$$P_{\tilde{Y}} = \left(\frac{MB}{H(1+t^*)}\right)\frac{dS}{d\tilde{Y}} - \left(\frac{P/r}{1+t^*}\right)\frac{dt}{d\tilde{Y}}.$$

Inserting a budget constraint helps to draw out the intuition of the problem by removing ambiguity about the relationship between $\tilde{Y}$ and $t$.

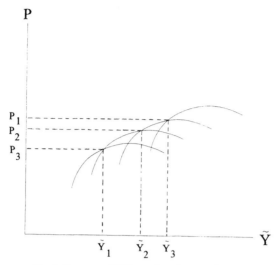

Fig. 2. Consensus bidding and sorting net of taxes.

Solving Eq. (2.5) for $t^*$ and substituting the result into Eq. (2.1) yields:

Maximize $\quad P = \dfrac{Y - Z}{H} - \dfrac{E[S(\tilde{Y}), \tilde{Y}]}{\bar{H}(\tilde{Y})}$

$H, Z$                                                                                                                       (2.6)

Subject to $\quad U[Z, H, S(\tilde{Y})] = U^0(Y).$

Another application of the envelope theorem now reveals that the slope of the bid function with respect to $\tilde{Y}$ is

$$P_{\tilde{Y}} = \left( \frac{1}{H} \frac{\mathrm{d}S}{\mathrm{d}\tilde{Y}} \right) \left( MB - MC \frac{H}{\bar{H}} \right) + \left( \frac{E}{\bar{H}^2} \frac{\mathrm{d}\bar{H}}{\mathrm{d}\tilde{Y}} \right) - \left( \frac{1}{\bar{H}} \frac{\partial E}{\partial \tilde{Y}} \right).$$ (2.7)

The second pair of parentheses marks the net benefit from additional services, that is, the excess of a household's marginal benefit from $S$ over its tax price, which equals $MC$ multiplied by the voters tax share, $H/\bar{H} = V/\bar{V}$. As illustrated in Fig. 2, this term, and hence $P_{\tilde{Y}}$, could be positive or negative.

The third pair of parentheses indicates the percentage increase in taxbase that accompanies an increase in $\tilde{Y}$ weighted by spending per unit of taxbase. This term measures a household's cost savings from moving to a jurisdiction where $\tilde{Y}$ is larger and hence its tax price is lower.[11] Finally, the fourth pair of paren-

---

[11] Ellickson (1971) was the first to identify this effect and to point out that it gives high income jurisdictions an incentive to keep out low income households. See also Hamilton (1975) and Henderson (1977).

theses marks the link between community characteristics and the cost of $S$. The evidence, discussed below, indicates that $\partial E/\partial \tilde{Y}$ is negative, so the cost savings from moving to a higher income jurisdiction serves to boost housing bids there.

Now consider two income classes that both live in the same jurisdiction. As shown in Figs. 1 and 2, this implies that they both have the same bid there or, to put it another way, pay the same $P$. However, the slopes of their bid functions with respect to $S$, described by Eq. (2.2) and Fig. 1, or with respect to $\tilde{Y}$, described by Eq. (2.7) and Fig. 2, may differ.[12] For "matched" sorting to occur, the class with the higher income must have a bid function with a steeper slope at all values of $S$; that is, the derivative of $P_{\tilde{Y}}$ with respect to $Y$ must be positive. From Eq. (2.7) this derivative is[13]

$$\frac{\partial P_{\tilde{Y}}}{\partial Y} = \left( \frac{MB}{YH} \frac{dS}{d\tilde{Y}} \right) (\epsilon - \theta), \tag{2.8}$$

where $\epsilon$ is the elasticity of $MB$ with respect to $Y$ and $\theta$ is the income elasticity of demand for $H$; this is known as the single-crossing condition. If $S$ is a normal good, matched sorting exists whenever $\epsilon$ is greater than $\theta$. This condition arises because willingness to pay for an increment in $S$ is spread out over the amount of $H$ consumed. If $H$ increases rapidly with income, the impact of an improved service-tax package on the bid per unit of $H$ may actually decline as income goes up.

Note that $\epsilon$ is not the same as the income elasticity of demand for $S$, say $\alpha$. Yinger (1995) shows, for example, that with a constant-elasticity demand function for public services, $\epsilon = -\alpha/\mu$, where $\mu$ is the price elasticity of demand for $S$.[14] Moreover, Wheaton (1993) shows that $\epsilon \cong -\alpha/\mu$ for any utility function. Thus, matched sorting occurs as long as $-\alpha/\mu > \theta$. According to the

---

[12] As shown by Yinger (1982), sorting is not affected by the property tax; after all, people at all income levels are willing to pay $1 to avoid $1 of property taxes. Thus, it is possible to analyze sorting with either Eqs. (2.2) or (2.7). As shown in the following footnote, the property tax appears in the condition derived from Eq. (2.2), but even in that case it only scales the expression and does not affect its sign—or its implications for sorting. Changes in $\bar{H}$ or $MC$ (in the last two terms in Eq. (2.7)) also do not affect income sorting because they are not functions of $Y$.

[13] This condition was first derived by Henderson (1977). It also appears in Wheaton (1993), although his formula is more complicated because he treats land and housing capital differently (see footnote 9). The no-budget-constraint result in footnote 10 leads to a version of Eq. (2.8) with $(1 + t^*)$ in the denominator. This term is positive and does not alter the elasticity condition in the text; that is, this condition holds in general regardless of the relationship between $S$ and $t$. Also, maximizing $P(1 + t^*)$, instead of $P$, as in Ellickson (1971) and Epple et al. (1983, 1984, 1993), leads to the same condition. With or without a budget constraint, $P(1 + t^*) = (Y - Z)/H$, and envelope theorem implies that $P_{\tilde{Y}} = (MB/H)(dS/d\tilde{Y})$. Equation (2.8) follows directly.

[14] If $S = AY^\alpha C^\mu$, where $C$ is the tax price of $S$, then the marginal benefit from $S$ can be written as $MB = C = (A/S)^{-1/\mu} Y^{-\alpha/\mu}$. Logarithmic differentiation yields the result in the text.

empirical literature, this is likely to be true; the best recent studies find that $\alpha$ probably exceeds $\theta$ and $|\mu|$ is close to zero.[15] Matched sorting obviously will not occur, however, for inferior public services (defined by $\alpha < 0$), perhaps including welfare programs.

Bid models are flexible and do not depend on the existence of property taxation. Bidding with an income tax, for example, has been considered by Goodspeed (1989), Pogodzinski and Sjoquist (1993) and Boije (1997). In the framework presented here, the household budget constraint becomes $Y(1 - y) = Z + PH$, where $y$ is the income tax rate, and the community budget constraint becomes $E = y\bar{Y}$. Making $S$ a function of $\tilde{Y}$ and solving for $y$, the bid problem analogous to Eq. (2.6) is

$$
\begin{array}{ll}
\text{Maximize} \\
H, Z
\end{array}
\quad
P = \frac{Y\left(1 - \dfrac{E[S(\tilde{Y}), \tilde{Y}]}{\bar{Y}}\right) - Z}{H}
\tag{2.9}
$$

Subject to $\quad U[Z, H, S(\tilde{Y})] = U^0(Y).$

From this problem, we find that

$$
P_{\tilde{Y}} = \left(\frac{1}{H}\frac{dS}{d\tilde{Y}}\right)\left(MB - MC\frac{Y}{\bar{Y}}\right) + \left(\frac{E}{\bar{Y}^2}\frac{Y}{H}\right) - \left(\frac{1}{H}\frac{\partial E}{\partial \tilde{Y}}\right).
\tag{2.10}
$$

This result is analogous to Eq. (2.7), but its derivative with respect to income is much more complicated because three terms are now functions of $Y$: the tax share, $Y/\bar{Y}$; the term in the third pair of parentheses, which reflects the benefits from moving to a community with a higher taxbase; and the last term, which reflects the gain from moving to a lower-cost community. Hence, the simple sorting rule in Eq. (2.8) no longer holds.[16]

*Hamilton's approach.* An alternative approach to sorting, which yields a Tiebout-like outcome with housing and a property tax, was proposed in a well-known article by Hamilton (1975). This approach adds three assumptions. First, the per-unit cost of $S$ is a constant, $g$; that is, $E(S) = gS$. This is a two-part assumption:

---

[15] The evidence on $\alpha$ and $\mu$ is reviewed in Section 3.2.1. Evidence on $\theta$ can be found in Mayo (1981) and Harmon (1988).

[16] This sorting rule is complicated, and its derivation is left to the reader. We do note, however, that differentiating Eq. (2.10) with respect to $Y$ does not lead to the formula in Goodspeed (1989), which is the same as Eq. (2.8). In his derivation he ignores the impact of $Y$ on the last three terms in Eq. (2.10).

each unit of $S$ costs $\$g$, and this cost is the same in all jurisdictions. The second part rules out public goods, for which the per-unit cost declines with population. Second, the supply of housing associated with any given service-tax package is perfectly elastic. Because the supply of housing cannot be elastic in a jurisdiction with fixed boundaries, this assumption requires that the boundaries of existing jurisdictions be flexible or that new jurisdictions can be costlessly created. Third, a jurisdiction can use zoning restrictions to set the consumption of $H$ at exactly the optimal level. In our framework, this assumption implies that $H$ is no longer a choice variable for a household in search of housing but is instead a function of $\tilde{Y}$. Note also that the third assumption has two parts: zoning must be exact, in the sense that it sets the same minimum value of $H$ for every household, and it must be set at the optimal level of $H$.

As shown earlier, a household's utility (and hence its housing bid) increases as a jurisdiction's average taxbase increases, that is, as its own tax share decreases. This result reflects the fact that with a property tax, households with relatively high $H$ (and hence a high tax share) cover some of the cost of $S$ for households with relatively low $H$ (and hence a low tax share). Hamilton's (1975) assumptions make it possible for high income households to prevent this type of subsidization. The assumption of perfectly elastic housing supply makes it possible for anyone to set up a homogeneous community with housing priced at $\bar{P}$, which is the marginal cost of $H$ when land is priced at the agricultural rental rate.[17] Moreover, exact zoning ensures that everyone consumes the same level of $H$ (because no household would voluntarily consume more than the minimum and therefore subsidize its neighbors) and perfect zoning ensures that this level of $H$ is optimal; thus, the community can keep out anyone who wants to consume less $H$ than the optimal level for current residents.

In formal terms, the Hamilton (1975) assumptions transform the household's problem into one in which the household knows that the value of $H$ it selects also will be the average value of $H$ in the jurisdiction (Epple et al., 1978). Thus, Eq. (2.1) becomes:

$$\text{Maximize}_{H, Z, S} \quad P = \frac{Y - Z - gS}{H}$$

(2.11)

$$\text{Subject to} \quad U(Z, H, S) = U^0(Y).$$

---

[17] Earlier work by Edel and Sclar (1974) predicted, like Hamilton (1975), that housing prices would not vary in the long run because the supply of housing is elastic. See also Epple et al. (1978) and Henderson (1977, 1985).

The first-order conditions of this problem imply that a household chooses $S$ and $H$ so that

$$MB = g \quad \text{and} \quad \frac{U_H}{U_Z} = P[= \bar{P}].$$ (2.12)

Do these assumptions result in a sorting equilibrium? We can answer this question by determining whether, or not, a household that selects a jurisdiction (called the base jurisdiction) according to the conditions in Eq. (2.12) will bid more for housing in a jurisdiction with a higher value of $\tilde{Y}$ (called the higher income jurisdiction); if so, an allocation with a price of $\bar{P}$ everywhere cannot be sustained. To keep the analysis general, suppose that $\hat{H}$ identifies the minimum housing consumption required by zoning and that $\hat{H}$, $\bar{H}$ and $g$ are all functions of $\tilde{Y}$.[18] Then the bidding problem becomes:

Maximize $\quad P = \dfrac{Y - Z}{\hat{H}(\tilde{Y})} - \dfrac{g(\tilde{Y})S(\tilde{Y})}{\bar{H}(\tilde{Y})}$

$Z$ (2.13)

Subject to $\quad U[Z, \hat{H}(\tilde{Y}), S(\tilde{Y})] = U^0(Y).$

Applying the envelope theorem and assuming that, to start with, everyone is in a jurisdiction where $\hat{H}$ equals $\bar{H}$, we find that

$$P_{\tilde{Y}} = \frac{1}{\hat{H}} \left[ \frac{\mathrm{d}S}{\mathrm{d}\tilde{Y}} (MB - g) + \frac{\mathrm{d}\hat{H}}{\mathrm{d}\tilde{Y}} \left( \frac{U_H}{U_Z} - P \right) + \frac{gS}{\hat{H}} \left( \frac{\mathrm{d}\bar{H}}{\mathrm{d}\tilde{Y}} - \frac{\mathrm{d}\hat{H}}{\mathrm{d}\tilde{Y}} \right) - S \frac{\mathrm{d}g}{\mathrm{d}\tilde{Y}} \right].$$

(2.14)

According to Eq. (2.12), the first two terms drop out; households place no value on the increases in $S$ and $H$ associated with moving to the higher income community. The third term drops out by the assumption that zoning is exact, so that everyone's $H$ is at the minimum allowable value. The final term drops out by the assumption that $g$ is fixed across communities. Thus, under Hamilton's (1975) assumptions, $P_{\tilde{Y}} = 0$ equals zero. This defines the situation first described by Pauley (1976), in which there is no capitalization because every household lives in the community where its bid is highest. This situation is illustrated in Fig. 3.

---

[18] This formulation assumes that if a household moves to a community with a higher value of $\tilde{Y}$, the zoning constraint there will be binding. A more general, but no more illuminating, version of the problem would allow $H$ to exceed $\hat{H}$.

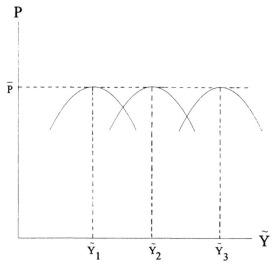

Fig. 3. Hamilton bidding and sorting.

This discussion not only confirms Hamilton's reasoning, but also reveals that each of Hamilton's (1975) assumptions is crucial. Without the ability to cost-lessly create new jurisdictions, the base community may have heterogeneity in housing consumption, the first part of Eq. (2.12) may not hold, and thus the first term in Eq. (2.14) may not equal zero.[19] Without zoning at the optimal level of housing consumption in the base community, the second part of Eq. (2.12) may not hold, and thus the second term in Eq. (2.14) may not equal zero. Without exact zoning, bids reflect the advantages of moving to a jurisdiction with a higher taxbase, and the third term is not zero. And if the cost of $S$ declines with income, households will bid up the price in the higher income—and hence lower cost—jurisdiction so that the last term is not zero.

The assumptions that lead to Hamilton's (1975) equilibrium appear extreme. First, as pointed out by Yinger (1982) and Rose-Ackerman (1983), the possibility for new jurisdictions is limited by transportation costs; one cannot bid land away from agriculture at great distances from employment concentrations.[20] Moreover, no one has provided any evidence that jurisdiction boundaries change to increase

---

[19] Conditions analogous to Eq. (2.12) with heterogenous housing (and a property tax) are derived in Section 4.1.3.

[20] This is one of the few points at which the logic of a spatial model, such as those cited in footnote 1, is brought into a multijurisdiction framework. For a more formal treatment of space with many jurisdictions, see Crampton (1996).

the supply of housing where housing bids are high.[21] Furthermore, the evidence, reviewed below, indicates that $g$ declines as a jurisdiction's income goes up.

Finally, the assumptions about zoning are very strong. Actual zoning tools, such as lot-size restrictions and set-back rules, appear far too blunt to control $H$ precisely, and indeed voters would have to be foresightful to set zoning barriers at exactly the optimal level of $H$. For example, if voters are myopic, in the sense that they take the existing value of $\bar{H}$ as given, then their perceived price of $H$ is $P(1 + t^*) = P + E(S)/\bar{H}$, and they select a level of $H$ that is too low due to this property tax distortion. To prevent subsidization of incoming residents, they will set the zoning level equal to their own preferred $H$, so that it, too, will be too low. In contrast, if voters' own houses are exempt from the zoning constraint they select, they have a strong incentive to set the constraint above their own $H$ so that future entrants will subsidize their taxes (White, 1975; Miceli, 1991, 1992). This incentive suggests that zoning constraints may be too strict, in the sense that they force people to consume more $H$ than they want, and may reduce property values.

Fischel (1992) argues that local zoning tools are varied and flexible and presents evidence that zoning ordinances are driven primarily by fiscal concerns. According to Fischel, this evidence supports the Hamilton (1975) model. In our view, however, the existence of fiscal zoning is consistent with many models, not just with the Hamilton model. Voters who do not understand that matched sorting may arise naturally may pass zoning ordinances to mimic what the market would do anyway. If the elasticity condition in Eq. (2.8) is not satisfied, communities may pass zoning ordinances that ensure matched sorting but do not eliminate capitalization.[22] Moreover, if public service costs decline with income, so that the last term in Eq. (2.14) is not zero, communities may set zoning above the optimal level of $H$ in order to keep out low income and, hence, high cost households.[23] Finally, communities may use zoning as a form of insurance against upward shifts in the bid functions of lower income groups due to immigration or natural population growth.

Thus, a test of Hamilton's model is not whether fiscal zoning exists, but whether, or not, fiscal zoning is set at exactly the optimal level of $H$. Moreover,

---

[21] As pointed out by Henderson (1985), jurisdiction boundaries change fairly often, particularly in the Southwest. However, Epple and Romer (1989) show that these changes do not involve expansions of high-bid groups into low-bid areas as the Hamilton and Henderson models imply.

[22] Henderson (1977), Wheaton (1993) and Yinger (1995) describe zoning rules that serve this function.

[23] This point is made by Oates (1977b), who presents survey evidence that cost-related fiscal zoning is far more important than the taxbase related fiscal zoning in the Hamilton approach. Fischel (1992) does not distinguish between these two types of fiscal zoning.

this model implies that the zoning restriction (or level of $H$) in one jurisdiction should be independent of the zoning decisions of surrounding jurisdictions; if every household obtains its optimal $H$, no resident has an incentive to move, and no voter needs to consider what other jurisdictions do.

The Hamilton model also predicts no capitalization, so that a house value regression will obtain zero coefficients for $S$ and $t$. This model does not imply that people do not care about $S$ and $t$, or even that $S$ and $t$ do not affect their housing bids, only that these effects cannot be observed. If $P$ (or $V$, holding $H$ constant) does not vary with $S$ and $t$ (or, equivalently, with factors that influence $S$ and $t$, summarized by $\tilde{Y}$ here), then an econometric analysis of $P$ has nothing to work with and will conclude that $S$ and $t$ have no impact on $P$.[24] If $P$ does vary with $S$ and $t$, so that coefficients for these two variables can be estimated, then the principal prediction of the Hamilton model, a constant $P$, can be rejected. Statistically significant capitalization of $S$ or $t$ therefore serves as a rejection of the Hamilton model.[25]

This conclusion can be clarified by distinguishing between the bid function of a particular class and the observed housing price function. As shown in Fig. 3, the Hamilton bid function for any class reaches a maximum at the $S$ in its own jurisdiction. This bid function reflects the willingness to pay both for higher $S$ and for lower $t$. If that bid function could be observed, its slope would be zero at that service quality. To put it another way, the Hamilton model predicts that the marginal impact of higher $S$ (due to higher $\tilde{Y}$) on that groups's bids is exactly offset by the marginal impact of a change in $t$ (due to higher $\tilde{Y}$). Because each class's bid function is observed at only one point, however, this prediction cannot be tested. A regression is based on the values of $P$ at different values of $\tilde{Y}$, which, according to Hamilton, should not differ.

Several scholars have argued that the Hamilton approach implies zero net capitalization, not no capitalization at all.[26] Zero net capitalization exists when the "border" household's willingness to pay to avoid the difference in $t$ between

[24] This argument does not require the use of $\tilde{Y}$. The Hamilton model assumes that any community can be costlessly replicated, so no community can possess an advantage over other communities in the production of $S$—an advantage that might, if it existed, show up in $P$.

[25] The argument in the text applies to interjurisdictional capitalization. A related argument can be made for intrajurisdictional capitalization: If differences in $S$ or $t$ exist within a jurisdiction (as demonstrated by their impact on property values) then the homogeneity predicted by the Hamilton model must not exist. Thus, statistically significant intrajurisdictional capitalization also constitutes evidence against the Hamilton model.

[26] See Sonstelie and Portney (1980) and Oates (1994). Hamilton himself originally believed that his approach involved no capitalization but then changed his mind. As he put it (1983b; p. 87), the precise link between taxes and public services in his approach "has unfortunately led some observers (see Hamilton, 1975) to refer to this case as zero capitalization rather than full capitalization, thus creating some confusion in the literature". As we show below, Hamilton's change of mind depends on another extreme assumption. As noted

two communities just equals its willingness to pay for the associated difference in $S$. In our judgement, this view confuses the bid function of a given household type with the observed housing price function. As shown above, it is indeed true that an infinitesimal increase in $\tilde{Y}$ leads to offsetting impacts on $P$ through $S$ and through $t$, but Fig. 3 clearly shows that this change in bids is not what is observed between two communities. Because the second derivative of $P$ with respect to $\tilde{Y}$ is negative, a class will bid less in a community other than in its own—unless the values of $\tilde{Y}$ in the two communities differ by only an infinitesimal amount. Hence, it cannot be said that there is zero net capitalization between jurisdictions 1 and 2 in Fig. 3; a household who lives in jurisdiction 1 is unwilling to pay enough for the increment in $S$ it would receive in jurisdiction 2 to cover what it would lose from higher $t$, so its (unobserved) bid in jurisdiction 2 is below the market price. With anything less than an infinite number of jurisdictions, therefore, it is the elastic supply of housing, not a balance between benefits and costs of $S$ for each household class, that keeps the price of housing constant in the Hamilton model.

In a later paper, Hamilton (1976) employs an assumption that ensures zero net capitalization without an infinite number of communities, namely, that the benefits from $S$ can be measured by local public spending. In particular, he examines a community that contains high and low income housing (designated HIH and LIH) and assumes that the price of HIH is given by $H_i = H' + (X - H_i t_i)D$, "where $H_i$ = the value of the HIH dwelling unit in community $i$; $H'$ = the value of the same structure in a homogeneous HIH community; $X$ = the per household expenditure on the local public service; $t_i$ = community $i$'s property tax rate; $D$ = the discount factor that converts a constant annual stream into a present value" (Hamilton, 1976: p. 746). In formal terms, this assumption implies that the marginal willingness to pay for (or marginal benefit from) $1 of public spending is $1. Because $1 of property taxes can finance exactly $1 of public spending, this assumption ensures that *every* household's willingness to pay for a difference in $S$ between *any* two communities is exactly offset by the associated property tax difference.

This assumption is extreme. Whereas a standard demand curve sets $MB = MB(Y, S)$, this assumption sets $MB = \$1$, which requires both the income and price elasticities of demand for $S$ to equal zero. This requirement is strongly contradicted by the evidence (discussed below). In short, without adding another extreme assumption (either infinite communities or zero income and price elas-

---

earlier, several other scholars are clear that the Tiebout or Hamilton assumptions imply no capitalization (Edel and Sclar, 1974; Epple et al., 1978).

ticities of demand for $S$), the Hamilton (1975) approach implies that neither $t$ nor $S$ has any effect on property values.[27] Moreover, even with one of these assumptions, one cannot distinguish empirically between zero net capitalization and no capitalization.[28]

This analysis also applies to zoning. Fischel (1992) argues that Hamilton's (1975) approach predicts a positive relationship between restrictive zoning controls and property values. As shown in Fig. 3, however, Hamilton zoning (along with his other assumptions) implies that the price of housing services equals $\bar{P}$; any link between zoning and property value implies a deviation from this prediction.[29]

The Hamilton model also implies homogeneity within a community in both $S$ and $H$. As observed by Goldstein and Pauly (1981), however, homogeneity in public service demands does not imply income homogeneity; a low income household with a strong taste for public services might demand the same $S$ as a high income household with a weak taste for public services. As shown below, these unobserved tastes for $S$ complicate both tests of the Hamilton (1975) model based on heterogeneity and the estimation of public service demand equations.

*Henderson's approach.* Henderson (1991) provides an alternative to Hamilton's (1975) approach in which sorting occurs and capitalization disappears without zoning. His model makes the assumptions of the consensus bidding model except that jurisdiction boundaries are flexible and the per-household cost of $S$ declines with population. In this case, communities may be heterogeneous because a given class of households may not be large enough to take advantage of economies of scale, but jurisdiction boundaries will adjust until housing price differences across jurisdictions disappear.

Henderson's model adds another dimension to empirical tests. Statistically significant capitalization leads to a rejection of both the Hamilton (1975) and Henderson (1991) models but supports the consensus bidding model. In con-

[27] Hamilton's (1976) equation for HIH and the equivalent one for LIH were designed primarily to introduce heterogeneity and capitalization into his framework and were one of the first attempts to introduce bidding notions into the Tiebout literature. Since the consensus bidding model does not require zero income and price elasticities for $S$, the Hamilton bidding model is not pursued here.

[28] With zero net capitalization, willingness to pay for $S$ is perfectly correlated with willingness to pay for a reduction in $t$, so coefficients for $S$ and $t$ cannot be estimated. If these two variables are not perfectly correlated, then one cannot claim zero net capitalization, even if at some value of $S$ the willingness to pay for an increase in $S$ exactly cancels the willingness to pay for the associated increase in $t$.

[29] Fischel (1992: p. 175) also argues that effective zoning to offset nuisances will not affect house values. The failure of some studies "to detect spillover effects can be taken as evidence that zoning works well in their jurisdictions, contrary to the more usual inference that zoning is not justified". We believe the same point applies to fiscal zoning; zoning set at the optimal $H$ should not affect housing prices.

trast, a finding of heterogeneity in demands for $S$ and $H$ leads to a rejection of Hamilton (1975), but is consistent with both the consensus model and Henderson.

## 2.2. *The impact of bidding and sorting on public service levels and property tax rates*

Unlike the literature on bidding and sorting, the literature on the determinants of local public service quality shows no signs of a consensus, largely because of the wide range of issues that must be considered. Many of these issues are complex and several of them involve questions of voters' perceptions about which we have little information. As a result, innumerable combinations of assumptions are possible, and no two scholars use the same model.

### 2.2.1. *Key questions in models of public service determination*
To be specific, an analysis of public service determination must address the following five questions:[30]

(1) *What is the public choice mechanism?* Decisions about public service levels and tax rates are made by communities, not individuals, so any model of these decisions must specify the public choice mechanism. Most of the literature reviewed here employs some version of a median-voter model, following the work of Bergstrom and Goodman (1973) and others.[31] As is well known, this approach requires some strong assumptions about preferences, the nature of public choices, and public institutions, but its convenience and usefulness in hundreds of empirical studies—some of which are reviewed below—have given it a corner on the market. In particular, this approach implies that decisions about public services and tax rates can be modeled as a standard utility maximization problem for the median voter, defined as the voter with median income and tax share. Models based on this approach answer the following questions through their specification of the median voter's utility function and budget constraint.

Although they are not pursued in this review, alternatives to the median-voter approach are available (see Wildasin, 1986; Inman, 1987), and are employed in a few models of public spending that include housing markets. Pogodzinski and Sjoquist (1991) explore the effect of reducing the cost of a public good in two bureaucratic models, one in which bureaucrats use the savings to increase the

---

[30] A sixth question, namely, how public services are distributed within a jurisdiction, has been neglected in this literature; virtually all studies assume an equal distribution.

[31] See Wildasin (1986) for a literature review. Romer and Rosenthal (1979) present a critique of the median-voter model, Holcombe (1989) evaluates evidence for it, and Aronsson and Wikstrom (1996) provide a recent test of it using data from Sweden.

budget and the other in which they use the savings to reduce property taxes. Konishi (1997) employs the $d$-majority voting rule developed by Greenberg (1979), which makes it possible to apply voting logic to decisions involving many local public goods.[32] Finally, public service levels may be determined by coalition (or jurisdiction) formation, a process in which all consumers in a coalition agree in advance to a level of public service provision; in equilibrium no subset of consumers has an incentive to form a new coalition.[33] The literature reviewed here does not consider highly centralized governmental arrangements in which public service outcomes are imposed by a central government.

(2) *Are voters owners or renters?* For two reasons, most of the research on local voting focuses on owners. First, almost two-thirds of households in the US are owners. Second, when housing bids are included in the analysis (which is a requirement to be considered in this review!) the median-voter framework breaks down for renters. Renters' voting incentives depend on the difference between their willingness to pay for public services (as expressed in housing bids), and those of renters moving into the community. If resident renters are identical to entering renters, then any benefit from increased public services is exactly offset by an increase in rents, and resident renters do not care about the public service level (Stiglitz, 1983; Yinger, 1985). If resident and entering renters are not identical, renters care about the level of public services, but one cannot specify their incentives without a simultaneous examination of voting and sorting, as in Epple and Romer (1991).[34]

(3) *Do voters understand that their decisions may affect housing prices?* This question is the first of two key questions about the extent to which voters are myopic. This question arises primarily because of capitalization; changes in $S$ and $t$ alter housing prices. Moreover, voters' perceptions about housing prices are important for at least four reasons. First, an increase in housing prices represents an increase in the opportunity cost of a voter's housing. Because a homeowner's mortgage payments are based on the price of his house at the time it was purchased, this increase may not show up in any observed market transaction,

---

[32] Greenberg (1979) shows that a necessary and sufficient condition for an equilibrium to exist is that the maximal set of winning coalitions in a community consists of all coalitions that contain more than $d/(d+1)$ of its residents, where $d$ is the number of dimensions over which public services are evaluated; $d = 1$ for the median-voter model.

[33] This choice mechanism is consistent with Hamilton's (1975) assumption of costless community formation. Wooders (1989) develops a model based on this choice mechanism, but the model does not include a land market.

[34] Epple et al. (1983, 1984, 1993) interpret their model as a renter model because households do not perceive capital gains or losses in their voting decisions, but it can also be interpreted as an owner model in which households do not perceive the effect of voting outcomes on the value of their property.

but it still represents a change in the voter's implicit market rent. Second, with flexible assessments, an increase in housing price leads to an increased property tax payment. Third, a change in housing price leads to a capital gain or loss for a homeowner, which represents a change in the voter's permanent income. Fourth, an increase in housing price alters the market value of houses in the community, and hence affects the community's budget constraint.[35] Voting outcomes may depend on whether or not voters recognize such effects.

(4) *Do voters understand that their decisions may affect housing consumption, both their own and that of other households in the community?* Changes in $S$ and $t$ also can influence housing consumption, primarily through changes in housing prices. The question is whether or not voters are aware that this might occur. Do voters know, for example, that they might want to adjust their own $H$ after a change in $S$ or $t$? In addition, changes in housing consumption affect the community budget constraint. If housing prices go up, for example, and other households cut back their $H$, then a voter's tax share could increase. Voters' decisions may be influenced by their perceptions of these possibilities.

(5) *What is the technology of public production?* Different scholars make different assumptions about the technology of public production. Three characteristics of this technology are particularly important: returns to service quality, the degree of publicness, and the impact of community characteristics.[36] As in the simple community budget constraints presented earlier, assumptions about technology typically appear in a cost function. A cost function that reflects all three of these characteristics can be written $E = E(S, N, A)$, where $N$ is the jurisdiction's population or number of pupils, and $A$ is a vector of community attributes that influence production costs (see Duncombe and Yinger, 1993).

The first characteristic is summarized by the elasticity of cost per unit of $S$ with respect to $S$. A zero (negative) [positive] value for this elasticity implies constant (increasing) [decreasing] returns to quality scale.[37] The vast majority of studies assume constant returns, although, as discussed in Section 3.2.2, the limited available evidence does not support this assumption.

The second characteristic is summarized by the elasticity of cost per capita with respect to $N$. A zero (negative) [positive] value for this elasticity implies

---

[35] Changes in the $S$ or $t$ could also alter the price of commercial and industrial property (Carroll and Yinger, 1994), but this effect is not considered here.

[36] A fourth aspect is returns to scope due to sharing of inputs across governmental activities. See, for example, Gyapong and Gyimah-Brempong (1988), Grosskopf and Yaisawaring (1990) or Duncombe and Yinger (1993).

[37] Duncombe and Yinger (1993) show that returns to quality scale depend on both technical returns to scale, which are measured by the elasticity of total costs with respect to $G$, and on the elasticity of $G$ with respect to $S$, which is influenced by community characteristics.

constant (increasing) [decreasing] returns to population scale.[38] Following Borcherding and Deacon (1972), the standard approach to population scale has been to specify a congestion function, usually of the form $S = GN^{-\gamma}$, where $\gamma$ equals zero for a pure public good, equals unity for a pure private good, and exceeds unity for a highly congested good. Most studies assume that $\gamma$ is constant across communities.

The third characteristic, namely $A$, first appeared in a well-known framework developed by Bradford et al. (1969). In this framework, $S$ is produced in a two-stage process. The first stage yields intermediate public outputs, $G$, using inputs, $I$, such as labor and capital; that is, $G = G(I)$. Examples of $G$ include police patrol hours or fire protection units. The cost function associated with this production function is $TC = c(G, W)$, where $TC$ is total cost and $W$ is a vector of input prices.[39] The second stage produces final outputs, $S$, as a function of $G$, $N$ and $A$; that is, $S = s(G, N, A)$. For example, controlling for $G$ and $N$, the amount of fire protection delivered might depend on the types of buildings in a community, and the amount of protection from crime might depend on the extent of poverty. The inverse of this second-stage production function is, $G = s^{-1}(S, N, A)$, which can be substituted into the first-stage cost function to yield $TC = c[s^{-1}(S, N, A), W]$.[40] The $E$ defined earlier equals $TC$ per household.

As we will see, $N$ and $A$ complicate models of local voting because they imply that the technology of public production, and hence voting outcomes, depends on the sorting process. In other words, these characteristics imply simultaneity between sorting and voting outcomes. Most conceptual models avoid this simultaneity by ignoring the role of $A$ and assuming that local governments provide goods that are, technically speaking, private goods.[41] This assumption is equivalent to setting $\gamma = 1$ in the congestion function. As discussed below,

---

[38] Duncombe and Yinger (1993) show that returns to population scale depend on technical returns to scale (defined in the previous footnote) and on the elasticity of $G$ with respect to $N$. The role of technical returns to scale is often missed.

[39] In production theory, cost functions are derived from production functions assuming cost minimization. Although local governments may not minimize costs, this assumption is also used to estimate public cost functions. A general treatment of cost functions under other assumptions is unavailable.

[40] Bradford et al. (1969) assume that community characteristics do not affect factor substitution in the first-stage production function. A more general form that allows for such an effect is $TC = c'[s^{-1}(S, N, A), W, A']$, where $A'$ is the set of community characteristics that affect factor substitution. See Duncombe and Yinger (1993).

[41] An exception is the bidding model of Epple and Romano (1997), that brings in $A$ by assuming that education costs depend on student ability. They examine the sorting of public school students by ability and income, derive conditions under which equilibria stratified by ability are expected to exist, and find that multiple equilibria exist under these conditions.

however, some empirical work uses this framework to estimate a comprehensive cost index that indicates the impact of $N$ and $A$ on $TC$, holding $S$ constant.

### 2.2.2. Examples of voting models

Many different combinations of these assumptions have appeared in the literature and many others could be formed.

*Epple et al.'s myopic voters.* One approach to voting, illustrated by the work of Epple et al. (1983, 1984, 1993), is to assume that voters are myopic in the sense that they do not know that their decisions about $S$ and $t$ will influence housing prices or the average housing consumption in their jurisdiction. A voter's perceptions about her own $H$ are not crucial; Epple et al. (1983) show that the equilibrium is the same whether, or not, the voter treats her own $H$ as fixed. In formal terms, the median voter maximizes her utility subject to her own and the community's budget constraint under the assumption that $P$ is fixed. Substituting the community budget constraint, $E(S) = t^* P \bar{H}$, into the household budget constraint, this problem becomes:

$$
\begin{aligned}
&\text{Maximize} \quad U(Z, H, S) \\
&\quad Z, H, S \\
&\text{Subject to} \quad Y = Z + \left( P + \frac{E(S)}{\bar{H}} \right) H.
\end{aligned}
\tag{2.15}
$$

The first-order conditions of this problem imply that voters set

$$
MB = MC \frac{H}{\bar{H}}
\tag{2.16a}
$$

and

$$
\frac{U_H}{U_Z} = P + \frac{E(S)}{\bar{H}} = P(1 + t^*).
\tag{2.16b}
$$

In this model, therefore, the median voter's decision about $S$ is influenced by her tax share and her decision about $H$ is influenced by the property tax.

Although this model is simple, it does not necessarily have an equilibrium. Epple et al. (1984) analyze "viable" within-community or internal equilibria, defined as ones in which the value of aggregate housing consumption at the equilibrium $t$ results in exactly the revenue necessary to finance the equilibrium $E$. Moreover, an equilibrium requires that an interactive process of voting and housing market adjustment converges to a viable outcome. If housing demand is less than supply for a particular voting equilibrium, for example, then the housing market adjustments will decrease the taxbase, which could result in a further decrease in housing demand, thereby causing the system to diverge from the viable equilibrium.

Epple et al. (1984) ensure convergence with strong assumptions about preferences and the public good technology.[42] Specifically, they assume that the slopes of the household bids are nonincreasing in both $P$ and $S$, are decreasing over at least one of these variables, approach infinity as $S$ approaches zero, and approach zero as $P$ approaches infinity. In addition, they assume that the price elasticity of housing demand is $\leq 1$ and that the technology for producing $S$ is linear in the product of $N$ and $S$. Rose-Ackerman (1979) demonstrates that this restriction on the relationship between the slope of the household bids and $P$ can be violated even with Cobb–Douglas preferences. If this restriction is satisfied, however, she proves that an internal equilibrium is ensured by increasing returns to quality scale in the production of $S$, a weaker assumption than the linearity assumption of Epple et al. (1984).

Epple et al. (1984) also point out that this convergence problem does not arise and the strong assumptions on preferences can be avoided if voters anticipate adjustments in $\bar{H}$.[43] This result has not led to models without myopic voters, however, because it is difficult to describe the characteristics of equilibrium in such models. Specifically, when voters are myopic, the tax price of $S$ equals $MC(H/\bar{H})$. With nonmyopic voters, however, the tax price also depends on the relationship between $S$ and $\bar{H}$, both directly and through migration.

It may be tempting to substitute Eq. (2.16a) into Eq. (2.7) and conclude that there will be zero net capitalization. In fact, however, Eq. (2.16a) refers to the median voter (or some other decisive voter) and Eq. (2.7) refers to the marginal household in a bidding model, which is the one indifferent between two communities. In general, these two households will not be the same; even with homogeneous communities, the marginal household could live outside a community and have preferences that differ from those of the (homogeneous) residents. Moreover, even when the marginal household and the median voter coincide, a house-value regression cannot distinguish between zero net capitalization and no

---

[42] Epple et al. (1984) is based on a general cost function for $S$, but the proof in Epple et al. (1993) depends on more restrictive assumptions about technology.

[43] Epple and Romer (1991) prove that, even without strong assumptions about preferences, an internal equilibrium exists in a model of income redistribution when voters anticipate the effect redistribution policy has on both housing stock and community population. They also demonstrate that an equilibrium is unlikely to exist in a redistributive public economy when voters are myopic.

capitalization at all: both possibilities are consistent with coefficients of zero for all tax and service variables. Equation (2.7) and its analog with zoning, namely Eq. (2.14), also reveal that one cannot isolate net capitalization without accounting for other fiscal factors that vary across jurisdictions and influence bids, including the taxbase and the cost of $S$. At best, therefore, a house-value regression can provide only a rough guide to the decision rule used by local voters.

*Perceptions of capitalization and capital gains.* Another possible approach is to assume that voters are aware that their decisions about $S$ and $t$ alter $P$ and, therefore, alter their own opportunity cost for housing and lead to gains or losses in the value of their houses. For example, Yinger (1982, 1985) combines this approach with the same myopia about $\bar{H}$ assumed by Epple et al. (1984). With this approach, the price of housing is written $P(S, t)$, the property tax payment is $t^* P(S, t) H$, and a voter's annualized capital gain is $[P(S, t) - P(S', t')]H$, where primes indicate values at the time her house was purchased. Solving the community budget constraint for $t^*$ (under the assumption that voters perceive the average property value in the community to be $P(S, t)\bar{H}/r$), substituting the result into the household budget constraint, and subtracting the capital gain from the expense side of this constraint, we find that:

$$
\begin{aligned}
Y &= Z + \left( P(S, t) + \frac{E(S)}{\bar{H}} \right) H - [P(S, t) - P(S', t')]H \\
&= Z + \left( P(S', t') + \frac{E(S)}{\bar{H}} \right) H.
\end{aligned}
\tag{2.17}
$$

This is equivalent to the budget constraint in Eq. (2.15); surprisingly, assuming complete voter awareness of capitalization leads to the same outcome, namely Eq. (2.16), as assuming complete voter ignorance of capitalization.

Complete awareness and complete ignorance of capitalization are not the only possibilities that lead to Eq. (2.16a). In fact, Yinger (1999) identifies two broad cases in which this outcome obtains. The first case arises whenever voters are: (1) equally aware that changes in $S$ and $t$ can lead to capital gains and can influence the opportunity cost of housing; (2) equally aware that changes in $S$ and $t$ can influence their property taxes and can influence $P$ for other properties, thereby affecting the property taxbase; but (3) are totally unaware that changes in $P$ caused by changes in $S$ and $t$ can induce other residents to alter their housing consumption, and thereby alter the property taxbase still more. The second case arises whenever: (1) $S$ and $t$ are capitalized to the same degree, and (2) the second condition for the first case holds. The first of these cases covers both the myopic voters of Epple et al. (1984) and Yinger's (1982, 1985) voters, who are aware of capitalization. The second case covers the voters in Crane (1988, 1990), who are aware only of the possibility that changes in $S$ and $t$ affect the opportunity cost of their housing.

Nevertheless, many plausible cases lead to different decision rules. Suppose, for example, that voters are aware of property tax capitalization, but are not aware that $S$ affects property values, and that they are aware of the impact of capitalization on either the value of their house or the opportunity cost of their housing, but not both. If they are aware of capital gains, voters perceive an added cost to increasing $S$, namely, the capital loss associated with the required higher $t$. By Eq. (2.4), the annualized capital loss, $d(rV)/dt$, is $r/(r+t)\%$ of $V$; to reflect this cost, the right side of Eq. (2.16a) must be multiplied by $[1 + r/(r+t)]$. In contrast, the higher $t$ associated with higher $S$ lowers the opportunity cost of housing, also $rV$, so an awareness of the opportunity cost, but not of capital gains, lowers the perceived cost of $S$, and the right side of Eq. (2.16a) must be multiplied by $[1 - r/(r+t)]$.

In short, many different assumptions about voter perceptions and capitalization lead to the same well-known decision rule, Eq. (2.16a). However, these perceptions are poorly understood, and reasonable alternative assumptions can lead to public service quality that is either above or below the level implied by Eq. (2.16a).

### 2.3. Models in which both housing and fiscal variables are endogenous

A household's choice of a community depends on $S$ and $t$. Collective decisions about $S$ depend on the characteristics of the voters in the community. It is natural, therefore, to ask whether or not models of sorting and models of voting are compatible, that is, whether or not there exist equilibria when both community choice and $S$ are made endogenous.[44]

#### 2.3.1. Epple, Filimon and Romer
Building on research by Ellickson (1971) and Westoff (1977), Epple et al. (1983, 1984, 1993) provide the only formal proof of equilibrium in a model with both

---

[44] An alternative literature, reviewed in Conley and Wooders (1998), examines the existence and nature of the core in economies with local public goods and no land market. Conley and Wooders (1997) show, for example, that in large economies with endogenous community formation, price taking equilibria exist and are nearly optimal.

voting and the consensus model of community choice.[45] As explained earlier, they assume that public services are chosen by a median voter who is myopic about the effect of her vote on the community housing stock. In addition, they assume that bid functions steepen with income, which is the elasticity condition in Eq. (2.8), and, as noted earlier, the internal equilibrium portion of their proof requires several strong assumptions about household preferences.

Epple et al. also make strong assumptions about the public good technology to avoid conflicts between voting and sorting. This type of conflict arises when the public spending decisions residents make are inconsistent with the implicit public service choices in the sorting process. With matched sorting, for example, this conflict arises if the $S$ selected by voters declines with community income. So long as $S$ is a normal good, the median voter in a low income community will not select a higher $S$ than the median voter in a high income community unless she faces a lower tax price. Lower tax prices in the low income community and, hence, potential conflicts between sorting and voting, can arise in three main cases.[46]

(1) *The public good has increasing returns to population scale and the high income community has a smaller population.* Suppose all communities have the same land area. If housing is a normal good, high income households will demand more $H$ and in equilibrium the high income community will have a smaller population. Increasing returns imply that the $MC$ of $S$ is higher in the high income community.[47] With a sufficiently high price elasticity of demand for $S$, say $\mu$, the selected level of $S$ could be lower in the high income community. In contrast, if the differences in community population result from differences in the community stock of land, a situation in which the high income community

---

[45] Pogodzinski and Sjoquist (1985, 1991, 1993) and Henderson (1991) provide informal proofs of equilibrium with specific functional forms and specific parameter values by showing that their simulation models have solutions.

[46] In principle, power equalizing grants also could cause trouble for equilibrium. These grants involve a higher matching rate for jurisdictions with lower wealth (and most likely lower income). See Ladd and Yinger (1994). One study (Feldstein, 1976b) argues that power-equalizing grants would lead to lower spending on education in higher wealth school districts. Nechyba (1996) introduces power-equalizing grants into a general equilibrium model with multiple communities and also finds a negative correlation between local spending and income. However, Feldstein's (1976b) estimated price elasticities are far higher than that obtained in the rest of the literature (discussed in Sections 3.2.1 and 4.2.1). Moreover, no state has implemented a pure form of a power-equalizing grant. See Reschovsky (1994). These grants are unlikely to cause disequilibrium!

[47] This problem cannot arise with decreasing returns to $N$ and equal land area. In this case, the high income community will have a higher $MC$ only if it has a larger $N$. A larger $N$ requires smaller per-household $H$, which in turn requires a higher $P$. A higher $P$ is possible, but only through capitalization, that is, only if $S$ is higher.

faces a higher $MC$ could be eliminated simply by having the two income classes trade communities.[48]

(2) *The marginal cost of delivering public services increases with community income.* Because $MC$ is part of the tax price, this case, like the previous one, could lead to lower demand for $S$ in the high income than in the low income community. Thus, to take advantage of the low tax price in the low income community, high income households might outbid low income households there. As high income households move in, however, $MC$ will rise, thereby preventing equilibrium. As we will see, the empirical evidence indicates that this case is unlikely.

(3) *The ratio of median to mean housing consumption (the median voter's tax share) increases with community income.* In this case, the median voter in the low income community faces a more favorable tax price for $S$ than does the median voter in the high income community, and might, therefore, demand more $S$. This case obviously depends on the underlying distribution of income and on sorting.[49]

Epple et al. (1983, 1984, 1993) prove that these conflicts between sorting and voting cannot arise when the cost of producing $S$ is linear in the product of $N$ and $S$ and the income elasticities of demand for $H$ and $S$ are positive. This assumption about public service technology restricts the extent of returns to population or quality scale and rules out variation in $MC$ with respect to community characteristics.[50] Moreover, the tax-share problem is eliminated by assuming linear costs and positive elasticities.[51]

We suspect that these assumptions are stronger than necessary to rule out these conflicts.[52] These assumptions are sufficient because they ensure that high income voters never face higher tax prices than lower income voters, but they

---

[48] This same switching logic could be used to eliminate situations in which jurisdictions vary by the technology for producing $H$ or $S$.

[49] As shown by Hanson and Kessler (1997), a similar issue arises when government spending is funded with an income tax. They examine a model with purely redistributive governments, following Epple and Romer (1991), but myopic voters, as in Epple et al. (1983, 1984, 1993). They prove that a stratification equilibrium will not exist unless the ratio of median-to-mean income in high income jurisdictions is less than this ratio in low income jurisdictions; otherwise, high income households have an incentive to move.

[50] Diminishing returns to $S$ cannot lead to this conflict. In this case, jurisdictions with higher $S$ have higher $MC$, but all jurisdictions still face the same price profile over values of $S$. Formally, in a homogeneous community, the demand function can be written $S = S[MC(S), Y]$. Totally differentiating this equation with respect to $S$ and $Y$ reveals that diminishing returns serve only to scale down the income effect and cannot fully offset it.

[51] Epple et al. (1984) also assume a uniform income distribution, which rules out case three, but the income distribution assumption is not necessary for existence given their other assumptions.

[52] These assumptions may be necessary, however, to assure that empty communities do not arise (Rose-Ackerman, 1979).

do not appear to be necessary because higher tax prices for high income voters do not lead to sorting-voting conflicts unless $\mu$ is fairly high. Moreover, these assumptions restrict some aspects of public service technology, such as decreasing returns to population scale or nonconstant returns to quality scale, that do not lead to sorting-voting conflicts. Further research on necessary conditions for equilibrium is warranted.

### 2.3.2. Other equilibrium proofs

Konishi (1997) and Nechyba (1997) use a different approach to establish the existence of equilibrium. To be specific, they provide general proofs of existence without first specifying the characteristics of the equilibrium. This approach has the advantage that many of the restrictive assumptions about preferences and public goods technology in Epple et al. (1983, 1984, 1993) can be avoided,[53] but it is not tractable in a system of jurisdictions with property taxes and malleable housing. Konishi (1997) employs a model in which $S$ is financed with an income tax, thereby avoiding the difficulties faced by Epple et al. in demonstrating the existence of an internal equilibrium.[54] However, he does not examine the necessary characteristics of such equilibria, such as whether the equilibrium is stratified or uniform (which implies identical communities).[55]

Nechyba (1997) assumes that housing is not malleable and that the housing stock is fixed.[56] Each household is endowed with an initial housing unit, but in equilibrium the household may reside in a different unit and even in a different jurisdiction. After proving that an equilibrium exists, Nebycha examines the characteristics of possible equilibria, particularly stratification. His stratification results do not require the elasticity condition in Eq. (2.8) because housing is not malleable.[57] Either all houses are the same, in which case the property tax is converted into a head tax, or houses vary, in which case houses that provide less $H$ in a given jurisdiction will have lower tax prices and the value of

---

[53] To avoid the problems raised by Rose-Ackerman (1979), both Konishi (1997) and Nechyba (1997) assume that no communities are empty in equilibrium. However, Konishi's proof recognizes that resident characteristics may influence the production function for $S$.

[54] When $S$ is financed with an income tax, land or currently existing housing stock can be treated like any other location-specific consumption good.

[55] Because he does not rule out uniform equilibria, Konishi (1997) must assume a finite number of communities and household types with an infinitely divisible number of households.

[56] This assumption converts the jurisdiction choice and housing demand decisions into an assignment problem.

[57] Nechyba (1997) emphasizes that an initial ranking of households based on income is not possible in his model because total wealth depends on equilibrium house values; however, this is not the driving factor behind the stratification results. The endogeneity of wealth only implies that the sorting condition must be evaluated at the final equilibrium prices.

their tax subsidy will be capitalized into their prices. This creates an incentive for homebuilders and landowners to change the composition of a community's housing stock. As a result, Nechyba's stratification may not persist in the long run unless it is associated with differences in site quality or exogenous location characteristics.

## 3. Empirical research

This section reviews empirical work in urban public finance. The focus is on studies that test hypotheses related to the consensus view of bidding and sorting, the Hamilton (1975) approach, and aspects of voting that are related to housing markets.[58]

### 3.1. The impact of public services on housing market outcomes

#### 3.1.1. Property tax capitalization
The clearest prediction of the consensus view of bidding is that property taxes will be capitalized into the price of housing according to Eq. (2.4).[59] Starting with Oates (1969), many studies, reviewed in Yinger et al. (1988), have tested this hypothesis for property tax variation both across and within jurisdictions. Although Eq. (2.4) appears straightforward, studies that estimate it must overcome four difficult methodological problems: (1) functional form; (2) the endogeneity of the tax rate; (3) controls for housing characteristics; and (4) the choice of a discount rate. Moreover, the literature often confuses two different notions of tax capitalization: the capitalization of current tax rate differences and the capitalization of the present value of the expected property tax stream. The role of expectations, which are hidden in Eq. (2.4), is crucial. The theory predicts that a $1 increase in the present value of future property taxes will lead to a $1 decline in house value, but it does not say that current tax differences will be fully capitalized *if they are not expected to persist.*

---

[58] An alternative review of the empirical literature is provided by Dowding et al. (1994). This review does not distinguish between bidding models and the Hamilton approach, but it does cover several topics that are omitted here. In particular, it examines studies of the US and the UK in which household mobility is affected by service quality or tax rates. However, most of this literature refers to intermetropolitan mobility, about which the models presented here make no predictions, and all of it ignores housing prices and therefore cannot test hypotheses from the models in this paper. One careful investigation of intrametropolitan mobility, Reschovsky (1979) finds that service quality affects moving decisions for high income but not for low income households.

[59] The derivative of Eq. (2.9) with respect to the income tax rate implies that local income taxes also are capitalized into house values. Stull and Stull (1991), using data from the Philadelphia area, and Boije (1997), using data from the Stockholm area, find evidence to support this prediction.

As defined by most studies, the degree of property tax capitalization, say $\beta$, is the extent to which current tax differences are capitalized into house values. It appears as the coefficient of tax payment, $T = tV$, in a standard asset-pricing model of housing or, equivalently, as the coefficient of $t$ in Eq. (2.4):[60]

$$V = \frac{\hat{P}H}{r} - \beta\left(\frac{T}{r}\right) = \frac{\hat{P}H}{r + \beta t}. \tag{3.1}$$

Despite its clear conceptual foundations, however, few studies make use of this equation's functional form. Many studies follow Oates (1969), for example, and approximate Eq. (3.1) by including $t$ or the logarithm of $t$ as an explanatory variable. When data on tax and house value changes over time are available, simple but exact functional forms are possible. Let subscripts indicate time periods, then Eq. (3.1) leads to

$$\frac{\Delta V}{V_1} = \frac{-\beta\Delta t}{r + \beta t_2} \quad \text{or} \quad \Delta V = \frac{-\beta\Delta T}{r}. \tag{3.2}$$

If $t_2$ is roughly constant (as it might be after a revaluation), then both of these equations reduce to a constant multiplied by the change in a tax variable.[61] The second equation can be estimated, for example, when tax payments undergo a large change (as with Proposition 13, a property tax limit in California; see Rosen, 1982). The estimating equation also should reflect the role of income tax deductions for property tax payments, which cannot be claimed by homeowners who do not itemize; Eisenberg (1996) and deBartolome and Rosenthal (in press) find that capitalization is significantly higher for itemizers than for nonitemizers.

The second methodological difficulty is that the property tax variable is endogenous. Assessed values, and hence tax payments, are based to some degree on market values, and effective tax rates are defined with market value as the denominator. As first pointed out by Oates (1969), capitalization equations therefore must be estimated with a simultaneous equations procedure. Moreover, the choice of instruments is important (see Pollakowski, 1973),[62] and the best studies formally model assessor behavior to identify appropriate instruments.

Because house values are affected by many factors other than $t$, careful controls are important to insulate capitalization estimates against omitted variable

---

[60] As stated in footnote 9, the form derived by Wheaton (1993) is somewhat different, but it has never been tested.

[61] Intrajurisdictional tax capitalization applies to deviations from the average tax rate. Redefining $t$ as a deviation from the community average, a constant effective tax rate after revaluation implies that $t_2 = 0$, so that this form reduces to $-\beta\Delta t/r$. See Yinger et al. (1988).

[62] Pollakowski (1973) is a comment on Oates (1969); Oates (1973) is the reply.

bias. Some studies avoid this bias with an extensive list of housing and neighbor-hood characteristics and public service measures, but other studies do not have adequate controls. Studies based on tax changes must control for changes in both housing and neighborhood characteristics.

Finally, the form of Eqs. (3.1) and (3.2) precludes separate estimation of $r$ and $\beta$. Most studies follow Oates (1969) in assuming a value for $r$, but in this case the value of $\beta$ depends on an untested assumption and different studies use different values of $r$. Yinger et al. (1988) point out that the appropriate $r$ is a real discount rate, defined as a nominal rate minus anticipated inflation; by subtracting a pre-diction of anticipated inflation from the nominal interest rate, they estimate $r$ to be about 3% in their sample period. Do and Sirmans (1994) claim to estimate $r$, but in fact, they simply reverse the usual procedure by assuming $\beta = 1$ and calculating the implied $r$.

Virtually all the literature estimates the capitalization of current property tax differences. Under the assumption that current differences will persist indefi-nitely, the theory behind Eq. (2.4) implies that these differences should be fully capitalized, that is, that $\beta = 1$. In fact, however, current differences may not be expected to persist. In this case, Yinger et al. (1988) show that the capitalization of current tax differences, the $\beta$ in Eq. (3.1), is related to the capitalization of the present value of the expected tax stream, say $\beta'$, as follows:

$$\beta = \beta'[1 - (1 + r)^{-N'}], \tag{3.3}$$

where $N'$ is the length of time current tax differences are expected to persist. The theory indicates that $\beta' = 1$, but the estimated $\beta$ clearly need not equal 1, and indeed need not equal the same value under all circumstances. In the case of intrajurisdictional tax differences, for example, if an upcoming revaluation is expected to eliminate current tax differences in 10 years and $r = 0.03$, then Eq. (3.3) implies that the estimated $\beta$ will be only 26% even if $\beta' = 1$.

Virtually every study of property tax capitalization finds a statistically sig-nificant negative impact of property taxes (or property tax changes) on house values.[63] The vast majority these studies use data from the US, but a few, includ-ing Chinloy (1978) and Hamilton (1979), use data from Canada. Estimates of $\beta$ vary widely, but if $r$ is set at 3%, the estimates of $\beta$ for the best studies fall between 15 and 60% (Yinger et al., 1988; deBartolome and Rosenberg, 1997). No study yet provides a definitive estimate of $\beta'$, but Yinger et al. (1988) and Eisenberg (1996) present some evidence that it is close to 100%. These results are

---

[63] All the studies that find no effect have serious methodological flaws. See Yinger et al. (1988).

consistent with the consensus bidding model, but contradict both the Hamilton and Henderson approaches.

### 3.1.2. Public service capitalization

As shown by Eq. (2.2), housing price, $\hat{P}$ in Eq. (3.1), is a function of public service quality, $S$. Several studies, again starting with Oates (1969), have tested the resulting prediction that higher $S$ leads to higher house values. Many of these studies follow Oates by using spending per capita as a measure of public service quality.[64] By the argument in Bradford et al. (1969), however, spending is a poor measure of $S$ because spending does not go as far in communities with relatively harsh environments. Several studies, including King (1973), McDougall (1976), Noto (1976), Rosen and Fullerton (1977), Harrison and Rubinfeld (1978), Judd and Watts (1981) and Haurin and Bresington (1996), use student test scores or other measure of actual public outputs in a house-value regression.[65] Moreover, a study of the impact of public service quality on the median apartment rent in a community (Carroll and Yinger, 1994), uses a public service cost index (defined above) to translate observed spending into a comprehensive measure of $S$. Virtually all of these studies find a positive, statistically significant impact of $S$ on house value (or rent). Rosen and Fullerton (1977) find, for example, that "being in the first rather than the last decile [on a fourth-grade reading score] would increase median property values by about \$4,300, other things being equal".

Two recent studies provide particularly compelling evidence about the capitalization of local public services. Bogart and Cromwell (1997) compare the values of houses located in the same municipality but in different school districts, a situation made possible by unusual jurisdiction boundaries in the Cleveland area. After controlling for a long list of housing and neighborhood characteristics, and accounting for the impact on $P$ of differences in school property taxes, they find that the annual willingness to pay for living in a better school district ranges from \$186–\$2171. Black (in press) controls for unobserved jurisdiction and neighborhood characteristics by comparing the market values of houses on opposite sides of attendance-zone boundaries in the same school district. She also finds that housing prices increase with school quality, but the magnitude of this impact is substantially smaller after accounting for neighborhood effects.

---

[64] The general equilibrium nature of the sorting problem causes difficulties for interpreting studies of service capitalization based on before-and-after data. See Pogodzinski and Sjoquist (1994).

[65] Alternative approaches, namely, bidding or random utility models (McFadden, 1974; Ellickson, 1981; Lerman and Kern, 1983), are used by Quigley (1985), Nechyba and Strauss (1998) and Chattopadhyay (1998) to estimate the impact of public spending on house values.

These results all support the key prediction of Eq. (2.2) and contradict the Hamilton and Henderson approaches. Far more work needs to be done, however, to obtain comprehensive measures of $S$ and to estimate the implied marginal benefit function in Eq. (2.2). Although the large literature on hedonic prices identifies several methods for estimating demand or marginal benefit functions (Follain and Jimenez, 1985; Epple, 1987; Chattopadhyay, 1998), only one study, Boije (1997), applies such methods to local public services; using data from Sweden with per capita local spending as a measure of $S$, Boije estimates income and price elasticities of demand for $S$ equal to 0.09 and $-0.89$, respectively.

Several studies have looked at net capitalization, which, as noted earlier, can provide a rough guide to local spending decisions. Oates (1973) calculates that, at average values for the explanatory variables, the negative impact on median $V$ of a property tax increase is roughly offset by the positive impact of the increased educational spending the resulting revenue could fund. He does not find zero net capitalization at all values of spending and $t$, however, so the implications for local voting are unclear. Brueckner (1979, 1982) solves the community budget constraint for $t$, substitutes the result into Eq. (3.1), and argues that to maximize its property values a community will increase $S$ up to the point where its marginal net impact on house values is zero, which is the same thing as zero net capitalization. Using a sample of communities in Massachusetts, Brueckner (1982) estimates this version of Eq. (3.1), finds that $S$ has a coefficient of zero, and concludes that communities maximize property values. We do not find this conclusion persuasive. Brueckner's procedure cannot distinguish between zero net capitalization everywhere (which is consistent with his argument), and zero net capitalization on average or no capitalization (which are not). Moreover, his data have severe limitations (Rubinfeld, 1987); for example, public service quality is measured by spending per capita, and the regression includes only one housing characteristic.

A promising new look at net capitalization is provided by Bradbury et al. (1997). They distinguish between towns that are constrained by Proposition $2\frac{1}{2}$, a property tax limit in Massachusetts, and those that are not, and find that house values increase with spending only in constrained towns. This result supports the view that these communities used a decision rule similar to Eq. (2.16a) and that Proposition $2\frac{1}{2}$ pulled them below their preferred spending level. Because of this forced drop in spending, the marginal benefit from increased spending exceeded the cost for a wide range of households, including the marginal household bidding for housing in these communities. Thus, according to Eq. (2.7), increases in spending resulted in higher house values.

### 3.1.3. Heterogeneity

Several scholars have argued that theories about local public finance can be tested by examining the extent to which communities are homogeneous. As shown above, the Hamilton model does not require homogeneity in income, but it does predict that individual jurisdictions should be substantially more homogenous in income than is a metropolitan area as a whole. Unfortunately, however, this prediction is not helpful for testing Hamilton's model, because the consensus bid framework yields the same prediction. In models with a fixed number of jurisdictions with fixed land areas, Epple et al. (1983, 1984, 1993) and Epple and Platt (1998) show that jurisdictions will not exhibit perfect income homogeneity, but will be more homogeneous than the urban area. In the Hamilton model with the Goldstein and Pauly (1981) amendment, income heterogeneity arises because of taste differences; in the Epple et al. (1983, 1984, 1993) models it arises because the population must be spread out among a fixed number of communities; and in Epple and Platt (1998) it arises for both of these reasons. But these differences in mechanisms do not lead to differences in predictions about heterogeneity.

As a result, most existing studies of community heterogeneity fail to provide tests of the Hamilton model. Pack and Pack (1977) find that individual jurisdictions are not homogenous by income or occupational status, but are considerably more homogeneous than the urban area in which they are located. Hamilton et al. (1975), Eberts and Gronberg (1981) and Munley (1982) all find that within-jurisdiction homogeneity increases with the number of jurisdictions in a metropolitan area. Heikkila (1996) examines heterogeneity over a broad range of socioeconomic characteristics and finds substantial homogeneity.[66] Finally, Gramlich and Rubinfeld (1982) analyze a survey of household attitudes toward the level of public services in their jurisdictions and conclude that households are grouped based on their unobservable tastes for public services. Although several of these authors interpret their results as evidence that Tiebout or Hamilton sorting is taking place, all of these results are consistent with both the Tiebout/Hamilton approach and the consensus bidding framework.

One possible way to distinguish between the Hamilton and bidding approaches is to examine homogeneity in $H$ and $S$. While Hamilton's model might be a reasonable representation of the world with something less than perfect homogeneity in $H$ and $S$, it does require that the within-jurisdiction heterogeneity in $H$

---

[66] Heikkila uses factor analysis to generate indexes of heterogeneity across characteristics and analysis of variance to test whether or not census tracts of similar types tend to be found in the same jurisdiction. This approach avoids the problem of statistically generated within-jurisdiction homogeneity that has been discussed by Dowding et al. (1994).

and $S$ be substantially less than the within-jurisdiction heterogeneity in income.[67] Some evidence on this point comes from a footnote in Pack and Pack (1977), who say that a heterogeneity calculation based on house value "yields values very similar to those of income" (p. 195).[68] In addition, Schmidt (1992) finds that income heterogeneity increases private school enrollment, which implies that income heterogeneity leads to heterogeneity in the demand for $S$. Both of these results reject the predictions of Hamilton's model, but not of Henderson's model.[69]

### 3.1.4. Zoning

According to the Hamilton (1975) model, each jurisdiction's zoning restrictions are entirely determined by the housing demand of residents and, therefore, should not be affected by the zoning choices of nearby jurisdictions. Using data from Connecticut, Lenon et al. (1996) find that each town's zoning, taxing, and spending policies are significantly and positively related to the corresponding policies of nearby towns. This result directly contradicts the Hamilton prediction.

Moreover, neither perfect zoning, in the Hamilton sense, nor zoning that simply ratifies a sorting outcome should have an impact on house values. Without the perfect sorting of the Hamilton model, however, communities with stricter zoning might be better protected from the entry of (and resulting subsidies to) low income households and therefore have higher property values. If this zoning is not very exact, households that do move in may be forced to consume more housing than they prefer, so zoning also might have a negative impact on a community's average house value.

The empirical literature often finds that zoning is not neutral, thereby contradicting the Hamilton prediction, but does not clearly indicate the role that zoning plays. Frech and Lafferty (1984), Katz and Rosen (1987) and Schwartz et al. (1986) provide evidence that increased growth controls raise property values, whereas, McMillen and McDonald (1991) find that zoning for single-family houses (but not apartments) tends to be neutral, that is, to follow the market.

---

[67] Hoyt and Rosenthal (1997) argue that a test of Hamilton's (1975) model can be derived from the premise that all residents of a jurisdiction should have the same marginal benefit from additional public services. Regardless of the merits of this argument, their empirical implementation does not provide a test of the Hamilton model because it examines heterogeneity within neighborhoods, which are likely to be far more homogeneous than jurisdictions. For a formal derivation of this point, see Epple and Romano (1997).

[68] Gramlich and Rubinfeld (1982) observe the extent of heterogeneity in demand for $S$, but do not compare their results with observed heterogeneity in income.

[69] Hamilton et al. (1975) found that a greater number of jurisdictions did not lead to more within-community homogeneity in house value. This result also contradicts the Hamilton model, which predicts that expanded opportunities for sorting will lead to more homogeneity in both $S$ and $H$.

The most recent study, Pogodzinski and Sass (1994), finds that property values decline with stricter land use controls.

## 3.2. The impact of bidding and sorting on public service outcomes

The enormous literature on local voting includes many studies that determine whether or not housing market outcomes influence public service choices. Several key conceptual issues have not been explored empirically, however, including voter perceptions about capitalization and about the property taxbase.

### 3.2.1. Income and price elasticities
One obvious link between sorting and voting is through the income and price elasticities of demand for $S$, $\alpha$ and $\mu$, respectively. The larger $\alpha$, the greater the difference between the $S$ provided in low and high income jurisdictions. The role of $\mu$ is more subtle. With homogeneous communities (and no nonresidential property), the tax share equals unity everywhere, and greater housing consumption by higher income households does not influence demand for $S$. With heterogeneous communities, however, the impact of variation in income on tax shares, and hence on voting outcomes, depends on the price elasticity of demand for $S$. Moreover, the marginal cost of $S$ may vary with community characteristics and the impact of this variation in $S$ depends on $\mu$.

A large literature exists on this topic, some of it based on jurisdiction-level data and the median-voter framework and the rest based on household or individual-level data, often with surveys of public service preferences. However, this literature has already been thoroughly reviewed elsewhere. Most of the median voter studies are reviewed in Inman (1979), and the household or individual studies are reviewed in Rubinfeld (1987).

The studies reviewed in Inman generally find values of $\alpha$ between 0.2 and 0.7 and of $\mu$ between $-0.1$ and $-0.5$. Some more recent community-based studies, including Schwab and Zampelli (1987) for police, Dynarski et al. (1989) for education, and Duncombe (1991) for fire, all estimate that $\alpha$ is greater than one. In contrast, some recent studies based on microdata find relatively small elasticities. Rubinfeld et al. (1987), for example, find that both $\alpha$ and $\mu$ for education equal about 0.1 in absolute value.

These results all apply to the US. Several scholars have adapted this general approach for other countries.[70] Pommerehene (1978) studies cities in Switzer-

---

[70] The best evidence we can find for the UK comes from Preston and Ridge (1995), who estimate a local service demand model using survey data. They find a (statistically insignificant) income elasticity of about 0.8 and indirect evidence that public service demand is price elastic.

land, including direct democracies, where the median-voter model should work particularly well, and representative democracies. The tax share term is based on the local income tax. For direct democracies, $\alpha$ is about 1.3 and $\mu$ is about $-0.75$. Both elasticities are somewhat smaller in absolute value for representative democracies. Borge and Rattsø (1995) examine spending in Norwegian municipalities. They estimate values of $\alpha$ near 1.0 and of $\mu$ that are mostly in the $-0.5$ to $-0.9$ range. Aronsson and Wikström (1996) estimate that $\alpha = 0.82$ and $\mu = -0.47$ for municipalities in Sweden. Sone (1993) estimates a model of expenditure determination for cities in Japan. He argues that municipal officials in Japan attempt to please the mean resident (not the median voter). Moreover, Sone develops a tax-share term designed to reflect the fact that the property tax is one of several taxes levied by Japanese cities and does not appear to be the marginal tax; this term is the mean household's tax payment divided by the city's total taxbase (with an adjustment for tax exporting). Using data for individual cities, Sone estimates this model for several types of spending and three different years. For overall spending, $\alpha$ falls between 0.5 and 0.7, and $\mu$ between $-0.6$ and $-1.1$. Values of $\alpha$ and $\mu$ for individual services exhibit greater variation.

### 3.2.2. Population and community characteristics

Another important link between sorting and voting operates through the technology of public production. As discussed earlier, production and cost for $S$ are functions of community population and of the social and economic characteristics of community residents—which are outcomes of sorting. A large literature now documents the importance of this link.

Studies that focus on production begin with some public output measure, say $S_i$, such as a school-test score, and regress it on inputs, population, and community characteristics, or $S_i = S_i(I, N, A)$. Statements about production can be translated into statements about cost. As discussed earlier, a cost function is $TC = c[s^{-1}(S, N, A), W]$, where $TC$ is total spending and $W$ is a vector of input prices.[71] If measures of $S$ are available, this function can be estimated directly, treating those measures as endogenous. The instruments for the simultaneous equations procedure are the determinants of demand for $S$, such as income and tax share. Alternatively, the demand function for $S$ can be substituted into this expression and a reduced-form cost function can be estimated with income, tax

---

[71] This formulation follows Bradford et al. (1969) in assuming that $A$ only influences the second stage of public production—the link between $G$ and $S$. As pointed out earlier, however, $A$ also may influence the production of $G$. Duncombe and Yinger (1993) find, for example, that population and building height affect the tradeoff between firetrucks and firefighters in providing fire-protection services.

share, and other demand variables on the right side, which is one method used to estimate $\alpha$ and $\mu$ with community-level data.[72]

Despite their analytical connection, production and cost studies have some important differences. Production studies focus on a single output, whereas cost studies cover all the outputs for a broad type of public spending, such as education, police or fire. Moreover, production and cost studies may apply to different units of observation. Educational production studies typically focus on the school or student level, for example, whereas educational cost studies typically focus on the school district.

Several studies have explored the role of $N$ in production or cost.[73] In the case of education, many cost studies find a U-shaped relationship between cost per pupil and the number of pupils in a district. Early studies are reviewed in Fox (1981); more recent studies include Downes and Pogue (1994) and Duncombe and Yinger (1997, 1998). A production study of fire services by Brueckner (1981) finds some degree of publicness; to use the term defined earlier, he finds that $\gamma < 1$. A cost study of fire services by Duncombe and Yinger (1993) finds that $\gamma = 1$. In the case of police services, both Schwab and Zampelli (1987) and Ladd and Yinger (1991) find that $\gamma > 1$. Pommerehene (1978) finds clear evidence of publicness in aggregate public spending in Swiss municipalities, with a value of $\gamma$ around 0.6. The study of Japanese cities by Sone (1993) finds that $\gamma$ is close to one, both for overall spending and for most subcategories.[74]

The importance of community characteristics in educational production and cost functions has been known since Coleman (1966) found that a student's achievement (as measured by test scores) depends heavily on the social and economic characteristics of the other students in her class. This result has been duplicated by many studies, many of which are reviewed in Hanushek (1986). A recent production study by Ferguson (1991), for example, finds that, all else being equal, a student's achievement test scores are higher if her classroom has a smaller share of students living in poverty, with limited English proficiency, or from female, single-parent families. These variables also are significant in recent

---

[72] This approach requires assumptions about the forms of the cost and demand functions. Most studies assume a form that implies constant returns to quality scale. Duncombe and Yinger (1993) use a general form to estimate the cost function directly controlling for $S$ and find strongly increasing returns to quality scale.

[73] As first pointed out by Hayes (1986), community characteristics may influence $\gamma$. Duncombe and Yinger (1993: p. 55) argue, for example, that "the cost of assuring a certain quality of fire service for a new household is likely to be higher in communities with poor building condition than in communities with good building condition". They find evidence to support this view.

[74] All of these results except those of Brueckner (1981) and Pommerehene (1978) contradict a key assumption of the Henderson (1991) model presented earlier.

educational cost studies by Downes and Pogue (1994) and Duncombe and Yinger (1997, 1998).

Community characteristics also affect the production and cost of other public services.[75] Duncombe (1991), for example, finds that building age, poverty, and the presence of commercial and industrial capital, all raise the cost of fire protection; Ladd and Yinger (1991) find that the costs of both police and fire services rise with a city's poverty rate; and Bradbury et al. (1984) find that the overall cost of local services rises with population density and housing age. Sone (1993) finds that several community characteristics influence public service costs in Japan; for example, the cost of fire services increases with population density.

### 3.2.3. Tiebout bias

The important article by Goldstein and Pauly (1981) argues that because of sorting, in which households cluster in communities according to their overall demand for $S$, unobserved tastes for $S$ could lead to biased estimates of $\alpha$ and $\mu$ and of other coefficients in a median-voter model of public spending. Even the Tiebout/Hamilton "homogeneous" communities may contain both higher income households with relatively weak tastes for $S$ and lower income households with relatively strong tastes for $S$. Under these circumstances, observed median income may not identify the median voter and parameter estimates may be biased.[76] Studies of the demand for $S$ cannot afford to ignore the sorting process!

Goldstein and Pauly (1981) also suggest a cure for this bias. Under the assumption of perfect Tiebout/Hamilton sorting, every individual in a community demands exactly the observed level of $S$. Unbiased estimates of $\alpha$, therefore, can be obtained using a random sample of households across all communities instead of a sample of communities—but with community $S$ still as the dependent variable. However, this suggestion has been criticized by several scholars (Rubinfeld et al., 1987; Reid, 1990), largely because, as shown earlier, Tiebout/Hamilton sorting is unlikely to be perfect. If it is not, a household's demand for $S$ may not equal the level delivered in its community.

---

[75] Hamilton (1983a) argues that community income is correlated with other community characteristics and suggests that this correlation explains the observed difference between estimates of the income elasticity of demand and of the spending elasticity of grants, the so-called flypaper effect. Wyckoff (1991) tests and rejects this argument; in fact, he finds that the inclusion of additional community characteristics increases the difference between these two estimated elasticities. Schwab and Zampelli (1987) pursue the Hamilton approach using functional form restrictions to try to separate the demand and cost roles of income. Other studies in the literature have focused on other community characteristics, including the poverty rate, as environmental cost factors and interpreted income as a demand variable.

[76] Using data from Sweden, Aronsson and Wikström (1996) test and reject the hypothesis that the resident with median income is the median voter.

These issues can be illustrated by considering community and individual demand equations for $S$. Community demand is

$$S_j = bY_j + v_j, \tag{3.4}$$

where the subscript $j$ indicates a jurisdiction, $b$ is a vector of coefficients to be estimated, $Y$ is a vector of observed characteristics of the resident with median income, and $v$ is an error term that includes unobserved taste variables. Individual demand is

$$S_{ij}^* = bY_{ij}^* + \eta_{ij}, \tag{3.5}$$

where the subscript $i$ indicates a voter; the asterisks indicate that a variable applies to an individual voter, not the community; and $\eta$ is a random error term. The Goldstein/Pauly argument is that $Y$ is correlated with $v$, so that Eq. (3.4) will lead to a biased estimate of $b$, but that with perfect Tiebout/Hamilton sorting, $S_j = S_{ij}^*$, so that Eq. (3.5), which does not lead to bias, can be estimated with observed levels of $S$.

If sorting is not perfect, however, the Goldstein/Pauly procedure involves estimating

$$S_j = bY_{ij}^* + \tilde{\eta}_{ij}, \tag{3.6}$$

where, by Eq. (3.4), $\tilde{\eta}_{ij} = v_j + b(Y_j - Y_{ij}^*)$. It follows that

$$E_X[Y_{ij}^*, v_j + b(Y_j - Y_{ij}^*)] = E_X[Y_{ij}^*, v_j] + (E_X[Y_{ij}^*, Y_j] - \text{Var}[Y_{ij}^*]), \tag{3.7}$$

where $E_X$ is the expectations operator. The bias suggested by Goldstein and Pauly (1981) remains and is represented by the first term on the right side of Eq. (3.7). In addition, a new bias, represented by the second term in Eq. (3.7), appears because the differences between the characteristics of the voter with median income and the randomly selected voters are buried in the error term. Reid (1990) calls this second bias "omitted-variables Tiebout bias"; to correct for it, he includes the difference between household income and community median income as a regressor, a step that substantially alters his estimate of $b$. As pointed out by Roberts (1992), however, Reid's (1990) approach does not correct for the original Goldstein/Pauly bias.[77]

---

[77] Roberts (1992) argues that Reid (1990) reinserted the original Goldstein/Pauly bias into his estimation by including the difference between household and median income. This bias is present, however, whenever sorting is not perfect; it is not caused by Reid's method.

The problem of imperfect sorting also affects Rubinfeld et al. (1987). They examine the difference between community and individual demand for public service, or the difference between Eqs. (3.4) and (3.5):

$$S_j - S_{ij}^* = b(Y_j - Y_{ij}^*) + v_j - \eta_{ij}. \tag{3.8}$$

They argue that a household will reside in a community that does not deliver their preferred level of $S$, only if no other community offers a closer level. Individuals with extreme values of $\eta$ will not live in communities with others who have similar incomes, and for the individuals within a community, the distribution of $\eta$ will be truncated at both ends. This truncation creates a correlation between $\eta$ and the explanatory variables. Rubinfeld et al. (1987) show how to correct for this correlation but also assume that $v$ and the explanatory variables are uncorrelated, which, as shown earlier, requires no sorting by tastes.

In short, the use of a household sample eliminates the Goldstein/Pauly bias only if Tiebout/Hamilton sorting is perfect, whereas standard median-voter estimation is unbiased only if there are no unobserved taste factors. The work following Goldstein and Pauly (1981) identifies additional biases that arise with a household sample when sorting is not perfect. However, none of these studies eliminates the original Goldstein/Pauly bias, which remains in place with imperfect sorting.[78] The only way to eliminate the original bias is to combine a method that identifies the true median voter within a jurisdiction (Reid, 1991; Aronsson and Wikström, 1996; Epple and Sieg, 1997) with an analysis of spending across jurisdictions.

## 4. Normative analysis

### 4.1. The efficiency of a system of local government

The lasting fame of Tiebout (1956) derives primarily from his claim that "voting with one's feet" is analogous to shopping for a commodity and leads to efficient provision of local public services. The literature has struggled with questions of efficiency ever since.

### 4.1.1. Efficiency in a Tiebout/Hamilton model
Although the Tiebout model did not incorporate either a housing market or a property tax, Hamilton (1975) shows that the same result can be obtained from a

---

[78] In addition, all existing papers ignore unobserved tastes for housing, which might influence the tax price or other variables in Eq. (3.6) and lead to additional biases.

model with these features, as long as the assumptions listed earlier are satisfied. In particular, the Hamilton assumptions imply that every community is homogeneous and that voters select the level of $S$ as if its price were $g$ per unit—thereby mimicking a private market and ensuring efficiency. Moreover, households select the optimal level of $H$, so the property tax does not cause any distortion and one can say that the property tax is a benefit tax. See also Hamilton (1983b).

The Hamilton approach has been widely cited as proof that our system of local governments is at least approximately efficient. In our judgement, the Hamilton approach is valuable because it establishes a set of sufficient conditions for efficiency. However, these conditions are extreme, even a priori,[79] and the empirical work reviewed above rejects every prediction that distinguishes the Hamilton model. Unlike Oates (1994), who concludes that it is "impossible to reject ... the benefits view" on the basis of available evidence, we conclude that the evidence against the benefits view is overwhelming.[80]

### 4.1.2. The efficient allocation of people to communities

Once we leave the Tiebout/Hamilton world in which communities are homogeneous and all choices are efficient, we discover that two distinct efficiency questions have appeared in the literature. The first question is whether or not people are allocated to communities in an efficient manner. The second is whether or not voters select the efficient level of local public services. Although these two questions are related, no study yet addresses them both in a general way. Instead, the literature provides necessary conditions for efficiency that are determined by asking one of the two questions. This approach requires the assumption that efficiency holds for the other question; if it does not, the theory of the second best applies. In particular, if the efficiency conditions for one of the questions does not hold, the standard efficiency conditions for the other question are no longer valid guides to optimality (Lipsey and Lancaster, 1956).

A comprehensive treatment of necessary conditions for efficiency in the allocation of households to communities is provided by Wildasin (1986). The

---

[79] Rose-Ackerman (1983: p. 62) makes a similar point: "Rather than showing the applicability of Tiebout's theory to a world with property taxes and a housing market, Hamilton has only demonstrated the unrealistic nature of the required assumptions'. Hamilton (1983b: p. 86) seems to be making a similar point himself when he writes that "the set of assumptions that necessarily yield perfection in the pricing mechanism strain credulity". However, even later in the same article (pp. 103–104), Hamilton leaves a very different impression when we writes "The combination of foot and ballot voting does a reasonably smooth job of getting households on their demand curves for local public services, and of setting supplies equal to demands at average cost prices".

[80] The benefits view also implies that variation in property taxes across communities must be fully borne by tenants, who receive public services, not by landlords, who do not. Carroll and Yinger (1994) show that this is not the case.

Wildasin analysis is very general because it recognizes a wide range of possibilities in public service technology, including publicness and congestion, as well as differential costs for serving different types of people.

Wildasin shows that the market allocation does not satisfy the necessary conditions for efficiency without the availability of very specific revenue instruments and/or strong assumptions about the technology of the public good. Specifically, in the case of a pure public good, a uniform head tax across all residents of all communities results in an efficient allocation.[81] In addition, if the publicly provided good has the technology of a private good, with constant per capita costs, a uniform head tax within each community results in an efficient allocation. With any other technology, efficient allocation is only obtained by a system of head taxes (and perhaps wage taxes) that distinguishes among household types. In no case, therefore, does the tax system necessary for efficiency involve a property tax or otherwise resemble local fiscal policies anywhere in the world,[82] and in many cases efficiency requires fiscal tools that identify household types, and therefore may not even be feasible. Even the British poll tax, which varied by jurisdiction but not by household, could not have ensured efficiency if, as seems likely, local services in Britain exhibit publicness or congestion or costs that depend on community composition.[83] On the basis of this analysis, therefore, there is no reason to believe that housing markets allocate people to jurisdictions in an efficient manner.[84]

One important efficiency issue concerns the allocation of households to communities when the production function for $S$ depends on the types of people in the community. In this case, as first pointed out by Oates (1977a) and Henderson et al. (1978), allocative efficiency may require that some communities be heterogeneous. In particular, suppose there are two types of people: The presence of type-1 people lowers the $S$ received by others, all else equal, whereas, the presence of type-2 people increases the $S$ others receive. With these two types of people, it may be efficient to place some type-1 into a community with type-2, if the added production they experience more than offsets the loss of production experienced by the established type-2 residents.

---

[81] If wages for a household type do not vary across jurisdictions, uniform wage and head taxes across all residents of all communities also results in efficiency.

[82] In fact, Flatters et al. (1974) show that even with pure public goods and no differential costs across types of households, voters will not select uniform head taxes across different communities.

[83] For a description of the British poll tax, see Besley et al. (1997).

[84] Under some conditions, intergovernmental grants might do it. See, for example, Schwab and Oates (1991).

The most complete formal treatment of this issue is provided by Schwab and Oates (1991).[85] In a model without land or housing, they derive explicit efficiency conditions and show that one must account not only for the production effects but also for the deadweight loss associated with heterogeneity (which is discussed later). They also confirm the Wildasin (1986) result that the only way to achieve an efficient outcome is to levy different head taxes on different types of people—with a higher tax on type-1 than on type-2 people. No article yet explores these important issues with a full treatment of housing markets.

### 4.1.3. *The efficient selection of local public services*

The literature has identified four principal reasons why local governments might not select the efficient level of local public services.[86] One of these reasons, that political institutions do not reflect the preferences of the median voter, has been treated at length elsewhere and is not considered here. See Wildasin (1986) and Inman (1987). The other three reasons are the property tax, public service capitalization, and community heterogeneity.

*The property tax and public service capitalization.* The first two sources of efficiency can be illuminated with a simple planner's problem for a homogeneous community (under the assumption that an efficient allocation of people to communities has been achieved).[87] The planner maximizes the utility of a representative resident subject to resource constraints and production technology. Suppose $Z$ is produced with capital, $K$, and that $H$ and $S$ are produced with $K$ and land, $L$.[88] Then the planner's problem is to allocate $K$ and $L$ so as to

$$\text{Maximize} \quad U[Z(K^Z), H(K^H, L^H), S(K^S, L^S)]$$
$$\text{Subject to} \quad K^Z + K^H + K^L = \bar{K} \tag{4.1}$$
$$L^H + K^K = \bar{L}.$$

This problem leads to the following efficiency conditions, where subscripts indicate partial derivatives:

$$\frac{U_H}{U_Z} = \frac{Z_K}{H_K}, \frac{U_S}{U_Z} = \frac{Z_K}{S_K} \quad \text{and} \quad \frac{U_S}{U_H} = \frac{H_K}{S_K} = \frac{H_L}{S_L}. \tag{4.2}$$

[85] This problem also appears in club models. See Brueckner and Lee (1989).

[86] Some other sources of inefficiency have been identified, but they are not central to the models developed in this paper. See Wildasin (1986) for a review.

[87] Adding heterogeneity would not alter the substance of this efficiency analysis.

[88] A more general formulation is provided by Yinger (1999).

How do these conditions compare to the outcome of a competitive market? Let $r$ be the price of $K$, and $R$ the price of $L$. Then a profit maximizing $Z$-firm sets $Z_K = r$, and a profit maximizing housing producer sets $PH_K = r$ and $PH_L = R$. Furthermore, a cost-minimizing local government sets $r/S_K = R/S_L = MC$. It follows that:

$$\frac{Z_K}{H_K} = P, \quad \frac{Z_K}{S_K} = MC \quad \text{and} \quad \frac{H_K}{S_K} = \frac{H_L}{S_L} = \frac{MC}{P}. \tag{4.3}$$

Moreover, regardless of voters' perceptions about capitalization, they respond to $P(1+t^*)$, not $P$ (see Eq. (2.16b)), so the property tax inserts a wedge between consumer and producer decisions, and the first condition in Eq. (4.2) is not met.[89] This is classic distortion from the property tax, which has been emphasized by Oates (1972) and Mieszkowsi and Zodrow (1989), among others. This distortion disappears only under the extreme Hamilton assumptions.

If voters have either complete awareness or complete ignorance of public service capitalization, then according to Eq. (2.16a) when $H = \bar{H}$, they treat $MC$ as if it were the price of $S$, and the second condition in Eq. (4.2) is satisfied. Several authors have claimed that decisions about $S$ are efficient because they meet this condition.[90] By the theory of the second best, however, this condition is not a valid guide to efficient provision of $S$ unless all other first-best efficiency conditions in the overall planning problem are satisfied. As shown earlier, markets are unlikely to satisfy the efficiency conditions for household allocation to communities and for housing consumption. The second condition in Eq. (4.2) illuminates the requirements for efficiency, but cannot by itself be used to show that efficient service provision is attained.

Furthermore, we do not know whether, or not, voter perceptions lead to the decision rule in Eq. (2.16a). As discussed earlier, this rule is consistent with many different assumptions about these perceptions, but some reasonable assumptions lead to different decision rules—and hence to outcomes that are not consistent with efficiency (Yinger, 1999). Awareness of capital gains (but not the opportunity cost of housing) and of property tax capitalization (but not of public service capitalization), for example, results in spending below the level defined by Eq. (2.16a). Moreover, switching to a head tax does not guarantee efficiency, even

---

[89] Recall, however, that with complete capitalization, $P(1+t^*)$ is constant, so with a fixed housing stock, the property tax causes no distortion in household choices between $H$ and $S$. The problem arises because households and firms respond to different prices.

[90] Perhaps the best known example is Brueckner (1979, 1982, 1983), who argues that communities maximize property values and that this behavior leads to efficiency. For both empirical reasons (discussed earlier) and the reason in the text, we disagree.

assuming an efficient allocation of households to jurisdictions; efficiency still requires that voters be equally aware of the impact of $S$ on both capital gains and the opportunity cost of housing. Hence, the lack of attention in the literature to voters' perceptions leaves a major gap in our knowledge about the efficiency of public service provision.

Finally, even if voters' preferences are consistent with Eq. (2.16a), a property tax limitation could pull a jurisdiction away from this outcome (Ladd, 1975). The results of Bradbury et al. (1997) are consistent with this argument, although, as noted earlier, they do not identify the exact public spending rule. This argument does not prove that public service levels would be efficient without a property tax limitation; as just explained Eq. (2.16a) is not a sufficient condition for efficiency.

*Heterogeneity.* As first pointed out by Barlow (1970), heterogeneity in demand for $S$ can lead to a divergence between the Samuelson (1954) condition for efficiency and the outcome of voting. An extensive literature has since appeared on this conclusion. See, for example, Edelson (1973), Barzel (1973), Bergstrom (1973), Akin and Young Day (1976) and Yinger (1985). The extensive heterogeneity documented in the empirical literature implies that this inefficiency may be pervasive.

The key point can be derived by rewriting Eq. (4.1) so that the planner maximizes the utility of one individual holding the utility of other individuals constant at a fixed level. In this problem, the same level of $S$ is provided to all individuals either because $S$ is a pure public good, so that no other outcome is possible, or because legal or philosophical constraints require equal service provision to all residents. In this case, the analog to the second condition of Eq. (4.2) is the Samuelson condition that the sum across households of the marginal benefits from public services equal the marginal cost. In other words, the mean marginal benefit, say $\overline{MB}$, must equal the marginal cost per household, $MC$.

According to Eq. (2.16a), the median voter sets the median marginal benefit, say $MB_m$, equal to $MC$ weighted by the median tax share, $V_m/\bar{V}$. Hence, as shown in Fig. 4, the voter's choice may not satisfy the efficiency condition. To be more specific, the voter picks the efficient level of $S$ only when:

$$\frac{MB_m}{\overline{MB}} = \frac{V_m}{\bar{V}} = \frac{(P(S,t)H_m)/r}{(P(S,t)\bar{H})/r} = \frac{H_m}{\bar{H}}. \tag{4.4}$$

Moreover, if the ratio of median to mean is greater for $MB$ than for $H$ (or in Fig. 4 if, at the efficient level of $S$, the vertical distance between the $MB$ curves is greater than the vertical distance between the $MC$ curves), the voter selects a

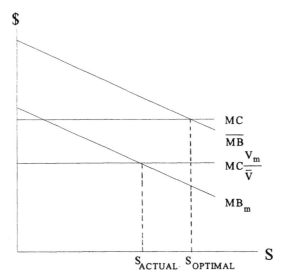

Fig. 4. Inefficiency due to heterogeneity.

level of $S$ that is below the efficient level. In effect, the efficiency rule gives more weight than does the median voter to the strong demand for $S$ from the highest income households.

Now suppose $\varphi$ is the ratio of median to mean income. Then with constant elasticity demand functions, the ratio of $MB_m$ to $\overline{MB}$ equals $\varphi^\epsilon$, where as before, $\epsilon$ is the income elasticity of $MB$. Similarly, the ratio of $V_m$ to $\overline{V}$ equals $\varphi^\theta$, where $\theta$ is the income elasticity of demand for housing. Thus, whenever $\varphi < 1$, which is always is true with a long upper tail for the income distribution, the elasticity condition that assures matched sorting, namely $\epsilon > \theta$, also assures that the level of $S$ will be below the efficient level in a heterogeneous community. A more general version of this result is provided by Bergstrom (1973), and matching grants to achieve efficiency in a heterogenous community are derived by Akin and Young Day (1976) and Yinger (1985).

### 4.1.4. Conclusion
In short, even with neutral political institutions, a general equilibrium analysis of housing and public services reveals four fundamental sources of inefficiency: misallocation of households to communities, the property tax, public service capitalization and heterogeneity. The empirical literature supports most of the key assumptions that lead to these types of inefficiency and leads to the strong presumption that our system of local governments is inefficient. Moreover, with

so many possible sources of inefficiency, the theory of the second best implies that efficiency cannot be inferred from a finding that one of the efficiency conditions is satisfied. The existing literature provides no information, however, on the magnitude of the excess burdens associated with all this efficiency and hence sheds no light on the potential gains from efficiency-enhancing policies.[91]

## 4.2. The fairness of local public spending

The analysis in this chapter points to several important issues of equity in a system of local governments, some associated with sorting and others associated with capitalization.

### 4.2.1. Sorting and equity

When local governments have considerable autonomy, as in the US, and sorting occurs, some jurisdictions have much higher incomes and taxbases than others and end up with much higher quality public services. This effect is magnified by environmental factors; high income jurisdictions tend to have favorable environments for providing public services and hence relatively low public service costs. Moreover, some jurisdictions have extensive commercial and industrial property, which lowers their tax price and thereby raises the quality of public services voters select.[92]

Because the system of local governments is established by higher levels of government, by the states in the US, for example, higher levels of government bear ultimate responsibility for the nature of this system. As a result, higher levels of government may be concerned with variation in local public services, and may want to compensate local governments for unfavorable fiscal factors that are largely outside their control, such as a low taxbase, high input prices, or a harsh environment.[93] This compensation by a state can take the form of intergovernmental aid programs that account for taxbase and cost differences across communities (Bradbury et al., 1984) or of institutional changes, such as regional taxbase sharing or allowing cities to tax suburban commuters (Reschovsky, 1980; Ladd and Yinger, 1991).

---

[91] In addition, little work has been done on second-best policies that take some constraints as given. One exception is Yinger (1985) who builds on the work of Atkinson and Stern (1974) to derive efficient conditions for service provision when a distortionary property tax is the only available revenue instrument.

[92] The impact of commercial and industrial property is quite complex, both because taxes on this property may be shifted to consumers (Ladd, 1975) and because the presence of this property may raise public service costs (Ladd and Yinger, 1991).

[93] For a contrary view, see Oakland (1994).

Fairness issues have long been recognized in the case of education, both by academics and policy-makers. Moreover, many American states, often in response to a court ruling, now provide higher grants per pupil to school districts with lower property values per pupil. See Downes (1992), Furman et al. (1993), Reschovsky (1994) and Courant and Loeb (1997). Some grant systems are designed to bring all school districts up to a minimum spending level, and others are designed to ensure that all districts that levy the same property tax rate will receive the same spending per pupil. No existing grant system eliminates the correlation between wealth and school spending, but some of them undoubtedly lower this correlation significantly.[94]

The role of educational costs is not widely understood, however, and most courts and grant systems focus on spending per pupil, not public output per pupil. At best, existing programs contain only limited, ad hoc adjustments for cost-related factors. This neglect is unfortunate; cost indexes can be estimated and included in aid formulas (LeGrand, 1975; Bradbury et al., 1984; Ladd and Yinger, 1994; Duncombe and Yinger, 1997, 1998). Because they also ignore variation in costs and taxbases, property tax limitation measures are likely to undermine equity by forcing high-cost, low-wealth school districts to make the largest tax cuts (Ladd and Wilson, 1985).

### 4.2.2. Capitalization and equity

The consensus bidding model implies that an unanticipated change in $S$ or $t$ in one jurisdiction relative to others leads to capital gains or losses for the owners of property there at the time of the change. In fact, if capitalization is complete, the capital gain or loss equals the present value of the stream of annual changes in service benefits or taxes, and these owners bear the entire burden of the change. Moreover, people who buy from them in the future bear no burden at all because these future buyers will be compensated for higher $t$ or lower $S$ in the form of lower housing prices. As a result, capitalization creates classes of households based on the timing of their home purchase, instead of their income or wealth. Some policies are unfair because they arbitrarily benefit or harm people in some of these time-dependent classes relative to others (Aaron, 1975; Feldstein, 1976a).

---

[94] Because grants alter recipient governments' behavior, a grant system that links spending per pupil to a district's taxbase, called a power-equalizing grant does not necessarily eliminate the positive correlation between spending and wealth (i.e., achieve wealth neutrality), and might lead to a negative correlation (Feldstein, 1976b; Nechyba, 1996). Recent evidence on the behavioral responses to grants indicates that power-equalizing grants do not bring this correlation down to zero (Duncombe and Yinger, 1998).

Consider, for example, a community in which poor assessing practices lead to assessment/sales ratios, and hence effective property tax rates, that vary widely from one house to another.[95] In this situation, an unanticipated revaluation that brings all houses to the same effective tax rate will result in capital losses for houses that were previously underassessed and to capital gains for houses that were previously overassessed. These gains and losses are largely arbitrary, and hence unfair; a long-time owner whose house was previously underassessed could be said to be paying back tax breaks in the form of a capital loss, but the same loss falls on a recent buyer who gained nothing at all from the past underassessment. One cannot avoid this problem, however, by retaining the poor assessing system, because such a system hands out regular, small, unannounced effective tax rate cuts or increases as it allows assessments to diverge from market values. The resulting incremental gains and losses also are arbitrary, and hence unfair. The only way out of this dilemma is to pay the one-time fairness cost of revaluation and then keep assessments up to date in the future (Yinger et al., 1988).

As shown by Wyckoff (1995), capitalization also can offset some or all of the equalizing impact of an equalizing grant program. Current homeowners and landlords in a jurisdiction that receives a higher intergovernmental grant will receive a capital gain, but anyone who moves into the jurisdiction in the future will have to pay a higher price or rent—which will offset some or all of the benefit from the increased public services or lower taxes there. This effect is not important if one is only concerned with equalizing service levels, but it is central if one wants to equalize household welfare over the long term. In the case of education, equalizing service quality for children appears to be a more compelling objective than equalizing welfare for parents. The issues are not so clear for police and fire. In any case, more work needs to be done on the appropriate equity objectives and on the extent to which capitalization undermines equalizing aid programs.

## 4.3. Welfare analysis

Few scholars have addressed issues of general welfare analysis in a system of local governments. One important exception is Bradford and Oates (1974), who calculate the excess burden (associated with heterogeneity, as discussed earlier) caused by moving from a system with many suburbs to a metropolitan government and discuss the tradeoff between this efficiency loss and the equity gain from eliminating variation in public services. There need not always be a tradeoff between equity and efficiency, however. An earlier section shows that large, het-

---

[95] By switching to an acquisition-value assessing system, Proposition 13 in California causes some large capital gains and losses with unusual equity implications. See O'Sullivan et al. (1995).

erogeneous jurisdictions are likely to underprovide public services on efficiency grounds. They are also likely to have low taxbases, high costs, and hence, low public service levels. As pointed out by Yinger (1985), therefore, intergovernmental grants to such jurisdictions may service to enhance both efficiency and equity.


## 5. Conclusions

The literature reviewed here raises important issues in local public finance for the US and many other countries, particularly those with decentralized governmental systems.

Bidding and sorting models have very general applicability. They do not require local governments to be autonomous but do require mobile households, a well functioning housing market, and some variation in local service levels and effective tax rates within a metropolitan area. For example, they could prove helpful in a country that sets spending levels for local governments without considering cost differences across jurisdictions. However, the extent of variation in local service levels and tax rates, and hence, the power of the bidding/sorting approach, is likely to be positively correlated with decentralization, which varies widely even among developed nations. Pommerhene (1977) shows, for example, that the US, Switzerland and Canada are very decentralized, whereas, at the other extreme, France reserves for the central government many services provided locally elsewhere, such as primary and secondary education. In addition, Oates (1972, 1993) finds that developing nations tend to be much less decentralized than developed nations.

Overall, bidding and sorting models are likely to be applicable in many countries, but most of the related empirical evidence comes from the US, and the usefulness of these models in a centralized country has never been tested. Moreover, the importance of these models is likely to increase over time as more countries move toward decentralized systems. For recent developments in fiscal decentralization, see Fraschini (1989) on Italy, Kojima (1992a) and Bahl and Nath (1986) on developing nations, Oh (1991) and Ito (1992) on Korea, Kojima (1992b) on China, and Leigland (1993) on Indonesia.

The generality of the bidding/sorting framework stands in sharp contrast to the dependence of collective choice models on institutional detail. The median-voter model, which is widely used in the literature reviewed here, implicitly assumes that all residents participate in and influence the collective choice process. This assumption appears to work well in some circumstances, such as voting in cities in Switzerland, especially those that are direct democracies, and in many local government contexts in the US. Evidence from Sone (1993) suggests that modified voter models also can be helpful in democracies, such as Japan, that give public officials considerable latitude.

The median-voter approach has obvious limits with more centralized decision-making and seems irrelevant in many developing nations where local fiscal decision-making is dominated by a select few (see Conyers, 1990). Moreover, Bahl and Linn (1992) document that local governments in developing countries rely heavily on property taxes, but they account for a small share of public revenue, and central decision-making greatly limits variation in public services across local governments. Although trends toward decentralization may increase their applicability in the future, the voting models explored here appear at present to be most helpful in developed countries with strong—and varied—local governments.

The literature reviewed here is rich and diverse but leaves plenty of room for future scholars. Many aspects of the voting models remain untested; little empirical research on bidding and sorting, or their impact on voting has been conducted for countries other than the US; and the implications of local government inefficiency for public policy remain largely unexplored.

# References

Aaron, H.J. (1975), Who Pays the Property Tax: A New View (The Brookings Institution, Washington, DC).

Akin, J.S. and D.J. Young Day (1976), "The efficiency of local school finance", Review of Economics and Statistics 58:255–258.

Arnott, R.J. and J.G. McKinnon (1977), "The effects of the property tax: A general equilibrium simulation", Journal of Urban Economics 4:389–407.

Aronsson, T. and M. Wikström (1996), "Local public expenditure in Sweden: a model where the median voter is not necessarily decisive", European Economic Review 40:1705–1716.

Atkinson, A.B. and N.H. Stern (1974), "Pigou, taxation, and public goods", Review of Economic Studies 41:119–128.

Bahl, R.W. and J.F. Linn (1992), Urban Public Finance in Developing Countries (Oxford University Press, Oxford).

Bahl, R.W. and S. Nath (1986), "Public expenditure decentralization in developing countries", Environment and Planning C: Government and Policy 4:405–418.

Barlow, R. (1970), "Efficiency aspects of local school finance", Journal of Political Economy 78:1028–1040.

Barzel, Y. (1973), "Private schools and public school finance", Journal of Political Economy 81:174–186.

Bentick, B.L. (1996), "The differential incidence of an urban land tax depends on the travel intensities of substitutes for land", Urban Studies 33:1729–1732.

Bergstrom, T. (1973), "A note on efficient taxation", Journal of Political Economy 81:187–191.

Bergstrom, T. and R. Goodman (1973), "Private demands for public goods", American Economic Review 63:280–296.

Besley, T., I. Preston and M. Ridge (1997), "Fiscal anarchy in the UK: modeling poll tax noncompliance", Journal of Public Economics 64:137–152.

Black, S.E. (in press), "Do better schools matter? Parental valuation of elementary education", Quarterly Journal of Economics.

Bogart, W.T. and B. Cromwell (1997), "How much more is a good school district worth?", National Tax Journal 50:215–232.

Boije, R. (1997), Capitalisation, Efficiency and the Demand for Local Public Services, Economic Studies 33 (Department of Economics, Uppsala University, Uppsala, Sweden).

Borcherding, T.E. and R.T. Deacon (1972), "The demand for services of non-federal governments", American Economic Review 62:891–901.

Borge, L.-E. and J. Rattsø (1995), "Demographic shift, relative costs, and the allocation of local public consumption in Norway", Regional Science and Urban Economics 25:705–724.

Bradbury, K.L., H.F. Ladd, M. Perrault, A. Reschovsky and J. Yinger (1984), "State aid to offset fiscal disparities across communities", National Tax Journal 37:151–170.

Bradbury, K.L., C.J. Mayer and K.E. Case (1997), "Property tax limits and local fiscal behavior: Did Massachusetts cities and towns spend too little on town services under Proposition $2\frac{1}{2}$", Working Paper No. 97-2 (Federal Reserve Bank of Boston, Boston).

Bradford, D.F., R.A. Malt and W.E. Oates (1969), "The rising cost of local public services: some evidence and reflections", National Tax Journal 22:185–202.

Bradford, D.F. and W.E. Oates (1974), "Suburban exploitation of central cities and government structure", in: H.M. Hochman and G.E. Peterson, eds., Redistribution Through Public Choice, pp. 43–92 (Columbia University Press, New York).

Brueckner, J.K. (1979), "Property values, local public expenditure, and economic efficiency", Journal of Urban Economics 11:223–246.

Brueckner, J.K. (1981), "Congested public goods: The case of fire protection", Journal of Public Economics 15:45–58.

Brueckner, J.K. (1982), "A test for allocative efficiency in the local public sector", Journal of Public Economics 14:311–332.

Brueckner, J.K. (1983), "Property value maximization and public sector efficiency", Journal of Urban Economics 14:1–16.

Brueckner, J.K. (1987), "The structure of urban equilibria: a unified treatment of the Muth–Mills model", in: E.S. Mills, ed, Handbook of Regional and Urban Economics, pp. 821–875 (North Holland, Amsterdam).

Brueckner, J.K. and K. Lee (1989), "Club theory with a peer-group effect", Regional Science and Urban Economics 19:399–420.

Carroll, R. and J. Yinger (1994), "Is the property tax a benefit tax? The case of rental housing", National Tax Journal 47:295–316.

Chattopadhyay, S. (1998), "An empirical investigation into the performance of Ellickson's random bidding model, with an application to air quality valuation", Journal of Urban Economics 43:292–314.

Chinloy, P. (1978), "Effective property taxes and tax capitalization", Canadian Journal of Economics 11:740–750.

Coleman, J. (1966), Equality of Educational Opportunity (US Government Printing Office, Washington, DC).

Conley, J. and M.H. Wooders (1998), "Anonymous pricing in Tiebout economies and economies with clubs", in: D. Pines, E. Sadka, and I. Zilcha, eds., Topics in Public Finance (Cambridge University Press, Cambridge).

Conley, J. and M.H. Wooders (1997), "Equivalence of the core and competitive equilibrium in a Tiebout economy with crowding types", Journal of Urban Economics 41:421–440.

Conyers, D. (1990), "Centralization and development planning: a comparative perspective", in: P. De Valk and K. Wekwete, eds., Decentralizing for Participatory Planning (Avebury, Aldershot, UK).

Courant, P.N. and S. Loeb (1997), "Centralization of school finance in Michigan", Journal of Policy Analysis and Management 16:114–136.

Crampton, G. (1996), "Local government structure and urban residential location", Urban Studies 33:1061–1076.

Crane, R. (1988), "Second-best property value capitalization", Economic Letters 26:175–178.

Crane, R. (1990), "Price specification and the demand for public goods", Journal of Public Economics 43:93–106.

deBartolome, C.A. and S.S. Rosenthal (in press), "Property tax capitalization in a model with tax deferred assets and standard deductions", Review of Economics and Statistics.

Do, A.Q. and C.F. Sirmans (1994), "Residential property tax capitalization: discount rate evidence from California", National Tax Journal 47:341–348.

Dowding, K., J. Peter and S. Biggs (1994), "Tiebout: a survey of empirical literature", Urban Studies 31:767–797.

Downes, T.A. (1992), "Evaluating the impact of school finance reform on the provision of public education: the California case", National Tax Journal 45:405–419.

Downes, T.A. and T.F. Pogue (1994), "Adjusting school aid formulas for the higher cost of educating disadvantaged students", National Tax Journal 47:89–110.

Duncombe, W. (1991), "Demand for local public services revisited: the case of fire protection", Public Finance Quarterly 19:412–436.

Duncombe, W. and J. Yinger (1993), "An analysis of returns to scale in public production, with an application to fire protection", Journal of Public Economics 52:49–72.

Duncombe, W. and J. Yinger (1997), "Why is it so hard to help central city schools?", Journal of Policy Analysis and Management 16:85–113.

Duncombe, W. and J. Yinger (1998), "School finance reform: aid formulas and equity objectives", National Tax Journal 51:239–262.

Dynarski, M., R. Schwab and E. Zampelli (1989), "Local characteristics and local production: the case of education", Journal of Urban Economics 26:250–263.

Eberts, R.W. and T.J. Gronberg (1981), "Jurisdictional homogeneity and the Tiebout hypothesis", Journal of Urban Economics 10:227–239.

Edel, M. and E. Sclar (1974), "Taxes, spending and property values: supply adjustments in a Tiebout–Oates model", Journal of Political Economy 82:941–954.

Edelson, N.M. (1973), "Efficiency aspects of local school finance: comments and extension", Journal of Political Economy 81:158–173.

Eisenberg, E.F. (1996), Intrajurisdictional Property Tax Capitalization Rates, unpublished PhD. Dissertation (Syracuse University, Syracuse, NY).

Ellickson, B. (1971), "Jurisdictional fragmentation and residential choice", American Economic Review 61:334–339.

Ellickson, B. (1981), "An alternative test of the hedonic theory of housing markets", Journal of Urban Economics 9:56–63.

Epple, D. (1987), "Hedonic prices and implicit markets: Estimating demand and supply functions for differential products", Journal of Political Economy 95:59–80.

Epple, D., R. Filimon, and T. Romer (1983), "Housing, voting, and moving: equilibrium in a model of local public goods with multiple jurisdictions", in: J.V. Henderson, ed., Research in Urban Economics, Vol. III, pp. 59–90 (JAI Press, Greenwich, CT).

Epple, D., R. Filimon, and T. Romer (1984), "Equilibrium among local jurisdictions: toward and integrated treatment of voting and residential choice", Journal of Public Economics 24:281–308.

Epple, D., R. Filimon, and T. Romer (1993), "Existence of voting and housing equilibrium in a system of communities with property taxes", Regional Science and Urban Economics 23:585–610.

Epple, D. and G.J. Platt (1998), "Equilibrium among jurisdictions when households differ by preferences and income", Journal of Urban Economics 43:23–51.

Epple, D. and R.E. Romano (1997), "School choice policies, household location, and property values", Department of Economics Working Paper No. 1997-93 (University of Florida, Gainesville, FL).

Epple, D. and T. Romer (1989), "On flexible municipal boundaries", Journal of Urban Economics 26:307–319.

Epple, D. and T. Romer (1991), "Mobility and redistribution", Journal of Political Economy 99:828–859.

Epple, D. and H. Sieg (1997), "Estimating equilibrium models of local jurisdictions", Graduate School of Industrial Administration Working Paper No. 1997-94 (Carnegie Mellon University, Pittsburgh, PA).

Epple, D., A. Zelenitz and M. Visscher (1978), "A search for testable implications of the Tiebout hypothesis", Journal of Political Economy 86:405–425.

Feldstein, M.S. (1976a), "On the theory of tax reform", Journal of Public Economics 6:77–104.

Feldstein, M.S. (1976b), "Wealth neutrality and public choice in local education", American Economic Review 65:75–89.

Ferguson, R. (1991), "Paying for public education: new evidence on how and why money matters", Harvard Journal on Legislation 28:465–498.

Fischel, W.A. (1992), "Property taxation and the Tiebout model: evidence for the benefit view from voting and zoning", Journal of Economic Literature 30:171–177.

Flatters, F., J.V. Henderson and P. Mieszkowski (1974), "Public goods, efficiency and regional fiscal equalization", Journal of Public Economics 3:99–112.

Follain, J.R. and E. Jimenez (1985), "Estimating the demand for housing characteristics: a survey and critique", Regional Science and Urban Economics 15:77–107.

Fox, W. (1981), "Reviewing economies of size in education", Journal of Education Finance 6:273–296.

Fraschini, A. (1989), "Local autonomy, accountability, and a new local tax: the Italian debate", Policy and Politics 17:155–163.

Frech, H.E., III and R.N. Lafferty (1984), "The effect of the California coastal commission on housing prices", Journal of Urban Economics 16:105–123.

Fuhrmann, S., R. Elmore and D. Massell (1993), "School reform in the United States: putting it into context", in S. Jacobson and R. Burne, eds., Reforming Education: The Emerging Systematic Approach, pp. 3–27 (Crown Press, Thousand Oakes, CA).

Goldstein, G.S. and M.V. Pauly (1981), "Tiebout bias on the demand for local public goods", Journal of Public Economics 16:131–144.

Goodspeed, T.J. (1989), "A re-examination of the use of ability to pay taxes by local governments", Journal of Public Economics 38:319–342.

Gramlich, E.M. and D.L. Rubinfeld (1982), "Micro estimates of public spending demand functions and tests of the Tiebout and median-voter hypotheses", Journal of Political Economy 90:536–560.

Greenberg, J. (1979), "Consistent majority rules over compact sets of alternatives", Econometrica 47:627–636.

Grosskopf, S. and S. Yaisawaring (1990), "Economics of scope in the provision of local public services", National Tax Journal 63:61–74.

Gyapong, A. and K. Gyimah-Brempong (1988), "Factor substitution, price elasticity of factor demand and returns to scale in police protection: Evidence from Michigan", Southern Economic Journal 54:863–878.

Hamilton, B.W. (1975), "Zoning and property taxation in a system of local governments", Urban Studies 12:205–211.

Hamilton, B.W. (1976), "Capitalization of intrajurisdictional differences in local tax prices", American Economic Review 22:743–753.

Hamilton, B.W. (1979), "Capitalization and the regressivity of the property tax: empirical evidence", National Tax Journal 32:169–180.

Hamilton, B.W. (1983a), "The flypaper effect and other anomalies", Journal of Public Economics 22:347–361.

Hamilton, B.W. (1983b), "A review: is the property tax a benefit tax?", in: G.R. Zodrow, ed., Local Provisions of Public Services: The Tiebout Model after Twenty-Five Years, pp. 85–108 (Academic Press, New York).

Hamilton, B.W., E.S. Mills and D. Puryear (1975), "The Tiebout hypothesis and residential income segregation", in E.S. Mills and W.E. Oates, eds., Fiscal Zoning and Land Use Controls, pp. 101–118 (Lexington Books, Lexington).

Hansen, N.A. and A.S. Kessler (1997), "The political geography of tax h(e)avens and tax hells", Discussion Paper No. A-541 (University of Bonn, Bonn).

Hanushek, E. (1986), "The economics of schooling: production and efficiency in public schools", Journal of Economic Literature 24:1141–1177.

Harmon, O.R. (1988), "The income elasticity of demand for single-family owner-occupied housing: an empirical reconciliation", Journal of Urban Economics 24:173–185.

Harrison, D. and D.L. Rubinfeld (1978), "Tiebout bias on the demand for local public goods", Journal of Environmental Economics and Management 5:81–102.

Haurin, D.R. and D. Brasington (1996), "School quality and real house prices: inter- and intrametropolitan effects", Journal of Housing Economics 5:351–368.

Haurin, D.R. (1980), "The effect of property taxes on urban areas", Journal of Urban Economics 7:384–396.

Hayes, K. (1986), "Local public good demands and demographic effects", Applied Economics 18:1039–1045.

Heikkila, E.J. (1996), "Are municipalities Tieboutian clubs?", Regional Science and Urban Economics 26:203–226.

Henderson, J.V. (1977), Economic Theory and the Cities (Academic Press, New York).

Henderson, J.V. (1985), "The Tiebout model: bring back the entrepreneurs", Journal of Political Economy 93:248–264.

Henderson, J.V. (1991), "Separating Tiebout equilibrium", Journal of Urban Economics 29:128–152.

Henderson, J.V., P. Mieszkowski and Y. Sauvageau (1978), "Peer group effects and education production functions", Journal of Public Economics 10:97–106.

Holcombe, R. (1989), "The median voter model in public choice theory", Public Choice 61:115–125.

Hoyt, W.H. and S.S. Rosenthal (1997), "Household location and Tiebout: Do families sort according to preferences for locational amenities?", Journal of Urban Economics 42:159–178.

Inman, R.P. (1979), "The fiscal performance of local governments: An interpretive review", in: P. Mieszkowski and M. Straszheim, eds., Current Issues in Urban Economics, pp. 270–321 (Johns Hopkins University Press, Baltimore).

Inman, R.P. (1987), "Markets, governments, and the 'new' political economy", in: A.J. Auerbach and M. Feldstein, eds., Handbook of Public Economics, Vol. II, pp. 647–778 (North-Holland, Amsterdam).

Ito, K. (1992), "The reinstatement of local fiscal autonomy in the Republic of Korea", Developing Economies 30:404–429.

Judd, G.D. and J.M. Watts (1981), "Schools and housing values", Land Economics 57:459–470.

Katz, L. and K.T. Rosen (1987), "The interjurisdictional effects of growth controls on housing prices", Journal of Law and Economics 30:149–160.

King, A.T. (1973), Property Taxes, Amenities, and Residential Land Values (Ballinger, Cambridge, MA).

Kojima, R. (1992a), "Central and local finances in developing countries—The trend toward decentralization: introduction", Developing Economies 30:311–314.

Kojima, R. (1992b), "The growing fiscal authority of provincial-level governments in China", Developing Economies 30:315–346.

Konishi, H. (1997), "Voting with ballots and feet: existence of equilibrium in a local public good economy", Journal of Economic Theory 68:480–509.

Ladd, H.F. (1975), "Local education expenditures, fiscal capacity, and the composition of the property tax base", National Tax Journal 28:145–158.

Ladd, H.F. and J. Boatright Wilson (1985), "Education and tax limitations: evidence from Massachusetts" Journal of Education Finance 10:281–296.

Ladd, H.F. and J. Yinger (1991), America's Ailing Cities: Fiscal Health and the Design of Urban Policy, updated edition (Johns Hopkins University Press, Baltimore).

Ladd, H.F. and J. Yinger (1994), "The case for equalizing aid", National Tax Journal 47:211–224.

LeGrand, J. (1975), "Fiscal equity and grants to local authorities", Economic Journal 85:531–547.

Leigland, J. (1993), "Decentralizing the development budget process in Indonesia: Progress and prospects", Public Budgeting and Finance 13:85–101.

Lenon, M., S.K. Chattopadhyay and D.R. Heffley (1996), "Zoning and fiscal interdependencies", Journal of Real Estate Finance and Economics 12:221–234.

Lerman, S.R. and C.R. Kern (1983), "Hedonic theory, bid rents, and willingness-to-pay: some extensions of Ellickson's results", Journal of Urban Economics 13:358–363.

Lipsey, R.G. and K. Lancaster (1956), "The general theory of the second best", Review of Economic Studies 24:11–32.

Mayo, S.K. (1981), "Theory and estimation in the economics of housing demand", Journal of Urban Economics 10:95–116.

McDougall, G.S. (1976), "Local public goods and residential property values: some insights and extensions", National Tax Journal 29:436–437.

McFadden, D. (1974), "Conditional logit analysis of qualitative choice", in: P. Zarembka, ed., Frontiers in Econometrics (Academic Press, New York).

McMillen, D.P. and J.F. McDonald (1991), "A simultaneous equations model of zoning and land values", Regional Science and Urban Economics 21:55–72.

Miceli, T.J. (1991), "Free riders and distortionary zoning by local communities", Journal of Urban Economics 30:112–122.

Miceli, T.J. (1992), "Optimal fiscal zoning when the local government is a discriminating monopolist", Regional Science and Urban Economics 22:579–596.

Mieszkowski, P. and G.R. Zodrow (1989), "Taxation and the Tiebout model", Journal of Economic Literature 27:1098–1146.

Munley, V.G. (1982), "An alternative test of the Tiebout hypothesis", Public Choice 38:211–217.

Nechyba, T.J. (1996), "A computable general equilibrium model of intergovernmental aid", Journal of Public Economics 62:363–398.

Nechyba, T.J. (1997), "Existence of equilibrium and stratification in local and hierarchical Tiebout economies with property taxes and voting", Economic Theory 10:277–304.

Nechyba, T.J. and R.P. Strauss (1998), "Community choice and local public services: a discrete choice approach", Regional Science and Urban Economics 28:51–74.

Noto, N.A. (1976), "The impact of the public sector on residential property values", Proceedings of the National Tax Association, pp. 192–200.

Oakland, W.H. (1994), "Fiscal equalization: an empty box?" National Tax Journal 47:211–224.

Oates, W.E. (1969), "The effects of property taxes and local public services on property values: an empirical study of tax capitalization and the Tiebout hypothesis", Journal of Political Economy 77:957–971.

Oates, W.E. (1972), Fiscal Federalism (Harcourt Brace, New York).

Oates, W.E. (1973), "The effects of property taxes and local spending on property values: a reply and yet further results", Journal of Political Economy 81:1004–1008.

Oates, W.E. (1977a), "An economist's perspective on fiscal federalism", in: W.E. Oates, ed., The Political Economy of Fiscal Federalism (Lexington Books, Lexington).

Oates, W.E. (1977b), "The use of local zoning ordinances to regulate population flows and the quality of local services", in: O.C. Ashenfelter and W.E. Oates, eds., Essays in Labor Market Analysis, pp. 201–220 (John Wiley and Sons, New York).

Oates, W.E. (1985), "Searching for Leviathan: An empirical study", American Economic Review 75:748–757.

Oates, W.E. (1993), "Fiscal decentralization and economic development", National Tax Journal 46:237–244.

Oates, W.E. (1994), "Federalism and government finance", in: J.S. Quigley and E. Smolensky, eds., Modern Public Finance, pp. 126–161 (Harvard University Press, Cambridge, MA).

Oh, Y.-C. (1991), "The allocation of tax bases between central and local governments in Korea", in: T. Prud'homme, ed., Public Finance with Several Levels of Government (Foundation Journal Public Finance, The Hague).

O'Sullivan, A., T.A. Sexton and S.M. Sheffrin (1995), Property Taxes and Tax Revolts: The Legacy of Proposition 13 (Cambridge University Press, New York).

Pack, H. and J.R. Pack (1977), "Metropolitan fragmentation and suburban homogeneity", Urban Studies 14:191–201.

Pasha, H.A. (1990), "The differential incidence of land taxation", Urban Studies 27:591–595.

Pasha, H.A. and A.F. Aisha Ghaus (1995), "General equilibrium effects of local taxes", Journal of Urban Economics 38:253–271.

Pauly, M.V. (1976), "A model of local government expenditure and tax capitalization", Journal of Public Economics 6:231–242.

Pogodzinski, J.M. (1988), "Amenities in an urban general equilibrium model", Journal of Urban Economics 24:260–278.

Pogodzinski, J.M. and T.R. Sass (1994), "The theory and estimation of endogenous zoning", Regional Science and Urban Economics 24:601–630.

Pogodzinski, J.M. and D.L. Sjoquist (1985), "A numerical approach to comparative statics in a Tiebout-median voter model", in: J.M. Quigley, ed., Perspectives on Local Public Finance and Public Policy, Vol. 2, pp. 31–58 (JAI Press, Greenwich, CT).

Pogodzinski, J.M. and D.L. Sjoquist (1991), "The effects of the social choice rule on local fiscal variables: a general equilibrium approach", Regional Science and Urban Economics 21:31–54.

Pogodzinski, J.M. and D.L. Sjoquist (1993), "Alternative tax regimes in a local public good model", Journal of Public Economics 50:115–141.

Pogodzinski, J.M. and D.L. Sjoquist (1994), "A note on the estimation of capitalization", Public Finance Quarterly 21:434–448.

Polinsky, A.M. and D.L. Rubinfeld (1978), "The long run effects of a residential property tax and local public services", Journal of Urban Economics 5:241–262.

Pollakowski, H.O. (1973), "The effects of property taxes and local public spending on property values: a comment and further results", Journal of Political Economy 5:119–129.

Pommerhene, W. (1977), "Quantitative aspects of federalism: a study of six countries", in: W.E. Oates, ed., The Political Economy of Fiscal Federalism (Lexington Books, Lexington).

Pommerhene, W. (1978), "Institutional approaches to public expenditure: empirical evidence from Swiss municipalities", Journal of Public Economics 9:255–280.

Preston, I. and M. Ridge (1995), "Demand for local public spending: evidence from the British social attitudes survey", The Economic Journal 105:644–660.

Quigley, J.M. (1985), "Consumer choice of dwelling, neighborhood, and public services", Journal of Urban Economics 15:41–63.

Reid, G. (1990), "The many faces of Tiebout bias in local education demand estimates", Journal of Urban Economics 27:232–254.

Reid, G. (1991), "Tests of institutional vs. non-institutional models of local public expenditure determination", Public Choice 70:315–333.

Reschovsky, A. (1979), "Residential choice and the local public sector: an alternative test of the Tiebout hypothesis", Journal of Urban Economics 4:501–520.

Reschovsky, A. (1980), "An evaluation of metropolitan area tax base sharing", National Tax Journal 33:55–66.

Reschovsky, A. (1994), "Fiscal equalization and school finance", National Tax Journal 47:185–198.

Roberts, J. (1992), "A comment on the many faces of Tiebout bias", Journal of Urban Economics 32:45–51.

Romer, T. and H. Rosenthal (1979), "The elusive median voter", Journal of Public Economics 12:143–170.

Rose-Ackerman, S. (1979), "Market models of local government: exit, voting, and the land market", Journal of Urban Economics 6:319–337.

Rose-Ackerman, S. (1983), "Beyond Tiebout: modeling the political economy of local government, in: G.R. Zodrow, ed., Local Provision of Public Services: The Tiebout Model after Twenty-Five Years, pp. 55–83 (Academic Press, New York).

Rosen, H.S. and D.J. Fullerton (1977), "A note on local tax rates, public benefit levels and property values", Journal of Political Economy 85:433–440.

Rosen, K.T. (1982), "The impact of Proposition 13 on house prices in northern California: a test of the interjurisdictional capitalization hypothesis", Journal of Political Economy 90:191–200.

Rubinfeld, D.L. (1987), "The economics of the local public sector", in: A.J. Auerbach and M. Feldstein, eds., Handbook of Public Economics, Vol. II, pp. 571–646 (North-Holland, New York).

Rubinfeld, D.L., P. Shapiro and J. Roberts (1987), "Tiebout bias and the demand for local public schooling", Review of Economics and Statistics 69:426–437.

Samuelson, P.A. (1954), "The pure theory of public expenditures", Review of Economics and Statistics 36:387–389.

Schmidt, A. (1992), "Private school enrollment in metropolitan areas", Public Finance Quarterly 20:298–320.

Schwab, R. and W.E. Oates (1991), "Community composition and the provision of local public goods: a normative analysis", Journal of Public Economics 44:217–237.

Schwab, R. and E. Zampelli (1987), "Untangling the demand function from the production function for local public services: the case of public safety", Journal of Public Economics 33:245–260.

Schwartz, S., P.M. Zorn and D.E. Hansen (1986), "Research design issues and pitfalls in growth control studies", Land Economics 62:223–233.

Sone, A. (1993), "An analysis of municipal government expenditures in Japan", unpublished PhD. Dissertation (Syracuse University, Syracuse, NY).

Sonstelie, J.C. and P.R. Portney (1980), "Gross rents and market values: testing the implications of Tiebout's hypothesis" Journal of Urban Economics 7:102–118.

Stiglitz, J.E. (1983), "The theory of local public goods twenty-five years after Tiebout: a perspective", in: G.S. Zodrow, ed., Local Provision of Public Services: The Tiebout Model after Twenty-Five Years, pp. 17–54 (Academic Press, New York).

Stull, W.J. and J.C. Stull (1991), "Capitalization of local income taxes", Journal of Urban Economics 29:182–190.

Sullivan, A.M. (1985), "The general equilibrium effects of the residential property tax: incidence and excess burden", Journal of Urban Economics 18:235–250.

Tiebout, C.M. (1956), "A pure theory of local expenditures", Journal of Political Economy 64:416–424.

Westoff, F. (1977), "Existence of equilibrium in economics with a local public good", Journal of Economic Theory 14:84–112.

Wheaton, W.C. (1993), "Land capitalization, Tiebout mobility, and the role of zoning regulations", Journal of Urban Economics 34:102–117.

White, M.J. (1975), "Fiscal zoning in fragmented metropolitan areas", in: E.S. Mills and W. Oates, eds., Fiscal Zoning and Land Use Controls, pp. 31–100 (Lexington Books, Lexington, MA).

Wildasin, D.E. (1986), Urban Public Finance (Harwood Academic Publishers, London).

Wooders, M.H. (1989), "A Tiebout theorem", Mathematical Social Sciences 18:33–35.

Wyckoff, P.G. (1991), "The elusive flypaper effect", Journal of Urban Economics 30:310–328.

Wyckoff, P.G. (1995), "Capitalization, equalization, and intergovernmental aid", Public Finance Quarterly 23:484–508.

Yinger, J. (1982), "Capitalization and the theory of local public finance", Journal of Political Economy 90:917–943.

Yinger, J. (1985), "Inefficiency and the median voter: Property taxes, capitalization, heterogeneity, and the theory of the second best", in: J.M. Quigley, ed., Perspectives on Local Public Finance and Public Policy, Vol. 2, pp. 3–30 (JAI Press, Greenwich, CT).

Yinger, J. (1995), "Capitalization and sorting: a revision", Public Finance Quarterly 23:217–225.

Yinger, J. (1999), "Capitalization and efficiency", in: A. Panagariya, P. Portney, and R. Schwab, eds., Environmental and Public Economics: Essays in Honor of W. E. Oates, pp. 310–26 (Edward Elgar Publishing Company, Cheltenham, UK).

Yinger, J., H.S. Bloom, A. Boersch-Supan and H.F. Ladd (1988), Property Taxes and House Values: The Theory and Estimation of Intrajurisdictional Property Tax Capitalization (Academic Press, New York).

# AUTHOR INDEX

Aaron, H.J., 1836, 2050
Abdel-Rahman, H.M., 1355, 1356, 1467, 1469, 1471, 1473
Abelson, P.W., 1443
Abercrombie, P., 1639
Aberg, Y., 1476
Acharya, B.P., 1841
Adair, A.S., 1656
Adams, D.W., 1921
Adelman, I., 1706, 1707, 1711
Ades, A.F., 1357, 1358, 1764
Agarwal, B., 1891
Agrawal, N., 1833
Ahlburg, D.A., 1899
Ahluwalia, M.S., 1880, 1900
Aina, T.A., 1734
Aisha Ghaus, A.F., 2004
Akin, J.S., 2047, 2048
Alabastro, S., 1890
Albon, R.P., 1582
Alchian, A.A., 1796
Alderman, H., 1892, 1893
Alexeev, M., 1803, 1833, 1841
Allen, G.R.P., 1343
Alonso, W., 1342, 1361, 1564
Alperovich, G., 1344, 1346–1348, 1352, 1355, 1356, 1540
Altaf, M.A., 1747
Altimir, O., 1927
Altshuler, A.A., 1946, 1954, 1972
American Automobile Manufacturers Association, 1942, 1944, 1945, 1963
American Public Transit Association, 1973, 1978
Anas, A., 1363, 1364, 1387, 1575, 1577, 1578, 1580, 1822, 1827, 1829, 1842
Anderson, D., 1942, 1954

Anderson, J.E., 1603, 1616
Andersson, A.E., 1361
Andersson, D.E., 1647
Andreev, E., 1723
Andres, M., 1576
Andrulis, J., 1506
Andrusz, G.D., 1804, 1820
Angel, S., 1793, 1808, 1817, 1824, 1925, 1943
Anglin, P.M., 1619
Annez, P., 1806, 1807
Apgar, W.C., 1578
Apogee Research, 1951
Appold, S.J., 1478
Arcelus, F., 1573
Arimah, B.C., 1801, 1802
Armstrong–Wright, A., 1742
Arnott, R.J., 1571, 1575, 1577, 1578, 1580, 1584, 1722, 1793, 1839, 1948, 1953, 2004
Arnould, R., 1967
Aronsson, T., 2019, 2038, 2040, 2042
Arriaga-Salinas, A.S., 1542
Arthur, W.B., 1901
Asabere, P.K., 1647, 1826, 1842
Aschauer, D.A., 1458
Asher, M., 1953
Asian Development Bank, 1822, 1883, 1886, 1887, 1890
Assadian, A., 1801, 1802
Atkinson, A.B., 1869, 1874, 1879, 2049
Auerbach, F., 1342
Ault, D.E., 1796, 1842
Ault, R., 1582
Ave, G., 1640, 1663
Awan, K., 1567
Awotona, A., 1842

# SUBJECT INDEX

Printed and bound by CPI Group (UK) Ltd, Croydon, CR0 4YY

08/05/2025

01864967-0004